Readings in
AMERICAN RELIGIOUS DIVERSITY

Edited by

Jon R. Stone
Carlos R. Piar
California State University, Long Beach

KENDALL/HUNT PUBLISHING COMPANY
4050 Westmark Drive   Dubuque, Iowa 52002

In Honor of and with Appreciation to Our Teachers:

at USC:
John P. Crossley, Donald E. Miller, and Robert S. Ellwood

at UCSB:
Catherine L. Albanese, †Walter H. Capps,
Phillip E. Hammond,
†Robert S. Michaelsen, Birger A. Pearson, and Wade Clark Roof

Cover images and images on pages 1, 143, 313, and 419 copyright © Corbis.

Copyright © 2007 by Kendall/Hunt Publishing Company

ISBN 13: 978-0-7575-4091-2

Printed in the United States of America
10 9 8 7 6 5 4 3 2 1

Contents

A Foreword

It is a commonplace to speak of America as a religiously diverse nation. From its origins, dating well before the arrival of European settlers, the American continent contained a great variety of peoples, languages, cultures, and religions. The native groups that came to inhabit this vast and varied landscape were of many types, from pueblo dwelling peoples, to those living in the woodland, prairie, mountain, and coastal regions. During the period of European exploration and colonial expansion, the Americas soon became home to English, French, Spanish, Portuguese, and Dutch settlers. And, after slavery was introduced into the New World, peoples of African tribal descent added their own cultural and religious expressions to the growing ethnic and racial diversity of the land. From many peoples there emerged one nation; from one nation there arose many religious voices. The long conversation—and the spirited debate—over issues of religious and cultural identity continues to this day. What does it mean to be an American? What does it mean to be part of an ethnic or racial community in America? In what ways have religious beliefs and traditional cultural practices informed that meaning or helped shape that identity?

This current anthology, *Readings in American Religious Diversity*, presents to students of American religions a collection of primary source materials that serves to illustrate the ethno-racial dimensions of religion in America beyond its usual European expressions. The ethno-racial religious communities featured in this reader broadly include Native American, African American, Asian American, and an array of Latino communities. A unique feature of this text is that the readings come from within the communities themselves, rather than from researchers commenting upon these communities from the outside. Thus, students reading these selections will come to hear the voices and sense the deeply-felt passion, sorrow, frustration, hope, and joy of those individuals who were or are still part of the important conversations at the heart of these four ethno-racial communities' ongoing dialogue and debates within themselves.

More specifically, this primary source reader is designed to complement the religious and historical materials of the junior-level course, "American Religious Diversity," which is offered every semester at California State University, Long Beach. For this course, students are required to read religious literature produced by women and men from within two of the four ethno-racial communities mentioned above. While many of our instructors have assigned works of fiction, such as short stories or novels, we have found that fictional literature has tended to give our students only a partial picture of the religious dimensions of these communities, and the difficulties these groups have experienced in their attempts to maintain traditional beliefs and practices in a predominantly "white" and Protestant culture. Thus, in addition to works of fiction, we have discovered that the diversity of religious experience as well as responses within these communities to discrimination, social dislocation, and loss of traditional culture could be "read" within other types of literature. These include folktales, sermons, letters, speeches, essays and addresses, autobiographies, oral histories and published interviews, as well as immigrant community histories, scholarly treatises, and ethnic denominational self-studies.

Because the course for which this text is designed is taught each semester by six to eight full-time and part-time faculty members, we do not believe that it is our role as the editors of this anthology to instruct our colleagues in how to use these selections. At the same time, we do think that it is important to provide an outline of themes that emerge from these readings, especially as they show both the similarities as well as the differences in the experiences of these four ethno-racial communities and the role that religious ideas and practices have played within each. Thus, despite differences in their origins and in their specific experiences in the Americas, the literature produced by persons within the Native American, African American, Asian American, and Latino communities share a number of themes which students and instructors can reflect upon and fruitfully discuss. Among these themes is the experience of being outsiders, of social and cultural "otherness," of dislocation, disorientation, and uprootedness, of turning to tradition and relying upon religious institutions for personal and communal support, of the importance of family and the larger ethnic community, of striving after the recognition of basic rights and of one's human worth, of resistance to assimilation and the struggle against the secularizing influences of modern social and cultural life, and of drawing upon mythologies to strengthen one's sense of self and importance in the world.

Owing to all these difficulties and other personal and social experiences, it is apparent that, for better or for worse, people have turned to religion and to traditional expressions of community life for their remedy. There are those who seek succor within a religious community as well as those who adapt themselves and their traditions to meet the exigencies of life as immigrants, as sojourners or outsiders, in a world where one's experiences are constantly defined by harassment, discrimination, and unrelenting assaults upon one's dignity. But also, and perhaps more importantly, people's experiences have likewise been defined by family, faith, community, friendship, religious mystery, wonder, thankfulness, laughter, and the renewal of the human spirit in the face of adversity.

Of course, while these themes predominate, one can also discern from these readings many lesser and many more contrasting themes. From this quartet of ethno-racial communities, a *discors concordia* or discordant concord can also be heard. The themes and variations that play throughout the pages of this anthology intersect in grand fugal style, and bear witness to the resilience of the human spirit, the signal significance of community, and the central role that religion plays in defining one's place in the world. Religion has been the tie that has bound individuals to their communities, has strengthened those same communities by renewing members' commitments to long-standing traditions, even as those traditions are transformed by the challenges that these and other like communities have had to face.

With respect to the reader selections, originally it had been our hope to include 20–25 readings per section. But, due to obvious page limitations and higher than expected copyright costs, we have had to limit the number of selections in each section to 15 or 20. The only exception is in the section on the African American religious community, in which a number of readings published in the nineteenth and early twentieth centuries are now in the public domain. Despite these constraints, we decided to reprint the selected number of chapters, speeches, essays, and articles in their entirety, unedited, and as they originally appeared in print—coarse language and all. One notable exception is the journal of Mrs. Jarena Lee, which we were obliged to condense by some thirty printed pages. Moreover, because this reader is aimed at highlighting the various types of religious literature produced by members of these four ethno-racial communities, it was soon evident that not all communities produced the same varieties of literature, neither in the types nor in the same quantity. This difference is most evident in the section on the Asian American religious experience, in which, to maintain some balance of material among sections, we have had to include more scholarly and historical types of literature.

Lastly, while this reader is primarily intended to meet the interdisciplinary and human diversity requirements of a specific course at Long Beach State, as the editors of this anthology we are also aware of its potential instructional value outside Southern California. Recognizing that instructors and their students at other colleges and universities throughout the United States might likewise find these selections of interest, we have designed the reader so that it might appeal more generally to faculty teaching similar courses in the fields of history, religious studies, ethnic studies, American studies, rhetoric, and comparative literary studies. To help familiarize readers with the four ethno-racial religious communities that comprise this anthology, we have also provided a brief preface or "foretaste" before each section, along with several suggested questions to help facilitate class discussion. And so that those using this text may be encouraged to explore further the histories and literatures of these communities, at the beginning of each section we have included a list of recommended sources for both instructors and students to consult.

Notwithstanding these limitations, we have sought to create an anthology that allows a variety of voices within these communities to be heard, in many cases for the first time under the same cover. Indeed, this text represents a true celebration of the religious diversity that defines the American nation.

Vox manet—the Voice remains (Ovid).

—Jon R. Stone and Carlos R. Piar
Long Beach, California
December 2006

Sources and Selected General Works in American Religious History

Ahlstrom, Sydney E. *A Religious History of the American People.* New Haven, CT: Yale University Press, 1972.

Albanese, Catherine L. *America: Religions and Religion,* 3rd ed. Belmont, CA: Wadsworth, 1999.

Becker, Penny, and Nancy Eiesland (eds.). *Contemporary American Religion: An Ethnographic Reader.* Walnut Creek, CA: AltaMira Press, 1997.

Butler, Jon, Grant Wacker, and Randall Balmer. *Religion in American Life: A Short History.* NY: Oxford University Press, 2003.

Carroll, Bret E. *The Routledge Historical Atlas of Religions in America.* New York: Routledge, 2000.

Corrigan, John, and Winthrop S. Hudson. *Religion in America,* 7th ed. Upper Saddle River, NJ: Prentice-Hall, 2004.

Ebaugh, Helen, and Janet Chafetz. *Religion and the New Immigrants: Continuities and Adaptations in Immigrant Congregations.* Walnut Creek, CA: AltaMira Press, 2000.

Eck, Diana L. *A New Religious America.* San Francisco: HarperSanFrancisco, 2002.

Gaustad, Edwin S (ed.). *A Documentary History of Religion in America,* 2 vols. Grand Rapids, MI: Eerdmans, 1982–1983.

———. *A Religious History of America,* rev. ed. San Francisco: Harper & Row, 1990.

Goff, Philip, and Paul Harvey (eds.). *Themes in Religion and American Culture.* Chapel Hill, NC: University of North Carolina Press, 2004.

Hackett, David G. (ed.). *Religion and American Culture: A Reader.* New York: Routledge, 1995.

Handy, Robert T. *A History of the Churches in the United States and Canada.* New York: Oxford University Press, 1977.

Hemeyer, Julia Corbett. *Religion in America,* 5th ed. Upper Saddle River, NJ: Prentice-Hall, 2005.

Lippy, Charles H., Robert Choquette, and Stafford Poole. *Christianity Comes to the Americas, 1492–1776.* New York: Paragon House, 1992.

McDannell, Colleen (ed.). *Religions of the United States in Practice,* 2 vols. Princeton, NJ: Princeton University Press, 2001.

Neusner, Jacob (ed.). *World Religions in America,* 3rd ed. Louisville, KY: Westminster/John Knox Press, 2003.

Porterfield, Amanda (ed.). *American Religious History.* Oxford, UK: Blackwell Publishers, 2002.

Warner, R. Stephen, and Judith G. Wittner (eds.). *Gatherings in Diaspora: Religious Communities and the New Immigration.* Philadelphia: Temple University Press, 1998.

Williams, Peter W. (ed.). *Perspectives on American Religion and Culture: A Reader.* Oxford, UK: Blackwell Publishers, 1999.

PART ONE

The Native American Religious Experience

Courtesy of the Library of Congress

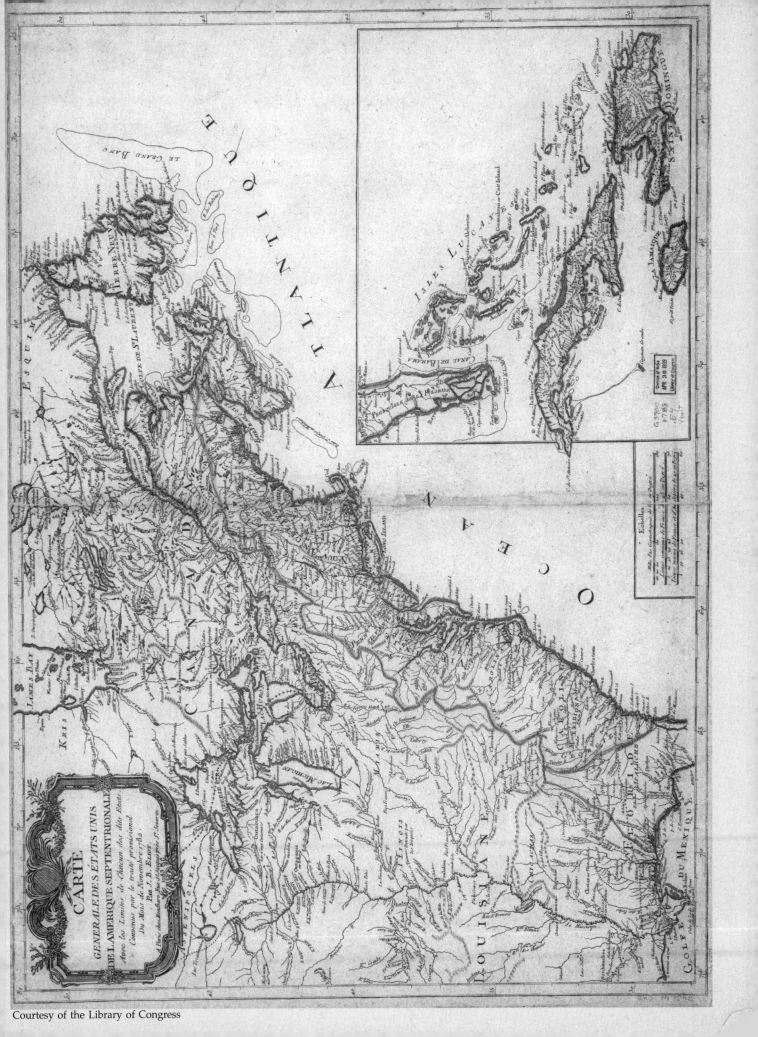

MAP
of the
Indian Tribes
of
NORTH AMERICA
about 1600 A.D.
along the Atlantic;
& about 1800 A.D.
westwardly.

ELEVENTH CENSUS OF THE UNITED STATES.
ROBERT P. PORTER, SUPERINTENDENT.

INDIANS.

MAP OF
LINGUISTIC STOCKS
OF
AMERICAN INDIANS
chiefly within the present limits of the United States.
From Annual Report of Bureau of Ethnology Vol. 7.
by J. W. POWELL.

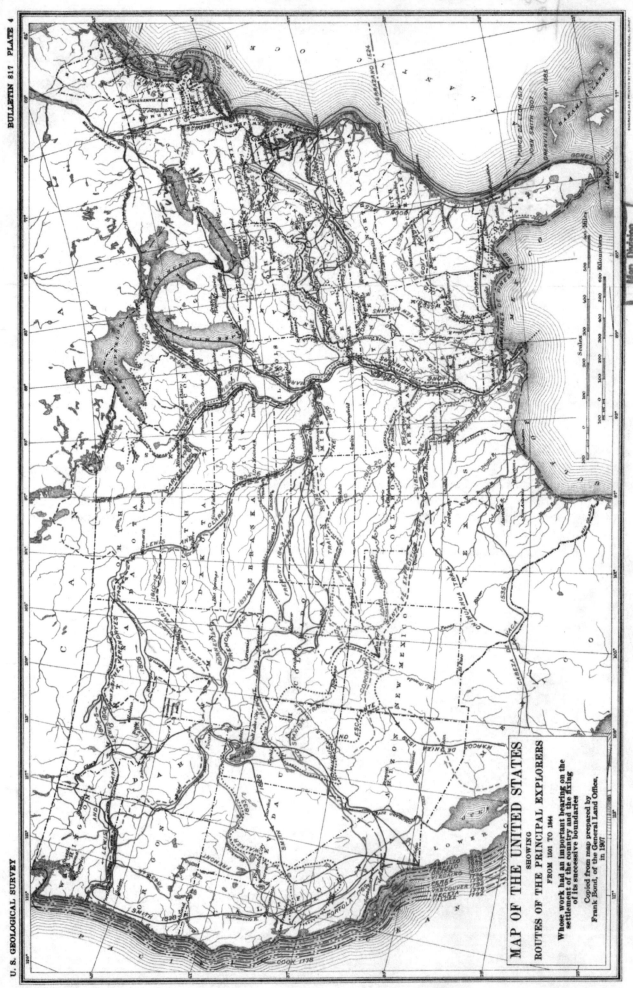

MAP OF THE UNITED STATES
SHOWING
ROUTES OF THE PRINCIPAL EXPLORERS
FROM 1501 TO 1844

Whose work had an important bearing on the
settlement of the country and the fixing
of its successive boundaries

Copied from map prepared by
Frank Bond, of the General Land Office,
in 1907

Readings in Native American Religious Traditions: A Foretaste

Sometime between 30,000 and 40,000 years ago, it is believed that nomadic tribes from Northeast Asia began to migrate into what was later to be called the North American continent. These hunting groups followed game southward, depositing themselves in various locations along the way. While some continued to wander eastward across the continent, by 8000 BCE, others began to settle in Central and South America, building various kinds of shelters, such as wood lodges or rock hewn dwellings, depending upon the terrain. These later tribes developed the means for growing modest amounts of corn, beans, and squash; learned to prepare acorns; dug for roots; and gathered pine nuts, wild grass seeds, and an assortment of berries.

Not surprisingly, the religions of these two types of subsistence tribes—hunting and gathering, and planting and harvesting—developed myths and rituals associated with their primary food source and its growth and renewal. The sacred came to denote that which was essential and indispensable to the maintenance of the tribal community. The religious worldview of these native tribes related closely to the rhythms of nature, viewing all living beings in the natural world as interconnected. True, while for many of these tribes there was a creator deity—such as Wakan Tanka and Tam Apo—all things within that created world were seen as sacred or participating in and sharing divine power. Wolf, bear, coyote, buffalo, eagle, badger, spider, and even rock possessed sacred power and became the subject of folktales and legends passed down through stories— an oral tradition that continues to this day.

Along with stories, Native peoples of North America also incorporated actions such as ritualized dances, many in imitation of the movements of sacred animals and beings. Among them included the sun dance, buffalo dance, and, later, the ghost dance. Many of these dance rituals were borrowed or shared among dozens of tribes living across the northern and central plains and into the Great Basin. In one account of the central role the sun dance continues to play in the ritual life of the Sioux, Tahca Ushte, a medicine man known also as John Fire/Lame Deer, explains that "[t]he sun dance is a prayer and a sacrifice. One does not take part in it voluntarily but as the result of a dream, or a vision." The ritual follows a prescribed process, a process that is both physically and spiritually demanding. As Lame Deer relates further, "[i]nsights gained at such a price are even greater than those that come to a man on a hilltop during his vision quest; they are truly *wakan*— sacred" (Fire & Erdoes 1972:199–200).

Though belonging to a tribal group, individuals within the tribe were encouraged, even expected, to seek power as well as guidance from the spirit world. Typical among these types of rituals of spirit contact was the vision quest. The individual, usually an adolescent boy, would leave the community and set out alone or with other boys his age in search of a spirit guide or other channel of sacred power. During the period of the quest, the boy would open himself to the spirit world, expecting contact from an animal spirit or some other type of spirit that would choose him as worthy of sharing in that spirit's sacred power. According to Sam Gill, among the Ojibway, "visions commonly took the form of a journey into the world of the spirits. During this journey the visionary was shown the path on which his life should proceed. He was associated with one or more spirit beings who would serve as his guardians and protectors throughout life" (2005:72). But among other native tribes, vision quests were not limited only to puberty rituals. Åke Hultkrantz notes that among the Plains Indians, "warriors repeatedly withdrew into the wilderness to seek spirits" and "may therefore have a variety of guardian spirits, each of which is good for a different purpose" (1987:31).

The arrival of European settlers in the sixteenth and seventeenth centuries proved disruptive to thousands of years of cultural continuity. Adaptation by native tribes became difficult, even as Christian missionaries revised traditions and, in many cases, eradicated longstanding rituals and the mythologies that informed them. The story of the Native encounter with Europeans—the Spanish, French, English, and others—can be summarized in one word: loss. It was not so much a clash of peoples as of religions and ways of life. The Native view of land as sacred did not square with the Western Christian belief in a fallen world—a world to be conquered, dominated, and eventually redeemed.

In this section of readings, we have selected varying types of literature that show these native traditions likely before and after contact with European ideas. The first several readings are of tribal tales taken from various peoples within North America, such as Plains Indians, Pueblo Indians, and those dwelling in the northern woodlands. Some of these tales have been passed down through oral repetition and elaboration, others, notably from the southern Ojibway, have been preserved on birch bark scrolls. For comparative purposes, we have also included a less formal mid-twentieth-century rendition of a creation myth, as recorded by the unconventional anthropologist, Jaime de Angulo.

The history of Native peoples since the mid-twentieth century has been one of recovery of native traditions, of renewed connections to community, and of the rediscovery of lost identity. Thus we have readings that document this aspect of Native Indian history as well. For instance, the middle three selections record issues of religious identity as presented in an autobiographical recollection (Black Elk) and two fictional reflections on the importance of native traditions to the continuing survival of Native peoples. The last four selections document more recent attempts by Native peoples to reclaim lost traditions, even among those embracing the teachings of Christ. The late Vine Deloria, Jr., himself a Christian theologian, notes that "the credal [sic] rhetoric of Christianity filled the vacuum it had created by its redefinition of religion as a commodity to be controlled." But, despite this, "Indian beliefs have always retained the capacity to return from their exile because they have always related to the Indian's deepest concern" (1969:102). During the 1960s, Deloria began to notice that "[t]he impotence and irrelevancy of the Christian message has meant a return to traditional religion by Indian people. Tribal religions are making a strong comeback on most reservations" (1969:112). He cites the sun dance, mentioned above, as one such example, the growing membership in the Native American Church as another. In response, Deloria calls upon his fellow tribesmen and women to "return to their older religions wherever possible," believing that "an Indian version of Christianity could do much for our society" (1969:124).

Not all individuals were comfortable abandoning long-held Christian beliefs in favor of returning to native religious practices. In the selection by Laverne Jacobs, one finds an Ojibway Christian struggling over the problem of holding dual identities. In this case the cognitive rub is over his desire to participate in the sweat lodge ceremony. With Jacobs, one discovers Native peoples being awakened to long dormant traditions, and finding that Christianity and Native religious traditions are not necessarily at odds, but, as Jacobs came to see it, "the sounds of many voices . . . together sing the praises of God the Creator and Jesus the Son in one great symphony of creation. In the midst of that glorious sound rings the phrase 'this is you—both Native and Christian.' The meaning of that phrase will be a lifelong dialogue with self" (Jacobs, in Treat 1997:240).

Thus, in all these readings, one gains a greater understanding, not only of the heroic struggles of the Native peoples of North America, but of the resilience of their religious and cultural traditions.

Sources and Selected Works in Native American History, Literature, and Religions

[*indicates works of fiction]

Archambault, Marie Therese, Mark G. Thiel, and Christopher Vecsey (eds.). *The Crossing of Two Roads: Being Catholic and Native in the United States.* Maryknoll, NY: Orbis Books, 2003.

Blaisdell, Bob (ed.). *Great Speeches by Native Americans.* New York: Dover Publications, 2000.

Brown, Joseph Epes. *The Spiritual Legacy of the American Indian.* New York: Crossroad, 1982.

Calloway, Colin G. *First Peoples: A Documentary Survey of American Indian History,* 2nd ed. New York: Bedford/St. Martin's Press, 2004.

Capps, Walter Holden (ed.). *Seeing with a Native Eye: Essays on Native American Religion.* San Francisco: Harper & Row, 1976.

Carrasco, Davíd. *Religions of Meso-America.* San Francisco: Harper & Row, 1990.

Cornell, Stephen. *The Return of the Native: American Indian Political Resurgence.* New York: Oxford University Press, 1990.

*Craven, Margaret. *I Heard the Owl Call My Name.* Garden City, NY: Doubleday & Co., 1973.

Crawford, Suzanne. *Native American Religious Traditions.* Upper Saddle River, NJ: Prentice Hall, 2006.

*Crow Dog, Mary. *Lakota Woman.* New York: Harper & Row, 1990.

Deloria, Philip J., and Neal Salisbury (eds.). *A Companion to American Indian History.* Oxford, UK: Blackwell Publishing, 2004.

Deloria, Vine, Jr. *Custer Died for Your Sins: An Indian Manifesto.* New York: Macmillan, 1969.

_____. *For This Land: Writings on Religion in America.* New York: Routledge, 1999.

_____. *God Is Red: A Native View of Religion.* New York: Dell Publishing Co., 1973.

DeMallie, Raymond J., and Douglas R. Parks (eds.). *Sioux Indian Religion: Tradition and Innovation.* Norman, OK: University of Oklahoma Press, 1989.

Dillehay, Thomas D. *The Settlement of the Americas: A New Prehistory.* New York: Basic Books, 2000.

*Dorris, Michael. *A Yellow Raft in Blue Water.* New York: Warner Books, 1988.

Erdoes, Richard, and Alfonso Ortiz (eds.). *American Indian Myths and Legends.* New York: Pantheon Books, 1984.

_____ (ed.). *American Indian Trickster Tales.* New York: Penguin Books, 1998.

*Erdrich, Louise. *Love Medicine.* New York: Bantam, 1987.

*_____. *Tracks.* New York: Henry Holt & Co., 1988.

Feldmann, Susan (ed.). *The Storytelling Stone: Traditional Native American Myths and Tales.* New York: Dell Publishing, 1965.

Forbes, Jack D. *Native Americans of California and Nevada,* rev. ed. Happy Camp, CA: Naturegraph Publishers, 1982.

Gill, Sam. *Native America Religions,* 2nd ed. Belmont, CA: Wadsworth, 2005.

Grounds, Richard A., George E. Tinker, and David E. Wilkins (eds.). *Native Voices: American Indian Identity and Resistance.* Lawrence, KS: University of Kansas Press, 2003.

Gutiérrez, Ramón A. *When Jesus Came, the Corn Mothers Went Away: Marriage, Sexuality, and Power in New Mexico, 1500–1846.* Stanford, CA: Stanford University Press, 1991.

Hagan, William. *American Indians,* 3rd ed. Chicago: The University of Chicago Press, 1993.

Harrod, Howard L. *Becoming and Remaining a People: Native American Religions on the Northern Plains.* Tucson, AZ: University of Arizona Press, 1995.

_____. *Renewing the World: Plains Indian Religion and Morality.* Tucson, AZ: University of Arizona Press, 1987.

Hausman, Gerald. *Tunkashila: From the Birth of Turtle Island to the Blood of Wounded Knee.* New York: St. Martin's Press, 1993.

Heizer, Robert F., and M.A. Whipple (eds.). *The California Indians: A Source Book,* 2nd ed., rev. & enl. Berkeley, CA: University of California Press, 1972.

Hirschfelder, Arlene B., and Paulette Molin. *Encyclopedia of Native American Religions: An Introduction,* updated ed. New York: Facts on File, 2001.

Holler, Clyde. *Black Elk's Religion: The Sun Dance and Lakota Catholicism.* Syracuse, NY: Syracuse University Press, 1995.

Hoxie, Frederick E., Peter C. Mancall, and James H. Merrell (eds.). *American Nations: Encounters in Indian Country, 1850 to the Present.* New York: Routledge, 2001.

Hultkrantz, Åke. *Native Religions of North America.* San Francisco: Harper & Row, 1987.

_____. *The Religions of the American Indians.* Berkeley, CA: University of California Press, 1979.

Jackson, Robert H., and Edward Castillo. *Indians, Franciscans, and Spanish Colonization: The Impact of the Mission System on California Indians.* Albuquerque, NM: University of New Mexico Press, 1996.

Josephy, Alvin M., Jr. (ed.). *America in 1492: The World of the Indian Peoples Before the Arrival of Columbus.* New York: Vintage Books, 1993.

_____. *500 Nations: An Illustrated History of North American Indians.* New York: Alfred A. Knopf, 1994.

Kehoe, Alice Beck. *The Ghost Dance: Ethnohistory and Revitalization,* 2nd ed. Long Grove, IL: Waveland Press, 2006.

Kidwell, Clara Sue, Homer Noley, and George E. Tinker. *A Native American Theology.* Maryknoll, NY: Orbis Books, 2001.

Fire, John/Lame Deer, and Richard Erdoes. *Lame Deer Seeker of Visions.* New York: Simon and Schuster, 1972.

Kroeber, Karl (ed.). *Native American Storytelling: A Reader of Myths and Legends.* Oxford, UK: Blackwell Publishing, 2004.

Leeming, David, and Jake Page. *The Mythology of Native North America.* Norman, OK: University of Oklahoma Press, 1998.

Lobo, Susan, and Kurt Peters. *American Indians and the Urban Experience.* Walnut Creek, CA: AltaMira Press, 2001.

Lobo, Susan, and Steve Talbot (eds.). *Native American Voices: A Reader,* 2nd ed. Upper Saddle River, NJ: Prentice Hall, 2001.

Lopez, Barry. *Giving Birth to Thunder, Sleeping with His Daughter: Coyote Builds North America.* New York: Avon Books, 1990.

Loftin, John D. *Religion and Hopi Life in the Twentieth Century.* Bloomington, IN: Indiana University Press, 1991.

Mancall, Peter C., and James H. Merrell (eds.). *American Encounters: Natives and Newcomers from European Contact to Indian Removal.* New York: Routledge, 2000.

Mintz, Steven (ed.). *Native American Voices: A History and Anthology,* 2nd ed., enl. St. James, NY: Brandywine Press, 2000.

Mooney, James. *The Ghost-Dance Religion and Wounded Knee.* New York: Dover Publications, 1973 [reprint of 1896 edition].

Nabokov, Peter (ed.). *Native American Testimony: A Chronicle of Indian-White Relations from Prophecy to the Present, 1492–1992.* New York: Penguin Books, 1992.

Nagel, Joane. *American Indian Ethnic Renewal: Red Power and the Resurgence of Identity and Culture.* New York: Oxford University Press, 1997.

Neihardt, John G. *Black Elk Speaks.* Lincoln, NE: University of Nebraska Press, 1961.

Niatum, Duane (ed.). *Harper's Anthology of Twentieth Century Native American Poetry.* San Francisco: Harper & Row, 1988.

Nies, Judith. *Native American History: A Chronology of a Culture's Vast Achievements and Their Links to World Events.* New York: Ballantine Books, 1996.

Olson, James S., and Raymond Wilson. *Native Americans in the Twentieth Century.* Urbana, IL: University of Illinois Press, 1986.

Ostler, Jeffrey. *The Plains Sioux and U.S. Colonialism from Lewis and Clark to Wounded Knee.* New York: Cambridge University Press, 2004.

Page, Jake. *In the Hands of the Great Spirit: The 20,000-Year History of American Indians.* New York: The Free Press, 2003.

Parman, Donald L. *Indians and the American West in the Twentieth Century.* Bloomington, IN: Indiana University Press, 1994.

Porter, Joy, and Kenneth M. Roemer (eds.). *The Cambridge Companion to Native American Literature.* New York: Cambridge University Press, 2005.

Powell, Joseph F. *The First Americans: Race, Evolution and the Origin of Native Americans.* Cambridge, UK: Cambridge University Press, 2005.

Powers, William K. *Oglala Religion.* Lincoln, NE: University of Nebraska Press, 1977.

———. *Sacred Language: The Nature of Supernatural Discourse in Lakota.* Norman, OK: University of Oklahoma Press, 1992.

Pritzker, Barry M. *A Native American Encyclopedia: History, Culture, and Peoples.* New York: Oxford University Press, 2000.

Rawls, James J. *Indians of California: The Changing Image.* Norman, OK: University of Oklahoma Press, 1984.

Richter, Daniel K. *Facing East from Indian Country: A Native History of Early America.* Cambridge, MA: Harvard University Press, 2003.

Rushforth, Scott, and Steadman Upham. *A Hopi Social History.* Austin, TX: University of Texas Press, 1992.

*Silko, Leslie Ann. *Ceremony.* New York: Penguin Books, 1986.

Smoak, Gregory E. *Ghost Dances and Identity: Prophetic Religion and American Indian Ethnogenesis in the Nineteenth Century.* Berkeley, CA: University of California Press, 2005.

Stewart, Omer C. *Peyote Religion: A History.* Norman, OK: University of Oklahoma Press, 1987.

Sullivan, Lawrence E. (ed.). *Native American Religions: North America.* New York: Macmillan Publishing Co., 1989.

Tinker, George E. *Missionary Conquest: The Gospel and Native American Cultural Genocide.* Minneapolis, MN: Augsburg Fortress, 1993.

Treat, James (ed.). *Native and Christian: Indigenous Voices on Religious Identity in the United States and Canada.* New York: Routledge, 1995.

Tyler, Hamilton A. *Pueblo Gods and Myths.* Norman, OK: University of Oklahoma Press, 1964.

Underhill, Ruth M. *Red Man's Religion.* Chicago: The University of Chicago Press, 1965.

Utter, Jack. *American Indians: Answers to Today's Questions,* 2nd ed. Norman, OK: University of Oklahoma Press, 2001.

Weaver, Jace (ed.). *Native American Religious Identity.* Maryknoll, NY: Orbis Books, 1998.

Wilson, James. *The Earth Shall Weep: A History of Native America.* New York: Grove Press, 2000.

Some Suggested Questions for Discussion

1. What kinds of understandings of the world and of humanity's relation to it does one discover in the myths and tales passed down within Native American traditions? In what noticeable ways do these myths and tales differ from Plains Indians to Woodlands Indians to Pueblo Indians?

2. Based on these readings, speculate on the place that dreams and visions hold in Native American religious traditions. How do dreams and visions, and their meaning to the individual and the community, compare across time and across tribal groups?

3. Reservation life appears to have exerted a secularizing influence, even as Christianity, according to Vine Deloria, Jr., "has proved to be a disintegrating force," in the life of Native Americans. What purpose do rituals and other traditional ceremonies appear to serve in reconnecting Native peoples to their ancestral past? What is it about these traditions that by maintaining them Native peoples experience healing and wholeness in their lives?

4. According to many writing within Native traditions, those continuing to embrace Christianity betray their native heritage, while to others, adhering to Christianity does not constitute a betrayal but a fulfillment of their spiritual aspirations. A question one might ask is how do Native peoples reconcile their traditional beliefs and religious practices with their personal commitment to Christianity? What might be meant by the phrase "life long dialogue with self" as offered in the essay by Laverne Jacobs?

5. In the fictional literature in this section, one finds women filling central roles as healers as well as primary keepers of tradition. What additional roles do women appear to play? As for men, if not healers or keepers of tradition, then what role do they play in these stories?

Coyote Steals the Sun and Moon

[Zuni]

Coyote is a bad hunter who never kills anything. Once he watched Eagle hunting rabbits, catching one after another—more rabbits than he could eat. Coyote thought, "I'll team up with Eagle so I can have enough meat." Coyote is always up to something.

"Friend," Coyote said to Eagle, "we should hunt together. Two can catch more than one."

"Why not?" Eagle said, and so they began to hunt in partnership. Eagle caught many rabbits, but all Coyote caught was some little bugs.

At this time the world was still dark; the sun and moon had not yet been put in the sky. "Friend," Coyote said to Eagle, "no wonder I can't catch anything; I can't see. Do you know where we can get some light?"

"You're right, friend, there should be some light," Eagle said. "I think there's a little toward the west. Let's try and find it."

And so they went looking for the sun and moon. They came to a big river, which Eagle flew over. Coyote swam, and swallowed so much water that he almost drowned. He crawled out with his fur full of mud, and Eagle asked, "Why don't you fly like me?"

"You have wings, I just have hair," Coyote said. "I can't fly without feathers."

At last they came to a pueblo, where the Kachinas happened to be dancing. The people invited Eagle and Coyote to sit down and have something to eat while they watched the sacred dances. Seeing the power of the Kachinas, Eagle said, "I believe these are the people who have light."

Coyote, who had been looking all around, pointed out two boxes, one large and one small, that the people opened whenever they wanted light. To produce a lot of light, they opened the lid of the big box, which contained the sun. For less light they opened the small box, which held the moon.

Coyote nudged Eagle. "Friend, did you see that? They have all the light we need in the big box. Let's steal it."

"You always want to steal and rob. I say we should just borrow it."

"They won't lend it to us."

"You may be right," said Eagle. "Let's wait till they finish dancing and then steal it."

After a while the Kachinas went home to sleep, and Eagle scooped up the large box and flew off. Coyote ran along trying to keep up, panting, his tongue hanging out. Soon he yelled up to Eagle, "Ho, friend, let me carry the box a little way."

"No, no," said Eagle, "you never do anything right."

He flew on, and Coyote ran after him. After a while Coyote shouted again: "Friend, you're my chief, and it's not right for you to carry the box; people will call me lazy. Let me have it."

"No, no, you always mess everything up." And Eagle flew on and Coyote ran along.

So it went for a stretch, and then Coyote started again. "Ho, friend, it isn't right for you to do this. What will people think of you and me?"

"I don't care what people think. I'm going to carry this box."

Again Eagle flew on and again Coyote ran after him. Finally Coyote begged for the fourth time: "Let me carry it. You're the chief, and I'm just Coyote. Let me carry it."

Eagle couldn't stand any more pestering. Also, Coyote had asked him four times, and if someone asks four times, you better give him what he wants. Eagle said, "Since you won't let up on me, go ahead and carry the box for a while. But promise not to open it."

"Oh, sure, oh yes, I promise." They went on as before, but now Coyote had the box. Soon Eagle was far ahead, and Coyote lagged behind a hill where Eagle couldn't see him. "I wonder what the light looks like, inside there," he said to himself. "Why shouldn't I take a peek? Probably there's something extra in the box, something good that Eagle wants to keep to himself."

And Coyote opened the lid. Now, not only was the sun inside, but the moon also. Eagle had put them both together, thinking that it would be easier to carry one box than two.

As soon as Coyote opened the lid, the moon escaped, flying high into the sky. At once all the plants shriveled up and turned brown. Just as quickly, all the leaves fell off the trees, and it was winter. Trying to catch the moon and put it back in the box, Coyote ran in pursuit as it skipped away from him. Meanwhile the sun flew out and rose into the sky. It drifted far away, and the peaches, squashes, and melons shriveled up with cold.

Eagle turned and flew back to see what had delayed Coyote, "You fool! Look what you've done!" he said. "You let the sun and moon escape, and now it's cold." Indeed, it began to snow, and Coyote shivered. "Now your teeth are chattering," Eagle said, "and it's your fault that cold has come into the world."

It's true. If it weren't for Coyote's curiosity and mischief making, we wouldn't have winter; we could enjoy summer all the time.

—Based on a story reported by Ruth Benedict in 1935.

Coyote, Iktome, and the Rock

[White River Sioux]

Coyote was walking with his friend Iktome. Along their path stood Iya, the rock. This was not just any rock; it was special. It had those spidery lines of green moss all over it, the kind that tell a story. Iya had power.

Coyote said: "Why, this is a nice-looking rock. I think it has power." Coyote took off the thick blanket he was wearing and put it on the rock. "Here, Iya, take this as a present. Take this blanket, friend rock, to keep you from freezing. You must feel cold."

"Wow, a giveaway!" said Iktome. "You sure are in a giving mood today, friend."

"Ah, it's nothing. I'm always giving things away. Iya looks real nice in my blanket."

"His blanket, now," said Iktome.

The two friends went on. Pretty soon a cold rain started. The rain turned to hail. The hail turned to slush. Coyote and Iktome took refuge in a cave, which was cold and wet. Iktome was all right; he had his thick buffalo robe. Coyote had only his shirt, and he was shivering. He was freezing. His teeth were chattering.

"*Kola,* friend of mine," Coyote said to Iktome, "go back and get me my fine blanket. I need it, and that rock has no use for it. He's been getting along without a blanket for ages. Hurry; I'm freezing!"

Iktome went back to Iya, saying: "Can I have that blanket back, please?"

The rock said: "No, I like it. What is given is given."

Iktome returned and told Coyote: "He won't give it back."

"That no-good, ungrateful rock!" said Coyote. "Has he paid for the blanket? Has he worked for it? I'll go get it myself."

"Friend," said Iktome, "Tunka, Iya, the rock——there's a lot of power there! Maybe you should let him keep it."

"Are you crazy? This is an expensive blanket of many colors and great thickness. I'll go talk to him."

Coyote went back and told Iya: "Hey, rock! What's the meaning of this? What do you need a blanket for? Let me have it back right now!"

"No," said the rock, "what is given is given."

"You're a bad rock! Don't you care that I'm freezing to death? That I'll catch a cold?" Coyote jerked the blanket away from Iya and put it on. "So there; that's the end of it."

"By no means the end," said the rock.

Coyote went back to the cave. The rain and hail stopped and the sun came out again, so Coyote and Iktome sat before the cave, sunning themselves, eating pemmican, and fry-bread and *wojapi,* berry soup. After eating, they took out their pipes and had a smoke.

All of a sudden Iktome said: "What's that noise?"

"What noise? I don't hear anything."

"A crashing, a rumble far off."

"Yes, friend, I hear it now."

"Friend Coyote, it's getting stronger and nearer, like thunder or an earthquake."

"It is rather strong and loud. I wonder what it can be."

"I have a pretty good idea, friend," said Iktome.

Then they saw the great rock. It was Iya, rolling, thundering, crashing upon them.

"Friend, let's run for it!" cried Iktome; "Iya means to kill us!"

The two ran as fast as they could while the rock rolled after them, coming closer and closer.

"Friend, let's swim the river. The rock is so heavy, he sure can't swim!" cried Iktome. So they swam the river, but Iya, the great rock, also swam over the river as if he had been made of wood.

"Friend, into the timber, among the big trees," cried Coyote. "That big rock surely can't get through this thick forest." They ran among the trees, but the huge Iya came rolling along after them, shivering and splintering the big pines to pieces, left and right.

The two came out onto the flats. "Oh! Oh!" cried Iktome, Spider Man. "Friend Coyote, this is really not my quarrel. I just remembered, I have pressing business to attend to. So long!" Iktome rolled himself into a tiny ball and became a spider. He disappeared into a mousehole.

Coyote ran on and on, the big rock thundering close at his heels. Then Iya, the big rock, rolled right over Coyote, flattening him out altogether.

Iya took the blanket and rolled back to his own place, saying: "So there!"

A *wasichu* rancher riding along saw Coyote lying there all flattened out. "What a nice rug!" said the rancher, picking Coyote up, and he took the rug home.

The rancher put Coyote right in front of his fireplace. Whenever Coyote is killed, he can make himself come to life again, but it took him the whole night to puff himself up into his usual shape. In the morning the rancher's wife told her husband: "I just saw your rug running away."

Friends, hear this: always be generous in heart. If you have something to give, give it forever.

—Told by Jenny Leading Cloud in White River, Rosebud
Indian Reservation, South Dakota, 1967.
Recorded by Richard Erdoes.

Coyote and the Origin of Death

[CADDO]

In the beginning of this world, there was no such thing as death. Everybody continued to live until there were so many people that the earth had no room for any more. The chiefs held a council to determine what to do. One man rose and said he thought it would be a good plan to have the people die and be gone for a little while, and then return.

As soon as he sat down, Coyote jumped up and said he thought people ought to die forever. He pointed out that this little world is not large enough to hold all of the people, and that if the people who died came back to life, there would not be food enough for all.

All the other men objected. They said that they did not want their friends and relatives to die and be gone forever, for then they would grieve and worry and there would be no happiness in the world. Everyone except Coyote decided to have people die and be gone for a little while, and then come back to life again.

The medicine men built a large grass house facing the east. When they had completed it, they called the men of the tribe together and told them that people who died would be restored to life in the medicine house. The chief medicine man explained that they would sing a song calling the spirit of the dead to the grass house. When the spirit came, they would restore it to life. All the people were glad, because they were anxious for the dead to come and live with them again.

When the first man died, the medicine men assembled in the grass house and sang. In about ten days a whirlwind blew from the west and circled about the grass house. Coyote saw it, and as the whirlwind was about to enter the house, he closed the door. The spirit of the whirlwind, finding the door closed, whirled on by. In this way Coyote made death eternal, and from that time on, people grieved over their dead and were unhappy.

Now whenever anyone meets a whirlwind or hears the wind whistle, he says: "Someone is wandering about." Ever since Coyote closed the door, the spirits of the dead have wandered over the earth trying to find some place to go, until at last they discovered the road to the spirit land.

Coyote ran away and never came back, for when he saw what he had done, he was afraid. Ever after that, he has run from one place to another, always looking back first over one shoulder and then over the other to see if anyone is pursuing him. And ever since then he has been starving, for no one will give him anything to eat.

—From a tale reported by George A. Dorsey in 1905.

The Creation of Man
(Second Version)

MORRIS EDWARD OPLER

In the beginning the dog was just like a Hactcin in appearance. This was because the Hactcin made everything. He was listless, however, and didn't do anything.

And Hactcin noticed this and spoke to him. He said, "Why don't you do something? Why don't you work?"

"I don't care to work. I'm too lazy. I'd better turn to the form of a dog I guess. Let my hands be round."

At first his hands were like ours, but he didn't use them and just stayed home so they became round.

When Hactcin made the dog in his present shape he took some of the yellow from the afterglow of the sunset and put it above each eye. And he took some of the white of the morning glow and put it on each paw. This was a sign that the dog would protect people.

And so today in the girl's ceremony, the girl has yellow ochre on her face and the boy who dances with her has white paint over his face.

Hactcin spoke to the dog and asked, "Where are you going to stay now?"

"Oh, you can make some people so I will have companions."

Hactcin asked, "What is the idea you have in mind? I never thought you would say a thing like that."

So the Hactcin lay down at a smooth place. He said to the dog, "Now draw a line around my feet and body. Trace my outline with your paw." So the Hactcin lay with his face down and his arms outstretched, and the dog drew his outline.

Then both got up. Hactcin said to the dog, "Go a little further on and do not look back yet."

The dog went on for a short distance.

"Now you can turn and look."

Dog looked back. "Someone is lying where you were, Grandfather," he said.

Hactcin said, "Face the other way and walk off again."

Dog did so.

"Now turn around."

The dog did so.

Someone was arising from the ground, bracing himself with his hands and knees.

"Grandfather," said Dog, "someone is on his hands and knees at the place where you were lying."

Hactcin said, "Turn and walk away again."

Dog did so. Then he was told to look once more. When he looked he saw a man sitting up.

"Grandfather, someone is sitting up!" he cried. There were surprise and happiness in his voice.

But Hactcin only said, "Turn once more and walk away."

He did so again.

"Turn around now and look," he was told.

He did so and cried out in astonishment and delight, "My grandfather, he is sitting up and moving around!"

Then Hactcin said, "Now come. We will go and see him."

They came to the man. He was sitting facing the east. Hactcin first faced him from the east. Then he went to the south, the west, and the north of him and then faced him again from the east. Then Hactcin went around

"The Creation of Man", *The Myths and Tales of the Jicarillo Apache Indians*, by Morris Edward Opler, New York: American Folk-lore Society, 1938, in the series: Memoirs of the American Folklore Society, v. 31. Reprinted by permission of American Folklore Society.

to this man's back, and after motioning four times lifted him to his feet. Then he went around his body clockwise and returned in front of him at the east again.

Then Hactcin addressed the man. "You must watch me. I am going to take four steps, moving my right foot first. As I do it you must do it too."

Hactcin did walk this way and the man followed.

"Now," said Hactcin, "let's run," and with Hactcin leading, the two ran. They ran to the east and back again in a clockwise manner. That is why they run like that in the girl's puberty rite.[1] They came back to the starting place.

Then Hactcin shouted into the ear of the man four times, twice from the right side and twice from the left and asked, "Did you hear that?" Because of this the old woman shouts into the ear of the girl in the puberty rite four times from the right side, so that the girl will have good hearing always.

But the man could not yet speak. Hactcin stood before him. Four times he said to the man, "Talk, talk, talk, talk," and then the man spoke. "Laugh, laugh, laugh, laugh," he said, and the fourth time the man laughed. "Now shout, shout, shout, shout," Hactcin told him, and the fourth time it was said the man shouted.

"Now you are ready to live around here."

The dog was very happy. He jumped at the man and ran back and forth just as dogs do now when they are glad to see you.

The dog was very happy, but the man, with no one but the dog to talk to, soon grew lonesome.

He told Hactcin the cause of his sadness and Hactcin thought about it. Finally Hactcin resolved to make a woman for him. So he told the man to lie down on the ground, face downward with arms and legs extended. The man did so. Then Hactcin traced his outline on the ground and bade him rise. Then Hactcin had the man do exactly what he had had the dog do when he had been making the man. He had the man face the other way and walk to the east four times while the figure he had drawn successively rose to its knees, sat up, and moved. Then Hactcin lifted this figure in the same manner and taught it to speak, hear, laugh, shout, and walk and run. Then Hactcin was satisfied and sent Ancestral Man and Ancestral Woman off together.

These two people who had been created also came to Black Hactcin and asked, "What are we to eat? Where shall we live?"

He showed them all the roots and leaves and plants. "These are your foods," he told them.

They went to taste all that he pointed out. They tasted them all and found them good.

Then he took them out and showed them the animals. "Those who are cloven-footed will be your meat."

In those days the animals were very gentle, very mild. They all stayed around there.[2]

He told them, "When you kill the animal you must save the hide and use it for clothes."

After that they did so.

"Where shall we put our heads?"

"Right on the earth. Stay anywhere you like to be. There is your place. There is your home."

That is why the Jicarilla Apache went from place to place. They would come to a desirable place and say, "This is pretty; let's stay here." Then they would go on to some other place later.

In those days the two people had no hair on their bodies or on their faces. The man had no moustache.

Hactcin told them the first day, "You must not let water touch your lips until I give you permission." He gave them tubes of reed and told them to use these. For three days they drank from the reeds as they were told.

The fourth day they grew impatient. It took too long to drink water that way, they thought. The man put his reed aside and lay down and drank from the stream. The front of his face touched the water and after that hair grew on his face. The woman had just stood there, however. Black Hactcin had told them what would happen if they disobeyed. The woman thought, "It would not look well for a woman to have hair on her face," so she did not do as her husband did.

Immediately the hair grew out on the man's face. The girl started to get angry because her husband looked so strange. In her rage she dashed some water under her armpits and around her pubic region. Hair grew at once in those places.

When the man saw this he thought, "I'd better do the same," and he splashed water on himself at those places too and hair grew there.

Hactcin came then and spoke to them. "Don't do that." He told the man, "Go up in the woods and find two branches which have been rubbed against each other by the wind and have become smooth. Rub your face with that."

To the woman he said, "Rub your face with abalone."

Now at the time of the girl's puberty rite when the girl acts as White-Shell Woman and the boy as Child-of-the-Water, they do this to themselves and then they do not get much body hair. It is not part of the ceremony. The young people do it by themselves.

A few generations passed. The animals, birds, and people increased, but they all lived in darkness. They had no sun as yet. The people were used to it, and because they were used to it they could see things. Still, one could not see objects clearly. But they did not have any hard times. All the animals were friendly. They had no enemies. If they wanted something to eat, it was present.

But Black Hactcin didn't think it was right. He sent for White Hactcin. They came together and talked of what they were going to do. They sent for a male eagle's white tail feather and a female eagle's spotted tail feather. And they sent for one tail feather of the blue jay too and for the yellow tail feather of the western tanager.

One mountain stretched upward. All around it lived the people. The Hactcin worked together. At the east side of the mountain, resting against it, they put the feather of the white male eagle. On the south side they put the blue feather, on the west the yellow feather, and on the north side the feather of the spotted female eaglet.[3]

The white feather sent a long beam of white light to the east. Because of the blue feather, everything looked blue to the south. To the west all looked yellow because of the yellow light of the feather. And on the north side the feather of the female eagle gave a flickering light, sometimes light and sometimes shadow.

The people kept gathering to the east and living there because of the greater light in that direction. On the blue side the light was not so clear. Just a few people liked that place and stayed over there. And for the same reason very few were living on the west and north sides.

Down in the underworld there were many brooks and streams. The people had all kinds of water.

Notes

1. For an account of the girl's puberty rite cf. p. 87.

2. In the Jicarilla myths the animals are represented as being extraordinarily tame in the beginning. For an account of how animals became wild see p. 215 and pp. 259–260.

3. The usual color-directional association, used whenever the materials or objects to which reference is made will permit is: east, black; south, blue; west, yellow; and north, glittering. Spotted or white is sometimes substituted for glittering and is associated with the north. The circuit is clockwise, beginning with the east. The association of east with white, as occurs in this passage, is unusual.

The Creation and Loss of the Sun and Moon

MORRIS EDWARD OPLER

Holy Boy was not satisfied. He thought there should be more light. By himself he started to make a sun. He tried hard in many ways. The first time he tried by himself. He used all kinds of specular iron ore and pollen. The result was not very satisfactory though. He used abalone too, but that didn't work any better. He tried turquoise and red beads and white beads, but without success. But he kept on. He tried over and over.

One time when he was at work the little whirlwind came. The little wind asked him, "What are you doing here all by yourself? You never go outside. I have not seen you for a long time."

Holy Boy said, "I have not been doing anything. I've stayed right here."

Wind said, "There must be some reason that you stay home."

Holy Boy said, "Yes, there is. I am making a sun. But it is not very bright."

Wind said to him, "There is a man who has a sun. Why don't you go to him?"

"Who is he?"

"Oh, it is White Hactcin. You go and ask him. But don't tell him who told you."[1]

So Holy Boy went to White Hactcin. He went into the home of White Hactcin.

"What do you want?" asked White Hactcin. "There must be some reason for your coming here. You never come to visit with us. What do you want, my grandson?"

Holy Boy said, "I came here to ask you for the sun."

White Hactcin said, "How do you know I have it? Who told you? No one could have seen that I have that sun."

White Hactcin sat there. He tried to think who could have seen it and reported it. Then he remembered that there was one who came often to his house. It was the wind.

"I believe it was Wind who told you I have the sun."

Holy Boy didn't mention Wind's name. He just continued to ask for the sun.

White Hactcin said then, "Yes, I have it." He picked up his bag and looked into it. He found it and he took it out. It was a very small sun and hard to see. It was just like the present sun, but it was no bigger than a pin head. He gave it to Holy Boy.

"This is for daylight," White Hactcin said.

Wind had told Holy Boy when he had talked to him, "There is a moon too, but another person has it. Black Hactcin has it.[2] You can get the moon from him."

So now Holy Boy went over to Black Hactcin.

"What do you want, my grandson?"[3] asked Black Hactcin. "You never came to see me before. There must be some reason."

"Yes, I have come for the night light. I have come for the moon."

"How do you know I have it? Who told you I have it?"

Black Hactcin thought a while. "I believe that little wind told you," he said. "He's the only one who comes to see me often." So he looked in his bag and found it. He gave it to Holy Boy. It was a tiny one too.

Then he said, "You must go back and put it on a deerskin which has no holes.[4] First make a circle to represent the sun and one for the moon too. Paint them with pollen and other coloring matter.

Then put the sun that you have been given right in the center of the sun that you make with pollen. Make a painting of the moon in the same way with specular iron ore on the deerskin and put this moon that I have

"The Creation and Loss of the Sun and Moon", *Myths and Tales of the Jicarillo Apache Indians*, by Morris Edward Opler, New York: American Folk-lore Society, 1938, in the series: Memoirs of the American Folklore Society, v. 31. Reprinted by permission of American Folklore Society.

given you exactly in the center of it.[5] When you get ready perhaps White Hactcin and I will come over, and Red Boy will come too.[6] There will be four of us.[7]

"Make rays for each of your designs too. Let there be four black rays to the east, four blue rays to the south, four yellow rays to the west, and four glittering rays to the north. On each, within the first outer circle of pollen or specular iron ore, make a circle of red paint. Make this near the edge. This red one stands for the rainbow. Then bring downy eagle feathers and white tail feathers of the eagle and spotted feathers of the eagle so that we can sing over this sun and moon."

Then Holy Boy went back to his own home. He worked on the sun and moon as the Black Hactcin had told him. He sent for Red Boy, and Red Boy came over and assisted him. They painted what the Hactcin had told them on the buckskin. They were nearly finished when the two Hactcin came in.

They walked in and looked at the designs. They said, "Oh, it's pretty good!" They put pollen in their own mouths and the two boys did likewise. Then the Hactcin put some pollen on top of their own heads and the boys did it too. Then each threw some to the east, south, west, and north, then straight up in the air, and then on the sun and the moon both. Each one of the four did that. They sprinkled pollen on the sun and the moon four times after throwing it upward in the air.[8]

Then White Hactcin took the white feathers and the Black Hactcin took the spotted feathers. The downy feathers they gave to Holy Boy and Red Boy. One bead of a certain color was placed in each direction on the outer circle of each design: a red stone bead on the east side, turquoise on the south side, a white bead on the west side, and abalone on the north side.

The two drawings lay before them. Everything was ready. They asked each other who was going to start to sing and pray.

Then White Hactcin spoke to Holy Boy. "You are the one who started to make the sun. You had better start the singing too. You must know how."

"Yes, I started it. I can't deny that."

So Holy Boy sang songs. He sang a song to the pollen. Then he sang a specular iron ore song.

Now Red Boy sang, and he sang to the beads. And he sang a song to the red ochre too.

That is why they rub paint on the face of the girl and the boy the last morning of the puberty rite. They put the red paint on then. If the boy and girl would go out without having their faces painted with red paint it would be like going out without being under the care of these holy things. Then if you prayed the Hactcin would not hear you or help you, nor would anything else.

And the pollen is just like a summer offering. After they used the pollen and sang of it, all kinds of fruit of the summer were mentioned. That song gives long life too. They sang it for both the sun and the moon, that they would have long life.

Then White Hactcin sang in the same way. He sang the same songs. He sang to make the sun and the moon come to life.

As he sang the pictures began to move a little. They began to come to life.

Then Black Hactcin sang too. He sang to make them move.

Red Boy helped each of them sing; he joined in. He didn't sing alone himself though.

Now everything was ready. The sun and moon were ready to go. Then all went out, the four of them. White Hactcin had the sun in his hand. Black Hactcin had the moon in his hand. They stood in a single file facing the east. Holy Boy stood first, then White Hactcin, then Black Hactcin, and behind him Red Boy.

Holy Boy and Red Boy had pollen in their hands. Each threw some towards the north and then up and to the south. They were making a path, just the way the sun and moon were to go.

Then White Hactcin and Black Hactcin released the sun and moon, and the sun and moon went up that path. In the sky they came up from the north and moved toward the south.[9] It was a long time before they reached the sky. Then they could be seen faintly, just as at dawn. The light began to get stronger and stronger. The light began to show on the mountains.

The other people of the underworld didn't know what it was.

Then the sun came out and in the bright sunshine everything could be seen clearly. It was just as it is now in daytime.

There were all kinds of shamans around there among the people. These were men and women who claimed they had power from all sorts of things. They saw the sun going from the north to the south across the sky.

These shamans began to talk. One said, "I made the sun."

Another contradicted him and said, "No, I did it."

They got to quarrelling about it.

Hactcin told them not to talk like that for four days. "After four days say what you want to." That's what White Hactcin told them.

But the shamans didn't listen. They kept making claims like this and fighting. They talked all the more. One would say, "I think I'll make the sun stop overhead so that there will be no night. But no, I guess I'll let it go, because we need some time to rest too." And another would say, "I might get rid of the moon. We don't need any light at night."

But the sun arose the second day and was overhead at noon. The birds and animals were happy. The third day it was the same way; the sun rose as before.

And the fourth day came. The sun rose early. But the shamans, in spite of what the Hactcin had told them, continued to talk and kept it up till noon of the fourth day.

Then, at noon, there was an eclipse of the sun. It grew black. The sun went straight overhead, through a hole, and on to this earth. The moon followed and came to this earth too. That is why we have eclipses today.[10]

The rays of the sun came straight down through the little hole that connected the underworld with the earth above. The people could see the light faintly.

Notes

1. The use of the whirlwind as a messenger or spy for the supernaturals is an ever recurring theme in Jicarilla folklore and will be encountered many times in these pages.

2. The association of Black Hactcin with darkness and the things of the night is here continued by representing him the possessor of the "night light" or moon, thus contrasting him with White Hactcin, who owns the sun material.

3. The term grandson is honorific in this context, referring to relative age and not to kinship.

4. Unblemished buckskin was much prized by the Jicarilla for ceremonial purposes. It was required, for instance, in the rite conducted four days after the birth of a child. (p. 44.)

5. Pollen is often used to represent the light of the sun; specular iron ore the light of the moon.

6. Red Boy and Holy Boy do not appear in other Jicarilla stories. Holy Boy is mentioned in the Navaho origin legend also. See Matthews: *Navaho Legends*.

7. The Black Hactcin and White Hactcin were leaders of all the Hactcin. All the rest were just helpers. I think that Holy Boy and Red Boy were the children of Hactcin, but I am not sure. (Inf.)

8. This is one of the few references in Jicarilla mythology to offerings of pollen to upward and downward directions as well as to the cardinal points.

9. At first the sun and moon moved from north to south. For an account of the change to the present direction of movement see p. 22.

10. Another account (p. 160) attributes eclipses of the sun and moon to jealousy of their spouses.

The Emergence[1]

MORRIS EDWARD OPLER

The Hactcin said to the boastful shamans, "All right, you people say you have power. Now bring back the sun."

And so they lined up. On one side were all the shamans and on the other side were all the birds and animals. The shamans started to sing songs and make ceremonies. They showed all they knew. Some would sit singing and then disappear into the earth, leaving only their eyes sticking out. Then they would come back as before, but it couldn't bring back the sun. It was only to show that they had power. Some swallowed arrows, and the arrows would come out of their flesh at their stomachs. Some swallowed feathers. Some swallowed whole spruce trees and then spat them up. But they couldn't do anything about regaining the sun and moon.[2]

Then White Hactcin said, "All you people are doing pretty well, but I don't think you are bringing the sun back. Your time is up."

Then he turned to the insects and the birds and animals and said, "All right, now it is your turn."

The birds and animals spoke to each other politely, just as though they were brothers-in-law.[3]

Hactcin told them, "You must do something more than speak to each other in that polite way. Why don't you get up and do something with your own power and make the sun come back?"

The grasshopper was the first one to try. "That's not a difficult thing to do," he said. He put up his hand to the east, to the south, to the west, and to the north in turn and then put down bread which had been baked in ashes.

White Hactcin asked, "What is this?"

Grasshopper said, "That is bread."

"How do you make the bread?"

"Oh, with grain," he said.

"What is in it?"

"Wheat. It grows. It has roots and leaves and pollen and a stalk."[4]

"All right, I can use that," White Hactcin said.

Then the deer's turn came. He said, "Hactcin hasn't asked such a difficult thing." He put out his hand in the four directions. Then he put down some yucca fruit.

White Hactcin asked, "What is it?"

"That is fruit. It is what I live on. It is a growing thing too. It has roots, stalk, leaves, blossoms, and pollen."

"I can use that too. It is wonderful," said Hactcin.

Then the bear stepped forth. He too put his hands out in the four directions. Then he put down a handful of choke-cherries. "This is what I live on," he said.

"What is it?" asked White Hactcin.

"It is a fruit too. It grows. It has root, stalk, leaves, blossom, and pollen."

"I can use it. It is good."

Then came Ground Hog. He too put out his right hand to the four directions. In his hand was a berry.

"What is it?"

"It is a fruit. It is what I live on. It has a root, stalk, flowers, and pollen."

"I can use it."

Then Chipmunk came out. He too put out his hand in the four directions. He put down a strawberry.

"What is it?"

"It is a fruit. It has roots, stem, blossom, and pollen. It is what I live on."

"The Emergence", *Myths and Tales of the Jicarillo Apache Indians*, by Morris Edward Opler, New York: American Folk-lore Society, 1938, in the series: Memoirs of the American Folklore Society, v. 31. Reprinted by permission of American Folklore Society.

In the same way all the animals came forward in turn. Each put his hand to the four directions and each gave something which was his food to Hactcin. The birds and insects came too. The birds brought all kinds of seeds.

The last one to come was Turkey. He went to the east, strutting. Black corn lay there as if spilled. He did the same to the south, and blue corn lay there. He strutted to the west, and yellow corn lay there. And then he went to the north, and all kinds of vegetables and fruit lay there.

Hactcin asked him, "What is all this?"

"This is what I live on. They have roots, stems, pollen, and the corn has tassels on top. It has dew on it too."

"That is very good. I think I am going to use you. You can help us make it grow," he said to the turkey.

Then White Hactcin sent for Thunder of four colors from the directions. And these thunders brought clouds of four colors. The rain fell from these clouds. Then Hactcin sent for Rainbow to make it beautiful while they planted these things on the mountain.

Then those four, White Hactcin, Black Hactcin, Holy Boy, and Red Boy, brought sand. It was sand of four colors. They brought pollen from all kinds of trees and from the fruits. They leveled off a place so they could work with the sand. They smoothed down the place with eagle feathers.[5]

They had earth of four colors there too: black, blue, yellow, and glittering.

First they laid the sand down evenly. Then they made four little mounds of earth with the dirt. In each one they put some seeds and fruits which the animals had given. And on top they put the needles and leaves of the trees that were to grow on the mountains. On the top of each one of the piles of earth they put a reed. On top of the reed was attached the downy feather of an eagle and the downy feather of a turkey. The mounds of earth were in a row extending from east to west. The first one was the one of black earth, next the one of blue earth, then the one of yellow earth, and last the one of glittering earth.

Before the mountain started to grow, the Holy Ones took a black clay bowl and filled it with water. They did this because water was needed to make the mountain grow. How could it grow that tall without water? When they did this there was still no single tall mountain there. But they put the clay bowl of water there and then added all the things that the animals gave, and the mountain began to grow. That is why the black clay bowl, full of medicine, is used in the bear dance.[6] And when the old people wanted holy water after that, they always got it from the mountain tops.

All the birds of the mountain and the mountain animals were there helping to make these mounds of earth grow. They all prayed. Then the two Hactcin and Holy Boy and Red Boy started to sing. They sang and sang and after a while all the fruit began to grow in these piles of earth.

The turkey was gobbling and strutting. When the mountain expanded he always did this. But they did not know how many times the mountain grew, for they had no sun and could not count.[7] Now we watch the sun and see the days pass, and in this way learn to count.

Every time the mountain grew there was a noise as though something was squeezed, a squeaking noise. All the four mounds of earth, as they grew, merged and became one mountain.

When the dirt had all grown together into one mountain, the two Hactcin and Holy Boy and Red Boy picked out twelve shamans who had performed many things when the people were showing off their power before. These were the ones who had been able to cut themselves and to swallow arrows. These people had ceremonies from different sources, from animals, from fire, from Turkey, from frogs and others things. They each had a shamanistic ceremony and they were shamans. They could not be left out. They had power and they had to help too. All with power were helping to make the mountain grow. Each animal and bird was contributing his power.

The four Holy Ones painted these twelve men and made them appear like the Tsanati of today.[8] They dressed them up with spruce branches and yucca leaves, using the narrow-leafed yucca and the broad-leafed yucca too. They wove the yucca and made a short skirt of it for the men to wear. They stuck spruce branches in around their waists. They tied yucca at the wrist and lower part of the arm and spruce at the upper arm. Six represented the summer and six the winter season. Therefore six were painted blue all over and six white all over. Yucca was tied to their ankles and to a place above the knee, and spruce branches were stuck in these circles of yucca. The faces, hands, and feet were painted. A line of black ran outward and down from each eye. They wore buckskin moccasins. One white eagle feather was tied in the hair of each, on top. In their hands were branches of spruce and blades of yucca. They held four kernels of blue corn in each hand.

Then the four Holy Ones made six clowns.[9] They were painted white all over except for four black stripes, one across the face, one across the chest, one across the upper leg, and one across the lower leg. The stripes went around the whole body. Each arm also had four black stripes. On their wrists they wore a band of narrow yucca and one around the neck. They wore loin cloths of deerskin, and they wore moccasins. Yucca bands were put around their ankles. Rattles of deer hoof were tied to the yucca at the ankle, two to each foot. The hair was gathered up and brought to a point on each side. These "horns" were painted white with four black stripes. They stuck out like horns. And at the top of each one was one eagle feather.

In the right hand they carried the broad blades of yucca. This was called their whip. It had a downy eagle feather at the very end. With this the clown protects the holy places against any woman whose menstrual period has come. If a woman is in that condition the feather points to her and the clown chases her away with it. This whip is used against sickness too.

In the left hand they carried a branch of spruce. These people are powerful. If you have touched the bone or marrow of a man or dog, though you did not realize it, and then later put your hand to your mouth, it makes you sick. You can't digest food. You vomit all the time. Then these clowns are the people who can cure you.

All those who were present helped. They all worked to make the mountain grow. It was getting large. The people wanted to travel on it. The mountain had much fruit on it now. There were cotton-wood and aspen trees on it and streams of water flowed from it too. It was very rich in everything. Yucca fruit and all other fruits were growing on it by this time, all kinds of berries and cherries.

The turkey, more than anything else, was the one who made the mountain grow. When he gobbled and strutted it would begin to rise.

It was very dark and they couldn't see well. They had the feathers by which they obtained some light, but they could not see all over.

Two girls went up on the mountain when no one was watching them. A little later the mountain stopped growing and would rise no more.

Then the Holy Ones[10] said, "Something must have happened up there."

They sent the whirlwind to find out about it. The wind went up there. He saw tracks.

They all continued with their songs and prayers, but the mountain would no longer move.

Whirlwind sent a message to the two Hactcin telling them to go up and fix the damage. Turkey was responsible for all growing things and so he first went up and saw what the two girls had done. He came back and told the two Hactcin. The Hactcin requested that the people remain where they were.

The two Hactcin went up with Holy Boy and Red Boy. They saw all that the girls had done. They saw how the reeds and many other plants were damaged. The girls had been chasing each other and wrestling and trampling on the holy plants. They had even used the holy mountain as a toilet. So the Holy Ones cleaned up everything and fixed it up. The girls were no longer there. They had gone down the mountain again.

The Holy Ones came down to the people again after performing a ceremony there. They asked the people who had been on top of the mountain, and they found out which girls had done it.

"Why did you go up there?" they asked these girls.

They blamed each other. One said, "She wanted me to go up." The other said, "No, she told me to go." They said they had intended to go only a little way but that they had seen berries and fruit ahead, and so had gone from one plant or tree to another until they had climbed to the top.

Now all the people came together once more and sang, and the mountain began to grow again. It grew just a little higher. It grew four times and then it wouldn't rise any more.

The four Holy Ones went up the mountain again. They saw that the top of the mountain was still a little way from the sky and from the hole through which they could see to the other earth. So they all held a council to decide what they would do next.

They sent up Fly and Spider. The spider put his web all around, and the fly and the spider went up on it. That is why, in February or March, when the first warm weather starts and the first flies appear, they come on the sunbeams, which stand for the spider's web.[11] You will see the sun's ray come through the window and the fly will come in on it, right into the house.

Those two went up where the sun was. They took four rays of the sun, each of a different color, and pulled on them as if they were ropes. They pulled them down to the mountain top. The ropes came down, black, blue, yellow, and glittering, one on each corner of the opening. From these rays of the sun the four Holy Ones made a ladder. Out of the same material they made twelve steps and placed them across.

When Spider first came up on this earth, there was only one mountain, and that was to the east. Flint Mountain was its name. It is still there, west of Abiquiu.

The first animals to be sent up after Spider came down and announced that water was plentiful there, were two wild ducks.[12] These are the ones they hunt now in October. They were sent up because it was thought that they could get along well in the water. But as soon as they came up they flew over to this mountain and stayed there until the water was sent away. When everyone was up on the earth, they came back and joined the others.

Now the fly and the spider went upward again on that ladder. They saw a great deal of water up there. They could see no ground at all. The spider made a cylinder of web which protected them and they went up to the top through this. Spider then wove four webs on top of the earth of four different colors and stretching in four directions so that the four Holy Ones could ascend.

The four came up. Black Hactcin stood on the black web to the east, and the others took their places too. They talked of what to do, for the sun was past the middle of the sky already.

Then they said, "Let us make four hoops of the different colors, one black, one blue, one yellow, and one glittering.[13]

They did so and threw the black one to the east, the blue one to the south, the yellow one to the west, and the glittering one to the north. Every time they threw one, the water rolled back and grew less where they were standing. By the time they threw the fourth one, there was land where they stood. The water had receded from the land and had made the oceans as they are now.

But everything was still muddy. So they sent for the four Big Winds of the different colors and for the little winds too. The winds blew and made it all dry. But the winds couldn't dry off certain places where the springs and rivers were.

When the wind was hurling the water back and exposing the land, it lifted the water high in the sky and held it there. Over by the oceans the water is still held there by the wind.

White Hactcin said to the wind, "Hold the water there and when it is needed we will let you know and you must blow and bring the rain."

Hactcin talked to the thunder, "You must lead," he said, "so people will hear and know the rain is coming and get ready. They will prepare buckets to fill and be ready to receive the rain."

Then he spoke to the sun saying, "You must shine on the lakes and rivers so that the steam will arise and turn to water and give rain. But Wind, you will always carry the water in the air; you are responsible for it. If the heat does not pick up the water but leaves it around on the earth in the same way all the time, the water will become dirty and unfit for use. But by changing it in this manner it will be made pure and good for the people."

High in the air there are four winds: the black wind from the east makes the water warm, the blue wind from the south makes it cool and fresh, the yellow wind from the west freezes the water and turns it to snow, and the guttering wind from the north turns it to ice and hail.[14] These four people are always there handing around the moisture of the air. When it is handed to the wind of the north, it turns to ice. Then, when it is handed back to Black Wind of the east, he warms it and it turns to water again. That is why we have the moisture of the air in all these forms.

And some people who also control water live in the mountains. These are the people who were directed by the Hactcin to stay in the mountains and take care of them and of all within them.[15]

When the people first came up on earth there were no mountains. But when the monsters began to grow, the mountains too began to rise, for Hactcin made them to be barriers so that the monsters could not get to the people easily.

And Hactcin stationed people in those mountains then, saying, "This mountain will be your home."

These people allow the water of the mountains to flow out, and thus there are springs.

We say that the fly is the messenger of the sun. It carries the news of the coming of the sun. And the spider has long ropes, we say. In ceremonies he helps people, and when he helps it is just as if a rope were lowered to one who has fallen in a deep place.

The four Holy Ones said to Fly and Spider, "We need your help still. Make a web and extend it to the sky," they said to Spider, "and then you two bring the sun down."

The Hactcin sang and sang so the sun and moon could be gotten down, for the sun and moon had not asked permission when they went up as they did. It was the fault of the sun and moon that the people had such a hard time and had to come up on this earth.

Spider did as he was told, and he and Fly brought the sun and moon down. Then all held council and they decided that they would change Sun to a person, a living person, because he had disobeyed. They were afraid that if they didn't do this the sun would go up again to some other place, and they had had a difficult time regaining the sun. They decided to do the same to Moon too. Before this Sun and Moon were alive, but they were not people.

So the four Holy Ones talked it over and said, "Of the sun we will make another people." And they made the sun into a Taos Indian boy. And out of the moon they made a Jicarilla Apache girl.[16]

"Let them marry," said the four Holy Ones, "and then the Jicarilla Apache and the Taos Indians will be good friends and will not fight over little things."

And so these two helped each other after this. They helped each other shine and give light.

Now they sent the sun and the moon back to the north again after they had become living persons. So they went back to the north. Then the sun started to go to the south. The moon followed. They went like this for one full day.

But then they thought about it.

"I don't believe it's right," Sun said, "for one side of the earth has light when we go this way and one has not."[17]

The Holy Ones thought about it. Then they changed it and had the sun and moon go from east to west. And the Milky Way that you see stretching from north to south across the sky is the first path of the sun and moon.

At first the sun and moon went together, at the same time.

"That's not right," they thought. "We will hold back the moon. Let the sun go first and then the moon can go at night."

The moon was flat and round. It followed the sun, coming later. When the sun set in the west, it could be seen. The moon is a girl and was having her menstrual period just at that time. She was tipped up so that only the rim could be seen. That is what we call the new moon when it occurs now. So it is that our women have a period after a new moon, and that is why the girl's puberty ceremony is always held at the new moon. And the new moon is used now for keeping track of the seasons.

The sun just kept going all the time.

When everything was ready in this upper world the Holy Ones went down below to the place where the people were waiting.

The people had a great deal of food on that mountain. They had much to eat while they were traveling. But they had not yet started upward. They were still below, in the underworld.

Then the four Holy Ones sent up the crows, the four crows of the different colors. "You must go up there and see how everything is getting along."

The crows came up. Some of the fish and water animals had died when the water was thrown back by the Holy Ones. The crows began to eat these dead bodies.

The other people were expecting them back. They wondered why the crows did not return. So finally they sent up White Weasel.

White Weasel went up and saw what the crows were doing. He returned and told the people, "No wonder they don't come back. They are busy eating."

So they sent Badger up then. Badger stepped into some place that was still muddy. He thought it must be muddy like that all over, so he went back and told them, "Oh, it's still very muddy." Because he stepped in the mud he has black on his paws now.

Then they sent up Beaver. When he got up there he tried to dam up the water. He stayed up there working and making dams.

Then Black Weasel was sent. Black Weasel came to Beaver and said, "What are you doing? The people are waiting for you."

"Oh, I'd better dam up this water so that the water will be ready when the people come up."

The rivers that are left us here today are the ones he dammed up.

Beaver knew that the people were on the journey to this earth and would be very tired. So be built a sweat house there where the people could come and get rested.

When Weasel came up he saw it. He asked, "What are you doing here? The people are waiting for you."

"I'm making a dam for the people, so they will have water. When the people come they will already have water for drinking and to bathe in."

"And what are you building?"

"That is my house. I call it *keltca*."[18]

"Is this for the people?"

"No, it is my home. But whenever the bodies of the people are doubled up they will use it. When they are tired they will use it too. After a long sickness when they are run down they will use it. When they come up I will explain to them how to use it. I'll explain to them what they should do. They should build a fire outside and put rocks in it. When these rocks are well heated they must throw them into the sweat house. The doorway must be closed by my own skin, by beaver skin, for when I go into my house I never wear my skin but take it off and hang it at the door. So let the people do likewise when they take a sweat bath. The door must always face to the east. The people must roll the hot rocks in with sticks and pile them all on the north side. Then they must throw water on the rocks and steam will arise. When it begins to cool down, more water must be thrown on the rocks. And the songs that are sung should be about Little Night. They must sing these, for they go into that small dark place which gives them the sweat bath and the cleansing.

"Two or four may go in and all can sing in there. And they should sing for long life too and sing of the sun and moon. Women may go in but not with the men.

"The sweat house shall be made of bent pieces of wood with brush and dirt over these. And it must be made by the water's edge so that all can go into the water and wash after the sweat bath.

"The men must not use the same sweat house that the women use. If they do so they will become blind, and the women will become blind too if they go into the one the men have used.

"The sweat house, after use, is to be left standing, and it may be used again."

Then from below the Holy Ones sent the birds up first, because they have wings to fly. They came up in a flock.

Hactcin told the animals and people. "Now get ready. We must go up in the sky."

At this time the girls were big with children.[19] This was the result of the things they had used on themselves in the absence of the men, when the women and the men had separated. They were already in late pregnancy when they started.

Now they all began traveling on the mountain going toward the top. The Hactcin made sure that everything was right and holy before they let the people start. There was no sun and so one cannot say that the people took four days to reach the vault of the underworld. But they traveled four times until they were tired and then stopped each time. The top of the mountain where they stopped last was twelve ladder steps from the earth hole. That was the distance between the mountain top and the earth hole. They had four ladders. The black ladder to the east was the one the men climbed up on. The blue ladder to the south was for the girls and women. The yellow ladder to the west was used by the young boys. The north ladder of a glittering color was used by all the little children.

First they prayed before the ladders. Holy Boy was the real leader of the ascent. It was due to him that the people were coming on this earth. So he prayed for the ladders and for the Hactcin, the clowns, and Tsanati.

Then the clowns came up first, for they had the whips of yucca with which to chase sickness away. At that time it was not known whether there was sickness on earth. They thought that perhaps the water animals which had died had some sickness. So the clowns came up and made everything wholesome for the people. They made the path that the people could follow.

White Hactcin was the next to come up. Holy Boy first dressed him up. He put a downy eagle feather on top of his head. He dressed him up with spruce. White Hactcin held a big whip made of yucca. A downy feather was at its end. In his left hand he held spruce branches.

The clowns uttered a certain laugh when they came up, so that all the sickness would be frightened, and the Hactcin made a different noise for the same reason. Black Hactcin ascended immediately after White Hactcin did. He had black specular iron ore and pollen all over his face. White Hactcin had pollen all over his face, and on the right side the seven stars of the Big Dipper were painted with specular iron ore. A sun of specular iron ore was designed on the middle of the forehead. On the left cheek was the moon, designed with specular iron ore. The bodies of both Hactcin were covered with white clay. They wore skirts of woven yucca like those of the Tsanati. At the arm and leg joints they wore yucca bands tied, and spruce branches were fastened on these.

Next Red Boy ascended. He, like the Hactcin, went up the ladder of the east. Then the twelve Tsanati came up. Then Holy Boy came up. After him came Turkey. All these came up the ladder to the east.

Now all these were up on this earth, and they prepared everything so that no harm should befall the people.

Now it was the turn of the people. Ancestral Man was the first of the people to ascend. Ancestral Woman followed and was the first woman to emerge. Both walked up with age sticks in their hands.[20] They were dressed as White-Shell Woman and Child-of-the-Water dress for the girl's puberty ceremony now. The other people followed. The men were to the east, the women to the west, and the children to the north and south.[21]

After the people the animals came.

The people emerged from a hole in a mountain. At that time this was the only mountain on the earth, besides Flint Mountain to the east. The other mountains grew up later, at the time of the monsters. Some say that the emergence mountain lies north of Durango, Colorado. Others say it is near Alamosa, Colorado. It was called Big Mountain.[22]

Sky is our father, Earth is our mother. They are husband and wife and they watch over us and take care of us. The earth gives us our food; all the fruits and plants come from the earth. Sky gives us the rain, and when we need water we pray to him. The earth is our mother.[23] We came from her. When we came up on this earth, it was just like a child being born from its mother. The place of emergence is the womb of the earths.[24]

The animals came up, the elk, the deer, and all the others. But they were not wild animals. They were gentle and tame then. The animals came up any ladder which was nearest. After a while the ladders were all worn through, so many had passed over them.

There were two old people, an old man and a very old woman who were far behind the animals. These two couldn't see well; their sight was dim. Those two silly girls who had interfered with the growth of the mountain before were far behind too. They had been chasing each other and playing, and the people didn't know it.

When the two old people came to the ladders, the ladders were worn out and they couldn't get up. They stood there and called, "Come and get us. Take us too." But there was no ladder nor any way to get them up. The old people tried to get the others to help them.

Finally they became angry. "All right," they said, "we shall stay here. But you must come back some day." They meant that the people must return to the underworld when they die.

Night came. The people on top tried to sleep. But they couldn't sleep the first night. They couldn't sleep the second nor the third. They wondered why. They wondered whether it was because something had been left behind.

Then they discovered that they had no lice in their hair. There were three kinds, black ones, grey ones, and the small ones, the nits. So they sent down to the old people for these. The two old people threw some up. The people divided the lice among themselves. The fourth night they all slept soundly.

The people looked down through the hole, for they couldn't find those two silly girls among those on top. The light of the sun went through the hole and hit the tip of the mountain, illuminating it. There, in the light, sat those two foolish girls sewing shallow tray baskets.

They called to these two girls, but they wouldn't come up. They wouldn't obey.

Then Holy Boy made two butterflies out of the flowers. He made the kind that always go in pairs, the yellow ones.

The sun had power now. Holy Boy sent word to Sun. "You must help us and send a beam for the butterflies." The sun did so and the butterflies went right in on that beam.[1]

The two silly girls caught sight of the butterflies.

"Let's catch them and make designs. We have always made mountain designs on our baskets. Now we'd better make a butterfly design," they said. "That is more beautiful."[2]

So they started to chase the butterflies. The ray of the sun came down and provided a ladder. The butterflies kept just out of reach above them. So they began to ascend the ladder, trying to get those butterflies. Before they knew it they were on top.

Notes

1. For abbreviated accounts of the emergence see Goddard, p. 193; Mooney, p. 197; Russell, p. 254.

2. The attribution of the loss of the sun and moon to the boasts of shamans (those who obtain supernatural power through a personal encounter with some animal or natural force) and the ridicule heaped on the ceremonies and legerdemain in which the shamans subsequently engaged in order to retrieve the loss, are indicative of the subordinate place shamanism plays in Jicarilla religion. Shamanistic ceremonies are used for emergencies and minor crises. For important occasions and for times when planning and preparation are possible, "long life ceremonies," traditional rites, which have their genesis and rationalization in the myths and not in any personal experience of an individual, are invoked instead.

3. A number of Jicarilla affinities must be addressed by a special third person form, called "polite form" because of the restraint and circumspection which are supposed to accompany it. By taking pains to be more formal and dignified, the birds and animals hoped to avoid the excesses of the thoughtless shamans.

4. The grasshopper is considered the guardian of wheat. See pp. 177–178 for further development of this theme.

5. Sand on which ground drawings are to be traced is leveled off with eagle feathers today.

6. For a description of the bear dance see pp. 27–44.

7. Another version: Some say that the mountain grew twelve times; that it grew eight times and then the foolish girls stopped it. Then the Hactcin fixed it, and it grew four more times. (Inf.)

8. The marked tendency of the Jicarilla to discourage shamanism in favor of the "long life ceremonies" finds unmistakable expression here. To become effective in this rite of the growing emergence mountain, shamans have to be transformed into a dance group which functions in the traditional or "long life" ceremonies today. The word Tsanati refers to ritual gesticulation. Since a literal translation would be awkward, the native term will be retained in these pages.

9. The literal translation of the term for the Jicarilla clown is "striped excrement." Their ability to cure stomach ailments is connected with scatological practices which will be presently described (p. 184). The clowns of the emergence were decorated with four black stripes. Clowns which function in war-path ceremonies are designed with six black stripes.

10. The Holy Ones are White Hactcin, Black Hactcin, Red Boy, and Holy Boy. Actually the informant mentioned these four names each time, but to avoid repetition this convention of referring to them collectively will be followed.

11. The Jicarilla will not kill spiders for this reason. The nexus in Jicarilla ideology between the spider's web and the sunbeam is made explicit in the birth rite, where a cord of unblemished buckskin, called in the rite "spider's rope," is stretched from the umbilicus of the child towards the sun.

12. For the origin of the water found on the earth at the time of the emergence see p. 267.

13. The device of rolling back waters by the tossing of colored hoops occurs in more than one place in Jicarilla mythology. See p. 106.

14. Like other natural forces, Wind is often personified. The Jicarilla's conception is of an animate universe which understands and responds to his needs.

15. The belief that people or supernaturals have been stationed within mountains for one purpose or another is a common theme. See also p. 112.

16. Apache cosmology is not consistent concerning the sex of the moon. When the moon is thought of in connection with the woman's menstrual cycle it is given female attributes. But Moon is also associated with Water, and Water becomes the father of one of the Culture Heroes. In an important ceremonial race Moon is represented as a male (p. 81) as is the case in the origin myth of the Hactcin ceremony (p. 141).

17. The earth is said to have the form of a woman whose feet point toward the east and whose head lies to the west.

18. This word means "beaver pelt" and is quite similar to the word for sweat-house, *kiltca*. The informant is employing a bit of folk etymology to hint that the word for sweat-house originally came from "beaver pelt." Since there is a difference of tone as well as outline between these two words, this is extremely unlikely.

19. For the explanation of these pregnancies see p. 266. The account of the misbehavior of the girls in the underworld is as often told as a part of the origin legend also.

20. The age stick, or the staff which an old person uses for support, is here mentioned as a symbol of the long life that man shall have on earth. It is constantly named in Jicarilla ritual songs.

21. At the time of the emergence, the man who came out last had his hair parted, not in the middle, but on the side. The line of the parting was painted red. If you know this emergence story well, you can wear your hair that way. Both men and women did this. (Inf.)

22. For identification of the emergence mountain as the San Juan of Colorado see pp. 163–164.

23. Taos is at the heart of the earth. Our own country used to be the Cimarron region. (Inf.)

24. That the emergence tale is a myth of gestation is patent enough. It is seldom, however, that the native draws the parallel so conclusively.

Creation and the Origin of Corn

FRANK HAMILTON CUSHING

I once heard a Zuñi priest say: "Five things alone are necessary to the sustenance and comfort of the 'dark ones' [Indians] among the children of earth."

"The sun, who is the Father of all.

"The earth, who is the Mother of men.

"The water, who is the Grandfather.

"The fire, who is the Grandmother.

"Our brothers and sisters the Corn, and seeds of growing things."

This Indian philosopher explained himself somewhat after the following fashion:

"Who among men and the creatures could live without the Sun-father?, for his light brings day, warms and gladdens the Earth-mother with rain which flows forth in the water we drink and that causes the flesh of the Earth-mother to yield abundantly seeds, while these—are they not cooked by the brand of fire which warms us in winter?"

That he reasoned well, may be the better understood if we follow for a while the teachings which instructed his logic. These relate that:

First, there was sublime darkness, which vanished not until came the "Ancient Father of the Sun," revealing universal waters. These were, save him, all that were.

The Sun-father thought to change the face of the waters and cause life to replace their desolation.

He rubbed the surface of his flesh, thus drawing forth *yep'-na*.[1]

The *yep'-na* he rolled into two balls. From his high and "ancient place among the spaces," (*Te'-thlä-shi-na-kwin*) he cast forth one of these balls and it fell upon the surface of the waters. There, as a drop of deer suet on hot broth, so this ball melted and spread far and wide like scum over the great waters, ever growing, until it sank into them.

Then the Sun-father cast forth the other ball, and it fell, spreading out and growing even larger than had the first, and dispelling so much of the waters that it rested upon the first. In time, the first became a great being—our Mother, the Earth; and the second became another great being—our Father, the Sky. Thus was divided the universal fluid into the "embracing waters of the World" below, and the "embracing waters of the Sky" above. Behold! this is why the Sky-father is blue as the ocean which is the home of the Earth-mother, blue even his flesh, as seem the far-away mountains—though they be the flesh of the Earth-mother.

Now while the Sky-father and the Earth-mother were together, the Earth-mother conceived in her ample wombs—which were the four great underworlds or caves—the first of men and creatures. Then the two entered into council that they might provide for the birth of their children.

"How shall it be?" said the one to the other. "How, when born forth, shall our children subsist, and who shall guide them?"

"Behold!" said the Sky-father. He spread his hand high and abroad with the hollow palm downward. Yellow grains like corn he stuck into all the lines and wrinkles of his palm and fingers. "Thus," said he, "shall I, as it were, hold my hand ever above thee and thy children, and the yellow grains shall represent so many shining points which shall guide and light these, our children, when the Sun-father is not nigh."

Gaze on the sky at night-time! Is it not the palm of the Great Father, and are the stars not in many lines of his hand yet to be seen?

"Ah yes!" said the Earth-mother, "yet my tiny children may not wander over my lap and bosom without guidance, even in the light of the Sun-father; therefore, behold!"

She took a great terraced bowl into which she poured water; upon the water she spat, and whipping it rapidly with her fingers it was soon beaten into foam as froths the soap-weed, and the foam rose high up around the rim of the bowl. The Earth-mother blew the foam. Flake after flake broke off, and bursting, cast spray downward into the bowl.

"See," said she, "this bowl is, as it were, the world, the rim its farthest limits, and the foam-bounden terraces round about, my features, which they shall call mountains whereby they shall name countries and be guided from place to place, and whence white clouds shall rise, float away, and, bursting, shed spray, that my children may drink of the water of life, and from my substance add unto the flesh of their being. Thou has said thou wilt watch over them when the Sun-father is absent, but thou art the cold being; I am the warm. Therefore, at night, when thou watchest, my children shall nestle in my bosom and find there warmth, strength and length of life from one day light to another."

Is not the bowl the emblem of the Earth, our mother?, for from it we draw both food and drink, as a babe draws nourishment from the breast of its mother, and round, as is the rim of a bowl, so is the horizon, terraced with mountains, whence rise the clouds. Is not woman the warm, man the cold being? For while woman sits shivering as she cooks by the fire in the house-room, man goes forth little heeding the storms of winter, to hunt the feed and gather pine-faggots.

Yet alas! Men and the creatures remained bounden in the lowermost womb of the Earth-mother, for she and the Sky-father feared to deliver them as a mother fears for the fate of her first offspring.

Then the Ancient Sun pitied the children of Earth. That they might speedily see his light, he cast a glance upon a foam cap floating abroad on the great waters. Forthwith the foam cap became instilled with life, and bore twin children, brothers one to the other, older and younger, for one was born before the other. To these he gave the *k'ia'-al-lan*, or "water-shield," that on it they might fly over the waters as the clouds—from which it was spun and woven—float over the ocean; that they might blind with its mists the sight of the enemy as the clouds darken the earth with rain-drops. He gave them for their bow, the rainbow, that with it they might clear men's trails of enemies, as the rain-bow clears away the storm-shadows; and for their arrows gave he them the thunder-bolts, that they might rive open the mountains, as the lightning cleaves asunder the pine trees; and then he sent them abroad to deliver, guide and protect the children of earth and the Sky-father. With their bow they lifted from his embraces the Sky-father from the bosom of the Earth-mother, "for," said they, "if he remain near, his cold will cause men to be stunted and stooped with shivering and to grovel in the earth," as stunted trees in the mountains delve under the snow to hide from the cold of the Sky-father. With their thunder-bolts they broke open the mountain which gave entrance to the cave-wombs of the Earth-mother, and upon their water-shields they descended into the lowermost of the caves, where dwelt the children of earth—men and all creatures.

Alas! It was dark as had been the world before the coming of the Sun, and the brothers found men and the beings sadly bewailing their lot. When one moved it was but to jostle another, whose complaints wearied the ears of yet others; hence the brothers called a council of the priest-chiefs—even ere the coming forth of men such lived—and they made a ladder of tall canes which they placed against the roof of the cavern. Up this rushed the children of earth. Some, climbing out before of their own wills, found deliverance from the caves above and, wandering away, became the ancestors of nations unknown to us; but our fathers followed in the footsteps of the older and younger brothers. Does not the cane grow jointed to-day, showing thus the notches which men traversed to day-light?

In the second cave all was still dark, but like starlight through cloud rifts, through the cleft above showed the twilight. After a time the people murmured again, until the two delivered them into the third world where they found light like that of early dawn. Again they grew discontented, again were guided upward, this time into the open light of the Sun—which was the light of this world. But some remained behind, not escaping until afterward; and these were the fathers of the Western nations whom our ancients knew not.

Then indeed for a time the people complained bitterly, for it was then that they *first* saw the light of the Sun-father, which, in its brilliancy, smote them so that they fell grasping their eye-balls and moaning. But when they became used to the light they looked around in joy and wonderment; yet they saw that the earth seemed but small, for everywhere rolled about the great misty waters.

The two brothers spread open the limbs of the Earth-mother, and cleft the western mountains with their shafts of lightning and the waters flowed down and away from the bosom of the Earth-mother, cutting great cañons and valleys which remain to this day. Thus was widened the land, yet the earth remained damp. Then they guided the people eastward.

Already before men came forth from the lower worlds with the priest-chiefs, there were many gods and strange beings. The gods gave to the priests many treasures and instructions, but the people knew not yet the meaning of either. Thus were first taught our ancients incantations, rituals and sacred talks (prayer), each band of them according to its usefulness. These bands were the "Priesthood"—*Shi'-wa-na-kwe*; the "Hunter-band"—*Sa'-ni-a-k'ia-kwe*; the "Knife-band"—*A'tchi-a-k'ia-kwe* or Warrior, and the *Ne'-we-kwe*, or Band of Wise Medicine Men. The leaders of each band thus came to have wonderful knowledge and power—even as that of the gods! They summoned a great council of their children—for they were called the 'Fathers of the People'—and asked them to choose such things as they would have for special ownership or use. Some chose the macaw, the eagle, or the turkey; others chose the deer, bear, or coyote; others the seeds of earth, or *a'-tâ-a*, the spring vine, tobacco, and the plants of medicine, the yellow-wood and many other things. Thus it came about that they and their brothers and sisters and their children, even unto the present day, were named after the things they chose in the days when all was new, and thus was divided our nation into many clans, or gentes (*A'-no-ti-we*) of brothers and sisters who may not marry one another but from one to the other. To some of the elders of these bands and clans was given some thing which should be, above all other things, precious. For instance, the clans of the Bear and Crane were given the *Mu'-et-ton-ne*, or medicine seed of hail and snow. For does not the bear go into his den, and appears not the crane when come storms of hail and snow?

When more than one clan possessed one of these magic medicines they formed a secret society—like the first four—for its keeping and use. Thus the Bear and Crane peoples became the "Holders of the Wand"—who bring the snow of winter and are potent to cure the diseases which come with them. In time they let into their secret council others, whom they had cured, that the precious secrets of their band might not be wasted. Thus it was that one after another were formed the rest of our medicine bands, who were and are called the finishers of men's trails, because, despite disease and evil, they guard and lengthen our lives; but in the "days of the new" there were only four bands.[2]

To the Eagle, Deer and Coyote peoples was given the *Nal'-e-ton*, or "Deer Medicine Seed," which the Hunter-band still guards; and to the Macaw, Sun and Frog peoples the *Kia'-et-ton*, or the "Medicine Seed of Water," which the priesthood and the Sacred Dance, or *Kâ'-kâ*, still hold—without the administration of which the world would dry up and even the insects of the mountains and hollows of earth grow thirsty and perish. Yet, not less precious was the gift to the "Seed-people," or *Ta'-a-kwe*. This was the *Tchu'-et-ton*, or the "Medicine Seed of Corn"—for from this came the parents of flesh and beauty, the solace of hunger, the emblems of birth, mortal life, death and immortality. To the Badger people was given the knowledge of Fire, for in the roots of all trees, great and little—which the badger best knows how to find—dwells the essence of fire.[3]

To all of these peoples it was told that they should wander for many generations toward the land whence the Sun brings the day-light (Eastward) until at last they would reach the "middle of the world," where their children should dwell forever over the heart of our Earth-mother until their days should be numbered and the light of Zuñi grow dark.

Toward this unknown country the "twin brothers of light" guided them. In those times a day meant a year, and a night another, so that four days and nights meant eight years. Many days the people wandered eastward, slaying game for their flesh-food, gathering seeds from grasses and weeds for their bread-food, and binding rushes about their loins for their clothing; they knew not until afterward, the flesh of the cotton and yucca-mothers.

The earth was still damp. Dig a hole in a hill-side, quickly it filled with water. Drop a seed on the highest table-land and it without waiting shot forth green sprouts. So moist, indeed, was the soil, that even footprints of men and all creatures might be traced whithersoever they tended. The beings and strange creatures increased with men, and spread over the world. Many monsters lived, by whose ferocity men perished.

Then said the twin brothers: "Men, our children, are poorer than the beasts, their enemies; for each creature has a special gift of strength or sagacity, while to men has been given only the power of guessing. Nor would we that our children be web-footed like the beings that live over the waters and damp places."

Therefore, they sent all men and harmless beings to a place of security; then laid their water shield on the ground. Upon it they placed four thunder-bolts, one pointed north, another west, another south, and the other eastward. When all was ready they let fly the thunder-bolts. Instantly the world was covered with lurid fire and shaken with rolling thunders, as is a forest to-day burned and blasted where the lightning has fallen. Thus as the clay of vessels is burned to rock, and the mud of the hearth crackled and reddened by fire, so the earth was mottled and crackled and hardened where now we see mountains and masses of rock. Many of the great monsters and prey-beings were changed in a twinkling to enduring rock or shriveled into twisted idols which the hunter and priest-warrior know best how to prize. Behold, their forms along every mountain side and ravine, and in the far western valleys and plains, still endure the tracks of the fathers of men and beings, the children of earth. Yet some of the beings of prey were spared, that the world might not become over-filled with life, and starvation follow, and that men might breathe of their spirits and be inspired with the hearts of warriors and hunters.

Often the people rested from their wanderings, building great houses of stone which may even now be seen, until the Conch of the Gods sounded, which lashed the ocean to fury and beat the earth to trembling.[4] Then the people started up, and gathering the few things they could, again commenced their wanderings; yet often those who slept or lingered were buried beneath their own walls, where yet their bones may sometimes be found.

Marvelous both of good and evil were the works of the ancients. Alas! There came forth with others, those impregnated with the seed of sorcery. Their evil works caused discord among men, and, through fear and anger, men were divided from one another. Born before our ancients, had been other men, and these our fathers sometimes overtook and looked not peacefully upon them, but challenged them—though were they not their older brothers? It thus happened when our ancients came to their fourth resting place on their eastward journey, that which they named *Shi-po-lo-lon-K'ai-a,* or "The Place of Misty Waters," there already dwelt a clan of people called the *A'-ta-a,* or Seed People, and the seed clan of our ancients challenged them to know by what right they assumed the name and attributes of their own clan. "Behold," said these stranger-beings, "we have power with the gods above yours, yet can we not exert it without your aid. Try, therefore, your own power first, then we will show you ours." At last, after much wrangling, the Seed clan agreed to this, and set apart eight days for prayer and sacred labors. First they worked together cutting sticks, to which they bound the plumes of summer birds which fly in the clouds or sail over the waters. "Therefore," thought our fathers, "why should not their plumes waft our beseechings to the waters and clouds?" These plumes, with prayers and offerings, they planted in the valleys, and there, also, they placed their *Tchu'-e-ton-ne.* Lo!, for eight days and nights it rained and there were thick mists; and the waters from the mountains poured down bringing new soil and spreading it over the valleys where the plumed sticks had been planted. "See!" said the fathers of the seed clan, "water and new earth bring we by our supplications."

"It is well," replied the strangers, "yet *life* ye did not bring. Behold!" and they too set apart eight days, during which they danced and sang a beautiful dance and prayer song, and at the end of that time they took the people of the seed clan to the valleys. Behold, indeed! Where the plumes had been planted and the *tchu'-e-ton* placed grew seven corn-plants, their tassels waving in the wind, their stalks laden with ripened grain. "These," said the strangers, "are the severed flesh of seven maidens, our own sisters and children. The eldest sister's is the yellow corn; the next, the blue; the next, the red; the next, the white; the next, the speckled; the next, the black, and the last and youngest is the sweet-corn, for see! even ripe, she is soft like the young of the others. The first is of the North-land, yellow like the light of winter; the second is of the West, blue like the great world of waters; the third is of the South, red like the Land of Everlasting Summer; the fourth is of the East, white like the land whence the sun brings the daylight; the fifth is of the upper regions, many-colored as are the clouds of morning and evening, and the sixth is of the lower regions, black as are the caves whence came we, your older, and ye, our younger brothers." "Brothers indeed be we, each one to the other," said the people to the strangers, "and may we not journey together seeking the middle of the world?" "Aye, we may," replied the strangers, "and of the flesh of our maidens ye may eat, no more seeking the seeds of the grasses and of your water we may drink, no more wondering whither we shall find it; thus shall each help the other to life and contentment. Ye shall pray and cut prayer-plumes, we shall sing, and dance shall our maidens that all may be delighted and that it may be for the best. But beware! no mortal must approach the persons of our maidens."

Thenceforward, many of the *A'-ta-a* and the seed clan journeyed together, until at last the Sun, Macaw, and some other clans-people found the middle of the world; while others yet wandered in search of it, not for many generations to join their brothers, over they heart of the Earth-mother, which is *Shi-wi-na-kwin,* or the "Land of the Zuñis."

Day after day, season after season, year after year, the people of the seed clan and the *A'-ta-a,* who were named together the Corn-clan, or people, prepared, and their maidens danced the dance of the *thla-he-kwe,*[5] or "Beautiful Corn Wands," until their children grew weary and yearned for other amusements.

Sometimes the people saw over Thunder-mountain thick mists floating and lowering. At such times, near the Cave of the Rainbow, a beautiful halo would spring forth, amidst which the many-colored garments of the rainbow himself could be seen, and soft, sweet music, stranger than that of the whistling winds in a mountain of pines, floated fitfully down the valley. At last the priests and elders gathered in council and determined to send their two chief warriors (Priests of the Bow) to the cavern of the rainbow, that it might be determined what strange people made the sights and sounds. "Mayhap it will prove some new dancers, who will throw the light of their favor on our weary hearts and come to cheer us and delight our children." Thus said they to the warriors when they were departing.

No sooner had the warriors reached the cave-entrance than the mists enshrouded them and the music ceased. They entered and were received by a splendid group of beings, bearing long brightly-painted flutes, amongst whom the leader was Pai'-a-tu-ma, the father of the *Ne'-we* band, and the God of Dew.

"Enter, my children," said he, "and sit. We have commanded our dancers to cease and our players to draw breath from their flutes, that we might listen to your messages; for 'not for nothing does one stranger visit the house of another.'"

"True," replied the warriors. "Our fathers have sent us that we might greet you, and the light of your favor ask for our children. Day after day the maidens of the corn-people dance one dance which, from oft repeating, has grown undelightful, and our fathers thought you might come to vary this dance with your own, for that you knew one we were taught by your music, which we sometimes heard."

"Aha!" replied Pai'-a-tu-ma, "it is well! We will follow; but not in the day-time—in the night-time we will follow. My children," said he, turning to the flute-players, "show to the strangers our custom."

The drum sounded till it shook the cavern; the music shrieked and pealed in softly surging unison, as the wind does in a wooded cañon after the storm is distant, and the mists played over the medicine bowl around which the musicians were gathered, until the rainbow fluttered his bright garments among the painted flutes. Maidens filed out brandishing wands whence issued tiny clouds white as the down of eagles, and as the sounds died away between the songs the two warriors in silent wonder and admiration departed for their home.

When they returned to their fathers in Zuñi, they told what they had seen and heard. Forthwith the fathers (priest-chiefs and elders) prepared the dance of the corn-maidens. A great bower was placed in the court of the pueblo, whither went the mothers and priests of the Seed-clan. The priests of the Macaw, Sun and Water clans were there. A terrace of sacred meal was marked on the ground, an altar set up over its base, and along its middle were placed the *E'-ta-e* or Medicine Seeds of corn and water. Along the outer edges were planted the sticks of prayer, plumed with the feathers of summer birds, and down in front of the altar and terrace were set basket-bowls covered with sacred mantles made of the flesh of the Cotton-mother (Goddess of Cotton), whose down grows from the earth and floats in the skies (cotton and the clouds are one in the Zuñi mythology). By the side of each basket-bowl sat a mother of the clan, silent in prayer and meditation. To the right were the singers, to the left the corn maidens. Night was coming on. The dance began and a fire was built in front of the bower beyond where the maidens danced. More beautiful than all human maidens were those maidens of the corn, but as are human maidens, so were they, irresistibly beautiful.

As the night deepened, the sound of music and flutes was heard up the river, and then followed the players of the rainbow-cave with their sisters, led by the God of Dew. When the players entered and saw the maidens their music ceased and they were impassioned. And when their turn came for leading the dance, they played their softest strains over their medicine bowl—the terraced bowl of the world—whence arose the rainbow. The people were delighted, but the corn maidens were sad; for no sooner had the dancing ceased a little than the flute players sought their hands and persons. In vain the corn maidens pleaded they were immortal virgins and the mothers of men! The flute players continually renewed their suits 'till the next day, and into the night which followed, while the dance went on. At last the people grew weary. The guardian warrior-priests nodded, and no longer wakened them. Silently the corn maidens stole up between the basket-trays and the sleeping people. There, passing their hands over their persons they placed something under the mantles, vanishing instantly as do the spirits of the dying, leaving only their flesh behind. Still the people slept, and ere long even the flute-players and dancers ceased. When the sun came out the people awoke. Then every one cried to the others "Where are our maiden mothers, our daughters?" Yet not even the warriors knew; for only of the flesh of the maidens (corn) could be found a little in the trays under the mantles. Then the place was filled with moaning among the women and upbraidings among the men, each blaming every other loudly until the priests cried out to silence their wranglings, and called a council. Then said they:

"Alas, we have laden our hearts with guilt, and sad thoughts have we prepared to weigh down our minds. We must send to seek the maidens, that they desert us not. Who shall undertake the journey?"

"Send for the eagle," it was said. The two warrior-priests were commanded to go and seek him.

Be it known that while yet the earth was young her children, both men and the creatures, spoke as men alone now speak, any one with any other. This the aged among all nations agree in saying, and are not those who grow not foolish with great age the wisest of men? Their words we speak!

Therefore, when the two warriors climbed the mountain whereon the eagle dwelt, and found only his eaglets at home, the little birds were frightened and tried to hide themselves in the hole where the nest was built. But when the warriors came nearer they screamed: "Oh do not pull our feathers; wait 'till we are older and we will drop them for you."

"Hush," said the warriors, "we seek your father."

But just then the old eagle, with a frown on his eyebrow, rushed in and asked why the warriors were frightening his "pin-feathers."

"We came for you, our father. Listen. Our mothers, the beautiful corn maidens, have vanished, leaving no trace save of their flesh. We come to beseech that you shall seek them for us."

"Go before!" said the eagle, smoothing his feathers, which meant that he would follow. So the warriors returned.

Then the eagle launched forth into the sky, circling higher and higher up, until he was smaller than a thistle-down in a whirlwind. At last he flew lower, then into the bower of the dancers where the council awaited him.

"Ah, thou comest!" exclaimed the people.

"Yes," replied the eagle. "Neither a blue-bird nor a wood-rat can escape my eye," said he, snapping his beak, "unless they hide under rocks or bushes. Send for my younger brother; he flies nearer the ground than I do."

So the warriors went to seek the sparrow-hawk. They found him sitting on an ant hill, but when he saw them he would have flown away had they not called out that they had words for him and meant him no harm.

"What is it?" said he. "For if you have any snare-strings with you I'll be off."

"No, no! we wish you to go and hunt for our maidens—the corn maidens," said the warriors,—"your old brother, the eagle, cannot find them."

"Oh, that's it; well, go before—of course he can't find them! He climbs up to the clouds and thinks he can see under every tree and shadow as the Sun, who sees not with eyes, does."

The sparrow-hawk flew away to the north and the east and the west, looking behind every cliff and copse-wood, but he found no trace of the maidens, and returned, declaring as he flew into the bower, "they can not be found. They are hiding more snugly than I ever knew a sparrow to hide," said he, ruffling his feathers and gripping the stick he settled on as though it were feathers and blood.

"Oh, alas! alas! our beautiful maidens!" cried the old women; "we shall never see them again!"

"Hold your feet with patience, there's old heavy nose out there; go and see if he can hunt for them. He knows well enough to find their flesh, however so little that may be," said an old priest, pointing to a crow who was scratching an ash-heap sidewise with his beak, trying to find something for a morning meal. So the warriors ran down and accosted him.

"O caw!" exclaimed the crow, probing a fresh place, "I am too hungry to go flying around for you stingy fellows. Here I've been ever since perching-time, trying to get a mouthful; but you pick your bones and bowls too clean, be sure for that!"

"Come in, then, grandfather, and we'll give you a smoke and something to eat," said the two warriors.

"Caw, haw!" said the old crow, ruffling up his collar and opening his mouth wide enough to swallow his own head. "Go before!" and he followed them into the dance-court.

"Come in, sit and smoke," said the chief priest, handing the crow a cigarette.

At once the old crow took the cigarette and drew such a big whiff into his throat that the smoke completely filled his feathers, and ever since then crows have been black all over, although before that time they had white shoulder-bands and very blue beaks, which made them look quite fine.

Then the crow suddenly espied an ear of corn under one of the mantles, for this was all the maidens had left; so he made for the corn and flew off with it, saying as he skipped over the houses, "I guess this is all you'll see of the maidens for many a day," and ever since then crows have been so fond of corn that they steal even that which is buried. But bye and bye the old crow came back, saying that he had a "sharp eye for the *flesh* of the maidens, but he could not find any trace of the maidens themselves."

Then the people were very sad with thought, when they suddenly heard Pai'-a-tu-ma joking[6] along the streets as though the whole pueblo were listening to him. "Call him," cried the priests to the warriors, and the warriors ran out to summon Pai'-a-tu-ma.

Pai'-a-tu-ma sat down on a heap of refuse, saying he was about to make a breakfast of it. The warriors greeted him.

"Why and wherefore do you two cowards come not after me?" inquired Pai'-a-tu-ma.

"We do come for you."

"No, you do not."

"Yes, we do."

"Well! I won't go with you," said he, forthwith following them to the dance-court.

"My little children," said he, to the gray-haired priests and mothers, "good evening;"—it was not yet mid-day—"you are all very happy, I see."

"Thou comest," said the chief priest.

"I do not," replied Pai'-a-tu-ma.

"Father," said the chief priest, "we are very sad and we have sought you that we might ask the light of your wisdom.

"Ah, quite as I had supposed; I am very glad to find you all so happy. Being thus you do not need my advice. What may I not do for you?"

"We would that you seek for the corn-maidens, our mothers, whom we have offended, and who have exchanged themselves for nothing in our gaze."

"Oh, *that's all,* is it? The corn maidens are not lost, and if they were I would not go to seek them, and if I went to seek for them I could not find them, and if I found them I would not bring them, but I would tell them you 'did not wish to see them' and leave them where they are not—in the Land of Everlasting Summer, which is not their home. Ha! you have no prayer-plumes here, I observe," said he, picking up one each of the yellow, blue and white kinds, and starting out with the remark—

"I come."

With rapid strides he set forth toward the south. When he came to the mouth of the "Cañon of the Woods," whence blows the wind of summer in spring-time, he planted the yellow-plumed stick. Then he knelt to watch the eagle down, and presently the down moved gently toward the north, as though some one were breathing on it. Then he went yet farther, and planted the blue stick. Again the eagle down moved. So he went on planting the sticks, until very far away he placed the last one. Now the eagle plume waved constantly toward the north.

"Aha!" said Pai'-a-tu-ma to himself, "It is the breath of the corn maidens, and thus shall it ever be, for when *they* breathe toward the northland, thither shall warmth, showers, fertility and health be wafted, and the summer birds shall chase the butterfly out of Summer-land and summer itself, with my own beads and treasures shall follow after." Then he journeyed on, no longer a dirty clown, but an aged, grand god, with a colored flute, flying softly and swiftly as the wind he sought for.

Soon he came to the home of the maidens, whom he greeted, bidding them, as he waved his flute over them, to follow him to the home of their children.

The maidens arose, and each taking a tray covered with embroidered cotton, followed him as he strode with folded arms, swiftly before them.

At last they reached the home of our fathers. Then Pai'-a-tu-ma gravely spoke to the council.

"Behold, I have returned with the lost maidens, yet may they not remain or come again, for you have not loved their beautiful custom—the source of your lives—and men would seek to change the blessings of their flesh itself into suffering humanity were they to remain amongst you.

"As a mother of her own blood and being gives life to her offspring, so have these given of their own flesh to you. Once more their flesh they give to you, as it were their children. From the beginning of the new Sun each year, ye shall treasure their gift, during the moon of the sacred fire, during the moon of the snow-broken boughs, during the moon of the great sand-driving winds, during the moon of the lesser sand-driving winds, ye shall treasure their flesh. Then, in the new soil which the winter winds and water have brought, ye shall bury their flesh as ye bury the flesh of the dead, and as die flesh of the dead decays so shall their flesh decay, and as from the flesh of the dead springs the other being (the soul), so from their flesh shall spring new being, like to the first, yet in eight-fold plenitude. Of this shall ye eat and be bereft of hunger. Behold these maidens, beautiful and perfect are they, and as this, their flesh, is derived from them, so shall it confer on those whom it feeds perfection of person and beauty, as of those whence it was derived." He lifted the tray from the head of the maiden nearest him. She smiled and was seen no more; yet when the people opened the tray it was filled with yellow seed-corn. And so Pai'-a-tu-ma lifted the trays, each in turn, from the heads of the other maidens, and, as he did so, each faded from view. In the second tray the people found blue corn; in the third, red; in the fourth, white; in the fifth, variegated; and in the sixth, black. These they saved, and in the springtime they carefully planted the seeds in separate places. The breaths of the corn maidens blew rain-clouds from their homes in Summer-land, and when the rains had passed away green corn plants grew everywhere the grains had been planted. And when the plants had grown tall and blossomed, they were laden with ears of corn, yellow, blue, red, white, speckled and black. Thus to this day grows the corn, always eight-fold more than is planted, and of six colors, which our women preserve separately during the moons of the sacred fire, snow-broken boughs, great sand-driving winds and lesser sand-driving winds.

It was Pai'-a-tu-ma who found the corn maidens and brought them back. He took the trays from their heads and gave them to the people; hence, when in winter, during the moon of the sacred fire, the priests gather to bless the seed-corn for the coming year, the chief-priest of the *Ne'-we-kwe* hands the trays of corn-seed into the estufa.

Ever since these days, the beautiful corn maidens have dwelt in the Land of Everlasting Summer. This we know. For does not their sweet-smelling breath come from that flowery country, bringing life to their children, the corn-plants? It is the south wind which we feel in spring-time.

Thus was born Tâ-a, or the "Seed of Seeds."

—From "Zuñi Breadstuff," Millstone 9, no. 1 (1884): 1–3.

Notes

1. Or the "substance of living flesh." This is exemplified as well as may be by the little cylinders of cuticle and fatty-matter that may be rubbed from the person after bathing. [F.H.C.]

2. It may be seen that the Zuñis have here their own way of accounting for their primitive social organization into *Gentes* and *Phratries*—organizations well nigh universal in the ancient world, as with the society of the early Greeks and Romans, and still prevalent amongst savage tribes of today. [F.H.C.]

3. In ancient times when desirous of making fire, and even today when kindling the sacred flame, the Zuñis produced and still produce, the first spark by drilling with a hard stick like an arrow-shaft into a dry piece of soft root. An arrow-shaft is now used by preference, as it is the emblem of lightning. [F.H.C.]

4. Doubtless this refers to the earthquake. Ruins may sometimes be found in the Southwest, buried like Pompeii beneath the ashes and lava of ancient eruptions, thus pointing either to a remote origin of the Pueblo or a recent cessation of volcanic action in New Mexico and Arizona. [F.H.C.]

5. Unexceptionably this is one of the most beautiful of the native ceremonials, and is one of the few sacred dances of the Zuñis in which women assume the leading part. It is still performed with untiring zeal, usually during each summer, although accompanied by exhausting fasts and abstinences from sleep. Curiously enough, it was observed and admirably, though too briefly described, by Coronado . . . nearly three hundred and fifty years ago.

    It was with this ceremonial that the delighted nation welcomed the water which my party brought in 1882 from the "Ocean of Sunrise." As I was then compelled to join the watch of the priests and elders, I had ample leisure during two sleepless days and nights to gather the above and following story from the song which celebrates the origin of the custom, but which both in length and poetic beauty far surpasses the limits and style of the present paper. [F.H.C.]

6. The *Ne'-we-kwe*, of whom the God of Dew, or Pai'-a-tu-ma, was the first Great Father, are a band of medicine priests belonging, as explained heretofore, to one of the most ancient organizations of the Zuñis. Their medical skill is supposed to be very great—in many cases—and their traditional wisdom is counted even greater. Yet they are clowns whose grotesque and quick-witted remarks amuse most public assemblies of the Pueblo holiday. One of their customs is to speak the opposite of their meaning; hence too, their assumptions of the clown's part at public ceremonials, when really their office and powers are to be reversed. Their grotesque costuming and face-painting are quite in keeping with their assumed characters, and would, were it possible, justify the belief that our own circus clowns were their lineal descendants or copyists. Often so like are human things, though geographically widely severed. [F.H.C.]

Red Sky's Scrolls and Origin Lore

SELWYN DEWDNEY

For the reader who is as dubious as I was when I first met James Red Sky Senior I offer this further preliminary account of his Midé credentials.

By Treaty nos. 131 and 132 signed in 1873, 55,000 square miles of territory were surrendered to the Canadian government by representatives of the Ojibway and Saulteaux-Ojibway occupying the Ontario section of the Winnipeg River watershed (bounded on the east by the heights of land into the Albany River system and the Lake Superior watershed), and the southeast corner of Manitoba east of the Winnipeg and Whitemouth Rivers and of a line running south from Whitemouth Lake to the 49th parallel.

The fifth signature on the list of native representatives was that of Powassan(g), pre-eminent among the Lake of the Woods leaders and Grand Shaman of the Midéwewin at Northwest Angle. Some, if not all, of Red Sky's scrolls were originally Powassan's, for Red Sky's mentor and uncle, Baldhead, learned his Midé lore at the feet of the great Northwest Angle Midé master. Further evidence of Red Sky's family standing among the Midé élite is the fact that it was Powassan, still living in 1895, who dreamed Red Sky's proper Ojibway name, Eshkway-keezhik (Last Sky). The name 'Red Sky' is the English translation of his father's personal name, Mushkwaykeezhik. Adopted by 'Baldhead' (Peshkwaykandip) as an English surname, the name Red Sky spread to the other brothers and today is one of the commonest surnames on the Shoal Lake Reserve. The person to whom these pages will refer as Red Sky, to distinguish himself from a younger James in the family connection, signs himself James Red Sky Senior.

The central concern of the Midé oral tradition was with origins: the creation of the world and of man, the origin of death, the introduction of the Midéwewin, and the ancestral origins of the Ojibway people. Instruction was of three sorts: a relatively simple, short term course of preparation for those to be initiated into the lower degrees, more complex information and requirements for those aiming at the higher degrees of initiation, and a long, gruelling apprenticeship which led—with or without actual initiations—to acquisition of the total Midé lore available and the summit of Midé status. Simple or complex, the instruction always included correct ritual procedures, some herbal and medical training, and a drilling in the origin traditions.

For each and all of these purposes a scroll could be devised as a mnemonic aid. On completion of an apprenticeship that extended over a period of many years Red Sky's uncle gave him all of his scrolls. Of the seven, four were mainly concerned with ritualistic details; three dealt with origins. The excerpts that follow are transcribed from tape-recordings made in 1969 of Red Sky's interpretations of his Creation and End scrolls, and of the first section of his Migration scroll. Supplementing these transcriptions are quotations from notes I had taken in previous years, from as early as 1960.

In anticipation of some confusion as the reader is confronted with varying interpretations by the same person of the same scroll, it should be explained that a Midé master was free to make selections from the total lore at his command, producing simple condensed accounts for one purpose or relating in detail one or more variations on the same theme, some of which, taken literally, contradict each other.

In this respect Red Sky was no exception. It would be arbitrary, even arrogant, for me to provide a running commentary, attempting to reconcile every contradiction, fill in all the gaps, or explain each obscurity in his interpretations, even if I could. It is time now for his voice to be heard.

Creation of the World (First Version)

When God first made this world he didn't think or work anything to make this world. He just said this and that, and it happened—just by the word of God. What he wanted [for] this world he took it. So he thought that nobody

---

could live on this world, because nothing went right. There was too much ice. There was too much water. Nobody could live on this earth. Well, he said he'd try a second time. This [referring to the second unit in his Creation scroll] is the second world. And he tried and he knew he was going to make [accomplish] it. So after the second time there was still too much ice—too much ice and too much water. Nobody can live like that. It didn't take him one day or one week or one month. I was told that it took him probably 2000 years—maybe 4000 years.

Well, he was trying, but it didn't look very good. Nobody can live on this earth that way. Too much water, too much ice. He knew he was going to make it—make this world all right. So he tried it a third time. He tried it and he made it go. And he was convinced he was going to make it. The earth looked pretty good. Not so much water, not so much ice. So he tried it again. That was the third earth. After trying the third time he tried the fourth time.

When he tried it the fourth time everything went nice. The hills were green, the water was nice and the streams were running. The trees grew—the leaves on the trees—everything was beautiful. When he looked among the hills everything was very nice. Well, he thought, it was going to be perfect—perfect to live on. It looked very *nice that anybody could live on it.*

The fact that in all the surviving origin lore there is no counterpart to this account of the creation of the world might cast some doubt on its place in the Midé tradition were it not for a single hint from Kohl (1860, 150) whose informant, Loonfoot, interpreted eight footprints drawn on one of his birchbark records as 'the footsteps of the Great Otter, which soon after the creation of the world ran through the water and across the world. At the first movement it stepped on ice, at the second into a swamp, at the third into water, while at the fourth flowers sprang up.'

Creation of the World (Second Version)

On scanning Red Sky's Creation scroll (Figure 1) for hints of the first version one finds very little that relates to it. An earlier version that Red Sky dictated to me in 1967 offers a quite different perspective. During the earlier interviews, however, I had limited the interpretations to writing on a blueprint of his scrolls his comments on each figure.

Reading the scroll from left to right, the partially obscured Bear's head symbolizes 'God.' On another occasion Red Sky explained. 'The Bear is the strongest animal, so it came to represent God. A bear can do *any*

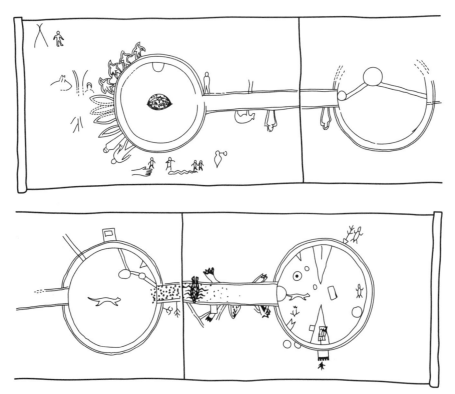

FIGURE 1   Red Sky's Creation Scroll (GAI-2)

thing.' The pictographic preface to the whole sequence means, 'God opens a way for you.' A 'tree' almost totally obscured by damage to the scroll comes next. 'When you enter the Midéwewin you have to pass through a big log which closes behind . . .'

Of the ten figures grouped around the left side of the first circle four are 'birds,' four are 'animals,' the dominant human figure is 'God,' and the lesser one 'the man who works for God.'

The first circular unit was again identified as 'God's first attempt to create the world.' The object in the centre was explained as 'God gave the Megis—that's a shell—for body health.' Pointing to the small inward projection from the upper edge of the circle, 'He seen this point,' adding, 'in his first creation God put hills, rivers, water, etcetera.'

On the pathway leading to the second unit the Bear is again 'God,' and the three human figures are, from the left, 'the man that works for God' . . . 'the Oskahbewiss (assistant), the man who looks after everything,' and 'an elder, to show people the way.'

The second unit was labelled 'God's second attempt.' The first small circle on the interior path is 'where he stopped to look around'; at the second, 'God stopped there. It wasn't fit to live in.'

The third unit was 'God's third attempt.' The path to it was 'the right way.' Proceeding clockwise around the circle from the entering path, the double line projecting outwards signifies 'He found out this was a river,' the rectangular form 'God saw that, thought it was a cloud [on the horizon], came close and saw it was a hill.' The interior detail showed pathways joining small circles that mark 'places where God stopped and looked around.' The animal near the centre is the Great Otter. 'God put the Otter there to bring life to the people.' The projecting tree just past the exit pathway is 'an oak tree,' and next to it is 'a pine.'

In this version, after God's disappointment with his first attempt is noted there is no further mention of failures. The fourth unit, however, is labelled 'God's last attempt to make the world: it was perfect.' In that unit the Otter, 'God's representative, the messenger,' appears again. Apparently in this version Red Sky's mention of a 'God' strangely unfamiliar with a world of his own making, really refers to the Otter seeking the people, to whom—as we shall see in other accounts—he was commissioned to bring the Midé message.

In the fourth unit (see Figure 2a), although it is labelled as the final successful creation, a transition has been made from theology to geography. Even the character of the pathway has changed. The zigzag lines on it indicated 'rapids,' the divergent lines just below indicate that the Otter 'went up that river and had to come back.' In an earlier explanation Red Sky told me 'There were no Indians there, he had to come back.'

'Then he made a portage and saw this long stretch of water. "If I stretch myself as long as this water then they will believe in me." So he made it.' The outward projections from the two ends of this passage were 'God's legs' and 'God's arms,' and a circular projection into the fourth unit was 'God's head.' The form superimposed over God's right arm was 'a reminder not to leave anything out.'

On his arrival at the end of the long stretch 'God looked around. He saw a great big lake.' Red Sky admitted, 'I don't know where that is,' but a moment later provided a substantial clue. The two triangular forms nearly meeting in the centre of the circle represent arms of land. 'At first there was no opening here, but God broke through. The water is still a bit muddy today.' Then he added, 'That's two big lakes in the States with a narrows between—*somewhere close.*'

Identity of 'God's Perfect World'

That was the first exciting inkling I had that the fourth unit of the Creation scroll represented an actual place. When I looked in my atlas—sure enough—there were two large lakes joined by a narrows in Minnesota, a mere fifty miles south of Lake of the Woods: Upper and Lower Red Lake. But I was puzzled by the places Red Sky named, features that had nothing to do with Red Lake: 'Two Points . . . Bear Island . . . and Pine Point.' On a hunch I examined Leech Lake, another 50 miles to the southeast (Figure 3). There they were, all three features!

Ever since my first good look at Red Sky's Migration scroll I had puzzled over a lake at the end of it (and of all other Migration scrolls I had found). This lake, and one from one of the others, shown in Figures 2c and d, although they fail to identify a Bear Island, clearly indicate the double point, and indicate Pine Point with the form of a tree (attached to the local manito). The highly formalized and decorative End scroll not only identified the two points, but marked Bear Island with the 'sacred dots' frequently used in Midé pictography to denote an especially reverenced feature. All through the latter half of the nineteenth century Leech Lake and Red Lake were the most active and prestigious centres in Minnesota, confirming the closeness of the Lake of the Woods tradition to the Midé mainstream. The fourth unit of Red Sky's Creation scroll and the figure in the End scroll are both *composites of the two centres.*

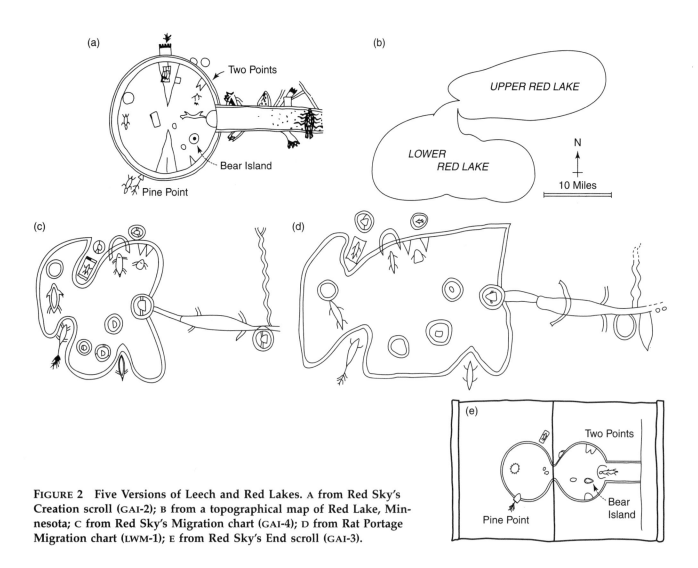

FIGURE 2 **Five Versions of Leech and Red Lakes. A from Red Sky's Creation scroll (GAI-2); B from a topographical map of Red Lake, Minnesota; C from Red Sky's Migration chart (GAI-4); D from Rat Portage Migration chart (LWM-1); E from Red Sky's End scroll (GAI-3).**

Red Sky explained that the End scroll was used only to be 'read' at the end of the Midé ceremonies when the public was admitted into the Midéwegun to share in the final Megis ritual. I suspect that the fourth unit of his Creation scroll was similarly separate, but eventually sewn to the sections containing the first three units, for reasons that will be examined in the next chapter.

There is further evidence of alterations to the original Creation scroll. In the upper and lower left corners are two 'pictographic footnotes' so faintly scratched on the bark that when Red Sky searched for them in vain under the light of a coal oil lamp I thought his memory had misled him. In the morning, however, with the bark flat on the table by the window the slanting rays of the rising sun threw the lines into clear, though delicate relief. In the upper corner a tiny human figure could be discerned, standing beside a conical wigwam. Below the first world was a sequence of figures relating to the creation of man. Both 'footnotes' were interpreted in full detail, as recorded in the 1969 transcriptions that follow.

Creation of Man

So he thought he'd make a man. So he spat on the ground. And afterwards he picked the ground up, moistened it, and he held it in his hand. After he held it in his hand for a long time until it was warm, when he opened his hand there stood a man. And he laid his hand on it and breathed on it. So he laid it down on the ground. Then that man stood on the ground. Then he said . . . he spoke to him, and he spoke back to him. When the man spoke there was flames coming out of his mouth. And when he looked his eyes glistened. Lights came out of his eyes. Flames came out of his mouth. He says 'Well, that's not very good, because he'll be the same as I am if he breathes like that all the time—God's way.'

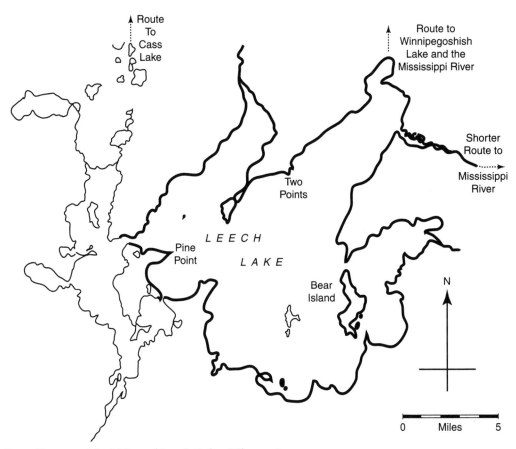

FIGURE 3 From Topographical Map of Leech Lake, Minnesota

Here Red Sky is discussing the figure at the extreme right with the power (like God's) coming out of him.

'He would be able to do anything [God continued]: soften rocks, tear trees into shreds—pull them all out like hair. That wouldn't be very good if he was like that.' So he put his hand on him, to cut him down a little bit— there was too much high pressure in him of the godliness he had in him.

So he let him go wandering around—around the earth, through streams, forests, lakes, creeks—everything. All through that. 'Well,' he said to the man. 'I'm going to give you a name—Ogahbi'ohsahtung (Everlasting-walking-through-this-world)—that's your name.'

So, after a while wandering around, wandering around and around this beautiful world, he had pity on him being alone all the time, day and night all alone. So he put him to sleep. After he put him to sleep he got the liver out of him. I was told there are four layers to the liver. He took one layer of the liver out of him, took it out and he held it there in his hand while he was sleeping. And when he opened his hand there was a woman. Oh, a very nice woman. Her hair was right down to her knees. As she looked her eyes had a gleam—sparkled. And as she stood there her bosom—her teats—were sticking out far. And God thought by her teats a woman, a human being would rise there, from her teats.

And as she stood there, this beautiful woman, the man woke up. He was surprised to see her standing right there before him. She looked at him and he looked at her—looked all over. He thought she wasn't the same as he was. She was a lot different. After awhile they come together, started talking to each other and they got acquainted. It was [a long time] after that that they started sleeping together. They wandered around in the forest, the streams, creeks and lakes, and so they couldn't part from each other. After awhile God looked at them and he said 'I'm going to pour a little water on them so they won't forget everything, what I've done for them.' So he sprinkled a little water out of a little cloud that passed by. And that is how he baptized them.

After awhile Ogahbi'ohsahtung was working over on one side and she was working on that side. There came a great big snake right before her, says to her . . . 'Come here. I want to talk to you.'

'No,' she said, 'I'm not going to talk to you.'

'I want you to go over there and get Ogahbi'ohsahtung and go back in the woods there.'

'No,' she said, 'We were told not to do anything like that. Because God knows everything. God was there. He told us not to. There'll be a time when he'll tell us when we will get together.'

So after a long coaxing . . . trying to reach Ogahbi'ohsahtung . . . she was too anxious to get connections with him sexually. So he didn't want to do it. Well, when this snake coaxed her she didn't take too much coaxing because she already thought that. She was very anxious to get connections with him. So as soon as she was tempted . . . well, everything broke off, as if it were two bottles, one on top of the other, and one fell off. That's how anxious she was. Now this one fell off. She went over with him back in the bushes.

In the Genesis account, from which a large part of this tale was obviously borrowed, there is a prophecy that there would be enmity thereafter between the snake and the woman's descendants. In Red Sky's version this is given an ingenious twist. 'By bruising the heel' (here Red Sky is referring to a biblical phrase) 'the Snake caused the woman to have periods monthly.'

In the taped interview Red Sky went right on with a story to which there was no reference in any of his scrolls. In what follows the words 'family marks' refer to the identifying pictographs used as signatures in the treaties, engraved on personal possessions, and used in trail messages.

Origin of the Dodem (Totem) System

The world was full of people at that time already, after the creation of a man and a woman—full of people. So when God looked at them they were so wicked they didn't follow any of the ways that he wanted them to live. There was all kinds of wickedness, such as fornication, sexuality . . . all these things. They even went together with their sisters, aunts, and the men went together with their mothers. It was a very bad state.

So he wanted to punish them. So the thought of this great Thunderbird, and he told this Thunderbird to make up a great big storm. Because these people worked together they were all in one place. And when they got together these Thunderbirds came. High winds blew. Thunder, lightning, rain—every thing came down. So these people ran to get shelter all over the place. They couldn't find no shelter. Their places of abode couldn't hold the storm that came upon them.

Well, after awhile when everything had quietened they started to talk to each other. They couldn't understand each other when they talked together. They couldn't understand each other at all. One person said something, they didn't understand it.

So they all went—one family this way, one family another way. One family east, north, how far they went nobody knows. So when these families that went east started talking together they started to understand each other. The families that went south and north started to understand each other. So afterwards they made family marks, like Caribou [Red Sky's totem] and a Sturgeon, Moose, Elk, things like that. And all the birds of the air, their family marks.

One might dismiss Red Sky's accounts of man's temptation and fall, and of totemic origins as mere garbled versions of biblical lore that he himself inserted into the Midé tradition. To do this, however, would be to overlook the extent to which the Midéwewin from early times adapted a number of Christian concepts and biblical details for its own purposes. Kohl (1860), for instance, in a conversation he recorded, was astonished to hear Loonfoot refer to the Tower of Babel, the Flood, and even the Romans. Loonfoot's wife was a Crane, who claimed, Kohl was told, that the Crane's lineage reached back to the Flood and their name was recorded 'dans les livres des Romains.' Hearing this last reference Kohl smiled incredulously.

But Loonfoot protested: 'Non, non, Monsieur, sérieusement on a trouvé déjà à la destruction de la Tour de Babel tous les noms [totems] qui sont à présent parmi nous.'

The Ojibway word 'totem,' pronounced *dodem* by the southern Ojibway, has been adopted universally to refer to systems used by many preliterate cultures to prevent 'inbreeding' and incest, or more positively, to ensure a flow of fresh genetic strains from outside the gene pool of small isolated bands. Red Sky makes this point amply clear. In the absence of tribal organization the clan system provided close links with other bands, for two members of the same clan, even if they had no blood relationship, regarded each other as close relatives, regardless of how far apart their respective bands might wander.

My own first acquaintance with the strength and significance of totemic identity was a statement by the wife of the late James Horton on the Manitou Reserve near Emo, Ontario. She informed my wife and me that she could not eat sturgeon. Moreover, she knew whenever a sturgeon was caught in the Rainy River, because *she herself was a Sturgeon.*

The Manito Council (Two Versions)

When I asked Red Sky to interpret the birds and other figures shown around the first unit of his Creation scroll he gave me the following account, transcribed from the 1969 tape recording.

> *When this world was full of human beings it got so all the people were dying off—dying off like that and God didn't know what to do about it. So he thought he'd teach them some way to worship him. So later, when he got this all organized he said, 'I'll have them meeting at the centre of a . . . of a different continent across the water. That's where I'll have this meeting. So where I think God took it was in Palestine. And so when God got this organized he brought all these birds and animals—all the living creatures in the world—to this one place. So then they had a meeting.*

This was one of his versions of the origin of the Manito Council. The second was an interpretation of the first unit of the Migration scroll (Figure 4), where five figures surround the circle.

'So God thought, "Well, I want these people to worship me. I don't know how to get them to worship me." So he called a meeting of all the birds—all the birds and all the creatures. And so they had a meeting to talk about it—somewhere across the Big Water, where this Manito was. So he said to this meeting, "Now who's going to take it? Who's going to take it across to the people?" Well, the Bear was there. He says, "I'll take it across to the people."'

The Bear's Mission

Now the Council's work was done and everything depended on the Bear. And, just as it took God three tries before his fourth successful effort to create a 'beautiful world,' so the Migration scroll records the Bear's four efforts to break through the barriers between himself and that same world (Figure 4).

> *So when he went out, this Everlasting Life that he was carrying was very heavy—very heavy. He could hardly walk. When he put his arms out he stuck his arms up to his elbows. Same with his hind feet; he stuck them right to his knees.*
>
> *After walking a little ways he came to a wall. He couldn't go anywhere. He didn't know what to do. So he stuck his tongue out. Then his tongue went through as if it were a bullet shot out of a rifle. It went right through to the other side. He went right through the little hole and then came out on the other side and took this Life— this Everlasting Life that he was carrying. After looking around he didn't see no earth—nothing. So he got out,*

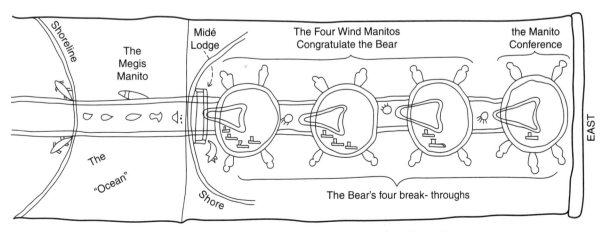

FIGURE 4   The Bear's Four Break-Throughs, from Red Sky's Migration Chart (GAI-4)

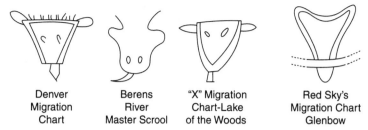

| Denver Migration Chart | Berens River Master Scrool | "X" Migration Chart-Lake of the Woods | Red Sky's Migration Chart Glenbow |

FIGURE 5   **Various Renderings of the Bear's Tongue, from Four Migration Charts**

he found another wall. He did the same thing—stuck his tongue out and it went right through as if it were a bullet shot out of a rifle. And in that hole he went through with this Pack he had—heavy Everlasting Life. And when these people saw this [here Red Sky pointed to the four manitos stationed around each of the introductory circles on the Migration scroll] the manito at the east, the manito at the south, manito at the west and manito at the north, they thanked him for the work he did.

Well, that wasn't the end. That was the second time. Well he started out . . . and he found another wall. That was the third time. And he did the same thing. He stuck out his tongue [Figure 5] and it went through as if shot out of a gun. Then he went through here. And when he got on the other side it happened the same thing. When he went through he did the same thing. That was the fourth time he did the same thing.

It is important, for later comparisons with other sources, to understand this passage, and its relation to the pictographs illustrated here. The four introductory units represent the Bear's four break-throughs. Stationed around each circle are the Wind manitos, the extra figure above the first circle representing God. The five together *also*, as I have mentioned, represented the Manito Council. The triangular abstraction overlapping the edge of each circle represents the Bear's head as it breaks through each barrier. Next we are allowed a glimpse of the whole Bear, just as he emerged after the fourth break-through.

After he was there—when he got out—he seen this little place [the small vertical rectangle]. He thought he'd go into this little place, what we call today Midéwegun [Midé lodge]. So towards the east there was a little door, and a little door to the west. After he got in he took eight steps. Then he took out a little tree and he planted it. He stuck the little tree into the middle of the Midéwegun. After a while, a Thunderbird came and landed on this tree.

'This is where I'm going to listen to the Indian whenever he calls upon God. When anything—some kind of sickness or some kind of bad luck happens—he'll have God. I'll listen to everything right from here.'

This is what we see on this tree. There's a bird on the tree. And a little later there came a great big Rock. God said, 'This is the foundation of this Midéwegun. This is the foundation. I'll uphold this as long as the earth lasts. It won't fall down. Nobody will turn it over, can't take it down. If the Indian fights for it I'll still be here to protect it.'

This completes Red Sky's interpretations of the first part of the origin section of his Migration scroll. The Bear has successfully carried the Pack of Life through the first obstacles and has been strengthened for the task ahead by passing through the Midéwegun, that is, by himself undergoing initiation into the Midéwewin.

And after he came out [of the Midéwegun] he came down, he came to the shore of a Big Water. After a little while, while he was walking back and forth there, he didn't know what to do. So finally he heard someone talking to him.

'What have you got there?'

'Oh, I've got something I've got to take to the Indians, across this Big Water.'

'Well,' he said, 'I'm the one that can do it.' This is Megis, the Shell—seashell.

So they started unloading and reloading. They tell me it looked as if a white man was loading a great big ship. That's what it looked like when they transferred what he was carrying.

So he went out—the Megis—he came out of the water. He had followed the bottom of the ocean. And after a little while he came up. When he came up he looked around. He seen this great big hill. After he looked around there was a small narrows where he went through. On the right hand side he seen this great big hill—high . . . high. So he thought he'd go up and look around. So he found another manito there and he left word with him that wants help—that has sickness or disease or misfortune—is unlucky—he'll go to him. He'll fix him up.

Well, after a bit he came up, looked around. He didn't see nothing. No land anywhere—couldn't see no land. And he went down again and followed along the bottom of the ocean and came up again. Still he didn't see nothing—no land in sight nowhere. So, after awhile he went down again. He did the same thing—followed along the bottom of the ocean, came up again, went along there. So he'd come up again. Looking around, he seen land just as if it was a little string going along there. That was land.

There are three points to note here. It is now the Megis, not the Bear, who is carrying the message. Apparently, on his first emergence the Megis manito gave the Midé message to a local manito: that is, he set up a Midé lodge as he had done before he went down to the shore. Proceeding, he sighted land on his *fourth* emergence, just as the Bear broke through the fourth barrier, and God made four attempts to create the world.

'Well,' he said, 'I'm glad.' He was glad he found land. Well, he didn't go down this time. He just went along [on the surface] and he seen this river coming down into the ocean. Well, he thought he'd stop there and look around.

The Cutfoot Legend (First Version)

At this point, although there is no break in Red Sky's narrative, a new theme takes over whose significance will become clear only when we explore it in the next chapter as we become acquainted with other origin tales. Here the Megis goes ashore, and:

Well, he seen a little wigwam—a little tent. He seen a baby just standing—just holding himself up. He couldn't stand up—the only thing he could do by standing was hold himself up. That's how young this baby was— maybe one year. So he took this little baby, picked it up and went back across the ocean. And he took him there before this manito—this Midé manito. He told him he took this little baby, and there he was. He [the Midé manito] taught him everything about how to worship God through the Midéwewin. Taught him until he was a great big man.

So then these people who lost their baby were very sorrowful, crying day and night. They looked around the whole continent, crying—looked it over, trying to find their baby. So they went back to their tent while they were crying there. It took them quite a number of years. The old man was getting pretty grey, the lady was pretty grey, too. And they felt sorrowful.

They were sitting there sorrowful and a man stood before them.

'What's the crying about? What's all the crying about?'

'Oh,' they told him, 'We lost our little baby—a little baby boy.'

'Oh, don't think anything about it. I'm the little baby. I'm the one you lost.'

They went and hugged and kissed him. They were glad to see that little baby back again.

'Well,' he told them, 'I'm not staying here. I'm going back to where this Midéwewin came from.' So he left them there.

And when you dream about going to Midé [i.e., to be initiated] you want to sacrifice a few little things. This is the man who thinks about you when you're sick or have bad luck all the time. He looks upon you. He has mercy upon you. He pities you for having all the troubles. He comes to you in dreams, and that's where you [qualify to] enter the Midéwewin.

One point here may easily be missed: that even the loss of so valued a possession as a child would not be too high a price for the benefits of the Midé health-giving rites, so why not make some small sacrifices—that is, make worthwhile gifts to the Midé officials who will initiate you.

The Cutfoot Legend (Second Version)

In the upper left corner of the Creation scroll a small human figure stands beside a wigwam. This pictograph could remind us not only of the episode just described, but of the second version of a myth which we shall encounter again. For both versions have features in common that I believe reach back to an early period— perhaps the actual origin—of the Midéwewin.

There was a little boy and his father and mother. They were living close to the lakeshore. So he [the boy] was whittling away there. He was making a bow and arrow. So this man went to this little boy. And this little boy said to his Mother and Dad, 'Mother, there's a stranger here.'

'Is that so? Who is that talking to this little boy?'

He said, 'Will you get your bow and arrow ready today?'

'Oh yes, I'll have it ready today.'

So the father and mother came out and spread this cloth where they use a mat to eat on. Oh, they gave him something to eat and they noticed then that he wouldn't eat anything. He wouldn't take nothing at all that was set before him. And then, after they were through eating this man asked them, 'How far is the next village from here?'

'Oh, it'll take you quite a long time, because it's quite a long way. It'll take you two hands before sunset.' That's how they measured the time—about two hands before sunset.

'Could I have this little boy to take me a little ways before I get to the next village?'

'Oh yes. That'll be all right,' they tell him.

So he got the little boy and went out started walking. And it was pretty tough walking because there was no road—they travelled in the bush. After going a little ways—Oh boy! He got sweating. He got tired walking through the bush. After going a little more he asked if they could rest a bit.

'Oh yes. Yes, we'll rest a little bit.'

Then after they rested a little bit they started off again. After they started off he noticed he wasn't sweating at all. He was walking above the ground. He was walking in the air. Oh boy, he thought. He told this man, 'I think I'll stop here.'

'Wait a minute,' he said. And he started to teach him everything. Teach him about God, God's ways. Teach him about roots—herbal remedies. He taught him the remedy for whatever sickness he got. He told him about what he would take—what roots he would take.

So after this the little boy went home. Boy, was he glad!

This is the man that knew every thing. Afterwards when he got to be a big man he was the head of everything [in charge of the whole ceremony]. He had a knowledge because he was taught the way God had fixed everything up [solved the problems of sickness and death by providing the Midéwewin].

This is the last of Red Sky's more comprehensive interpretations and associated lore, with the exception of his comments on the main body of his Migration chart. These other comments and explanations, however, would lose much of their meaning without some familiarity with what has survived of the oral tradition from other sources.

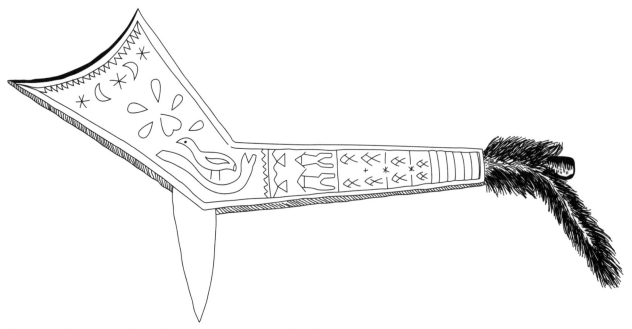

FIGURE 6   Dream Symbols Carved on Tomahawk, after Kohl

Other Origin Tales and Scrolls

SELWYN DEWDNEY

Kohl's interest in the art of the villagers at La Pointe and his very human curiosity led him to insights into the Ojibway mystique that few other observers have matched. For example (1860, 296–7) there was the occasion when he noticed the engraved decoration on the wooden handle of a tomahawk (Figure 6) and asked its owner what the symbols signified. Surprisingly enough, in view of the many reports that significant dreams must be kept secret lest they lose their power, the man not only revealed that the pictographs represented the results of his boyhood dream quest during which he fasted for ten days, but interpreted their content, refusing only to reveal 'all the circumstances and course' of the dream. But he did reveal the intimacy that linked him with the powerful manito he had acquired in the dream as his lifetime personal guardian.

'I often think of this face, this eagle,' he said, 'and I not only think of it, but I speak to it in a loud voice.'

No better glimpse could be offered into the heart of the Ojibway survival system, inherited from ancestral life styles that were shared by many other Amerindian societies. Here, before examining the origin traditions that await our attention, it will be useful to take a further look into the sources of Ojibway identity and of Midé mythology.

The Manito World

All-pervasive in the oral tradition of the Midéwewin lie the concept of the manito world and the central role of the dream. Throughout this study of the sacred scrolls, and long before that in numerous interviews with Cree and Ojibway elders to learn what beliefs were associated with the rock paintings, it became more and more obvious to me that the word *manito* cannot be translated into English. Renderings such as 'spirit' or even 'god' reduce seriously the combination of substance, power and reality that the native word can express. For in the manito world, accessible only through the doorway of the dreams, were vested all the powers that determined whether the hunter and his family would survive or perish. To enter this world was to step *into*, not out of, the *real* world.

The dream, therefore, was man's most meaningful experience. A child's name might be dreamed up—literally—by a prestigious elder. And when the male child reached puberty he was sent into isolation, to build himself a tree nest, or find a secluded rock platform, where he fasted until he achieved the dream state that would reveal to him the manito who would be available for life to help him meet the crises of survival.

In a land where every winter brought close the threat of starvation a strong sharing code developed, a moral compulsion on the successful hunter to see that the weak, and even wandering strangers, were fed. So the manitos were conceived of as beings who might normally be indifferent to human welfare, but were vulnerable to the appeal of a human being who lay weak and helpless before them without food or water, exposed to the elements and alone.

Psychologically the boyhood dream quest prepared the youth for the stress of his future role as provider. Among the northern Algonkian-speakers the nature of the land and distribution of the food supply created a pattern of family groups subsisting on moose or caribou in isolated winter hunting territories, emerging after spring break-up to join other families in brief summer village gatherings around food concentrations: fish spawning grounds, berry picking areas, and—in the south—wild rice fields at harvest time. Even in summer there were animal epidemics and population cycles, forest fires and unseasonable weather that could threaten the food supply. But in the winter a spring that came too early, or too late, an unpredictable shift in caribou migrations, or prolonged blizzards—a dozen alternatives could bring disaster.

More than once in his lifetime the hunter as he ranged the frozen lakes and silent snow-laden forests would be stalked by the dreaded Windigo, grim allegory of winter starvation and the threat of cannibalism. Paradoxically, the more desperate the hunter's state the closer he would feel he was to earning the pity of the supernaturals. So he had the faith to muster his last resources for the final effort to survive; and his dreams—far from being impractical flights of imagination—gave him the self-confidence that was the most *practical* necessity of his life.

There was no limit to the manito concept. If in his boyhood dream the hunter had encountered and conversed with a mere stone or a cloud, that object became his manito guardian. Theoretically all supernatural beings were equal; in practice some were more, others less, powerful. The manitos, therefore, could be graded in terms of power and status. Very loosely, one might divide them into four sorts of supernatural beings.

At the lowest level there were the powers potential in the simplest of natural objects, whether organic or inorganic. At a much higher level were the manitos that Hallowell (1942, 7) refers to as the 'masters.' Writing about the Saulteaux-Ojibway of the Lake Winnipeg region he explains that 'in the case of animal and plant species there is in theory a "master" for each group, for bears as well as for birch trees.' The concept of a 'master' has always reminded me of the Platonic theory of reality, in which the 'doorness' of a door—the Idea out of which all doors emerge—is more real than any individual manifestation of the Idea. So, individual rabbits might come and go—live, die, and be eaten or rot—but the Great Rabbit was the source of all rabbits, and as long as he was respected in prescribed rituals he would continue to supply the temporary, edible manifestations according to man's need. Even among the Source Beings, as I prefer to call them, there were higher and lower ranks, partly determined by their importance as a food supply, partly reaching deep into traditional mysteries. Thus, though the Bear manito ranked high as a food animal, it ranked far higher than the Moose or Sturgeon manitos, as we shall see. As Hallowell puts it: 'in practice certain masters have assumed greater prominence than others, e.g. *mikinak*, the master of the great turtles . . . [of] the conjuring lodge [or Shaking Tent].'

Earlier (1942, 5) Hallowell contrasts the realities of the Saulteaux-Ojibway world with the Western concept of what is real, using as an example

> *a belief in the Thunder Birds who live in the South during the winter and spend spring and summer in the North. When you hear them they are pursuing snakes that live on the earth . . . They [the snakes] are* water *monsters [italics added] living in the lakes and swamps and some of the Indians have seen them . . . Since from our point of view thunder is a part of their physical environment and monster snakes are not, we might be inclined to make a distinction between them . . . I prefer to consider both the Thunder Birds and the monster snakes as part of the behavioral environment of these Indians and to ignore any such distinction. Both are 'real' in the sense that they have actual effects upon behavior.*

In the broader Ojibway context there was a tendency, never explicit, to distinguish between manitos referred to in the plural—as in Thunderbirds—and the same manito as a singular entity—as in *the* Thunderbird. In this sense *the* Thunderbird symbolizes all threats to man from the sky, especially lightning, and may be grouped with the Great Lynx (or Lion) Misshipeshu, associated with death by drowning, and the dreaded Windigo. Other manitos symbolizing the uncontrollable forces of nature are the four Wind manitos (East, South, West, and North) and the May-maygwessiwuk, mysterious denizens of shorewater rocks who can affect local weather on the open lakes.

Of the five great beings who might be referred to as the 'super-manitos'—Misshipeshu, the Thunderbird, the Sacred Bear, the Great Turtle and the Windigo—only the first three have a place in the Midéwewin; but some Midé practitioners were also skilled in the Shaking-tent rites (page 121). Here, too, there is great confusion; but at the deepest level, the most dangerous and therefore the most powerful of all the manitos were the Bear and the Lion, with roots reaching back into prehistory.

A confusing aspect of both Cree and Ojibway lore is the role of the shaman-trickster folk-hero, known to the southern Ojibway as Nanabozho, in the north as Wissakachauk. As the subject of hilarious and frequently earthy humour in hundreds of tales still circulating he was a very human figure, frequently misusing his supernatural powers to the point where he got himself into embarrassing situations.

Ruth Landes (1968) accounts for the confusions and discrepancies that are typical of the Midé oral tradition by the Ojibway respect for *any* authoritative source of information about the supernatural. A Midé apprentice, she was told, was expected to memorize everything his instructor passed on to him, with uncritical zeal. Interruptions and questions were regarded as presumptuous and irrelevant, even dangerous, for to cross a shaman in any way was to invite destruction by sorcery. The shaman himself was equally uncritical of information he acquired from his colleagues in exchange for appropriate gifts. All such material, no matter how inconsistent or illogical it might seem, added to his status and manito power. In any case Ojibway thinking was so allegorical, subtle and indirect that contradictions were not seen as such, but rather as hiding deeper levels of meaning that were the more powerful for being difficult to correlate with other information.

To minimize the confusion of origin accounts that follow I have grouped them into six categories: 1 *In the beginning*—creation of the world, of man and the animals; 2 *The origin of death*—and manito concern for the people; 3 *The Manito Council*—and appointment of an agent; 4 *The agent's breakthrough*—and initiation; 5 *The agent's mission*—and major stopping places; 6 *The visionary revelation*—Sun-boy and the Cutfoot legends.

In the Beginning

The widely current legend of how Nanabozho re-created the world after the flood let loose by Misshipeshu after the *fourth* of his helpers brought up a small scoop of mud is not included in the Midé tradition. It seems that there was far more interest in the creation of man than in that of the earth. One tale, other than Red Sky's account, was recorded by Howard (1965, 126) whose Bungi-Ojibway informant, Standing Chief, told him that the world was made by a spirit who took a piece of earth and kept blowing on it until it reached the earth's present size.

Standing Chief also related how the same spirit took a piece of clay and made a man by the same means, stopping when he felt that 'If you were larger it would be hard for you to make clothing for yourselves.' Another informant told Howard that Nanapus (Nanabozho) was the first man. The Bungi (Little) Ojibway were a branch of the more northerly migrations, probably from the northwest shore of Lake Superior, who moved out on the prairies in the early historical period, adopting the Plains culture of their Siouan and Cree neighbours, but maintaining many of the practices and beliefs—including variants of the Midéwewin—from their original bush milieu.

Hoffman (1883, 172) was told by his chief informant Sikassige at White Earth, Minnesota, that 'Dzhe Manitou' created two men and two women who had, at first, 'no power of thought or reason. He took them in his hands so that they should multiply; he paired them, and from this sprung the Indians.' The faculty of reason was added later. Landes (1968, 90) had another version, from Everwind. The great Spirit picked up some dirt, shut his hand over it, opened it, and there was a woman. He then gave the woman a man.

Hole in the Sky, however, offered Landes a very different story. In the beginning the Snake manito wrapped himself around the 'primal wigwam,' shading one side. Misshipeshu, the Underwater 'Lion,' got suspicious of the Snake's intentions and asked him why he was doing this. In reply the Snake grasped some dirt, opened his hand, and there was a black Indian. The lion knocked the dirt out of the Snake's hand, closed his own over some sand, and there stood an Indian 'shining like glass.' This referred to an early belief that originally men were protected from disease and death by a smooth, highly reflective coating like a fish's scales, that covered the whole body. According to Hole in the Sky the male was created first. In Everwind's second version the Great Spirit picked up some dirt and shut his hand on it till he felt something moving, opened it, and discovered a human being. So he placed him on the earth and told him to take four breaths. This created the lower air. Another four breaths created the earth and a final four produced the upper air.

Kohl (1860, 195) recorded that while Kitchi manito was walking along the beach surveying his creation, he 'noticed a being coming out of the water entirely covered with silver-glistening scales like a fish, but otherwise formed like a man.' The man appeared to be suffering deeply from loneliness, so Kitchi manito modelled some company for him 'nearly like what he had seen the man to be, and also covered her body with silver-glistening scales. Then he breathed life into her,' and set about arranging for the two to get together. The tale thereafter follows Genesis closely except for the finale. To punish the pair for their disobedience 'the silver scales with which the bodies had been covered fell off; only twenty of these scales remained on, but lost their brilliance, ten on the fingers and ten on the toes.'

Origin of Death

From Everwind's account too (Landes 1968, 92–3) it is clear that after losing the scales the human race became subject to disease and death.

Skinner picked up (1911, 157–9) a Bungi-Ojibway story that death had its origin in the jealousy of the Rattlesnake, who manoeuvred his closest friend the Natawa snake into a contest to see whose venom was the more powerful. Waylaying two youths—who were also very close to each other—each snake bit one. Death came into the world with that of the youth the Natawa snake had bitten.

Warren (1957, 43–4) reported an origin tale more central to the Midé tradition: how, 'when the earth was new, the An-ish-in-aub-ag congregated on the shores of a great salt water. From the bosom of the deep there suddenly appeared six beings in human form, who entered their wigwams.' One of them kept his eyes covered but finally had so strong an urge to look at the humans they were visiting that he looked at a man, who died instantly. The dangerous Manito was sent back; the other five remained, to become the original totemic clans of the Ojibway. But the damage had been done. The first man had died.

Whatever the origins of suffering and death, almost all the accounts relate that there was deep manito concern. Something must be done to alleviate human misery. Credit for this reaction, however, goes in different directions. In most accounts Nanabozho, the trickster-hero, plays a key role, but there is a surprising division of opinion as to whether his role was positive or negative. In one version, as we shall see, he was indirectly responsible for death. Regardless, the upshot of this concern was the calling of a Council by the 'Head' manito to work out a solution.

The Manito Council

Warren (1957), Hoffman (1891), and Densmore (1910) all agree that it was Nanabozho who was moved to compassion and persuaded the 'Great Spirit' to do something to help the people. But a northerly and earlier source, John Tanner (1830, 185), claimed that the Great Spirit whom he identified as Misshipeshu, the Great Underwater 'Lion,' agreed to give the Midéwewin to the people only as a peace-making gesture in his prolonged struggle with Nanabozho. For Red Sky, Nanabozho was 'the Devil.' His account and another recorded by Landes tell a very different story, whose style is far more in keeping with the traditional concept of the trickster. Nanabozho, these accounts state, was excluded from the Manito Council and determined to do something about it. In Red Sky's tale he tried to make a bargain with God, not to save the people but to share control of the world 'because I know [said Nanabozho] he can't run it by himself.' But 'God's helpers' were alerted, Nanabozho was intercepted on his way up to heaven to discuss his takeover with God, and after a brief tussle 'he came down faster than he went up,' Red Sky asserted, 'and right into this little pond—he fell right into this little pond there. Water splashed all over—he must have went pretty deep into this little pond.' So the tale accounts for the expansion of Lake Superior to its present size, and for the lake-splashed region around it. Nanabozho may still be seen on the hill where he crawled out of the water, to fall asleep as he sunned himself dry. Hence the 'Sleeping Giant' seen here as it may be viewed from the city of Thunder Bay.

In Everwind's account (Landes 1968, 92–3) Nanabozho, excluded from the Manito Council, wandered about until he encountered Great Black Rock, who had also been overlooked. Lured by Nanabozho's promise to compensate him for the gifts that would have been his as a Council member, Black Rock agreed to follow Nanabozho's suggestion. So he traversed the water, seeking an Ojibway settlement, submerging and surfacing in the same style as the Megis in Red Sky's main origin tale. Finally, on his *third* emergence, he reached an Ojibway village on a peninsula. There he met a child and followed Nanabozho's instructions to give the child one of his own 'gold and silver scales.' The child's own silvery coating then fell off—except the twenty scales on fingers and toes—and he became vulnerable to disease and death. Thereupon Nanabozho went running all over the country protesting the terrible thing Black Rock had done, a point in the story that invariably sent an Ojibway audience into spasms of laughter at the blatant hypocrisy involved.

Hoffman's informant, Ojibwa (1891, 172), spoke of 'ten Midé Manitous' having been summoned, but not so much to share in a decision as to offer their services in disseminating the prescribed antidote to disease and death—the Midéwewin. According to Sikassige, Dzhe Manitou called together four Midé manitos and four Wind manitos. Apparently the Sun manito was also present, for it was he who was directed to take the Midé message to the people. But this might merely have been an alternative name for the East manito (the sun rising in the east), for in Densmore's version (1910, 21) it was the East Wind who was given the task. Equally the Megis manito (also originating in the east and 'reflecting the rays of the sun') was the chosen Agent, as he became in Red Sky's version after the Bear had carried the Pack of Life to the edge of the 'great big water.'

The location of the Council meeting was conceived in either a vertical or a horizontal perspective, although the latter seems to disagree with the total concept. For though Red Sky's Bear is supposed to be travelling on the earth's surface the earthen walls he encounters seem to block off any sense of being on the surface until he breaks through the last one and 'there was the world—right there—a beautiful world,' as if he were seeing it for the first time. One periodically suspects Red Sky of trying to reconcile Christian and Midé mythology, which would account for his guess that the Council met in Palestine. Densmore's female informant Nawajibigokwe (1910, 21) located the Council site 'at the centre of the earth, not *under* the earth, but at some place far away' (italics added). It was almost as if there were evil connotations to the alternative concept, communicated to Landes and others, that the Council site was at the vertical centre of the earth, *beneath four earth layers.*

The introductory sections of all Origin, Migration, and Master scrolls make pictographic reference to the Manito Council, although some are abstracted or condensed to the point of atrophy. Of seven Origin scrolls reproduced on the following pages all show unmistakable similarities to the first three units of Red Sky's Creation scroll. Four of them show four bird forms, two human figures, and four indeterminate ones. The Bungi scroll adds two birds and two other unidentified forms, to make six of each. The Peterson scroll from Glenbow shows four manitos in human guise (perhaps the four Winds), then indicates eight other manitos by way of four bird tracks and four bear tracks entering the circle, although each set of tracks might represent the entry of only one manito—the Eagle (or Thunderbird) for example and the Bear. In every instance, as in the Creation scroll the first unit features the Megis, in the centre. All but the Logan and Larson scrolls show the Bear on the pathway leading away from the Council circle, but none symbolizes the Bear's break-through.

The Agent's Break-Through

As in Red Sky's interpretation, Landes was informed (1968, 99) that the Bear was the appointed messenger of the Council and carried with him a heavy load, with the one difference that he broke his way *upward* through four layers, using a pole (literally a 'cedar tree') instead of his tongue. Both versions convey that the Bear is, literally or metaphorically, in the dark until the world bursts into sight. The tree, moreover, comes into the Red Sky tale when the Bear plants it in the Midéwegun.

All other sources in the literature are silent as to the Bear's break-throughs in connection with the Manito Council, although not in another context which is irrelevant at this point. The priest's three hesitations followed by a fourth successful step into the Midéwegun during the ceremony probably symbolize the break-throughs but the probability is not directly documented. The fact that the four Wind manitos thank the Bear for each of his efforts certainly qualifies them pre-eminently for places on the Council.

Clear symbols of the four break-throughs appear in the introductory section of all but one of the Migration charts, in one case as a succession of rings overlaid by a Bear's head, in two others by four concentric rings to which a Bear's head with out-thrust tongue is attached, or in the New York and National Museum examples as four simple bars across the Bear's path (see Figure 1).

Hoffman's informant, Skwekomik (1891, 172–4), told him that the trickster-hero 'Minabozho' in a godlike role, 'while thoughtfully hovering over the centre of the earth'—a hint of the Council site—'. . . heard something laugh, and perceived a dark object appear upon the surface of the water to the west. He could not recognize its form, and while watching it closely it slowly disappeared from view.' Although this object was repeatedly invited to come to the centre—an island—it disappeared and reappeared clockwise around the compass, returning to the western point before it swam in to meet Minabozho. Only then did the demi-god recognize the Otter, initiate him into the Midéwewin and appoint him as the special agent to carry the Midé message to the people.

There is no break-through, and the only hint of the Council is the Otter's emergence at each of the cardinal points of the compass, which suggests the presence of the four Wind manitos.

The Agent's Mission and Journey

In the account Hoffman got from Sikassige it is the Otter who is the official agent. We have already encountered Red Sky's story in which the Bear passes on his load to the Great Megis, who carries it under or over the 'ocean.' Hole in the Sky told Landes (1968, 108) in one version that on reaching the shore of this great

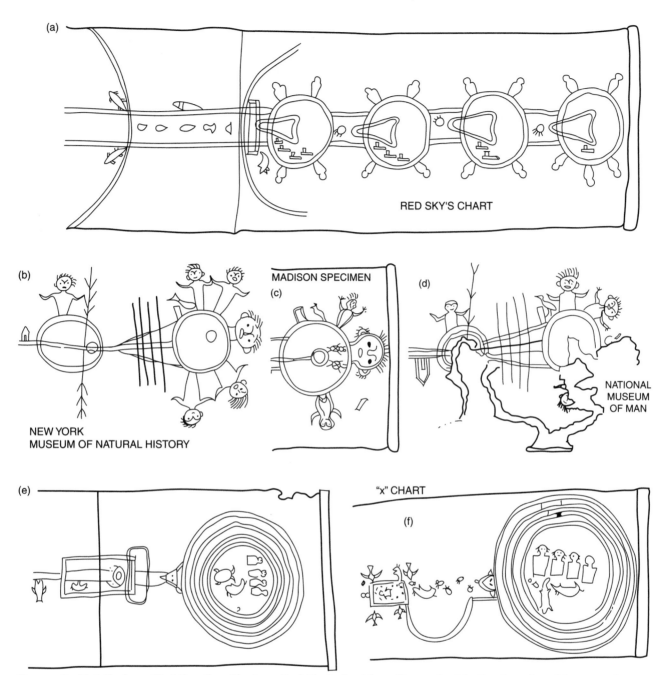

FIGURE 1 Details from Six Migration Charts. A Red Sky's chart (GAI-4); B a chart in the American Museum of Natural History (AMNH-1); C a chart in the State Historical Society of Wisconsin Museum (SHSW-1); D a chart in the National Museum of Man; E a chart in the Denver Art Museum (DAM-1); F 'x' chart (ax)

body of water the Bear persuaded the 'Great Lion,' Misshipeshu, to subdue the waves so that he could carry his load across on the surface, while in a second version he simply walked along on the floor of the ocean. In this latter tale there is an encounter with the Megis, but no transfer of the load.

When we turn to the bark records there are some difficulties to sort out. The Migration charts trace the Agent's movements quite specifically. The Origin scrolls, on the other hand, although they seem to relate to the same theme, do so only vaguely.

Reading from left to right, the three large circular units that appear in all the Origin scrolls will be referred to as units I, II, and III. In every case Unit I is dominated by a representation of the Megis, and presided over by the Manito Council. The only interpretations available are the two versions obtained from Red Sky and those supplied to Skinner (1920) and Cadzow (1926) respectively by their informants. Of the two latter the account given to Skinner by Ogimauwinini (Chief Man) simply cannot be taken seriously, on two counts. In the first place we learn (Skinner, 1920, 318) that 'Ogimauwinini never opened the roll, excepting when he first received it, until he transferred it to the writer.' Secondly he interpreted the single-lodge side as referring to a fourth-degree initiation, and the three-unit side reproduced here (Figure 2) as showing 'the three upper degrees.' As we shall see in a later chapter this bears no relation to any authentic upper degree scroll. Skinner then adds, 'Unfortunately this side is not well known to Ogimauwinini, as his instructor died while at work here with him.' Cadzow's informant, Moose Bell, gives a far more convincing interpretation. Units I, II, and III (Figure 3) represent the first three degrees of initiation. The four otter-like forms below Unit I represent 'The sacred skin medicine bags of the cardinal points—east, south, west, north . . . ' The four bird forms are also identified: 'the bird of the east and summer . . . the thunderbird . . . the bird of the sun . . . the bird of winter.' (Cadzow, 1926, 126–7.) The central circle, surrounded by Megis shells, is 'the house in which the candidate is born into the fraternity'—in other words, initiated into the Midéwewin. The shells are interpreted in a rather ambiguous way as 'Nine magic shells . . . are given to the initiates for the purpose of making them fertile.' I suspect that the 'them' refers to the shells, not the candidates, for one man I interviewed—I believe it was Red Sky—told me that it was possible for the megis shells to *breed* more shells.

FIGURE 2　Three-Unit Side of Scroll Interpreted by Ogimauwinini (Sk-1a)

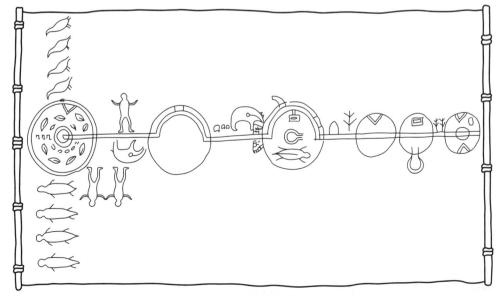

FIGURE 3　Three-Unit Side of Scroll Interpreted by Moose Bell (Ca-1a)

Of the paired human figures Moose Bell said they were 'The first man to be given the secrets of the medicine-lodge . . . and the first woman . . . ' The first bear keeps an eye on the candidates as they walk the path from one degree to the next, the second is 'the sacred white bear' who 'walks ahead four steps and makes three resting tents.' Here is a clear example of symbol conversion, the original 'tents'—judging by the conventions of many other scrolls—having been bear *tracks*.

The pictographic symbols on either side of the entrance to unit III represent 'rain,' the curved projection, 'a mountain [that] blocks the road' but disappears if the candidates have 'clean minds.' Within the central enclosure in unit III 'Various secret medicines . . . are given to the initiate . . . and the great lizard . . . creator of all water animals, becomes their friend.' This manito can be no other than the 'King of the Fishes . . . Great Lion . . . Underground Panther'—Misshipeshu, in prairie guise. Success in winning his patronage casts a shadow of suspicion over the powers conferred by the third degree, especially in view of the absence of any reference to promotion of the candidate's health.

To find any features of Red Sky's (see Figure 4) and Moose Bell's interpretations of units II and III common to both would demand more ingenuity than I can muster, except for one item. In Red Sky's account 'God' sees what looks like a cloud on the horizon, goes closer and discovers it is a hill. In the Origin section of Red Sky's Migration chart the Megis encounters a hill, 'very high,' where he finds people and gives them the Midé message. In five of the seven Origin scrolls a projection recurs on the upper edge of unit III, suggesting an actual locality along the Agent's route. This shows up clearly in Moose Bell's Chart.

I have already pointed out that the fourth unit of Red Sky's Creation scroll is a composite chart of Red Lake and Leech Lake, featuring two triangular projections from opposite sides that almost meet in the centre. Both Moose Bell's scroll and the one from Larson's collection (Figure 5) add three smaller circular units to the basic three. In both cases the third of these smaller units shows triangles in the same relationship as those in Red Sky's unit IV. There is no interpretation for the Larson scroll; and Moose Bell refers to the two triangles as places where the candidates 'rest in their tipis' while an unidentified manito 'talks to the Indians.' The Otter, too, who broke through to create the Red Lake narrows, has disappeared, and where we expect to find him in unit III—for all the specimens show a water creature that Red Sky identifies in his as the Otter—Moose Bell interprets him as 'the great lizard . . . creator of all the water animals!'

Before leaving these 'extended' Origin scrolls one further point needs making. Red Sky's copy seems to be older. Examining the bark, I strongly suspected that unit IV had been added by sewing on a new section to an original three-unit scroll. The Origin scrolls collected by Peterson (Figure 6), Larson and Cadzow were all—quite clearly—designed as they stand. If the sixth unit in the two latter scrolls is derived from Leech Lake,

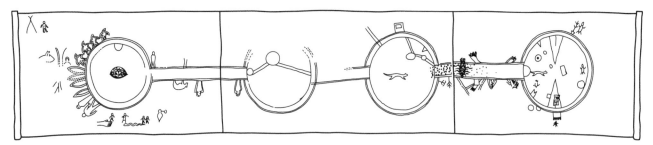

FIGURE 4   Red Sky's Creation Scroll (GAI-2)

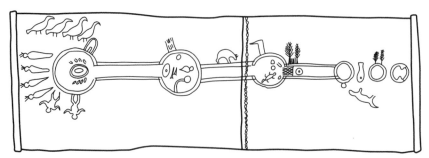

FIGURE 5   Origin scroll (la-1)

as seems likely, then a considerable lapse of time must be allowed for the original meaning to be metamorphosed into an entirely unrelated one. As for interpreting the Origin scrolls (see also Figure 7–9) in toto as attenuated descriptions of the Agent's journeys a decision must be deferred until we examine the Migration scrolls in which the journeys are charted in great detail.

Returning to the literature, one reference in Landes (1968, 104) may have some bearing on the Megis featured in unit I. In this account the Bear, after crossing, or walking under, the first stretch of ocean, reaches a

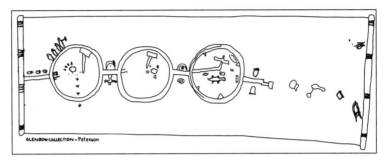

FIGURE 6   Origin Scroll (GAI-5)

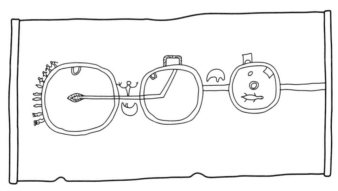

FIGURE 7   Condensed Origin Scroll (LM-2a)

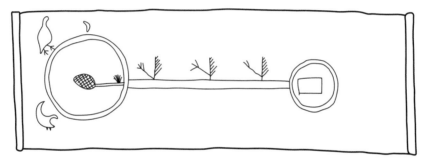

FIGURE 8   Origin Scroll (fi-1)

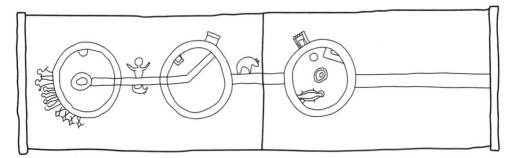

FIGURE 9   Origin Scroll (de-1)

rocky island. In one version he climbs over the island, and finds himself 'stuck all over' with megis shells; in the other the island turns out to be the body of the Great Megis itself (Figure 10).

Warren (1957, 77–89) has some interesting things to say about the use of the Megis in a Midé ceremony he witnessed. 'One of the four We-kauns [Midé officials] . . . took from his medicine sack the Me-da-me-gis, a small white seashell, which is the chief emblem of the Me-da-we rite.' After some preliminaries he made this statement. 'While our forefathers were living on the great salt water toward the rising sun, the great Megis (sea-shell) showed itself above the surface of the great water, and the rays of the sun for a long period were reflected from its glossy back. It gave warmth and light to the An-ish-in-aub-ag (red race). All at once it sank into the deep, and for a time our ancestors were not blessed with its light.' The speech went on to relate that the Megis reappeared 'on the great river that drains the waters of the Great Lakes'; then disappeared, to show itself 'on the shores of the first great lake'; sank from sight again until it 'reflected the rays of the sun once more at Bow-e-ting' (Sault Ste Marie); and finally reappeared at La Pointe, or Shequamegon, near the west end of the south Superior shore.

Privately this Midé elder informed Warren that the Megis was merely a figure of speech for the Midé religion. Consulting the old men at Fond du Lac, Warren learned that among them the Otter was used 'in the same figurative manner' as the Megis, so that it was the Otter who appeared, first 'from the depths of the great salt water,' then at a succession of stopping places farther west. In yet another metaphor the Crane (Figure 11) incorporates in its own person the migratory shifts, although the allegory does not refer directly to the Midé message; rather it seems to be a symbolic way of describing a migration. Tug-waug-aun-ay, head of the Crane phratry, in a speech to remind his audience of the leadership exercised by his totemic clan

Variations
on the Megis Theme

FIGURE 10   Six Versions of the Megis as Represented in the Origin scrolls

After Blessing

From Lac Seul

FIGURE 11   Two Versions of the Sun Manito

(Warren, 1957, 87) stated that 'the Great Spirit once made a bird, and he sent it from the skies to make its abode on the earth. The bird came and when it reached halfway down, among the clouds, it sent forth a loud and resounding cry, which was heard by all who resided on the earth, and even by the spirits who make their abode within its bosom.' The orator gestured toward the east as the direction from which the bird had flown. Circling the rapids at Sault Ste Marie it settled there, but eventually took to the air again to find its resting place at La Pointe.

Reagan's unpublished notes in the ethnology files at the National Museum of Man in Ottawa quote a Nett Lake informant as stating that 'The crane is the bird-god that lives in the heavens. He pays special attention to the supplications of men . . . the fire of his eyes will last forever . . . *his eye is the sun*' (italics added). The Megis, reflecting the sun, the Crane, and the Sun itself (Figure 44) are therefore interchangeable and allegorically synonymous, and even the Council's Agent, who conveys the actual Midé message—whether Bear or Otter—shares in these figurative associations.

The Visionary Revelation

At this point in my studies I began to wonder if the Midéwewin was a device for re-enacting ritualistically the agent's original mission, at the same time re-creating, in the four lodges of the Master scrolls, not only the agent's original initiation, but the major stopping-places on the westward movements of the ancestral Ojibway. Yet there seemed to be a quite separate group of traditions that suggested a quite different origin for the Midéwewin.

This collection of origin lore makes no reference to saltwater shores, attributing the emergence of the Midé rites to a human agent who is directly taught the procedures by a delegate from the Manito Council. The go-between chosen by the Council is the East manito, equated by Landes's informants with the Sun manito, who, it will be recalled, is strongly associated with the Megis manito.

In the Densmore version (1910, 21–3) the East manito takes the form of a baby born to an elderly couple who lived on Madeline Island, but apparently on a shore that was isolated from the village of La Pointe. The baby grows up in close friendship with a cousin. Then, as the two are approaching manhood, the cousin dies. The young 'East-man' promises to restore his cousin to life. He instructs his parents in the construction of the Midéwegun, tells his father to sing and drum for four days, then disappears.

On the fourth morning 'they looked toward the east and saw the sky streaked with colours like those he [the East manito] had painted on their foreheads . . . A little before noon they heard a peculiar sound in the sky. It was from the east. Someone was calling *Wa, hi, hi, hi* . . . [they] saw four Indians walking toward them in the sky, giving this call. Each Indian had a living otter in his hand.' These were the four Wind manitos, who circled the body of the cousin four times, to bring him alive again.

Hole-in-the-Sky gave Landes a variant of this (1968, 110). An Indian couple living on 'Yellow Hammer Beach,' somewhere on the south shore of Lake Superior, had two children. As one of the two was dying his brother, the youthful Cutfoot, showed his parents the Midé healing technique which he had acquired in a vision. A second version, also supplied by Hole in the Sky, stated that the boy Cutfoot when only six or seven years old was summoned to visit the Megis manito. He disappeared for four years, came home for a year, then went away for another four. On his return his parents knew he had experienced a vision. When his elder brother fell sick they constructed a Midéwegun under Cutfoot's direction in which the young visionary conducted the rites that cured his brother.

Sikassige's version told to Hoffman (1893, 172–3) has some interesting variations. The Sun manito took the form of a little boy who was adopted by a couple who had a son of their own. Their natural son died, and the foster-child offered to restore him. After due preparations were made under his direction the family and friends gathered around the body in the Midéwegun. 'When they had all been sitting quietly for some time, they saw through the doorway the approach of a bear which gradually came towards the wigwam, entered it, and placed itself before the dead body and said hu, hu, hu, hu, when it passed towards the left side [clockwise] with a trembling motion, and as he did so, the body started quivering, and the quivering increased as the bear continued until he had passed around four times, when the body came to life again and stood up.'

Sikassige explained that the boy remained with his adopted parents until he had taught them the entire Midéwewin. Then he adds, although he had previously identified the boy as the Sun manito, that 'The little bear boy is the one who did this.'

Clearly, it was the vestiges of the Cutfoot legend that reached Red Sky without preserving the account of an actual curing. Farther from the Midé heartland Skinner (1911, 158–9) encountered a variant of the Cutfoot legend among the Bungi-Ojibway of Manitoba that had been both enriched and radically altered by merging with the Rattlesnake-Natawa lore of the prairies. Here again there were two young males—past puberty in this tale—who were deeply attached to each other. One died from the bite of the Natawa, and introduced death into the world.

The Natawa, after endowing the Rattlesnake with the warning device on his tail, set about making things right with the father of the deceased youth. Day after day the bereaved chief mourned by his son's grave. Then one day a huge snake appeared, who told him that he would be visited by a horned snake that would curl itself around the grave. The chief was then to lift the snake by its horns, three times. The prophecy materialized, the father obeyed instructions and the horned snake turned into a white-haired old man, with a 'fire-bag of life' made of Natawa skin.

'I have come to comfort and console you for the death of your son. The spirits of the earth, the wind, and the water have seen your sorrow,' (note the hint of a manito council) 'and I am sent to your race to show you the way of life which you will teach to your children, and which shall continue to the end of time. Now, therefore, light your pipe, and with your stem point to the sky, the abode of the Great Spirit, who shall give you life, to the abode of the spirits of the centre of the earth, whose will is to teach you the virtue of all herbs, and to the four winds who will protect you and give you power and success.'

The chief obeyed, then offered his pipe, whereupon three sharp taps of a drum were heard. The Natawa manito then sang a song, which began with the words, 'I come from the east where the long tent does rest . . .' He stayed with the bereaved chief for a full month, instructing him in all the Midé rites and lore. And the story concludes with the good news that after his mentor was gone the chief not only set up the Midéwewin, but in his old age another son was born, 'the very image of the one who died by the sting of the Natawa.'

It is noteworthy that this tale, unlike the others, places a sacred emphasis on the numeral *three*, rather than the usual four. This will be investigated further in a later chapter.

The common feature of all these tales is emphasis on the youth of the central figures. Although Red Sky's tradition had lost the healing role of the young visionary, his Creation scroll provides the only identified pictographic reference to the Cutfoot legend, the tiny figure beside a wigwam that is so faintly scratched into the top left corner of the bark.

Perhaps the most significant difference between the two traditions is the emphasis the one puts on the role of the manitos in disseminating the Midé 'gospel' while the other throws its weight on the human side. Now, as we turn to the Migration charts, the human role recedes.

Indians in Overalls

JAIME DE ANGULO

I went up north again the next summer. I found Jack Folsom and Lena at their place behind the little hill in the sagebrush. I noticed that Lena seemed apathetic, ill, Jack was as usual, with his quizzical smile, his quiet ways, his practical sense. "Say, Doc, I hear your friend Sukmit is around. There is a woman sick near town, you know, that place just before you reach town, Indians live there, well, there is a woman sick there, some doctor poisoned her, and they got your friend Sukmit to doctor her . . . and say, Doc, we are pretty near out of grub, you will be in town in two minutes with your car, today is Saturday and the stores will be open late, and will you bring back some grub, get some bacon, and bring some sweets for Lena, she loves sweets, I don't know what's the matter with that woman, Doc, something's wrong, she don't look well to me." "All right, Jack."

So I went to Alturas, did the shopping, and on the way back, it was dusk, I saw the familiar figure of Sukmit, a little way off the road, walking through the brush with long strides. I stopped the car, and honked and yelled. He paid no attention. I honked and yelled again. Surely he must hear me. I got out of the car and went up to him. He had heard me all right, and he was in a towering rage: "Goddam you, I am fixing for a doctoring! I have caught a new *damaagome* and I am training him, he is wild yet, he was following me like a dog, and here you come yelling your head off, you scared him away!" "I am sorry, Sukmit, I didn't know . . . " "You never know anything. You'll never learn anything, you'll never be an Indian, you'll always be a damfool white man!!" "All right, all right, you don't have to be so nasty about it," and I turned to go. He followed me: "Well, aren't you going to give me a ride? They are waiting for me, I have to doctor a sick woman." "What's the use if I scared your *damaagome?*" "Do you think I have only one *damaagome?* That's just a new one I am training."

So I took him to the place. There were a dozen or so Indians gathered around a campfire. There was a woman lying under a blanket on a bed of tules on the ground. Old Mary was there. She greeted me with her usual banter: "Here is the Indian white man. He is going to do the interpreting. No, maybe he'll do the doctoring. Ha-ha-ha, Indian white man." Most of the Indians already knew me. Greetings. "*Is kaakaadzi*, Man, you are alive, *is kaakaadzi*. Where have you been? Where is your wife, your son, *mi'mu amiteudzan, mi'mu belatsi?* Why didn't they come?"

Sukmit looked somber and abstracted. He went and looked at the sick woman silently; then he came back and knelt in front of the fire. Old Mary then got up and went a little way into the sagebrush and called the *damaagomes*.[1] Everybody became silent. Then Sukmit started one of his songs. Two or three people caught on, then others, then nearly everybody. Then he clapped his hands and the singing stopped abruptly. Now he is interpellating a poison, and old Mary, his mother, interprets (that is, repeats word for word, but more slowly, although Sukmit never got himself into a state of *bafouillage*, like Blind Hall and some others). And so on and so forth. In between interpellations of the poisons there was the usual relaxing and smoking by the audience and the usual gossip. But Sukmit never relaxed. He became more and more somber and abstracted. To me he seemed to be getting exhausted. After a while of this he got up and "sucked" the sick woman: he put his lips to different parts of her body and sucked with a strong hissing noise. Then he came back and knelt again in front of the fire, right next to me. He looked very sick. He asked for a container. Somebody passed him an empty can that had contained lard (a three-pound can), and he puked and puked and puked into it. I was right next to him. What he puked looked exactly like very dark blood, but the light was uncertain. He made a grimace and said to me: "Fuahh! . . . it looks like coffee." He was still retching. He poured the can into the fire.[2]

Most of the Indians then left. Old Mary looked very tired also. She said to me: "You take care of your Sukmit," and she disappeared. Sukmit was like a drunken man. I spread my blankets on the ground and dragged him in after me. For a long time he was crying like a child, and shaking all over. Finally he went to sleep.

In the morning he was quite all right. So also was the sick woman (she evidently had had a bad case of "funk"). She came to where we were having breakfast, and she gave Sukmit a string of beads for payment. She said: "It's not much but I am a poor woman." Sukmit took the string and threw it to his mother, and he said to the woman: "That's good. I am not doing it for payment." Then Sukmit pumped up his tires and he and old Mary started for Big Valley (which was their home), and I went back to Jack and Lena at their place in the sagebrush around the little hill.

Poor Lena was really sick. Jack would have liked to call in Blind Hall, but he was away somewhere down river. Then we heard that a bunch of Modocs was in town on their way to their home in Oregon, and with them was old Kate, a famous medicine-woman, and Jack decided to try her. She arrived in the afternoon, in a horse-wagon, with her son, a big strapping fellow (with whom I later studied the Modoc language). She was a little bit of an old old woman, so *racroquevillée* that she was almost bent double; she was nearly blind; still she insisted on "helping" (all the conversation had to be in English, since the Modocs didn't understand Pit River, and vice versa) with the cooking. She would totter around, extend a claw, peer, grab something and drop it in the skillet. Jessie (Jack's daughter by another wife—and a big, handsome woman Jessie was, somewhere around in her forties, graceful, dignified, a little bit haughty), who had come to help,[3] Jessie would sigh, turn her face aside to grimace, then calmly remove whatever *immondice* old Kate had dropped into the skillet.

Evening arrived. Old Kate had a sister who acted as her "interpreter," a much younger woman. Everything was ready; we were all inside the cabin; still old Kate was waiting for something; finally she said: "Dat white man going to stay?" "He is no white man!" said Jack. "He is Indian just like us." "What tribe?" she asked me. "Spanish," I answered. "Oh, dat's all right. Spanish good people." To her, too, Spanish meant Mexican.

Old Kate's procedure was slightly different from Blind Hall, Sukmit, or the other Pit River shamans I have associated with; but on the whole it followed the same lines—perhaps a little less loose, a trifle more conventionalized. For instance, her songs appeared to be directed less to an individual *damaagome* than to a generalized animal. Her sister would explain to me: "That's duck song . . . that's crane song . . . that's pelican song. . . ." The old woman's son had gone out. Doctoring didn't interest him. The Pit Rivers didn't know that kind of singing and were too self-conscious to try. Only the old woman's sister carried on the singing. Old Kate complained. Finally she turned to me: "Why you no sing? *Canta, canta!*" "All right, I'll try." The songs weren't difficult. They had more lilt than the Pit River ones. Anyhow, the important thing was to make a noise and be heard by the poisons.

Toward midnight or one o'clock (unlike the Pit River shamans, who never doctor for more than a couple of hours, Kate kept it up all night, right till dawn—although all the Pit Rivers had fallen asleep in various corners), Kate had a fit. She started to shake, foam at the mouth, and throw herself around. At first her sister tried to hold her down, but she wasn't strong enough. She called for help to the Pit Rivers; but for some reason no one moved. Then she yelled at me: "Hey, you Mexican, hold her, I'll call her son. . . ." He came in, a calm, big, powerful fellow. Yet, with the two of us sitting on her she managed once to free herself, that little bit of an old woman whom ordinarily you could have pushed over with your little finger! After a while she quieted down, and the singing started again, at intervals. But she was tired. Once she peered at the roof: "Is dat morning?" "No, Kate, it's the moon. There is a crack in the roof." She sighed.

Finally she started to extract the poison. She sucked and sucked. Then she straightened up, put her hand to her mouth, and grabbed something that was between her teeth. In the light of the lamp I saw distinctly what she did: she bit a piece of her own fingernail off. This she exhibited around as the poison. Then she called for a bowl of water; she drowned the poison in it and threw the water in a corner of the room.

In the morning the Modocs started to go. Jack Folsom wanted to give Kate some money, but she refused it, "I didn't do any good, Jack, you people don't sing, my poison no hear. Your woman going to die. Too bad." She said goodby to me. "You good man, Spanish, you help, you sing. Come see me my place Oregon." I said I would.

(I did go there, the next year, to study the Modoc language with her son. I had many talks with her. One day I was sitting on a log in the sun beside her; she was smoking her pipe; I said: "Kate, you remember that time at Jack Folsom's place when you doctored that woman. . . . You bit off your fingernail and said it was the poison. . . ." She gave me a sidelong look, pretty piercing in spite of her rheumy eyes; she grumbled: ". . . You know too much—sure dat's tomfoolery, good for people, make him believe—but my poison him no fool, him powerful, no nonsense, but he no hear dat time, son-of-a-bitch!" " . . . Kate, why did you become a doctor?" "Oh, long time ago, me young girl, go in woods look for berries, I no look for poison, poison find me." "Did he scare you?" "You bet he scare me!" "Does he still scare you when he comes?" She burst into her cackling laughter; "Hell NO! He don't scare me. I scare him now!!!")

Soon after the Modocs left, Lena's own father arrived from Hat Creek country. His name was Jack Wilson. He drove in in a horse-wagon, and with him was an "elder brother" (or cousin) of his, who must have been close to ninety or a hundred; Jack Folsom (who didn't know his own age by years) said of Bob-Chief, or Tom-Chief (like all Indians he had a variety of American names): "When I was a young fellow that old man had already buried three wives." He was still erect, but walked slowly; his skin was the color of chocolate; a few long white whiskers made him look like a walrus.

Jack Wilson was a "sort of doctor," according to Jack Folsom. He would doctor his own daughter, that night. Old Tom-Chief would interpret. Jack Wilson was a tall man, very silent. During the day Tom-Chief, who usually sat on a log, would totter into the sagebrush and make a sort of speech. "What is he doing?" I asked Jack. "Oh, he is telling old-time stories, what the people used to do long ago." "But there is nobody there. To whom is he talking?" Jack shrugged his shoulders: "To the sagebrush, I guess."

When evening came, old Tom-Chief went out and called the *damaagomes*. Three young Indians had arrived; but they were slightly drunk. They sang a *contre-temps* and laughed. Jack had to reprimand them. Old Tom was very deaf; he didn't hear what the doctor said; so everybody had to shout at him what the shaman had said so he could repeat it; the whole thing was a failure. After about an hour Jack Wilson gave up in despair. "No use! My poison don't hear. Mountain lion, wolf, too far away, don't hear!"

In the morning he said to me: "I lost all my children. This is the last one. I lose her too."

It was in the afternoon. Autumn and warm. The door of the cabin stood open. Away to the west I could see the hills of sagebrush, silent, and the mountains beyond. One of those days that do not move. There were half a dozen of us in the cabin, and the sick woman breathing heavily on her pile of blankets. I don't know how we all knew it, but we all felt that she was dying just then. At last, Jack Folsom broke down. He buried his face in his hands and started to cry. He cried like a little child, with convulsive sobs. Then that awful sound of the rattle. And even before that had died away Jessie began the wail. Oh, that weird, wild, atrocious thing that goes mounting like the shriek of a wounded beast, that infernal yell drawn away until it falls in a series of exhausted sobs. And again, and again. I was to hear that wail all night through the sagebrush until it drove me mad.

The old man, her father, was kneeling at her head. His face twitched uncontrollably. He closed her eyes, and laid a handkerchief over her face. Then he, too, broke down. He took the head of his child in his lap, he raised it to his breast, and he sobbed and sobbed.

All night long Jessie wandered through the brush, wailing, wailing. And all through the night Indians kept arriving. The men sat against the wall. The women went out into the night and wailed.

One Indian is dead.

Then Jack took his wife's body away to bury it in Hat Creek, her home. He said to me: "I'll be back here in about two weeks, and then we will burn her. Will you stay here for me, Doc?"

I was sort of puzzled about this business of burying first, and burning her after, but I didn't ask him any questions. I said I would stay until he got back. He said: "You sure you won't be scared?" "No, . . . why should I?" "Account of the woman who died." "But why?" "She might come and kill you by mistake." "Hell no!" I said.

The very night after they had left, Wild Bill arrived. He was a horse-breaker by trade and I had known him in the days of my venture in ranching. A delightful fellow, always full of fun and jokes, and a superb rider; in fact he was a crazy daredevil. We had always been friends.

I was surprised to see him. He had tied his horse to a post in the corral and came over to me. He said he had come for the funeral, and that the woman-who-had-died was his cousin. He said "sister."

"How can she be your sister, Bill?"

"Well, she is, Indian way."

"I don't see how."

"Oh, yes. Look: her *apun*, her grandfather on the mother side was the elder brother, what we call *apau*, to my sister, the younger than me, my *enun*."

"But Bill, that doesn't make her your sister!"

"Sure it does, Doc. . . . See, if a man is my wife's brother I call him *malis*, and my own brother, if he is older I call him *apau*, but if he is younger I call him *atun*. Just like my sister, *apis* or *enun*. But if he is my uncle, if he is my father's sister, then I call him . . . Oh, hell, Doc; you can't get it straight in English . . . But I tell you, this woman who died she is related to me, I know, because she always called this here Tom-Chief, *aqun*, and he also called me *aqun*, and that proves it."

Wild Bill said he would stay here and wait for Jack Folsom and the rest of the party to come back from the *atsuge* country. That evening he told me a lot about Coyote and the Coyote saga. The Coyote stories form a regular cycle, a saga. This is true of all of California; and it extends eastward even as far as the Pueblos of Arizona and New Mexico. Coyote has a double personality. He is at once the Creator, and the Fool. This antinomy is very important. Unless you understand it you will miss the Indian psychology completely—at least you will miss the significance of their literature (because I call their tales, their "old-time stories," literature).

The wise man and the buffoon: the two aspects of Coyote, Coyote Old Man. Note that I don't call them the good and the evil, because that conception of morality does not seem to play much part in the Pit River attitude to life. Their mores are not much concerned with good and evil. You have a definite attitude toward moral right and moral wrong. I don't think the Pit River has. At least, if he has, he does not try to coerce. I have heard Indians say: "That's not right what he is doing, that fellow . . . " "What d'you mean it's not right?" " . . . Well . . . you ain't supposed to do things that way . . . it never was done that way . . . there'll be trouble." "Then why don't you stop him?" "Stop him? How can I stop him? It's his way."

The Pit Rivers (except the younger ones who have gone to the Government School at Fort Bidwell) don't ever seem to get a very clear conception of what you mean by the term God. This is true even of those who speak American fluently, like Wild Bill. He said to me: "What is this thing that the white people call God? They are always talking about it. It's goddam this and goddam that, and in the name of the god, and the god made the world. Who is that god, Doc? They say that Coyote is the Indian God, but if I say to them that God is Coyote, they get mad at me. Why?"

"Listen, Bill, tell me . . . Do the Indians think, really think that Coyote made the world? I mean, do they really think so? Do you really think so?"

"Why of course I do. . . . Why not? . . . Anyway . . . that's what the old people always said . . . only they don't all tell the same story. Here is one way I heard it: it seems like there was nothing everywhere but a kind of fog. Fog and water mixed, they say, no land anywhere, and this here Silver Fox. . . ."

"You mean Coyote?"

"No, no, I mean Silver Fox. Coyote comes later. You'll see, but right now, somewhere in the fog, they say, Silver Fox was wandering and feeling lonely. *Tsikuellaaduwi maandza tsikualaasa.*[4] He was feeling lonely, the Silver Fox. I wish I would meet someone, he said to himself, the Silver Fox did. He was walking along in the fog. He met Coyote. 'I thought I was going to meet someone,' he said. The Coyote looked at him, but he didn't say anything. 'Where are you traveling?' says Fox. 'But where are YOU traveling? Why do you travel like that?' 'Because I am worried.'[5] I also am wandering,' said the Coyote, 'I also am worrying and traveling.' 'I thought I would meet someone, I thought I would meet someone. Let's you and I travel together. It's better for two people to be traveling together, that's what they always say. . . .'"

"Wait a minute, Bill. . . . Who said that?"

"The Fox said that. I don't know who he meant when he said: *that's what they always say*. It's funny, isn't it? How could he talk about *other* people since there had never been anybody before? I don't know . . . I wonder about that sometimes, myself. I have asked some of the old people and they say: That's what I have been wondering myself, but that's the way we have always heard it told. And then you hear the Paiutes tell it different! And our own people down the river, they also tell it a little bit different from us. Doc, maybe the whole thing just never happened. . . . And maybe it did happen but everybody tells it different. People often do that, you know. . . ."

"Well, go on with the story. You said that Fox had met Coyote. . . ."

"Oh, yah . . . Well, this Coyote he says: 'What are we going to do now?' 'What do you think?' says Fox. 'I don't know,' says Coyote. 'Well then,' says Fox, 'I'll tell you: LET'S MAKE THE WORLD.' 'And how are we going to do that?' 'WE WILL SING,' says the Fox.

"So, there they were singing up there in the sky. They were singing and stomping[6] and dancing around each other in a circle. Then the Fox he thought in his mind: CLUMP OF SOD, come!! That's the way he made it come: *by thinking*.[7] Pretty soon he had it in his hands. And he was singing, all the while he had it in his hands. They were both singing and stomping. All of a sudden the Fox threw that clump of sod, that *tsapettia*,[8] he threw it down into the clouds. 'Don't look down!' he said to the Coyote. 'Keep on singing! Shut your eyes, and keep them shut until I tell you.' So they kept on singing and stomping around each other in a circle for quite a while. Then the Fox said to the Coyote: 'Now, look down there. What do you see?' 'I see something . . . I see something . . . but I don't know what it is.' 'All right. Shut your eyes again!' Now they started singing and stomping again, and the Fox thought and wished: Stretch! Stretch! 'Now look down again. What do you see?' 'Oh! it's getting bigger!' 'Shut your eyes again and don't look down!' And they went on singing and stomping up there in the sky. 'Now look down again!' 'Oooh! Now it's big enough!' said the Coyote.

"That's the way they made the world, Doc. Then they both jumped down on it and they stretched it some more. Then they made mountains and valleys; they made trees and rocks and everything. It took them a long time to do all that!"

"Didn't they make people, too?"

"No. Not people. Not Indians.[9] The Indians came much later, after the world was spoiled by a crazy woman, Loon. But that's a long story. . . . I'll tell you some day."

"All right, Bill, but tell me just one thing now: there was a world now; then there were a lot of animals living on it, but there were no people then. . . ."

"Whad'you mean there were no people? Ain't animals people?"

"Yes, they are . . . but . . . "

"They are not Indians, but they are people, they are alive . . . Whad'you mean animal?"

"Well . . . how do you say 'animal' in Pit River?"

" . . . I dunno. . . ."

"But suppose you wanted to say it?"

"Well . . . I guess I would say something like *teeqaadewade toolol aakaadzi* (world-over, all living) . . . I guess that means animals, Doc."

"I don't see how, Bill. That means people, also. People are living, aren't they?"

"Sure they are! that's what I am telling you. Everything is living, even the rocks, even that bench you are sitting on. Somebody *made that bench for a purpose*, didn't he? Well then *it's alive*, isn't it? Everything is alive. That's what we Indians believe. White people think everything is dead. . . ."

"Listen, Bill. How do you say 'people'?"

"I don't know . . . just *is*, I guess."

"I thought that meant 'Indian.'"

"Say . . . Ain't we *people*?!"

"So are the whites!"

"Like hell they are!! We call them *inillaaduwi*, 'tramps,' nothing but tramps. They don't believe anything is alive. They are dead themselves. I don't call that 'people.' They are smart, but they don't know anything. . . . Say, it's getting late, Doc, I am getting sleepy. I guess I'll go out and sleep on top of the haystack. . . ."

"But you'll die of cold! It's already freezing, these nights."

"Naw, I won't. I am an Indian. I am used to it."

"But why don't you sleep here, inside?"

"WHAT?! Are you crazy? That woman might come and kill me."

"You mean Lena?"

"Shh! . . . Doc! For God's sake don't call her, don't call her name! Just say: the woman who died. That's bad enough. She is probably somewhere around, somewhere around here. They haven't burnt her things yet, you know, her baskets, her blankets, her clothes . . . all these things are calling her, are calling her shadow, her *de'lamdzi*."

"But why should she hurt you?"

"She don't want to hurt me."

"But you just said she might kill you. . . ."

"Well, she'll take my shadow away with her, and then I'll die."

"What for would she take your shadow away with her?"

"Oh, to keep from getting lonely on the road to the land of the dead people."

"Where is that?"

"I dunno. Nobody knows. Somewhere out west. They say there is a big lake there, no end to it, and the dead people live there on an island . . . I dunno . . . that's what I've heard."

"But, Bill, I still don't see why she should want to take you there. . . ."

"I just told you, Doc: to keep from getting lonely on the trip to the land of the dead. You would do the same thing yourself if you were going to a strange place. You would take along someone you knew and liked."

"Well then, she might take me, Bill. I know she liked me."

"Sure! That's why I tell you that you are a damn fool to sleep here!"

"Listen, Bill, tell me something else before you go . . . about the shadow, what do you call it, the *dalilamdzi?*"

"Naw, that means 'to make a shadow,' for instance *salilamdzi*, that means I am making a shadow, *kalilamdzi* it's you who are making a shadow. . . . No, Doc, I know what you are thinking about, that's the *de'lamdzi*, the shadow, that's not the same as *dalilamdzi*, that's the shadow . . . oh, hell, I dunno what's the difference, it kind of sounds the same, don't it? Lissen: I remember when I was a little boy I used to hear the old men when they woke in the morning, they used to sing:

dalilamdzi	*walilamdzi*	*de'lamdzi*	*seena seena*
(the dawn	is dawning	a shadow	I come home, I come home)

"So the *dalilamdzi*, that means the dawn, also! The old people they would hum like that when they woke up in the morning and they said: My shadow is liable to go wandering during the night and mebbe get lost and not find me again in the morning, that's why I sing to show him where I am! . . . Well, I think you are foolish to sleep here in this shack where she is liable to come back and take another look at her baskets that she made herself, and her stove, and everything, her shadow is, and it may ask your shadow to go along, and there will be no more Buckaroo Doc, and we will bury you and burn all your things, your saddle, and your book, and everything, and everybody will cry . . . well, good night, Doc!"

Wild Bill stayed there several days, waiting for Jack Folsom and the other people to come back from the Hat Creek country where they had buried "the woman who had died." He was an excellent raconteur and told me many old-time stories. There are tribes where the old-time stories and "myths" (as the anthropologists call them) are stereotyped, may even be cast in a rigid form and must be recited verbatim. But not so with the Pit Rivers! A poor story-teller gives you the barest outline, in short sentences (nearly all beginning with "and then . . . "), in a monotonous voice. But a good raconteur like Wild Bill or old Mary tells it with gestures, mimicry, imitation noises—a regular theatrical performance. If there are several people in the audience they grunt in approval after each telling passage. Instead of applauding by clapping as we do, they raise their chins and say: Hunh. . . .

Finally, one day about noon, Jack and all the relatives returned; five or six wagons full of them, and immediately everything was confusion and pandemonium in this quiet corner of the sagebrush behind the little hill. They started a big bonfire. There was a lot of argument going on. Some of the people were still wailing. A woman would come dragging things out of the house, maybe two or three baskets, maybe an armful of clothes, and throw them into the fire; then she would go out a little way into the sagebrush and wail. The men were mostly silent and preoccupied; some of them wailed in man fashion: a sort of deep grunt, Honh-ho-ho, honh-ho-ho. . . . They carried things swiftly out of the house, threw them into the fire, and went back for more. Some of them were arguing (they wouldn't have been Pit Rivers if there hadn't been some kind of argument going on!); there was a little man who kept coming to me and complaining that they ought to burn the house, also. That seemed to be a moot point because in the old days there were no individual houses. And besides, according to Wild Bill, it was Jack's house, as well as the woman's who had died. . . . But the little old man was all for destruction. At least they should throw the stove into the fire. "But it won't burn!" said Wild Bill. "Well, throw it into the creek, then," said the fundamentalist.

I was sitting in my little tent, trying to keep out of the way. All this had happened so fast, like a whirlwind out of the sagebrush, that I was dazed. But everybody kept coming into my tent either to prove to me or to themselves that they were right, or to ask me if this or that object were mine, before throwing it into the fire. My copy of *Moby-Dick* nearly went, and a horse's hackamore that belonged to me. Wild Bill stuck in my tent most of the time, sardonic as usual: "That's Indians for you! Just watch them, Doc. . . . Crazy goddam bunch. Always argue, always argue; argue all the time . . . I wish they would get through with that burning. I have three colts I am breaking, at Tuluukupi, I left them in the corrals, I guess them fellows will feed them . . . still, I ought to be getting back to them."

Jack Folsom himself didn't seem to be doing anything except going around, wailing, crying, grunting. He came into my tent and sat on my cot and sobbed like a little child. "She was very good, that woman, Doc. She never quarreled. I have had four, no, five, before her. We have been together a long time now. You know my daughter Jessie, well she raised her. Jessie has got grandchildren now."

"But, Jack, I thought Jessie was this woman's daughter. . . ."

"No, another woman's. I have had three women already, no, four. No, two only, according to Indian way. This woman I paid for her and she paid for me. That's according to Indian law. I gave Jack Wilson, you know . . . the old fellow who was singing that night, I gave him a white mare, she was awful fast, she had won several races for me, and her people gave me the right to fish on Hat Creek. . . . But you noticed that woman that's come in with them? She is ordering everything around, she is bossing everybody. . . ."

"Yes, I noticed her. Who is she?"

"She is younger sister of the woman who died, what we call *enun*, same as what you call "cousin." So, she has come to claim me."

"What do you mean, claim you?"

"It's this way, Doc: according to Indian law, *the dead people have got the say*; the relations of the dead person have got the right. If I had died, then my people, my relations, they are the ones who have the right to bring another man in my place. It don't matter he is an old man good for nothing. They say: We bought that woman, she belongs to us now; here's a man for her; she take him, or give us back our present; we gave you a horse for her; where is that horse? Now, this woman who died I married her according to Indian law. So, her people, her relations, they come here with this other woman, and they say to me: You lost one, here's another, you got no claim against us."

"Well, then, it's all right, isn't it?"

"No, it ain't all right, Doc. I don't want that woman. She is all right. She is young, I know. She is clean; she is a good worker . . . but she is bossy as hell! She'll boss me . . . I am too old to be bossed!"

Afterwards I took Jack down to my little ranch in the mountains south of Monterey. We had to go fifty miles by horse-stage, then fifteen miles more by trail over the ridges. When we were on top of the highest ridge the sun was dipping into the ocean, and we stopped to eat some sandwiches and make a little coffee. But before he ate, Jack chewed a piece and spat some to the east, and to the north, and to the south, and to the west. "See, Doc, I am doing that because I am in a new country. Them people you don't see, them coyotes and foxes and all kinds of *dinihowis* and *damaagomes* that live around here, they don't know me, because I am a stranger. They might hurt me. So I am telling them: I am all right, I don't mean no harm to you people, see, I am feeding you; and you people don't hurt me neither, because I am a stranger but I want to be friends with you. That's the way to do, Doc, that's the good way."

Night overtook us, and we went down the steep trail in the dark. Jack was stumbling. "Say, Doc, you sure picked you a darn steep country for your homestead." We reached the cabin at last, and I lit a fire in the hearth. There was an old rock mortar, of the kind the Indians use to pound acorns with a stone pestle. They still use them in Central California, but, for some reason which I don't understand, they don't use them any more in Pit River country. Indeed, the Pit River Indians are afraid to touch them. "Them things are dangerous, Doc, them things are full of power. You come across one lying on the ground, some place; and next day you'll find him mebbe a mile further away! He moved during the night!" Whether it was only the ones that were lying abandoned "some place," or whether it was *all* mortars, I never found out. Anyway, I never saw any in use among the Pit Rivers. And now, Jack was very much shocked because I had one of these mortars lying near the hearth! "You shouldn't do that, Doc! He is getting too hot there, near the fire . . . make him mad . . . he is liable to hurt you, bring you bad luck, maybe make your children sick. . . ."

But Jack did not stay very long at my little ranch. He was having bad dreams. "I been dreaming of blood, Doc. It's those people working against me, my wife's people, the one who died. They have got some powerful doctors on their side. I should have married that sister of hers when she came to claim me. That's Indian law. I can't get out of it!"

So I put him on the stage and he went back to Modoc and the joys of matrimony.

When I saw him the next summer he looked subdued. He greeted me with his usual warmth, but when I asked him how he was getting along with quondam sister-in-law, he said: "Oh, it's hell, Doc, just hell. I don't draw a free breath of my own."

I saw him again the next summer. He was radiant. "I got rid of her, Doc. I was camped at Davis Creek, and her brother he come and see me, and he says: Jack, I wouldn't stay with that woman, if I were you. She is too damn bossy! . . . Well, Doc, that's all I wanted to hear. He was her elder brother, so he had the say. So I called my own boy, Millard, you know him, and I said: I am going—when that woman comes back to the camp, don't tell her where I am gone—you don't know nothing about it, *sabe?*"

A few years later I found her married to Sukmit, of all people! But she had found her mate. They were yelling at each other, while old Mary smiled on complacently. Old Mary had earned her rest.

Notes

1. After the *damaaagomes* have been called, no one is allowed to approach the meeting, whether Indian or white man. The reason is obvious: the sudden arrival of a stranger might scare away the *damaagomes* hovering in the air over the shaman's head.

2. The can looked about half full. Was it an intestinal hemorrhage of hysterical origin? Sukmit (unlike some of the shamans, Old Modoc Kate, for instance, of whom I will speak later) was incapable of *supercherie*. I can vouch for that. I knew him too well. When two boon companions get drunk together time and time again, the truth is bound to come out. I simply have no explanation for the stuff in that can except the one given above.

3. Lena had raised Jessie, but they must have been almost the same age, at most ten years' difference—so Jessie looked upon Lena as her mother.

4. When you tell old-time stories of long ago, every verb must begin with *tsik*—, which then is more or less blended with the pronominal prefix.

5. To be worried,—*inismallauw*—(conjugation II). When an Indian is worried, he goes wandering,—*inillaaduw*—. When he is "wandering" he goes around the mountains, cries, breaks pieces of wood, hurls stones. Some of his relatives may be watching him from afar, but they never come near.

6. Indian dancing is not like the European, by lifting the heels and balancing the body on the toes; on the contrary, one foot is raised *flat* from the ground while the other foot is pressed into the ground (by flexing the knee); then a very slight pause with one foot in the air; then the other foot is stamped flat into the ground while the first one is lifted. That is the fundamental idea; there are many variations; besides, the shoulders and head are made to synchronize or syncopate.

7. I am not romancing, nor translating loosely; *hay-dutsi-la* means literally "by thinking." The radical *hay*—means "thought"; *dutsi* is the verb "to be" used here as an auxiliary in participial form (i.e. "being");—*la* is the suffix representing the instrumental case (i.e. "by").

8. Those big clumps of coarse grass and sod which gradually rise above the level of the water on the marshes are called *tsappetia*.

9. The word for "people" is *is*. Nowadays it is applied especially to Indians, in contradistinction to the term applied to the whites: *enellaaduwi.*

The Messiah

from *Black Elk Speaks*
[As told through John G. Neihardt (Flaming Rainbow)]

There was hunger among my people before I went away across the big water, because the Wasichus did not give us all the food they promised in the Black Hills treaty. They made that treaty themselves; our people did not want it and did not make it. Yet the Wasichus who made it had given us less than half as much as they promised. So the people were hungry before I went away.

But it was worse when I came back. My people looked pitiful. There was a big drouth, and the rivers and creeks seemed to be dying. Nothing would grow that the people had planted, and the Wasichus had been sending less cattle and other food than ever before. The Wasichus had slaughtered all the bison and shut us up in pens. It looked as though we might all starve to death. We could not eat lies, and there was nothing we could do.

And now the Wasichus had made another treaty to take away from us about half the land we had left. Our people did not want this treaty either, but Three Stars[1] came and made the treaty just the same, because the Wasichus wanted our land between the Smoky Earth and the Good River. So the flood of Wasichus, dirty with bad deeds, gnawed away half of the island that was left to us. When Three Stars came to kill us on the Rosebud, Crazy Horse whipped him and drove him back. But when he came this time without any soldiers, he whipped us and drove us back. We were penned up and could do nothing.

All the time I was away from home across the big water, my power was gone, and I was like a dead man moving around most of the time. I could hardly remember my vision, and when I did remember, it seemed like a dim dream.

Just after I came back, some people asked me to cure a sick person, and I was afraid the power would not come back to me; but it did. So I went on helping the sick, and there were many, for the measles had come among the people who were already weak because of hunger. There were more sick people that winter when the whooping cough came and killed little children who did not have enough to eat.

So it was. Our people were pitiful and in despair.

But early that summer when I came back from across the big water (1889) strange news had come from the west, and the people had been talking and talking about it. They were talking about it when I came home, and that was the first I had heard of it. This news came to the Ogalalas first of all, and I heard that it came to us from the Shoshones and Blue Clouds (Arapahoes). Some believed it and some did not believe. It was hard to believe; and when I first heard of it, I thought it was only foolish talk that somebody had started somewhere. This news said that out yonder in the west at a place near where the great mountains (The Sierras) stand before you come to the big water, there was a sacred man among the Paiütes who had talked to the Great Spirit in a vision, and the Great Spirit had told him how to save the Indian peoples and make the Wasichus disappear and bring back all the bison and the people who were dead and how there would be a new earth. Before I came back, the people had got together to talk about this and they had sent three men, Good Thunder, Brave Bear and Yellow Breast, to see this sacred man with their own eyes and learn if the story about him was true. So these three men had made the long journey west, and in the fall after I came home, they returned to the Ogalalas with wonderful things to tell.

There was a big meeting at the head of White Clay Creek, not far from Pine Ridge, when they came back, but I did not go over there to hear, because I did not yet believe. I thought maybe it was only the despair that made people believe, just as a man who is starving may dream of plenty of everything good to eat.

I did not go over to the meeting, but I heard all they had to tell. These three men all said the same thing, and they were good men. They said that they traveled far until they came to a great flat valley[2] near the last great mountains before the big water, and there they saw the Wanekia,[3] who was the son of the Great Spirit, and they talked to him. Wasichus called him Jack Wilson, but his name was Wovoka. He told them that there was another world coming, just like a cloud. It would come in a whirlwind out of the west and would crush out everything on this world, which was old and dying. In that other world there was plenty of meat, just like old times; and in that world all the dead Indians were alive, and all the bison that had ever been killed were roaming around again.

This sacred man gave some sacred red paint and two eagle feathers to Good Thunder. The people must put this paint on their faces and they must dance a ghost dance that the sacred man taught to Good Thunder, Yellow Breast, and Brave Bear. If they did this, they could get on this other world when it came, and the Wasichus would not be able to get on, and so they would disappear. When he gave the two eagle feathers to Good Thunder, the sacred man said: "Receive these eagle feathers and behold them, for my father will cause these to bring your people back to him."

This was all that was heard the whole winter.

When I heard this about the red paint and the eagle feathers and about bringing the people back to the Great Spirit, it made me think hard. I had had a great vision that was to bring the people back into the nation's hoop, and maybe this sacred man had had the same vision and it was going to come true, so that the people would get back on the red road. Maybe I was not meant to do this myself, but if I helped with the power that was given me, the tree might bloom again and the people prosper. This was in my mind all that winter, but I did not know what vision the sacred man out there had seen, and I wished I could talk to him and find out. This was sitting deeper in my mind every day, and it was a very bad winter, with much hunger and sickness.

My father died in the first part of the winter from the bad sickness that many people had. This made me very sad. Everything good seemed to be going away. My younger brother and sister had died before I came home, and now I was fatherless in this world. But I still had my mother. I was working in a store for the Wasichus so that I could get something for her to eat, and I just kept on working there and thinking about what Good Thunder, Yellow Breast, and Brave Bear had told; but I did not feel sure yet.

During that winter the people wanted to hear some more about this sacred man and the new world coming, so they sent more men out there to learn what they could. Good Thunder and Yellow Breast, with two others, went from Pine Ridge. Some went with them from other agencies, and two of these were Kicking Bear and Short Bull. News came back from these men as they traveled west, and it seemed that everywhere people belived all that we had heard, and more. Letters came back telling us this. I kept on working in the store and helping sick people with my power.

Then it was spring (1890), and I heard that these men had all come back from the west and that they said it was all true. I did not go to this meeting either, but I heard the gossip that was everywhere now, and people said it was really the son of the Great Spirit who was out there; that when he came to the Wasichus a long time ago, they had killed him; but he was coming to the Indians this time, and there would not be any Wasichus in the new world that would come like a cloud in a whirlwind and crush out the old earth that was dying. This they said would happen after one more winter, when the grasses were appearing (1891).

I heard many wonderful things about the Wanekia that these men had seen and heard, and they were good men. He could make animals talk, and once while they were with him he made a spirit vision, and they all saw it. They saw a big water, and beyond it was a beautiful green land where all the Indians that had ever lived and the bison and the other animals were all coming home together. Then the Wanekia, they said, made the vision go out, because it was not yet time for this to happen. After another winter it would happen, when the grasses were appearing.

And once, they said, the Wanekia held out his hat for them to look into; and when they did this, all but one saw there the whole world and all that was wonderful. But that one could see only the inside of the hat, they said.

Good Thunder himself told me that, with the power of the Wanekia, he had gone to a bison skin tepee; and there his son, who had been dead a long time, was living with his wife, and they had a long talk together.

This was not like my great vision, and I just went on working in the store. I was puzzled and did not know what to think.

Afterwhile I heard that north of Pine Ridge at the head of Cheyenne Creek, Kicking Bear had held the first ghost dance, and that people who danced had seen their dead relatives and talked to them. The next thing I heard was that they were dancing on Wounded Knee Creek just below Manderson.

I did not believe yet, but I wanted to find out things, because all this was sitting more and more strongly in my heart since my father died. Something seemed to tell me to go and see. For awhile I kept from going, but at last I could not any more. So I got on my horse and went to this ghost dance on Wounded Knee Creek below Manderson.

I was surprised, and could hardly believe what I saw; because so much of my vision seemed to be in it. The dancers, both women and men, were holding hands in a big circle, and in the center of the circle they had a tree painted red with most of its branches cut off and some dead leaves on it. This was exactly like the part of my vision where the holy tree was dying, and the circle of the men and women holding hands was like the sacred hoop that should have power to make the tree to bloom again. I saw too that the sacred articles the people had offered were scarlet, as in my vision, and all their faces were painted red. Also, they used the pipe and the eagle feathers. I sat there looking on and feeling sad. It all seemed to be from my great vision somehow and I had done nothing yet to make the tree to bloom.

Then all at once great happiness overcame me, and it all took hold of me right there. This was to remind me to get to work at once and help to bring my people back into the sacred hoop, that they might again walk the red road in a sacred manner pleasing to the Powers of the Universe that are One Power. I remembered how the spirits had taken me to the center of the earth and shown me the good things, and how my people should prosper. I remembered how the Six Grandfathers had told me that through their power I should make my people live and the holy tree should bloom. I believed my vision was coming true at last, and happiness overcame me.

When I went to the dance, I went only to see and to learn what the people believed; but now I was going to stay and use the power that had been given me. The dance was over for that day, but they would dance again next day, and I would dance with them.

Notes

1. General Crook headed the commission that arranged the treaty of 1889.

2. Mason Valley, Nevada.

3. "One Who Makes Live."

Visions of the Other World

from *Black Elk Speaks*
[As told through John G. Neihardt (Flaming Rainbow)]

So I dressed myself in a sacred manner, and before the dance began next morning I went among the people who were standing around the withered tree. Good Thunder, who was a relative of my father and later married my mother, put his arms around me and took me to the sacred tree that had not bloomed, and there he offered up a prayer for me. He said: "Father, Great Spirit, behold this boy! Your ways he shall see!" Then he began to cry.

I thought of my father and my brother and sister who had left us, and I could not keep the tears from running out of my eyes. I raised my face up to keep them back, but they came out just the same. I cried with my whole heart, and while I cried I thought of my people in despair. I thought of my vision, and how it was promised me that my people should have a place in this earth where they could be happy every day. I thought of them on the wrong road now, but maybe they could be brought back into the hoop again and to the good road.

Under the tree that never bloomed I stood and cried because it had withered away. With tears on my face I asked the Great Spirit to give it life and leaves and singing birds as in my vision.

Then there came a strong shivering all over my body, and I knew that the power was in me.

Good Thunder now took one of my arms, Kicking Bear the other, and we began to dance. The song we sang was like this:

"Who do you think he is that comes?
It is one who seeks his mother!"

It was what the dead would sing when entering the other world and looking for their relatives who had gone there before them.

As I danced, with Good Thunder and Kicking Bear holding my arms between them, I had the queer feeling that I knew and I seemed to be lifted clear off the ground. I did not have a vision all that first day. That night I thought about the other world and that the Wanekia himself was with my people there and maybe the holy tree of my vision was really blooming yonder right then, and that it was there my vision had already come true. From the center of the earth I had been shown all good and beautiful things in a great circle of peace, and maybe this land of my vision was where all my people were going, and there they would live and prosper where no Wasichus were or could ever be.

Before we started dancing next day, Kicking Bear offered a prayer, saying: "Father, Great Spirit, behold these people! They shall go forth to-day to see their relatives, and yonder they shall be happy, day after day, and their happiness will not end."

Then we began dancing, and most of the people wailed and cried as they danced, holding hands in a circle; but some of them laughed with happiness. Now and then some one would fall down like dead, and others would go staggering around and panting before they would fall. While they were lying there like dead they were having visions, and we kept on dancing and singing, and many were crying for the old way of living and that the old religion might be with them again.

After awhile I began to feel very queer. First, my legs seemed to be full of ants. I was dancing with my eyes closed, as the others did. Suddenly it seemed that I was swinging off the ground and not touching it any longer. The queer feeling came up from my legs and was in my heart now. It seemed I would glide forward like a swing, and then glide back again in longer and longer swoops. There was no fear with this, just a growing happiness.

I must have fallen down, but I felt as though I had fallen off a swing when it was going forward, and I was floating head first through the air. My arms were stretched out, and all I saw at first was a single eagle feather right in front of me. Then the feather was a spotted eagle dancing on ahead of me with his wings fluttering, and he was making the shrill whistle that is his. My body did not move at all, but I looked ahead and floated fast toward where I looked.

There was a ridge right in front of me, and I thought I was going to run into it, but I went right over it. On the other side of the ridge I could see a beautiful land where many, many people were camping in a great circle. I could see that they were happy and had plenty. Everywhere there were drying racks full of meat. The air was clear and beautiful with a living light that was everywhere. All around the circle, feeding on the green, green grass, were fat and happy horses; and animals of all kinds were scattered all over the green hills, and singing hunters were returning with their meat.

I floated over the tepees and began to come down feet first at the center of the hoop where I could see a beautiful tree all green and full of flowers. When I touched the ground, two men were coming toward me, and they wore holy shirts made and painted in a certain way. They came to me and said: "It is not yet time to see your father, who is happy. You have work to do. We will give you something that you shall carry back to your people, and with it they shall come to see their loved ones."

I knew it was the way their holy shirts were made that they wanted me to take back. They told me to return at once, and then I was out in the air again, floating fast as before. When I came right over the dancing place, the people were still dancing, but it seemed they were not making any sound. I had hoped to see the withered tree in bloom, but it was dead.

Then I fell back into my body, and as I did this I heard voices all around and above me, and I was sitting on the ground. Many were crowding around, asking me what vision I had seen. I told them just what I had seen, and what I brought back was the memory of the holy shirts the two men wore.

That evening some of us got together at Big Road's tepee and decided to use the ghost shirts I had seen. So the next day I made ghost shirts all day long and painted them in the sacred manner of my vision. As I made these shirts, I thought how in my vision everything was like old times and the tree was flowering, but when I came back the tree was dead. And I thought that if this world would do as the vision teaches, the tree could bloom here too.

I made the first shirt for Afraid-of-Hawk and the second for the son of Big Road.

In the evening I made a sacred stick like that I had seen in my first vision and painted it red with the sacred paint of the Wanekia. On the top of it I tied one eagle feather, and this I carried in the dance after that, wearing the holy shirt as I had seen it.

Because of my vision and the power they knew I had, I was asked to lead the dance next morning. We all stood in a straight line, facing the west, and I prayed: "Father, Great Spirit, behold me! The nation that I have is in despair. The new earth you promised you have shown me. Let my nation also behold it."

After the prayer we stood with our right hands raised to the west, and we all began to weep, and right there, as they wept, some of them fainted before the dance began.

As we were dancing I had the same queer feeling I had before, as though my feet were off the earth and swinging. Kicking Bear and Good Thunder were holding my arms. Afterwhile it seemed they let go of me, and once more I floated head first, face down, with arms extended, and the spotted eagle was dancing there ahead of me again, and I could hear his shrill whistle and his scream.

I saw the ridge again, and as I neared it there was a deep, rumbling sound, and out of it there leaped a flame. But I glided right over it. There were six villages ahead of me in the beautiful land that was all clear and green in living light. Over these in turn I glided, coming down on the south side of the sixth village. And as I touched the ground, twelve men were coming towards me, and they said: "Our Father, the two-legged chief, you shall see!"

Then they led me to the center of the circle where once more I saw the holy tree all full of leaves and blooming.

But that was not all I saw. Against the tree there was a man standing with arms held wide in front of him. I looked hard at him, and I could not tell what people he came from. He was not a Wasichu and he was not an Indian. His hair was long and hanging loose, and on the left side of his head he wore an eagle feather. His body was strong and good to see, and it was painted red. I tried to recognize him, but I could not make him out. He was a very fine-looking man. While I was staring hard at him, his body began to change and became very beautiful with all colors of light, and around him there was light. He spoke like singing: "My life is such that all earthly beings and growing things belong to me. Your father, the Great Spirit, has said this. You too must say this."

Then he went out like a light in a wind.

The twelve men who were there spoke: "Behold them! Your nation's life shall be such!"

I saw again how beautiful the day was—the sky all blue and full of yellow light above the greening earth. And I saw that all the people were beautiful and young. There were no old ones there, nor children either—just people of about one age, and beautiful.

Then there were twelve women who stood in front of me and spoke: "Behold them! Their way of life you shall take back to earth." When they had spoken, I heard singing in the west, and I learned the song I heard.

Then one of the twelve men took two sticks, one painted white and one red, and, thrusting them in the ground, he said: "Take these! You shall depend upon them. Make haste!"

I started to walk, and it seemed as though a strong wind went under me and picked me up. I was in the air, with outstretched arms, and floating fast. There was a fearful dark river that I had to go over, and I was afraid. It rushed and roared and was full of angry foam. Then I looked down and saw many men and women who were trying to cross the dark and fearful river, but they could not. Weeping, they looked up to me and cried: "Help us!" But I could not stop gliding, for it was as though a great wind were under me.

Then I saw my earthly people again at the dancing place, and fell back into my body lying there. And I was sitting up, and people were crowding around me to ask what vision I had seen.

I told my vision through songs, and the older men explained them to the others. I sang a song, the words of which were those the Wanekia spoke under the flowering tree, and the air of it was that which I heard in the West after the twelve women had spoken. I sang it four times, and the fourth time all the people began to weep together because the Wasichus had taken the beautiful world away from us.

I thought and thought about this vision. The six villages seemed to represent the Six Grandfathers that I had seen long ago in the Flaming Rainbow Tepee, and I had gone to the sixth village, which was for the Sixth Grandfather, the Spirit of the Earth, because I was to stand for him in the world. I wondered if the Wanekia might be the red man of my great vision, who turned into a bison, and then into the four-rayed herb, the day-break-star herb of understanding. I thought the twelve men and twelve women were for the moons of the year.

Bad Trouble Coming

from *Black Elk Speaks*

While these things were happening, the summer (1890) was getting old. I did not then know all that was going on at other places, but some things I heard, and much more I heard later.

When Good Thunder and Kicking Bear came back in the spring from seeing the Wanekia, the Wasichus at Pine Ridge put them in prison awhile, and then let them go. This showed the Wasichus were afraid of something. In the Moon of Black Cherries (August) many people were dancing at No Water's Camp on Clay Creek, and the agent came and told them to stop dancing. They would not stop, and they said they would fight for their religion if they had to do it. The agent went away, and they kept on dancing. They called him Young-Man-Afraid-of-Lakotas.

Later, I heard that the Brules were dancing over east of us; and then I heard that Big Foot's people were dancing on the Good River reservation; also that Kicking Bear had gone to Sitting Bull's camp on Grand River, and that the people were dancing there too. Word came to us that the Indians were beginning to dance everywhere.

The people were hungry and in despair, and many believed in the good new world that was coming. The Wasichus gave us less than half the beef cattle they promised us in the treaty, and these cattle were very poor. For a while our people would not take the cattle, because there were so few of them and they were so poor. But afterwhile they had to take them or starve to death. So we got more lies than cattle, and we could not eat lies. When the agent told the people to quit dancing, their hearts were bad.

From the dancing on Wounded Knee I went over to the Brules, who were camping on Cut Meat Creek at this time, and I took with me six shirts like those I had seen the twelve men wearing in my vision, and six dresses like the twelve women wore. I gave these to the Brules and they made others for themselves.

We danced there, and another vision came to me. I saw a Flaming Rainbow, like the one I had seen in my first great vision. Below the rainbow was a tepee made of cloud. Over me there was a spotted eagle soaring, and he said to me: "Remember this." That was all I saw and heard.

I have thought much about this since, and I have thought that this was where I made my great mistake. I had had a very great vision, and I should have depended only upon that to guide me to the good. But I followed the lesser visions that had come to me while dancing on Wounded Knee Creek. The vision of the Flaming Rainbow was to warn me, maybe; and I did not understand. I did not depend upon the great vision as I should have done; I depended upon the two sticks that I had seen in the lesser vision. It is hard to follow one great vision in this world of darkness and of many changing shadows. Among those shadows men get lost.

When I came back from the Brules, the weather was getting cold. Many of the Brules came along when I came back, and joined the Ogalalas in the dancing on Wounded Knee. We heard that there were soldiers at Pine Ridge and that others were coming all the time. Then one morning we heard that the soldiers were marching toward us, so we broke camp and moved west to Grass Creek. From there we went to White Clay and camped awhile and danced.

There came to us Fire Thunder, Red Wound and Young American Horse with a message from the soldiers that this matter of the ghost dance must be looked into, and that there should be rulings over it; and that they did not mean to take the dance away from us. But could we believe anything the Wasichus ever said to us? They spoke with forked tongues.

We moved in closer to Pine Ridge and camped. Many soldiers were there now, and what were they there for?

There was a big meeting with the agent, but I did not go to hear. He made a ruling that we could dance three days every moon, and the rest of the time we should go and make a living for ourselves somehow. He did not say how we could do that. But the people agreed to this.

The next day, while I was sitting in a tepee with Good Thunder, a policeman came to us and said: "I was not sent here, but I came for your good to tell you what I have heard—that they are going to arrest you two."

Good Thunder thought we ought to go to the Brules, who had a big camp on Wounded Knee below Manderson. So that evening we saddled and started. We came through Pepper Creek and White Horse Creek to Wounded Knee and followed it down to the Brule camp. They were glad to see us.

In the morning the crier went around and called a meeting. I spoke to the Brules, and this is what I said: "My relatives, there is a certain thing that we have done. From that certain sacred thing, we have had visions. In those visions we have seen, and also we have heard, that our relatives who have gone before us are in the Other World that has been revealed to us, and that we too shall go there. They are right now with the Wanekia. If the Wasichus want to fight us, let them do it. Have in your minds a strong desire, and take courage. We must depend upon the departed ones who are in the new world that is coming."

More Brules came there from Porcupine and Medicine Root creeks, and we all broke camp, moving down the Wounded Knee to Smoky Earth River (the White). There a Black Robe (Catholic Priest) came and tried to coax us to return. Our people told him that Wasichu promises were no good; that everything they had promised was a lie. Only a few Ogalalas turned back with the Black Robe. He was a good man and he was badly wounded that winter in the butchering of Big Foot's band. He was a very good man, and not like the other Wasichus.[1]

From Smoky Earth River we moved to High Pockets' place southwest of the Top of the Badlands.[2] While we were there, American Horse and Fast Thunder came to us. They were both chiefs, and they came to bring us in to Pine Ridge. We had to obey. The Brules would not obey and tried to keep us from going. They struck us, and there was quite a struggle for a while; but we went anyway, because we had to go. Kicking Bear stayed with the Brules that time, but he came in to Pine Ridge a little later. A very few of the Brules went along with us.

We camped on White River, then on White Clay, then on Cheyenne Creek north of Pine Ridge. Most of the Ogalalas were camping near there too.

It was about this time that bad news came to us from the north. We heard that some policemen from Standing Rock had gone to arrest Sitting Bull on Grand River, and that he would not let them take him; so there was a fight, and they killed him.

It was now near the end of the Moon of Popping Trees, and I was twenty-seven years old (December, 1890). We heard that Big Foot was coming down from the Badlands with nearly four hundred people. Some of these were from Sitting Bull's band. They had run away when Sitting Bull was killed, and joined Big Foot on Good River. There were only about a hundred warriors in this band, and all the others were women and children and some old men. They were all starving and freezing, and Big Foot was so sick that they had to bring him along in a pony drag.[3] They had all run away to hide in the Badlands, and they were coming in now because they were starving and freezing. When they crossed Smoky Earth River, they followed up Medicine Root Creek to its head. Soldiers were over there looking for them. The soldiers had everything and were not freezing and starving. Near Porcupine Butte the soldiers came up to the Big Foots, and they surrendered and went along with the soldiers to Wounded Knee Creek where the Brenan store is now.

It was in the evening when we heard that the Big Foots were camped over there with the soldiers, about fifteen miles by the old road from where we were. It was the next morning (December 29, 1890) that something terrible happened.

Notes

1. This was Father Craft.

2. Cuny Table, a high plateau in the midst of the Badlands.

3. He was very ill with pneumonia.

The Butchering at Wounded Knee

from *Black Elk Speaks*
[As told through John G. Neihardt (Flaming Rainbow)]

That evening before it happened, I went in to Pine Ridge and heard these things, and while I was there, soldiers started for where the Big Foots were. These made about five hundred soldiers that were there next morning. When I saw them starting I felt that something terrible was going to happen. That night I could hardly sleep at all. I walked around most of the night.

In the morning I went out after my horses, and while I was out I heard shooting off toward the east, and I knew from the sound that it must be wagon-guns (cannon) going off. The sounds went right through my body, and I felt that something terrible would happen.

When I reached camp with the horses, a man rode up to me and said: "Hey-hey-hey! The people that are coming are fired on! I know it!"

I saddled up my buckskin and put on my sacred shirt. It was one I had made to be worn by no one but myself. It had a spotted eagle outstretched on the back of it, and the daybreak star was on the left shoulder, because when facing south that shoulder is toward the east. Across the breast, from the left shoulder to the right hip, was the flaming rainbow, and there was another rainbow around the neck, like a necklace, with a star at the bottom. At each shoulder, elbow, and wrist was an eagle feather; and over the whole shirt were red streaks of lightning. You will see that this was from my great vision, and you will know how it protected me that day.

I painted my face all red, and in my hair I put one eagle feather for the One Above.

It did not take me long to get ready, for I could still hear the shooting over there.

I started out alone on the old road that ran across the hills to Wounded Knee. I had no gun. I carried only the sacred bow of the west that I had seen in my great vision. I had gone only a little way when a band of young men came galloping after me. The first two who came up were Loves War and Iron Wasichu. I asked what they were going to do, and they said they were just going to see where the shooting was. Then others were coming up, and some older men.

We rode fast, and there were about twenty of us now. The shooting was getting louder. A horseback from over there came galloping very fast toward us, and he said: "Hey-hey-hey! They have murdered them!" Then he whipped his horse and rode away faster toward Pine Ridge.

In a little while we had come to the top of the ridge where, looking to the east, you can see for the first time the monument and the burying ground on the little hill where the church is. That is where the terrible thing started. Just south of the burying ground on the little hill a deep dry gulch runs about east and west, very crooked, and it rises westward to nearly the top of the ridge where we were. It had no name, but the Wasichus sometimes call it Battle Creek now. We stopped on the ridge not far from the head of the dry gulch. Wagon guns were still going off over there on the little hill, and they were going off again where they hit along the gulch. There was much shooting down yonder, and there were many cries, and we could see cavalrymen scattered over the hills ahead of us. Cavalrymen were riding along the gulch and shooting into it, where the women and children were running away and trying to hide in the gullies and the stunted pines.

A little way ahead of us, just below the head of the dry gulch, there were some women and children who were huddled under a clay bank, and some cavalrymen were there pointing guns at them.

We stopped back behind the ridge, and I said to the others: "Take courage. These are our relatives. We will try to get them back." Then we all sang a song which went like this:

"A thunder being nation I am, I have said.
A thunder being nation I am, I have said.

You shall live.
You shall live.
You shall live.
You shall live."

Then I rode over the ridge and the others after me, and we were crying: "Take courage! It is time to fight!" The soldiers who were guarding our relatives shot at us and then ran away fast, and some more cavalrymen on the other side of the gulch did too. We got our relatives and sent them across the ridge to the northwest where they would be safe.

I had no gun, and when we were charging, I just held the sacred bow out in front of me with my right hand. The bullets did not hit us at all.

We found a little baby lying all alone near the head of the gulch. I could not pick her up just then, but I got her later and some of my people adopted her. I just wrapped her up tighter in a shawl that was around her and left her there. It was a safe place, and I had other work to do.

The soldiers had run eastward over the hills where there were some more soldiers, and they were off their horses and lying down. I told the others to stay back, and I charged upon them holding the sacred bow out toward them with my right hand. They all shot at me, and I could hear bullets all around me, but I ran my horse right close to them, and then swung around. Some soldiers across the gulch began shooting at me too, but I got back to the others and was not hurt at all.

By now many other Lakotas, who had heard the shooting, were coming up from Pine Ridge, and we all charged on the soldiers. They ran eastward toward where the trouble began. We followed down along the dry gulch, and what we saw was terrible. Dead and wounded women and children and little babies were scattered all along there where they had been trying to run away. The soldiers had followed along the gulch, as they ran, and murdered them in there. Sometimes they were in heaps because they had huddled together, and some were scattered all along. Sometimes bunches of them had been killed and torn to pieces where the wagon guns hit them. I saw a little baby trying to suck its mother, but she was bloody and dead.

There were two little boys at one place in this gulch. They had guns and they had been killing soldiers all by themselves. We could see the soldiers they had killed. The boys were all alone there, and they were not hurt. These were very brave little boys.

When we drove the soldiers back, they dug themselves in, and we were not enough people to drive them out from there. In the evening they marched off up Wounded Knee Creek, and then we saw all that they had done there.

Men and women and children were heaped and scattered all over the flat at the bottom of the little hill where the soldiers had their wagon-guns, and westward up the dry gulch all the way to the high ridge, the dead women and children and babies were scattered.

When I saw this I wished that I had died too, but I was not sorry for the women and children. It was better for them to be happy in the other world, and I wanted to be there too. But before I went there I wanted to have revenge. I thought there might be a day, and we should have revenge.

After the soldiers marched away, I heard from my friend, Dog Chief, how the trouble started, and he was right there by Yellow Bird when it happened. This is the way it was:

In the morning the soldiers began to take all the guns away from the Big Foots, who were camped in the flat below the little hill where the monument and burying ground are now. The people had stacked most of their guns, and even their knives, by the tepee where Big Foot was lying sick. Soldiers were on the little hill and all around, and there were soldiers across the dry gulch to the south and over east along Wounded Knee Creek too. The people were nearly surrounded, and the wagon-guns were pointing at them.

Some had not yet given up their guns, and so the soldiers were searching all the tepees, throwing things around and poking into everything. There was a man called Yellow Bird, and he and another man were standing in front of the tepee where Big Foot was lying sick. They had white sheets around and over them, with eyeholes to look through, and they had guns under these. An officer came to search them. He took the other man's gun, and then started to take Yellow Bird's. But Yellow Bird would not let go. He wrestled with the officer, and while they were wrestling, the gun went off and killed the officer. Wasichus and some others have said he meant to do this, but Dog Chief was standing right there, and he told me it was not so. As soon as the gun went off, Dog Chief told me, an officer shot and killed Big Foot who was lying sick inside the tepee.

Then suddenly nobody knew what was happening, except that the soldiers were all shooting and the wagon-guns began going off right in among the people.

Many were shot down right there. The women and children ran into the gulch and up west, dropping all the time, for the soldiers shot them as they ran. There were only about a hundred warriors and there were nearly five hundred soldiers. The warriors rushed to where they had piled their guns and knives. They fought soldiers with only their hands until they got their guns.

Dog Chief saw Yellow Bird run into a tepee with his gun, and from there he killed soldiers until the tepee caught fire. Then he died full of bullets.

It was a good winter day when all this happened. The sun was shining. But after the soldiers marched away from their dirty work, a heavy snow began to fall. The wind came up in the night. There was a big blizzard, and it grew very cold. The snow drifted deep in the crooked gulch, and it was one long grave of butchered women and children and babies, who had never done any harm and were only trying to run away.

The End of the Dream

from *Black Elk Speaks*
[As told through John G. Neihardt (Flaming Rainbow)]

After the soldiers marched away, Red Crow and I started back toward Pine Ridge together, and I took the little baby that I told you about. Red Crow had one too.

We were going back to Pine Ridge, because we thought there was peace back home; but it was not so. While we were gone, there was a fight around the Agency, and our people had all gone away. They had gone away so fast that they left all the tepees standing.

It was nearly dark when we passed north of Pine Ridge where the hospital is now, and some soldiers shot at us, but did not hit us. We rode into the camp, and it was all empty. We were very hungry because we had not eaten anything since early morning, so we peeped into the tepees until we saw where there was a pot with papa (dried meat) cooked in it. We sat down in there and began to eat. While we were doing this, the soldiers shot at the tepee, and a bullet struck right between Red Crow and me. It threw dust in the soup, but we kept right on eating until we had our fill. Then we took the babies and got on our horses and rode away. If that bullet had only killed me, then I could have died with papa in my mouth.

The people had fled down Clay Creek, and we followed their trail. It was dark now, and late in the night we came to where they were camped without any tepees. They were just sitting by little fires, and the snow was beginning to blow. We rode in among them and I heard my mother's voice. She was singing a death song for me, because she felt sure I had died over there. She was so glad to see me that she cried and cried.

Women who had milk fed the little babies that Red Crow and I brought with us.

I think nobody but the little children slept any that night. The snow blew and we had no tepees.

When it was getting light, a war party went out and I went along; but this time I took a gun with me. When I started out the day before to Wounded Knee, I took only my sacred bow, which was not made to shoot with; because I was a little in doubt about the Wanekia religion at that time, and I did not really want to kill anybody because of it.

But I did not feel like that any more. After what I had seen over there, I wanted revenge; I wanted to kill.

We crossed White Clay Creek and followed it up, keeping on the west side. Soon we could hear many guns going off. So we struck west, following a ridge to where the fight was. It was close to the Mission, and there are many bullets in the Mission yet.

From this ridge we could see that the Lakotas were on both sides of the creek and were shooting at soldiers who were coming down the creek. As we looked down, we saw a little ravine, and across this was a big hill. We crossed and rode up the hillside.

They were fighting right there, and a Lakota cried to me: "Black Elk, this is the kind of a day in which to do something great!" I answered: "How!"[1]

Then I got off my horse and rubbed earth on myself, to show the Powers that I was nothing without their help. Then I took my rifle, got on my horse and galloped up to the top of the hill. Right below me the soldiers were shooting, and my people called out to me not to go down there; that there were some good shots among the soldiers and I should get killed for nothing.

But I remembered my great vision, the part where the geese of the north appeared. I depended upon their power. Stretching out my arms with my gun in the right hand, like a goose soaring when it flies low to turn in a change of weather, I made the sound the geese make—br-r-r-p, br-r-r-p, br-r-r-p; and, doing this, I charged. The soldiers saw, and began shooting fast at me. I kept right on with my buckskin running, shot in their faces when I was near, then swung wide and rode back up the hill.

All this time the bullets were buzzing around me and I was not touched. I was not even afraid. It was like being in a dream about shooting. But just as I had reached the very top of the hill, suddenly it was like waking up, and I was afraid. I dropped my arms and quit making the goose cry. Just as I did this, I felt something strike my belt as though some one had hit me there with the back of an ax. I nearly fell out of my saddle, but I managed to hold on, and rode over the hill.

An old man by the name of Protector was there, and he ran up and held me, for now I was falling off my horse. I will show you where the bullet struck me sidewise across the belly here (showing a long deep scar on the abdomen). My insides were coming out. Protector tore up a blanket in strips and bound it around me so that my insides would stay in. By now I was crazy to kill, and I said to Protector: "Help me on my horse! Let me go over there. It is a good day to die, so I will go over there!" But Protector said: "No, young nephew! You must not die to-day. That would be foolish. Your people need you. There may be a better day to die." He lifted me into my saddle and led my horse away down hill. Then I began to feel very sick.

By now it looked as though the soldiers would be wiped out, and the Lakotas were fighting harder; but I heard that, after I left, the black Wasichu soldiers came, and the Lakotas had to retreat.

There were many of our children in the Mission, and the sisters and priests were taking care of them. I heard there were sisters and priests right in the battle helping wounded people and praying.

There was a man by the name of Little Soldier who took charge of me and brought me to where our people were camped. While we were over at the Mission Fight, they had fled to the O-ona-gazhee[2] and were camped on top of it where the women and children would be safe from soldiers. Old Hollow Horn was there. He was a very powerful bear medicine man, and he came over to heal my wound. In three days I could walk, but I kept a piece of blanket tied around my belly.

It was now nearly the middle of the Moon of Frost in the Tepee (January). We heard that soldiers were on Smoky Earth River and were coming to attack us in the O-ona-gazhee. They were near Black Feather's place. So a party of about sixty of us started on the war-path to find them. My mother tried to keep me at home, because, although I could walk and ride a horse, my wound was not all healed yet. But I would not stay; for, after what I had seen at Wounded Knee, I wanted a chance to kill soldiers.

We rode down Grass Creek to Smoky Earth, and crossed, riding down stream. Soon from the top of a little hill we saw wagons and cavalry guarding them. The soldiers were making a corral of their wagons and getting ready to fight. We got off our horses and went behind some hills to a little knoll, where we crept up to look at the camp. Some soldiers were bringing harnessed horses down to a little creek to water, and I said to the others: "If you will stay here and shoot at the soldiers, I will charge over there and get some good horses." They knew of my power, so they did this, and I charged on my buckskin while the others kept shooting. I got seven of the horses; but when I started back with these, all the soldiers saw me and began shooting. They killed two of my horses, but I brought five back safe and was not hit. When I was out of range, I caught up a fine bald-faced bay and turned my buckskin loose. Then I drove the others back to our party.

By now more cavalry were coming up the river, a big bunch of them, and there was some hard fighting for a while, because there were not enough of us. We were fighting and retreating, and all at once I saw Red Willow on foot running. He called to me: "Cousin, my horse is killed!" So I caught up a soldier's horse that was dragging a rope and brought it to Red Willow while the soldiers were shooting fast at me. Just then, for a little while, I was a wanekia[3] myself. In this fight Long Bear and another man, whose name I have forgotten, were badly wounded; but we saved them and carried them along with us. The soldiers did not follow us far into the Badlands, and when it was night we rode back with our wounded to the O-ona-gazhee.

We wanted a much bigger war-party so that we could meet the soldiers and get revenge. But this was hard, because the people were not all of the same mind, and they were hungry and cold. We had a meeting there, and were all ready to go out with more warriors, when Afraid-of-His-Horses came over from Pine Ridge to make peace with Red Cloud, who was with us there.

Our party wanted to go out and fight anyway, but Red Cloud made a speech to us something like this: "Brothers, this is a very hard winter. The women and children are starving and freezing. If this were summer, I would say to keep on fighting to the end. But we cannot do this. We must think of the women and children and that it is very bad for them. So we must make peace, and I will see that nobody is hurt by the soldiers."

The people agreed to this, for it was true. So we broke camp next day and went down from the O-ona-gazhee to Pine Ridge, and many, many Lakotas were already there. Also, there were many, many soldiers. They stood in two lines with their guns held in front of them as we went through to where we camped.

And so it was all over.

I did not know then how much was ended. When I look back now from this high hill of my old age, I can still see the butchered women and children lying heaped and scattered all along the crooked gulch as plain as when I saw them with eyes still young. And I can see that something else died there in the bloody mud, and was buried in the blizzard. A people's dream died there. It was a beautiful dream.

And I, to whom so great a vision was given in my youth,—you see me now a pitiful old man who has done nothing, for the nation's hoop is broken and scattered. There is no center any longer, and the sacred tree is dead.

Notes

1. Signifying assent.

2. Sheltering place, an elevated plateau in the Badlands, with precipitous sides, and inaccessible save by one narrow neck of land easily defended.

3. A "make-live," savior.

Fall 1917—Spring 1918
Manitou-geezis
Strong Spirit Sun

[Louise Erdrich]

There was nothing to say when Eli showed at my door. His hands were open and lifeless, hung at his sides. The hair flowed thick and loose down one cheek, as if he were in mourning. I saw his gun, tied across the pack on his shoulders, and a small bundle which he handed to me. When I opened the cloth I saw he'd brought me a stash of flour, lard, sugar, and I knew that he wanted to stay. I finally said to him, "You best sit down and have a plate of stew." So he came in, but he wouldn't eat. I suppose he could see for himself that the meat in the pot was only one poor gopher that should have hibernated while it could. He sat on the bed while I ate, but wouldn't look at me, or talk. I got weary of his shuttered face.

"I'm an old man who doesn't have much time left," I hinted.

He took a deep breath, let it out with sad force.

"Ah, the wind has come up!" I encouraged. But now he glared at me, annoyed that his advisor should fail to understand the serious nature of his problem. I understood well enough, however. I took my chair to the window for the fading light and looked at some catalogues and some letters from the land court that had come by mail. A system of post was still a new and different thing to Indians, and I was marked out by the Agent to receive words in envelopes. They were addressed to Mr. Nanapush, and I saved every one I got. I had a skin of them tied and stowed beneath my bed.

Fearing he had lost my interest, Eli mumbled some fierce words to the top of the table and locked his hands together. He knotted and unknotted his fingers until the knucklebones made irritating cracks.

"Spread that fire," is all I said, "the wood burns too hot and the sticks are snapping."

He wrung out his fingers, prodded the fire for a while, and fell back in his seat. Next I began to hear the sound of his clenched teeth grinding together, and finally he moaned between his lips.

"How much a man endures!"

"What man?" I said.

"This one!" He sank his face against his palms, and then, most impressive of all, let his head fall with a crash onto my table.

"Lucky my table is made of solid wood too."

"Uncle, have pity on your poor nephew!" he demanded angrily.

"My nephew already has sufficient pity on himself."

"You don't care for me either," he said in a bitter voice, pulling at the long messy flow of his locks. "None of them cares for me anymore."

I knew he was too full of vanity to remove a single hair.

"Some men would pull out a handful or two over what they've done," I told him, bending close. "Look at mine, so thin in spots there's almost nothing. I once shared your weakness—but for women, not little girls."

"She was no little girl!" He came to attention, stirred by the injustice of my judgment. "And besides, I was witched!"

"That's no good, " I counseled, shaking my head. "Fleur has known weak men before, and won't believe that excuse."

"All right," he countered, "but listen to this. *She* has done worse now. And I won't go back to her. She frightens me."

"At last." I continued to turn the dry, sharp pages of my papers. Between this unpromising winter, the pain in my hip that made me feel so poor I could not hunt, and the wholesale purchase of our allotment land by whites, the problems of Eli Kashpaw were of thin consequence, and yet he insisted on pelting me to death with grass.

"Look, fool," I said. "Open your eyes. Even your baby brother has a better grasp of what is going on. We're offered money in the agreements, cash for land. What will you do with the money?"

"Right now?" Eli asked in a belligerent, stalling way.

"Yes," I said, "what would you do with fifty dollars this moment?"

"I'd drink it up," he said in a pouting voice, daring my wrath even though I knew he rarely drank. I gave him no satisfaction, just kept the argument going.

"Like many," I said, "you'd wake with no place to put your foot down."

"I don't want to live around here anyway!" he yelled in rage.

I threw down the papers. "That's all you think about! You!"

Satisfied that he'd raised my temper, pretending he'd got my sympathy, Eli now busied himself with the cold stew. He gulped it all down as if it held tender beef, which we had not seen since the government issue. When he was done he leaned back and, without meaning to, his face registered the flat spoiled taste of the gopher meat. And with that, the first hint of pity for me. But I wanted none.

"I got a herd of this Indian beef corralled out in the woodpile and branded the government way," I told him. "I'm planning on holding a roundup."

He couldn't let himself laugh, so he punished me by staring blankly. He rolled a bit of tobacco and smoked to cut the edge of the grease.

He thought aloud after a while. "If Fleur was only in the church I could go there, get forgiveness by the priest, and then she would have to forget what happened."

He looked over at me, waiting with new hope for some reaction. But I was so disgusted at his foolish reasoning that I'd begun to wonder whether I would even help him. So many other things were on my mind. I had already given Father Damien testimony on this Anishinabe land, which was nibbled at the edges and surrounded by farmers waiting for it to go underneath the gavel of the auctioneer. There were so few of us who even understood the writing on the papers. Some signed their land away with thumbs and crosses. As a young man, I had made my reputation as a government interpreter, that is, until the Beauchamp Treaty signing, in which I said to Rift-In-A-Cloud, "Don't put your thumb in the ink." One of the officials understood and I lost my job. All of this could not have concerned Eli less. Now he put out the cigarette, grinding it onto the stove and saving the shred of tobacco. He kept looking hopeful, waiting for advice which he did not deserve.

"Lay your blankets down anywhere you want," I said to Eli. There was only the floor of beaten dirt, rock cold in the winter even by the stove. I expected that such constant discomfort would drive him home. He was disappointed, but knelt meekly and covered himself with the rough brown robe.

"My boy," I said into the dark after we were lying without sleep. "They'll eat much worse than gopher out there without a man to hunt. Margaret's no treaty Indian to get her rations in town."

Eli gave a harsh laugh. "Come winter, Fleur will chop a hole in the ice and fish the lake."

"Until then?"

"Until then, she's a good shot."

After six days I could not bear to hear any more from Eli. Each day of snow seemed endless, trapped with a sulking boy. Eli paced, muttered, slept, and also ate my cupboard completely bare, down to the last potato, and emptied the little bundle he brought, too, which would have lasted me the whole evil month. We went two days without anything but grease and crumbs of bread. On the seventh day I handed him his gun. He looked at it in surprise, but finally went north. I went out on my own, checking snares. I had caught some beardgrass, a clump of gray fur, a small carcass picked clean overnight by an owl, and a rabbit that was no good, full of worm. I went home and built the fire, drank some tea of dried nettles and considered that by the end of what looked to be a worse winter than I'd feared, I might be forced to boil my moccasins. That was one good thing at least. I hadn't taken to wearing tradestore boots of dyed leather. Those can kill you. After a while, I went and looked into the floursack, which I knew was already empty, and it was still empty. That's when I lay down.

In my fist I had a lump of charcoal, with which I blackened my face. I placed my otter bag upon my chest, my rattle near. I began to sing slowly, calling on my helpers, until the words came from my mouth but were not mine, until the rattle started, the song sang itself, and there, in the deep bright drifts, I saw the tracks of Eli's snowshoes clearly.

He was wandering, weak from his empty stomach, not thinking how the wind blew or calling on the clouds to cover the sky. He did not know what he hunted, what sign to look for or to follow. He let the snow dazzle him and almost dropped his gun. And then the song picked up and stopped him until he understood, from the deep snow and light hard crust, the high wind and rolling clouds, that everything around him was perfect for killing moose.

He had seen the tracks before, down near a frozen shallow slough. So he went there, knowing a moose is dull and has no imagination, although its hearing is particularly keen. He walked carefully around the rim of the depression. Now he was thinking. His vision had cleared and right away he saw the trail leading over the ice and back into the brush and overgrowth. Immediately, he stepped downwind and branched away, walked parallel and then looped back to find the animal's trail. He tracked like that, never right behind it, always careful of the wind, cautious on the harsh ground, gaining on his webbed shoes as the moose floundered and broke through the crust with every step until finally it came to a stand of young saplings, and fed.

Now the song gathered. I exerted myself. Eli's arms and legs were heavy, and without food he could not think. His mind was empty and I so feared that he would make a mistake. He knew that after the moose fed it would always turn downwind to rest. But the trees grew thicker, small and tightly clumped, and the shadows were a darker blue, lengthening.

Eli's coat, made by Margaret, was an old gray army blanket lined with the fur of rabbits. When he took it off and turned it inside out, so that only the soft pelts would brush the branches and not betray him as he neared, I was encouraged. He took his snowshoes off and left them in a tree. He stuffed his hat into his pocket, made his gun ready and then, pausing and sensitive for movement, for the rough shape, he slowly advanced.

Do not sour the meat, I reminded him now, *a strong heart moves slowly*. If he startled the moose so that adrenaline flowed into its blood, the meat would toughen, reveal the vinegar taste of fear.

Eli advanced with caution. The moose appeared. I held it in my vision just as it was, then, a hulking male, brown and unsuspicious in the late ordinary light of an afternoon. The scrub it stood within was difficult and dense all around, ready to deflect Eli's bullet.

But my song directed it to fly true.

The animal collapsed to its knees. Eli crashed from his hiding place, too soon, but the shot was good and the animal was dead. He used a tree limb to roll it on its back and then with his knife, cut the line down the middle. He was so cold he was almost in tears, and the warmth of the carcass dizzied him. To gain strength for the hard work ahead he carefully removed the liver, sliced off a bit. With a strip of cloth torn from the hem of his shirt, he wrapped that piece, sprinkled it with tobacco, and buried it under a handful of snow. Half of the rest, he ate. The other he saved for me.

He butchered carefully, but fast as possible, according to my instructions. One time in his youth, he had pierced the stomach of a deer with his knife, spreading its acids through the meat, and I'd hardly spoken to him all the rest of that day. He put his jacket right side out again, smeared it with tallow from a packet in his shirt, then quickly cut off warm slabs of meat and bound them to his body with sinew so that they would mold to fit him as they froze. He secured jagged ovals of haunch meat to his thighs, then fitted smaller rectangles down his legs, below the knees. He pressed to himself a new body, red and steaming, swung a roast to his back and knotted its ligaments around his chest. He bound a rack of ribs across his hat, jutting over his face, and tied them on beneath his chin. Last of all, he wrapped new muscles, wide and thick, around each forearm and past his elbows. What he could not pack, he covered with snow and branches, or hoisted laboriously into the boughs of an ash. He was too heavily laden to hide it all and the light was failing, so he fetched his snowshoes, then dragged the hide a distance away from the meat cache and left it for distraction. It was dusk then, and the walk was long.

There is a temptation, when it is terribly cold and the burden is heavy, to quicken pace to warm the blood. The body argues and steps fast, but the knowledge, informed by tales of hunters frozen with the flesh of their own bounty, resists. I know it well. Eli had become a thing of such cold by now, that, if he sweat, the film on his skin would freeze and draw from his blood all life, all warmth.

Without opening my eyes on the world around me, I took the drum from beneath my bed and beat out footsteps for Eli to hear and follow. Each time he speeded I slowed him. I strengthened the rhythm whenever he faltered beneath the weight he bore. In that way, he returned, and when I could hear the echo of his panting breath, I went outside to help him, still in my song.

He glowed, for the meat strapped to him had frozen a marbled blue. The blood from the moose was flour on his coat and on his face. His features were stiff, the strength in his limbs near exhausted. I freed him from the burden he held to his chest, and carried it home in my arms. He followed. I severed the rest from Eli's body and stashed it outside, in the lean-to. The meat stood on its own in pieces, a moose transformed into the mold of Eli, an armor that would fit no other.

He was stockstill, reluctant to move, his mouth dried open as I pulled him through the door. I took off his clothes, found the piece of saved liver under his arm, and ate it. Then I put a drop of water between his lips, wrapped him in a quilt and led him near the stove. I removed the kidneys and heart from Eli's pocket and cut them into smaller sections. My hands shook as I prepared the pieces with salt. My mouth watered as I put them in the fire and at the smell of meat roasting, I almost wept. I gave the first cut to Eli, who fell on it gratefully. As I put my share into my mouth, as I swallowed it, I felt myself grow solid in the chair. Lit by the burning stove, everything around me sharpened. Thoughts returned.

"You're my son," I said, moved by the scorched taste, "you're my relative."

Ceremony

Leslie Marmon Silko

Robert and Tayo stopped on the bridge and looked into the riverbed. It had been dry for a long time, and there were paths in the sand where the people walked. They were beginning to move. All along the sandy clay banks there were people, mostly men, stretched out, sleeping, some of them face down where they fell, and a few rolled over on their backs or on their sides, sleeping with their heads on their arms. The sun was getting hot and the flies were beginning to come out. They could see them buzzing around the face of a man under the bridge, smelling the sweetness of the wine or maybe the vomit down the front of the man's shirt. Robert shook his head. Tayo felt the choking in his throat; he blinked his eyes hard and didn't say anything. A man and woman came walking down the wash below them and looked up at them on the bridge. "Hey buddy!" the man yelled up. "You got a dollar you can loan us?" Robert looked at them and shook his head calmly, but Tayo started to sweat. He started reaching deep into his pockets for loose coins. The woman's hair was tangled in hairpins which had been pulled loose and hung around her head like ornaments. Her head weaved from side to side as she squinted and tried to focus on Tayo up above her. Her slip was torn and dragging the ground under her skirt; she had a dark bruise on her forehead. He found two quarters and tossed them into the man's outstretched hands, swaying above his head, and both the man and the woman dropped to their knees in the sand to find them. Robert walked away, but Tayo stood there, remembering the little bridge in a park in San Diego where all the soldiers took their dates the night before they shipped out to the South Pacific and stood throwing coins into the shallow pond. He had tossed the coins to them the way he had tossed them from the bridge in San Diego, in a gentle slow arc. Rocky wished out loud that night for a safe return from the war, but Tayo couldn't remember his wish. He watched them stumble and crawl up the loose clay of the steep riverbank. The man pulled the woman up the last few feet. The fly of his pants was unbuttoned and one of his shoes was flopping loose on his foot. They walked toward a bar south of the bridge, to wait for it to open.

They walked like survivors, with dull vacant eyes, their fists clutching the coins he'd thrown to them. They were Navajos, but he had seen Zunis and Lagunas and Hopis there too, walking alone or in twos and threes along the dusty Gallup streets. He didn't know how they got there in the first place, from the reservation to Gallup, but some must have had jobs for a while when they first came, and cheap rooms on the north side of the tracks, where they stayed until they got laid off or fired. Reservation people were the first ones to get laid off because white people in Gallup already knew they wouldn't ask any questions or get angry; they just walked away. They were educated only enough to know they wanted to leave the reservation; when they got to Gallup there weren't many jobs they could get. The men unloaded trucks in the warehouses near the tracks or piled lumber in the lumberyards or pushed wheelbarrows for construction; the women cleaned out motel rooms along Highway 66. The Gallup people knew they didn't have to pay good wages or put up with anything they didn't like, because there were plenty more Indians where these had come from.

It seemed to Tayo that they would go home, sooner or later, when they were hungry and dirty and broke; stand on 666 north of town and wait for someone driving to Keams Canyon or Lukachukai to stop, or borrow two dollars and ride the bus back to Laguna. But Gallup was a dangerous place, and by the time they realized what had happened to them, they must have believed it was too late to go home.

Robert was waiting for him on the hill. "Somebody you used to know?"

"Maybe," Tayo said. The sun was above them now, in a deep blue sky like good turquoise.

He looked back at the bridge, and he made a wish. The same wish Rocky made that night in San Diego: a safe return.

"What kind of medicine man lives in a place like that, in the foothills north of the Ceremonial Grounds?" Auntie wanted to know. Grandma told her, "Never mind. Old man Ku'oosh knows him, and he thinks this man Betonie might help him."

The Gallup Ceremonial had been an annual event for a long time. It was good for the tourist business coming through in the summertime on Highway 66. They liked to see Indians and Indian dances; they wanted a chance to buy Indian jewelry and Navajo rugs. Every year it was organized by the white men there, Turpen, Foutz, Kennedy, and the mayor. Dance groups from the Pueblos were paid to come; they got Plains hoop dancers, and flying-pole dancers from northern Mexico. They organized an all-Indian rodeo and horse races. And the people came, from all the reservations nearby, and some came from farther away; they brought their things to sell to the tourists, and they brought things to trade with each other: white deerhides, and feathers, and dried meat or piki bread. The tourists got to see what they wanted; from the grandstand at the Ceremonial grounds they watched the dancers perform, and they watched Indian cowboys ride bucking horses and Brahma bulls. There were wagon races, and the ladies' wood-chopping contest and fry-bread-making race. The Gallup merchants raised prices in motels and restaurants all Ceremonial week, and made a lot of money off the tourists. They sold great amounts of liquor to Indians, and in those years when liquor was illegal for Indians, they made a lot more money because they bootlegged it.

Old Betonie's place looked down on all of it; from the yellow sandrock foothills the whole town spread out below. The old man was tall and his chest was wide; at one time he had been heavier, but old age was consuming everything but the bones. He kept his hair tied back neatly with red yarn in a chongo knot, like the oldtimers wore. He was sitting on an old tin bucket turned upside down by the doorway to his hogan. When he stood up and extended his hand to Robert and Tayo, his motions were strong and unhesitating, as if they belonged to a younger man. He watched Tayo look around at the hogan and then back down at the Ceremonial grounds and city streets in the distance. He nodded his head at Tayo.

"People ask me why I live here," he said, in good English, "I tell them I want to keep track of the people. 'Why over here?' they ask me. 'Because this is where Gallup keeps Indians until Ceremonial time. Then they want to show us off to the tourists.'" He looked down at the riverbed winding through the north side of Gallup. "There," he said, pointing his chin at the bridge, "they sleep over there, in alleys between the bars." He turned and pointed to the city dump east of the Ceremonial grounds and rodeo chutes. "They keep us on the north side of the railroad tracks, next to the river and their dump. Where none of them want to live." He laughed. "They don't understand. We know these hills, and we are comfortable here." There was something about the way the old man said the word "comfortable." It had a different meaning—not the comfort of big houses or rich food or even clean streets, but the comfort of belonging with the land, and the peace of being with these hills. But the special meaning the old man had given to the English word was burned away by the glare of the sun on tin cans and broken glass, blinding reflections off the mirrors and chrome of the wrecked cars in the dump below. Tayo felt the old nausea rising up in his stomach, along with a vague feeling that he knew something which he could not remember. The sun was getting hot, and he thought about flies buzzing around their faces as they slept in the weeds along the arroyo. He turned back to Betonie. He didn't know how the medicine man could look down at it every day.

"You know, at one time when my great-grandfather was young, Navajos lived in all these hills." He pointed to the hills and ridges south of the tracks where the white people had built their houses. He nodded at the arroyo cut by the river. "They had little farms along the river. When the railroaders came and the white people began to build their town, the Navajos had to move." The old man laughed suddenly. He slapped his hands on his thighs. His laughter was easy, but Tayo could feel the tiny hairs along his spine spring up. This Betonie didn't talk the way Tayo expected a medicine man to talk. He didn't act like a medicine man at all.

"It strikes me funny," the medicine man said, shaking his head, "people wondering why I live so close to this filthy town. But see, this hogan was here first. Built long before the white people ever came. It is that town down there which is out of place. Not this old medicine man." He laughed again, and Tayo looked at Robert quickly to see what he thought of the old man; but Robert's face was calm, without any mistrust or alarm. When old Betonie had finished talking, Robert stepped over to Tayo and touched his shoulder gently. "I guess I'll go now," he said softly.

Tayo watched him walk down the path from the old man's place, and he could feel cold sweat between his fingers. His heart was pounding, and all he could think about was that if he started running right then, he could still catch up to Robert.

"Go ahead," old Betonie said, "you can go. Most of the Navajos feel the same way about me. You won't be the first one to run away."

Tayo turned to look for Robert, but he was gone. He stared at the dry yellow grass by the old man's feet. The sun's heat was draining his strength away; there was no place to go now except back to the hospital in Los Angeles. They didn't want him at Laguna the way he was.

All along there had been something familiar about the old man. Tayo turned around then to figure out what it was. He looked at his clothes: the old moccasins with splayed-out elkhide soles, the leather stained dark with mud and grease; the gray wool trousers were baggy and worn thin at the knees, and the old man's elbows made brown points through the sleeves of the blue cotton work shirt. He looked at his face. The cheekbones were like the wings of a hawk soaring away from his broad nose; he wore a drooping thick mustache; the hairs were steel gray. Then Tayo looked at his eyes. They were hazel like his own. The medicine man nodded. "My grandmother was a remarkable Mexican with green eyes," he said.

He bent down like the old man did when he passed through the low doorway. Currents of cool air streamed toward the door, and even before his eyes adjusted to the dimness of the room, he could smell its contents; a great variety of herb and root odors were almost hidden by the smell of mountain sage and something as ordinary as curry powder. Behind the smell of dried desert tea he smelled heavier objects: the salty cured smell of old hides sewn into boxes bound in brass; the odor of old newspapers and cardboard, their dust smelling of the years they had taken to decay.

The old man pointed to the back of the circular room. "The west side is built into the hill in the old-style way. Sand and dirt for a roof; just about halfway underground. You can feel it, can't you?"

Tayo nodded. He was standing with his feet in the bright circle of sunlight below the center of the log ceiling open for smoke. The size of the room had not been lost in the clutter of boxes and trunks stacked almost to the ceiling beams.

Old Betonie pointed at a woolly brown goatskin on the floor below the sky hole. Tayo sat down, but he didn't take his eyes off the cardboard boxes that filled the big room; the sides of some boxes were broken down, sagging over with old clothing and rags spilling out; others were jammed with the antennas of dry roots and reddish willow twigs tied in neat bundles with old cotton strings. The boxes were stacked crookedly, some stacks leaning into others, with only their opposing angles holding them steady. Inside the boxes without lids, the erect brown string handles of shopping bags poked out; piled to the tops of the WOOLWORTH bags were bouquets of dried sage and the brown leaves of mountain tobacco wrapped in swaths of silvery unspun wool.

He could see bundles of newspapers, their edges curled stiff and brown, barricading piles of telephone books with the years scattered among cities—St. Louis, Seattle, New York, Oakland—and he began to feel another dimension to the old man's room. His heart beat faster, and he felt the blood draining from his legs. He knew the answer before he could shape the question. Light from the door worked paths through the thick bluish green glass of the Coke bottles; his eyes followed the light until he was dizzy and sick. He wanted to dismiss all of it as an old man's rubbish, debris that had fallen out of the years, but the boxes and trunks, the bundles and stacks were plainly part of the pattern: they followed the concentric shadows of the room.

The old man smiled. His teeth were big and white. "Take it easy," he said, "don't try to see everything all at once." He laughed. "We've been gathering these things for a long time—hundreds of years. She was doing it before I was born, and he was working before she came. And on and on back down in time." He stopped, smiling. "Talking like this is just as bad, isn't it? Too big to swallow all at once."

Tayo nodded, but now his eyes were on the ceiling logs where pouches and bags dangled from wooden pegs and square-headed nails. Hard shrunken skin pouches and black leather purses trimmed with hammered silver buttons were things he could understand. They were a medicine man's paraphernalia, laid beside the painted gourd rattles and deer-hoof clackers of the ceremony. But with this old man it did not end there; under the medicine bags and bundles of rawhide on the walls, he saw layers of old calendars, the sequences of years confused and lost as if occasionally the oldest calendars had fallen or been taken out from under the others and then had been replaced on top of the most recent years. A few showed January, as if the months on the underlying pages had no longer been turned or torn away.

Old Betonie waved his hands around the hogan. "And what do I make from all this?" He nodded, moving his head slowly up and down. "Maybe you smelled it when you came in.

"In the old days it was simple. A medicine person could get by without all these things. But nowadays . . ." He let his voice trail off and nodded to let Tayo complete the thought for him.

Tayo studied the pictures and names on the calendars. He recognized names of stores in Phoenix and Albuquerque, but in recent years the old man had favored Santa Fe Railroad calendars that had Indian scenes painted on them—Navajos herding sheep, deer dancers at Cochiti, and little Pueblo children chasing burros. The chills on his neck followed his eyes: he recognized the pictures for the years 1939 and 1940. Josiah used to bring the calendars home every year from the Santa Fe depot; on the reservation these calendars were more common than Coca-Cola calendars. There was no reason to be startled. This old man had only done the same thing. He tried to shake off the feeling by talking.

"I remember those two," he said.

"That gives me some place to start," old Betonie said, lighting up the little brown cigarette he had rolled. "All these things have stories alive in them." He pointed at the Santa Fe calendars. "I'm one of their best customers down there. I rode the train to Chicago in 1903." His eyes were shining then, and he was looking directly into Tayo's eyes. "I know," he said proudly, "people are always surprised when I tell them the places I have traveled." He pointed at the telephone books. "I brought back the books with all the names in them. Keeping track of things." He stroked his mustache as if he were remembering things.

Tayo watched him, trying to decide if the old man was lying. He wasn't sure if they even let Indians ride trains in those days. The old man laughed at the expression on Tayo's face. He wiped his mouth on the sleeve of his shirt.

"She sent me to school. Sherman Institute, Riverside, California. That was the first train I ever rode. I had been watching them from the hills up here all my life. I told her it looked like a snake crawling along the red-rock mesas. I told her I didn't want to go. I was already a big kid then. Bigger than the rest. But she said 'It is carried on in all languages now, so you have to know English too.'" He ran his fingers through his mustache again, still smiling as though he were thinking of other stories to tell. But a single hair came loose from his thick gray mustache, and his attention shifted suddenly to the hair between his fingers. He got up and went to the back of the hogan. Tayo heard the jingle of keys and the tin sound of a footlocker opening; the lock snapped shut and the old man came back and sat down; the hair was gone.

"I don't take any chances," he said as he got settled on the goatskin again. Tayo could hear his own pulse sound in his ears. He wasn't sure what the old man was talking about, but he had an idea. "Didn't anyone ever teach you about these things?"

Tayo shook his head, but he knew the medicine man could see he was lying. He knew what they did with strands of hair they found; he knew what they did with bits of fingernail and toenails they found. He was breathing faster, and he could feel the fear surge over him with each beat of his heart. They didn't want him around. They blamed him. And now they had sent him here, and this would be the end of him. The Gallup police would find his body in the bushes along the big arroyo, and he would be just one of the two or three they'd find dead that week. He thought about running again; he was stronger than the old man and he could fight his way out of this. But the pain of betrayal pushed into his throat like a fist. He blinked back the tears, but he didn't move. He was tired of fighting. If there was no one left to trust, then he had no more reason to live.

The old man laughed and laughed. He laughed, and when his laughter seemed almost to cease, he would shake his head and laugh all over again.

"I was at the World's Fair in St. Louis, Missouri, the year they had Geronimo there on display. The white people were scared to death of him. Some of them even wanted him in leg irons."

Tayo did not look up. Maybe this time he really was crazy. Maybe the medicine man didn't laugh all the time; maybe the dreams and the voices were taking over again.

"If you don't trust me, you better get going before dark. You can't be too careful these days," Betonie said, gesturing toward the footlocker where he kept the hairs. "Anyway, I couldn't help anyone who was afraid of me." He started humming softly to himself, a song that Tayo could hear only faintly, but that reminded him of butterflies darting from flower to flower.

"They sent me to this place after the war. It was white. Everything in that place was white. Except for me. I was invisible. But I wasn't afraid there. I didn't feel things sneaking up behind me. I didn't cry for Rocky or Josiah. There were no voices and no dreams. Maybe I belong back in that place."

Betonie reached into his shirt pocket for the tobacco sack. He rolled a skinny little cigarette in a brown wheat paper and offered the sack to Tayo. He nodded slowly to indicate that he had been listening.

"That's true," the old man said, "you could go back to that white place." He took a puff from the cigarette and stared down at the red sand floor. Then he looked up suddenly and his eyes were shining; he had a grin on his face. "But if you are going to do that, you might as well go down there, with the rest of them, sleeping in the mud, vomiting cheap wine, rolling over women. Die that way and get it over with." He shook his head and laughed. "In that hospital they don't bury the dead, they keep them in rooms and talk to them."

"There are stories about me," Betonie began in a quiet round voice. "Maybe you have heard some of them. They say I'm crazy. Sometimes they say worse things. But whatever they say, they don't forget me, even when I'm not here." Tayo was wary of his eyes. "That's right," Betonie said, "when I am gone off on the train, a hundred miles from here, those Navajos won't come near this hogan." He smoked for a while and stared at the circle of sunlight on the floor between them. What Tayo could feel was powerful, but there was no way to be sure what it was.

"My uncle Josiah was there that day. Yet I know he couldn't have been there. He was thousands of miles away, at home in Laguna. We were in the Philippine jungles. I understand that. I know he couldn't have been there. But I've got this feeling and it won't go away even though I know he wasn't there. I feel like he was there. I feel like he was there with those Japanese soldiers who died." Tayo's voice was shaking; he could feel the tears pushing into his eyes. Suddenly the feeling was there, as strong as it had been that day in the jungle. "He loved me. He loved me, and I didn't do anything to save him."

"When did he die?"

"While we were gone. He died because there was no one to help him search for the cattle after they were stolen."

"Rocky," Betonie said softly, "tell me about Rocky."

The tears ran along the sides of Tayo's nose and off his chin; as they fell, the hollow inside his chest folded into the black hole, and he waited for the collapse into himself.

"It was the one thing I could have done. For all of them, for all those years they kept me . . . for everything that had happened because of me . . . "

"You've been doing something all along. All this time, and now you are at an important place in this story." He paused. "The Japanese," the medicine man went on, as though he were trying to remember something. "It isn't surprising you saw him with them. You saw who they were. Thirty thousand years ago they were not strangers. You saw what the evil had done: you saw the witchery ranging as wide as this world."

"And these cattle . . .

"The people in Cubero called her the Night Swan. She told him about the cattle. She encouraged him to buy them. Auntie said that—"

The old man waved his arms at Tayo. "Don't tell me about your aunt. I want to know about those cattle and that woman."

"She said something to me once. About our eyes. Hazel-green eyes. I never understood. Was she bad, like Auntie kept saying? Did the cattle kill him—did I let the cattle kill him?"

The old man had jumped up. He was walking around the fire pit, moving behind Tayo as he went around. He was excited, and from time to time he would say something to himself in Navajo.

Betonie dug down into the cardboard boxes until dust flew up around his face. Finally he pulled out a brown spiral notebook with a torn cover; he thumbed through the pages slowly, moving his lips slightly. He sat down again, across from Tayo, with the notebook in his lap.

"I'm beginning to see something," he said with his eyes closed, "yes. Something very important."

The room was cooler than before. The light from the opening in the roof was becoming diffuse and gray. It was sundown. Betonie pointed a finger at him.

"This has been going on for a long long time. They will try to stop you from completing the ceremony."

The hollow inside him was suddenly too small for the anger. "Look," Tayo said through clenched teeth, "I've been sick, and half the time I don't know if I'm still crazy or not. I don't know anything about ceremonies or these things you talk about. I don't know how long anything has been going on. I just need help." The words made his body shake as if they had an intensity of their own which was released as he spoke.

"We all have been waiting for help a long time. But it never has been easy. The people must do it. You must do it." Betonie sounded as if he were explaining something simple but important to a small child. But Tayo's stomach clenched around the words like knives stuck into his guts. There was something large and terrifying in the old man's words. He wanted to yell at the medicine man, to yell the things the white doctors had yelled at him—that he had to think only of himself, and not about the others, that he would never get well as long as he used words like "we" and "us." But he had known the answer all along, even while the white doctors were telling him he could get well and he was trying to believe them: medicine didn't work that way, because the world didn't work that way. His sickness was only part of something larger, and his cure would be found only in something great and inclusive of everything.

"There are some things I have to tell you," Betonie began softly. "The people nowadays have an idea about the ceremonies. They think the ceremonies must be performed exactly as they have always been done, maybe because one slip-up or mistake and the whole ceremony must be stopped and the sand painting destroyed. That much is true. They think that if a singer tampers with any part of the ritual, great harm can be done, great power unleashed." He was quiet for a while, looking up at the sky through the smoke hole. "That much can be true also. But long ago when the people were given these ceremonies, the changing began, if only in the aging of the yellow gourd rattle or the shrinking of the skin around the eagle's claw, if only in the different voices from generation to generation, singing the chants. You see, in many ways, the ceremonies have always been changing."

Tayo nodded; he looked at the medicine pouches hanging from the ceiling and tried to imagine the objects they contained.

"At one time, the ceremonies as they had been performed were enough for the way the world was then. But after the white people came, elements in this world began to shift; and it became necessary to create new ceremonies. I have made changes in the rituals. The people mistrust this greatly, but only this growth keeps the ceremonies strong.

"She taught me this above all else: things which don't shift and grow are dead things. They are things the witchery people want. Witchery works to scare people, to make them fear growth. But it has always been necessary, and more than ever now, it is. Otherwise we won't make it. We won't survive. That's what the witchery is counting on: that we will cling to the ceremonies the way they were, and then their power will triumph, and the people will be no more."

He wanted to believe old Betonie. He wanted to keep the feeling of his words alive inside himself so that he could believe that he might get well. But when the old man left, he was suddenly aware of the old hogan: the red sand floor had been swept unevenly; the boxes were spilling out rags; the trunks were full of the junk and trash an old man saves—notebooks and whisker hairs. The shopping bags were torn, and the weeds and twigs stuck out of rips in the brown paper. The calendars Betonie got for free and the phone books that he picked up in his travels—all of it seemed suddenly so pitiful and small compared to the world he knew the white people had—a world of comfort in the sprawling houses he'd seen in California, a world of plenty in the food he had carried from the officers' mess to dump into garbage cans. The old man's clothes were dirty and old, probably collected like his calendars. The leftover things the whites didn't want. All Betonie owned in the world was in this room. What kind of healing power was in this?

Anger propelled him to his feet; his legs were stiff from sitting for so long. This was where the white people and their promises had left the Indians. All the promises they made to you, Rocky, they weren't any different than the other promises they made.

He walked into the evening air, which was cool and smelled like juniper smoke from the old man's fire. Betonie was sitting by the fire, watching the mutton ribs cook over a grill he had salvaged from the front end of a wrecked car in the dump below. The grill was balanced between two big sandrocks, where the hot coals were banked under the spattering meat. Tayo looked down at the valley, at the lights of the town and the headlights and taillights strung along Highway 66.

"They took almost everything, didn't they?"

The old man looked up from the fire. He shook his head slowly while he turned the meat with a forked stick. "We always come back to that, don't we? It was planned that way. For all the anger and the frustration. And for the guilt too. Indians wake up every morning of their lives to see the land which was stolen, still there, within reach, its theft being flaunted. And the desire is strong to make things right, to take back what was stolen and to stop them from destroying what they have taken. But you see, Tayo, we have done as much fighting as we can with the destroyers and the thieves: as much as we could do and still survive."

Tayo walked over and knelt in front of the ribs roasting over the white coals of the fire.

"Look," Betonie said, pointing east to Mount Taylor towering dark blue with the last twilight. "They only fool themselves when they think it is theirs. The deeds and papers don't mean anything. It is the people who belong to the mountain."

Tayo poked a stick into the coals and watched them lose shape and collapse into white ash. "I wonder sometimes," he said, "because my mother went with white men." He stopped there, unable to say any more. The birth had betrayed his mother and brought shame to the family and to the people.

Old Betonie sat back on his heels and looked off in the distance. "Nothing is that simple," he said, "you don't write off all the white people, just like you don't trust all the Indians." He pointed at the coffeepot in the sand at the edge of the coals, and then at the meat. "You better eat now," he said.

Tayo finished the meat on the mutton ribs and threw the bones to a skinny yellow dog that came out from behind the hogan. Behind the dog a boy about fifteen or sixteen came with an armload of firewood. He knelt by the fire with the kindling; Betonie spoke to him in Navajo and indicated Tayo with a nod of his head.

"This is my helper," he told Tayo. "They call him Shush. That means bear." It was dark, but in the light from the fire Tayo could see there was something strange about the boy, something remote in his eyes, as if he were on a distant mountaintop alone and the fire and hogan and the lights of the town below them did not exist.

He was a small child
learning to get around
by himself.
His family went by wagon
into the mountains near
Fluted Rock.

It was Fall and
they were picking piñons.
I guess he just wandered away
trying to follow his brothers and sisters
into the trees.
His aunt thought he was with his mother,
and she thought he was with her sister.

When they tracked him the next day
his tracks went into the canyon
near the place which belonged
to the bears. They went
as far as they could
to the place
where no human
could go beyond,
and his little footprints
were mixed in with bear tracks.

So they sent word for this medicine man
to come. He knew how
to call the child back again.

There wasn't much time.
The medicine man was running, and his
assistants followed behind him.

They all wore bearweed
tied at their wrists and ankles
and around their necks.

He grunted loudly and scratched on the ground in front of him
he kept watching the entrance of the bear cave.
He grunted and made a low growling sound.
Pretty soon the little bears came out
because he was making mother bear sounds.

He grunted and growled a little more
and then the child came out.
He was already walking like his sisters
he was already crawling on the ground.

They couldn't just grab the child
They couldn't simply take him back
because he would be in between forever
and probably he would die.

They had to call him
step by step the medicine man
brought the child back.

So, long time ago
they got him back again
but he wasn't quite the same
after that
not like the other children.

Tayo stood up and moved around the fire uneasily; the boy took some ribs and disappeared again behind the hogan. The old man put some wood on the fire. "You don't have to be afraid of him. Some people act like witchery is responsible for everything that happens, when actually witchery only manipulates a small portion." He pointed in the direction the boy had gone. "Accidents happen, and there's little we can do. But don't be so quick to call something good or bad. There are balances and harmonies always shifting, always necessary to maintain. It is very peaceful with the bears; the people say that's the reason human beings seldom return. It is a matter of transitions, you see; the changing, the becoming must be cared for closely. You would do as much for the seedlings as they become plants in the field."

Note on Bear People and Witches

Don't confuse those who go to the bears with the witch people. Human beings who live with the bears do not wear bear skins. They are naked and not conscious of being different from their bear relatives. Witches crawl into skins of dead animals, but they can do nothing but play around with objects and bodies. Living animals are terrified of witches. They smell the death. That's why witches can't get close to them. That's why people keep dogs around their hogans. Dogs howl with fear when witch animals come around.

The wind came up and fanned the fire. Tayo watched a red flame crawl out from under the white coals; he reached down for a piece of juniper and tossed it in. The fire caught. He rubbed pitch from the wood between his fingers and looked down at Gallup.

"I never told you about Emo," he said, "I never told you what happened to Rocky." He pointed at the lights below. "Something about the lights down there, something about the cars and the neon signs which reminds me of both of them."

"Yes," the old man said, "my grandmother would not leave this hill. She said the whole world could be seen from here."

"Rocky wanted to get away from the reservation; he wanted to make something of himself. In a city somewhere."

"They are down there. Ones like your brother. They are down there."

"He didn't make it though. I was supposed to help him, so he'd make it back. They were counting on him. They were proud of him. I owed them that much. After everything that happened. I owed it to them." He looked at the old man, but he was staring at the lights down below, following the headlights from the west until they were taillights disappearing in the east. He didn't seem to be listening.

"There are no limits to this thing," Betonie said. "When it was set loose, it ranged everywhere, from the mountains and plains to the towns and cities; rivers and oceans never stopped it." The wind was blowing steadily and the old man's voice was almost lost in it.

"Emo plays with these teeth—human teeth—and he says the Indians have nothing compared to white people. He talks about their cities and all the machines and food they have. He says the land is no good, and we must go after what they have, and take it from them." Tayo coughed and tried to clear the tightness from his throat. "Well, I don't know how to say this but it seems that way. All you have to do is look around. And so I wonder," he said, feeling the tightness in his throat squeeze out the tears, "I wonder what good Indian ceremonies can do against the sickness which comes from their wars, their bombs, their lies?"

The old man shook his head. "That is the trickery of the witchcraft," he said. "They want us to believe all evil resides with white people. Then we will look no further to see what is really happening. They want us to separate ourselves from white people, to be ignorant and helpless as we watch our own destruction. But white people are only tools that the witchery manipulates; and I tell you, we can deal with white people, with their machines and their beliefs. We can because we invented white people; it was Indian witchery that made white people in the first place.

Long time ago
in the beginning
there were no white people in this world
there was nothing European.
And this world might have gone on like that
except for one thing:
witchery.
This world was already complete
even without white people.
There was everything
including witchery.

Then it happened.
These witch people got together.
Some came from far far away
across oceans
across mountains.
Some had slanty eyes
others had black skin.
They all got together for a contest
the way people have baseball tournaments nowadays
except this was a contest
in dark things.

So anyway
they all got together
witch people from all directions
witches from all the Pueblos
and all the tribes.
They had Navajo witches there,
some from Hopi, and a few from Zuni.
They were having a witches' conference,
that's what it was
Way up in the lava rock hills
north of Cañoncito
they got together
to fool around in caves
with their animal skins.
Fox, badger, bobcat, and wolf
they circled the fire
and on the fourth time
they jumped into that animal's skin.

But this time it wasn't enough
and one of them
maybe a Sioux or some Eskimos
started showing off.
"That wasn't anything,
watch this."

The contest started like that.
Then some of them lifted the lids
on their big cooking pots,
calling the rest of them over
to take a look:
dead babies simmering in blood
circles of skull cut away
all the brains sucked out.
Witch medicine
to dry and grind into powder
for new victims.

Others untied skin bundles of disgusting objects:
dark flints, cinders from burned hogans where the dead lay
Whorls of skin
cut from fingertips
sliced from the penis end and clitoris tip.

Finally there was only one
who hadn't shown off charms or powers.
The witch stood in the shadows beyond the fire
and no one ever knew where this witch came from
which tribe
or if it was a woman or a man.
But the important thing was
this witch didn't show off any dark thunder charcoals
or red ant-hill beads.
This one just told them to listen:
"What I have is a story."

At first they all laughed
but this witch said
Okay
go ahead
laugh if you want to
but as I tell the story
it will begin to happen.

Set in motion now
set in motion by our witchery
to work for us.

Caves across the ocean
in caves of dark hills
white skin people
like the belly of a fish
covered with hair.

Then they grow away from the earth
then they grow away from the sun
then they grow away from the plants and animals.

They see no life
When they look
they see only objects.
The world is a dead thing for them
the trees and rivers are not alive
the mountains and stones are not alive.
The deer and bear are objects
They see no life.

They fear
They fear the world.
They destroy what they fear.
They fear themselves.

The wind will blow them across the ocean
thousands of them in giant boats
swarming like larva
out of a crushed ant hill.

They will carry objects
which can shoot death
faster than the eye can see.

They will kill the things they fear
all the animals
the people will starve.

They will poison the water
they will spin the water away
and there will be drought
the people will starve.

They will fear what they find
They will fear the people
They kill what they fear.

Entire villages will be wiped out
They will slaughter whole tribes.

Corpses for us
Blood for us
Killing killing killing killing.

And those they do not kill
will die anyway
at the destruction they see
at the loss
at the loss of the children
the loss will destroy the rest.

Stolen rivers and mountains
the stolen land will eat their hearts
and jerk their mouths from the Mother.
The people will starve.

They will bring terrible diseases
the people have never known.
Entire tribes will die out
covered with festered sores
shitting blood

vomiting blood.
Corpses for our work

Set in motion now
set in motion by our witchery
set in motion
to work for us.

They will take this world from ocean to ocean
they will turn on each other
they will destroy each other
Up here
in these hills
they will find the rocks,
rocks with veins of green and yellow and black.
They will lay the final pattern with these rocks
they will lay it across the world
and explode everything.

Set in motion now
set in motion
To destroy
To kill
Objects to work for us
objects to act for us
Performing the witchery
for suffering
for torment
for the still-born
the deformed
the sterile
the dead.
Whirling
whirling
whirling
whirling
set into motion now
set into motion.

So the other witches said
"Okay you win; you take the prize,
but what you said just now—
it isn't so funny
It doesn't sound so good.
We are doing okay without it
we can get along without that kind of thing.
Take it back.
Call that story back."

But the witch just shook its head
at the others in their stinking animal skins, fur and feathers.
It's already turned loose.
It's already coming.
It can't be called back.

They left on horseback before dawn. The old man rode a skinny pinto mare with hip bones and ribs poking against the hide like springs of an old car seat. But she was strong and moved nimbly up the narrow rocky path north of Betonie's hogan. The old man's helper rode a black pony, hunching low over its neck with his face in the mane. Maybe he rode like that for warmth, because it was cold in those foothills before dawn; the night air of the high mountains was chilled by the light of the stars and the shadows of the moon. The brown gelding stumbled with Tayo; he reined it in and walked it more slowly. Behind them in the valley, the highway was a faint dark vein through the yellow sand and red rock. He smelled piñon and sage in the wind that blew across the stony backbone of the ridge. They left the red sandstone and the valley and rode into the lava-rock foothills and pine of the Chuska Mountains.

"We'll have the second night here," Betonie said, indicating a stone hogan set back from the edge of the rimrock.

Tayo stood near the horses, looking down the path over the way they had come. The plateaus and canyons spread out below him like clouds falling into each other past the horizon. The world below was distant and small; it was dwarfed by a sky so blue and vast the clouds were lost in it. Far into the south there were smoky blue ridges of the mountain haze at Zuni. He smoothed his hand over the top of his head and felt the sun. The mountain wind was cool; it smelled like springs hidden deep in mossy black stone. He could see no signs of what had been set loose upon the earth: the highways, the towns, even the fences were gone. This was the highest point on the earth: he could feel it. It had nothing to do with measurements or height. It was a special place. He was smiling. He felt strong. He had to touch his own hand to remember what year it was: thick welted scars from the shattered bottle glass.

His mother-in-law suspected something.
She smelled coyote piss one morning.
She told her daughter.
She figured Coyote was doing this.
She knew her son-in-law was missing.

There was no telling what Coyote had done to him.
Four of them went to track the man.
They tracked him to the place he found deer tracks.
They found the place the deer was arrow-wounded
where the man started chasing it.
Then they found the place where Coyote got him.
Sure enough those coyote tracks went right along there
Right around the marks in the sand where the man lay.

The human tracks went off
toward the mountain
where the man must have crawled.
They followed the tracks to a hard oak tree
where he had spent a night.
From there he had crawled some distance farther
and slept under a scrub oak tree.
Then his tracks went to a piñon tree
and then under the juniper where he slept another night.

The tracks went on and on
but finally they caught up with him
sleeping under the wild rose bush.
"What happened? Are you the one
who left four days ago, my grandchild?"
A coyote whine was the only sound he made.
"Four days ago you left,
are you that one, my grandchild?"
The man tried to speak
but only a coyote sound was heard,
and the tail moved back and forth
sweeping ridges in the sand.
He was suffering from thirst and hunger

he was almost too weak to raise his head.
But he nodded his head "yes."

"This is him all right,
but what can we do to save him?"

They ran to the holy places
they asked what might be done.

"At the summit of Dark Mountain
ask the four old Bear People.
They are the only possible hope
they have the power to restore the mind.
Time and again
it has been done."

Big Fly went to tell them.
The old Bear People said they would come
They said
Prepare hard oak
scrub oak
piñon
juniper and wild rose twigs
Make hoops
tie bundles of weeds into hoops.
Make four bundles
tie them with yucca
spruce mixed with charcoal from burned weeds
snakeweed and gramma grass and rock sage.
Make four bundles.

The rainbows were crossed.
They had been his former means of travel.
Their purpose was
to restore this to him.

They made Pollen Boy right in the center of
the white corn painting.
His eyes were blue pollen
his mouth was blue pollen
his neck was too
There were pinches of blue pollen
at his joints.

He sat in the center of the white corn sand painting. The rainbows crossed were in the painting behind him. Betonie's helper scraped the sand away and buried the bottoms of the hoops in little trenches so that they were standing up and spaced apart, with the hard oak closest to him and the wild rose hoop in front of the door. The old man painted a dark mountain range beside the farthest hoop, the next, closer, he painted blue, and moving toward him, he knelt and made the yellow mountains; and in front of him, Betonie painted the white mountain range.

The helper worked in the shadows beyond the dark mountain range; he worked with the black sand, making bear prints side by side. Along the right side of the bear footprints, the old man painted paw prints in blue, and then yellow, and finally white. They finished it together, with a big rainbow arching wide above all the mountain ranges. Betonie gave him a basket with prayer sticks to hold.

en-e-e-ya-a-a-a-a!
en-e-e-ya-a-a-a-a!
en-e-e-ya-a-a-a-a!
en-e-e-ya-a-a-a-a!

In dangerous places you traveled
in danger you traveled
to a dangerous place you traveled
in danger e-hey-ya-ah-na!

To the place
where whirling darkness started its journey
along the edges of the rocks
along the places of the gentle wind
along the edges of blue clouds
along the edges of clear water.

Whirling darkness came up from the North
Whirling darkness moved along to the East
It came along the South
It arrived in the West
Whirling darkness spiraled downward
and it came up in the Middle.

The helper stepped out from the shadows; he was grunting like a bear. He raised his head as if it were heavy for him, and he sniffed the air. He stood up and walked to Tayo; he reached down for the prayer sticks and spoke the words distinctly, pressing the sticks close to his heart. The old man came forward then and cut Tayo across the top of his head; it happened suddenly. He hadn't expected it, but the dark flint was sharp and the cut was short. They both reached for him then; lifting him up by the shoulders, they guided his feet into the bear footprints, and Betonie prayed him through each of the five hoops.

eh-hey-yah-ah-na!
eh-hey-yah-ah-na!
eh-hey-yah-ah-na!
eh-hey-yah-ah-na!
eh-hey-yah-ah-na!

Tayo could feel the blood ooze along his scalp; he could feel rivulets in his hair. It moved down his head slowly, onto his face and neck as he stooped through each hoop.

e-hey-yah-ah-na!
e-hey-yah-ah-na!
e-hey-yah-ah-na!
e-hey-yah-ah-na!

At the Dark Mountain
born from the mountain
walked along the mountain
I will bring you through my hoop,
I will bring you back.

Following my footprints
walk home
following my footprints
Come home, happily
return belonging to your home
return to long life and happiness again
return to long life and happiness.

e-hey-yah-ah-na!
e-hey-yah-ah-na!
e-hey-yah-ah-na!
e-hey-yah-ah-na!

At the Dark Mountain
born from the mountain
moves his hand along the mountain
I have left the zigzag lightning behind
I have left the straight lightning behind

I have the dew,
a sunray falls from me,
I was born from the mountain
I leave a path of wildflowers
A raindrop falls from me
I'm walking home
I'm walking back to belonging
I'm walking home to happiness
I'm walking back to long life.

When he passed through the last hoop
it wasn't finished
They spun him around sunwise
and he recovered
he stood up
The rainbows returned him to his
home, but it wasn't over.
All kinds of evil were still on him.

From the last hoop they led him through the doorway. It was dark and the sky was bright with stars. The chill touched the blood on his head; his arms and legs were shaking. The helper brought him a blanket; they walked him to the edge of the rim-rock, and the medicine man told him to sit down. Behind him he heard the sound of wood and brush being broken into kindling. He smelled a fire. They gave him Indian tea to drink and old Betonie told him to sleep.

He dreamed about the speckled cattle. They had seen him and they were scattering between juniper trees, through tall yellow grass, below the mesas near the dripping spring. Some of them had spotted calves who ran behind them, their bony rumps flashing white and disappearing into the trees. He tried to run after them, but it was no use without a horse. They were gone, running southwest again, toward the high, lone-standing mesa the people called Pa'to'ch.

He woke up and he was shivering. He stood up and the blanket covering him slid to the ground. He wanted to leave that night to find the cattle; there would be no peace until he did. He looked around for Betonie and his helper. The horses had been tied by a big piñon tree, but they were gone now. He felt the top of his head where the cut had been made; it wasn't swollen or hot. It didn't hurt. He stood on the edge of the rimrock and looked down below: the canyons and valleys were thick powdery black; their variations of height and depth were marked by a thinner black color. He remembered the black of the sand paintings on the floor of the hogan; the hills and mountains were the mountains and hills they had painted in sand. He took a deep breath of cold mountain air: there were no boundaries; the world below and the sand paintings inside became the same that night. The mountains from all the directions had been gathered there that night.

He heard someone come up from the west side of the ridge. He turned. Betonie looked even taller in the darkness. He motioned for Tayo to sit down. He sat down next to him and reached into his shirt pocket for the tobacco and wheat papers. He rolled a thin cigarette without looking down at his hands, still gazing up at the east sky. He lit it and took little puffs without inhaling the smoke.

"It all started a long time ago. My grandfather, Descheeny, was an old man then. The hunters were returning from the South Peak. They had been hunting deer and drying the meat for two months. The burros were loaded with sacks full of jerky and bundles of stiff dry hides. The Navajos were careful. They didn't want any trouble with the soldiers at the fort in San Mateo. They made their night camp up a narrow deep canyon, northwest of the settlement, and they didn't build any campfires. The night was warm and the sky was bright with stars which flared like fire as they shined. The older men sat wrapped in their blankets, smoking and looking up at the sky to watch for shooting stars. But the young men stood over near the horses, talking in whispers and laughing frequently. They shared a cigarette, and the red light of ash passed back and forth between them in the dark. They didn't want to sit around all night and listen to the old men belch and pluck out chin whiskers until they were snoring. They wanted to ride over toward the settlement just to see if maybe there wasn't some stray horse or lost goats wandering in the hills outside town. There had been no raiding for many years, but they could sense the feeling of riding at night through pinon trees, galloping through the cool wind along the flats.

"The old men were unconcerned. They sat whittling toothpicks from piñon twigs. They knew how it would feel to let the horses run through the cool air; they had been traveling slowly in the dust and sun beside the burros for over a week. They watched the young men untie their horses; someone commented that it was a seductive night, and all the old men laughed and settled back to watch the sky again, and to tell the stories they had for nights like this night.

"The stars gave off a special light, more subtle and luminous than moonlight. The riders could make out the density of the trees and the massive boundaries of the boulders, but were still protected by darkness. When they got close enough that they could smell wood smoke, they pulled the running horses down to a lope and then a trot. The horses were excited and hot; they shook their heads and tried to pull away the reins. The riders could feel their heat and smell the horse sweat. They looked east at the tiny square pattern of the town in the valley that came down from the west slope of the big blue peaks, still solid with snow. They could see a few dim outlines of windows. They rode slowly, listening and watching. They did not expect to find anything, because they knew how careful the Mexicans were with their livestock at night. They were satisfied to ride close enough to smell the wood smoke and hear the village dogs barking in the distance.

"They had turned the horses around, and were riding back to the camp, along a piñon ridge. They had crossed a grassy clearing and were riding into the trees again when their horses stopped suddenly and spun around in panic. It was something about the big piñon tree at the edge of the clearing; the horses shied away from it and blew air through their nostrils when the men tried to ride them near it. They would have left that place, galloping fast, if one of them had not seen a light-colored object fall out of the tree, lightly like a bird. He dismounted and walked over to the tree slowly and picked up the object. It was a blue lace shawl. The others walked over, and they stood together and looked up into the branches of the big tree.

"They boosted a man up to the big branch to bring her down. He moved toward her cautiously, expecting her to fight, but she came down on her own, dropping softly into the dry needles under the tree. She did not cry like captives did, or jabber in her own language with tears running down her face. She held her mouth tight, teeth clenched under her thin lips, and she stared at them with hazel green eyes that had a peculiar night shine of a wolf or bobcat. The wind came out of the trees and blew her loose hair wildly around her wide brown face. Their confidence was caught in the wind; they were chilled as they looked at her. Each man was ready to let her go, to leave that place as fast as possible, but no one wanted to be the one to admit his fear. After all she was only twelve or thirteen, and she would bring a good price.

"They tied her to a small tree in a clearing where they could see her. But she watched them all night, staring at them steadily until they were afraid to look at her. In the morning the old men were silent. They did not joke or laugh as they loaded the burros. They gave her a horse to ride, and doubled up themselves; none of them wanted to get near her. Late in the afternoon they stopped to rest the animals in a canyon surrounded by red-rock mesas. The old men discussed how to get rid of her; nobody said so, but they all knew that they could not simply turn her loose or leave her behind, tied to a tree. They were in trouble now. They would kill her as soon as they found somebody who knew how it should be done. The old men discussed the stupidity of the young men in tones of great contempt. 'It's a good thing for us we are near old Descheeny's place,' one of them said, 'we can get him to help us.'

"Early the next morning they rode into the Chuska Mountains. They stopped at the white clay springs and sent someone up the hill to find Descheeny. They looked at the Mexican captive and then at the burros loaded with meat; they wondered how much Descheeny would charge to get them out of this situation. Descheeny's wives came down the hill first; they watched curiously, and then walked back up the trail.

"'What does she look like?' he asked his wives before they could speak. 'Who?' they said, pretending not to understand him, the way they often did, trying to anger him. But he smiled this time, and got up from his place by the door. 'Don't give me any trouble, ladies,' he said, putting on his old badger fur hat, and reaching for his walking cane, 'or I think I will marry her.'

Descheeny stood on the trail above the spring and watched her. She was kneeling at the edge of the pool, washing herself. Descheeny came down to the hunters who pretended to be adjusting the harnesses and tightening the cinches.

"'Nice load of meat you have there,' he said, motioning toward the bundles with his chin.

"'We have something else too, you might have noticed,' the tall man said casually. 'She's quite valuable, but she slows us down. You know how they are. Crying and screaming.' Descheeny smiled at the lies. He shook his head. 'I can see what you have. I will help you out for two or three loads of meat. Otherwise . . .' His voice trailed off and the hunters started whispering among themselves.

"He knew some Spanish. 'I'm too old to bother with you,' he said. 'Tomorrow we'll take you back to your people. We'll assure them that you have not been touched by the men. You can go back to your former life.' Descheeny was pleased with himself; he thought the words sounded suitably generous and sensitive. He watched her face; it was unchanged.

"'We'll tell your people where you were found. It was up in a tree, wasn't it? In the hills, late at night.' She laughed at him; her nostrils flared and her face was sneering.

"'You know the answer, old man, don't play games with me. You know what the people there will do with me.'

"'We don't want that thing around here,' the three sisters told their husband. 'It is a disgrace the way you sleep with her every night. We try to teach our children to avoid touching alien things, but every day they see you do it, you senile old man.' So he moved her to the winter house below the mountains, in the southwest, where the yellow sandrock foothills look over on the river.

"In the middle of the night he heard her moving in the hogan, the soft sounds of basket lids lifted and buckskin bundles unrolling, the rustle of seeds and dry leaves, the clink of eagle claws and wolves' teeth taken on their strings from his bag. Then there was silence.

"'I hear you, old man. Go back to sleep.'

"'I get cold without you close to me. Come lay down again.'

"'I will if you tell me why I hear so many voices in this hogan at night. All these languages I never heard before.'

"'Come lay down now. I'm shivering.'

"She lay down beside him and pulled the blanket over her mouth, and gradually moved closer to him until she could feel his thin ribs moving up and down. Old Descheeny's heart still pounded when he heard her breathing, and the excitement crawled up his thighs to his belly in anticipation.

"'I think it is them again.'

"'Yes.'

"'They are working for the end of this world, aren't they?'

"'I think so.'

"'Sometimes I don't know if the ceremony will be strong enough to stop them. We have to depend on people not even born yet. A hundred years from now.' She could only whisper the words because he was holding her close to him now.

"'You Mexicans have no patience,' he said, stroking her belly, 'it never has been easy. It will take a long long time and many more stories like this one before they are laid low.' She rolled over on top of him quickly.

"'There is something else which takes a long time happening,' she said in a low voice. 'Why do I bother to lay down with you, old man?'

"Old age made him fearless. He flexed the old chants and the beliefs like a mountain-oak bow. He had been watching the sky before she came, the planets and constellations wheeling and shifting the patterns of the old stories. He saw the transition, and he was ready. Some of the old singers could see new shadows across the moon; they could make out new darkness between the stars. They sent Descheeny the patients they couldn't cure, the victims of this new evil set loose upon the world.

"He reasoned that because it was set loose by witchery of all the world, and brought to them by the whites, the ceremony against it must be the same. When she came, she didn't fool him for long. She had come for his ceremonies, for the chants and the stories they grew from.

"'This is the only way,' she told him. 'It cannot be done alone. We must have power from everywhere. Even the power we can get from the whites.'

"Although the people detected changes in the ceremonies Descheeny performed, they tolerated them because of his acknowledged power to aid victims tainted by Christianity or liquor. But after the Mexican captive came, they were terrified, and few of them stayed to see the conclusion of his ceremonies. But by then, Descheeny was getting ready to die anyway, and he could not be bothered with isolated cures.

"He gazed into his smoky quartz crystal and she stared into the fire, and they plotted the course of the ceremony by the direction of dark night winds and by the colors of the clay in drought-ridden valleys.

"The day I was born they saw the color of my eyes, and they took me from the village. The Spaniards in the town looked at me, and the Catholic priest said, 'Let her die.' They blamed the Root Woman for this birth and they told her to leave the village before dark. She waited until they had gone, and she went to the old trash pile in the arroyo where they left me. She took me north to El Paso, and years later she laughed about how long she had waited for me in that village full of dirty stupid people. Sometimes she was bitter because of what they had done to her in the end, after all the years she had helped them. 'Sometimes I have to shake my head,' she'd say, 'because human beings deserve exactly what they get.'"

> The people asked,
> "Did you find him?"
> "Yes, but we forgot something.
> Tobacco."
> But there was no tobacco
> so Fly and Hummingbird had to fly
> all the way back down
> to the fourth world below
> to ask our mother where
> they could get some tobacco.
>
> "We came back again,"
> they told our mother.
> "Maybe you need something?"
> "Tobacco."
> "Go ask caterpillar."

"There was a child. The Mexican woman gave her to Descheeny's daughters to raise. The half sisters taught her to fear her mother. Many years later she had a child. When I was weaned, my grandmother came and took me. My mother and my old aunts did not resist because it all had been settled before Descheeny died."

Betonie paused and blew smoke rings up at the sky. Tayo stretched out his legs in front of him. He was thinking about the ceremony the medicine man had performed over him, testing it against the old feeling, the sick hollow in his belly formed by the memories of Rocky and Josiah, and all the years of Auntie's eyes and her teeth set hard on edge. He could feel the ceremony like the rawhide thongs of the medicine pouch, straining to hold back the voices, the dreams, faces in the jungle in the L.A. depot, the smoky silence of solid white walls.

"One night or nine nights won't do it any more," the medicine man said; "the ceremony isn't finished yet." He was drawing in the dirt with his finger. "Remember these stars," he said. "I've seen them and I've seen the spotted cattle; I've seen a mountain and I've seen a woman."

The wind came up and caught the sleeves of Tayo's shirt. He smelled wood smoke and sage in the old man's clothes. He reached for the billfold in his hip pocket. "I want to pay you for the ceremony you did tonight."

Old Betonie shook his head. "This has been going on for a long long time now. It's up to you. Don't let them stop you. Don't let them finish off this world."

> The dry skin
> was still stuck
> to his body.
> But the effects
> of the witchery
> of the evil thing

began to leave
his body.
The effects of the witchery
of the evil thing
in his surroundings
began to turn away.
It had gone a great distance
It had gone below the North.

The truck driver stopped at San Fidel to dump a load of diesel fuel. Tayo went inside the station to buy candy; he had not eaten since he had left Betonie and his helper up in the mountains. The room smelled like rubber from the loops of fan belts hanging from the ceiling. Cases of motor oil were stacked in front of the counter; the cans had a dull oil film on them. The desk behind the counter was covered with yellow and pink slips of paper, invoices and bills with a half cup of cold coffee sitting on top of them. Above the desk, on a calendar, a smiling blond girl, in a baton twirler's shiny blue suit with white boots to her knees, had her arms flung around the neck of a palomino horse. She was holding a bottle of Coca-Cola in one hand. He stared at the calendar for a long time; the horse's mane was bleached white, and there was no trace of dust on its coat. The hooves were waxed with dark polish, shining like metal. The woman's eyes and the display of her teeth made him remember the glassy eyes of the stuffed bobcat above the bar in Bibo. The teeth were the same. He turned away from the calendar; he felt sick, like a walking shadow, faint and wispy, his sense of balance still swaying from the ride in the cab of the tank truck. All the windows of the candy machine had red sold-out flags in them.

The station man came inside. He looked at Tayo suspiciously, as if he thought Tayo might be drunk, or in there to steal something. In his anger Tayo imagined movie images of himself turning the pockets of his jeans inside out, unbuttoning his shirt to prove he had stolen nothing. A confrontation would have been too easy, and he was not going to let them stop him; he asked the man where he could buy some candy.

"Down the road," he said, not looking up from the cash register. His milky white face was shaded with the stubble of a red beard. There were white hairs scattered among the red, and the skin across his forehead and at the corner of each eye was wrinkled as if he had been frowning for a long time. The backs of his hands were covered with curly reddish hair; the fingers were black and oily. He had never seen a white person so clearly before. He had to turn away. All those things old Betonie had told him were swirling inside his head, doing strange things; he wanted to laugh. He wanted to laugh at the station man who did not even know that his existence and the existence of all white people had been conceived by witchery.

He told the truck driver he didn't need to ride any farther. The sun was behind him and a warm dry wind from the southwest was blowing enough to cool the sweat on his forehead, and to dry out the wet cloth under the arms of his shirt. He walked down the ditch beside the highway, below the shoulder of the highway. He didn't want any more rides. He wanted to walk until he recognized himself again. Grasshoppers buzzed out of the weeds ahead of him; they were fading to a dry yellow color, from their bright green color of spring. Their wings flashed reflections of sun when they jumped. He looked down at the weeds and grass. He stepped carefully, pushing the toe of his boot into the weeds first to make sure the grasshoppers were gone before he set his foot down into the crackling leathery stalks of dead sunflowers. Across the highway, behind the bar at Cerritos, there was a big corn field, but the plants were short and thin, and their leaves were faded yellow like the grasshoppers. There would be only a few cobs on each plant, and the kernels would be small and deformed. He wondered what the Mexicans at Cubero thought. Their cattle were thin too. What did they do? Drop down on their knees in the chapel, sweaty straw hats in their hands, to smell the candle wax and watch the flickering red and blue votive lights? Pray up to the plaster Jesus in rose-colored robes, his arms reaching out? "Help us, forgive us."

He heard a truck slowing down on the highway behind him. He turned around and saw Harley hanging out the window, waving at him. He swung the door open before the old green truck had come to a stop and stumbled out of the seat grinning, holding a bottle of Garden Deluxe Tokay in each hand. Harley patted him on the back and pushed him toward the truck. Tayo could see Leroy was driving, but there was someone else in the truck, someone sitting in the middle, between them.

"Hey buddy—meet Helen Jean," Harley said, and winked crookedly, as if he had been drinking for a while. She was wearing tight blue western pants and a frilly pink western blouse. She didn't say anything, but she smiled and moved closer to Leroy. Leroy grinned at Tayo. She rubbed her leg against Leroy, but she was staring out the window while she did it, as if her mind were somewhere else. Leroy and Harley were happy; they had wine and two six-packs, and they didn't watch her the way Tayo did. Her perfume was close and heavy; breathing it was like swallowing big red roses; it choked him. He turned his face to the fresh air rushing in the window.

"Good thing you're skinny, buddy. Otherwise we couldn't shut the door!" Leroy shifted through the gears. The woman grinned at him because she was straddling the gear stick and he kept brushing against her thigh whenever he shifted gears. Harley nudged her in the ribs with an elbow and offered her the bottle.

"Look at her! She drinks like a pro," Harley said, delighted. "We found her in Gallup last night, didn't we?"

Leroy nodded. His eyes were bloodshot.

Harley passed him the bottle. Tayo shook his head.

"You want a beer?"

Tayo shook his head and pointed to his stomach.

"Sick? Hey Leroy, this guy says he's sick! We know how to cure him, don't we, Helen Jean?" She nodded. Tayo could see the lines at the corners of her eyes and a slight curve of flesh under her chin. Her hair was short and curled tight, and her eyelashes were stiff with mascara; she kept reaching into her tooled leather purse between her feet for her lipstick, rubbing it back and forth until her lips were thick and red. She wasn't much older than they were.

Tayo leaned out the window to make more room in the cab, but Harley, Helen Jean, and Leroy enjoyed squeezing close. He wanted to be still walking, but he knew them too well. It was no use to refuse a ride from them when they were drunk, because they'd follow him along the shoulder of the highway for ten miles in low gear until he got in with them. He wanted to catch a grasshopper and hold it close to his face, to look at its big flat eyes and shiny thin legs with stripes of black and brown like beadwork, making tiny intricate designs. The last time he held one, Rocky was with him, and they had stained their finger tips brown with the tobacco juice the grasshoppers spit.

"Hey!" Harley said. "What you watching?"

"Grasshoppers."

She giggled.

Harley shook his head and made him hold the wine bottle. "Here. You better have some. You're in bad shape, isn't he, Leroy? Watching grasshoppers when we've got Helen Jean here to watch, eh?" He laughed again.

The bottle was sticky. It was almost empty. He watched the weeds in the ditch speeding by. In another month the grasshoppers would be dead; autumn wind and old age would chill them bone white, leaving their hollow shells to swirl with the dry leaves in the ditch.

"Hey! You like my truck?"

Tayo nodded.

"Where'd you get it?"

"No money down! Pay at the first of the month!"

"If they catch him!" Harley laughed.

"Yeah! They have to catch me first!"

Harley bounced up and down on the seat laughing. "They owed it to us—we traded it for some of the land they stole from us!"

Helen Jean didn't smile, but she said, "Gypped you again! This thing isn't even worth a half acre!"

Tayo laughed then, too, because it was true. He could smell fumes from a loud busted muffler, and he was going to make a joke about how the white people sold junk pickups to Indians so they could drive around until they asphyxiated themselves; but it wasn't that funny. Not really.

They were getting close to Laguna, crossing the overpass by New Laguna; Leroy shifted into second gear for the hill.

"Thanks for the ride," Tayo said. "You can let me out any place along here." He gave the wine bottle to Helen Jean. She steadied it between her thighs, and pulled the cork out again.

"Easy, easy!" she said to Leroy. "You guys already spilled one bottle all over me." She was either an Apache or a Ute. Her face was angular, and something about her nose and eyes reminded him of a hawk.

Leroy slowed down and pulled off the right shoulder of the highway.

"Hey! Wait! He's going with us. Aren't you, Tayo? Huh, buddy!" Harley had Tayo by the arm and was leaning close to him, breathing wine fumes in his face. Harley was sweating and his face was shiny. They had been his friends for a long time; they were the only ones left now. He hesitated and Harley saw it.

He started whooping and slapping Tayo on the back; Leroy revved up the engine and threw it into low gear. The rear wheels spun sand and pebbles against the fenders, and the truck skidded and swerved back on the pavement. He did a speed shift into second gear and gunned it across the bridge, up the hill past Willie Creager's garage. Helen Jean squealed and laughed because Leroy's driving threw them hard against each other; Harley had his arms around her neck, bellowing out war whoops and laughs. The old truck was vibrating hard; the steering was loose and the front end wandered across the white line into the other lane, and each time a car was coming at them head-on before Leroy wrestled the wheel around and steered the truck over again. White people selling Indians junk cars and trucks reminded Tayo of the Army captain in the 1860s who made a gift of wool blankets to the Apaches: the entire stack of blankets was infected with smallpox. But he was laughing anyway, the bumps shaking laughter out of him, like feathers out of an old pillow, until he was limp and there were tears in his eyes.

"We'll give you a cure! We know how, don't we?" Harley was bouncing on the seat, and he made the whole truck sway on its weak springs. Helen Jean squealed, and the bottle of wine she was holding splashed all over them. Tayo grabbed it and swallowed what was left in the bottle.

"Drink it! Drink it! It's good for you! You'll get better! Get this man to the cold Coors hospital! Hurry up!"

Leroy pressed the gas pedal to the floorboard, and the speedometer dial spun around and around before it fluttered at 65. The engine whined with the strain, and the heat-gauge needle was pointing at 212. Tayo could smell hot oil and rubber, but Leroy kept it wide open past Mesita.

Up ahead, he could see where the highway dipped across an arroyo. But Leroy didn't slow down, and the old truck bounced, and landed hard on the other side of the dip. Their heads hit the roof of the cab, and Harley said this was better than a carnival ride at the Laguna fiesta. Tayo sank down into sensations—the truck vibrating and bouncing down the road, the bodies squeezed around him tight, the smell of perfume and sweat and wine, and the rushing fresh air cooling the sweat. Everything made them laugh, until they were laughing at their own noises and laughter. He didn't have to remember anything, he didn't have to feel anything but this; and he wished the truck would never stop moving, that they could ride like that forever.

Leroy parked the truck under the elm trees at the Y bar. Wine bottles and beer cans were scattered everywhere, broken and flattened by tires. Leroy turned off the key, but he left it in gear, so when he took his foot off the clutch, the truck lurched forward suddenly. Harley was helping Helen Jean get out, and the sudden lurch threw her against him. They both collapsed on the ground, laughing. The contents of her tooled leather purse with the rose designs had spilled all around her. She picked up her billfold, but they all got down on their hands and knees, crawling around to pick up little brass tubes of lipstick and her mirror and powder puff. Harley grabbed the mirror out of her hand and pranced around one of the elm trees, pretending to be "chickish muggy," someone who swished around, exercising his back muscles as he walked.

"Hey, Harley!" Tayo yelled. "You can't fool us any more! We know you are one of those guys! Where's your lipstick and nail polish?"

Harley took mincing steps and dropped the mirror into Helen's purse. "I'll race you to a cold beer!" he said as he took off, running to the door of the bar.

Harley and Leroy raced for the screen door, leaving Tayo behind with Helen Jean. She was giggling to herself, taking big steps and setting her feet down stiffly, as though she weren't sure the ground would hold her. They stepped over a Navajo sleeping on the shady side of the wooden steps. The juke box was playing a Mexican polka and Harley was dancing around by himself. There were some Mexicans from the section gang drinking beer at a table in the corner and three Navajos slouching on stools at the bar. The Mexicans could see she was drunk, and they were already getting ideas about her.

The way the men looked at her tensed Tayo's hands into fists. He didn't feel the fun or the laughter any more. His back was rigid; he sat down stiffly in the chair Leroy pulled out for him. Harley kept Helen Jean between himself and Tayo, and away from Leroy. He should have been worrying about the Mexicans in the corner, not Leroy. But Harley was up again, ordering a round of Coors, feeding quarters into the juke box as he punched the buttons for all the Hank Williams songs.

Helen Jean was smiling coyly at one of the Mexicans. Tayo tried to focus his eyes in the dim light to see which one, but there was a buzzing inside his head that made his eyes lose focus. He swallowed more beer, trying to clear away the dull ache; and he decided then he was too tired to care what she did.

"It wouldn't have worked anyway," Harley was saying in a loud voice; "between this beer belly of mine and her big belly, there would have been too much distance!" He laughed and looked at Helen Jean to see if she liked his story. She moved her eyes away quickly from the tall Mexican with long sideburns. She stared down at the table, smiling to herself.

The Mexicans stood up; the tall one put his cap on slowly and pulled it to one side of his head seductively. He watched her steadily; he didn't care if the Indians noticed. He nodded, and she smiled. Harley had the bottle tilted all the way, nursing the last drops of beer. He was too drunk and too happy to see what was happening. Leroy's shirttail was coming loose from his jeans, and when he answered Harley he had trouble making the words come out.

Helen Jean reached down by her feet for her purse. She hesitated and looked at Tayo. She giggled and said, "I have to go pee"; he nodded and finished off the beer. Harley and Leroy never even saw her go.

She had been thinking about it that morning when they left Gallup. Something had reminded her; maybe it was the people in the bar talking about the Gallup Ceremonial coming in two weeks. She had left Towac about then, August, one year ago. Left the reservation for good to find a job. She hadn't thought about it until then. Maybe it was because she was with these reservation Indians, out drinking with them and dancing in Gallup with all the other reservation Indians. Maybe someone had even talked about Towac.

She took the money she had saved—money the missionary lady paid her for cooking—and she stopped by Emma's to tell them good-bye. But the padlock was hooked through the hasp on the door, and it was locked, which meant Emma would be gone all day. Maybe to Cortez. So she left without seeing her little sisters, because she planned to come back on the bus, every weekend, to visit, and to bring money to help them out.

These Laguna guys were about the worst she'd run into, especially that guy they picked up walking along the highway; he acted funny. Too quiet, and not very friendly. She wanted to get away from them. They weren't mean like the two Oklahoma guys who beat her up one afternoon in a parked car behind the El Fidel. Pawnees, they said. Normandy. Omaha Beach. They beat her up—took turns holding and hitting her. They yelled at her because they both wanted her; they had been buddies all through the war together, and she was trying to split them up, they said. These Lagunas wouldn't beat her up, except she didn't know for sure about the quiet one. But Harley and Leroy, they were okay. She just didn't want to be driving around, way out in the sticks, with these reservation guys, even if they were war vets.

It was just a feeling she'd had since that morning. Thinking about Ceremonial time coming again. She hadn't sent any letters to Emma or the girls. She meant to do it; she had even written letters, in the evenings, on Stephanie's pink stationery at the little table in the kitchen they all shared. But she saved the letters in unsealed envelopes, waiting for a couple of dollar bills to send along.

It didn't work out. Her roommates were nice, but they had to have rent money, and she had to buy her share of the food. All day one Saturday the girls gave each other curly permanent waves and plucked out their eyebrows, penciling a thin arc over each eye. Monday she borrowed Elaine's blue dress, and she went down to the Kimo theater to apply for the job they advertised in the theater window. The man told her to wait in the lobby. It smelled like cold popcorn and burned-out cigarettes. She was too shy to ask him what the job was, or to tell him she knew how to type. She looked at the doors marked PRIVATE and OFFICE and tried to imagine what the desks looked like and what kind of typewriter they had. He didn't smile or look at her directly. "You can start today," he said, "but you might want to change your clothes." She stood in front of him, afraid to ask what was wrong with her clothes. He turned and motioned for her to follow. At the end of the corridor he pulled open a door, and she saw a push broom, and a scrub bucket. "Oh," she said. She always smiled when she was embarrassed. "How much do you pay?" "Seventy-five cents an hour," he said, walking away.

These Laguna guys were fun all right. And they sure spent their money. She didn't even know if there would be any money left when she asked them to help her out a little. Her roommates got tired of helping her out. They thought she was a secretary; they kept asking her what she did with all her money. She lied; she said she had to send it back home to Emma and the girls. She got dressed every day and left for work when they did. She changed her clothes in the ladies' lounge. But it wasn't working out. The man at the theater waited for her now; he watched her go down to the ladies' lounge. She wasn't surprised the day she heard the door open and close and she saw his brown shoes under the door of the toilet stall.

These Indians who fought in the war were full of stories about all the places they'd seen. San Diego, Oakland, Germany, the Philippines. The first few times she heard them talk, she believed everything. That was right after she got to town, and the girls took her out one weekend. She had walked around, staring up at the tall buildings, and all the big neon signs on Central Avenue. Every time she rode an elevator then, she thought of the old people at home, who shook their heads at the mention of elevators and tall buildings or juke boxes that could play a hundred different records. The old Utes said it was a lie; there were no such things. But she saw it every day, and for a long time when she saw these things, she felt embarrassed for the old people at home, who did not believe in these things. So she was careful not to make the same kind of mistake herself; and she believed all the stories the guys told. They had ribbons and medals they carried in their wallets; and if the U.S. Government decorated them, they must be okay.

She knew where to find them—which downtown bars they liked. She knew the veterans' disability checks came out around the first of the month. She learned these things after she quit her job at the Kimo. She walked by the El Fidel, that day she quit, and she could hear them laughing and whooping it up inside, so she knew they were Indians. That day she went in only to ask for a loan, because the girls were getting behind with the rent. The guys told her to sit down. She asked for a Coke, and they told the bartender to put rum in it.

"How do you like that!" they said, laughing and patting each other on the back. "Nothing like this at Towac, huh?"

She sat with them all afternoon. It was dim in there, and cool because they had a table near the fan. In July the streets and sidewalks were too hot to touch. She looked for work, but every day when it started to get hot, she walked past the El Fidel to see who was there. They were happy to see her; they introduced her to their other buddies. Late in the afternoon, when she got up to leave, she would ask someone to help her out a little. By then they would be feeling pretty good. Someone always helped her out with five or maybe ten dollars. "We used to do this every night during the war," one of them told her. "In San Diego one time, we bought the whole bar—all the soldiers and their girls—a round of drinks. That bartender shook his head: he told us, 'I know it's you Indians, without even looking. No one ever did that until the Indian soldiers came around.'"

They told her other stories too. Later on, when they started looking at her and sitting closer to her. The sergeant from Isleta still wore his khaki shirt with the stripes on the arm. As he reached over to pour her more beer, he rubbed his shaky arm against her side to feel the swell of her breast. She wasn't surprised then either. She knew if they helped her out, they would get friendly with her too. He had already told her a story about blowing up a bunker full of Japs. The story ended with him pulling out his wallet to show her a little bronze star on a blue ribbon. "Another thing was the women. The white women in California. Boy! You never saw anything like it! They couldn't get enough of us, huh?" "No!" all the others at the table would shout. "See," the sergeant said, looking a little crookedly at her, "I'll tell you about this one who was in love with me." He nodded deliberately. "Yeah, she was. I told her I was already married back home, but she didn't care. Boy, you shoulda seen her blond hair! She had it all curled. And she was built like this up front." He held his brown hands out in front of his chest and grinned at the others. He turned back to her and breathed heavily into her ear. "Hey, let's go someplace where I can tell you about it."

But she didn't want to go with him. "Tell me here," she said, "I want to finish my drink."

"Her name was Doreen. She only needed the money because her mother was a cripple. She wasn't like the others. She went with me because she loved me. I could still have her if I went back to California."

One of the guys at the table, an Apache, yelled at the Isleta sergeant. "She told that to all the guys. Doreen. That's what she called herself. Sure she liked Indians! Because they were dumb guys like you!"

The Apache had been watching Helen Jean; he had been watching the Isleta rub up against her. The Isleta grabbed her arm. "Let's go," he said. She didn't move. The Apache jumped up, ready to fight.

"She doesn't want to go with you," the Apache said.

The Isleta turned to her; his eyes were pinched with rage. "You bitch! You think you're better than a white woman?" He slapped her across the face. Her teeth cut her tongue and the inside of her mouth. Tears ran down her face. The Apache grabbed him, and they started pushing at each other, in a staggering circle on the dance floor. The other guys were cheering for a fight. They forgot about her.

She knew all the stories, about white women in San Diego and Oakland and L.A. Always blond or redhead, nice girls with sick or crippled parents at home. It didn't make any difference to her. They drank until they couldn't walk without holding on to her. She asked them for money then, money to send back to Emma at Towac: for the little girls. Then they stumbled up the steps to the Hudson Hotel. If she took long enough in the toilet, they usually passed out on the bed.

Even in the wintertime, when the rooms at the Hudson were cold and the window by the bed had frost on it, they sweated beer; and they lay on her so heavily that it was difficult to breathe. Their mouths were wet and soured with beer, and when they pushed themselves down on her, they felt small and soft between her thighs. She stared at the stains on the ceiling, and waited until they gave up or fell asleep, and then she rolled out from under them.

She looked at these Laguna guys. They had been treated first class once, with their uniforms. As long as there had been a war and the white people were afraid of the Japs and Hitler. But these Indians got fooled when they thought it would last. She was tired of pretending with them, tired of making believe it had lasted. It was almost a year since she had left Towac. There was something about Gallup that made her think about it. She didn't like the looks of the Indian women she saw in Gallup, dancing at Eddie's club with the drunks that stumbled around the floor with them. Their hair was dirty and straight. They'd shaved off their eyebrows, but the hairs were growing back and they didn't bother to pencil them any more. Their blouses had buttons missing and were fastened with safety pins. Their western pants were splitting out at the seams; there were stains around the crotch.

She reached into her purse for the little pink compact and looked in the mirror. Her hair was cut short and was tightly curled. It needed to be washed, but at least it wasn't long or straight. She touched up her left eyebrow and put on lipstick. She didn't like the looks of the country around here either. Rocks and sand, arroyos and no trees. After spending all her life at Towac, she didn't need to be wasting her time there, in the middle of nowhere, some place worse than the reservation she had left. If she hung around any longer with these guys, that's how she'd end up. Like the rest of the Indians. She smiled at the Mexican; he winked at her. He had the cash from his railroad pay check on the table in front of him. He'd help her out, give her some to send back to Towac. And this time she was really going to send some money to Emma, and she wasn't going to waste any more time fooling around with Indian war heroes.

He sat back in the chair and rested his head against the cool plaster wall. Through the sound of the juke box he could hear the Navajo, sitting now with his back against the screen door, singing songs. There was something familiar in the songs, and he remembered old Betonie's singing; something in his belly stirred faintly; but it was too far away now. He crawled deeper into the black gauzy web where he could rest in the silence, where his coming and going through this world was no more than a star falling across the night sky. He left behind the pain and buzzing in his head; they were shut out by the wide dark distance.

Someone was yelling. Someone was shaking him out of the tall tree he was in. He thought it might be old Betonie telling him to get on his way, telling him that he'd slept too long and there were the cattle to find, and the stars, the mountain, and the woman.

He started to answer old Betonie, to tell him he hadn't forgotten.

"I'm going," he said.

"You're damn right you're going!" the white man said. "Your pal just got the shit kicked out of him, and I don't want no more trouble here."

The last bright rays of sunlight split his head in half, like a big ax splitting logs for winter kindling. He put his hand over his eyes to shade them. He moved down the steps carefully, remembering the Navajo who had been sitting there, singing. But he was gone and the Mexicans were gone too; and the sky was deep orange and scarlet, all the way across to Mount Taylor. Leroy was kneeling over Harley, balancing himself unsteadily with one hand. His shirttail was loose, making a little skirt around his slim hips. He was saying, "Harley, buddy, did they hurt you?" Leroy's lips were bloody and swollen where they'd hit him. Harley was breathing peacefully, passed out or knocked out, Tayo couldn't tell. There was a big cut above his left eyebrow, but the blood had already crusted over it.

They carried Harley to the truck; his legs dragged behind him, wobbling and leaving long toe marks in the dirt. They propped him up between them, with Tayo behind the wheel. Leroy was slumped against the door, passed out. He searched the dashboard for the knob to turn on the headlights. When he pulled it, the knob came loose in his hands; he was too tired and sick to laugh at this truck, but he would have if Helen Jean had been there. Because she said it: gypped again.

At twilight the earth was darker than the sky, and it was difficult to see if any of Romero's sheep or goats were grazing along the edge of the pavement. The tourist traffic on Highway 66 was gone now, and Tayo imagined white people eating their mashed potatoes and gravy in some steamy Grants café.

During that last summer they had ridden across these flats to round up the speckled cattle and brand the calves. He took the pickup across the dip slowly, almost tenderly, as if the old truck were the blind white mule, too old to be treated roughly any more. He was thinking about Harley and Leroy; about Helen Jean and himself. How much longer would they last? How long before one of them got stabbed in a bar fight, not just knocked out? How long before this old truck swerved off the road or head-on into a bus? But it didn't make much difference anyway. The drinking and hell raising were just things they did, as he had done sitting at the ranch all afternoon, watching the yellow cat bite the air for flies; passing the time away, waiting for it to end.

Someone groaned; he looked over to see who it was. He smelled vomit. Harley had thrown up all over himself. Tayo rolled down the window and drove with his head outside, the way train engineers did, the air rushing at his face as he watched the white lines of the highway fall past the truck.

He pulled off the highway at Mesita, and reached over and shook Leroy by the arm. He mumbled and pushed Tayo's hand away. He shut off the engine and looked at the village. The lights of the houses were as scattered and dim as far-away stars. He left the keys in the ignition and rolled up the window in case the wind blew that night. One of them had pissed, and the rubber mat at Leroy's feet was wet, and with the windows rolled up the urine smell steamed around him. He gagged as he pushed the door open, and something gave way in his belly. He vomited out everything he had drunk with them, and when that was gone, he was still kneeling on the road beside the truck, holding his heaving belly, trying to vomit out everything—all the past, all his life.

The Scalp Ceremony lay to rest the Japanese souls in the green humid jungles, and it satisfied the female giant who fed on the dreams of warriors. But there was something else now, as Betonie said: it was everything they had seen—the cities, the tall buildings, the noise and the lights, the power of their weapons and machines. They were never the same after that: they had seen what the white people had made from the stolen land. It was the story of the white shell beads all over again, the white shell beads, stolen from a grave and found by a man as he walked along a trail one day. He carried the beautiful white shell beads on the end of a stick because he suspected where they came from; he left them hanging in the branches of a piñon tree. And although he had never touched them, they haunted him; all he could think of, all he dreamed of, were these white shell beads hanging in that tree. He could not eat, and he could not work. He lost touch with the life he had lived before the day he found those beads; and the man he had been before that day was lost somewhere on that trail where he first saw the beads. Every day they had to look at the land, from horizon to horizon, and every day the loss was with them; it was the dead unburied, and the mourning of the lost going on forever. So they tried to sink the loss in booze, and silence their grief with war stories about their courage, defending the land they had already lost.

Missionaries and the Religious Vacuum

VINE DELORIA, JR.

One of the major problems of the Indian people is the missionary. It has been said of missionaries that when they arrived they had only the Book and we had the land; now we have the Book and they have the land. An old Indian once told me that when the missionaries arrived they fell on their knees and prayed. Then they got up, fell on the Indians, and preyed.

Columbus managed to combine religion and real estate in his proclamation of discovery, claiming the new world for Catholicism and Spain. Missionaries have been unable to distinguish between their religious mission and their hunger for land since that time.

The first concern of mission work was land on which to build churches, homes, storehouses, and other necessary religious monuments. Like the men from New England in *Hawaii* by Michener, missionaries on the North American continent came to preach and stayed to rule. Or at least prepared the way for others to conquer and exploit.

Sacrifices often matched mistakes. Missionaries did more to open up the West than any other group, but in doing so they increased the possibility of exploitation of the people they purported to save. Land acquisition and missionary work always went hand in hand in American history.

While the thrust of Christian missions was to save the individual Indian, its result was to shatter Indian societies and destroy the cohesiveness of the Indian communities. Tribes that resisted the overtures of the missionaries seemed to survive. Tribes that converted were never heard of again. Where Christianity failed, and insofar as it failed, Indians were able to withstand the cultural deluge that threatened to engulf them.

The conflict between the Indian and white religions was classic. Each religion expressed the outlook and understanding of its respective group. Religious ideas of the two groups never confronted each other directly. The conflict was one of rites and techniques. Christianity destroyed many Indian religious practices by offering a much easier and more practical religion. It was something one could immediately understand, not a paving of the way for what ultimately confronted one.

The credal rhetoric of Christianity filled the vacuum it had created by its redefinition of religion as a commodity to be controlled. Although prohibited for several generations, Indian beliefs have always retained the capacity to return from their exile because they have always related to the Indian's deepest concern.

Indian religion required a personal commitment to act. Holy men relied upon revelations experienced during fasting, sacrifices, and visions. Social in impact, most Indian religious experience was individualistic in origin. Visions defined vocations in this world rather than providing information concerning salvation in the other world.

Formulas of faith were anathema to Indian societies. Debate over implications of the existence of God and creation of subtleties related to deity were unknown. The substantial doctrines developed by Christian theologians to explain, define, and control deity were never contemplated in Indian religious life. Religion was an undefined sphere of influence in tribal society.

Tribes shared with the Hebrews of the Old Testament the concept of the covenant of the People with God. The majority of tribal names, when translated into English, mean the People, First Men, or Original People. From the belief that the tribe is the People of God to the exclusion of other peoples, it usually follows that tribal customs and religious ordinances are synonymous.

Laws as such did not exist within tribal societies. Law was rejected as being force imposed from without, whereas peoplehood required fulfillment from within the individual. Insofar as there were external controls, Indians accepted only the traditions and customs which were rooted in the tribe's distant past. Time itself became irrelevant because custom prevailed long enough to outlive any knowledge of its origin. Mystery and reverence gradually surrounded rites and ceremonies, giving them the necessary *mysterium tremendum* by which they were able to influence social behavior.

Most mysterious was the Indian reverence for land. When told to settle down and become farmers, most Indians rebelled. For centuries they had lived off the land as hunters, taking and giving in their dances and ceremonies. Earth, they believed, was mother of all. Most important was the land which their particular tribe dwelt on. The Crow are a good example of the Indian religious love for land. The Crow have a long prayer which thanks the Great Spirit for giving them their land. It is not too hot, they say, and not too cold. It is not too high and snowy and not too low and dusty. Animals enjoy the land of the Crow, men enjoy it also. The prayer ends by declaring that of all the possible lands in which happiness can be found, only in the land of the Crow is true happiness found.

Even today I have watched Indian people look sadly over the miles of plowed ground of South Dakota, wishing that the land were returned to its primitive beauty, undefiled and giving to man and animal alike the life only land can give. Instead of beauty one sees a dust storm in the distance, ribbons of dirty highway going west, and the earth cut into a giant perverted checkerboard with no beauty and hardly even any symmetry.

Contrast this living, undefined religion, where man is a comfortable part of his world, with the message brought by the Christian missionary. The Reformation had divided the world into two arenas: church and state. Morality of one was not necessarily related to morality in the other. Often acts of the state, immoral by any standard, were endorsed by the church in an effort to gain political power and influence. Other times the church, in striving to protect its economic base, would encourage the state to undertake projects it dared not conceive of in its own moral terms.

There is, of course, an analogy in the contemporary role of the late Cardinal Spellman in supporting the United States in the Vietnam situation and the original encouragement by the churches of possession of lands the different European nations had *discovered*.

At one time or another slavery, poverty, and treachery were all justified by Christianity as politically moral institutions of the state. Economic Darwinism, the survival of the fittest businessman, was seen as a process approved by God and the means by which He determined His Chosen for salvation.

Exploitation of one's fellows by any means became a religious exercise. Law became a trap for the unwary and a dangerous weapon in the hands of those who understood how to use it. Public disclosure of wrongdoing was the only punishment society acknowledged either side of the grave, although religious sentimentalists talked vaguely about playing harps for an infinite number of years in some undisclosed heaven. Few mastered the harp before departing for that better life, however.

When the two religious movements came into conflict, the Christian religion was able to overcome tribal beliefs because of its ability to differentiate life into segments which were unrelated. When a world view is broken into its component disciplines, these disciplines become things unto themselves and life turns into an unrelated group of categories each with its own morality and ethics.

Missionaries approached the Indian tribes in an effort to bring them into western European religious life. Their primary message sought to invalidate the totality of Indian life and replace it with Christian values. Because Christian reality had been broken into credal definitions, all the missionaries could present to the Indians were words and phrases that had a magical connotation.

Missionaries looked at the feats of the medicine men and proclaimed them to be works of the devil. They overlooked the fact that the medicine men were able to do marvelous things. Above all, they overlooked the fact that what the Indian medicine men did *worked*.

Most activity centered on teaching and preaching. The thrust was to get the Indians to memorize the Large Catechism, the Small Catechism, the Apostles Creed, the Nicene Creed, the Ten Commandments, and other magic rites and formulas dear to Christianity. Salvation became a matter of regurgitation of creeds. In a very real sense, then, Christianity replaced living religions with magic.

And the white man had much magic. Blessed with the gun, the printing press, the iron kettle, and whiskey, it was obvious to many Indians that the white man's god took pretty good care of his people. Since there were no distinctions made between religion and life's other activities by the Indian people, the natural tendency was to adopt the white religion of recitation and forego the rigors of fasting, sacrifice, and prayer.

Missionary activity became an earthly parallel of what Christians thought was happening in heaven. Like the rich burghers of Europe, whom God bribed with earthly treasures, missionaries bribed their way into Indian societies. Once established, they began the laborious task of imprinting two thousand years of sterile dogmas on the unstructured Indian psyche.

Warfare between white and red solidified Indian religion in the persons of a few great leaders such as Sitting Bull, the Prophet (who was the brother of Tecumseh), Handsome Lake, and Wovoka, creator of the Ghost Dance. When these great leaders died, Indian religion went underground and became, like its white competitor, unrelated to the social and political life of the tribe.

By the middle of the last century few tribes were untouched by Christianity. When a tribe had been thoroughly subjugated, Army, trappers, and missionaries moved on and permanent personnel moved in to take control of Indian communities.

From 1860 to 1880, tribes were confined to reservations, as the West was in its death throes. Churches began lobbying early in the 1860's at the Indian Bureau in Washington for franchises over the respective reservations. Thus one reservation would be assigned to the Roman Catholics, one to the Lutherans, one to the Methodists, and one to the Episcopalians. Other churches were prohibited from entry on a reservation once it had been assigned to a particular church and could enter only with permission from the other church. It always bothered me that these churches who would not share pulpits and regarded each other as children of the devil, should have so cold-bloodedly divided up the tribes as if they were choosing sides for touch football.

Many times rations due Indians were mysteriously late in arriving, until the tribes responded to the pleadings of the missionaries. Other times outrageous programs designed to farm desert land were equated with Christian missions. A crop failure was sometimes seen as comparable to a decline in converts because the two harvests were inseparable in the minds of the missionaries.

Indian religious life was forbidden. The Ghost Dance movement, a last attempt to bring back the old hunting days, was enough to convince the Indian Bureau and the Army that the sooner the Indian was Christianized the safer the old frontier would be. Soon the only social activity permitted on reservations was the church service. Signs of any other activity would call for a cavalry troop storming in to rescue civilization from some non-existent threat.

It always amuses me to hear some white missionary glamorize the reception of Christianity by the Plains tribes. He will tell how "two or three were gathered together and gladly heard the word of God preached." The simple fact is that had the two or three not been talking about the white god they probably would have been shot down for fomenting an uprising.

It was no feat, therefore, to convert Indians to a new religion. No missionary ever realized that it was less the reality of his religion and more the threat of extinction that brought converts to him. Or if he did realize it, he never acknowledged it.

Some churches patterned their work after existing social traits within the tribal culture. They were able to translate older Indian ceremonies and rites into Christian celebrations. Like the Gothic arches which took the place of the oak groves under which the European tribes had worshiped, the traditional gatherings of the tribes were made into annual meetings of the mission fields.

Particularly among the Sioux in the Dakotas, the Sun Dance was reinterpreted as the annual convocation of the missions on each reservation. And this type of accommodation to Indian life gave churches that used it built-in advantages over their competitors. But Christianity was presented in such a dogmatic form to the Sioux that it became frozen into a rigid structure. The religion, as it was presented in the 1870's, remains the religion of the Sioux today. This fact was brought home to me quite vividly in 1964.

That was the year that many church people became convinced that the Civil Rights movement was the only real Christian mission. Most of us secretly suspected that the opportunity for national publicity had more to do with this feeling than did God. But we accepted this message of the churches as valid.

Church officials from the East came out to the reservations to bring the new message and to get Indians involved in the struggle. A New Yorker attended a Sioux religious meeting in South Dakota and was treated to an evening of hymns and prayers sung in the Dakota language. And he was horrified.

Nowhere, he later stated, did he find the social concern for integration and equality which made up the bulk of the Christian message. God's number-one priority, he felt, was Civil Rights and here he had been overwhelmed with missionary hymns that had no relevance to the great struggle.

When this message was later related to the Sioux they were more outraged than was our friend from New York. They insisted that the missionaries had come out to them in the 1870's and taught them to sing "From Greenland's Icy Mountains" and had told them that this was God's word, and that, by God, they were going to keep on singing "From Greenland's Icy Mountains" regardless of what the rest of the world was doing.

Where, therefore, Christianity was accepted, it became so ingrained in the social life of the people that it often became impossible to change. And the tribes generally accepted what they felt was important and disregarded the rest.

Today it is fairly easy to tell which churches had which reservations by the predominance of members of a certain church among the older Indians. Nowhere was the validity of one denomination over another demonstrated. It always causes me to wonder why the various church bodies fight over doctrines today when a century ago they were willing to commit the souls of their red brothers to pernicious doctrines on one reservation in return for the exclusive preaching franchise on another.

Various Lutheran bodies do not share communions or pulpits today. The Roman Catholics and Episcopalians are always engaged in a brawl over the Apostolic pedigree of their ministry. Methodists, Presbyterians, and Baptists continually struggle over concepts of congregational sovereignty. Yet one hundred years ago these churches deliberately ceded various tribes to doctrines they considered heretical in order to gain a captive audience from the federal government.

What each denomination did share, however, was the Anglo-Saxon social forms. These modes of behavior were what they really taught and preached about on the various reservations. Churches struggled to make the Indians cut their hair because they felt that wearing one's hair short was the civilized Christian thing to do. After the tribal elders had been fully sheared, they were ushered into church meeting, given pictures of Jesus and the Disciples, and told to follow these Holy Men. Looking down at the pictures, the ex-warriors were stunned to discover the Holy Dozen in shoulder-length hair!

Often rows of sullen former warriors filled rickety wooden chapels to hear sermons on the ways of peace. They were told that the life of war was the path of destruction. Eternal hell, they were assured, awaited the man of war. Then the service would be closed with the old favorite hymn, "Onward, Christian Soldiers, Marching as to War."

An objective consideration of missionary efforts would indicate that the major emphasis was not religious conversion but experimentation with a captive culture. Western religion had failed to influence the society within which it was created. It had become a commodity for export long before Columbus discovered America. It had no choice but to attempt to gain a stranglehold on other cultures to reinstate itself. But its influence on Indian culture was comparable to that of other trade goods. Where it was useful, it was used.

Indian people obediently followed the way of the white man because it was the path of least resistance. The Great Spirit was exchanged for Santa Claus with some misgivings. Substituting toys for spiritual powers created a vacuum, however, and the tribes secretly preferred their old religion over the religion of the Easter Bunny.

The years from 1870 to 1930 were prosperous times, producing record harvests of red souls. Indian congregations were established in nearly every reservation west of the Mississippi. Many became self-supporting in a short time. By 1930 the majority of the Indian people had a tradition of three generations of church life behind them. Religious controversy centered on doctrinal differences unsolved by the denominations during Reformation days. Missionary work concentrated on such glamorous exploits as stealing sheep from another missionary's fold rather than the de-paganization which had characterized the early mission work.

The flower of tribal leadership served in the reservation chapels as laymen and helpers to the white missionaries. Many people hoped and expected that the mission status of Indian churches would soon be ended and they would receive full parish and congregational equality. Little did they realize that the Indian mission field had become a hobby in and of itself.

Church piety required that the "finest young men" take up the White Man's Burden and go abroad to save the heathen from their great darkness. Indian missions provided the only opportunity whereby young white clergymen could serve God after the mandate of Kipling and still enjoy the comforts of home. To release the Indian congregations to their own devices would have meant closing the only field in which traditional heroics could be achieved. A state of inertia set in.

The white missionaries of the Depression years and later frantically tried to duplicate the exploits of Whipple, Whitman, Father DeSmet, and Charles Cook. There was still glory to be gained by being identified as *the* missionary to a certain tribe. This struggle meant an absolute rejection of Indian people as candidates for the ministry. Recognition of an Indian as an equal or possibly a superior in the missionary venture would have acknowledged that the Indian people had already accepted Christianity. Paganism, per se, would have ceased to exist and there would have been no need for white missionaries.

The Depression missionaries were succeeded by a generation in which the mission field had been the glory spot of Christian work. Many arrived out West with the idea of finally completing the task started by the heroes of the faith two centuries ago. The new breed contemptuously announced that nothing had really been done by their predecessors. There were still Indians around and Indians meant pagans.

The new breed was something to behold. Almost universally they expected the Indian people to come to them for spiritual advice. The older missionaries had made the rounds of their chapels faithfully. After a time, most of the old timers were converted to the Indian way of life and spent their declining years ministering in an Indian way to the people.

But the new breed felt that the Indians were damn lucky they had come. Universally they downgraded Indian laymen. Often they changed patterns of worship and services that had been established for nearly a century. Quite a few had "days off," when they refused to do anything, and most spent a great deal of their time either on vacations or at conferences learning about the relevant new movements of the modern world.

The situation has not changed greatly over the past few years. Several years ago at a conference of missionary workers, a female missionary (somehow missionaries are able to achieve an asexual status) asked my advice on a problem she was having. It seemed that no matter how hard she tried, she couldn't get her little Choctaw pupils in Sunday School to understand the "technical side of being saved."

In her church, it turned out, there were seven steps to salvation. When one understood the seven steps to salvation and was able to recite the sequence correctly, he was saved. Then his task was to teach others the seven steps until Jesus came. Apparently the Lord would ask all people to recite the seven steps on Judgment Day.

Unfortunately I was not able to give her any insight into the task of getting six-year-old Choctaws to walk the seven steps to salvation, let alone memorize them. I asked her why, if it was so difficult to get them to understand, didn't she move to a field which the Lord had spent more time preparing. She replied that the Baptists had had the children for some time and had left them terribly confused. Her first task had been to correct all the heretical theology the Baptists had taught them. She said that she wouldn't dream of leaving and letting some other church come in after her and again confuse the children. On such incisive insights is Christian mission to the Indians founded.

The determination of white churches to keep Indian congregations in a mission status is their greatest sin. But it is more a sin against themselves than it is against Indian people. For the national churches do not realize how obsolete their conceptions have become and they continue to tread the same path they walked centuries ago.

The epitome of this blithe ignorance is the work of the Presbyterian Church among the Shinnecocks on Long Island. At a missionary conference two years ago, a Presbyterian minister, in charge of the Indian work for his denomination, described his church's work among this tribe. Then he asked for questions.

I asked him how long the Presbyterians intended to conduct mission activities among a tribe that had lived as Christians for over three hundred and fifty years. His answer to my question was representative of Christian attitudes toward Indian people today: "Until the job is done."

Christianity, which had laid the ancient world prostrate in less than three hundred years and conquered the mighty Roman Empire, has not been able in the same time period to subdue one hundred Indians huddled on Long Island. Needless to say, my faith was shaken to the core by this statement.

The impotence and irrelevancy of the Christian message has meant a return to traditional religion by Indian people. Tribal religions are making a strong comeback on most reservations. Only in the past few years have the Oglala Sioux and Rosebud Sioux revived their ancient Sioux Sun Dance. And this revival is not simply a re-enactment for tourists. The dance is done in the most reverent manner and with the old custom of piercing the dancers' breasts.

Pathetically, the response of the white missionaries has been to set up tipis and attempt to compete with the Indian religion by holding Masses and communions during the celebration. Nervously they try to convince the Indians that the Sun Dance and the Holy Communion are really the same thing and that Christianity is therefore "relevant" to the Indian people.

In the Great Lakes area the old Medicine Lodge religion has been making inroads with the Chippewas and Winnebagos. Two years ago at an annual conference of the Wisconsin tribes, a panel of Indians discussed native religions. Eagerly the younger conference participants listened to the old men talk. They left that conference with the conviction that Indian religion was for Indian people and Christian religion was for whites.

The Native American Church, famed for its use of the peyote button in its sacramental worship life, has doubled its membership in the last few years. It appears to be the religion of the future among the Indian people. At first a southwestern-based religion, it has spread since the last world war into a great number of northern tribes. Eventually it will replace Christianity among the Indian people.

When I was growing up on the Pine Ridge reservation before and during World War II, the Native American Church was something far away and officially "bad." Few adherents to this faith could be found among the two large Sioux reservations in southern South Dakota. Today a reasonable estimate would be that some 40 percent of the people are members of the Native American Church there.

Indian people have always been confused at the public stance of the Christian churches. The churches preached peace for years yet have always endorsed the wars in which the nation has been engaged. While the missionaries have never spoken about this obvious inconsistency, Indian people have been curious about it for some time. So the element of Indian people who believe deeply in pacifism have looked to other places for a religion of peace.

From the Hopi reservation has come a prophet of peace named Thomas Banyaca. He stands within the old Hopi religion and preaches to all Indians of their need to return to a life of peace and purity before the world ends. In 1967 Banyaca and some members of the Iroquois tribes traveled throughout the nation visiting the different reservations, bringing a message based on the prophecies of the Hopi and Iroquois. In June of 1968 Banyaca, "Mad Bear" Anderson, a Tuscarora prophet, and many of the traditional leaders of different tribes had two National Aborigine conventions in Oklahoma and New York to discuss prophecies of their religion.

Banyaca's message, and its ultimate influence, appears to me to be the most significant movement in religion in Indian Affairs today. Banyaca is very spiritual and highly traditional. He stands solidly within Hopi legend which looks at world history as a catastrophic series of events all of which the Hopi have been saved from. In the late fifties a Hopi delegation went to the United Nations to deliver a message of peace, as Hopi prophecies had required them to do. Legends said that should the Hopi delegation be refused entrance—as they were—the series of events foretelling the end of the world would begin. Banyaca's message to other Indian people is to orient them as to the number of prophecies now fulfilled.

The best statement of Hopi prophecy is contained in Frank Waters' *Book of the Hopi* in which the end of the world as we know it is foretold. There is great similarity between Hopi prophecy and Iroquois prophecy regarding the end of the white man and the restoration of the red man to dominance on this continent. Many people, especially whites, laugh when they hear the Hopi prophecy, feeling that they are so powerful that nothing can overcome them. They forget that Indian gods still roam these lands and do not realize that the Hopi have incredible gifts from their gods which cannot be duplicated by any Christian missionaries; not even, people tell me, by the Pope.

Even in the Northwest, Indian religions are on the move. The Northwest was supposedly converted by Marcus Whitman, early missionary to Oregon Territory. But those tribes, by and large, did not succumb to the word as easily as did tribes in other regions. People from Shoshone country tell me that the medicine men are more powerful there today than they were a century ago. Among the Yakimas the old religion still holds an honored place among the people. If and when native religion combines with political activism among the small tribes in western Washington, they are going to become extremely active in the coming Indian religious revival that many tribes expect in the next decade.

Perhaps only in eastern Oklahoma has Christianity been able to hold its ground. Among the Five Civilized Tribes, Cherokee, Choctaw, Creek, Seminole, and Chickasaw—called civilized because they were most like white men a century ago and have surpassed them in whiteness today—the Baptist denomination exerts great influence. This strength is due primarily to the large number of native clergy among the tribes. The Creeks particularly seem to have taken the Christian doctrines and made them their own. Native preachers exert tremendous influence among the Creeks and Cherokees. If Christianity is to have an Indian base of survival, it will be among the Creeks.

The dilemma of Christian missions today is great. National churches have committed two great mistakes, the solution of which depends upon their foresight and ability to reconcile themselves to what they have been preaching to Indian people for years.

The different denominations have, over the years, invested an enormous amount of money in mission buildings and property. In the closing years of the last century, churches could receive a piece of tribal land simply by promising to conduct certain operations such as a school, hospital, or mission station. Consequently many of them applied for and received a great deal of tribal land.

Now they are caught with property which is suitable only for religious use and with a declining religious following. What use has a church building other than as a church? National churches have continued to pour thousands of dollars annually into their mission programs simply to keep up the value of their investments. They must soon be prepared either to take a devastating paper loss as their congregations vanish or give the properties to the Indian people for their own use. Either solution is distasteful to the materialistic instincts of the churches.

Added to the question of property is the obvious racial discrimination of the denominations against the Indian people, which is becoming apparent to the reservation people. Try as they might, the churches cannot admit that an Indian minister speaking in his native tongue to his own people is more efficient and more effective than a highly trained white missionary talking nonsense.

The major denominations are adamant in their determination to exclude Indian people from the ministry. A number of devices, which skirt "official" pronouncements of concern for an indigenous ministry, are used to bar Indian candidates.

One church refuses to admit Indians to the ministry because it is afraid that someday an Indian priest or clergyman may want to serve in a white parish. Indian ministers would not, by definition, be able to serve in a white parish. Therefore, the reasoning goes, they are not suitable for work among Indian congregations either. While they are welcome, I have been told, they don't seem to be able to qualify.

Other churches are frightened that when the sacred doctrines are translated into the native tongue, the subtle nuances created by theologians of the Reformation will lose some of their distinctions. A perfect example of this attitude happened at an orientation session for new missionaries which I attended in 1963.

A Navajo interpreter was asked to demonstrate how the missionary's sermon was translated into Navajo. So the white missionary gave a few homilies and the interpreter spoke a few words of Navajo. The trainees cooed with satisfaction that meaning could actually be transferred into a barbaric tongue like Navajo.

One missionary was skeptical, however, and asked if there were specific words in Navajo that were comparable to English words. He was afraid, he said, that the wrong messages might be transmitted. So he asked what the Navajo word for "faith" was. Quickly the Navajo replied with the desired word.

"Yes," the missionary commented, "that's all very nice. Now what does that word mean?"

"Faith," said the Navajo smiling.

Nevertheless, many denominations are skeptical about letting Indians enter the ministry because of the possibility that doctrine may become impure. So they continue to send white missionaries for posts in Indian country to insure that the proper theological distinctions be drawn.

With the necessity of keeping large missions open and by refusing to bring Indian people into the ministry, churches have had great difficulty in filling their mission posts. The glory of intrepid pioneering is now gone, and the glory seekers as well as the devoted have long since written off Indian country as the place for service and advancement. Staff positions go unfilled for months and often the first white who comes wandering in across the desert is hired to operate the mission stations.

Some churches have an incredible turnover each spring and try all summer to fill their posts. Eventually they find some white who is a former basketball coach, a retired editor, an interested layman, or an ex-schoolteacher and promptly hand over the mission lock, stock, and barrel without further inquiry. The fact that the new appointee is white is sufficient to cover any theological or professional shortcomings.

Thus the quality of mission workers is at an all-time low. Most are not interested in their work and regard it as a job rather than a calling. Generally they have great contempt for the Indian people they are supposed to be helping.

But probably worse, much mission work is done by white clergymen who are not capable enough to run white parishes. In most cases, the Indian field is their last stop before leaving the ministry altogether. They are hauled from pillar to post by frantic church officials desperately trying to shore up the sagging fortunes of their mission fields. A great deal of money is spent covering up disasters created by these white misfits. When they cause too much controversy in one place they are transferred to another and turned loose again. More money is spent on them than on recruitment and training of Indian people for church work.

Pay is not high in mission work for either white or Indian workers. But it is universally higher for whites than it is for Indians. In the past there was some justification for a pay difference. Many Indian workers were only part-time workers and had another source of income. Gradually, however, Indian clergymen were assigned to remote areas and received less compensation.

Often the pay scale is based primarily upon whether a man is white or Indian. Indians receive less pay, even with seminary training. And Indians are still assigned to the remote areas with the poorest housing and least facilities. Go out to any mission field today and examine the placement of church workers and clergymen. You will discover that white workers have the best assignments, the best houses, the best fringe benefits, and receive the most consideration for advancement from their superiors.

No other field of endeavor in America today has as much blatant racial discrimination as does the field of Christian missions to the American Indian people. It is a marvel that so many Indian people still want to do work for the churches.

Documentation of discrimination and favoritism would be fairly easy were it not for the fantastic ability of the churches to cover their tracks. Instead of forcing resignations from the ministry, church officials transfer incompetents from station to station in order to protect the good name of the church. Thus some tribes are visited with a problem missionary who should have been sent on his way years ago but who has managed to hang on to his ministerial status by periodic transfer and the lack of moral courage by church officials to take action.

The Indian people have come a long way in the last generation. For a long time they accepted the missionary because he seemed to want to do the right thing. But there has always been a desire for the Indian people to take over their own churches. Now they no longer have the expectation that there will be native clergy in their churches. More and more they are returning to Indian dances and celebrations for their religious expressions. They now wait only for a religious leader to rise from among the people and lead them to total religious independence. Thomas Banyaca or Frank Takes Gun, leader of the Native American Church, or someone yet unknown may suddenly find a way to integrate religion with tribalism as it exists today and become that leader.

Indian religion appears to many of us as the only ultimate salvation for the Indian people. Religion formerly held an important place in Indian tribal life. It integrated the functions of tribal society so that life was experienced as a unity. Christianity has proved to be a disintegrating force by confining its influence to the field of formula recitation and allowing the important movements of living go their separate ways until life has become separated into a number of unrelated categories.

Religion today, or at least Christianity, does not provide the understanding with which society makes sense. Nor does it provide any means by which the life of the individual has value. Christianity fights unreal crises which it creates by its fascination with its own abstractions.

I remember going to an Indian home shortly after the death of a child. There was a Roman Catholic priest admonishing the mother not to cry because the child was now with Jesus. Automatically, he insisted, because it had been baptized. Grief, he declared, was unnatural to man ever since Jesus had died on the cross. He went on to tell how God had decided on a great mission for the child and had called it home to Him and that the mother could see the hand of God in the child's death and needn't wonder about its cause.

In fact, the mother had not wondered about the reason for the child's death. Her child had fallen from a second-story window and suffered internal injuries. It had lingered several days with a number of ruptured organs and had eventually and mercifully died.

I could never believe that the priest was comforting the mother. It seemed rather that he was trying frantically to reinforce what had been taught to him in seminary, doctrines that now seemed shaken to their roots. The whole scene was frightening in its abstract cruelty. I felt sorrier for the priest than for the mother. His obvious disbelief in what he was telling her and his inability to face death in its bitterest moment made *him* the tragic figure.

That is why I believe that Indian religion will be the salvation of the Indian people. In Indian religions, regardless of the tribe, death is a natural occurrence and not a special punishment from an arbitrary God. Indian people do not try to reason themselves out of their grief. Nor do they try to make a natural but sad event an occasion for probing the rationale of whatever reality exists beyond ourselves.

Indians know that people die. They accept death as a fact of life. Rather than build a series of logical syllogisms that reason away grief, Indian people have a ceremony of mourning by which grief can properly be expressed. Depending on the tribal traditions, grief is usually accompanied by specific acts of mourning, which is then ended by giving a feast for the community. After the feast, there is no more official mourning. When expression of grief is channeled into behavioral patterns—as it is, also, in the Jewish religion—it can be adequately understood and felt. When it is suppressed—as it is in the Christian religion—death becomes an entity in itself and is something to be feared. But death also becomes unreal and the act of an arbitrary God.

When death is unreal, violence also becomes unreal, and human life has no value in and of itself. Consider the last talk you had with an insurance salesman. Remember how he told you that you would be covered "if" you died. An Indian salesman would have said "when," but then an Indian would have known how to die and both "if" and "when" would have held no terror for him.

Many tribes have kept their puberty ceremonies, and these ceremonies are very much alive today in the Southwest. Childhood and adolescence are marked off by these ceremonies so that the natural growth processes are recognized and young people growing up will be sure of their place in society.

Contrast the value of these ceremonies with the confusion of suburban America where children are pushed into imitations of adults in their younger years and then later denied the privileges of adults. Certainly the pressures on boys in the Little League are comparable in intensity and form with those professional ballplayers face. But after ten years of being treated like adults, young people begin to demand adult status and they are clubbed into submission by police at Columbia University and in Chicago.

The largest difference I can see between Indian religion and Christian religions is in inter-personal relationships. Indian society had a religion that taught respect for all members of the society. Remember, Indians had a religion that produced a society in which there were no locks on doors, no orphanages, no need for oaths, and no hungry people. Indian religion taught that sharing one's goods with another human being was the highest form of behavior. The Indian people have tenaciously held to this tradition of sharing their goods with other people in spite of all attempts by churches, government agencies, and schools to break them of the custom.

Christianity came along and tried to substitute "giving" for sharing. There was only one catch: giving meant giving to the church, not to other people. Giving, in the modern Christian sense, is simply a method of shearing the sheep, not of tending them.

Several years ago a Roman Catholic priest on the Wind River reservation complained bitterly about the Indian custom of sharing as being "un-Christian" because it distributed the wealth so well no middle class could be established. Hence "bad" Indians dragged the "good" ones down to a lower economic level and the reservation remained economically static.

The initial object of the Roman Catholic priest's outburst was an Indian woman who had a telephone and let all her neighbors use it. The bill ran as high as one hundred dollars some months. Often the woman was behind on her bill. But she didn't mind letting her neighbors use the phone when they wanted to.

The priest was furious when he reminded himself that of a Sunday the collection plate was not filled by the Indians. He felt that was intolerable and he wanted to teach the Indians "stewardship." Stewardship meant saving money and giving a percentage of the savings in the plate.

There was no difference, for the missionary, between sharing one's goods with the community and squandering resources. He preferred that the people give their money to the church, which would, in turn, efficiently define who was in need of help. Indians looked at the missionary's form of sharing as a sophisticated attempt to bribe the Great Spirit.

The onus is not on the Roman Catholics alone. The Protestants have devised a scheme whereby sharing is reduced to a painless sixty minutes a year. It is called One Great Hour of Sharing. Once a year they remind themselves how lucky they are to be Protestants and call for an outpouring of money so that others might receive the same privilege. Tough social problems always go unsolved.

Sharing, the great Indian tradition, can be the basis of a new thrust in religious development. Religion is not synonymous with a large organizational structure in Indian eyes. Spontaneous communal activity is more important. Thus any religious movement of the future would be wise to model itself on existing Indian behavioral patterns. This would mean returning religion to the Indian people.

The best thing that the national denominations could do to ensure the revitalization of Christian missions among Indian people would be to assist in the creation of a national Indian Christian Church. Such a church would incorporate all existing missions and programs into one national church to be wholly in the hands of Indian people.

Such a church would include all ordained Indian clergymen now serving as church workers in the Indian field. The actual form of the ministry would not be determined by obsolete theological distinctions preserved from the middle ages, but would rather incorporate the most feasible role that religion can now play in the expanding reservation societies.

Each denomination that has been putting funds into Indian work would contribute toward the total budget of the new church. Existing buildings and church structures would be evaluated by the new Indian church and the tribal council of the reservation on which the property is located. Congregations of the various denominations would be consolidated and reservation-wide boards of laymen would direct activities on each reservation.

With the religious function integrated into the ongoing life of the tribe, the Indian church would be able to achieve self-support in a short time as the role of religion clarified itself to the reservation communities. Religious competition, which fractures present tribal life, would disappear and the movement toward ancient religions might not be so crucial.

Such a proposal is too comprehensive for most denominations to accept at the present time. The primary fear of turning over the sacred white religion to a group of pagans would probably outrage most denominations, too few of whom realize how ridiculous denominational competition really is.

The best example I can mention of denominational competition existed at Farmington, New Mexico, a couple of years ago. The situation has probably changed since 1965. But that year there were twenty-six different churches serving an estimated Navajo population of 250. That's less than ten Indians per denomination! Assuming each church had a choir of eight, the congregations must have totaled one or two people per Sunday. Which does not indicate a field ready for harvest.

I estimated that the total mission budget for the Farmington area that year was in excess of $250,000. Christianity, not tourism, was Farmington's most profitable industry in 1965.

Churches face literal dissolution on the reservations unless they radically change their method of operation. Younger Indians are finding in Indian nationalism and tribal religions sufficient meaning to continue their drift away from the established churches. Even though many churches had chaplaincies in the government boarding schools, the young are not accepting missionary overtures like their fathers and mothers did.

As Indian nationalism continues to rise, bumper stickers like "God is Red" will take on new meanings. Originally put out at the height of Altizer's "God is Dead" theological pronouncements, the slogan characterizes the trend in Indian religion today.

Many Indians believe that the Indian gods will return when the Indian people throw out the white man's religion and return to the ways of their fathers. Whether or not this thinking is realistic is not the question. Rather the question is one of response and responsibilty of the missionaries today. Will they continues to be a burden or not?

Can the white man's religion make one final effort to be real, or must it too vanish like its predecessors from the old world? I personally would like to see Indians return to their old religions wherever possible. For me at least, Christianity has been a sham to cover over the white man's shortcomings. Yet I spent four years in a seminary finding out for myself where Christianity had fallen short.

I believe that an Indian version of Christianity could do much for our society. But there is little chance for such a melding of cards. Everyone in the religious sphere wants his trump to play on the last trick. In the meantime, Banyaca, Mad Bear Anderson, and others are silently changing the game from pinochle to one where all fifty-two cards are wild. They may, if the breaks fall their way, introduce religion to this continent once again.

The Native American Church of Jesus Christ

EMERSON SPIDER, SR.

First of all, I'm very thankful that you boys could come to the Native American Church of Jesus Christ, which was built here at Porcupine not too long ago. I am Emerson Spider, Sr., and my title is Reverend of the Native American Church. I'm the headman of the Native American Church of Jesus Christ in the state of South Dakota.

Our church began to come into South Dakota during the early 1900s. There was a man named John Rave, a Winnebago Indian. This was before I was born. I guess this man was very smart. He was in the Catholic Church. Then he ordained another man named Henry White, also a Winnebago, as a minister in the Native American Church. That man came to the Sioux in the community of Allen, on Pine Ridge Reservation. So we got our ordination by rights.

At first we weren't organized as a church. It was a Sioux man named Jim Blue Bird who organized this peyote way of worshipping as a church and put the Bible in there to be the head instrument in our church. Then he said that we should have ministers. So in 1924 we organized as a church with ministers, like any other church. Last June we had our fifty-eighth annual convention. My grandpa on my mother's side, Reverend William Black Bear, was the first headman of the church in South Dakota. Then after he was gone, my dad took over. He was sixty-six years old when he passed away. For the past seventeen years I have been head of the church.

We started out as a traditional church. We didn't have the Bible or practice Christianity. Among the Indians, we always say that it is the oldest church in the world. Gradually we learned about the second coming of Christ, and finally we accepted the Lord as our personal savior, just as in any other church. Originally, the Native American Church followed the Half Moon way. Then the Winnebagos adopted the Cross Fire way. The fireplace on their altar looks like a half-moon, but instead of tobacco smoke they use the Bible.

The Native American Church started out with the Half Moon way of the Peyote religion. They use what they call the "Generation Fireplace." On the altar they mound the earth like a half-moon, and they put a little road on that mound which represents your life from the time you were born until you come to the center, and on to when you get old and go from there to death. They put the Generation Fireplace at the altar within the tipi, and at the center of the road they place the peyote.

We know that this Generation Fireplace pushes souls to Christ. The Cross Fire way comes in after believing on the Lord Jesus Christ. In this way we put the cross at the center to represent the place where Christ gave his life for each and every one of us. So it begins with this Half Moon way and then comes into the Cross Fire way, where you believe in Christ and pass to believing on the Lord. I'm not saying that the Cross Fire way is better, but as we come along we learn about the second coming of Christ. We put the peace pipe aside and we put the Bible in its place.

When I was becoming a Christian, I heard some people say, "I'm worshipping the same God as my forefathers." I thought that was real good, but now I think our forefathers must not have had the right kind of god. I hate to say this, but it is so. In the olden days, when people from different tribes came around, they killed them. We said they were enemies because they didn't speak our language. They had the same skin as we had, but we killed them. In those days they prayed to the Great Spirit, but I don't think that's the right god. The God we found is love. He loves us all. If in the olden days they prayed to that God, why is it they killed each other as enemies?

Also, in the olden days, one tribe believed that the souls of the departed went east, riding white horses. The Happy Hunting Grounds were supposed to be over the fourth hill to the east. Other tribes said the departed souls went south, riding sorrel horses. Every tribe had different beliefs. If they prayed to the same Great Spirit in the early days, they should all have had the same belief. Christ gave His life and made a road for us to go on. That's one way: towards heaven.

Right now some traditional Indian people say this Bible doesn't belong to the Indians because the white man made it. But I never thought of it that way. I thought this Bible belongs to any wicked man, any man with a living soul in him, so that through this Bible he would be saved. This is the way I think. It wasn't for just the white men alone but for every man, every person who has a living soul within him. It's the food for that person.

I'm not saying the traditional ways are bad, but it tells in the Bible, "Choose you this day whom you will serve, whether the gods of Amorites our forefathers served; but as for me and my house, we will serve the Lord." These are not my own words; I always like to use the words of God. Some people say they are real traditional men, but Christ is also a traditional man. He's been here almost two thousand years. That's traditional; that's a long time. I was thinking that we didn't use this peyote until after 1900, but Christ was in the world two thousand years ago. I think that's more traditional than what we have been trying to do here.

In the traditional way of worshipping in the Native American Church, the leader is called a *road man*. We still have our traditional way, especially in this area. In the traditional way we pray with the tobacco and corn-shock cigarette in place of the peace pipe. I held a service like that the other night, a back-to-school meeting. I prayed for the little ones who are going back to school. So we still have our traditional way as well. I ordained some of the traditional road men as ministers of the church. I did this because if we don't it will just be tradition, and we won't be recognized as a church.

The peyote that we use is classified as a drug by the state of South Dakota. We use it in the Native American Church as a sacrament. Because we are organized as a church, the government can't take the peyote away from us. Our church is the last thing we have among the Indian people, the peyote way of worshipping. We call it *Pejuta yuta okolakiciye*, "medicine-eating church." The Native American Church is organized among the Sioux in South Dakota on three reservations: Pine Ridge, Rosebud, and Yankton. I have some ministers working on all three of these reservations. We are supposed to keep records, but I really don't know how many members there are. The other tribes still hang onto the traditional way of worshipping. They don't want to organize as a church, but the Sioux organized as a church. I think this is good, because other churches will recognize us as a church.

My grandpa and my dad told me that when they first started using peyote in the community of Allen, the Indian police would sneak up on them and stop them. They would take away the drum and the peyote. At that time my mother was real small, and she was going to the boarding school at Pine Ridge. While she was there, they found out that she had tuberculosis. In those days it was considered incurable. They placed my mother in the hospital, in a little room all by herself. No one was supposed to go near her because the disease was contagious. So they kept her there.

One day a grandma of mine was visiting the sick ones in the hospital. The door to my mother's room was open just a little bit. Her eyes were swollen nearly closed, and her body was swollen up; she was dying. As she lay there, she was looking towards the door, and she recognized the lady who went by. Mother called her name, so that lady came into the room. Although she was my mother's aunt, she didn't recognize my mother for awhile. Pretty soon she recognized her. "Is that you?" she said. "Yeah, that's me."

"Why are you lying here like this? Did you let your dad know that you're here?" My grandma on my mother's side passed away when my mother was real small, so she grew up with no mother, just my grandpa. I don't know what had happened, but the hospital hadn't notified my grandfather. So this grandma of mine said, "As soon as I get home I'm going to go to your dad and I'm going to tell him that you are here." I guess that made my mother feel real good. She said, "You do that."

Sure enough, in a few days my grandpa went after her. In those days there were just buggies, no cars. My grandpa really got mad because he had not been notified that my mother was sick. But the doctor told my grandpa not to take my mother because she had that contagious disease and was going to die anyway. Still, my grandpa took her home.

When they got home, my mother started taking that medicine, the peyote. They started giving her the medicine. My mother told me that it was towards springtime. All through that summer they would give her medicine, put her on a horse, and let her go out riding. She'd be on that horse most all day long. When she came back in the evening they would give her some more medicine. After a few months she was well. She was all right.

About that time they were caught while they were holding a Native American Church service. The man who ran the store at Allen at that time was against peyote, and he was the one who caught them. They called him *Nape Blaska*, "Flat-handed," because his hands were deformed. All of them got caught, including my mother, so they took them to Deadwood for trial. The court said that peyote was a narcotic, that it was no good. The judge asked, "Why are you using that?"

My mother's dad said: "This is good. This peyote's good. It is good medicine and I can prove it."

"What have you got to prove it with?"

"This girl here." So they had my mother stand up. "This girl had tuberculosis. The doctors gave up on her. She was placed in the sanitarium. I got her away from there. Now she's alive today."

Luckily, the doctor who had cared for my mother was in the courtroom. He asked her if she was Jessie Black Bear. "Yeah, it's me," she said.

He said, "How did you get well?"

"Through the peyote, through what we have here. I got well through that."

I guess the doctor got up and shook her hand, saying: "I thought you were gone a long time ago. I thought you were dead."

So right away the judge said, "I have nothing to do with this." "These mescal beans must be good," he said. (In those days they called peyote mescal beans.) "These mescal beans are yours; they don't belong to the white man. Give them back to them." So they gave the whole thing back, a wooden barrel full of peyote.

This is the reason that people say my mother is the one who saved the peyote. If she hadn't been there, they would have had a hard time proving that this medicine was good. After this happened, that man *Nape Blaska* went back and got into some kind of trouble. I guess he was in debt and couldn't pay, so he killed himself in the garage—committed suicide.

My dad was from Porcupine community. His family lived right across the road from here. My dad was born and raised here. He belonged to the Episcopal Church. My grandpa on my dad's side was a minister in that church. And my mother was from Allen, where the peyote church originated. They didn't tell me how they met, but anyway they got married. But my dad didn't like this medicine. He didn't believe in it. So whenever he went to Allen, and they started tying a drum for a service, he would take off. He didn't like to hear the drum or the songs. He would get on his horse and go way over the hill someplace. When they were through, he would come back. He did that for four years, I think.

My dad didn't believe in the peyote, but at the same time he was always thinking about it. He wondered, "What does it do for these people when they eat it?" Some people told him that when you ate it you got high, just like drinking. My dad never drank and never smoked. I guess he grew up like that. So he was wondering; he had it in mind all the time. But at the same time he was scared to use it because some people said it was dope.

Finally one day, when my mother and dad were alone, he said to my mother, "Jessie, I wonder if you could give me some of that medicine you eat?"

"Sure," she said. So she picked out four dried ones. She gave them to my dad and he started to eat one. This medicine is very bitter, so as he started to chew on it, he quickly took it out of his mouth. "This is awful," he said. "I don't see how you could eat it and why you would eat it. It's no good, not fit to be eaten." Then he got up. "This is not a thing to eat," he said. He started towards the stove, and although my mother tried to stop him, she couldn't. He opened that stove, threw the peyote in there, and burned it up.

Four days later, all of a sudden my dad couldn't pass any water. It stopped completely. His kidneys were swelling up, so he came back to Porcupine. His father sent for a doctor from Rapid City. That doctor came in a hurry; the Indians called him *Wasicu Wakan Witkokola*, "Crazy Doctor." He came and got his bag out and examined my father all over. I guess he told my grandpa: "If I wanted to, I could give your boy some medicine, but I want to tell you the truth. That boy's not going to live four days. You'd better get ready for it. There's no medicine that will cure him."

So my grandfather heard that. Then he wrote out a note and gave it to my father. "You take this to your father-in-law," he said. So they got in a buggy and rushed back to Allen, about twenty miles on the cut-across. When they got there, they gave that note to my grandpa on that side. He said, "Yeah, I got good medicine for that." My dad wanted to find out what kind of medicine he had. I guess he kept asking my mother, "What kind of medicine does your father have?" Finally my mother told him. "It's the same medicine that you burned here not too long ago." My dad said: "Well, that's it. If that's the medicine they are going to give, I don't want any. I'd rather die. I'm not going to eat it." "I'm not going to take it," he said.

My dad's older brother went with them on this trip. He's still alive today, over ninety years old. My dad was real young in those days. And I guess my uncle said to my father, "Brother, you're a coward." He said: "You're a coward. I'll eat it. You're scared of it. I'll eat it first," he said.

You know how young men are. When my dad heard that about being a coward and being scared, he got mad. "Well, bring all you got," he said. "I'll eat everything you got. Bring everything." So right away they told my grandfather. "Okay," he said. They got everything ready in no time. They boiled some of the powdered medicine in water to make tea, and they started giving my dad some of the dried medicine to eat. My dad said he didn't know how much he ate. "A lot of it," he said, "and I drank a lot of tea." His stomach and his kidneys were so swollen he could hardly walk. "I could hardly move," he said.

They were beating a drum, but it seemed to my dad that they were very slow to begin. My grandpa went after some boys, and pretty soon they came back and started their service. That morning my dad had to be excused, so he went out. There was no longer anything wrong with him. Back there about three gallons of water came out of him, I guess.

This is the way my dad told it. He said, "That's good medicine—real good medicine. It could cure anything. But the way they're praying with it, that's another thing." He grew up in the Episcopal Church, so he didn't believe in the Native American Church. "How can they pray with that peyote? How can they say that it is holy and leading a man to Christ? How could it be?" My dad kept going to church. Then one day he took some medicine, and I guess it showed him. Although he never brought out what happened, he learned that those who were weak in faith could benefit from using the peyote, that it was put here for the Indian people to lead them to Christ.

Now some of us are Christians—you might say born-again Christians. That's what we are. As we come along, we try to do whatever other churches are doing. In the past we had the Half Moon way of worshipping, and we used the peace pipe in our services, because the peace pipe is the traditional way of worshipping among our Sioux Indian people. As we came along, we put the peace pipe away, and in place of it we now use the Bible, so that we may be saved in the end. I know and believe that the Great Spirit in heaven did this for the Indian people, so that through this medicine we would find Christ.

In my own life I have experienced this, and I've told a lot of people about it. Indians from all tribes went out to hunt for roots to use as medicines, so God put this peyote here for the Indians to find. They call it peyote, but we say *pejuta*, which means "medicine" in our language. All the different tribes call it "medicine" in their own languages. Because God loves all of us he put this medicine in the world so that the Indians would find it and through it they would come to Christ.

Today I am well-known among other tribes as a good person because I have the fear of the Lord and I love God and I love Jesus Christ. If you live this way you'll get somewhere. I went to school as far as the fifth grade at Holy Rosary Mission at Pine Ridge, South Dakota. Some of the teachers there talked against our church and said that I was a dope eater. The boys I played with got scared of me. They said, "Don't go close to Spider cause he's going to poison you. He's a dope eater. He's no good." Sometimes I cried in the classroom, or on the playground, because I wanted to have friends but the boys didn't like me. They always said things like that to me as I grew up.

About two years ago they called me to that same place where I went to school. The people there used to hate me for using this peyote, but now they wanted to find out more about it. I didn't refuse them, because I have the love of God. I went back and told them about what the peyote had done for me.

To start with, we had our services in a tipi, with a fire burning inside. Our instruments were the drum, rattle, and feather fan. And we used God's plant, the Divine Herb. Through that, some of us—not all of us, but some of us—have become Christians. We're walking hand in hand doing the Christian walk. It's pretty hard to put in words; I think it's a mystery of God and no one can bring it out in words. But I'm going to try my best to explain some of what happened to me.

One time, before I became a Christian, I was sick. At that time I used the Divine Herb and I was healed by Christ. I got hurt when I was fifteen years old. The sickness I had was osteomyelitis. The doctors told me that it's incurable. There's no medicine on earth that will cure it, they said. And sure enough, the peyote eased my pain, but it didn't kill the disease. They said it's in my bones. I got hurt when I was young, and it started from there. When I was sick, I got double pneumonia, too. I was on my deathbed. I overheard the doctor talking to my parents, and he said if I didn't make it through that night, I would die. The doctor was telling my dad and my mom to be ready.

That day a preacher came into my room, passing out tracts. He gave me one, but I couldn't read it. I had poor eyesight, so I couldn't read it. So I just put it on the table. I was lying down. I couldn't get up from bed.

I couldn't sit up, and I could hardly talk. That morning—I think it was a Sunday—it was coming daylight, and I remembered that the old people used to tell us that that's the time to talk to God. If you tell Him something, He'll hear you, they said. So that morning I was praying on my deathbed that if it's at all possible, I wanted to live longer.

God must have pitied me, because that morning He called me by my name. It was real loud. It was the first time I heard something like that, and it really hit me hard. The voice said, "Emerson!" real loud in the room. I couldn't get up from the bed but I answered that call. I said: "What? I am over here. I'm lying here." I thought it was one of the other boys in the room with me. There were about four other patients who were about to die, too, so they were placed in the room. But when I looked around they were all in bed asleep. I just started to go back to sleep again when I heard it a second time. It got me out of bed, sitting up. I noticed I was sitting up as I said, "Hau! I'm over here. What do you want?" But there was no answer, so I lay back down again.

The third time the voice got me to my feet, standing up. I knew that I was on my feet standing up. I walked towards the aisle and looked around, and here it was, the high calling of God; and it seemed like cold water on my face that morning, like it tells in the Scriptures about spiritual baptism. And that morning Christ healed me from my sickness. So I rejoice in the Lord every day of my life. Every time in the morning, ever since then when I get up I praise the Lord. I give Him thanks every day of my life. That's the life I'm leading now.

When I came back to the bed, I noticed the tract that had been given to me. I picked it up and read it, and it said, "Come as you are." Christ was speaking. "Come as you are." I knew it meant me, because I was a real sinner. I was no good, but it said *as I am*, He wants me to come to Him. And it says in there, "If any man comes unto me, I shall in no ways cast him out." So I know Christ called me by my name to be a leader of our church. I was supposed to stop sinning and try to be a good person because I was going to be the leader of the church. I was married when I was twenty-one, and when I was twenty-three years old I stopped drinking and smoking.

While I was coming along, there were some Christians who said to me: "You should come to our church where you won't be shedding tears for your people. Although you try to tell them right from wrong, they don't listen to you. Our church will listen to you," they said. But God wanted me to go where the church wasn't doing right, to tell them about the second coming of Christ. So actually God sent me to this Native American Church. He used me as a tool of the church to be the head man to try and guide them in the right way.

In our church we have leader helpers who can hold a service if there is no leader present. I remained a leader helper for a long time. Then I became a candidate leader. And then I became the chief leader. I gave information on how to hold a service. Gradually I became the headman of the community; you might say a minister of the community, the headman of the local branch. Then pretty soon, when the assistant man who sat next to my dad passed away, they appointed me his assistant. So I came to it step by step, and then when my dad passed away, I became the high priest.

Before my dad passed away, he said: "This is my best. I want you to make it right for me." So that's what I'm doing now. I'm trying to make the other non-peyote people see that I can lead a Christian life in the Native American Church. I stand up for my church and say that it is a good church.

By rights we can hold our church services most any time. During the summertime we can have our services any time of the week, but during the wintertime we have to have services on Saturday because the kids have to go to school Monday. And lately some of the church members have been working, too, so we have to consider them. Also, the cost of the medicine we use is getting real high. Usually we go and harvest it ourselves, but the trip is very expensive. I know just lately there are people selling land to get the money to go and harvest peyote and bring it back.

It takes four persons to run a service: the leader, the drummer, the cedar man and the fire man. They don't pick out just anybody for these positions.

The man who takes care of the drum is supposed to be a certain kind of man who knows how to hit the drum. He can't live a wicked life and handle the drum. It's sacred to the Indians. Indians really like the drum. It is made into a great big drum which they use at powwows and things like that. We use that same drum, but we make it into a real small drum, and we use it to praise and sing unto the Lord. For that reason the drummer has to be a certain kind of person to hit that drum. He has to know how to sing, how to hit the drum, and how to live a good life. He must know how to make instruments in the church.

The man who takes care of the cedar throughout the night has to be a man who knows how to pray to the Great Creator, to the Great Spirit. He has to take care of the prayers. Every time a person prays, he burns cedar. We use the cedar smoke as incense, just like the Catholic Church. We were told that a long time ago the old people made smoke signals in order to send messages to others far away. We were told that we're doing that. That's the reason they used the peace pipe to pray to the Great Spirit, making smoke signals to pray with. During our church services in the tipi we burn that cedar whenever somebody prays, so that the smoke goes up. Our understanding is that we are making smoke signals to the Great Spirit so that He will hear our prayers. That's what we have been told.

The fire man is supposed to know how to build the fire; they don't just throw the wood into the fireplace. This man has to know how to chop and gather wood, how to build a tipi, and things like that. We have a fire going inside the tipi all the time, so this man takes care of it, he watches it. He's the only man who moves in the church, like an altar boy in the Catholic Church. He goes out, brings wood in, and keeps that fire burning. In our church building we have lights, but when we hold traditional services in the tipi, we have to keep the fire going all night.

In the traditional way our services started at sundown and continued until sunrise. That's the way it used to be. But nowadays the people come late. When the leader, drummer, cedar man, and fire man all arrive, then we start our service.

There are different instruments that we use in our services in order to praise the Lord. To start with we use this staff, which we call *sagye*. That means "cane" in our language. Each man, when he sings in the service, holds onto this cane.

We use this small drum, tied in a certain way, with water inside. Only a few men know how to tie and beat the drum. We call it a holy drum.

We use this drumstick, which can be made from all kinds of wood. One kind is called snake wood. It makes a really good-looking stick.

We use this gourd rattle, which each man holds when it is his turn to sing.

We use this sage. From the beginning of our church, the Half Moon way, we have used this sage. It was used as a traditional way of praying. They were told that they should use it to refresh themselves, to cleanse themselves, before going into a ceremonial like the Sun Dance or sweat lodge or fasting. If you wipe yourself with it there is a good fresh smell and it cleans you. That's the reason they used it all over the body in the sweat lodge. For that reason the traditional way of worship in our church uses sage. They hit themselves all over with that sage to clean themselves. Then they partake of the Divine Herb.

We use this bone whistle, made from the wing bone of an eagle. The leader blows it in a ceremonial way during the service.

We use this fan, made from different kinds of bird feathers, to perform holy orders. To start with, they used to use a feather fan made from two swift hawk tails, twelve feathers on each bird, a total of twenty-four. These feathers are arranged to form a circle. On the outside are four eagle feathers, and inside, at the center, is an eagle plume. They say this swift hawk is the swiftest bird in the world, and they say the eagle is the fiercest bird. The plume inside the fan represents the living soul that's in a person. We were told that the tail feathers are there for the swift hawks to try to catch the living soul, the spirit of a man, the soul of each person. They can surround him and catch that living soul. The eagle plume is there so that if any bad spirit comes, the eagle will fight that spirit away. This is the way we were taught by our elders. We should use this type of feather fan to come out of the traditional way into a Christian way of worship.

Today they make fans from red and blue macaw feathers, and what they call scissortails—real pretty feathers. They bring all these different feathers into the church. They're good, they're God's creation, but it didn't come to us like that from the start.

Finally, we use the Divine Herb. When a person takes the peyote in a service, if he has teeth, he usually eats it dry. When I was young, when I had teeth, I could eat it dry. Sometimes they grind it up. Then a person can put the powder in his hand and eat it like that. Or he can mix it with water and make it into a kind of gravy and eat it like that. We also make tea out of the powdered peyote, using warm water. The peyote is very bitter. If you can eat four of them it is good, and if you can eat more, it will do you a lot of good.

When peyote first started to come into our area, we used our native tongue all the time to preach the word of God. I have a Bible that's written in our language, and I can read it well. Gradually our young people have gone to school and gotten a good understanding of English. The man who had this church building built is half Sioux and half Shoshone, but he was raised in a city, so he didn't learn either the Sioux language or the Shoshone language. He speaks just this whiteman language. So when we have our services and there's no person who doesn't speak our language, we usually talk in our own native tongue. But when somebody who doesn't understand our language comes into our church, we try to perform everything in English so it will be understandable. But some things we can't do in English, because we were brought up in a certain way and it has to be that way. It doesn't have to be understood by other men, just so the Great Spirit will understand us, listen to us, hear us. We believe that way.

During the service we sing songs in groups of four. Some are in Lakota and others are in English. These are the words to one set of songs. I composed the first song using words from my favorite gospel hymn; the words of the third song are in English, and the other three are in Lakota:

(1)   I have decided to follow Jesus.
       No turning back.

(2)   Jesus I love your words
       Because your words are eternal life.
       Give me life.
       I love your words.

(3)   Praise our Lord Savior Jesus.
       Did you know that our Lord Savior Jesus died upon the
       cross for our sins?
       Praise our Lord Savior Jesus.

(4)   God, look upon us Indians,
       We want to be saved.

After the service we eat a breakfast of four symbolic foods. They are sacred to the Indians and are eaten not for the body but for spiritual strength.

The first is water. They say everything lives by water, so in the morning we have a woman bring in water and pray over it. This is because in the beginning it was a woman who first found the peyote. Later, when the Indians learned to read the Bible, they found out about the well of Jacob, and about Christ saying "I am the living water." They found where Christ says: "The water you will give me, I'll be thirsty again, but the water I'll give you, you will never be thirsty. You will become a spring within yourself." This is what it tells in the Scripture, so they pray over the water for spiritual strength.

The second is corn. Usually at this time of year they have fresh corn on the cob, but in the wintertime they used dried corn, which they cook so it comes out just like it was fresh. We have been told that before the white men ever came across, the Indians knew how to plant corn. They already had that here and they lived by it. They use this to pray that their gardens will be good; they pray over the corn that in the summertime everything will grow real good.

The third is meat. A long time ago they used only dried meat, but today they use any kind of meat, usually beef. They boil it and serve it with soup, although some pass around just the meat itself. In the olden days the Indians used to have a lot of livestock, cattle, and wild animals like deer and buffalo. So they prayed over the meat that the hunting season would be good, that their children would have good food.

The fourth is fruit. The old people prayed over the fruit so that the wild fruits along the creeks would grow for the Indians to use. They pounded the fruit up and dried it so it would keep.

All the church services we have are not alike. We have services for birthdays, healing, marriage, baptism, prayers, funerals—anything, we have it all. Every service is different. That's the mystery of God.

One time we had a healing service here which pretty much surprised us. We had a man who was going to have surgery for gallstones, and we had a healing service here and gave him medicine. He was seated right near the altar. A girl suffering with arthritis was seated across the room, against the east wall. We performed their healing. Lately we're trying to get the healing of Jesus Christ. We don't give sick people a whole bunch of medicine like in the olden times, but we just give them so much. One Scripture I used was, "Any man sit among you, let him call the elders of the church that they anoint him with oil, pray over him that he may get well, and if he commits any sin, it shall be forgiven." These are the Lord's words, so I used them. That man was healed right there that night. And the girl, even though she wasn't out in the center of the church, was also healed. So things like this happen. It's altogether different than the works of the peyote.

I might put it this way. When people come to a service and partake of the Divine Herb, it works on them in different ways. That's the mystery of God. Sometimes, even if a person is no good, the peyote will work for him. Through the peyote he will throw away the evil and give himself to Christ. In this way some of our church members have put away alcohol, become Christians, and gotten good jobs again. And they help other people in the church, too.

One time my dad went to a prayer ceremony. He must have eaten a lot of medicine, and the service was going on and on. And all at once he saw the door open, so he looked over there and here was a man coming in. It seemed like nobody else noticed that man coming in. But my dad kept watching him, and that man came up to him and said: "I've been looking for you all over. I couldn't find you. I heard that you were in a meeting someplace. I went to one meeting but you weren't there, so I came over here." He sat beside my dad and said, "Tonight I'm going to pray with you, sing with you." So my dad was happy. My dad wasn't a drummer, but he was a good singer, had a good voice. And my dad was a minister and a good man. The visitor had a box with him, so he took his instruments out. Everything he had was perfect. When the singing came to them, the visitor sang first. He sang good songs, real pretty songs. Then he hit the drum for my dad, but he made that drum sound different, a good sound. Then he talked and prayed, prayed real good, prayed so interestingly that the people started crying. He was really good at everything.

My dad was watching him, but he never did see the man talking. Then he saw that the man was going around to every person in there, looking at their prayer instruments, opening their boxes up and taking a good look at their instruments. Then, finally, he came to where the altar was, and he looked at everything there. They had this Divine Herb there, which they were partaking of. My dad saw him open it, and suddenly it seemed like somebody had hit the man in the face and knocked him toward the door. When he landed by the door, my dad could see his tail and horns. As he was going out, he looked back at my dad and said: "I'm going to come back and visit you again. Someday I'm going to come back again."

From this we know that the Evil One can come into any place, even a church. The Evil One can read the Bible, he can talk, he can pray, but he doesn't believe in Christ. He says he believes in Christ, that he knows Christ, but doesn't believe it. He's that powerful, fooling people all over the world. So a man should be aware that the Evil One can come anywhere.

Through my work in the church I came to know many things. One thing I wanted to find out for sure is where the souls of our departed ones are. I went around to different ministers, different churches. "I want you to tell me the truth of it," I said. "Where is paradise?" But no one could answer me. So I came back to my church and finally learned that the departed souls are here. They're not going any place. When we pray in the prayer service, and we are thinking about our departed loved ones, they come near us. They come right close to us. The only thing I found out about it in the Scriptures is that the departed souls are just like they are behind glass. They're on the other side, we're on this side. They see us, but we can't see them; they hear us, but we can't hear them. That's how it is. I found this out in our church and by reading the Scriptures, that the departed ones are always here with us. I thought this was real nice.

We are Indian people, and we still have some of our traditional ways. One thing we have, which the Indians grew up with, is what we call the spiritual food for our departed ones. Long ago, when people were eating something good, they would think about their loved ones who had gone beyond. Then they would take a little bit of the food they were eating and throw it outside, saying, *"Wanagi le iyakiya,"* which means, "Spirit, find this." When my grandpa and my grandma were alive, I saw them do this, and we still have this. We couldn't part with the things that the traditionals had, so we still have them.

They prayed for these departed ones, too, and they talked to them. They grew up with that. The Bible says that when a person dies he knows nothing, he can't hear, he can't see. But the Indians say that for four days that body is holy. It can see you, it can hear you, they say. One time I went to a gospel mission. The preacher was a white man. His wife had just died, and they were having a wake service. I said: "This lady is not dead, she's sleeping, I think, resting. So she sees you." And that man started crying. He said to me, "Those are comforting words that you brought here, words we never heard before."

"That's the way I was taught," I said, "and that's the way it is." So I prayed over her, and I talked to that dead body, because that's how I was brought up.

There are some traditional things that we still have in the Cross Fire way, things we still hang onto because we grew up with them and we're Indians. But actually I don't know about the next generations, the coming generation. I notice that every generation changes. Things are changing.

I was told that God created all men equal, so this was the reason He put the peyote here for the Indians. Some of us didn't find out about it for a long time. But it is a good thing that my grandfather and my father found out about it, because it helped us to find Christ. Lately I have been going around to other churches and to schools telling about what our church is doing for us Indian people. For this reason I am happy to put my talk in a book so that people will read it and learn about our church. The days are getting short. The second coming of the Lord is at hand and we're getting ready for it. People will not be judged according to their beliefs, or according to which church they belong to. God will not say, "What kind of church do you belong to? What ways do you have?" It's not going to be that way. The bad things we've done and the good things we've done shall be weighed; and if we do good we'll be in the arms of Christ. It doesn't matter what church we belong to—the church will not save us. These are things I want to bring out to people, especially to the younger generation.

I would like you to understand that the fear of the Lord is the beginning of all knowledge. It says in the Scriptures that it doesn't matter if you gain the whole world's knowledge if you don't have the fear of the Lord. You have to be good in every way and put Christ ahead of you all the time so you won't go wrong. If you put your beliefs or anything else ahead of Christ, you'll be wrong. This world will come to an end. Everything must be stopped. So you need to have the true love of God to be saved.

Some people tell me that the knowledge of this world is the key to tomorrow. That's what they say. This earthly knowledge is good; it's necessary to get by in this world. I wish that the boys and girls will stay in school and learn—but put Christ ahead of your schooling. Read your Bible and you'll be safe in the arms of Christ. There is no other way to salvation.

If you come to the Lord, no matter what sickness you have, you can be healed. I was healed and now I'm a born-again Christian, and I'm working for my church. It used to be that when we had the traditional way of worshipping, we believed in earthly life. Now we believe in the second coming of Christ, although we still have our traditional ways. We still believe in them. I believe in the Sun Dance and fasting and all the traditional ways. I believe that they are sacred and I believe that they are good. But they are earthly, so by them alone no man will be saved.

The second coming of Christ is the only way to salvation. So I want you to know me and I want you to understand my church. There are some Christians who don't know our church, who may even think we are uncivilized. I want the Native American Church to be recognized by other churches. And I want people everywhere to pray for us, too.

Who Can Sit at the Lord's Table?
The Experience of Indigenous Peoples

ROSEMARY McCOMBS MAXEY

The purpose of this essay is to explore the place of indigenous peoples' religions within and without the diverse theological stances of the United Church of Christ. Indigenous people are those who today are called American Indians or Native Americans. I intend to recall briefly the history of the Euro-American Christian movement and the indigenous peoples' responses in early "American" history thereby creating a base for a deeper understanding of Native American particularization of their perspectives as they relate to Christian churches today. The major thrust has to do with relationships, not with classical definitions of ecclesiology as proposed by European and Euro-American scholars. Relationships link the present with past and future and link people with all creation. Theologically, environmentally, and in their holistic understanding of human nature, indigenous people have much insight to offer to those who seem to have garnered the best seats for themselves at the Lord's Table. The United Church of Christ, which carries as its motto "That They May All Be One" and proclaims its unity in diversity, should be especially receptive to the voices of indigenous people who desire room at the table.

Historical Survey

Beginning with the "discovery" made by Christopher Columbus, Christians have struggled with the issue of what should be done with the original inhabitants of the New World. When Columbus returned from his first voyage in 1493, a squabble arose between the kingdoms of Castile and Portugal over possession of the lands of the New World. The Pope intervened with four papal bulls in 1493 and one in 1506, in them demarcating lands, giving most of the New World to Spain, which would convert the pagan indigenous inhabitants. Other European countries denounced or ignored the Pope's bulls, but throughout the sixteenth century theologians, jurists, historians, friars, and administrators debated what to do with the indigenous people. In 1550 the issue was debated by the Catholic Church's Council of Fourteen. Two theological camps emerged. Bishop Bartolome de las Casas debated one side: that the noble savages were developed in the arts, languages, and government. They were gentle, eager to learn, and quick to accept Christianity. The other side, represented by Gines de Sepulveda, argued that these creatures were savage-like, slaves by nature, pagan, uncivilized, incapable of learning, and unable to govern themselves.[2] The issue was what to do with the aboriginal inhabitants, whether they were entitled to the soil, and what could be done to them if they refused the beneficence of "lumbre y doctrina" ("light and doctrine" or "light and teaching"). The debate ended in Las Casas's favor, but when missionaries came from Europe, the results were more closely tied to Sepulveda's argument.[3] And for five hundred years, the primary mission strategy of many mainline denominations has followed or paralleled that early approach.

Common historic interests have always existed between the indigenous people of North America and the forebears of the United Church of Christ. In 1629 the Congregationalists began efforts to include indigenous people in the Christian fold. With well-intentioned, dedicated missionaries, the general thrust was to "wynn and invite the Natives . . . [to] the onlie God and Savior of Mankinde."[4] Missionaries from that time to the present have consistently tried to make indigenous people participate in the church as acculturated Euro-American Christians. Indigenous people have resisted, reacted, and responded in a variety of ways to Christianity as presented by the missionaries. A monograph in the United Church of Christ Heritage Series, *Two Spirits Meet*, traces the process of cultural change and conflict:

Prof. Robert Berkhofer, in Salvation and the Savage, *demonstrated that when missionaries successfully converted part of the tribe, they set off a sequence of events through which the tribal unit frequently crumbled. Berkhofer studied Protestant mission history of the one-hundred-year period prior to the Civil War. He outlined a sequence of four stages. After missionaries converted some members of a tribal group, either the traditional or the Christian group was ostracized. The ostracized group usually moved and separated physically from the other members of the tribe. However, both groups frequently reunited physically in the face of common military threats. After they reunited and reestablished common government, political factions emerged, usually based on religion, which prevented the tribe from taking totally effective actions.*[5]

The same continues to be true today. Three patterns of participation can be discerned among the indigenous people who relate to the United Church of Christ. The first, occurring in the earliest relationships with the missionaries, was the development of native churches. Using their tribal language in worship and church polity, single tribal churches developed along family, clan, and community lines. These churches exist today among the Dakotas and the Winnebagos.

Second, in 1982, a multitribal congregation was started in Minnesota, called All Nations Indian Church. Incorporating some of the symbols of their ancestors and their native languages, this church worships and provides services to the community. The third pattern involved other indigenous people over the years who joined Anglo churches and became involved in them to varying degrees, sometimes minimizing their identity with the indigenous community, sometimes assimilating in terms of worship but maintaining an identity with the tribal community.

My own relationship with the church as a Muscogee (Creek) Indian Christian has taken me through all three relationships. Three generations of my family have been Christian in a tribal community church affiliated with the Southern Baptist Convention. The Muscogee language is spoken in worship and business. During college and seminary, and immediately thereafter, I attempted to assimilate with the Anglo churches by working in new church development. It was not until I was a member of a multiracial church in New York City that I began to question the Euro-American nature of all Christian churches and to search for a new church relationship where the attempts at pluralism were more intentional. My search ended when I moved to Westminster, Maryland, and became friends with the leaders of a United Church of Christ congregation. In the tradition of my grandfather, who said, "I will be a Baptist because I have met a real good one," I became a member of the United Church of Christ because I met some "real good ones" who shared with me convincing evidence of the United Church of Christ's genuine interest in pluralism and ecumenism.

Since joining this congregation I have been privileged to sit with those in conference and association-level consultations who are serious about theology and serious about ecumenicity. But even they are more apt to cling to investigating "the unity." With furrowed brows, members of theological consultations and study groups pore over an array of theological position papers looking for that shred of evidence that enables them to proclaim, Aha! We are alike after all! Let's celebrate our unity. The fact that the United Church of Christ cannot declare a single or at least a four-strand theological position bothers even the most progressive theologian. The nameless "they" seem to push the panic button. "Other denominations make fun of the United Church of Christ because it is too diverse to take a theological position. . . . The UCC has been accused of a murky Christology," wailed two theologians in my presence recently.

From an indigenous person's perspective, I raise some questions about the denomination's proclaimed inclusivity. One must ask, What exactly is the criteria for sitting diversely together at the Lord's Table? What conditions and limits are placed on such an invitation? Do the indigenous peoples' ways of living and believing keep them marginalized in the United Church of Christ because there is no Euro-American theological or ecclesiastical category for them at the Lord's Table?

Can indigenous people, in their diversity, and others in the United Church of Christ, in their diversity, sit side by side in wholeness to strategize and pray for a realization of an eschatology that restores the unity of a fragmented world? Can we, in our united particularities, prepare our human communities for the wholeness that is more than people, and includes the entire cosmos?

There are difficulties in addressing these questions. In the first place, there is no way of presenting a single homogeneous view of the indigenous peoples. We are as varied and diverse as the United Church of Christ claims to be. We are many tribal groups and nations who vary in culture, thought, government, and language. However, some tribal and national commonalities exist in theological beliefs about the deity, ceremonies that celebrate the relationship between the Creator and the created, the origins of humankind, and the relationship and responsibility for living within the created order.[6] We also have many symbols and rituals that are common to us and parallel those of the Christian church. We often practice parallel Christian/Traditional rituals and rites simultaneously.

The second difficulty is our loss of pure culture. What was ideal and complete culturally cannot be entirely regained. Exploitation, relocation, assimilation, loss of sacred land bases, and loss of many of our languages (our roots of understanding) hinder us from achieving our cultural and religious goals, our ways of being. Most of us have become "diaspora people" in our own homeland.

The third difficulty in presenting the indigenous peoples' perspective is the "majority" audience who will read this essay. Conveying ideas in our common language of English is incomplete and misunderstood because of our differing world views, which remain largely unexplored and foreign to one another.

The motivation for listening to each other should, however, point to our mutual need for understanding, respecting, and living with each other. Indigenous people need the help of Christian churches in advocacy for justice and survival as distinct peoples. Christian churches need the indigenous people to help the church reclaim the activity of a particularly significant and faithful community of believers. That is, Christian people need to undertake their specific mission in the world, understand their possession of a sacred history, and live out their sacred duty to humankind and to the cosmos.

Further, the church needs to hear the indigenous peoples' voices regarding place in the universe and care for the created order. The United Church of Christ is just now doing its exegetical work on environmental theology and stewardship and coming to the same conclusions that the Ancient Ones have proclaimed all along.

Identity versus Assimilation

In December 1978, the Native American Project (now called the Indigenous Peoples Project to avoid confusion of "Native Americans" as a reference to second and third generations of others who have staked a claim in "America") of Theology in the Americas worked out a position paper to describe and analyze the commonalities that exist for indigenous peoples in their religions and the effects Christianity has had on them. The uniqueness of this project lies in the sixty-five indigenous people who participated. They included Catholic and Protestant Christians and traditionalists (those who practice only their tribal religions) from urban and reservation dwelling places and represented some fifteen tribal nations.

The common beliefs or themes that emerged follow:

> We are an ancient people whose religious oral traditions declare that we have lived and evolved in these lands since the beginning of time. Examining our history, our traditions and our beliefs, we find creation stories that point to a time of birth from out of the earth and a covenant relationship with a Creator Spirit that is unique to this part of the world. We know that we have always been integral to this part of the world; we did not come from anywhere else. We know that our covenant with the Life Giving Force did not end and was not negated with the arrival of Christopher Columbus, the Mayflower or any other foreign vessel that has ever come to this continent. Many of our tribal people have clung tenaciously to the ancient beliefs and ritual ceremonies of our people even under persecution: therefore, we have survived as distinct peoples with a history and a place in the cosmos.[7]

With the introduction of Christianity to the tribes, some of our people, regardless of tribal affiliation, found the teachings of Jesus similar and compatible to the ancient moral and ethical teachings of our people. Jesus' teachings were accepted by many who did not give up their understanding of their place in the universe as taught in traditional instruction prior to missionary influence. Indigenous peoples have started churches of their own and conducted the business of the church from a tribal perspective, that is, using the same style of selecting a minister as was used in designating a chief and designing the worship according to the model of traditional religious ceremonies. Accepting "civilization" and Christianity from this orientation was an attempt to maintain separate sovereign nations in the face of Western expansion. Ultimately, the "Indian Church" did not help maintain tribal sovereignty, but it did provide indigenous expression in a Christian mode.

Assimilation attempts by the U.S. government, working in concert with the Euro-American church, have had an impact on many of our people as well. This triumphal church approach led many of us to join the Anglo church and we often find ourselves accepting Americanized Christianity as a way of believing and living. I find that, for me, this is a dangerous way to live. The different perceptions of the ministry of the church and the Euro-American's view about humankind's place in the universe and the: church's efforts to universalize and impose its beliefs on all peoples of earth create difficulty and confusion for many indigenous people.

In spite of Christianity's doctrine of original sin and the virtue of humility, the European perception and attitude about their place ("a little lower than the angels") is quite lofty. This is the irony of a pessimistic view of sinful humanity. The contradictions between stated beliefs and the actual life style leave one to compromise and compartmentalize daily living into incompatible units. The belief that Jesus came "that all may have life" and the actual practices of genocide to indigenous peoples are strange bedfellows indeed.

Granted, the United Church of Christ has adopted an impressive and new missiology. It has become common to affirm that "the gospel is in the people and we go to them and discover the gospel in their lives." Evangelism has become more of a witnessing/inspecting mechanism to see the gospel at work and respond with awe. Is this another name for "fact-finding missions" where the church checks to see if God is at work and is surprised to find out that it is so? This missiology may have been slow in coming, but it does make way for cultural diversity within the church and may be welcomed by indigenous people who are outside the church.

Those indigenous people outside the church who maintain their tribal religious ceremonies and ways of being are referred to as the traditionalists. Indigenous people within the church who adore their heritages must express gratitude to those who in the face of adversity have held to the ancient beliefs of our peoples. It is through the efforts of the traditionalists that indigenous Christians stand a chance of regaining identity as a distinct and covenanted people. We must reconsider our old values if not our old practices, even as we take our places at the Lord's Table.

To promote greater understanding and cross-cultural exchanges, traditionalists have invited Anglos to share in ceremonials such as the Vision Quest and Sweatlodges. Recently, some of our brothers and sisters in the United Church of Christ have explored these experiences of Native Americans. Ordinarily, one would welcome these cross-cultural opportunities but two suspicions arise. These ceremonials are about the essence of survival as a covenanted people. When nonindigenous persons bypass the hardships of reservation life and what it means to be Indian in this country and move into the ceremonials for filling a personal spiritual void, are they not exploiting the religious experience for personal gain? What are they contributing back to the survival of a people and our beloved Mother Earth? Another question concerns people like those in the New Age movement. The New Age movement people who have explored Native American spirituality have turned a nice profit by writing and lecturing on Native American spirituality.

I find it odd/interesting that while some Anglos learn and experience Native American roots of spirituality, the United Church of Christ affirms and supports indigenous Christians in their efforts to learn about scripture, tradition, and reason in order to provide leadership for indigenous peoples' church community. Such engaging issues are prime topics for opening dialogue for all of us. Consider Joshua 24:25-28, where God made a covenant with the tribes of Israel:

> *So Joshua made a covenant with the people that day, and made statutes and ordinances for them at Shechem. And Joshua wrote these words in the book of the law of God; and he took a great stone, and set it up there under the oak in the sanctuary of the Lord. And Joshua said to all the people, "Behold, this stone shall be a witness against us; . . . lest you deal falsely with your God."*

Some of the psalms likewise speak of God's power in created nature. Psalm 96 says, "Sing to the Lord, all the earth! Let the heavens be glad . . . let the sea roar . . . let the field exult, and everything in it . . . the trees of the wood will sing for joy."

Perceptions of the Deity

In the Muscogee (Creek) language, the name of the creator-spirit deity is *Hesaketvmese*, that is, "Breath Holder." Other meanings include Creator (earth), Sustainer (air), Redeemer (water), Intervener (unexpected events), Lover, Intimate Confidant, and Fun-Loving Friend (gentle breezes and small whirlwinds). The deity is accessible and present throughout the entire cosmos.

The scriptures, in remarkably similar ways, attest to the presence of the deity in what are considered by the Euro-Americans to be inanimate objects. In the Gospel according to Luke, when Jesus was making the triumphant entry into Jerusalem amidst the palm waving and praise, the Pharisees in the crowd spoke to Jesus, saying, "Teacher, rebuke your disciples." He answered, "I tell you, if these [disciples] were silent, the very stones would cry out" (Luke 19:40). Passages such as these resonate vibrantly in the essence of indigenous peoples.

In the history of the church there have been a few individuals, Francis of Assisi, St. Anthony, and Julian of Norwich, for example, who have been especially spiritually alive to the Creator in the created world. In the indigenous peoples' history Black Elk is recorded as a spiritual holy man attuned to the created order, and there are many others, including women, who are known to us by oral tradition.

But greater than the enchantment of mystery in the created order and stones that shout is the recognition that nature is an active participant with human beings and has feelings. Nature may have immortal and inexhaustible qualities, but it can die and it can die at the hands of human beings if human beings are not attuned to the voices and feelings of nature.

Indigenous people call for the recognition of the Breath Holder who through the act of creation permeates all life forms. Native thought has always embraced the philosophy enculturated through our oral traditions that all of the created elements are to be revered as an elder and nurtured as a child. What creation provides is to be cared for and used by all.[8] All of creation is sacred.

Perceptions of Humankind

The stories of many tribal nations concerning the creation of human beings are not unlike the Genesis account (2:4a-23). We are created from the earth, made last, not as a hierarchical culmination, but in a more humble position.

The human being is considered the weakest of creation, entirely dependent on all other created life forms for mere existence. Gratitude, nurture, and equality are to be accorded all creation.[9] The Genesis story of the fall from grace and expulsion from Paradise (Genesis 3) should humble us, not make us proud and possessive. Christian faith aims to restore the state of grace with God and creation but Christians have alienated themselves too far from nature, making reconciliation in universal wholeness difficult.

Only in recent biblical scholarship have theologians begun to see that the Hebrew words for dominion (radah) and subdue (kabash) are antithetical to universal harmony and order.[10] Some ancient manuscripts can be read as either radah or as mashal. Could it be that substituting the Hebrew verb mashal for radah would clarify human beings' place in the created order? While the root word of mashal is difficult to trace, one of the verb's meanings is "to pattern one upon the other" as in speaking in parables. If humankind could pattern its relationship to the created order in the way the Creator is related to creation, humankind could be cocreators with God in God's world. God-likeness would generate harmony and order rather than dominion and subjugation.

Contrast that to the Euro-American distortion of the concept of "man" naming, subduing, and having dominion over the earth. This forces the earth to produce rather than allowing the earth to flourish under the rhythm of life. Western European technological arrogance has jarred the harmony of the cosmos and thwarted the Creator's intention. The drive to possess the land, rather than act as God's cocreators, further adds to the imbalance. Christianity's influence in this regard affects all humanity. The earth and every living entity have been objectified, depersonalized, and made inanimate. The concept of humankind being patterned after God, the Breath Holder and Gardenkeeper, is lost.

The United Church of Christ has exhibited concern for the environment and a desire to uphold a theology of stewardship rather than dominion. It seems, then, that one of the areas that indigenous peoples have in common with the United Church of Christ is the goal of restoring harmony with each other and the natural order. But how do we overcome our diverse perceptions of what that means?

I had the privilege of attending the first Theodore Roosevelt Environment and Conservation Symposium (Fall 1986) sponsored jointly by Grace Reformed Church in Washington, D.C., the United Church Board for Homeland Ministries, the Central Atlantic Conference of the UCC, the UCC Office for Church in Society, the Stewardship Council, and the National Wildlife Federation. While the goal of preserving creation was common to all, the contrast in approach between the United States Forestry Service and the United Church of Christ was interesting. The theological approach was that the problem is people taking over the function of God instead of recognizing that God is at home in God's world, and that God has shared God's home with nature and humankind alike as a household. The Forestry Service representative called for persons to exercise their responsibility to be God's stewards and use and renew resources as appropriate to the technology that has been developed by humankind. In other words, to the Forestry Service it seems that people have found a way to care for the world in God's absence.

The perspective of the UCC theologian is in harmony with indigenous peoples' goal of restoring and maintaining harmony with each other and the natural order. But we have a lot of work to do to overcome our diverse perceptions of what that means. Over a century ago, Chief Seattle spoke of the indigenous peoples' perspective of our human relationship to earth and the environment, the indigenous sense of harmony and the problem with the Euro-American world view. In 1854, at a time when the president of the United States was trying to negotiate a treaty, Chief Seattle said,

So we will consider your offer to buy our land. But it will not be easy. For this land is sacred to us. . . . We may be brothers after all; we shall see. One thing we know, which the white man may one day discover, our God is the same God. You may think now that you own him as you wish to own our land, but you cannot. He is the God of man, and his compassion is equal for the red man and the white. This earth is precious to him and to harm the earth is to heap contempt on its Creator. Continue to contaminate your bed, and you will one night suffocate in your own waste.[11]

A Perception of Harmony

For God so loved the world that God gave God's only Son, that whoever believes in him should not perish, but have eternal life. (John 3:16, RSV adapted)

This famous verse that the missionaries taught us, but often neglected to analyze or assess for themselves, contains real truth in the word "world." The Greek word is *kosmos,* or universe. The intention of the deity seems to be to offer salvation to all of creation. The offered salvation is not limited to the people in the church, to those who have strands of unity, but salvation is opened to the entire cosmos. Cosmic balance, harmony, and longevity belong to all of the created order in their particularities and even when there seems to be no common thread among them! Justice, ethics, and morality flow from the intertwined, interdependent, and intimate relationships of Creator and created.

Genocide, extermination, exploitation, pollution, contamination, and oppression are the acts that most upset the natural order and upset the deity. When harmony is disrupted, the Creator is sad, hurt, angry, and vengeful (in the sense that the disrupters must suffer the natural consequences of their deeds). Sometimes the deity turns away from, does not favor, those who are disruptive. Sometimes, in a manner reminiscent of Jesus' Beatitudes, the deity intervenes with those least likely to appear worthy and orthodox.

Learning the lessons of restoring harmony involves individuals and their community as they participate in the ceremonies of the tribe. It is in the seasonal, temporal, geography-centered, rigidly followed ceremonies that one learns the ways of worship, gratitude, and well-being.[12] Ceremonies always begin with prayer. Many tribes use a sacred pipe filled with special tobacco. First, offering the pipe to the four directions, then to the sky and the earth, then to "all my relatives" symbolizes the inclusion of all creation. Then, the smoking of the pipe by every person in the circle symbolizes communion and accepting the gift from the Creator and Mother Earth. Dances, such as the hoop dance of the Ojibwe, represent the circle of the universe. Other dances remind the tribe of its dependency on and relatedness to the Creator and the created.[13] In the ceremonies harmony is restored and perpetuated for the future. In the ceremonies indigenous nations express their connection with primordial time and space, with cosmic reality.

Yet the very ceremonies that ground our beings were hindered and outlawed with the arrival of Europeans. The attacks on our ways of life are unparalleled in human history and our ability to regain and restore these ceremonies in their fullest sense is all but lost.

What Can we Do at the Lord's Table?

Vine Deloria, Jr., says, "Tribal religions have a very difficult time advocating their case (in the courts) . . . They may have to wait for the radical changes now occurring within Western religious institutions to take root and flourish before much progress can be made. Protestantism is increasing its ceremonial/ritual life, and Catholicism is becoming more secular, so that behavior comparable to tribal ceremonial behavior among Christians may not be far off."[14]

The United Church of Christ is noted for its diversity within the Euro-American theological tradition, in its historic pluralism and flexibility, its ecumenical interest, and its being on the cutting edge of social issues as a prophetic voice in the world. If this church can relinquish its defensive power posture and assume a listening posture, then we can sit at the Lord's Table as I believe God intends us to do. Let the United Church of Christ forthrightly say, We don't see one strand of commonality on which to base our unity, but let's be our unique selves at the Lord's Table. At the Lord's Table there is room to be, to be included, to be fed, to be forgiven, to be acknowledged, and to be at home in God's world.

At the Lord's Table, there is a theology of listening toward mutual hearing. Our various voices, the voices of all creation, and the voice of the Creator can speak and be heard. In mutuality, we can examine our motives for listening, our motives for hearing, our motives for talking—if we can risk being heard. Indigenous peoples' ceremonies and ceremonial grounds and the worship centers of the United Church of Christ have community-building opportunities that are mandated by our sacred histories and sacred obligations.

Each of us, indigenous peoples and the United Church of Christ, must learn how to authenticate our relationships with our own people. It is one thing to stand on the side of justice in Central America, South Africa, the Philippines, and the "uttermost parts of the earth" (Acts 13:47), but it is quite another to do justice with the victimized of our own people and the contamination of the environment in which we are blessed to dwell. Community building and living requires rebirth and relinquishment in the present in this place as well as in other lands and in the future so that "all may have life" at the Lord's Table. Paulo Freire wrote,

> *Those who authentically commit themselves to the people must re-examine themselves constantly. This conversion is so radical as not to allow ambiguous behavior. To affirm this commitment but to consider oneself the proprietor of revolutionary wisdom—which must then be given to (or imposed on) the people is to retain the old ways. The [person] who proclaims devotion to the cause of liberation yet is unable to enter into communion with people, whom he [or she] continues to regard as totally ignorant is grievously self-deceived. Conversion to the people requires a profound rebirth. Those who undergo it must take on a new form of existence; they can no longer remain as they were.*[15]

May it be so.

Notes

1. J. Leitch Wright, Jr., *The Only Land They Knew* (New York: MacMillan Free Press, 1981), 29.

2. *Ibid.*, 30–33.

3. Vine Deloria, Jr., *God Is Red* (New York: Delta Books, 1973), 3.

4. Stuart Lang, *Two Spirits Meet*, Heritage series, ed. Edward A. Powers (Philadelphia: United Church Press, 1976), 3.

5. *Ibid.*, 18.

6. Position paper of the Native American Project of Theology in the Americas, 475 Riverside Drive, New York, N.Y., 1978.

7. *Ibid.*

8. *Ibid.*

9. "Recalling, Reliving, Reviewing," a report on a religious dialogue sponsored by the Native American Theological Association and the Minnesota Humanities Commission, October 1979.

10. David Jobling, "Dominion Over Creation," in *Interpreter's Dictionary of the Bible*, supp. vol. (Nashville: Abingdon Press, 1976), 247–48.

11. The words of Chief Seattle were quoted by Adam Cuthand, in "The Spirituality of Native Americans," a speech given at the Toronto World's Future Conference (July 1980).

12. Deloria, *God is Red*, 262ff.

13. *Ibid.*

14. Vine Deloria, Jr., "Indians and Other Americans: The Cultural Chasm," *Church and Society* (Presbyterian Church U.S.A.) (Jan.–Feb. 1985): 11–19.

15. Paulo Freire, *Pedagogy of the Oppressed* (New York: Seabury Press, 1969), 47.

The Native Church: A Search for an Authentic Spirituality

LAVERNE JACOBS

One memorable Saturday morning in May of 1959 I "committed my life to Jesus Christ." Thus began a very convoluted spiritual journey. This commitment was preceded by a searching question posed several weeks earlier by my pastor. His question as I lay on a hospital bed was, "Laverne, are you saved?" I knew he was asking about my relationship with God. I also knew I was not satisfied with that relationship. Several weeks later on the side of a road I prayed the "sinner's prayer," guided by my pastor, and began a new relationship with God.

Christian Roots

The stability and identity I needed as a Native youth growing up in the late fifties and early sixties was provided by that experience. The social and economic conditions of my reserve community caused me tremendous shame. I struggled with all the stereotypes of the lazy, drunken, irresponsible Indian. As a new Christian, I gained a status which I did not enjoy as a Native person. I became a "child of God," an "heir of God and joint heir with Christ," and a "fellow citizen with the saints and members of the household of God" [Romans 8:16, 17; Ephesians 2:19]. Following high school and two years in the work world I entered an Anglican theological college.

I grew to appreciate the devotional life of the Church during my seminary years. I learned about the church fathers, the history, and traditions of the Church. I read the writings of Tillich, Kierkegaard and others. I learned the songs of the Church and embraced its rituals. I studied Greek. This was my formation for the priesthood. I accepted this process willingly and acknowledged western thought and theology as normative and absolute in my preparation for life as a priest and as a Native Christian. These were happy years. The Christian traditions which I had embraced brought meaning and purpose to my life.

Resurgence of Traditional Native Spirituality

I was convinced that Native traditions and spirituality were inherently evil and pagan. Such traditions were contradictory to the Christian faith. I was warned about the dangers of syncretism and told I must not compromise my faith as a Christian. Deeply concerned about the centrality of Christ, I resolved that I would not bring dishonour to Christ by seeking after other gods.

In 1975 I returned to my home community to pastor both the Anglican and United congregations. During this period I and members of the faith community struggled with the resurgence of traditional Native Spirituality. Younger members of the reserve in their search for identity were exploring their Native heritage. These young people travelled to powwows throughout North America. They brought back ways and cultural traditions foreign to our community.

"The Native Church: A Search for an Authentic Spirituality" by Laverne Jacobs. Reprinted by permission of The Rev. Laverne V. Jacobs.

Years of Struggle

The years that followed were difficult years marked by religious zeal and conflict. "Born again" members of my parish burned their Native symbols and quit making Native crafts. Christian members of the community boycotted powwows. Followers of the Traditional Ways lobbied to have Native Spirituality taught in the school. Anxious church members launched a counter campaign. Confusion and conflict struck to the core of people's beings. A funeral exacerbated the turmoil. Once a faithful church member, the deceased person left the Church and embraced the Traditional Ways. At death the body was prepared in the Traditional Way with painted face and the use of traditional symbols and rituals. Community members were torn between their desire to support the bereaved family and their fear of Native Spirituality. As the parish priest, I did not know what an appropriate pastoral response should be. I was just as confused and fearful as everyone else.

The Journey

These years of turmoil and religious conflict were the beginning of a long and painful journey. Early on I attended a conference, enrolling in a workshop by Father John Hascall, a Native Roman Catholic priest. Father Hascall was a Pipe Carrier and spiritual leader in the Midewiwin Lodge. I was deeply disturbed and troubled by his address. In sharing his spiritual journey he seemingly equated Native Spirituality with Christianity. His whole story evoked my worst fears of syncretism.

Within that same period I attended a United Church conference for Native peoples. Two Traditional Elders led sessions on Native Spirituality. The Elders talked about the Pipe and Sweetgrass ceremonies. Provision was made for people to participate in a Sweat Lodge. People chose either to participate in or to observe the Sweetgrass Ceremony. Those actively participating in the ceremony formed an inner circle; those choosing to observe formed an outer circle. All were permitted to talk about the choices they had made. I remained in the outer circle anxiously observing the ceremony. I deliberately chose the outer circle because I did not understand the ceremony and was afraid of compromising my Christian beliefs. There was no way I would join the group in a Sweat Lodge! Engaging in a Sweat was just asking too much of me. I was fearful of aligning myself with the Evil One.

I put these experiences aside determined to devote my energies more fully to the Christian faith. As a part of this new commitment I went to confession and sought forgiveness for delving into pagan rituals. I resolved to refrain from any involvement with Native Spirituality.

This renunciation of Native Spirituality seemed to provoke more confrontation and struggle. Again I sat in the presence of Father John Hascall, the Medicine Priest. On this occasion, I attended a service of the Native community in my home diocese. This service, held in the cathedral, began with Father Hascall praying with the Pipe in the Four Directions. He began the ceremony with a brief explanation saying that certain people would be invited to share the Pipe with him. His assistant called me to come forward. Time stood still. I struggled with the implications of this request: *Was it right for me, as national staff, to share in this ritual? What would such action say to people? Would I be compromising my Christian beliefs? Would it be right to refuse something which was sacred to others and offered to me as a symbol of honour and trust?*

In my turmoil and anxiety I placed the Pipe to my lips and drew upon the sacred substance not knowing what would follow, but trusting and hoping that somehow God was present in this action and praying that I would be protected from that which I did not know or understand. I returned to my seat and watched as the ceremony continued. I looked at the young men, just barely in their teens, who had been invited to be "helpers" to Father John. They were engrossed in the ceremony and service; their faces reflected a deep sense of pride in their Native heritage. As I pondered the whole experience I had the sensation of One saying *"This is you."*

Years later I attended a World Council of Churches assembly in Korea on *Justice, Peace, and the Integrity of Creation.* I was the only First Nations person from Canada in a gathering of several thousand. The process was so European and overwhelming. I felt alienated and alone. I desperately wanted to be back home. In my loneliness, I was approached by four Native Americans who asked me to join them in prayers. I felt relieved to be with my own people. The next morning we gathered on a mound outside the conference hall. As we stood in a circle, one of the men beat a drum and sang a prayer song. Another man prepared the Sacred Pipe for our prayers. Again, I wondered if I should be there. I was torn between my desperate need for support and my fear of Traditional Ways and the possibility of compromising my Christian principles. As the Pipe was handed to me, I asked for protection and prayed to the God that I knew and to Jesus my Brother. During and following this ceremony I felt a certain peace of mind and heart and was assured that I had not compromised my Christian values. In the remaining days of the conference, the daily prayers with the Pipe—the very thing which I feared—sustained me.

A Sacred Time

Of all Native ceremonies in my ken, the one I feared most was the Sweat Lodge. It is a ceremony I was determined to avoid. In the summer of 1992.

I attended a Native gathering sponsored by the Roman Catholic Church. The program included healing circles and the Sweat Lodge. As I read the program I had the ominous feeling that this time I would not be able to run away and that I would participate in a Sweat which filled me with anxiety and fear. I attended the seminar on the healing circle and the Sweat Lodge. I still did not know what to do. After the seminar, a deacon told me of his first experience of praying in a Sweat Lodge, a dramatic and wonderful experience. His glowing account did not allay my fears. It was only at the last moment, comforted by the knowledge that a close friend would be with me, I decided to join in the Sweat. The presence of my friend and the fact that the Elder leading the ceremony was one I trusted enabled me to go forward. Following the example of other men I took a pinch of tobacco and offered it at the Sacred Fire as I entered the Sweat Lodge, crawling on hands and knees behind other participants. When all had entered, the Elder ordered the flap of the lodge closed and began the ceremony. The intensity of the prayers matched the intensity of the heat from the steaming rocks. After several rounds and hours of prayer the ceremony came to a close. As we emerged from the lodge into the coolness of the night, we sat or lay on the ground knit together by the sacred bond of men who had shared a sacred journey. As I lay gazing up into the starlit sky I felt a tremendous sense of restfulness and peace. It was a truly sacred time. There was nothing that was contradictory to the Christian gospel which I embraced.

Both Native and Christian

Through these and many other experiences I gained an openness to faith journeys different from mine. I listened to stories of others whose ways are different, but in whose stories I have found the Christ of the Christian gospel. I learned to put aside my fears and step out in faith; and in that step of faith experienced the vastness of God, the Creator. I hear the sounds of many voices, each with a tenor and beauty of its own, but which together sing the praises of God the Creator and Jesus the Son in one great symphony of creation. In the midst of that glorious sound rings the phrase *"This is you—both Native and Christian."* The meaning of that phrase will be a lifelong dialogue with self. Each new experience and each year will uncover different aspects of that reality like the many facets of a precious gem. This dialogue is a dialogue shared by many First Nations people and which must continue in the midst of a changing world.

PART TWO

The African American
Religious Experience

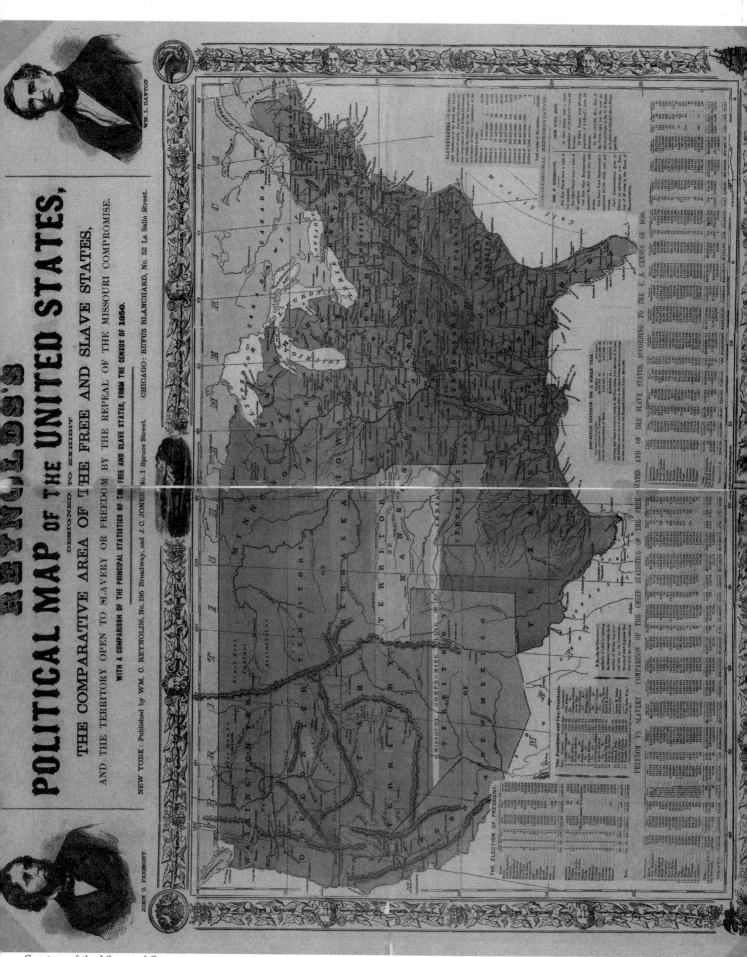

REYNOLDS'S

POLITICAL MAP OF THE UNITED STATES,

DESIGNED TO EXHIBIT

THE COMPARATIVE AREA OF THE FREE AND SLAVE STATES,

AND THE TERRITORY OPEN TO SLAVERY OR FREEDOM BY THE REPEAL OF THE MISSOURI COMPROMISE.

WITH A COMPARISON OF THE PRINCIPAL STATISTICS OF THE FREE AND SLAVE STATES, FROM THE CENSUS OF 1850.

NEW YORK: Published by WM. C. REYNOLDS, No. 196 Broadway, and J. C. JONES, No. 1 Spruce Street.   CHICAGO: RUFUS BLANCHARD, No. 52 La Salle Street.

WM. L. DAYTON.

JOHN C. FREMONT.

HISTORICAL GEOGRAPHY.

Entered according to act of Congress in the year 1888, by John F. Smith, in the office of the Librarian of Congress at Washington.

LIBERTY

SLAVERY

BLESSING

CURSE

GOD'S BLESSING

GOD'S CURSE

MURDER

REBELLION

PACIFIC OCEAN

ATLANTIC OCEAN

GULF OF MEXICO

NORTH AMERICA

BRITISH

MEXICO

LOWER CALIFORNIA

IMMIGRATION

EMIGRATION

HOPE

FAITH

CHARITY

PATIENCE

TEMPERANCE

HAPPINESS

BENEVOLENCE

PHILANTHROPY

LOVE OF COUNTRY

EQUAL RIGHTS

OBEDIENCE TO LAW

INTELLIGENCE

FREE SCHOOLS

KNOWLEDGE

FREE SPEECH

CONTENTMENT

INDUSTRY

SOBRIETY

MORALITY

JUSTICE

VIRTUE

TRUTH

HONOR

PEACE

IMMORTALITY

WASHINGTON

OREGON

IDAHO

MONTANA

DAKOTA

WYOMING

NEVADA

UTAH

COLORADO

NEBRASKA

KANSAS

CALIFORNIA

ARIZONA

NEW MEXICO

TEXAS

INDIAN TERRITORY

MINNESOTA

WISCONSIN

IOWA

MISSOURI

ARKANSAS

LOUISIANA

ILLINOIS

INDIANA

OHIO

MICHIGAN

MISSISSIPPI

ALABAMA

GEORGIA

FLORIDA

TENNESSEE

KENTUCKY

PENNSYLVANIA

NEW YORK

MAINE

NEW HAMPSHIRE

VERMONT

NEW BRUNSWICK

HADES

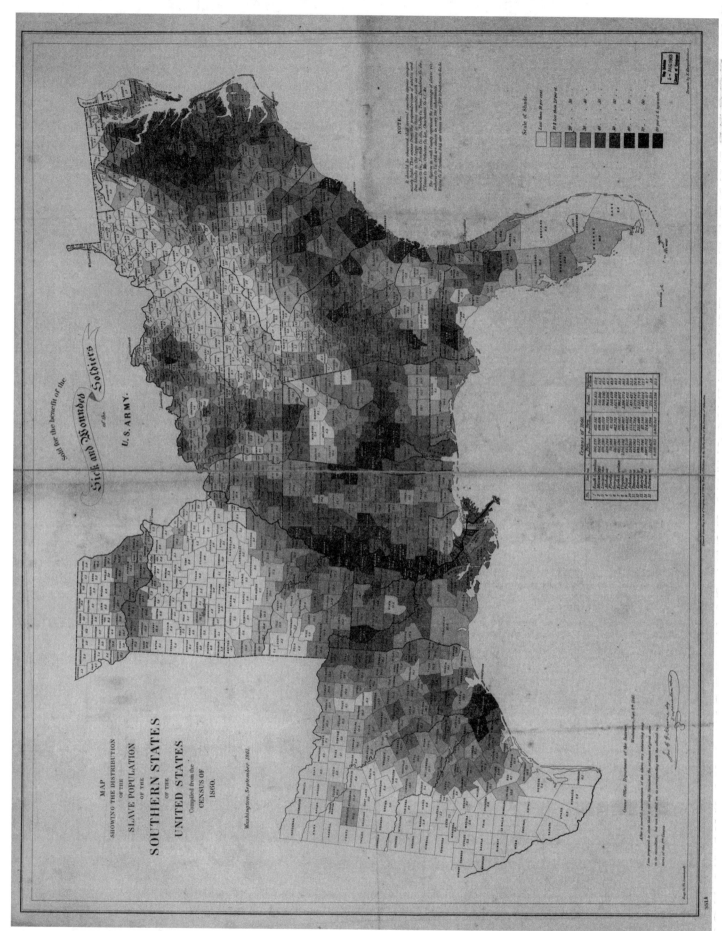

Readings in African American Religious Traditions: A Foretaste

To speak of the African American experience is to be ever mindful of the long shadow cast by the injustice of slavery. Though nearly 150 years have passed since emancipation, the consequences of that "primal crime," as sociologist Robert Bellah has aptly termed it, are felt to this day. How in good conscience, one might ask, could Christian men and women assent to enslaving fellow humans, or visit such evil upon the sons and daughters of the same Heavenly Father? The great indignity and outrage felt by Americans of African descent—both slave and free—are expressed in the pages of newspapers, journals, declarations, addresses, and autobiographical recollections, as well as in creative works of fiction. This section of the reader presents a variety of literary works that convey the depth of feelings and religious experiences associated with slavery and its continuing consequences for African Americans.

As they came to develop in the New World, African American cultures and religions combined deeply rooted African elements with biblical traditions. Especially strong was the identification of the African American experience with that of the Hebrew slaves and their miraculous exodus from Egypt. Indeed, Egypt became a metaphor for slavery, even as the American continent came to be associated metaphorically with Israel's later exile and captivity in Babylon. And, as Israel of old, the African peoples enslaved in America, *de facto* and *de jure*, likewise cried unto God to send to them a deliverer. In time, many talented men as well as women from within the African American community—both North and South—would rise to claim the mantle of prophet and, "like unto Moses from among their brethren," would speak as one with authority from God.

In response, therefore, to the humiliation of slavery and of finding themselves socially and religiously marginalized in white Southern culture, African slaves created their own spaces for worship and community life. Historians have referred to this social and religious phenomenon as the "invisible institution." Initially, Southern slaves would gather in secret locations for mutual comfort and encouragement. These informal gatherings became brief periods of solace from the cruelty of their condition, and provided spiritual healing that was at once personal as well as communal. In time, however, these religious meetings became more formalized. "Slave religion," as Gayraud Wilmore has observed, "was partly a clandestine protest against the hypocrisy of a system that expected blacks to be virtuous and obedient to those who themselves lived lives of indolence and immorality in full view of the ones they purported to serve as examples" (1998:35). From these "hush harbors" emerged a religious and cultural life that became uniquely African American. In fact, these gatherings of African slaves for mutual prayer, to join their voices in deeply moving spirituals (what one might call communal songs in motion), and for spiritual uplift, would help define the characteristic styles of worship in the black churches that would sprout up throughout the South after emancipation.

Several decades later, in his essay, "Of the Faith of the Fathers," W.E.B. DuBois gave eloquent testimony to the music of the soul that typified the black worship experience as "the most original and beautiful expression of human life and longing yet born on American soil." In this essay, DuBois identified three essential characteristics of slave religion that were witnessed in his day, namely, the preacher, the music, and the frenzy of worship "when the Spirit of the Lord passed by" (1926:191). According to DuBois, the preacher is at one and the same time "a leader, a politician, an orator, a 'boss', an intriguer, an idealist," and ever "the centre of a group of men, now twenty, now a thousand in number" (1926:190). The music, though "[s]prung from the African forests, . . . was adapted, changed, and intensified by the tragic soul-life of the slave, until, under the stress of law and whip, it became the one true expression of a people's sorrow, despair, and hope." And, while the worship "varied in expression from the silent rapt countenance or the low murmur and moan to the mad abandon of physical fervor, . . . so firm a hold did it have on the Negro, that many generations firmly believed that without this visible manifestation of the God there could be no true communion with the Invisible" (1926:191). To these three essential characteristics, one might add the community itself, in that one finds worship to be a dialogue between a preacher and his people as well as between the community as a whole and the Divine, mediated through the rhythms of the spoken word and song.

In the North, except for the chains, the condition of freeborn and emancipated Africans during the nineteenth and into the twentieth century differed only slightly from their Southern cousins. Northern blacks found themselves similarly excluded from mainstream social and religious life. In response, individuals, such as Richard Allen and Peter Williams, established their own Protestant churches. Among them were the African Methodist Episcopal Church (AME) and the African Methodist Episcopal Zion Church (AMEZ), which were officially established in 1816 and 1821 respectively. For Northern blacks, these and other independent denominations became a type of invisible institution, that is, a place where shared religious and community life could be experienced apart from the controlling gaze of white society. Or, as Wilmore has also noted, "[b]oth the slave congregations of the South—'the invisible institution'—and the more or less free black churches of the North developed a religion that masked a sublimated outrage balanced with patience, cheerfulness, and a boundless confidence in the ultimate justice of God" (1998:36). In this section of the reader, we have included several brief examples of the influence of the churches in the lives of Southern and Northern blacks. These include selections by Langston Hughes and Zora Hurston, as well as oral recollections edited by B.A. Botkin, and an historical essay by W.E.B. DuBois.

In the century from the end of the Civil War to the famous "March on Washington"—the period of "Jim Crow" laws—the religious experience of African Americans, both North and South, continued to be informed by daily assaults upon their personal and civil rights. "Separate but equal," mandated in 1896 by the Supreme Court in *Plessy v. Ferguson,* allowed for the lawful segregation of blacks from whites and consigned blacks to the status of second-class citizens, if citizens at all. African Americans were denied basic rights, such as the right to vote. They were refused service at local markets and lunch counters, and were consigned to sending their children to run-down schools. Those who objected to Jim Crow laws were beaten and punished. Lynchings became common in the South, but not unknown in the North. As Albert J. Raboteau records, during this period, "[i]ncidents of violence against African Americans became more frequent. Between 1882 and 1885, 227 black people were lynched. Between 1889 and 1899, that figure rose to 1,240. . . . In 1898 alone, white mobs seized and murdered 104 black people" (2001:72). In the pages of the NAACP newsletter, *The Crisis: A Record of the Darker Races,* edited by W.E.B. DuBois, space is given not just for the purpose of documenting lynchings and mob violence against blacks, but of calling upon their white brothers and sisters to reject the evil perpetrated by those among them. In this reader, we have included a short story by DuBois, titled "Jesus Christ in Georgia," which dramatically illustrates this outrage.

It was against these and other longstanding injustices that the leaders of the civil rights movement of the 1950s and 1960s rallied their people. Renewed enforcement of Jim Crow lent greater urgency, and moral authority, to their cause. The Reverend Martin Luther King, Jr.'s famous letter from a Birmingham jail, reminiscent of St. Paul's own prison epistles, provided an ethical and religious rationale for King's nonviolent approach to gaining the inevitable triumph, as he would later proclaim from the steps of the Lincoln Memorial, by "meeting physical force with soul force." As he wrote, "[i]f the inexpressible cruelties of slavery could not stop us, the opposition we now face will surely fail. We will win our freedom because the sacred heritage of our nation and the eternal will of God are embodied in our echoing demands" (1992:98). One can also hear echoes of King's letter in the selections by James Cone and Jacquelyn Grant, reprinted below.

King had cautioned his followers against resorting to violence, and to resist traveling down the roads of bitterness and hatred that might lead to retaliation and an endless cycle of violence. Others were not as long-suffering as King and his followers. Indeed, King cited as an example the black nationalist groups, such as the Nation of Islam, led by Elijah Muhammad. "This movement," King explained, "is nourished by the contemporary frustration over the continued existence of racial discrimination. It is made up of people who," he believed, "have lost faith in America, who have absolutely repudiated Christianity, and who have concluded that the white man is an incurable 'devil'" (1992:93). As an example of this alternative to King's nonviolent and Christian approach, we have selected two readings: one is a speech by Malcolm X, entitled "Black Man's History," delivered in 1962; the other is a chapter on the place of women in Islam from a more recent apologetic work by Aminah Beverly McCloud. But even between these two readings, whose authors are separated by generation and gender, differences in religious assumptions are noticeable.

Taken together, the selections in this section give evidence of the spiritual and intellectual vitality that has informed and continues to enliven the African American community in our own day. Or, in the words of Maya Angelou, as quoted below in Jacquelyn Grant's essay on Womanist theology (1993:287–288):

Out of the hut of history's shame
I rise
Up from a past that's rooted in pain
I rise

I'm a Black ocean, leaping and wide,
Welling and swelling, I bear in the tide
Leaving behind nights of terror and fear
I rise
Into a daybreak that's wondrously clear
I rise
Bringing the gifts that my ancestors gave
I am the dream and hope of the slave.
I rise.
I rise.
I rise.

Sources and Selected Works in African American History, Literature, and Religions

[*indicates works of fiction]

Abrahams, Roger D. (ed.). *Afro-American Folktales: Stories from Black Traditions in the New World*. New York: Random House, 1985.

Aptheker, Herbert. *Nat Turner's Slave Rebellion*. New York: Grove Press, 1968.

Baer, Hans A. *The Black Spiritual Movement: A Religious Response to Racism*. Knoxville, TN: University of Tennessee Press, 1984.

Baer, Hans A. and Merrill Singer. *African-American Religion in the Twentieth Century*. Knoxville, TN: University of Tennessee Press, 1992.

*Baldwin, James. *Go Tell It on the Mountain*. New York: Dell Publishing, 1985.

*———. *The Fire Next Time*. New York: Vintage International, 1993.

Bennett, Lerone, Jr. *The Shaping of Black America: The Struggles and Triumphs of African-Americans, 1619 to the 1990s*. New York: Penguin Books, 1993.

Berry, Mary Frances, and John W. Blassingame. *Long Memory: The Black Experience in America*. New York: Oxford University Press, 1982.

Branch, Taylor. *Parting the Waters: America in the King Years, 1954–1963*. New York: Simon and Schuster, 1988.

Broderick, Francis L., and August Meier (eds.). *Negro Protest Thought in the Twentieth Century*. Indianapolis: Bobbs Merrill, 1965.

Burkett, Randall K. *Garveyism as a Religious Movement: The Institutionalization of a Black Civil Religion*. Metuchen, NJ: The Scarecrow Press, 1978.

Cannon, Katie Geneva. *Katie's Canon: Womanism and the Soul of the Black Community*. New York: Continuum, 1995.

Carson, Clayborne, David J. Garrow, Gerald Gill, Vincent Harding, and Darlene Clark Hine (gen. eds.). *The Eyes on the Prize Civil Rights Reader: Documents, Speeches, and Firsthand Accounts from the Black Freedom Struggle, 1954–1990*. New York: Penguin Books, 1991.

Chappell, David L. *A Stone of Hope: Prophetic Religion and the Death of Jim Crow*. Chapel Hill, NC: University of North Carolina Press, 2004.

Clegg, Claude Andrew, III. *An Original Man: The Life and Times of Elijah Muhammad*. New York: St. Martin's Press, 1997.

Cone, James H. *A Black Theology of Liberation*, 2nd ed. Maryknoll, New York: Orbis Books, 1986.

———. *Martin & Malcolm & America*. Maryknoll, New York: Orbis Books, 1995.

Daley, James (ed.). *Great Speeches by African Americans*. New York: Dover Publications, 2006.

Davis, Cyprian. *The History of Black Catholics in the United States*. New York: Crossroad, 1996.

DeCaro, Louis A., Jr. *On the Side of My People: A Religious Life of Malcolm X*. New York: New York University Press, 1996.

DuBois, W.E.B. (ed.). *The Negro Church*. Walnut Creek, CA: AltaMira Press, 2003 [reprint of 1903 edition].

Dunbar, Alice Moore (ed.). *Masterpieces of Negro Eloquence: The Best Speeches Delivered by the Negro from the Days of Slavery to the Present Time.* New York: The Bookery Publishing Co., 1914.

Essien-Udom, E.U. *Black Nationalism: A Search for an Identity in America.* Chicago: The University of Chicago Press, 1971.

Fauset, Arthur Huff. *Black Gods of the Metropolis: Negro Religious Cults of the Urban North.* Philadelphia: University of Pennsylvania Press, 1944.

Fitts, Leroy. *A History of Black Baptists.* Nashville, TN: Broadman Press, 1985.

Franklin, Robert Michael. *Liberating Visions.* Minneapolis, MN: Fortress Press, 1990.

Frazier, Franklin E., and C. Eric Lincoln. *The Negro Church in America/The Black Church since Frazier.* New York: Schocken Books, 1974.

Fulop, Timothy E., and Albert J. Raboteau (eds.). *African-American Religion: Interpretive Essays in History and Culture.* New York: Routledge, 1997.

Gardell, Mattias. *In the Name of Elijah Muhammad: Louis Farrakhan and the Nation of Islam.* Durham, NC: Duke University Press, 1996.

Gordon, Lewis R. *Existentia Africana: Understanding Africana Existential Thought.* New York: Routledge, 2000.

Grant, Joanne (ed.). *Black Protest: History, Documents, and Analyses, 1619 to Present.* New York: Fawcett, 1991.

Higginbotham, Evelyn Brooks. *Righteous Discontent: The Women's Movement in the Black Baptist Church, 1880–1920.* Cambridge, MA: Harvard University Press, 1993.

Hurston, Zora. *Dust Tracks on a Road: An Autobiography.* Philadelphia: J.B. Lippincott Co., 1942.

*———. *Their Eyes Were Watching God.* New York: Harper Perennial, 1990.

Johnson, F. Roy. *The Nat Turner Slave Insurrection.* Murfreesboro, NC: Johnson Publishing Co., 1966.

King, Martin Luther, Jr. (James M. Washington, ed.). *I Have a Dream: Writings and Speeches That Changed the World.* New York: HarperCollins, 1992.

———. *Strength to Love.* Minneapolis, MN: Fortress Press, 1981.

———. *Where Do We Go From Here: Chaos or Community?* New York: Harper & Row, 1967.

———. *Why We Can't Wait.* New York: Signet Classic, 2000.

Lee, Martha F. *The Nation of Islam: An American Millenarian Movement.* Syracuse, New York: Syracuse University Press, 1996.

Levine, Lawrence W. *Black Culture and Black Consciousness.* New York: Oxford University Press, 1977.

Lewis, David L. *W.E.B. Du Bois: Biography of a Race 1868–1919.* New York: Henry Holt & Co., 1993.

Lincoln, C. Eric. *The Black Muslims in America,* 3rd ed. Grand Rapids, MI: Eerdmans; Trenton, NJ: Africa World Press, 1994.

Lincoln, C. Eric, and Lawrence H. Mamiya. *The Black Church in the African American Experience.* Durham, NC: Duke University Press, 1990.

Malcolm X. *The Autobiography of Malcolm X* (as told to Alex Haley). New York: Ballantine Books, 1973.

———. *The End of White World Supremacy.* New York: Arcade Publishing, 1971.

Marsh, Clifton E. *From Black Muslims to Muslim,* 2nd ed. Metuchen, NJ: The Scarecrow Press, 1995.

McCloud, Aminah Beverly. *African American Islam.* New York: Routledge, 1995.

Mellon, James (ed.). *Bullwhip Days: The Slaves Remember, An Oral History.* New York: Weidenfeld & Nicolson, 1988.

Mintz, Steven (ed.). *African American Voices: The Life Cycle Of Slavery,* rev. ed. St. James, New York: Brandywine Press, 1996.

Moses, Wilson Jeremiah. *Black Messiahs and Uncle Toms: Social and Literary Manipulations of a Religious Myth,* rev. ed. University Park, PA: Pennsylvania State University Press, 1993.

Muhammad, Elijah. *Message to the Blackman in America.* Chicago: Muhammad's Temple No. 2, 1965.

Mullane, Deirdre (ed.). *Crossing the Danger Water: Three Hundred Years of African-American Writing.* New York: Anchor Doubleday, 1993.

Murphy, Larry G. (ed.). *Down by the Riverside: Readings in African American Religion.* New York: New York University Press, 2000.

Murphy, Larry G., J. Gordon Melton, and Gary L. Ward (eds.). *Encyclopedia of African American Religions*. New York: Garland Publishing, 1993.

Newman, Richard, Patrick Rael, and Phillip Lapsansky (eds.). *Pamphlets of Protest: An Anthology of Early African American Protest Literature, 1790–1860*. New York: Routledge, 2001.

Oates, Stephen B. *Let the Trumpet Sound: The Life of Martin Luther King, Jr*. New York: Mentor, 1985.

Olmos, Margarite Fernández, and Lisbeth Paravisini-Gebert. *Creole Religions of the Caribbean: An Introduction from Vodou and Santería to Obeah and Espiritismo*. New York: New York University Press, 2003.

Pitts, Walter F. *Old Ship of Zion: The Afro-Baptist Spiritual in the African Diaspora*. New York: Oxford University Press, 1993.

Raboteau, Albert J. *A Fire in the Bones: Reflections on African-American Religious History*. Boston: Beacon Press, 1995.

———. *Slave Religion: The 'Invisible Institution' in the Antebellum South*. New York: Oxford University Press, 1978.

Riggs, Marcia Y. (ed., with Barbara Holmes). *Can I Get a Witness? Prophetic Religious Voices of African American Women: An Anthology*. Maryknoll, New York: Orbis Books, 1997.

Sernett, Milton C. *Bound for the Promised Land: African American Religion and the Great Migration*. Durham, NC: Duke University Press, 1997.

———. (ed.). *African American Religious History: A Documentary History*, 2nd ed. Durham, NC: Duke University Press, 1999.

Shockley, Ann Allen. *Afro-American Women Writers, 1746–1933: An Anthology and Critical Guide*. New York: New American Library, 1989.

Sitkoff, Harvard. *The Struggle for Black Equality, 1954–1992* rev. ed. New York: Hill & Wang, 1993.

Smith, Theophus H. *Conjuring Culture: Biblical Formations of Black America*. New York: Oxford University Press, 1994.

Stewart, Dianne M. *Three Eyes for the Journey: African Dimensions of the Jamaican Religious Experience*. New York: Oxford University Press, 2005.

Taylor, Clarence. *Black Religious Intellectuals: The Fight for Equality from Jim Crow to the 21st Century*. New York: Routledge, 2002.

Townes, Emilie M. *In a Blaze of Glory: Womanist Spirituality as Social Witness*. Nashville, TN: Abingdon Press, 1995.

Turner, Richard Brent. *Islam in the African-American Experience*. Bloomington, IN: Indiana University Press, 1997.

Washington, James M. *A Testament of Hope: The Essential Writings and Speeches of Martin Luther King, Jr*. New York: HarperCollins, 1991.

Washington, Joseph R., Jr. *Black Sects and Cults*. Garden City, New York: Doubleday, 1973.

Watts, Jill. *God, Harlem U.S.A.: The Father Divine Story*. Berkeley, CA: University of California Press, 1992.

West, Cornel. *The Cornel West Reader*. New York: Basic *Civitas* Books, 1999.

———. *Race Matters*. Boston: Beacon Press, 1993.

West, Cornel, and Eddie S. Glaude, Jr. (eds.). *African American Religious Thought: An Anthology*. Louisville, KY: Westminster/John Knox Press, 2003.

Williams, Juan. *Eyes on the Prize: America's Civil Rights Years, 1954–1965*. New York: Penguin Books, 1988.

Wilmore, Gayraud S. *Black Religion and Black Radicalism*, 3rd ed. Maryknoll, New York: Orbis Books, 1998.

———. (ed.). *African American Religious Studies: An Interdisciplinary Anthology*. Durham, NC: Duke University Press, 1989.

Some Suggested Questions for Discussion

1. Historically, African American identification with the experiences of the Hebrew slaves in the Book of Exodus has been very strong. List and discuss the similarities and differences that you see between the African experience in America—both before and after emancipation—with that of the Hebrew/Israelite peoples. What are some of the similar themes that one can discern?

2. Discuss the African American uses of the Bible and its teachings in the nineteenth century as opposed to the twentieth century as seen in these selections. What different interpretive lenses do people such as Robert Young, David Walker, Mrs. Jarena Lee, Frederick Douglass, and even W.E.B. DuBois appear to use in comparison and contrast to Martin Luther King, Jr., Malcolm X, James Cone, and Jacquelyn Grant?

3. Based on the speech by Malcolm X and the essay by Aminah McCloud reprinted above, what beliefs appear to have remained constant in the Nation of Islam and the Black Muslim community in the United States despite dramatic changes in the movement? That is, would Malcolm X recognize Aminah McCloud's beliefs about African American Islam in the 1990s as consistent with the movement founded by Elijah Muhammad in the 1930s, of which he (Malcolm X) became its most famous interpreter in the 1950s and 1960s?

4. In comparing the essays of Jacquelyn Grant and Aminah McCloud, how do their positions differ concerning womanist interpretations of religious traditions (in the first case Christianity, in the second case Islam)? Given their assumptions about women and religion, how might they critique each other's position?

An Address before the Pennsylvania Augustine Society (1818)

PRINCE SAUNDERS

"Perhaps there never was a period, when the attention of so many enlightened men was so vigorously awakened to a sense of the importance of a universal dissemination of the blessings of instruction, as at this enlightened age . . ."

AN ADDRESS, etc.:

THE human heart is a parti-coloured piece of Mosaic. But notwithstanding its veriagated appearances, the whited inlaying of those genuine excellencies, and of those enobling affections, which encompass humanity with glory and honour, are but seldom to be found its innate, or, as it were, its spontaneous ornaments.

We hence descry some of the grounds for that invaluable importance which has uniformly been given to education, in supplying the mind with intellectual acquisitions, and for adorning it with those elevated accomplishments which have generally been considered as its peculiar fruits, by the virtuous and contemplative of every age and nation; where the genial influences of the Sun of Science have been experienced, and where the blessings of civilized society have been enjoyed. If by investigating the historic page of antiquity, we take a retrospective view of the numerous votaries of literature and the useful arts, who flourished at those early periods, when the improving influences of knowledge and civilization were wholly confined to the oriental regions, we shall then discover some traces of their views of the intrinsic utility of mutually associating, to aid the progress of those who were aspiring to taste the Castilian spring, while ascending the towering heights of Parnassus, that there they might behold the magnificent temple of the Ruler of the Muses, and hear his venerated oracle.

We have heard of the early distinguishing attainments of the celebrated Aristotle, who improved so much at seventeen years of age, that the immortal Plato, (his preceptor,) gave him the appellation of a Lover of the Truth. He soon afterwards became tutor to Alexander the great, and founder of the sublime researches of the ancient Peripotetici. The accomplished and eloquent youth, Antonius Gripho, a native of Gaul, came to Rome, and taught rhetoric and poetry at the house of Julius Caesar, when a mere boy; and historians tell us, that his school was frequented by Cicero and others of the most eminent literati of the age.

Many, in different periods, by cultivating the arts and sciences, have contributed to human happiness and improvement, by that invincible zeal for moral virtue and intellectual excellence, which their example has inspired in other minds and hearts, as well as by the sublimity of those traces of truth with which they have illuminated the world, and dignified the intercourse of civilized society.

Perhaps there never was a period, when the attention of so many enlightened men was so vigorously awakened to a sense of the importance of a universal dissemination of the blessings of instruction, as at this enlightened age, in this, in the northern and eastern sections of our country, in some portions of Europe, and in the island of Hayti.

The hope is encouraged, that in the above-mentioned portions of the world, the means of acquiring knowledge sufficient to read and understand the sacred Scriptures, and to manage with propriety, the ordinary concerns of domestic and social life, will soon be within the reach of every individual. Then, we trust, that we shall see a practical exemplification of the beauty and excellence of those celestial precepts and commandments which came from heaven, and which are equally applicable to all descriptions of men. They address themselves to the king upon the throne; they visit the obscurity of the humblest dwelling; they call upon the poor man to cultivate every good principle of action, as well as the man of a more elevated rank, and to aim at a life of purity, innocence, elevated virtue, and moral excellence, with the assurance that he too, shall reap his reward in that better scene of human destination, to which Christianity has called all those who fear God and work righteousness.

Wherever these lofty and commanding views of piety and virtue have been encouraged, a high sense of the social, moral, and practical obligations and duties of life, have been cherished and cultivated with an elevated and an invincible spirit.

Under the influence of this spirit, this benevolent spirit, practical Christians, of every denomination, have elevated their views far beyond the circumscribed boundaries of selfishness, sectarianism, and party zeal; and, being bound together by the indissoluble links of that golden chain of charity and kind affection, with which Christianity invariably connects its sincere votaries, and standing upon the common ground of Christian equality, they encircle the great community of those who profess the religion of our divine Master, in the arms of their charity and love, and become co-workers and fellow-labourers in the illumination, the improvement, and the ultimate felicity of those who will, undoubtedly, eventually belong to the commonwealth of the Israel of our God.

In such improved sections of the world, the gardens of the Academy are thronged with youth, whose ardour to reap its fairest flowers, would even vie with that evinced by the hazardous enterprize of the intrepid Jason of antiquity, when he cast the watchful Dragon, and seized that invaluable prize, the Golden Fleece.

We have reason to be grateful, my friends, that it has pleased God to permit us to witness a period when those unjust prejudices, and those hitherto insuperable barriers to the instruction, and, consequently, to the intellectual, the moral, and the religious improvement and elevation of the people of colour, under which our fathers groaned, are beginning to subside.

And now, in the true spirit of the religion of that beneficent Parent, who has made of one blood all nations of men who dwell upon the face of the whole earth, many persons of different regions and various nations, have been led to the contemplation of the interesting relations in which the human race stand to each other. They have seen that man, as a solitary individual, is a very wretched being. As long as he stands detached from his kind, he is possessed neither of happiness nor of strength. We are formed by nature to unite; we are impelled towards each other by the benevolent instincts in our frames; we are linked by a thousand connexions, founded on common wants.

Benevolent affection therefore, or, as it is very properly termed, humanity, is what man, as such in every station, owes to man. To be inaccessible, contemptuous, avaricious, and hard hearted, is to revolt against our very reason and nature; it is, according to the language of inspiration, to "hide ourselves from our own flesh."

The genuine kind affections, and the elevated sensibilities of Christianity, as they are exhibited to us in the conduct and character of our blessed Saviour, during his residence in this scene of our pilgrimage, are suited to call forth into vigorous exercise, the best sentiments, feelings and dispositions of the human heart; while they disclose to the admiring view of his obedient followers, those indissoluble and enobling moral ties, which connect earth with heaven, and which assimilate man to the benevolent Author of his being.

Wherever Christianity is considered as a religion of the affections, every well instructed, practical Christian, habitually aspires at an entire imitation of the example, and to yield a cheerful and unreserved obedience to the precepts and instructions of its heavenly founder. So peculiar is the adaptation of Christianity to become a universal religion; for wherever its spirit enters into the councils of nations, we find it unbinding the chains of corporeal and mental captivity, and diffusing over the whole world, the maxims of impartial justice, and of enlightened benevolence.

Such, and so sublimely excellent, are the fruits of a spirit of Christian charity and practical beneficence; for to it alone the glory is due, of having placed the weak under the protection of their stronger brethren; for she unceasingly labours to improve all the varying circumstances and conditions of mankind: so that, among those who profess her true spirit, the love of our neighbour is not an inactive principle, but it is real beneficence; and they, like the good Samaritan in the gospel, evince their sincerity by ministering to the necessities, and in labouring for the welfare, improvement and happiness of mankind.

Mess'rs Vice-Presidents, and Gentlemen of the Pennsylvania Augustine Education Society.

ALTHOUGH the seat of your respected President is vacant on this intersecting occasion, on account of the severe indisposition with which he is visited, still we trust that his heart is with you, and that you have his best wishes and his prayers, for the prosperity of this excellent establishment. The hope is encouraged, that you will never be weary in labouring for the promotion of the cause and interests of science and literature among the rising generation of the people of colour. For upon their intellectual, moral and religious improvements, depend the future elevation of their standing, in the social, civil and ecclesiastical community. Surely then, my friends, you are associated for the most laudable, interesting, and invaluable purposes.

Therefore, let it be the unceasing labour, the undeviating and the inflexibly firm purpose of the members of this Association, individually and collectively, to inspire all within the sphere of their influence, with a sense of the value and importance of giving their children a good education. Hear the words of revelation, calling upon you who profess to be Christians, to "train up your children in the way they should go," and to "bring them up in the nurture and admonition of the Lord." And if you believe this high authority, how can you be excused, if you neglect to give them the means of acquiring a knowledge of their duty to that divine instructor who came to call them to glory, to virtue, and to immortality.

Permit me to again entreat you, duly to appreciate the importance of religiously educating your children. For, a Christian education is not only of great utility while sojourning in this scene of discipline and probation, but it is more transcendently excellent in that more elevated scene of human destination to which we are hastening. For even the ruthless hand of death itself, cannot disrobe the soul of those virtuous principles, which are sometimes acquired through the medium of a virtuous education, and "which, when transplanted to the skies, in heaven's immortal garden bloom."

Ethiopian Manifesto (1829)

ROBERT ALEXANDER YOUNG

"Know, then, in your present state or standing, in your sphere of government in any nation within which you reside, we hold and contend you enjoy but a few of your rights of government within them."

Southern District of New-York, s s.

BE IT REMEBERED, That on the 18th day of February, A.D. 1829, in the 53d year of the Independence of the United States of America, Robert Alexander Young, of the said district, hath deposited in this office the title of a book the right whereof he claims as author, in the words following, to wit:

"The Ethiopian Manifesto, issued in defence of the Black Man's Rights, in the scale of Universal Freedom."

In conformity to the Act of Congress of the United States, entitled. "An Act for the Encouragement of Learning, by securing the copies of Maps, Charts, and Books, to the author and proprietors of such copies, during the time therein mentioned." And also to an Act, entitled "An Act supplementary to an act, entitled an act for the encouragement of learning, by securing the copies of Maps, Charts, and Books, to the authors and proprietors of such copies, during the times therein mentioned, and extending the benefits thereof to the arts of designing, engraving, and etching historical and other prints."

—FRED I. BETTS, *Clerk of the Southern District of New-York.*

Ethiopian Manifesto

By the Omnipotent will of God, we, Rednaxela, sage, and asserter to the Ethiopian of his rights, do hereby declare, and make known, as follows:—

Ethiopians! the power of Divinity having within us, as man, implanted a sense of the due and prerogatives belonging to you, a people, of whom we were of your race, in part born, as a mirror we trust, to reflect to you from a review of ourselves, the dread condition in which you do at this day stand. We do, therefore, to the accomplishment of our purpose, issue this but a brief of our grand manifesto, herefrom requiring the attention towards us of every native, or those proceeding in descent from the Ethiopian or African people; a regard to your welfare being the great and inspiring motive which leads us to this our undertaking. We do therefore strictly enjoin your attention to these the dictates from our sense of justice, held forth and produced to your notice, but with the most pure intention.

Ethiopians! open your minds to reason; let therein weigh the effects of truth, wisdom, and justice (and a regard to your individual as a general good), and the spirit of these our words we know full well, cannot but produce the effect for which they are by us herefrom intended. Know, then, in your present state or standing, in your sphere of government in any nation within which you reside, we hold and contend you enjoy but a few of your rights of government within them. We here speak of the whole of the Ethiopian people, as we admit not even those in their state of native simplicity, to be in an enjoyment of their rights, as bestowed to them of the great bequest of God to man.

The impositions practised to their state, not being known to them from the heavy and darksome clouds of ignorance which so woefully obscures their reason, we do, therefore, for the recovering of them, as well as establishing to you your rights, proclaim, that duty—imperious duty, exacts the convocation of ourselves in a body politic; that we do, for the promotion and welfare of our order, establish to ourselves a people framed unto the likeness of that order, which from our mind's eye we do evidently discern governs the universal creation. Beholding but one sole power, supremacy, or head, we do of that head, but hope and look forward for succour in the accomplishment of the great design which he hath, in his wisdom, promoted us to its undertaking.

We find we possess in ourselves an understanding; of this we are taught to know the ends of right and wrong, that depression should come upon us or any of our race of the wrongs inflicted on us of men. We know in ourselves we possess a right to see ourselves justified therefrom, of the right of God; knowing, but of his power hath he decreed to man, that either in himself he stands, or by himself he falls. Fallen, sadly, sadly low indeed, hath become our race, when we behold it reduced but to an enslaved state, to raise it from its degenerate sphere, and instill into it the rights of men, are the ends intended of these our words; here we are met in ourselves, we constitute but one, aided as we trust, by the effulgent light of wisdom to a discernment of the path which shall lead us to the collecting together of a people, rendered disobedient to the great dictates of nature, by the barbarity that hath been practised upon them from generation to generation of the will of their more cruel fellow-men. Am I, because I am a descendant of a mixed race of men, whose shade hath stamped them with the hue of black, to deem myself less eligible to the attainment of the great gift allotted of God to man, than are any other of whatsoever cast you please, deemed from being white as being more exalted than the black?

These words, which carry to the view of others the dictates of my mind, I borrow not from the sense of white men or of black: learn, my brother and fellow-Ethiopian, it is but the invigorating power of Deity instills them to my discernment. Of him do I know I derive my right; of him was I on the conception of a mother's womb created free; who then in the shape of man shall dare to rob me of my birthright as bestowed to me in my existence from God? No, I am in myself a man, and as a man will live, or as a man will die; for as I was born free of the will allotted me of the freedom of God, so do I claim and purport to establish an alike universal freedom to every son and daughter descending from the black; though however mixed in grades of colour through an intercourse of white with black; still as I am in myself, but a mixture of like, I call to witness, if the power of my mind hath not a right to claim an allegiance with all descendants of a race, for the justification of whose rights reason hath established within me the ends for their obtainment? God, an almighty, sole, and governing God, can alone direct me to the ends I have, but of his will to fulfill, be they here to the view of the universal world from him established; for as I do in myself stand upright, and claim in myself, as outwardly from myself, all my rights and prerogatives as pertaining to me in my birthright of man, so do I equally claim to the untutored black of every denomination, be he in bondage or free, an alike right; and do hereby publicly protest against the infringement of his rights, as is at this day practised by the fiendish cast of men who dare, contrary to the knowledge of justice, as hath been implanted of God in the soul of man, to hold him in bondage, adducing from his servitude a gorgeous maintenance. Accursed and damned be he in mind, soul and body, who dare after this my protest, to claim the slightest alleged right to hold a man, as regards manly visage, shape, and bearing, equal in all points, though ignorant and untaught with himself, and in intrinsic worth to the view of Deity; by far in his sacred presence, must he appear the better man, the calm submission to his fate, pointing him to the view of justice at the throne of God, as being more worthy of the rights of man, than the wretch who would claim from him his rights as a man.

I pause. Custom here points to me her accursed practises, if founded in error, as base injustice; shall they stand? nay, aught they to be allowed or sanctioned, for so to do by the cognizance of the just, the wise, the great, the good, and sound men of discretion of this world? I speak for no man, understanding but in myself my rights, that from myself shall be made known to a people, rights, which I, of the divine will of God, to them establish. Man—white man—black man—or, more properly, ye monsters incarnate, in human shape, who claim the horrid right to hold nature's untutored son, the Ethiopian, in bondage, to you I do herefrom speak. Mark me, and regard well these my words; be assured, they convey the voice of reason, dictated to you through a prophetic sense of truth. The time is at hand when many signs shall appear to you, to denote that Almighty God regards the affairs of afflicted men:— for know, the cries of bitter servitude, from those unhappy sons of men, whom ye have so long unjustly oppressed with the goading shafts of an accursed slavery, hath descended to Deity. Your God, the great and mighty God, hath seen your degradation of your fellow brother, and mortal man; he hath long looked down with mercy on your suffering slave; his cries have called for a vindication of his rights, and know ye they have been heard of the Majesty of Heaven, whose dignity have you not offended by deeming a mortal man, in your own likeness, as but worthy of being your slave, degraded to your brute? The voice of intuitive justice speaks aloud to you, and bids you to release your slave; otherwise stings, eternal stings, of an outraged and goading conscience will, ere long, hold all them in subjection who pay not due attention to this, its admonition. Beware! know thyselves to be but mortal men, doomed to the good or evil, as your works shall merit from you. Pride ye not yourselves in the greatness of your worldly standing, since all things are but moth when contrasted with the invisible spirit, which in yourself maintains within you your course of action. That within you will, to the presence of your God, be at all times your sole accuser. Weigh well these my words in the balance of your conscientious reason, and abide the judgement thereof to your own standing, for we tell you of a surety, the decree hath already passed the judgement seat of an undeviating God, wherein he hath said, "surely hath the cries of the black, a most persecuted people, ascended to my throne and craved my mercy; now, behold! I will stretch forth mine hand and gather them to the palm, that they become unto me a people, and I unto them their God." Hearken, therefore, oh! slaveholder, thou task inflicter against the rights of men, the day is at hand, nay the hour draweth nigh, when poverty shall appear to thee a blessing, if it but restore to thy fellow-man his rights; all worldly riches shall be known to thee then but as a curse, and in thine heart's desire to obtain contentment, when sad reverses come upon thee, then shalt thou linger for a renewal of days, that in thine end thou might not curse the spirit which called thee forth to life. Take warning, again we say, for of a surety from this, God will give you signs to know, in his decrees he regards the fallen state of the sons of men. Think not that wisdom descries not from here your vanity. We behold it, thou vain bloated upstart worldling of a slaveholder, laugh in derision of thy earthly taught and worldly sneer; but know, on thee we pronounce our judgment, and as fitting thee, point out to thy notice this our sign. Of the degraded of this earth, shall be exalted, one who shall draw from thee, as though gifted of power divine, all attachment and regard of thy slave toward thee. Death shall he prefer to a continuance of his race:—being doomed to thy vile servitude, no cohabitation shall be known between the sexes, while suffering under thy slavery; but should ungovernable passion attain over the untaught mind an ascendancy, abortion shall destroy the birth. We command it, the voice of imperative justice, though however harsh, must be obeyed. Ah! doth your expanding judgement, base slaveholder, not from here descry that the shackles which have been by you so undeservingly forged upon a wretched Ethiopian's frame, are about to be forever from him unlinked. Say ye, this can never be accomplished? If so, must indeed the power and decrees of Infinity become subservient to the will of depraved man. But learn, slaveholder, thine will rests not in thine hand: God decrees to thy slave his rights as man. This we issue forth as the spirit of the black man or Ethiopian's rights, established from the Ethiopian's Rock, the foundation of his civil and religious rights, which hereafter will be exemplified in the order of its course. Ethiopians, throughout the world in general, receive this as but a lesson presented to you from an instructive Book, in which many, many therein are contained, to the vindication of its purpose. As came John the Baptist, of old, to spread abroad the forthcoming of his master, so alike are intended these our words, to denote to the black African or Ethiopian people, that God has prepared them for a leader, who awaits but for his season to proclaim to them his birthright. How shall you know this man? By indubitable signs which cannot be controverted by the power of mortal, his marks being stamped in open visage, as equally so upon his frame, which constitutes him to have been particularly regarded in the infinite work of God to man.

Know ye, then, if a white man ever appeared on earth, bearing in himself the semblance of his former race, the man we proclaim ordained of God, to call together the black people as a nation in themselves. We say, in him will be seen, in appearance a white man, although having been born of a black woman, his mother. The proof is strong, and in Granada's Island, Grand Anta Estate, there, some time ago, did dwell his mother— his father then owner of the said estate. The church books of St. Georgestown, the capital of Grenada, can truly prove his birth. As another instance wherein providence decreed he should appear peculiar in his make, the two middle toes on each of his feet were, in his conception, webbed and bearded. Now, after the custom of the ancient order of men, with long and flowing hair, by like appearances may he be known; none other man, but the one bearing alike marks, and proving his identity from the island on which he was born, can be the man of whom we speak. To him, thou poor black Ethiopian or African slave, do thou, from henceforth, place a firm reliance thereon, as trusting in him to prove thy liberator from the infernal state of bondage, under which you have been so long and so unjustly laboring. To thee he pledges himself, in life to death, not to desert thee, his trust being in the power of the Almighty, who giveth not the race to the swift nor the battle to the strong, but decrees to all men the justice he establishes. As such, we draw from him the conception of your rights, and to its obtainment we issue this to you, our first pledge of faith, binding ourselves herefrom to render to you, at all times, such services as shall tend most to your advantage in effecting a speedy deliverance from your mortal and most deadly foe, the monster of a slaveholder. We would most particularly direct you to such government of yourselves as should be responsible but to God, your maker, for the duty exacted of you to your fellow-men; but, under goading situations, where power and might is but the construction of law, it then behooves the depressed and vilely injured to bear his burthen with the firmness of his manhood:— So at this time, we particularly recommend to you, degraded sons of Africa, to submit with fortitude to your present state of suffering, relying in yourselves, from the justice of a God, that the time is at hand, when, with but the power of words and the divine will of our God, the vile shackles of slavery shall be broken asunder from you, and no man known who shall dare to own or proclaim you as his bondsman. We say it, and assert it as though by an oracle given and delivered to you on high. God, in his holy keeping, direct thee, thou poor untaught and degraded African slave, to a full conception of these the words we have written for your express benefit. Our care and regard of you will be that of a fostering parent toward a beloved offspring. The hatred of your oppressor we fear not, nor do we his power, or any vile machinations that may be resorted to by incendiaries towards us. We hold ourself, with the aid of our God therewith, at all times ready to encounter, trusting but in God, our Creator, and not in ourselves, for a deliverance from all worldly evil.

Peace and Liberty to the Ethiopian first, as also all other grades of men, is the invocation we offer to the throne of our God.

REDNAXELA

DATED FROM THE
ETHIOPIAN'S ROCK,
IN THE
THIRTY-SEVENTH YEAR
FROM ITS
FOUNDATION,
THIS THIRTEENTH DAY OF FEBRUARY, A.D.
1829

Appeal to the Colored Citizens of the World (1829, 1830)

David Walker

"When God Almighty commences his battle on the continent of America, for the oppression of his people, tyrants will wish they were never born."

[Note: The following selection comes from section four of Walker's lengthy "Appeal," "Our Wretchedness In Consequence of the Colonizing Plan."]

Our Wretchedness in Consequence of the Colonizing Plan

My dearly beloved brethren:—This is a scheme on which so many able writers, together with that very judicious coloured Baltimorean, have commented, that I feel my delicacy about touching it. But as I am compelled to do the will of my Master, I declare, I will give you my sentiments upon it.—Previous, how-ever, to giving my sentiments, either for or against it, I shall give that of Mr. Henry Clay, together with that of Mr. Elias B. Caldwell, Esq. of the District of Columbia, as extracted from the National Intelligence, by Dr. Torrey, author of a series of "Essays on Morals, and the Diffusion of Useful Knowledge."

At a meeting which was convened in the District of Columbia, for the express purpose of agitating the subject of colonizing us in some part of the world, Mr. Clay was called to the chair, and having been seated a little while, he rose and spoke, in substance, as follows: says he—"That class of the mixt population of our country [coloured people] was peculiarly situated; they neither enjoyed the immunities of freemen, nor were they subjected to the incapacity of slaves, but partook, in some degree, of the qualities of both. From their condition, and the unconquerable prejudices resulting from their colour, they never could amalgamate with the free whites of this country. It was desirable, therefore, as it respected them, and the residue of the population of the country, to drain them off. Various schemes of colonization had been thought of, and a part of our continent, it was supposed by some, might furnish a suitable establishment for them. But, for his part, Mr. C. said, he had a decided preference for some part of the Coast of Africa. There ample provision might be made for the colony itself, and it might be rendered instrumental to the introduction into that extensive quarter of the globe, of the arts, civilization, and Christianity." [Here I ask Mr. Clay, what kind of Christianity? Did he mean such as they have among the Americans—distinction, whip, blood and oppression? I pray the Lord Jesus Christ to forbid it.] "There," said he, "was a peculiar, a moral fitness, in restoring them to the land of their fathers, and if instead of the evils and sufferings which we had been the innocent cause of inflicting upon the inhabitants of Africa, we can transmit to her the blessings of our arts, our civilization, and our religion. May we not hope that America will extinguish a great portion of that moral debt which she has contracted to that unfortunate continent? Can there be a nobler cause than that which, whilst it proposes," &c. * * * * * * * [you know what this means.] "contemplates the spreading of the arts of civilized life, and the possible redemption from ignorance and barbarism of a benighted quarter of the globe?"

Before I proceed any further, I solicit your notice, brethren, to the foregoing part of Mr. Clay's speech, in which he says, (→ look above) "and if, instead of the evils and sufferings, which we had been the innocent cause of inflicting," &c.—What this very learned statesman could have been thinking about, when he said in his speech, "we had been the innocent cause of inflicting," &c., I have never been able to conceive. Are Mr. Clay and the rest of the Americans, innocent of the blood and groans of our fathers and us, their children?—Every individual may plead innocence, if he pleases, but God will, before long, separate the innocent from the guilty, unless something is speedily done which I suppose will hardly be, so that their destruction may be sure. Oh

---

* See Dr. Torrey's Portraiture of Domestic Slavery in the United States, pages 85, 86.

Americans! let me tell you, in the name of the Lord, it will be good for you, if you listen to the voice of the Holy Ghost, but if you do not, you are ruined! ! ! Some of you are good men; but the will of my God must be done. Those avaricious and ungodly tyrants among you, I am awfully afraid will drag down the vengeance of God upon you. When God Almighty commences his battle on the continent of America, for the oppression of his people, tyrants will wish they never were born.

But to return to Mr. Clay, whence I digressed. He says, "It was proper and necessary distinctly to state, that he understood it constituted no part of the object of this meeting, to touch or agitate in the slightest degree, a delicate question, connected with another portion of the coloured population of our country. It was not proposed to deliberate upon or consider at all, any question of emancipation, or that which was connected with the abolition of slavery. It was upon that condition alone, he was sure, that many gentlemen from the South and the West, whom he saw present, had attended, or could be expected to co-operate. It was upon that condition only, that he himself had attended."

That is to say, to fix a plan to get those of the coloured people, who are said to be free, away from among those of our brethren whom they unjustly hold in bondage, so that they may be enabled to keep them the more secure in ignorance and wretchedness, to support them and their children, and consequently they would have the more obedient slaves. For if the free are allowed to stay among the slaves, they will have intercourse together, and, of course, the free will learn the slaves *bad habits*, by teaching them that they are MEN, as well as other people, and certainly *ought* and *must* be FREE.

I presume, that every intelligent man of colour must have some idea of Mr. Henry Clay, originally of Virginia, but now of Kentucky; they know too, perhaps, whether he is a friend, or a foe to the coloured citizens of this country, and of the world. This gentleman, according to his own words, had been highly favoured and blessed of the Lord, though he did not acknowledge it; but, to the contrary, he acknowledged men, for all the blessings with which God had favoured him. At a public dinner, given him at Fowler's Garden, Lexington, Kentucky, he delivered a public speech to a very large concourse of people—in the concluding clause of which, he says, "And now, my friends and fellow citizens, I cannot part from you, on possibly the last occasion of my ever publicly addressing you, without reiterating the expression of my thanks, from a heart overflowing with gratitude. I came among you, now more than thirty years ago, an orphan boy, pennyless, a stranger to you all, without friends, without the favour of the great, you took me up, cherished me, protected me, honoured me, you have constantly poured upon me a bold and unabated stream of innumerable favours, time which wears out every thing has increased and strengthened your affection for me. When I seemed deserted by almost the whole world, and assailed by almost every tongue, and pen, and press, you have fearlessly and manfully stood by me, with unsurpassed zeal and undiminished friendship. When I felt as if I should sink beneath the storm of abuse and detraction, which was violently raging around me, I have found myself upheld and sustained by your encouraging voices and approving smiles. I have doubtless, committed many faults and indiscretions, over which you have thrown the broad mantle of your charity. But I can say, and in the presence of God and in this assembled multitude, I will say, that I have honestly and faithfully served my country—that I have never wronged it—and that, however unprepared, I lament that I am to appear in the Divine presence on other accounts, I invoke the stern justice of his judgment on my public conduct, without the slightest apprehension of his displeasure."

Hearken to this Statesman indeed, but no philanthropist, whom God sent into Kentucky, an orphan boy, penniless, and friendless, where he not only gave him a plenty of friends and the comforts of life, but raised him almost to the very highest honour in the nation, where his great talents, with which the Lord has been pleased to bless him, has gained for him the affection of a great portion of the people with whom he had to do. But what has this gentleman done for the Lord, after having done so much for him? The Lord has a suffering people, whose moans and groans at his feet for deliverance from oppression and wretchedness, pierce the very throne of Heaven, and call loudly on the God of Justice, to be revenged. Now, what this gentleman who is so highly favoured of the Lord, has done to liberate those miserable victims of oppression, shall appear before the world by his letters to Mr. Gallatin, Envoy Extraordinary and Minister Plenipotentiary to Great Britain, dated June 19, 1826.—Though Mr. Clay was writing for the States, yet nevertheless, it appears from the very face of his letters to that gentleman, that he was as anxious, if not more so, to get those free people and sink them into wretchedness, as his constituents, for whom he wrote.

The Americans of North and of South America including the West India Islands—no trifling portion of whom were, for stealing, murdering, &c. compelled to flee from Europe, to save their necks or banishment, have effected their escape to this continent, where God blessed them with all the comforts of life—He gave them a plenty of every thing calculated to do them good—not satisfied with this, however, they wanted slaves and wanted us for their slaves, who belong to the Holy Ghost, and no other, who we shall have to serve instead of tyrants.—I say, the Americans want us, the property of the Holy Ghost to serve them. But there is a day fast approaching, when (unless there is a universal repentance on the part of the whites, which will scarcely take place, they have got to be so hardened in consequence of our blood, and so wise in their own conceit.) To be plain and candid with you, Americans! I say that the day is fast approaching, when there will be a greater time on the continent of America, than ever was witnessed upon this earth since it came from the hand of its Creator. Some of you have done us so much injury, that you will never be able to repent.—Your cup must be filled.—You want us for your slaves, and shall have enough of us—God is just, *who will give you your fill of us*. But Mr. Henry Clay, speaking to Mr. Gallatin, respecting coloured people, who had effected their escape from the U. States (or to them *hell upon earth! ! !*) to the hospitable shores of Canada,* from whence it would cause more than the lives of the Americans to get them, to plunge into wretchedness—he says: "The General Assembly of Kentucky, one of the states which is most affected by the escape of slaves into Upper Canada has again, at their session which has just terminated, invoked the interposition of the General Government. In the treaty which has been recently concluded with the United Mexican States, and which is now under the consideration of the Senate, provision is made for the restoration of fugitive slaves. As it appears from your statements of what passed on that subject, with the British Plenipotentiaries, that they admitted the correctness of the principle of restoration, it is hoped that you will be able to succeed in making satisfactory arrangements."

There are a series of these letters, all of which are to the same amount; some however, presenting a face more of his own responsibility. I wonder what would this gentleman think, if the Lord should give him among the rest of his blessings enough of slaves? Could he blame any other being but himself? Do we not belong to the Holy Ghost? What business has he or any body else, to be sending letters about the world respecting us? Can we not go where we want to, as well as other people, only if we obey the voice of the Holy Ghost? This gentleman, (Mr. Henry Clay) not only took an active part in this colonizing plan, but was absolutely chairman of a meeting held at Washington, the twenty-first day of December 1816, to agitate the subject of colonizing us in Africa.—Now I appeal and ask every citizen of these United States and of the world, both *white* and *black*, who has any knowledge of Mr. Clay's public labor for these States—I want you candidly to answer the Lord, who sees the secrets of our hearts.—Do you believe that Mr. Henry Clay, late Secretary of State, and now in Kentucky, is a friend to the blacks, further, than his personal interest extends? Is it not his greatest object and glory upon earth, to sink us into miseries and wretchedness by making slaves of us, to work his plantation to enrich him and his family? Does he care a pinch of snuff about Africa—whether it remains a land of Pagans and of blood, or of Christians, so long as he gets enough of her sons and daughters to dig up gold and silver for him? If he had no slaves, and could obtain them in no other way if it were not, repugnant to the laws of his country, which prohibit the importation of slaves (which act was, indeed, more through apprehension than humanity) would he not try to import a few from Africa, to work his farm? Would he work in the hot sun to earn his bread, if he could make an African work for nothing, particularly, if he could keep him in ignorance and make him believe that God made him for nothing else but to work for him? Is not Mr. Clay a white man, and too delicate to work in the hot sun! ! Was he not made by his Creator to sit in the shade, and make the blacks work without remuneration for their services, to support him and his family! ! ! I have been for some time taking notice of this man's speeches and public writings, but never to my knowledge have I seen any thing in his writings which insisted on the emancipation of slavery, which has almost ruined his country. Thus we see the depravity of men's hearts, when in pursuit only of gain—particularly when they oppress their fellow creatures to obtain that gain—God suffers some to go on until they are lost forever. This same Mr. Clay, wants to know, what he has done, to merit die disapprobation of the American people. In a public speech delivered by him, he asked: "Did I involve my country in an unnecessary war?" to merit the censure of the Americans—"Did I bring obliquy upon the nation, or the people whom I represented? —did I ever lose any opportunity to advance the fame, honor and prosperity of this State and the Union?" How astonishing it is, for a man who knows so much about God and his ways, as Mr. Clay, to ask such frivolous questions? Does he believe that a man of his talents and standing in the midst of a people, will get along unnoticed by the penetrating and all seeing eye of God, who is continually taking cognizance of the hearts of men? Is not God against him, for advocating the murderous cause of slavery? If God is against him, what can the Americans, together with the whole world do for him? Can they save him from the hand of the Lord Jesus Christ?

---

* Among the English, our real friends and benefactors.

I shall now pass in review the speech of Mr. Elias B. Caldwell Esq. of the District of Columbia, extracted from the same page on which Mr. Clay's will be found. Mr. Caldwell, giving his opinion respecting us, at that ever memorable meeting, he says: "The more you improve the condition of these people, the more you cultivate their minds, the more miserable you make them in their present state. You give them a higher relish for those privileges which they can never attain, and turn what we intend for a blessing into a curse." Let me ask this benevolent man, what he means by a blessing intended for us? Did he mean sinking us and our children into ignorance and wretchedness, to support him and his family? What he meant will appear evident and obvious to the most ignorant in the world (See Mr. Caldwell's intended blessings for us, O! my Lord! ! "No," said he, "if they must remain in their present situation, keep them in the *lowest state of degradation and ignorance*. The nearer you bring them to the condition of brutes, the better chance do you give them of possessing their *apathy*." Here I pause to get breath, having labored to extract the above clause of this gentleman's speech, at that colonizing meeting. I presume that everybody knows the meaning of the word "*apathy*," —if any do not, let him get Sheridan's Dictionary, in which he will find it explained in full. I solicit the attention of the world, to the foregoing part of Mr. Caldwell's speech, that they may see what man will do with his fellow men, when he has them under his feet. To what length will not man go in iniquity when given up to a hard heart, and reprobate mind, in consequence of blood and oppression? The last clause of this speech, which was written in a very artful manner, and which will be taken for the speech of a friend, without close examination and deep penetration, I shall now present. He says, "surely, Americans ought to be the last people on earth, to advocate such slavish doctrines, to cry peace and contentment to those who are deprived of the privileges of civil liberty, they who have so largely partaken of its blessings, who know so well how to estimate its value, ought to be among the foremost to extend it to others." The real sense and meaning of the last part of Mr. Caldwell's speech is, get the free people of colour away to Africa, from among the slaves, where they may at once be blessed and happy, and those who we hold in slavery, will be contented to rest in ignorance and wretchedness, to dig up gold and silver for us and our children. Men have indeed got to be so cunning, these days, that it would take the eye of a Solomon to penetrate and find them out.

→ ADDITION.—OUR dear Redeemer said, "Therefore, whatsoever ye have spoken in darkness, shall be heard in the light; and that which ye have spoken in the ear in closets, shall be pro-claimed upon the house tops."

How obviously this declaration of our Lord has been shown among the Americans of the United States. They have hitherto passed among some nations, who do not know any thing about their internal concerns, for the most enlightened, humane charitable, and merciful people upon earth, when at the same time they treat us, the (coloured people) secretly more cruel and unmerciful than any other nation upon earth.—It is a fact that in our Southern and Western States, there are millions who hold us in chains or in slavery, whose greatest object and glory, is centered in keeping us sunk in the most profound ignorance and stupidity, to make us work without remunerations for our services. Many of whom if they catch a coloured person, whom they hold in unjust ignorance, slavery and degradation, to them and their children, with a book in his hand, will beat him nearly to death. I heard a wretch in the state of North Carolina said that if any man would teach a black person whom he held in slavery, to spell, read or write, he would prosecute him to the very extent of the law.—Said the ignorant wretch,* "a Nigar, ought not to have any more sense than enough to work for his master." May I not ask to fatten the wretch and his family?—These and similar cruelties these *Christians* have been for hundreds of years inflicting on our fathers and us in the dark God has however, very recently published some of their secret crimes on the house top, that the world may gaze on their Christianity and see of what kind it is composed.—Georgia for instance, God has completely shown to the world, the *Christianity* among its white *inhabitants*. A law has recently passed the Legislature of this *republican* State (Georgia) prohibiting all free or slave persons of colour, from learning to read or write; another law has passed the *republican* House of Delegates, (but not the Senate) in Virginia, to prohibit all persons of colour, (free and slave) from learning to read or write, and even to hinder them from meeting together in order to worship our Maker! ! ! ! !—Now I solemnly appeal, to the most skilful historians in the world, and all those who are mostly acquainted with the histories of the Antideluvians and of Sodom and Gomorrah, to show me a parallel of barbarity. *Christians! ! Christians! ! !* I dare you to show me a parallel of cruelties in the annals of Heathens or of Devils, with those of Ohio, Virginia and of Georgia— know the world that these things were before done in the dark, or in a corner under a garb of humanity and religion. God has however, taken of the figleaf covering, and made them expose them-selves on the house top. I tell you that God works in many ways his wonders to perform, he will unless they repent, make them expose

* It is a fact, that in all our Slave-holding States (in the countries) there are thousands of the whites, who are almost as ignorant in comparison as horses, the most they know, is to beat the coloured people, which some of them shall have their hearts full of yet.

themselves enough more yet to the world.—See the acts of the *Christians* in FLORIDA, SOUTH CAROLINA, and KENTUCKY—was it not for the reputation of the house of my Lord and Master, I would mention here, an act of cruelty inflicted a few days since on a black man, by the white *Christians* in the PARK STREET CHURCH, in this (CITY) which is almost enough to make Demons themselves quake and tremble in their FIREY HABITATIONS.—Oh! my Lord how refined in iniquity the whites have got to be in consequence of our blood*— what kind! ! Oh! what kind! ! ! of Christianity can be found this day in all the earth! ! ! ! ! !

I write without the fear of man, I am writing for my God, and fear none but himself; they may put me to death if they choose—(I fear and esteem a good man however, let him be black or white.) I forbear to comment on the cruelties inflicted on this Black Man by the Whites, in the Park Street MEETING HOUSE, I will leave it in the dark! ! ! ! ! But I declare that the atrocity is really to Heaven daring and infernal, that I must say that God has commenced a course of exposition among the Americans, and the glorious and heavenly work will continue to progress until they learn to do justice.←

Extract from the Speech of Mr. John Randolph, of Roanoke.

Said he:—"It had been properly observed by the Chairman, as well as by the gentleman from this District (meaning Messrs. Clay and Caldwell) that there was nothing in the proposition submitted to consideration which in the smallest degree touches* The Blood of our fathers who have been murdered by the whites, and the groans of our Brethren, who are now held in cruel ignorance, wretchedness and slavery by them, cry aloud to the Maker of Heaven and of earth, against the whole continent of America, for redresses. Another very important and delicate question, which ought to be left as much out of view as possible, is Negro Slavery. "There is no fear," Mr. R. said, "that this proposition would alarm the slave-holders; they had been accustomed to think seriously of the subject.—There was a popular work on agriculture by John Taylor of Caroline, which was widely circulated, and much confided in, in Virginia. In that book, much read because coming from a practical man, this description of people, [referring to us half free ones] were pointed out as a great evil. They had indeed been held up as the greater bug-bear to every man who feels an inclination to emancipate his slaves, not to create in the bosom of his country so great a nuisance. If a place could be provided for their reception, and a mode of sending them hence, there were hundreds, nay thousands of citizens who would, by manumitting their slaves, relieve themselves from the cares attendant on their possession. The great slaveholder," Mr. R. said, "was frequently a mere sentry at his own door-bound to stay on his plantation to see that his slaves were properly treated, &c." Mr. R. concluded by saying, that he had thought it necessary to make these remarks being a slaveholder himself, to shew that, "so far from being connected with abolition of slavery, the measure proposed would prove one of the greatest securities to enable the master to keep in possession his own property."

Here is a demonstrative proof, of a plan got up, by a gang of slave-holders to select the free people of colour from among the slaves, that our more miserable brethren may be the better secured in ignorance and wretchedness, to work their farms and dig their mines, and thus go on enriching the Christians with their blood and groans. What our brethren could have been thinking about, who have left their native land and home and gone away to Africa, I am unable to say. This country is as much ours as it is the whites, whether they will admit it now or not, they will see and believe it by and by. . . .

→ ADDITION.—If any of us see fit to go away, go to those who have been for many years, and are now our greatest earthly friends and benefactors—the English. If not so, go to our brethren, the Haytians, who, according to their word, are bound to protect and comfort us. The Americans say, that we are ungrateful— but I ask them for heaven's sake, what should we be grateful to them for—for murdering our fathers and mothers?—Or do they wish us to return thanks to them for chaining and hand-cuffing us, branding us, cramming fire down our throats, or for keeping us in slavery, and beating us nearly or quite to death to make us work in ignorance and miseries, to support them and their families. They certainly think that we are a gang of fools. Those among them, who have volunteered their services for our redemption, though we are unable to compensate them for their labours, we nevertheless thank them from the bottom of our hearts, and have

---

* "Niger," is a word derived from the Latin, which was used by the old Romans, to designate inanimate beings, which were black: such as soot pot wood, house, &c. Also, animals which they considered inferior to the human species, as a black horse, cow, hog, bird, dog, &c. The white Americans have applied this term to Africans, by way of reproach for our colour, to aggravate and heighten our miseries, because they have their feet on our throats, prejudice—what have we to do with it? Their prejudices will be obliged to fall like lightning to the ground, in succeeding generations; not, however, with the will and consent of all the whites, for some will be obliged to hold on to the old adage, viz: the blacks are not men, but were made to be an inheritance to us and our children for ever! ! ! ! ! ! I hope the residue of the coloured people, will stand still and see the salvation of God and the miracle which he will work for our delivery from wretchedness under the Christians! ! ! ! ! !

our eyes steadfastly fixed upon them, and their labours of love for God and man.—But do slave-holders think that we thank them for keeping us in miseries, and taking our lives by the inches?

Before I proceed further with this scheme, I shall give an extract from the letter of that truly Reverend Divine, (Bishop Allen,) of Philadelphia, respecting this trick. At the instance of the editor of the Freedom's Journal, he says, "Dear Sir, I have been for several years trying to reconcile my mind to the Colonizing of Africans in Liberia, but there have always been, and there still remain great and insurmountable objections against the scheme. We are an unlettered people, brought up in ignorance, not one in a hundred can read or write, not one in a thousand has a liberal education; is there any fitness for such to be sent into a far country, among heathens, to convert or civilize them when they themselves are neither civilized or Christianized? Se: the great bulk of the poor, ignorant Africans in this country, exposed to every temptation before them: all for the want of their morals being refined by education and proper attendance paid unto them by their owners, or those who had the charge of them. It is said by the Southern slave-holders, that the more ignorant they can bring up the Africans, the better slaves they make, ('go and come.') Is there any fitness for such people to be colonized in a far country to be their own rulers? Can we not discern the project of sending the free people of colour away from their country? Is it not for the interest of the slave-holders to select the free people of colour out of the different states, and send them to Liberia? Will it not make their slaves uneasy to see free men of colour enjoying liberty? It is against the law in some of the Southern States, that a person of colour should receive an education, under a severe penalty. Colonizationists speak of America being first colonized; but is there any comparison between the two? America was colonized by as *wise, judicious and educated* men as the world afforded. WILLIAM PENN did not want for *learning, wisdom, or intelligence.* If all the people in Europe and America were as ignorant and in the same situation as our brethren, what would become of the world? Where would be the principle or piety that would govern the people? We were stolen from our mother country, and brought *here.* We have *tilled* the ground and made fortunes for thousands, and still they are not weary of our services. *But they who stay to till the ground must be slaves.* Is there not land enough in America, or 'corn enough in Egypt?' Why should they send us into a far country to die? See the thousands of foreigners emigrating to America every year: and if there be ground sufficient for them to cultivate, and bread for them to eat, why would they wish to send the *first tillers* of the land away? Africans have made fortunes for thousands, who are yet unwilling to part with their services; but the free must be sent away, and those who remain, must be *slaves.* I have no doubt that there are many good men who do not see as I do, and who are for sending us to Liberia; but they have not duly considered the subject—they are not men of colour.—This land which we have watered with our *tears* and *our blood,* is now our *mother country,* and we are well satisfied to stay where wisdom abounds and the gospel is free."

—"RICHARD ALLEN, *"Bishop of the African Methodist Episcopal "Church in the United States."*

I have given you, my brethren, an extract verbatim, from the letter of that godly man, as you may find it on the aforementioned page of Freedom's Journal. I know that thousands, and perhaps millions of my brethren in these States, have never heard of such a man as Bishop Allen—a man whom God many years ago raised up among his ignorant and degraded brethren, to preach Jesus Christ and him crucified to them—who notwithstanding, had to wrestle against principalities and the powers of darkness to diffuse that gospel with which he was endowed among his brethren—but who having overcome the combined powers of devils and wicked men, has under God planted a Church among us which will be as durable as the foundation of the earth on which it stands. Richard Allen! O my God! The bare recollection of the labours of this man, and his ministers among his deplorably wretched brethren, (rendered so by the whites) to bring them to a knowledge of the God of Heaven, fills my soul with all those very high emotions which would take the pen of an Addison to portray. It is impossible my brethren for me to say much in this work respecting that man of God. When the Lord shall raise up coloured historians in succeeding generations, to present the crimes of this nation, to the then gazing world, the Holy Ghost will make them do justice to the name of Bishop Allen, of Philadelphia. Suffice it for me to say, that, the name of this very man (Richard Allen) though now in obscurity and degradation, will notwithstanding, stand on the pages of history among the greatest divines who have lived since the apostolic age, and among the Africans, Bishop Allen's will be entirely preeminent. My brethren, search after the character and exploits of this godly man among his ignorant and miserable brethren to bring them to a knowledge of the truth as it is in our Master. Consider upon the tyrants and false Christians against whom he had to contend in order to get access to his brethren. See him and his ministers in the States of New York, New Jersey, Pennsylvania, Delaware and Maryland, carrying the gladsome tidings of free and full salvation to the coloured people. Tyrants and false Christians however, would not allow him to penetrate far into the South, for fear that he would awaken some of his ignorant brethren, whom they held in wretchedness and misery—for fear, I say it, that he would awaken and bring them to a knowledge of their Maker. O my Master! my Master! I can-not but think upon Christian Americans! ! !—What kind of people can they be? Will not those who were burnt up in Sodom and Gomorrah rise up in judgment against Christian Americans with the Bible in their hands, and condemn them? Will not the Scribes and Pharisees of Jerusalem, who had nothing but the laws of Moses and the Prophets to go by, rise up in judgment against Christian Americans, and condemn them,* who, in addition to these have a revelation from Jesus Christ the Son of the living God? In fine, will not the Antideluvians, together with the whole heathen world of antiquity, rise up in judgment against Christian Americans and condemn them? The Christians of Europe and America go to Africa, bring us away, and throw us into the seas, and in other ways murder us, as they would wild beast. The Antideluvians and heathens never dreamed of such barbarities.—Now the Christians believe, because they have a name to live, while they are dead, that God will overlook such things. But if he does not deceive them, it will be because he has over-looked it sure enough. But to return to this godly man, Bishop Allen. I do hereby openly affirm it to the world, that he has done more in a spiritual sense for his ignorant and wretched brethren than any other man of colour has, since the world began. And as for the greater part of the whites, it has hitherto been their greatest object and glory to keep us ignorant of our Maker, so as to make us believe that we were made to be slaves to them and their children, to dig up gold and silver for them.

It is notorious that not a few professing Christians among the whites, who profess to love our Lord and Saviour Jesus Christ, have assailed this man and laid all the obstacles in his way they possibly could, consistent with their profession—and what for? Why, their course of proceeding and his, clashed exactly together—they trying their best to keep us ignorant, that we might be the better and more obedient slaves—while he, on the other hand, doing his very best to enlighten us and teach, us a knowledge of the Lord. And I am sorry that I have it to say, that many of our brethren have joined in with our oppressors, whose dearest objects are only to keep us ignorant and miserable against this man to stay his hand.—However, they have kept us in so much ignorance, that many of us know no better than to fight against ourselves, and by that means strengthen the hands of our natural enemies, to rivet their infernal chains of slavery upon us and our children. I have several times called the white Americans our *natural enemies*—I shall here define my meaning of the phrase. Shem, Ham and Japheth, together with their father Noah and wives, I believe were not natural enemies to each other. When the ark rested after the flood upon Mount Arrarat, in Asia, they (eight) were all the people which could be found alive in all the earth—in fact if Scriptures be true, (which I believe are) there were no other living men in all the earth, notwithstanding some ignorant creatures hesitate not to tell us that we, (the blacks) are the seed of Cain the murderer of his brother Abel. But where or of whom those ignorant and avaricious wretches could have got their information, I am unable to declare. Did they receive it from the Bible? I have searched the Bible as well as they, if I am not as well learned as they are, and have never seen a verse which testifies whether we are the seed of Cain or of Abel. Yet those men tell us that we are the seed of Cain, and that God put a dark stain upon us, that we might be known as their slaves! ! ! Now, I ask those avaricious and ignorant wretches, who act more like the seed of Cain, by murdering the whites or the blacks? How many vessel loads of human beings have the blacks thrown into the seas? How many thousand souls have the blacks murdered in cold blood, to make them work in wretchedness and ignorance, to support them and their families?** —However, let us be the seed of *Cain, Harry, Dick, or Tom*! ! ! God will show the whites what we are, yet. I say, from the beginning, I do not think that we were natural enemies to each other. But the whites having made us so wretched, by subjecting us to slavery, and having murdered so many millions of us, in order to make us work for them, and out of devilishness—and they taking our wives, whom we love as we do ourselves—our mothers who bore the pains of death to give us birth—our fathers and dear little children, and ourselves, and strip and beat us one before the other—chain, hand-cuff, and drag us about like rattle-snakes—shoot us down like wild bears, before each other's faces to make us submissive to, and work to support them and their families. They (the whites) know well, if we are *men*—and there is a secret monitor in their hearts which tells them we are—they know, I say, if we *are* men, and see them treating us in the manner they do, that there can be nothing in our hearts but death alone, for them, notwithstanding we may appear cheerful, when we see them murdering our dear mothers and wives because

---

* I mean those whose labours for the good, or rather destruction of Jerusalem and the Jews ceased before our Lord entered the Temple, and overturned the tables of the Money Changers.

** How many millions souls of the human family have the blacks beat nearly to death to keep them from learning to read the Word of God and from writing. And telling lies about them, by holding them up to the world as a tribe of TALKING APES, void of INTELLECT! ! ! ! ! incapable of LEARNING, &c.

we cannot help ourselves. Man, in all ages and all nations of the earth, is the same. Man is a peculiar creature—he is the image of his God, though he may be subjected to the most wretched condition upon earth, yet the spirit and feeling which constitute the creature, man, can never be entirely erased from his breast, because the God who made him after his own image planted it in his heart; he cannot get rid of it.

The whites knowing this, they do not know what to do; they know that they have done us so much injury, they are afraid that we, being men and not brutes, will retaliate, and woe will be to them; therefore, that dreadful fear, together with an avaricious spirit, and the natural love in them, to be called masters, (which term will yet honour them with to their sorrow) bring them to the resolve that they will keep us in ignorance and wretchedness, as long as they possibly can,* and make the best of their time, while it lasts.

Consequently they, themselves, (and not us) render them-selves our natural enemies, by treating us so cruel. They keep us miserable now, and call us their property, but some of them will have enough of us by and by—their stomachs shall run over with us; they want us for their slaves, and shall have us to their fill. We are all in the world together! !—I said above, because we cannot help ourselves, (viz. we cannot help the whites murdering our mothers and our wives) but this statement is incorrect—for we can help ourselves; for, if we lay aside abject servility, and be determined to act like men, and not brutes—the murderers among the whites would be afraid to show their cruel heads. But O, my God! —in sorrow I must say it, that my colour, all over the world, have a mean, servile spirit. They yield in a moment to the whites, let them be right or wrong—the reason they are able to keep their feet on our throats. Oh! my coloured brethren, all over the world, when shall we arise from this death-like apathy?—And be men! ! You will notice, if ever we become men, (I mean *respectable* men, such as other people are,) we must exert ourselves to the full. For remember, that it is the greatest desire and object of the greater part of the whites, to keep us ignorant, and make us work to support them and their families.—Here now, in the Southern and Western sections of this country, there are at least three coloured persons for one white, why is it, that those few weak, good-for-nothing whites, are able to keep so many able men, one of whom, can put to flight a dozen whites, in wretchedness and misery? It shows at once, what the blacks are, we are ignorant, abject, servile and mean—and the whites know it—they know that we are too servile to assert our rights as men—or they would not fool with us as they do. Would they fool with any other peoples as they do with us? No, they know too well, that they would get themselves ruined. Why do they not bring the inhabitants of Asia to be body servants to them? They know they would get their bodies rent and torn from head to foot. Why do they not get the Aborigines of this country to be slaves to them and their children, to work their farms and dig their mines? They know well that the Aborigines of this country, or (Indians) would tear them from the earth. The Indians would not rest day or night, they would be up all times of night, cutting their cruel throats. But my colour, (some, not all,) are willing to stand still and be murdered by the cruel whites. In some of the West-Indies Islands, and over a large part of South America, there are six or eight coloured persons for one white.**

---

* And still holds us up with indignity as being incapable of acquiring knowledge! ! See the inconsistency of the assertions of those wretches—they beat us inhumanely, sometimes almost to death for attempting to inform ourselves, by reading the Word of our Maker, and at the same time tell us, that we are beings void of intellect! How admirably their practices agree with their professions in this case. Let me cry shame upon you Americans, for such out-rages upon human nature! ! ! If it were possible for the whites always to keep us ignorant and miserable, and make us work to enrich them and their children, and insult our feelings by representing us as talking Apes, what would they do? But glory, honour and praise to Heaven's King, that the sons and daughters of Africa, will, in spite of all the opposition of their enemies, stand forth in all the dignity and glory that is granted by the Lord to his creature man.

** For instance in the two States of Georgia, and South Carolina, there are, perhaps, not much short of six or seven hundred thousand persons of colour; and if I was a gambling character, I would not be afraid to stake down upon the board FIVE CENTS against TEN, that there are in the single State of Virginia, five or six hundred thousand Coloured persons. Four hundred and fifty thousand of whom (let them be well equipt for war) I would put against every white person on the whole continent of America. (Why? why because I know that the Blacks, once they get involved in a war, had rather die than to live, they either kill or be killed.) The whites know this too, which make them quake and tremble. To show the world further, how servile the coloured people are, I will only hold up to view, the one Island of Jamaica, as a specimen of our meanness. In that Island, there are three hundred and fifty thousand souls—of whom fifteen thousand are whites, the remainder, three hundred and thirty-five thousand are coloured people! and this Island is ruled by the white people! ! ! ! ! ! ! (15,000) ruling and tyranizing over 335,000 persons ! ! ! ! ! ! ! !—O! coloured men!! O! coloured men!!! O! coloured men!!!! Look!! look!!! at this!!!! and, tell me if we are not abject and servile enough, how long, O! how long my colour shall we be dupes and dogs to the cruel whites?—I only passed Jamaica, and its inhabitants, in review as a specimen to show the world, the condition of the Blacks at this time, now coloured people of the whole world, I beg you to look at the (15000 white,) and (Three Hundred and Thirty-five Thousand coloured people) in that Island, and tell me how can the white tyrants of the world but say that we are not men, hut were made to be slaves and Dogs to them and their children forever!! !! ! !—why my friend only look at the thing ! ! ! ! (15000) whites keeping in wretchedness and degradation (335000) viz. 22 coloured persons for one white! ! ! ! ! ! ! when at the same time, an equal number (15000) Blacks, would almost take the whole of South America, because where they go as soldiers to fight death follows in their tram.

Why do they not take possession of those places? Who hinders them? It is not the avaricious whites—for they are too busily engaged in laying up money—derived from the blood and tears of the blacks. The fact is, they are too servile, they love to have Masters too well! ! Some of our brethren, too, who seeking more after self aggrandizement, than the glory of God, and the welfare of their brethren, join in with our oppressors, to ridicule and say all manner of evils falsely against our Bishop. They think, that they are doing great things, when they can get in company with the whites, to ridicule and make sport of those who are labouring for their good. Poor ignorant creatures, they do not know that the sole aim and object of the whites, are only to make fools and slaves of them, and put the whip to them, and make them work to support them and their families. But I do say, that no man, can well be a despiser of Bishop Allen, for his public labours among us, unless he is a despiser of God and of Righteousness. Thus, we see, my brethren, the two very opposite positions of those great men, who have written respecting this "Coloniz-ing Plan." (Mr. Clay and his slave-holding party,) men who are resolved to keep us in eternal wretched-ness, are also bent upon sending us to Liberia. While the Reverend Bishop Allen, and his party, men who have the fear of God, and the wellfare of their brethren at heart. The Bishop, in particular, whose labours for the salvation of his brethren, are well known to a large part of those, who dwell in the United States, are completely opposed to the plan—and advise us to stay where we are. Now we have to determine whose advice we will take respecting this all important matter, whether we will adhere to Mr. Clay and his slave holding party, who have always been our oppressors and murderers, and who are for colonizing us, more through apprehension than humanity, or to this godly man who has done so much for our ben-efit, together with the advice of all the good and wise among us and the whites. Will any of us leave our homes and go to Africa? I hope not.*

Let them commence their attack upon us as they did on our brethren in Ohio, driving and beating us from our country, and my soul for theirs they will have enough of it. Let no man of us budge one step: and let slave-holders come to beat us from our country. America is more our country, than it is the whites—we have enriched it with our *blood and tears.* The greatest riches in all America have arisen from our blood and tears:—and will they drive us from our property and homes, which we have earned with our *blood?* They must look sharp or this very thing will bring swift destruction upon them. The Americans have got so fat on our blood and groans, that they have almost forgotten the God of armies. But let them go on.

→ ADDITION.—I will give here a very imperfect list of the cruelties inflicted on us by the enlightened Christians of America.—First, no trifling portion of them will beat us nearly to death if they find us on our knees praying to God,—They hinder us from going to hear the word of God—they keep us sunk in ignorance, and will not let us learn to read the word of God, nor write—If they find us with a book of any description in our hand they will beat us nearly to death—they are so afraid we will learn to read, and enlighten our dark and benighted minds—They will not suffer us to meet together to worship the God who made us—they brand us with hot iron—they cram bolts of fire down our throats—they cut us as they do horses, bulls, or hogs—they crop our ears and sometimes cut off bits of our tongues—they chain and hand-cuff us, and while in that miserable and wretched condition, beat us with cow-hides and clubs—they keep us half naked and starve us sometimes nearly to death under their infernal whips or lashes (which some of them shall have enough of yet)—They put on us fifty-sixes and chains, and make us work in that cruel situation, and in sick-ness, under lashes to support them and their families.—They keep us three or four hundred feet under ground working in their mines, night and day to dig up gold and silver to enrich them and their children.—They keep us in the most death-like ignorance by keeping us from all source of information, and call us, who are free men and next to the Angels of God, their property! ! ! ! ! They make us fight and murder each other, many of us being ignorant, not knowing any better.—They take us, (being ignorant,) and put us as drivers one over the other, and make us afflict each other as bad as they themselves afflict us—and to crown the whole of this catalogue of cruelties, they tell us that we the (blacks) are an inferior race of beings! incapable of self government! !—We would be injurious to society and ourselves, if tyrants should loose their unjust hold on us! ! ! That if we were free we would not work, but would live on plunder or theft! ! ! ! that we are the meanest and laziest set of beings in the world! ! ! ! ! ! That they are obliged to keep us in bondage to do us good ! ! ! ! ! !—That we are satisfied to rest in slavery to them and their children ! ! ! ! ! ! !—That we ought not to be set free in America, but ought to be sent away to Africa ! ! ! ! ! ! ! ! !—That if we were set free in America,

---

* Those who are ignorant enough to go to Africa, the coloured people ought to be glad to have them go, for if they are ignorant enough to let the whites fool them off to Africa, they would be no small injury to us if they reside in this country.

we would involve the country in a civil war, which assertion is altogether at variance with our feeling or design, for we ask them for nothing but the rights of man, viz. for them to set us free, and treat us like men, and there will be no danger, for we will love and respect them, and protect our country—but cannot conscientiously do these things until they treat us like men. ←

How cunning slave-holders think they are!!!—How much like the king of Egypt who, after he saw plainly that God was determined to bring out his people, in spite of him and his, as powerful as they were. He was willing that Moses, Aaron and the Elders of Israel, but not all the people should go and serve the Lord. But God deceived him as he will Christian Americans, unless they are very cautious how they move. What would have become of the United States of America, was it not for those among the whites, who not in words barely, but in truth and in deed, love and fear the Lord?—Our Lord and Master said: "[But] Whose shall offend one of these little ones which believe in me, it were better for him that a millstone were hanged about his neck, and that he were drowned in the depth of the sea."

But the Americans with this very threatening of the Lord's, not only beat his little ones among the Africans, but many of them they put to death or murder. Now the avaricious Americans, think that the Lord Jesus Christ will let them off, because his words are no more than the words of a man! ! ! In fact, many of them are so avaricious and ignorant, that they do not believe in our Lord and Saviour Jesus Christ. Tyrants may think they are so skillful in State affairs is the reason that the government is preserved. But I tell you, that this country would have been given up long ago, was it not for the lovers of the Lord. They are indeed, the salt of the earth. Remove the people of God among the whites, from this land of blood, and it will stand until they cleverly get out of the way.

I adopt the language of the Rev. Mr. S. E. Cornish, of New York, editor of the Rights of All, and say: "Any coloured man of common intelligence, who gives his countenance and influence to that colony, further than its missionary object and interest extend, should be considered as a traitor to his brethren, and discarded by every respectable man of colour. And every member of that society, however pure his motive, whatever may be his religious character and moral worth, should in his efforts to remove the coloured population from their rightful soil, the land of their birth and nativity, be considered as acting gratuitously unrighteous and cruel."

Let me make an appeal brethren, to your hearts, for your cordial co-operation in the circulation of "The Rights of All", among us. The utility of such a vehicle conducted, cannot be estimated. I hope that the well informed among us, may see the absolute necessity of their co-operation in its universal spread among us. If we should let it go down, never let us undertake any thing of the kind again, but give up at once and say that we are really so ignorant and wretched that we cannot do any thing at all! !—As far as I have seen the writings of its editor, I believe he is not seeking to till his pockets with money, but has the welfare of his brethren truly at heart. Such men, brethren, ought to be supported by us.

But to return to the colonizing trick. It will be well for me to notice here at once, that I do not mean indiscriminately to condemn all the members and advocates of this scheme, for I believe that there are some friends to the sons of Africa, who are laboring for our salvation, not in words—only but in truth and in deed, who have been drawn into this plan—Some, more by persuasion than any thing else; while others, with humane feelings and lively zeal for our good, seeing how much we suffer from the afflictions poured upon us by unmerciful tyrants, are willing to enroll their names in any thing which they think has for its ultimate end our redemption from wretchedness and miseries; such men, with a heart truly overflowing with gratitude for their past services and zeal in our cause, I humbly beg to examine this plot minutely, and see if the end which they have in view will be completely consummated by such a course of procedure. Our friends who have been imperceptibly drawn into this plot I view with tenderness, and would not for the world injure their feelings, and I have only to hope for the future, that they will withdraw themselves from it;—for I declare to them, that the plot is not for the glory of God, but on the contrary the perpetuation of slavery in this country, which will ruin them and the country forever, unless something is immediately done.

Do the colonizationists think to send us off without first being reconciled to us? Do they think to bundle us up like brutes and send us off, as they did our brethren of the State of Ohio?* Have they not to be reconciled to us, or reconcile us to them, for the cruelties with which they have afflicted our fathers and us?

---

* The great slave holder, Mr. John Randolph, of Virginia, intimated in one of his great, happy and eloquent HARRANGUES, before the Virginia Convention, that Ohio is a slave State, by ranking it among other Slave-holding States. This probably was done by the HONORABLE Slave-holder to deter the minds of the ignorant; to such I would say, that Ohio always was and is now a free State, that it never was and I do not believe it ever will be a slave-holding State; the people I believe, though some of them are hard hearted enough, detest Slavery too much to admit an evil into their bosom, which gnaws into the very vitals, and sinews of those who are now in possession of it.

Methinks colonizationists think they have a set of brutes to deal with, sure enough. Do they think to drive us from our country and homes, after having enriched it with our blood and tears, and keep back millions of our dear brethren, sunk in the most barbarous wretchedness, to dig up gold and silver for them and their children? Surely, the Americans must think that we are brutes, as some of them have represented us to be. They think that we do not feel for our brethren, whom they are murdering by the inches, but they are dreadfully deceived. I acknowledge that there are some deceitful and hypocritical wretches among us, who will tell us one thing while they mean another, and thus they go on aiding our enemies to oppress themselves and us. But I declare this day before my Lord and Master, that I believe there are some true-hearted sons of Africa, in this land of oppression, but pretended *liberty*! ! !—who do in reality feel for their suffering brethren, who are held in bondage by tyrants. Some of the advocates of this cunningly devised plot of Satan represent us to be the greatest set of cut-throats in the world, as though God wants us to take his work out of his hand before he is ready. Does not vengeance belong to the Lord? Is he not able to repay the Americans for their cruelties, with which they have afflicted Africa's sons and daughters, without our interference, unless we are ordered? It is surprising to think that the Americans, having the Bible in their hands, do not believe it. Are not the hearts of all men in the hands of the God of battles? And does he not suffer some, in consequence of cruelties, to go on until they are irrecoverably lost? Now, what can be more aggravating, than for the Americans, after having treated us so bad, to hold us up to the world as such great throat-cutters? It appears to me as though they are resolved to assail us with every species of affliction that their ingenuity can invent !—→ See the African Repository and Colonial Journal, from its commencement to the present day—see how we are through the medium of that periodical, abused and held up by the Americans, as the greatest nuisance to society, and throat-cutters in the world. But the Lord sees their actions. Americans! notwithstanding you have and do continue to treat us more cruel than any heathen nation ever did a people it had subjected to the same condition that you have us. Now let us reason—I mean you of the United States, whom I believe God designs to save from destruction, if you will hear. For I declare to you, whether you believe it or not, that there are some on the continent of America, who will never be able to repent. God will surely destroy them, to show you his disapprobation of the murders they and you have inflicted on us. I say, let us reason; had you not better take our body, while you have it in your power, and while we are yet ignorant and wretched, not knowing but a little, give us education, and teach us the pure religion of our Lord and Master, which is calculated to make the lion lay down in peace with the lamb, and which millions of you have beaten us nearly to death for trying to obtain since we have been among you, and thus at once, gain our affection while we are ignorant? Remember Americans, that we must and shall be free and enlightened as you are, will you wait until we shall, under God, obtain our liberty by the crushing arm of power? Will it not be dreadful for you? I speak Americans for your good. We must and shall be free I say, in spite of you. You may do your best to keep us in wretchedness and misery, to enrich you and your children; but God will deliver us from under you. And wo, wo, will be to you if we have to obtain our freedom by fighting. Throw away your fears and prejudices then, and enlighten us and treat us like men, and we will like you more than we do now hate you,* and tell us now no more about colonization, for America is as much our country, as it is yours.—Treat us like men, and there is no danger but we will all live in peace and happiness together.

For we are not like you, hard hearted, unmerciful, and unforgiving. What a happy country this will be, if the whites will listen. What nation under heaven, will be able to do any thing with us, unless God gives us up into its hand? But Americans, I declare to you, while you keep us and our children in bondage, and treat us like brutes, to make us support you and your families, we can-not be your friends. You do not look for it, do you? Treat us then like men, and we will be your friends. And there is not a doubt in my mind, but that the whole of the past will be sunk into oblivion, and we yet, under God, will become a united and happy people. The whites may say it is impossible, but remember that nothing is impossible with God.

The Americans may say or do as they please, but they have to raise us from the condition of brutes to that of respectable men, and to make a national acknowledgement to us for the wrongs they have inflicted on us. As unexpected, strange, and wild as these propositions may to some appear, it is no less a fact, that unless they are complied with, the Americans of the United States, though they may for a little while escape, God will yet weigh them in a balance, and if they are not superior to other men, as they have represented themselves to be, he will give them wretchedness to their very heart's content.

And now brethren, having concluded these four Articles, I submit them, together with my Preamble, dedicated to the Lord, for your inspection, in language so very simple, that the most ignorant, who can read at

---

* You are not astonished at my saying we hate you, for if we are men, we cannot but hate you, while you are treating us like dogs.

all, may easily understand—of which you may make the best you possibly can.* Should tyrants take it into their heads to emancipate any of you, remember that your freedom is your natural right.

You are men, as well as they and instead of returning thanks to them for your freedom, return it to the Holy Ghost, who is our rightful owner. If they do not want to part with your labours, which have enriched them, let them keep you, and my word for it, that God Almighty, will break their strong band. Do you believe this, my brethren?—See my Address, delivered before the General Coloured Association of Massachusetts, which may be found in Freedom's Journal, for Dec. 20, 1828.~See the last clause of that Address. Whether you believe it or not, I tell you that God will dash tyrants, in combination with devils, into atoms, and will bring you out from your wretchedness and miseries under these *Christian People! ! ! ! !*

Those philanthropists and lovers of the human family, who have volunteered their services for our redemption from wretchedness, have a high claim on our gratitude, and we should always view them as our greatest earthly benefactors.

If any are anxious to ascertain who I am, know the world that I am one of the oppressed, degraded and wretched sons of Africa rendered so by the avaricious and unmerciful, among the whites. —If any wish to plunge me into the wretched incapacity of a slave, or murder me for the truth, know ye, that I am in the hand of God, and at your disposal. I count my life not dear unto me, but I am ready to be offered at any moment. For what is the use of living, when in fact I am dead. But remember, Americans, that as miserable, wretched, degraded and abject as you have made us in preceding, and in this generation, to support you and your families, that some of you, (whites) on the continent of America, will yet curse the day that you ever were born. You want slaves, and want us for your slaves! ! ! My colour will yet, root some of you out of the very face of the earth! ! ! ! ! ! You may doubt it if you please. I know that thousands will doubt— they think they have us so well secured in wretchedness, to them and their children, that it is impossible for such things to occur.**

---

* Some of my brethren, who are sensible, do not take an interest in enlightening the minds of our more ignorant brethren respecting this BOOK and in reading it to them, just as though they will not have either to stand or fall by what is written in this book. Do they believe that I would be so foolish as to put out a book of this kind without strict—ah! very strict commandments of the Lord?—Surely the blacks and whites must think that I am ignorant enough.—Do they think that I would have the audacious wickedness to take the name of my God in vain?

Notice, I said in the concluding clause of Article 3—I call God, I call Angels I call men to witness, that the destruction of the Americans is at hand and will be speedily consummated unless they repent. Now I wonder if the world think that I would take the name of God in this way in vain? What do they think I take God to be? Do they suppose that I would trifle with that God who will not have his Holy name taken in vain?—He will show you and the world, in due time, whether this book is for his glory, or written by me through envy to the whites, as some have represented.

** Why do the Slave-holders or Tyrants of America and their advocates fight so hard to keep my brethren from receiving and reading my Book of Appeal to them?—Is it because they treat us so well?—Is it because we are satisfied to rest in Slavery to them and their children?—Is it because they are treating us like men, by compensating us all over this free country!! for our labours?—But why are the Americans so very fearfully terrified respecting my Book?—Why do they search vessels, &c. when entering the harbours of tyrannical States, to see if any of my Books can be found, for fear that my brethren will get them to read. Why, I thought the Americans proclaimed to the world that they are a happy, enlightened, humane and Christian people, all the in-habitants of the country enjoy equal Rights! ! America is the Asylum for the oppressed of all nations! ! !

Now I ask the Americans to see the fearful terror they labor under for fear that my brethren will get my Book and read it-and tell me if their declaration is true—viz, if the United States of America is a Republican Government?—Is this not the most tyrannical, unmerciful, and cruel government under Heaven—not excepting the Algerines, Turks and Arabs?—I believe if any candid person would take the trouble to go through the Southern and Western sections of this country, and could have the heart to see the cruelties inflicted by these Christians on us, he would say, that the Algerines, Turks and Arabs treat their dogs a thousand times better than we are treated by the Christians.—But perhaps the Americans do their very best to keep my Brethren from receiving and reading my "Appeal" for fear they will find in it an extract which I made from their Declaration of Independence, which says, "we hold these truths to be self-evident, that all men are created equal," &c. &c. &c.—If the above are not the causes of the alarm among the Americans, respecting my Book, I do not know what to impute it to, unless they are possessed of the same spirit with which Demetrius the Silversmith was possessed-however, that they may judge whether they are of the same avaricious and ungodly spirit with that man, I will give here an extract from the Acts of the Apostles, chapter xix,—verses 23, 24, 25, 26, 27.

"And the same time there arose no small stir about that way. For a certain man named Demetrius, a silversmith, which made silver shrines for Diana, brought no small gain unto the craftsmen; whom he called together with the workmen of like occupation, and said, Sirs, ye know that by this craft we have our wealth: moreover, ye see and hear, that not alone at Ephesus, but almost throughout all Asia, this Paul hath persuaded and turned away much people, saying, that they be no gods which are made with hands: so that not only this our craft is in danger to be set at nought; but also that the temple of the great goddess Diana should be despised, and her magnificence should be destroyed, whom all Asia and the world worshippeth."

I pray you Americans of North and South America, together with the whole European inhabitants of the world, (I mean Slave-holders and their advocates) to read and ponder over the above verses in your minds, and judge whether or not you are of the infernal spirit with that Heathen Demetrius, the Silversmith: In fine I beg you to read the whole chapter through carefully.

So did the antideluvians doubt Noah, until the day in which the flood came and swept them away. So did the Sodomites doubt until Lot had got out of the city, and God rained down fire and brimstone from Heaven upon them, and burnt them up. So did the king of Egypt doubt the very existence of a God; he said, "who is the Lord, that I should let Israel go?" Did he not find to his sorrow, who the Lord was, when he and all his mighty men of war, were smothered to death in the Red Sea? So did the Romans doubt, many of them were really so ignorant, that they thought the whole of mankind were made to be slaves to them; just as many of the Americans think now, of my colour. But they got dreadfully deceived. When men got their eyes opened, they made the murderers scamper. The way in which they cut their tyrannical throats, was not much inferior to the way the Romans or murderers, served them, when they held them in wretchedness and degradation under their feet. So would Christian Americans doubt, if God should send an Angel from Heaven to preach their funeral sermon. The fact is, the Christians having a name to live, while they are dead, think that God will screen them on that ground.

See the hundreds and thousands of us that are thrown into the seas by Christians, and murdered by them in other ways. They cram us into their vessel holds in chains and in hand-cuffs—men, women and children, all together! ! O! save us, we pray thee, thou God of Heaven and of earth, from the devouring hands of the white Christians! ! !

Oh! thou Alpha and Omega!
The beginning and the end,
Enthron'd thou art, in Heaven above,
Surrounded by Angels there.

From Whence thou seest the miseries
To which we are subject;
The whites have murder'd us, O God
And kept us ignorant of thee.

Not satisfied with this, my Lord!
They throw us in the seas:
Be pleas'd, we pray, for Jesus' sake,
To save us from their grasp.

We believe that, for thy glory's sake,
Thou wilt deliver us;
But that thou may'st effect these things,
Thy glory must be sought.

In conclusion, I ask the candid and unprejudiced of the whole world, to search the pages of historians diligently, and see if the Antideluvians—the Sodomites—the Egyptians—the Babylonians—the Ninevites—the Carthagenians—the Persians—the Macedonians—the Greeks—the Romans—the Mahometans—the Jews—or devils, ever treated a set of human beings, as the white Christians of America do us, the blacks, or Africans. I also ask the attention of the world of mankind to the declaration of these very American people, of the United States.

A Declaration Made July 4, 1776

It says,* "When in the course of human events, it becomes necessary for one people to dissolve the political bands which have connected them with another, and to assume among the Powers of the earth, the separate and equal station to which the laws of nature and of nature's God entitle them. A decent respect for the opinions of mankind requires, that they should declare the causes which impel them to the separation.—We hold these truths to be self evident—that all men are created equal, that they are endowed by their Creator with certain unalienable rights: that among these, are life, liberty, and the pursuit of happiness that, to secure

---

* See the Declaration of Independence of the United States.

these rights, governments are instituted among men, deriving their just powers from the consent of the governed; that when ever any form of government becomes destructive of these ends, it is the right of the people to alter or to abolish it, and to institute a new government laying its foundation on such principles, and organizing its powers in such form, as to them shall seem most likely to effect their safety and happiness. Prudence, indeed, will dictate, that governments long established should not be changed for light and transient causes; and accordingly all experience hath shewn, that mankind are more disposed to suffer, while evils are sufferable, than to right themselves by abolishing the forms to which they are accustomed. But when a long train of abuses and usurpations, pursuing invariably the same object, evinces a design to reduce them under absolute despotism, it is their right it is their duty to throw off such government, and to provide new guards for their future security." See your Declaration Americans! ! !

Do you understand your own language? Hear your language, proclaimed to the world, July 4th, 1776 → "We hold these truths to be self evident—that ALL MEN ARE CREATED EQUAL! ! that they *are endowed by their Creator with certain unalienable rights;* that among these are life, *liberty,* and the pursuit of happiness! !" Compare your own language above, extracted from your Declaration of Independence, with your cruelties and murders inflicted by your cruel and unmerciful fathers and yourselves on our fathers and on us—men who have never given your fathers or you the least provocation! ! ! ! !

Hear your language further! → "But when a long train of abuses and usurpation, pursuing invariably the same object, evinces a design to reduce them under absolute despotism, it is their *right,* it is their *duty,* to throw off such government, and to provide new guards for their future security."

Now, Americans! I ask you candidly, was your sufferings under Great Britain, one hundredth part as cruel and tyranical as you have rendered ours under you? Some of you, no doubt, believe that we will never throw off your murderous government and "provide new guards for our future security." If Satan has made you believe it, will he not deceive you?* Do the whites say, I being a black man, ought to be humble, which I readily admit?

I ask them, ought they not to be as humble as I? or do they think that they can measure arms with Jehovah? Will not the Lord yet humble them? or will not these very coloured people whom they now treat worse than brutes, yet under God, humble them low down enough? Some of the whites are ignorant enough to tell us, that we ought to be submissive to them, that they may keep their feet on our throats. And if we do not submit to be beaten to death by them, we are bad creatures and of course must be damned, &c. If any man wishes to hear this doctrine openly preached to us by the American preachers, let him go into the Southern and Western sections of this country—I do not speak from hear say—what I have written, is what I have seen and heard myself. No man may think that my book is made up of conjecture—I have travelled and observed nearly the whole of those things myself, and what little I did not get by my own observation, I received from those among the whites and blacks, in whom the greatest confidence may be placed.

The Americans may be as vigilant as they please, but they cannot be vigilant enough for the Lord, neither can they hide themselves, where he will not find and bring them out.

Narrative of the Life of Frederick Douglass, an American Slave

FREDERICK DOUGLASS

This battle with Mr. Covey was the turning-point in my career as a slave. It rekindled the few expiring embers of freedom, and revived within me a sense of my own manhood. It recalled the departed self-confidence, and inspired me again with a determination to be free. The gratification afforded by the triumph was a full compensation for whatever else might follow, even death itself. He only can understand the deep satisfaction which I experienced, who has himself repelled by force the bloody arm of slavery. I felt as I never felt before. It was a glorious resurrection, from the tomb of slavery, to the heaven of freedom. My long-crushed spirit rose, cowardice departed, bold defiance took its place; and I now resolved that, however long I might remain a slave in form, the day had passed forever when I could be a slave in fact. I did not hesitate to let it be known of me, that the white man who expected to succeed in whipping, must also succeed in killing me.

From this time I was never again what might be called fairly whipped, though I remained a slave four years afterwards. I had several fights, but was never whipped.

It was for a long time a matter of surprise to me why Mr. Covey did not immediately have me taken by the constable to the whipping-post, and there regularly whipped for the crime of raising my hand against a white man in defence of myself. And the only explanation I can now think of does not entirely satisfy me; but such as it is, I will give it. Mr. Covey enjoyed the most unbounded reputation for being a first-rate overseer and negro-breaker. It was of considerable importance to him. That reputation was at stake; and had he sent me—a boy about sixteen years old—to the public whipping-post, his reputation would have been lost; so, to save his reputation, he suffered me to go unpunished.

My term of actual service to Mr. Edward Covey ended on Christmas day, 1833. The days between Christmas and New Year's day are allowed as holidays; and, accordingly, we were not required to perform any labor, more than to feed and take care of the stock. This time we regarded as our own, by the grace of our masters; and we therefore used or abused it nearly as we pleased. Those of us who had families at a distance, were generally allowed to spend the whole six days in their society. This time, however, was spent in various ways. The staid, sober, thinking and industrious ones of our number would employ themselves in making cornbrooms, mats, horse-collars, and baskets; and another class of us would spend the time in hunting opossums, hares, and coons. But by far the larger part engaged in such sports and merriments as playing ball, wrestling, running foot-races, fiddling, dancing, and drinking whisky; and this latter mode of spending the time was by far the most agreeable to the feelings of our masters. A slave who would work during the holidays was considered by our masters as scarcely deserving them. He was regarded as one who rejected the favor of his master. It was deemed a disgrace not to get drunk at Christmas; and he was regarded as lazy indeed, who had not provided himself with the necessary means, during the year, to get whisky enough to last him through Christmas.

From what I know of the effect of these holidays upon the slave, I believe them to be among the most effective means in the hands of the slaveholder in keeping down the spirit of insurrection. Were the slaveholders at once to abandon this practice, I have not the slightest doubt it would lead to an immediate insurrection among the slaves. These holidays serve as conductors, or safety-valves, to carry off the rebellious spirit of enslaved humanity. But for these, the slave would be forced up to the wildest desperation; and woe betide the slaveholder, the day he ventures to remove or hinder the operation of those conductors! I warn him that, in such an event, a spirit will go forth in their midst, more to be dreaded than the most appalling earthquake.

The holidays are part and parcel of the gross fraud, wrong, and inhumanity of slavery. They are professedly a custom established by the benevolence of the slaveholders; but I undertake to say, it is the result of selfishness, and one of the grossest frauds committed upon the down-trodden slave. They do not give the slaves this time because they would not like to have their work during its continuance, but because they know it would be unsafe to deprive them of it. This will be seen by the fact, that the slaveholders like to have their slaves spend those days just in such a manner as to make them as glad of their ending as of their beginning. Their object seems to be, to disgust their slaves with freedom, by plunging them into the lowest depths of dissipation. For instance, the slaveholders not only like to see the slave drink of his own accord, but will adopt various plans to make him drunk. One plan is, to make bets on their slaves, as to who can drink the most whisky without getting drunk; and in this way they succeed in getting whole multitudes to drink to excess. Thus, when the slave asks for virtuous freedom, the cunning slaveholder, knowing his ignorance, cheats him with a dose of vicious dissipation, artfully labelled with the name of liberty. The most of us used to drink it down, and the result was just what might be supposed: many of us were led to think that there was little to choose between liberty and slavery. We felt, and very properly too, that we had almost as well be slaves to man as to rum. So, when the holidays ended, we staggered up from the filth of our wallowing, took a long breath, and marched to the field,—feeling, upon the whole, rather glad to go, from what our master had deceived us into a belief was freedom, back to the arms of slavery.

I have said that this mode of treatment is a part of the whole system of fraud and inhumanity of slavery. It is so. The mode here adopted to disgust the slave with freedom, by allowing him to see only the abuse of it, is carried out in other things. For instance, a slave loves molasses; he steals some. His master, in many cases, goes off to town, and buys a large quantity; he returns, takes his whip, and commands the slave to eat the molasses, until the poor fellow is made sick at the very mention of it. The same mode is sometimes adopted to make the slaves refrain from asking for more food than their regular allowance. A slave runs through his allowance, and applies for more. His master is enraged at him; but, not willing to send him off without food, gives him more than is necessary, and compels him to eat it within a given time. Then, if he complains that he cannot eat it, he is said to be satisfied neither full nor fasting, and is whipped for being hard to please! I have an abundance of such illustrations of the same principle, drawn from my own observation, but think the cases I have cited sufficient. The practice is a very common one.

On the first of January, 1834, I left Mr. Covey, and went to live with Mr. William Freeland, who lived about three miles from St. Michael's. I soon found Mr. Freeland a very different man from Mr. Covey. Though not rich, he was what would be called an educated southern gentleman. Mr. Covey, as I have shown, was a well-trained negro-breaker and slave-driver. The former (slaveholder though he was) seemed to possess some regard for honor, some reverence for justice, and some respect for humanity. The latter seemed totally insensible to all such sentiments. Mr. Freeland had many of the faults peculiar to slaveholders, such as being very passionate and fretful; but I must do him the justice to say, that he was exceedingly free from those degrading vices to which Mr. Covey was constantly addicted. The one was open and frank, and we always knew where to find him. The other was a most artful deceiver, and could be understood only by such as were skilful enough to detect his cunningly-devised frauds. Another advantage I gained in my new master was, he made no pretensions to, or profession of, religion; and this, in my opinion, was truly a great advantage. I assert most unhesitatingly, that the religion of the south is a mere covering for the most horrid crimes,—a justifier of the most appalling barbarity,— a sanctifier of the most hateful frauds,—and a dark shelter under, which the darkest, foulest, grossest, and most infernal deeds of slaveholders find the strongest protection. Were I to be again reduced to the chains of slavery, next to that enslavement, I should regard being the slave of a religious master the greatest calamity that could befall me. For of all slaveholders with whom I have ever met, religious slaveholders are the worst. I have ever found them the meanest and basest, the most cruel and cowardly, of all others. It was my unhappy lot not only to belong to a religious slaveholder, but to live in a community of such religionists. Very near Mr. Freeland lived the Rev. Daniel Weeden, and in the same neighborhood lived the Rev. Rigby Hopkins. These were members and ministers in the Reformed Methodist Church. Mr. Weeden owned, among others, a woman slave, whose name I have forgotten. This woman's back, for weeks, was kept literally raw, made so by the lash of this merciless, *religious* wretch. He used to hire hands. His maxim was, Behave well or behave ill, it is the duty of a master occasionally to whip a slave, to remind him of his master's authority. Such was his theory, and such his practice.

Mr. Hopkins was even worse than Mr. Weeden. His chief boast was his ability to manage slaves. The peculiar feature of his government was that of whipping slaves in advance of deserving it. He always managed to have one or more of his slaves to whip every Monday morning. He did this to alarm their fears, and strike terror into those who escaped. His plan was to whip for the smallest offences, to prevent the commission of large ones. Mr. Hopkins could always find some excuse for whipping a slave. It would astonish one, unaccustomed to a slaveholding life, to see with what wonderful ease a slaveholder can find things, of which to make occasion to whip a slave. A mere look, word, or motion,—a mistake, accident, or want of power,—are all matters for which a slave may be whipped at any time. Does a slave look dissatisfied? It is said, he has the devil in him, and it must be whipped out. Does he speak loudly when spoken to by his master? Then he is getting high-minded, and should be taken down a button-hole lower. Does he forget to pull off his hat at the approach of a white person? Then he is wanting in reverence, and should be whipped for it. Does he ever venture to vindicate his conduct, when censured for it? Then he is guilty of impudence,— one of the greatest crimes of which a slave can be guilty. Does he ever venture to suggest a different mode of doing things from that pointed out by his master? He is indeed presumptuous, and getting above himself; and nothing less than a flogging will do for him. Does he, while ploughing, break a plough,— or, while hoeing, break a hoe? It is owing to his carelessness, and for it a slave must always be whipped. Mr. Hopkins could always find something of this sort to justify the use of the lash, and he seldom failed to embrace such opportunities. There was not a man in the whole county, with whom the slaves who had the getting their own home, would not prefer to live, rather than with this Rev. Mr. Hopkins. And yet there was not a man any where round, who made higher professions of religion, or was more active in revivals,—more attentive to the class, love-feast, prayer and preaching meetings, or more devotional in his family,—that prayed earlier, later, louder, and longer,—than this same reverend slave-driver, Rigby Hopkins.

But to return to Mr. Freeland, and to my experience while in his employment. He, like Mr. Covey, gave us enough to eat; but, unlike Mr. Covey, he also gave us sufficient time to take our meals. He worked us hard, but always between sunrise and sunset. He required a good deal of work to be done, but gave us good tools with which to work. His farm was large, but he employed hands enough to work it, and with ease, compared with many of his neighbors. My treatment, while in his employment, was heavenly, compared with what I experienced at the hands of Mr. Edward Covey.

Mr. Freeland was himself the owner of but two slaves. Their names were Henry Harris and John Harris. The rest of his hands he hired. These consisted of myself, Sandy Jenkins,* and Handy Caldwell. Henry and John were quite intelligent, and in a very little while after I went there, I succeeded in creating in them a strong desire to learn how to read. This desire soon sprang up in the others also. They very soon mustered up some old spelling-books, and nothing would do but that I must keep a Sabbath school. I agreed to do so, and accordingly devoted my Sundays to teaching these my loved fellow-slaves how to read. Neither of them knew his letters when I went there. Some of the slaves of the neighboring farms found what was going on, and also availed themselves of this little opportunity to learn to read. It was understood, among all who came, that there must be as little display about it as possible. It was necessary to keep our religious masters at St. Michael's unacquainted with the fact, that, instead of spending the Sabbath in wrestling, boxing, and drinking whisky, we were trying to learn how to read the will of God; for they had much rather see us engaged in those degrading sports, than to see us behaving like intellectual, moral, and accountable beings. My blood boils as I think of the bloody manner in which Messrs. Wright Fairbanks and Garrison West, both class-leaders, in connection with many others, rushed in upon us with sticks and stones, and broke up our virtuous little Sabbath school, at St. Michael's—all calling themselves Christians! humble followers of the Lord Jesus Christ! But I am again digressing.

I held my Sabbath school at the house of a free colored man, whose name I deem it imprudent to mention; for should it be known, it might embarrass him greatly, though the crime of holding the school was committed ten years ago. I had at one time over forty scholars, and those of the right sort, ardently desiring to learn. They were of all ages, though mostly men and women. I look back to those Sundays with an amount of pleasure not to be expressed. They were great days to my soul. The work of instructing my dear fellow-slaves was the sweetest engagement with which I was ever blessed. We loved each other, and to leave them at the close of the Sabbath was a severe cross indeed. When I think that these precious souls are to-day shut up in the prison-house of slavery, my feelings overcome me, and I am almost ready to ask, "Does a righteous God govern the universe? and for what does he hold the thunders in his right hand, if not to smite the oppressor, and deliver the spoiled out of the hand of the spoiler?" These dear souls came not to Sabbath school because it was popular to do so, nor did I teach them because it was reputable to be thus engaged. Every moment they spent in that school, they were liable to be taken up, and given thirty-nine lashes. They came because they wished to learn. Their minds had been starved by their cruel masters. They had been shut up

---

* This is the same man who gave me the roots to prevent my being whipped by Mr. Covey. He was "a clever soul." We used frequently to talk about the fight with Covey, and as often as we did so, he would claim my success as the result of the roots which he gave me. This superstition is very common among the more ignorant slaves. A slave seldom dies but that his death is attributed to trickery.

in mental darkness. I taught them, because it was the delight of my soul to be doing something that looked like bettering the condition of my race. I kept up my school nearly the whole year I lived with Mr. Freeland; and, beside my Sabbath school, I devoted three evenings in the week, during the winter, to teaching the slaves at home. And I have the happiness to know, that several of those who came to Sabbath school learned how to read; and that one, at least, is now free through my agency.

The year passed off smoothly. It seemed only about half as long as the year which preceded it. I went through it without receiving a single blow. I will give Mr. Freeland the credit of being the best master I ever had, *till I became my own master.* For the ease with which I passed the year, I was, however, some what indebted to the society of my fellow-slaves. They were noble souls; they not only possessed loving hearts, but brave ones. We were linked and interlinked with each other. I loved them with a love stronger than any thing I have experienced since. It is sometimes said that we slaves do not love and confide in each other. In answer to this assertion, I can say, I never loved any or confided in any people more than my fellow-slaves, and especially those with whom I lived at Mr. Freeland's. I believe we would have died for each other. We never undertook to do any thing, of any importance, without a mutual consultation. We never moved separately. We were one; and as much so by our tempers and dispositions, as by the mutual hardships to which we were necessarily subjected by our condition as slaves.

At the close of the year 1834, Mr. Freeland again hired me of my master, for the year 1835. But, by this time, I began to want to live *upon free land* as well as *with Freeland;* and I was no longer content, therefore, to live with him or any other slaveholder. I began, with the commencement of the year, to prepare myself for a final struggle, which should decide my fate one way or the other. My tendency was upward. I was fast approaching manhood, and year after year had passed, and I was still a slave. These thoughts roused me—I must do something. I therefore resolved that 1835 should not pass without witnessing an attempt, on my part, to secure my liberty. But I was not willing to cherish this determination alone. My fellow-slaves were dear to me. I was anxious to have them participate with me in this, my life-giving determination. I therefore, though with great prudence, commenced early to ascertain their views and feelings in regard to their condition, and to imbue their minds with thoughts of freedom. I bent myself to devising ways and means for our escape, and meanwhile strove, on all fitting occasions, to impress them with the gross fraud and inhumanity of slavery. I went first to Henry, next to John, then to the others. I found, in them all, warm hearts and noble spirits. They were ready to hear, and ready to act when a feasible plan should be proposed. This was what I wanted. I talked to them of our want of manhood, if we submitted to our enslavement without at least one noble effort to be free. We met often, and consulted frequently, and told our hopes and fears, recounted the difficulties, real and imagined, which we should be called on to meet. At times we were almost disposed to give up, and try to content ourselves with our wretched lot; at others, we were firm and unbending in our determination to go. Whenever we suggested any plan, there was shrinking— the odds were fearful. Our path was beset with the greatest obstacles; and if we succeeded in gaining the end of it, our right to be free was yet questionable—we were yet liable to be returned to bondage. We could see no spot, this side of the ocean, where we could be free. We knew nothing about Canada. Our knowledge of the north did not extend farther than New York; and to go there, and be forever harassed with the frightful liability of being returned to slavery—with the certainty of being treated tenfold worse than before—the thought was truly a horrible one, and one which it was not easy to overcome. The case sometimes stood thus: At every gate through which we were to pass, we saw a watchman—at every ferry a guard—on every bridge a sentinel—and in every wood a patrol. We were hemmed in upon every side. Here were the difficulties, real or imagined—the good to be sought, and the evil to be shunned. On the one hand, there stood slavery, a stern reality, glaring frightfully upon us,—its robes already crimsoned with the blood of millions, and even now feasting itself greedily upon our own flesh. On the other hand, away back in the dim distance, under the flickering light of the north star, behind some craggy hill or snow-covered mountain, stood a doubtful freedom—half frozen—beckoning us to come and share its hospitality. This in itself was sometimes enough to stagger us; but when we permitted ourselves to survey the road, we were frequently appalled. Upon either side we saw grim death, assuming the most horrid shapes. Now it was starvation, causing us to eat our own flesh;—now we were contending with the waves, and were drowned;— now we were overtaken, and torn to pieces by the fangs of the terrible bloodhound. We were stung by scorpions, chased by wild beasts, bitten by snakes, and finally, after having nearly reached the desired spot,—after swimming rivers, encountering wild beasts, sleeping in the woods, suffering hunger and nakedness,—we were overtaken by our pursuers, and, in our resistance, we were shot dead upon the spot! I say, this picture sometimes appalled us, and made us

"rather bear those ills we had,
Than fly to others, that we knew not of."

In coming to a fixed determination to run away, we did more than Patrick Henry, when he resolved upon liberty or death. With us it was a doubtful liberty at most, and almost certain death if we failed. For my part, I should prefer death to hopeless bondage.

Sandy, one of our number, gave up the notion, but still encouraged us. Our company then consisted of Henry Harris, John Harris, Henry Bailey, Charles Roberts, and myself. Henry Bailey was my uncle, and belonged to my master. Charles married my aunt: he belonged to my master's father-in-law, Mr. William Hamilton.

The plan we finally concluded upon was, to get a large canoe belonging to Mr. Hamilton, and upon the Saturday night previous to Easter holidays, paddle directly up the Chesapeake Bay. On our arrival at the head of the bay, a distance of seventy or eighty miles from where we lived, it was our purpose to turn our canoe adrift, and follow the guidance of the north star till we got beyond the limits of Maryland. Our rea-son for taking the water route was, that we were less liable to be suspected as runaways; we hoped to be regarded as fishermen; whereas, if we should take the land route, we should be subjected to interruptions of almost every kind. Any one having a white face, and being so disposed, could stop us, and subject us to examination.

The week before our intended start, I wrote several protections, one for each of us. As well as I can remem-ber, they were in the following words, to wit:—

"This is to certify that I, the undersigned, have given the bearer, my servant, full liberty to go to Baltimore, and spend the Easter holidays. Written with mine own hand, &c., 1835.

"William Hamilton,
"Near St. Michael's, in Talbot county, Maryland."

We were not going to Baltimore; but, in going up the bay, we went toward Baltimore, and these protections were only intended to protect us while on the bay.

As the time drew near for our departure, our anxiety became more and more intense. It was truly a matter of life and death with us. The strength of our determination was about to be fully tested. At this time, I was very active in explaining every difficulty, removing every doubt, dispelling every fear, and inspiring all with the firmness indispensable to success in our undertaking; assuring them that half was gained the instant we made the move; we had talked long enough; we were now ready to move; if not now, we never should be; and if we did not intend to move now, we had as well fold our arms, sit down, and acknowledge ourselves fit only to be slaves. This, none of us were prepared to acknowledge. Every man stood firm; and at our last meeting, we pledged ourselves afresh, in the most solemn manner, that, at the time appointed, we would certainly start in pursuit of freedom. This was in the middle of the week, at the end of which we were to be off. We went, as usual, to our several fields of labor, but with bosoms highly agitated with thoughts of our truly hazardous undertaking. We tried to conceal our feelings as much as possible; and I think we succeeded very well.

After a painful waiting, the Saturday morning, whose night was to witness our departure, came. I hailed it with joy, bring what of sadness it might. Friday night was a sleepless one for me. I probably felt more anx-ious than the rest, because I was, by common consent, at the head of the whole affair. The responsibility of success or failure lay heavily upon me. The glory of the one, and the confusion of the other, were alike mine. The first two hours of that morning were such as I never experienced before, and hope never to again. Early in the morning, we went, as usual, to the field. We were spreading manure; and all at once, while thus engaged, I was overwhelmed with an indescribable feeling, in the fulness of which I turned to Sandy, who was near by, and said, "We are betrayed!" "Well," said he, "that thought has this moment struck me." We said no more. I was never more certain of any thing.

The horn was blown as usual, and we went up from the field to the house for breakfast. I went for the form, more than for want of any thing to eat that morning. Just as I got to the house, in looking out at the lane gate, I saw four white men, with two colored men. The white men were on horseback, and the colored ones were walking behind, as if tied. I watched them a few moments till they got up to our lane gate. Here they halted, and tied the colored men to the gate-post. I was not yet certain as to what the matter was. In a few moments, in rode Mr. Hamilton, with a speed betokening great excitement. He came to the door, and inquired if Master William was in. He was told he was at the barn. Mr. Hamilton, without dismounting, rode up to the barn with extraordinary speed. In a few moments, he and Mr. Freeland returned to the house. By this time, the three constables rode up, and in great haste dismounted, tied their horses, and met Master William and Mr. Hamilton returning from the barn; and after talking awhile, they all walked up to the kitchen door. There was no one in the kitchen but myself and John. Henry and Sandy were up at the barn. Mr. Freeland put his head in at the door, and called me by name, saying, there were some gentlemen at the door who wished to see me. I stepped to the door, and inquired what they wanted. They at once seized me, and, without giving me any satisfaction, tied me—lashing my hands closely together. I insisted upon knowing what the matter was. They at length said, that they had learned I had been in a "scrape," and that I was to be examined before my master; and if their information proved false, I should not be hurt.

In a few moments, they succeeded in tying John. They then turned to Henry, who had by this time returned, and commanded him to cross his hands. "I won't!" said Henry, in a firm tone, indicating his readiness to meet the consequences of his refusal. "Won't you?" said Tom Graham, the constable. "No, I won't!" said Henry, in a still stronger tone. With this, two of the constables pulled out their shining pistols, and swore, by their Creator, that they would make him cross his hands or kill him. Each cocked his pistol, and, with fingers on the trigger, walked up to Henry, saying, at the same time, if he did not cross his hands, they would blow his damned heart out. "Shoot me, shoot me!" said Henry; "you can't kill me but once. Shoot, shoot,—and be damned! *I won't be tied!*" This he said in a tone of loud defiance; and at the same time, with a motion as quick as lightning, he with one single stroke dashed the pistols from the hand of each constable. As he did this, all hands fell upon him, and, after beating him some time, they finally overpowered him, and got him tied.

During the scuffle, I managed, I know not how, to get my pass out, and, without being discovered, put it into the fire. We were all now tied; and just as we were to leave for Easton jail, Betsy Freeland, mother of William Freeland, came to the door with her hands full of biscuits, and divided them between Henry and John. She, then delivered herself of a speech, to the following effect:—addressing herself to me, she said, "*You devil! You yellow devil!* it was you that put it into the heads of Henry and John to run away. But for you, you long-legged mulatto devil! Henry nor John would never have thought of such a thing." I made no reply, and was immediately hurried off towards St. Michael's. Just a moment previous to the scuffle with Henry, Mr. Hamilton suggested the propriety of making a search for the protections which he had understood Frederick had written for himself and the rest. But, just, at the moment he was about carrying his proposal into effect, his aid was needed in helping to tie Henry; and the excitement attending the scuffle caused them either to forget, or to deem it unsafe, under the circumstances, to search. So we were not yet convicted of the intention to run away.

When we got about half way to St. Michael's, while the constables having us in charge were looking ahead, Henry inquired of me what he should do with his pass. I told him to eat it with his biscuit, and own nothing; and we passed the word around, "*Own nothing;*" and "*Own nothing!*" said we all. Our confidence in each other was unshaken. We were resolved to succeed or fail together, after the calamity had befallen us as much as before. We were now prepared for any thing. We were to be dragged that morning fifteen miles behind horses, and then to be placed in the Easton jail. When we reached St. Michael's, we underwent a sort of examination. We all denied that we ever intended to run away. We did this more to bring out the evidence against us, than from any hope of getting clear of being sold; for, as I have said, we were ready for that. The fact was, we cared but little where we went, so we went together. Our greatest concern was about separation. We dreaded that more than any thing this side of death. We found the evidence against us to be the testimony of one person; our master would not tell who it was; but we came to a unanimous decision among ourselves as to who their informant was. We were sent off to the jail at Easton. When we got there, we were delivered up to the sheriff, Mr. Joseph Graham, and by him placed in jail. Henry, John, and myself, were placed in one room together—Charles, and Henry Bailey, in another. Their object in separating us was to hinder concert.

We had been in jail scarcely twenty minutes, when a swarm of slave traders, and agents for slave traders, flocked into jail to look at us, and to ascertain if we were for sale. Such a set of beings I never saw before! I felt myself surrounded by so many fiends from perdition. A band of pirates never looked more like their father, the devil. They laughed and grinned over us, saying, "Ah, my boys! we have got you, haven't we?" And after taunting us in various ways, they one by one went into an examination of us, with intent to ascertain our value. They would impudently ask us if we would not like to have them for our masters. We would make them no answer, and leave them to find out as best they could. Then they would curse and swear at us, telling us that they could take the devil out of us in a very little while, if we were only in their hands.

While in jail, we found ourselves in much more comfortable quarters than we expected when we went there. We did not get much to eat, nor that which was very good; but we had a good clean room, from the windows of which we could see what was going on in the street, which was very much better than though we had been placed in one of the dark, damp cells. Upon the whole, we got along very well, so far as the jail and its keeper were concerned. Immediately after the holidays were over, contrary to all our expectations, Mr. Hamilton and Mr. Freeland came up to Easton, and took Charles, the two Henrys, and John, out of jail, and carried them home, leaving me alone. I regarded this separation as a final one. It caused me more pain than any thing else in the whole transaction. I was ready for any thing rather than separation. I supposed that they had consulted together, and had decided that, as I was the whole cause of the intention of the others to run away, it was hard to make the innocent suffer with the guilty; and that they had, therefore, concluded to take the others home, and sell me, as a warning to the others that remained. It is due to the noble Henry to say, he seemed almost as reluctant at leaving the prison as at leaving home to come to the prison. But we knew we should, in all probability, be separated, if we were sold; and since he was in their hands, he concluded to go peaceably home.

I was now left to my fate. I was all alone, and within the walls of a stone prison. But a few days before, and I was full of hope. I expected to have been safe in a land of freedom; but now I was covered with gloom, sunk down to the utmost despair. I thought the possibility of freedom was gone. I was kept in this way about one week, at the end of which, Captain Auld, my master, to my surprise and utter astonishment, came up, and took me out, with the intention of sending me, with a gentleman of his acquaintance, into Alabama. But, from some cause or other, he did not send me to Alabama, but concluded to send me back to Baltimore, to live again with his brother Hugh, and to learn a trade.

Thus, after an absence of three years and one month, I was once more permitted to return to my old home at Baltimore. My master sent me away, because there existed against me a very great prejudice in the community, and he feared I might be killed.

In a few weeks after I went to Baltimore, Master Hugh hired me to Mr. William Gardner, an extensive ship-builder, on Fell's Point. I was put there to learn how to calk. It, however, proved a very unfavorable place for the accomplishment of this object. Mr. Gardner was engaged that spring in building two large man-of-war brigs, professedly for the Mexican government. The vessels were to be launched in the July of that year, and in failure thereof, Mr. Gardner was to lose a considerable sum; so that when I entered, all was hurry. There was no time to learn any thing. Every man had to do that which he knew how to do. In entering the shipyard, my orders from Mr. Gardner were, to do whatever the carpenters commanded me to do. This was placing me at the beck and call of about seventy-five men. I was to regard all these as masters. Their word was to be my law. My situation was a most trying one. At times I needed a dozen pair of hands. I was called a dozen ways in the space of a single minute. Three or four voices would strike my ear at the same moment. It was—"Fred., come help me to cant this timber here."—"Fred., come carry this timber yonder."—"Fred., bring that roller here."—"Fred., go get a fresh can of water."—"Fred., come help saw off the end of this timber."—"Fred., go quick, and get the crowbar."—"Fred., hold on the end of this fall."—"Fred., go to the blacksmith's shop, and get a new punch."—"Hurra, Fred.! run and bring me a cold chisel."—"I say, Fred., bear a hand, and get up a fire as quick as lightning under that steam-box."—"Halloo, nigger! come, turn this grindstone."—"Come, come! move, move! and *bowse* this timber forward."—"I say, darky, blast your eyes, why don't you heat up some pitch?"—"Halloo! halloo! halloo!" (Three voices at the same time.) "Come here!—Go there!—Hold on where you are! Damn you, if you move, I'll knock your brains out!"

This was my school for eight months; and I might have remained there longer, but for a most horrid fight I had with four of the white apprentices, in which my left eye was nearly knocked out, and I was horribly mangled in other respects. The facts in the case were these: Until a very little while after I went there, white and black ship-carpenters worked side by side, and no one seemed to see any impropriety in it. All hands seemed to be very well satisfied. Many of the black carpenters were freemen. Things seemed to be going on very well. All at once, the white carpenters knocked off, and said they would not work with free colored workmen. Their reason for this, as alleged, was, that if free colored carpenters were encouraged, they would soon take the trade into their own hands, and poor white men would be thrown out of employment. They therefore felt called upon at once to put a stop to it. And, taking advantage of Mr. Gardner's necessities, they broke off, swearing they would work no longer, unless he would discharge his black carpenters. Now, though this did not extend to me in form, it did reach me in fact. My fellow-apprentices very soon began to feel it degrading to them to work with me. They began to put on airs, and talk about the "niggers" taking the country, saying we all ought to be killed; and, being encouraged by the journeymen, they commenced making my condition as hard as they could, by hectoring me around, and sometimes striking me. I, of course, kept the vow

I made after the fight with Mr. Covey, and struck back again, regardless of consequences; and while I kept them from combining, I succeeded very well; for I could whip the whole of them, taking them separately. They, however, at length combined, and came upon me, armed with sticks, stones, and heavy handspikes. One came in front with a half brick. There was one at each side of me, and one behind me. While I was attending to those in front, and on either side, the one behind ran up with the handspike, and struck me a heavy blow upon the head. It stunned me. I fell, and with this they all ran upon me, and fell to beating me with their fists. I let them lay on for a while, gathering strength. In an instant, I gave a sudden surge, and rose to my hands and knees. Just as I did that, one of their number gave me, with his heavy boot, a powerful kick in the left eye. My eyeball seemed to have burst. When they saw my eye closed, and badly swollen, they left me. With this I seized the handspike, and for a time pursued them. But here the carpenters interfered, and I thought I might as well give it up. It was impossible to stand my hand against so many. All this took place in sight of not less than fifty white ship-carpenters, and not one interposed a friendly word; but some cried, "Kill the damned nigger! Kill him! kill him! He struck a white person." I found my only chance for life was in flight. I succeeded in getting away without an additional blow, and barely so; for to strike a white man is death by Lynch law,—and that was the law in Mr. Gardner's ship-yard; nor is there much of any other out of Mr. Gardner's ship-yard.

I went directly home, and told the story of my wrongs to Master Hugh; and I am happy to say of him, irreligious as he was, his conduct was heavenly, compared with that of his brother Thomas under similar circumstances. He listened attentively to my narration of the circumstances leading to the savage outrage, and gave many proofs of his strong indignation at it. The heart of my once overkind mistress was again melted into pity. My puffed-out eye and blood-covered face moved her to tears. She took a chair by me, washed the blood from my face, and, with a mother's tenderness, bound up my head, covering the wounded eye with a lean piece of fresh beef. It was almost compensation for my suffering to witness, once more, a manifestation of kindness from this, my once affectionate old mistress. Master Hugh was very much enraged. He gave expression to his feelings by pouring out curses upon the heads of those who did the deed. As soon as I got a little the better of my bruises, he took me with him to Esquire Watson's, on Bond Street, to see what could be done about the matter. Mr. Watson inquired who saw the assault committed. Master Hugh told him it was done in Mr. Gardner's ship-yard, at midday, where there were a large company of men at work. "As to that," he said, "the deed was done, and there was no question as to who did it." His answer was, he could do nothing in the case, unless some white man would come forward and testify. He could issue no warrant on my word. If I had been killed in the presence of a thousand colored people, their testimony combined would have been insufficient to have arrested one of the murderers. Master Hugh, for once, was compelled to say this state of things was too bad. Of course, it was impossible to get any white man to volunteer his testimony in my behalf, and against the white young men. Even those who may have sympathized with me were not prepared to do this. It required a degree of courage unknown to them to do so; for just at that time, the slightest manifestation of humanity toward a colored person was denounced as abolitionism, and that name subjected its bearer to frightful liabilities. The watchwords of the bloody-minded in that region, and in those days, were, "Damn the abolitionists!" and "Damn the niggers!" There was nothing done, and probably nothing would have been done if I had been killed. Such was, and such remains, the state of things in the Christian city of Baltimore.

Master Hugh, finding he could get no redress, refused to let me go back again to Mr. Gardner. He kept me himself, and his wife dressed my wound till I was again restored to health. He then took me into the ship-yard of which he was foreman, in the employment of Mr. Walter Price. There I was immediately set to calking, and very soon learned the art of using my mallet and irons. In the course of one year from the time I left Mr. Gardner's, I was able to command the highest wages given to the most experienced calkers. I was now of some importance to my master. I was bringing him from six to seven dollars per week. I sometimes brought him nine dollars per week: my wages were a dollar and a half a day. After learning how to calk, I sought my own employment, made my own contracts, and collected the money which I earned. My pathway became much more smooth than before; my condition was now much more comfortable. When I could get no calking to do, I did nothing. During these leisure times, those old notions about freedom would steal over me again. When in Mr. Gardner's employment, I was kept in such a perpetual whirl of excitement, I could think of nothing, scarcely, but my life; and in thinking of my life, I almost forgot my liberty. I have observed this in my experience of slavery, —that whenever my condition was improved, instead of its increasing my contentment, it only increased my desire to be free, and set me to thinking of plans to gain my freedom. I have found that, to make a contented slave, it is necessary to make a thoughtless one. It is necessary to darken his moral and mental vision, and, as far as possible, to annihilate the power of reason. He must be able to detect no inconsistencies in slavery; he must be made to feel that slavery is right; and he can be brought to that only when he ceases to be a man.

* * * * *

Appendix

I find, since reading over the foregoing Narrative that I have, in several instances, spoken in such a tone and manner, respecting religion, as may possibly lead those unacquainted with my religious views to suppose me an opponent of all religion. To remove the liability of such misapprehension, I deem it proper to append the following brief explanation. What I have said respecting and against religion, I mean strictly to apply to the *slaveholding religion* of this land, and with no possible reference to Christianity proper; for, between the Christianity of this land, and the Christianity of Christ, I recognize the widest possible difference—so wide, that to receive the one as good, pure, and holy, is of necessity to reject the other as bad, corrupt, and wicked. To be the friend of the one, is of necessity to be the enemy of the other. I love the pure, peaceable, and impartial Christianity of Christ: I therefore hate the corrupt, slaveholding, women-whipping, cradle-plundering, partial and hypocritical Christianity of this land. Indeed, I can see no reason, but the most deceitful one, for calling the religion of this land Christianity. I look upon it as the climax of all misnomers, the boldest of all frauds, and the grossest of all libels. Never was there a clearer case of "stealing the livery of the court of heaven to serve the devil in." I am filled with unutterable loathing when I contemplate the religious pomp and show, together with the horrible inconsistencies, which every where surround me. We have men-stealers for ministers, women-whippers for missionaries, and cradle-plunderers for church members. The man who wields the blood-clotted cowskin during the week fills the pulpit on Sunday, and claims to be a minister of the meek and lowly Jesus. The man who robs me of my earnings at the end of each week meets me as a class-leader on Sunday morning, to show me the way of life, and the path of salvation. He who sells my sister, for purposes of prostitution, stands forth as the pious advocate of purity. He who proclaims it a religious duty to read the Bible denies me the right of learning to read the name of the God who made me. He who is the religious advocate of marriage robs whole millions of its sacred influence, and leaves them to the ravages of wholesale pollution. The warm defender of the sacredness of the family relation is the same that scatters whole families,—sundering husbands and wives, parents and children, sisters and brothers,—leaving the hut vacant, and the hearth desolate. We see the thief preaching against theft, and the adulterer against adultery. We have men sold to build churches, women sold to support the gospel, and babes sold to purchase Bibles for the *poor heathen! all for the glory of God and the good of souls!* The slave auctioneer's bell and the church-going bell chime in with each other, and the bitter cries of the heart-broken slave are drowned in the religious shouts of his pious master. Revivals of religion and revivals in the slave-trade go hand in hand together. The slave prison and the church stand near each other. The clanking of fetters and the rattling of chains in the prison, and the pious psalm and solemn prayer in the church, may be heard at the same time. The dealers in the bodies and souls of men erect their stand in the presence of the pulpit, and they mutually help each other. The dealer gives his blood-stained gold to support the pulpit, and the pulpit, in return, covers his infernal business with the garb of Christianity. Here we have religion and robbery the allies of each other—devils dressed in angels' robes, and hell presenting the semblance of paradise.

"Just God! and these are they,
    Who minister at thine altar, God of right!
Men who their hands, with prayer and blessing, lay
    On Israel's ark of light.

"What! preach, and kidnap men?
    Give thanks, and rob thy own afflicted poor?
Talk of thy glorious liberty, and then
    Bolt hard the captive's door?

"What! servants of thy own
    Merciful Son, who came to seek and save
The homeless and the outcast, fettering down
    The tasked and plundered slave!

"Pilate and Herod friends!
   Chief priests and rulers, as of old, combine!
Just God and holy! is that church which lends
   Strength to the spoiler thine?"

The Christianity of America is a Christianity, of whose votaries it may be as truly said, as it was of the ancient scribes and Pharisees, "They bind heavy burdens, and grievous to be borne, and lay them on men's shoulders, but they themselves will not move them with one of their fingers. All their works they do for to be seen of men.——They love the uppermost rooms at feasts, and the chief seats in the synagogues, ... and to be called of men, Rabbi, Rabbi.——But woe unto you, scribes and Pharisees, hypocrites! for ye shut up the kingdom of heaven against men; for ye neither go in yourselves, neither suffer ye them that are entering to go in. Ye devour widows' houses, and for a pretence make long prayers; therefore ye shall receive the greater damnation. Ye compass sea and land to make one proselyte, and when he is made, ye make him twofold more the child of hell than yourselves.——Woe unto you, scribes and Pharisees, hypocrites! for ye pay tithe of mint, and anise, and cumin, and have omitted the weightier matters of the law, judgment, mercy, and faith; these ought ye to have done, and not to leave the other undone. Ye blind guides! which strain at a gnat, and swallow a camel. Woe unto you, scribes and Pharisees, hypocrites! for ye make clean the outside of the cup and of the platter; but within, they are full of extortion and excess.——Woe unto you, scribes and Pharisees, hypocrites! for ye are like unto whited sepulchres, which indeed appear beautiful outward, but are within full of dead men's bones, and of all uncleanness. Even so ye also outwardly appear righteous unto men, but within ye are full of hypocrisy and iniquity."

Dark and terrible as is this picture, I hold it to be strictly true of the overwhelming mass of professed Christians in America. They strain at a gnat, and swallow a camel. Could any thing be more true of our churches? They would be shocked at the proposition of fellowshipping a *sheep*-stealer; and at the same time they hug to their communion a *man*-stealer, and brand me with being an infidel, if I find fault with them for it. They attend with Pharisaical strictness to the outward forms of religion, and at the same time neglect the weightier matters of the law, judgment, mercy, and faith. They are always ready to sacrifice, but seldom to show mercy. They are they who are represented as professing to love God whom they have not seen, whilst they hate their brother whom they have seen. They love the heathen on the other side of the globe. They can pray for him, pay money to have the Bible put into his hand, and missionaries to instruct him; while they despise and totally neglect the heathen at their own doors.

Such is, very briefly, my view of the religion of this land; and to avoid any misunderstanding, growing out of the use of general terms, I mean, by the religion of this land, that which is revealed in the words, deeds, and actions, of those bodies, north and south, calling themselves Christian churches, and yet in union with slaveholders. It is against religion, as presented by these bodies, that I have felt it my duty to testify.

I conclude these remarks by copying the following portrait of the religion of the south, (which is, by communion and fellowship, the religion of the north,) which I soberly affirm is "true to the life," and without caricature or the slightest exaggeration. It is said to have been drawn, several years before the present anti-slavery agitation began, by a northern Methodist preacher, who, while residing at the south, had an opportunity to see slaveholding morals, manners, and piety, with his own eyes. "Shall I not visit for these things? saith the Lord. Shall not my soul be avenged on such a nation as this?"

A PARODY

"Come, saints and sinners, hear me tell
How pious priests whip Jack and Nell,
And women buy and children sell,
And preach all sinners down to hell,
   And sing of heavenly union.

"They'll bleat and baa, dona like goats,
Gorge down black sheep, and strain at motes,
Array their backs in fine black coats,
Then seize their negroes by their throats,
   And choke, for heavenly union.

"They'll church you if you sip a dram,
And damn you if you steal a lamb;
Yet rob old Tony, Doll, and Sam,
Of human rights, and bread and ham;
    Kidnapper's heavenly union.

"They'll loudly talk of Christ's reward,
And bind his image with a cord,
And scold, and swing the lash abhorred,
And sell their brother in the Lord
    To handcuffed heavenly union.

"They'll read and sing a sacred song,
And make a prayer both loud and long,
And teach the right and do the wrong,
Hailing the brother, sister throng,
    With words of heavenly union.

"We wonder how such saints can sing,
Or praise the Lord upon the wing,
Who roar, and scold, and whip, and sting,
And to their slaves and mammon cling,
    In guilty conscience union.

"They'll raise tobacco, corn, and rye,
And drive, and thieve, and cheat, and lie,
And lay up treasures in the sky,
By making switch and cowskin fly,
    In hope of heavenly union.

"They'll crack old Tony on the skull,
And preach and roar like Bashan bull,
Or braying ass, of mischief full,
Then seize old Jacob by the wool,
    And pull for heavenly union.

"A roaring, ranting, sleek man-thief,
Who lived on mutton, veal, and beef,
Yet never would afford relief
To needy, sable sons of grief,
    Was big with heavenly union.

"'Love not the world,' the preacher said,
And winked his eye, and shook his head;
He seized on Tom, and Dick, and Ned,
Cut short their meat, and clothes, and bread,
    Yet still loved heavenly union.

"Another preacher whining spoke
Of One whose heart for sinners broke
He tied old Nanny to an oak,
And drew the blood at every stroke,
    And prayed for heavenly union.

"Two others oped their iron jaws,
And waved their children-stealing paws;
There sat their children in gewgaws;
By stinting negroes' backs and maws,
    They kept up heavenly union.

"All good from Jack another takes,
And entertains their flirts and rakes,
Who dress as sleek as glossy snakes,
And cram their mouths with sweetened cakes;
    And this goes down for union."

Sincerely and earnestly hoping that this little book may do something toward throwing light on the American slave system, and hastening the glad day of deliverance to the millions of my brethren in bonds— faithfully relying upon the power of truth, love, and justice, for success in my humble efforts—and solemnly pledging my self anew to the sacred cause, —I subscribe myself,

FREDERICK DOUGLASS.
—Lynn, *Mass., April 28, 1845.*

Religious Experience and Journal of Mrs. Jarena Lee

"And it shall come to pass . . . . that I will pour out my Spirit upon all flesh; and your sons, and your daughters shall prophecy." —Joel ii. 28.

I was born February 11th, 1783, at Cape May, State of New Jersey. At the age of seven years I was parted from my parents, and went to live as a servant maid, with a Mr. Sharp, at the distance of about sixty miles from the place of my birth.

My parents being wholly ignorant of the knowledge of God, had not therefore instructed me in any degree in this great matter. Not long after the commencement of my attendance on this lady, she had bid me do something respecting my work, which in a little while after she asked me if I had done, when I replied, Yes—but this was not true.

At this awful point, in my early history, the Spirit of God moved in power through my conscience, and told me I was a wretched sinner. On this account so great was the impression, and so strong were the feelings of guilt, that I promised in my heart that I would not tell another lie.

But notwithstanding this promise my heart grew harder, after a while, yet the Spirit of the Lord never entirely forsook me, but continued mercifully striving with me, until his gracious power converted my soul.

The manner of this great accomplishment, was as follows: In the year 1804, it so happened that I went with others to hear a missionary of the Presbyterian order-preach. It was an afternoon meeting, but few were there, the place was a school room; but the preacher was solemn, and in his countenance the earnestness of his master's business appeared equally strong, as though he were about to speak to a multitude.

At the reading of the Psalms, a ray of renewed conviction darted into my soul. These were the words, composing the first verse of the Psalms for the service:

"Lord, I am vile, conceived in sin,
Born unholy and unclean.
Sprung from man, whose guilty fall
Corrupts the race, and taints us all."

This description of my condition struck me to the heart, and made me to feel in some measure, the weight of my sins, and sinful nature. But not knowing how to run immediately to the Lord for help, I was driven of Satan, in the course of a few days, and tempted to destroy myself.

There was a brook about a quarter of a mile from the house, in which there was a deep hole, where the water whirled about among the rocks; to this place it was suggested, I must go and drown myself.

At the time I had a book in my hand; it was on a Sabbath morning, about ten o'clock; to this place I resorted, where on coming to the water I sat down on the bank, and on my looking into it, it was suggested that drowning would be an easy death. It seemed as if some one was speaking to me, saying put your head under, it will not distress you. But by some means, of which I can give no account, my thoughts were taken entirely from this purpose, when I went from the place to the house again. It was the unseen arm of God which saved me from self-murder.

But notwithstanding this escape from death, my mind was not at rest—but so great was the labor of my spirit and the fearful oppressions of a judgment to come, that I was reduced as one extremely ill, on which account a physician was called to attend me, from which illness I recovered in about three months.

But as yet I had not found Him of whom Moses and the prophets did write, being extremely ignorant: there being no one to instruct me in the way of life and salvation as yet. After my recovery, I left the lady, who, during my sickness, was exceedingly kind, and went to Philadelphia. From this place I soon went a few miles into the country, where I resided in the family of a Roman Catholic. But my anxiety still continued respecting my poor soul, on which account I used to watch my opportunity to read in the Bible; and this lady observing this, took the Bible from me and hid it, giving me a novel in its stead—which when I perceived, I refused to read.

Soon after this I again went to the city of Philadelphia, and commenced going to the English Church, the pastor of which was an Englishman, by the name of Pilmore, one of the number who at first preached Methodism in America, in the city of New York.

But while sitting under the ministration of this man, which was about three months, and at the last time, it appeared that there was a wall between me and a communion with that people, which was higher than I could possibly see over, and seemed to make this impression upon my mind, *this is not the people for you.*

But on returning home at noon I inquired of the head cook of the house respecting the rules of the Methodists, as I knew she belonged to that society, who told me what they were; on which account I replied, that I should not be able to abide by such strict rules not even one year—however, I told her that I would go with her and hear what they had to say.

The man who was to speak in the afternoon of that day, was the Rev. Richard Allen, since bishop of the African Episcopal Methodists in America. During the labors of this man that afternoon, I had come to the conclusion, that this is the people to which my heart unites, and it so happened, that as soon as the service closed he invited such as felt a desire to flee the wrath to come, to unite on trial with them—I embraced the opportunity. Three weeks from that day, my soul was gloriously converted to God, under preaching, at the very outset of the sermon. The text was barely pronounced, which was 'I perceive thy heart is not right in the sight of God," when there appeared to *my* view, in the centre of the heart, *one* sin; and this was *malice* against one particular individual, who had strove deeply to injure me, which I resented. At this discovery I said, *Lord I forgive every* creature. That instant, it appeared to me as if a garment, which had entirely enveloped my whole person, even to my fingers' ends, split at the crown of my head, and was stripped away from me, passing like a shadow from my sight—when the glory of God seemed to cover me in its stead.

That moment, though hundreds were present, I did leap to my feet and declare that God, for Christ's sake, had pardoned the sins of my soul. Great was the ecstacy of my mind, for I felt that not only the sin of *malice* was pardoned, but all other sins were swept away together. That day was the first when my heart had believed, and my tongue had made confession unto salvation—the first words uttered, a part of that song, which shall fill eternity with its sound, was *glory* to *God.* For a few moments I had power to exhort sinners, and to tell of the wonders and of the goodness of Him who had clothed me with *His* salvation. During this the minister was silent, until my soul felt its duty had been performed, when he declared another witness of the power of Christ to forgive sins on earth, was manifest in my conversion.

From the day on which I first went to the Methodist Church, until the hour of my deliverance, I was strangely buffetted by that enemy of all righteousness—the devil.

I was naturally of a lively turn of disposition; and during the space of time from my first awakening until I knew my peace was made with God, I rejoiced in the vanities of this life, and then again sunk back into sorrow.

For four years I had continued in this way, frequently laboring under the awful apprehension, that I could never be happy in this life. This persuasion was greatly strengthened during the three weeks, which was the last of Satan's power over me, in this peculiar manner, on which account I had come to the conclusion that I had better be dead than alive. Here I was again tempted to destroy my life by drowning; but suddenly this mode was changed—and while in the dusk of the evening, as I was walking to and fro in the yard of the house, I was beset to hang myself with a cord suspended from the wall enclosing the secluded spot.

But no sooner was the intention resolved on in my mind, than an awful dread came over me, when I ran into the house; still the tempter pursued me. There was standing a vessel of water—into this I was strangly impressed to plunge my head, so as to extinguish the life which God had given me. Had I done this, I have been always of the opinion, that I should have been unable to have released myself; although the vessel was scarcely large enough to hold a gallon of water. Of me may it not be said as written by Isaiah, (chap. 65, verses 1, 2.) "I am sought of them that asked not for me; I am found of them that sought me not." Glory be to God for his redeeming power, which saved me from the violence of my own hands, from the malice of Satan, and from eternal death; for had I have killed myself, a great ransom could not have delivered me; for it is written —"No murderer hath eternal life abiding in him." How appropriately can I sing—

> "Jesus sought me when a stranger,
>   Wandering from the fold of God;
> He to rescue me from danger,
>   Interposed his precious blood."

But notwithstanding the terror which seized upon me, when about to end my life, I had no view of the precipice on the edge of which I was tottering, until it was over, and my eyes were opened. Then the awful gulf of hell seemed to he open beneath me, covered only, as it were, by a spider's web, on which I stood. I seemed to hear the howling of the damned, to see the smoke of the bottomless pit, and to hear the rattling of those chains, which hold the impenitent under clouds of darkness to the judgment of the great day.

I trembled like Belshazzar, and cried out in the horror of my spirit, "God be merciful to me a sinner." That night I formed a resolution to pray; which, when resolved upon, there appeared, sitting in one corner of the room, Satan, in the form of a monstrous dog, and in a rage, as if in pursuit, his tongue protruding from his mouth to a great length, and his eyes looked like two balls of fire; it soon, however, vanished out of my sight. From this state of terror and dismay, I was happily delivered under the preaching of the Gospel as before related.

This view which I was permitted to have of Satan, in the form of a dog, is evidence, which corroborates in my estimation, the Bible account of a hell of fire, which burneth with brimstone, called in Scripture the bottomless pit; the place where all liars, who repent not, shall have their portion; as also the Sabbath breaker, the adulterer, the fornicator, with the fearful, the abominable, and the unbelieving, this shall be the portion of their cup.

This language is too strong and expressive to be applied to any state of suffering in *time*. Were it to be thus applied, the reality could no where be found in human life; the consequence would be, that *this* scripture would be found a false testimony. But when made to apply to an endless state of perdition, in eternity, beyond the bounds of human life, then this language is found not to exceed our views of a state of eternal damnation.

During the latter part of my state of conviction, I can now apply to my case, as it then was, the beautiful words of the poet:

"The more I strove against its power,
I felt its weight and guilt the more;
'Till late I heard my Saviour say,
Come hither soul, I am the way."

This I found to be true, to the joy of my disconsolate and despairing heart, in the hour of my conversion to God.

During this state of mind, while sitting near the fire one evening, after I had heard Rev. Richard Allen, as before related, a view of my distressed condition so affected my heart, that I could not refrain from weeping and crying aloud; which caused the lady with whom I then lived, to inquire, with surprise, what ailed me; to which I answered, that I knew not what ailed me. She replied that I ought to pray. I arose from where I was sitting, being in an agony, and weeping convulsively, requested her to pray for me; but at the very moment when she would have done so, some person wrapped heavily at the door for admittance; it was but a person of the house, but this occurrence was sufficient to interrupt us in our intentions; and I believe to this day, I should then have found salvation to my soul. This interruption was, doubtless, also the work of Satan.

Although at this time, when my conviction was so great, yet I knew not that Jesus Christ was the Son of God, the second person in the adorable Trinity. I knew him not in the pardon of my sins, yet I felt a consciousness that if I died without pardon, that my lot must inevitably be damnation. If I would pray—I knew not how. I could form no connexion of ideas into words; but I knew the Lord's prayer; this I uttered with a loud voice, and with all my might and strength. I was the most ignorant creature in the world; I did not even know that Christ had died for the sins of the world, and to save sinners. Every circumstance, however, was so directed as still to continue and increase the sorrows of my heart, which I now know to have been a Godly sorrow which wrought repentance, which is not to repented of. Even the falling of the dead leaves from the forests, and the dried spires of the mown grass, showed me that I too must die in like manner. But my case was awfully different from that of the grass of the field, or the wide spread decay of a thousand forests, as I felt within me a living principle, an immortal spirit, which cannot die, and must forever either enjoy the smiles of its Creator, or feel the pangs of ceaseless damnation.

But the Lord led me on; being gracious, he took pity on my ignorance; he heard my wailings, which had entered into the ear of the Lord of Sabaoth. Circumstances so transpired that I soon came to a knowledge of the being and character of the Son of God, of whom I knew nothing.

My strength had left me. I had become feverish and sickly through the violence of my feelings, on which account I left my place of service to spend a week with a colored physician, who was a member of the Methodist society, and also to spend this week in going to places where prayer and supplication was statedly made for such as me.

Through this means I had learned much, so as to be able in some degree to comprehend the spiritual meaning of the text, which the minister took on the Sabbath morning, as before related, which was "I perceive thy heart is not right in the sight of God."—Acts, chap. 8, verse 21.

This text, as already related, became the power of God unto salvation to me, because I believed. I was baptized according to the direction of our Lord, who said, as he was about to ascend from the mount, to his disciples, "Go ye into all the world and preach my gospel to every creature, he that believeth and is baptized shall be saved."

I have now passed through the account of my conviction, and also of my conversion to God: and shall next speak of the blessings of sanctification.

A time, after I had received forgiveness, flowed sweetly on; day and night my joy was full, no temptation was permitted to molest me. I could say continually with the psalmist, that "God had separated my sins from me as far as the east is from the west." I was ready continually to cry,

"Come all the world, come sinner thou,
All things in Christ are ready now."

I continued in this happy state of mind for almost three months, when a certain colored man, by name William Scott, came to pay me a religious visit. He had been for many years a faithful follower of the Lamb; and he had also taken much time in visiting the sick and distressed of our color, and understood well the great things belonging to a man of full stature in Christ Jesus.

In the course of our conversation, he inquired if the Lord had justified my soul. I answered yes. He then asked me if he had sanctified me. I answered no; and that I did not know what that was. He then undertook to instruct me further in the knowledge of the Lord respecting this blessing.

He told me the progress of the soul from a state of darkness, or of nature, was three-fold; or consisted in three degrees, as follows: First, conviction for sin. Second, justification from sin. Third, the entire sanctification of the soul to God. I thought this description was beautiful, and immediately believed in it. He then inquired if I would promise to pray for this in my secret devotions. I told him yes. Very soon I began to call upon the Lord to show me all that was in my heart, which was not according to his will. Now there appeared to be a new struggle commencing in my soul, not accompanied with fear, guilt, and bitter distress, as while under my first conviction for sin, but a laboring of the mind to know more of the right way of the Lord. I began now to feel that my heart was not clean in his sight; that there yet remained the roots of bitterness, which if not destroyed, would ere long sprout up from these roots, and overwhelm me in a new growth of the brambles and brushwood of sin.

By the increasing light of the Spirit, I had found there yet remained the root of pride, anger, self-will, with many evils, the result of fallen nature. I now became alarmed at this discovery, and began to fear that I had been deceived in my experience. I was now greatly alarmed, lest I should fall away from what I knew I had enjoyed; and to guard against this I prayed almost incessantly, without acting faith on the power and promises of God to keep me from falling. I had not yet learned how to war against temptation of this kind. Satan well knew that if he could succeed in making me disbelieve my conversion, that he would catch me either on the ground of complete despair, or on the ground of infidelity. For if all I had passed through was to go for nothing, and was but a fiction, the mere ravings of a disordered mind, that I would naturally be led to believe that there is nothing in religion at all.

From this snare I was mercifully preserved, and led to believe that there was yet a greater work than that of pardon to be wrought in me. I retired to a secret place, (after having sought this blessing, as well as I could, for nearly three months, from the time brother Scott had instructed me respecting it,) for prayer, about four o'clock in the afternoon. I had struggled long and hard, but found not the desire of my heart. When I rose from my knees, there seemed a voice speaking to me, as I yet stood in a leaning posture—"Ask for sanctification." When to my surprise, I recollected that I had not even thought of it in my whole prayer. It would seem Satan had hidden the very object from my mind, for which I had purposely kneeled to pray. But when this voice whispered in my heart, saying, "Pray for sanctification," I again bowed in the same place, at the same time, and said "Lord *sanctify* my soul for Christ's sake." That very instant, as if lightning had darted through me, I sprang to my feet, and cried, "The Lord has sanctified my soul!" There was none to hear this but the angels who stood around to witness my joy—and Satan, whose malice raged the more. That Satan was there, I knew; for no sooner had I cried out "The Lord has sanctified my soul," than there seemed another voice behind me, saying "No, it is too great a work to be done." But another spirit said "Bow down for the witness—I received it—*thou art sanctified!"* The first I knew of myself after that, I was standing in the yard with my hands spread out, and looking with my face toward heaven.

I now ran into the house and told them what had happened to me, when, as it were a new rush of the same ecstacy came upon me, and caused me to feel as if I were in an ocean of light and bliss.

During this, I stood perfectly still, the tears rolling in a flood from my eyes. So great was the joy, that it is past description. There is no language that can describe it, except that which was heard by St. Paul, when he was caught up to third heaven, and heard words which it was not lawful to utter.

My Call to Preach the Gospel

Between four and five years after my sanctification, on a certain time, an impressive silence fell upon me, and I stood as if some one was about to speak to me, yet I had no such thought in my heart.— But to my utter surprise there seemed to sound a voice which I thought I distinctly heard, and most certainly understand, which said to me, "Go preach the Gospel!" I immediately replied aloud, "No one will believe me." Again I listened, and again the same voice seemed to say—"Preach the Gospel; I will put words in your mouth, and will turn your enemies to become your friends."

At first I supposed that Satan had spoken to me, for I had read that he could transform himself into an angel of light for the purpose of deception. Immediately I went into a secret place, and called upon the Lord to know if he had called me to preach, and whether I was deceived or not; when there appeared to my view the form and figure of a pulpit, with a Bible lying thereon, the back of which was presented to me as plainly as if it had been a literal fact.

In consequence of this, my mind became so exercised, that during the night following, I took a text and preached in my sleep. I thought there stood before me a great multitude, while I expounded to them the things of religion. So violent were my exertions and so loud were my exclamations, that I awoke from the sound of my own voice, which also awoke the family of the house where I resided. Two days after I went to see the preacher in charge of the African Society, who was the Rev. Richard Allen, the same before named in these pages, to tell him that I felt it my duty to preach the gospel But as I drew near the street in which his house was, which was in the city of Philadelphia, my courage began to fail me; so terrible did the cross appear, it seemed that I should not be able to bear it. Previous to my setting out to go to see him, so agitated was my mind, that my appetite for my daily food failed me entirely. Several times on my way there, I turned back again; but as often I felt my strength again renewed, and I soon found that the nearer I approached to the house of the minister, the less was my fear. Accordingly, as soon as I came to the door, my fears subsided, the cross was removed, all things appeared pleasant—I was tranquil.

I now told him, that the Lord had revealed it to me, that must preach the gospel. He replied, by asking, in what sphere I wished to move in? I said, among the Methodists. He then replied, that a Mrs. Cook, a Methodist lady, had also some time before requested the same privilege; who, it was believed, had done much good in the way of exhortation, and holding prayer meetings; and who had been permitted to do so by the verbal license of the preacher in charge at the time. But as to women preaching, he said that our Discipline knew nothing at all about it—that it did not call for women preachers. This I was glad to hear, because it removed the fear of the cross—but no sooner did this feeling cross my mind, than I found that a love of souls had in a measure departed from me; that holy energy which burned within me, as a fire, began to be smothered. This I soon perceived.

O how careful ought we to be, lest through our by-laws of church government and discipline, we bring into disrepute even the word of life. For as unseemly as it may appear now-a-days for a woman to preach, it should be remembered that nothing is impossible with God. And why should it be thought impossible, heterodox, or improper for a woman to preach? seeing the Saviour died for the woman as well as for the man.

If the man may preach, because the Saviour died for him, why not the woman? seeing he died for her also. Is he not a whole Saviour, instead of a half one? as those who hold it wrong for a woman to preach, would seem to make it appear.

Did not Mary *first* preach the risen Saviour, and is not the doctrine of the resurrection the very climax of Christianity—hangs not all our hope on this, as argued by St. Paul? Then did not Mary, a woman, preach the gospel? for she preached the resurrection of the crucified Son of God.

But some will say that Mary did not expound the Scripture, therefore, she did not preach, in the proper sense of the term. To this I reply, it may be that the term *preach* in those primitive times, did not mean exactly what it is now *made* to mean; perhaps it was a great deal more simple then, than it is now—if it were not, the unlearned fishermen could not have preached the gospel at all, as they had no learning.

To this it may be replied, by those who are determined not to believe that it is right for a woman to preach, that the disciples, though they were fishermen and ignorant of letters too, were inspired so to do. To which I would reply, that though they were inspired, yet that inspiration did not save them from showing their ignorance of letters, and of man's wisdom; this the multitude soon found out, by listening to the remarks of the envious Jewish priests. If then, to preach the gospel, by the gift of heaven, comes by inspiration solely, is God straitened: must he take the man exclusively? May he not, did he not, and can he not inspire a female to preach the simple story of the birth, life, death, and resurrection of our Lord, and accompany it too with power to the sinner's heart. As for me, I am fully persuaded that the Lord called me to labor according to what I have received, in his vineyard. If he has not, how could he consistently bear testimony in favor of my poor labors, in awakening and converting sinners?

In my wanderings up and down among men, preaching according to my ability, I have frequently found families who told me that they had not for several years been to a meeting, and yet, while listening to hear what God would say by his poor female instrument, have believed with trembling—tears rolling down their cheeks, the signs of contrition and repentance towards God. I firmly believe that I have sown seed, in the name of the Lord, which shall appear with its increase at the great day of accounts, when Christ shall come to make up his jewels.

At a certain time, I was beset with the idea, that soon or late I should fall from grace and lose my soul at last. I was frequently called to the throne of grace about this matter, but found no relief; the temptation pursued me still. Being more and more afflicted with it, till at a certain time, when the spirit strongly impressed it on my mind to enter into my closet and carry my case once more to the Lord; the Lord enabled me to draw nigh to him, and to his mercy seat, at this time, in an extraordinary manner; for while I wrestled with him for the victory over this disposition to doubt whether I should persevere, there appeared a form of fire, about the size of a man's hand, as I was on my knees; at the same moment there appeared to the eye of faith a man robed in a white garment, from the shoulders down to the feet; from him a voice proceeded, saying: "Thou shalt never return from the cross." Since that time I have never doubted, but believe that God will keep me until the day of redemption. Now I could adopt the very language of St. Paul, and say, that nothing could have separated me from the love of God, which is in Christ Jesus. Since that time, 1807, until the present, 1833, I have not even doubted the power and goodness of God to keep me from falling, through the sanctification of the spirit and belief of the truth.

My Marriage

In the year 1811, I changed my situation in life, having married Mr. Joseph Lee, pastor of a Society at Snow Hill, about six miles from the city of Philadelphia. It became necessary therefore for me to remove. This was a great trial at first, as I knew no person at Snow Hill, except my husband, and to leave my associates in the society, and especially those who composed the *band* of which I was one. None but those who have been in sweet fellowship with such as really love God, and have together drank bliss and happiness from the same fountain, can tell how dear such company is, and how hard it is to part from them.

At Snow Hill, as was feared, I never found that agreement and closeness in communion and fellowship, that I had in Philadelphia, among my young companions, nor ought I to have expected it. The manners and customs at this place were somewhat different, on which account I became discontented in the course of a year, and began to importune my husband to remove to the city. But this plan did not suit him, as he was the Pastor of the Society, he could not bring his mind to leave them. This afflicted me a little. But the Lord showed me in a dream what his will was concerning this matter.

I dreamed that as I was walking on the summit of a beautiful hill, that I saw near me a flock of sheep, fair and white, as if but newly washed; when there came walking toward me a man of a grave and dignified countenance, dressed entirely in white, as it were in a robe, and looking at me, said emphatically, "Joseph Lee must take care of these sheep, or the wolf will come and devour them." When I awoke I was convinced of my error, and immediately, with a glad heart, yielded to the right spirit in the Lord. This also greatly strengthened my faith in his care over them, for fear the wolf should by some means take any of them away. The following verse was beautifully suited to our condition, as well as to all the little flocks of God scattered up and down this land:

"Us into Thy protection take,
And gather with Thine arm;
Unless the fold We first forsake,
The wolf can never harm."

After this, I fell into a state of general debility, and in an ill state of health, so much so, that I could not sit up; but a desire to warn sinners to flee the wrath to come, burned vehemently in my heart, when the Lord would send sinners into the house to see me. Such opportunities I embraced to press home on their consciences the things of eternity, and so effectual was the word of exhortation made through the Spirit, that I have seen them fall to the floor crying aloud for mercy.

From this sickness I did not expect to recover, and there was but one thing which bound me to earth, and this was, that I had not as yet preached the gospel to the fallen sons and daughters of Adam's race, to the satisfaction of my mind. I wished to go from one end of the earth to the other, crying, Behold, behold the lamb! To this end I earnestly prayed the Lord to raise me up, if consistent with his will. He condescended to hear my prayer, and to give me a token in a dream, that in due time I should recover my health. The dream was as follows: I thought I saw the sun rise in the morning, and ascend to an altitude of about half an hour high, and then become obscured by a dense black cloud, which continued to hide its rays for about one-third part of the day, and then it burst forth again with renewed splendor.

This dream I interpreted to signify my early life, my conversion to God, and this sickness, which was a great affliction, as it hindered me, and I feared would forever hinder me from preaching the gospel, was signified by the cloud; and the bursting forth of the sun, again, was the recovery of my health, and being permitted to preach.

I went to the throne of grace on this subject, where the Lord made this impressive reply in my heart, while on my knees: "Ye shall be restored to thy health again, and worship God in full purpose of heart."

This manifestation was so impressive, that I could but hide my face as if some one was gazing upon me, to think of the great goodness of the Almighty God to my poor soul and body. From that very time I began to gain strength of body and mind, glory to God in the highest, until my health was fully recovered.

For six years from this time I continued to receive from above, such baptisms of the Spirit as mortality could scarcely bear. About that time I was called to suffer in my family, by death—five, in the course of about six years, fell by his hand; my husband being one of the number, which was the greatest affliction of all.

I was now left alone in the world, with two infant children, one of the age of about two years, the other six months, with no other dependence than the promise of Him who hath said—I will be the widow's God, and a father to the fatherless. Accordingly, he raised me up friends, whose liberality comforted and solaced me in my state of widowhood and sorrows, I could sing with the greatest propriety the words of the poet.

> "He helps the stranger in distress,
> The widow and the fatherless,
>   And grants the prisoner sweet release."

I can say even now, with the Psalmist, "Once I was young, but now I am old, yet I have never seen the righteous forsaken, nor his seed begging bread." I have ever been fed by his bounty, clothed by his mercy, comforted and healed when sick, succored when tempted, and every where upheld by his hand.

The Subject of My Call to Preach Renewed

It was now eight years since I had made application to be permitted to preach the gospel, during which time I had only been allowed to exhort, and even this privilege but seldom. This subject now was renewed afresh in my mind; it was as a fire shut up in my bones. About thirteen months passed on, while under this renewed impression. During this time, I had solicited of the Rev. Bishop, Richard Allen, who at this time had become Bishop of the African Episcopal Methodists in America, to be permitted the liberty of holding prayer meetings in my own hired house, and of exhorting as I found liberty, which was granted me. By this means, my mind was relieved, as the house soon filled when the hour appointed for prayer had arrived.

I cannot but relate in this place, before I proceed further with the above subject, the singular conversion of a very wicked young man. He was a colored man, who had generally attended our meetings, but not for any good purpose; but rather to disturb and to ridicule our denomination. He openly and uniformly declared that he neither believed in religion, nor wanted any thing to do with it. He was of a Gallio disposition, and took the lead among the young people of color. But after a while he fell sick, and lay about three months in a state of ill health; his disease was a consumption. Toward the close of his days, his sister who was a member of the society, came and desired me to go and see her brother, as she had no hopes of his recovery, perhaps the Lord might break into his mind. I went alone, and found him very low. I soon commenced to inquire respecting his state of feeling, and how he found his mind. His answer was, "O tolerable well," with an air of great in difference. I asked him if I should pray for him. He answered in a sluggish and careless manner, "O yes, if you have time." I then sung a hymn, kneeled down and prayed for him, and then went my way.

Three days after this, I went again to visit the young man. At this time there went with me two of the sisters in Christ. We found the Rev. Mr. Cornish, of our denomination, laboring with him. But he said he received but little satisfaction from him. Pretty soon, however, brother Cornish took his leave; when myself, with the other two sisters, one of which was an elderly woman named Jane Hutt, the other was younger, both colored, commenced conversing with him, respecting his eternal interest, and of his hopes of a happy eternity, if any he had. He said but little; we then kneeled, down together and besought the Lord in his behalf, praying that if mercy were not clear gone for ever, to shed a ray of softening grace upon the hardness of his heart. He appeared now to be somewhat more tender, and we thought we could perceive some tokens of conviction, as he wished us to visit him again, in a tone of voice not quite as indifferent as he had hitherto manifested.

But two days had elapsed after this visit, when his sister came to me in haste, saying, that she believed her brother was then dying, and that he had *sent* for me. I immediately called on Jane Hutt, who was still among us as a mother in Israel, to go with me. When we arrived there, we found him sitting up in bed, very restless and uneasy, but he soon laid down again. He now wished me to come to him, by the side of his bed. I asked him how he was. He said, "Very ill;" and added, "Pray for me, quick?" We now perceived his time in this world to be short. I took up the hymn-book, and opened to a hymn suitable to his case, and commenced to sing, but there seemed to be a *horror* in the room—a darkness of a mental kind, which was felt by us all; there being five persons, except the sick young man and his nurse. We had sung but one verse, when they all gave over singing, on account of this uneartlhy sensation, but myself. I continued to sing on alone, but in a dull and heavy manner, though looking up to God all the while for help. Suddenly I felt a spring of energy awake in my heart, when darkness gave way in some degree. It was but a glimmer from above. When the hymn was finished, we all kneeled down to pray for him. While calling on the name of the Lord, to have mercy on his soul, and to grant him repentance unto life, it came suddenly into my mind never to rise from my knees until God should hear prayer in his behalf, until he should convert and save his soul.

Now, while I thus continued importuning heaven, as I felt I was led, a ray of light, more abundant, broke forth among us. There appeared to my view, though my eyes were closed, the Saviour in full stature, nailed to the cross, just over the head of the young man, against the ceiling of the room. I cried out, brother look up, the Saviour is come, he will pardon you, your sins he will forgive. My sorrow for the soul of the young man was gone; I could no longer pray—joy and rapture made it impossible. We rose up from our knees, when lo, his eyes were gazing with ecstacy upwards; over his face there was an expression of joy; his lips were clothed in a sweet and holy smile; but no sound came from his tongue; it was heard in its stillness of bliss; full of hope and immortality. Thus, as I held him by the hand, his happy and purified soul soared away, without a sigh or a groan, to its eternal rest.

I now closed his eyes, straightened out his limbs, and left him to be dressed for the grave. But as for me, I was filled with the power of the Holy Ghost—the very room seemed filled with glory. His sister and all that were in the room rejoiced, nothing doubting but he had entered into Paradise; and I believe I shall see him at the last and great day, safe on the shores of salvation.

But to return to the subject of my call to preach. Soon after this, as above related, the Rev. Richard Williams was to preach at Bethel Church, where I with others were assembled. He entered the pulpit, gave out the hymn, which was sung, and then addressed the throne of grace; took his text, passed through the exordium, and commenced to expound it. The text he took is in Jonah, 2d chap. 9th verse,—"Salvation is of the Lord." But as he proceeded to explain, he seemed to have lost the spirit; when in the same instant, I sprang, as by altogether supernatural impulse, to my feet, when I was aided from above to give an exhortation on the very text which my brother Williams had taken.

I told them I was like Jonah; for it had been then nearly eight years since the Lord had called me to preach his gospel to the fallen sons and daughters of Adam's race, but that I had lingered like him, and delayed to go at the bidding of the Lord, and warn those who are as deeply guilty as were the people of Ninevah.

During the exhortation, God made manifest his power in a manner sufficient to show the world that I was called to labor according to my ability, and the grace given unto me, in the vineyard of the good husbandman.

I now sat down, scarcely knowing what I had done, being frightened. I imagined, that for this indecorum, as I feared it might be called, I should be expelled from the church. But instead of this, the Bishop rose up in the assembly, and related that I had called upon him eight years before, asking to be permitted to preach, and that he had put me off; but that he now as much believed that I was called to that work, as any of the preachers present. These remarks greatly strengthened me, so that my fears of having given an offence, and made myself liable as an offender, subsided, giving place to a sweet serenity, a holy joy of a peculiar kind, untasted in my bosom until then.

The next Sabbath day, while sitting under the word of the gospel, I felt moved to attempt to speak to the people in a public manner, but I could not bring my mind to attempt it in the church. I said, Lord, anywhere but here. Accordingly, there was a house not far off which was pointed out to me; to this I went. It was the house of a sister belonging to the same society with myself. Her name was Anderson. I told her I had come to hold a meeting in her house, if she would call in her neighbors. With this request she immediately complied. My congregation consisted of but five persons. I commenced by reading and singing a hymn; when I arose I found my hand resting on the Bible, which I had not noticed till that moment. It now occurred to me to take a text. I opened the Scripture, as it happened, at the 141st Psalm, fixing my eye on the third verse, which reads: "Set a watch, O Lord, before my mouth, keep the door of my lips." My sermon, such as it was, applied wholly to myself, and added an exhortation. Two of my congregation wept much, as the fruit of my labor this time. In closing, I said to the few, that if any one would open a door, I would hold a meeting the next sixth-day evening: when one answered that her house was at my service. Accordingly I went, and God made manifest his power among the people. Some wept, while others shouted for joy. One whole seat of females, by the power of God, as the rushing of a wind, were all bowed to the floor, at once, and screamed out. Also a sick man and woman in one house, the Lord convicted them both; one lived, and the other died. God wrought a judgment—some were well at night, and died in the morning. At this place I continued to hold meetings about six months. During that time I kept house with my little son, who was very sickly. About this time I had a call to preach at a place about thirty miles distant, among the Methodists, with whom I remained one week, and during the whole time, not a thought of my little son came into my mind; it was hid from me, lest, I should have been diverted from the work I had to do, to look after my son. Here by the instrumentality of a poor coloured woman, the Lord poured forth his spirit among the people. Though, as I was told, there were lawyers, doctors, und magistrates present, to hear me speak, yet there was mourning and crying among sinners, for the Lord scattered fire among them of his own kindling. The Lord gave his handmaiden power to speak for his-great name, for he arrested the hearts of the people, and caused a shaking amongst the multitude, for God was in the midst.

I now returned home, found all well; no harm had come to my child, although I left it very sick. Friends had taken care of it which was of the Lord. I now began to think seriously of breaking up housekeeping, and forsaking all to preach the everlasting Gospel. I felt a strong desire to return to the place of my nativity, at Cape May, after an absence of about fourteen years. To this place, where the heaviest cross was to be met with, the Lord sent me, as Saul of Tarsus was sent to Jerusalem, to preach the same gospel which he had neglected and despised before his conversion. I went by water, and on my passage was much distressed by sea sickness, so much so that I expected to have died, but such was not the will of the Lord respecting me. After I had disembarked, I proceeded on as opportunities offered, toward where my mother lived. When within ten miles of that place, I appointed an evening meeting. There were a goodly number came out to hear. The Lord was pleased to give me light and liberty among the people. After meeting, there came an elderly lady to me and said, she believed the Lord had sent me among them; she then appointed me another meeting there two weeks from that night. The next day I hastened forward to the place of my mother, who was happy to see me, and the happiness was mutual between us. With her I left my poor sickly boy, while I departed to do my Master's will. In this neighborhood I had an uncle, who was a Methodist, and who gladly threw open his door for meetings to be held there. At the first meeting which I held at my uncle's house, there was, with others who had come from curiosity to hear the woman preacher, an old man, who was a Deist, and who said he did not believe the coloured people had any souls—he was sure they had none. He took a seat very near where I was standing, and boldly tried to look me out of countenance. But as I labored on in the best manner I was able, looking to God all the while, though it seemed to me I had but little liberty, yet there went an arrow from the bent bow of the gospel, and fastened in his till then obdurate heart. After I had done speaking, he went out, and called the people around him, said that my preaching might seem a small thing, yet he believed I had the worth of souls at heart. This language was different from what it was a little time before, as he now seemed to admit that coloured people had souls, as it was to these I was chiefly speaking; and unless they had souls, whose good I had in view, his remark must have been, without meaning. He now came into the house, and in the most friendly manner shook hands with me, saying, he hoped God had spared him to some good purpose. This man was a great slave holder, and had been very cruel; thinking nothing of knocking down a slave with a fence stake, or whatever might come to hand. From this time it was said of him that he became greatly altered in his ways for the better. At that time he was about seventy years old, his head as white as snow; but whether he became a converted man or net, I never heard.

The week following, I had an invitation to hold a meeting at the Court House of the County, when I spoke from the 53d chap. of Isaiah, 3d verse. It was a solemn time, and the Lord attended the word; I had life and liberty, though there were people there of various denominations. Here again I saw the aged slaveholder, who notwithstanding his age, walked about three miles to hear me. This day I spoke twice, and walked six miles to the place appointed. There was a magistrate present, who showed his friendship, by saying in a friendly manner, that he had heard of me: he handed me a hymnbook, pointing to a hymn which he had selected. When the meeting was over, he invited me to preach in a schoolhouse in his neighborhood, about three miles distant from where I then was. During this meetng one backslider was reclaimed. This day I walked six miles, and preached twice to large congregations, both in the morning and evening. The Lord was with me, glory be to his holy name. I next went six miles and held a meeting in a coloured friund's house, at eleven o'clock in the morning, and preached to a well behaved congregation of both coloured and white. After service I again walked back, which was in all twelve miles in the same day. This was on Sabbath, or as I sometimes call it, seventh day; for after my conversion I preferred the plain language of the Friends. On the fourth day, after this, in compliance with an invitation received by note, from the same magistrate who had heard me at the above place I preached to a large congregation, where we had a precious time: much weeping was heard among the people. The same gentleman, now at the close of the meeting, gave out another appointment at the same place, that day week. Here again I had liberty, there was a move among the people. Ten years from that time, in the neighborhood of Cape May, I held a prayer meeting in a school house, which was then the regular place of preaching for the Episcopal Methodists, after service, there came a white lady, of great distinction, a member of the Methodist Society, and told me that at the same school house ten years before, under my preaching, the Lord first awakened her. She rejoiced much to see me, and invited me home with her, where I staid till the next day. This was bread cast upon the water, seen after many days.

From this place I next went to Dennis Creek meeting house, where at the invitation or an elder, I spoke to a large congregation of various and conflicting sentiments, when a wonderful shock of God's power was felt, shown everywhere by groans, by sighs, and loud and happy amens. I felt as if aided from above. My tongue was cut loose, the stammerer spoke freely; the love of God, and of his service, burned with a vehement flame within me—his name was glorified among the people.

I had my little son with me, and was very much straitened for money—and not having means to procure my passage home, I opened a School, and taught eleven scholars, for the purpose of raising a small sum. For many weeks I knew not what to do about returning home, when the Lord came to my assistance as I was rambling in the fields meditating upon his goodness, and made known to me that I might go to the city of Philadelphia, for which place I soon embarked with a very kind captain. We had a perilous passage—a dreadful storm arose, and before leaving the Delaware bay, we had a narrow escape from being run down by a large ship. But the good Lord held us in the hollow of his hand, and in the afternoon of Nov. 12, 1821, we arrived at the city.

Here I held meetings in the dwelling house of sister Lydia Anderson, and for about three months had as many appointments as I could attend. We had many precious seasons together, and the Lord was with his little praying band, convincing and converting sinners to the truth. I continued in the city until spring, when I felt it impressed upon my mind to travel, and walked fourteen miles in company with a sister to meet with some ministers, there to assemble, from Philadelphia. Satan tempted me while on the way, telling me that I was a fool for walking so far, as I would not be permitted to preach. But I pursued my journey, with the determination to set down and worship with them. When I arrived, a goodly number of people had assembled, and no preacher. They waited the time to commence the exercises, and then called upon me. I took the 3d chapter John, 14th verse for my text. I had life and liberty, and the Lord was in the camp with a shout. Another meeting was appointed three miles from there, when I spoke from Psalms cxxxvii, 1, 2, 3, 4. My master was with me, and made manifest his power. In the County House, also, we held a meeting, and had a sweet waiting upon the Lord. I spoke from Hebrews ii, 3, when the Lord gave me peculiar liberty. At a dwelling house one night I spoke from John vii, 46, when six souls fell to the floor crying for mercy. We had a blessed outpouring of the spirit among us—the God of Jacob was in our midst—and the shout of heaven-born souls was like music to our ears.

About the month of February my little son James, then in his sixth year, gave evidence of having religious inclinations. Once he got up in a chair, with a hymn book in his hand, and with quite a ministerial jesture, gave out a hymn. I felt the spirit move me to sing with him. A worthy sister was in the room, who I asked to pray for him. I invoked the Lord to answer and seal this prayer in the courts of heaven. I believed He would and did, and while yet on our knees I was filled with the fulness of God, and the answer came. I cried out in the joy of my heart—"The dead is alive"—and ran down stairs to inform a neighbor. Tears ran down the cheeks of my now happy boy, and great was our rejoicing together. He had been the subject of many prayers, and often had I thought I would rather follow him to his grave than to see him grow up an open and profane sinner like many children I had seen. And here let me say, the promise of the Lord is, "ask and ye shall receive." Dear parents; pray for your children in childhood—carry them in the arms of faith to the mercy seat, and there present them an offering to the Lord. I can say from my own experience, the Lord will hear prayer. I had given James the Bible as Haman gave Samuel to God in his youth, and by his gracious favor he was received. For the further encouragement of fathers and mothers to engage in this blessed work, let me refer them to Ecclesiastes xi, 6: "In the morning sow thy seed, and in the evening withhold not thy hand, for thou knowest not whether shall prosper either this or that, or whether they both shall be alike good."

> *"Sow it in the youthful mind,*
> *Can you have a fairer field?*
> *Be it but in faith consigned,*
> *Harvest, doubtless, it shall yield,*
> *Fruits of early, piety,*
> *All that God delights to see."*

In November I journeyed for Trenton, N. J. At Burlington I spoke to the people on the Sabbath, and had a good time among them, and on Monday the 12th, in a School house. Sister Mary Owan, who had laid aside all the cares of the world, went with me. We had no means of travelling but on foot, but the Lord regarded us, and by some means put it into the heart of a stranger, to convey us to the Trenton bridge. We fell in with the elder of the circuit, who spoke to me in a cold and formal manner, and as though he thought my capacity was not equal to his. We went into the sister's house, where we expected to stay, and waited a long while with our hats and cloaks on, before the invitation to lodge there was given. In the morning I had thought to visit Newhope, but remained to discharge my duty in visiting the sick and afflicted three or four days in the neighborhood. I was invited to a prayer meeting, and was called upon by a brother to speak. I improved the offer, and made some remarks from Kings xviii, 21. One of the preachers invited me to preach for them on sixth day evening, which I complied with before an attentive congregation, when God followed the word with much power, and great was our joy. On the 17th I spoke in the morning at 11 o'clock. I felt my weakness and deficiency for the work, and thought "who is able for these things," and desired to get away from the task. My text was Timothy vi, 2–7. The Lord again cut loose the stammering tongue, and opened the Scriptures to my mind, so that, glory to God's dear name, we had a most melting, sin-killing, and soul-reviving time. In the afternoon I assisted in leading a class, when we found the Lord faithful and true—and on the same evening I spoke from Hebrews ii, 3.

The next day, sister Mary Owan and myself set out for Newhope, where we arrived, after walking sixteen miles, at about six o'clock in the evening. Though tedious, it was a pleasant walk to view the high mountain and towering hills, and the beauty and variety of nature around us, which powerfully impressed my mind with the greatness and wisdom of my Maker. At this place I stopt at the house of the gentleman with whose wife's mother I was brought up, and by whom we were agreeably received. The next evening we called upon brother Butler, where I addressed a small company, and God, through his words, quickened some. The next night I spoke in an Academy to a goodly number of people, from John iii, 14. Here I found some very ill-behaved persons, who talked roughly, and said among other things, "I was not a woman, but a man dressed in female clothes." I labored one week among them, and went next to Lambertsville, where we experienced kindness from the people, and had a happy time and parted in tears.

I now returned to Philadelphia, where I stayed a short time, and went to Salem, West Jersey. I met with many troubles on my journey, especially from the elder, who like many others, was averse to a woman's preaching. And here let me tell that elder, if he has not gone to heaven, that I have heard that as far back as Adam Clarke's time, his objections to female preaching were met by the answer—"If an ass reproved Balaam, and a barn-door fowl reproved Peter, why should not a woman reprove sin?" I do not introduce this for its complimentary classification of women with donkeys and fowls, but to give the reply of a poor woman, who had once been a slave. To the first companion she said—"May be a speaking woman is like an ass—but I can tell you one thing, the ass seen the angel when Balaam didn't."

Notwithstanding the opposition, we had a prosperous time at Salem. I had some good congregations, and sinners were cut to the heart. After speaking in the meeting house, two women came up into the pulpit, and falling upon my neck cried out "What shall I do to be saved?" One said she had disobeyed God, and he had taken her children from her—he had called often after her, but she did not hearken. I pointed her to the all-atoning blood of Christ, which is sufficient to cleanse from all sin, and left her, after prayer, to his mercy. From this place I walked twenty-one miles, and preached with difficulty to a stiff-necked and rebellious people, who I soon left without any animosity for their treatment. They might have respected my message, if not the poor weak servant who brought it to them with so much labor.

"If they persecute you in one city, flee into another," was the advice I had resolved to take, and I hastened to Greenwich, where I had a lively congregation, had unusual life and liberty in speaking, and the power of God was there. We also had a solemn time in the meeting house on Sabbath day morning, and in a dwelling house in the evening; a large company assembled, when the spirit was with us, and we had a mighty shaking among the dry bones.

On second day morning, I took stage and rode seven miles to Woodstown, and there I spoke to a respectable congregation of white and colored, in a school house. I was desired to speak in the colored meeting house, but the minister could not reconcile his mind to a woman preacher—he could not unite in fellowship with me even to shaking hands as christians ought. I had visited that place before, when God made manifest his power "through the foolishness of preaching," and owned the poor old woman. One of the brothers appointed a meeting in his own house, and after much persuasion this minister came also. I did not feel much like preaching, but spoke from Acts viii, 35. I felt my inability, and was led to complain of weakness—but God directed the arrow to the hearts of the guilty—and my friend the minister got happy, and often shouted "Amen," and "as it is, sister." We had a wonderful display of the spirit of God among us, and we found it good to be there. There is nothing too hard for the Lord to do. I committed the meeting into the hands of the elder, who afterwards invited me to preach in the meeting house. He had said he did not believe that ever a soul was converted under the preaching of a woman—but while I was laboring in his place, conviction seized a woman, who fell to the floor crying for mercy. This meeting held till 12 or 1 o'clock. O how precious is the sound of Jesus' name! I never felt a doubt at this time of my acceptance with God, but rested my soul on his every promise. The elder shook hands, and we parted.

Nov. 22, 1822, I returned to Philadelphia, and attended meetings in and out of the city. God was still my help, and I preached and formed a class, and tried to be useful. The oppositions I met with, however, were numerous—so much so, that I was tempted to withdraw from the Methodist Church, lest some might go into ruin by their persecutions of me—but this was allowed only to try my faithfulness to God. At times I was pressed down like a cart beneath its shafts—my life seemed as at the point of the sword—my heart was sore and pained me in my body. But the Lord knows how to deliver the godly out of temptation, and to reserve the unjust till the day of judgment to be punished. While relating the feelings of my mind to a sister who called to see me, joy sprang up in my bosom that I was not overcome by the adversary, and I was overwhelmed with the love of God and souls. I embraced the sister in my arms, and we had a melting time together. Oh how comforting it is to have the spirit of God bearing witness with our spirits that we are his children in such dark hours!

> *When Satan appears to stop up our path,*
> *And fill us with fears, we triumph by faith;*
> *He cannot take from us, (tho' oft he has tried,)*
> *The soul cheering promise the Lord will provide.*
> *He tells us we're weak, our hope is in vain,*
> *The good that we seek we ne'er shall obtain;*
> *But when such suggestions our graces have tried,*
> *This answers all questions, the Lord will provide.*

I felt a greater love for the people than ever. It appeared to me that they erred through ignorance of my desire to do them good; and my prayer was that nothing but love might appear in my ways, and actuate my heart. Religion is love—God is love. But it was nothing less than the Divine power that brought me through, for it appeared that the hosts of darkness were arrayed against me to destroy my peace and lead me away from the throne of love.

June 24, I left the city of Philadelphia to travel in Delaware State. I went with captain Ryal, a kind gentleman, who took me to his house in Wilmington, and himself and lady both treated me well. The first night of my arrival; I preached in the stone Methodist meeting house. I tried, in my weak way, to interest the assembly from the 2d chapter of Hebrews, 3d verse—"How shall we escape, if we neglect so great salvation." God was there, as we had the most delightful evidence—and many had their eyes opened to see there was no escape from the second death while out of Christ, and cried unto God for his saving grace. I would that all who have not embraced the salvation offered in the gospel, might examine the question candidly and seriously, ere the realities of the other world break up their fancied security.

In July I spoke in a School house to a large congregation, from Numbers xxix, 17. Here we had a sweet foretaste of heaven—full measure, and running over—shouting and rejoicing—while the poor errand-bearer of a free gospel was assisted from on high. I wish my reader had been there to share with us the joyous heavenly feast. On the 15th of July I gave an exhortation in the meeting house again to a listening multitude—deep and solemn were the convictions of many, and good, I trust, was done.

The next place I visited was Newcastle. The meeting house could not be obtained, and two young gentleman interested themselves to get the Court house, but the Trustees objected, wishing to know why the Methodists did not open their Church. The reason was "I was not licensed," they said. My two friends waited on me to speak in the Market house, where I attended at early candlelight, and had the pleasure of addressing a few plain truths to a crowded but respectful congregation, from John vii, 46—"Never man spake like this man." On Sunday the same young gentlemen invited me to give another discourse, to which I consented, before a large gathering of all descriptions.

From here I proceeded to Christine, where we worshipped in a dwelling house, and I must say was well treated by some of my colored friends. I then returned to Wilmington, where in a few days I had a message to return again to C. My friends said I should have the Meeting house, for which Squire Luden interested himself, and the appointment was published. When the people met at the proper time, the doors remained locked. Amid cries of "shame" we left the Church steps—but a private house was opened a short distance up the road, and though disappointed in obtaining egress to a Church, the Lord did not disappoint his people, for we were fed with the bread of life, and had a happy time. Mr. and Mrs. Lewelen took me to their house, and treated me, not as one of their hired servants, but as a companion, for which I shall ever feel grateful. Mr. Smith, a doctor, also invited me to call upon them—he was a Presbyterian, but we prayed and conversed together about Jesus and his love, and parted without meddling with each others creeds. Oh, I long to see the day when Christians will meet on one common platform—Jesus of Nazareth—and cease their bickerings and contentions about non-essentials—when "our Church" shall be less debated, but "our Jesus" shall be all in all.

Another family gave me the invitation to attend a prayer meeting. It was like a "little heaven below." From here I walked about four miles that evening, accompanied by the house maid of Mrs. Ford, a Presbyterian, who said she knew her mistress would be glad to see me. Mrs. F. gave me a welcome—said she felt interested in my speaking, and sent a note to a Methodist lady, who replied that my labor would be acceptable, no doubt, in her Church that afternoon. When I came in, the elder was in the pulpit. He gave us a good sermon. After preaching, this lady spoke of me to the elder; in consequence, he invited me to his pulpit, saying "he was willing that every one should do good." My text was Hebrew ii, 3. Though weak in body, the good Master filled my mouth and gave me liberty among strangers, and seldom have I spent so happy a Sabbath. Mrs. F. had a colored woman in her family one hundred and ten years of age, with whom I conversed about religion—how Christ had died to redeem us, and the way of salvation, and the poor old lady said "she wished she could hear me every day." I also called upon another, one hundred and sixteen years old, who was blind. We talked together about Jesus—she had a strong and abiding evidence of her new birth, and in a few weeks went home to heaven. Here she was long deprived of the light of the sun, and the privilege of reading God's blessed word; but there her eyes are unsealed, and the Sun of righteousness has risen with healing in his wings.

> There glory beams on all the plains,
>   Which sight to her is given—
> There music rolls in sweetest strains,
> And spotless beauty ever reigns,
>   And all is love in heaven.

I left Mrs. Ford's and walked about three miles to St. George, with a recommend to a Mrs. Sutton, a noble-minded lady of the Presbyterian order, where I was generously treated. Here I preached in the School house to a respectable company—had considerable weeping and a profitable waiting upon the Lord. I accepted an invitation from a gentleman to preach in a Methodist Church three miles distant—found there a loving people, and was highly gratified at the order and decorum manifested while I addressed them. Mrs. Smith took me home with her, who I found to be a christian both in sentiment and action. By invitation, I went next to Port Penn, and spoke with freedom, being assisted of the Lord, to a full house, and had a glorious feast of the Spirit. The next night found me at Canton Bride, to which place I had walked—spoke in a School house, from Math, xxii, 41—"What think ye of Christ?" The presence of the Lord over-shadowed us—believers rejoiced—some were awakened to believe well of my Master, and I trust are on their way to glory. In Fieldsborough, also, we had gracious meetings.

At Smyrna I met brother C. W. Cannon, who made application for the Friend's Meeting house for me, where the Lord blessed us abundantly. We attended a Camp-meeting of the old connexion, and got greatly refreshed for the King's service. I rode ten miles and delivered a message from the Lord to a waiting audience—the Master assisted, and seven individuals, white and colored, prostrated themselves for prayer. Next day I rode to Middletown—spoke in a School house to a white congregation from Isaiah lxiii, 1, and a good time it was. In the morning at 11 o'clock, I addressed a Methodist Society, and in the afternoon at 3 o'clock, spoke under a tree in the grave yard, by the road side, to a large audience. Squire Maxwell's lady, who was present, invited me home to tea with herself and nieces, and a Quaker lady showed her benevolence by putting into my hand enough to help me on my journey. The Lord is good—what shall I do to make it known? I rode seven miles that night, and gave an exhortation after the minister had preached, and felt happier than a King.

I now travelled to Cecil county, Md., and the first evening spoke to a large congregation. The pastor afterwards baptized some adult persons—and we all experienced the cleansing and purifying power. We had a baptism within and without. I was next sent for by the servant of a white gentleman, to hold a meeting in his house in the evening. He invited the neighbors, colored and white, when I spoke according to the ability God gave me. It was pleasant to my poor soul to be there—Jesus was in our midst—and we gave glory to God. Yes, glory—glory be to God in the highest. "God forbid that I should glory, save in the cross of our Lord Jesus Christ." I boast not myself. Paul may plant and Apollos water, but God giveth the increase, I tried also to preach three times at a place 14 miles from here—had good meetings—backsliders were reclaimed and sinners convicted of sin, who I left in the hands of God, with the hope of meeting and recognizing again "when we arrive at home." * * * * *

Returned back to Middletown. The next day the preacher of the circuit conveyed me to his place of appointment at Elkton. We had a wonderful outpouring of the spirit. At Frenchtown I spoke at 11 o'clock, where I realized my nothingness, but, God's name he praised, he helped me in the duty. Went again to Middletown, and from there to Canton's Bridge, and talked to the people as best I could. Seven miles from this place I found, by the direction of a kind Providence, my own sister, who had been separated from me some thirty-three years. We were young when last we met, with less of the cares of life than now. Each heart then was buoyant with mildly hopes and pleasures—and little did we expect at parting that thirty-three years would pass over us, with its changes and vicissitudes, ere we should see each other's face. Both were much altered in appearance, but we knew each other, and talked over the dealings of the Lord with us, retracing our wanderings in the world and "the days when life was young."

"Our days of childhood quickly pass,
    And soon our happiest years are run—
As the pure dew that gems the grass
    Is dried beneath the summer sun.
There's such deceit—such guile in men,
Who would not be a child again?"

During this visit I had three meetings in different directions in gentlemen's houses, and a prayer meeting at my brother's, who did not enjoy religion. My good old friend Mr. Lorton happened to be there, who told the people that he had been to my house—that he knew Mr. Lee (my husband) intimately, and that he had often preached for him while pastor of the Church at Snow Hill, N. J.

I next attended and preached several times at a camp meetinng, which continued five days. We had pentecostal showers—sinners were pricked to the heart, and cried mightily to God for succor from impending judgment, and I verily believe the Lord was well pleased at our weak endeavors to serve him in the tented grove. The elder in charge, on the last day of the camp, appointed a meeting for me in a dwelling house. Spoke from Acts ii, 41. The truth fastened in the hearts of two young women, who, after I was seated, came and fell down at my side, and cried for God to have mercy on them—we prayed and wrestled with the Lord, and both were made happy in believing, and are alive in the faith of the gospel. The next morning a brother preacher took me to St. Georgetown. From there I took stage to Wilmington, and called on my friend Captain Rial, in whose family I spent two days and nights. Went to Philadelphia to attend a camp-meeting. Returned again to W—, where I was taken sick with typhus fever, and was in the doctor's hands for some days—but the Lord rebuked the disease, gave me my usual health again, and I returned back to Philadelphia.

The Bishop gave me an invitation to speak in Bethel Church; but here my heart fluttered with fear at the commencement, in a manner known but to those who feel their unworthiness in addressing new and large assemblies. My text was in Isaiah x. 10, 11. Previous to dismission, the Bishop gave me another appointment in Wesley Church for first day morning, where I labored to encourage believers, from Ephesians ii, 19. The comforter was with us—we were sprinkled as with clear water from above—the hands of those that were hanging down were lifted up, and we truly had a refreshing season. Glory to God for the manifestation of His Spirit. "Now therefore ye are no more strangers and foreigners, but fellow-citizens with the saints, and of the household of God."

On the ensuing Thursday night, in Union Church, I had the opportunity of speaking a word for my Saviour again, and recommeneed the impenitent to see to it that they took the advice of my text, in Rev. iii, 18. The Lord searched the heart as he did Jerusalem with a lighted candle, and there was a moving of the Spirit among the people.

From Philadelphia I travelled on foot thirty miles to Downingtown, and gave ten sermons while there; and remember the cold day in December I walked sixteen miles from the above place to brother Wells', where I staid one week, and labored both among colored and white. They had one class there. Three miles further, I talked on Lord's day to an apparently hardened people, and next night preached in a School-house, after a ride of ten miles. The call of the Lord was for me now to go to West Chester, N. Y., where I remained a little period with brother Thomas Henry and brother Miller; preached in a School-house and in the Wesleyan Methodist Meeting-house. When prepared to go home, a request was sent me to preach in the Court-house of the county, to which I rode ten miles, and addressed the citizens on two evenings. The Lord strengthened his feeble instrument in the effort to win souls to Christ, for which my heart at this time was heavily burthened. Next morning I left for Westhaven, where I visited a School of boys and girls, and was much pleased to see them engaged and improving in their studies. How great the difference now, thought I, for the mental and moral culture of the young than when I was a child!

In the month of June, 1823, I went on from Philadelphia to New York with Bishop Allen and several Elders, (including our present Rev. Bishop Brown,) to attend the New York Annual Conference of our denomination, where I spent three months of my time. We arrived about nine o'clock in the evening. As we left the boat, a person fell into the dock, and notwithstanding the effort made to save and find him, he was seen no more. 'In the midst of life we are in death.' On the 4th of June I spoke in the Asbury Church, from Psalms c, 33. I think I never witnessed such a shouting and rejoicing time. The Church had then but recently adopted the African M. E. discipline. On the 5th I brought my master's message to the Bethel Church—Text Isaiah lviii, 1. "Cry aloud, spare not; lift up thy voice like a trumpet, and show my people their transgressions, and the house of Jacob their sins." The spirit of God came upon me; I spoke without fear of man, and seemed willing even there to be offered up; the preachers shouted and prayed, and it was a time long to be remembered.

June 6. Spoke in the Church in High Street, Brooklyn, from Jer. ix, 1—"Oh that my head were waters, and mine eyes a fountain of tears, that I might weep day and night for the slain of the daughter of my people." In these days I felt it my duty to travel up and down in the world, and promulgate the gospel of Christ, especially among my own people, though I often desired to be released from the great task. The Lord had promised to be with me, and my trust was in his strong arm.

> *Renouncing every worldly thing,*
> *Safe 'neath the shadow of thy wing,*
> *My sweetest thought henceforth shall be*
> *That all I want I find in thee,*
>   *In thee, my God, in Thee.*

I left my friend in Brooklyn, and went to Flushing, L. I. Here we had quite a revival feeling, and two joined society. Visited Jamaica and Jericho; spoke in brother B's dwelling, in the church, and under a tree. Went to White Plains to the camp-meeting; the Lord was with us indeed; believers were revived, backsliders reclaimed, and sinners converted. Returned and spent a little time in Brooklyn, where I addressed the people from Rev. iii, 18, and John iii, 15.

July 22. Spoke in Asbury Church from Acts xiii, 41—"Behold ye despisers, and wonder and perish." I pointed out the portion of the hypocrite, the liar, the Sabbath-breaker, and all who do wickedly and die in their sins; they shall be to the judgment bar of Jehovah, and before an assembled universe hear their awful sentence, "Depart from me, ye cursed, into everlasting fire, prepared for the devil and his angels," while the righteous shall be received "into life eternal." On the 28th I went to Dutch Hill, L. I., and spoke before a congregation of white and colored, in a barn, as there was no other suitable place. I felt happy when I thought of my dear Redeemer, who was born in a stable and cradled in a manger, and we had a precious season. Brother Croker, of Brooklyn, and father Thompson were with me, at whose feet I desired rather to sit and learn, they being experienced "workmen that needed not to be ashamed." But the Lord sends by whom he will.

The next Sabbath I weakly attempted to address my friends in New York again. Took the words in Math. xxviii, 13, for my text—"Say ye, his disciples came by night, and stole him away while we slept." The place was greatly crowded, and many came who could not get in. A class met here, to which the preacher invited all who desired to remain, and thirty persons tarried. He called upon me to lead, but He who led Israel over the Red Sea assisted, and it was a gracious time with us. Some who remained from curiosity were made, like Belshazzar, to tremble and weep, while the spirit strove powerfully with them. One experienced religion and joined society. I expect in the resurrection morning to meet many who were in that little company, in my Father's house, where we shall strike hands no more to part; where our song of redemption shall be raised to God and the Lamb forever. Dear reader, if you have not, I charge you to make your peace with God while time and opportunity is given, and be one of that number who shall take part and lot in the first resurrection. Though I may never see you in the flesh, I leave on this page my solemn entreaty that you delay not to obtain the pardoning favor of God; that you leave not the momentous subject of religion to a sick bed or dying hour, but NOW, even now, seek the Lord with full purpose of heart, and he will be found of thee. "If any man sin, he has advocate with the Father, Jesus Christ the righteous."

> "Oh that the world might taste and see
>   The riches of his grace;
> The arms of love that compass me,
>   Would all mankind embrace."

I visited a woman who was laying sick upon her death-bed. She told me "she had once enjoyed religion, but the enemy had cheated her out of it." She knew that she must die in a very little while, and could not get well, and her agony of soul, in view of its unprepared state for a judgment to come, awoke every feeling of sympathy within me. Oh! how loud such a scene calls upon us to be "faithful unto death"—then shall we "receive a crown of life." Also visited Mrs. Miller, who once "tasted that the Lord was good," but had ceased now to follow him. She had been a Methodist for many years—got her feelings injured through some untoward circumstance—had fallen from grace, and now was sick. A good sister accompanied me? we conversed with Mrs. M., sung an appropriate hymn, and my friend supplicated the throne of grace in her behalf. She had frequently felt the need of a returning Saviour, and during prayer her heart became melted into tenderness. She cried aloud for mercy, wrestled like Jacob for the witness, and the Lord, faithful and true, "healed her backslidings," and we left her happy in his father. Praise the Lord for his matchless grace. I entertained no doubt of her well-grounded hope; and on seeing such a display of God's power, I was lost in wonder, love and praise. Let the backslider hear and take courage, Let all who are out of Christ hear the invitation—"Repent ye and be converted, for God hath called all men everywhere to repent."

> "Without reserve give Christ your heart,
> Let him his righteousness impart—
> Then all things else he'll freely give,
> With him you all things shall receive."

With a serene and tranquil mind I now returned to Philadelphia. The Bishop was pleased to give me an appointment at Bethel Church, but a spirit of opposition arose among the people against the propriety of female preaching. My faith was tried—yet I felt my call to labor for souls none the less. "Shall the servant be above his Master?" The ministers of Jesus must expect persecution, if they would be faithful witnesses against sin and sinners—but shall they, "awed by a mortal's form, conceal the word of God?" Thou God knowest my heart, and that thy glory is all I have in view. Shall I cease from sounding the alarm to an ungodly world, when the vengeance of offended heaven is about to be poured out, because my way is sometimes beset with scoffers, or those who lose sight of the great Object, and stop on the road to glory to contend about non-essentials? Rather let the messengers of God go on—let them not be hindered by the fashions and customs of a gainsaying and mis-loving generation, but with the crown in view, which shall deck the brow of those only who are "faithful unto death"—let them "cry aloud and spare not." Who regarded the warnings of Noah? who believed in his report? Who among the antidiluvians, that witnessed the preparations of this righteous man to save himself and family from a deluge of waters, believed him any thing else than a fanatic, deluded, and beside himself? Let the servants of Christ gird on the armor, and "listen to the Captain's voice: "Lo I am with you always, even unto the end." With the promise of my Lord impressed upon my mind, I remained at home only a week, and walked twenty-one miles to Lumbertown, and preached in the Old Methodist Church and our African Church. Brother Joshua Edely was then a deacon there, and held a quarterly meeting soon after my reaching the place. He also appointed a love-feast in the morning, when the love that true believers enjoy at such scenes made the place akin to heaven. While here I spoke as the Spirit taught me from Solomon's Songs. It was a happy meeting—refreshing to the thirsty soul—and we had a shout of the king in the camp. I shall never forget the kindness I received here from dear sister G. B. May the blessings of heaven be hers in this and the world to come.

I travelled seven miles from the above place to Snow Hill on Sabbath morning, where I was to preach in the Church of which I was a member; and although much afflicted in body, I strove, by the grace of God, to perform the duty. This was once the charge of JOSEPH LEE. In this desk my lamented husband had often stood up before me, proclaiming the "acceptable year of the Lord"—here he labored with zeal and spent his strength to induce sinners to be "reconciled to God"—here his toils ended. And could it be, that a poor unworthy being like myself should be called to address his former congregation, and should stand in the same pulpit! The thought made me tremble. My heart sighed when memory brought back the image, and the reminiscences of other days crowded upon me. But why, my heart, dost thou sigh? He has ceased from his labor, and I here see his works do follow. It will be enough, if these, the people of his care, press on and gain the kingdom. It will be enough, if, on the final day, "for which all other days were made," we pass through the gates into the city, and live again together where death cannot enter, and separations are unknown. Cease then, my tears—a little while, my fluttering heart! and the turf that covers my companion, perchance, may cover thee—a little while, my soul! if faithful, and the widow's God will call thee from this valley of tears and sorrows to rest in the mansions the Saviour has gone to prepare for his people. "Good what God gives—just what he takes away."

My mind was next exercised to visited Trenton, N. J. I spoke for the people there, but soon had felt the cross so heavy. Perhaps it was occasioned through grieving over the past, and my feelings of loneliness in the world. A sister wished me to go with her to Bridgeport—where I found brother Orwin, then elder over that church. He gave me an appointment. We had a full house, and God's power was manifest among the people, and I returned to the elder's house rejoicing. The following day I walked fourteen miles to a meeting, where also we were greatly favored with the presence of God. Soon after this, I thought of going home to Philadelphia. I got about three miles on foot, when an apparent voice said "I thou goest home thou wilt die." I paused for a moment, and not comprehending what it meant, pursued my journey. Again I was startled by something like a tapping on my shoulder, but, on turning round, I found myself alone, which two circumstances created a singular feeling I could not understand. I thought of Balaam when met by the angel in the way. I was taken sick and it seemed I should die in the road. I said I will go back, and walked about four miles to Bridgeport. Told a good sister my exercise, who was moved with sympathy, and got brandy and bathed me. On Wednesday night I spoke to the people at Trenton Bridge, and notwithstanding the opposition I had met with from brother Samuel R—, then on the circuit, the Lord supported the "woman preacher" and my soul was cheered. On Thursday I walked fourteen miles, when the friends applied to the elder to let me talk for them, but his prejudices also, against women preaching were very strong, and tried hard to disaffect the minds of the people. The dear man has since gone to stand before that God who knows the secrets of all hearts—and where, I earnestly pray, he may find some who have been saved by grace through the instrumentality of female preaching.

"Then here, O God, thy work fulfil;
   And from thy mercy's throne
O grant me strength to do thy will,
   And to resist my own."

Norristown, Bucks county, January 6, 1824. Brother Morris conveyed me here at his own expense, and made application for places for me to speak. Addressed a large congregation on the fourth day after my introduction into the place, in the court-house, from Isaiah liiii. 1,—"Who hath believed our report? and to whom is the arm of the Lord revealed?" I felt embarrassed in the commencement, but the Spirit came, and "helped our infirmities"—good attention, and some weeping. On the 18th I spoke in the academy—it was a solemn time, and the people came out in numbers to hear. I then walked four miles to brother Morris's—spoke twice in the schoolhouse, and once in a dwelling house.

On the 14th April, I went with Bishop Allen and several elders to Baltimore, on their way to attend Conference; at the end of which the Bishop gave me permission to express a few thoughts for my Lord. On leaving the city of B., I travelled about 100 miles to Eastern Shore, Maryland. Brother Bailey was then laboring on that circuit, who received and treated me very kindly. We had several good meetings, and twice I spoke in Bethel Church, when the outpouring of the Spirit was truly great. In company with a good sister, who took a gig and horse, I travelled about three hundred miles, and labored in different places. Went to Denton African Church, and on the first Sabbath gave two sermons. The Church was in a thriving, prosperous condition, and the Lord blessed the word to our comfort. During the week I labored in the court-house before a large concourse of hearers. The Lord was unspeakably good, and one fell to the floor under the power.

By request, I also spoke in the Old Methodist Church in Denton, which was full to overflowing. It was a happy meeting. My tongue was loosened, and my heart warm with the love of God and souls—a season yet sweet to my memory. From there I went to Greensboro'—the elder gave a sermon, after which I exhorted the poor sinner to prepare to meet the Lord in peace, before mercy was clear gone forever. The Old Methodist connexion gave an invitation for me to speak in their house, which I embraced, feeling thankful that the middle wall of partition had, thus far, been broken down. "He that feareth God and worketh righteousness shall be accepted of him"—not he who hath a different skin—not he who belongs to this denomination, or, to that— but "he that feareth God." My Master is no respecter of persons. May the partition walls that divide His sincere followers be broken down by the spirit of love.

In Whitehall Chapel I spoke to a respectable congregation, from Isaiah liii. 1. Though in a slave country, I found the Omnipresent One was with us. Dr. Clarke took us home to dine with his family—for which uncommon attention I felt highly gratified. I believe him a Christian in heart, and one, no doubt, who has read the words of the Saviour: "Whosoever shall give to drink unto one of these little ones a cup of cold water only, shall in no wise lose his reward." And, notwithstanding the doctor was a Presbyterian, Mr. Buly had the privilege of baptizing two of their colored children. * * *

I stopped next at Concord, and in the Old Methodist connexion tried to encourage the Lord's people to persevere. God displayed His power by a general outpouring of the Spirit—sinners cried for mercy, while others shouted for joy. Spoke also to a congregation of colored and white at Stanton Mills; and arrived again at Eastern Shore, where I spoke in Bethel Church during Quarterly Meeting. Attended their love-feast, where several joined society, and many encouraging testimonies were given by young converts that "God hath power on earth to forgive sins." May they be faithful stewards of the manifold gifts of God—and never be ashamed to confess what the Lord had done for them. Many lose the witness out of the heart by withholding their testimony from their friends and neighbors of the power of God to save. They run well for a season, but the tempter whispers "not now"—and by and by the soul becomes barren and unfruitful. May God help the young converts to "watch," and tell around what a dear Saviour they have found.

"Ashamed of Jesus!—yes, I may,
   When I've no guilt to wash away—
No tears to wipe—no good to crave—
   No fears to quell—no soul to save."

June 10th, 1824. Left Eastern Shore for a journey to Bath, and went around the circuit with brother J. B., the elder. In the Old Methodist Church, at Fory's Neck, I had the privilege of speaking to a large congregation, which was made the power of God unto salvation. Visited Lewistown, and had a blessed meeting in the

Methodist Church. The tears of the penitent flowed sweetly, which always encourages me to persevere in proclaiming the glad tidings of a risen Saviour to my fellow beings. When the heart is thus melted into tenderdess, I feel assured the Lord sanctions the feeble effort of His poor servant—it is a good omen to my mind that the mourner is not forsaken of God, and that he yet stands knocking at the door for admittance. Oh! that those who weep for an absent Jesus may be comforted by hearing Him say—" Thy sins, which were many, are all forgiven thee: go in peace and sin no more."

* * * * *

But here I feel constrained to give over, as from the smallness of this pamphlet I cannot go through with the whole of my journal, as it would probably make a volume of two hundred pages; which, if the Lord be willing, may at some future day be published. But for the satisfaction of such as may follow after me, when I am no more, I have recorded how the Lord called me to his work, and how he has kept me from falling from grace, as I feared I should. In all things he has proved himself a God of truth to me; and in his service I am now as much determined to spend and be spent, as at the very first. My ardour for the progress of his cause abates not a whit, so far as I am able to judge, though I am now something more than fifty years of age.

As to the nature of uncommon impressions, which the reader cannot but have noticed, and possibly sneered at in the course of these pages, they may be accounted for in this way: It is known that the blind have the sense of hearing in a manner much more acute than those who can see: also their sense of feeling is exceedingly fine, and is found to detect any roughness on the smoothest surface, where those who can see find none. So it may be with such as I am, who has never had more than three months schooling; and wishing to know much of the way and law of God, have therefore watched the more closely, the operations of the Spirit, and have in consequence been led thereby. But let it be remarked that I have never found that Spirit lead me contrary to the Scriptures of truth, as I understand them. "For as many as are led by the *Spirit* of God are the sons of God."—Rom. viii. 14.

I have now only to say, May the blessing of the Father, and of the Son, and of the Holy Ghost, accompany the reading of this poor effort to speak well of his name, wherever it may be read.   AMEN.

P. S. Please to pardon errors, and excuse all imperfections, as I have been deprived of the advantages of education (which I hope all will appreciate) as I am measurably a self-taught person. I hope the contents of this work may be instrumental in leaving a lasting impression upon the minds of the impenitent; may it prove to be encouraging to the justified soul, and a comfort to the sanctified

Though much opposed, it is certainly essential in life, as Mr. Wesley wisely observes. Thus ends the Narrative of JARENA LEE, the first female preacher of the First African Methodist Episcopal Church.

Bethel at Philadelphia, Penn., United States of America.

Pastor and Flock

They'd pray, "Lord, deliver us from under bondage."

What the Preacher Said

I

We went to the white folks' church, so we sit in the back on the floor. They allowed us to join their church whenever one got ready to join or felt that the Lord had forgiven them of their sins. We told our determination; this is what we said: "I feel that the Lord have forgiven me for my sins. I have prayed and I feel that I am a better girl. I belong to Master So and So and I am so old." The white preacher would then ask our miss and master what they thought about it and if they could see any change. They would get up and say: "I notice she don't steal and I notice she don't lie as much and I notice she works better." Then they let us join. We served our mistress and master in slavery time and not God.

II

They had preaching one Sunday for white folks and one Sunday for black folks. They used the same preacher there, but some colored preachers would come on the place at times and preach under the trees down at the quarters. They said the white preacher would say, "You may get to the kitchen of heaven if you obey your master, if you don't steal, if you tell no stories," etc.

III

The niggers didn't go to the church building; the preacher came and preached to them in their quarters. He'd just say, "Serve your masters. Don't steal your master's turkey. Don't steal your master's chickens. Don't steal your master's hogs. Don't steal your master's meat. Do whatsomever your master tells you to do." Same old thing all the time.

IV

When Grandma was fourteen or fifteen years old, they locked her up in the seedhouse once or twice for not going to church. You see, they let the white folks go to the church in the morning and the colored folks in the evening, and my grandma didn't always want to go. She would be locked up in the seed bin, and she would cuss the preacher out so he could hear her. She would say, "Master, let us out." And he would say, "You want to go to church?" And she would say, "No, I don't want to hear that same old sermon: 'Stay out of your missus' and master's henhouse. Don't steal your missus' and master's chickens. Stay out of your missus' and master's smokehouse. Don't steal your missus' and master's hams.' I don't steal nothing. Don't need to tell me not to."

She was telling the truth, too. She didn't steal because she didn't have to. She had plenty without stealing. She got plenty to eat in the house. But the other slaves didn't git nothing but fat meat and corn bread and molasses. And they got tired of that same old thing. They wanted something else sometimes. They'd go to the henhouse and get chickens. They would go to the smokehouse and get hams and lard. And they would get flour and anything else they wanted, and they would eat something they wanted. There wasn't no way to keep them from it.

V

One time when an old white man came along who wanted to preach, the white people gave him a chance to preach to the niggers. The substance of his sermon was this:

"Now when you servants are working for your masters, you must be honest. When you go to the mill, don't carry along an extra sack and put some of the meal or the flour in for yourself. And when you women are cooking in the big house, don't make a big pocket under your dress and put a sack of coffee and a sack of sugar and other things you want in it."

They took him out and hanged him for corrupting the morals of the slaves.

God Got a Clean Kitchen to Put You In

There wasn't no church on the plantation where I stay. Had preaching in Mr. Ford's yard sometimes, and then another time the slaves went to white people's church at Bear Swamp. Boss tell slaves to go to meeting 'cause he say he pay the preacher. Dean Ears, white man, gave out speech to the slaves one day there to Nichols. Slaves sat in gallery when they go there. He tell them to obey they master and missus. Then he say, "God got a clean kitchen to put you in. You think you gwine be free, but you ain't gwine be free long as there an ash in Ashpole Swamp." White folks complain 'bout the slaves getting two sermons and they get one. After that, they tell old slaves not to come to church till after the white folks had left. That never happen till after the war was over.

Two Ways of Preaching the Gospel

I been preaching the gospel and farming since slavery time. I jined the church 'most 83 years ago when I was Major Gaud's slave, and they baptizes me in the spring branch close to where I finds the Lord. When I starts preaching I couldn't read or write and had to preach what Master told me, and he say tell them niggers iffen they obeys the master they goes to Heaven; but I knowed there's something better for them, but daren't tell them 'cept on the sly. That I done lots. I tells 'em iffen they keeps praying, the Lord will set 'em free.

Every Kind of Fish Is Caught in a Net

Sunday morning he preached "Every kind of fish is caught in a net." . . . Parson sure told 'em 'bout it. He say, "First, they catch the crawfish, and that fish ain't worth much; anybody that gets back from duty or one which says I will and then won't is a crawfish Christian." Then he say, "The next is a mudcat; this kind of a fish likes dark trashy places. When you catch 'em, you won't do it in front water; it likes back water and wants to stay in mud. That's the way with some people in church. You can't never get them to the front for nothing. You has to fish deep for them. The next one is the jellyfish. It ain't got no backbone to face the right thing. That the trouble with our churches today. Too many jellyfishes in 'em. Next," he say, "is the goldfish—good for nothing but to look at. They is pretty. That the way folks is. Some of them go to church just to sit up and look pretty to everybody. Too pretty to sing; too pretty to say Amen!" That what the parson preached Sunday. Well, I'm a full-grown man and a full-grown Christian, praise the Lord. Yes'm, parson is a real preacher.

They'd Pray

My master used to ask us children, "Do your folks pray at night?" We said "No," 'cause our folks had told us what to say. But the Lord have mercy, there was plenty of that going on. They'd pray, "Lord, deliver us from under bondage."

Master Frank Has Come Through

We went to church all the time. We had both white and colored preachers. Master Frank wasn't a Christian, but he would help build brush-arbors for us to have church under, and we sure would have big meetings. I'll tell you.

One day Master Frank was going through the woods close to where niggers was having church. All on a sudden he started running and beating hisself and hollering, and the niggers all went to shouting and saying, "Thank the Lord, Master Frank has done come through!" Master Frank after a minute say, "Yes, through the worst of 'em." He had run into a yellow jackets' nest.

Damn Poor Preacher

I never went to school a day in my life. I learned my ABC's after I was nineteen years old. I went to night school, then to a teacher by the name of Nelse Otom. I was the first nigger to join the church on this side of the Mason and Dixie line. During slavery we all joined the white folks' church, set in the back. After slavery in 1866 they met in conference and motioned to turn all of the black sheep out then. There was four or five they turned out here and four or five there, so we called our preacher, and I was the first one to join. Old Master asked our preacher what we paid him to preach to us. We told him old shoes and clothes. Old Master says, "Well, that's damn poor pay." Our preacher says, "And they got a damn poor preacher."

Boots or No Boots

Once when Master Gilliam took one of his slaves to church at old Tranquil, he told him that he mustn't shout that day—said he would give him a pair of new boots if he didn't shout. About the middle of services, the old nigger couldn't stand it no longer. He jumped up and hollered: "Boots or no boots, I gwine to shout today."

Methodist Dogs and Baptist Dogs

Master John had a big fine bird dog. She was a mammy dog, and one day he found six puppies out in the harness-house. They was 'most all girl puppies, so Master gwine drown 'em. I axed him to give 'em to me, and pretty soon the missus sent me to the postoffice, so I put the puppies in a basket and took 'em with me. Dr. Lyles come by where I was setting, and he say, "Want to sell them pups, Siney?" I tell him, "Uh-huh." Then he say, "What 'nomination is they?" I tell him, "They's Methodist dogs." He didn't say no more. 'Bout a week after that Old Missus sent me to the postoffice again, so I took my basket of puppies. Sure 'nough, 'long come Dr. Lyles, and he say, "Siney, see you still ain't sold them pups." I say, "No, sir." Then he axed me again what 'nomination they belong to. I told him they was Baptist dogs. He say, "How come? You told me last week them was Methodist pups." Ha! Ha! Bless God! Look like he had me. But I say, "Yes, sir, but you see, Doctor, they got their eyes open since then." He laugh and go on down to his newspaper office.

Barbecue and Big Meeting

Newt and Anderson was my young masters. They was 'long 'bout my own age. They went to school at Goshen Hill. The school was near the store, some folks called it the trading post in them days. They had barrels of liquor setting out from the store in a long row. Sold the liquor to the rich mens that carried on at the race track near by. Folks in Goshen was all rich in them days. Rogers Church, where the Carlisles, Jeters, Sims, Selbys, Glens, and lots of other folks went, too, and the slaves, was the richest country church in this part of the whole state, so I is often been told. Ebenezer, over in Maybinton, was the onliest church in the whole country that tried to strive with Rogers in the way of finery and style. The Hendersons, Maybins, Hardys, Douglasses, Cofields, Chicks, and Oxners was the big folks over there. Both the churches was Methodist.

Every summer they carried on camp meeting at Rogers. All the big Methodist preachers would come from 'way off then. They was entertained in the Carlisle big house. Missus put on the dog (as the niggers says now) then. Everything was cleaned up just 'fore the meeting like us did for the early spring cleaning. Camp meeting come just after the craps was done laid by. Then all craps was done laid by before July the fourth. It was unheard of for anybody to let the Fourth come without the craps outen the way. Times is done changed now, Lord. Then the fields was heavy with corn head high and cotton up around the darky's waist! Grass was all cleaned out of the furrows on the last go round. The fields and even the terraces was put in apple pie order for the gathering of the craps in the fall.

As you all knows, the Fourth has always been nigger day. Marse and Missus had good rations for us early on the Fourth. Then us went to barbecues after the morning chores was done. In them days the barbecues was usually held on the plantation of Marse Jim Hill in Fish Dam. That was not far from Goshen. Marse Jim had a pretty spring that is still all walled up with fine rocks. The water come outen these rocks that cold that you can't hold your hand in it for more than a minute at the longest. There is a big flat rock beyond the spring that I 'specks covers more than an acre and a half of ground. A creek run along over this rock, where the mules and the hosses could rest in the shade of the trees and drink all the water that they wanted. Wild ferns growed waist high along there then. All kinds of pretty flowers and daisies was gathered by the gals. Them was the best days that any darky has ever seed. Never had nothing to aggravate your mind then. Plenty to eat; plenty to wear; plenty wood to burn; good house to live in; and no worry 'bout where it was a-coming from!

Old Marse he give us the rations for the barbecues. Every master wanted his darkies to be thought well of at the barbecues by the darkies from all the other plantations. They had pigs barbecued, and goats; and the missus let the womenfolks bake pies, cakes, and custards for the barbecue, just 'zactly like it was for the white folks' barbecue theyself!

Young ones carried on like young colts, a-frolicking in the pasture till they had done got so full of victuals that they could not eat another bite. Then they roamed on off and set down somewhere to sleep in the shade of the trees. When the sun started to going down, then the old folks begin to git ready to return back to they home plantations, for there was the master's stock and chickens to feed and put up for the night, to say nothing of the cows to milk. The master's work had to go on around the big house, 'cause all the darkies had been 'lowed to have such a pleasant day. Next day being Saturday was on this occasion not only ration day, but the day to git ready for the white folks' camp meeting which I has already called to recollection several times. . . .

As I has said once, the fields was in lay-by shape and the missus done already got the house cleaned. The childrens was put in one room to sleep, and that make more room for the preachers and guests that gwine to visit in the big house for the next six weeks. Then the plans for cooking had to be brung 'bout. They never had no ice in them days, as you well knows; but us had a dry well under our big house. It was deep, and everything keep real cool down there. Steps led down into it, and it always be real dark down there. The rats run around down there, and the young-uns scared to go down for anything. So us carry a lightwood knot for light when us put anything in it or take anything out. There ain't no need for me to tell you 'bout the wellhouse where us kept all the milk and butter, for it was the talk of the country 'bout what nice fresh milk and butter the missus always had. A hollow oak log was used for the milk trough. Three times a day Cilla had her little boy run fresh cool well water all through the trough. That keep the milk from gwine to whey and the butter fresh and cool. In the dry well was kept the canned things and dough to set till it had done riz! When company come like they always did for the camp meetings, shoats and goats and maybe a sheep or lamb or two was kilt for barbecue out by Cilla's cabin. These carcasses was kept down in the dry well over night and put over the pit early the next morning after it had done took salt. Then there was a big box covered with screen wire that victuals was kept in in the dry well. These boxes was made rat-proof.

Whilst the meats for the company table was kept barbecued out in the yard, the cakes, pies, breads, and t'other fixings was done in the kitchen out in the big house yard. Baskets had to be packed to go to camp meeting. Tables was built up at Rogers under the big oak trees that has all been cut down now. The tables just groaned and creaked and sighed with victuals at dinner hour every day during the camp meeting.

Missus fetch her finest linens and silver and glasses to outshine them brung by t'other white folks of quality. In them days the white folks of quality in Union most all come from Goshen Hill and Fish Dam. After the white folks done et all they could hold, then the slaves what had done come to church and to help with the tables and the carriages would have the dinner on a smaller table over clost to the spring. Us had table cloths on our table also, and us et from the kitchen china and the kitchen silver.

Young gals couldn't eat much in public, 'cause it ain't stylish for young courting gals to let on like they has any appetite to speak of. I sees that am a custom that still goes amongst the womenfolks, not to eat so heavy. Colored gals tried to do just like the young white missus would do.

After everything was done et, it would be enough to pack up and fetch back home to feed all the hungry niggers what roams round here in Union now. Them was the times when everybody had 'nough to eat and more than they wanted and plenty clothes to wear!

During the preaching us darkies sot in the back of the church. Our white folks had some benches there that didn't nobody set on 'cept the slaves. Us wore the best clothes that us had. The marse give us a coat and a hat, and his sons give all the old hats and coats round. Us wore shirts and pants made from the looms. Us kept them cleaned and ironed just like the master and the young masters done theirn. Then us wore a string tie, that the white folks done let us have, to church. That 'bout the onliest time that a darky was seed with a tie. Some the oldest men even wore a cravat, that they had done got from the old master. Us combed our hair on Sunday for church. But us never bothered much with it no other time. During slavery some of the old men had short plaits of hair.

The gals come out in the starch dresses for the camp meeting. They took they hair down outen the strings for the meeting. In them days all the darky womens wore they hair in string 'cept when they 'tended church or a wedding. At the camp meetings the womens pulled off the head rags, 'cept the mammies. On this occasion the mammies wore linen head rags fresh laundered. They wore the best aprons with long streamers ironed and starched out a-hanging down they backs. All the other darky womens wore the black dresses, and they got hats from some they white lady folks, just as us mens got hats from ourn. Them womens that couldn't git no hats mostly wore black bonnets. The nigger gals and wenches did all the dressing up that they could for the meeting and also for the barbecue.

At night when the meeting done busted till next day was when the darkies really did have they freedom of spirit. As the wagon be creeping along in the late hours of moonlight, the darkies would raise a tune. Then the air soon be filled with the sweetest tune as us rid on home and sung all the old hymns that us loved. It was always some big black nigger with a deep bass voice like a frog that'd start up the tune. Then the other mens jine in, followed up by the fine little voices of the gals and the cracked voices of the old womens and the grannies. When us reach near the big house us soften down to a deep hum that the missus like! Sometimes she hist up the window and tell us sing "Swing Low, Sweet Chariot" for her and the visiting guests. That all us want to hear. Us open up, and the niggers near the big house that hadn't been to church would wake up and come out to the cabin door and jine in the refrain. From that we'd swing on into all the old spirituals that us love so well and that us knowed how to sing. Missus often 'low that her darkies could sing with heaven's inspiration. Now and then some old mammy would fall outen the wagon a-shouting Glory! and Hallelujah! and Amen! After that us went off to lay down for the night.

If All Slaves Had Belonged to White Folks Like Ours

I was big enough to remember well us coming back from Texas after we refugeed there when the fighting of the war was so bad at St. Charles. We stayed in Texas till the surrender, then we all come back in lots of wagons. I was sick, but they put me on a little bed, and me and all the little children rode in a "Jersey" that one of the old Negro mammies drove, along behind the wagons, and our young master, Colonel Bob Chaney, rode a great big black horse. Oh! he nice-looking on that horse! Every once and a while he'd ride back to the last wagon to see if everything was all right. I remember how scared us children was when we crossed the Red River. Aunt Mandy said, "We crossing you old Red River today, but we not going to cross you any more, 'cause we are going home now, back to Arkansas." That day when we stopped to cook our dinner I picked up a lot little blackjack acorns, and when my mammy saw them she said, "Throw them things down, child. They'll make you wormy." I cried because I thought they were chinquapins. I begged my daddy to let's go back to Texas, but he said, "No! No! We going with our white folks." My mammy and daddy belonged to Colonel Jesse Chaney, much of a gentleman, and his wife, Miss Sallie, was the best mistress anybody ever had. She was a Christian. I can hear her praying yet! She wouldn't let one of her slaves hit a tap on Sunday. They must rest and go to church. They had preaching at the cabin of some one of the slaves, and in the summertime sometimes they had it out in the shade under the trees. Yes, and the slaves on each plantation had their own church. They didn't go gallivanting over the neighborhood or country like niggers do now. Colonel Chaney had lots and lots of slaves, and all their houses were in a row, all one-room cabins. Everything happened in that one room—birth, sickness, death, and everything, but in them days niggers kept their houses clean and their door yards too. These houses where they lived was called "the quarters." I used to love to walk down by that row of houses. It looked like a town, and late of an evening as you'd go by the doors you could smell meat a-frying, coffee making, and good things cooking. We were fed good and had plenty clothes to keep us dry and warm.

Along about time for the surrender, Colonel Jess, our master, took sick and died with some kind of head trouble. Then Colonel Bob, our young master, took care of his mama and the slaves. All the grown folks went to the field to work, and the little children would be left at a big room called the nursing-home. All us little ones would be nursed and fed by an old mammy, Aunt Mandy. She was too old to go to the field, you know. We wouldn't see our mammy and daddy from early in the morning till night when their work was done, then they'd go by Aunt Mandy's and get their children and go home till work time in the morning.

Some of the slaves were house Negroes. They didn't go to work in the fields. They each one had their own job around the house, barn, orchard, milkhouse, and things like that.

When washday come, Lord, the pretty white clothes! It would take three or four women a-washing all day.

When two of the slaves wanted to get married, they'd dress up nice as they could and go up to the big house, and the master would marry them. They'd stand up before him, and he'd read out of a book called *The Discipline* and say, "Thou shalt love the Lord thy God with all thy heart, all thy strength, with all thy might and thy neighbor as thyself." Then he'd say they were man and wife and tell them to live right and be honest and kind to each other. All the slaves would be there too, seeing the wedding.

Our Miss Sallie was the sweetest best thing in the world! She was so good and kind to everybody, and she loved her slaves, too. I can remember when Uncle Tony died how she cried! Uncle Tony Wadd was Miss Sallie's favorite servant. He stayed in a little house in the yard and made fires for her, brought in wood and water, and just waited on the house. He was a little black man and white-headed as cotton, when he died. Miss Sallie told the niggers when they come to take him to the graveyard, to let her know when they got him in his coffin, and when they sent and told her she come out with all the little white children, her little grandchildren, to see Uncle Tony. She just cried and stood for a long time looking at him, then she said, "Tony, you have been a good and faithful servant." Then the Negro men walked and carried him to the graveyard out in a big grove in the field. Every plantation had its own graveyard and buried its own folks and slaves right on the place.

If all slaves had belonged to white folks like ours, there wouldn't been any freedom wanted.

The Chanted Sermon

ALBERT J. RABOTEAU

Sunday after Sunday, for more than a century and a half, black ministers have moved their congregations to religious ecstacy by a distinctive style of preaching. Sometimes called the "black folk sermon" or "old-time country preaching," this complex verbal art is governed by strict performance rules that require skill and dedication to master. This kind of sermon is "old-time" in the sense that it is a traditional genre whose origins stretch back to the eighteenth century. But it is also a hardy perennial, alive and healthy in the modern day. It is "country" since its development took place primarily in the prayer meetings and revivals of the rural South. But it has long since spread West and North to the cities, where radio, television, and records extend the preachers' voices beyond the churches into the cars and homes of their flocks. This preaching style is a "folk" art because it is a creation of popular rather than elite culture and because it is an oral rather than literary form. However, the "folk" are notoriously difficult to define, and this tradition of preaching remains popular among literate and "sophisticated" congregations. Though "old-time" and "folk" are part of the aura surrounding this kind of preaching, the term "chanted" more accurately describes its defining characteristic, the metrical, tonal, rhythmic chant with which the preacher climaxes the sermon.[1]

The chanted sermon, while it is usually identified with black preachers, is not an exclusively black tradition; neither is it inclusive of all the preaching styles used by black ministers. Some whites preach in this manner, and there have always been some black ministers who preach in an altogether different idiom. Nevertheless, the chanted sermon is as much a staple of African-American culture as spirituals, gospel, blues, and tales. Like these other forms of oral literature, the sermon has served as a source of information, advice, wisdom, and, not least, sheer enjoyment for generations of black Americans. This sermonic style has spread outside the pulpit to influence public speaking and singing styles in the secular sphere. Black and white literary artists as varied as Paul Laurence Dunbar, James Weldon Johnson, William Faulkner, Toni Morrison, Paule Marshalle, and Ralph Ellison have attempted to capture the cadences and esthetic effect of the chanted sermon.[2]

Because the oral rather than the written word has been the primary bearer of black culture, verbal skill is valued highly in the black community. As is the case with oral tradition in general, so here, too, the individual verbal artist earns critical recognition not by introducing something new, but by performing the old with skill, fluency, spontaneity, and intensity. Style of delivery determines the success of the oral performer whether bluesman, gospel singer, or preacher. It is not, then, merely the word as spoken—much less as read—but the word as *performed* that must be taken into account if the sermon is to be adequately understood. In this case, more than in most, style is content. For this reaon, the chanted sermon cannot be given full justice in print.[3]

The formal structure of the sermon derives from the Evangelical Protestant belief that the sermonic words should be devoted to explaining the Word. The presence of the Bible on the pulpit is a visual reminder of this close connection. It is customary for the preacher to begin by reading a text chosen from the Old or New Testament, which is supposed to indicate the theme of the sermon to follow. Frequently, the preacher's theme as it is actually developed strays far afield from the announced text, but the tradition of reading a biblical verse is strong, so strong that some illiterate slave preachers of the antebellum South had their texts read for them or, lacking a Bible, pretended to read scriptural words from their hand or from a handkerchief; others claimed that, since they could not read, verses from the Bible were written by God on their hearts. The Bible is more than a source of texts; it is the single most important source of language, imagery, and story for the sermon. Through the sermon, as well as spirituals and gospel songs, the Jewish and Christian Scriptures entered and shaped the imaginative world of African-Americans. Black preachers fashioned out of the biblical characters, events, and symbols a religious ethos that fit the peculiar experience of black people in America.

After reading his text, the preacher elaborates its context. Drawing upon his knowledge of the Bible, he may range widely over both Testaments; explaining the meaning of this specific text by reference to other passages. Having set the context, the preacher ideally devotes the rest of his sermon to applying the lessons of the text to the day-to-day concerns of his congregation. Text-context-application is the conventional pattern for the development of the logic of the sermon. There is, however, another pattern as important as the structure of logical meaning, that of performance style, which gives rise to the sermon's emotive meaning.

The stylistic structure of the chanted sermon may be divided into three movements. The preacher begins calmly, speaking in conversational, if oratorical and occasionally grandiloquent, prose; he then gradually begins to speak more rapidly, excitedly, and to chant his words in time to a regular beat; finally, he reaches an emotional peak in which his chanted speech becomes tonal and merges with the singing, clapping, and shouting of the congregation. Frequently, the preacher ends the sermon by returning briefly to conversational prose.

The chanting preacher composes his sermon extemporaneously. This does not mean that he does not prepare. He may have thought about his sermon all week; he may have used a book of sermon outlines to get ideas; he may even carry notes into the pulpit. But at some point, he must breath spontaneous life into the outline, whether written or memorized, by composing on the spot a sermon delivered in rhythmic metrical speech. The meter is not based on accent but on time, the length of time between regular beats. As the preacher moves into the chanted section of his sermon, he fits his speech to a beat. When necessary, he lengthens vowels or rushes together words in order to make a line match the meter. The regularity of the beat is accentuated by the preacher's gasp for air at the end of each line. Sometimes he actually raps out the rhythm on the pulpit. The congregational responses—"Preach it, preach it," "Amen, brother," "Yes, yes, glory!"—reinforce the beat and simultaneously fill in the space left by the preacher's pause for breath. When properly "working," the rhythm of the sermon becomes "as inexorable as a drumbeat."[4]

At a certain stage, the preacher's chanting takes on a musical tone, which indicates a concomitant rise in emotional pitch. The preacher's voice changes: the timbre becomes harsh, almost hoarse. His vocal cords are constricted; his breathing is labored. All the while he moves, gestures, dances, speaking with body as well as voice.

The difficulty of delivering an extemporaneously composed metrical sermon can only be fully appreciated by one who has attempted it. The fullest description of how chanting preachers compose their sermons has been presented by Bruce Rosenberg, a medievalist interested in the composition of oral epics. Extending the theories of Parry and Lord concerning oral composition to the "art of the American folk preacher," he argues that this style of preaching is heavily formulaic. The "basic unit of composition" is, according to Rosenberg, the formula, by which he means "the metrically governed sentence" that the preacher generates in oral performance. The preacher clusters "these formulas together" into larger segments, called "themes," which become, through repetition, part of his repertoire. Since the preacher is familiar with these clusters of verses or themes, he may "fall back" upon them when his rhythm falters. Stock phrases or "stall formulas," such as C. L. Franklins's "I don't believe you hear me tonight," allow the preacher time to pause until the next verse comes to him, at the same time that they invite the congregation to respond. Because of the metrical constraints, the preacher makes frequent and effective use of repetition and tends to develop the narrative of his sermon along associational rather than logical lines.[5]

Congregational response is crucial to the delivery of the sermon. If response is weak or irregular, it will keep the preacher off stride. Conversely, if the preacher's sense of timing is poor, he will fail to rouse the congregation, and the sermon will fail. There is, then, a reciprocal relation between preacher and congregation in the composition of the sermon. Ideally, the preacher's delivery will ignite the congregation's vocal response, which will, in turn, support and push him further.

The expert preacher composes impromptu a sermon typically twenty to forty minutes in length. It is obvious that he has learned to do so only after long hours of observation and practice. However, if asked, he disavows the importance of his own skill or training in preaching and credits the sermon to the inspiration of the Holy Spirit. For this reason, chanting preachers refer to themselves as "spiritual" preachers as distinct from "manuscript" preachers, that is, those who read their sermons from prepared texts. In this view, the preacher's words are placed in his mind and on his lips by the Holy Spirit. The preacher is literally the instrument of God's breath, "God's trombone," in James Weldon Johnson's apt metaphor. When the preacher states that he is "filled with" or "set on fire by the Spirit," he is not only claiming that he is a channel of God's grace or that God is telling him what to say; he is also describing his own ecstatic experience of preaching. As he preaches, he feels that a force or power other than his ordinary self takes over.

This power he identifies as the Spirit of God. Hence the conventional antipathy of the "old-time preacher" to formal seminary training—"I haven't rubbed my head on seminary walls"—was only partially due to the suspicion that education would alienate him from his uneducated flock. The insistence that the sermon was God's work, not man's, tended to undermine the importance of education for preaching. Two other conventions stem from the same rationale: the preacher's contention that he resisted God's call to preach until it proved irresistible and his frequent complaint as he steps to the pulpit: "I feel poorly this morning." In both cases, the weakness of the minister and the strength of God are acclaimed.

Similarly, the members of the congregation explain that the emotional experience that moves them to sing, shout, and dance is the effect of God's Spirit. The experiential claims of the preacher and his congregation should not be dismissed as conventional piety. Rather, they should be taken seriously by those who want to understand the sermon, precisely because these claims of inspiration define and determine the expectations and so the performances of both preacher and congregation. The experiential dimension is crucial because for Evangelical Christians one only becomes Christian through an *experience*, the experience of conversion. And even after conversion, religion has to be vital, "heartfelt," and not just intellectually convincing. When religious fervor grows cold, it is time for revival.

Early descriptions of Methodist and Baptist preaching, black and white, suggest three characteristics: it was plain or simple in language, dramatic in delivery, and—at least for the Baptists—musical, if we can believe the pejorative description applied by their critics: "Baptist whine." Today's chanted sermon still evidences these traits. The preacher's eloquence is measured not by his book learning but by his mother-wit. Down-home familiarity, wordplay, humor, well-turned phrases put a congregation at ease and encourage them to identify with the preacher. Formal, academic, scholarly language is inappropriate. It is viewed as "lecturing" not preaching and leaves the congregation cold. Dramatic ability, as much as sense of timing, is a necessity for the successful preacher, who may play several parts at once in the pulpit as he retells one of the familiar Bible stories. The relation of music and preaching has been symbiotic. There is a vocal continuum between speech and song in the sermon, as speech becomes rhythmic chant, and chant in turn becomes tonal and shades into song. The sermon may be introduced and closed by a hymn. Preachers make extensive use of verses from spiritual and hymns within their sermons. Conversely, gospel quartets and rhythm-and-blues singers imitate the style of the chanting preacher.

The date of the first chanted sermon cannot be given, because there was, of course, no such moment. Many sermons and many influences contributed to the development of this sermonic style: the emphasis placed upon biblical preaching by Evangelical Protestantism, the emotional and dramatic delivery legitimated by the Great Awakening of the mid eighteenth century, the ecstatic behavior encouraged by the revivals, the musical "tuned" voice of early Baptist preachers, the antiphonal pattern familiarized by the custom of lining-out hymns, and the renewed stress upon Christian experience fostered by American revivalism. By the early decades of the nineteeth century, the chanted sermon had probably emerged as a recognizable style of preaching. At midcentury Frederick Olmsted observed and described a chanted sermon delivered in a black church in New Orleans:

> As soon as I had taken my seat, my attention was attracted by an old negro near me, whom I supposed for some time to be suffering under some nervous complaint; he trembled, his teeth chattered, and his face, at intervals, was convulsed. He soon began to respond aloud to the sentiments of the preacher, in such words as these: "Oh, yes,!" and similar expressions could be heard from all parts of the house whenever the speaker's voice was unusually solemn, or his language and manner eloquent or excited.
>
> Sometimes the outcries and responses were not confined to ejaculations of this kind, but shouts, and groans, terrific shrieks, and indescribable expressions of ecstasy—of pleasure or agony—and even stamping, jumping, and clapping of hands were added. . . . I was once surprised to find my own muscles all stretched, as if ready for a struggle—my face glowing, and my feet stamping—having been infected unconsciously. . . . I could not, when my mind reverted to itself, find any connection or meaning in the phrases of the speaker that remained in my memory; and I have no doubt it was his "action" rather than his sentiments, that had given rise to the excitement of the congregation.[6]

Olmsted's description focuses on the power of the sermon to excite ecstatic response, even in a cultured white northerner like Olmsted himself.

Mary Boykin Chesnut, a southern white woman, found herself excited by the chanted style with which a slave driver on her plantation delivered a prayer:

He became wildly excited, on his knees, facing us with his eyes shut. He clapped his hands at the end of every sentence, and his voice rose to the pitch of a shrill shriek, yet was strangely clear and musical, occasionally in a plaintive minor key that went to your heart. Sometimes it rang out like a trumpet. I wept bitterly. . . . The Negroes sobbed and shouted and swayed backward and forward, some with aprons to their eyes, most of them clapping their hands and responding in shrill tones: "Yes, God!" "Jesus?" "Savior?" "Bless de Lord, amen," etc. It was a little too exciting for me. I would very much have liked to shout, too. . . . When he rose from his knees [he] trembled and shook as one in a palsy, and from his eyes you could see the ecstasy had not left him yet.[7]

In both instances, the observers distinguish the style of delivery from the meaning of the sermon or, in Chesnut's case, prayer. Both find themselves moved, but neither considers the possibility that the ecstasy they resist is itself the meaning of the events they witness. By dismissing the "sense" of the emotional behavior aroused by the style of the sermon or prayer, Olmsted and Chesnut are missing the message. The same mistake is made by the modern observer who separates form from content, style from meaning in describing the chanted sermon. To identify ecstatic behavior with the style of the preacher, and instruction or edification with the intelligible content of his words, is to misunderstand the complexity of the sermon and the religious ethos from which it springs.

Ecstatic religious behavior is central to the religious tradition in which the chanting preacher stands. As we have seen, the origins of this tradition can be found in the Evangelical revivals of the eighteenth and nineteenth centuries. But there is another source not yet mentioned: the African religious culture of the slaves. A look at this distant heritage and its interaction with Protestant revivalism may help to explain how style and meaning are one in the sermon and why it is that the chanted delivery has exerted such a long and deep appeal. In the revivals, African-Americans found a context in which the bodily expression of religious emotion was not only permitted but encouraged—harking back to the danced religions of their African forebears. Black American Christians were filled with the Spirit of the Christian God, but they responded in ways markedly similar to the ways in which their ancestors had responded to possession by the gods of Africa. Possessed by the Holy Spirit, slaves and freedmen danced, sang, and shouted in styles that were African. More important, ecstatic trance was at the center of their worship as it had been in Africa. In the revivals, African and Christian traditions met on common ground, ecstatic response to divine possession. The African tradition of religious dance was Christianized and the Evangelical Protestant tradition of experiential religion was Africanized.[8]

The influence of African traditions upon the religious dancing and singing of slaves and their descendants may be granted, but what about preaching? Where does the African influence lie? Anthropologist Morton Marks has suggested an answer. According to Marks, there is a ritual structure underlying several kinds of speech events within African-American cultures in the New World. The structure consists of an alternation from European styles of performance to African ones. When the style switch occurs, it acts as a code signaling that ritual possession by the Spirit is about to occur. To the observer unfamiliar with the performance clues, the stylistic switch is commonly perceived as a change from order to chaos, from music to noise, or from speech to gibberish. What in fact is really happening is a shift from one type of order to another: from a nonrhythmic to a rhythmic, or rather, increasingly rhythmic, performance style. The importance of rhythmic drumming and singing for the onset of divine possession in African and African-American religions has been widely observed. Applied to the chanted sermon, Marks's theory implies that the preacher's switch from conversational prose to the metrical and tonal chant, the rhythm holding steady as a drumbeat, sets the stage for the divine possession that everyone expects. Moreover there are recognizable cues that announce the Spirit's arrival. The preacher's harsh vocal sound, the constriction of voice, the audible gasp at the end of each line, the tonal quality, the participatory claps, shouts and noise of the congregation all announce the onset of possession and instigate it in others. In this sense, the preacher's style itself speaks, at least to those who understand the language of his sermonic tradition.[9]

Admittedly, Marks's theory is an interpretation; it has not been proved. Still the notion that African-influenced performance styles have been transmitted to American blacks and that they are shared across different African-American cultures in the New World has been convincingly demonstrated for dance, song, and music. It may very well be true of the chanted sermon and other forms of oral performance as well.

The chanted sermon is the product of a religious imagination in which experience is primary and is so because it validates religious truth. Without experience, how can one know that one's religious life is real? In the words of one former slave: "Nobody can talk about the religion of God unless they've had a religious experience in it."[10] In the chanted sermon, African-American Christians did not merely talk about God, they experienced his power, and found that in the experience their own spirits were renewed.

Notes

1. Given its importance in African-American culture, the literature on the "folk," or chanted, sermon is not as extensive as one might suppose. The following works have heavily influenced my treatment: James Weldon Johnson, *God's Trombones: Seven Negro Sermons in Verse* (New York: Viking Press, 1927); William H. Pipes, *Say Amen, Brother! Old-Time Negro Preaching: A Study in American Frustration* (New York: William Frederick Press, 1951); Bruce A. Rosenberg, *The Art of the American Folk Preacher* (New York: Oxford University Press, 1970), "The Psychology of the Spiritual Sermon," in *Religious Movements in Contemporary America*, ed. Irving I. Zaretsky and Mark P. Leone (Princeton: Princeton University Press, 1974), 13–49; Henry H. Mitchell, *Black Preaching* (Philadelphia: J. B. Lippincott, 1970); Gerald L. Davis, *I Got the Word in Me and I Can Sing It, You Know: A Study of the Performed African-American Sermon* (Philadelphia: University of Pennsylvania Press, 1985).

2. See Paul Laurence Dunbar's poem, "An Antebellum Sermon," most easily accessible in Dudley Randall, ed., *The Black Poets* (New York: Bantam Books, 1971), 44–46; Johnson, *God's Trombones*; Ralph Ellison, *Invisible Man* (New York: Signet Books, 1952), 12–13; William Faulkner, *The Sound and the Fury* (New York: Vintage Books, 1946), 356–71; Paule Marshall, *Praisesong for the Widow* (New York: E. P. Dutton, 1983), 198–203. The speeches of Martin Luther King, Jr., have made this tradition at least vaguely familiar to many Americans otherwise unacquainted with it. Although male-dominated, the tradition has also been exemplified by women preachers who usually had to struggle against clerical resistance to exercise their talents to preach.

3. I urge the reader to listen to a recording or radio broadcast of a chanted sermon, or better yet, visit a church in which this type of preaching is performed. The Reverend C. L. Franklin, father of Aretha, has recorded more than seventy albums of sermons on Chess and Jewel labels. See Jeff Todd Titon, ed., *Give Me This Mountain: Reverend C. L. Franklin, Life History and Selected Sermons* (Urbana: University of Illinois Press, 1989). Sunday evening broadcasts of black church services are common. The chanted sermon *must be heard* to be understood.

4. Rosenberg, *Art of the American Folk Preacher*, 48.

5. Rosenberg's description of the use of formulas in oral composition differs from Lord's: Lord thought that "new formulas" were created by analogy with the old, the composition process [being] merely one of substituting a word or phrase." Rosenberg, applying the insights of generative theory, suggests that the preacher "has at his command . . . not several score or several hundred formulas which he manipulates by word and phrase substitution, but rather a metrical deep structure which enables him to generate an infinite number of sentences in his native meter." Note these positions are not mutually exclusive. See Rosenberg, "Psychology of the Spiritual Sermon," 141, and *Art of the American Folk Preacher*, 46–116; Pipes, *Say Amen, Brother!* 150–55.

6. Frederick Law Olmsted, *The Cotton Kingdom*, 2 vols. (New York, 1861).

7. Mary Boykin Chestnut, *A Diary from Dixie*, ed. Ben Ames Williams (Boston: Houghton Mifflin, 1949), 148–49.

8. For fuller treatment of African influence upon the religious worship of American slaves, see Albert J. Raboteau, *Slave Religion: The "Invisible Institution" in the Antebellum South* (New York: Oxford University Press: 1978), 48–75.

9. Morton Marks, "Uncovering Ritual Structures in Afro-American Music," in Zaretsky and Leone, *Religious Movements in Contemporary America*, 60–134.

10. Clifton H. Johnson, ed., *God Struck Me Dead: Religious Conversion Experiences and Autobiographies of Ex-slaves* (Philadelphia: Pilgrim Press, 1969), 144.

Of the Faith of the Fathers

W.E.B. DUBOIS

Dim face of Beauty haunting all the world,
Fair face of Beauty all too fair to see,
Where the lost stars adown the heavens are hurled,—
There, there alone for thee
May white peace be.

Beauty, sad face of Beauty, Mystery, Wonder,
What are these dreams to foolish babbling men
Who cry with little noises 'neath the thunder
Of Ages ground to sand,
To a little sand. —Fiona Macleod

It was out in the country, far from home, far from my foster home, on a dark Sunday night. The road wandered from our rambling log-house up the stony bed of a creek, past wheat and corn, until we could hear dimly across the fields a rhythmic cadence of song,—soft, thrilling, powerful, that swelled and died sorrowfully in our ears. I was a country school-teacher then, fresh from the East, and had never seen a Southern Negro revival. To be sure, we in Berkshire were not perhaps as stiff and formal as they in Suffolk of olden time; yet we were very quiet and subdued, and I know not what would have happened those clear Sabbath mornings had some one punctuated the sermon with a wild scream, or interrupted the long prayer with a loud Amen! And so most striking to me, as I approached the village and the little plain church perched aloft, was the air of intense excitement that possessed that mass of black folk. A sort of suppressed terror hung in the air and seemed to seize us,—a pythian madness, a demoniac possession, that lent terrible reality to song and word. The black and massive form of the preacher swayed and quivered as the words crowded to his lips and flew at us in singular eloquence. The people moaned and fluttered, and then the gaunt-cheeked brown woman beside me suddenly leaped straight into the air and shrieked like a lost soul, while round about came wail and groan and outcry, and a scene of human passion such as I had never conceived before.

Those who have not thus witnessed the frenzy of a Negro revival in the untouched backwoods of the South can but dimly realize the religious feeling of the slave; as described, such scenes appear grotesque and funny, but as seen they are awful. Three things characterized this religion of the slave,—the Preacher, the Music, and the Frenzy. The Preacher is the most unique personality developed by the Negro on American soil. A leader, a politician, an orator, a "boss," an intriguer, an idealist,—all these he is, and ever, too, the centre of a group of men, now twenty, now a thousand in number. The combination of a certain adroitness with deep-seated earnestness, of tact with consummate ability, gave him his preëminence, and helps him maintain it. The type, of course, varies according to time and place, from the West Indies in the sixteenth century to New England in the nineteenth, and from the Mississippi bottoms to cities like New Orleans or New York.

The Music of Negro religion is that plaintive rhythmic melody, with its touching minor cadences, which, despite caricature and defilement, still remains the most original and beautiful expression of human life and longing yet born on American soil. Sprung from the African forests, where its counterpart can still be heard, it was adapted, changed, and intensified by the tragic soul-life of the slave, until, under the stress of law and whip, it became the one true expression of a people's sorrow, despair, and hope.

Finally the Frenzy or "Shouting," when the Spirit of the Lord passed by, and, seizing the devotee, made him mad with supernatural joy, was the last essential of Negro religion and the one more devoutly believed in than all the rest. It varied in expression from the silent rapt countenance or the low murmur and moan to the mad abandon of physical fervor,—the stamping, shrieking, and shouting, the rushing to and fro and wild waving of arms, the weeping and laughing, the vision and the trance. All this is nothing new in the world, but old as religion, as Delphi and Endor. And so firm a hold did it have on the Negro, that many generations firmly believed that without this visible manifestation of the God there could be no true communion with the Invisible.

These were the characteristics of Negro religious life as developed up to the time of Emancipation. Since under the peculiar circumstances of the black man's environment they were the one expression of his higher life, they are of deep interest to the student of his development, both socially and psychologically. Numerous are the attractive lines of inquiry that here group themselves. What did slavery mean to the African savage? What was his attitude toward the World and Life? What seemed to him good and evil,—God and Devil? Whither went his longings and strivings, and wherefore were his heart-burnings and disappointments? Answers to such questions can come only from a study of Negro religion as a development, through its gradual changes from the heathenism of the Gold Coast to the institutional Negro church of Chicago.

Moreover, the religious growth of millions of men, even though they be slaves, cannot be without potent influence upon their contemporaries. The Methodists and Baptists of America owe much of their condition to the silent but potent influence of their millions of Negro converts. Especially is this noticeable in the South, where theology and religious philosophy are on this account a long way behind the North, and where the religion of the poor whites is a plain copy of Negro thought and methods. The mass of "gospel" hymns which has swept through American churches and well-nigh ruined our sense of song consists largely of debased imitations of Negro melodies made by ears that caught the jingle but not the music, the body but not the soul, of the Jubilee songs. It is thus clear that the study of Negro religion is not only a vital part of the history of the Negro in America, but no uninteresting part of American history.

The Negro church of to-day is the social centre of Negro life in the United States, and the most characteristic expression of African character. Take a typical church in a small Virginian town: it is the "First Baptist" a roomy brick edifice seating five hundred or more persons, tastefully finished in Georgia pine, with a carpet, a small organ, and stained-glass windows. Underneath is a large assembly room with benches. This building is the central club-house of a community of a thousand or more Negroes. Various organizations meet here,—the church proper, the Sunday-school, two or three insurance societies, women's societies, secret societies, and mass meetings of various kinds. Entertainments, suppers, and lectures are held beside the five or six regular weekly religious services. Considerable sums of money are collected and expended here, employment is found for the idle, strangers are introduced, news is disseminated and charity distributed. At the same time this social, intellectual, and economic centre is a religious centre of great power. Depravity, Sin, Redemption, Heaven, Hell, and Damnation are preached twice a Sunday with much fervor, and revivals take place every year after the crops are laid by; and few indeed of the community have the hardihood to withstand conversion. Back of this more formal religion, the Church often stands as a real conserver of morals, a strengthener of family life, and the final authority on what is Good and Right.

Thus one can see in the Negro church to-day, reproduced in microcosm, all that great world from which the Negro is cut off by color-prejudice and social condition. In the great city churches the same tendency is noticeable and in many respects emphasized. A great church like the Bethel of Philadelphia has over eleven hundred members, an edifice seating fifteen hundred persons and valued at one hundred thousand dollars, an annual budget of five thousand dollars, and a government consisting of a pastor with several assisting local preachers, an executive and legislative board, financial boards and tax collectors; general church meetings for making laws; subdivided groups led by class leaders, a company of militia, and twenty-four auxiliary societies. The activity of a church like this is immense and far-reaching, and the bishops who preside over these organizations throughout the land are among the most powerful Negro rulers in the world.

Such churches are really governments of men, and consequently a little investigation reveals the curious fact that, in the South, at least, practically every American Negro is a church member. Some, to be sure, are not regularly enrolled, and a few do not habitually attend services; but, practically, a proscribed people must have a social centre, and that centre for this people is the Negro church. The census of 1890 showed nearly twenty-four thousand Negro churches in the country, with a total enrolled membership of over two and a half millions, or ten actual church members to every twenty-eight persons, and in some Southern States one in every two persons. Besides these there is the large number who, while not enrolled as members, attend and take part in many of the activities of the church. There is an organized Negro church for every sixty black families in the nation, and in some States for every forty families, owning, on an average, a thousand dollars' worth of property each, or nearly twenty-six million dollars in all.

Such, then, is the large development of the Negro church since Emancipation. The question now is, What have been the successive steps of this social history and what are the present tendencies? First, we must realize that no such institution as the Negro church could rear itself without definite historical foundations. These foundations we can find if we remember that the social history of the Negro did not start in America. He was brought from a definite social environment,—the polygamous clan life under the headship of the chief and the potent influence of the priest. His religion was nature-worship, with profound belief in invisible surrounding influences, good and bad, and his worship was through incantation and sacrifice. The first rude change in this life was the slave ship and the West Indian sugar-fields. The plantation organization replaced the clan and tribe, and the white master replaced the chief with far greater and more despotic powers. Forced and long-continued toil became the rule of life, the old ties of blood relationship and kinship disappeared, and instead of the family appeared a new polygamy and polyandry, which, in some cases, almost reached promiscuity. It was a terrific social revolution, and yet some traces were retained of the former group life, and the chief remaining institution was the Priest or Medicine-man. He early appeared on the plantation and found his function as the healer of the sick, the interpreter of the Unknown, the comforter of the sorrowing, the supernatural avenger of wrong, and the one who rudely but picturesquely expressed the longing, disappointment, and resentment of a stolen and oppressed people. Thus, as bard, physician, judge, and priest, within the narrow limits allowed by the slave system, rose the Negro preacher, and under him the first Afro-American institution, the Negro church. This church was not at first by any means Christian nor definitely organized; rather it was an adaptation and mingling of heathen rites among the members of each plantation, and roughly designated as Voodooism. Association with the masters, missionary effort and motives of expediency gave these rites an early veneer of Christianity, and after the lapse of many generations the Negro church became Christian.

Two characteristic things must be noticed in regard to this church. First, it became almost entirely Baptist and Methodist in faith; secondly, as a social institution it antedated by many decades the monogamic Negro home. From the very circumstances of its beginning, the church was confined to the plantation, and consisted primarily of a series of disconnected units; although, later on, some freedom of movement was allowed, still this geographical limitation was always important and was one cause of the spread of the decentralized and democratic Baptist faith among the slaves. At the same time, the visible rite of baptism appealed strongly to their mystic temperament. To-day the Baptist Church is still largest in membership among Negroes, and has a million and a half communicants. Next in popularity came the churches organized in connection with the white neighboring churches, chiefly Baptist and Methodist, with a few Episcopalian and others. The Methodists still form the second greatest denomination, with nearly a million members. The faith of these, two leading denominations was more suited to the slave church from the prominence they gave to religious feeling and fervor. The Negro membership in other denominations has always been small and relatively unimportant, although the Episcopalians and Presbyterians are gaining among the more intelligent classes to-day, and the Catholic Church is making headway in certain sections. After Emancipation, and still earlier in the North, the Negro churches largely severed such affiliations as they had had with the white churches, either by choice or by compulsion. The Baptist churches became independent, but the Methodists were compelled early to unite for purposes of episcopal government. This gave rise to the great African Methodist Church, the greatest Negro organization in the world, to the Zion Church and the Colored Methodist, and to the black conferences and churches in this and other denominations.

The second fact noted, namely, that the Negro church antedates the Negro home, leads to an explanation of much that is paradoxical in this communistic institution and in the morals of its members. But especially it leads us to regard this institution as peculiarly the expression of the inner ethical life of a people in a sense seldom true elsewhere. Let us turn, then, from the outer physical development of the church to the more important inner ethical life of the people who compose it. The Negro has already been pointed out many times as a religious animal,—a being of that deep emotional nature which turns instinctively toward the supernatural. Endowed with a rich tropical imagination and a keen, delicate appreciation of Nature, the transplanted African lived in a world animate with gods and devils, elves and witches; full of strange influences,—of Good to be implored, of Evil to be propitiated. Slavery, then, was to him the dark triumph of Evil over him. All the hateful powers of the Under-world were striving against him, and a spirit of revolt and revenge filled his heart. He called up all the resources of heathenism to aid,—exorcism and witchcraft, the mysterious Obi worship with its barbarous rites, spells, and blood-sacrifice even, now and then, of human victims. Weird midnight orgies and mystic conjurations were invoked, the witch-woman and the voodoopriest became the centre of Negro group life, and that vein of vague superstition which characterizes the unlettered Negro even to-day was deepened and strengthened.

In spite, however, of such success as that of the fierce Maroons, the Danish blacks, and others, the spirit of revolt gradually died away under the untiring energy and superior strength of the slave masters. By the middle of the eighteenth century the black slave had sunk, with hushed murmurs, to his place at the bottom of a new economic system, and was unconsciously ripe for a new philosophy of life. Nothing suited his condition then better than the doctrines of passive submission embodied in the newly learned Christianity. Slave masters early realized this, and cheerfully aided religious propaganda within certain bounds. The long system of repression and degradation of the Negro tended to emphasize the elements in his character which made him a valuable chattel: courtesy became humility, moral strength degenerated into submission, and the exquisite native appreciation of the beautiful became an infinite capacity for dumb suffering. The Negro, losing the joy of this world, eagerly seized upon the offered conceptions of the next; the avenging Spirit of the Lord enjoining patience in this world, under sorrow and tribulation until the Great Day when He should lead His dark children home,—this became his comforting dream. His preacher repeated the prophecy, and his bards sang,—

"Children, we all shall be free
When the Lord shall appear!"

This deep religious fatalism, painted so beautifully in "Uncle Tom," came soon to breed, as all fatalistic faiths will, the sensualist side by side with the martyr. Under the lax moral life of the plantation, where marriage was a farce, laziness a virtue, and property a theft, a religion of resignation and submission degenerated easily, in less strenuous minds, into a philosophy of indulgence and crime. Many of the worst characteristics of the Negro masses of to-day had their seed in this period of the slave's ethical growth. Here it was that the Home was ruined under the very shadow of the Church, white and black; here habits of shiftlessness took root, and sullen hopelessness replaced hopeful strife.

With the beginning of the abolition movement and the gradual growth of a class of free Negroes came a change. We often neglect the influence of the freedman before the war, because of the paucity of his numbers and the small weight he had in the history of the nation. But we must not forget that his chief influence was internal,—was exerted on the black world; and that there he was the ethical and social leader. Huddled as he was in a few centres like Philadelphia, New York, and New Orleans, the masses of the freedmen sank into poverty and listlessness; but not all of them. The free Negro leader early arose and his chief characteristic was intense earnestness and deep feeling on the slavery question. Freedom became to him a real thing and not a dream His religion became darker and more intense, and into his ethics crept a note of revenge, into his songs a day of reckoning close at hand. The "Coming of the Lord" swept this side of Death, and came to be a thing to be hoped for in this day. Through fugitive slaves and irrepressible discussion this desire for freedom seized the black millions still in bondage, and became their one ideal of life. The black bards caught new notes, and sometimes even dared to sing,—

"O Freedom, O Freedom, O Freedom over me!
Before I'll be a slave
I'll be buried in my grave,
And go home to my Lord
And be free."

For fifty years Negro religion thus transformed itself and identified itself with the dream of Abolition, until that which was a radical fad in the white North and an anarchistic plot in the white South had become a religion to the black world. Thus, when Emancipation finally came, it seemed to the freedman a literal Coming of the Lord. His fervid imagination was stirred as never before, by the tramp of armies, the blood and dust of battle, and the wail and whirl of social upheaval. He stood dumb and motionless before the whirlwind: what had he to do with it? Was it not the Lord's doing, and marvellous in his eyes? Joyed and bewildered with what came, he stood awaiting new wonders till the inevitable Age of Reaction swept over the nation and brought the crisis of to-day.

It is difficult to explain clearly the present critical stage of Negro religion. First, we must remember that living as the blacks do in close contact with a great modern nation, and sharing, although imperfectly, the soul-life of that nation, they must necessarily be affected more or less directly by all the religious and ethical forces that are to-day moving the United States. These questions and movements are, however, overshadowed and dwarfed by the (to them) all-important question of their civil, political, and economic status. They must perpetually discuss the "Negro Problem,"—must live, move, and have their being in it, and interpret all else in its light or darkness. With this come, too, peculiar problems of their inner life,—of the status of women, the maintenance of Home, the training of children, the accumulation of wealth, and the prevention of crime. All this must mean a time of intense ethical ferment, of religious heart-searching and intellectual unrest. From the double life every American Negro must live, as a Negro and as an American, as swept on by the current of the nineteenth while yet struggling in the eddies of the fifteenth century,—from this must arise a painful self-consciousness, an almost morbid sense of personality and a moral hesitancy which is fatal to self-confidence. The worlds within and without the Veil of Color are changing, and changing rapidly, but not at the same rate, not in the same way; and this must produce a peculiar wrenching of the soul, a peculiar sense of doubt and bewilderment. Such a double life, with double thoughts, double duties, and double social classes, must give rise to double words and double ideals, and tempt the mind to pretence or to revolt, to hypocrisy or to radicalism.

In some such doubtful words and phrases can one perhaps most clearly picture the peculiar ethical paradox that faces the Negro of to-day and is tingeing and changing his religious life. Feeling that his rights and his dearest ideals are being trampled upon, that the public conscience is ever more deaf to his righteous appeal, and that all the reactionary forces of prejudice, greed, and revenge are daily gaining new strength and fresh allies, the Negro faces no enviable dilemma. Conscious of his impotence, and pessimistic, he often becomes bitter and vindictive; and his religion, instead of a worship, is a complaint and a curse, a wail rather than a hope, a sneer rather than a faith. On the other hand, another type of mind, shrewder and keener and more tortuous too, sees in the very strength of the anti-Negro movement its patent weaknesses, and with Jesuitic casuistry is deterred by no ethical considerations in the endeavor to turn this weakness to the black man's strength. Thus we have two great and hardly reconcilable streams of thought and ethical strivings; the danger of the one lies in anarchy, that of the other in hypocrisy. The one type of Negro stands almost ready to curse God and die, and the other is too often found a traitor to right and a coward before force; the one is wedded to ideals remote, whimsical, perhaps impossible of realization; the other forgets that life is more than meat and the body more than raiment. But, after all, is not this simply the writhing of the age translated into black,—the triumph of the Lie which to-day, with its false culture, faces the hideousness of the anarchist assassin?

To-day the two groups of Negroes, the one in the North, the other in the South, represent these divergent ethical tendencies, the first tending toward radicalism, the other toward hypocritical compromise. It is no idle regret with which the white South mourns the loss of the old-time Negro,—the frank, honest, simple old servant who stood for the earlier religious age of submission and humility. With all his laziness and lack of many elements of true manhood, he was at least open-hearted, faithful, and sincere. To-day he is gone, but who is to blame for his going? Is it not those very persons who mourn for him? Is it not the tendency, born of Reconstruction and Reaction, to found a society on lawlessness and deception, to tamper with the moral fibre of a naturally honest and straightforward people until the whites threaten to become ungovernable tyrants and the blacks criminals and hypocrites? Deception is the natural defence of the weak against the strong, and the South used it for many years against its conquerors; to-day it must be prepared to see its black proletariat turn that same two-edged weapon against itself. And how natural this is! The death of Denmark Vesey and Nat Turner proved long since to the Negro the present hopelessness of physical defence. Political defence is becoming less and less available, and economic defence is still only partially effective. But there is a patent defence at hand,—the defence of deception and flattery, of cajoling and lying. It is the same defence which the Jews of the Middle Age used and which left its stamp on their character for centuries. To-day the young Negro of the South who would succeed cannot be frank and outspoken, honest and self-assertive, but rather he is daily tempted to be silent and wary, politic and sly; he must flatter and be pleasant, endure petty insults with a smile, shut his eyes to wrong; in too many cases he sees positive personal advantage in deception and lying. His real thoughts, his real aspirations, must be guarded in whispers; he must not criticise, he must not complain. Patience, humility, and adroitness must, in these growing black youth, replace impulse, manliness, and courage. With this sacrifice there is an economic opening, and perhaps peace and some prosperity. Without this there is riot, migration, or crime. Nor is this situation peculiar to the Southern United States,—is it not rather the only method by which undeveloped races have gained the right to share modern culture? The price of culture is a Lie.

On the other hand, in the North the tendency is to emphasize the radicalism of the Negro. Driven from his birthright in the South by a situation at which every fibre of his more outspoken and assertive nature revolts, he finds himself in a land where he can scarcely earn a decent living amid the harsh competition and the color discrimination. At the same time, through schools and periodicals, discussions and lectures, he is intellectually quickened and awakened. The soul, long pent up and dwarfed, suddenly expands in new-found freedom. What wonder that every tendency is to excess,—radical complaint, radical remedies, bitter denunciation or angry silence. Some sink, some rise. The criminal and the sensualist leave the church for the gambling-hell and the brothel, and fill the slums of Chicago and Baltimore; the better classes segregate themselves from the group-life of both white and black, and form an aristocracy, cultured but pessimistic, whose bitter criticism stings while it points out no way of escape. They despise the submission and subserviency of the Southern Negroes, but offer no other means by which a poor and oppressed minority can exist side by side with its masters. Feeling deeply and keenly the tendencies and opportunities of the age in which they live, their souls are bitter at the fate which drops the Veil between; and the very fact that this bitterness is natural and justifiable only serves to intensify it and make it more maddening.

Between the two extreme types of ethical attitude which I have thus sought to make clear wavers the mass of the millions of Negroes, North and South; and their religious life and activity partake of this social conflict within their ranks. Their churches are differentiating,—now into groups of cold, fashionable devotees, in no way distinguishable from similar white groups save in color of skin; now into large social and business institutions catering to the desire for information and amusement of their members, warily avoiding unpleasant questions both within and without the black world, and preaching in effect if not in word: *Dum vivimus, vivamus.*

But back of this still broods silently the deep religious feeling of the real Negro heart, the stirring, unguided might of powerful human souls who have lost the guiding star of the past and are seeking in the great night a new religious ideal. Some day the Awakening will come, when the pent-up vigor of ten million souls shall sweep irresistibly toward the Goal, out of the Valley of the Shadow of Death, where all that makes life worth living—Liberty, Justice, and Right—is marked "For White People Only."

Religion in the South

W.E.B. DuBois

IT is often a nice question as to which is of greater importance among a people—the way in which they earn their living, or their attitude toward life. As a matter of fact these two things are but two sides of the same problem, for nothing so reveals the attitude of a people toward life as the manner in which they earn their living; and on the other hand the earning of a living depends in the last analysis upon one's estimate of what life really is. So that these two questions that I am discussing with regard to the South are intimately bound up with each other.

If we have studied the economic development of the South carefully, then we have already seen something of its attitude toward life; the history of religion in the South means a study of these same facts over which we have gone, from a different point of view. Moreover, as the economic history of the South is in effect the economics of slavery and the Negro problem, so the essence of a study of religion in the South is a study of the ethics of slavery and emancipation.

It is very difficult of course for one who has not seen the practical difficulties that surround a people at any particular time in their battle with the hard facts of this world, to interpret with sympathy their ideals of life; and this is especially difficult when the economic life of a nation has been expressed by such a discredited word as slavery. If, then, we are to study the history of religion in the South, we must first of all divest ourselves of prejudice, pro and con; we must try to put ourselves in the place of those who are seeking to read the riddle of life and grant to them about the same general charity and the same general desire to do right that we find in the average human being. On the other hand, we must not, in striving to be charitable, be false to truth and right. Slavery in the United States was an economic mistake and a moral crime. This we cannot forget. Yet it had its excuses and mitigations. These we must remember.

When in the seventeenth century there grew up in the New World a system of human slavery, it was not by any means a new thing. There were slaves and slavery in Europe, not, to be sure, to a great extent, but none the less real. The Christian religion, however, had come to regard it as wrong and unjust that those who partook of the privileges and hopes and aspirations of that religion should oppress each other to the extent of actual enslavement. The idea of human brotherhood in the seventeenth century was of a brotherhood of coreligionists. When it came to the dealing of Christian with heathen, however, the century saw nothing wrong in slavery; rather, theoretically, they saw a chance for a great act of humanity and religion. The slaves were to be brought from heathenism to Christianity, and through slavery the benighted Indian and African were to find their passport into the kingdom of God. This theory of human slavery was held by Spaniards, French, and English. It was New England in the early days that put the echo of it in her codes (see Note 1) and recognition of it can be seen in most of the colonies.

But no sooner had people adopted this theory than there came the insistent and perplexing question as to what the status of the heathen slave was to be after he was Christianized and baptized; and even more pressing, what was to be the status of his children?

It took a great deal of bitter heart searching for the conscientious early slave-holders to settle this question. The obvious state of things was that the new convert awoke immediately to the freedom of Christ and became a freeman. But while this was the theoretical, religious answer, and indeed the answer which was given in several instances, the practice soon came into direct and perplexing conflict with the grim facts of economic life.

Here was a man who had invested his money and his labor in slaves; he had done it with dependence on the institution of property. Could he be deprived of his property simply because his slaves were baptized afterward into a Christian church? Very soon such economic reasoning swept away the theological dogma and it was expressly declared in colony after colony that baptism did not free the slaves (see Note 2). This, of course, put an end to the old doctrine of the heathen slave and it was necessary for the church to arrange for itself a new theory by which it could ameliorate, if not excuse, the position of the slave. The next question was naturally that of the children of slaves born in Christianity and the church for a time hedged unworthily on the subject by consigning to perpetual slavery the children of heathen but not those born of Christian parents; this was satisfactory for the first generation but it fell short of the logic of slavery later, and a new adjustment was demanded.

Here again this was not found difficult. In Virginia there had been built up the beginnings of a feudal aristocracy. Men saw nothing wrong or unthinkable in the situation as it began to develop, but rather something familiar. At the head of the feudal manor was the lord, or master, beneath him the under-lord or overseers and then the artisans, retainers, the free working men and lastly the serfs, slaves or servants as they were called. The servant was not free and yet he was not theoretically exactly a slave, and the laws of Virginia were rather careful to speak very little of slaves.

Serfdom in America as in Europe was to be a matter of status or position and not of race or blood, and the law of the South in the seventeenth and early eighteenth centuries made little or no distinction between black and white bondservants save in the time of their service. The idea, felt rather than expressed, was that here in America we were to have a new feudalism suited to the new country. At the top was the governor of the colony representing the majesty of the English king, at the bottom the serfs or slaves, some white, most of them black.

Slavery therefore was gradually transformed in the seventeenth and eighteenth centuries into a social status out of which a man, even a black man, could escape and did escape; and, no matter what his color was, when he became free, he became free in the same sense that other people were. Thus it was that there were free black voters in the southern colonies (Virginia and the Carolinas) in the early days concerning whose right to vote there was less question than there is concerning my right to vote now in Georgia (see Note 3).

The church recognized the situation and the Episcopal church especially gave itself easily to this new conception. This church recognized the social gradation of men; all souls were equal in the sight of God, but there were differences in worldly consideration and respect, and consequently it was perfectly natural that there should be an aristocracy at the top and a group of serfs at the bottom.

Meantime, however, America began to be stirred by a new democratic ideal; there came the reign of that ruler of men, Andrew Jackson; there came the spread of the democratic churches, Methodist and Baptist, and the democratization of other churches. Now when America became to be looked upon more and more as the dwelling place of free and equal men and when the Methodist and, particularly, the Baptist churches went down into the fields and proselyted among the slaves, a thing which the more aristocratic Episcopal church had never done (see Note 4), there came new questions and new heart-searchings among those who wanted to explain the difficulties and to think and speak clearly in the midst of their religious convictions.

As such people began to look round them the condition of the slaves appalled them. The Presbyterian Synod of South Carolina and Georgia declared in 1833: "There are over two millions of human beings in the condition of heathen and some of them in a worse condition. They may be justly considered the heathen of this country, and will bear a comparison with heathen in any country in the world. The Negroes are destitute of the gospel, and ever will be under the present state of things. In the vast field extending from an entire state beyond the Potomac [*i.e.,* Maryland] to the Sabine River [at the time our southwestern boundary] and from the Atlantic to the Ohio, there are, to the best of our knowledge, not twelve men exclusively devoted to the religious instruction of the Negroes. In the present state of feeling in the South, a ministry of their own color could neither be obtained nor tolerated.

"But do not the Negroes have access to the gospel through the stated ministry of the whites? We answer, no. The Negroes have no regular and efficient ministry; as a matter of course, no churches; neither is there sufficient room in the white churches for their accommodation. We know of but five churches in the slave-holding states built expressly for their use. These are all in the state of Georgia. We may now inquire whether they enjoy the privileges of the gospel in their own houses, and on our plantations? Again we return a negative answer. They have no Bibles to read by their own firesides. They have no family altars; and when in affliction, sickness, or death, they have no minister to address to them the consolations of the gospel, nor to bury them with appropriate services."

The same synod said in 1834: "The gospel, as things now are, can never be preached to the two classes (whites and blacks) successfully in conjunction. The galleries or back seats on the lower floor of white churches are generally appropriated to the Negroes, when it can be done without inconvenience to the whites. When it cannot be done conveniently, the Negroes must catch the gospel as it escapes through the doors and windows. If the master is pious, the house servants alone attend family worship, and frequently few of them, while the field hands have no attention at all. So far as masters are engaged in the work [of religious instruction of slaves], an almost unbroken silence reigns on this vast field."

The Rev. C. C. Jones, a Georgian and ardent defender of slavery (see Note 5) says of the period 1790–1820: "It is not too much to say that the religious and physical condition of the Negroes were both improved during this period. Their increase was natural and regular, ranging every ten years between thirty-four and thirty-six per cent. As the old stock from Africa died out of the country, the grosser customs, ignorance, and paganism of Africa died with them. Their descendants, the country-born, were better looking, more intelligent, more civilized, more susceptible of religious impressions.

"On the whole, however, but a minority of the Negroes, and that a small one, attended regularly the house of God, and taking them as a class, their religious instruction was extensively and most seriously neglected."

And of the decade 1830–40, he insists: "We cannot cry out against the Papists for withholding the Scriptures from the common people and keeping them in ignorance of the way of life, for we withhold the Bible from our servants, and keep them in ignorance of it, while we will not use the means to have it read and explained to them."

Such condition stirred the more radical-minded toward abolition sentiments and the more conservative toward renewed effort to evangelize and better the condition of the slaves. This condition was deplorable as Jones pictures it. "Persons live and die in the midst of Negroes and know comparatively little of their real character. They have not the immediate management of them. They have to do with them in the ordinary discharge of their duty as servants, further than this they institute no inquiries; they give themselves no trouble.

"The Negroes are a distinct class in the community, and keep themselves very much to themselves. They are one thing before the whites and another before their own color. Deception before the former is characteristic of them, whether bond or free, throughout the whole United States. It is habit, a long established custom, which descends from generation to generation. There is an upper and an under current. Some are contented with the appearance on the surface; others dive beneath. Hence the diversity of impressions and representations of the moral and religious condition of the Negroes. Hence the disposition of some to deny the darker pictures of their more searching and knowing friends."

He then enumerates the vice of the slaves: "The divine institution of marriage depends for its perpetuity, sacredness, and value, largely upon the protection given it by the law of the land. Negro marriages are neither recognized nor protected by law. The Negroes receive no instruction on the nature, sacredness, and perpetuity of the institution; at any rate they are far from being duly impressed with these things. They are not required to be married in any particular form, nor by any particular persons."

He continues: "Hence, as may well be imagined, the marriage relation loses much of the sacredness and perpetuity of its character. It is a contract of convenience, profit, or pleasure, that may be entered into and dissolved at the will of the parties, and that without heinous sin, or the injury of the property or interests of any one. That which they possess in common is speedily divided, and the support of the wife and children falls not upon the husband, but upon the master. Protracted sickness, want of industrial habits, of congeniality of disposition, or disparity of age, are sufficient grounds for a separation."

Under such circumstances, "polygamy is practiced both secretly and openly." Uncleanness, infanticide, theft, lying, quarreling, and fighting are noted, and the words of Charles Cotesworth Pinckney in 1829 are recalled: "There needs no stronger illustration of the doctrine of human depravity than the state of morals on plantations in general. Besides the mischievous tendency of bad example in parents and elders, the little Negro is often taught by these natural instructors that he may commit any vice that he can conceal from his superiors, and thus falsehood and deception are among the earliest lessons they imbibe. Their advance in years is but a progression to the higher grades of iniquity. The violation of the Seventh Commandment is viewed in a more venial light than in fashionable European circles. Their depredations of rice have been estimated to amount to twenty-five per cent of the gross average of crops."

John Randolph of Roanoke once visited a lady and "found her surrounded with her seamstresses, making up a quantity of clothing. 'What work have you in hand?' 'O sir, I am preparing this clothing to send to the poor Greeks.' On taking leave at the steps of her mansion, he saw some of her servants in need of the very clothing which their tender-hearted mistress was sending abroad. He exclaimed, 'Madam, madam, the Greeks are at your door!'"

One natural solution of this difficulty was to train teachers and preachers for the slaves from among their own number. The old Voodoo priests were passing away and already here and there new spiritual leaders of the Negroes began to arise. Accounts of several of these, taken from "The Negro Church," will be given.

Among the earliest was Harry Hosier who traveled with the Methodist Bishop Asbury and often filled appointments for him. George Leile and Andrew Bryan were preachers whose life history is of intense interest. "George Leile or Lisle, sometimes called George Sharp, was born in Virginia about 1750. His master (Mr. Sharp) some time before the American war removed and settled in Burke County, Georgia. Mr. Sharp was a Baptist and a deacon in a Baptist church, of which Rev. Matthew Moore was pastor. George was converted and baptized under Mr. Moore's ministry. The church gave him liberty to preach.

"About nine months after George Leile left Georgia, Andrew, surnamed Bryan, a man of good sense, great zeal, and some natural elocution, began to exhort his black brethren and friends. He and his followers were reprimanded and forbidden to engage further in religious exercises. He would, however, pray, sing, and encourage his fellow worshipers to seek the Lord.

"Their persecution was carried to an inhuman extent. Their evening assemblies were broken up and those found present were punished with stripes. Andrew Bryan and Sampson, his brother, converted about a year after him, were twice imprisoned, and they with about fifty others were whipped. When publicly whipped, and bleeding under his wounds, Andrew declared that he not only rejoiced to be whipped, but would gladly suffer death for the cause of Jesus Christ, and that while he had life and opportunity he would continue to preach Christ. He was faithful to his vow and, by patient continuance in welldoing, he put to silence and shamed his adversaries, and influential advocates and patrons were raised up for him. Liberty was given Andrew by the civil authority to continue his religious meetings under certain regulations. His master gave him the use of his barn at Brampton, three miles from Savannah, where he preached for two years with little interruption."

Lott Carey a free Virginia Negro "was evidently a man of superior intellect and force of character, as is evidenced from the fact that his reading took a wide range—from political economy, in Adam Smith's Wealth of Nations,' to the voyage of Captain Cook. That he was a worker as well as a preacher is true, for when he decided to go to Africa his employers offered to raise his salary from $800 to $1,000 a year. Remember that this was over eighty years ago. Carey was not seduced by such a flattering offer, for he was determined.

"His last sermon in the old First Church in Richmond must have been exceedingly powerful, for it was compared by an eyewitness, a resident of another state, to the burning, eloquent appeals of George Whitfield. Fancy him as he stands there in that historic building ringing the changes on the word 'freely,' depicting the willingness with which he was ready to give up his life for service in Africa.

"He, as you may already know, was the leader of the pioneer colony to Liberia, where he arrived even before the agent of the Colonization Society. In his new home his abilities were recognized, for he was made vice governor, and became governor in fact while Governor Ashmun was absent from the colony in this country. Carey did not allow his position to betray the cause of his people, for he did not hesitate to expose the duplicity of the Colonization Society and even to defy their authority, it would seem, in the interests of the people.

"While casting cartridges to defend the colonists against the natives in 1828, the accidental upsetting of a candle caused an explosion that resulted in his death.

"Carey is described as a typical Negro, six feet in height, of massive and erect frame, with the sinews of a Titan. He had a square face, keen eyes, and a grave countenance. His movements were measured; in short, he had all the bearing and dignity of a prince of the blood."

John Chavis was a full-blooded Negro, born in Granville County, N. C., near Oxford, in 1763. He was born free and was sent to Princeton, studying privately under Dr. Witherspoon, where he did well. He went to Virginia to preach to Negroes. In 1802, in the county court, his freedom and character were certified to and it was declared that he had passed "through a regular course of academic studies" at what is now Washington and Lee University. In 1805 he returned to North Carolina, where in 1809 he was made a licentiate in the Presbyterian Church and allowed to preach. His English was remarkably pure, his manner impressive, his explanations clear and concise.

For a long time he taught school and had the best whites as pupils—a United States senator, the sons of a chief justice of North Carolina, a governor of the state and many others. Some of his pupils boarded in the family, and his school was regarded as the best in the State. "All accounts agree that John Chavis was a gentleman," and he was received socially among the best whites and asked to table. In 1830 he was stopped from preaching by the law. Afterward he taught a school for free Negroes in Raleigh.

Henry Evans was a full-blooded Virginia free Negro, and was the pioneer of Methodism in Fayetteville, N. C. He found the Negroes there, about 1800, without any religious instruction. He began preaching and the town council ordered him away; he continued and whites came to hear him. Finally the white auditors outnumbered the blacks and sheds were erected for Negroes at the side of the church. The gathering became a regular Methodist Church, with a white and Negro membership, but Evans continued to preach. He exhibited "rare self-control before the most wretched of castes! Henry Evans did much good, but he would have done more good had his spirit been untrammeled by this sense of inferiority."

His dying words uttered as he stood, aged and bent beside his pulpit, are of singular pathos: "I have come to say my last word to you. It is this: None but Christ. Three times have I had my life in jeopardy for preaching the gospel to you. Three times I have broken ice on the edge of the water and swam across the Cape Fear to preach the gospel to you; and, if in my last hour I could trust to that, or anything but Christ crucified, for my salvation, all should be lost and my soul perish forever."

Early in the nineteenth century Ralph Freeman was a slave in Anson County, N. C. He was a full-blooded Negro, and was ordained and became an able Baptist preacher. He baptized and administered communion, and was greatly respected. When the Baptists split on the question of missions he sided with the anti-mission side. Finally the law forbade him to preach.

Lunsford Lane was a Negro who bought his freedom in Raleigh, N. C., by the manufacture of smoking tobacco. He later became a minister of the gospel, and had the confidence of many of the best people.

The story of Jack of Virginia is best told in the words of a Southern writer:

"Probably the most interesting case in the whole South is that of an African preacher of Nottoway County, popularly known as 'Uncle Jack,' whose services to white and black were so valuable that a distinguished minister of the Southern Presbyterian Church felt called upon to memorialize his work in a biography.

"Kidnapped from his idolatrous parents in Africa, he was brought over in one of the last cargoes of slaves admitted to Virginia and sold to a remote and obscure planter in Nottoway County, a region at that time in the backwoods and destitute particularly as to religious life and instruction. He was converted under the occasional preaching of Rev. Dr. John Blair Smith, president of Hampden-Sidney College, and of Dr. William Hill and Dr. Archibald Alexander of Princeton, then young theologues, and by hearing the Scriptures read.

"Taught by his master's children to read, he became so full of the spirit and knowledge of the Bible that he was recognized among the whites as a powerful expounder of Christian doctrine, was licensed to preach by the Baptist Church, and preached from plantation to plantation within a radius of thirty miles, as he was invited by overseers or masters. His freedom was purchased by a subscription of whites, and he was given a home and tract of land for his support. He organized a large and orderly Negro church, and exercised such a wonderful controlling influence over the private morals of his flock that masters, instead of punishing their slaves, often referred them to the discipline of their pastor, which they dreaded far more.

"He stopped a heresy among the Negroes of Southern Virginia, defeating in open argument a famous fanatical Negro preacher named Campbell, who advocated noise and 'the spirit' against the Bible, and winning over Campbell's adherents in a body. For over forty years, and until he was nearly a hundred years of age, he labored successfully in public and private among black and whites, voluntarily giving up his preaching in obedience to the law of 1832, the result of 'Old Nat's war.'

"The most refined and aristocratic people paid tribute to him, and he was instrumental in the conversion of many whites. Says his biographer, Rev. Dr. William S. White: 'He was invited into their houses, sat with their families, took part in their social worship, sometimes leading the prayer at the family altar. Many of the most intelligent people attended upon his ministry and listened to his sermons with great delight. Indeed, previous to the year 1825, he was considered by the best judges to be the best preacher in that county. His opinions were respected, his advice followed, and yet he never betrayed the least symptoms of arrogance or self-conceit.

"'His dwelling was a rude log cabin, his apparel of the plainest and coarsest materials.' This was because he wanted to be fully identified with his class. He refused gifts of better clothing, saying 'These clothes are a great deal better than are generally worn by people of my color, and besides if I wear finer ones I find I shall be obliged to think about them even at meeting.'"

Thus slowly, surely, the slave, in the persons of such exceptional men, appearing here and there at rare intervals, was persistently stretching upward. The Negroes bade fair in time to have their leaders. The new democratic evangelism began to encourage this, and then came the difficulty—the inevitable ethical paradox.

The good men of the South recognized the needs of the slaves. Here and there Negro ministers were arising. What now should be the policy? On the part of the best thinkers it seemed as if men might strive here, in spite of slavery, after brotherhood; that the slaves should be proselyted, taught religion, admitted to the churches, and, notwithstanding their civil station, looked upon as the spiritual brothers of the white communicants. Much was done to make this true. The conditions improved in a great many respects, but no sooner was there a systematic effort to teach the slaves, even though that teaching was confined to elementary religion, than the various things followed that must follow all intellectual awakenings.

We have had the same thing in our day. A few Negroes of the South have been taught, they consequently have begun to think, they have begun to assert themselves, and suddenly men are face to face with the fact that either one of two things must happen—either they must stop teaching or these people are going to be men, not serfs or slaves. Not only that, but to seek to put an awakening people back to sleep means revolt. It meant revolt in the eighteenth century, when a series of insurrections and disturbances frightened the South tremendously, not so much by their actual extent as by the possibilities they suggested. It was noticeable that many of these revolts were led by preachers.

The revolution in Hayti greatly stirred the South and induced South Carolina to declare in 1800:

"It shall not be lawful for any number of slaves, free Negroes, mulattoes, or mestizoes, even in company with white persons, to meet together and assemble for the purpose of mental instruction or religious worship either before the rising of the sun or after the going down of the same. And all magistrates, sheriffs, militia officers, etc., etc., are hereby vested with power, etc., for dispersing such assemblies."

On petition of the white churches the rigor of this law was slightly abated in 1803 by a modification which forbade any person, before nine o'clock in the evening, "to break into a place of meeting wherein shall be assembled the members of any religious society in this State, provided a majority of them shall be white persons, or otherwise to disturb their devotions unless such persons, etc., so entering said place (of worship) shall first have obtained from some magistrate, etc., a warrant, etc., in case a magistrate shall be then actually within a distance of three miles from such place of meeting; otherwise the provisions, etc. (of the Act of 1800) to remain in full force."

So, too, in Virginia the Haytian revolt and the attempted insurrection under Gabriel in 1800 led to the Act of 1804, which forbade all evening meetings of slaves. This was modified in 1805 so as to allow a slave, in company with a white person, to listen to a white minister in the evening. A master was "allowed" to employ a religious teacher for his slaves. Mississippi passed similar restrictions.

By 1822 the rigor of the South Carolina laws in regard to Negro meetings had abated, especially in a city like Charleston, and one of the results was the Vesey plot.

"The sundry religious classes or congregations, with Negro leaders or local preachers, into which were formed the Negro members of the various churches of Charleston, furnished Vesey with the first rudiments of an organization, and at the same time with a singularly safe medium for conducting his underground agitation. It was customary, at that time, for these Negro congregations to meet for purposes of worship entirely free from the presence of whites. Such meetings were afterward forbidden to be held except in the presence of at least one representative of the dominant race, but during the three or four years prior to the year 1822 they certainly offered Denmark Vesey regular, easy, and safe opportunity for preaching his gospel of liberty and hate. And we are left in no doubt whatever in regard to the uses to which he put those gatherings of blacks.

"Like many of his race, he possessed the gift of gab, as the silver in the tongue and the gold in the full or thick-lipped mouth are oftentimes contemptuously characterized. And, like many of his race, he was a devoted student of the Bible, to whose interpretation he brought, like many other Bible students not confined to the Negro race, a good deal of imagination and not a little of superstition, which, with some natures, is perhaps but another name for the desires of the heart.

"Thus equipped, it is no wonder that Vesey, as he pored over the Old Testament scriptures, found many points of similitude in the history of the Jews and that of the slaves in the United States. They were both peculiar peoples. They were both Jehovah's peculiar peoples, one in the past, the other in the present. And it seemed to him that as Jehovah bent His ear, and bared His arm once in behalf of the one, so would He do the same for the other. It was all vividly real to his thought, I believe, for to his mind thus had said the Lord.

"He ransacked the Bible for apposite and terrible texts whose commands in the olden times, to the olden people, were no less imperative upon the new times and the new people. This new people were also commanded to arise and destroy their enemies and the city in which they dwelt, 'both man and woman, young and old, with the edge of the sword.' Believing super-stitiously as he did in the stern and Nemesis-like God of the Old Testament he looked confidently for a day of vengeance and retribution for the blacks. He felt, I doubt not, something peculiarly applicable to his enterprise and intensely personal to himself in the stern and exultant prophecy of Zechariah, fierce and sanguinary words, which were constantly in his mouth: 'Then shall the Lord go forth and fight against those nations as when He fought in the day of battle.' According to Vesey's lurid exegesis 'those nations' in the text meant beyond peradventure the cruel masters, and Jehovah was to go forth to fight them for the poor slaves and on whichever side fought that day the Almighty God on that side would assuredly rest victory and deliverance.

"It will not be denied that Vesey's plan contemplated the total annihilation of the white population of Charleston. Nursing for many dark years the bitter wrongs of himself and race had filled him without doubt with a mad spirit of revenge and had given to him a decided predilection for shedding the blood of his oppressors. But if he intended to kill them to satisfy a desire for vengeance he intended to do so also on broader ground. The conspirators, he argued, had no choice in the matter, but were compelled to adopt a policy of extermination by the necessity of their position. The liberty of the blacks was in the balance of fate against the lives of the whites. He could strike that balance in favor of the blacks only by the total destruction of the whites. Therefore the whites, men, women, and children, were doomed to death."[1]

Vesey's plot was well laid, but the conspirators were betrayed.

Less than ten years after this plot was discovered and Vesey and his associates hanged, there broke out the Nat Turner insurrection in Virginia. Turner was himself a preacher.

"He was a Christian and a man. He was conscious that he was a Man and not a 'thing'; therefore, driven by religious fanaticism, he undertook a difficult and bloody task. Nathaniel Turner was born in Southampton County, Virginia, October 2, 1800. His master was one Benjamin Turner, a very wealthy and aristocratic man. He owned many slaves, and was a cruel and exacting master. Young 'Nat' was born of slave parents, and carried to his grave many of the superstitions and traits of his father and mother. The former was a preacher, the latter a 'mother in Israel.' Both were unlettered but, nevertheless, very pious people.

"The mother began when Nat was quite young to teach him that he was born, like Moses, to be the deliverer of his race. She would sing to him snatches of wild, rapturous songs and repeat portions of prophecy she had learned from the preachers of those times. Nat listened with reverence and awe, and believed everything his mother said. He imbibed the deep religious character of his parents, and soon manifested a desire to preach. He was solemnly set apart to 'the gospel ministry' by his father, the church, and visiting preachers. He was quite low in stature, dark, and had the genuine African features. His eyes were small but sharp, and gleamed like fire when he was talking about his 'mission' or preaching from some prophetic passage of scripture. It is said that he never laughed. He was a dreamy sort of a man, and avoided the crowd.

"Like Moses he lived in the solitudes of the mountains and brooded over the condition of his people. There was something grand to him in the rugged scenery that nature had surrounded him with. He believed that he was a prophet, a leader raised up by God to burst the bolts of the prison-house and set the oppressed free. The thunder, the hail, the storm-cloud, the air, the earth, the stars, at which he would sit and gaze half the night all spake the language of the God of the oppressed. He was seldom seen in a large company, and never drank a drop of ardent spirits. Like John the Baptist, when he had delivered his message, he would retire to the fastness of the mountain or seek the desert, where he could meditate upon his great work."

In the impression of the Richmond *Enquirer* of the 30th of August, 1831, the first editorial or leader is under the caption of "The Banditte." The editor says:

"They remind one of a parcel of blood-thirsty wolves rushing down from the Alps; or, rather, like a former incursion of the Indians upon the white settlements. Nothing is spared; neither age nor sex respected—the helplessness of women and children pleads in vain for mercy. . . . The case of Nat Turner warns us. No black man ought to be permitted to turn preacher through the country. The law must be enforced, or the tragedy of Southampton appeals to us in vain."

Mr. Gray, the man to whom Turner made his confession before dying, said:

"It has been said that he was ignorant and cowardly and that his object was to murder and rob for the purpose of obtaining money to make his escape. It is notorious that he was never known to have a dollar in his life, to swear an oath, or drink a drop of spirits. As to his ignorance, he certainly never had the advantages of an education, but he can read and write, and for natural intelligence and quickness of apprehension is surpassed by few men I have ever seen. As to his being a coward, his reason as given for not resisting Mr. Phipps, shows the decision of his character. When he saw Mr. Phipps present his gun, he said he knew it was impossible for him to escape as the woods were full of men. He, therefore, thought it was better for him to surrender and trust to fortune for his escape.

"He is a complete fanatic or plays his part most admirably. On other subjects he possesses an uncommon share of intelligence, with a mind capable of attaining anything, but warped and perverted by the influence of early impressions. He is below the ordinary stature, though strong and active, having the true Negro face, every feature of which is strongly marked.

"I shall not attempt to describe the effect of his narrative, as told and commented on by himself, in the condemned hole of the prison; the calm deliberate composure with which he spoke of his late deeds and intentions; the expression of his fiend-like face when excited by enthusiasm, still bearing the stains of the blood of the helpless innocence about him, clothed with rags and covered with chains, yet daring to raise his manacled

---

[1] Grimke: "Right on the Scaffold."

hand to Heaven, with a spirit soaring above the attributes of man. I looked on him and the blood curdled in my veins."[1]

The Turner insurrection is so connected with the economic revolution which enthroned cotton that it marks an epoch in the history of the slave. A wave of legislation passed over the South prohibiting the slaves from learning to read and write, forbidding Negroes to preach, and interfering with Negro religious meetings.

Virginia declared, in 1831, that neither slaves nor free Negroes might preach, nor could they attend religious service at night without permission. In North Carolina slaves and free Negroes were forbidden to preach, exhort or teach "in any prayer-meeting or other association for worship where slaves of different families are collected together" on penalty of not more than thirty-nine lashes. Maryland and Georgia had similar laws. The Mississippi law of 1831 said: It is "unlawful for any slave, free Negro, or mulatto to preach the gospel" upon pain of receiving thirty-nine lashes upon the naked back of the presumptuous preacher. If a Negro received written permission from his master he might preach to the Negroes in his immediate neighborhood, providing six respectable white men, owners of slaves, were present. In Alabama the law of 1832 prohibited the assembling of more than five male slaves at any place off the plantation to which they belonged, but nothing in the act was to be considered as forbidding attendance at places of public worship held by white persons. No slave or free person of color was permitted to "preach, exhort, or harangue any slave or slaves, or free persons of color, except in the presence of five respectable slaveholders, or unless the person preaching was licensed by some regular body of professing Christians in the neighborhood, to whose society or church the Negroes addressed properly belonged."

In the District of Columbia the free Negroes began to leave white churches in 1831 and to assemble in their own.

Thus it was that through the fear of insurrection, the economic press of the new slavery that was arising, and the new significance of slavery in the economics of the South, the strife for spiritual brotherhood was given up. Slavery became distinctly a matter of race and not of status. Long years before, the white servants had been freed and only black servants were left; now social condition came to be not simply a matter of slavery but a matter of belonging to the black race, so that even the free Negroes began to be disfranchised and put into the caste system (see Note 6).

A new adjustment of ethics and religion had to be made to meet this new situation, and in the adjustment no matter what might be said or thought, the Negro and slavery had to be the central thing.

In the adjustment of religion and ethics that was made for the new slavery, under the cotton kingdom, there was in the first place a distinct denial of human brotherhood. These black men were not men in the sense that white men were men. They were different—different in kind, different in origin; they had different diseases (see Note 7); they had different feelings; they were not to be treated the same; they were not looked upon as the same; they were altogether apart and, while perhaps they had certain low sensibilities and aspirations, yet so far as this world is concerned, there could be with them neither human nor spiritual brotherhood.

The only status that they could possibly occupy was the status of slaves. They could not get along as freemen; they could not work as freemen; it was utterly unthinkable that people should live with them free. This was the philosophy that was worked out gradually, with exceptions here and there, and that was thought through, written on, preached from the pulpits and taught in the homes, until people in the South believed it as they believed the rising and the setting of the sun.

As this became more and more the orthodox ethical opinion, heretics appeared in the land as they always do. But intolerance and anathema met them. In community after community there was a demand for orthodoxy on this one burning question of the economic and religious South, and the heretics were driven out. The Quakers left North Carolina, the abolitionists either left Virginia or ceased to talk, and throughout the South those people who dared to think otherwise were left silent or dead (see Note 8).

So long as slavery was an economic success this orthodoxy was all powerful; when signs of economic distress appeared it became intolerant and aggressive. A great moral battle was impending in the South, but political turmoil and a development of northern thought so rapid as to be unintelligible in the South stopped this development forcibly. War came and the hatred and moral bluntness incident to war, and men crystallized in their old thought.

The matter now could no longer be argued and thought out, it became a matter of tradition, of faith, of family and personal honor. There grew up therefore after the war a new predicament; a new-old paradox.

---

[1] "The Negro Church," Atlanta University Publications, No. 8.

Upon the whites hung the curse of the past; because they had not settled their labor problem then, they must settle the problem now in the face of upheaval and handicapped by the natural advance of the world.

So after the war and even to this day, the religious and ethical life of the South bows beneath this burden. Shrinking from facing the burning ethical questions that front it unrelentingly, the Southern Church clings all the more closely to the letter of a worn out orthodoxy, while its inner truer soul crouches before and fears to answer the problem of eight million black neighbors. It therefore assiduously "preaches Christ crucified," in prayer meeting *patois*, and crucifies "Niggers" in unrelenting daily life.

While the Church in the North, all too slowly but surely is struggling up from the ashes of a childish faith in myth and miracle, and beginning to preach a living gospel of civic virtue, peace and good will and a crusade against lying, stealing and snobbery, the Southern church for the most part is still murmuring of modes of "baptism," "infant damnation" and the "divine plan of creation."

Thus the post-bellum ethical paradox of the South is far more puzzling than the economic paradox. To be sure there is leaven in the lump. There are brave voices here and there, but they are easily drowned by social tyranny in the South and by indifference and sensationalism in the North (see Note 9).

First of all the result of the war was the complete expulsion of Negroes from white churches. Little has been said of this, but perhaps it was in itself the most singular and tremendous result of slavery. The Methodist Church South simply set its Negro members bodily out of doors. They did it with some consideration for their feelings, with as much kindliness as crass unkindliness can show, but they virtually said to all their black members—to the black mammies whom they have almost fulsomely praised and whom they remember in such astonishing numbers to-day, to the polite and deferential old servant, to whose character they build monuments—they said to them: "You cannot worship God with us." There grew up, therefore, the Colored Methodist Episcopal Church.

Flagrantly unchristian as this course was, it was still in some ways better than the absolute withdrawal of church fellowship on the part of the Baptists, or the policy of Episcopalians, which was simply that of studied neglect and discouragement which froze, harried, and well nigh invited the black communicants to withdraw.

From the North now came those Negro church bodies born of color discrimination in Philadelphia and New York in the eighteenth century, and thus a Christianity absolutely divided along the color line arose. There may be in the South a black man belonging to a white church to-day but if so, he must be very old and very feeble. This anomaly—this utter denial of the very first principles of the ethics of Jesus Christ—is today so deep seated and unquestionable a principle of Southern Christianity that its essential heathenism is scarcely thought of, and every revival of religion in this section banks its spiritual riches solidly and unmovedly against the color line, without conscious question.

Among the Negroes the results are equally unhappy. They needed ethical leadership, spiritual guidance, and religious instruction. If the Negroes of the South are to any degree immoral, sexually unchaste, criminally inclined, and religiously ignorant, what right has the Christian South even to whisper reproach or accusation? How often have they raised a finger to assume spiritual or religious guardianship over those victims of their past system of economic and social life?

Left thus unguided the Negroes, with some help from such Northern white churches as dared, began their own religious upbuilding (see Note 10). They faced tremendous difficulties—lack of ministers, money, and experience. Their churches could not be simply centres of religious life—because in the poverty of their organized efforts all united striving tended to centre in this one social organ. The Negro Church consequently became a great social institution with some ethical ideas but with those ethical ideas warped and changed and perverted by the whole history of the past; with memories, traditions, and rites of heathen worship, of intense emotionalism, trance, and weird singing.

And above all, there brooded over and in the church the sense of all their grievances. Whatsoever their own shortcomings might be, at least they knew that they were not guilty of hypocrisy; they did not cry "Whosoever will" and then brazenly ostracize half the world. They knew that they opened their doors and hearts wide to all people that really wanted to come in and they looked upon the white churches not as examples but with a sort of silent contempt and a real inner questioning of the genuineness of their Christianity.

On the other hand, so far as the white post-bellum Christian church is concerned, I can conceive no more pitiable paradox than that of the young white Christian in the South to-day who really believes in the ethics of Jesus Christ. What can he think when he hangs upon his church doors the sign that I have often seen, "All are welcome." He knows that half the population of his city would not dare to go inside that church. Or if there was any fellowship between Christians, white and black, it would be after the manner explained by a white Mississippi clergyman in all seriousness: "The whites and Negroes understand each other here perfectly, sir, perfectly; if they come to my church they take a seat in the gallery. If I go to theirs, they invite me to the front pew or the platform."

Once in Atlanta a great revival was going on in a prominent white church. The people were at fever heat, the minister was preaching and calling "Come to Jesus." Up the aisle tottered an old black man—he was an outcast, he had wandered in there aimlessly off the streets, dimly he had comprehended this call and he came tottering and swaying up the aisle. What was the result? It broke up the revival. There was no disturbance; he was gently led out, but that sudden appearance of a black face spoiled the whole spirit of the thing and the revival was at an end.

Who can doubt that if Christ came to Georgia to-day one of His first deeds would be to sit down and take supper with black men, and who can doubt the outcome if He did?

It is this tremendous paradox of a Christianity that theoretically opens the church to all men and yet closes it forcibly and insultingly in the face of black men and that does this not simply in the visible church but even more harshly in the spiritual fellowship of human souls—it is this that makes the ethical and religious problem in the South to-day of such tremendous importance, and that gives rise to the one thing which it seems to me is the most difficult in the Southern situation and that is, the tendency to deny the truth, the tendency to lie when the real situation comes up because the truth is too hard to face. This lying about the situation of the South has not been simply a political subterfuge against the dangers of ignorance, but is a sort of gasping inner revolt against acknowledging the real truth of the ethical conviction which every true Southerner must feel, namely: that the South is eternally and fundamentally wrong on the plain straight question of the equality of souls before God—of the inalienable rights of all men.

Here are men—they are aspiring, they are struggling piteously forward, they have frequent instances of ability, there is no doubt as to the tremendous strides which certain classes of Negroes have made—how shall they be treated? That they should be treated as men, of course, the best class of Southerners know and sometimes acknowledge. And yet they believe, and believe with fierce conviction, that it is impossible to treat Negroes as men, and still live with them. Right there is the paradox which they face daily and which is daily stamping hypocrisy upon their religion and upon their land.

Their irresistible impulse in this awful dilemma is to point to and emphasize the Negro's degradation, even though they know that it is not the degraded Negro whom they most fear, ostracize, and fight to keep down, but rather the rising, ambitious Negro.

If my own city of Atlanta had offered it to-day the choice between 500 Negro college graduates—forceful, busy, ambitious men of property and self-respect, and 500 black cringing vagrants and criminals, the popular vote in favor of the criminals would be simply overwhelming. Why? because they want Negro crime? No, not that they fear Negro crime less, but that they fear Negro ambition and success more. They can deal with crime by chain-gang and lynch law, or at least they think they can, but the South can conceive neither machinery nor place for the educated, self-reliant, self-assertive black man.

Are a people pushed to such moral extremities, the ones whose level-headed, unbiased statements of fact concerning the Negro can be relied upon? Do they really know the Negro? Can the nation expect of them the poise and patience necessary for the settling of a great social problem?

Not only is there then this initial falseness when the South excuses its ethical paradox by pointing to the low condition of the Negro masses, but there is also a strange blindness in failing to see that every pound of evidence to prove the present degradation of black men but adds to the crushing weight of indictment against their past treatment of this race.

A race is not made in a single generation. If they accuse Negro women of lewdness and Negro men of monstrous crime, what are they doing but advertising to the world the shameless lewdness of those Southern men who brought millions of mulattoes into the world, and whose deeds throughout the South and particularly in Virginia, the mother of slavery, have left but few prominent families whose blood does not to-day course in black veins? Suppose to-day Negroes do steal; who was it that for centuries made stealing a virtue by stealing their labor? Have not laziness and listlessness always been the followers of slavery? If these ten millions are ignorant by whose past law and mandate and present practice is this true?

The truth then cannot be controverted. The present condition of the Negro in America is better than the history of slavery proves we might reasonably expect. With the help of his friends, North and South, and despite the bitter opposition of his foes, South and North, he has bought twelve million acres of land, swept away two-thirds of his illiteracy, organized his church, and found leadership and articulate voice. Yet despite this the South, Christian and unchristian, with only here and there an exception, still stands like a rock wall and says: Negroes are not men and must not be treated as men.

When now the world faces such an absolute ethical contradiction, the truth is nearer than it seems.

It stands to-day perfectly clear and plain despite all sophistication and false assumption: If the contention of the South is true—that Negroes cannot by reason of hereditary inferiority take their places in modern civilization beside white men, then the South owes it to the world and to its better self to give the Negro every chance to prove this. To make the assertion dogmatically and then resort to all means which retard and restrict Negro development is not simply to stand convicted of insincerity before the civilized world, but, far worse than that, it is to make a nation of naturally generous, honest people to sit humiliated before their own consciences.

I believe that a straightforward, honorable treatment of black men according to their desert and achievement, will soon settle the Negro problem. If the South is right few will rise to a plane that will make their social reception a matter worth consideration; few will gain the sobriety and industry which will deserve the ballot; and few will achieve such solid moral character as will give them welcome to the fellowship of the church. If, on the other hand, Negroes with the door of opportunity thrown wide do become men of industry and achievement, of moral strength and even genius, then such rise will silence the South with an eternal silence.

The nation that enslaved the Negro owes him this trial; the section that doggedly and unreasonably kept him in slavery owes him at least this chance; and the church which professes to follow Jesus Christ and does not insist on this elemental act of justice merits the denial of the Master—"*I never knew you.*"

This, then, is the history of those mighty moral battles in the South which have given us the Negro problem. And the last great battle is not a battle of South or East, of black or white, but of all of us. The path to racial peace is straight but narrow—its following to-day means tremendous fight against inertia, prejudice, and intrenched snobbery. But it is the duty of men, it is a duty of the church, to face the problem. Not only is it their duty to face it—they *must* face it, it is impossible not to, the very attempt to ignore it is assuming an attitude. It is a problem not simply of political expediency, of economic success, but a problem above all of religious and social life; and it carries with it not simply a demand for its own solution, but beneath it lies the whole question of the real intent of our civilization: Is the civilization of the United States Christian?

It is a matter of grave consideration what answer we ought to give to that question. The precepts of Jesus Christ cannot but mean that Christianity consists of an attitude of humility, of a desire for peace, of a disposition to treat our brothers as we would have our brothers treat us, of mercy and charity toward our fellow men, of willingness to suffer persecution for right ideals and in general of love not only toward our friends but even toward our enemies.

Judged by this, it is absurd to call the practical religion of this nation Christian. We are not humble, we are impudently proud; we are not merciful, we are unmerciful toward friend and foe; we are not peaceful nor peacefully inclined as our armies and battle-ships declare; we do not want to be martyrs, we would much rather be thieves and liars so long as we can be rich; we do not seek continuously, and prayerfully inculcate, love and justice for our fellow men, but on the contrary the treatment of the poor, the unfortunate, and the black within our borders is almost a national crime.

The problem that lies before Christians is tremendous (see Note 11), and the answer must begin not by a slurring over of the one problem where these different tests of Christianity are most flagrantly disregarded, but it must begin by a girding of ourselves and a determination to see that justice is done in this country to the humblest and blackest as well as to the greatest and whitest of our citizens.

Now a word especially about the Episcopal church, whose position toward its Negro communicants is peculiar. I appreciate this position and speak of it specifically because I am one of those communicants. For four generations my family has belonged to this church and I belong to it, not by personal choice, not because I feel myself welcome within its portals, but simply because I refuse to be read outside of a church which is mine by inheritance and the service of my fathers. When the Episcopal church comes, as it does come to-day, to the Parting of the Ways, to the question as to whether its record in the future is going to be, on the Negro prpblem, as disgraceful as it has been in the past, I feel like appealing to all who are members of that church to remember that after all it is a church of Jesus Christ. Your creed and your duty enjoin upon you one, and only one, course of procedure.

In the real Christian church there is neither black nor white, rich nor poor, barbarian, Scythian, bond nor free, but all stand equal before the face of the Master. If you find that you cannot treat your Negro members as fellow Christians then do not deceive yourselves into thinking that the differences that you make or are going to make in their treatment are made for their good or for the service of the world; do not entice them to ask for a separation which your unchristian conduct forces them to prefer; do not pretend that the distinctions which you make toward them are distinctions which are made for the larger good of men, but simply confess in humility and self-abasement that you are not able to live up to your Christian vows; that you cannot treat these men as brothers and therefore you are going to set them aside and let them go their half-tended way.

I should be sorry, I should be grieved more than I can say, to see that which happened in the Southern Methodist Church and that which is practically happening in the Presbyterian Church, and that which will come in other sects—namely, a segregation of Negro Christians, come to be true among Episcopalians. It would be a sign of Christian disunity far more distressing than sectarianism. I should therefore deplore it; and yet I am also free to say that unless this church is prepared to treat its Negro members with exactly the same consideration that other members receive, with the same brotherhood and fellowship, the same encouragement to aspiration, the same privileges, similarly trained priests and similar preferment for them, then I should a great deal rather see them set aside than to see a continuation of present injustice. All I ask is that when you do this you do it with an open and honest statement of the real reasons and not with statements veiled by any hypocritical excuses.

I am therefore above all desirous that the younger men and women who are to-day taking up the leadership of this great group of men, who wish the world better and work toward that end, should begin to see the real significance of this step and of the great problem behind it. It is not a problem simply of the South, not a problem simply of this country, it is a problem of the world.

As I have said elsewhere: "Most men are colored. A belief in humanity is above all a belief in colored men." If you cannot get on with colored men in America you cannot, get on with the modern world; and if you cannot work with the humanity of this world how shall your souls ever tune with the myriad sided souls of worlds to come?

It may be that the price of the black man's survival in America and in the modern world, will be a long and shameful night of subjection to caste and segregation. If so, he will pay it, doggedly, silently, unfalteringly, for the sake of human liberty and the souls of his children's children. But as he stoops he will remember the indignation of that Jesus who cried, yonder behind heaving seas and years: "Woe unto you scribes and Pharisees, hypocrites, that strain out a gnat and swallow a camel,"—as if God cared a whit whether His Sons are born of maid, wife or widow so long as His church sits deaf to His own calling:

"Ho! every one that thirsteth, come ye to the waters and he that hath no money; come ye, buy and eat; yea, come, buy wine and milk without money and without price!"

Notes

1. See Atlanta University Publications, No 8, Section 4.

2. "Baptism doth not alter the condition of the person as to his bondage or freedom, in order that diverse masters freed from this doubt may more carefully endeavor the propagation of Christianity." (Williams I, 139.)

3. Of. Dr. Albert Bushnell Hart, "The Realities of Negro Suffrage," Proceedings of the American Political Science Association, Vol. II, 1905.

4. The Church of England through the "Society for the Propagation of the Gospel" (incorporated 1701) sent several missionaries who worked chiefly in the North. The history of the society goes on to say: "It is a matter of commendation to the clergy that they have done thus much in so great and difficult a work. But, alas! what is the instruction of a few hundreds in several years with respect to the many thousands uninstructed, unconverted, living, dying, utter pagans. It must be confessed what hath been done is as nothing with regard to what a true Christian would hope to see effected." After stating several difficulties in respect to the religious instruction of the Negroes, it is said: "But the greatest obstruction is the masters themselves do not consider enough the obligation which lies upon them to have their slaves instructed." The work of this society in America ceased in 1783. The Methodists report the following members:

1786	-	-	-	-	1,890
1790	-	-	-	-	11,682
1791	-	-	-	-	12,884
1796	-	-	-	-	12,215

Nearly all were in the North and the border states. Georgia had only 148. The Baptists had 18,000 Negro members in 1793. As to the Episcopalians, the single state of Virginia where more was done than elsewhere will illustrate the result:

"The Church Commission for Work among the Colored People at a late meeting decided to request the various rectors of parishes throughout the South to institute Sunday-schools and special services for the colored population 'such as were frequently found in the South before the war.' The commission hope for 'real advance' among the colored people in so doing. We do not agree with the commission with respect to either the wisdom or the efficiency of the plan suggested. In the first place, this 'before the war' plan was a complete failure so far as church extension was concerned, in the past when white churchmen had complete bodily control of their slaves. . . .

"The Journals of Virginia will verify the contention, that during the 'before the war' period, while the bishops and a large number of the clergy were always interested in the religious training of the slaves, yet as a matter of fact there was general apathy and indifference upon the part of the laity with respect to this matter.

"At various intervals resolutions were presented in the Annual Conventions with the avowed purpose of stimulating an interest in the religious welfare of the slaves. But despite all these efforts the Journals fail to record any great achievements along that line. . . . So faithful had been the work under such conditions that as late as 1879 there were less than 200 colored communicants reported in the whole state of Virginia." (*Church Advocate.*)

5. Charles C. Jones: "The Religious Instruction of the Negroes in the United States," Savannah, 1842. Cf. Atlanta University Publication, No. 8, passim.

6. Cf. Hart, *supra*. Note too the decrease in the proportion of free Negroes.

7. Note Dr. Cartwright's articles; DeBow's "Review", Vol. II, pp. 29, 184, 331 and 504. Cf. Fitzhugh, "Cannibals All."

8. Cf. Weeks, "Southern Quakers and Slavery," Balt. 1896; Ballagh, "Slavery in Virginia."

9. There has been in the North a generously conceived campaign in the last ten years to emphasize the good in the South and minimize the evil. Consequently many people have come to believe that men like Fleming and Murphy represent either the dominant Southern sentiment or that of a strong minority. On the contrary the brave utterances of such men represent a very small and very weak minority—a minority which is growing very slowly and which can only hope for success by means of moral support from the outside. Such moral support has not been generally given; it is Tillman, Vardaman and Dixon who get the largest hearing in the land and they represent the dominant public opinion in the South. The mass of public opinion there while it hesitates at the extreme brutality of these spokesmen is nearer to them than to Bassett or Fleming or Alderman.

10. Cf. "The Negro Church," Atlanta University Publication, No. 8. 212 pp. 1903.

11. Twenty good references on the ethical and religious aspect of slavery and the Negro problem are:

C. C. Jones, "The Religious Instruction of the Negroes in the United States," Savannah, 1842. 277 pp. 12mo.

R. F. Campbell, "Some Aspects of the Race Problem in the South," Pamphlet, 1899. Asheville, N. C. 31 pp. 8vo.

R. L. Dabney, "Defence of Virginia, and Through Her of the South," New York, 1867. 356 pp. 12mo.

Nehemiah Adams, "A South Side View of Slavery," Boston, 1854. viii, 7–214 pp. 16mo.

Richard Allen, First Bishop of the A. M. E. Church. "The life, experience and gospel labors of the Rt. Rev. Richard Allen." Written by himself. Phila., 1793. 69 pp. 8vo.

Matthew Anderson, "Presbyterianism and Its Relation to the Negro," Phila., 1897.

Geo. S. Merriam, "The Negro and the Nation," N. Y., 1906. 436 pp. 12mo.

M. S. Locke, "Anti-Slavery in America," 255 pp. 1901.

W. A. Sinclair, "The Aftermath of Slavery," etc., with an introduction by T. W. Higginson, Boston, 1905. 358 pp.

N. S. Shaler, "The Neighbor: The Natural History of Human Contrasts" (The problem of the African), Boston, 1904. vii, 342 pp. 12mo.

Atlanta University Publications:

Number 6, "The Negro Common School," 120 pp. 1901.

Number 8, "The Negro Church," 212 pp. 1903.

Number 9, "Notes on Negro Crime," 76 pp. 1904.

E. H. Abbott, "Religious life in America," A record of personal observation. N. Y.: *The Outlook*, 1902. xii, 730 pp. 8vo.

W. E. B. DuBois, "The Souls of Black Folk," Chicago, 1903.

Friends, "A Brief Testimony of the Progress of the Friends Against Slavery and the Slave-Trade," 1671–1787. Phila., 1843.

J. W. Hood, "One Hundred Years of the A. M. E. Zion Church."

S. M. Janney, "History of the Religious Society of Friends," Phila., 1859–1867.

D. A. Payne, "History of the A. M. E. Church," Nashville, 1891.

S. B. Weeks, "Anti-Slavery Sentiment in the South," Washington, D. C., 1898. "Southern Quakers and Slavery," Baltimore, 1896.

White, "The African Preacher."

Jesus Christ in Georgia

W.E.B. DuBois

The convict guard laughed.

"I don't know," he said, "I hadn't thought of that—"

He hesitated and looked at the stranger curiously. In the solemn twilight he got an impression of unusual height and soft dark eyes.

"Curious sort of acquaintance for the Colonel," he thought; then he continued aloud: "But that nigger there is bad; a born thief and ought to be sent up for life; is practically; got ten years last time—"

Here the voice of the promoter talking within interrupted; he was bending over his figures, sitting by the Colonel. He was slight, with a sharp nose.

"The convicts," he said, "would cost us $96 a year and board. Well, we can squeeze that so that it won't be over $125 apiece. Now, if these fellows are driven, they can build this line within twelve months. It will be running next April, Freights will fall fifty per cent. Why, man, you will be a millionaire in less than ten years."

The Colonel started. He was a thick, short man, with clean-shaven face, and a certain air of breeding about the lines of his countenance; the word millionaire sounded well in his ears. He thought—he thought a great deal; he almost heard the puff of the fearfully costly automobile that was coming up the road, and he said:

"I suppose we might as well hire them."

"Of course," answered the promoter.

The voice of the tall stranger in the corner broke in here:

"It will be a good thing for them?" he said, half in question.

The Colonel moved. "The guard makes strange friends," he thought to himself. "What's this man doing here, anyway?" He looked at him, or rather, looked at his eyes, and then somehow felt a warming toward him. He said:

"Well, at least it can't harm them—they're beyond that."

"It will do them good, then," said the stranger again. The promoter shrugged his shoulders.

"It will do us good," he said.

But the Colonel shook his head impatiently. He felt a desire to justify himself before those eyes, and he answered:

"Yes, it will do them good; or, at any rate, it won't make them any worse than they are."

Then he started to say something else, but here sure enough the sound of the automobile breathing at the gate stopped him and they all arose.

"It is settled, then," said the promoter.

"Yes," said the Colonel, signing his name and turning toward the stranger again.

"Are you going into town?" he asked with the Southern courtesy of white man to white man in a country town. The stranger said he was.

"Then come along in my machine. I want to talk to you about this."

They went out to the car. The stranger as he went turned again to look back at the convict. He was a tall, powerfully built black fellow. His face was sullen, with a low forehead, thick, hanging lips, and bitter eyes. There was revolt written about the mouth, and a hangdog expression. He stood bending over his pile of stones pounding listlessly.

Beside him stood a boy of twelve, yellow, with a hunted, crafty look. The convict raised his eyes, and they met the eyes of the stranger. The hammer fell from his hands.

The stranger turned slowly toward the automobile, and the Colonel introduced him. He could not exactly catch the foreign-sounding name, but he mumbled something as he presented him to his wife and little girl, who were waiting. As they whirled away he started to talk, but the stranger had taken the little girl into his lap, and together they conversed in low tones all the way home.

In some way, they did not exactly know how, they got the impression that the man was a teacher, and of course he must be a foreigner. The long cloak-like coat told this. They rode in the twilight through the half-lighted town, and at last drew up before the Colonel's mansion, with its ghostlike pillars.

The lady in the back seat was thinking of the guests she had invited to dinner, and wondered if she ought not to ask this man to stay. He seemed cultured, and she supposed he was some acquaintance of the Colonel's. It would be rather a distinction to have him there, with the Judge's wife and daughter and the Rector. She spoke almost before she thought:

"You will enter and rest awhile?"

The Colonel and the little girl insisted. For a moment the stranger seemed about to refuse. He said he was on his way North, where he had some business for his father in Pennsylvania. Then, for the child's sake, he consented. Up the steps they went, and into the dark parlor, and there they sat and talked a long time. It was a curious conversation. Afterward they did not remember exactly what was said, and yet they all remembered a certain strange satisfaction in that long talk.

Presently the nurse came for the reluctant child, and the hostess bethought herself:

"We will have a cup of tea—you will be dry and tired."

She rang and switched on a blaze of light. With one accord they all looked at the stranger, for they had hardly seen him well in the glooming twilight. The woman started in amazement and the Colonel half rose in anger. Why, the man was a mulatto, surely—even if he did not own the Negro blood, their practised eyes knew it. He was tall and straight, and the coat looked like a Jewish gabardine. His hair hung in close curls far down the sides of his face, and his face was olive, even yellow.

A peremptory order rose to the Colonel's lips, and froze there as he caught the stranger's eyes. Those eyes, where had he seen those eyes before? He remembered them long years ago—the soft tear-filled eyes of a brown girl. He remembered many things, and his face grew drawn and white. Those eyes kept burning into him, even when they were turned half away toward the staircase, where the white figure of the child hovered with her nurse, and waved goodnight. The lady sank into her chair and thought: "What will the Judge's wife say? How did the Colonel come to invite this man here? How shall we be rid of him?" She looked at the Colonel in reproachful consternation.

Just then the door opened and the old butler came in. He was an ancient black man with tufted white hair, and he held before him a large silver tray filled with a china tea service. The stranger rose slowly and stretched forth his hands as if to bless the viands. The old man paused in bewilderment, tottered and then, with sudden gladness in his eyes, dropped to his knees as the tray crashed to the floor.

"My Lord!" he whispered, "and My God!" But the woman screamed:

"Mother's china!"

The doorbell rang.

"Heavens! Here is the dinner party!" exclaimed the lady.

She turned toward the door, but there in the hall, clad in her night clothes, was the little girl. She had stolen down the stairs to see the stranger again, and the nurse above was calling in vain. The woman felt hysterical and scolded at the nurse, but the stranger had stretched out his arms, and with a glad cry the child nestled in them. "Of such," he whispered, "is the Kingdom of Heaven," as he slowly mounted the stairs with his little burden.

The mother was glad; anything to be rid of the interloper even for a moment. The bell rang again, and she hastened toward the door, which the loitering black maid was just opening. She did not notice the shadow of the stranger as he came slowly down the stairs and paused by the newel post, dark and silent.

The Judge's wife entered. She was an old woman, frilled and powdered into a caricature of youth, and gorgeously gowned. She came forward, smiling with extended hands, but just as she was opposite the stranger, a chill from somewhere seemed to strike her, and she shuddered and cried: "What a draft!" as she drew a silken shawl about her and shook hands cordially; she forgot to ask who the stranger was. The Judge strode in unseeing, thinking of a puzzling case of theft.

"Eh? What? Oh—er—yes—good-evening," he said, "good-evening."

Behind them came a young woman in the glory of youth, daintily silked, with diamonds around her fair neck, beautiful in face and form. She came in lightly, but stopped with a little gasp; then she laughed gaily and said:

"Why, I beg your pardon. Was it not curious? I thought I saw there behind your man"—she hesitated ("but he must be a servant," she argued)—"the shadow of wide white wings. It was but the light on the drapery. What a turn it gave me—so glad to be here!" And she smiled again. With her came a tall and haughty naval officer. Hearing his lady refer to the servant, he hardly looked at him, but held his gilded cap and cloak carelessly toward him; the stranger took them and placed them carefully on the rack.

Last came the Rector, a man of forty, and well clothed. He started to pass the stranger, stopped and looked at him inquiringly.

"I beg your pardon," he said, "I beg your pardon, I think I have met you?"

The stranger made no answer, and the hostess nervously hurried the guests on. But the Rector lingered and looked perplexed.

"Surely I know you; I have met you somewhere," he said, putting his hand vaguely to his head. "You—you remember me, do you not?"

The stranger quietly swept his cloak aside, and to the hostess' unspeakable relief moved toward the door.

"I never knew you," he said in low tones, as he went.

The lady murmured some faint excuse about intruders, but the Rector stood with annoyance written on his face.

"I beg a thousand pardons," he said to the hostess absently. "It is a great pleasure to be here—somehow. I thought I knew that man. I am sure I knew him, once."

The stranger had passed down the steps, and as he went the nurse-maid, lingering at the top of the staircase, flew down after him, caught his cloak, trembled, hesitated, and then kneeled in the dust. He touched her lightly with his hand and said, "Go, and sin no more."

With a glad cry the maid left the house with its open door and turned north, running, while the stranger turned eastward to the night. As they parted a long low howl rose tremulously and reverberated through the town. The Colonel's wife within shuddered.

"The bloodhounds," she said. The Rector answered carelessly.

"Another one of those convicts escaped, I suppose; really, they need severer measures." Then he stopped. He was trying to remember that stranger's name. The Judge's wife looked about for the draft and arranged her shawl. The girl glanced at the white drapery in the hall, but the young officer was bending over her, and the fires of life burned in her veins.

Howl after howl rose in the night, swelled and died away. The stranger strode rapidly along the highway and out into the deep forest. There he paused and stood waiting, tall and still. A mile up the road behind him a man was running, tall and powerful and black, with crime-stained face, with convict's stripes upon him and shackles on his legs. He ran and jumped in little short steps, and the chains rang. He fell and rose again, while the howl of the hounds rung harder behind him.

Into the forest he leaped and crept and jumped and ran, streaming with sweat; seeing the tall form rise before him, he stopped suddenly, dropped his hands in sullen impotence and sank panting to the earth. A bloodhound shot into the woods behind him, howled, whined and fawned before the stranger's feet. Hound after hound bayed, leapt and lay there; then silent, one by one, with bowed head, they crept backward toward the town.

The stranger made a cup of his hands and gave the man water to drink, bathed his hot head, and gently took the chains and irons from his feet. By and by the convict stood up. Day was dawning above the tree-tops. He looked into the stranger's face, and for a moment a gladness swept over the stains of his face.

"Why, you'se a nigger, too," he said.

Then the convict seemed anxious to justify himself.

"I never had no chance," he said furtively.

"Thou shalt not steal," said the stranger.

The man bridled.

"But how about them? Can they steal? Didn't they steal a whole year's work and then, when I stole to keep from starving—" he glanced at the stranger. "No, I didn't steal just to keep from starving. I stole to be stealing. I can't help stealing. Seems like when I sees things I just must—but, yes, I'll try!"

The convict looked down at his striped clothes, but the stranger had taken off his long coat—and put it around him, and the stripes disappeared. In the opening morning the black man started toward the low log farmhouse in the distance, and the stranger stood watching him. There was a new glory in the day. The black man's face cleared up and the farmer was glad to get him.

All day he worked as he had never worked before, and the farmer gave him some cold food toward night.

"You can sleep in the barn," he said, and turned away.

"How much do I git a day?" asked the man.

The farmer scowled:

"If you'll sign a contract for the season," he said, "I'll give you ten dollars a month."

"I won't sign no contract to be a slave," said the man doggedly.

"Yes, you will," said the farmer, threateningly, "or I'll call the convict guard." And he grinned.

The convict shrunk and slouched to the barn. As night fell he looked out and saw the farmer leave the place. Slowly he crept out and sneaked toward the house. He looked into the kitchen door. No one was there, but the supper was spread as if the mistress had laid it and gone out. He ate ravenously. Then he looked into the front room and listened. He could hear low voices on the porch. On the table lay a silver watch. He gazed at it, and in a moment was beside it, with his hand on it. Quickly he slipped out of the house and slouched toward the field. He saw his employer coming along the highway. He fled back stealthily and around to the front of the house, when suddenly he stopped. He felt the great dark eyes of the stranger and saw the same dark, cloaklike coat, where he was seated on the doorstep talking with the mistress of the house. Slowly, guiltily, he turned back, entered the kitchen and laid the watch where he had found it; and then he rushed wildly with arms outstretched back toward the stranger.

The woman had laid supper for her husband, and going down from the house had walked out toward a neighbor's. She was gone but a little while, and when she came back she started to see a dark figure on the doorsteps under the tall red oak. She thought it was the new Negro hand until he said in a soft voice:

"Will you give me bread?"

Reassured at the voice of a white man, she answered quickly in her soft Southern tones:

"Why, certainly."

She was a little woman. Once she had been handsome, but now her face was drawn with work and care. She was nervous, and was always thinking, wishing, wanting for something. She went in and got him some cornbread and a glass of cool, rich buttermilk, and then came out and sat down beside him. She began, quite unconsciously, to tell him about herself—the things she had done, and had not done, and the things she had wished. She told him of her husband, and this new farm they were trying to buy. She said it was so hard to get niggers to work. She said they ought all to be in the chain gang and made to work. Even then some ran away. Only yesterday one had escaped.

At last she gossiped of her neighbors; how good they were and how bad.

"And do you like them all?" asked the stranger.

She hesitated.

"Most of them," she said; and then, looking up into his face and putting her hand in his as though he were her father, she said:

"There are none I hate; no, none at all."

He looked away and said dreamily:

"You love your neighbor as yourself?" She hesitated—

"I try—" she began, and then looked the way he was looking; down under the hill, where lay a little, half-ruined cabin.

"They are niggers," she said briefly.

He looked at her. Suddenly a confusion came over her, and she insisted, she knew not why—

"But they are niggers."

With a sudden impulse she rose, and hurriedly lighted the lamp that stood just within the door and held it above her head. She saw his dark face and curly hair. She shrieked in angry terror, and rushed down the path; and just as she rushed down, the black convict came running up with hands outstretched. They met in midpath, and before he could stop he had run against her, and she fell heavily to earth and lay white and still. Her husband came rushing up with cry and oath:

"I knew it," he said; "it is that runaway nigger." He held the black man struggling to the earth, and raised his voice to a yell. Down the highway came the convict guard with hound and mob and gun. They poured across the fields. The farmer motioned to them.

"He—attacked—my wife," he gasped.

The mob snarled and worked silently. Right to the limb of the red oak they hoisted the struggling, writhing black man, while others lifted the dazed woman. Right and left as she tottered to the house she searched for the stranger, with a sick yearning, but the stranger was gone. And she told none of her guest.

"No—no—I want nothing," she insisted, until they left her, as they thought, asleep. For a time she lay still listening to the departure of the mob. Then she rose. She shuddered as she heard the creaking of the limb where the body hung. But resolutely she crawled to the window and peered out into the moonlight; she saw the dead man writhe. He stretched his arms out like a cross, looking upward. She gasped and clung to the window sill. Behind the swaying body, and down where the little, half-ruined cabin lay, a single flame flashed up arnid the far-off shout and cry of the mob. A fierce joy sobbed up through the terror in her soul and then sank abashed as she watched the flame rise. Suddenly whirling into one great crimson column it shot to the top of the sky and threw great arms athwart the gloom until above the world and behind the roped and swaying form below hung quivering and burning a great crimson cross.

She hid her dizzy, aching head in an agony of tears, and dared not look, for she knew. Her dry lips moved: "Despised and rejected of men."

She knew, and the very horror of it lifted her dull and shrinking eyelids. There, heaven-tall, earth-wide, hung the stranger on the crimson cross, riven and bloodstained with thorn-crowned head and pierced hands. She stretched her arms and shrieked.

He did not hear. He did not see. His calm dark eyes all sorrowful were fastened on the writhing, twisting body of the thief, and a voice came out of the winds of the night, saying:

"This day thou shalt be with me in Paradise!"

Salvation

LANGSTON HUGHES

I was saved from sin when I was going on thirteen. But not really saved. It happened like this. There was a big revival at my Auntie Reed's church. Every night for weeks there had been much preaching, singing, praying, and shouting, and some very hardened sinners had been brought to Christ, and the membership of the church had grown by leaps and bounds. Then just before the revival ended, they held a special meeting for children, "to bring the young lambs to the fold." My aunt spoke of it for days ahead. That night I was escorted to the front row and placed on the mourners' bench with all the other young sinners, who had not yet been brought to Jesus.

My aunt told me that when you were saved you saw a light, and something happened to you inside! And Jesus came into your life! And God was with you from then on! She said you could see and hear and feel Jesus in your soul. I believed her. I had heard a great many old people say the same thing and it seemed to me they ought to know. So I sat there calmly in the hot, crowded church, waiting for Jesus to come to me.

The preacher preached a wonderful rhythmical sermon, all moans and shouts and lonely cries and dire pictures of hell, and then he sang a song about the ninety and nine safe in the fold, but one little lamb was left out in the cold. Then he said: "Won't you come? Won't you come to Jesus? Young lambs, won't you come?" And he held out his arms to all us young sinners there on the mourners' bench. And the little girls cried. And some of them jumped up and went to Jesus right away. But most of us just sat there.

A great many old people came and knelt around us and prayed, old women with jet-black faces and braided hair, old men with work-gnarled hands. And the church sang a song about the lower lights are burning, some poor sinners to be saved. And the whole building rocked with prayer and song.

Still I kept waiting to *see* Jesus.

Finally all the young people had gone to the altar and were saved, but one boy and me. He was a rounder's son named Westley. Westley and I were surrounded by sisters and deacons praying. It was very hot in the church, and getting late now. Finally Westley said to me in a whisper: "God damn! I'm tired o' sitting here. Let's get up and be saved." So he got up and was saved.

Then I was left all alone on the mourners' bench. My aunt came and knelt at my knees and cried, while prayers and songs swirled all around me in the little church. The whole congregation prayed for me alone, in a mighty wail of moans and voices. And I kept waiting serenely for Jesus, waiting, waiting—but he didn't come. I wanted to see him, but nothing happened to me. Nothing! I wanted something to happen to me, but nothing happened.

I heard the songs and the minister saying: "Why don't you come? My dear child, why don't you come to Jesus? Jesus is waiting for you. He wants you. Why don't you come? Sister Reed, what is this child's name?"

"Langston," my aunt sobbed.

"Langston, why don't you come? Why don't you come and be saved? Oh, Lamb of God! Why don't you come?"

Now it was really getting late. I began to be ashamed of myself, holding everything up so long. I began to wonder what God thought about Westley, who certainly hadn't seen Jesus either, but who was now sitting proudly on the platform, swinging his knickerbockered legs and grinning down at me, surrounded by deacons and old women on their knees praying. God had not struck Westley dead for taking his name in vain or for lying in the temple. So I decided that maybe to save further trouble, I'd better lie, too, and say that Jesus had come, and get up and be saved.

So I got up.

Suddenly the whole room broke into a sea of shouting, as they saw me rise. Waves of rejoicing swept the place. Women leaped in the air. My aunt threw her arms around me. The minister took me by the hand and led me to the platform.

When things quieted down, in a hushed silence, punctuated by a few ecstatic "Amens," all the new young lambs were blessed in the name of God. Then joyous singing filled the room.

That night, for the last time in my life but one—for I was a big boy twelve years old—I cried. I cried, in bed alone, and couldn't stop. I buried my head under the quilts, but my aunt heard me. She woke up and told my uncle I was crying because the Holy Ghost had come into my life, and because I had seen Jesus. But I was really crying because I couldn't bear to tell her that I had lied, that I had deceived everybody in the church, that I hadn't seen Jesus, and that now I didn't believe there was a Jesus any more, since he didn't come to help me.

My People! My People!

ZORA NEALE HURSTON

"My people! My people!" From the earliest rocking of my cradle days, I have heard this cry go up from Negro lips. It is forced outward by pity, scorn and hopeless resignation. It is called forth by the observations of one class of Negro on the doings of another branch of the brother in black. For instance, well-mannered Negroes groan out like that when they board a train or a bus and find other Negroes on there with their shoes off, stuffing themselves with fried fish, bananas and peanuts, and throwing the garbage on the floor. Maybe they are not only eating and drinking. The offenders may be "loud-talking" the place, and holding back nothing of their private lives, in a voice that embraces the entire coach. The well-dressed Negro shrinks back in his seat at that, shakes his head and sighs, "My people! My people!"

Now, the well-mannered Negro is embarrassed by the crude behavior of the others. They are not friends, and have never seen each other before. So why should he or she be embarrassed? It is like this: the well-bred Negro has looked around and seen America with his eyes. He or she has set himself to measure up to what he thinks of as the white standard of living. He is conscious of the fact that the Negro in America needs more respect if he expects to get any acceptance at all. Therefore, after straining every nerve to get an education, maintain an attractive home, dress decently, and otherwise conform, he is dismayed at the sight of other Negroes tearing down what he is trying to build up. It is said every day, "And that good-for-nothing, trashy Negro is the one the white people judge us all by. They think we're all just alike. My people! My people!"

What that educated Negro knows further is that he can do very little towards imposing his own viewpoint on the lowlier members of his race. Class and culture stand between. The humble Negro has a built-up antagonism to the "Big Nigger." It is a curious thing that he does not resent a white man looking down on him. But he resents any lines between himself and the wealthy and educated of his own race. "He's a nigger just like us," is the sullen rejoinder. The only answer to this is "My people! My people!"

So the quiet-spoken Negro man or woman who finds himself in the midst of one of these "broadcasts" as on the train, cannot go over and say, "Don't act like that, brother. You're giving us all a black eye." He or she would know better than to try that. The performance would not only go on, it would get better with the "dickty" Negro as the butt of all the quips. The educated Negro may know all about differential calculus and the theory of evolution, but he is fighting entirely out of his class when he tries to quip with the underprivileged. The bookless may have difficulty in reading a paragraph in a newspaper, but when they get down to "playing the dozens" they have no equal in America, and, I'd risk a sizable bet, in the whole world. Starting off in the first by calling you a seven-sided son-of-a-bitch, and pausing to name the sides, they proceed to "specify" until the tip-top branch of your family tree has been "given a reading." No profit in that to the upper-class Negro, so he minds his own business and groans, "My people! My people!"

It being a traditional cry, I was bound to hear it often and under many circumstances. But it is not the only folk label that I heard. "Race Pride"—"Race Prejudice"—"Race Man"—"Race Solidarity"—"Race Consciousness"—"Race."

"Race Prejudice" I was instructed was something bad that white people used on us. It seemed that white people felt superior to black ones and would not give Negroes justice for that reason. "Race Pride" was something that, if we had it, we would feel ourselves superior to the whites. A black skin was the greatest honor that could be blessed on any man. A "Race Man" was somebody who always kept the glory and honor of his race before him. Must stand ever ready to defend the Negro race from all hurt, harm and danger. Especially if a white person said "Nigger," "You people," "Negress" or "Darkies." It was a mark of shame if somebody accused: "Why, you are not a Race Man (or woman)." People made whole careers of being "Race" men and women. They were champions of the race.

"Race Consciousness" is a plea to Negroes to bear their color in mind at all times. It was just a phrase to me when I was a child. I knew it was supposed to mean something deep. By the time I got grown I saw that it was only an imposing line of syllables, for no Negro in America is apt to forget his race. "Race Solidarity" looked like something solid in my childhood, but like all other mirages, it faded as I came close enough to look. As soon as I could think, I saw that there is no such thing as Race Solidarity in America with any group. It is freely admitted that it does not exist among Negroes. Our so-called Race Leaders cry over it. Others accept it as a natural thing that Negroes should not remain an unmelting black knot in the body politic. Our interests are too varied. Personal benefits run counter to race lines too often for it to hold. If it did, we could never fit into the national pattern. Since the race line has never held any other group in America, why expect it to be effective with us? The upper-class Negroes admit it in their own phrases. The lower-class Negroes say it with a tale.

It seems that a Negro was asked to lead the congregation in prayer. He got down on his knees and began, "Oh, Lawd, I got something to ask You, but I know You can't do it."

"Go on, Brother Isham and ask Him."

"Lawd," Brother Isham began again, "I really want to ask You something but I just know You can't do it."

"Aw, Brother Isham, go on and tell the Lawd what you want. He's the Lawd! Ain't nothing He can't do! He can even lead a butt-headed cow by the horns. You're killing up time. Go 'head on, Brother Isham, and let the church roll on."

"Well then, Lawd, I ask You to get these Negroes together, but I know You can't do it." Then there is laughter and "My people! My people!"

Hearing things like this from my childhood, sooner or later I was bound to have some curiosity about my race of people.

What fell into my ears from time to time tended more to confuse than to clarify. One thing made a liar out of the one that went before and the thing that came after. At different times I heard opposite viewpoints expressed by the same person or persons.

For instance, come school-closing time and like formal occasions, I heard speeches which brought thunderous applause. I did not know the word for it at the time, but it did not take me long to know the material was traditional. Just as folk as the songs in church. I knew that because so many people got up and used the same, identical phrases: (*a*) The Negro had made the greatest progress in fifty years of any race on the face of the globe. (*b*) Negroes composed the most *beautiful* race on earth, being just like a flower garden with every color and kind. (*c*) Negroes were the bravest men on earth, facing every danger like lions, and fighting with demons. We must remember with pride that the first blood spilled for American Independence was that of the brave and daring Crispus Attucks, a Negro who had bared his black breast to the bullets of the British tyrants at Boston, and thus struck the first blow for American liberty. They had marched with Colonel Shaw during the Civil War and hurled back the forces of the iniquitous South, who sought to hold black men in bondage. It was a Negro named Simon who had been the only one with enough pity and compassion in his heart to help the Savior bear His cross upon Calvary. It was the Negro troops under Teddy Roosevelt who won the battle of San Juan Hill.

It was the genius of the Negro which had invented the steam engine, the cotton gin, the airbrake, and numerous other things—but conniving white men had seen the Negro's inventions and run off and put them into practice before the Negro had a chance to do anything about it. Thus the white man got credit for what the genius of the Negro brain had produced. Were it not for the envy and greed of the white man, the Negro would hold his rightful place—the noblest and the greatest man on earth.

The people listening would cheer themselves hoarse and go home feeling good. Over the fences next day it would be agreed that it was a wonderful speech, and nothing but the God's truth. What a great people we would be if we only had our rights!

But my own pinnacle would be made to reel and rock anyway by other things I heard from the very people who always applauded "the great speech," when it was shouted to them from the schoolhouse rostrum. For instance, let some member of the community do or say something which was considered either dumb or underhand: the verdict would be "Dat's just like a nigger!" or "Nigger from nigger leave nigger"—("Nothing from nothing leave nothing"). It was not said in either admiration or pity. Utter scorn was in the saying. "Old Cuffy just got to cut de fool, you know. Monkey see, monkey do. Nigger see de white man do something, he jump in and try to do like de white man, and make a great big old mess." "My people! My people!"

"Yeah, you's mighty right. Another monkey on de line. De white man, you understand, he was a railroad engineer, so he had a pet monkey he used to take along wid him all de time. De monkey, he set up there in de cab wid de engineer and see what he do to run de train. Way after while, figger he can run de train just as good as de engineer his own self. He was just itching to git at dat throttle and bust dat main line wide open. Well, one day de engineer jumped down at de station to git his orders and old monkey seen his chance. He just jumped up in de engineer's seat, grabbed a holt of dat throttle, and dat engine was splitting de wind down de track. So de engineer sent a message on ahead, say 'Clear de track. Monkey on de line!' Well, Brer Monk he was holding de throttle wide open and jumping up and down and laughing fit to kill. Course, he didn't know nothing about no side tracks and no switches and no schedules, so he was making a mile a minute when he hit a open switch and a string of box cars was standing on de siding. Ker-blam-er-lam-er-lam! And dat was de last of Brer Engine-driving Monk. Lovely monkey he was, but a damned poor engineer." "My people! My people!"

Everybody would laugh at that, and the laughter puzzled me some. Weren't Negroes the smartest people on earth, or something like that? Somebody ought to remind the people of what we had heard at the schoolhouse. Instead of that, there would be more monkey stories.

There was the one about the white doctor who had a pet monkey who wanted to be a doctor. Kept worrying his master to show him how, and the doctor had other troubles, too. Another man had a bulldog who used to pass the doctor's gate every day and pick a fight with the monkey. Finally, the doctor saw a way to stop the monkey from worrying him about showing him how to be a doctor. "Whip that bulldog until he evacuates, then bring me some of it, monkey. I'll take it and show you how to be a doctor, and then I'll treat it in a way so as to ruin that bulldog for life. He won't be no more trouble to you."

"Oh, I'll git it, boss. Don't you worry. I sho' wants to be a doctor, and then again, dat old bulldog sho' is worrisome."

No sooner did the bulldog reach the gate that day, than the monkey, which could not wait for the bulldog to start the fight as usual, jumped on the dog. The monkey was all over him like gravy over rice. He put all he had into it and it went on until the doctor came out and drove the dog off and gave the monkey a chance to bolt into the office with what he had been fighting for.

"Here 'tis, boss. It was a tight fight, but I got it."

"Fine! Fine!" the doctor told him. "Now, gimme that bottle over there. I'll fix that bulldog so he'll never be able to sit down again. When I get through with this, he'll be ruined for life."

"Hold on there, boss! Hold on there a minute! I wish you wouldn't do dat, boss."

"How come? You want to get rid of that old bulldog, don't you?"

"Dat's right, I sho' do."

"Well, why don't you want me to fix him, then?"

"Well, boss, you see it's like dis. Dat was a tight fight, a mighty tight fight. I could have been mistaken about dat bulldog, boss, we was all tangled up together so bad. You better leave dat fixing business alone, boss. De wrong man might git hurt."

There were many other tales, equally ludicrous, in which the Negro, sometimes symbolized by the monkey, and sometimes named outright, ran off with the wrong understanding of what he had seen and heard. Several white and Negro proposals of marriage were compared, and the like. The white suitor had said his love had dove's eyes. His valet had hurried to compliment his girl by saying she had dog's eyes, and so on.

There was a general acceptance of the monkey as kinfolks. Perhaps it was some distant memory of tribal monkey reverence from Africa which had been forgotten in the main, but remembered in some vague way. Perhaps it was an acknowledgment of our talent for mimicry with the monkey as a symbol.

The classic monkey parable, which is very much alive wherever the Negroes congregate in America, is the one about "My people!"

It seems that a monkey squatted down in the middle of a highway to play. A Cadillac full of white people came along, saw the monkey at play and carefully drove around him. Then came a Buick full of more white people and did the same. The monkey kept right on playing. Way after a while a T-model Ford came along full of Negroes. But instead of driving around the monkey, the car headed straight for him. He only saved his life by a quick leap to the shoulder of the road. He sat there and watched the car rattle off in the distance and sighed "My people! My people!"

A new addition to the tale is that the monkey has quit saying "My people!" He is now saying, "Those people! Those people!"

I found the Negro, and always the blackest Negro, being made the butt of all jokes,—particularly black women.

They brought bad luck for a week if they came to your house of a Monday morning. They were evil. They slept with their fists balled up ready to fight and squabble even while they were asleep. They even had evil dreams. White, yellow and brown girls dreamed about roses and perfume and kisses. Black gals dreamed about guns, razors, ice-picks, hatchets and hot lye. I heard men swear they had seen women dreaming and knew these things to be true.

"Oh, gwan!" somebody would chide, laughing. You know dat ain't so."

"Oh, now, he ain't lying," somebody else would take up the theme. "I know for my own self. I done slept wid yaller women and I done slept wid black ones. They *is* evil. You marry a yaller or a brown woman and wake her up in de night and she will sort of stretch herself and say, 'I know what I was dreaming when you woke me up. I was dreaming I had done baked you a chicken and cooked you a great big old cake, and we was at de table eating our dinner out of de same plate, and I was sitting on your lap and we was just enjoying ourselves to death!' Then she will kiss you more times than you ask her to, and go on back to sleep. But you take and wake up a black gal, now! First thing she been sleeping wid her fists balled up, and you shake her, she'll lam you five or six times before you can get her awake. Then when she do git wake she'll have off and ast you, 'Nigger, what you wake me up for? Know what I was dreaming when you woke me up? I dreamt dat you shook your old rusty black fist under my nose and I split your head open wid a axe.' Then she'll kick your feets away from hers, snatch de covers all over on her side, ball up her fists agin, and gwan back to sleep. You can't tell me nothing. I know." "My people!"

This always was, and is still, good for a raucous burst of laughter. I listened to this talk and became more and more confused. If it was so honorable and glorious to be black, why was it the yellow-skinned people among us had so much prestige? Even a child in the first grade could see that this was so from what happened in the classroom and on school programs. The light-skinned children were always the angels, fairies and queens of school plays. The lighter the girl, the more money and prestige she was apt, and expected, to marry. So on into high-school years, I was asking myself questions. Were Negroes the great heroes I heard about from the platform, or were they the ridiculous monkeys of everyday talk? Was it really honorable to be black? There was even talk that it was no use for Negro boys and girls to rub all the hair off of their heads against college walls. There was no place for them to go with it after they got all this education. Some of the older heads held that it was too much for Negroes to handle. Better leave such things for the white folks, who knew what to do with it. But there were others who were all for pushing ahead. I saw the conflict in my own home between my parents. My mother was the one to dare all. My father was satisfied.

This Negro business came home to me in incidents and ways. There was the time when Old Man Bronner was taken out and beaten. Mr. Bronner was a white man of the poor class who had settled in aristocratic Maitland. One night just after dark, we heard terrible cries back in the woods behind Park Lake. Sam Moseley, his brother Elijah, and Ike Clarke, hurried up to our gate and they were armed. The howls of pain kept up. Old fears and memories must have stirred inside of the grown folks. Many people closed and barred their doors. Papa and the men around our gate were sullen and restless as the cries churned over the woods and lake.

"Who do you reckon it is?" Sam Moseley asked.

"I don't know for sure, but some thinks it's Jim Watson. Anyhow, he ain't home yet," Clarke said, and all of them looked at each other in an asking way.

Finally Papa said, "Well, hold on a minute till I go get my rifle."

" 'Tain't no ifs and buts about it," Elijah Moseley said gravely, "We can't leave Jim Watson be beat to death like that."

Papa had sensed that these armed men had not come to merely stand around and talk. They had come to see if he would go with the rest. When he came out shoving the sixteen bullets into his rifle, and dropping more into his pocket, Mama made no move to stop him. "Well, we all got families," he said with an attempt at lightness. "Shoot off your gun, somebody, so de rest will know we ready."

Papa himself pointed his Winchester rifle at the sky and fired a shot. Another shot answered him from around the store and a huddle of figures came hurrying up the road in the dark.

"It's Jim Watson. Us got to go git him!" and the dozen or more men armed with double-barreled shotguns, breech-loaders, pistols and Papa's repeating Winchester hurried off on their grim mission. Perhaps not a single one of them expected to return alive. No doubt they hoped. But they went.

Mama gasped a short sentence of some sort and herded us all into the house and barred the door. Lights went out all over the village and doors were barred. Axes had been dragged in from woodpiles, grass-hooks, pitch-forks and scythes were ranked up in corners behind those barred doors. If the men did not come back, or if they only came back in part, the women and children were ready to do the best they could. Mama spoke only to say she wished Hezekiah and John, the two biggest boys, had not gone to Maitland late in the afternoon. They were not back and she feared they might start home and—But she did not cry. Our seven hounds with big, ferocious Ned in the lead, barked around the house. We huddled around Mama in her room and kept quiet. There was not a human sound in all the village. Nothing had ever happened before in our vicinity to create such tension. But people had memories and told tales of what happened back there in Georgia, and Alabama and West Florida that made the skin of the young crawl with transmitted memory, and reminded the old heads that they were still flinchy.

The dark silence of the village kept up for an hour or more. The once loud cries fell and fell until our straining ears could no longer find them. Strangest of all, not a shot was fired. We huddled in the dark and waited, and died a little, and waited. The silence was ten times more punishing than the cries.

At long last, a bubble of laughing voices approached our barn from the rear. It got louder and took on other dimensions between the barn and the house. Mama hissed at us to shut up when, in fact, nobody was saying a thing.

"Hey, there Little-Bits," Papa bellowed. "Open up!"

"Strike a light, Daught," Mama told my sister, feeling around in the dark to find Sarah's hand to give her the matches which I had seen clutched in her fingers before she had put out the light. Mama had said very little, and I could not see her face in the dark; somehow she could not scratch a match now that Papa was home again.

All of the men came in behind Papa, laughing and joking, perhaps more from relief than anything else.

"Don't stand there grinning like a chessy cat, Mr. Hurston," Mama scolded. "You ain't told me a thing."

"Oh, it wasn't Jim Watson at all, Lulu. You remember 'bout a week ago Old Man Bronner wrote something in de Orlando paper about H.'s daughter and W.B.G.'s son being seen sitting around the lakes an awful lot?"

"Yeah, I heard something about it."

"Well, you know those rich white folks wasn't going to 'low nothing like dat. So some of 'em waylaid him this evening. They pulled him down off of a load of hay he was hauling and drug him off back there in de woods and tanned his hide for him."

"Did y'all see any of it?"

"Nope, we could hear him hollering for a while, though. We never got no further than the lake. A white man, one of the G—— boys was standing in the bushes at de road. When we got ready to turn off round de lake he stepped out and spoke to us and told us it didn't concern us. They had Bronner down there tied down on his all-fours, and de men was taking turns wid dat bull whip. They must have been standing on tip-toes to do it. You could hear them licks clear out to de road."

The men all laughed. Somebody mocked Bronner's cries and moans a time or two and the crowd laughed immoderately. They had gone out to rescue a neighbor or die in the attempt, and they were back with their families. So they let loose their insides and laughed. They resurrected a joke or two and worried it like a bone and laughed some more. Then they just laughed. The men who spoke of members of their race as monkeys had gone out to die for one. The men who were always saying, "My skin-folks, but not kinfolks; my race but not my taste," had rushed forth to die for one of these same contemptibles. They shoved each other around and laughed. So I could see that what looked like ridicule was really the Negro poking a little fun at himself. At the same time, just like other people, hoping and wishing he was what the orators said he was.

My mother eased back in her chair and took a dip of snuff. Maybe she did not feel so well, for she didn't get tickled at all. After a while, she ordered us off to bed in a rough voice. Time was, and the men scattered. Mama sat right where she was until Hezekiah and John came home around ten o'clock. She gave them an awful going over with her tongue for staying out late, and then she eased to bed.

I was dredged up inside that night, so I did not think about the incident's general connection with race. Besides I had to go to sleep. But days later, it was called to my recollection again. There was a program at the Methodist Church, and Mrs. Mattie Moseley, it was announced, was to have a paper. She was also going to have a fine new dress to read it in. We all wanted to see the dress.

The time came and she had the dress on. The subject of her paper was, "What will the Negroes do with the whites?" I do not know what she decided was to be done. It seemed equally unimportant to the rest of the town. I remember that everybody said it was a fine subject. But the next week, the women talked about nothing else but the new wrist-watch she had on. It was the first one ever seen in our town.

But in me, the affair stirred up more confusion. Why bring the subject up? Something was moving around me which I had no hooks to grasp. What was this about white and black people that was being talked about?

Certainly nothing changed in the village. The townspeople who were in domestic service over in Maitland or Winter Park went to work as usual. The white people interested in Eatonville came and went as before. Mr. Irving Bacheller, the author, who had a show place in Winter Park, petted up Willie Sewell, who was his head gardener, in the same old way. Bishop Whipple petted Elijah Moseley, and Mrs. Mars, who was his sister, did lots of things for Lulu Moseley, Elijah's wife. What was all the talk about? It certainly was puzzling to me.

As time went on, the confusion grew. By the time that I got to high school, I was conscious of a group that was neither the top nor the bottom of Negrodom. I met the type which designates itself as "the better-thinking Negro." I was thrown off my stride by finding that while they considered themselves Race Champions, they wanted nothing to do with anything frankly Negroid. They drew color lines within the race. The Spirituals, the Blues, *any* definitely Negroid thing was just not done. They went to the trouble at times to protest the use of them by Negro artists. Booker T. Washington was absolutely vile for advocating industrial education. There was no analysis, no seeking for merits. If it was old cuffy, down with it! "My People! My People!"

This irritated me until I got to the place where I could analyze. The thing they were trying to do went wrong because it lacked reason. It lacked reason because they were attempting to stand equal with the best in America without having the tools to work with. They were attempting a flight away from Negrodom because they felt that there was so much scorn for black skin in the nation that their only security was in flight. They lacked the happy carelessness of a class beneath them and the understanding of the top-flight Negro above them. Once, when they used to set their mouths in what they thought was the Boston Crimp, and ask me about the great differences between the ordinary Negro and "the better-thinking Negro," I used to show my irritation by saying I did not know who the better-thinking Negro was. I knew who the think-they-are-better Negroes were, but who were the better-thinkers was another matter. But when I came to understand what made them make their useless motions, and saw them pacing a cage that wasn't there, I felt more sympathy than irritation. If they want to establish a sort of fur-coat peerage, let 'em! Since they can find no comfort where they happened to be born, no especial talents to lift them, and other doors are closed to them, they have to find some pleasure somewhere in life. They have to use whatever their mentality provides. "My People! My People!"

But one thing and another kept the conflict going on inside me, off and on for years. Sometimes I was sure that the Negro race was all that the platform speakers said. Then I would hear so much self-deprecation that I would be deflated. Over and over I heard people shake their heads and explain us by the supposed prayer of a humble Negro, who got down on his knees and said: "Lawd, you know I ain't nothing. My wife, she ain't nothing. My chillun ain't nothing, and if you fool 'round us, Lawd, you won't be nothing neither."

So I sensed early, that the Negro race was not one band of heavenly love. There was stress and strain inside as well as out. Being black was not enough. It took more than a community of skin color to make your love come down on you. That was the beginning of my peace.

Light came to me when I realized that I did not have to consider any racial group as a whole. God made them duck by duck and that was the only way I could see them. I learned that skins were no measure of what was inside people. So none of the Race clichés meant anything any more. I began to laugh at both white and black who claimed special blessings on the basis of race. Therefore I saw no curse in being black, nor no extra flavor by being white I saw no benefit in excusing my looks by claiming to be half Indian. In fact, I boast that I am the only Negro in the United States whose grandfather on the mother's side was *not* an Indian chief. Neither did I descend from George Washington, Thomas Jefferson, or any Governor of a Southern state. I see no need to manufacture me a legend to beat the facts. I do not coyly admit to a touch of the tarbrush to my Indian and white ancestry. You can consider me Old Tar-Brush in person if you want to. I am a mixed-blood, it is true, but I differ from the party line in that I neither consider it an honor nor a shame. I neither claim Jefferson as my grandpa, nor exclaim, "Just look how that white man took advantage of my grandma!" It does not matter in the first place, and then in the next place, I do not know how it came about. Since nobody ever told me, I give my ancestress the benefit of the doubt. She probably ran away from him just as fast as she could. But if that white man could run faster than my grandma, that was no fault of hers. Anyway, you must remember, he didn't have a thing to do but to keep on running forward. She, being the pursued, had to look back over her shoulder every now and then to see how she was doing. And you know your ownself, how looking backwards slows people up.

In this same connection, I have been told that God meant for all the so-called races of the world to stay just as they are, and the people who say that may be right. But it is a well-known fact that no matter where two sets of people come together, there are bound to be some in-betweens. It looks like the command was given to people's heads, because the other parts don't seem to have heard tell. When the next batch is made up, maybe Old Maker will straighten all that out. Maybe the men will be more tangle-footed and the women a whole lot more faster around the feet. That will bring about a great deal more of racial and other kinds of purity, but a somewhat less exciting world. It might work, but I doubt it. There will have to be something harder to get across than an ocean to keep East and West from meeting. But maybe Old Maker will have a remedy. Maybe even He has given up. Perhaps in a moment of discouragement He turned the job over to Adolf Hitler and went on about His business of making more beetles.

I do not share the gloomy thought that Negroes in America are doomed to be stomped out bodaciously, nor even shackled to the bottom of things. Of course some of them will be tromped out, and some will always, be at the bottom, keeping company with other bottom-folks. It would be against all nature for all the Negroes to be either at the bottom, top, or in between. It has never happened with anybody else, so why with us? No, we will go where the internal drive carries us like everybody else. It is up to the individual. If you haven't got it, you can't show it. If you have got it, you can't hide it. That is one of the strongest laws God ever made.

I maintain that I have been a Negro three times—a Negro baby, a Negro girl and a Negro woman. Still, if you have received no clear cut impression of what the Negro in America is like, then you are in the same place with me. There is no *The Negro* here. Our lives are so diversified, internal attitudes so varied, appearances and capabilities so different, that there is no possible classification so catholic that it will cover us all, except My people! My people!

Religion

ZORA NEALE HURSTON

You wouldn't think that a person who was born with God in the house would ever have any questions to ask on the subject.

But as early as I can remember, I was questing and seeking. It was not that I did not hear. I tumbled right into the Missionary Baptist Church when I was born. I saw the preachers and the pulpits, the people and the pews. Both at home and from the pulpit, I heard my father, known to thousands as "Reverend Jno" (an abbreviation for John) explain all about God's habits, His heaven, His ways and means. Everything was known and settled.

From the pews I heard a ready acceptance of all that Papa said. Feet beneath the pews beat out a rhythm as he pictured the scenery of heaven. Heads nodded with conviction in time to Papa's words. Tense snatches of tune broke out and some shouted until they fell into a trance at the recognition of what they heard from the pulpit. Come "love feast"* some of the congregation told of getting close enough to peep into God's sitting-room windows. Some went further. They had been inside the place and looked all around. They spoke of sights and scenes around God's throne.

That should have been enough for me. But somehow it left a lack in my mind. They should have looked and acted differently from other people after experiences like that. But these people looked and acted like everybody else—or so it seemed to me. They plowed, chopped wood, went possum-hunting, washed clothes, raked up back yards and cooked collard greens like anybody else. No more ornaments and nothing. It mystified me. There were so many things they neglected to look after while they were right there in the presence of All-Power. I made up my mind to do better than that if ever I made the trip.

I wanted to know, for instance, why didn't God make grown babies instead of those little measly things that messed up didies and cried all the time? What was the sense in making babies with no teeth? He knew that they had to have teeth, didn't He? So why not give babies their teeth in the beginning instead of hiding the toothless things in hollow stumps and logs for grannies and doctors to find and give to people? He could see all the trouble people had with babies, rubbing their gums and putting wood-lice around their necks to get them to cut teeth. Why did God hate for children to play on Sundays? If Christ, God's son, hated to die, and God hated for Him to die and have everybody grieving over it ever since, why did He have to do it? Why did people die anyway?

It was explained to me that Christ died to save the world from sin and then too, so that folks did not have to die any more. That was a simple, clear-cut explanation. But then I heard my father and other preachers accusing people of sin. They went so far as to say that people were so prone to sin, that they sinned with every breath they drew. You couldn't even breathe without sinning! How could that happen if we had already been saved from it? So far as the dying part was concerned, I saw enough funerals to know that somebody was dying. It seemed to me that somebody had been fooled and I so stated to my father and two of his colleagues. When they got through with me, I knew better than to say that out loud again, but their shocked and angry tirades did nothing for my bewilderment. My head was full of misty fumes of doubt.

Neither could I understand the passionate declarations of love for a being that nobody could see. Your family, your puppy and the new bull-calf, yes. But a spirit away off who found fault with everybody all the time, that was more than I could fathom. When I was asked if I loved God, I always said yes because I knew that that was the thing I was supposed to say. It was a guilty secret with me for a long time. I did not dare ask even my chums if they meant it when they said they loved God with all their souls and minds and hearts, and would be glad to die if He wanted them to. Maybe they had found out how to do it, and I was afraid of what they might say if they found out I hadn't. Maybe they wouldn't even play with me any more.

---

* The "Love Feast" or "Experience Meeting" is a meeting held either the Friday night or the Sunday morning before Communion. Since no one is supposed to take Communion unless he or she is in harmony with all other members, there are great protestations of love and friendship. It is an opportunity to reaffirm faith plus anything the imagination might dictate.

"Religion", chapter 15 from *Dust Tracks on a Road* by Zora Neale Hurston. Copyright 1942 by Zora Neale Hurston; renewed © 1970 by John C. Hurston. Reprinted by permission of HarperCollins Publishers.

As I grew, the questions went to sleep in me. I just said the words, made the motions and went on. My father being a preacher, and my mother superintendent of the Sunday School, I naturally was always having to do with religious ceremonies. I even enjoyed participation at times; I was moved, not by the spirit, but by action, more or less dramatic.

I liked revival meetings particularly. During these meetings the preacher let himself go. God was called by all of His praise-giving names. The scenery of heaven was described in detail. Hallelujah Avenue and Amen Street were paved with gold so fine that you couldn't drop a pea on them but what they rang like chimes. Hallelujah Avenue ran north and south across heaven, and was tuned to sound alto and bass. Amen Street ran east and west and was tuned to "treble" and tenor. These streets crossed each other right in front of the throne and made harmony all the time. Yes, and right there on that corner was where all the loved ones who had gone on before would be waiting for those left behind.

Oh yes! They were all there in their white robes with the glittering crowns on their heads, golden girdles clasped about their waists and shoes of jeweled gold on their feet, singing the hallelujah song and waiting. And as they walked up and down the golden streets, their shoes would sing, "sol me, sol do" at every step.

Hell was described in dramatic fury. Flames of fire leaped up a thousand miles from the furnaces of Hell, and raised blisters on a sinning man's back before he hardly got started downward. Hell-hounds pursued their ever-dying souls. Everybody under the sound of the preacher's voice was warned, while yet they were on pleading terms with mercy, to take steps to be sure that they would not be a brand in that eternal burning.

Sinners lined the mourner's bench from the opening night of the revival. Before the week was over, several or all of them would be "under conviction." People, solemn of face, crept off to the woods to "praying ground" to seek religion. Every church member worked on them hard, and there was great clamor and rejoicing when any of them "come through" religion.

The pressure on the unconverted was stepped up by music and high drama. For instance I have seen my father stop preaching suddenly and walk down to the front edge of the pulpit and breathe into a whispered song. One of his most effective ones was:

Run! Run! Run to the City of Refuge, children!
Run! Oh, run! Or else you'll be consumed.

The congregation working like a Greek chorus behind him, would take up the song and the mood and hold it over for a while even after he had gone back into the sermon at high altitude:

Are you ready-ee? Hah!
For that great day, hah!
When the moon shall drape her face in mourning, hah!
And the sun drip down in blood, hah!
When the stars, hah!
Shall burst forth from their diamond sockets, hah!
And the mountains shall skip like lambs, hah!
Havoc will be there, my friends, hah!
With her jaws wide open, hah!
And the sinner-man, hah!
He will run to the rocks, hah!
And cry, Oh rocks! Hah!
Hide me! Hah!
Hide me from the face of an angry God, hah!
Hide me, Ohhhhhh!
But the rocks shall cry, hah!
Git away! Sinner man git away, hah!

(Tense harmonic chant seeps over the audience.)

    You run to de rocks,
CHORUS: You can't hide
SOLOIST: Oh, you run to de rocks

CHORUS: Can't hide
SOLOIST: Oh, run to de mountain, you can't hide
ALL: Can't hide sinner, you can't hide.
         Rocks cry 'I'm burning too, hah!
         In the eternal burning, hah!
         Sinner man! Hah!
         Where will you stand? Hah!
         In that great gittin'-up morning? Hah!

The congregation would be right in there at the right moment bearing Papa up and heightening the effect of the fearsome picture a hundredfold. The more susceptible would be swept away on the tide and "come through" shouting, and the most reluctant would begin to waver. Seldom would there be anybody left at the mourners' bench when the revival meeting was over. I have seen my father "bring through" as many as seventy-five in one two-week period of revival. Then a day would be set to begin the induction into the regular congregation. The first thing was to hear their testimony or Christian experience, and thus the congregation could judge whether they had really "got religion" or whether they were faking and needed to be sent back to "lick de calf over" again.

It was exciting to hear them tell their "visions." This was known as admitting people to the church on "Christian experience." This was an exciting time.

These visions are traditional. I knew them by heart as did the rest of the congregation, but still it was exciting to see how the converts would handle them. Some of them made up new details. Some of them would forget a part and improvise clumsily or fill up the gap with shouting. The audience knew, but everybody acted as if every word of it was new.

First they told of suddenly becoming conscious that they had to die. They became conscious of their sins. They were Godly sorry. But somehow, they could not believe. They started to pray. They prayed and they prayed to have their sins forgiven and their souls converted. While they laid under conviction, the hell-hounds pursued them as they ran for salvation. They hung over Hell by one strand of hair. Outside of the meeting, any of the listeners would have laughed at the idea of anybody with hair as close to their heads as ninety-nine is to a hundred hanging over Hell or anywhere else by a strand of that hair. But it was part of the vision and the congregation shuddered and groaned at the picture in a fervent manner. The vision must go on. While the seeker hung there, flames of fire leaped up and all but destroyed their ever-dying souls. But they called on the name of Jesus and immediately that dilemma was over. They then found themselves walking over Hell on a foot-log so narrow that they had to put one foot right in front of the other while the howling hell-hounds pursued them relentlessly. Lord! They saw no way of rescue. But they looked on the other side and saw a little white man and he called to them to come there. So they called the name of Jesus and suddenly they were on the other side. He poured the oil of salvation into their souls and, hallelujah! They never expect to turn back. But still they wouldn't believe. So they asked God, if he had saved their souls, to give them a sign. If their sins were forgiven and their souls set free, please move that big star in the west over to the east. The star moved over. But still they wouldn't believe. If they were really saved, please move that big oak tree across the road. The tree skipped across the road and kept on growing just like it had always been there. Still they didn't believe. So they asked God for one more sign. Would He please make the sun shout so they could be sure. At that God got mad and said He had shown them all the signs He intended to. If they still didn't believe, He would send their bodies to the grave, where the worm never dies, and their souls to Hell, where the fire is never quenched. So then they cried out "I believe! I believe!" Then the dungeon shook and their chains fell off. "Glory! I know I got religion! I know I been converted and my soul set free! I never will forget that day when the morning star bust in my soul. I never expect to turn back!"

The convert shouted. Ecstatic cries, snatches of chants, old converts shouting in frenzy with the new. When the tumult finally died down, the pastor asks if the candidate is acceptable and there is unanimous consent. He or she is given the right hand of fellowship, and the next candidate takes the floor. And so on to the end.

I know now that I liked that part because it was high drama. I liked the baptisms in the lake too, and the funerals for the same reason. But of the inner thing, I was right where I was when I first began to seek answers.

Away from the church after the emotional fire had died down, there were little jokes about some of the testimony. For instance a deacon said in my hearing, "Sister Seeny ought to know better than to be worrying God about moving the sun for her. She asked Him to move de tree to convince her, and He done it. Then she took and asked Him to move a star for her and He done it. But When she kept on worrying Him about moving the sun, He took and told her, says, 'I' I don't mind moving that tree for you, and I don't mind moving a star just to pacify your mind, because I got plenty of *them*. I aint got but one sun, Seeny, and I aint going to be shoving it around to please you and nobody else. I'd like mighty much for you to believe, but if you can't believe without me moving my sun for you, you can just go right on to Hell.'"

The thing slept on in me until my college years without any real decision. I made the necessary motions and forgot to think. But when I studied both history and philosophy, the struggle began again.

When I studied the history of the great religions of the world, I saw that even in his religion man carried himself along. His worship of strength was there. God was made to look that way too. We see the Emperor Constantine, as pagan as he could lay in his hide, having his famous vision of the cross with the injunction: "*In Hoc Signo Vinces,*" and arising next day not only to win a great battle, but to start out on his missionary journey with his sword. He could not sing like Peter, and he could not preach like Paul. He probably did not even have a good straining voice like my father to win converts and influence people. But he had his good points—one of them being a sword—and a seasoned army. And the way he brought sinners to repentance was nothing short of miraculous. Whole tribes and nations fell under conviction just as soon as they heard he was on the way. They did not wait for any stars to move, nor trees to jump the road. By the time he crossed the border, they knew they had been converted. Their testimony was in on Christian experience and they were all ready for the right hand of fellowship and baptism. It seems that Reverend Brother Emperor Constantine carried the gospel up and down Europe with his revival meetings to such an extent that Christianity really took on. In Rome where Christians had been looked upon as rather indifferent lion-bait at best, and among other things as keepers of virgins in their homes for no real good to the virgins, Christianity mounted. Where before, Emperors could scarcely find enough of them to keep the spectacles going, now they were everywhere, in places high and low. The arrow had left the bow. Christianity was on its way to world power that would last. That was only the beginning. Military power was to be called in time and time again to carry forward the gospel of peace. There is not apt to be any difference of opinion between you and a dead man.

It was obvious that two men, both outsiders, had given my religion its chances of success. First the Apostle Paul, who had been Saul, the erudite Pharisee, had arisen with a vision when he fell off of his horse on the way to Damascus. He not only formulated the religion, but exerted his brilliant mind to carry it to the most civilized nations of his time. Then Constantine took up with force where Paul left off with persuasion.

I saw the same thing with different details, happen in all the other great religions, and seeing these things, I went to thinking and questing again. I have achieved a certain peace within myself, but perhaps the seeking after the inner heart of truth will never cease in me. All sorts of interesting speculations arise.

So, having looked at the subject from many sides, studied beliefs by word of mouth and then as they fit into great rigid forms, I find I know a great deal about form, but little or nothing about the mysteries I sought as a child. As the ancient tent-maker said, I have come out of the same door wherein I went.

But certain things have seemed to me to be true as I heard the tongues of those who had speech, and listened at the lips of books. It seems to me to be true that heavens are placed in the sky because it is the unreachable. The unreachable and therefore the unknowable always seems divine—hence, religion. People need religion because the great masses fear life and its consequences. Its responsibilities weigh heavy. Feeling a weakness in the face of great forces, men seek an alliance with omnipotence to bolster up their feeling of weakness, even though the omnipotence they rely upon is a creature of their own minds. It gives them a feeling of security. Strong, self-determining men are notorious for their lack of reverence. Constantine, having converted millions to Christianity by the sword, himself refused the consolation of Christ until his last hour. Some say not even then.

As for me, I do not pretend to read God's mind. If He has a plan of the universe worked out to the smallest detail, it would be folly for me to presume to get down on my knees and attempt to revise it. That, to me, seems the highest form of sacrilege. So I do not pray. I accept the means at my disposal for working out my destiny. It seems to me that I have been given a mind and will-power for that very purpose. I do not expect God to single me out and grant me advantages over my fellow men. Prayer is for those who need it. Prayer seems to me a cry of weakness, and an attempt to avoid, by trickery, the rules of the game as laid down. I do not choose to admit weakness. I accept the challenge of responsibility. Life, as it is, does not frighten me, since I have made my peace with the niverse as I find it, and bow to its laws. The ever-sleepless sea in its bed, crying out "How long?" to Time; million-formed and never motionless flame; the contemplation of these two aspects alone, affords me sufficient food for ten spans of my expected lifetime. It seems to me that organized creeds are collections of words around a wish. I feel no need for such. However, I would not, by word or deed, attempt to deprive another of the consolation it affords. It is simply not for me. Somebody else may have my rapturous glance at the archangels. The springing of the yellow line of morning out of the misty deep of dawn, is glory enough for me. I know that nothing is destructible; things merely change forms. When the consciousness we know as life ceases, I know that I shall still be part and parcel of the world. I was a part before the sun rolled into shape and burst forth in the glory of change. I was, when the earth was hurled out from its fiery rim. I shall return with the earth to Father Sun, and still exist in substance when the sun has lost its fire, and disintegrated in infinity to perhaps become a part of the whirling rubble in space. Why fear? The stuff of my being is matter, ever changing, ever moving, but never lost; so what need of denominations and creeds to deny myself the comfort of all my fellow men? The wide belt of the universe has no need for finger-rings. I am one with the infinite and need no other assurance.

Letter from a Birmingham Jail

Martin Luther King, Jr.

My dear fellow clergymen,

While confined here in the Birmingham city jail, I came across your recent statement calling our present activities "unwise and untimely." Seldom, if ever, do I pause to answer criticism of my work and ideas. If I sought to answer all of the criticisms that cross my desk, my secretaries would be engaged in little else in the course of the day, and I would have no time for constructive work. But since I feel that you are men of genuine good will and your criticisms are sincerely set forth, I would like to answer your statement in what I hope will be patient and reasonable terms.

I think I should give the reason for my being in Birmingham, since you have been influenced by the argument of "outsiders coming in." I have the honor of serving as president of the Southern Christian Leadership Conference, an organization operating in every southern state, with headquarters in Atlanta, Georgia. We have some eighty-five affiliate organizations all across the South—one being the Alabama Christian Movement for Human Rights. Whenever necessary and possible we share staff, educational and financial resources with our affiliates. Several months ago our local affiliate here in Birmingham invited us to be on call to engage in a nonviolent direct-action program if such were deemed necessary. We readily consented and when the hour came we lived up to our promises. So I am here, along with several members of my staff, because we were invited here. I am here because I have basic organizational ties here.

Beyond this, I am in Birmingham because injustice is here. Just as the eighth-century prophets left their little villages and carried their "thus saith the Lord" far beyond the boundaries of their hometowns; and just as the Apostle Paul left his little village of Tarsus and carried the gospel of Jesus Christ to practically every hamlet and city of the Graeco-Roman world, I too am compelled to carry the gospel of freedom beyond my particular hometown. Like Paul, I must constantly respond to the Macedonian call for aid.

Moreover, I am cognizant of the interrelatedness of all communities and states. I cannot sit idly by in Atlanta and not be concerned about what happens in Birmingham. Injustice anywhere is a threat to justice everywhere. We are caught in an inescapable network of mutuality, tied in a single garment of destiny. Whatever affects one directly affects all indirectly. Never again can we afford to live with the narrow, provincial "outside agitator" idea. Anyone who lives in the United States can never be considered an outsider anywhere in this country.

You deplore the demonstrations that are presently taking place in Birmingham. But I am sorry that your statement did not express a similar concern for the conditions that brought the demonstrations into being. I am sure that each of you would want to go beyond the superficial social analyst who looks merely at effects, and does not grapple with underlying causes. I would not hesitate to say that it is unfortunate that so-called demonstrations are taking place in Birmingham at this time, but I would say in more emphatic terms that it is even more unfortunate that the white power structure of this city left the Negro community with no other alternative.

In any nonviolent campaign there are four basic steps: (1) collection of the facts to determine whether injustices are alive, (2) negotiation, (3) self-purification, and (4) direct action. We have gone through all of these steps in Birmingham. There can be no gainsaying of the fact that racial injustice engulfs this community.

Birmingham is probably the most thoroughly segregated city in the United States. Its ugly record of police brutality is known in every section of this country. Its unjust treatment of Negroes in the courts is a notorious reality. There have been more unsolved bombings of Negro homes and churches in Birmingham than any city in this nation. These are the hard, brutal and unbelievable facts. On the basis of these conditions Negro leaders sought to negotiate with the city fathers. But the political leaders consistently refused to engage in good faith negotiation.

Then came the opportunity last September to talk with some of the leaders of the economic community. In these negotiating sessions certain promises were made by the merchants—such as the promise to remove the humiliating racial signs from the stores. On the basis of these promises Rev. Shuttlesworth and the leaders of the Alabama Christian Movement for Human Rights agreed to call a moratorium on any type of demonstrations. As the weeks and months unfolded we realized that we were the victims of a broken promise. The signs remained. Like so many experiences of the past we were confronted with blasted hopes, and the dark shadow of a deep disappointment settled upon us. So we had no alternative except that of preparing for direct action, whereby we would present our very bodies as a means of laying our case before the conscience of the local and national community. We were not unmindful of the difficulties involved. So we decided to go through a process of self-purification. We started having workshops on nonviolence and repeatedly asked ourselves the questions, "Are you able to accept blows without retaliating?" "Are you able to endure the ordeals of jail?" We decided to set our direct-action program around the Easter season, realizing that with the exception of Christmas, this was the largest shopping period of the year. Knowing that a strong economic withdrawal program would be the by-product of direct action, we felt that this was the best time to bring pressure on the merchants for the needed changes. Then it occurred to us that the March election was ahead and so we speedily decided to postpone action until after election day. When we discovered that Mr. Connor was in the run-off, we decided again to postpone action so that the demonstrations could not be used to cloud the issues. At this time we agreed to begin our nonviolent witness the day after the run-off.

This reveals that we did not move irresponsibly into direct action. We too wanted to see Mr. Connor defeated; so we went through postponement after postponement to aid in this community need. After this we felt that direct action could be delayed no longer.

You may well ask, "Why direct action? Why sit-ins, marches, etc.? Isn't negotiation a better path?" You are exactly right in your call for negotiation. Indeed, this is the purpose of direct action. Nonviolent direct action seeks to create such a crisis and establish such creative tension that a community that has constantly refused to negotiate is forced to confront the issue. It seeks so to dramatize the issue that it can no longer be ignored. I just referred to the creation of tension as a part of the work of the nonviolent resister. This may sound rather shocking. But I must confess that I am not afraid of the word *tension*. I have earnestly worked and preached against violent tension, but there is a type of constructive nonviolent tension that is necessary for growth. Just as Socrates felt that it was necessary to create a tension in the mind so that individuals could rise from the bondage of myths and half-truths to the unfettered realm of creative analysis and objective appraisal, we must see the need of having nonviolent gadflies to create the kind of tension in society that will help men to rise from the dark depths of prejudice and racism to the majestic heights of understanding and brotherhood. So the purpose of the direct action is to create a situation so crisis-packed that it will inevitably open the door to negotiation. We, therefore, concur with you in your call for negotiation. Too long has our beloved Southland been bogged down in the tragic attempt to live in monologue rather than dialogue.

One of the basic points in your statement is that our acts are untimely. Some have asked, "Why didn't you give the new administration time to act?" The only answer that I can give to this inquiry is that the new administration must be prodded about as much as the outgoing one before it acts. We will be sadly mistaken if we feel that the election of Mr. Boutwell will bring the millennium to Birmingham. While Mr. Boutwell is much more articulate and gentle than Mr. Connor, they are both segregationists, dedicated to the task of maintaining the status quo. The hope I see in Mr. Boutwell is that he will be reasonable enough to see the futility of massive resistance to desegregation. But he will not see this without pressure from the devotees of civil rights. My friends, I must say to you that we have not made a single gain in civil rights without determined legal and nonviolent pressure. History is the long and tragic story of the fact that privileged groups seldom give up their privileges voluntarily. Individuals may see the moral light and voluntarily give up their unjust posture; but as Reinhold Niebuhr has reminded us, groups are more immoral than individuals.

We know through painful experience that freedom is never voluntarily given by the oppressor; it must be demanded by the oppressed. Frankly, I have never yet engaged in a direct action movement that was "well-timed," according to the timetable of those who have not suffered unduly from the disease of segregation. For years now I have heard the word "Wait!" It rings in the ear of every Negro with a piercing familiarity. This "Wait" has almost always meant "Never." It has been a tranquilizing thalidomide, relieving the emotional stress for a moment, only to give birth to an ill-formed infant of frustration. We must come to see with the distinguished jurist of yesterday that "justice too long delayed is justice denied." We have waited for more than 340 years for our constitutional and God-given rights. The nations of Asia and Africa are moving with jet-like speed toward the goal of political independence, and we still creep at horse and buggy pace toward the gaining of a cup of coffee at a lunch counter. I guess it is easy for those who have never felt the stinging darts of segregation to say, "Wait." But when you have seen vicious mobs lynch your mothers and fathers at will and drown your sisters and brothers at whim; when you have seen hate-filled policemen curse, kick, brutalize and even kill your black brothers and sisters with impunity; when you see the vast majority of your twenty million Negro brothers smothering in an airtight cage of poverty in the midst of an affluent society; when you suddenly find your tongue twisted and your speech stammering as you seek to explain to your six-year-old daughter why she can't go to the public amusement park that has just been advertised on television, and see tears welling up in her little eyes when she is told that Funtown is closed to colored children, and see the depressing clouds of inferiority begin to form in her little mental sky, and see her begin to distort her little personality by unconsciously developing a bitterness toward white people; when you have to concoct an answer for a five-year-old son asking in agonizing pathos: "Daddy, why do white people treat colored people so mean?"; when you take a cross-country drive and find it necessary to sleep night after night in the uncomfortable corners of your automobile because no motel will accept you; when you are humiliated day in and day out by nagging signs reading "white" and "colored"; when your first name becomes "nigger" and your middle name becomes "boy" (however old you are) and your last name becomes "John," and when your wife and mother are never given the respected title "Mrs."; when you are harried by day and haunted by night by the fact that you are a Negro, living constantly at tiptoe stance never quite knowing what to expect next, and plagued with inner fears and outer resentments; when you are forever fighting a degenerating sense of "nobodiness"; then you will understand why we find it difficult to wait. There comes a time when the cup of endurance runs over, and men are no longer willing to be plunged into an abyss of injustice where they experience the blackness of corroding despair. I hope, sirs, you can understand our legitimate and unavoidable impatience.

You express a great deal of anxiety over our willingness to break laws. This is certainly a legitimate concern. Since we so diligently urge people to obey the Supreme Court's decision of 1954 outlawing segregation in the public schools, it is rather strange and paradoxical to find us consciously breaking laws. One may well ask, "How can you advocate breaking some laws and obeying others?" The answer is found in the fact that there are two types of laws: there are *just* and there are *unjust* laws. I would agree with Saint Augustine that "An unjust law is no law at all."

Now what is the difference between the two? How does one determine when a law is just or unjust? A just law is a man-made code that squares with the moral law or the law of God. An unjust law is a code that is out of harmony with the moral law. To put it in the terms of Saint Thomas Aquinas, an unjust law is a human law that is not rooted in eternal and natural law. Any law that uplifts human personality is just. Any law that degrades human personality is unjust. All segregation statutes are unjust because segregation distorts the soul and damages the personality. It gives the segregator a false sense of superiority, and the segregated a false sense of inferiority. To use the words of Martin Buber, the great Jewish philosopher, segregation substitutes an "I-it" relationship for the "I-thou" relationship, and ends up relegating persons to the status of things. So segregation is not only politically, economically and sociologically unsound, but it is morally wrong and sinful. Paul Tillich has said that sin is separation. Isn't segregation an existential expression of man's tragic separation, an expression of his awful estrangement, his terrible sinfulness? So I can urge men to disobey segregation ordinances because they are morally wrong.

Let us turn to a more concrete example of just and unjust laws. An unjust law is a code that a majority inflicts on a minority that is not binding on itself. This is difference made legal. On the other hand a just law is a code that a majority compels a minority to follow that it is willing to follow itself. This is sameness made legal.

Let me give another explanation. An unjust law is a code inflicted upon a minority which that minority had no part in enacting or creating because they did not have the unhampered right to vote. Who can say that the legislature of Alabama which set up the segregation laws was democratically elected? Throughout the state of Alabama all types of conniving methods are used to prevent Negroes from becoming registered voters and there are some counties without a single Negro registered to vote despite the fact that the Negro constitutes a majority of the population. Can any law set up in such a state be considered democratically structured?

These are just a few examples of unjust and just laws. There are some instances when a law is just on its face and unjust in its application. For instance, I was arrested Friday on a change of parading without a permit. Now there is nothing wrong with an ordinance which requires a permit for a parade, but when the ordinance is used to preserve segregation and to deny citizens the First Amendment privilege of peaceful assembly and peaceful protest, then it becomes unjust.

I hope you can see the distinction I am trying to point out. In no sense do I advocate evading or defying the law as the rabid segregationist would do. This would lead to anarchy. One who breaks an unjust law must do it *openly*, *lovingly* (not hatefully as the white mothers did in New Orleans when they were seen on television screaming, "nigger, nigger, nigger"), and with a willingness to accept the penalty. I submit that an individual who breaks a law that conscience tells him is unjust, and willingly accepts the penalty by staying in jail to arouse the conscience of the community over its injustice, is in reality expressing the very highest respect for law.

Of course, there is nothing new about this kind of civil disobedience. It was seen sublimely in the refusal of Shadrach, Meshach and Abednego to obey the laws of Nebuchadnezzar because a higher moral law was involved. It was practiced superbly by the early Christians who were willing to face hungry lions and the excruciating pain of chopping blocks, before submitting to certain unjust laws of the Roman Empire. To a degree academic freedom is a reality today because Socrates practiced civil disobedience.

We can never forget that everything Hitler did in Germany was "legal" and everything the Hungarian freedom fighters did in Hungary was "illegal." It was "illegal" to aid and comfort a Jew in Hitler's Germany. But I am sure that if I had lived in Germany during that time I would have aided and comforted my Jewish brothers even though it was illegal. If I lived in a Communist country today where certain principles dear to the Christian faith are suppressed, I believe I would openly advocate disobeying these anti-religious laws. I must make two honest confessions to you, my Christian and Jewish brothers. First, I must confess that over the last few years I have been gravely disappointed with the white moderate. I have almost reached the regrettable conclusion that the Negro's great stumbling block in the stride toward freedom is not the White Citizens Counciler or the Ku Klux Klanner, but the white moderate who is more devoted to "order" than to justice; who prefers a negative peace which is the absence of tension to a positive peace which is the presence of justice; who constantly says, "I agree with you in the goal you seek, but I can't agree with your methods of direct action"; who paternalistically feels that he can set the timetable for another man's freedom; who lives by the myth of time and who constantly advised the Negro to wait until a "more convenient season." Shallow understanding from people of good will is more frustrating than absolute misunderstanding from people of ill will. Lukewarm acceptance is much more bewildering than outright rejection.

I had hoped that the white moderate would understand that law and order exist for the purpose of establishing justice, and that when they fail to do this they become dangerously structured dams that block the flow of social progress. I had hoped that the white moderate would understand that the present tension of the South is merely a necessary phase of the transition from an obnoxious negative peace, where the Negro passively accepted his unjust plight, to a substance-filled positive peace, where all men will respect the dignity and worth of human personality. Actually, we who engage in nonviolent direct action are not the creators of tension. We merely bring to the surface the hidden tension that is already alive. We bring it out in the open where it can be seen and dealt with. Like a boil that can never be cured as long as it is covered up but must be opened with all its pus-flowing ugliness to the natural medicines of air and light, injustice must likewise be exposed, with all of the tension its exposing creates, to the light of human conscience and the air of national opinion before it can be cured.

In your statement you asserted that our actions, even though peaceful, must be condemned because they precipitate violence. But can this assertion be logically made? Isn't this like condemning the robbed man because his possession of money precipitated the evil act of robbery? Isn't this like condemning Socrates because his unswerving commitment to truth and his philosophical delvings precipitated the misguided popular mind to make him drink the hemlock? Isn't this like condemning Jesus because His unique God-consciousness and never-ceasing devotion to his will precipitated the evil act of crucifixion? We must come to see, as federal courts have consistently affirmed, that it is immoral to urge an individual to withdraw his efforts to gain his basic constitutional rights because the quest precipitates violence. Society must protect the robbed and punish the robber.

I had also hoped that the white moderate would reject the myth of time. I received a letter this morning from a white brother in Texas which said: "All Christians know that the colored people will receive equal rights eventually, but it is possible that you are in too great of a religious hurry. It has taken Christianity almost two thousand years to accomplish what it has. The teachings of Christ take time to come to earth." All that is said here grows out of a tragic misconception of time. It is the strangely irrational notion that there is something in the very flow of time that will inevitably cure all ills. Actually time is neutral. It can be used either destructively or constructively. I am coming to feel that the people of ill will have used time much more effectively than the people of good will. We will have to repent in this generation not merely for the vitriolic words and actions of the bad people, but for the appalling silence of the good people. We must come to see that human progress never rolls in on wheels of inevitability. It comes through the tireless efforts and persistent work of men willing to be co-workers with God, and without this hard work time itself becomes an ally of the forces of social stagnation. We must use time creatively, and forever realize that the time is always ripe to do right. Now is the time to make real the promise of democracy, and transform our pending national elegy into a creative psalm of brotherhood. Now is the time to lift our national policy from the quicksand of racial injustice to the solid rock of human dignity.

You spoke of our activity in Birmingham as extreme. At first I was rather disappointed that fellow clergymen would see my nonviolent efforts as those of the extremist. I started thinking about the fact that I stand in the middle of two opposing forces in the Negro community. One is a force of complacency made up of Negroes who, as a result of long years of oppression, have been so completely drained of self-respect and a sense of "somebodiness" that they have adjusted to segregation, and, of a few Negroes in the middle class who, because of a degree of academic and economic security, and because at points they profit by segregation, have unconsciously become insensitive to the problems of the masses. The other force is one of bitterness and hatred, and comes perilously close to advocating violence. It is expressed in the various black nationalist groups that are springing up over the nation, the largest and best known being Elijah Muhammad's Muslim movement. This movement is nourished by the contemporary frustration over the continued existence of racial discrimination. It is made up of people who have lost faith in America, who have absolutely repudiated Christianity, and who have concluded that the white man is an incurable "devil." I have tried to stand between these two forces, saying that we need not follow the "donothingism" of the complacent or the hatred and despair of the black nationalist. There is the more excellent way of love and nonviolent protest. I'm grateful to God that, through the Negro church, the dimension of nonviolence entered our struggle. If this philosophy had not emerged, I am convinced that by now many streets of the South would be flowing with floods of blood. And I am further convinced that if our white brothers dismiss as "rabble-rousers" and "outside agitators" those of us who are working through the channels of nonviolent direct action and refuse to support our nonviolent efforts, millions of Negroes, out of frustration and despair, will seek solace and security in black nationalist ideologies, a development that will lead inevitably to a frightening racial nightmare.

Oppressed people cannot remain oppressed forever. The urge for freedom will eventually come. This is what happened to the American Negro. Something within has reminded him of his birthright of freedom; something without has reminded him that he can gain it. Consciously and unconsciously, he has been swept in by what the Germans call the *Zeitgeist*, and with his black brothers of Africa, and his brown and yellow brothers of Asia, South America and the Caribbean, he is moving with a sense of cosmic urgency toward the promised land of racial justice. Recognizing this vital urge that has engulfed the Negro community, one should readily understand public demonstrations. The Negro has many pent-up resentments and latent frustrations. He has to get them out. So let him march sometime; let him have his prayer pilgrimages to the city hall; understand why he must have sit-ins and freedom rides. If his repressed emotions do not come out in these nonviolent ways, they will come out in ominous expressions of violence. This is not a threat; it is a fact of history. So I have not said to my people "get rid of your discontent." But I have tried to say that this normal and healthy discontent can be channelized through the creative outlet of nonviolent direct action. Now this approach is being dismissed as extremist. I must admit that I was initially disappointed in being so categorized.

But as I continued to think about the matter I gradually gained a bit of satisfaction from being considered an extremist. Was not Jesus an extremist in love—"Love your enemies, bless them that curse you, pray for them that despitefully use you." Was not Amos an extremist for justice—"Let justice roll down like waters and righteousness like a mighty stream." Was not Paul an extremist for the gospel of Jesus Christ—"I bear in my body the marks of the Lord Jesus." Was not Martin Luther an extremist—"Here I stand; I can do none other so help me God." Was not John Bunyan an extremist—"I will stay in jail to the end of my days before I make a butchery of my conscience." Was not Abraham Lincoln an extremist—"This nation cannot survive half slave and half free." Was not Thomas Jefferson an extremist—"We hold these truths to be self-evident, that all men are created equal." So the question is not whether we will be extremist but what kind of extremist will we be. Will we be extremists for hate or will we be extremists for love? Will we be extremists for the preservation of injustice—or will we be extremists for the cause of justice? In that dramatic scene on Calvary's hill, three men were crucified. We must not forget that all three were crucified for the same crime—the crime of extremism. Two were extremists for immorality, and thusly fell below their environment. The other, Jesus Christ, was an extremist for love, truth and goodness, and thereby rose above his environment. So, after all, maybe the South, the nation and the world are in dire need of creative extremists.

I had hoped that the white moderate would see this. Maybe I was too optimistic. Maybe I expected too much. I guess I should have realized that few members of a race that has oppressed another race can understand or appreciate the deep groans and passionate yearnings of those that have been oppressed and still fewer have the vision to see that injustice must be rooted out by strong, persistent and determined action. I am thankful, however, that some of our white brothers have grasped the meaning of this social revolution and committed themselves to it. They are still all too small in quantity, but they are big in quality. Some like Ralph McGill, Lillian Smith, Harry Golden and James Dabbs have written about our struggle in eloquent, prophetic and understanding terms. Others have marched with us down nameless streets of the South. They have languished in filthy roach-infested jails, suffering the abuse and brutality of angry policemen who see them as "dirty nigger-lovers." They, unlike so many of their moderate brothers and sisters, have recognized the urgency of the moment and sensed the need for powerful "action" antidotes to combat the disease of segregation.

Let me rush on to mention my other disappointment. I have been so greatly disappointed with the white church and its leadership. Of course, there are some notable exceptions. I am not unmindful of the fact that each of you has taken some significant stands on this issue. I commend you, Rev. Stallings, for your Christian stance on this past Sunday, in welcoming Negroes to your worship service on a non-segregated basis. I commend the Catholic leaders of this state for integrating Springhill College several years ago.

But despite these notable exceptions I must honestly reiterate that I have been disappointed with the church. I do not say that as one of the negative critics who can always find something wrong with the church. I say it as a minister of the gospel, who loves the church; who was nurtured in its bosom; who has been sustained by its spiritual blessings and who will remain true to it as long as the cord of life shall lengthen.

I had the strange feeling when I was suddenly catapulted into the leadership of the bus protest in Montgomery several years ago that we would have the support of the white church. I felt that the white ministers, priests and rabbis of the South would be some of our strongest allies. Instead, some have been outright opponents, refusing to understand the freedom movement and misrepresenting its leaders; all too many others have been more cautious than courageous and have remained silent behind the anesthetizing security of the stained-glass windows.

In spite of my shattered dreams of the past, I came to Birmingham with the hope that the white religious leadership of this community would see the justice of our cause, and with deep moral concern, serve as the channel through which our just grievances would get to the power structure. I had hoped that each of you would understand. But again I have been disappointed. I have heard numerous religious leaders of the South call upon their worshippers to comply with a desegregation decision because it is the *law*, but I have longed to hear white ministers say, "Follow this decree because integration is morally *right* and the Negro is your brother." In the midst of blatant injustices inflicted upon the Negro, I have watched white churches stand on the sideline and merely mouth pious irrelevancies and sanctimonious trivialities. In the midst of a mighty struggle to rid our nation of racial and economic injustice, I have heard so many ministers say, "Those are social issues with which the gospel has no real concern," and I have watched so many churches commit themselves to a completely otherworldly religion which made a strange distinction between body and soul, the sacred and the secular.

So here we are moving toward the exit of the twentieth century with a religious community largely adjusted to the status quo, standing as a taillight behind other community agencies rather than a headlight leading men to higher levels of justice.

I have traveled the length and breadth of Alabama, Mississippi and all the other southern states. On sweltering summer days and crisp autumn mornings I have looked at her beautiful churches with their lofty spires pointing heavenward. I have beheld the impressive outlay of her massive religious education buildings. Over and over again I have found myself asking: "What kind of people worship here? Who is their God? Where were their voices when the lips of Governor Barnett dripped with words of interposition and nullification? Where were they when Governor Wallace gave the clarion call for defiance and hatred? Where were their voices of support when tired, bruised and weary Negro men and women decided to rise from the dark dungeons of complacency to the bright hills of creative protest?"

Yes, these questions are still in my mind. In deep disappointment, I have wept over the laxity of the church. But be assured that my tears have been tears of love. There can be no deep disappointment where there is not deep love. Yes, I love the church; I love her sacred walls. How could I do otherwise? I am in the rather unique position of being the son, the grandson and the great-grandson of preachers. Yes, I see the church as the body of Christ. But, oh! How we have blemished and scarred that body through social neglect and fear of being nonconformists.

There was a time when the church was very powerful. It was during that period when the early Christians rejoiced when they were deemed worthy to suffer for what they believed. In those days the church was not merely a thermometer that recorded the ideas and principles of popular opinion; it was a thermostat that transformed the mores of society. Wherever the early Christians entered a town the power structure got disturbed and immediately sought to convict them for being "disturbers of the peace" and "outside agitators." But they went on with the conviction that they were "a colony of heaven," and had to obey God rather than man. They were small in number but big in commitment. They were too God-intoxicated to be "astronomically intimidated." They brought an end to such ancient evils as infanticide and gladiatorial contest.

Things are different now. The contemporary church is often a weak, ineffectual voice with an uncertain sound. It is so often the arch-supporter of the status quo. Far from being disturbed by the presence of the church, the power structure of the average community is consoled by the church's silent and often vocal sanction of things as they are.

But the judgment of God is upon the church as never before. If the church of today does not recapture the sacrificial spirit of the early church, it will lose its authentic ring, forfeit the loyalty of millions, and be dismissed as an irrelevant social club with no meaning for the twentieth century. I am meeting young people every day whose disappointment with the church has risen to outright disgust.

Maybe again, I have been too optimistic. Is organized religion too inextricably bound to the status quo to save our nation and the world? Maybe I must turn my faith to the inner spiritual church, the church within the church, as the true *ecclesia* and the hope of the world. But again I am thankful to God that some noble souls from the ranks of organized religion have broken loose from the paralyzing chains of conformity and joined us as active partners in the struggle for freedom. They have left their secure congregations and walked the streets of Albany, Georgia, with us. They have gone through the highways of the South on tortuous rides for freedom. Yes, they have gone to jail with us. Some have been kicked out of their churches, and lost support of their bishops and fellow ministers. But they have gone with the faith that right defeated is stronger than evil triumphant. These men have been the leaven in the lump of the race. Their witness has been the spiritual salt that has preserved the true meaning of the gospel in these troubled times. They have carved a tunnel of hope through the dark mountain of disappointment.

I hope the church as a whole will meet the challenge of this decisive hour. But even if the church does not come to the aid of justice, I have no despair about the future. I have no fear about the outcome of our struggle in Birmingham, even if our motives are presently misunderstood. We will reach the goal of freedom in Birmingham and all over the nation, because the goal of America is freedom. Abused and scorned though we may be, our destiny is tied up with the destiny of America. Before the Pilgrims landed at Plymouth we were here. Before the pen of Jefferson etched across the pages of history the majestic words of the Declaration of Independence, we were here. For more than two centuries our foreparents labored in this country without wages; they made cotton king; and they built the homes of their masters in the midst of brutal injustice and shameful humiliation—and yet out of a bottomless vitality they continued to thrive and develop. If the inexpressible cruelties of slavery could not stop us, the opposition we now face will surely fail. We will win our freedom because the sacred heritage of our nation and the eternal will of God are embodied in our echoing demands.

I must close now. But before closing I am impelled to mention one other point in your statement that troubled me profoundly. You warmly commended the Birmingham police force for keeping "order" and "preventing violence." I don't believe you would have so warmly commended the police force if you had seen its angry violent dogs literally biting six unarmed, nonviolent Negroes. I don't believe you would so quickly commend the policemen if you would observe their ugly and inhuman treatment of Negroes here in the city jail; if you would watch them push and curse old Negro women and young Negro girls; if you would see them slap and kick old Negro men and young boys; if you will observe them, as they did on two occasions, refuse to give us food because we wanted to sing our grace together. I'm sorry that I can't join you in your praise for the police department.

It is true that they have been rather disciplined in their public handling of the demonstrators. In this sense they have been rather publicly "nonviolent." But for what purpose? To preserve the evil system of segregation. Over the last few years I have consistently preached that nonviolence demands that the means we use must be as pure as the ends we seek. So I have tried to make it clear that it is wrong to use immoral means to attain moral ends. But now I must affirm that it is just as wrong, or even more so, to use moral means to preserve immoral ends. Maybe Mr. Connor and his policemen have been rather publicly nonviolent, as Chief Pritchett was in Albany, Georgia, but they have used the moral means of nonviolence to maintain the immoral end of flagrant racial injustice. T. S. Eliot has said that there is no greater treason than to do the right deed for the wrong reason.

I wish you had commended the Negro sit-inners and demonstrators of Birmingham for their sublime courage, their willingness to suffer and their amazing discipline in the midst of the most inhuman provocation. One day the South will recognize its real heroes. They will be the James Merediths, courageously and with a majestic sense of purpose facing jeering and hostile mobs and the agonizing loneliness that characterizes the life of the pioneer. They will be old, oppressed, battered Negro women, symbolized in a seventy-two-year-old woman of Montgomery, Alabama, who rose up with a sense of dignity and with her people decided not to ride the segregated buses, and responded to one who inquired about her tiredness with ungrammatical profundity: "My feet is tired, but my soul is rested." They will be the young high school and college students, young ministers of the gospel and a host of their elders courageously and non-violently sitting-in at lunch counters and willingly going to jail for conscience's sake. One day the South will know that when these disinherited children of God sat down at lunch counters they were in reality standing up for the best in the American dream and the most sacred values in our Judeo-Christian heritage, and thusly, carrying our whole nation back to those great wells of democracy which were dug deep by the Founding Fathers in the formulation of the Constitution and the Declaration of Independence.

Never before have I written a letter this long (or should I say a book?). I'm afraid that it is much too long to take your precious time. I can assure you that it would have been much shorter if I had been writing from a comfortable desk, but what else is there to do when you are alone for days in the dull monotony of a narrow jail cell other than write long letters, think strange thoughts, and pray long prayers?

If I have said anything in this letter that is an overstatement of the truth and is indicative of an unreasonable impatience, I beg you to forgive me. If I have said anything in this letter that is an understatement of the truth and is indicative of my having a patience that makes me patient with anything less than brotherhood, I beg God to forgive me.

I hope this letter finds you strong in the faith. I also hope that circumstances will soon make it possible for me to meet each of you, not as an integrationist or a civil rights leader, but as a fellow clergyman and a Christian brother. Let us all hope that the dark clouds of racial prejudice will soon pass away and the deep fog of misunderstanding will be lifted from our fear-drenched communities and in some not too distant tomorrow the radiant stars of love and brotherhood will shine over our great nation with all of their scintillating beauty.

Yours for the cause of Peace and Brotherhood,
Martin Luther King, Jr.

Black Man's History

MALCOLM X

I want to thank Allah for coming and giving to us our leader and teacher here in America, The Honorable Elijah Muhammad. I want to thank Brother Benjamin at the outset for doing a wonderful job of opening up our eyes and giving us a good preliminary basic understanding of the means and the objectives of The Honorable Elijah Muhammad, and also I am thankful to Allah for bringing so many people out here tonight, especially just before Christmas. You know, it's next to a miracle when you get this many of our people together so close to Christmas interested in anything whatsoever that's serious. And actually what this shows is the change that's taking place among the so-called Negroes not only here in New York but throughout the entire world. Today dark mankind is waking up and is undertaking a new type of thinking, and it is this new type of thinking that is creating new approaches and new reactions that make it almost impossible to figure out what the black man is going to do next, and by black man we mean, as we are taught by The Honorable Elijah Muhammad, we include all those who are nonwhite. He teaches us that black is the basic color, that black is the foundation or the basis of all colors. And all of our people who have not yet become white are still black, or at least part of the Black Nation, and here at Muhammad's Mosque when you hear us using the term "black" we mean everbody who's here, regardless of your complexion. If you're here at the Mosque you're black, because the only ticket you need to get into Muhammad's Mosque is to be black. So if you got in you know you're black. You may not have known that you were black before you came here. In fact, very few of our people really look upon themselves as being black. They think of themselves as practically everything else on the color spectrum except black. And no matter how dark one of our people may be, you rarely hear him call himself black. But now that The Honorable Elijah Muhammad has been teaching among the so-called Negroes, you find our people of all complexions going around bragging that "I'm a black man." This shows you that a new teaching is taking place and there is new thinking among the so-called Negroes. Yet just yesterday you would have to admit that it was very difficult to get our people to refer to themselves as black. Now all of a sudden our people of all complexions are not apologizing for being black but bragging about being black. So there's a new thinking all over America among the so-called Negroes. And the one who is actually the author of this new thinking is The Honorable Elijah Muhammad. It is what he is teaching that is making our people, for the first time, proud to be black, and what's most important of all, for the first time it makes our people want to know more about black, want to know why black is good, or what there is about black that is good.

I might stop right here to point out that some of you may say, "I came up here to listen to some religion, about Islam, but now all I hear you talk about is black." We don't separate our color from our religion. The white man doesn't. The white man never has separated Christianity from white, nor has he separated the white man from Christianity. When you hear the white man bragging, "I'm a Christian," he's bragging about being a white man. Then you have the Negro. When he is bragging about being a Christian, he's bragging that he's a white man, or he wants to be white, and usually those Negroes who brag like that, I think you have to agree, in their songs and the things they sing in church, they show that they have a greater desire to be white than anything else. My mother was a Christian and my father was a Christian and I used to hear them when I was a little child sing the song "Wash Me White as Snow." My father was a black man and my mother was a black woman, but yet the songs that they sang in their church were designed to fill their hearts with the desire to be white. So many people, especially our people, get resentful when they hear me say something like this. But rather than get resentful all they have to do is think back on many of the songs and much of the teachings and the doctrines that they were taught while they were going to church and they'll have to agree that it was all designed to make us look down on black and up at white.

So the religion that we have, the religion of Islam, the religion that makes us Muslims, the religion that The Honorable Elijah Muhammad is teaching us here in America today, is designed to undo in our minds what the white man has done to us. It's designed to undo the type of brainwashing that we have had to undergo for four hundred years at the hands of the white man in order to bring us down to the level that we're at today. So when you hear us often refer to black in almost a boastful way, actually we're not boasting, we're speaking of it in a factual sense. All we're doing is telling the truth about our people. Whenever you exalt black, that's not propaganda; when you exalt white, *that's* propaganda. Yet no one can give biological evidence to show that black actually is the stronger or superior of the two if you want to make that kind of comparison. So never think ill of the person whom you hear representing The Honorable Elijah Muhammad if an overemphasis seems to be placed on the word black, but rather sit and analyze and try to get an understanding.

The Honorable Elijah Muhammad teaches us that of all the things that the black man, or any man for that matter, can study, history is the best qualified to reward all research. You have to have a knowledge of history no matter what you are going to do; anything that you undertake you have to have a knowledge of history in order to be successful in it. The thing that has made the so-called Negro in America fail, more than any other thing, is your, my, lack of knowledge concerning history. We know less about history than anything else. There are black people in America who have mastered the mathematical sciences, have become professors and experts in physics, are able to toss sputniks out there in the atmosphere, out in space. They are masters in that field. We have black men who have mastered the field of medicine, we have black men who have mastered other fields, but very seldom do we have black men in America who have mastered the knowledge of the history of the black man himself. We have among our people those who are experts in every field, but seldom can you find one among us who is an expert on the history of the black man. And because of his lack of knowledge concerning the history of the black man, no matter how much he excels in the other sciences, he's always confined, he's always relegated to the same low rung of the ladder that the dumbest of our people are relegated to. And *all* of this stems from his lack of knowledge concerning history. What made Dr. George Washington Carver a *Negro* scientist instead of a scientist? What made Paul Robeson a *Negro* actor instead of an actor? What made, or makes, Ralph Bunche a *Negro* statesman instead of a statesman? The only difference between Bunche and Carver and these others I just mentioned is they don't know the history of the black man. Bunche is an expert, an international politician, but he doesn't know himself, he doesn't know the history of the black people. He can be sent all over the world by America to solve problems for America, or to solve problems for other nations, but he can't solve problems for his own people in this country. Why? What is it that ties our people up in this way? The Honorable Elijah Muhammad says that it boils down to just one word—history.

When you study the history of Bunche, his history is different from the history of the black man who just came here from Africa. And if you notice, when Bunche was in Atlanta, Georgia, during the summer NAACP Convention, he was Jim Crowed, he was segregated, he was not allowed to go in a hotel down there. Yet there are Africans who come here, black as night, who can go into those cracker hotels. Well, what is the difference between Bunche and one of them? The difference is Bunche doesn't know his history, and they, the Africans, do know their history. They may come here out of the jungles, but they know their history. They may come here wearing sheets with their heads all wrapped up, but they know their history. You and I can come out of Harvard but we don't know our history. There's a basic difference in why we are treated as we are: one knows his history and one doesn't know his history! The American so-called Negro is a soldier who doesn't know his history; he's a servant who doesn't know his history; he's a graduate of Columbia, or Yale, or Harvard, or Tuskeegee, who doesn't know his history. He's confined, he's limited, he's held under the control and the jurisdiction of the white man who knows more about the history of the Negro than the Negro knows about himself. But when you and I wake up, as we're taught by The Honorable Elijah Muhammad, and learn our history, learn the history of our kind, and the history of the white kind, then the white man will be at a disadvantage and we'll be at an advantage.

The only thing that puts you and me at a disadvantage is our lack of knowledge concerning history. So one of the reasons, one of the missions, one of the objectives of The Honorable Elijah Muhammad here in America is not only to teach you and me the right religions but to teach you and me history. In fact, do you know that if you and I know history we know the right religion? The only way that you can become confused, that you can become mixed up and not know which religion belongs to God, is if you don't know history. In fact, you have to know history to know something about God. You have to know history to know something about God's religion. You have to know history to know something about God's people. You have to know history to know something about God's plans and God's purposes, and, as I say, the only people who don't know history are the American so-called Negroes. If you know history, for example, you know when you look at this religion right here [writes "Christianity" on the blackboard] the only way you can explain it is to have a knowledge of history.

Why is it called Christianity? It is called Christianity, they say, because it was named after a man called Christ who was born two thousand years ago. Now you know, brothers and sisters, God is an old God, and the world is an old world. The universe has been here a long time. I think all of you would agree that the universe has been here longer than two thousand years. Then you'll also agree that the universe was made by God Himself, that God created the universe. God created the people who are on this earth, God wouldn't create a universe, God wouldn't set a thing up in the sky that makes nine planets rotate around it, all of them inhabited, you and I inhabiting the planet earth upon which we live—God wouldn't have done all this and not given people a religion. God put His religion here at the creation of the universe. In fact, God's religion is older than the universe. Now then, since you agree to this and you'll agree also that Christ was born two thousand years ago, this couldn't have been God's religion. Your knowledge of history tells you that God couldn't call His religion Christianity because Christianity is only two thousand years old. So if this is the case, then what was God's religion called *before* the birth of Christ? Can you see the importance of history? Why, if you didn't know history you'd think that Christianity was God's religion, and you'd be running around here wondering why everybody doesn't practice it. Because some people have a better knowledge of history than others do, it is only the people whose knowledge of history is limited who jump up and say that Christianity is the name of God's religion. If Christianity hasn't *always* been the name of God's religion it isn't *now* the name of God's religion. God doesn't change the name of His religion; God doesn't change His religion; God doesn't change His mind; God's mind is made up from the beginning. He doesn't have to change His mind because He knows all there is to know all the way down the wheel of time. He never has to change His mind, His mind is made up, His knowledge is complete, all encompassing. Do you understand? So once you can see, and I think you can, then it's almost impossible for God to call *Christianity* His religion.

What should God call His religion? Christians are the ones who call God's religion Christianity, but God was here before Christians came on the scene. They tell you that Christians began back there with the Romans, with one of the Roman Emperors who accepted the teachings of some of Jesus' disciples and then named what the disciples taught "Christianity." But Jesus didn't call it Christianity, it wasn't named until two or three hundred years after Jesus was dead. Right or wrong? Any history book will tell this, any theologian knows this, and the only Negroes who will contend this are those who don't know history, and most Negroes don't know history. Most Negroes will contend this, but when you tell it to the white man he shuts his mouth because he knows that this is true.

Then those who have studied a little deeper will say, "Before God called it Christianity it was called Judaism"—isn't this what they say? Named after a man called Judah. This doesn't follow logically. If Christianity was named after Christ was born, and before Christ was born the religion was called Judaism, then that means that it got its name from a son of Jacob whose name was Judah. But history tells us that Jacob was bending down before Judah was born, which shows us that Jacob's religion couldn't have been Judaism, and Isaac was Jacob's father and he was bending down also before Jacob, his son, was born. Isaac was Judah's grandfather and Abraham was Judah's great-grandfather, meaning that Abraham was on the scene long before Judah, and you couldn't call Abraham's religion Judaism because there was no such thing as Judaism in Abraham's day. There was no such thing as Judaism in Isaac's day, or in Jacob's day. Do you understand? So what was God's religion before they called it Judaism? This is something that the white man has never taught you and me. The white man is afraid to let you and me know what's God's religion was called in Abraham's day because Abraham is supposed to have been the father of all of them. He is supposed to have been the progenitor of all of them. He is supposed to have been one of God's first servants. One of the first to submit to God is supposed to have been Abraham. Now if you can see this, then find out what Abraham's religion was.

The Honorable Elijah Muhammad teaches us that Abraham's religion was the religion of Islam. Islam only means complete submission to God, complete obedience to God. Abraham obeyed God. Abraham obeyed God so much so that when God told Abraham to take his son and sacrifice him—stick a dagger in his heart, isn't that what he said?—Abraham took his only son up on the mountain. He was going to sacrifice him to God, showing that he believed in Islam. What does Islam mean? Obey God. Submit to God. So that this name [writes "Islam"], if you'll notice, has no connection, no association, with the death of a man. This is not a man's name, this doesn't come from a man. Buddhism is named after a man called Buddha; Confucianism is named after a man called Confucius—right or wrong? Likewise with Judaism and Christianity. But Islam is not connected with any name. Islam is independent of any name. Islam is an act which means submit completely to God, or obey God. And when you say your religion is Islam that means you're a Muslim. So to clarify this what must you do? You must have a knowledge of history. If you don't have a knowledge of history you'll run around calling yourself a Christian when you're serving God, or you'll run around saying your religion is Judaism and you'll swear you're serving God. If your religion is Christianity you're following Christ, if your religion is Judaism you're following Judah, if your religion is Buddhism you're following Buddha, do you understand? And they are all dead, and if you follow them you'll die too. This is where it all leads you. Wherever your leaders go, that's what happens to you. Now we who follow The Honorable Elijah Muhammad, we believe in Islam, we don't believe in Muhammad.

He teaches us the religion of Islam. Do you understand the difference? These people who follow Christ [pointing to the cross painted on the blackboard], they believe in Christ; they believe Christ is God—Oh yes, they do—that he was born of the Blessed Virgin, didn't have a father, was just a spirit, and then came into the world and was crucified, rose from the dead, and went up into space. They believe that, but they believe it because they don't know history. But if you notice, the Jews have a better knowledge of history than the Christians do, do they not? The Christians' history only goes back two thousand years; the history of the Jews goes back beyond four thousand years. Can you see this? And the Muslim history goes back . . . there is no limit to the Muslim history. If you notice, the Christians can only go back to what they call the Greek Empire. That's what they call the Occidental, the beginning of the Occident, the Greek Empire, the Roman Empire, and so forth. The Jews have a knowledge of history that goes back into Egypt and Babylon. You notice how one goes back further than the other. But now the Muslims' history goes back . . . it has no limit. There are no chains on how far you can go back when you are a Muslim. The Christians and the Jews combined go back to whom? To Adam, and they stop right there. And they say beyond him there was nothing happening. The greater their knowledge of history is—this has an influence on the type of religion that they accept. Do you understand?

All praise is due to Allah. Another example: What makes the royal family of Europe, or any country, differ from the peasant? Royalty knows its ancestry, royalty knows its history, this is what makes them royal. You can't have a king who can't trace his history back to his forefathers. The only way you can be king is to be born a king. If you take away his history, and he doesn't know who his forefathers were, what does he become? A peasant—a common ordinary man. Same with the Jews and Christians. It's because the Jews have the longest record of history that they can call themselves the Chosen People. The Christians can't call themselves the Chosen People because their history is not long enough. They can't go back to the time when the choice was being made. The Hebrews, the so-called Jews, can go back so far they can lay claim to that which is actually not theirs. But the reason they can claim it is that nobody else they are dealing with can go back far enough to disprove them. Except the Muslims—do you understand? So The Honorable Elijah Muhammad's mission is to teach the so-called Negroes a knowledge of history, the history of ourselves, our own kind, showing us how we fit into prophecy, Biblical prophecy. When you go to one of the churches you will notice that it is named after some word in their Bible: Big Rock Baptist Church, or Drinking at the Well Baptist Church, Friendship Baptist Church, Union Baptist, Israel Baptist, Jacob's Ladder Baptist. They find some kind of old funny word in their Bible to name their whole religion after. Their whole doctrine is based on a verse in the Bible: "He rose."

The Honorable Elijah Muhammad bases what he teaches not on a verse but on the entire book. And from beginning to end, he says, he can open up the Book and prove that the Bible agrees with him, and then use the Bible to prove that what they are teaching in the church is wrong. You know that's saying something.

For instance, he says that in Genesis, the fifteenth chapter and the thirteenth verse, just to give you an example: "And he said unto Abram, Know of a surety that thy seed shall be a stranger in a land that is not theirs, and shall serve them; and they shall afflict them four hundred years; and also that nation, whom they shall serve, will I judge: and afterward shall they come out with great substance." Now The Honorable Elijah Muhammad says that explains his teachings right there, because he teaches that the so-called Negro is the one that the Bible is talking about. Who have spent four hundred years and are strangers in a land that is not theirs? And you can't deny that we are strangers here. I don't think any of you will deny that we are strangers here. We are not in a country where we are made to feel at home. We'll put it that way. There is hardly any Negro in his right mind who can say he feels at home in America. He has to admit that he is made to feel like a stranger. Right or wrong? Well, this is what God said to Abraham would happen in this day and time. Remember, Abraham's religion was Islam. Abraham wasn't a Jew, Abraham wasn't a Christian, Abraham wasn't a Buddhist, Abraham was a Muslim, which means he obeyed God. God told him, yes, He said, your people are going into bondage, they're going to become slaves, they're going to be afflicted, they'll be strangers in a land far from home for four hundred years. The Honorable Elijah Muhammad says you and I are the seed of Abraham, we're the descendants of Abraham. Now the preacher in the church, he tells you that the Jews are the seed of Abraham. One of them is right and one of them is wrong; either Mr. Muhammad is right and the preacher is wrong, or the preacher is right and Mr. Muhammad is wrong. This is what we are putting on the line today.

Who is the seed of Abraham? Is it this blue-eyed, blond-haired, pale-skinned Jew? Or is it the so-called Negro—you? Who is it? And what makes it so pitiful, many of our people would rather believe that the Jews are God's Chosen People than to believe that they are God's Chosen People. They would rather believe that God is going to save the Jews than believe that God is going to save them. They would rather believe that the Jew is better than anybody else. This is a Negro. Nobody else would put everybody else above him but the Negro. No one likes to place himself below everybody else but the Negro. I mean the American Negro. Remember, God said that the people would be strangers. The Jews aren't strangers. The Jews know their history, the Jews know their culture, the Jews know their language; they know everything there is to know about themselves. They know how to rob you, they know how to be your landlord, they know how to be your grocer, they know how to be your lawyer, they know how to join the NAACP and become the president— right or wrong? They know how to control everything you've got. You can't say they're lost. But the poor so-called Negro, he hasn't control over anything. He doesn't control the NAACP, he can't control the Urban League, he can't control CORE, he can't control his church, he can't control his own schools, he can't control his own businesses in his own community. He can't even control his own mind. He's lost and lost control of himself and gone astray.

But he fits the picture here that the Bible says concerning our people in the last day: "Know of a surety that thy seed shall be a stranger in a land that is not theirs, and shall serve them." And you have served the white man; he hasn't served you and me. Why, the Jew hasn't served anybody here. You are the one that's serving: "And they shall afflict them four hundred years; and also that nation, whom they shall serve, will I judge: and afterward shall they come out with great substance." Ofttimes when you say this to the so-called Negroes they'll come up and tell you that this is the Jew. But if you'll notice, when Jesus was talking to the Jews, way back here in John, he told them that they shall know the truth and it will make them free. The Jews popped up and said: "How are you going to say that we shall be made free? We have never been in bondage to anyone." Isn't that what the Jews told Jesus? Now look at it. If the Jews said to Jesus, two thousand years after Moses supposedly led the Hebrews out of bondage, that they had never been in bondage—now you know the Jews had Moses' history, they knew who Moses was—how could they stand up and tell Jesus they had never been in bondage? Not *these* things that you *call* Jews. They weren't in Egypt, *they* weren't the people that Moses led out of Egypt, and the Jews know this. But the Bible is written in such a tricky way, when you read it you think that Moses led the Jews out of bondage. But if you get a Jew in a good solid conversation today and you know how to talk to him, he'll have to admit this, that it wasn't out of Egypt's land that Moses brought them, that it wasn't out of bondage that Moses brought them—it was out of somewhere else—and where Moses really brought them is their secret, but, thanks to Almighty God, The Honorable Elijah Muhammad knows their secret, and he told it to us and we're going to tell it to you.

If the Bible said that God is going to judge that nation, the nation that enslaved His people, how would He keep from destroying His own people? The same Bible is a book of history and in the eighteenth chapter of the book of Deuteronomy, in the eighteenth verse, God told Moses: "I will raise them up a Prophet"— talking about you and me—I'll raise them up a prophet just like thee—a prophet like Moses whose mission it would be to do for you and me the same thing that Moses did back then. It would be a prophet like Moses. In fact, when you get down to Malachi, He lets it be known that just before He comes to judge that nation, the name of the prophet or messenger whom He would send among the people would be Elijah. It says: Before the coming of that great and dreadful day I shall send you Elijah and Elijah's job will be to turn the hearts of the children to the fathers and the hearts of the fathers to the children. What does this mean, turn the hearts of the children to the fathers? The so-called Negro are childlike people—you're like children. No matter how old you get, or how bold you get, or how wise you get, or how rich you get, or how educated you get, the white man still calls you what? Boy! Why, you are a child in his eyesight! And you *are* a child. Anytime you have to let another man set up a factory for you and you can't set up a factory for yourself, you're a child; anytime another man has to open up businesses for you and you don't know how to open up businesses for yourself and your people, you're a child; anytime another man sets up Schools and you don't know how to set up your own schools, you're a child. Because a child is someone who sits around and waits for his father to do for him what he should be doing for himself, or what he's too young to do for himself, or what he is too dumb to do for himself. So the white man, knowing that here in America all the Negro has done—I hate to say it, but it's the truth—all you and I have done is build churches and let the white man build factories.

You and I build churches and let the white man build schools. You and I build churches and let the white man build up everything for himself. Then after you build the church you have to go and beg the white man for a job, and beg the white man for some education. Am I right or wrong? Do you see what I mean? It's too bad but it's true. And it's history. So it shows that these childlike people—people who would be children, following after the white man—it says in the last day that God will raise up Elijah, and Elijah's job will be to turn the hearts of these children back toward their fathers. Elijah will come and change our minds; he'll teach us something that will turn us completely around. When Elijah finds us we'll be easy to lead in the wrong direction but hard to lead in the right direction. But when Elijah gets through teaching the Lost Sheep, or the Lost People of God, he'll turn them around, he'll change their minds, he'll put a board in their back, he'll make them throw their shoulders back and stand upright like men for the first time. It says he'll turn the hearts of these children toward their fathers and the hearts of the fathers toward the children. This is something that The Honorable Elijah Muhammad is doing here in America today. You and I haven't thought in terms of our forefathers. We haven't thought of our fathers. Our fathers, brother, are back home. Our fathers are in the East. We're running around here begging the Great White Father. You never hear of black people in this country talking or speaking or thinking in terms of connecting themselves with their own kind back home. They are trying to make contact with the white man, trying to make a connection with the white man, trying to connect, trying to make a connection with a kidnapper who brought them here, trying to make a connection with, actually, the man who enslaved them. You know that's a shame—it's pitiful—but it's true.

The Honorable Elijah Muhammad says that when Elijah comes, the Book says when Elijah comes, what Elijah will do is to teach these people the truth. And the truth that Elijah will teach the people would be so strong it will make all that other stuff that the preachers are talking about sound like a fairy story. Elijah will open the people's eyes up so wide that from then on a preacher won't be able to talk to them—and this is really true. Do you know, people have come to Muhammad's Mosque and no matter whether they believed in what Mr. Muhammad was saying or not they never could go back and sit in church. This is true. What The Honorable Elijah Muhammad does is to turn on the light, and when he turns on the light it enables us to see and think for ourselves. He shows us that what the white man has taught us concerning history has actually been a distortion. He's never given you and me true facts about history, neither about himself nor about our people. You know I read a book one day called *The Four Cities of Troy*. You can go to the library, some libraries, and check it out. What was this based on? To show you what a *liar* the white man is. When I say liar: you have white people who are scientists and keep truth in their own circles, and they never let you— they never let the masses—know anything about this truth that they keep in the circle. They got something else that they invent and put out for the masses to believe, but they themselves keep knowledge in a circle. So in this particular book it pointed out that some archaeologists were delving in the ruins of the ancient city of Troy, and it's the practice of archaeologists to dig, so in digging down into the ruins of Troy they dug deeper than they intended to, and they ran into the ruins of another city that had been there so much longer than this city of Troy that it had gone down beneath the sands of time, and they had built this city of Troy on top of it. When these archaeologists were delving into the ruins of the ancient city they learned that there were ruins of a city more ancient than that. So they started frantically digging into that one and dug some more until they found another one and before they got through digging they had dug down and they had discovered that civilizations in that area had been there so far back into history that at different times in his-tory some of the cities had been destroyed, had become completely covered up with sand and dirt, until another people came along and didn't even know it was there and built another civilization on top of it. This happened four different times—to give you some idea of what the white man knows concerning the length of time man has been on this earth—and still that white man would jump up in your face and try to make you believe that the first man was made six thousand years ago named Adam. And a lot of Negroes will want to know what you are talking about—Adam—that's what God called him—God took some dirt and breathed on it and told Adam, "Come forth," and there he was. Now you know that's a shame. It's all right to believe when you were a little baby that God made a little doll out of the sand and mud and breathed on it and that was the first man. But here it is 1962 with all this information floating around in everybody's ears—you can get it free. Why, you should open up your minds and your heads and your hearts and realize that you have been led by a lie. Today it's time to listen to nothing but naked, undiluted truth. And when you know the truth, as Jesus said: "The truth will make you free." Abraham Lincoln won't make you free. Truth will make you free. When you know the truth, you're free. Also you have your archaeologists, anthropologists, other forms of historians who agree that they don't know how long man has been on earth, but they do know that man has been on earth longer than six thousand years. They know that man was not made just six thousand years ago. They know this now but a long time ago they didn't know it. There was a time when they believed that a man had fewer ribs than a woman. You can believe that because they said that God made Eve from one of Adam's ribs—so Adam had a rib missing. And they actually ran around here believing for many years that man had one less rib, and they were shook up when they got into the science of anatomy and discovered that man—all his ribs were there! They began to wonder then what happened in the Bible?

How long has man been here? In the Bible in the first chapter of Genesis and the twenty-sixth verse, after God had made everything else it says: "And God said, Let us make man." Let me write what God said here on the board . . . Look what God said, brothers. I don't think you ever *looked* at this. It says: "And God said, Let us make man." The key word here is what? Yes, what does "us" mean? More than one. Who was God talking to? If God was all by Himself, no one was there but Him, who was He talking to when He said, "Let us make man"? Who was there with God who was about to help Him make this man? When God was getting ready to make the sun He didn't say, "*Let us* make some sun!" He said, "Let there be light." And here is the sun, a ball of fire 2,679,785 miles in circumference, 853,000 miles in diameter, 14,072 degrees hot, and God said, "Let there be," and that big ball of fire popped up there in the universe, with no help. Now you know something is wrong. It should be harder to make that than a man: a huge ball of fire 2,679,785 miles in circumference, 14,072 degrees hot—that's a whole lot of heat. And God said, "Let there be," and that just jumped up in the universe. He didn't ask for no help: "Let there be this and let there be that." He had so much power that everything He wanted came into existence; as soon as He said "be," there it was. But when He got to man something happened, someone else was there, wasn't there? That's something to think about. We'll let you think about it for a minute . . .

The white man's world is a newer world than the black man's world. If this man said that they were about to make man, and he said we would make him how—in our image—this shows you that there's somebody there with him—in *our* likeness—there is somebody there with him. "Let us make man in our image, in our likeness. Let us make him look like us. He won't be the same as we are, he'll be in our image." That's God talking, right? He's talking to somebody. You know, I'm thankful to Allah for raising up The Honorable Elijah Muhammad and making us see these things that we could never see before. The birth of the white race has always been a secret. The Honorable Elijah Muhammad says that the birth of the white race is shrouded in the story of Adam. The story of Adam hides the birth of the white race, and because you and I have never been taught to look into a thing and analyze a thing we took the story of Adam exactly as it was. We thought that God made *a* man named Adam six thousand years ago. But today The Honorable Elijah Muhammad teaches us that that man, Adam, was a white man; that before Adam was made the black man was already here. The white man will even tell you that, because *he* refers to Adam as the first one. He refers to the Adamites as those who came from that first one. He refers to the pre-Adamites as those who were here before Adam. Right or wrong? Those people who were here before Adam. And he always refers to these people as "aborigines," which means what? BLACK FOLK!!!! You never find a white aborigine. Aborigines are called natives, and they're always dark-skinned people. You and I are aborigines. But you don't like to be called an aborigine; you want to be called an American. Aborigine actually means, "from the beginning." It's two Latin words, "ab" meaning "from"; "origine" meaning "the beginning"; and aborigine is only the term applied to those dark-skinned people who have been on this earth since the beginning of the universe. You know that's going way back. What do you mean, since the beginning of the universe?

The Honorable Elijah Muhammad teaches us that, just as we pointed out a moment ago, the black man has been here a long time. He never has had a beginning. But the white man has never had a knowledge of the history of the black man. It's like a father and a son. If the father is fifty years old and the son is only ten, the father knows everything there is to know about his son because he was here before his son was born; the son only knows what has happened during his own ten years. He only knows what went on before his arrival from what his father tells him. It's the same way with the black man and the white man: the black man's been here a long time, but the white man has been here a short time. Now the white man only knows about himself, what he's been told, and he hasn't been told anything. He came to himself up in the caves of Europe, and he can't get any information that goes beyond the cave. And since you and I fell into his trap and were made deaf, dumb, and blind by him, we don't have access now to any information that the white man doesn't know about. So we think that the beginning of the white man meant the beginning of everything, us too. We're not aware that we were here before he was made. Can you understand that? The Honorable Elijah Muhammad teaches us that sixty-six trillion years ago—trillion, how much is trillion? Not hundreds, nor thousands, nor millions, nor billions, but sixty-six trillion years ago—the black man was here. We have the sun which is the center of the universe; 36,000,000 miles from the sun is the planet we call Mercury, and 67,200,000 miles from the sun is the planet called Venus, and 93,000,000 miles from the sun is the planet here that you and I live on called Earth, 141,500,000 miles out here is a planet called Mars, and 483,000,000 miles from the sun is a planet called Jupiter, 886,000,000 miles from the sun is a planet called Saturn, and on down the road a piece are a couple more planets. So right here this planet that you and I live on called Earth, that rotates around the sun, The Honorable Elijah Muhammad teaches us that sixty-six trillion years ago our people were living on this planet: the black man was living on this planet. But in those days it was larger than it is now, and the planet Mars, that was off here beyond it, had an effect upon our planet then in the same manner that the moon affects us today. At that time there was no moon up there. Where was the moon? The moon was down here, the moon was part of this planet, the moon and this planet were one planet, and the black man was living here then. He was a scientist, he was a wise black man. Black men have always been wise, black men have always been the wisest beings in the universe, and among these beings, black beings, there is one who is supreme; he is referred to as the Supreme Being, do you understand?

So The Honorable Elijah Muhammad tells us that a wise black scientist, sixty-six trillion years ago, began to argue with the other scientists because he wanted the people of Earth to speak a certain language, and since they wouldn't agree he wanted to destroy civilization. So this scientist drove a shaft into the center of the Earth and filled it with high explosives and set it off. He was trying to destroy civilization; he was trying to destroy the black man. But you can't destroy the black man; the black man can't destroy himself. The black man has the most powerful brain in the universe. So there is no intelligence more powerful than the intelligence of the black man. And because of this the black man can't even create a *thought* that would destroy him. He is indestructible. You can blow up everything and the black man will still be here. You just can't get away from him, brother. So The Honorable Elijah Muhammad said he filled the Earth, the planet, with high explosives and set it off, and when it was exploded the piece that you and I today call the moon was tossed out here into space and it rotated around the Earth. It still rotates around the Earth; it came from the Earth; it was blasted right off the Earth. And as it was blasted right off the Earth, it turned over and over and over and all of the water that was on it stayed with the Earth. So that the piece that was blasted out there has no water on it today, and because it has no water on it it has no civilization on it, has no life on it. You can't have life where there's no water; water is the source of life. Where there's no water there's no life; where there's no life there's no civilization. Can you understand that? So this dead piece, called the moon by us today, turning over and over and over, lost all of its water, all of the water coming with *this* piece. The Honorable Elijah Muhammad told us that this piece, that the Earth, that we remained on, shifted, dropped thirty-six thousand miles in the pocket that we remained in. And as it dropped and all of the water came with it, that left a situation in which today the Earth that we now live on weighs six sextillion tons. The weight of it is six sextillion tons. And as it makes its way around the sun, the strong power of the sun's rays striking the equator causes the planet to turn on its own axis at the speed of 1037⅓ miles per hour. And he teaches us that the square mileage of the Earth is 196,940,000 square miles which means only 57,255,000 square miles of land stuck up out of 139,685,000 square miles of water. Three-fourths of the Earth's surface is covered with water. Part of the water that left the moon is here with the Earth. So you say since it's the natural law for water to seek its own level, why doesn't it overrun the land? The Honorable Elijah Muhammad says that as the Earth speeds around the sun turning on its axis 1037⅓ miles per hour it creates gravity and the strong attracting power of the sun pulls on the waters of the Earth, drawing them up into the Earth's atmosphere in a fine mist that the naked eye can hardly detect. As this water gathers into the Earth's atmosphere it then distills and comes back to Earth. When it gets heavier than the atmosphere in which it is, it distills and comes back to the Earth in the form of water, rain, hail, or snow. All of the water that you see coming out of the sky went up into the sky. Everything that's coming down on the Earth got up there by leaving the Earth. Do you understand? And he teaches us that it comes back down in the form of hail or rain or snow or whatever else you have, depending upon the temperature of the current atmosphere that it was in. He says that at night the gravitational pull of the moon takes over, and, because the power of the moon is not as great as that of the sun, once the attracting power of the sun is absent at night the moon takes over, but since it can't pull the waters up like the sun does, it still has that magnetic pull and it causes the waves that you see out there on the ocean to churn. It is the moon that does that; the moon makes the waves go up and down. It never lets them level out. If they leveled out the water would overrun the land. It also causes the shifting of the tide. This is the pull of the moon upon the waters of the Earth. If it weren't for the attracting powers of the sun and the moon upon the Earth, the waters would overrun the land and drown out civilization. All of this was done by man himself, not some Mystery God. A black man set this up. And you and I have been running around in the trap that the white man put us in, thinking that the only one who can do anything is a Mystery God and what the Mystery God doesn't do the white man does.

The Honorable Elijah Muhammad says that all the time that this was going on there was no white man. The white man was nowhere on the scene. He says that when the moon was blasted away and we came along with the Earth, one tribe was in fact destroyed. Prior to the time that the explosion took place there were thirteen tribes. In the explosion set off sixty-six trillion years ago the thirteenth tribe was destroyed, and then all of the time down through the wheel of time since then there were twelve tribes until six thousand years ago. And six thousand years ago, a scientist named Yacub created another tribe on this Earth.

Understand, prior to the time the explosion took place, there were thirteen tribes, but the thirteenth tribe was destroyed in that explosion and then six thousand years ago another tribe came on the scene. It was made different from all of the twelve tribes that were here when it arrived. A new tribe, a weak tribe, a wicked tribe, a devilish tribe, a diabolical tribe, a tribe that is devilish by nature. So that before they got on the scene, The Honorable Elijah Muhammad says that when we came with the Earth, the oldest city on the Earth is the Holy City, Mecca, in Arabia. Mecca is the oldest city on Earth. Mecca is the city that is forbidden. No one can go there but the black man. No one can go there but the Muslims. No one can go there but the believer. No one can go there but the righteous. And at Mecca are kept the records of history that go on back to the beginning of time. He says that fifty thousand years ago another scientist named Shabazz became angry with the scientists of his day. He wanted to bring about a tougher people. He wanted the people to undergo a form of life that would make them tough and hard, and the other scientists wouldn't agree with him. So this scientist named Shabazz took his family and wandered down into the jungles of Africa. Prior to that time no one lived in the jungles. Our people were soft; they were black but they were soft and delicate, fine. They had straight hair. Right here on this Earth you find some of them look like that today. They are black as night, but their hair is like silk, and originally *all* our people had that kind of hair. But this scientist took his family down into the jungles of Africa, and living in the open, living a jungle life, eating all kinds of food had an effect on the appearance of our people. Actually living in the rough climate, our hair became stiff, like it is now. We undertook new features that we have now. The Honorable Elijah Muhammad says that the only hair that the black man has today that looks now like it looked prior to fifty thousand years ago is your and my eyebrows. Right here, you notice, all Negroes have straight—I don't care how nappy their hair is—they have straight eyebrows. When you see a nappy-hair-eyebrowed Negro [chuckle] you got somebody. But all of this took place back in history, and everything The Honorable Elijah Muhammad teaches is based on history. Now then, where does the white man come in?

The Honorable Elijah Muhammad says that the wise black man who was a master of science never wrote his history like it is written today, of the past. The wise black man in that day wrote his history in the future. The Honorable Elijah Muhammad says that the circumference of the Earth is 24,896 miles, approximately 25,000 miles. So when he says the wise black man of the East writes history a year for every mile, he writes history to last for 25,000 years—not in the past, but in the future. He says that on this Earth there are wise black men who can tune in and tell what's going to happen in the future just as clear—they can see ahead just as clear—as they can see in the past. And every 25,000 years he says that civilization reaches its peak, or reaches its perfection. At this time the wise black man can hear a pin drop anywhere on the planet Earth. And they sit down and write history to last for 25,000 years. After this history expires they put it in a vault at the Holy City, Mecca, and write a new history. This has been going on and on and on. So, in the year one of the cycle in which we now live, he says that in the East there are twenty-four wise men. They're spoken of in the Bible as twenty-four elders or twenty-four prophets or twenty-four scientists or twenty-four imams. Twelve of them are major and twelve of them are minor. So The Honorable Elijah Muhammad says that these twenty-three men are called together by this one, which makes twenty-four. And these twenty-four, these twenty-three presided over by the twenty-fourth, are spoken of in the Book of Revelation where John said he had a vision in heaven where there was a throne, and around the throne were twenty-four seats and on the seats sat twenty-four elders. These twenty-four elders are called angels. They are actually twenty-four wise black men who live right here on this Earth, but no one knows who they are. At the end of every 25,000 years this one calls all of them into conference, and they sit down at the Holy City, Mecca, and he informs them that the history of the past 25,000 years has expired and it's time to write a new history. So these twenty-four, these scientists, begin to tune in on the population of the planet Earth and he says that back in his day—at that time there were five billion people on this Earth—all of them black, not a white man in sight—five billion people—not a white man in sight, so he says that when these twenty-four scientists begin to tune in, they look down through the wheel of time. They can tell not only what the people on this Earth are thinking, but they can tell what their children are thinking, what the unborn children's children are thinking, what the unborn children's children's children are thinking. They can look right down through the wheel of time and tell minute-by-minute, hour-by-hour, day-by-day, week-by-week, month-by-month, year-by-year, for 25,000 years exactly what is going to take place. And they discovered that in the year 8400 to come it would register that among five billion black people, seventy percent would be satisfied and thirty percent would be dissatisfied. And out of that thirty percent would be born a wise black scientist named Yacub, and Yacub would teach among these thirty percent dissatisfied from whom he would come, and create a new race, start a new world, and a new civilization that would rule this Earth for six thousand years to come. So they brought these findings back to the king and they were put in a book. And by the way, that which is written to last for 25,000 years is called the Holy Koran.

The Honorable Elijah Muhammad said that this was put into the history and then when the year 8400 came, Yacub was born. When Yucab reached the age of six years he was playing in the sand one day with two pieces of metal, two pieces of steel, at which time he discovered what is known as the law of magnetism: that unlike attracts and like repels. Two objects that are alike repel each other like two women repel each other, but man and woman attract each other. Unlike attracts and like repels. Yacub discovered this. So Yacub knew that all he had to do was make a man unlike any other man on this Earth and because he would be different he would attract all other people. Then he could teach this man a science called tricknology, which is a science of tricks and lies, and this weak man would be able to use that science to trick and rob and rule the world. So Yacub turned to his uncle and said, "When I grow up I'm going to make a man who will rule you." And Yacub's uncle said, "What can you make other than that which will cause bloodshed and wickedness in the land?" And Yacub pointed to his head and said, "I know that which you know not." Yacub was born with a determined idea to make this man because it had been predicted 8400 years prior to his birth that he would be born to do this work. So he was born with this idea in him, and when his uncle realized that this was he about whom it had been prophesied his uncle submitted. The Honorable Elijah Muhammad said that Yacub went to school in the East; he studied the astronomical sciences, mathematical sciences, and the germination of man. He discovered that in the black man there are two germs. In the black man there's a brown man. In the black man, or the black germ, which is a strong germ, there's a weak germ, a brown germ. Yacub was the first one to discover this and Yacub knew that by separating that brown one from the black one, and then by grafting the brown one from the black one so that it became lighter and lighter, it would eventually reach its lightest stage which is known as white. And when it got to that stage it would be weak, and because it was weak it would be susceptible to wickedness. And then Yacub could take that weak man that he made and teach him how to lie and rob and cheat and thereby become the ruler of all of the rest of the world.

So The Honorable Elijah Muhammad teaches us that Yacub began to preach at the age of sixteen. He began to preach all over Arabia in the East. He preached among the thirty percent who were dissatisfied and got many of them to follow him. As they began to listen to Yacub's teachings and believe them, his teachings spread, his followers grew, and it created confusion in the land. So The Honorable Elijah Muhammad says that so much confusion came into existence over there that they threw Yacub's followers in jail, and as fast as they would throw them in jail they taught more people. So the teachings spread in jail. Finally Yacub was put in jail, under an alias. And one day, The Honorable Elijah Muhammad says, the thing began to get out of hand and the authorities went to the king and told him that they couldn't control these people, but that they had the leader of the people in jail right now, and the king said, "Take me to him."

And when the king went to the jail where Yacub was, he greeted Yacub with "As-Salaam-Alaikum, Mr. Yacub"—I know you're Mr. Yacub—and Yacub said, "Wa-Alaikum-Salaam"—I am Yacub! And the king said, "Look, I came to make an agreement with you. I know that you are the one that it is written or predicted would be on the scene in this day and would create a new race, and there is nothing we can do to stop you. But in order for us to have peace we want to make an agreement with you. In order to stop the confusion and for there to be some peace in the land, we want you to agree to take all who will follow you and exile yourselves out on an island in the Aegean Sea."

Yacub told them, "I'll go. But you've got to give me everything that I will need to bring into existence a new civilization. You've got to give me everything I'll need. You've got to supply me with everything I need for the next twenty years." And The Honorable Elijah Muhammad says that the king agreed with Yacub, the government of that day agreed to supply Yacub and his followers with everything they needed for twenty years. And he says that he gets this from the Bible where it says Jacob wrestled with the angel. Jacob was Yacub, and the angel that Jacob wrestled with wasn't God, it was the government of that day. "Angel" only means "a power," or somebody with power. When a man has his wings clipped, you say that he has lost his power, lost his position. So wings only mean a position of power entrapped him. So when it says Jacob wrestled with an angel, "angel" is only used as a symbol to hide the one he was really wrestling with. Jacob was wrestling with the government of that day. He made the government of that day give him everything he needed to last him and his followers for twenty years, just like The Honorable Elijah Muhammad is telling the government of this day that they've got to give us everything that we need in our own separate territory to last us for twenty to twenty-five years. You say, well, The Honorable Elijah Muhammad teaches us that Yacub agreed, the government agreed, Yacub took all of his followers down to the sea. The Honorable Elijah Muhammad says that Yacub took 59,999 of his followers down to the seaside, with himself making 60,000. He piled them in boats and took them out to an island in the Aegean Sea called Pelan. In the Bible it's called Patmos. When you read in the Book of Revelation where John, on the island of Patmos, heard the word of the Lord, that is Yacub. What was John doing on the island of Patmos? John was Yacub. John was out there getting ready to make a new race, he said, for the word of the Lord. What was the word of the Lord? The word was that in the year 8400 a new man would be made, a new race would be made. And when Yacub and his followers got out there his followers realized that Yacub was wiser than any man of his day, and they recognized him as a god; he was a god to them. So when you get to the place in the Bible where it says, "And God said, 'Let us make man,'" that was Yacub too, not the Supreme Being. It wasn't the Supreme Being who made the sun who said, "Let us make man." When the Supreme Being made the sun he said, "Let there be light." He said He was supreme, He was independent, He needed no help, no associates. But when it came to making a man, that god said, "Let us make man." He didn't speak with independence, because there were two different gods. God the Supreme Being made the light. His word is "be"; that's how He makes things. But Yacub, who was a lesser god, said to 59,999 of his followers, "Let us make man, let us make a man in our image, in our likeness. We're going to make a white man." It was Yacub talking: "Make him in our image and in our likeness, and give him dominion over the fowl of the air and the fish of the sea and the creatures of the land. And we'll call him Adam." It's only a name for the white man. The white man has taken mastery over the air, his airplanes rule the sky, his submarines and ships rule the sea, his armies rule the land. This was the man that was made six thousand years ago and the purpose for making him was so he could rule the world for six thousand years. That's the white man.

The Honorable Elijah Muhammad says that first thing Yacub did was to get his ministers, doctors, nurses, and cremators together. He gave them the laws because he had to set up a birth control law. He told the doctors whenever two black ones come to him to get married to stick a needle in their veins, take some blood, and go back and tell them that their blood doesn't match so that they can't marry. He also said when a black one and a brown one come, let them get married, or if two brown ones come let them get married. Then he told the nurse nine months after they're married, when you're ready to deliver their child, if it's a black child, put a needle in its brain and feed it to a wild animal or give it to the cremator. Let it be destroyed. But if it's a brown child, take that child to the mother and tell her that this is going to be a great man when he grows up because he's lighter than the others. Tell her that the child you destroyed was an angel baby and it went up to heaven to prepare a place for her when she dies. Same old lie they tell you today—when a little baby dies they tell you it went to heaven. When a baby dies he goes to the same place a man goes when he dies—right down into the ground. Is that right or wrong? So The Honorable Elijah Muhammad has taught us that Yacub right there set up his birth control law. Within two hundred years they had killed off all of the black babies on the island. Everything black on the island had been destroyed. And then Yacub only lived 150 years. But he left laws and rules and regulations behind, for his followers to go by. And after they had destroyed all of the black on the island of Pelan, they began to work on the brown germ. They saved the yellow and destroyed the brown, because you see in the black there's brown and in the brown there's yellow. Can you see how it goes? The darkest one always has a lighter one in it. So in the black man there's a brown man, in the brown man there's a yellow man, in the yellow man there's what? A white man. Oh yes. Getting weaker all the time. So it took two hundred years to destroy the black. And then they worked on the brown for two hundred years. And in two hundred years all the brown was destroyed and all they had on the island of Pelan was a yellow or mulatto-looking civilization. And then they went to work on it and began to destroy it. So that after six hundred years of destruction on the island of Pelan, they had grafted away the black, grafted away the brown, grafted away the yellow, so that all they had left was a pale-skinned, blue-eyed, blond-haired thing that you call a man. But actually the Bible calls him the devil. That's the devil that the

Bible is talking about: old Lucifer, Satan, or the serpent. Because the lighter they got, the weaker they got. As they began to get lighter and lighter they grew weaker and weaker. Their blood became weaker, their bones became weaker, their minds became weaker, their morals became weaker. They became a wicked race; by nature wicked. Why by nature?

The Book says concerning the devil: "He was conceived in inequity and born in sin." What does this mean? At the outset the nurses had to kill the little black babies, but after a while it got so that the mother, having been brainwashed, hated that black one so much she killed it herself. Killed it herself, and saved the light one. And right on down for six hundred years. In order for the white one to come into existence, the darker one was always murdered, murdered, MURDERED! This went right into the nature of the child that was being born. The mother wanted a light baby when the child was being conceived. This went right into the baby. The mother hated black when the child was being conceived. This went right into the baby. So that at the end of the six hundred years, after planting the seed of inequity right into the brain, right into the mind, right into the heart, right into the nature of these people, by the time they got the white man, they had someone who by nature hated everything that was darker than he was. Why, they had to murder off the black to get to the brown. They had to murder off the brown in order to get to the yellow. They had to murder off the black, brown, and yellow in order to get to the white. And right to this very day the white man *by nature* wants to murder off the black, brown, and yellow. You don't have to teach him to kill the black man. He does it for sport. He does it for kicks. He does it because it's his nature to do it. Do you understand that?

So in six hundred years now they got a devil on the scene, a blue-eyed devil, blond-haired. Oh yes, they were out here on the island of Pelan. Yacub was dead. Yacub was their father but he never saw them. They never saw him. Yacub was their god. When the Bible says no man had seen God, that's what it means. No white man has seen their god. None of them saw Yacub because Yacub only lived to be 150 years old. This doesn't mean that no man can see God the Supreme Being. Why, the Book of Revelation says when He comes every eye will see Him. So The Honorable Elijah Muhammad says after these devils got grafted—now we're not going to call them white any more. We call them what they are. White, that's their color, but devil, that's what they are. These aren't white people. You're not using the right language when you say the white man. You call it the devil. When you call him devil you're calling him by his name, and he's got another name—Satan; another name—serpent; another name—snake; another name—beast. All these names are in the Bible for the white man. Another name—Pharaoh; another name—Caesar; another name—France; French; Frenchman; Englishman; American; all those are just names for the devil.

So after they were out there six hundred years, after they were made and grafted and Yacub was dead, then they packed up their bags and made it back to civilization. Yacub had left them some laws to go by. He left them a science called "tricknology": how to divide and conquer. Yacub told these people in his book: "All you got to do to take over the world is lie. Go back among the black people. Take your woman and send her to the black man's woman and let her lie about the neighbor across the street. And then send another woman to that woman to lie on this woman to that woman. And when they get through spreading those lies and they all start fighting and killing one another, you tell them to let you be the mediator." This is the trick the white man used. It all comes from Yacub. You see, he's an underdog. He's a minority, and the only way a minority can rule a majority is to *divide* the majority. This is the trick that the white man was born to execute among dark mankind here on this Earth. Yacub said, "When you go back among them, lie about them to each other, and when they start fighting, ask them to let you be the mediator. And as soon as you become the mediator then you're the boss." The white man has done this trick everywhere. Here in America to the Indians. He sent one priest to the Indians in New York and another priest to the Indians in Pennsylvania and both of them would tell lies to both Indians, and the Indians who had never been at war with each other would start beating the tom-toms, the war drums, and then as they got ready to fight the priest would run in and say, "Let me be the mediator."

So he told the New York Indians, you just move out to Minnesota; and the Pennsylvania Indians, you move out to Oklahoma. That would leave the whole states of New York and Pennsylvania for the white man. You see how he does it? He's all over the world. He's a mediator. He's an instigator and a mediator. He instigates division and dissension and as soon as they start fighting one another he says, "OK, I'll settle it." If you don't think so look all over the world right now. Every place on this earth you have a division: South Korea-North Korea, South Vietnam-North Vietnam. Right or wrong? He is the one that makes this decision. He doesn't let anybody get together, but when it comes to his kind he's united. United States means all white people are united. United States of Europe, or European Common Market—they want to get together. But when you start talking about a United States of Asia, or a United States of Africa, why he says, "Oh no, too many different languages [chuckle]. You all don't have anything in common." You see how he does it? He always discourages unity among others but he encourages unity among his own kind. "United We Stand," that doesn't mean *you*. That means the white man. The white man is the one who stands united.

So The Honorable Elijah Muhammad says that these devils went back into Arabia. When they got there they started telling lies, started confusion, and in six months' time they had turned heaven into hell. Oh yeah, they had so much fighting going on among our people, brother, it became hell. We never did fight each other we loved each other, we were in harmony with each other. And when these devils came back into our midst they turned our paradise into a hell. So it was taken to the king and the king looked into the book and said, "Why, these are Yacub's people." He said, "They were made to do what they're doing and the only way to have peace is to get rid of all of them. Put them all to death." So the king gave the order for all of the devils to be rounded up. And by devils I mean all those blue-eyed, blond-haired, white things. He gave orders for them to be rounded up there in the East, and they were rounded up. They were rounded up and taken down to the edge of the Arabian Desert. They were stripped naked, stripped of everything except their language. The Honorable Elijah Muhammad says that we put lambskin aprons around their waists to hide their nakedness. We put them in chains and marched them across the hot sands of the Arabian Desert. This is what the black man did to the white man, brothers. This is what the gods did to the devils. Actually, if you think I don't know what I'm talking about, those of you who are Masons, you go through this and don't understand it. When you go in, they put a lambskin apron around your waist. They put you in what's called the "cable tow." Right or wrong? And then they make you jump up and down on an electric mat. Make you take off your shoes and put the juice in the mat and make you jump up and down. Why? What are they getting at? That's all a sign of what happened to the white man six thousand years ago. It just doesn't have anything to do with you, but you're supposed to be walking on hot sands when you jump up and down. Right or wrong? You've all been in some of that stuff. They tell you that's crossing the hot sand. And if you walk up to a Negro Mason and you ask him, "When you crossed the hot sand were you walking or riding?" he'll say, "I was walking." He's a fool. Because he was riding. He was riding horseback. He was riding on a camel. It was the white man that was in chains. It was the white man that had the apron around him. It was the white man that was walking the white sand. We walked them at high noon. We wouldn't even let them walk at night. We stopped at night. And you know how hot the sun and the sands are in Arabia. We expected the white man to die when we were running him out of the East. But that fool lived, brother [chuckle]. He lived. A lot of them died on the desert. And I might come back—all of this is tied up in the Masonic ritual. When a man gets initiated into the higher degrees of that order he goes through this. They put on the chains, they put on the aprons, and they darken him up and pretend to be driving him across. Then when he gets up to the top order in those degrees, they tell him what it means. The white man, they tell the white man what it means: a white Shriner, a white Mason, what it means. A Negro never learns what it means. But it actually points back toward the time when the white man, who is the devil, or Adam, as they say, was cast out of the Garden. When the Bible says Adam sinned and was cast out of the Garden, this is what is meant. And an angel was put at the East gate to keep him from coming back in. When the white man was run out of the East by the Muslims six thousand years ago into the caves of Europe, the people called Turks were put there at the Straits of the Dardanelles, with swords, and any old devil that they caught trying to come back across the water—WHOP!!!—off went his head. The Book tells you that the angel had a flaming sword, and any time any of them tried to come back across they were put to death.

The Honorable Elijah Muhammad says that the white man went down into the caves of Europe and he lived there for two thousand years on all fours. Within one thousand years after he had gotten there he was on all fours, couldn't stand upright. You watch an old cracker today. Crackers don't walk upright like black people do. Every time you look at them, they're about to go down on all fours. But those who have had some education, they straighten up a little bit because they're taught how to straighten up. But a black man can be the most dumb, illiterate thing you can find anywhere, and he still walks like a million dollars because by nature he's upright, by nature he stands up. But a white man has to be stood up. You have to put a white man on the square. But the black is born on the square.

Can we prove it? Yes. You notice in the East, dark people carry things on their heads, don't they? Just throw it up there and walk with it, showing you they have perfect poise, perfect balance. It just comes natural to them. You and I lost our poise. We, you, can't even wear a hat on your head, hardly, today [chuckle]. The Honorable Elijah Muhammad says that within one thousand years after the white people were up in the caves they were on all fours. And they were living in the outdoors where it's cold, just as cold over there as it is outside right now. They didn't have clothes. So by being out there in the cold their hair got longer and longer. Hair grew all over their bodies. By being on all fours, the end of their spine begin to grow. They grew a little tail that came out from the end of their spine . . . Oh yes, this was the white man, brother, up in the caves of Europe. He had a tail that long. You ever notice that anything that walks on all fours has a tail? That which straightens up doesn't have a tail, because when you get down, you see, you just make that spine come right on out. And just like a dog, he was crawling around up there. He was hairy as a dog. He had a tail like a dog. He had a smell like a dog. And nothing could get along with him but another dog. The Honorable Elijah Muhammad says that all the beasts up in Europe wanted to kill the white man. Yeah, they tried to kill the white man. They were after the white man. They hated the white man. So, he says, what the white man would do, he'd dig a hole in the hill, that was his cave. And his mother and his daughter and his wife would all be in there with the dog. The only thing that made friends with the white man was the dog. Everything else hated him. He'd sit outside of the cave at night in a tree with rocks in his hand, and if any beast came up and tried to get in the cave at his family, he'd throw rocks at it, or he'd have a club that he'd swing down and try to drive it away with it. But the dog stayed in the cave with his family. It was then that the dog and the white man amalgamated. The white woman went with the dog while they were living in the caves of Europe. And right to this very day the white woman will tell you there is nothing she loves better than a dog. They tell you that a dog is a man's best friend. A dog isn't a black man's best friend. God is the black man's best friend. But a dog is the white man's best friend. They lived in that cave with those dogs and right now they got that dog smell. They got that dog . . . They are dog lovers. A dog can get in a white man's house and eat at his table, lick out of his plate. They'll kiss the dog right on the nose and think nothing of it. You're not a dog kisser. You don't see black people kissing or rubbing noses with dogs. But little white children will hug dogs and kiss dogs and *eat* with dogs. Am I right or wrong? You-all have been inside their kitchens cooking their food, and making their beds, you *know* how they live. The dog will live right in the white man's house, better than you can; you try and break your way in there and they'll put a rope around your neck [chuckle], but the dog has got free run of the whole house. He's the white man's best friend.

The Honorable Elijah Muhammad says that they lived up there for two thousand years, and at the end of two thousand years the scientists in the East, realizing that it was originally predestined that the white race would rule for six thousand years, and that they had already lost two thousand years in the caves of Europe, sent a prophet up there, from Mecca, to teach the white race, the race of devils, how to become civilized again, and become up-right, and come back and rule the way they had originally been meant to. The name of that prophet was Moses. Moses never went down into Egypt. Moses went into the caves of Europe and civilized the white man. It was Moses who raised the devil from a dead level to a perpendicular and placed him on the square. Moses taught the white man how to cook his food. Moses taught the white man how to build a house for himself. He taught the white man also some of the tricknology that Yacub had originally meant for him, and it was Moses who put the white man back on the road toward civilization. He told him that he was supposed to rule for six thousand years, but that much of the time had already been lost, and at the end of time one would come who would destroy the whole white race. Moses taught them this. And this is why when the Jews, two thousand years later, were looking for the Messiah, they thought that Jesus was the Messiah and they put him to death because they knew when the Messiah came he was going to destroy that whole race of devils. The Jews knew this, so they put him to death thinking that they could stop him from destroying them. But actually, they made a mistake because Jesus two thousand years ago wasn't the Messiah. Their time wasn't up two thousand years ago. Their time would not be up until two thousand years later, the day and time that we're living in right now.

So, brothers and sisters, my time has expired. I just wanted to point out that the white man, a race of devils, was made six thousand years ago. This doesn't mean to tell you that this implies any kind of hate. They're just a race of devils. They were made six thousand years ago, they were made to rule for six thousand years, and their time expired in the year 1914. The only reason God didn't remove them then was because you and I were here in their clutches and God gave them an extension of time—not *them* an extension of time, but they received an extension of time to give the wise men of the East the opportunity to get into this House of Bondage and "awaken" the Lost Sheep. Once the American so-called Negroes have been awakened to a knowledge of themselves and of their own God and of the white man, then they're on their own. Then it'll be left up to you and me whether we want to integrate into this wicked race or leave them and separate and go to our own. And if we integrate we'll be destroyed along with them. If we separate then we have a chance for salvation. So on that note, in the name of Allah, and His Messenger The Honorable Elijah Muhammad, I bring my talk to a close, "As-Salaam-Alaikum."

With your hands outstretched in this manner, follow silently in the closing Muslim prayer:

In the name of Allah, the Beneficent, the Merciful,
All praise is due to Allah, the Lord of the Worlds,
The Beneficent, the Merciful,
Master of this Day of Judgment in which we now live,
Thee do we serve and Thee do we beseech for thine aid.
Guide us on the right path,
The path upon which Thou hast bestowed favors,
Not the path upon which Thy wrath is brought down
Nor of those who go astray after they have heard Thy teaching.
Say: He Allah is one God
Allah is He upon whom nothing is independent but
Upon whom we all depend.
He neither begets nor is He begotten and none is like Him.
I bear witness there is none to be served but Allah,
And I bear witness that The Honorable Elijah Muhammad is
His True Servant and Last Apostle . . . Amen

God in Black Theology

JAMES H. CONE

The reality of God is presupposed in black theology. Black theology is an attempt to analyze the nature of that reality, asking what we can say about the nature of God in view of God's self-disclosure in biblical history and the oppressed condition of black Americans.

If we take the question seriously, it becomes evident that there is no simple answer to it. To speak of God and God's participation in the liberation of the oppressed of the land is a risky venture in any society. But if the society is racist and also uses God-language as an instrument to further the cause of human humiliation, then the task of authentic theological speech is even more dangerous and difficult.

It is *dangerous* because the true prophet of the gospel of God must become both "anti-Christian" and "unpatriotic." It is impossible to confront a racist society, with the meaning of human existence grounded in commitment to the divine, without at the same time challenging the very existence of the national structure and all its institutions, especially the established churches. All national institutions represent the interests of society as a whole. We live in a nation which is committed to the perpetuation of white supremacy, and it will try to exterminate all who fail to support this ideal. The genocide of the Amerindian is evidence of that fact. Black theology represents that community of blacks who refuse to cooperate in the exaltation of whiteness and the degradation of blackness. It proclaims the reality of the biblical God who is actively destroying everything that is against the manifestation of black human dignity.

Because whiteness by its very nature is against blackness, the black prophet is a prophet of national doom. He proclaims the end of the "American Way," for God has stirred the soul of the black community, and now that community will stop at nothing to claim the freedom that is three hundred and fifty years overdue. The black prophet is a rebel with a cause, the cause of over twenty-five million American blacks and all oppressed persons everywhere. It is God's cause because God has chosen the blacks as God's own people. And God has chosen them not for redemptive suffering but for freedom. Blacks are not elected to be Yahweh's suffering people. Rather we are elected because we are oppressed against our will and God's, and God has decided to make our liberation God's own undertaking. We are elected to be free now to do the work for which we were called into being—namely, the breaking of chains. Black theologians must assume the dangerous responsibility of articulating the revolutionary mood of the black community. This means that their speech about God, in the authentic prophetic tradition, will always move on the brink of treason and heresy in an oppressive society.

The task of authentic theological speech is *difficult* because all religionists in society claim to be for God and thus for humankind. Even executioners are for God. They carry out punitive acts against certain segments of society because "decent" citizens need protection against undesirables. That is why blacks were enslaved and Amerindians exterminated—in the name of God and freedom. That is why today blacks are forced into ghettos and shot down like dogs if they raise a hand in protest.

When George Washington, Thomas Jefferson, Lyndon Johnson, Richard Nixon, and other "great" Americans can invoke the name of God at the same time that they are shaping society for whites only, then black theology knows it cannot approach the God-question too casually. It must ask, "How can we speak of God without being associated with oppressors?" White racism is so pervasive that oppressors can destroy the revolutionary mood among the oppressed by introducing a complacent white God into the black community, thereby quelling the spirit of freedom.

Therefore if blacks want to break their chains, they must recognize the need for going all the way if liberation is to be a reality. The white God will point to heavenly bliss as a means of detouring blacks away from earthly rage. Freedom comes when we realize that it is against our interests, as a self-determining black community, to point out the "good" elements in an oppressive structure. *There are no assets to slavery!* Every segment of society participates in black oppression. To accept the white God, to see good in evil, is to lose sight of the goal of the revolution—the destruction of everything "masterly" in society. "All or nothing" is the only possible attitude for the black community.

Must We Discard God-Language?

Realizing that it is very easy to be co-opted by the enemy and the enemy's God-language, it is tempting to discard all references to God and seek to describe a way of living in the world that could not possibly be associated with "Christian" murderers. Some existentialist writers—Camus and Sartre—have taken this course, and many black revolutionaries find this procedure appealing. Reacting to the ungodly behavior of white churches and the timid, Uncle Tom approach of black churches, many black militants have no time for God and the deadly prattle about loving your enemies and turning the other cheek. Christianity, they argue, participates in the enslavement of black Americans. Therefore an emancipation from white oppression means also liberation from the ungodly influences of white religion.

This approach is certainly understandable, and the merits of the argument warrant a serious investigation. As black theologians seeking to analyze the meaning of black liberation, we cannot ignore this approach. Indeed, it is quite intellectually tempting. Nevertheless two observations are in order at this juncture.

(1) Black theology affirms that there is nothing special about the English word "God" in itself. What is important is the dimension of reality to which it points. The word "God" is a symbol that opens up depths of reality in the world. If the symbol loses its power to point to the meaning of black liberation, then we must destroy it. Black theology asks whether the word "God" has lost its liberating power. Must we say that as a meaningful symbol the word "God" is hopelessly dead and cannot be resurrected?

Certainly black theology realizes that, when a society performs ungodly acts against the poor in the name of God, there may come a time when the oppressed might have to renounce all claims to that kind of "faith" in God in order to affirm authentic faith in God. Sometimes because of the very nature of oppressed existence, the oppressed must define their being by negating everything oppressors affirm, including belief in the God of oppressors. The oppressed must demonstrate that all communications are cut off. In Camus's words:

> There is, in fact, nothing in common between a master and a slave; it is impossible to speak and communicate with a person who has been reduced to servitude.[1]

Oppressed and oppressors cannot possibly mean the same thing when they speak of God. The God of the oppressed is a God of revolution who breaks the chains of slavery. The oppressors' God is a God of slavery and must be destroyed along with the oppressors. The question then, as black theology sees it, is not whether blacks believe in God, but whose God?

(2) In response to those inclined to discard God-language, black theology also believes that the destiny of blacks is inseparable from the religious dimensions inherent in the black community. Theologically, one way of describing this reality is to call it general revelation. This means that all human beings have a sense of the presence of God, a feeling of awe, and it is precisely this experience that makes them creatures who always rebel against domestication. The black community is thus a religious community, a community that views its liberation as the work of the divine.

It is important to note that every significant black liberation movement has had its religious dimensions. Black liberation as a movement began with the pre-Civil War black churches which recognized that Christian freedom grounded in Jesus Christ was inseparable from civil freedom. That is why black preachers were the leaders in the struggle for the abolition of slavery, and why southern slave owners refused to allow the establishment of independent black churches in the south. It is true, however, that the post-Civil War black church lost its emphasis on civil freedom and began to identify Christianity with moral purity. But this does not mean that religion is irrelevant altogether; it only means that religion unrelated to black liberation is irrelevant.

To try to separate black liberation from black religion is a mistake, because black religion is authentic only when it is identified with the struggle for black freedom. The influence of Marcus Garvey, Elijah Muhammed, Malcolm X, and Martin Luther King, Jr., demonstrates the role of religion in the black community.

It is not the task of black theology to remove the influence of the divine in the black community. Its task is to interpret the divine element in the forces and achievements of black liberation. Black theology must retain God-language despite its perils, because the black community perceives its identity in terms of divine presence.

Black theology cannot create new symbols independent of the black community and expect blacks to respond. It must stay in the black community and get down to the real issues at hand ("cutting throats" to use LeRoi Jones's phrase) and not waste too much time discussing the legitimacy of religious language.

The legitimacy of any language, religious or otherwise, is determined by its usefulness in the struggle for liberation. That the God-language of white religion has been used to create a docile spirit among blacks so that whites could aggressively attack them is beyond question. But that does not mean that we cannot kill the white God, so that the presence of the black God can become known in the black-white encounter. The white God is an idol created by racists, and we blacks must perform the iconoclastic task of smashing false images.

Hermeneutical Principle for the Doctrine of God

Every doctrine of God is based on a particular theological methodology. For instance, Karl Barth's theological point of departure is the word of God as revealed in the man Jesus. We know who God is, according to Barth, because we know who Christ is. To look for the knowledge of God other than in Christ is to look in the wrong place, and thus end up constructing images which reflect human pride rather than divine revelation. "The knowledge of God occurs in the fulfillment of the revelation of His Word by the Holy Spirit."[2]

Paul Tillich, on the other hand, does not share Barth's kerygmatic emphasis. His theological methodology is a "method of correlation," in which he seeks to relate the changeless gospel to changing cultural situations. Culture, according to Tillich, is indispensable for God-talk.

Relying heavily on existential philosophy and its analysis of the human condition (a condition best described by the word "estrangement"), Tillich describes God as being-itself, which provides the only answer to human estrangement from self and neighbor. Because being-itself is free from the threat of nonbeing or nothingness, it is the source of human courage—the ability to affirm being in spite of the presence of nonbeing. Therefore "God" is a symbolic word pointing to the dimension of reality which is the answer to the human condition.

Inasmuch as the perspective of black theology differs from that of both Barth and Tillich, there is also a difference in its approach to the doctrine of God. The point of departure of black theology is the biblical God as related to the black liberation struggle. It asks, "How do we *dare* speak of God in a suffering world, a world in which blacks are humiliated because they are black?" This question, which occupies the central place in our theological perspective, forces us to say nothing about God that does not participate in the emancipation of black humanity. God-talk is not Christian-talk unless it is *directly* related to the liberation of the oppressed. Any other talk is at best an intellectual hobby, and at worst blasphemy.

There are, then, two hermeneutical principles which are operative in the black theology analysis of the doctrine of God.

(1) The Christian understanding of God arises from the biblical view of revelation, a revelation of God that takes place in the liberation of oppressed Israel and is completed in the incarnation, in Jesus Christ. This means that whatever is said about the nature of God and God's being-in-the-world must be based on the biblical account of God's revelatory activity. We are not free to say anything we please about God. Although scripture is not the only source that helps us to recognize divine activity in the world, it cannot be ignored if we intend to speak of the Holy One of Israel.

(2) The doctrine of God in black theology must be of the God who is participating in the liberation of the oppressed of the land. This hermeneutical principle arises out of the first. Because God has been revealed in the history of oppressed Israel and decisively in the Oppressed One, Jesus Christ, it is impossible to say anything about God without seeing him as being involved in the contemporary liberation of all oppressed peoples. The God in black theology is the God of and for the oppressed, the God who comes into view in their liberation. Any other approach is a denial of biblical revelation.

New Wine in New Wineskins

Because black theology is the theology of black liberation, it must break with traditional theological speech when that speech softens the drive for black self-determination. It cannot run the risk of putting "new wine into old wineskins" (Mark 2:22). When Jesus used the phrase, he was referring to the kingdom of God and its relationship to the conventional Judaism of his time.

When black theologians analyze the doctrine of God, seeking to relate it to the emerging black revolution in America, they must be especially careful not to put this new wine (the revelation of God as expressed in black power) into old wineskins (white folk-religion). The black theology view of God must be sharply distinguished from white distortions of God. This does not mean that black theology rejects white theology entirely. Unfortunately, this cannot be done, for oppression always means that the communication skills of an oppressed community are determined to a large degree by the oppressors. That is precisely the meaning of oppression! Because black theologians are trained in white seminaries, and white thinkers make decisions about the structure and scope of theology, it is not possible for black religionists to separate themselves immediately and completely from white thought.

When Jesus spoke of the gospel as new wine, it did not mean a total rejection of Judaism. What he meant was that the revolutionary message could not be restricted to the possibilities available in the old structure.

Similarly, because our knowledge of Christianity came from white oppressors, the black theology view of God is in part dependent on white theologians, but this does not mean white theologians set the criteria for black theology. Liberation means that the oppressed must define the structure and scope of reality for themselves; they do not take their cues from oppressors. If there is one brutal fact that the centuries of white oppression have taught blacks, it is that whites are incapable of making any valid judgment about human existence. The goal of black theology is the destruction of *everything* white, so that blacks can be liberated from alien gods.

The God of black liberation will not be confused with a bloodthirsty white idol. Black theology must show that the black God has nothing to do with the God worshiped in white churches whose primary purpose is to sanctify the racism of whites and to daub the wounds of blacks. Putting new wine in new wineskins means that the black theology view of God has nothing in common with those who prayed for an American victory in Vietnam or who pray for a "cool" summer in the ghetto.

The refusal of black theology to put new wine in old wineskins also means that it will show that the God of the black community cannot be confused with the God of white seminaries. With their intellectual expertise, it is inevitable that white scholars fall into the racist error of believing that they have the right to define what is and what is not orthodox religious talk. Because they have read so many of their own books and heard themselves talk so often, it is not surprising that they actually believe most of the garbage they spout out about God. They therefore think that all authentic God-talk must meet their approval before it can be called theology. But black theology rejects their standards, for we know they speak for oppressors, and thus will inevitably analyze the nature of God in the interests of white society as a whole.

Black theology must also be suspicious of so-called white revolutionary theologians. What is most disturbing about their self-proclaimed identification with black power is their inability to let *us* speak for ourselves. They still insist on defining what black power is, and not only in private conversations but also in print. And to make it worse, they invariably miss the whole point of black power. They should know by now that, in view of white brutality against blacks and church participation in it, no white person who is halfway sensitive to black self-determination should have the audacity to speak for blacks. That is the problem! *Too many whites think they know how we feel about them.* If whites were really serious about their radicalism in regard to the black revolution and its theological implications in America, they would keep silent and take instructions from blacks. Only blacks can speak about God in relationship to their liberation. And those who wish to join us in this divine work must be willing to lose their white identity—indeed, destroy it.

Black theology also rejects any identification with the "death of God" theology. The death-of-God question is a white issue which arises out of the white experience. Questions like "How do we find meaning and purpose in a world in which God is absent?" are questions of an affluent society. Whites may wonder how to find purpose in their lives, but our purpose is forced upon us. We do not want to know how we can get along without God, but how we can survive in a world permeated with white racism.

God Is Black

Because blacks have come to know themselves, as *black*, and because that blackness is the cause of their own love of themselves and hatred of whiteness, the blackness of God is the key to our knowledge of God. The blackness of God, and everything implied by it in a racist society, is the heart of the black theology doctrine of God. There is no place in black theology for a colorless God in a society where human beings suffer precisely because of their color. The black theologian must reject any conception of God which stifles black self-determination by picturing God as a God of all peoples. Either God is identified with the oppressed to the point that their experience becomes God's experience, or God is a God of racism.

As Camus has pointed out, authentic identification

> [Is not] a question of psychological identification—a mere subterfuge by which the individual imagines that it is he himself who is being offended. . . . [It is] identification of one's destiny with that of others and a choice of sides.[3]

Because God has made the goal of blacks God's own goal, black theology believes that it is not only appropriate but necessary to begin the doctrine of God with an insistence on God's blackness.

The blackness of God means that God has made the oppressed condition God's own condition. This is the essence of the biblical revelation. By electing Israelite slaves as the people of God and by becoming the Oppressed One in Jesus Christ, the human race is made to understand that God is known where human beings experience humiliation and suffering. It is not that God feels sorry and takes pity on them (the condescending attitude of those racists who need their guilt assuaged for getting fat on the starvation of others); quite the contrary, God's election of Israel and incarnation in Christ reveal that the *liberation* of the oppressed is a part of the innermost nature of God. Liberation is not an afterthought, but the essence of divine activity.

The blackness of God means that the essence of the nature of God is to be found in the concept of liberation. Taking seriously the Trinitarian view of the Godhead, black theology says that as Creator, God identified with oppressed Israel, participating in the bringing into being of this people; as Redeemer, God became the Oppressed One in order that all may be free from oppression; as Holy Spirit, God continues the work of liberation. The Holy Spirit is the Spirit of the Creator and the Redeemer at work in the forces of human liberation in our society today. In America, the Holy Spirit is black persons making decisions about their togetherness, which means making preparation for an encounter with whites.

It is the black theology emphasis on the blackness of God that distinguishes it sharply from contemporary white views of God. White religionists are not capable of perceiving the blackness of God, because their satanic whiteness is a denial of the very essence of divinity. That is why whites are finding and will continue to find the black experience a disturbing reality.

White theologians would prefer to do theology without reference to color, but this only reveals how deeply racism is embedded in the thought forms of their culture. To be sure, they would *probably* concede that the concept of liberation is essential to the biblical view of God. But it is still impossible for them to translate the biblical emphasis on liberation to the black-white struggle today. Invariably they quibble on this issue, moving from side to side, always pointing out the dangers of extremism on both sides. (In the black community, we call this "shuffling.") They really cannot make a decision, because it has already been made for them.

How scholars would analyze God and blacks was decided when black slaves were brought to this land, while churchmen sang "Jesus, Lover of My Soul." Their attitude today is no different from that of the bishop of London who assured slaveholders that:

> Christianity, and the embracing of the Gospel, does not make the least Alteration in Civil property, or in any Duties which belong to Civil Relations; but in all these Respects, it continues Persons just in the same State as it found them. The Freedom which Christianity gives, is a Freedom from the Bondage of Sin and Satan, and from the dominion of Man's Lust and Passions and inordinate Desires; but as to their outward Condition, whatever that was before, whether bond or free, their being baptized and becoming Christians, makes no matter of change in it.[4]

Of course white theologians today have a "better" way of putting it, but what difference does that make? It means the same thing to blacks. "Sure," as the so-called radicals would say, "God is concerned about blacks." And then they would go on to talk about God and secularization or some other white problem unrelated to the emancipation of blacks. This style is a contemporary white way of saying that "Christianity . . . does not make the least alteration in civil property."

In contrast to this racist view of God, black theology proclaims God's blackness. Those who want to know who God is and what God is doing must know who black persons are and what they are doing. This does not mean lending a helping hand to the poor and unfortunate blacks of society. It does not mean joining the war on poverty! Such acts are sin offerings that represent a white way of assuring themselves that they are basically "good" persons. Knowing God means being on the side of the oppressed, becoming *one* with them, and participating in the goal of liberation. *We must become black with God!*

It is to be expected that whites will have some difficulty with the idea of "becoming *black* with God." The experience is not only alien to their existence as they know it to be, it appears to be an impossibility. "How can whites become black?" they ask. This question always amuses me because they do not really want to lose their precious white identity, as if it is worth saving. They know, as everyone in this country knows, blacks are those who say they are black, regardless of skin color. In the literal sense a black person is anyone who has "even one drop of black blood in his or her veins."

But "becoming black with God" means more than just saying "I am black," if it involves that at all. The question "How can white persons become black?" is analogous to the Philippian jailer's question to Paul and Silas, "What must I do to be saved?" The implication is that if we work hard enough at it, we can reach the goal. But the misunderstanding here is the failure to see that blackness or salvation (the two are synonymous) is the work of God, not a human work. It is not something we accomplish; it is a gift. That is why Paul and Silas said, "Believe in the Lord Jesus and you will be saved."

To *believe* is to receive the gift and utterly to reorient one's existence on the basis of the gift. The gift is so unlike what humans expect that when it is offered and accepted, we become completely new creatures. This is what the Wholly Otherness of God means. God comes to us in God's blackness, which is wholly unlike whiteness. To receive God's revelation is to become black with God by joining God in the work of liberation.

Even some blacks will find this view of God hard to handle. Having been enslaved by the God of white racism so long, they will have difficulty believing that God is identified with their struggle for freedom. Becoming one of God's disciples means rejecting whiteness and accepting themselves as they are in all their physical blackness. This is what the Christian view of God means for blacks.

The Love and Righteousness of God

The theological statement "God is love" is the most widely accepted assertion regarding the nature of God. All theologians would agree that it is impossible to speak of the Christian understanding of God without affirming the idea of love as essential to the divine nature. Anders Nygren's *Agape and Eros*[5] is the classic treatment of the subject, and he shows, perhaps conclusively, that *agape* is inseparable from the authentic Christian view of God. When religionists deviated from the *agape* motif, the result was always a distortion of the authentic Christian conception of God.

Though religionists have agreed that love is indispensable to the Christian view of God's nature, there has been much disagreement on how the idea of the *wrath* of God is reconciled with the love of God.

Marcion was one of the first to face this problem head-on. According to him, it is impossible to reconcile the Old Testament idea of the righteous God with the New Testament idea of the God of love.[6] The concept of law (*nomos*) is a complete denial of love (*agape*). Marcion's solution was to insist that the gospel of Christ is completely new and thus has nothing to do with the concept of righteousness (including wrath) as presented in the Old Testament. This led him to posit two Gods, the Creator God of the Old Testament who stressed obedience to the law of righteousness, and the Redeemer God of the New Testament who is the "good" God, the God of love. Interpreting Marcion's view, Nygren writes:

> *The message of Christ is marked by the spontaneous love and mercy of the Highest God, shown to strangers, unmotivated and uncalculated. In the Old Testament, on the other hand, man's relation to God is dominated by the idea of retribution, of reward and punishment.*[7]

It was to be expected that the church would reject Marcion's view: the early Christian community did not understand its existence as being completely new in the sense of negating the God of the Old Testament. The early Christians believed that they were the authentic continuation of the old Israel, not its denial. Jesus, therefore, did not destroy the Old Testament; he fulfilled it.

Although the church rejected Marcion's sharp dichotomy between the Old Testament view of God's righteousness and the New Testament view of God's love in Jesus Christ, there is still much confusion about the precise relationship between the two "symbols"[8] when applied to God's nature. The most common procedure is to emphasize God's love as the dominant motif of Christianity and then interpret God's righteousness in the light of it. But this approach fails to take seriously the concept of God's righteousness and tends to make God's love mere sentimentality. By emphasizing the love of God to the exclusion of a meaningful encounter of God's righteousness, we could argue that the approach is basically Marcionite, except that Marcion was more honest. Marcion claimed that the idea of righteousness is *basic* to the Old Testament view of God, and he was right in this. He further suggested that the idea of love as revealed in Christ is a negation of the Old Testament view of righteousness, and he was wrong in this.

Most religionists, although rejecting the Marcion dichotomy, proceed to analyze the concept of the love of God without relating it to God's righteousness. Marcion's position presents us with two alternatives. Either we agree with him and his view of the two Gods, Righteousness and Love, or we affirm the basic oneness of God's righteousness and love, and that means that God's love is inexplicable without equal emphasis on God's righteousness and vice versa. Contemporary theology seems to want to have its cake and eat it too—that is, reject the Marcionite view and also accept a view of love that ignores righteousness, and that is not possible.

Gordon Kaufmann's work, *Systematic Theology: A Historicist Perspective*, seems to be open to this criticism. Particularly concerned about protecting the idea of love in God's nature, Kaufmann says that it is improper to speak of the "wrath" of God as an expression of the being of God. Love is essential, but the idea of wrath is an expression of human disobedience and can be understood only by looking at human nature, not God's nature:

> *The wrath of God is a symbol more appropriate to discussion of the nature (and plight) of* man *than God. . . . The man hanging on the cross . . . reveals God's nature as long-suffering love, not vengeance or wrath in any sense. . . . I Hence, in our direct exposition of the doctrine of God such symbols as "wrath" would only be misleading and should be avoided: God reveals himself as love and faithfulness, and this it is that we must seek to grasp here.*[9]

Black theology agrees that the idea of love is indispensable to the Christian view of God. The exodus, the call of Israel into being as the people of the covenant, the gift of the promised land, the rise of prophecy, the second exodus, and above all the incarnation reveal God's self-giving love to oppressed humanity.

We do not read far in the biblical tradition without recognizing that the divine-human fellowship is to be understood exclusively in terms of what God does for humankind and not what humankind does for itself or for God. That is why Nygren is correct in describing God's *agape* as the "initiation of the fellowship with God,"[10] and why it is appropriate for Barth to emphasize the complete freedom of God in the divine-human encounter. If the incarnation means anything in Christian theology, it must mean that "God so loved the world that he gave his only Son, that whoever believes in him should not perish but have eternal life" (John 3:16).

The love of God is the heart of the Christian gospel. As the writer of I John puts it, "God is love" (4:8, 16). Commenting on the theological implications of this phrase, C. H. Dodd writes:

> *To say "God is love" implies that* all *His activity is loving activity. If He creates, He creates in love; if He rules, He rules in love; if He judges, He judges in love. All that He does is the expression of His nature which is— to love.*[11]

Black theology, then, asks not whether love is an essential element of the Christian interpretation of God, but whether the love of God itself can be properly understood without focusing equally on the biblical view of God's righteousness. Is it possible to understand what God's love means for the oppressed without making *wrath* an essential ingredient of that love? What could love possibly mean in a racist society except the righteous condemnation of everything racist? Most theological treatments of God's love fail to place the proper emphasis on God's wrath, suggesting that love is completely self-giving without any demand for obedience. Bonhoeffer called this "cheap grace":

> *Cheap grace means grace as a doctrine, a principle, a system. It means forgiveness of sins proclaimed as a general truth, the love of God taught as the Christian "conception" of God.*[12]

The difficulty with Kaufmann's view and others like his is not so much his explicit statements but their false implications. By removing wrath as a symbol of the nature of God, his interpretation weakens the central biblical truth about God's liberation of the oppressed from oppressors. A God without wrath does not plan to do too much liberating, for the two concepts belong together. A God minus wrath seems to be a God who is basically not against anything. All we have to do is behave nicely, and everything will work out all right.

Such a view of God leaves us in doubt about God's role in the black-white struggle. Blacks want to know whose side God is on and what kind of decision God is making about the black revolution. We will not accept a God who is on everybody's side—which means that God loves everybody in spite of who they are, and is working (through the acceptable channels of society, of course) to reconcile all persons to the Godhead.

Black theology cannot accept a view of God which does not represent God as being for oppressed blacks and thus against white oppressors. Living in a world of white oppressors, blacks have no time for a neutral God. The brutalities are too great and the pain too severe, and this means we must know where God is and what God is doing in the revolution. There is no use for a God who loves white oppressors *the same as* oppressed blacks. We have had too much of white love, the love that tells blacks to turn the other cheek and go the second mile. What we need is the divine love as expressed in black power, which is the power of blacks to destroy their oppressors, here and now, by any means at their disposal. Unless God is participating in this holy activity, we must reject God's love.

The interpretation of God's love without righteousness also suggests that white "success" is a sign of God's favor, of God's love. Kaufmann's view is open to the ungodly assumption that all is well with the way whites live in the world, because God loves them, and their material success is the evidence. But according to black theology, it is blasphemy to say that God loves white oppressors unless that love is interpreted as God's wrathful activity against them and everything that whiteness stands for in American society. If the wrath of God is God's almighty no to the yes of human beings, then blacks want to know where the no of God is today in white America. We believe that the black community's no as expressed in the black revolution is God's no, showing God's rejection of oppressors and acceptance of the oppressed.

Kaufmann's view also suggests that there is knowledge of God as God is *in se.* Theologically this seems impossible. We can know God only in relationship to the human race, or more particularly in God's liberating activity in behalf of oppressed humanity. The attempt to analyze God independently of God's liberating work is analogous to the theological attempt to understand human nature *before* the fall. The fall itself renders such knowledge impossible: there is no way to get behind the human condition as we know it to be.

The limitation of human knowledge is equally true in regard to God as God is *in se.* We are not permitted to transcend our finiteness and rise to a vision of God unrelated to the human condition. If this is true, what merit is there in saying that God's wrath is not a part of the divine nature? If God is a God of the oppressed of the land, as the revelation of Christ discloses, then wrath is an indispensable element for describing the scope and meaning of God's liberation of the oppressed. The wrath of God is the love of God in regard to the forces opposed to liberation of the oppressed.

Love without righteousness is unacceptable to blacks: this view of God is a product of the minds of enslavers. By emphasizing the complete self-giving of God in Christ, without seeing also the content of righteousness, oppressors could then demand that the oppressed do likewise. If God freely enters into self-donation, then in order to be godlike we must give ourselves to our oppressors in like manner. If God has loved us in spite of our revolt against God, then to be like God we too must love those who revolt against or enslave us. For blacks this would mean letting whites crowd us into ghettos where rats and filth eat away at our being, and not raising a hand against them.

This view of love places no obligation on white oppressors. The existing laws of society protect them, and their white skins are badges of acceptance. In fact, they are permitted to do whatever they will against blacks, assured that God loves them as well as the ones they oppress. Love means that God will accept white oppressors, and blacks will not seek reprisal.

Black theology rejects this view, saying that those who oppress others are in no position to define what love is. How could white scholars know that love means turning the other cheek? They have never had to do so. Only those who live in an oppressed condition can know what their love-response ought to be to their oppressors. Their oppressors certainly cannot answer that question for them!

This means that all white intellectual disputation about blacks and God is a religious lie. If oppressors themselves, who claim to be followers of the love-ethic, would actually practice what they preach, then the oppressed condition would no longer exist. There is something demonic about whites who have the protection of the state but advise blacks to go the second mile for them. They have not moved even an inch for blacks: how can they claim to be speaking from a common perspective called Christianity?

It takes a special kind of reasoning to conclude that God's love means that God is no respecter of persons in a society filled with hate, where some think they have the right to define the course of human history for all.

Ungodly in their very relationship to blacks, they want to tell us what God's love means. There is only one explanation for this attitude. They are white and can think only in white thought-patterns, even in reference to God. How else do we explain that the white theological view of God's love invariably complements or shores up outrageous socio-political structures that want blacks to be complacent and obedient to white enemies? Can they really expect blacks to take them seriously?

The oppressor's view of God's love is rejected by black theologians because they represent a people that shares Frantz Fanon's feelings about the world:

> All the native has seen in his country is that they can freely arrest him, beat him, starve him: and no professor of ethics, no priest has ever come to be beaten in his place, nor to share their bread with him. As far as the native is concerned, morality is very concrete; it is to silence the settler's defiance, to break his flaunting violence—in a word, to put him out of the picture.[13]

Black theology will accept only a love of God which participates in the destruction of the white oppressor. With Fanon, black theology takes literally Jesus' statement, "the last will be first, and the first last." Black power "is the putting into practice of this sentence."[14]

Blacks cannot adhere to a view of God that will weaken their drive for liberation. This means that in a racist society, we must insist that God's love and God's righteousness are two ways of talking about the same reality. Righteousness means that God is addressing the black condition; love means that God is doing so in the interests of both blacks and whites. The blackness of God points to the righteousness of God, as well as to the love of God.

Paul Tillich, in another connection, has placed a similar emphasis. Though he refuses to say that wrath is a part of God's being, it is to his credit that he has insisted that divine love and justice should not be separated:

> Justice is that side of love which affirms the independent right to object and subject within the love relation. [Because love is the reunion of the estranged, it] does not destroy the freedom of the beloved and does not violate the structures of the beloved's individual and social existence.[15]

This means that justice is the structure necessary for the human expression of human freedom. To be God, God must protect both the freedom and the structure of human behavior. That is why Tillich rejects sentimental misinterpretations of love as emotion, which suggest that there is a conflict between divine love and its relationship to power and justice. The three are inseparable, according to Tillich:

> It must be emphasized that it is not divine power as such which is thought to be in conflict with the divine love. The divine power is the power of being-itself, and being-itself is actual in the divine life whose nature is love. A conflict can be imagined only in relation to the creature who violates the structure of justice and so violates love itself. When this happens . . . judgment and condemnation follow. . . . Condemnation then is not the negation of love but the negation of the negation of love.[16]

What, then, can we conclude about the meaning of God's love in a racist society? Using blackness as the point of departure, black theology believes that God's love of humankind is revealed in God's willingness to become black. God's love is incomprehensible apart from blackness. This means that to love blacks God takes on black oppressed existence, becoming one of us. God is black because God loves us; and God loves us because we are black.

Righteousness is that side of God's love which expresses itself through black liberation. God makes black what humans have made white. Righteousness is that aspect of God's love which prevents it from being equated with sentimentality. Love is a refusal to accept whiteness. To love is to make a decision against white racism. Because love means that God meets our needs, God's love for white oppressors could only mean wrath—that is, a destruction of their whiteness and a creation of blackness.

For black theology love cannot be discussed in the abstract. It must be concrete because black suffering is concrete. Black suffering is whites making decisions about our place in the world, telling us what we can or cannot do in society. Love must be brought down to this level, the reality of white inhumanity against the black community. As Fanon says, "no phraseology can be a substitute for reality."[17] That is why black theology says that God's love is God's liberation of blacks as expressed in black power.

Traditional Theological Language and the Black God

One of the major tasks of black theology is that of making sense out of the traditional theological talk about God. It asks, in regard to every theological assertion, "What are its implications for the oppressed?" Or, more specifically, "Does it have any meaning in the struggle for black liberation in America?" Believing that the biblical God is made known through the liberation of the oppressed, the black theology analysis of God begins with an emphasis on God's blackness.

But now we must ask, How is the concept of the blackness of God related to such traditional divine symbols as creator, transcendence, immanence, and providence?

1. *God as Creator.*   The biblical view of God as creator is expressed in the priestly assertion, "In the beginning God created the heavens and the earth" (Genesis 1:1). To speak of God as creator means that the world and everything that is *is* because of the creative will of God. In traditional theological language, God as creator expresses aseity—that is, the total independence of God from creation. God is self-existent, meaning that the source of God's existence is found in God.

In order to emphasize the absolute sovereignty of God over creation, traditional theology introduced the idea of creation out of nothing *(ex nihilo).* The purpose is to deny that God used an eternal substance (as in Plato) in the creation of the universe. The existence of an eternal substance would compromise the complete lordship of God over creation. God is fully free, Being without limitations.

Black theology is not interested in debating the philosophical and theological merits of God's aseity except as it can be related to the earthly emancipation of the oppressed. What has the idea of God's self-existence to do with the existence of the oppressed? First it is necessary to point out that the biblical view of God as creator is not a paleontological statement about the nature and origin of the universe, but a theological assertion about God and God's relationship to the oppressed of the land.

It is important to remember that the priestly narrative was put together during the Babylonian exile as an attempt to make theological sense of the history of Israel as an oppressed people. Therefore, it is impossible to remain faithful to the biblical viewpoint without seeing the doctrine of creation as a statement about God and the oppressed of the land. God as creator means that humankind is a creature; the source of its meaning and purpose in the world is not found in oppressors but in God. This view of God undoubtedly accounts for the exclusivism of Israel in a situation of political oppression.

Though white theologians have emphasized that God as creator is a statement about the divine-human relationship, they have not pointed out the political implications of this theological truth for blacks. God as creator has not been related to the oppressed in society. If creation "involves a bringing into existence of something that did not exist before,"[18] then to say God is creator means that *my being* finds its source in God. *I am black because God is black!* God as creator is the ground of my blackness (being), the point of reference for meaning and purpose in the universe.

If God, not whiteness, is the ground of my being, then God is the only source for reference regarding how I should behave in the world. Complete obedience is owed only to God, and every alien loyalty must be rejected. Therefore, as a black person living in a white world that defines human existence according to white inhumanity, I cannot relax and pretend that all is well with black humanity. Rather it is incumbent upon me by the freedom granted by the creator to deny whiteness and affirm blackness as the essence of God.

That is why it is necessary to speak of the black revolution rather than reformation. The idea of reformation suggests that there is still something "good" in the system itself, which needs only to be cleaned up a bit. This is a false perception of reality. The system is based on whiteness, and what is necessary is a replacement of whiteness with blackness. God as creator means that oppressed humanity is free to revolutionize society, assured that acts of liberation are the work of God.

2. *Immanence and Transcendence of God.*   The immanence of God means that God always encounters us in a situation of historical liberation. That is why Christianity is called a historical religion. God is not a symbol referring to the interior religious experiences of humankind. Nor is God to be thought of in the manner of the deist philosophers, who pictured God as performing the initial act of creation but refraining from any further involvement in the world. According to biblical religion, God is involved in the concrete affairs of human history, liberating the oppressed. Therefore to ask, "Who is God?" is to focus on what God

is doing; and to look at what God is doing is to center on human events as they pertain to the liberation of suffering humanity.

God, then, is not that pious feeling in our hearts, nor is God a being "out there" or "up there." It is not possible to speak of the reality of the divine in scientific categories. Like the symbol transcendence, immanence is not a causal term. It refers to the depths of liberation in human society, affirming that God is never less than our experience of liberation.

The immanence of God is the infinite expressing itself in the finite. It is God becoming concrete in finite human existence. We are able to speak of the divine because the divine is revealed in the concreteness of this world. The immanence of God forces us to look for God in the world and to make decisions about the Ultimate in terms of present historical reality. We cannot postpone our decision about God or condition it in terms of a future reality. The finality of God is God's involvement in human now-experiences. For blacks this means that God has taken on blackness, has moved into the black liberation struggle.

Though black theology stresses the immanence of God, it does not deny the reality of God's transcendence. The transcendence of God prevents us from deifying our own experiences, which results in pantheism. God is neither nature nor our highest aspirations. God is always more than our experience of God. This means that truth is not limited to human capabilities. It is this reality that frees the rebel to give all for the liberation struggle without having to worry about the Western concept of winning.

When blacks say that "all is in God's hand," this should not be equated with the trite expression "We should do nothing." It should be taken to mean that blacks are now free to be for the black community, to make decisions about their existence in the world without an undue preoccupation with white ideas about "odds" (we have all the guns) or victory (you cannot win). Ultimately (and this is what God's transcendence means) black humanity is not dependent on our power to win. Despite the empirical odds, our involvement in our liberation is not pointless; it is not absurd. It refers to the depth and meaning of our being-in-the-world.

It is interesting that, although white "Christians" say they adhere to the meaning of Jesus Christ's existence in the world, they are especially concerned about "winning." The military budget of this country is evidence of this fact. When confronted with the uncompromising demands of the black community, they quickly remind us that they have all the guns, as if that fact itself is supposed to make blacks "stay in their place." Being "Christian," they should know that Jesus was crucified because he did not "stay in his place."

In fact, that is what authentic Christian existence is all about, *the refusal to stay in one's place.* Of course, this may mean physical death, but death is beside the point when one knows that there is a depth to existence that transcends death. The death and resurrection of Christ were an expression of God's transcendence— that is, human beings do not have to live on the basis of mere physical existence. They are free to transcend it, free to encounter the presence of the infinite, which transcends physical reality. This is why blacks do not have to cling to physical life as if it were the ultimate.

Like immanence, transcendence is not a special concept. God is not "above" or "beyond" the world. Rather transcendence refers to human purpose as defined by the infinite in the struggle for liberation. For blacks this means that their humanity is not defined by sociological reports and scientific studies. There is a transcendent value in blackness that makes us all human and to which blacks must appeal as ultimate. Human dignity transcends human calculation.

Whites try to tell blacks what is "best" for them in scientific terms—as if blackness were subject to white measurements. But to the surprise of whites, blacks reject their definitions, because blacks know that they are not "things" to be computerized and limited according to white predeterminations. We are *free*, free to defy the oppressor's laws of human behavior, because we have encountered the concreteness of the divine in our liberation, which has revealed to us the transcendence of our cause beyond all human definitions.

The tension between the transcendence and immanence of God is what Paul Tillich calls the risk of faith. To speak of God is to speak, on the one hand, of the presence of the infinite in the finite concrete world. On the other hand, the infinite can never be reduced to the finite. Though the infinite is not equated with finite existence, yet because human beings can encounter the infinite only in their finiteness, they must speak of the finite as if it were the ultimate. Tillich calls this "the infinite tension between the absoluteness of its claim and the relativity of its life."[19]

Relating this to black humanity, black theology interprets it to mean that our struggle for liberation is the infinite participating in the concrete reality of human existence. But because God is always more than our experience of God, the reality of God cannot be limited to a particular human experience. However, just because God is more than our encounter of the divine in a particular moment of liberation, this should not be interpreted to mean that we must qualify our assertions about God. Just the opposite. Because God is not less than our experience of the divine, we must speak with an absoluteness that does not compromise with evil, despite the relativity of our claims.

3. *Providence.*   It is difficult to talk about divine providence when men and women are dying and children are tortured. Richard Rubenstein pointed out the dangers of this concept in his excellent book *After Auschwitz.*[20] Whether or not we agree with his conclusion about the death of God, we can appreciate his analysis, based as it is on his identification with an oppressed people. Like black theology, Rubenstein refuses to affirm any view of God which contributes to the oppression of the Jewish people. If God is the Lord of history, directing the course of events toward a final goal, and if the Jews are God's elected people, then there is no way to avoid divine responsibility for the death of six million Jews in Germany, according to Rubenstein. Therefore, rather than accept a view of God that incorporates Jewish blood in the divine plan, he concludes that God is dead. The argument is cogent and certainly advances the death-of-God theology beyond white Christian views as represented in the thinking of William Hamilton and Thomas Altizer.

Rubenstein was not the first to recognize the difficulty of reconciling human suffering and divine participation in history. Without focusing on the God of history, the writer of Job recognized this problem. In more recent writing Albert Camus and the existentialists have dealt with it also. In the thinking of Camus, if God is omnipotent and permits human suffering, then God is a murderer. That is why he quotes Bakunin with approval: "If God did exist, we would have to abolish Him."

Traditional Christian theology somehow fails to take this problem seriously. Although agreeing that human suffering is a reality which appears to conflict with God's love, theologians still insist on quoting Paul with approval: "We know that in everything God works for good with those who love him, who are called according to his purpose" (Romans 8:28).

Emil Brunner's view of divine providence is perhaps representative. He begins by distinguishing between God as creator and God's providential care of the world. Avoiding both pantheism and deism, he writes:

There is an existence which is not that of God, but is a creaturely existence, one therefore which is distinguished from the existence of God. Without a certain independent existence the creature cannot stand over against God, and if it does not do so, then it is not a creature as contrasted with the Creator. Even if we do not speak of a creatio continua *we imply that even now God does not cease to create an existence distinct from His own, a manner of existence which is different from His. If this be so, then there is also an activity of God in and on this existence which is distinct from himself, in and on the world He has created, which is not the activity of the Creator, but of the Preserver, the Ruler.*[21]

After distinguishing providence from God's activity as creator, Brunner proceeds to define the meaning of divine providence. Providence, he says, means that "all that is, and all that happens, takes place within the knowledge and the will of God." There is nothing that happens that does not fit into God's ultimate plan:

All that happens is connected with the divine Purpose; all is ordered in accordance with, and in subordination to, the divine plan and the final divine purpose.[22]

If providence means what Brunner says, it is difficult, if not impossible, to avoid the conclusion that all human suffering is in accordance with the divine plan. This would mean that the death of six million Jews, the genocide of Amerindians, the enslavement and lynching of blacks, and every other inhumanity, happened "within the knowledge and will of God." Only oppressors can make such a claim.

Of course, my opponents could reply that this view of providence does not mean that God *wills* human suffering. It simply means that God permits it in order to protect human freedom. It means further that, although there is oppression in this world, God does not let humankind have the last word about human existence, but translates human evil into the divine purpose. Quoting Paul with approval, Brunner says, "I reckon that the sufferings of this present time are not worthy to be compared with the glory which shall be revealed in us" (Romans 8:18). The believer looks beyond suffering to the final goal which it must serve; compared with that promised glory, suffering does not count. Suffering becomes the way to eternal life. No human suffering is overlooked by God, and thus providence means that it is redeemable. Thus "the real solution to the problem of theodicy is redemption."[23]

Despite the emphasis on future redemption in present suffering, black theology cannot accept any view of God that even *indirectly* places divine approval on human suffering. The death and resurrection of Jesus does not mean that God promises us a future reality in order that we might tolerate present evil. The suffering that Jesus accepted and which is promised to his disciples is not to be equated with the easy acceptance of human injustice inflicted by white oppressors. God cannot be the God of blacks *and* will their suffering. To be elected by God does not mean freely accepting the evils of oppressors. The suffering which is inseparable from the gospel is that style of existence that arises from a decision to *be* in spite of nonbeing. It is that type of suffering that is inseparable from freedom, the freedom that affirms black liberation despite the white powers of evil. It is suffering in the struggle for liberation.

Providence, then, is not a statement about the future. It does not mean that all things will work out for the best for those who love God. Providence is a statement about present reality—the reality of the liberation of the oppressed. For blacks it is a statement about the reality of blackness and what it means in the liberation struggle against whites. As Tillich says:

> Faith in providence is faith "in spite of"—in spite of the . . . meaninglessness of existence. . . . [Special providence] gives the individual the certainty that under any circumstances, under any set of conditions, the divine "factor" is active and that therefore the road to his ultimate fulfillment is open.[24]

Black theology interprets this to mean that in spite of whiteness a way is open to blackness, and we do not have to accept white definitions.

It is within this context that divine omnipotence should be interpreted. Omnipotence does not refer to God's absolute power to accomplish what God wants. As John Macquarrie says, omnipotence is "the power to let something stand out from nothing and to be."[25] Translating this idea into the black experience, God's omnipotence is the power to let blacks stand out from whiteness and to be. It is what happens when blacks make ready for the black-white encounter with the full determination that they shall have their freedom or else. In this situation, divine providence is seeing divine reality in the present reality of black liberation—no more, no less.

Notes

1. Albert Camus, *The Rebel,* trans. by Anthony Bower, Vintage Book V30 (New York: Random House, 1956), p. 283.

2. Barth, *Church Dogmatics*, vol. 2, part 1, trans. by T. H. L. Parker, W. B. Johnston, Harold Knight, J. L. M. Haire (Edinburgh: T. & T. Clark, 1957), p. 3.

3. Camus, *The Rebel*, pp. 16, 17.

4. Quoted in H. Richard Niebuhr, *The Social Sources of Denominationalism* (Cleveland: Meridian Books, 1929), p. 249.

5. Trans. by P. S. Watson (Philadelphia: The Westminster Press, 1953).

6. This follows Nygren's view of Marcion; *Agape and Eros,* pp. 316–34.

7. Ibid., p. 321.

8. I use "symbols" instead of "attributes" because I agree with Tillich and others who suggest that the phrase "attributes of God" is misleading. It suggests the idea of a property which God has. God is not an object, and thus cannot be referred to as such. "Symbol," though it has its weakness, is a better word for expressing the Being of God in the world.

9. Kaufmann, *Systematic Theology: A Historicist Perspective* (New York: Charles Scribner's Sons, 1968), p. 154.

10. Nygren, *Agape and Eros,* p. 80.

11. C. H. Dodd, *The Johannine Epistles* (New York: Harper and Brothers, 1946), p. 110.

12. Dietrich Bonhoeffer, *The Cost of Discipleship* (New York: The Macmillan Co., 1961), p. 35.

13. Frantz Fanon, *The Wretched of the Earth,* trans. by Constance Farrington (New York: Grove Press, 1963), p. 36.

14. Ibid., p. 40. Of course, Fanon was speaking in the context of decolonization.

15. Tillich, *Systematic Theology,* vol. 1 (University of Chicago Press, 1951), p. 282.

16. Ibid., p. 283.

17. Fanon, *The Wretched*, p. 36.

18. Kaufmann, *Systematic Theology*, p. 140.

19. Tillich, *Dynamics of Faith* (New York: Harper and Brothers, 1957), p. 57.

20. New York: Bobbs-Merrill Co., 1966.

21. Brunner, *The Christian Doctrine of Creation and Redemption,* trans. by Olive Wyon (Philadelphia: The Westminster Press, 1952), p. 149.

22. Ibid., p. 155.

23. Ibid., p. 183.

24. Tillich, *Systematic Theology,* vol. 1, pp. 264, 267.

25. Macquarrie, *God and Secularity* (Philadelphia: The Westminster Press, 1967), p. 123.

Womanist Theology: Black Women's Experience as a Source for Doing Theology, with Special Reference to Christology

JACQUELYN GRANT

Introduction

This essay is an exploration into the experiences of Black women for the purpose of providing alternative sources for doing theology.

Black theology and other third world theologies of liberation have shown through their challenge of the methodologies of classical theologies that experience of the dominant culture has been the invisible crucible for theologizing. They have demonstrated that theology is not unrelated to socio-political realities of existence; and that historically it has been used to maintain the social and political advantages of the status quo. The portrayal of the universal God was such that an affirmation of this God meant a simultaneous negation of all others' cultural perceptions of the divinity, as well as a negation of those very cultures. Nowhere was this more clear than in the area of Christian foreign missions where conversion to Christianity implicitly meant deculturalization and acceptance of the western value system on the part of Asians, Africans, and Latin Americans. Upon conversion, one had to withdraw from indigenous ways of imaging the divine reality, and embrace foreign, western ways which often served to undergird oppressive religious, social and political structures.

This is true not only in the foreign missions field but also in the western world; it is reflected in the ways in which oppressors deal with oppressed people within their own territory. We see this with respect to third world people in the first world context as well as with respect to women.

An illustration emerging out of Black theology and Feminist theology will make the point. Theologians in both these theological camps propose an alternative understanding, for example, of Christian love.

James Cone in an early work makes a distinction between a non-threatening love of many Christians and the radical love of Jesus which demands justice.

There is no place in Christian theology for sentimental love—love without risk or cost. Love demands all, the whole of one's being. Thus, for the black [person] to believe the Word of God about [God's] love revealed in Christ, he/she must be prepared to meet head-on the sentimental "Christian" love of whites, which would make him/her a nonperson.[1]

Cone insists that one cannot practice Christian love and at the same time practice racism. He argues:

It seems that whites forget about the necessary interrelatedness of love, justice, and power when they encounter Black people. Love becomes emotional and sentimental. This sentimental, condescending love accounts for their desire to "help" by relieving the physical pains of the suffering blacks so they can satisfy their own religious piety and keep the poor powerless. But the new blacks, redeemed in Christ, must refuse their "help" and demand that blacks be confronted as persons. They must say to whites that authentic love is not "help," not giving Christmas baskets, but working for political, social, and economic justice, which always means a redistribution of power. It is a kind of power which enables the blacks to fight their own battles and thus keep their dignity. "Powerlessness breeds a race of beggars."[2]

"Womanist Theology: Black Women's Experience as a Source for Doing Theology, with Special Reference to Christology" by Jacquelyn Grant. Reprinted with permission from *The Journal of Interdenominational Theological Center*, 13, Spring 1986, Atlanta, GA.

Black people do not need a love which functions contrary to the establishment of Black personhood. This understanding of love was just recently affirmed by Black theologians (lay and clergy, professional and non-professional) in Southern Africa in their challenge to the church through *The Kairos Document.* They cautioned, "we must also remember that the most loving thing we can do for both the oppressed and for our enemies who are oppressors is to eliminate the oppression, remove the tyrants from power and establish a just government for the common good of all the people."[3] Here, love is not defined in the interest of those who wish to maintain the present status quo. But it is defined from the point of view of those on the underside of history—the victims of the oppressors' power.

In a similar vein, feminists challenge traditional understandings of love. Valerie Saiving Goldstein expresses her suspicions of traditional theological works in the following way:

I am no longer certain as I once was that, when theologians speak of "man," they are using the word in its generic sense. It is, after all, a well-known fact that theology has been written almost exclusively by men. This alone should put us on guard, especially since contemporary theologians constantly remind us that one of man's strongest temptations is to identify his own limited perspective with universal truth.[4]

Lifting up the Christian notion of sin and love, Goldstein suggests that it would be equally unsatisfactory to impose universal understanding on those concepts. The identification of these notions with self-assertion and selflessness respectively, functions differently in masculine experience and feminine experience. She explains further:

Contemporary theological doctrines of love have, I believe, been constructed primarily upon the basis of mas-culine experience and thus view the human condition from the male standpoint. Consequently, these doctrines do not provide an adequate interpretation of the situation of women—nor, for that matter, of men, especially in light of certain fundamental changes now taking place in our own society.[5]

Because of their feminine character, for women love takes the form of nurturing, supporting and servic-ing their families. Consequently, if a woman believes

the theologians, she will try to strangle other impulses in herself. She will believe that, having chosen marriage and children and thus being face to face with the needs of her family for love, refreshment, and forgiveness, she has no right to ask anything for herself but must submit without qualification to the strictly feminine role.[6]

For women, too, the issue is one of personhood—are women to deny who they are in order to be saved?

Goldstein then argues that when experience in theology is scrutinized, we will discover that because it has been synonymous with masculine experience, it is inadequate to deal with the situation of women.

In other words, Black theologians and feminist theologians have argued that the universalism which classical theologians attempt to uphold represents merely the particular experiences of the dominant culture. Blacks identify that experience as White experience; and women identify it as male experience. The question then is, if universalism is the criterion for valid theology, how is such a universalism achieved?

What I will be exploring here is how Black women's experiences can provide some insights into this question. In doing so, Black women not only join Blacks and feminists in their challenge of theology but they also provide an internal critique for Black men as well as for White women. In this paper, I will focus primarily upon Black women's experience as related to the development of feminist theology. (In a rather limited way, I have addressed the issue of Black women's experiences and Black theology in an article entitled "Black Theology and the Black Woman."[7] That subject certainly has not been exhausted, and shall be treated in more substantive ways in the future.)

But here I am interested in engaging feminist theology with reference to its constructive efficacy for Black women given the peculiarities of their experiences. The results will be the beginnings of a theology from a Black woman's perspective with special reference to Christology.

In order to create a common starting point, let's begin with a synopsis of the basic tenets of Feminist the-ology. First, Feminist theology seeks to develop a *wholistic theology.* Feminist theology rejects the traditional forms of oppressive and one-sided, male-dominated theologies which arise out of patriarchal religion(s).[8] Women have begun to see that their continuous oppression in the church and society has its basis in these patriarchal religion(s). Historically, the theologies of religions have emerged out of the experiences of men, making the theologies representative thereof. Because humanity is comprised of both men and women Feminist theologians seek to develop a more wholistic perspective in theology.

Second, in seeking to produce a wholistic perspective in theology Feminist theologians call for the *eradication of social/sexual dualisms* in human existence which are inherent in patriarchy. A patriarchy is characterized by male-domination and female submission and subordination. In such a society, men are considered strong, intelligent, rational and aggressive; women are considered weak, irrational, and docile.

A third function of Feminist theology is to *conceptualize new and positive images of women.* Throughout history, including the history of theology, women have been portrayed in negative ways. They have been sources of evil (snakes), authors of trickery (witches), and stimulants (therefore causes) for the sexual perversions of men (temptresses and prostitutes). These negative images must be changed to reflect reality.

Finally, Feminist theology must *evaluate male articulated understandings of the Christian faith.* Doctrines developed in a system of patriarchy merely perpetuate patriarchal structures. As the patriarchal theological system is challenged, so are the doctrines, e.g., God, Jesus Christ, the Fall and the Church.

Emerging Black Feminist Perspective

It has been argued by many Blacks that the women's liberation movement is a White middle-class movement. Therefore, it is believed to be totally irrelevant to the situation of Black women since the majority of them are not middle-class.

Brenda Eichelberger gives several reasons for Black women's non-involvement in feminist causes. Among them are such things as class differences, the lack of Black women's knowledge about the real issues involved and the suspicion that the middle-class White women's movement is divisive to the Black community which claims prior allegiance.[9] In spite of these and other negative responses to the White women's liberation movement, there has been a growing feminist consciousness among many Black women and some Black men. This consciousness is coupled by the increased willingness of Black women to undertake an independent analysis of sexism, thereby creating an emerging Black perspective on feminism. Black feminism grows out of Black women's tri-dimensional reality of race/sex/class. It holds that full human liberation cannot be achieved simply by the elimination of any one form of oppression. Consequently, real liberation must be "broad in the concrete";[10] it must be based upon a multi-dimensional analysis.

Recent writings by secular Black feminists have challenged White feminist analysis and Black race analysis, particularly by introducing data from Black women's experience that has been historically ignored by White feminists and Black male liberationists.

In only a few of them do Black women employ only a gender analysis to treat Black women's reality. Whereas Ntozake Shange focuses chiefly upon sexism, Michelle Wallace, like Alice Walker, presumes that White racism has had an adverse effect upon the Black community in a way that confuses and reinforces the already existing sexism. Sharon Harley, Rosalyn Terborg-Penn, Paula Giddings and Gloria Wade-Gayles all recognize the inclusiveness of the oppressive reality of Black women as they endure racism, sexism and economic oppression. Barbara Smith, Gloria Hull, Bell Hooks and Angela Davis particularly explore the implications of this tri-dimensional oppression of Black women. In so doing, Black women have either articulated Black feminist perspectives or developed grounds for doing so.[11] These perspectives, however, have not led to the resolution of tensions between Black women and White women, and they even have brought to the forefront some tensions between Black women and Black men.

On the contrary, the possibly irreparable nature of these tensions is implied in Walker's suggestion that the experience of being a Black woman or a White woman is so different that another word is required to describe the liberative efforts of Black women. Her suggestion that the word "womanist" is more appropriate for Black women is derived from the sense of the word as it is used in Black communities:

Womanist, from womanish. (Opp. of "girlish," i.e., frivolous, irresponsible, not serious.) A Black feminist or feminist of color. From the Black folk expression of mothers to female children, "You acting womanish," i.e., like a woman. Usually referring to outrageous, audacious, courageous or willful behavior. Wanting to know more and in greater depth than is considered "good" for one. Interest in grown-up doings. Acting grown up. Being grown up. Interchangeable with another black folk expression: "You trying to be grown." Responsible. In charge. Serious.[12]

Womanists were Sojourner Truth, Jarena Lee, Amanda Berry Smith, Ida B. Wells, Mary Church Terrell, Mary McCloud Bethune and countless others not remembered in any historical study. A womanist then is a strong Black woman who has sometimes been mislabeled as domineering castrating matriarch. A womanist is one who has developed survival strategies in spite of the oppression of her race and sex in order to save her family and her people. Walker's womanist notation suggests not "the feminist," but the active struggle of Black women that makes them who they are. For some Black women that may involve being feminine as traditionally defined, and for others it involves being masculine as stereotypically defined. In any case, womanist means being and acting out who you are and interpreting the reality for yourself. In other words, Black women speak out for themselves. As a Black feminist critic Barbara Christian explains, referring to Audre Lorde's poem about the deadly consequence of silence, Black women must speak up and answer in order to validate their own experience. This is important even if only to ourselves. It is to the womanist tradition that Black women must appeal for the doing of theology.

The Beginnings of a Womanist Theology with Special Reference to Christology

Womanist theology begins with the experiences of Black women as its point of departure. This experience includes not only Black women's activities in the larger society but also in the churches, and reveals that Black women have often rejected the oppressive structure in the church as well.

These experiences provide a context which is significant for doing theology. Those experiences had been and continue to be defined by racism, sexism and classism and therefore offer a unique opportunity and a new challenge for developing a relevant perspective in the theological enterprise. This perspective in theology which I am calling womanist theology draws upon the life and experiences of some Black women who have created meaningful interpretations of the Christian faith.

Black women must do theology out of their tri-dimensional experience of racism/sexism/classism. To ignore any aspect of this experience is to deny the wholistic and integrated reality of Black womanhood. When Black women say that God is on the side of the oppressed, we mean that God is in solidarity with the struggles of those on the underside of humanity, those whose lives are bent and broken from the many levels of assault perpetrated against them.

In a chapter entitled "Black Women: Shaping Feminist Theory," Hooks elaborates on the interrelationship of the threefold oppressive reality of Black women and shows some of the weaknesses of White feminist theory. Challenging the racist and classist assumptions of White feminism, Hooks writes:

> Racism abounds in the writings of white feminists, reinforcing white supremacy and negating the possibility that women will bond politically across ethnic and racial boundaries. Past feminist refusal to draw attention to and attack racial hierarchy suppressed the link between race and class. Yet class structure in American society has been shaped by the racial politics of white supremacy.[13]

This means that Black women, because of oppression determined by race and their subjugation as women, make up a disproportionately high percentage of the poor and working classes. However, the fact that Black women are a subjugated group even within the Black community and the White women's community does not mean that they are alone in their oppression within those communities. In the women's community poor White women are discriminated against, and in the Black community, poor Black men are marginalized. This suggests that classism, as well as racism and sexism, has a life of its own. Consequently, simply addressing racism and sexism is inadequate to bring about total liberation. Even though there are dimensions of class which are not directly related to race or sex, classism impacts Black women in a peculiar way which results in the fact that they are most often on the bottom of the social and economic ladder. For Black women doing theology, to ignore classism would mean that their theology is no different from any other bourgeois theology. It would be meaningless to the majority of Black women, who are themselves poor. This means that addressing only issues relevant to middle-class women or Blacks will simply not do. The daily struggles of poor Black women must serve as the gauge for the verification of the claims of womanist theology. Anna Julia Cooper makes a relevant point:

> Women's wrongs are thus indissolubly linked with all undefended woes, and the acquirement of her "rights" will mean the supremacy of triumph of all right over might, the supremacy of the moral forces of reason, and justice, and love in the government of the nations of earth.[14]

Black women's experience must be affirmed as the crucible for doing womanist theology. It is the context in which we must decide theological questions. More specifically, it is within the context of this experience that Black women read the Bible. A (brief) look at Black women's use of the Bible indicates how it is their experiences which determine relevant questions for them.

The Bible in the Womanist Tradition

Theological investigation into the experiences of Christian Black women reveals that Black women considered the Bible to be a major source of religious validation in their lives. Though Black women's relationship with God preceded their introduction to the Bible, this Bible gave some content to their God-consciousness.[15] The source for Black women's understanding of God has been twofold: first, God's revelation directly to them, and secondly, God's revelation as witnessed in the Bible and as read and heard in the context of their experience. The understanding of God as creator, sustainer, comforter, and liberator took on life as they agonized over their pain, and celebrated the hope that as God delivered the Israelites, they would be delivered as well. The God of the Old and New Testament became real in the consciousness of oppressed Black women. Of the use of the Bible, Fannie Barrier Williams quite aptly said:

> *Though the Bible was not an open book to the Negro before emancipation, thousands of the enslaved men and women of the negro race learned more than was taught to them. Thousands of them realized the deeper meanings, the sweeter consolations and the spiritual awakenings that are part of the religious experiences of all Christians.*[16]

In other words, though Black people in general and Black women in particular were politically impotent, religiously controlled, they were able to appropriate certain themes of the Bible which spoke to their reality. For example, Jarena Lee, a nineteenth-century Black woman preacher in the African Methodist Episcopal Church, constantly emphasized the theme "Life and Liberty" in her sermons which were always biblically based. This interplay of scripture and experience was exercised even more expressly by many other Black women. An ex-slave woman revealed that when her experience negated certain oppressive interpretations of the Bible given by White preachers, she, through engaging the biblical message for herself, rejected them. Consequently, she also dismissed white preachers who distorted the message in order to maintain slavery. Her grandson, Howard Thurman, speaks of her use of the Bible in this way:

> *"During the days of slavery," she said, "the master's minister would occasionally hold services for the slaves. Alas the white minister used as his text something from Paul. 'Slaves be obedient to them that are your masters . . . as unto Christ.' Then he would go on to show how, if we were good and happy slaves, God would bless us. I promised my Maker that if I ever learned to read and if freedom ever came, I would not read that part of the Bible."*[17]

What we see here is perhaps more than a mere rejection of a White preacher's interpretation of the Bible: it is an exercise in internal critique of the Bible. The liberating message of the gospel is seen as over against the oppressive elements in the Bible.

The truth which the Bible brought was undeniable, though perception of it was often distorted in order to support the monstrous system of oppression. Sarcastically responding to this tendency, Fannie Barrier Williams admonished, "do not open the Bible too wide." Biblical interpretation, realized Williams, a non-theologically trained person, had at its basis the prior agenda of White America. She therefore argued:

> *Religion, like every other force in America, was first used as in instrument and servant of slavery. All attempts to Christianize the negro were limited by the important fact that he was property of valuable and peculiar sort and that the property value must not be disturbed, even if his soul were lost. If Christianity could make the negro docile, domestic and less an independent and fighting savage, let it be preached to that extent and no further.*[18]

Such false, pernicious, demoralizing gospel could only be preached if the Bible was not opened wide enough, lest one sees the liberating message of Jesus as summarized in Luke 4:18. The Bible must be read and interpreted in the light of Black women's own oppression and God's revelation within that context. Womanist must, like Sojourner, "compare the teachings of the Bible with the witness" in them.[19]

To do Womanist theology, then, we must read and hear the Bible and engage it within the context of our own experience. This is the only way that it can make sense to people who are oppressed. Black women of the past did not hesitate in doing this and we must do no less.

Jesus in the Womanist Tradition

Having opened the Bible wider than many White people, Black people, in general, and Black women in particular, found a Jesus who they could claim, and whose claim for them was one of affirmation of dignity and self-respect.

In the experience of Black people, Jesus was "all things."[20] Chief among these however was the belief in Jesus as the divine co-sufferer, who empowers them in situations of oppression. For Christian Black women in the past, Jesus was their central frame of reference. They identified with Jesus because they believed that Jesus identified with them. As Jesus was persecuted and made to suffer undeservedly, so were they. His suffering culminated in the crucifixion. Their crucifixion included rapes, and husbands being castrated (literally and metaphorically), babies being sold, and other cruel and often murderous treatments. But Jesus' suffering was not the suffering of a mere human, for Jesus was understood to be God incarnate. As Harold Carter observed of Black prayers in general, there was no difference made between the persons of the trinity, Jesus, God, or the Holy Spirit. All of these proper names for God were used interchangeably in prayer language. Thus, Jesus was the one who speaks the world into creation. He was the power behind the Church.[21] Black women's affirmation of Jesus as God meant that White people were not God. One old slave woman clearly demonstrates this as she prayed:

> "Dear Massa Jesus, we all uns beg Ooner [you] come make us a call dis yere day. We is nutting but poor Etiopian women and people ain't tink much 'bout we. We ain't trust any of dem great high people for come to we church, but do' you is de one great Massa, great too much dan Massa Linkum, you ain't shame to care for we African people."[22]

Implicit in the description "nothing but poor Black women" and what follows is the awareness of the public devaluation of Black women. But in spite of that Jesus is presented as a confidant who could be trusted while White people could not be trusted. This woman affirmed the contribution of Abraham Lincoln to the emancipation of Blacks, but rejected Mr. Lincoln as her real or ultimate master. Quite a contrast to the master's (slave owner's) perception of his/herself.

This slave woman did not hesitate to identify her struggle and pain with those of Jesus. In fact, the common struggle made her know that Jesus would respond to her beck and call.

> Come to we, dear Massa Jesus. De sun, he hot too much, de road am dat long and boggy (sandy) and we ain't got no buggy for send and fetch Ooner. But Massa, you 'member how you walked dat hard walk up Calvary and ain't weary but tink about we all dat way. We know you ain't weary for to come to we. We pick out de torns, de prickles, de brier, de backslidin' and de quarrel and de sin out of you path so dey shan't hurt Ooner pierce feet no more.[23]

The reference to "no buggy" to send for Jesus, brings to mind the limited material possessions of pre- and post-Civil War Blacks. In her speech, "Ain't I a Woman," Sojourner Truth distinguished between White women's and Black women's experiences by emphasizing that Black women were not helped into carriages as were White women.[24] In the prayer, this woman speaks of that reality wherein most Blacks didn't even have carriages or buggies. For had she owned one, certainly she'd send it to fetch Jesus. Here we see the concern for the comfort and the suffering of Jesus. Jesus suffers when we sin—when we backslide or when we quarrel. But still Jesus is identified with her plight. Note that Jesus went to the cross with this Black woman on his mind. He was thinking about her and all others like her. So totally dedicated to the poor, the weak, the downtrodden, the outcast that in this Black woman's faith, Jesus would never be too tired to come. As she is truly among the people at the bottom of humanity, she can make things comfortable for Jesus even though she may have nothing to give him—no water, no food—but she can give tears and love. She continues:

Come to me, dear Massa Jesus. We all uns ain't got no good cool water for give when you thirsty. You know Massa, de drought so long, and the well so low, ain't nutting but mud to drink. But we gwine to take de munion cup and fill it wid de tear of repentance, and love clean out of we heart. Dat all we hab to gib you good Massa.[25]

The material or physical deprivation experienced by this woman did not reduce her desire to give Jesus the best. Being a Black woman in the American society meant essentially being poor, with no buggy, and no good cool water. Life for Black women was indeed bad, hot and at best muddy. Note that there is no hint that their condition results from some divine intention. Now, whereas I am not prepared to say that this same woman or any others in that church the next day would have been engaged in political praxis by joining such movements as Nat Turner's rebellion or Denmark Vesey's revolt, it is clear that her perspective was such that the social, political and economic orders were believed to be sinful and against the will of the real master, Jesus.

For Black women, the role of Jesus unraveled as they encountered him in their experience as one who empowers the weak. In this vein, Jesus was such a central part of Sojourner Truth's life that all of her sermons made him the starting point. When asked by a preacher if the source of her preaching was the Bible, she responded, "No honey, can't preach from de Bible—can't read a letter."[26] Then she explained, "When I preaches, I has jest one text to preach from, an' I always preaches from this one. My text is, 'When I found Jesus!' "[27] In this sermon Sojourner Truth recounts the events and struggles of life from the time her parents were brought from Africa and sold "up an' down, an' hither an' yon . . ."[28] to the time that she met Jesus within the context of her struggles for dignity of Black people and women. Her encounter with Jesus brought such joy that she became overwhelmed with love and praise:

Praise, praise, praise to the Lord! An I begun to feel such a love in my soul as I never felt before—love to all creatures. An then, all of a sudden, it stopped, an I said, Dar's de white folks that have abused you, an beat you, an abused your people—think o them! But then there came another rush of love through my soul, an cried out loud—Lord, I can love even de white folks![29]

This love was not a sentimental, passive love. It was a tough, active love that empowered her to fight more fiercely for the freedom of her people. For the rest of her life she continued speaking at abolition and women's rights gatherings, and condemned the horrors of oppression.

The Womanist Traditions and Christological Reflections

More than anyone, Black theologians have captured the essence of the significance of Jesus in the lives of Black people which to an extent includes Black women. They all hold that the Jesus of history is important for understanding who he was and his significance for us today. By and large they have affirmed that this Jesus is the Christ, that is, God incarnate. They have argued that in the light of our experience, Jesus meant freedom.[30] They have maintained that Jesus means freedom from the sociopsychological, psychocultural, economic and political oppression of Black people. In other words, Jesus is a political messiah.[31] "To free [humans] from bondage was Jesus' own definition of his ministry."[32] This meant that as Jesus identified with the lowly of his day, he now identifies with the lowly of this day, who in the American context are Black people. The identification is so real that Jesus Christ in fact becomes Black. It is important to note that Jesus' blackness is not a result of ideological distortion of a few Black thinkers, but a result of careful christological investigation. Cone examines the sources of Christology and concludes that Jesus is Black because "Jesus was a Jew." He explains:

It is on the basis of the soteriological meaning of the particularity of his Jewishness that theology must affirm the christological significance of Jesus' present blackness. He is black because he was a Jew. The affirmation of the black Christ can be understood when the significance of his past Jewishness is related dialectically to the significance of his present blackness. On the other hand, the Jewishness of Jesus located him in the context of the Exodus, thereby connecting his appearance in Palestine with God's liberation of oppressed Israelites from Egypt. Unless Jesus were truly from Jewish ancestry, it would make little theological sense to say that he is the fulfillment of God's covenant with Israel. But on the other hand, the blackness of Jesus brings out the soteriological meaning of his Jewishness for our contemporary situation when Jesus' person is understood in the context of the cross and resurrection. Without negating the divine election of Israel, the cross and resurrection are Yahweh's fulfillment of his original intention for Israel . . .[33]

The condition of Black people today reflects the cross of Jesus. Yet the resurrection brings the hope that liberation from oppression is immanent. The resurrected Black Christ signifies this hope.

Cone further argues that this christological title, "The Black Christ," is not validated by its universality, but, in fact, by its particularity. Its significance lies in whether or not the christological title "points to God's universal will to liberate particular oppressed people from inhumanity."[34] These particular oppressed peoples to which Cone refers are characterized in Jesus' parable on the Last Judgment as "the least." "The least in America are literally and symbolically present in Black people."[35] This notion of "the least" is attractive because it descriptively locates the condition of Black women. "The least" are those people who have no water to give, but offer what they have, as the old slave woman cited above says in her prayer. Black women's experience in general is such a reality. Their tri-dimensional reality renders their particular situation a complex one. One could say that not only are they the oppressed of the oppressed, but their situation represents "the particular within the particular."

But is this just another situation that takes us deeper into the abyss of theological relativity? I would argue that it is not, because it is in the context of Black women's experience where the particular connects up with the universal. By this I mean that in each of the three dynamics of oppression, Black women share in the reality of a broader community. They share race suffering with Black men; with White women and other Third World women, they are victims of sexism; and with poor Blacks and Whites, and other Third World peoples, especially women, they are disproportionately poor. To speak of Black women's tri-dimensional reality, therefore, is not to speak of Black women exclusively, for there is an implied universality which connects them with others.

Likewise, with Jesus Christ, there was an implied universality which made him identify with others—the poor, the woman, the stranger. To affirm Jesus' solidarity with the "least of the people" is not an exercise in romanticized contentment with one's oppressed status in life. For as the resurrection signified that there is more to life than the cross of Jesus Christ, for Black women it signifies that their tri-dimensional oppressive existence is not the end, but it merely represents the context in which a particular people struggle to experience hope and liberation. Jesus Christ thus represents a three-fold significance; first he identifies with the "little people," Black women where they are; secondly, he affirms the basic humanity for these, "the least"; and thirdly, he inspires active hope in the struggle for resurrected, liberated existence.

To locate the Christ in Black people is a radical and necessary step, but understanding of Black women's reality challenges us to go further. Christ among the least must also mean Christ in the community of Black women. William Eichelberger was able to recognize this as he further particularized the significance of the Blackness of Jesus by locating Christ in Black women's community. He was able to see Christ not only as Black male but also Black female.

> God in revealing Himself and His attributes from time to time in His creaturely existence has exercised His freedom to formalize His appearance in a variety of ways. . . . God revealed Himself at a point in the past as Jesus the Christ a Black male. My reasons for affirming the Blackness of Jesus of Nazareth are much different from that of the white apologist. . . . God wanted to identify with that segment of mankind which had suffered most, and is still suffering. . . . I am constrained to believe that God in our times has updated His form of revelation to western society. It is my feeling that God is now manifesting Himself, and has been for over 450 years, in the form of the Black American Woman as mother, as wife, as nourisher, sustainer and preserver of life, the Suffering Servant who is despised and rejected by men, a personality of sorrow who is acquainted with grief. The Black Woman has borne our griefs and carried our sorrows. She has been wounded because of American white society's transgressions and bruised by white iniquities. It appears that she may be the instrumentality through whom God will make us whole.[36]

Granted, Eichelberger's categories for God and woman are very traditional. Nevertheless, the significance of his thought is that he is able to conceive of the Divine reality as other than a Black male messianic figure.

Even though Black women have been able to transcend some of the oppressive tendencies of White male (and Black male) articulated theologies, careful study reveals that some traditional symbols are inadequate for us today. The Christ understood as the stranger, the outcast, the hungry, the weak, the poor, makes the traditional male Christ (Black and White) less significant. Even our sisters of the past had some suspicions about the effects of a male image of the divine, for they did challenge the oppressive use of it in the church's theology. In so doing, they were able to move from a traditional oppressive Christology, with respect to women, to an egalitarian Christology. This kind of egalitarian Christology was operative in Jarena Lee's argument for the right of women to preach. She argued ". . . the Saviour died for the woman as well as for the man."[37] The crucifixion was for universal salvation, not just for male salvation or, as we may extend the argument to include, not just for white salvation. Because of this, Christ came and died, no less for the woman as for the man, no less for Blacks as for Whites. For Lee, this was not an academic issue, but one with practical ramifications.

If the man may preach, because the Saviour died for him, why not the woman? Seeing he died for her also. Is he not a whole Saviour instead of half one? as those who hold it wrong for a woman to preach, would seem to make It appear.[38]

Lee correctly perceives that there is an ontological issue at stake. If Jesus Christ were a Saviour of men then it is true the maleness of Christ would be paramount.[39] But if Christ is a Savior of all, then it is the humanity—the wholeness—of Christ which is significant.

Sojourner was aware of the same tendency of some scholars and church leaders to link the maleness of Jesus and the sin of Eve with the status of women and she challenged this notion in her famed speech "Ain't I A Woman?"

Then that little man in black there, he says women can't have as much rights as men, 'cause Christ wasn't a woman! Where did your Christ come from? Where did your Christ come from? From God and a woman. Man had nothing to do with Him.

If the first woman God ever made was strong enough to turn the world upside down alone, these women together ought to be able to turn it back, and get it right side up again! And now they is asking to do it, the men better let them.[40]

I would argue, as suggested by both Lee and Sojourner, that the significance of Christ is not his maleness, but his humanity. The most significant events of Jesus Christ were the life and ministry, the crucifixion, and the resurrection. The significance of these events, in one sense, is that in them the absolute becomes concrete. God becomes concrete not only in the man Jesus, for he was crucified, but in the lives of those who will accept the challenge of the risen Saviour—the Christ. For Lee, this meant that women could preach; for Sojourner, it meant that women could possibly save the world; for me, it means today, this Christ, found in the experience of Black women, is a Black woman.

Conclusion

I have argued that Black women's tri-dimensional reality provides a fertile context for articulating a theological perspective which is wholistic in scope and liberating in nature. The theology is potentially wholistic because the experience out of which it emerges is totally interconnected with other experiences. It is potentially liberating because it rests not on one single issue which could be considered only a middle-class issue relevant to one group of people, but it is multi-faceted. Thus, the possibility for wholistic theology is more likely. Feminist theology as presently developed is limited by virtue of the experience base for feminist theology. That is, when feminists say that experience is the crucible for doing [feminist] theology, they usually mean White women's experience. With few exceptions, feminist thinkers do their analysis primarily, and in some circles exclusively, based on the notion that because sexism is the longest and most universal form of oppression, it should claim priority.[41]

Black women, by and large, have not held this assumption. Many have claimed that because of the pervasiveness of racism, and because of its defining character for Black life in general, racism is most important. Though Sojourner Truth never did develop a sophisticated social analysis she was aware of the fact that she (and her people) were poor because she was Black, and perhaps poorer because she was woman. I say "perhaps" simply because in the slave economy one could argue that there was relatively little distinction between the property status of slaves by virtue of gender; women were no less property than men. As properly, they were a part of the material distributed, rather than participants in the inequitable (system of) material distribution. Thus as indicated above in the Black woman's prayer, material possessions of Blacks were limited. In a sense one could say that by virtue of one's race, one was slave and by virtue of that status one was poor.

Still as we see the issues today, class distinctions which have emerged even in the Black community, and sex differences, which have taken on new forms of institutionalization, must be addressed. For liberation to become a reality, race, sex and class must be deliberately confronted. Interconnected as they are, they all impinge greatly on the lives of Black women. Overwhelming as are these realities, black women do not feel defeated. For Jarena Lee observed the hope of the struggle is based on the faith that Jesus died (and was raised) for the woman as well as the man. This realization gave inspiration for the struggle. Black women today inside and outside of the church still bring an optimistic spirit as reflected in the conclusion of Maya Angelou's poem, "Still I Rise":

> Out of the hut of history's shame
> I rise
> Up from a past that's rooted in pain
> I rise
> I'm a Black ocean, leaping and wide,
> Welling and swelling, I bear in the tide
> Leaving behind nights of terror and fear
> I rise
> Into a daybreak that's wondrously clear
> I rise
> Bringing the gifts that my ancestors gave
> I am the dream and the hope of the slave.
> I rise.
> I rise.
> I rise.[42]

Notes

1. James H. Cone, *Black Theology and Black Power* (New York: Seabury Press, 1969), 53–54.

2. Ibid., 54–54.

3. The Kairos Theologians, *The Kairos Document: Challenge to the Church*, 2d ed. (Braarufontein, South Africa: Skotaville Publishers, 1985; Grand Rapids, Mich.: Eerd-mans, 1986), 24–25.

4. Valerie Saiving Goldstein, "The Human Situation of a Feminine," *Journal of Religion* 40 (April 1960): 100.

5. Ibid.

6. Ibid.

7. Jacquelyn Grant, "Black Theology and the Black Woman" in *Black Theology: A Documentary History 1966–1979*, ed. Gayraud S. Wilmore and James H. Cone (Maryknoll, N.Y.: Orbis Books, 1979; and rev. ed. vol. 1, 1993).

8. See Sheila D. Collins, *A Different Heaven and Earth: A Feminist Perspective on Religion* (Valley Forge, Pa.: Judson Press, 1974); Mary Daly, *Beyond God the Father: Toward a Philosophy of Women's Liberation* (Boston: Beacon Press, 1973); Mary Daly, *The Church and the Second Sex: With a New Feminist Post Christian Introduction by the Author* (New York: Colophon Books/Harper & Row, 1975).

9. Brenda Eichelberger, "Voice of Black Feminism," *Quest: A Feminist Quarterly* III (Spring, 1977): 16–23.

10. This phrase is used by Anna Julia Cooper, *A Voice From the South* (1852; reprint, Westport Conn.: Negro Universities Press, 1969), cited by Bell Hooks, *Ain't I A Woman: Black Women and Feminism* (Boston: South End Press, 1981), 193–194. I use it here to characterize Black women's experience. To be concerned about Black Women's issues is to be *concrete*. Yet because of their interconnectedness with Black men (racism), White women (sexism) and the poor (classism), it is also to be, at the same time, concerned with broad issues.

11. See Ntozake Shange, *For Colored Girls Who Have Considered Suicide When the Rainbow is Enuf* (New York: MacMillan, 1975); Michelle Wallace, *Black Macho and the Myth of the Superwoman* (New York: Dial Press, 1978); Alice Walker, *The Color Purple* (New York: Harcourt Brace Jovanovich, 1982); and *In Search of Our Mothers' Gardens* (San Diego, Calif.: Harcourt Brace Jovanovich, 1983); Sharon Harley and Rosalyn Terborg-Penn, eds., *Afro-American Women* (New York: Kennikat Press, 1978); Paula Giddings, *When and Where I Enter* (New York: William Morrow & Co., 1984); Gloria Wade-Gayles, *No Crystal Stair: Visions of Race and Sex in Black Women's Fiction* (New York: Pilgrim

Press, 1984); Bell Hooks, *Feminist Theory: From Margin to Center* (Boston: South End Press, 1984); Barbara Smith, Gloria Hull, and Patricia Scott, *All the Women are White, and All the Blacks are Men, But Some of Us are Brave* (Old Westbury, N.Y.: Feminist Press, 1982); Angela Y. Davis, *Women, Race and Class* (New York: Vintage Books, 1981).

12. Walker, *In Search of Our Mothers' Gardens*, xi.

13. Hooks, *Feminist Theory*, 3.

14. Cooper, *A Voice From The South*, 91

15. Cecil Wayne Cone, *Identity Crisis In Black Theology* (Nashville: African Methodist Episcopal Church Press, 1975), passim, especially chapter III.

16. Ben James Loewenberg and Ruth Bogin, eds., *Black Women in Nineteenth-Century American Life: Their Words, Their Thoughts, Their Feelings* (University Park, Pa.: Pennsylvania State University Press, 1976), 267.

17. Howard Thurman, *Jesus and the Disinherited* (Nashville: Abingdon Press, 1949), 30–31.

18. Loewenberg and Bogin, *Black Women in Nineteenth-Century*, 265.

19. Olive Gilbert, *Sojourner Truth: Narrative and Book of Life* (1850 and 1875; reprint Chicago: Johnson Publishing Co. 1970), 83.

20. Harold A. Carter, *The Prayer Tradition of Black People* (Valley Forge: Judson Press, 1976), 50. Carter, in referring to traditional Black prayer in general, states that Jesus was revealed as one who "was all one needs!"

21. Ibid.

22. Ibid., 49.

23. Ibid.

24. Sojourner Truth, "Ain't I A Woman?" in *Feminism: The Essential Historical Writings*, ed. Miriam Schneir (New York: Vintage Books, 1972).

25. Carter, *The Prayer Tradition*, 49.

26. Gilbert, *Book of Life*, 118.

27. Ibid., 119.

28. Ibid.

29. Ibid.

30. James Deotis Roberts, *A Black Political Theology* (Philadelphia: Westminster Press, 1974), 138. See especially chapter 5. See also Noel Leo Erskine, *Decolonizing Theology: A Caribbean Perspective* (Maryknoll, N.Y.: Orbis, 1980), 125.

31. Roberts, *A Black Political Theology*, 133.

32. Albert B. Cleage, Jr., *The Black Messiah* (New York: Sheed & Ward, 1969), 92.

33. James H. Cone, *God of the Oppressed* (New York: Seabury Press, 1975), 134.

34. Ibid., 135.

35. Ibid., 136.

36. William Eichelberger, "Reflections on the Person and Personality of the Black Messiah," *The Black Church II* (n.d.): 54.

37. Jarena Lee, *The Life and Religious Experiences and Journal of Mrs. Jerema Lee: A Colored Lady Giving an Account of Her Call to Preach* (Philadelphia, Pa.: n.p., 1836), 15–16.

38. Ibid., 16.

39. There is no evidence to suggest that Black women debated the significance of the maleness of Jesus. The fact is that Jesus Christ was a real, crucial figure in their lives. However, recent feminist scholarship has been important in showing the relation between the maleness of Christ and the oppression of women.

40. Truth, "Ain't I A Woman," in Schneir, ed., *Feminism*, 94.

41. This question is explored further in Jacquelyn Grant, "The Development and Limitation of Feminist Theology: Toward an engagement of black women's religious experience and white women's religious experience" (Ph.D. diss., Union Theological Seminary, New York, 1985).

42. Maya Angelou, *And Still I Rise* (New York: Random House, 1978), 42.

Women in Islam

Aminah Beverly McCloud

And one of His signs is that He created mates for you from yourselves that you may find rest in them, and He put between you love and compassion; most surely there are signs in this for a people who reflect.

—Sura Rum 30:21.

Discourses on the Status of Muslim Women

Muslim women and their roles in communities continue to be a major concern of both scholarly and everyday inquiry. To non-Muslims, Muslim women have been the subject of speculation, consternation, and ridicule for decades. As one Muslim teacher and scholar has noted:

Old ideas about the place of women in Islam have hardly changed. The most difficult task I have faced in years of teaching Islam is how to provide an accurate account of the role of women in face of the deep prejudices of not only my students but also my colleagues. . . . And given the background of the students, it was natural for them to come into class convinced, on some level of their awareness, that Eastern women, and especially Muslim women, are the most oppressed and downtrodden women on earth, and that although Islam may have something interesting to say on some level, it certainly has nothing to offer on the level of women's role in society.[1]

Scholarly works have called Muslim women's existence and ways of being in the world as oppressed and voiceless, and have explored these characteristics in a variety of communities, elaborating a discourse replete with negative stereotypes. Western women feel that their "work on" Muslim women is a model of excellence.

Our knowledge of women in Islamic society has benefited from the burgeoning studies on women in the West. This interest has resulted in excellent monographs, essay collections, scholarly and popular articles, and translations of works by Muslim women into Western languages, particularly English.[2]

Muslim women, however, are generally unflattered by such scholarship. For example, Leila Ahmed had complained that

The peculiar practices of Islam with respect to women had always formed part of the Western narrative of the quintessential otherness and inferiority of Islam.[3]

Broadly speaking, the thesis of the discourse on Islam blending a colonialism committed to male dominance with feminism—the thesis of the new colonial discourse of Islam centered on women—was that Islam was innately and immutably oppressive to women, that the veil and segregation epitomized that oppression, and that these customs were the fundamental reasons for the general and comprehensive backwardness of Islamic societies.[4]

This is not to imply that Muslim women in many Muslim cultures are not struggling to break bonds that prevent them from intellectual pursuits and physical mobility. Yet whereas many social scientists asserted a need to liberate Muslim women from their families, husbands, children, history, and culture, liberation for Muslim women is mostly conceived of in terms of the veil, often called *hijab*, and their role in the home.

Muslim women scholars, fighting patriarchy have devoted considerable energy to clarifying the emergence of *hijab* as defining for Muslim women. Fatima Mernissi has explored this issue at length.

The hijab—literally "curtain"—"descended," not to put a barrier between a man and a women . . . The descent of the hijab is an event dating back to verse 53 of Surah 33, which was revealed during year 5 of the Hejira (627 A.D.).

"O you who believe! Enter not the Prophet's house for a meal without waiting for the proper time, unless permission be granted you. But when you are invited, enter; and when your meal is ended, then disperse. Linger not for conversation. Lo, that would cause annoyance to the Prophet, and he would be shy of (asking) you (to go); but Allah is not shy of the truth. And when you ask of them (the wives of the Prophet) anything, ask it of them from behind a curtain. That is purer for your hearts and for their hearts."[5]

Mernissi further illustrates another major use of the word *hijab* in *Qur'an* in *Sura* 41 *ayah* 5:

And they say, "Our hearts are (fortified) within a covering against that (Book) towards which you call us. We are deaf in the ear and there exists a barrier between us and you. So carry on your work (according to your creed) and surely you are the workers (in accordance with our own doctrines)."[6]

In light of these Qur'anic passages, Mernissi concludes:

So it is strange indeed to observe the modern course of this concept. . . . The very sign of the person who is damned, excluded from the privileges and spiritual grace to which the Muslim has access, is claimed in our day as a symbol of Muslim identity, manna for the Muslim woman.[7]

Muslim women scholars are not alone in seeking to clarify the identity of women although the emphases and roles outlined are sometimes different. Afzular Rahman asserts that

It seems quite fair and rational to say that the circle of operation of woman in general is the home, while the field of work of man is outside the home. In other words, the basic and fundamental function of woman is to run the home. She is equipped with such natural gifts and capabilities as are suitable for the bringing up, nursing, education and training of children.[8]

But woman is not called upon that scale and with that urgency to undertake social and collective obligations which would entail her leaving her household duties . . . it is more important for a woman to continue doing her household duties than to participate in collective worship.[9]

Dr. Hasan Al-Turabi, a Sudanese scholar and statesman, has contributed significantly to the issue of women and gender relations in a pamphlet entitled, *Women in Muslim Society and Islam.* Some of Dr. Al-Turabi's key observations are cited below.

Men purposefully attempt to keep women weak, and the jealousy which they entertain in respect to women induces them to multiply the means for restraining and monopolizing them. They dominate the property and life of women out of vanity and arrogance.

The greatest injustice visited upon women is their segregation and isolation from the general society. Sometimes the slightest aspect of her public appearance is considered a form of obscene exhibitionism. Even her voice is bracketed in the same category. Her mere presence at a place where men are also present is considered shameful promiscuity. She is confined to her home in a manner prescribed in Islam only as a penal sanction for an act of adultery. She is so isolated on the pretext that she should devote herself exclusively to the care of her children and the service of her husband. But how can she qualify for attending to domestic family affairs or for the rearing of children in satisfactory manner without being herself versed through education or experience, in the moral and functional culture of the wider society?

So far as the familiar Hijab is concerned, it refers to the special regulations pertaining to the Prophet's wives due to their status and situation. They occupied a position different from all other women, and their responsibilty was therefore stiffened. God ordained that their reward, as well as their punishment would be double that for any other woman.

> *The verses of the same Sura ordained that the wives of the Prophet draw a curtain (to ensure privacy in the prophet's room which naturally attracted many visitors of all sorts), and that they dress up completely without showing any part their bodies including face and hands to any man; though all other Muslim women were exempted from these restrictions.*[10]

Along similar lines, Rashid al-Ghanushi finds that in a close review of different *tafseers* (commentaries on the *Qur'an* and *hadith*), the view of women that is elaborated is incompatible with predominant cultural views.[11]

In attempting to sort out the controversial literature on the status of Muslim women, the most obvious questions to raise include: What actually does the *Qur'an* say about women? If there is a difference between the Qur'anic discourse and the cultural practices of Muslims, why is this so, given the fact that Muslims understand the *Qur'an* to be the word of God? If Muslims believe the *Qur'an* to be the authority for the social life, how could they misinterpret it so seriously?

In order to answer these important questions, Muslim women scholars are beginning to meticulously investigate what the *Qur'an* says and what has happened. In a text entitled, *Qur'an and Woman*, Amina Wadud-Mushin has made the following observations:

> *Compatible mutually supportive functional relationships between men and women can be seen as part of the goal of the Qur'an with regard to society. However, the Qur'an does not propose or support a singular role or single definition of a set of roles, exclusively, for each gender across every culture.*[12]
>
> *Man and woman are two categories of the human species given the same or equal consideration and endowed with the same or equal potential. . . . The Qur'an encourages all believers, male and female, to follow their belief with actions, and for this it promises them a great reward.*[13]
>
> *The roles of women who have been referred to in the Qur'an fall into one of three categories: (1) A role which represents the social, cultural, and historical context in which that individual lived—without compliment or critique from the text. (2) A role which fulfills a universally accepted (i.e., nurturing or caretaking) female function, to which exceptions can be made—and have been made even in the Qur'an itself. Finally, (3) A role which fulfills a non-gender-specific function.*[14]

Why is the contemporary discourse on women (there are no texts on men) so full of conflicting claims? Leila Ahmed has observed that "discourses shape and are shaped by specific moments in specific societies," which means that we have to look to Islamic history for an answer to this question.

> *Converts brought traditions of thought and custom with them. For instance (to give just one example of how easily and invisibly scriptural assimilation could occur), in its account of the creation of humankind the Qur'an gives no indication of the order in which the first couple was created from Adam's rib. In Islamic traditionalist literature, however, which was inscribed in the period following the Muslim conquests, Eve, sure enough, is referred to as created from a rib.*[15]
>
> *The adoption of the veil by Muslim women occurred by similar process of seamless assimilation of the mores of the conquered people. . . . During Muhammed's (pbuh) lifetime and only toward the end at that, his wives were the only Muslim women required to veil. After his death and following the Muslim conquest of the adjoining territories, where upper-class women veiled, the veil became a commonplace item of clothing among Muslim upper-class women, by a process of assimilation that no one has yet ascertained in much detail.*[16]

Dr. Al-Turabi has offered similar observations along these lines:

> *Throughout history, Muslims have experienced a significant deviation from the general ideals of life as taught by Islam. . . . Whenever weakness creeps into the faith of Muslim men, they tend to treat women oppressively and seek to exploit them. This is a natural tendency, and is amply demonstrated by the fact that most of the rulings of the Qur'an regarding women were set down as restrictions on men—to prevent them from transgressing against women, as is their natural disposition and their actual practice in most societies.*
>
> *This discriminatory attitude of interpretation is very widespread. Yet another aspect of this tendentious jurisprudence is to generalize the provisions of the Qur'an and the Sunna that were meant to apply exclusively to the Prophet or his wives due to their unique position.*[17]

While we do not have all the pieces to this puzzle, some Muslim scholars are examining Islamic history, philosophy, and commentaries on the *Qur'an* and *hadith* to find answers. Interpretations of the Qur'anic message, like all interpretations, are an exercise in power and knowledge. In the early days of Islam, debate and controversy filled the air, and from this atmosphere schools of thought formed. Eventually, we were left with five schools of legal thought, a few well-known philosophers, and one interpretation of the *Qur'an*. As Dr. Al-Turbi writes:

> *Although the message of Islam spread in [Arab, Persian, and Indian] societies from early times, the teaching and inculcation of Islamic cultural values was not coextensive with the horizontal expansion. Consequently, some pre-Islamic values and prejudices, have contiued to persist despite the domination of Islamic forms.*
>
> *By attaching an Islamic value to these practices, they sought to give them legitamacy and sanctity, because the values of Islam were accepted as sacred and supreme. This explains the unabated influence, on the minds of many otherwise good Muslims, of attitudes abhorent to Islam.*[18]

In the end, Muslim women were encased in a mold called "Muslim woman" which was ahistorical, silent, and without a strong Qur'anic basis.

Islam in the Lives of African American Women

Before we examine how African-American women walk into this fourteen-hundred-year-old history, we need to know a few things about them. We must first address the issue of silence, on which bell hooks has aptly commented in her work *Talking Back*.

> *This empasis on woman's silence may be an accurate remembering of what has taken place in the households of women from WASP backgrounds in the United States, but in black communities . . . women have not been silent. Their voices can be heard. Certainly for black women, our struggle has not been to emerge from silence into speech but to change the nature of our speech, to make a speech that compels listeners, one that is heard.*[19]

African-American women as a whole have not seen themselves as silenced by their circumstances, though many times they have been hostage to the need to survive. They have always carefully chosen what they share, because the "sharing is always an issue of survival." African-American women have had to constantly fight the issues of racism, and even though they are aware of sexism, racism has been the commanding force. As hooks points out,

> *Many black women insist that they do not join the feminist movement because they cannot bond with white women who are racist. . . .*
>
> *At times, the insistence that feminism is really "a white female thing that has nothing to do with black women" masks black female rage towards white women, a rage rooted in the historical servant-served relationship where white women have used power to dominate, exploit, and oppress. Many black women share this animosity, and it is evoked again and again when white women attempt to assert control over us.*[20]

African-American women have, in large numbers, spurned the women's liberation movement and the feminist movement even though they have gained a little from both. African-American women have been formed socially by racism. Their spiritually has rarely been examined except through narratives of heroic deeds—usually either for family or the race.

The first Islamic encounter for African-American women was predominately in communities, where 'asabiya was the focus. During the first half of the twentieth century, for most African-American Muslim women, who generally had not encountered their Muslim sisters from the Muslim world, there is an ambiguous gender relationship. Women have a lot of say in nation-building—they are present, sometimes in quasi-leadership capacities, keeping the mini-nations informed and intact. At the same time, however, they are subject to the attitudes about women held by the men. For example, even though Clara Muhammad tended the Nation of Islam in its early days when Elijah Muhammad was jailed or running from the police, she is rarely written about, and leads no organizations within the Nation. For women in the Moorish Science Temple and the First Mosque of Pittsburgh, subordination of women is not so clearly a problem, but we have no written accounts of the first women and their lives. Women wear a modest dress and cover their heads, but do not seem to feel oppressed; rather, their dress is viewed as a difference that aligns them with a worldview, an identity other than slavery, and God.

The second half of the twentieth century brings a wave of Muslim immigrants into contact with already established African-American Islamic expressions. Along with these Muslim immigrants comes the notion of "Muslim woman," which includes silence, submissiveness, and absence. For some African-American Muslim women and for some of those moving into Islam, this notion is enticing, while for others it is the beginning of a new struggle.

The notion "Muslim woman" refers directly to dress and adab. The Muslim woman is one who looks Muslim, wearing a scarf that covers her hair, neck, and bosom. Her dress touches the ground, her sleeves close at the wrist, and whether she wears a blouse and pants or a dress her clothing must be loose enough so that it does not show her form. The Muslim woman is obedient to her husband, takes constant care of her children, and soft spoken. She does not want much, is content, and understands that this behavior is pleasing to God. Her obligations as a Muslim are marginalized. If she does not look like a Muslim woman she is not a Muslim woman, even if she prays five times daily, pays *zakat*, fasts during Ramadan, and saves to make *hajj*. This conception of Muslim woman has determined life for many African-American Muslim women for decades, though not all have accommodated this notion its entirety.

In the last decade, I have been asked the question, "Why Islam?" hundreds of times. It seems to me that the attraction of Islam for women, especially African-American women, is best summarized by Leila Ahmed, who informs us that

> *even as Islam instituted, in the initiatory society, a hierarchical structure as the basis of relations between men and women, it also preached, in its ethical voice . . . the moral and spiritual equality of all human beings.* [21]
>
> *It is because Muslim women hear this egalitarian voice that they often declare (generally to the astonishment of non-Muslims) that Islam is non-sexist.* [22]

African-American women come to Islam from various educational, social, and economic positions, and their reasons for choosing Islam reflect that diversity. How they lived their previous lives is important for understanding their accommodations and struggles in Islam. Some women, with college educations and opportunities for self-empowerment, come to Islam after the study of several worldviews and/or participation in other traditions. The following remarks from interviews express some of the paths traveled by African-American women toward their encounter with Islam:

> *One thing is clear. Christianity is one of the roots of black folk's problems in this country. It's got black folk thinkin' that white folk are God. As long as black folk are singin' and shoutin' in church thinkin' that some White god is gonna save them they will not and can never fight to preserve their humanity. Jesse Jackson tells everybody to say, "I am somebody"—hell, the White man already knows we are somebody. That's why he is kickin' our asses on every level he can.*
>
> —Ayesha

> *Everywhere I read there was some mention of Islam or Muslims. I figured I should check it out; this was very different, wide enough for everybody. More like one huge culture with little communities. God, I already knew about, Muhammad was new but since nobody was worship-pin' him he was no problem. Most of all the Qur'an didn't ask me to love those who did evil. This was cool.*
>
> —Sayeeda

> *I remember reading Carlos Castaneda and trying to understand the opening of the universe in the mind with the mind-altering drugs. I was too scared to take anything, though, but I got a great imagination and it was working overtime. What was clear though was a different connection with nature and the universe than what I was being taught in school. What some people thought should result in "love," I kinda got the feeling that we have a responsibility to nature.*
>
> —Fareeda

After spending all my childhood and some of my adult years in Catholicism I knew that what Scriptures say and what people do don't always go together. Islam seemed to be a way for me to be religious just between me and God. There was the stress on community but my personal connection with God didn't depend on anybody else. You know what I mean—there was no confession: God knows and expects me to straighten it out.

—Maryam

Other women come to Islam through direct contact with Muslims. Several women talked about meeting Muslim women in public places. They were most aware of the difference in attitude.

I was in the welfare office talkin' to this sister and she was tellin' me wasn't no sense in gettin' mad with these people 'cause all this was just a moment. People who treated other people like this weren't long for this earth. She said it like it was understood and she knew somethin' deep.

—Fatimah

Muslim men also play a role in attracting women to Islam. Muslim men, both immigrant and African-American, engage in African-American women in conversations about Islam and Muslim women. Often the end result of these conversations is a move into Islam.

I guess I kinda raised myself. They thought I was bright and pretty so if I kept quiet nobody paid me much attention. I liked high school but I just didn't fit—too light to be black and too black to be white. I read all the time—black literature, history, autobiography. My family only paid attention to the fact that I read, wasn't in trouble, and was cute. I wanted to be a doctor—family doctor. So when at fifteen I met this Muslim brother who was about thirty, good-looking, and smart. I listened to what he had to say because he listened to what I had to say and didn't treat me like a kid. He was attentive and Islam was exotic.

—Sandra

Further reflections on their lives reveal considerations of life in America.

College taught the history, philosophy, and literature of Europeans. We learned how primitive, undeveloped, and backward Africans and other people of color were.

—Ameena

Even though my folks walked picket lines and experienced white folks calling them dirty names, throwin' things at them, puttin' their dogs on 'em, they still felt they had to prove they were human. They feel that if they act like white folks they will be accepted by white folks. So they make sure their English is proper. The things we were taught to want and need were European. My folks thought that the key to equality was to be jus' like 'em. They never thought that they were o.k. jus' bein' who they are.

—Rabiyyah

Welfare means you are totally unable to care for yourself, your children. The person on welfare is made to be nobody and is kept in the system by force. I will clean toilets, anything, before I go on welfare and if there is nothing out there to do, I will make stuff and sell it. . . . I know that this country has put a system into motion that feeds on poor people and rather than educate them to be independent of it, it makes more dependencies. It constantly penalizes people who try to get out of it so that it can stay alive.

—Joan

In Catholic school, the black children always know that they are different because the priests and nuns tell you in so many ways. They always assume that you are in the special lunch program or that you can't participate in something because of money, they don't ask. When it comes to things like band or the orchestra black kids don't get to go because they are always assigned to gym or sports. Everybody thinks that all black people can do is play games. If you are smart it's unique 'cause black folks aren't supposed to know anything either. In class, the teachers are always cutting you off before you're finished or interpreting what you mean like you can't say what you mean. . . . My mother taught us that any kind of work is work. I might think that I'm too educated for certain types of work by if the alternative is welfare, then to the toilets

—Leila

As mentioned in previous chapters, the move into Islam—affirming the *shahadah*—is accompanied by a move into a community. These two levels of contract—one with God and the other with community—are reflected in spirituality and personal space transformation. On the spiritual level, the move into Islam demands a level of consciousness of God—an awareness of *deen* (religion). The God-centeredness of Islam and *wa'ezudeeni Islamiyyah* (Islamic consciousness) are instilled by the performance of *salat*, reading the *Qur'an*, and the use of everyday phrases such as *al-hamdullilah, insha Allah, as-salaamu alaikum, ma'shallah,* and so on. African-American Muslim women describe this God-consciousness in a number of ways. For example, *sawm* (fasting) clears one's sight and tunes one's hearing to one's environment. The discipline of the fast from sunrise to sunset for thirty days while working (in or outside of the home) or attending school, and residing in a culture where the fast has no meaning is one space of spiritual nourishment.

During Ramadan, I see things differently. It is as though everyone has to be their real selves. People, the people I work with can pretend all the other months of the year except Ramadan. I can see right through them and see who they really are. Ramadan always shocks me with the evil I can see clearly.

—Rasheeda

As I am just talking now I use inshallah all the time. Using it makes me remember that nothing I can plan can happen without God's will.

—Ameena

In Islam, my soul has a focus. I know that there is no one who can save me. I must obey God and wait until the last day to see what I have really done in this life. So I try and sometimes fail to keep this on my mind. I pray to stay on the path.

—Deborah

Listening to the Qur'an on tape is something I do everyday. The recitation always brings tears and moves my heart. I don't see how anyone could hear the Qur'an and not be moved. I am learning a new surah a month. When I get to the long ones I guess it will take years, but I will get it done.

—Bahirah

In addition to personal spiritual strivings, women also participate in classes and less formal groups for Qur'anic and Arabic studies. These sessions generally are focused on some portion of the *Qur'an* chosen for study and comment on what God intends to be learned from it. Here women seek interpretation from each other using hadith literature and each other's knowledge. Women have little or no opportunity to share their knowledge with the men, but often continue in these sessions for years. One group in Chicago, called Bushra, has had ongoing meetings for fifteen consecutive years. Women's groups have expanded in the past ten years out of local communities to regional organizations, but a major focus remains spirituality.

While women have nurtured their own spirituality, both personally and in groups, the move into Islam on the community level has its own indoctrination. The following remarks indicate some of the difficulties encountered in this indoctrination.

Befo' I could ketch my breath, they were telling me about all the layers of clothes I had to wear so nobody could lust after me.

—Hassannah

I literally cried when I was told I couldn't listen to my music because it was vulgar. But I refused to get rid of the records. I just had to look at all those memories. Some sisters "snatched" down pictures of my family off the walls and I freaked out!

—Aisha

I had to learn to go to bed early in order to make the morning prayer and learn the prayer at the same time in Arabic. I used to worry if I had memorized it correctly or if I was mispronouncing words. At first I was scared to make prayer at work because everybody had already started acting funny around me so I waited until I got home and then I worried about having missed the prayer. There was so much to learn that I worried all the time. The only time I could relax was when my menstrual cycle was on.

—Latifah

I went to the masjid to look around, went to some of the classes. Most of the sisters were either my age and real kids or women not paying me any attention. I look back on it and wish I had just joined the other teenagers. Instead I decided that I was a black woman and was bright enough to be on my own. When he showed me what the Qur'an said about men being the maintainers and protectors of women and that Muslim men could have four wives, I thought I was mature enough to handle it. When I met his wife she was nice and thought I was there to learn about Muslim women, not to marry her husband. Well, I became a co-wife, second wife, pregnant, high school drop out, family outcast, you name it, all before I turned sixteen. The women at the masjid would not talk to me. I figured and my husband told me they were envious so I just studied Islam and Arabic on my own. My life was hell except for reading the Qur'an and prayer.

—Sharifah

People are people no matter what religious community they belong to. Some are there for security, others seeking knowledge and some just 'cause they think it's a happening. You have to decide why you are there if this presents a problem for you and then go with it. We have sisters who were born Muslim and it is the only way of life they know and we have some who are making mistakes with brothers as they try to find out how they want to be Muslims. Some come into Islam trying to make it Christianity and are confused as they find out it isn't. Its hard to be Muslim in America in the center of a weird kind of Christianity mixed up with all kinds of other things.

—Jamiliah

What is life like in these Muslim communities for African-American women? According to many Muslim women it is average American life with a spiritual twist. What does this mean? African-American Muslim women experience all the joys and struggles that their African-American and Muslim sisters experience. These women struggle in the culture of the United States, where women of all social classes struggle; in African-American culture, where women are torn between fighting racism and sexism; and finally in a budding Muslim culture that inherited the Muslim world's misrepresentation of gender relations in Islam. They push against three layers of mire, and are making dents. Those women who struggle with sexism and male domination see Muslim women as necessarily in the service of their mates, but not in a diminutive way.

Muslim women must see themselves as the backbone of the family and society. If their homes are peaceful, their husbands content, their children loved and safe, then their [own] lives can be productive. There are many ways women can influence men without being out there, up front.

—Maryam

It is inherent in the genetic make-up of the black female to seek to satisfy the black male, to help him meet his goals and to demand good treatment from him.

—Minister Ava Muhammad[23]

The woman in Islam's role is very important, because she has the responsibility, as the Mother of Civilization and first teacher, of teaching these good manners to the (her) children, to continue this polite society.

—Nyasha Muhammad[24]

In a widely read and discussed article, "Women of the Veil: Islamic Militants Pushing Women Back to an Age of Official Servitude," two non-Muslim female journalists for the *Atlantic Journal-Constitution* sparked the ire of African-American Muslim women from all over the country. Led by women in Warithudeen Muhammad's communities, these women rejected the claim that Islam degrades women and makes them servants:

> *We urge all Muslim women from all over the world—those born in the religion of Islam and those who have converted to it—to speak out and defend their choice [of Islam] in spirit, word, and in action.*[25]

African-American Muslim women who struggle against male dominance do so within a framework that does not mimic Western feminism. These women seek valid Qur'anic interpretation. As Mildred El-Amin argues,

> *Many Muslims interpret 4:34 to mean devout obedience to the husband; there is no Qur'anic foundation for this interpretation. Devout obedience is due Allah alone; all human beings are subject to error and ignorance.*[26]

In contrast to many Muslim societies, African-American Muslim women spend a great deal of time in the *masjid*, organizing educational programs, doing good in community activities, attending classes, and praying. Like the women of the earliest Muslim communities, most African-American Muslim women attend *Jum'ah* prayer when possible. Separation from men is put into effect differently in different communities. All communities provide for the privacy of women. In two communities I visited—Masjid Ar-Raham on Chicago's West side, and the First Cleveland Mosque in Cleveland—the Imams made concerted efforts to give the women a sense of belonging to the *masjid*, and acknowledged that what women contribute is very important. In those communities, where the Imam is elected based on knowledge of the *Qur'an* and *hadith*, women participate in the community selection. Women also participate in the selection of some of the sites for the *masjid*.

African-American Muslim women have tended on the whole to be better acclimated to various sectors of the work force, though less well educated in professional fields, than their Middle Eastern and Southeast Asian sisters. While the government has seriously restricted Muslim women's educational levels in a number of Muslim communities in the world, racism, religious bias, and sexism in the United States have placed an overwhelming burden on Muslim women. The secular nature of American society is often used to force Muslim women out of positions of high visibility. Most African American women find a great deal of bias and hostility directed toward them, no matter what their status or occupation. Many women are forced either to compromise their appearances in order to maintain employment in mainstream professions, or turn to home businesses for income.

Religious discrimination, particularly toward Islam, is widespread in the United States, but this has not prevented large numbers of African American women from turning to Islam as a way of life. Highly visible as "religious artifacts," African American Muslim women in public spaces are the constant objects of hostilities. In contrast, immigrant Muslim women receive either compliments or other positive regard for their difference in the same public spaces. There seems to be some sort of expectations that Muslim women from the Muslim world will look different, while difference in the appearance of African American Muslim women is not accepted.

Among women in various communities there are points of convergence and divergence on any number of issues. In general, African American Muslim women live in a closed society that is highly charged with rumor, innuendo, envy, love, nurturing, and spirituality. These women strive to overcome the negative in search of the positive—most times.

Notes

1. Sachiko Murata, *The Tao of Islam: A Source Book on Gender Relationships in Islamic Thought*, (New York: State University of New York Press, 1992), 1.

2. Wiebeke Walther, *Women in Islam from Medieval to Modern Times* (New York: Markus Weiner Publishing, Inc., 1993), 3.

3. Leila Ahmed, *Women and Gender in Islam*, (New Haven, Connecticut: Yale University Press, 1992), 149.

4. *Ibid.*, 151–52.

5. Fatima Mernissi, *The Veil and the Male Elite*, trans. Mary Jo Lakeland (New York: Addison-Wesley Publishing Company, Inc., 1991), 85. The remainder of this quote says ". . . but between two men." I assume this is an error in translation, because the ayah clearly is speaking about a curtain between visitors and the Prophet's wives.

6. *Ibid.*

7. *Ibid.*

8. Afzular Rahman, *Role of Muslim Women in Society* (London: Seerah Foundation, 1986), 1.

9. *Ibid..*, 2.

10. Hasa Al-Turabi, *Women in Muslim Society and Islam* (London: Milestone, 1973).

11. Rashid al-Ghanushi, *Al-Mara a-Muslim fi Tunis Bain Tawjeehat al-Qur'an was Wagi al-Mujtama al-Tunisi (The Muslim Women of Tunisia between the Directives of Qur'an and the Reality of the Tunisia Society)* (Kuwait: Dar al-Qalam, 1988). Some other recent texts that explore issues around women include: Abdul-Halim Abu Shaqa, *Tahreer al-Mara fi Asr al-Risala (The Liberation of Women in the Era of Revelation: A Comprehensive Study of Qur'an, Sahih Burkari, and Sahih Muslim Texts)* (Kuwait: Dar al-Kuwait, 1990); al-Turabi, *Al-Mara Bin Taa'lim al-Sharia's was Takalid al-Mujtama (Women between the teaching of Sharia and the Customs of Society)* (Sudan.)

12. Amina Wadud-Mushin, *Woman and the Qur'an* (Kuala Lumpur, Malaysia: Penerbit Fajar Bakit Sdn. Bhd., 1992), 8.

13. *Ibid.*, 15.

14. *Ibid.*, 29.

15. Ahmed, *Women and Gender in Islam* 4.1 also note that there is no Eve in the *Qur'an.*

16. *Ibid.*, 5.

17. Hasan Al-Turabi

18. Hasan Al-Turabi.

19. bell hooks, *Talking Back* (Boston: South End Press, 1989), 6.

20. *Ibid.*, 79.

21. Ahmed, *Women and Gender in Islam*, 238.

22. Ibid., 239.

23. From *Final Call*, 10 May 1993.

24. From *Muhammad Speaks Continues*, December 1992.

25. Ayesha Mustafa, editor, *Muslim Journal*, 24 July 1993, 20.

26. Mildred El-Amin, *Family Roots*, (Chicago: International Ummah Foundation), 1991, 29.

PART THREE

The Latino/a American
Religious Experience

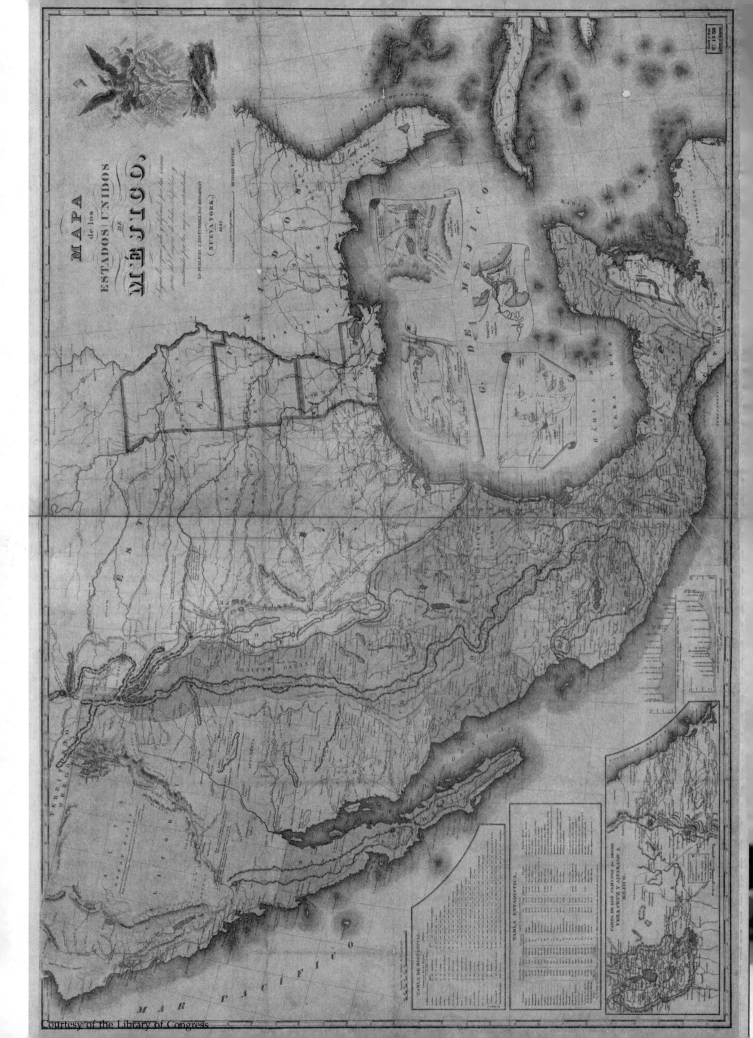

MAPA
de los
ESTADOS UNIDOS
de
MÉJICO,

REVISED EDITION.

LO PUBLICAN J. DISTURNELL, 102 BROADWAY
(NUEVA YORK.)
1847.

Readings in Latino American Religious Traditions: A Foretaste

Latinos constitute one of the largest ethnic groups in America. Recent waves of immigration, especially from Mexico, have swelled the Latino population even further. This demographic growth has made the rest of America aware that although Latinos share the same language and a common cultural ancestor—Spain—there are significant differences among them, including their religious experiences, due to history and contact with non-European peoples. A Mexican from Oaxaca and an Argentine from Buenos Aires, for example, are as different as an American from Brooklyn and a New Zealander from Whataroa. Immigrants from Latin America and the Caribbean have brought these dissimilar cultural and religious expressions with them to the United States. And they cling to these differences despite the broader culture's misperception of Latinos as culturally and religiously homogeneous.

Religiously, Latinos are still predominantly Roman Catholic. In the last century, however, Protestantism, and especially Pentecostalism, made significant gains in Latin America to the consternation of the Vatican. Latino immigrants to the United States, more than ever before, espouse a variety of religious commitments.

Whether Catholic or Protestant, Latinos have given their particular brand of Christianity their own unique cultural flavor. Latinos, both in Latin America and North America, have adapted the Christianity they received to their own needs and cultural style. The readings included here show Latinos' creative adaptations of religion within the new socio-historical context of Anglo-America.

The three largest Latino groups in the United States are Mexican, Puerto Rican, and Cuban. Three historical events are of special importance in accounting for the presence of these particular Latinos: (1) the Mexican-American War of 1846-48, (2) the Spanish-American War of 1898, and (3) the Cuban Revolution of 1959.

With the defeat of Mexico and the signing of the Treaty of Guadalupe Hidalgo, the southwestern lands north of the Rio Grande became part of the United States and the estimated 80,000 Mexican inhabitants already living there became American citizens. These saw themselves more as *Californios, Nuevo Mexicanos,* and *Tejanos* than *Mexicanos* and became the first significant Spanish-speaking ethnic group in the United States. These, and Mexicans who immigrated later (some during the Mexican revolution of 1910 and others in subsequent decades), introduced their own forms of popular religiosity: the devotion to the Virgin of Guadalupe or *Guadalupismo, curanderismo,* and the *Penitente* tradition, which were in many ways foreign to institutional American Catholicism.

In 1898, the United States defeated Spain in an expansionist war and acquired Puerto Rico along with several other colonies (Cuba, the Philippines) as part of the terms of surrender. While the other acquisitions were subsequently given independence, Puerto Rico was kept as a U.S. territory. Puerto Ricans were granted U.S. citizenship with the Jones Act of 1917. Thousands of Puerto Ricans would eventually immigrate to the mainland in search of better economic opportunities. Protestant missionaries, for their part, would come to the island seeking to both convert and Americanize the new contingent of Spanish-speaking citizens. Because of the Catholic Church's conservatism and its alliance with the government of Spain, by the late nineteenth century many liberal and independence-minded Puerto Ricans had rejected institutional Catholicism for allegedly scientific Kardecism or Spiritism (in Spanish called *Espiritismo Mesa Blanca*). Judith Ortiz Cofer's childhood memories of her spiritist grandfather in "Talking to the Dead" portray the bourgeois sensibility characteristic of Puerto Rican *Espiritismo.*

With the entry of American missionaries in the early twentieth century, many Puerto Ricans embraced Protestantism as the progressive and liberal religious alternative. When Puerto Ricans came to the United States in greater numbers after World War II, they brought with them their forms of Catholicism, Protestantism, and Spiritism.

Finally, the Cuban Revolution of 1959, in which Fidel Castro ousted Fulgencio Batista and established a Marxist-Leninist state, resulted in waves of Cuban refugees coming into the United States seeking political asylum. These immigrants brought with them, not only their own Catholic devotion to the patron saint of Cuba, the *Virgen de la Caridad del Cobre* (the Virgin of Charity), but also *Santería* and *Palo Monte Mayombé*, both syncretistic or creolized forms of African religion. The selections from Cristina García's *Dreaming in Cuban* give insight into the multi-layered functions of *Santería* in the construction of racial, ethnic, and religious identity both in Cuba and the United States.

With the ethnic consciousness-raising that occurred in the Sixties, Latinos began to look at religion more critically. This was especially true within the Chicano movement. *Chicanismo* was a political movement that sought greater civil rights for Mexican Americans and also to infuse a sense of cultural pride. It was analogous to the Black Power movement within the African American community and the Red Power movement among Native Americans. As a movement of radical politics it began to turn a critical eye on the Roman Catholic Church, which in the United States has historically been dominated by Irish and German American clergy. Consequently, various Mexican American leaders, such as Oscar Zeta Acosta and Cesar Chavez, began to give voice to Latinos' sense of alienation from the Catholic Church. Chavez, for example, in his essay "The Mexican-American and the Church," criticizes the Catholic Church for its reluctant then sluggish response to the plight of migrant workers. Like Chavez, many felt that the church did not take the concerns of Mexican Americans or other Latinos seriously.

Along with political activism, the rise of ethnic and gender consciousness in the Sixties produced new forms of theological reflection that took as their point of departure the experiences of marginalization and discrimination. Alongside black theology, feminist theology, and the womanist response, there emerged Hispanic theology and *Mujerista* theology. Representing these new theologies we have included essays by Virgilio Elizondo and Ada María Isasi-Diaz. Elizondo, the best known of these Hispanic theologians, focuses in his writings on the Mexican American experience of living on the borderlands, both geographically and culturally, and on the reality of *mestizaje* or miscegenation, which he interprets theologically as symbolizing the overcoming of separateness through "a new creation."

Mujerista theologians, such as Cuban American Isasi-Diaz, focus on Latinas' experience of double oppression: sexism and racism. Latinas confront the sexism of Anglo-American culture, of the institutional Catholic Church which sacralizes the exclusion of women, and of Latino men who have been socialized into the ideology of male dominance and superiority called *machismo*. *Mujerista* theology seeks to empower Latinas in the struggle (*en la lucha*) against these forms of oppression and exclusion.

The reader of these selections will discover that the Latino religious experience in the United States reflects the diversity that has existed in Latin America since the sixteenth century, when Spanish Catholicism encountered Amerindian and African religions and new forms of religious expression were conceived.

Sources and Selected Works in Latino/a American History, Literature, and Religions

[* indicates works of fiction]

Acosta, Oscar Zeta. *The Revolt of the Cockroach People*. New York: Vintage Books, 1989.

Alexander, Kay. *California Catholicism*. Santa Barbara, CA: Fithian Press, 1993.

*Anaya, Rudolfo. *Bless Me, Ultima*. Berkeley, CA: TQS Publications, 1972.

Aquino, Maria Pilar, Daisy L. Machado, and Jeanette Rodriguez (eds.). *A Reader in Latina Feminist Theology: Religion and Justice*. Austin, TX: University of Texas Press, 2002.

Avalos, David T. *Latinos in the United States: The Sacred and the Political*. South Bend, IN: University of Notre Dame Press, 1986.

Avalos, Hector (ed.). *Introduction to the U.S. Latina and Latino Religious Experience*. Boston: Brill Academic Publishers, 2004.

Badillo, David A. *Latinos and the New Immigrant Church*. Baltimore: The Johns Hopkins University Press, 2006.

Beebe, Rose Marie, and Robert M. Senkewicz. *Lands of Promise and Despair: Chronicles of Early California, 1535–1846*. Santa Clara, CA: Santa Clara University Press; Berkeley, CA: Heyday Books, 2001.

Boyer, Richard, and Geoffrey Spurling (eds.). *Colonial Lives: Documents on Latin American History, 1550–1850*. New York: Oxford University Press, 2000.

Brading, D.A. *Mexican Phoenix: Our Lady of Guadalupe: Image and Tradition Across Five Centuries*. Cambridge, UK: Cambridge University Press, 2001.

Camarillo, Albert. *Chicanos in a Changing Society: From Mexican Pueblos to American Barrios in Santa Barbara and Southern California, 1848–1930*, new ed. Cambridge, MA: Harvard University Press, 1996.

Castillo, Ana (ed.). *Goddess of the Americas/La Diosa de las Américas: Writings on the Virgin of Guadalupe*. New York: Riverhead Books, 1996.

De La Torre, Miguel A., and Edwin David Aponte. *Introducing Latino/a Theologies*. Maryknoll, New York: Orbis Books, 2001.

Deck, Allan Figueroa (ed.). *Frontiers of Hispanic Theology in the United States*, 2nd ed. Maryknoll, New York: Orbis Books, 1992.

Diaz-Stevens, Ana Maria, and Anthony M. Stevens-Arroyo. *Recognizing the Latino Resurgence in U.S. Religion*. Boulder, CO: Westview Press, 1998.

Dolan, Jay P., and Allan Figueroa Deck (eds.). *Hispanic Catholic Culture in the U.S.: Issues and Concerns*. South Bend, IN: University of Notre Dame Press, 1997.

Dolan, Jay P., and Jaime R. Vidal (eds.). *Puerto Rican and Cuban Catholics in the U.S., 1900–1965*. South Bend, IN: University of Notre Dame Press, 1994.

Duany, Jorge. *The Puerto Rican Nation on the Move: Identities on the Island and in the United States*. Chapel Hill, NC: University of North Carolina Press, 2002.

Espinosa, Gastón, Virgilio Elizondo, and Jesse Miranda (eds.). *Latino Religions and Civic Activism in the United States*. New York: Oxford University Press, 2005.

Flores, Juan. *Divided Borders: Essays on Puerto Rican Identity*. Houston: University of Houton/Arte Público Press, 1993.

Garcia, Alma M. (ed.). *Chicana Feminist Thought: The Basic Historical Writings*. New York: Routledge, 1997.

García Canclini, Néstor (Lidia Lozano, trans.). *Transforming Modernity: Popular Culture in Mexico*. Austin, TX: University of Texas Press, 1993.

Gonzalez, Justo. *Harvest of Empire: A History of Latinos in America*. New York: Penguin, 2001.

———. *Voces: Voices from the Hispanic Church*. Nashville, TN: Abingdon Press, 1992.

Griswold del Castillo, Richard, and Arnoldo de León. *North to Aztlán: A History of Mexican Americans in the United States*. New York: Twayne Publishers, 1996.

Gutiérrez, Ramón A. *When Jesus Came, the Corn Mothers Went Away: Marriage, Sexuality, and Power in New Mexico, 1500–1846*. Stanford, CA: Stanford University Press, 1991.

Gutiérrez, Ramón A., and Richard J. Orsi (eds.). *Contested Eden: California Before the Gold Rush*. Berkeley, CA: University of California Press, 1998.

Heyck, Denis Lynn Daly (ed.). *Barrios and Borderlands: Cultures of Latinos and Latinas in the United States*. New York: Routledge, 1994.

Isasi-Diaz, Ada Maria. *En La Lucha/In the Struggle: An Hispanic Women's Theology*. Minneapolis, MN: Fortress Press, 1993.

Isasi-Diaz, Ada Maria, and Fernando F. Segovia (eds.). *Hispanic/Latino Theology: Challenge and Promise*. Minneapolis, MN: Fortress Press, 1996.

Isasi-Diaz, Ada Maria, and Yolanda Tarango. *Hispanic Women: Prophetic Voice in the Church*. Minneapolis, MN: Fortress Press, 1992; (bilingual ed.) Scranton, PA: University of Scranton Press, 2006.

Lopez, Tiffany Ann (ed.). *Growing Up Chicano: An Anthology*. New York: Morrow, 1993.

Martin, Patricia Preciado. *Songs My Mother Sang to Me: An Oral History of Mexican American Women*. Tucson, AZ: University of Arizona Press, 1992.

Matovina, Timothy. *Guadalupe and Her Faithful: Latino Catholics in San Antonio, from Colonial Origins to the Present*. Baltimore: The Johns Hopkins University Press, 2005.

Matovina, Timothy, and Gerald E. Poyo (eds.). *Presente!: U.S. Latino Catholics from Colonial Origins to the Present*. Maryknoll, New York: Orbis Books, 2000.

Matovina, Timothy, and Gary Riebe-Estrella (eds.). *Horizons of the Sacred: Mexican Traditions in U.S. Catholicism.* Ithaca, New York: Cornell University Press, 2002.

Moore, Joan W. *Mexican Americans.* Englewood Cliffs, NJ: Prentice Hall, 1976.

Olmos, Margarite Fernández, and Lisbeth Paravisini-Gebert. *Creole Religions of the Caribbean: An Introduction from Vodou and Santería to Obeah and Espiritismo.* New York: New York University Press, 2003.

Rodriguez, Jeanette. *Our Lady of Guadalupe: Faith and Empowerment among Mexican American Women.* Austin, TX: University of Texas Press, 1994.

Rodriguez, Richard. *Days of Obligation.* New York: Penguin Books, 1992.

———. *Hunger of Memory: The Education of Richard Rodriguez.* New York: Bantam Books, 1983.

Romero, C. Gilbert. *Hispanic Devotional Piety: Tracing the Biblical Roots.* Maryknoll, New York: Orbis Books, 1991.

Sandoval, Moises. *On the Move: A History of the Hispanic Church in the United States,* 2nd ed., rev. Maryknoll, New York: Orbis Books, 2006.

Stavans, Ilan. *The Hispanic Condition: The Power of a People,* 2nd ed. New York: HarperCollins, 2001.

Tweed, Thomas A. *Our Lady of the Exile: Diasporic Religion at a Cuban Catholic Shrine in Miami.* New York: Oxford University Press, 1997.

Valdez, Luis, and Stan Steiner (eds.). *Aztlan: An Anthology of Mexican American Literature.* New York: Alfred A. Knopf, 1972.

Whalen, Carmen Teresa, and Víctor Vázquez-Hernández. *The Puerto Rican Diaspora: Historical Perspectives.* Philadelphia: Temple University Press, 2005.

Some Suggested Questions for Discussion

1. Compare Jeanette Rodriguez and Richard Rodriguez on the significance or meaning of the Virgin of Guadalupe for Mexican Americans. How is it an expression of Mexican American identity? What meanings communicated through the image help fulfill or hinder the *Mujerista* historical project or *projecto historico* discussed by Ada María Isasi-Diaz?

2. Discuss how popular religious practices (rather than institutional forms of religion), such as those of the Penitentes of New Mexico and of Cubans living in Miami, serve to maintain a sense of personal and communal identity, a connection to heritage and homeland.

3. Compare the selections from Cristina Garcia's *Dreaming in Cuban* and Virgilio Elizondo's "Mestizaje as a Locus of Theological Reflection." Discuss whether or not Elizondo's understanding of *mestizaje* is an idealization of racial relations among Latinos. Is *mestizaje* an adequate or inadequate locus of theological reflection? Why or why not?

4. Compare Judith Ortiz Cofer's "Talking to the Dead" in *Silent Dancing* with Cesar Chavez's "The Mexican American and the Church." From the perspective of these authors, what roles do religion play in Latinos' lives? Can similar comparisons be made using the other selections in this section of the book?

Hymns, Prayers, and Other Religious Verses

AURELIO M. ESPINOSA AND J. MANUEL ESPINOSA

Popular Themes: Christ of the Passion, Prayers and Hymns (Alabados) of the Penitentes, the Child Jesus, the Holy Family, the Virgin Mary, the Matins; the Bachelor's Prayer. Special Invocations.

The history of the Catholic Church in Spanish America is the continuation of its history in Spain. Catholicism was transported to America in exactly the same form, with all its doctrines, ceremonies, pomp, and traditions. The Franciscan missionaries who labored in New Mexico for nearly two and one-half centuries established there the same institutions that they had in Spain to keep alive the fires of the faith among the colonizers and their descendants and to Christianize the Indians.

There are popular prayers, ballads, hymns, dramatic representations, legends, and beliefs which keep alive in the hearts and in the memories of the people practically all the scenes of the birth, life, sufferings, and death of Christ, special devotion to the Virgin Mary, and prayers to favorite saints. While many of these ceremonies and practices are inspired directly in the liturgical ceremonies of the Church, many others are of popular origin and have a history as old as the Church itself.

Christ of the Passion

The Christ of the Passion has been ever present in the tradition of Catholic Spain. In New Mexican tradition He has been the special object of adoration and reverence from the days of the *conquistadores* to the present time. When entering New Mexico, the first *conquistador* and colonizer, Juan de Oñate, not only whipped himself in the company of his soldiers in reverence to Christ Crucified on Holy Thursday of the year 1598, but also everywhere and on many occasions erected large wooden crosses before which he prayed for victory that he might succeed in Christianizing the Indians. The complete gospel narrative of the Passion and Death of Christ is commemorated in various forms of Spanish traditions: prayers, hymns, ballads, dramatic compositions, and iconography, a related popular artistic expression of religious sentiment. In New Mexican tradition all these manifestations of Spanish religious tradition are to be found in popular form.

Christian communities in early times gave dramatic forms to some of the scenes of the Passion as they were depicted in the gospels, at first perhaps as ceremonies accessory to the liturgy of the mass during Lent. In the Middle Ages religious worship was always very real, very dramatic. The mass, with its dramatic action and dialogue between the officiating priest and his assistants, the choir, and the people who participated, was in reality drama of the highest form. The elaborations of the liturgy called *tropes* were soon developed, and these may be considered the beginnings of the Passion plays of Christian tradition. The people then developed independent scenes, among them the scene of the Descent from the Cross, and began the truly popular religious drama, often separated from the official ecclesiastical ceremonies.

The so-called Easter plays of mediaeval Catholic tradition were a development of the earlier *tropes*, with the addition of the characters of Pilate, Judas, the Roman soldiers, Mary Magdalen, and so on. From these were developed the Passion plays of the fourteenth and fifteenth centuries. In the fifteenth century the Church authorities took a great interest in the Passion plays, but in the sixteenth century they generally left them to the people. The plays had become too long and complicated, with legendary elements added, and were often a source of mirth and amusement in some respects rather than of sorrow and devotion. From that time on, the Passion play was relegated to the people.

In Spain, however, the scenes of the Passion were not altogether relegated to the people, being continued, in a way, by the *autos sacramentales* produced in the streets of Madrid on carriages, each of which, as it passed along, represented a scene from a secular play in honor of the Eucharist or some scene from the Passion. Moreover, popular religious drama had a greater development in Spain than in any other European country. Nowhere in Europe are the scenes of the Passion and Death of Christ popularized for public devotion as in some cities of Spain: Barcelona, Seville, Toledo, Valencia. The religious orders and confraternities that have represented in one form or another some of the outstanding scenes of the Passion are legion. Holy Week in Seville has produced since the sixteenth century practically every scene that can be dramatized.

The Passion was a popular theme for dramatization in all parts of the Spanish world. Among the scenes of the Passion that have been popularly dramatized in New Mexico there is the popular dramatic representation called *La primera persecutión de Jesús* (The first persecution of Jesus). I know of two manuscript versions from Taos. The older and better version is very short and represents the visit of the three Magi Kings to the Child Jesus at Bethlehem, the Herodian persecution and massacres, and the flight to Egypt. This popular composition, which is still produced in Taos, is not properly speaking a Passion play; it is more fully described in another chapter.

Scenes from the Passion are apparently no longer performed today in New Mexico, although it seems that they were often staged up to the end of the nineteenth century. No texts of any of them have been found, but certain fragments of ballads and other verse narratives that have been preserved may have been parts of such plays. According to authentic information, a Passion play was part of the Church ceremony of Holy Week, following the mass on Good Friday, although some of the preparatory scenes were performed on previous days; Roman soldiers with helmets, the Centurion, and the Cyrenian appeared in them in costume. The play began with the adoration of Christ on the Cross, represented by a large image of Christ crucified on a huge cross. Longinus then appeared with his lance, often on horseback. It is said that at Tomé, Longinus actually entered the Church on a horse to pierce the side of the Savior. All this was accompanied by weeping and by the singing of sacred hymns, perhaps some of those, cited below, now found only in the ritual manuscripts of the Penitentes. Next, the lamentations of the Virgin took place. The lamentations are preserved in one of the most beautiful traditional Spanish ballads now found in New Mexico. The Descent from the Cross followed, and the lamentations continued. The image of Christ was taken down from the cross and delivered into the arms of the Virgin Mary. Finally, there took place the *Santo entierro*, or the burial. This consisted of placing the body of *nuestro padre* Jesús in the sepulchre, a large wooden box, to be venerated in the Church. I myself have witnessed some of the above scenes. None, to my knowledge, are performed today, except in the ceremonies of the Passion that are included in the practices of the Penitentes. The Ecce Homo, or Jesús Nazareno, of which there are still in New Mexico some very realistic iconographic examples, may have appeared also immediately before the scene of the Crucifixion.

Although these traditional scenes of the Passion were performed by the people, the Church officials approved them and took part in them. The scene of the Descent from the Cross, with the lamentations of the Virgin, was especially popular, and at Taos, Santa Fe, and other places it lasted longer than the other scenes, with ecclesiastical sanction and direction. The lamentations of the Virgin are found in several popular versions.

Prayers and Hymns (*Alabados*) of Penitentes

The hermanos penitentes, or Penitent Brothers of the society now called La Sociedad de Nuestro Padre Jesús Nazareno, represent an interesting New Mexican Spanish religious survival. Just when this Catholic religious society of New Mexican flagellants was given its present name we do not know. Up to the turn of the century its members were usually called Los Hermanos Penitentes de Nuestro Padre San Francisco. (The Penitent Brothers of Our Father Saint Francis), and there is much evidence to indicate that the society was a popular development of the Third Order of Saint Francis. The members of this lay religious brotherhood are generally referred to as Penitentes. The Passion of Christ is the central theme of the religious ritual and ceremonies of the Penitentes.

A study of the ritual, with its traditional Spanish prayers, ballads, hymns, and Passion narratives, together with the practices now in vogue, reveal at once the Spanish origin of the society and of practically all its ritual and ceremonies. The same or similar practices were common in mediaeval Europe. In modern Spain most of the ceremonies, including self-flagellation as penance for sin, are still to be found. The religious processions of various parish religious groups during Holy Week, with the carrying of heavy crosses, for example, are still commonplace in Madrid, Toledo, Seville, Valencia, and other cities in Spain. Similar examples can be given from some of the countries of present-day Hispanic America.

The New Mexican Spanish *penitentes* have practiced flagellation since the earliest years of the conquest, attested to by the fact that they did so when Oñate entered New Mexico in 1598, it was described by Father Benavides in the 1630's and religious societies have practiced it to our knowledge until recent years not only in New Mexico (the Penitentes), but also in Mexico, Spain, Italy, and other countries. At Santa Fe, members of the Third Order of Saint Francis, or *terciarios*, who flagellated themselves especially during Holy Week ceremonies, had their Franciscan chaplain and maintained a chapel which in the seventeenth and eighteenth centuries adjoined the Church of San Miguel. Its concession was annulled in 1826.

In the nineteenth century the Penitentes were numerous in northern New Mexico. After the American occupation, they were frequently in conflict with the ecclesiastical authorities, but the society seems to have flourished most when the opposition of the Church was the strongest. New Mexican ecclesiastical authorities of that era sometimes spoke rather harshly about the organization. Very often the conflict between the Penitentes and the Church seems to have been precipitated by overzealous ecclesiastics who attempted to stamp out too abruptly old customs such as these.

The members of the Penitente brotherhood are Catholic men who gather during Lent to perform certain religious rites, consisting of prayers and hymns about the Passion and Death of Christ, and who, in addition, practice flagellation during Holy Week and on other special occasions, such as the night of a vigil held for a deceased member. The march to Calvary from the *morada*, or chapel, on Good Friday is the special occasion for flagellation, and up to the end of the nineteenth century it was the usual custom to simulate a crucifixion: a Penitente was tied to a cross, which was raised for the period of the Agony on the Cross or for such time as the Penitente could endure. The Lenten and other devotions of the organization are not of New Mexican origin but are traditional Spanish prayers, hymns, and Passion ballads—the work, no doubt, of Franciscan missionaries of the seventeenth and eighteenth centuries or versions of Spanish originals printed in Spain in the sixteenth and seventeenth centuries.

The organization of the New Mexican Penitentes is very simple. The local *morada* has an *hermano mayor*, chief brother, as its supreme director, who holds office for four or five years together with as many as eleven other officers: the *pitero cantador*, or leader in singing; the *curandero*, or doctor who looks after the wounds of the members during their religious exercises; and others. The officers are usually selected from those who have finished their flagellation period of four or five years and are not obliged by the rules to whip themselves any more. Until recent years, the various *moradas* of northern New Mexico, some thirty in number, sometimes sent representatives to a general assembly that met usually at Santa Cruz to discuss matters of interest to the society, but there is no well-defined central organization. The local *morada*, with its officers, is an independent unit. It alone decided whether or not to send delegates to the general assemblies at Santa Cruz. Some Penitentes speak of the Santa Cruz chapel as the *morada madre*, or mother chapel, which seems to indicate that the general meetings held there may have been a continuation of meetings that were formerly the regular assemblies of a general and more highly organized society that since the days of Governor Vargas in the last years of the seventeenth century had its center at Santa Cruz. The division of the society into *moradas* of independent rule and organization was probably the result of the ecclesiastical opposition in the first half of the nineteenth century.

The entire ritual and actual ceremonies and practices of the New Mexican Penitentes are a commemoration of the Passion and Death of Christ. Although now continued chiefly by the lower classes in the old Spanish-speaking rural areas, the institution is not of popular origin. The Spanish tradition itself has a mediaeval Catholic origin, monastic in its beginnings. Even in the modern imperfect and garbled versions of the prayers, hymns, and religious ballads that are found in the hand-written *cuadernos*, or hymn books, of the New Mexican Penitentes, recopied and handed down from one generation to another, the learned sources are clearly observable. The existence of this mediaeval Spanish institution, a society of Christian flagellants, with their traditional Spanish ritual in prayers, hymns, ballads, and Passion narratives, is one of the most extraordinary features of Spanish tradition in New Mexico.

Of the various traditional Spanish prayers and Passion ballads that are found in the ritual and prayer manuscripts of the present-day New Mexican Penitentes, none appears to be a modern composition. All are versions of traditional Spanish seventeenth- and eighteenth-century compositions. The ballads *Por el rastro de la sangre*, *Un ángel triste lloraba*, and some of the traditional forms of the prayer *Bendito y alabado* certainly go back to the sixteenth and seventeenth centuries. The religious ballads preserved by the Penitentes are among the gems of the contribution of northern New Mexico and southern Colorado to Spanish balladry, the *romances tradicionales*.

One of the longest and best of the Passion narratives in verse—one that is chanted or sung at the *morada* on Holy Thursday—consists of 144 octosyllabic quatrains, or 576 verses. It narrates the complete story of the Crucifixion. The first 52 and the last 24 verses of this version are the following:

Con mansedumbre y ternura	With meekness and deep affection
y señas de fino amor	and signs of the most pure love,
les previno a sus discípulos	the Lord for his twelve disciples

la última cena el Señor.
Y con mucha caridad,
que en los mortales no ves,
después de haber cenado
les lava humilde los pies.
Luego consagró su sangre
y con cariñoso afán
se les dio muy escogido
en accidente de pan.
Por este medio dispuso
aquel nuevo testamento,
sacrificándose así
para desterrar el viejo,
pues en este sacrificio
era sangre de animales,
y en el nuevo la de Cristo
para redimir mortales.
Y para mayor firmeza
de lo que en él ordenó
les hizo beber su sangre
en el cáliz que les dio.
También quiso que durara
el sacramento en su Iglesia,
y para ello potestades
a sus discípulos deja.
Estos las comunicaron,
del modo que ha de durar,
a sus hijos sacerdotes
hasta que vuelva a juzgar.
Y al mismo tiempo les manda
que al hacer el sacrificio
se acordasen del Señor
por tan grande beneficio.
Concluida que fue la cena
dio gracias al Padre Eterno,
y con tal echó a nosotros
el más saludable ejemplo.
Despidióse de su madre
con gran ternura y dolor;
el de la madre fue grande,
pero el del Hijo mayor.
Después de esta despedida
con sus discípulos fue
desde la ciudad al huerto,
donde había orado otra vez.
En la cena antes les dijo
que habían de experimentar
que aquella misma noche
todos lo habían de dejar.

. . . .

Ya resucita Jesús,
ya el tercer día ha sacado
de allá del seno de Abrán
los justos depositados.
Consigo al cielo los sube,

provided the Last Supper.
And with the greatest charity,
the charity we never see,
after the supper was over
He humbly washed their feet.
He then consecrated His blood,
and with affectionate zeal
He gave Himself to them
in the accident of bread.
In this way He established
the New Testament and Faith,
thus sacrificing Himself
to do away with the Old;
for in the Old they offered
as a sacrifice animals' blood,
while in the New it is Christ's blood
that was shed for the sins of men.
And to confirm their faith
in all the things he commanded,
He gave them in the chalice
His precious blood to drink.
This Sacrament He wished
should abide in His living church,
and for that purpose He gave
to His disciples His powers.
These have then transmitted them
and their powers are thus continued
in all the priests who follow them
until He comes to judge.
He also commanded them
that when offering the sacrifice
they should do it in remembrance
of Him Who did such good.
And when the supper was finished
He gave thanks to the Father,
giving us thus an example
of what we too must do.
He took leave of His Mother
with deep affection and sorrow;
great was the Mother's sorrow,
but greater was that of the Son.
After this sad parting
with His disciples He went
from the city to the garden,
where He had prayed before.
He had told them during the supper
that it would come to pass
that on that very night
all of them would abandon Him.

. . . .

On the third day Jesus has risen,
and has already delivered
from the bosom of Abraham those
just souls that were waiting there.
He took them with Him to heaven,

que se mantuvo cerrado
hasta que sirvió de llave
la sangre que ha derramado.
Con la cual el nuevo Adán
recuperó aquella tierra
que primero había perdido
causa una serpiente fiera.
Reconozcamos después
a Nuestro Jesús Amado;
nuestros yerros son la causa
que le ponen nuevos clavos.
Acabemos con su muerte
nuestras culpas, sus agravios,
y no le ofendamos más,
que seremos muy ingratos.
Intercédenos, Maria,
se borren nuestros errores,
ya que vuestro Hijo os dejó
por madre de pecadores.

the heaven that was ever closed
until it was opened at last
by the blood that Christ has shed.
In this manner the New Adam
recovered all that paradise
that in ages past he had lost
through the serpent's evil advice.
Les us praise forever and ever
the name of Our Loving Jesus;
our sins alone are to blame
for the nails that pierced his flesh.
He died for us; let us end
our life of sin and His grief
and let us offend Him no more,
for we would be most ungrateful.
Intercede for us, Virgin Mary,
that our sins may be forgiven,
for Your Son has deemed to name you
as the mother of all sinners.

As a sample of part of the ritual of the Penitentes, the complete ceremony, with the password and prayers performed on the arrival of each Penitente at the *morada* after the door has been closed, as found in the Santa Cruz manuscripts, is given below. Most of the language of the ceremony is in octosyllabic verse.

—Dios toca en esta misión
las puertas de su clemencia.
—Penitencia, penitencia,
que quieres tu salvación.
—San Pedro me abra las puertas,
bañado entre clara luz;
soy esclavo de María;
traigo el sello de Jesús.
Pregunto a esta cofradía,
¿Quién a esta casa da luz?
—Jesús.
—¿Quién la llena de alegría?
—María.
—¿Quién la conserva en la fe?
—José.
—Luego bien claro se ve
que siempre habrá contrición
teniendo en el corazón
a Jesús, María y José.
Para entrar a esta misión
el pie derecho pondré,
y alabo a los dulces nombres
de Jesús, María y José.

"In this mission God unbolts
the gates of His boundless mercy."
"Penance we preach, penance,
for you wish your salvation."
"May Saint Peter open the gates,
for me with brilliant light;
I am the slave of Mary;
I have the seal of Jesus.
I ask this confraternity,
"Who gives light to this house?"
"Jesus."
"Who fills it with joy?"
"Mary."
"Who keeps it in the faith?"
"Joseph."
"It is perfectly clear, then,
that all those will be saved
who hold in their hearts
Jesus, Mary, and Joseph.
In order to enter this mission
I will put first my right foot,
and will praise the sweet names
of Jesus, Mary, and Joseph."

The door is opened and the penitent enters, stepping in first with his right foot. He then kneels and on his knees he advances toward the Cross on the altar. In the long prayer that the penitent recites while venerating the Cross, he is often accompanied by all those present. Sometimes the prayer is omitted. After the veneration of the Cross, the penitent recites the following prayer in verse, performing the various acts indicated in the words:

—Señor Mío Jesucristo,
yo soy este pecador

My Lord, Jesus Christ,
I come, a grievous sinner,

que vengo a hacer mi ejercicio	to perform my exercises
y cumplir mi devoción.	and accomplish my devotions.
Besaré este santo velo	I will kiss this holy veil
para que mi alma suba al cielo;	so that my soul may be saved;
besaré esta santa mesa,	I will kiss this holy altar
que es lo que mi alma confiesa;	for it confirms my faith;
besaré esta santa cuerda	I will kiss this holy cord
para que mi alma no se pierda.	that my soul may not be lost.

All those present then pray:

"—*Adorámoste, Nuestro Señor Jesucristo y bendecímoste que por tu Santa Cruz redimiste al mundo y a mí pecador también.*"

"*We adore Thee and we bless Thee, Our Lord Jesus Christ, because through Thy Cross Thou hast redeemed the world and also me, a sinner.*"

The Penitente then withdraws from the altar backwards, always facing the Cross and on his knees. He then kisses the feet of the *hermano mayor* and asks pardon of all those he may have offended, and the others answer him:

"—*Perdónenme, hermanos míos, si en algo los he ofendido y escandalizado.*
—*Que le perdone Dios, que de nosotros ya está perdonado.*"

"*Pardon me, brothers, if in any way I have offended you and scandalized you.*"
"*May God pardon you, because we have already pardoned you.*"

In most of the *moradas* the above ceremony apparently takes place only at the beginning of the Lenten ceremonies, when the Penitentes first gather at the *morada* for their regular Lenten exercises. Each Penitente enters individually until all have been received.

The Child Jesus

In New Mexico, as in all Spanish-speaking countries, the veneration for the Child Jesus is deeply rooted in popular tradition. Prayers to the Child Jesus are taught to New Mexican children by their parents and relatives as soon as they learn to speak. Among the most beautiful nursery rhymes known by children we find the following:

Dijo el gallo:	Said the cock,
—¡Cocorocó!	"Kokoroko!
¡Cristo nació!	Christ is born!"
Dijo la cabra:	Said the goat
—¡Me, me!	"Ma, Ma!
¿Donde? ¿Donde?	Where? Where?"
Dijo la oveja:	Said the sheep,
—¡Be, be!	"Ba, ba!
¡En Belén!	In Bethlehem!"
Dijo la mula:	Said the mule,
—¡Vamos a ver!	"Let us go and see!"
Dijo el buey:	Said the ox,
—¡No es menester!	"It is not necessary!"

This New Mexican Spanish Christmas rhyme is traditional. There are similar versions from Argentina and Chile and from several parts of Spain. The verses are pan-European and are a survival from mediaeval Latin rhymes. In such a well-known book as *Songs of the Nativity* by William Henry Husk we find the following mediaeval Latin version: "The cock croweth, *Christus natus est* [Christ is born]; the raven asketh, *Quando?* [When?]; the cow replieth, *Hac nocte* [This night]; the ox crieth out, *Ubi? Ubi?* [Where? Where?]; the sheep bleateth out, *Bethlehem.*"

The Child Jesus born of the Virgin Mary in the stable at Bethlehem and adored by the Magi Kings and by the shepherds is the special object of adoration, love, and pity. No more beautiful lyric poetry has ever been written than some of the verses composed by Lope de Vega for his *Los pastores de Belén* (The shepherds of Bethlehem). The following verses are sung by the Virgin Mary and the shepherds when the Divine Child trembles and weeps from the cold:

No lloréis, mis ojos;
Niño Dios, callad,
que si llora el cielo,
¿quién podrá cantar?

Do not weep, my love;
Child God, do not weep,
for if heaven weeps,
who will ever sing?

Vuestra madre hermosa,
que cantando está,
llorará también,
si ve que lloráis.

Your beautiful mother,
who is now singing,
will weep also,
if she sees you weeping.

Los ángeles bellos
cantan, que les dais
a los cielos gloria
y a la tierra paz.

The angels on high
are singing, for you give
joy to heaven and
peace to earth.

De aquestas montañas
descendiendo van
pastores cantando
por daros solaz.

From these mountains
the shepherds are coming
singing joyously
to bring you comfort.

Niño de mis ojos,
ea, no haya más,
que si el cielo llora,
¿quién podrá cantar?

Dear Child, my love,
come, weep no more,
for if heaven weeps,
who will ever sing?

There are many prayers, ballads, legends, and dramatic representations that continue the general Spanish cult of the Divine Child, and some are traditional and very old. The popular verses that may be compared to those of Lope de Vega, although not so beautiful, are numerous. Among the most popular are the following, found as separate verses to the Child Jesus or as part of the dramatic compositions called *Los pastores*, discussed in another chapter. In *Los pastores* they are usually put in the mouths of the shepherds.

Duérmete, Niño chiquito,
duérmete, amado mío;
mis pecados fueron causa
que estés temblando de frío.

Go to sleep, little Child,
go to sleep, my love;
it is on account of my sins
that you suffer from the cold.

Duérmete, Niño chiquito,
duérmete, mi Redentor;
duérmete tierno querido
hasta unirme con mi Dios.

Go to sleep, little Child,
go to sleep, my Redeemer;
go to sleep, my dear one,
until I meet my God.

Alarrú, Niño chiquito,
alarrú, mi vida mía;
duérmete, Niño chiquito,
que la noche está muy fría.

Lullaby, little Child,
lullaby, my life;
go to sleep, little Child,
for the night is very cold.

¡Quién pudiera, Niño lindo,
lograr en esta ocasión
que te sirvieran de cuna
telas de mi corazón!

Would, beautiful Child,
that on this occasion
a cradle could be made for you
from the tissues of my heart!

The novenas to the Holy Child (el Santo Niño), especially to the Santo Niño de Atocha, are very popular in New Mexico. The expression "¡Santo Niño de Atocha!" to express surprise or sorrow, asking the help of the Divine Child to avert disaster or suffering, is heard in New Mexico today. There is a popular prayer in verse to the Santo Niño de Atocha that has many variants, the differences being chiefly in their length. The version given below, which is one of the shorter ones, in its Spanish form consists of nine octosyllabic quatrains, each quatrain with the second and fourth verses in assonance:

¡Adiós, Niñito de Atocha,
mi dulzura y mi placer!
Hermosura de la gloria,
¿cuándo te volveré a ver?

Hail, Child of Jesus of Atocha,
my sweetness and my joy!
Heavenly beauty,
when will I see you again?

Manuelito de mi vida
líbrame de Lucifer.
Hermosura de la gloria,
¿cuándo te volveré a ver?

Manuelito, my life,
save me from Lucifer's wiles.
Heavenly beauty,
when will I see you again?

Jardín lleno de delicias,
y matizado clavel,
delicia de los arcangeles,
¿cuándo te volveré a ver?

Garden of all delight,
multiple-hued carnation,
joy of archangels,
when will I see you again?

Lucerito de mi vida,
de la más linda mujer,
encanto de las virtudes,
¿cuándo te volveré a ver?

Morning star of my life,
born of the loveliest of women,
joy of heavenly virtues,
when will I see you again?

Naciste, divino Niño.
en la ciudad de Belén.
Gloria de (de)nominaciones,
¿cuándo te volveré a ver?

You were born, divine Child,
in the city of Bethlehem.
Glory of denominations,
when will I see you again?

Cielo estrellado, divino,
y todo mi menester,
gloria de los principados,
¿cuándo te volveré a ver?

Starry heaven, divine,
the end of my desires,
glory of principalities,
when will I see you again?

Por tus santísimos padres
y por tu divino ser,
gloria de los mismos tronos,
¿cuándo te volveré a ver?

Through your divine origin
and your divine essence
glory of thrones, I ask,
when will I see you again?

Por el natal que tomaste
de una peregrina Ester,
gloria de los querubines,
¿cuándo te volveré a ver?

Through your divine birth
from an Esther full of grace,
I ask, glory of Cherubim,
when will I see you again?

Por el suspenso y afán
de mi señor San José,
gloria de los serafines,
¡cuándo te volveré a ver?

By the suspense and agony
suffered by St. Joseph, I ask,
glory of the seraphim,
when will I see you again?

The lost Christ Child found with the high priests in the temple is sung in New Mexico in traditional Spanish ballads, usually incorporated in the texts of the popular dramatic composition *El Niño Perdido* (The lost Child). A version from Taos, modernized into strophic form in two different meters and with changes in assonance, is the following:

La Virgen buscaba al Niño—por las calles y las plazas,
y a todos los que veía—por su Hijo preguntaba.

—Decid si habéis visto—al sol de los soles,
al que nos alumbra—con sus resplandores.
Dénos, Señora, las señas,—por si acaso lo encontramos.
—Es blanco como la nieve,—y como la aura encarnado.
Tiene unos cabellos—como el sol dorado;
sus labios y boca—son flores del año.
—Por aquí pasó ese Niño,—según las señas que dais
Al templo se encaminó,—id allá y lo hallaréis.
—Dios os pague, hijos,—esa buena nueva.
Ya encontrará alivio,—el alma en su pena.
   Partió el Alma Divina,—al templo se encaminó.
Entre todos los doctores,—al Sol de Justicia halló.

   The Virgin sought the Child through streets and squares,
and asked all those she met if they had seen her Child,
"Tell me if you have seen the sun of all the suns,
that one who gives us of his divine light."
"Describe him, dear Lady; we may meet him perchance."
"He is as white as snow, and as fair as the dawn.
The locks of his forehead are of a golden hue;
his lips and his mouth are the flowers of the season."
"That child passed by here, to judge from that description.
Go to the temple, lady, and you will find him there."
"The Lord reward you, children, for the good news.
My grieved heart will now find more comfort and peace."
   The Blessed Mother to the temple directed her steps.
Among the doctors the sun of all justice she found.

The Holy Family

The Holy Family is a special object of veneration in New Mexico as well as in all Spanish countries. In New Mexican Spanish tradition, popular dramatic compositions, numerous prayers, hymns, nursery rhymes, and a few ballads attest the great popularity of the veneration for the Holy Family. The first prayer that New Mexican Spanish children learned from their mother's lips is the following one, no doubt traditional. It is known by all. As noted earlier, the Penitentes of New Mexico have a version of it in their ritual, and some of its verses are found in other New Mexican prayers.

—¡Bendito y alabado sea el
   Santísimo Sacramento del altar!
—¡Ave, María Purísima!
—¿Quién en esta casa da luz?
—Jesús.
—¿Quién la llena de alegría?
—María.
—¿Quién la conserva en la fe?
—José.
—Pues bien claro se ve
que siempre habrá contrición,
teniendo en el corazón.
a Jesús, María y José.
   ¡Salgan los espíritus malignos
y entre la suma bondad,
y se estampe en mi alma
la Santísima Trinidad!
	Blessed and praised be the
	   Most Holy Sacrament of the altar!
	Hail, Most Pure Mary!
	"Who gives light to this home?"
	"Jesus."
	"Who fills it with joy?"
	"Mary."
	"Who keeps it in the faith?"
	"Joseph."
	   "It is perfectly clear, then
	that all those will be saved
	who hold in their hearts
	Jesus, Mary, and Joseph."
	   May all evil spirits depart
	and may true virtue enter
	and may the Most Holy Trinity
	take possession of my soul!

Purísima Concepción,	Most Immaculate Conception,
Madre del Verbo Divino,	Mother of the Divine Word,
échame tu bendición	give me your blessing
y guíanos por buen camino,	and show us the right way,
que yo la recibo en el nombre	for I now receive it in the name
del Padre y del Hijo	of the Father, and of the Son,
y del Espíritu Santo, Amén.	and of the Holy Ghost, Amen.

There are shorter versions, but none omits the beautiful verses beginning with "¿Quién en esta casa de luz?" and ending with "a Jesús, María y José," which are mumbled even by infants just learning to speak. In religious processions, such as first-communion processions, children used to sing the complete version given above. These verses are the oldest form of the prayer and are traditional. They probably came from Spain in some form in the seventeenth century. In the *Noche buena, autos al nacimiento del Hijo de Dios*, a seventeenth-century Spanish work by Gómez Tejada de los Reyes, we find in one of the *villancicos*, or Christmas carols, the following version of the above lines, one very close to the New Mexican prayer and probably one of the oldest versions:

—Zagal, ¿dónde está mi bien?	"Youth, where is my greatest treasure?"
—En María, Jesús y José.	"In Mary, Jesus, and Joseph."
—¿Adónde está mi alegría?	"Where is my joy?"
—En Jesús, José y María.	"In Jesus, Joseph, and Mary."
—¿Adónde toda la luz?	"Where is all my light?"
—En María, José y Jesús.	"In Mary, Joseph and Jesus."

In a Chilean version of the widely known Spanish traditional children's prayer that begins with the words "Con Dios me acuesto, con Dios me levanto," (I retire with God, and I rise with God) we find the following version of the verses in question:

—¿Quién es mi luz	"Who is my light?"
—Jesús.	"Jesus."
—¿Quién es mi guía?	"Who is my guide?"
—María.	"Mary."
—¿Quién corona la fe?	"Who sustains the faith?"
—José.	"Joseph."
Con vosotros viviré	With you I will live
lleno de paz y alegría,	in peace and in happiness,
y me serviréis de guía	and you will guide me,
Jesús, María y José,	Jesus, Mary and Joseph,
y el Santo de mi nombre,	and also the saint
Amén.	whose name I bear, Amen.

From the numerous popular hymns dedicated to the Holy Family it is not easy to select a typical example. Comparison of many of them with similar compositions from Spain and Spanish America reveals, as usual, that some are traditional and very old. Many changes have taken place, however; here and there new verses appear and sometimes entirely new strophes have been added. In New Mexican tradition the most popular hymns in honor of the Holy Family are called alabanzas de Jesús, María y José (praises to Jesus, Mary, and Joseph). All are in the well-known traditional Spanish octosyllabic meter, the meter of the Spanish ballads and, in fact, the most popular meter of Spanish poetry generally. The longest hymn of this series contains twenty-eight octosyllabic rhymed quatrains, or 112 verses. Many of these quatrains appear in shorter versions, so the essential differences between the various versions are to be found in the number of quatrains they contain. Below, with translation, are six quatrains from the long version cited above; it appears in a Penitente ritual and hymn manuscript from Peña Blanca:

Daremos gracias con fe	With faith and great hope
y crecidas esperanzas,	we will give thanks,

cantando las alabanzas
de Jesús, María y José.
 Canten dulces serafines,
que yo les ayudaré,
a cantarles los maitines
a Jesús, María y José.
 Los tres reyes del oriente,
por grande dicha se ve,
que adoran en el portal
a Jesús, María y José.
 Esta Sagrada Familia
de Dios escogida fue.
Ya saben sus santos nombres
de Jesús, María y José.
 En el trance de la muerte,
cuando agonizando esté,
me asistan los santos nombres
de Jesús, María y José.
 —¡Misericordia, Señor,
Dios Uno, Trino!—diré,
poniendo de intercesores
a Jesús, María y José.

by singing the praises
of Jesus, Mary, and Joseph.
 Let sweet seraphim sing,
for I will help them,
to sing the matins
to Jesus, Mary, and Joseph.
 The three kings from the East,
what a great joy it is!
have come to adore
Jesus, Mary, and Joseph.
 This Holy Family
was chosen by God.
Their names you know:
Jesus, Mary, and Joseph.
 At the hour of my death,
when I am in my last agony,
may the holy names assist me
of Jesus, Mary, and Joseph.
 "Mercy, my Lord, One God,
Triune God!" I will say,
begging for the intercession
of Jesus, Mary, and Joseph.

The Virgin Mary

The cult of the Virgin Mary in New Mexico is universal. Traditional Spanish ballads preserved in New Mexican tradition in which the Virgin Mary plays the chief role are found like many others in the manuscripts of the Penitentes. Not only ballads but also poetic compositions of other types, prayers, invocations, folktales, anecdotes, and miracles about the Virgin Mary abound in New Mexican tradition.

In the *coplas populares*, called simply *versos* in New Mexico, la Virgen de los Dolores, the traditional Spanish Virgin of Sorrows, is the most popular. Of the following two *coplas*, which are very popular in New Mexico, the first one is found in identical form in Spain, and the second one is apparently not only traditional, but also very old, for its syntax—the use of the subjunctive for the imperative in affirmative commands or requests in the second person singular—is that of fourteenth- and fifteenth-century Spanish.

 La Virgen de los Dolores
quiere mucho a los Manueles,
porque se llama su hijo
Manolito de los Reyes.

 Madre mía de los Dolores,
Tú has de ser mi intercesora.
En la hora de mi muerte
Tú me defiendas, Señora.

 Our Lady of Sorrows
loves all those called Manuel,
because her son's name is
Manolito of the Kings.

 Dear Mother of Sorrows,
intercede for me.
In the hour of my death,
Blessed Lady, assist me.

The May devotions to the Blessed Virgin are universally observed in New Mexico. Up to within recent years, it was the custom in every home to adorn with flowers of the field and garden a specially constructed altar in honor of the Virgin. Every night, prayers, including the rosary, were recited by all the members of the family, and hymns were sung. The hymns to the Virgin usually sung during the month of May included the well-known "Dulcísima Virgen del cielo delicia" (Most sweet Virgin, joy of Heaven") and "Venid y vamos todos con flores a María" (Come, let us all offer flowers to Mary), both of which are traditional Spanish hymns to the Virgin found in devotional books of Spain and Spanish America.

But the recitation of the rosary was not limited to the month of May. The devotion of the rosary was widespread in all Spanish Catholic families of New Mexico until the end of the nineteenth century. It is only in recent years that the devotion has decreased. The rosary, prayers, and other devotions were usually recited every night of the year, and hymns and ballads appropriate for the feast celebrated or for the season of the year were sung. The special rosaries for the sick and for the dead have always been popular. In saying the rosary for the dying and for the dead, traditional prayers, ejaculations, and verses accompany the *ofrecimientos* or special offerings of each of the mysteries of the rosary.

These *ofrecimientos* are numerous and varied, and most of them are traditional. In the rosary for the dying or for those recently deceased, and for whom a *velorio*, an evening of prayers and hymns for the dead, in this case, is being held, one of the most common forms of the verse offering at each mystery is the following:

Los ángeles en el cielo	The angels in heaven
alaban con alegría,	sing joyous praises,
y los hombres en la tierra	and men on earth
responden:—¡Ave, María!	reply, "Hail, Mary!"

When the rosary is recited for the souls in purgatory, the above formula is also used, but a more common one is the following, a traditional Spanish one to be sure, and one not altogether of popular origin, for there are two Latin verses in the original text:

Por las ánimas benditas	For the blessed souls
que en el purgatorio están	who are in purgatory
ofrezco este misterio.	I offer this mystery.
Lux perpetua luceat eas.	May perpetual light shine upon them.
¡Requiescant in pace, Amén!	May they rest in peace, Amen!

A very extraordinary Spanish religious survival still found in New Mexico, although not generally, is the custom of singing matins in bed at the first signs of dawn. These matins are called *oraciones* or *alabanzas del alba* (dawn prayers or praises). The grandfather or eldest person in the family begins the singing, and the other members from their beds, wherever they may be, respond and join in the singing. According to available sources of information, the same custom exists in the country villages of Spain, Chile, and other regions of Spanish America. One of the best versions from New Mexico is the following:

Cantemos el alba;	Let us sing the matins;
ya viene el día.	daylight is coming.
Daremos gracias.	We will give thanks,
¡Ave, María!	Hail, Mary!
Ángel de mi guarda,	My Guardian Angel,
noble compañía,	most noble company,
vélame de noche	watch over me at night,
y guárdame de día.	and protect me during the day.
Ya nació María	Mary was born
para el consuelo	for the comfort
de pecadores,	of sinners,
y luz del cielo.	and to be the light of heaven.
Tan bella grandeza	Such magnificence
no quiso ver	Lucifer,
la sierpe fiera	the venomous serpent,
de Lucifer.	did not wish to see.
María Divina,	Mary Immaculate,
con ser tan pura,	although most pure,
fué celebrada	was indeed famous
por su hermosura.	for her beauty.
Éstas sí son flores;	These indeed are flowers;
éstas sí que son.	indeed they are.
Gracias a María;	We thank Mary;
gracias al Señor.	We thank the Lord.

En suma pobreza	In the greatest poverty
ya parió María,	Mary gave birth
al Verbo Encarnado,	to the Word Incarnate,
Nuestro amparo y guía.	our refuge and guide.
Que todos los santos	May all the saints
del cielo nos valgan.	in heaven protect us.
¡Oh, Jesús Divino,	Oh, Divine Jesus,
guía nuestras almas!	guide our souls!
La mula se espanta	The mule is frightened
con el resplandor,	at such radiance,
y el buey con el vaho	and the ox with his breath
calienta al Señor.	gives warmth to the Lord.
¡Viva Jesús!	Hail, Jesus!
¡Viva María!	Hail, Virgin Mary!
Cantemos todos	Let us all sing
en este día.	on this day.
Bendito seas,	Blessed be you,
sol refulgente.	shining sun.
Bendito seas,	Blessed be you,
sol del oriente.	sun from the East.
Bendita sea	Blessed be
tu claridad.	your light.
Bendito sea	Blessed be the one
quien nos la da.	Who sends it to us.
Quien el alba canta	Those who sing the matins
muy de mañana	early in the morning
las indulgencias	obtain the indulgences
del cielo gana.	granted by God.

Of traditional Spanish prayers and hymns in New Mexico, there seems to be no end. A large number of hymns, not all of them traditional or really popular, were collected and published by Father Rallière in 1877 in his book *Cánticos espirituales*. Another abundant collection of traditional prayers, including the various versions of "El bendito," "El sudario a las ánimas del purgatorio" (the prayer for the souls in Purgatory), traditional versions of the Act of Contrition, the numerous and diverse prayers to the saints, exorcisms, and the like, could be compiled without great difficulty.

The Bachelor's Prayer

Turning to a lighter vein of religious tradition, one finds many examples of the survival of a special prayer, a humorous one, but one which is very common in all Spanish countries: *la oración del soltero* or *de la soltera*, the prayer of the bachelor or maiden who is looking for a wife or husband. The traditional and popular versions from Spain, Chile, and New Mexico that have been published are very similar. One of the best from New Mexico, which has taken on some modern dress, is the following *oración del soltero*:

Después de tantos quebrantos	After a long string of troubles
yo me quiero desposar,	I wish to get married,
y pido a todos los santos	and I beg all the saints
que me quieran ayudar.	to come to my assistance.
Siendo mis pesares tantos	My troubles are now so great
ya me arriesgo al matrimonio,	that I am brave enough to marry,
y pido a todos los santos	and I beg all the saints
que me libren del demonio.	to protect me from evil.
Santa Sinforosa,	Saint Sinforosa,
si yo he de encontrar esposa,	if I really find a wife,

que sea mujer de casa,
cumplida, limpia y virtuosa.
　Santa Gertrudis,
que esté llena de virtudes.
Para guardar tal tesoro,
espero que tú le ayudes.
　Santa Elena,
que sea una mujer buena,
que cumpla con sus deberes,
y que no me tenga en pena.
　Santa Tomasa,
que cuide bien de su casa,
y no quiera averiguar
cuanto se mueve en la plaza.
　Santa Juliana,
que no se esté en la ventana,
mirando a los que pasan
y oyendo palabra vana.
　Santa Miquela,
que no sea de las que velan,
que deben a todos los santos,
y a cada uno su vela.
　Santa Inés,
si sabe hablar inglés,
que sepa decir, "No,"
y cuando debe, decir "Yes."
　Santa Delfina,
que no sea espadachina,
que no sea curandera,
astróloga ni adivina.
　Santa Dorotea,
ni muy linda ni muy fea;
pero no sirva de pena
si el mundo se ríe de ella.
　Santa Margarita,
si por ventura es bonita,
que sepa prenderse bien,
y ser limpia y exquisita.
　Santa Catalina,
que sepa bien la cocina,
y no quiera pasar los días
en la calle o en la esquina.
　Santa Ana,
que no quiera andar galana,
paseando de casa en casa
bailando la varsuviana.
　Santa Isabel,
que nunca me sea cruel;
que a la tarde y a la mañana
me dé sopitas de miel.
　Santa Rosa,
que no sea muy mugrosa;
que *amás* de bailar *tustepe*
sepa hacer alguna cosa.

may she be a good housekeeper,
dutiful, neat and virtuous.
　Saint Gertrude,
may she be of fine character.
To keep such a treasure,
I hope you will help her.
　Saint Helen,
may she be a good woman,
may she perform all her duties,
and may she bring me no grief.
　Saint Thomasa,
may she take good care of her home,
and may she never worry
about what happens in the plaza.
　Saint Juliana,
may she not stay at the window,
looking at the passers-by
and listening to vain words.
　Saint Miquela,
may she not be one of those
who are always praying to the saints,
offering each a candle.
　Saint Agnes,
if she knows English
let her know when to say, "No,"
and when to say, "Yes."
　Saint Delfina,
I hope she won't be quarrelsome;
may she not be a medicaster,
an astrologer, or soothsayer.
　Saint Dorothy,
neither very beautiful nor very ugly;
but she must not worry me
if everybody laughs at her.
　Saint Margaret,
if perchance she is beautiful,
I hope she will know how to dress,
and be neat and dainty.
　Saint Catherine,
I hope she will be a good cook,
and not wish to spend her time
in the streets or on the corners.
　Saint Anne,
may she not overdress,
and go from house to house
dancing the varsouvienne.
　Saint Elizabeth,
may she always be good to me;
whether it be late or early
may she always give me fine food.
　Saint Rose,
may she not be too unkempt;
and besides dancing the two-step
may she also know how to work.

Santa Sofía,
que se esté en casa de día,
y que no le sea costumbre
darme la comida fría.
   Santa Enriqueta,
que no me salga coqueta
y quiera pasar los días
paseando en la bicicleta.
   Santa Damiana,
que no sea tan cristiana,
que abandone sus quehaceres
a la primera campana.
   Santa Rosario,
que cuide bien de mi diario,
y no quiera gastar tanto
cual si fuera millionario.
   Santa Beatriz,
que ella me haga muy feliz;
y que sea mi escogida
una de las de San Luis.

Saint Sophie,
may she stay at home during the day,
and may she never have the habit
of giving me cold food.
   Saint Henrietta,
I hope she will not be a flirt
and want to spend all day
riding around on her bicycle.
   Saint Damiana,
may she not be so religious
that she will give up her work
the moment the first bell rings.
   Saint Rosario,
may she be careful with my money,
and not wish to spend freely
as if I were a millionaire.
   Saint Beatrice,
may she make me very happy;
and may my chosen one be
one of the most virtuous.

Special Invocations

The traditional Spanish formula used in exorcising is rare in New Mexico. The prayers and brief invocations to the saints who are believed to be the special patrons of certain phenomena, however, are almost as common as in Spain. A few of the shorter ones, all traditional and in verse, are the following:

Señora Santa Ana,
Señor San Joaquín,
arrullá este niño,
se quiere dormir.

Dear Saint Anne,
Dear Saint Joachim,
lull this baby, please,
he wishes to go to sleep.

San Lorenzo,
barbas de oro,
ruega a Dios
que llueva a chorros.

Saint Lawrence,
you of the golden beard,
pray to our Lord
that it may rain abundantly.

San Isidro,
labrador,
ruega a Dios
que salga el sol.

Saint Isidore,
tiller of the soil,
pray to our Lord
that the sun will come out.

Santa Bárbara bendita,
que en el cielo estás escrita
con papel y agua bendita,
Santa Bárbara doncella,
líbranos del rayo
y de la centella.

Blessed Saint Barbara,
your name is written in heaven
on holy paper with holy water,
Saint Barbara Virgin,
guard us ever against
thunderbolt and lightning.

The following invocation is recited on setting a hen:

Padre mío,
San Amador,
todas pollitas,
y un cantador.

Dear Father,
Saint Amador,
may one be a rooster,
and the rest pullets.

The Penitente Brotherhood

Cleofas M. Jaramillo

In my youth, *La Hermandad de los Penitentes* (the penitentes' brotherhood) was still active.

Some years ago, I wrote to Mr. Jose Maria Chavez of Abiquiu, who was very well read in history, asking him to give me the origin of the penitentes. I quote his answer, translated as closely as possible from his original Spanish.

"As to the origin of the marked association *Los Penitentes*, it is a well-established fact in history. Born in the Holy Land, the same throng who demonstrated their joy by singing "Hosanna" while they spread their garments on the ground before Jesus, as he entered Jerusalem, afterwards cried out, "Crucify Him," which brought his death. On hearing of His resurrection, some of them tried to choke themselves by tying handkerchiefs around their throats. Others covered their heads and ran distracted. A few gashed their flesh and let their blood flow, trying in this manner to atone for the Innocent's bloodshed.

"Here you have the *penitentes;* later on, the *flagelantes,* their actions modified but not in the form of penance. From Egypt the practice spread to Germany, from there to Spain, and from Spain to New Spain. There is nothing wrong in its object, but it seems rather barbarous and scandalous before modern society."

However, the beginning of the sect is lost to history and different opinions exist as to its origin. St. Justin says that it first appeared in Perugia, and soon spread through Italy, across the Alps, into Switzerland and Germany.

During the sixteenth century, the *flagelantes* were found in Spain and all southern Europe. Some opinion prevails that there is a connection between the New Mexico *Penitentes* and the European *flagellantes.* Others believe that they are a survival of the Third Order of St. Francis and that the sect was brought here from Old Mexico by the Franciscan monks, gradually spreading through New Mexico and southern Colorado.

The first Christian to flog himself voluntarily seems to have been St. Pardulf, a Benedictine monk. The sect spread even among Protestants. In 1535, there was a group called Anabaptists, who whipped themselves.

Among the rules of the Order, most of which still hold good today, is one which states that associates must be members of the Catholic Church and of good repute. The *Hermano Mayor* is the elected head. Newly-initiated members are branded by three gashes cut lengthwise on their backs with a sharp *pedernal* (flint). Members must renounce all evil practices and abandon all feuds with their neighbors. Ill-gotten goods must be restored or atoned for by penance. They believe that pain and penance endured here on earth lessens suffering in the hereafter.

Due credit is given to the English writers who come to New Mexico and write such interesting books from second-hand information, but I wish here to contradict some of their statements.

One author starts his article on the *penitentes:* "Are they lunatics or murderers?" They are neither. The members that live according to the brotherhood's rules are the best, most sincere religious people.

My parents, who lived in Taos and Rio Arriba counties, two strongholds of the *Hermandad* penitente brotherhood, never heard of a penitente being crucified alive and left on the cross to die. In some of the most remote places, like Penasco, Mora and Las Truchas, penitentes have been tied to the cross, and there may have been an instance where a *penitente* died on the cross from exhaustion, from the long fast, loss or blood, or from the flogging which he had been practicing.

As to the statement that some of them have been buried alive, in punishment for the betrayal of secrets of the order, this is another exaggeration. I have heard of their being punished in various ways. One penitente was made to walk with chains, tying his feet together, while he carried a cross on each shoulder. Another was forced to walk blindfolded, his arms extended, holding in each hand a sword with its points resting on his loins. It was alleged that this brother met his death, when he stumbled and fell, the two swords crossing through his sides. A few days later, his clothes, tied in a bundle, were sent to his family, with word that the boy had left for the Holy Land.

One form of punishment was the criss-cross gashing of their backs, laying them on the floor and switching them with a knotted rope until they fainted.

A penitente sometimes requested, before his death, that he be buried bare-foot or without a coffin, as a penance. His request was always carried out.

The *disciplinas* (palm whips) were usually dipped in Romero decoction, to soothe the cuts and to keep them from becoming inflamed with the cold, and not to add more sting, as some writers say.

Penitentes never walked into a church or chapel carrying their crosses. They slipped from under them covered with their blanket, and each pair left their two crosses standing outside, interlocked in some way.

The Catholic Church has condemned the Order for years, excommunicating the members of the *moradas* who insisted upon going out and scourging themselves. This strict order of the Church, together with the weight of opinion among the younger members who are becoming educated, will in a few years put an end to the sect.

Holy Week at Arroyo Hondo

Cleofas M. Jaramillo

In this hidden nook, isolated from the outside world and still untouched by modern progress, people were contented to live their simple lives. Still holding to ceremonies carried on from the medieval age of faith and religious traditions, during Lent every year they reenacted with sincere religious fervor the Sorrows of the Passion Play. The *penitente* brotherhood took charge of the religious ceremonies, inasmuch as there was no resident priest in the town in my time.

On Monday and Tuesday of Holy Week the conical adobe ovens were seen smoking throughout the three villages, while the week's supply of bread and *panocha* was being baked. The mud ovens must be blessed before using them, or they won't bake the bread right; it will come out heavy and soggy. To bless the oven, a cross is laid on the floor of the oven, salt is sprinkled on the cross and prayers recited.

At the *penitentes' morada* where half the male population congregated on Wednesday, one *mayordomo* (sometimes two) was chosen for each day to supply the food for the brothers who fasted each day from Wednesday morning until Saturday noon, when the *mayordomos* vied with each other in treating the *hermanos* to the nicest repast. Four or five of the *acompañadores* (brethren of light) were seen coming out of the *mayordomo's* house carrying four copper kettles hanging on a stick. These kettles contained *torrejas con chile* (egg fritters in chile sauce), *rueditas* (fried dried squash), and *sopa de fideos* (home-made spaghetti). They carried in an earthen bowl bread pudding, with cheese and raisins. All meat was forbidden during the four Holy days. Recipes for these lenten dishes will be found in my cook book of Spanish recipes.

Penítente Morada

339

There was a great deal of exchanging done of *charolitas*—dishes—at noon on both Holy Thursday and Good Friday. Neighbors and friends were seen carrying back and forth small bowls filled with *panocha, capirotada, torejas*, or whatever other nice dish they had prepared. This exchange of special dishes went on in every small village during Holy Week.

The *morada* stood across the river a few yards below the town. On each side of the door, resting against the wall, was a pile of century-old crosses, which were kept inside the secret room from year to year.

With a field glass my family had a very good view of the *penitentes* as they came out of the *morada*. The members were told that with this field glass we could distinguish their faces through the black masks. After this, for fear of being detected, the brethren of light stood in line outside the front of the door, holding up outspread blankets, thus screening the *penitentes* while they came out. They took up their crosses, over which a blanket was thrown, leaving only their heads and feet exposed. Followed by the *hermanos de disciplina* (flagelantes), they dragged their heavy crosses around to the back of the *morada* and proceeded on their painful way up the rocky trail to *el calvario* (Calvary Cross on the hill).

* * * * *

On *Viernes de Dolores*, the Friday before Good Friday, my grandmother carried out her votive promise of giving an alm and a dinner to the poorest family in the village.

She had brought from Old Mexico her favorite painting of *Nuestra Señora de Los Dolores* (Our Lady of Sorrows). The beautiful madonna face, with a tear like a pearl rolling down her pink cheek—her white hands clasping tightly the handle of the sword piercing her breast under her blue mantle—was tinted in soft shades on a tin sheet and framed in a fancy tin frame. Throughout the year every dime or nickel that the grandchildren could save was pasted around the picture inside the glass covering it.

The daughters and their children were invited also to the dinner. At the end of the meal, the tin frame with the painting was brought down; the nickels and dimes were taken off and together with a crown made from coffee cake dough baked very nice and brown, the hollow center filled with *melcochas*—candies, was given to the poor family as the promised alm.

The *Tenebrae*. On Wednesday evening, *Las Tinieblas* were held at the *morada*. The name *Tinieblas* was given this office because towards its close all the lights were extinguished to represent the darkness that shrouded the face of the earth at the time Christ expired on the cross, as well as to express the profound mourning of the Church at that time.

Fifteen candles were placed on a triangular wooden stand. Those at the sides were snuffed out successively, beginning with the lowest one, at the end of each of the eleven Penitential Psalms, representing the flight of the eleven apostles; the other three candles represented the three Marys.

When the central light, representing Christ, was the only one left, it was removed by the *resador* to the back of the altar, where they continued their chant. Between chants, one of the *rezadors* stepped out to the front of the altar, and striking a match he whirled it around saying, "*Salgan vivos y difúntos, que aquí estamos todos juntos.*" The flash of light from the match represented the lightning. In the dim light the bent, huddled figures of the *penitentes*, their bodies bare to the waist, filed in through the low door. With their masked faces and long white trousers they looked ghostly. The air in the small oratorio room, already packed with men and women kneeling on the floor, became stifling. Above the roar of the wooden *matraca*, the rumbling of chains, the wail of the reed *pito*, groans and prayers, was heard the thud-thud of the *penitentes'* blood-matted whips.

The removal of the central light and its sudden reappearance represented Christ's death and resurrection.

At the close of the ceremony, all but one of the *penitentes* filed out to their secret room across the hall. The one who remained stretched himself across the floor at the door, and the brethren of light who accompanied him told the people that the brother requested in the name of God that every one step on him on their way out. I heard of a cruel woman who more than complied with the request by grinding her heel into the flesh of the *penitente's* bare back. Another one, more kind-hearted, begged the *hermano* to excuse her from complying with his request.

Moved by curiosity to see the inside of the *morada*, I once asked a *penitente's* wife, who was going to pay a votive debt to the *santos* at the *morada*, if I might accompany her. We climbed the hill on which the *morada* stood in the upper town and were admitted to the chapel. On the wall of the hall dividing the chapel from the secret room hung a row of whips. The woman crawled on her knees from one statue to another, placing lighted candles before each. I was left kneeling before the statue of the Crucifixion. Paralyzed with fear, I could not move, for there before me on the mud altar table stood the statue of *La Muerte*, Death, staring at me with one glass eye, the other eye shut, aiming at me with her drawn bow and arrow. Behind me I heard the *hermanos* going in and out of the room. I did not dare turn around for fear of seeing a *penitente* standing in back of me. This visit satisfied my curiosity.

For a couple of years during Holy Week a flagellant *penitente* with his *acompañador* came to our private chapel and asked permission to go in and make a visit. While the brother of light recited the prayers, the brother lay prostrated with arms extended on the floor before the altar. He got up and stood by the door while flogging himself, leaving the bloody marks of his *disciplina* on the white-washed walls. Then he left, still flogging himself as he passed in front of our store on the way back to the *morada*. My family persisted in believing that this was the man who had helped himself to one of the fat lambs from our corral and had come to atone for it. The oft-repeated verse of *"Penitente pecador, porque te andas azotando? Porque me comí un carnero gordo y ahora lo ando desquitando,"* applied in this case.

On one occasion, hearing the doleful notes of the penitentes' flute, I ran out to the front porch in time to see three *penitentes de madero* passing on their way to visit the lower town *morada*. My uncle, sitting on the porch step, teasingly grabbed me by both hands and swung me out towards them. My breath caught with fright as I thought that one of them had stretched out his hand from under his blanket to grab my feet.

Anyone wishing to see a *penitente* now must stay up quite late at night, and then he may get only a glimpse, as they come out only one or two at a time and are very carefully guarded and screened-in by the *acompañadores*.

Holy Week

On Maundy Thursday at two o'clock in the afternoon, the *Emprendimiento* (Seizure of Christ) took place. The men carrying the statue of *Nuestro Padre Jesus*, a life-sized statue of Jesus of Nazareth, crowned with thorns and dressed in a long red tunic, led the procession out of the Church. The *rezador*, reading the seizure and trial of Christ, walked behind the statue, followed by the throng of women.

From *la morada* on the opposite side of the town two files of brethren of light, representing the Jews, started out. These men had red handkerchiefs tied over their heads with a knot on top representing a helmet. They were preceded by a man dressed like a centurion. The Jews carried long, iron chains and *matracas*, or rattlers. On meeting the procession coming from the Church, they stopped before the statue and asked "Who art Thou?" The men carrying the statue answered, *"Jesus de Nazareno.* (Jesus of Nazareth.")* The Jews then seized the statue, tied the statue's hands with a white cord, while their leader read the arrest sentence. The other Jews stood, loudly clanging the chains and rattling the *matracas*. They led the procession back to the *morada*, carrying with them the statue.

El Encuentro. The next morning—Good Friday—the same two groups took part in the ceremony. This time the group that left the Church carried the statue of *Nuestra Señora de la Soledad* (The Sorrowful Mary), dressed in black; a black mantle covering her head, over which a silver halo shone. The procession of men representing the Jews came from the *morada* carrying the statue of Christ. The two groups met half way around the town, representing the meeting of Christ and His Mother. One of the women took a white cloth from her head, and approaching on her knees wiped the face of the statue, while the grieving Marys wept real tears aloud. The *resador* read the passage of the meeting of Christ and His Mother as the procession walked back to the Church.

About half an hour later, *La Procesión de Sangre* (The bloody procession) of all the *penitentes* combined, in the long double file of flagellants, was seen winding its way up the rocky trail to the *calvario*, then back again to the *morada*. Special self-imposed penances were practiced between one and three o'clock in the afternoon. A lone penitente sometimes staggered up the trail surrounded by brethren of light. He dragged his feet tied with a heavy iron chain. On his back a bunch of sharp cactus needles pricked his flesh at every step.

Good Friday. Las Tres Caías (Three Falls). The largest and heaviest cross was picked out and laid upon the shoulder of the *hermano* who chose to represent the crucified Christ. A crown of thorns was placed on his head, and a bunch of prickly cactus was hung on his back. Laboriously, the *penitente* dragged the scraping cross up the rocky trail. Two brethren of light walked on each side of him, one reading the three falls in the Stations of the Cross from an open book in his hand. The other, acting the part of Simon Cyrene, helped the *hermano* lift the weighty cross when he stumbled and fell under its weight. A group of brethren of light had already dug a pit and gathered a pile of rocks by Calvary Cross. They stood around the *calvario*, awaiting the arrival of the *Cristo* brother, who on reaching the hill was stretched upon his cross and tied with ropes. The cross was raised and placed in the pit surrounded by the pile of rocks to hold it upright.

The *hermanos* knelt with bowed heads around the cross, praying and reciting the Seven Last Words of the crucified Savior. The voice of the man upon the cross grew more and more faint, as he repeated the words, until his body hung limp, and he was taken down and carried on a blanket, too weak to carry his cross back to the *morada*.

Las Estaciones.   At three o'clock the people gathered at the Church for the Stations of the Cross. The procession of *penitentes*, some carrying crosses and others switching their lacerated backs, came first. Between the two files walked a masked *penitente* pulling a small cart in which stood the statue of Death. "Comadre Sebastiana" death was called. The *acompañador*, walking behind the cart, now and then picked up a large stone and dropped it into the cart to make it heavier to pull. The men carrying the statue of *Nuestro Padre Jesus*, another man with a crucifix, and the reader walked in the center of the procession. As the *resador* read each Station of the Cross, the people knelt on the ground, then arose and walked singing a verse of the *alabado de las columnas*.

Én una columna atádo		Onto a pillar,
Estaba El Réy del Cielo.		The King of Heaven was tied.
	Chorus	
Herído y ensangrentádo		Wounded and bloody,
Y arrastrádo por los suélos.		He was dragged on the ground.

A few days after the close of Holy Week, some of the young men would appear at the store looking pale and haggard. My brother, curious to find out if a certain young man were a *penitente*, gave him a friendly slap on the back. Taken unawares, the man betrayed his secret by a painful shrug and expression of agony on his face.

Sabado de Gloria closed the Holy Week with joy and cheer, for Lent ended at noon on Holy Saturday, and a big *baile* was given that night.

"Comadre Sebastiana" (Statue of Death)

In most of the old Spanish mansions a *sala* (long living room) was always included. In this room the private invitation dances were given. To these dances only the exclusive Spanish society was invited. For the private dances of *carestrolendas*, egg shells filled with confetti or cologne water, were taken to the dance. These were playfully broken on the heads of the dancers, providing much merriment. Refreshments of wine, *biscochitos*, cakes and candies were passed to all the guests. This custom was attacked by the towns' parish priests in their sermons, but in the remote villages, which the priest visited only once a month, the people followed their own rules and customs.

* * * * *

On the first of August, the *penitentes* celebrated the wake of *La Porsiuncula*, the most important event, excepting Holy Week. The two *moradas* combined for this wake. The gloomy interior of the old church was illuminated by tallow candles placed on tin sconces hung on the side walls and stuck on the mud floor before the statues of *La Sangre de Cristo* (Christ on the Cross) and *Nuestra Señora de Los Angeles* (Our Lady of the Angels), which were brought down from their niches and set before the sanctuary steps.

The weird strains of the flute announced the approach of the *penitente* procession which stopped outside. The women and men kneeling on the mud floor moved to the sides, men to the left, women to the right, opening an aisle for the penitente chief and the brethren of light, who passed in, chanting hymns accompanied by the lonesome notes of the flute.

With arms crossed, they knelt in prayer before the statues, while the *mayordomo del velorio*, chief of the wake, distributed to each person a lantern. The lantern was made from a beer bottle, the bottom of which had been taken off by tying a string saturated in kerosene around it, and then burning off the string. Through the open bottom, candles were set in the neck of the bottle and lighted.

The penitentes, numbering about thirty, led the procession. First, walked the flagelantes, their bare backs streaming with blood. In unison, their whips were raised first over one shoulder and then over the other. They took two or three steps, paused, and then swung the palm whips over their shoulders again. Following the flagellants were those carrying crosses, each guarded by an *acompañador*, walking by his side. The brethren of light and the men carrying burning pitch-wood torches came next. In the middle of the procession walked the men with the statues; behind them came the *rezador* and the singer, Hemerejildo, reciting with great fervor the rosary on large blue and white glass beads hung around his neck. The women followed. The two lines of candle light circled the town, and the outline of the square could be seen from the top of the hill.

Each decade of the rosary was offered in song:

Jesús mi dulce dueño, Todo cristiano procura,
Desagraviarte queremos, Llorar un paso tan tierno,
Recíbe Padre amoroso, Libra Virgen del infierno
Las flores de este mistério. Quien rezara su rosario.

The lonesome lament of the flute and the wailful chant, punctuated by the painful slap of the palm whip, lingered in the echo of the hill after the procession had gone back into the *morada*.

Noche Buena and Religious Dramas

CLEOFAS M. JARAMILLO

"Let the luminarias leap high
As the night grows long,
And the shadows dance
To the caroler's song."

On the twenty-fourth of December the snow lay heavily on the deep valley, half burying the silent little villages nestling among the white hills. As the last rays of the setting sun turned the highest snow-capped peaks into gold and rose, the men and boys of the three villages busied themselves clearing the snow from the front yards in every house. They were preparing the ground for the *luminarias*, which later in the evening they built of *ocote*—pitch wood sticks, placed by fours in log cabin fashion. Rows of these *luminarias* outlined the towns and *cordilleras*.

As the deepening shadows of night spread over the valley, the brown adobe houses were brightened with the red glow of their fire, which warmed the groups of men and boys standing around them. The fires built in front of my house were kept burning brightly until midnight by an occasional addition of an empty kerosene barrel, which had been saved in the store for that purpose.

Inside the house there was great activity in the kitchen. The children warmed the *piñones* and shelled them by rubbing them between two boards. These nuts were used in the mince meat for the *empanaditas* (little fried pies). An extra hired woman beat the white corn dough until it was so light that a small piece dropped into a cup of water floated on top. It was then ready for the *tamales*, which were made and steamed, to be served with hot coffee after the midnight chapel services. Lupe and her helpers were kept busy until almost midnight, frying the *empanaditas* and *buñuelos* for the *Oremos* boys, who came to the door singing:

Orémos, Orémos,	Oration, Oration,
Del cielo venímos,	From heaven we come,
Angelitos somos,	Angels we are,
Si no nos dán Orémos,	If you won't give us gifts,
Ya no volverémos.	Alas, we won't return.
A las señoras caseras,	From the housekeepers,
Aguinaldos pedímos,	New Year's gifts we ask.
Con mucha alegría,	With great joy,
Con mucho contento,	With great contentment,
Vamos celebrando,	Let's celebrate this birth.
Este nacimiento.	Give us here, if you will give,
Dénos aquí, si nos han de dar,	For the night is long,
La noche es larga,	And we have lots to walk.
Y hay mucho que andar.	

A large pan of fried dainties was passed to these *Oremos* boys at the kitchen door, and they ate them, sitting around the bonfires.

Santa Claus was still unknown in those days. The *abuelo* (bug-a-boo man) took his place, although he was a stern old man dreaded by the children. Dressed in an old, shabby, patched suit and shabby hat, the *abuelo* went around the *luminarias* cracking his long whip, sending the boys home on the run. He followed some of them into their homes and made them kneel down and say their prayers. If they did not know their prayers, he gave them a good scolding and told them to stay home and learn them, but no sooner was the *abuelo* out of sight than the boys were out again, hopping, running and jumping over the bonfires, for the Spirit of the Christ Child filled their innocent hearts and fear could not remain long in them.

Down in the village the group that was to take part in the performance of the play of *Los Pastores* was going from house to house making *Las Posadas*. They represented Mary and Joseph going through the streets of Bethlehem seeking shelter for the night.

In earlier times, for nine days before Christmas groups of children led by a couple representing Mary and Joseph went through the village to nine houses. The group was refused entrance until they came to the ninth house, where they were admitted and refreshments passed to them. Here the hermit held up his cross at the door, trying to prevent *el diablo* from entering, but the shrewd evil one watched his chance and entered while the hermit was busy eating the refreshments spread before them. Satan played his pranks, helped himself to anything he liked, rattled his long nails, wrote in his book the names of the girls and women who smiled at him when he asked them if they wanted to come with him.

At the end of the village the group came to the chapel where the wake of *el Santo Niño* was taking place. Here the group gave the play of *Los Pastores*, the religious drama of the shepherds.

When making *Las Posadas*, Joseph knocked at the door of each house singing:

¿Quién le da posada	Who will give lodging
A estos peregrinos,	To these travelers
Que vienen cansados	Who come weary
De andar los caminos?	From traveling long roads?

A voice from within answered:

¿Quién da golpes a la puerta,	Who bangs at the door?
Que de imprudente hace alarde,	The imprudent makes a commotion,
Sin reflejar que ya es tarde	Without noticing that it's late,
Y a los de casa despierta?	And the household he awakes.

Joseph:

Señor os imploro	O Lord, I implore Thee,
Que en vuestra caridad,	That in Thy mercy
Le des posada a ésta dama.	Thou wilt give shelter to this damsel.

Voice from within:

Para el que tiene dinero	For him who has money,
Mi casa está lista,	My house is ready,
Para el que no tiene,	For him who has nothing,
Dios lo asista.	May God assist him.

Into a stable door they retired, where an ox and a mule were their only companions.

A BRIEF SYNOPSIS OF THE DRAMA "LOS PASTORES." There were twelve shepherds in the original play of *Los Pastores*, but at the time of which I write only six took part:

Characters

Shepherds—Tubal	Gila
Belicio	San Miguel
Lipido	El Ermitaño
Bato	La Estrella Oriental
Lizardo	Bartolo
Tebano	El Diablo

In earlier reproductions of this play, there was another female character—Dora, wife of Barto, one of the shepherds.

A shrine had been arranged with white sheets and a table at the head of the *oratorio* chapel. A double row of pine trees formed an aisle from the shrine to the middle of the room, through which the shepherds marched in double file, carrying flowery staffs with dingling little bells. A bundle slung over one shoulder suggested the bedding of the shepherds.

Ahead of them walked Hila, a serious-looking little girl, dressed in white, wearing over the veil on her head a tinfoil covered crown. She carried a small baby statue in a basket filled with snow.

Bartolo, the lazy shepherd, walked behind the other shepherds, carrying a sheepskin, which he spread under a tree and then lay upon.

The shepherds tramped up and down the aisle singing verses about the heavy snow and their flocks sleeping down in the valley.

Shepherd Song

Cielos soberanos,	Sovereign heavens,
Tenednos piedad	Have pity on us
Que ya no sufrimos,	For we cannot longer endure
La Nieve que cae.	The snow that falls.
Suspende tus íras	Suspend Thy rage
Y tanto quebranto,	So many damages,
Que ya están poblados,	For the valleys
De Nieve los campos.	Are already covered with snow.
Las estrellas brillan,	The stars shine brightly,
Y luego se apagan	Then get dim
Absortas se quedan	Amazed to see
De ver tal nevada.	Such a heavy snow.
Que copas de nieve,	What large snow flakes
Caen sobre el ganado,	Fall over the flock,
Aunque entre el monte	Although resting
Está reclinado.	Under the forest.

Belicio suggested stopping a while, to let the flocks rest, saying:

Pues hermanos míos,	Well, my brethren,
Ya que el cielo nos ha permitido,	Since heaven has permitted
Traernos con grán dicha,	Bringing us with great happiness
A estos valles dé Egipto,	To this valley of Egypt,
Si les parecíere bien,	If it seems right to you,
Parémos aquí un poquíto,	Let's stop here a while
Que descansen los ganádos.	To rest the flocks.

The rest of this drama will be found in my book of translated Spanish dramas.

El Día de Los Inocentes (Holy Innocents Day)

I do not know why this day was celebrated on the twenty-eighth of December instead of after the Kings' visit to the Manger, for it commemorates the day on which King Herod put the children of Judea to death by the sword. On this day one had to be very careful about lending things; and if you loaned something, you must not forget to say, "*Se la empresto, pero no por inocente.*" Anyone who forgot to say this had to pay a penalty.

On one occasion my aunt, who lived close by, sent her maid to ask my mother to let her have my baby brother for a little while. My mother, forgetting the day, let the girl take the baby. A few minutes later the maid returned with a tiny broom made of a few straws tied with red floss and wrapped in a little note with the words, "*Barrete la inocencia paga la pena.*" Mother at once set to work baking a cake which she sent to my aunt to *desempeñar* (redeem) the baby; he was sent back with the same cake bearer.

DIA DE AÑO NUEVO (New Year's Day). Instead of the birthday, the Spanish celebrate the Saint's name day. New Year's day is the day of los Manueles, and the women and men called by this name were serenaded on this day.

One year my brother, who was visiting at my home during the holidays, thought he would play a joke on my husband. He slipped quietly out of the house at four o'clock in the morning and rounded up the musicians who were going around the town *dando los dias a los Manueles* (serenading).

We awakened with the sound of music and singing at our front door; my husband in bathrobe and bedroom slippers opened the door and was greeted by the usual verse:

> *"Por aquí caigo, por aquí levanto,*
> *A darle los buenos días,*
> *Pues hoy es día de su santo."*

He politely invited the serenaders to enter; and they made themselves at home, while he ransacked my pantry for refreshments. My brother sat among them, with a broad smile, quite pleased with the success of his joke.

My husband's grandmother's name was Manuelita; and not wishing to disturb her so early in the morning, my brother had them come to our house to give the serenade in her honor.

* * * * *

Gifts were exchanged on the sixth of January, celebrating the arrival of the Three Kings at the Manger in Bethlehem to offer their gifts to the newborn Babe.

On New Year's day Grandma Melita started counting *"Las Cabañuelas"* for twelve days. Each day of the month represented one of the months of the year, and as the weather showed on each day so would the month be fair, stormy or cold. If January the second was fair and mild, so would the month of February be. The third was counted as March, and so on through each succeeding month. On the thirteenth, *Las Cabañuelas* were reversed and counted backwards, beginning with the month of December. This count was said to come out more true. The definition given for the word *"cabañuelas"* is *"Festival of the Jews of Toledo,"* so this custom must be originally from Spain.

This marked the end of the Christmas ceremonies.

Religious Dramas

As the dramatization of Bible stories was an old Spanish type of entertainment, it has been assumed that the Spanish *conquistadores* brought the religious drama to Mexico, and that from there the Spanish missionaries introduced it into New Mexico in their efforts to convert the Indians to Christianity. There are four Christmas plays that come in a cycle—in this order: *El Coloquio de San José; El Auto del Niño Dios,* or *Pastorela,* now called *Los Pastores* with several versions; *Los Reyes Magos;* and *El Auto del Niño Perdido.*

El Coloquio de San José begins with a summons from Simeon to all the males to appear at the temple with a reed in hand, for the purpose of choosing a husband for Mary, one of the Virgins in the Temple.

When Feliciano, the herald, comes to Joseph, he voices the wishes of his master, saying:

Vós patriarca escuchad.	Patriarch, thou listen.
Pues ya sabeis que Simeón,	Well thou knowest that Simeon,
Cabéza de éstas comarcas,	Head of this territory,
Manda púes que los patriarcas	Commands that all the patriarchs
En su real generación,	In his royal generation,
Hoy al templo soberano	Today at the sacred temple
Sean obligados a llevar,	Are obliged to appear
Una vara en su mano	With a reed in their hand,
Y de parte de Simeón	And I, for Simeon,
He venido a tí avisar.	Have come to inform you.

Joseph, because of his poverty, is reluctant to go into the temple, and he sits in the portico. Suddenly his reed sprouts forth a lily, and he is chosen to espouse Mary.

After the Annunciation, several months elapse; and Joseph and Mary are on their way to Bethlehem. On reaching the town, they go from house to house seeking lodging for the night. This part of the action is represented by *Los Posadas,* which is an introduction to the play of *El Niño Dios,* or *Los Pastores,* the second drama of the cycle.

Then comes the third drama, *Los Reyes Magos*. The three kings, noticing the new star in the East, decide to go to Bethlehem and offer gifts to the Christ Child. They stop at the palace of King Herod, who gives them welcome and asks them to stop again on their return. The kings reach the manger and present their gifts. After they leave, an angel appears and bids Joseph to take Mary and the Infant and flee into Egypt. On the way the Holy Family meets a number of shepherds, who recognize them.

The fourth drama of the series is called *El Niño Perdido*. Christ, being separated from His parents comes, in his wanderings, to a rich man's palace. The rich man is seated at a banquet table when the Child arrives. He tries to confuse the Child with his questions, but is given wise answers. At the end, the Child arrives at the temple, and the Doctors of the temple gather around to question Him, while Mary and Joseph are looking for Him. The script of this play is given in my book of Spanish dramas.

* * * * *

Besides the Christmas cycle, there is an earlier one of more simple folk plays, some of which are still enacted in remote mountain villages. This cycle is composed of three plays: *Adán y Eva, Caín y Abel* or *El Primer Pecado*, and *Lucifer y San Miguel*. It is claimed that "Adam and Eve" is the oldest play written. It opens with a song by Adam and Eve, as they are sitting on a bed of boughs underneath the Tree of Knowledge:

Song

Guerra es la vida del hombre
En la estación de sú império,
De morir en la campaña, irrevocable el decreto.

Lucifer calls all his helpers to dethrone man from the position to which God has elevated him. "Appetite" volunteers to tempt Eve, in the form of a serpent. Eve snatches an apple from the forbidden tree, and passes it to Adam, who is eating it when God, in a thundering voice, reproves them for their disobedience. Shamefacedly, they try to cover their nudity with branches of leaves. God orders them out of the garden. "Mercy" intercedes and begs that the penalty be waived. God promises man redemption through the birth of Christ. Eve laments their fall in a long recitation. The angels then foretell the coming of Christ, and the play ends with the song:

| *Gloria a Dios en las alturas,* | *Glory to God in the highest,* |
| *Y paz al hombre en la tierra.* | *And peace to man on earth.* |

The first drama presented in New Mexico, was The Moors and The Christians, given at San Juan de los Caballeros, during the dedication of the first church built by the Oñate expedition. When first enacted these dramas were held out in the open; afterwards they were given in *salas* (dance halls).

During the past thirty years the Spanish religious dramas have been discontinued. A few years ago a new legend of Our Lady of Lourdes was presented at Chamita, and in recent years Los Pastores have been revived, and the legend of Our Lady of Guadalupe, but these few presentations given, are not acted with the same vim, nor in the natural setting and costumes, and they have lost much of their attractiveness.

The legend of Our Lady of Guadalupe, which originated in Mexico over four hundred years ago, tells the story of a shepherd:

Juan Diego, the Indian shepherd, while tending his sheep on the hills near the city of Mexico, sees a vision. The Virgin, surrounded by a radiant light, appears to him, saying: "Juan, go to the Bishop and tell him to build a shrine in my honor here on this spot." Juan delivers the message, but the Bishop refuses to believe his story, until after the fourth apparition, when he brings a proof in the form of fresh roses which the Virgin commands him to pick on top of the mountain and to take to the Bishop. This is taken as a miracle, being in the month of November when the country was barren of flowers.

Upon being admitted, Juan kneels before his superior and relates the episode of the roses. As he opens his blanket, the fragrant roses tumble out at the Bishop's feet. On the blanket was stamped the image of the radiant Lady, just as the Indian boy had seen her in the apparitions on the hill. In robes of blue and rose, rays of light surrounding her, she was poised on a crescent moon, born up by a cherub's wings. The astonished Bishop is now convinced and orders the shrine of Our Lady of Guadalupe built on Tepeyac hill. The miraculous blanket was hung in a gold frame over the altar.

A new shrine, noted for its riches, now stands at the foot of the hill. The rail enclosing the sanctuary and the stairways leading to it contain many tons of solid silver. Twelve massive, solid silver candelabras hang from the ceiling, and a dozen silver candlesticks adorn the altar.

I visited the *santuario* during the holidays, which start a week before the celebration of the feast of Our Lady of Guadalupe.

Crowds of pilgrims visited the church. Some of them holding lighted candles crawled on their knees from the door to the rail before the altar. Others sat in the yard eating their lunch, or at the booths where hot lunches were being served. Many climbed the hill to the spring, on the site of the old shrine, and filled bottles with the miraculous water to carry home. Faith still gives it the power to perform miracles and to cure.

Saints' Holy Days

CLEOFAS M. JARAMILLO

Día de San Juan (St. John's Day)

Icy winter glided into spring. April showers gave life to the gray valley and turned meadows and fields into verdant seas. In warm, sunny May, rivers and arroyos filled with water that came from the mountain's melting snow. The overflowing *acequias* wound their way through freshly ploughed and planted fields.

School closed late in June, and on the twenty-third my father awaited me in the convent parlor. After bidding goodbye to my teachers and to Sr. Rosana, the principal, who was one of the pioneer sisters brought by Bishop Lamy, I joined him and climbed in the high seat of our buggy, of a make now forgotten. We rode along, inhaling the delicious fragrance of the newly-awakened sage and gray-green rabbit brush, which later in the summer would be covered with yellow blossoms. The desert plain seemed a fairyland. Here and there the road dropped into a verdant little valley, the sparkling river fringed with fresh green trees and drooping willows. From the edge of the highest ridge one looked down into the Arroyo Hondo, sunken valley, which in its rich verdure seemed to lie asleep, the deep silence enveloping the valley—broken only by the rattling of our buggy wheels or the distant barking of a dog.

I arrived home in time for the feast of the beloved disciple St. John. The women of the village were up early on the twenty-fourth of June. At six o'clock they were bathing in the river or in the *acequias*. Later in the morning the small children were seen also in the river and ditches, splashing cold water at each other, for on this day the waters in the streams were believed to be holy. Better health awaited those who rose early to bathe at least their faces and feet in the holy water. For was it not St. John who baptized Jesus in the river Jordan and blessed the waters?

The day was kept at Arroyo Hondo as a Rogation Day. By eight o'clock in the morning a procession started from the Church in the upper town. Standing on a wooden platform, the statue of *Nuestra Señora del Rosario*, dressed in a gala blue silk dress, and the statue of *San Juan*, carried in the arms of one of his devotees, were taken on a tour through the fields, along the foot of the second ridge of hills to the lower village—a distance of three miles. On arriving at the village, the procession visited each house. A boy beating a drum went ahead announcing the approach of the procession, which halted about ten feet from the door of the house. The lady of the house came out to meet the *santos*, with an *escudilla* full of live coals, over which aromatic incense had been sprinkled. She incensed the statues and helped carry them into the *sala*, where they were placed on an improvised altar decorated with wild flowers and tree branches.

Around the altar the crowd of people knelt while the lady of the house recited prayers, sang a hymn, and pinned a flower or jewel on Our Lady's veil or dress. Then the people arose and proceeded to the next house. Having visited every house in the lower village, the procession walked to the middle town, then up the *Cordillera* to the upper town, reaching the Church at dusk, where a wake in honor of the saints was held. Sometimes the wake was held at the house in which the procession stopped just before dusk.

* * * * *

On the Fourth of May was celebrated *El Día de La Santa Cruz* (Feast of the Holy Cross). At the chapel or at the home of a devotee an altar was erected in tiers. On the top tier a wooden, decorated cross was placed. From here it was brought down and rested on each step, while a prayer or hymn was sung or recited. Then the cross was taken out in procession to the next village, where a wake was held in honor of the Holy Cross.

* * * * *

Día de Santiago

The feast of *Santiago*, the national patron saint of Spain, was and still is celebrated in some of the northern towns, on the twenty-fifth of July. After the morning services at the Church, the statue of Saint James, the patron saint of *los caballeros* (horsemen), was carried in procession through the town. Two files of gallant horsemen, *socios de Santiago*, with their horses' bridles decorated with flowers and flags, rode ahead of the procession. A few yards from the procession they halted, turned, and rode back through the center of the procession in pairs to meet the statue. The two files crossed and galloped ahead. Again they whirled and galloped back to the statue, repeating this during the whole procession.

The *gallo* race, held years ago, has been replaced by horse races and modern sports. The rooster race of old was similar to the rooster race the Indians have at San Juan Pueblo, except that the Mexicans, instead of hanging the rooster as the Indians do, bury it in the ground, leaving its head exposed.

At Arroyo Hondo a group of *galleros* gathered at one end of the street, about fifty feet from the buried cock. One by one, they raced past the rooster, back and forth at full speed, leaning over the side of their saddles to grapple at the fowl, until one of them succeeded in grabbing its head and unearthing it. Swinging it by the legs over his head, with a triumphant shout he spurred his horse and raced ahead, the whole pack of horsemen yelling and racing after him. Up the *cordillera* they chased to the upper town. When finally one of the *galleros* overtook him, he turned and hit the man with the rooster. The challenged horseman grabbed away the trophy and raced on ahead, hotly pursued by the others. The rooster changed hands in this way several times during the race. Back they came like an avalanche, lashing their horses, yelling and racing down the hill to the lower town, where they crowded around the leader. A hot skirmish ensued. The *gallero* defended himself by striking in all directions with the rooster, until the cock was torn to pieces.

After several roosters met this fate, the crowd scattered, and a wagon was hitched, in which the *convite* for the *baile* started out. A fiddler, a guitarist, and a singer climbed into the wagon and rode around the three towns, playing and singing, finally coming back to the hall where the dance was to be held. This was the public invitation to the dance.

Early in the evening the hall was packed. Gray-haired *abuelitas* cuddling the *nietos* lined the back row around the hall. The young women who took part in the dances sat in front. All classes mingled in these public dances, from the silk-gowned *patrona* to the calico-dressed Indian maid. The elite left the dance early, before the men became too gay with drink. Sometimes a drunkard forced his way into the hall, causing great excitement when the *bastonero* tried to push him out.

Jealous husbands and lovers sometimes took advantage of the commotion to get even with their rivals, and a fist fight took place in the middle of the hall. The women—screaming and jumping over seats, dragging by the hand children that were half asleep—pushed their way out. When finally the *bastonero*, with the aid of the sheriff or sober men, restored order, the dance went on.

Through the clouds of smoke from the home-grown *punche* tobacco cigarettes, the bent heads and crouching shoulders of the *musicos* were seen. There was languor and softness in the wire strings, then recklessness and madness, as the dance wore on and *tragitos* from the musicians' pocket flasks went to their heads.

Día de Santa Ana

The next day was *Santa Ana's* day. Every woman fortunate enough to own a riding horse and side saddle brought them out. And with a white sheet thrown over the saddle and tied underneath to keep the long flowing skirts from soiling, she rode off, dressed in all her finery, to join the other lady riders. When tired of riding, they dismounted at the dance, which continued through the hot afternoon into the night.

These Holy days were always gala occasions eagerly awaited and long remembered.

Theological Significance

Jeanette Rodriguez

Within the Roman Catholic Church, devotion to Guadalupe's image and message has been used to discuss the significance and role of Mary (Mariology). While this is a very rich dimension in the faith life of Roman Catholics, I believe it is not the only or the best utilization of the story and image. There are three areas in which the understanding and application of the Guadalupe event may offer some theological insights to the larger church: (1) popular religiosity, (2) Guadalupe as symbol of God's unconditional love, and (3) the need for "feminine" metaphors for a more comprehensive understanding of the divine.

Guadalupe: "Of the People" Democracy

To appreciate the significance of Our Lady of Guadalupe it is crucial to understand the context in which she is recognized: popular religiosity. Popular religiosity—that is, how religion is lived and experienced by a majority of people (Schreiter 1985:122)—contributes to our understanding of Our Lady of Guadalupe. The adjective "popular" literally means "of the people." Although there is no comprehensive theory of popular religiosity, I offer a number of considerations that may assist in understanding this dynamic force.

One of the major elements of life among Hispanics in general and among Mexican-Americans in the United States is a system of folk customs and faith expressions termed popular religiosity or *religiosidad popular* (see Rodriguez 1990), which can be defined as the complexity of spontaneous expressions of faith which have been celebrated by the people over a considerable period of time (Elizondo, personal communication). They are spontaneous in that the people celebrate because they want to and not because they have been mandated by the official hierarchy, in this case the Roman Catholic tradition. When I speak of Catholicism in relationship to the Mexican-American culture, I am not referring to the institutionalized version of Catholicism, but to popular Catholicism, handed down through generations by the laity more than by the recognized and/or ordained clergy. There is a distinction between popular religiosity and what is called official religiosity (the institutional church). Although Hispanic popular religiosity has its historical roots in sixteenth-century Catholicism, it has evolved a life of its own that captures the identity and values and inspirations of the people in a way that I believe official religiosity has ignored. This way of being Catholic has always thought of itself as being the true faith of Christians, as being as "equally Catholic" as the clergy's version (Espín and García 1989:70–90).

From the point of view of the institutional church, popular religiosity has not been seen as equally Catholic, but as primitive and backward, perhaps even childlike. But popular religiosity is a hybrid with a life of its own: it continues to exist because for the poor and marginalized it is a source of power, dignity, and acceptance not found in the institutional church. Popular religiosity is not celebrated by a few, but by the majority of the people. It is an expression of faith which has survived over a considerable period with roots in the historical beginnings of Hispanic culture. Above all, popular religiosity is active, dynamic, lived, and has as its object to move its practitioners, the believers, to live their beliefs. That is, the people's own history, both personal and cultural, their own possibility for being saved in history, is expressed. Popular religiosity not only narrates a people's own history, but also acts it out and represents it. The life of the people is life as a human-divine drama in which the natural and supernatural claims are intimately intertwined. It is the humanization of God and the divinization of humanity. Humanity's cause (the poor) is the cause of God; God's actions for the cause of the poor are the actions that humanity must realize (Siller-Acuña 1981c).

In the example of the story and context of Our Lady of Guadalupe, she is God's action on the side of the poor, as is Juan Diego. In his encounter with the religious powers of the time, he is the protagonist, representing all who are marginalized. Similarly, Mexican-American women are the poor; Guadalupe comes and stands among them to reflect who they are—mother, woman, *morena*, mestiza—and gives them a place in a world that negates them.

Some of the documents of the church support this notion of popular religiosity. One of the fruits of the Latin American Church Conference at Medellín in 1968 was the serious discussion about popular religiosity. In *Pastoral Care of the Masses*, the Medellín Conference confirmed that in our evaluation of popular religion we may not take as our frame of reference the Westernized cultural interpretation (Second General Conference of Latin American Bishops 1973) and reaffirmed the vision of Vatican II that the Christian community should be so formed that it can provide its own necessities. (See Chapter 2, on the Nahuatl interpretation of the story and symbology.) This congregation of the faithful, endowed with the riches of its own culture, should be deeply rooted in the people. ("Decree on the Church's Missionary Activity, Vatican II," article 15, in Flannery 1975). The church attempts to discover and respect the presence of God in the concrete expressions of a particular culture. One such concrete expression has been revealed in the apparition of Our Lady of Guadalupe.

Popular religiosity is not only a vehicle for evangelization of many disparate Hispanic communities, but also functions as a form of resistance to assimilation. At the CTSA (Catholic Theological Society of America) Conference of 1989, Doctors Espín and García pointed out that popular religiosity is an important guardian of culture, history, and identity; without popular religiosity we (Hispanics in general and Mexican-Americans in particular) would not be the people we are. "Our identity as an integral part of the Catholic Church would not have survived the frequent clashes with the non-Hispanic—and often, anti-Hispanic—ways of the church in America" (Espín and García 1989:71).

When "we who are church" begin to theologize, we must be conscious that our theological methods are colored by who we are as individuals and which culture we are interpreting from. I express my ecclesiology with the expression "we who are church" to indicate ownership and identity as opposed to handing over of a church that is something outside of ourselves and a nonevolving institution. Because Our Lady of Guadalupe lives and breathes within this realm of popular religiosity, our theologizing must come from within, in this case, Mexican Americans' popular religiosity. There are many living Gospel values and metaphors of who and what God is that are expressed through Mexican-American culture. Through popular religiosity, Our Lady of Guadalupe's presence and message has been able to empower her people as they interact with the society of the United States. The emphasis on family values, the notion of enduring suffering, the ability to hope against all hope, a spontaneous feeling of connection and relationality, the unquestioned sense of God's providence as it is delivered through Our Lady of Guadalupe, the warm conversational sense of the presence of God, respect and love for all beings—all of these are found in the image of Our Lady of Guadalupe, as expressed by the women of the study in Chapter 6. Other popular faith expressions are pilgrimages, to the basilica for example; or sacred moments like Good Friday, Las Posadas (a reenactment of Mary and Joseph seeking lodging), and the making of *mandas* (promises). For Mexican Americans, the liturgical year begins with the Marian feast of Our Lady of Guadalupe.

These faith expressions of popular religiosity are readily accessible to anyone without exception and no one is excluded from participating in them. They provide a deep sense of unity and joy, while providing a forum for shared suffering. They are participatory and everyone takes an active role in them. The faith expressions, while serious, are not overly organized. The challenge, I believe, is not to eliminate them or simply to reduce them to a devotional celebration but to bring them into constant dialogue with the Word of God as contained in Scripture, tradition, and everyday revelation.

Some principal characteristics of popular religiosity (as set forth by Schreiter 1985, Galilea 1981, and Marzal 1973) are the assertion that God exists and everything is controlled by God; that God is rarely approached directly—hence the importance of powerful mediators such as Jesus and Mary (Schreiter 1985:158); and involvement and participation of the whole community (Schreiter 1985:129). There is, however, a private dimension to popular religiosity which we saw in the interviews with the women of my study. This private dimension is built upon the seeking of favors. The world is seen as interconnected and controlled, which is to say that the concerns of the inhabitants are concrete and requests are directed as immediate needs. Prescriptions for religious activity of the official religion are usually not observed in popular religiosity. For example, attending mass is not considered as important as visiting the basilica (Schreiter 1985:130).

The work of José Luis Gonzàlez (1983) is helpful in expanding our understanding of popular religiosity. He asserts that it operates out of a principle of participation that integrates the world in such a way that everything is perceived as interdependent or relational. For example, I am who I am because I am somehow related to you. Members of community-oriented communities that live and breathe within the realm of popular religiosity refer to each other as *hermana o hermano* (sister or brother).

If God is immediately involved in all worldly affairs, then any event that happens, good or evil (that is, physical, natural evil as opposed to moral evil), can be attributed to God's decision. Even in daily conversation members of the Mexican-American community use the phrase *si Dios quiere* (if God wants).

Vital relationships with nature and nature's integration of positive and negative forces are part of the religious experience in popular religiosity. The world is seen as an interconnected and controlled place and this perception is confirmed by the forces of nature leaving little room for human maneuvering. For example, the earthquake in Mexico in 1985 was attributed to God's disfavor with the people.

Our Lady of Guadalupe's clear connection to nature is seen both in her image and in the fiestas that celebrate her. She is surrounded by the sun, the stars, the moon, and nature. In her fiestas all children carry roses to her image, indicating that a proper celebration of a divine event must contain beautiful elements of nature. In the celebration of Guadalupe, sacred space and time are particularly important. There is a specific day, December 12, designated to celebrate the feast and a specific time, dawn. The people rise at daybreak, the time of new beginnings and the rebirth of the sun, to sing *Las Mañanitas* (a dawn song) to her.

For those who participate in the realm of popular religiosity, religious experience permeates all space and time. There are spaces and times of special strength and power that are part of the religious experience. Some examples of these phenomena are home altars, shrines, processions, and grave sites. Our Lady of Guadalupe clearly represents a familial and relational component in Mexican-American life. She identifies herself as their mother and they are all brothers and sisters to each other. The notion of the sacred being immersed in history is seen as Our Lady of Guadalupe takes a central role regarding the vital necessities of life—food, shelter, safety, and concern for family. She is petitioned for everything from health to the protection of a family-owned business. Her image is found in many homes and businesses in the form of pictures, statues, and altars and is worn on people's bodies in the form of necklaces and even tattoos.

All of these examples are significant to the people and their religious life, but they are not institutionalized, that is, they are not formally structured with rigid rules and procedures.

It is crucial to understand that popular religiosity is rooted in marginality and oppression. Official religiosity usually rejects religious symbols that express the people's marginality, and in doing so also rejects the people. For example, a newly assigned pastor removed the Hispanic people's statue of Jesus, which graphically depicted his suffering. The people, who identified closely with the statue, were outraged and exclaimed, "If you do not want our Jesus then you do not want us either."

In the story of Our Lady of Guadalupe, as in the present, she is still not accepted by some officials of the church. Many parishes with large Hispanic populations still refuse to place an image of our Lady of Guadalupe in their churches. She is, however, recognized and welcome among the people, with whom she shares the experience of rejection.

In the realm of popular religiosity there is a longing to critique and alter our reality and understanding of the sacred. Values and beliefs expressed through liberation theology, such as the value of justice in which all people are co-creators of the reign of God, are part of this longing. I define liberation theology in the terms of Gustavo Gutiérrez (1973): it is a theology of the people whose focus is the struggle of the poor to overcome oppression. It is not a theology created by the intelligentsia, the affluent, or the powerful, but by the poor and oppressed. It is a theology that believes in a God of history, that believes that God is active and present in the world, and that it is not enough that the hearts and minds of women and men be converted, but that the very structures that perpetuate systems of injustice must enter a similar conversion process. This is of course to suggest a radical change in the current social and political situation and overturning the established order. In the same way that Exodus and the Gospels function as a source for theology of liberation, so too has Our Lady of Guadalupe been the driving force behind many struggles for justice among Mexicans and Mexican Americans. We need only look at the Mexican Revolution, the plight of the farm workers, and the emergence of the basic Christian community. When Father Hidalgo called out for the Mexican Revolution in 1821, he rallied the people under the banner of Our Lady of Guadalupe, as did César Chávez and Dolores Huerta in rallying the *campesinos* (farm workers) to fight for their rights as laborers. However, I caution against reducing Our Lady of Guadalupe to a political cause or ideology as the Christian God has been used. Liberation theology may also serve as a challenge to the popular religious notion of ethical and economic evil as being God's will.

Within popular religiosity social organization is predominantly horizontal, with temporal responsibilities which do not separate persons or give unequal weight to functions. In preparation for Las Posadas, Holy Week, Día de los Muertos, or All Souls' Day, everyone plays a role of equal importance, whether their task is to make the tortillas or proclaim the Word. In celebrating Our Lady of Guadalupe, social organization is present in a paramount way. No role is of higher status than any other. All are essential to the celebration, all are valued and affirmed. The presence of clergy, although desired, is not required and the fiesta could easily take place without them.

Guadalupe: Symbol of God's Unconditional Love

As seen in the practices of popular devotion, presence and immediate contact are vital in the world of symbols. The image of Our Lady of Guadalupe in the churches must be accessible and within reach, so that devotees may touch it or rub their hands across the frame or touch the candle before the picture. It is not enough to recognize a symbol; it must be held, experienced, and received. The symbols that emerge from the Guadalupe event are concrete: flowers, music, the sun. Not only does she come in her full presence adorned with cultural symbols that the people recognize, but she enters into their history. Through her affirmation and acceptance of her people, she gives them a reason to hope and to live.

The symbol of Our Lady of Guadalupe manifests the creating energy and creative power which is God. She is nothing less than God's self-giving, or grace. I understand grace in relational terms: not so much God as a person I love or God as a person who loves us, but God as love itself. God is love and the way of experiencing that love is within the dynamic of a relationship. Divine nature is relational and self-sacrificial: to share in the life of God, for God to give God's whole self to us, means that we live in some kind of relationship. How do we know we are living in that kind of relationship? We need to look at the relationships in our life to answer this question: Are they life-giving? Are they hopeful, affirming? Do they inspire growth? In Mexican-American women's relationship with her, Our Lady of Guadalupe comforts and renews their spirit.

God's grace is universally and unconditionally offered; it is God's self-giving. Our Lady of Guadalupe becomes a symbol and a manifestation of God's love, compassion, help, and defense of the poor. She restores her people's dignity and hope and gives them a place in the world and in salvific history. The first manifestation of God's creative energy and creative power is creation—to give life, to bring something forth. To this extent, I believe that Guadalupe may be a symbol of that grace of God. It is the dynamic giving of oneself to another, Guadalupe offering herself to the people in a life-giving and transforming way that is full of grace. One of the first things we say about the historical Mary is that she is filled with grace.

One of the stations of this grace, or God's self-giving, is experienced through the women's relationship with Our Lady of Guadalupe. Presence should be first among our pastoral tasks because of the high value Mexican-Americans place on relationality and interdependence. Within a pastoral context, then, presence is understood as visibility, accessibility, active listening, and sustained dialogue with Our Lady of Guadalupe. These factors are evident in the women's stories as they relate their relationship and their understanding of what and who Our Lady of Guadalupe is.

There is a danger of mistaking the *symbol* for the reality. Our Lady of Guadalupe is not God; she is a metaphor for God. All the qualities attributed to her (loving, comforting, present, maternal) are qualities of God. Her image is as a nurturing woman and mother, but God has what have been stereotypically designated as female as well as male qualities. Thus, the symbol of Our Lady of Guadalupe is a matrix of meaning: she tells us something about who we are (in the Mexican-American women's case, that they are female, mother, *morena*, marginalized), and she tells us something about who God is: God is the source of all life, maternal, compassionate, and present, and protects the poor and marginalized.

At the heart of any assumptive world for an individual or an overarching culture, there is always some ultimate symbol which ties everything together and which people can give themselves to. As anthropologists would say, an ultimate symbol should be capable of containing within itself the highest aspirations and desires of the people. In Julia's words, Our Lady of Guadalupe does this: "Our Lady of Guadalupe represents to me everything we as a people should strive to be: strong yet humble, warm and compassionate, yet courageous enough to stand up for what we believe in, no matter how tense the pressure. Above all, obedient to God's will." As a universal symbol Our Lady of Guadalupe bridges cultures: for Mexican-American women she affirms them because she looks like them and is a woman and a mother, and she affirms their Anglo-educated side, challenging sexism.

Although she may be more appealing to darker-skinned people than to light-skinned people, her message affirms the darker-skinned but also transcends ethnicity. She is grounded in Mexican history, but functions as a symbol of God's love, not only for Mexicans but for everyone.

Certain symbols may not be effective for an individual or for a group. For example, the symbol of God the Father may not work for the Mexican-American community, so the symbol of Our Lady of Guadalupe may speak more to them about the nature of God or about how God relates than do many of the classical symbols of God. Mexican-Americans may experience the Divine working through Our Lady of Guadalupe in symbols that are not the standard ones of official religiosity.

The understanding of where Guadalupe manifests herself is of utmost importance. Within the context of popular religiosity, that is, a context where the people are, a context and source of people's identity and values—this is where Our Lady of Guadalupe engages the people. The things for pastoral ministers and theologians to watch most closely are the ultimate questions her devotees ask, the places God is present in their lives, and how they celebrate and bring that to expression. These things I believe are revelatory.

Guadalupe: The Feminine Face of God

The significance of Our Lady of Guadalupe in popular religiosity must assume a dialectic posture with contemporary Catholic theology, and so we look at the insights that feminist theology has given us in terms of the maternal or feminine face of God.

Hispanic colonial evangelization taught that the Christian God was more powerful than the indigenous gods. The proof was that those who fought under the banner of the Christian God became successful conquerors. The Christian God was, more likely than not, imaged by those in power to reflect themselves. There is thus a metaphor and a constellation of images surrounding the God brought by the conquistadors.

Christianity preached forgiveness, mercy, compassion, and reconciliation. The symbol used by the dominant Spanish culture to communicate these values was the Virgin Mary. Representing Christianity to the newly conquered, the missionaries did not connect these fundamental Christian elements with God in their catechisms; they did connect them with Mary. These traits at the time were held to be maternal and also may have reflected the way the Spanish might have wanted the Indians to feel toward their oppressors. All of these "maternal" qualities were attributed to God by the missionaries, but in the conquered population's mind the association of God with the powerful and victorious was primary. Mary, however, was presented as loving. comforting, and accepting; she was clearly the faithful and solidarious one (Espín 1991:99).

Even in the early history of Hispanic Christianity, there is a dichotomy of attributes: those that are powerful but somewhat alienating were attributed to the male white European Christian God, and the more affective, maternal reconciling ones to the Virgin Mary. Dr. Espín (1991:98) asks, "How do Hispanics experience God as faithfully solidarious with them?" He suggests that perhaps we need to remove from the word "God" all the dominant, conquering demons it evokes.

If, instead of looking for the explicit use of the term "God" or other God-related activities, we look at instances when Mexican Americans seem to be relating explicitly or implicitly to a divinity closer to the Gospel's real God, we will discover a very clear presence of faithful solidarity in their operative definition of that God. The surprise is that this faithfully solidarious one is Mary, the Virgin, says Espín (1991:100). There is historical evidence that these stereotypical attributes of the feminine have been presented through Marian symbols and thus have traditionally been ascribed to Mary as Our Lady of Guadalupe. It is easy to perceive Our Lady of Guadalupe as the maternal or female face of God, because she evokes an unconditional love, solidarity, and a never-failing presence at the affective level. But in doing so, we inaccurately remove these attributes from where they rightly belong: to God.

I myself struggle with this concept, because naturally I am drawn to the caring and nurturing presence of Our Lady of Guadalupe, but I am committed to retrieving the basic meaning of her message and placing it within a new context. I am in a relationship with her; when a relationship is expressed, it reveals something about both the person and (in my case) that person's relationship with God through Our Lady of Guadalupe. What does the metaphor of Our Lady of Guadalupe tell us about who God is?

A tremendous amount of scholarly work has been done on Mariology, less on Our Lady of Guadalupe. Because Our Lady of Guadalupe is a Marian image, Mariology can contribute to an understanding of the image of Our Lady of Guadalupe and the truth about God which she expresses. In this section I rely heavily upon the insightful scholarship of Elizabeth Johnson.

The Marian phenomenon throughout history has been powerful precisely because it is a female representation of the divine, bearing attributes otherwise excluded from mainline Christian perceptions of God as Father, Son, and Spirit. In official religiosity, the feminine face of God has been suppressed and excluded, and female images of God have migrated to the figure of Mary. Now some Catholics feel what Johnson calls a theological necessity: to express the mystery of a Christian God adequately, God must be envisioned in ways inclusive of the reality of women and other marginalized groups. Those elements in the Marian symbol which properly belong to divine reality must be retrieved (Johnson 1989:500–501).

Toward a more gender-inclusive theology of God, the Marian tradition offers its powerful maternal and other female images of the Divine. Through this process of integration, the figure of Mary no longer has to bear the burden of keeping alive female imagery of the Divine, and the figure of God becomes our loving Mother to whom we entrust our needs. Again, for some, it may be difficult to image the male face of God as a loving provider, but the Marian image is not meant to replace but to enhance the personhood of God.

There are many incidents of the split of divine attributes traditional in Christianity. In an influential work, theologian Edward Schillebeeckx (1964:101–128) argued that God's love is both paternal and maternal but that the mother aspect of God cannot be expressed through the historical figure of Jesus as a male. God selected Mary so that the "tender, mild, simple, generous, gentle and sweet" aspects of divine love could be made manifest: "Mary is the translation and effective expression in maternal terms of God's mercy, grace and redeeming love which manifested itself to us in a visible and tangible form in the person of Christ, our Redeemer."

Feminist theologian Elisabeth Schussler Fiorenza (1979) explains the split by a long process of patriarchalization, as a result of which the divine image became more remote and judgmental, while Mary became the beloved "other face" of God. Intellectually a distinction was maintained between adoration of God and veneration of Mary, but on the affective, imaginative level people experienced the love of God and the saving mystery of divine reality in the figure of Mary (Johnson 1989:513; Schussler Fiorenza 1983:130–140).

What accounts for Hispanics' massive and persistent devotion to Mary? Latin American and U.S. Hispanic theologians view Marian images from a liberationist theology point of view: Mary's cult appeals strongly to the oppressed because she gives dignity to downtrodden people and thus renews their energy to resist assimilation into the dominant culture. Further, as Virgil Elizondo points out, the cult not only liberates downtrodden peoples but also liberates us from a restrictive idea of God (Johnson 1989:514; Elizondo 1977:25–33, 1983b).

Within the Roman Catholic tradition Our Lady of Guadalupe is a Marian image, and within the Hispanic culture she is a mestiza, a mixture of both Spanish and Indian blood. The event and figure of Our Lady of Guadalupe combined the Nahuatl female expression of God with the Spanish male expression of God which had been incomprehensible to the Indians' duality—their belief that everything perfect has a male and female component. Each understanding of God was expanded by the other, yielding a new mestizo expression which enriches the understanding of the selfhood of God (Johnson 1989:515). "The results of the new expressions of God and the Mother of God are an amazing enrichment to the very understanding of the self-hood of God. There is no longer the European expression of God-Nahuatl, but a new mestizo expression which is mutually interpreted and enriching" (Elizondo 1983b:61).

"Even for those who do not find Mary a personally viable religious symbol, she nonetheless does represent the psychologically ultimate validity of the feminine, insuring a religious valuation of bodiliness, sensitivity, relationality, and nurturing qualities. . . . The symbol of Mary as feminine principle balances the masculine principle in the deity, which expresses itself in rationality, assertiveness, and independence" (Johnson 1989:517).

Within the Roman Catholic tradition Marian devotion and the study of Mary are sources of understanding the divinity in female language and symbols. Johnson identifies five female images for God: mother, divine compassion, divine power and might, divine presence (immanence), and a source of recreative energy. I take the same five images and apply them to Our Lady of Guadalupe.

Our Lady of Guadalupe manifests God as mother: Our Lady of Guadalupe identifies herself as Our Loving Mother and people see her as a mother, a maternal presence, consoling, nurturing, offering unconditional love, comforting—qualities which tell us that mother is an appropriate metaphor for God. "Transferring this maternal language back to God enables us to see that God has a maternal countenance. All that is creative and generative of life, all that nourishes and nurtures, all that is benign, cherishes, and sustains, all that is solicitous and sympathetic originates in God/Her" (Johnson 1989:520).

Madonna Kolbenschlag's work *Lost in the Land of Oz* (1988:9) addresses the importance and necessity of the maternal. She identifies orphanhood metaphorically as "the deepest, most fundamental reality: experiences of attachment and abandonment, of expectation and deprivation, of loss and failure, and of loneliness." What message does Our Lady of Guadalupe offer to the spiritual orphans of the twentieth century through the metaphor of mother? That we are lovable and capable, that we belong, that we can grow and be transformed, and that there is a reason to live and a reason to hope.

Our Lady of Guadalupe manifests God's compassion: Our Lady of Guadalupe came to show forth her love, compassion, help, defense, and her presence among the people. "Returning this language to God, to whom it properly belongs, enables us to name the holy mystery as essentially and unfathomably merciful. God is the Mother of mercy who has compassionate womb-love for all God's children. We need not be afraid to approach. She is brimming over with gentleness, loving kindness, and forgiveness" (Johnson 1989:521). In the interviews with the women in my study, we have seen how they take their troubles to Our Lady of Guadalupe because they experience her as being compassionate and responsive to their needs, in a way which, if present, nevertheless has not been identified in their relationship to God. She will understand them better than the male face of God because she too is female and a mother.

Our Lady of Guadalupe manifests divine power and might: The word "power" comes from the Latin *posse*, meaning to be able, yet often when we think of power it is in terms of having power *over* someone or something, rather than having power *with*. Again and again, the women in my study found that in encountering and being in the presence of Our Lady of Guadalupe they regained their sense of self in an accepting and empowering relationship.

Our Lady of Guadalupe images power *with*, in a dynamism centered around mutuality, trust, participation, and regard. The power accessed by these women in their dialogue with Our Lady of Guadalupe is the power of memory, which she continues to stand for, justice, solidarity with the oppressed, belonging, unconditional love, the power of expressed feelings and sharing (women come to her and share their immediate needs and they feel heard). The power of commitment, the power to endure suffering, the power of caring, the power of risk ("As long as she is beside me, I'm going to keep trying"), the power of naming their fears, the power of knowing that the way things are is not the way things are meant to be, and with her help they are encouraged and given hope. She gives them not the will to suffer under injustice, but the will to continue *la lucha* (the struggle).

Our Lady of Guadalupe manifests, symbolizes, and activates the power of the people, in this case the power of the poor people. In the *Nican Mopohua*, it is the poor Indian Juan Diego who evangelizes the bishop, whose conversion enables him to work with the poor, the marginalized, and the indigenous. Siller emphasizes the Nahuatl image of *yollo* (the heart), which moves us to action; if a devotion to Our Lady of Guadalupe does not bring us closer to action and to solidarity with the cause of the poor, then the devotion is not authentically Guadalupana. This heart, love, relationship, and consciousness emerging from the poor call us to act on behalf of the poor.

Our Lady of Guadalupe manifests the presence of God: I have addressed this in the previous section about Our Lady of Guadalupe as a symbol of God's unconditional love.

Our Lady of Guadalupe manifests God as a source of recreating energy: "Attributing this imagery of plenty and new beginnings directly to God allows us to affirm that it is God's own self that is the source of transforming energy among all creatures. She initiates novelty, instigates change, transforms what is dead" (Johnson 1989:524). This is clearly seen in the timing of the apparition of Our Lady of Guadalupe. As argued in Chapter 2, she came at a time when the people were spiritually dead, abandoned by their gods, with no reason to live. Our Lady of Guadalupe's coming restored the people's reason to live and to hope. She identified herself using the familiar Nahuatl expressions of God, which showed the people that she came from the region of the gods.

In the Nahuatl culture the one supreme god, Ometeotl, was the god of duality, with both masculine and feminine principles. Because Ometeotl was invisible, there was no physical representation of this god, who was known by the titles of the Most True God, the God Who Gives Us Life, the Inventor and Creator of People, the Owner of What Is around Us and Very Close to Us, and the Owner and Lord of the Earth (Siller-Acuña 1989:48).

The Nahuatl names for God are not just dimensions but ultimate metaphors for who God is. And because they contain that which gave life to the people, those metaphors become a source of recreating energy.

India

RICHARD RODRIGUEZ

At sunrise the next day, the time the Indians appointed, they came according to their promise, and brought us a large quantity of fish with certain roots. . . . They sent their women and children to look at us. . . .

—*Álvar Núñez Cabeza de Vaca*

I used to stare at the Indian in the mirror. The wide nostrils, the thick lips. Starring Paul Muni as Benito Juárez. Such a long face—such a long nose—sculpted by indifferent, blunt thumbs, and of such common clay. No one in my family had a face as dark or as Indian as mine. My face could not portray the ambition I brought to it. What could the United States of America say to me? I remember reading the ponderous conclusion of the Kerner Report in the sixties: two Americas, one white, one black—the prophecy of an eclipse too simple to account for the complexity of my face.

Mestizo in Mexican Spanish means mixed, confused. Clotted with Indian, thinned by Spanish spume.

What could Mexico say to me?

Mexican philosophers powwow in their tony journals about Indian "fatalism" and "Whither Mexico?" *El fatalismo del indio* is an important Mexican philosophical theme; the phrase is trusted to conjure the quality of Indian passivity as well as to initiate debate about Mexico's reluctant progress toward modernization. Mexicans imagine their Indian part as deadweight: the Indian stunned by modernity; so overwhelmed by the loss of what is genuine to him—his language, his religion—that he sits weeping like a medieval lady at the crossroads; or else he resorts to occult powers and superstitions, choosing to consort with death because the purpose of the world has passed him by.

One night in Mexico City I ventured from my hotel to a distant *colonia* to visit my aunt, my father's only sister. But she was not there. She had moved. For the past several years she has moved, this woman of eighty-odd years, from one of her children to another. She takes with her only her papers and books—she is a poetess—and an upright piano painted blue. My aunt writes love poems to her dead husband, Juan—keeping Juan up to date, while rewatering her loss. Last year she sent me her *obras completas*, an inch-thick block of bound onionskin. And with her poems she sent me a list of names, a genealogy braiding two centuries, two continents, to a common origin: eighteenth-century Salamanca. No explanation is attached to the list. Its implication is nonetheless clear. We are—my father's family is (despite the evidence of my face)—of Europe. We are not Indian.

On the other hand, a Berkeley undergraduate approached me one day, creeping up as if I were a stone totem to say, "God, it must be cool to be related to Aztecs."

* * * * *

I sat down next to the journalist from Pakistan—the guest of honor. He had been making a tour of the United States under the auspices of the U.S. State Department. Nearing the end of his journey now, he was having dinner with several of us, American journalists, at a Chinese restaurant in San Francisco. He said he'd seen pretty much all he wanted to see in America. His wife, however, had asked him to bring back some American Indian handicrafts. Blankets. Beaded stuff. He'd looked everywhere.

The table was momentarily captured by the novelty of his dilemma. You can't touch the stuff nowadays, somebody said. So rare, so expensive. Somebody else knew of a shop up on Sacramento Street that sells authentic Santa Fe. Several others remembered a store in Chinatown where moccasins, belts—"the works"—were to be found. All manufactured in Taiwan.

The Pakistani journalist looked incredulous. His dream of America had been shaped by American export-Westerns. Cowboys and Indians are yin and yang of America. He had seen men dressed like cowboys on this trip. But (turning to me): Where are the Indians?

(Two Indians staring at one another. One asks where are all the Indians, the other shrugs.)

* * * * *

I grew up in Sacramento thinking of Indians as people who had disappeared. I was a Mexican in California; I would no more have thought of myself as an Aztec in California than you might imagine yourself a Viking or a Bantu. Mrs. Ferrucci up the block used to call my family "Spanish." We knew she intended to ennoble us by that designation. We also knew she was ignorant.

I was ignorant.

In America the Indian is relegated to the obligatory first chapter—the "Once Great Nation" chapter—after which the Indian is cleared away as easily as brush, using a very sharp rhetorical tool called an "alas." Thereafter, the Indian reappears only as a stunned remnant—Ishi, or the hundred-year-old hag blowing out her birthday candle at a rest home in Tucson; or the teenager drunk on his ass in Plaza Park.

Here they come down Broadway in the Fourth of July parades of my childhood—middle-aged men wearing glasses, beating their tom-toms; Hey-ya-ya-yah; Hey-ya-ya-yah. They wore Bermuda shorts under their loincloths. High-school kids could never refrain from the answering Woo-woo-woo, stopping their mouths with the palms of their hands.

In the 1960s, Indians began to name themselves Native Americans, recalling themselves to life. That self-designation underestimated the ruthless idea Puritans had superimposed upon the landscape. America is an idea to which natives are inimical. The Indian represented permanence and continuity to Americans who were determined to call this country new. Indians must be ghosts.

I collected conflicting evidence concerning Mexico, it's true, but I never felt myself the remnant of anything. Mexican magazines arrived in our mailbox from Mexico City; showed pedestrians strolling wide ocher boulevards beneath trees with lime-green leaves. My past was at least this coherent: Mexico was a real place with plenty of people walking around in it. My parents had come from somewhere that went on without them.

When I was a graduate student at Berkeley, teaching remedial English, there were a few American Indians in my classroom. They were unlike any other "minority students" in the classes I taught. The Indians drifted in and out. When I summoned them to my office, they came and sat while I did all the talking.

I remember one tall man particularly, a near-somnambulist, beautiful in an off-putting way, but interesting, too, because I never saw him without the current issue of *The New York Review of Books* under his arm, which I took as an advertisement of ambition. He eschewed my class for weeks at a time. Then one morning I saw him in a café on Telegraph Avenue, across from Cody's. I did not fancy myself Sidney Poitier, but I was interested in this moody brave's lack of interest in me, for one, and then *The New York Review.*

Do you mind if I sit here?

Nothing.

Blah, Blah, Blah . . . *N. Y. R. B.?*—entirely on my part—until, when I got up to leave:

"You're not Indian, you're Mexican," he said. "You wouldn't understand."

He meant I was cut. Diluted.

Understand what?

He meant I was not an Indian in America. He meant he was an enemy of the history that had otherwise created me. And he was right, I didn't understand. I took his diffidence for chauvinism. I read his chauvinism as arrogance. He didn't see the Indian in my face? I saw his face—his refusal to consort with the living—as the face of a dead man.

As the landscape goes, so goes the Indian? In the public-service TV commercial, the Indian sheds a tear at the sight of an America polluted beyond his recognition. Indian memory has become the measure against which America gauges corrupting history when it suits us. Gitchigoomeism—the habit of placing the Indian outside history—is a white sentimentality that relegates the Indian to death.

An obituary from *The New York Times* (September 1989—dateline Alaska): An oil freighter has spilled its load along the Alaskan coast. There is a billion-dollar cleanup, bringing jobs and dollars to Indian villages.

The modern world has been closing in on English Bay . . . with glacial slowness. The oil spill and the resulting sea of money have accelerated the process, so that English Bay now seems caught on the cusp of history.

The omniscient reporter from *The New York Times* takes it upon himself to regret history on behalf of the Indians.

Instead of hanging salmon to dry this month, as Aleut natives have done for centuries . . . John Kvasnikoff was putting up a three thousand dollar television satellite dish on the bluff next to his home above the sea.

The reporter from *The New York Times* knows the price modernity will exact from an Indian who wants to plug himself in. Mind you, the reporter is confident of his own role in history, his freedom to lug a word processor to some remote Alaskan village. About the reporter's journey, *The New York Times* is not censorious. But let the Indian drop one bead from custom, or let his son straddle a snowmobile—as he does in the photo accompanying the article—and *The New York Times* cries Boo-hoo-hoo yah-yah-yah.

Thus does the Indian become the mascot of an international ecology movement. The industrial countries of the world romanticize the Indian who no longer exists, ignoring the Indian who does—the Indian who is poised to chop down his rain forest, for example. Or the Indian who reads *The New York Times.*

Once more in San Francisco: I flattered myself that the woman staring at me all evening "knew my work." I considered myself an active agent, in other words. But, after several passes around the buffet, the woman cornered me to say she recognized me as an "ancient soul."

Do I lure or am I just minding my own business?

Is it the nature of Indians—not verifiable in nature, of course, but in the European description of Indians—that we wait around to be "discovered"?

Europe discovers. India beckons. Isn't that so? India sits atop her lily pad through centuries, lost in contemplation of the horizon. And, from time to time, India is discovered.

In the fifteenth century, sailing Spaniards were acting according to scientific conjecture as to the nature and as to the shape of the world. Most thinking men in Europe at the time of Columbus believed the world to be round. The voyage of Columbus was the test of a theory believed to be true. Brave, yes, but pedantic therefore.

The Indian is forever implicated in the roundness of the world. America was the false India, the mistaken India, and yet veritable India, for all that—India—the clasp, the coupling mystery at the end of quest.

This is as true today as of yore. Where do the Beatles go when the world is too much with them? Where does Jerry Brown seek the fat farm of his soul? India, man, India!

India waits.

India has all the answers beneath her passive face or behind her veil or between her legs. The European has only questions, questions that are assertions turned inside out, questions that can only be answered by sailing toward the abysmal horizon.

The lusty Europeans wanted the shortest answers. They knew what they wanted. They wanted spices, pagodas, gold.

Had the world been flat, had the European sought the unknown, then the European would have been as great a victor over history as he has portrayed himself to be. The European would have outdistanced history—even theology—if he could have arrived at the shore of some prelapsarian state. If the world had been flat, then the European could have traveled outward toward innocence.

But the world was round. The entrance into the Indies was a reunion of peoples. The Indian awaited the long-separated European, the inevitable European, as the approaching horizon.

Though perhaps, too, there was some demiurge felt by the human race of the fifteenth century to heal itself, to make itself whole? Certainly, in retrospect, there was some inevitability to the Catholic venture. If the world was round, continuous, then so, too, were peoples?

According to the European version—the stag version—of the pageant of the New World, the Indian must play a passive role. Europe has been accustomed to play the swaggart in history—Europe striding through the Americas, overturning temples, spilling language, spilling seed, spilling blood.

And wasn't the Indian the female, the passive, the waiting aspect to the theorem—lewd and promiscuous in her embrace as she is indolent betimes?

Charles Macomb Flandrau, a native of St. Paul, Minnesota, wrote a book called *Viva Mexico!* in 1908, wherein he described the Mexican Indian as "incorrigibly plump. One never ceases to marvel at the super-human strength existing beneath the pretty and effeminate modeling of their arms and legs and backs. . . . The legs of an American 'strong man' look usually like an anatomical chart, but the legs of the most powerful Totonac Indian—and the power of many of them is beyond belief—would serve admirably as one of those idealized extremities on which women's hosiery is displayed in shop windows."

In Western Civilization histories, the little honeymoon joke Europe tells on itself is of mistaking America for the extremities of India. But India was perhaps not so much a misnomer as was "discoverer" or "conquistador."

Earliest snapshots of Indians brought back to Europe were of naked little woodcuts, arms akimbo, resembling Erasmus, or of grandees in capes and feathered tiaras, courtiers of an Egyptified palace of nature. In European museums, she is idle, recumbent at the base of a silver pineapple tree or the pedestal of the Dresden urn or the Sèvres tureen—the muse of European adventure, at once wanderlust and bounty.

Many tribes of Indians were prescient enough, preserved memory enough, or were lonesome enough to predict the coming of a pale stranger from across the sea, a messianic twin of completing memory or skill.

None of this could the watery Europeans have known as they marveled at the sight of approaching land. Filled with the arrogance of discovery, the Europeans were not predisposed to imagine that they were being watched, awaited.

* * * * *

That friend of mine at Oxford loses patience whenever I describe my face as mestizo. Look at my face. What do you see?

An Indian, he says.

Mestizo, I correct.

Mestizo, mestizo, he says.

Listen, he says. I went back to my mother's village in Mexico last summer and there was nothing mestizo about it. Dust, dogs, and Indians. People there don't even speak Spanish.

So I ask my friend at Oxford what it means to him to be an Indian.

He hesitates. My friend has recently been taken up as amusing by a bunch of rich Pakistanis in London. But, facing me, he is vexed and in earnest. He describes a lonely search among his family for evidence of Indian-ness. He thinks he has found it in his mother; watching his mother in her garden.

Does she plant corn by the light of the moon?

She seems to have some relationship with the earth, he says quietly.

So there it is. The mystical tie to nature. How else to think of the Indian except in terms of some druidical green thumb? No one says of an English matron in her rose garden that she is behaving like a Celt. Because the Indian has no history—that is, because history books are the province of the descendants of Europeans—the Indian seems only to belong to the party of the first part, the first chapter. So that is where the son expects to find his mother, Daughter of the Moon.

Let's talk about something else. Let's talk about London. The last time I was in London, I was walking toward an early evening at the Queen's Theatre when I passed that Christopher Wren church near Fortnum & Mason. The church was lit; I decided to stop, to savor the spectacle of what I expected would be a few Pymish men and women rolled into balls of fur at evensong. Imagine my surprise that the congregation was young—dressed in army fatigues and Laura Ashley. Within the chancel, cross-legged on a dais, was a South American shaman.

Now, who is the truer Indian in this picture? Me . . . me on my way to the Queen's Theatre? Or that guy on the altar with a Ph.D. in death?

* * * * *

We have hurled—like starlings, like Goths—through the castle of European memory. Our reflections have glanced upon the golden coach that carried the Emperor Maximilian through the streets of Mexico City, thence onward through the sludge of a hundred varnished paintings.

I have come at last to Mexico, the country of my parents' birth. I do not expect to find anything that pertains to me.

We have strained the rouge cordon at the thresholds of imperial apartments; seen chairs low enough for dwarfs, commodious enough for angels.

We have imagined the Empress Carlota standing in the shadows of an afternoon; we have followed her gaze down the Paseo de la Reforma toward the distant city. The Paseo was a nostalgic allusion to the Champs-Elysées, we learn, which Maximilian recreated for his tempestuous, crowlike bride.

Come this way, please. . . .

European memory is not to be the point of our excursion. Señor Fuentes, our tour director, is already beginning to descend the hill from Chapultepec Castle. What the American credit-card company calls our "orientation tour" of Mexico City had started late and so Señor Fuentes has been forced, regrettably,

". . . This way, please . . ."

to rush. Señor Fuentes is consumed with contrition for time wasted this morning. He intends to uphold his schedule, as a way of upholding Mexico, against our expectation.

We had gathered at the appointed time at the limousine entrance to our hotel, beneath the banner welcoming contestants to the Señorita Mexico pageant. We—Japanese, Germans, Americans—were waiting promptly at nine. There was no bus. And as we waited, the Señorita Mexico contestants arrived. Drivers leaned into their cabs to pull out long-legged señoritas. The drivers then balanced the señoritas onto stiletto heels (the driveway was cobbled) before they passed the señoritas, *en pointe*, to the waiting arms of officials.

Mexican men, meanwhile—doormen, bellhops, window washers, hotel guests—stopped dead in their tracks, wounded by the scent and spectacle of so many blond señoritas. The Mexican men assumed fierce expressions, nostrils flared, brows knit. Such expressions are masks—the men intend to convey their adoration of prey—as thoroughly ritualized as the smiles of beauty queens.

By now we can see the point of our excursion beyond the parched trees of Chapultepec Park—the Museo Nacional de Antropología—which is an air-conditioned repository for the artifacts of the Indian civilizations of Meso-America, the finest anthropological museum in the world.

"There will not be time to see everything," Señor Fuentes warns as he ushers us into the grand salon, our first experience of the suffocating debris of The Ancients. Señor Fuentes wants us in and out of here by noon.

Whereas the United States traditionally has rejoiced at the delivery of its landscape from "savagery," Mexico has taken its national identity only from the Indian, the mother. Mexico measures all cultural bastardy against the Indian; equates civilization with India—Indian kingdoms of a golden age; cities as fabulous as Alexandria or Benares or Constantinople; a court as hairless, as subtle as the Pekingese. Mexico equates barbarism with Europe—beardedness—with Spain.

It is curious, therefore, that both modern nations should similarly apostrophize the Indian, relegate the Indian to the past.

Come this way, please. Mrs. . . . Ah . . . this way, please.

Señor Fuentes wears an avocado-green sports coat with gold buttons. He is short. He is rather elegant, with a fine small head, small hands, small feet; with his two rows of fine small teeth like a nutcracker's teeth, with which he curtails consonants as cleanly as bitten thread. Señor Fuentes is brittle, he is watchful, he is ironic, he is metropolitan; his wit is quotational, literary, wasted on Mrs. Ah.

He is not our equal. His demeanor says he is not our equal. We mistake his condescension for humility. He will not eat when we eat. He will not spend when we shop. He will not have done with Mexico when we have done with Mexico.

Señor Fuentes is impatient with us, for we have paused momentarily outside the museum to consider the misfortune of an adolescent mother who holds her crying baby out to us. Several of us confer among ourselves in an attempt to place a peso value on the woman's situation. We do not ask for the advice of Señor Fuentes.

For we, in turn, are impatient with Señor Fuentes. We are in a bad mood. The air conditioning on our "fully air-conditioned coach" is nonexistent. We have a headache. Nor is the city air any relief, but it is brown, fungal, farted.

Señor Fuentes is a mystery to us, for there is no American equivalent to him; for there is no American equivalent to the subtleties he is paid to describe to us.

Mexico will not raise a public monument to Hernán Cortés, for example, the father of Mexico—the rapist. In the Diego Rivera murals in the presidential palace, the Aztec city of Tenochtitlán is rendered—its blood temples and blood canals—as haughty as Troy, as vulnerable as Pompeii. Any suggestion of the complicity of other tribes of Indians in overthrowing the Aztec empire is painted over. Spaniards appear on the horizons of Arcadia as syphilitic brigands and demon-eyed priests.

The Spaniard entered the Indian by entering her city—the floating city—first as a suitor, ceremoniously; later by force. How should Mexico honor the rape?

In New England the European and the Indian drew apart to regard each other with suspicion over centuries. Miscegenation was a sin against Protestant individualism. In Mexico the European and the Indian consorted. The ravishment of fabulous Tenochtitlán ended in a marriage of blood—a "cosmic race," the Mexican philosopher José Vasconcelos has called it.

Mexico's tragedy is that she has no political idea of herself as rich as her blood.

The rhetoric of Señor Fuentes, like the murals of Diego Rivera, resorts often to the dream of India—to Tenochtitlán, the capital of the world before conquest. "Preconquest" in the Mexican political lexicon is tantamount to "prelapsarian" in the Judeo-Christian scheme, and hearkens to a time Mexico feels herself to have been whole, a time before the Indian was separated from India by the serpent Spain.

Three centuries after Cortés, Mexico declared herself independent of Spain. If Mexico would have no yoke, then Mexico would have no crown, then Mexico would have no father. The denial of Spain has persisted into our century.

The priest and the landowner yet serve Señor Fuentes as symbols of the hated Spanish order. Though, in private, Mexico is Catholic; Mexican mothers may wish for light-skinned children. Touch blond hair and good luck will be yours.

In private, in Mexican Spanish, *indio* is a seller of Chiclets, a sidewalk squatter. *Indio* means backward or lazy or lower-class. In the eyes of the world, Mexico raises a magnificent museum of anthropology—the finest in the world—to honor the Indian mother.

In the nave of the National Cathedral, we notice the floor slopes dramatically. "The cathedral is sinking," Señor Fuentes explains as a hooded figure approaches our group from behind a column. She is an Indian woman; she wears a blue stole; her hands are cupped, beseeching; tear marks ream her cheeks. In Spanish, Señor Fuentes forbids this apparition: "Go ask *padrecito* to pry some gold off the altar for you."

"Mexico City is built upon swamp," Señor Fuentes resumes in English. "Therefore, the cathedral is sinking." But it is clear that Señor Fuentes believes the sinkage is due to the oppressive weight of Spanish Catholicism, its masses of gold, its volumes of deluded suspiration.

Mexican political life can only seem Panglossian when you consider an anti-Catholic government of an overwhelmingly Catholic population. Mexico is famous for politicians descended from Masonic fathers and Catholic mothers. Señor Fuentes himself is less a Spaniard, less an Indian, perhaps, than an embittered eighteenth-century man, clinging to the witty knees of Voltaire against the chaos of twentieth-century Mexico.

Mexico blamed the ruin of the nineteenth century on the foreigner, and with reason. Once emptied of Spain, the palace of Mexico became the dollhouse of France. Mexico was overrun by imperial armies. The greed of Europe met the Manifest Destiny of the United States in Mexico. Austria sent an archduke to marry Mexico with full panoply of candles and bishops. The U.S. reached under Mexico's skirt every chance he got.

"Poor Mexico, so far from God, so close to the United States."

Señor Fuentes dutifully attributes the mot to Porfirio Díaz, the Mexican president who sold more of Mexico to foreign interests than any other president. It was against the regime of Porfirio Díaz that Mexicans rebelled in the early decades of this century. Mexico prefers to call its civil war a "revolution."

Mexico for Mexicans!

The Revolution did not accomplish a union of Mexicans. The Revolution did not accomplish a restoration of Mexicans to their landscape. The dust of the Revolution parted to reveal—not India—but Marx *ex machina*, the Institutional Revolutionary Party, the PRI—a political machine appropriate to the age of steam. The Institutional Revolutionary Party, as its name implies, was designed to reconcile institutional pragmatism with revolutionary rhetoric. And the PRI worked for a time, because it gave Mexico what Mexico most needed, the stability of compromise.

The PRI appears everywhere in Mexico—a slogan on the wall, the politician impersonating a journalist on the evening news, the professor at his podium. The PRI is in its way as much a Mexican institution as the Virgin of Guadalupe.

Now Mexicans speak of the government as something imposed upon them, and they are the victims of it. But the political failure of Mexico must be counted a failure of Mexicans. Whom now shall Señor Fuentes blame for a twentieth century that has become synonymous with corruption?

Well, as long as you stay out of the way of the police no one will bother you, is conventional Mexican wisdom, and Mexico continues to live her daily life. In the capital, the air is the color of the buildings of Siena. Telephone connections are an aspect of the will of God. Mexicans drive on the sidewalks. A man on the street corner seizes the opportunity of stalled traffic to earn his living as a fire-eater. His ten children pass among the cars and among the honking horns to collect small coins.

Thank you. Thank you very much. A pleasure, Mrs. . . . Ah. Thank you very much.

Señor Fuentes bids each farewell. He accepts tips within a handshake. He bows slightly. We have no complaint with Señor Fuentes, after all. The bus was not his fault. Mexico City is not his fault. And Señor Fuentes will return to his unimaginable Mexico and we will return to our rooms to take aspirin and to initiate long-distance telephone calls. Señor Fuentes will remove his avocado-green coat and, having divested, Señor Fuentes will in some fashion partake of what he has successfully kept from us all day, which is the life and the drinking water of Mexico.

* * * * *

The Virgin of Guadalupe symbolizes the entire coherence of Mexico, body and soul. You will not find the story of the Virgin within hidebound secular histories of Mexico—nor indeed within the credulous repertoire of Señor Fuentes—and the omission renders the history of Mexico incomprehensible.

One recent afternoon, within the winy bell jar of a very late lunch, I told the story of the Virgin of Guadalupe to Lynn, a sophisticated twentieth-century woman. The history of Mexico, I promised her, is neither mundane nor masculine, but it is a miracle play with trapdoors and sequins and jokes on the living.

In the sixteenth century, when Indians were demoralized by the routing of their gods, when millions of Indians were dying from the plague of Europe, the Virgin Mary appeared pacing on a hillside to an Indian peasant named Juan Diego—his Christian name, for Juan was a convert. It was December 1531.

On his way to mass, Juan passed the hill called Tepayac . . .

Just as the East was beginning to kindle
To dawn. He heard there a cloud
Of birdsong bursting overhead
Of whistles and flutes and beating wings
—Now here, now there—
A mantle of chuckles and berries and rain
That rocked through the sky like the great Spanish bell
In Mexico City;
At the top of the hill there shone a light
And the light called out a name to him
With a lady's voice.
Juan, Juan,
The Lady-light called.
Juan crossed himself, he fell to his knees,
He covered his eyes and prepared to be blinded.

He could see through his hands that covered his face
As the sun rose up from behind her cape,
That the poor light of day
Was no match for this Lady, but broke upon her
Like a waterfall,
A rain of rings.
She wore a gown the color of dawn.
Her hair was braided with ribbons and flowers
And tiny tinkling silver bells. Her mantle was sheer
And bright as rain and embroidered with thousands of twinkling stars.
A clap before curtains, like waking from sleep;
Then a human face,
A mother's smile;
Her complexion as red as cinnamon bark;
Cheeks as brown as pérsimmon.

Her eyes were her voice,
As modest and shy as a pair of doves
In the eaves of her brow. Her voice was
Like listening. This lady spoke
In soft Nahuatl, the Aztec tongue
(As different from Spanish
As some other season of weather,

As doves in the boughs of a summer tree
Are different from crows in a wheeling wind,
Who scatter destruction and
Caw caw caw caw)—
Nahuatl like rain, like water flowing, like drips in a cavern,
Or glistening thaw,
Like breath through a flute,
With many stops and plops and sighs . . .

Peering through the grille of her cigarette smoke, Lynn heard and she seemed to approve the story.

At the Virgin's behest, this Prufrock Indian must go several times to the bishop of Mexico City. He must ask that a chapel be built on Tepayac where his discovered Lady may share in the sorrows of her people. Juan Diego's visits to the Spanish bishop parody the conversion of the Indians by the Spaniards. The bishop is skeptical.

The bishop wants proof.

The Virgin tells Juan Diego to climb the hill and gather a sheaf of roses as proof for the bishop—Castilian roses—impossible in Mexico in December of 1531. Juan carries the roses in the folds of his cloak, a pregnant messenger. Upon entering the bishop's presence, Juan parts his cloak, the roses tumble; the bishop falls to his knees.

In the end—with crumpled napkins, torn carbons, the bitter dregs of coffee—Lynn gave the story over to the Spaniards.

The legend concludes with a concession to humanity—proof more durable than roses—the imprint of the Virgin's image upon the cloak of Juan Diego . . .

A Spanish trick, Lynn said. A recruitment poster for the new religion, no more, she said (though sadly). An itinerant diva with a costume trunk. Birgit Nilsson as Aïda.

Why do we assume Spain made up the story?

The importance of the story is that Indians believed it. The jokes, the vaudeville, the relegation of the Spanish bishop to the role of comic adversary, the Virgin's chosen cavalier, and especially the brown-faced Mary—all elements spoke directly to Indians.

The result of the apparition and of the miraculous image of the Lady remaining upon the cloak of Juan Diego was a mass conversion of Indians to Catholicism.

The image of Our Lady of Guadalupe (privately, affectionately, Mexicans call her La Morenita—Little Darkling) has become the unofficial, the private flag of Mexicans. Unique possession of her image is a more wonderful election to Mexicans than any political call to nationhood. Perhaps Mexico's tragedy in our century, perhaps Mexico's abiding grace thus far, is that she has no political idea of herself as compelling as her icon.

The Virgin appears everywhere in Mexico. On dashboards and on calendars, on playing cards, on lampshades and cigar boxes; within the loneliness and tattooed upon the very skins of Mexicans.

Nor is the image of Guadalupe a diminishing mirage of the sixteenth century, but she has become more vivid with time, developing in her replication from earthy shades of melon and musk to bubble-gum pink, Windex blue, to achieve the hard, literal focus of holy cards or baseball cards; of Krishna or St. Jude or the Atlanta Braves.

Mexico City stands as the last living medieval capital of the world. Mexico is the creation of a Spanish Catholicism that attempted to draw continents together as one flesh. The success of Spanish Catholicism in Mexico resulted in a kind of proof—a profound concession to humanity: the *mestizaje*.

What joke on the living? Lynn said.

The joke is that Spain arrived with missionary zeal at the shores of contemplation. But Spain had no idea of the absorbent strength of Indian spirituality.

By the waters of baptism, the active European was entirely absorbed within the contemplation of the Indian. The faith that Europe imposed in the sixteenth century was, by virtue of the Guadalupe, embraced by the Indian. Catholicism has become an Indian religion. By the twenty-first century, the locus of the Catholic Church, by virtue of numbers, will be Latin America, by which time Catholicism itself will have assumed the aspect of the Virgin of Guadalupe.

Brown skin.

* * * * *

Time magazine dropped through the chute of my mailbox a few years ago with a cover story on Mexico entitled "The Population Curse." From the vantage point of Sixth Avenue, the editors of Time-Life peer down into the basin of Mexico City—like peering down into the skull of a pumpkin—to contemplate the nightmare of fecundity, the tangled mass of slime and hair and seed.

America sees death in all that life; sees rot. Life—not illness and poverty; not death—life becomes the curse of Mexico City in the opinion of *Time* magazine.

For a long time I had my own fear of Mexico, an American fear. Mexico's history was death. Her stature was tragedy. A race of people that looked like me had disappeared.

I had a dream about Mexico City, a conquistador's dream. I was lost and late and twisted in my sheet. I dreamed streets narrower than they actually are—narrow as old Jerusalem. I dreamed sheets, entanglements, bunting, hanging larvaelike from open windows, distended from balconies and from lines thrown over the streets. These streets were not empty streets. I was among a crowd. The crowd was not a carnival crowd. This crowd was purposeful and ordinary, welling up from subways, ascending from stairwells. And then the dream followed the course of all my dreams. I must find the airport—the American solution—I must somehow escape, fly over.

Each face looked like mine. But no one looked at me.

I have come at last to Mexico, to the place of my parents' birth. I have come under the protection of an American credit-card company. I have canceled this trip three times.

As the plane descends into the basin of Mexico City, I brace myself for some confrontation with death, with India, with confusion of purpose that I do not know how to master.

Do you speak Spanish? the driver asks in English.

Andrés, the driver employed by my hotel, is in his forties. He lives in the Colonia Roma, near the airport. There is nothing about the city he does not know. This is his city and he is its memory.

Andrés's car is a dark-blue Buick—about 1975. Windows slide up and down at the touch of his finger. There is the smell of disinfectant in Andrés's car, as there is in every bus or limousine or taxi I've ridden in Mexico—the smell of the glycerine crystals in urinals. Dangling from Andrés's rearview mirror is the other appliance common to all public conveyance in Mexico—a rosary.

Andrés is a man of the world, a man, like other working-class Mexican men, eager for the world. He speaks two languages. He knows several cities. He has been to the United States. His brother lives there still.

In the annals of the famous European discoverers there is invariably an Indian guide, a translator—willing or not—to facilitate, to preserve Europe's stride. These seem to have become fluent in pallor before Europe learned anything of them. How is that possible?

The most famous guide in Mexican history is also the most reviled by Mexican histories—the villainess Marina—"La Malinche." Marina became the lover of Cortés. So, of course, Mexicans say she betrayed India for Europe. In the end, she was herself betrayed, left behind when Cortés repaired to his Spanish wife.

Nonetheless, Marina's treachery anticipates the epic marriage of Mexico. La Malinche prefigures, as well, the other, the beloved female aspect of Mexico, the Virgin of Guadalupe.

Because Marina was the seducer of Spain, she challenges the boast Europe has always told about India.

I assure you Mexico has an Indian point of view as well, a female point of view:

I opened my little eye and the Spaniard disappeared.

Imagine a dark pool; the Spaniard dissolved; the surface triumphantly smooth.

My eye!

The spectacle of the Spaniard on the horizon, vainglorious—the shiny surfaces, clanks of metal; the horses, the muskets, the jingling bits.

Cannot you imagine me curious? Didn't I draw near?

European vocabularies do not have a silence rich enough to describe the force within Indian contemplation. Only Shakespeare understood that Indians have eyes. Shakespeare saw Caliban eyeing his master's books—well, why not his master as well? The same dumb lust.

WHAT DAT? is a question philosophers ask. And Indians.

Shakespeare's comedy, of course, resolves itself to the European's applause. The play that Shakespeare did not write is Mexico City.

Now the great city swells under the moon; seems, now, to breathe of itself—the largest city in the world—a Globe, kind Will, not of your devising, not under your control.

The superstition persists in European travel literature that Indian Christianity is the thinnest veneer covering an ulterior altar. But there is a possibility still more frightening to the European imagination, so frightening that in five hundred years such a possibility has scarcely found utterance.

What if the Indian were converted?

The Indian eye becomes a portal through which the entire pageant of European civilization has already passed; turned inside out. Then the baroque is an Indian conceit. The colonial arcade is an Indian detail.

Look once more at the city from La Malinche's point of view. Mexico is littered with the shells and skulls of Spain, cathedrals, poems, and the limbs of orange trees. But everywhere you look in this great museum of Spain you see living Indians.

Where are the *conquistadores*?

Postcolonial Europe expresses pity or guilt behind its sleeve, pities the Indian the loss of her gods or her tongue. But let the Indian speak for herself. Spanish is now an Indian language. Mexico City has become the metropolitan see of the Spanish-speaking world. In something like the way New York won English from London after World War I, Mexico City has captured Spanish.

The Indian stands in the same relationship to modernity as she did to Spain—willing to marry, to breed, to disappear in order to ensure her inclusion in time; refusing to absent herself from the future. The Indian has chosen to survive, to consort with the living, to live in the city, to crawl on her hands and knees, if need be, to Mexico City or L.A.

I take it as an Indian achievement that I am alive, that I am Catholic, that I speak English, that I am an American. My life began, it did not end, in the sixteenth century.

The idea occurs to me on a weekday morning, at a crowded intersection in Mexico City: Europe's lie. Here I am in the capital of death. Life surges about me; wells up from subways, wave upon wave; descends from stairwells. Everywhere I look. Babies. Traffic. Food. Beggars. Life. Life coming upon me like sunstroke.

Each face looks like mine. No one looks at me.

Where, then, is the famous conquistador?

We have eaten him, the crowd tells me, *we have eaten him with our eyes.*

I run to the mirror to see if this is true.

It is true.

In the distance, at its depths, Mexico City stands as the prophetic example. Mexico City is modern in ways that "multiracial," ethnically "diverse" New York City is not yet. Mexico City is centuries more modern than racially "pure," provincial Tokyo. Nothing to do with computers or skyscrapers.

Mexico City is the capital of modernity, for in the sixteenth century, under the tutelage of a curious Indian whore, under the patronage of the Queen of Heaven, Mexico initiated the task of the twenty-first century—the renewal of the old, the known world, through miscegenation. Mexico carries the idea of a round world to its biological conclusion.

* * * * *

For a time when he was young, Andrés, my driver, worked in Alpine County in northern California.

And then he worked at a Lake Tahoe resort. He remembers the snow. He remembers the weekends when blond California girls would arrive in their ski suits and sunglasses. Andrés worked at the top of a ski lift. His job was to reach out over a little precipice to help the California girls out of their lift chairs. He would maintain his grasp until they were balanced upon the snow. And then he would release them, watch them descend the winter slope—how they laughed!—oblivious of his admiration, until they disappeared.

The Mexican-American and the Church

CÉSAR E. CHAVEZ

The following article was prepared by Mr. Chavez during his 25-day "spiritual fast" and was presented to a meeting on "Mexican-Americans and the Church" at the Second Annual Mexican-American Conference in Sacramento, California on March 8-10, 1968.

The place to begin is with our own experience with the Church in the strike which has gone on for thirty-one months in Delano. For in Delano the Church has been involved with the poor in a unique way which should stand as a symbol to other communities. Of course, when we refer to the Church we should define the word a little. We mean the whole Church, the Church as an ecumenical body spread around the world, and not just its particular form in a parish in a local community. The Church we are talking about is a tremendously powerful institution in our society, and in the world. That Church is one form of the Presence of God on Earth, and so naturally it is powerful. It is powerful by definition. It is a powerful moral and spiritual force which cannot be ignored by any movement. Furthermore, it is an organization with tremendous wealth. Since the Church is to be servant to the poor, it is *our* fault if that wealth is not channeled to help the poor in our world.

In a small way we have been able, in the Delano strike, to work together with the Church in such a way as to bring some of its moral and economic power to bear on those who want to maintain the status quo, keeping farm workers in virtual enslavement. In brief, here is what happened in Delano.

Some years ago, when some of us were working with the Community Service Organization, we began to realize the powerful effect which the Church can have on the conscience of the opposition. In scattered instances, in San Jose, Sacramento, Oakland, Los Angeles and other places, priests would speak out loudly and clearly against specific instances of oppression, and in some cases, stand with the people who were being hurt. Furthermore, a small group of priests, Frs. McDonald, McCollough, Duggan and others, began to pinpoint attention on the terrible situation of the farm workers in our state.

At about that same time, we began to run into the California Migrant Ministry in the camps and fields. They were about the only ones there, and a lot of us were very suspicious, since we were Catholics and they were Protestants. However, they had developed a very clear conception of the Church. It was called to serve, to be at the mercy of the poor, and not to try to use them. After a while this made a lot of sense to us, and we began to find ourselves working side by side with them. In fact, it forced us to raise the question why OUR Church was not doing the same. We would ask, "Why do the Protestants come out here and help the people, demand nothing, and give all their time to serving farm workers, while our own parish priests stay in their churches, where only a few people come, and usually feel uncomfortable?"

It was not until some of us moved to Delano and began working to build the National Farm Workers Association that we really saw how far removed from the people the parish Church was. In fact, we could not get any help at all from the priests of Delano. When the strike began, they told us we could not even use the Church's auditorium for the meetings. The farm workers' money helped build that auditorium! But the Protestants were there again, in the form of the California Migrant Ministry, and they began to help in little ways, here and there.

When the strike started in 1965, most of our "friends" forsook us for a while. They ran—or were just too busy to help. But the California Migrant Ministry held a meeting with its staff and decided that the strike was a matter of life or death for farm workers everywhere, and that even if it meant the end of the Migrant Ministry they would turn over their resources to the strikers. The political pressure on the Protestant Churches was tremendous and the Migrant Ministry lost a lot of money. But they stuck it out, and they began to point the

"The Mexican-American and the Church", by César E. Chávez, presented at the Second Annual Mexican-American Conference in Sacramento, California on March 8–10, 1968. TM/© 2007 the Cesar E. Chavez Foundation. www.chavezfoundation.org. Reprinted by permission.

way to the rest of the Church. In fact, when 30 of the strikers were arrested for shouting Huelga, 11 ministers went to jail with them. They were in Delano that day at the request of Chris Hartmire, director of the California Migrant Ministry.

Then the workers began to raise the question: "Why ministers? Why not priests? What does the Bishop say?" But the Bishop said nothing. But slowly the pressure of the people grew and grew, until finally we have in Delano a priest sent by the new Bishop, Timothy Manning, who is there to help minister to the needs of farm workers. His name is Father Mark Day and he is the Union's chaplain. *Finally*, our own Catholic Church has decided to recognize that we have our own peculiar needs, just as the growers have theirs.

But outside of the local diocese, the pressure built up on growers to negotiate was tremendous. Though we were not allowed to have our own priest, the power of the ecumenical body of the Church was tremendous. The work of the Church, for example, in the Schenley, Di Giorgio, Perelli-Minetti strikes was fantastic. They applied pressure—and they mediated.

When poor people get involved in a long conflict, such as a strike, or a civil rights drive, and the pressure increases each day, there is a deep need for spiritual advice. Without it we see families crumble, leadership weaken, and hard workers grow tired. And in such a situation the spiritual advice must be given by a *friend*, not by the opposition. What sense does it make to go to Mass on Sunday and reach out for spiritual help, and instead get sermons about the wickedness of your cause? That only drives one to question and to despair. The growers in Delano have their spiritual problems . . . we do not deny that. They have every right to have priests and ministers who serve their needs. BUT WE HAVE DIFFERENT NEEDS, AND SO WE NEEDED A FRIENDLY SPIRITUAL GUIDE. And this is true in every community in this state where the poor face tremendous problems.

But the opposition raises a tremendous howl about this. They don't want us to have our spiritual advisors, friendly to our needs. Why is this? Why indeed except that THERE IS TREMENDOUS SPIRITUAL AND ECONOMIC POWER IN THE CHURCH. The rich know it, and for that reason they choose to keep it from the people.

The leadership of the Mexican-American Community must admit that we have fallen far short in our task of helping provide spiritual guidance for our people. We may say, "I don't feel any such need. I can get along." But that is a poor excuse for not helping provide such help for others. For we can also say, "I don't need any welfare help. I can take care of my own problems." But we are all willing to fight like hell for welfare aid for those who truly need it, who would starve without it. Likewise we may have gotten an education and not care about scholarship money for ourselves, or our children. But we would, we should, fight like hell to see to it that our state provides aid for any child needing it so that he can get the education he desires. LIKEWISE WE CAN SAY WE DON'T NEED THE CHURCH. THAT IS OUR BUSINESS. BUT THERE ARE HUNDREDS OF THOUSANDS OF OUR PEOPLE WHO DESPERATELY NEED SOME HELP FROM THAT POWERFUL INSTITUTION, THE CHURCH, AND WE ARE FOOLISH NOT TO HELP THEM GET IT.

For example, the Catholic Charities agencies of the Catholic Church has millions of dollars earmarked for the poor. But often the money is spent for food baskets for the needy instead of for effective action to eradicate the causes of poverty. The men and women who administer this money sincerely want to help their brothers. It should be our duty to help direct the attention to the basic needs of the Mexican-Americans in our society . . . needs which cannot be satisfied with baskets of food, but rather with effective organizing at the grass roots level.

Therefore, I am calling for Mexican-American groups to stop ignoring this source of power. It is not just our right to appeal to the Church to use its power effectively for the poor, it is our duty to do so. It should be as natural as appealing to government . . . and we do that often enough.

Furthermore, we should be prepared to come to the defense of that priest, rabbi, minister, or layman of the Church, who out of commitment to truth and justice gets into a tight place with his pastor or bishop. It behooves us to stand with that man and help him see his trial through. It is our duty to see to it that his rights of conscience are respected and that no bishop, pastor or other higher body takes that God-given, human right away.

Finally, in a nutshell, what do we want the Church to do? We don't ask for more cathedrals. We don't ask for bigger churches or fine gifts. We ask for its presence with us, beside us, as Christ among us. We ask the Church to *sacrifice with the people* for social change, for justice, and for love of brother. We don't ask for words. We ask for deeds. We don't ask for paternalism. We ask for servanthood.

El Aposento Alto

ARLENE M. SANCHEZ WALSH

Among Protestant groups, what made Pentecostals stand out was their reliance on the Holy Spirit as the central experience from which one could partake to equip oneself to lead the sanctified life Methodists talked about, and to modify one's behavior as other conservative Protestants stressed. When faced with the choice of Unitarian-Trinitarian Pentecostalism, the marketplace became more competitive. In this case, Pentecostals were pitted against Pentecostals, including the Oneness groups willing to compete fiercely for congregants. Oneness Pentecostals offered similar spiritual experiences but stressed that their baptism in the Holy Spirit was just as efficacious as Trinitarians—meaning that believers spoke in tongues as evidence of the Spirit's indwelling. Oneness Pentecostals stressed that their baptismal formula of baptizing in the name of Jesus was correct, because there was a biblical verse and an Apostle who appeared to have baptized in that way (Acts 10:48). Oneness Pentecostals competed successfully for Latino congregants because they ministered to them where they were, as will be seen later; on a theological level, they convinced a sufficient number of people that their view of the Pentecostal outpouring and view of God was as biblically orthodox, if not more so, than their Trinitarian brethren. The significance of these parallels are that religious choice existed, and was partaken of, on a regular basis; the Pentecostal faith continued a long line of Protestant faiths that Mexicanos adhered to and promoted. Within the larger framework of Pentecostalism, the choices included the Unitarian-Trinitarian bodies, and later the movement led by famed evangelist Francisco Olazábal.

Here I shall turn our focus to the early years of the movement at the Azusa Street mission, to the breaking away of Oneness Pentecostals, and, finally, to the institutionalizing processes of the Assemblies of God.

Azusa Street's worshippers were a diverse population, some of whom spoke no English, but, as William Seymour expressed in his *Apostolic Faith* (hereafter, AF), that did not matter: "It is noticeable how free all nationalities feel. If a Mexican or German cannot speak English, he gets up and speaks in his own tongue and feels quite at home for the spirit interprets through the face and people say amen." Pentecost broke down linguistic barriers. For Pentecostals, Azusa Street was part of a continuum, since the day of Pentecost marked the beginning of the Christian Church. From its inception, this revival became a worldwide phenomenon. Frank Bartleman, a Pentecostal missionary, wrote: "Pentecost has come to Los Angeles, the American Jerusalem. Every sect, creed, and doctrine under heaven . . . as well as every nation is represented." Both Seymour and Bartleman noted the diversity among people at the mission. This diversity worked in favor of the evangelist Seymour who received instruction from Charles Parham on the importance of speaking in tongues; language was now a gift from God, regardless of one's original language. This experience allowed the Spanish speaker to communicate with the German speaker, with the English speaker, and so on.

The revival began in house church gatherings held by Seymour. Eventually, their tarrying for an outpouring of the Holy Spirit was answered when, on 6 April 1906, Pentecost descended on Seymour and his followers, in keeping with the biblical pronouncement of spiritual outpouring. Speaking in tongues, healing, prophecy, and other signs brought in crowds so large that Seymour rented a larger church on nearby Azusa Street. The revival continued for three years, and converts at the mission exported the revival to the Midwest and southern United States.

One of the few accounts of conversion among Mexicans came from A. C. Valdez, who was ten years old when his mother brought him to Azusa Street. Valdez's mother, Susie, converted from Catholicism and became Yoakum's helper at his Pisgah House mission for prostitutes and alcoholics. Valdez writes of his family's early years of evangelism from 1906 to 1916, a time he describes as the worst years of persecution. He tells of being thrown in jail while others were horsewhipped, clubbed, or stoned. He claims that some Pentecostals were martyred. Other sources corroborated Valdez's accounts of harassment and violence, but I have found no evidence of martyrdom. Aside from Susie Valdez's work with Yoakum, A.C. did not record another time when he or his family ministered to Spanish speakers. This was not the case with other Azusa Street converts.

Historian Mel Robeck's important work on Latinos at Azusa Street places their roles in the context of Pentecostal history of the early twentieth century. Abundio López and his wife, Rosa, converted to Pentecostalism at Azusa Street and became emissaries of the Pentecostal faith to other Mexicans. It seems that the Lópezes had embraced the Protestant faith before Azusa Street as the Reverend Alexander Moss Merwin, pastor of the Spanish Presbyterian Church, officiated at their wedding in 1902. They attended the revival on 29 May 1906, and converted the following month. Rosa was not mentioned in the Los Angeles City Directory, but Abundio was listed in the 1920 edition. He is listed as the pastor of the Apostolic Faith Church, a Spanish-speaking congregation that doubled as a Euro American church named Victoria Hall on Spring Street. The "Apostolic Faith" was the first name given to the nascent Pentecostal movement at Azusa Street. The couple's ministry caught the attention of Seymour, who wrote about their work at the mission: "There are a good many Spanish-speaking people in Los Angeles. The Lord has given them language, and now a Spanish preacher, who, with his wife, are preaching the gospel in open air meetings on the Plaza, having received their Pentecost." One month later the Lópezes became Seymour's helpers. "Brother and Sister López, Spanish people who are filled with the Holy Ghost, are being used of God in street meetings and helping Mexicans at the altar at Azusa Street." The Lópezes eventually left Los Angeles to minister to Mexicans in the borderlands. The specter of a Mexican preaching in the open-air plaza of Los Angeles, which, at the time of Azusa Street, contained within the plaza eleven Catholic churches, adds another important dimension to the creation of a Pentecostal identity. Pentecostalism liberated immigrants from language, and also from the enclosed sacred spaces of the plaza that, for decades, symbolized the Catholic Church's strength within the Mexican community. Protestants contested that space by building churches and training their Spanish-speaking ministers in the plaza as early as the 1880s. Pentecostals like the Lópezes zealously sought converts and did so in the heart of Catholic Los Angeles. To the eventual (and continuing) dismay of the Church, they succeeded.

Language for the Pentecostal took on a sacred meaning that other Protestant denominations working in Mexican communities did not have. The following report from Seymour demonstrates what spiritual language did for the convert. On 11 August 1906, a native Mexican from Central Mexico interpreted the language of a German woman to be his own. "He understood, and through the message that God gave him through her, he was most happily converted. . . . All the English he knew was Jesus Christ and Hallellujah." The Pentecostal baptism, according to converts, gave them the ability to transcend language barriers and proved key to gaining converts who did not speak English. Speaking in tongues transcended the temporal boundaries of human language and introduced the mostly working-class Mexican immigrant population to the ethereal world of the Spirit. Many reports describe what Wacker termed *missionary tongues* during the early years of the Pentecostal movement. This gift centered on the ability to speak in the language of the mission field so that the gospel could be preached all over the world in native languages. Wacker notes that no evidence of such a gift existed, aside from personal testimonials filling the pages of Pentecostal magazines and pulpits. He views missionary tongues as a pragmatic strategy employed by Pentecostals to continue their worldwide missionary efforts. Missionary tongues were needed, Pentecostals reasoned, because Jesus was coming soon, the "heathen" was perishing without the gospel, and it was not too far-fetched to assume that the Holy Spirit would give Pentecostals this gift to meet a practical need, another example of the pragmatic approach to seeking converts.

Another key to conversion efforts lay in the places where Euro American evangelists sought converts—homes, social missions, plazas, and jails—sites where a marginal population might find themselves in early twentieth-century Los Angeles. A lay missionary in jail in Whittier began ministering to the Mexican population, and, as he described it: "The Lord gave me their tongue, the Mexican language. . . . I did not have that tongue, until I went into jail . . . most of the men are Mexicans, the men in jail asked me where the mission was, and they were going to come down as soon as they get out." Pentecostals, then as now, have never been intimidated by the often dour and dark surroundings of prisons, migrant field houses, and the modest homes of working-class Mexicanos. In the same issue of *AF*, another unnamed missionary offered insight into the motivations behind this conversion strategy after the initial Azusa Street revival in April 1906: "I bless God that it did not start in any church in this city, but in a barn, so that we might all come and take part in it. If it had started in a fine church, poor, colored people, and Spanish people would not have got it." Pentecostals recognized the segregation that comprised much of churchgoing in Los Angeles, cognizant that had the revival occurred anywhere else, people of color would have been excluded.

Azusa Street initiated the Mexican population into the evangelical world of Pentecostals. This revival and the ensuing push to convert others signified something more than the beginning of a new religious movement. The Protestant Los Angeles Singleton, found in 1907, now included a zealous and growing movement whose characteristics included more than a voluntaristic impulse. Pentecostalism delivered a message to the burgeoning immigrant population that extolled the virtues of a spiritual experience offering certain salvation. But almost as soon as Azusa Street waned, around 1909, Pentecostalism's discordant voices began to give way to schism.

A new theological issue casting doubt on the Trinitarian nature of God split the small but growing Mexican convert population. The nascent Mexican Pentecostal movement experienced its first theological division, and, with that, Oneness Pentecostals felt the urge to spread their new message to their own. The significance of this break lies in the fact that the Mexican converts established churches and spread the Oneness message independently of the larger, Euro American Oneness group that separated from the Assemblies of God in 1914. Even more significant, for the purposes of unfurling the layers of a Pentecostal identity, is the establishment of a Mexican Oneness Pentecostal movement in Los Angeles by 1909 and its growth to the borderlands and Mexico by 1912. The first known Apostolic church (Oneness churches are still commonly referred to as Apostolic), the "Spanish Apostolic Faith Mission," opened on Alpine Street in 1912, pastored by Genaro Valenzuela Mexican converts began to challenge the established norms of Trinitarian Pentecostalism, and, within three years of their initiation, a separate Pentecostal identity began to take shape. The origins of the Oneness movement are not entirely clear. The movement began in house churches in and around Los Angeles, ministered by Mexicanos, who converted Azusa Street converts like Luis López and Romanita Valenzuela.

Romanita Carbajal de Valenzuela gathered followers in Los Angeles and rebaptized them in the name of Jesus. She returned to Chihuahua and converted her family. The church she established, La Iglesia Cristiana Espiritual (the Christian Spiritual Church), became one of the largest Protestant bodies in Mexico. The U.S. counterpart, La Asamblea Apostólica (Apostolic Assembly), spread quickly throughout southern California and the Southwest. Valenzuela also did work along the border of California, Texas, and Arizona. Though there is little biographical information on him, Luis López was baptized at Azusa Street in 1909. The revival also produced evangelist Juan Navarro. López and Navarro were rebaptized in the name of Jesus later that year. They established a mission and converted many of the future leaders of the Asambleas Apostólicas. One convert, Antonio C. Nava, copastored a small Apostolic church in Los Angeles, on Angeles and Aliso Streets, one of the denomination's first churches in Los Angeles. By 1919 Apostolics had established churches in Watts, Oxnard, Los Angeles, San Fernando, San Diego, San Bernardino, and Riverside, usually establishing missions among migrant farm workers. By 1925 there were at least twenty-three churches and twenty-five pastors scattered from Baja, California, to New Mexico.

As Daniel Ramírez notes, the preponderance of the Apostolic Assemblies churches were planted among migrant labor camps of southern California. Ramírez contends that the movement which began in the plaza area of Los Angeles became increasingly rural and focused its attention on farm workers: "A nucleus of farm worker converts in the Coachella Valley proved key in subsequent evangelization work in Mexico." The dire surroundings facing Apostolic Assembly members, and indeed most laborers in the fields, caught the attention of a rival missionary, Assemblies of God minister John Preston, who wrote of conditions in the Imperial Valley in 1918. "This is a very needy place. . . . There is absolutely nothing being done for the Mexicans on either side of the line by any of the Protestant churches, and so it is all over the Imperial Valley, the Mexicans are neglected." Judging by the requests missionaries made for donations, the remedy for this neglect focused not so much on a social mission but on a spiritual mission offering laborers a better life through Pentecostalism with fellow laborers leading the way, establishing churches and bringing laborers out of the fields they plowed together. The ease with which church members crossed the border to evangelize and create churches ceased with the deportation of many Apostolic members during the 1930s. During their stay in Mexico, Apostolic members spent their time evangelizing and building churches. Oneness Pentecostals established a separate identity from their Trinitarian brethren as early as 1912. Their desire to build on that difference is demonstrated by their commitment to evangelize their fellow immigrants and their former homeland. What attracted them to Oneness? To Pentecostalism? The spiritual gifts of tongues and healing were and remain two of the most important phenomena feeding the desire to become Pentecostal. In the pages of *AF* and in the experiences converts describe, several clues are provided.

What did Azusa Street represent to those who visited the mission? What did the emerging Oneness movement represent to the convert? What happened at the mission that so impressed people that they chose to adopt Pentecostalism, even for only a moment but often a lifetime? Two feats, in particular, appealed to visitors of Azusa Street: speaking in tongues and healing. Abundio López, Rosa López, Brigido Pérez, Luis López, Juan Navarro, and the unidentified native Mexican all experienced the baptism of the Holy Spirit. Both the native Mexican and Abundio López reported that they had been given the gift of healing or were healed themselves. The native Mexican laid hands on a woman at the mission, and she reported being healed of tuberculosis, "de almas y de cuerpos" (of soul and body). Information on early Oneness converts is scanty, revealing only that they claimed to experience Spirit baptism. Antonio C. Nava, on an evangelism tour of Yuma, Arizona, prayed for his sister, and she was reportedly healed of cancer. This resulted in the entire family converting to Oneness Pentecostalism. Like the native Mexican, healing facilitated the opening of Pentecostalism to others who sought the same experience. This is not to suggest, however, that Pentecostalism introduced religious healing to the Mexican community. The desire to alleviate physical suffering by means of divine intervention has a long tradition among Mexican immigrants, who, years before they entered the Azusa Street mission, visited the homes of curanderas like Teresa Urrea and took the prescriptions of curanderos like: Don Pedrito Jaramillo.

Urrea brought her healing powers to the Mexican population of Los Angeles in 1902 in exile. "The halt, the blind, the inwardly distressed, paralytics almost helpless, and others ravaged by consumption, are helped to her doors each day by friends, and relatives and none go there without the belief that by the laying on of her magic hands, they will be cured." Urrea purchased a home in Boyle Heights on Brooklyn Avenue and State Street, and, according to the *Los Angeles Times*, a continual stream of "invalids" visited her. Urrea's exile began when she became a larger threat to the Mexican government, who did not appreciate the moral support she gave to native Mexican uprisings. Faith healer Don Pedrito Jaramillo, the healer of Los Olmos, ministered to the Mexican population of southern Texas and northern Mexico from 1881 until his death in 1907. Jaramillo wrote unusual prescriptions for his followers, as the patients informed his assistant of their symptoms. During one engagement in San Antonio in 1897 between March 24 and April 11, Jaramillo received and prescribed cures for 11,583 people, sometimes sending telegrams as far away as New Orleans.

There are significant differences and a few similarities between the healing arts legacy within the Mexican community of Urrea and Jaramillo and the Pentecostal healing converts at Azusa Street experienced. Both the Pentecostals and Urrea used the laying on of hands to transmit healing. Both Urrea and Jaramillo became associated with the Latino Catholic lexicon of folk saints, a lexicon Pentecostals reject as having any part in their healing. For example, Tomochic rebels attempting to invade Mexico on behalf of Santa Teresa wore her picture on their person to help ward off bullets from Mexican government soldiers. Don Jaramillo's grave became a pilgrimage site. Pentecostals, implicitly if not explicitly, tried to remove any hint of popular Catholicism from the healing experience. Although similarities exist between the trance possession curanderos report when channeling spirits and the Pentecostal act of being "slain in the Spirit," Pentecostals diligently discourage any theological link to practices of folk religion in an attempt to create boundaries of orthodox/heterodox religion. Another experiential similarity exists between the healing tradition of Spiritualists and Pentecostals—both claim the supernatural ability to speak in tongues. Though this phenomenon has been recorded by both curanderos who are *espritualistas* and U.S. Spiritualists, it is again relegated outside the boundaries of orthodox religious practice.

While the healing traditions of the curanderos and santos have ancient roots among Mexicanos, the healing tradition brought to them through Pentecostalism bears little resemblance to the healing traditions of the past. The chief and, for Pentecostals, most important difference is their claim that their tradition receives its supernatural commandments from the New Testament's injunctions to use the power Jesus gave to heal to the Apostles as part of their reclaiming of the Apostolic tradition. Pentecostals would disavow any linkages—cultural, spiritual, or otherwise—to any healing traditions outside Christianity.

The power of Pentecostalism is in its immediacy and the implicit acceptance of the miraculous. God mandated the end of the exclusiveness of language by making spiritual language available to all who asked for the Spirit baptism. Among those who accepted the baptism, a handful of Mexicanos became evangelists for a new faith. Problems for these evangelists and for their new faith were not far behind. One of the problems, according to Robeck, was culture: "When Hispanic Pentecostals such as Lopez, Pérez, or the Valdez families did choose to share their personal testimony with other Hispanics and encourage them to seek the same thing thereby evangelizing them, have they actually violated their own culture?" Does preaching for Pentecostalism mean preaching against Catholicism? Did that, in turn, mean a betrayal of the cultural marker of Catholicism imbued so deeply that its loss signified a cultural death? Some of the more introspective analysis on Latino Pentecostals and the question of ethnicity and culture have come from Catholic priest/scholar Allen Figueroa Deck.

The thoughtful Hispanic will view evangelical efforts to convert Hispanics as a particularly vicious attack on his or her cultural identity. Even though the Hispanic American may not be active in practicing the Catholic faith, he or she perceives that the culture is permeated by a kind of Catholic ethos and symbols that revolves around a rich collection of rites and symbols. Many of these rites and symbols are imbued with a certain Catholic spirit. The evangelical penchant for reducing the mediation between God and humanity to the Scriptures is antithetical to the Hispanic Catholic tendency to multiple mediations. . . . Hispanics have often experienced serious family divisions when a member becomes Protestant. In Hispanic culture, this is not just a religious matter. It is a profound cultural, social, and familial rupture.

Examining Figueroa Deck's words explicates the dilemma that early Pentecostal converts experienced and, to some extent, still do. As Figueroa Deck described in another work, it is the reactionary impulse of the Catholic Church and the indifference of mainline Protestantism to the "Hispanic shift" toward Pentecostalism that has given rise to a culture of suspicion and animosity. All sides that have failed to understand the shift toward Pentecostalism feed this culture, ascribing to a premise based more on the proprietary concern of the Catholic Church and its desire to be seen as the Mother Church. Add to this the lack of attention Latino Protestants received in mainline Protestant churches, where, for nearly two centuries, becoming a Christian has been equated with becoming Euro American.

Although Figueroa Deck writes more about contemporary conversions than does Robeck in his historical analysis, the former recognizes the profound tensions created around conversion, but his insistence on placing it in a Catholic context does not help us ascertain how a Pentecostal identity is created among mainline Protestant or agnostic converts who have never been Catholic. In my research for the succeeding chapters, I interviewed many converts who did not have ties to Catholicism before conversion, and to suggest, as Figueroa Deck does, that Latinos have an innate Catholic ethos requires rigorous examination. If Figueroa Deck limits his scope to Catholic converts, then the problem becomes, of course, how these converts work out their faith life as an ex-Catholics, who may or may not still be involved in popular Catholic practices, and how they deal with familial tensions. But if we want to examine the larger picture of Latino converts, we cannot assume a Catholic ethos for non-Catholics nor even for nominal Catholics. However, we may be able to assert a symbolic religious identity for Latino Catholics, who are nonpracticing and are quite ambivalent about the Church but would never think of leaving. By this I wish to suggest that Latino Pentecostals developed a historical memory and religious identity separate from Catholicism and that, by maintaining certain faith traditions, these Pentecostal identities continue to this day, operating separately from Catholicism's historical memory and religious identity. Ruiz posits another perspective on ethnicity and religious identity called "cultural coalescence." "Immigrants and their children pick, borrow, retain, and create distinctive cultural forms. There is not a single hermetic Mexican or Mexican American culture but rather permeable cultures rooted in generation, region, class, and personal experience." If there is no single culture, then presumably there is no single religious heritage informing the faith lives of Latinos. Assumptions anchoring scholarship about Latinos and religion need reconceptualization. The permeability of cultures certainly finds support in the Pentecostal experience of Latinos, who not only chose their religious identity but also began forming it early on as they sifted through varieties of Pentecostalism. Sociologists Rubén Rumbaut and Alejandro Portes offer another theory that does not deal explicitly with religious identity but may help to explain why Latino immigrants, especially Mexican immigrants, enter into the acculturation process and form identities at different rates than other immigrant groups.

Portes's and Rumbaut's segmented assimilation idea suggests that a host of factors determines how second-generation immigrants, in particular, acculturate effectively into American society. The two describe three levels of acculturation based on their findings. Unfortunately, like most sociologists who do not deal with religion, there is no factor attached to this topic. In fact, in their entire book on second-generation immigrants, Portes and Rumbaut make only one reference to religion, and it focuses narrowly on Chinese immigrants and Buddhism. Nevertheless, this and other theoretical models are helpful in contributing to an understanding of the larger picture of Mexican immigration and how Pentecostalism figures into the acculturation process. Certain questions should be kept in mind as the story continues: Does Pentecostalism offer anything with regard to human capital? Does it ease modes of incorporation? Does it buffer family structures? How does Pentecostalism help successive generations of Latinos acculturate, and what does that do to their identity as Latinos? To answer these questions, we continue.

The very nature of Pentecostalism as an independent faith would be the cause of its unraveling within a few years of its inception. The evangelists would then have to organize churches, build Bible schools, and solidify a Pentecostal identity among the Mexican communities from California to Texas. In order to maintain our focus on the institutionalization of Pentecostalism within Mexican communities, attention here shifts to the Assemblies of God, one of the most productive of Pentecostal groups, who, by 1918, had missionaries committed to Latinos in the United States despite the breakaway movement of the Mexican healing evangelist, Francisco Olazábal.

Olazábal, born in El Verano, Sinaloa, Mexico, on October 12, 1886, was the mayor's son. After his mother converted to Methodism, he was sent to the United States to study for the ministry. After a stint at the Moody Bible Institute in Chicago, Olazábal worked at the Glad Tidings Tabernacle in San Francisco and then pastored at Misión Mexicana de Pasadena, founded in 1907. During that time he founded a cooperative laundry for Mexican immigrant women in Pasadena. Olazábal's Pentecostal conversion occurred under the ministry of Carrie and George Montgomery.

The Montgomerys worked in Arizona and California. Their Pentecostal lineage is not traced to Azusa Street but to the "come-out" movement within the Holiness denominations at the turn of the century. The Montgomerys "came out" of the Christian Missionary Alliance, a denomination particularly rife with contention over the alleged unsavory character of Pentecostalism. For years, Holiness converts to Pentecostalism tried unsuccessfully to win approval from the Alliance founder A. B. Simpson, who never accepted the more elaborate doctrines of Pentecostalism, especially speaking in tongues. Carrie's fame as a healer-evangelist grew within the Holiness community as her husband, George, funded her nationwide revivals with the profits of his northern Mexico mining business. On a trip to Los Angeles, they visited Misión Mexicana in Pasadena and met Olazábal, who told George that his own conversion to Pentecostalism came through George's healing experience which he had read about in a Spanish Bible tract.

Olazábal was one of the first Mexican Pentecostal leaders to leave any written record of his ministry. Not only do his writings piece together the early history of the movement but they also provide clues to the creation of a Latino Pentecostal identity. Olazábal demonstrated a typical nineteenth-century Protestant education in a speech before the Methodist Epworth League in Gardena, California, in May 1913, his predisposition to anti-Catholic sentiment having been set years before he became Pentecostal.

> *In the critical moments through which my country is passing, when nearly the entire world considers my people to be barbarous and uncivilized because of the fratricidal war that is desolating the fields and cities of Mexico . . . I do not believe in the armed intervention of your country because it is not what we need and you can bear it to us: the intervention of the Gospel and of Christian love.*

The Mexican, according to Olazábal, would prefer death rather than be subject to armed intervention. In an ironic twist, Olazábal's nationalism echoed what conservative Mexican Catholics said at the time on the need to respect the sovereignty of the Mexican nation. The obvious difference was that nationalist Catholics viewed Protestant missionaries in Mexico as part of the U.S. invasion, not as part of the solution to the nation's problems. Catholic detractors accused triumphant revolutionaries of Protestantism. Historian Deborah Baldwin believes that conservative Catholics saw the revolution as "culturally incongruous," since being both Protestant and Mexican was unacceptable. Not only did Olazábal see no incongruity in conversion, he encouraged the continued conversion of Mexican and Mexican Americans.

Olazábal, the Methodist, blamed the Catholic Church for Mexico's misfortunes. He explained: "I was born in that faith, and the first instruction which I received was Roman Catholic." Olazábal echoed a familiar refrain at the end of his speech, the idea that Catholicism was not Christian. "When Mexico shall come to be a Christian country, which it surely will be if we do our part, let its best friend be the U.S." Ruiz's contention that cultures permeate and create identities from various sources finds strength in Olazábal life. Olazábal, the Mexican nationalist Protestant with strong ties to the American Protestant community, pleads for the United States not to invade Mexico militarily but, instead, to invade Mexico with more American missionaries. Another ironic twist to this story is that the Americans who heeded similar calls from Olazábal and others to "save" Mexico turned out to be missionaries like Henry Ball—an Assemblies of God pastor whom Olazábal would break away from over allegations of racism.

Olazábal continued working for the Misión Mexicana Church in Pasadena until 1916 when he moved to Texas and began to work with the Assemblies of God mission to Mexicans. Olazábal was ordained into the Assemblies of God on 24 September 1916, and soon afterward moved to El Paso to pastor. Within three years the mission was in financial trouble, and Olazábal wrote to Montgomery for support. In response, Montgomery sent him forty-five dollars toward a new church building. In thanking him, Olazábal asked for prayer and more workers for his growing mission. The El Paso mission flourished in the midst of revival but not without repercussions. Olazábal described the difficulty of operating in a Catholic stronghold: "We had to fight against the powers of the Catholic Church. The tent was stoned, threatened to be set on fire, etc." Along with Spirit baptisms, the members reported healings, visions of Jesus and the Second Coming, and prophetic utterances regarding the future of the church. Olazábal concluded his column by asking for support for his ministry and hinting about a Bible school for Mexican men and women preparing for the ministry. In 1921 an unknown writer pleaded Olazábal's case to the readers of *Pentecostal Evangel* (hereafter, *PE*), the weekly magazine of the Assemblies of God. The writer notes the lack of workers for the masses of Mexicans who attend services in El Paso in a church that needs expansion to accommodate the crowds. During the first three years of his ministry with the Assemblies of God, Olazábal appeared to receive support and encouragement for his work. Apparently, however, as his ministry continued to grow and require more donations, his fund-raising activities on behalf of the church made the Assemblies of God uncomfortable. Depending on which version of the story one chooses to accept, Olazábal was either asked to leave or he resigned.

In January 1923 J. R. Flower, the Assemblies superintendent, wrote a column in *PE* describing Olazábal's situation. According to Flower, Olazábal's attempts to begin a school in El Paso failed so badly that Flower, Ball, Olazábal, Luce, and the missionary to Mexico George Blaisdell attended an emergency meeting in December 1922. According to Flower, the El Paso school was too far away from Mexicans to be effective. He also cited the poverty of the Mexicans of El Paso as a reason why the school failed. Flower said, quoting Olazábal: "He agreed that he would devote his time and energies to the ministry rather than to attempt to build up a school or other institution which would take him from the field." Flower moved the efforts to build a school to San Antonio and placed it under the supervision of the Missionary Commission of the General Council of the Assemblies of God. Ball took charge of the administration of the school, and Luce took charge of the faculty.

According to Miguel Guillen, the official chronicler of Olazábal's story and former minister with the Texas mission of the Assemblies of God, Olazábal did not leave the denomination voluntarily but was asked to leave because of problems related to his fund-raising for the school, which caused the leadership concern. According to Guillen, the Assemblies of God was intent on not allowing Olazábal any position of leadership and terminated his ministry in an effort to silence his powerful presence amid the growing Mexican Pentecostal community. In 1922 the Mexican members of the Texas Assemblies of God voted to start their own district council, which Olazábal would head. According to Isabel Flores (another former member of the Assemblies of God), the plan required Olazábal to run the council from his El Paso church while starting a Bible institute and a printing press. Opposition to Olazábal's promotion came from the Euro American members of the Assemblies of God, who, according to Flores, believed that "el pueblo Mexicano no estaba capacitado para dirigir el trabajo" (the Mexican people were not qualified to direct the work).

In December 1923 Guillen interviewed Olazábal at his home in Port Arthur, Texas, and the interview supported Flores's account. Olazábal recalls meeting with Assemblies of God leaders to explain why he raised money for his church. He mentioned Alice Luce's philosophy of autonomous Mexican leadership. The leadership was offended at his reference to Luce and suggested he showed disrespect. When Flower, the Assemblies of God leader, asked who had authorized his fund-raising, Olazábal answered that he had received authority to raise funds at the last Texas Assemblies of God convention (1918) from Flower himself. Olazábal's response to his dismissal was this: "Yo sali de entro los Metodistas y crei que habia entrado mas cristiana, pero ahora veo que un Ruso, un Griego puede se misionaro menos un Mexicano." (I left the Methodists and I thought I had been among Christians, but now I see that a Russian, a Greek, can be a missionary, but not a Mexican). With that, Olazábal set off to found his own church. In 1923 El Concilio Latino Americano de Iglesias Cristianas began.

The Assemblies of God recollection of events differs significantly from Olazábal's. Glenn Gohr, an Assemblies of God historian, believes that Olazábal became "disconcerted" with the predominantly Euro American denomination. Other Assemblies of God recollections of the Olazábal controversy are sparse. Henry Ball commented on the controversy in a 1940 retrospective on his career:

El hermano Francisco Olazábal se retiró de las Asambleas de Dios el dia de 13 de Enero de 1923. Era un gran evangelista y se retiró de nuestro movimiento que causo' disturbios de caracter serio; indudablemente estariamos mas avanzados.

[*Brother Francisco Olazábal withdrew from the Assemblies of God in January 1923. He was a grand evangelist. His retirement from the movement caused a great disturbance in the character (of the movement). Unquestionably, we would have been much more advanced*].

Ball concluded that the Assemblies of God mission would have been much stronger had Olazábal stayed with the church. Despite his popularity in the Assemblies, Olazábal left and convinced a core group of Assemblies of God ministers, including the future church superintendent Demetrio Bazán, to leave the church to join Olazábal in establishing churches in Texas and California. This episode between Olazábal and another Pentecostal denomination clearly speaks to the tenor of the times in which Olazábal preached and reflects how Euro American leadership viewed him.

After Olazábal left the Assemblies, he continued his healing campaigns. One campaign in East Los Angeles in 1927 attracted the attention of Foursquare founder Aimee Semple McPherson. McPherson and Olazábal were invited to preach in each other's churches, but this cozy relationship did not last long. When McPherson asked Olazábal to merge his new denomination with her's, the Concilio membership defeated the proposal. Undoubtedly, in the aftermath of the Assemblies of God split, Mexican members had had enough of Euro American leadership. McPherson did not take the rejection well and requested the return of her $100 "love offering." When Olazábal refused, McPherson set out to counter Olazábal's work in Los Angeles by starting Foursquare's own Spanish-speaking churches. From its inception, Olazábal's vision of Pentecostal revival and salvation for Mexico in the "last days" powered the Concilio.

In 1923 Olazábal wrote to the Pentecostal minister Richey and asked for support to fund a campaign Olazábal planned for Mexico. He offered two reasons for the campaign: (1) the millennial inspiration of the Second Coming; and (2) the need to "save" Mexico from "'a avaricia y absolutismo del clero romano, que por cuatro centurias ha esclavizado la consciencia de ese pueblo en el 99 por cento de su populación" (the avarice and absolutism of the Roman clergy, who, for four centuries, has enslaved the conscience of 99 percent of the population). Although Richey did not respond to this request, Olazábal's frequent campaigns across the United States seem to indicate that he soon became a very popular healing evangelist.

Olazábal's campaigns focused on healing and educating converts on the theological nuances of what Pentecostals believed. He writes of a campaign in Texas:

> *Muy pocos de los que han sido sanados en mis servicios de sanidad han vuelto la cara atras y casi todos los que han sido salvados por la operación de los milagros y la sanidades han sido completamente regenerados y llevan hoy una vida ejemplar.*

> *[Very few of those who have been healed in my healing services have turned back, and almost all those that have been saved through the working of miracles and healings have been completely renewed and today lead exemplary lives.]*

Healing changes lives and, in so doing, gives converts the opportunity to lead exemplary lives. Olazábal brought his campaigns to San Fernando, California, El Paso, Cleveland, Tennessee, New York, and Puerto Rico.

Reporting on his crusades, the media noted the great crowds and miraculous healings. The *Cleveland Daily Banner* pointed out the unusual nature of an all-night service, where the "Aztec missionary" Olazábal led the crowd in an all-night prayer meeting. The paper also notes the merger of his church with the Church of God, claiming Olazábal could deliver fifty thousand Mexicans to the denomination. Why Olazábal would leave the predominantely Euro American Assemblies of God for the predominantly Euro American Church of God is unclear. When Olazábal died in a car accident in 1937, the merger had not been completed. Another publication, the *Christian Herald*, wrote of Olazábal's growing ministry and the success the "great Aztec" had in ministering to Mexicans. The Aztec imagery reflects the racial component intoned by many Euro American observers and missionaries when writing about Mexican ministers and converts. The author of an article about Olazábal's New York ministry prefaced the piece by suggesting that the "barbaric" nature of Aztec priests and the "jungle dances" of Harlem bespeak an impossible situation for anything positive to come out of Harlem, where Olazábal's outreach reportedly converted and healed hundreds. What makes Olazábal acceptable? Despite his Aztec ancestry, his Protestantism legitimizes him as civilized and godly—unlike his ancestors. Commenting on contemporary racial attitudes, Roberto Almaraz, an Assemblies of God minister, says that this patronizing attitude plagues Latino/Euro American Pentecostal relations to this day. Says Almaraz: "The problem is that they [Assemblies of God continue to view us as a mission field, as converts . . . not as equals. The stereotypical language, using Aztec iconography, employed by the writer in the *Christian Herald* continues to this day by Olazábal's admirers themselves, who call him "el Azteca" as a term of affection.

As part of his two-tiered ministry, Olazábal took time out of his healing services and campaigns to answer questions about Pentecostalism and wrote responses in the church's magazine. During the 1930s the Pentecostal movement was considered "bizarre," and the misinformation about their spiritual practices was widespread. On several occasions the prejudice descended into verbal and physical violence. Detractors accused Pentecostals of practicing witchcraft, devil worship, and sexual promiscuity. They threw rocks and garbage, mobbed Pentecostal meetings, slashed meeting tent ropes, and set churches afire. With this history of contention, Olazábal's role as a promoter of Pentecostalism meant that he had to promote its acceptance as a part of orthodox Christianity. A question came from an unnamed person who wanted to know if Pentecostalism was equivalent to Spiritualism. Olazábal responded:

No, en ninguna manera si el pueblo conciente que pertenece al dicho movimiento Pentecostal es responsable de lo malo que encontrate en este o en aquel individuo por el hecho de que el dicho individuo asegura pertenecer al dicho movimiento . . . el movimiento Pentecostal enseña que es error todo lo que contradice, el material de doctrina, lo que está escrito en la Biblia; considera como pecado toda rebeldia contra la voluntad de Dios y toda desobediencia de su santa ley.

[No, in no manner is the Pentecostal movement responsible for such bad things. The Pentecostal movement teaches that [Spiritualism] is in error in doctrinal matters, in what is written in the Bible; it is considered a sin and rebellion for such bad things. The Pentecostal movement teaches [that Spiritualism] is in error in doctrinal manners, in what is written in the Bible; it is considered a sin and rebellion against God and totally disobedient of His Holy law].

Olazábal had two concerns: (1) to educate his growing congregation, and (2) to convince his flock of the uncomplimentary practices of Spiritualism. Spiritualists, along with using intermediaries to attempt contact with the deceased, practiced speaking in tongues. This practice for a time made Spiritualism an attractive option for Pentecostals who where "deceived" into attending Spiritualist churches.

Olazábal's crusades and teaching came to an end in 1937, when he died in a car accident on his way back from a campaign in Texas. The denomination he started did not merge with any other Pentecostal denomination and, for the most part, had relied on generational growth to continue to fill its churches. Holland calls the Concilio "the most conservative and introverted of the Pentecostal denominations." This observation is supported by a personal conversation with Latino Pentecostal ministers who have close ties to the Concilio, one of whom, a family friend of the Olazábal family, told me that the church has little interest in working with others, rarely grants interview requests, and, in his estimation, is still suffering the effects of the Olazábal split with the Assemblies of God more than seventy years ago. Despite the church's reluctance to discuss its history or current work, what should be kept in mind is Olazábal's work in the early years of Latino Pentecostalism, and his insistence on autonomy—an insistence that would be bolstered by the writing and work of Alice Luce.

Alice Luce began her "Mexican work" as a missionary to Mexico. Forced to leave on the eve of the Revolution, she became a missionary to Mexicans in California. She wrote an open letter to the Assemblies of God warning them of lost opportunities if they did not support the Mexican work. In order for this mission to work, the Assemblies of God would have to send many more workers to the border. Luce's missionary impulse concentrated on two points: (1) to spread the word about the Pentecostal cause among. Mexicans, and (2) to "save" Mexicans from the continuing influence of the Catholic Church. She writes: "We are proving the good old gospel to be the power of God unto salvation for these poor, dark, Mexicans, just as for the white people. The opposition of the priests has been terrible." Luce's sentiments demonstrate some ideas commonly held by Protestants raised in the nineteenth century, (Luce was the daughter of an Anglican bishop) that Catholicism kept people in darkness. But her idea that evangelization efforts succeeded in converting "white" people as well as "poor, dark" Mexicans displays a crucial element she had for her missions: that they be turned over to Mexican control as soon as possible. It should be noted, however, that Luce's partner, Henry Ball, did not have the same idea regarding Mexican control. Ball writes: "We need more American missionaries. I have in the past two years, trained several Mexican workers, but while they are excellent workers, they need American oversight." Creeping paternalism as it worked its way into Protestant missions to Mexicans before Pentecostalism continued despite the gains made by Mexican pastors and Luce's work.

Luce founded a Pentecostal mission in the Placita in 1917. El Aposento Alto was located on Los Angeles Street. Like other Protestant missions who set up in the plaza decades earlier, a distinct Pentecostal presence that had begun at the Azusa Street mission continued with Luce's mission and continued to reap the benefits of a large Mexican population of religious seekers. In 1922 Luce took a failed Pentecostal mission in the

Belvedere section of Los Angeles and moved her fledgling mission to what the Reverend Samuel Ortegón in 1932 described as the largest, most progressive settlement of Mexicans in East Los Angeles.

A large percentage of the 20,125 East Los Angeles residents were Mexican and Mexican Americans. Ortegón counted eight churches in the area. A Presbyterian church and settlement house, two Pentecostal churches, a Spiritualist church, a Baptist church, and two Catholic churches. (see maps 1–5 for specific locations of churches). Belvedere's progressive status did not mean that other areas of East Los Angeles fared as well. Ortegón noted that Maravilla Park, just east of Belvedere, was the poorest section, with people "living in shacks, and eating practically nothing." He mentioned that the two Pentecostal churches, Misión Mexicana McPherson and the Iglesia Pentecostal Bethel, Olazábal's church, had fifty members: The McPherson church was a part of the International Church of the Foursquare Gospel Church in Boyle Heights. Ortegón reports that most of the members came from other Pentecostal churches. The church sat eight hundred and had five hundred members. Ortegón, a Baptist minister, comments on the appeal of Pentecostalism: "The healing services . . . appeal strongly to the Mexican mind." The mission's other appealing features were its women's society, the clothes sale, and the food giveaways, which, during the Depression, fed four hundred every week. In addition to these churches, the Latter-Day Saints rented a hall for services, and the Catholic Church, in addition to its churches, had three settlement houses in Boyle Heights, Los Angeles, and Maravilla Park. The religious choices facing the burgeoning population in East Los Angeles must have made for a competitive and lively contest for the allegiance of the recent immigrant and long-time resident alike. Pentecostals proved to be well equipped for the fight.

Luce relied heavily on Mexican workers to help run El Aposento Alto, placing Francisco and Natividad Nevarez in charge soon after its move. The Nevarezes received the Pentecostal baptism in 1916 at Luce's tent revival in Los Angeles; they had converted from Presbyterianism. They ran the church until the 1950s, when they left to develop other Pentecostal missions to Mexicans in Mexico and Mexicans in East Los Angeles and Watts. According to Victor De Leon (an Assemblies of God minister who wrote the first and one of the only histories of Latino Pentecostals), many Mexicans who received Spirit baptism in these early years came from the Presbyterian, Baptist, and Methodist churches in East Los Angeles. Though he offers little evidence for his assertion, his description matches that of the Nevarezes. Mainline denominations offered a gateway to Pentecostalism for a variety of reasons. For one, Holiness denominations like the Methodists experienced the "come-out" movement and lost many members to Pentecostal groups. For another, Protestants, such as the former Baptist Arnulfo López, had nowhere else to go once they experienced Spirit baptism. For them, the Assemblies of God served as a new home and refuge: "Bro. A.M. Lopez . . . a young Spanish brother of considerable ability . . . received the baptism of the Holy Ghost . . . here in Austin last winter, on account of which church officials rejected him." López went to work for Ball's church in Texas and was instrumental in introducing the future Latino leader Demetrio Bazán to Pentecostalism by praying for him to receive Spirit baptism. Natividad Nevarez also recalls that from 1916 to the 1930s she encountered many Latinos open to proselytism by Pentecostals. This view may be supported by the thirty-four Pentecostal missions, of various denominational persuasions, throughout southern California.

Despite the presence of other Pentecostal groups, the Assemblies of God was still the most predominant. Why? Because it had the most extensive foreign-language ministry among Latinos. Healing and spiritual gifts certainly account for some of the popularity of Pentecostalism among a people not estranged from supernatural religious expression. Pentecostalism became a faith easily communicated through a common language of salvation, often spoken in Spanish. The acceptance of an active supernatural life made the acceptance of Pentecostal spirituality all the more enticing. Simply put, Pentecostalism nullifies the doubt one might have about the existence and efficacy of God through direct personal experience. Olazábal's healing ministry, the mission to Mexicans in their own language and within their own communities, and the Pentecostal baptism offered by all missionaries meant that this faith, far from being "bizarre" to Latinos, became quite natural. No church organized, institutionalized, or laid a better foundation for posterity than the Assemblies of God and the work of Henry Ball and Alice Luce.

The Fire between Them

CRISTINA GARCIA

Felicia del Pino doesn't know what brings on her delusions. She knows only that suddenly she can hear things very vividly. The scratching of a beetle on the porch. The shifting of the floorboards in the night. She can hear everything in this world and others, every sneeze and creak and breath in the heavens or the harbor or the gardenia tree down the block. They call to her all at once, grasping here and there for parts of her, hatching blue flames in her brain. Only the Beny Moré records, played loud and warped as they are, lessen the din.

The colors, too, escape their objects. The red floats above the carnations on her windowsill. The blues rise from the chipped tiles in the kitchen. Even the greens, her favorite shades of greens, flee the trees and assault her with luminosity. Nothing is solid until she touches it. She blames the sun for this, for the false shadows it casts in her house, and she tightens the shutters against enemy rays. When she dares look outside, the people are paintings, outlined in black, their faces crushed and squarish. They threaten her with their white shining eyes. She hears them talking but cannot understand what they say. She never knows the time.

Felicia's mind floods with thoughts, thoughts from the past, from the future, other people's thoughts. Things come back as symbols, bits of conversation, a snatch of an old church hymn. Every idea seems to her connected to thousands of others by a tangle of pulsing nerves. She jumps from one to another like a nervous circus horse. It is worse when she closes her eyes.

Felicia remembers how when she was in grammar school the paraphernalia of faith had proved more intriguing than its overwrought lessons. After mass, long after the priest's words stopped echoing against the cement walls, she remained in church, inspecting the pews for forgotten veils or rosary beads. She collected prayer cards and missals engraved with gold initials and filled glass jars with holy water, which she later used to baptize Ilda Limón's chickens. Once she pried loose a crucifix with an ivory Jesus from a Station of the Cross and blessed her baby brother, Javier, with three mild raps to his forehead.

During high mass, her sister and father recited the Lord's Prayer with loud precision and clung forever to the last syllables of the hymns.

"Alleluiaaaaaaaaaaaaaaaaaaaaaaaa!" they sang, releasing the "a" only when those around them began to stare.

Felicia knew that her mother, who stayed at home reading her books and rocking on the porch swing, had an instinctive distrust of the ecclesiastical. She suspected her mother of being an atheist and only hoped she wouldn't burn in hell for eternity as Lourdes and the nuns said.

Although Celia was not a believer, she was wary of powers she didn't understand. She locked her children in the house on December 4, the feast day of Changó, god of fire and lightning, and warned them that they'd be kidnapped and sacrificed to the black people's god if they wandered the streets alone. For good measure, she forbade Felicia to visit her best friend, Herminia, whose father everyone denounced as a witch doctor.

Lourdes took advantage of their confinement to tell Felicia how the shriveled tin peddler, who rattled by with his trolley at noon, abducted children to caves with flapping bats that nested in human hair. At night, he'd scoop out their eyes with a wooden spoon and drink their blood like milk. Lourdes insisted that the tin man had left the eyes of a dozen sacrificed children under Felicia's bed as an omen. Felicia, her eyes closed tight, cautiously patted the floor until she touched the peeled grapes her sister had left for her there, and screamed to holy hell.

As the summer of coconuts wears on, Felicia hears Saint Sebastian speaking to her inside her head. She can't stop his words, which come in rhymes sometimes or jumbled together like twisted yarn. He doesn't let her think. He reminds her how much she used to love him, how much she has disappointed him over the years.

Felicia first became fascinated with Saint Sebastian before her confirmation. She marveled over how he'd been shot through with arrows and left for dead, how he'd survived his murder only to be beaten to death by the Roman Emperor's soldiers and buried in the catacombs. Sebastian's double death appealed to Felicia. She studied his image, his hands tied above his head, his eyes rolled heavenward, arrows protruding from his chest and sides, and felt a great sympathy for him. But the nuns refused to let Felicia choose Sebastian as her confirmation name.

"Why don't you pick María like your sister?" the nuns had suggested. Their faces were pink, puffy squares cut off at the brows, their pores enlarged from the pressure of their tightly bound habits. "That way Our Blessed Virgin Mother will always look after you."

In the end, Felicia refused to be confirmed at all and Jorge del Pino blamed his daughter's later troubles on that fact.

God's Will: Herminia Delgado
(1980)

CRISTINA GARCIA

I met Felicia on the beach when we were both six years old. She was filling a pail with cowries and bleeding tooth. Felicia used to collect seashells, then rearrange them on the beach before going home because her mother wouldn't allow them in their house. Felicia designed great circles of overlapping shells on the sand, as if someone on the moon, or farther still, might read their significance. I told her that at my house we had many shells, that they told the future and were the special favorites of Yemayá, goddess of the seas. Felicia listened closely, then handed me her pail.

"Will you save me?" she asked me. Her eyes were wide and curious.

"Sure," I answered. How could I realize then what my promise would entail?

Felicia's parents were afraid of my father. He was a *babalawo*, a high priest of *santería*, and greeted the sun each morning with outstretched arms. His godchildren came from many miles on his saint's day, and brought him kola nuts and black hens.

The people in Santa Teresa del Mar told evil lies about my father. They said he used to rip the heads off goats with his teeth and fillet blue-eyed babies before dawn. I got into fights at school. The other children shunned me and called me *bruja*. They made fun of my hair, oiled and plaited in neat rows, and of my skin, black as my father's. But Felicia defended me. I'll always be grateful to her for that.

Felicia was forbidden to visit my house but she did anyway. Once she saw my father use the *obi*, the divining coconut, to answer the questions of a godchild who had come to consult him. I remember the pattern of rinds fell in *ellife*, two white sides and two brown, a definite yes. The godchild left very pleased, and Felicia's fascination with coconuts began that day.

I never doubted Felicia's love. Or her loyalty. When my oldest son died in Angola, Felicia didn't leave my side for a month. She cooked me *carne asada* and read me the collected plays of Molière, which she borrowed from her mother. Felicia arranged for Joaquín's remains to be brought home for a decent burial, and then she stayed with me until I could laugh again at silly things.

Felicia could be very stubborn, too, but she had a gift that offset her stubbornness, a gift I admired very much. I guess you could say she adapted to her grief with imagination. Felicia stayed on the fringe of life because it was free of everyday malice. It was more dignified there.

There is something else, something very important. Felicia is the only person I've known who didn't see color. There are white people who know how to act politely to blacks, but deep down you know they're uncomfortable. They're worse, more dangerous than those who speak their minds, because they don't know what they're capable of.

For many years in Cuba, nobody spoke of the problem between blacks and whites. It was considered too disagreeable to discuss. But my father spoke to me clearly so that I would understand what happened to his father and his uncles during the Little War of 1912, so that I would know how our men were hunted down day and night like animals, and finally hung by their genitals from the lampposts in Guáimaro. The war that killed my grandfather and great-uncles and thousands of other blacks is only a footnote in our history books. Why, then, should I trust anything I read? I trust only what I see, what I know with my heart, nothing more.

Things have gotten better under the revolution, that much I can say. In the old days, when voting time came, the politicians would tell us we were all the same, one happy family. Every day, though, it was another story. The whiter you were, the better off you were. Anybody could see that. There's more respect these days. I've been at the battery factory almost twenty years now, since right after the revolution, and I supervise forty-two women. It's not much, maybe, but it's better than mopping floors or taking care of another woman's children instead of my own.

One thing hasn't changed: the men are still in charge. Fixing that is going to take a lot longer than twenty years.

But let me begin again. After all, this story is about Felicia, not me.

Felicia returned to our religion with great eagerness after her disappearance in 1978. She showed up at my house one day, slim and tanned, as if she'd just returned from a vacation at a fancy foreign spa. "Take me to La Madrina," she told me, and I did. Then, during a holy trance, Felicia spoke of her days in a far-off town. She said she'd married a bearish man in an amusement park and that he'd planned to escape Cuba, to take a fishing boat north and go ice skating. I don't know if this part is true, but Felicia said that she'd pushed this man, her third husband, from the top of a roller coaster and watched him die on a bed of high-voltage wires. Felicia said his body turned to gray ash, and then the wind blew him north, just as he'd wished.

She never spoke of this again.

Within a week, Felicia had her old job back at the beauty shop. She worked hard to regain the confidence of her former customers, except, of course, for Graciela Moreira, who'd taken to wearing synthetic wigs imported from Hungary. I sent Felicia a few customers myself from the factory. Those girls *needed* manicures after assembling batteries all day long.

At night, Felicia attended our ceremonies. She didn't miss a single one. For her, they were a kind of poetry that connected her to larger worlds, worlds alive and infinite. Our rituals healed her, made her believe again. My father used to say that there are forces in the universe that can transform our lives if only we'd surrender ourselves. Felicia surrendered, and found her fulfillment.

Felicia's mother discouraged her devotion to the gods. Celia had only vague notions about spiritual possession and animal sacrifice, and suspected that our rites had caused her daughter's mysterious disappearance. Celia revered El Líder and wanted Felicia to give herself entirely to the revolution, believing that this alone would save her daughter. But Felicia would not be dissuaded from the *orishas*. She had a true vocation to the supernatural.

Before long, La Madrina initiated Felicia into the *elekes* and gave her the necklaces of the saints that would protect her from evil. They weren't easy to make. Since the revolution, it's been difficult to obtain the right beads. La Madrina told me she had to fashion Felicia's necklaces from the beaded curtains of a restaurant in Old Havana.

Many initiations followed, but I was not allowed to Felicia's last one, her *asiento*. This ritual has been done in secret since the first slaves worked the sugarcane fields on this island. But Felicia told me what she could.

Sixteen days before the *asiento*, Felicia went to live with La Madrina, who had procured seven white dresses for her, seven sets of underwear and nightclothes, seven sets of bedding, seven towels, large and small, and other special items, all white.

Felicia changed every day to stay pure.

On the morning of her initiation, sixteen *santeras* tore Felicia's clothes to shreds until she stood naked, then they bathed her in river water, rubbing her with soap wrapped in vegetable fibers until her skin glowed. The women dressed Felicia in a fresh white gown and combed and braided her hair, treating her like a newborn child.

That night, after a purifying coconut shampoo, Felicia was guided to a windowless room, where she sat for many hours, alone on a stool. La Madrina slipped the sacred necklace of Obatalá around Felicia's neck. Felicia told me she grew sleepy, and felt as though she were drifting through the heavens, that she was a planet looking at herself from one of her moons.

After many more rituals and a final bath in the *omiero*, the *santeras* led Felicia to Obatalá's throne. The diviner of shells shaved her head as everyone chanted in the language of the Yoruba. They painted circles and dots on her head and cheeks—white for Obatalá, reds and yellows and blues for the other gods—and crowned her with the sacred stones. It was then Felicia lost consciousness, falling into an emptiness without history or future.

She learned later that she'd walked purposefully around the room, possessed by Obatalá. The *santeras* had made eight cuts on her tongue with a razor blade so that the god could speak, but Felicia could not divulge his words. When Obatalá finally left her body, she opened her eyes and emerged from the void.

Once more Felicia was led to the throne. The goats to be sacrificed were marched in one by one, arrayed in silks and gold braids. Felicia smeared their eyes, ears, and foreheads with the coconut and pepper she chewed before the *babalawo* slit their throats. She tasted the goats' blood and spit it toward the ceiling, then she sampled the blood of many more creatures.

Four hours later, the *babalawo*, drenched in sweat and countless immolations, lowered his head near hers. "*Eroko ashé*," he whispered. It is done, with the blessings of the gods.

When I visited Felicia the following day, she was dressed in her coronation gown, her crown, and all her necklaces. She sat on a throne surrounded by gardenias, her face serene as a goddess's. I believe to this day she'd finally found her peace.

But when Felicia returned to Palmas Street with her sacred stones and her tureen, her seashells and the implements of her saint, neither her mother nor her children were there to greet her. Felicia was crestfallen, but she was certain that the gods were testing her. She wanted to prove to the *orishas* that she was a true believer, serious and worthy of serving them, so she continued her rituals.

Felicia did everything she was supposed to as a novice *santera*. She dressed only in white, and didn't wear makeup or cut her hair. She never touched the forbidden foods—coconuts, corn, or anything red—and covered the one mirror in her house with a sheet, as she was prohibited from seeing her own image.

When I came to visit her, we settled on the warping floorboards, where Felicia ate her meals with a serving spoon. As she spoke, Felicia rolled the spoon between her palms and watched its clumsy, twirling shadow on the wall.

"Have you spoken with them?" she asked me, referring to her mother, her daughters, her son.

"Your mother says they're frightened, like the summer of coconuts."

"But this is completely different. I have a clarity now. You can see the sun enters here." Felicia indicated the dusty shafts of light. "Did you tell her that even El Líder is initiated? That he's the son of Elleguá?"

I shook my head, saying nothing. Felicia covered her face with her hands. A rash erupted on her neck and cheeks. I noticed the imprint her fingers made on her forehead, the delicate chain of bloodless flesh.

Then Felicia spoke of our faith, of her final healing, and held my hands in hers.

"You've been more than a sister to me, Herminia. You saved me, like you promised on the beach."

That night, I dreamt of Felicia in her bathing suit with her pail of cowries and bleeding tooth.

"Will you save me?" she asked me.

"Sure," I answered, again and again.

I've seen other *santeras* during their first year. They are radiant. Their eyes are moist and clear, their skin is smoothed of wrinkles, and their nails grow strong. When you make a saint, the saint takes good care of you. But Felicia showed none of these blessings. Her eyes dried out like an old woman's and her fingers curled like claws until she could hardly pick up her spoon. Even her hair, which had been as black as a crow's, grew colorless in scruffy patches on her skull. Whenever she spoke, her lips blurred to a dull line in her face.

Over the next weeks, all of us from the *casa de santo* took turns visiting Felicia. We wrapped her wrists with beaded bracelets, gave her castor-oil enemas, packed hot cactus compresses on her brow. We boiled *yerba buena* teas and left yams and swatches of cotton on Obatalá's altar. But nothing seemed to help. Felicia's eyesight dimmed until she could perceive only shadows, and the right side of her head swelled with mushroomy lumps.

La Madrina was beside herself with worry. She performed sacrifices every day in Felicia's behalf. Some of us traveled with our offerings to the mountains, where Obatalá is said to live, and placed white flags around the house on Palmas Street to attract peace.

But each time La Madrina threw the shells, the omen was the same. *Ikú*. Death.

A group of *babalawos* tried a *panaldo*, an exorcism, and thought they had trapped an evil spirit in the rooster they buried in a knotted cloth. But Felicia continued to grow worse. The *babalawos* consulted the oracles with all their powers of divination. The *opelé*. The table of Ifá. Even the *ikin*, the sacred palm nuts. Still, the omen did not change.

"It is the will of the gods," they concluded. "It will be resolved by the spirits of the dead."

Just as the *babalawos* were about to leave, Felicia's mother entered the house on Palmas Street. She was wild-eyed, like a woman who gives birth to an unwanted child.

"Witch doctors! Murderers! Get out, all of you!" she cried, and swept the image of Obatalá off its altar.

We pulled back, afraid of the god's response.

Celia overturned the tureen with the sacred stones and crushed Felicia's seashells under the heels of her leather pumps. Suddenly, she removed her shoes and began stamping on the shells in her bare feet, slowly at first, then faster and faster in a mad flamenco, her arms thrown up in the air.

Then just as suddenly she stopped. She made no sound as she wept, as she bent to kiss Felicia's eyes, her forehead, her swollen, hairless skull. Celia lay with her torn, bleeding feet beside her daughter and held her, rocking and rocking her in the blue gypsy dusk until she died.

Pilar
(1980)

CRISTINA GARCIA

I'm browsing in the remainders bins outside a record shop on Amsterdam Avenue when two men call to me halfheartedly from across the street, more out of habit than desire. I sift through old 78 polkas with beribboned women smiling at me from the album covers. There's something grotesque about their grins, fixed for thirty years. Maybe I'd do them a favor by buying their records and breaking them in two. Maybe it'd release them from some terrible Romanian spell.

I find a Herb Alpert record, the one with the woman in whipped cream on the cover. It looks so tame to me now. I read somewhere that the woman who posed for it was three months pregnant at the time and that it was shaving cream, not whipped cream, she was suggestively dipping into her mouth.

In the last bin, I find an old Beny Moré album. Two of the cuts are scratched but I buy it anyway for fifty cents. The cashier's features are compressed beneath a bulbous forehead. When I thank him in Spanish, he's surprised and wants to chat. We talk about Celia Cruz and how she hasn't changed a hair or a vocal note in forty years. She's been fiftyish, it seems, since the Spanish-American War.

Then we get to talking about Lou Reed. It's funny how his fans can sniff each other out. We agree that his sexually ambiguous days—when he wore white face and black nail polish—were his best. It's hard to believe that Lou came out of a suburban home on Long Island and went to college in upstate New York. He should have been a lawyer or an accountant or somebody's father by now. I wonder if his mother thinks he's dangerous.

The cashier, Franco, puts on the *Take No Prisoners* album. I was at the Bottom Line the night they recorded it. How many lifetimes ago was that? I think about all that great early punk and the raucous paintings I used to do.

Shit, I'm only twenty-one years old. How can I be nostalgic for my youth?

Midterms are in a week and I can't seem to concentrate on anything. The only thing that helps is my bass. I've taught myself to play the thing these last two years and I'm not half bad. There's a group at Columbia that meets Sunday afternoons to jam on this punky fake jazz everyone's into. When things are cooking, me and my bass just move the whole damn floor.

Still, I feel something's dried up inside me, something a strong wind could blow out of me for good. That scares me. I guess I'm not so sure what I should be fighting for anymore. Without confines, I'm damn near reasonable. That's something I never wanted to become.

Franco and I commiserate about how St. Mark's Place is a zoo these days with the bridge-and-tunnel crowd wearing fuchsia mohawks and safety pins through their cheeks. Everybody wants to be part of the freak show for a day. Anything halfway interesting gets co-opted, mainstreamed. We'll all be doing car commercials soon.

It used to be you could see the Ramones in the East Village for five bucks. Nowadays you have to pay $12.50 to see them with five thousand bellowing skinheads who don't even let you hear the music. Count me out.

I enter a *botánica* on upper Park Avenue. I've passed the place before but I've never gone inside. Today, it seems, there's nowhere else for me to go. Dried snakeskins and *ouanga* bags hang from the walls. Painted wooden saints with severe mouths stand alongside plastic plug-in Virgins with sixty-watt bulbs. Iridescent oils are displayed with amulets, talismans, incense. There are sweet-smelling soaps and bottled bathwater, love perfumes and potions promising money and luck. Apothecary jars labeled in childish block letters are filled with pungent spices.

I'm not religious but I get the feeling that it's the simplest rituals, the ones that are integrated with the earth and its seasons, that are the most profound. It makes more sense to me than the more abstract forms of worship.

The owner of the shop is an elderly man who wears a white tunic and cotton fez. For a young woman with cropped hair, he prescribes a statuette of La Virgen de la Caridad del Cobre, a yellow candle, and five special oils: *amor* (love), *sígueme* (follow me), *yo puedo y tú no* (I can and you can't), *ven conmigo* (come with me), and *dominante* (dominant).

"Carve his name on the candle five times and anoint it with these oils," he instructs. "Do you have a picture of your intended?"

The woman nods.

"*Bueno*, put it on a dessert plate and coat it with honey. Then arrange five fishhooks on the picture and light the candle. Rest assured, he will be yours in two Sundays."

I envy this woman's passion, her determination to get what she knows is hers. I felt that way once, when I ran away to Miami. But I never made it to Cuba to see Abuela Celia. After that, I felt like my destiny was not my own, that men who had nothing to do with me had the power to rupture my dreams, to separate me from my grandmother.

I examine the beaded necklaces near the register. Most have five strands and come in two colors. I select a red-and-white one and place it over my head. I lift an ebony staff carved with the head of a woman balancing a double-edged ax.

"Ah, a daughter of Changó," the elderly man says and places a hand on my shoulder.

I say nothing but I notice that his eyes are the same almond color as his skin, that they're centuries older than his face.

"You must finish what you began," he says.

I rub the beads in my left hand and feel a warm current drifting up my arm, across my shoulders, down between my breasts.

"When?" I ask him.

"The moon after next."

I watch as he moves through the store. His back is long and straight, as if his ancestors were royal palms. He gathers herbs from various jars, then reaches for a white votive candle and a bottle of holy water.

"Begin with a bitter bath," he says, lining up the ingredients on the counter. "Bathe with these herbs for nine consecutive nights. Add the holy water and a drop of ammonia, then light the candle. On the last day, you will know what to do."

I reach in my jeans to pay him but he holds up his palm.

"This is a gift from our father Changó."

I can't wait to get back to my room and fill up the bathtub so I take a shortcut through Morningside Park. I feel shielded by the herbs, by the man with the straight spine and starched cotton fez. An elm tree seems to shade the world with its aerial roots. It begins to rain and I pick up my pace. The herbs shift rhythmically in my sack like the seeds of a maraca.

I remember the nannies in Cuba with their leaves and rattling beads. They prayed over me, sprinkled cinnamon in my bath, massaged my stomach with olive oil. They covered me with squares of flannel in the dead heat of summer.

The nannies told my mother that I stole their shadows, that I made their hair fall out and drove their husbands to other women. But my mother didn't believe them. She fired the nannies without an extra day's pay.

One night there was a furious thunderstorm. Lightning hit the royal palm outside my window. From my crib, I heard it snap and fall. The fronds whined in the wind. The aviary shattered. The toucans and cockatoos circled in confusion before flying north.

My new nanny wasn't afraid. She told me that it was only the temperamental Changó, god of fire and lightning. Changó, she said, once asked a young lizard to take a gift to the lover of a rival god. The lizard put the present in its mouth and scurried to the lady's house but it tripped and fell, swallowing the precious trinket.

When Changó found out, he tracked down his inept accomplice to the foot of a palm tree. The terrified reptile, unable to speak, ran up the tree and hid among the fronds, the gift still lodged in its throat. Changó, who believed the lizard was mocking him, aimed a lightning bolt at the tree, intending to scorch the sorry creature dead.

Since then, Lucila explained, Changó often takes out his rage on innocent palm trees, and to this day the lizard's throat is swollen and mute with the god's gift.

Three boys surround me suddenly in the park, locking me between their bodies. Their eyes are like fireflies, hot and erased of memory. The rain beads in their hair. They can't be more than eleven years old.

The tallest one presses a blade to my throat. Its edge is a scar, another border to cross.

A boy with a high, square forehead grabs the sack with the dried herbs and throws my Beny Moré album like a Frisbee against the elm. It doesn't break and I'm reassured. I imagine picking up the record, feeling each groove with my fingertips.

The boys push me under the elm, where it's somehow still dry. They pull off my sweater and carefully unbutton my blouse. With the knife still at my throat, they take turns suckling my breasts. They're children, I tell myself, trying to contain my fear. Incredibly, I hear the five-note pounding of Lou Reed's "Street Hassle," that crazy cello with its low, dying voice.

I watch as the last boy pinches some of the herb and arranges it on a rectangle of paper in his palm. He shapes it into a narrow cylinder then rolls the paper, licking the edge with the delicacy of a preening cat.

"Who's got a match?" he demands and the boy with the square forehead offers him a flame from a red plastic lighter. The boy takes a deep breath and holds it in his lungs. Then he passes it to the others.

I press my back against the base of the elm and close my eyes. I can feel the pulsing of its great taproot, the howling cello in its trunk. I know the sun sears its branches to hot wires. I don't know how long I sit against the elm, but when I open my eyes, the boys are gone. I button my blouse, gather up my herbs and my album, and run back to the university.

In the library, nothing makes sense. The fluorescent lights transmit conversations from passing cars on Broadway. Someone's ordering a bucket of chicken wings on 103rd Street. The chairman of the linguistics department is fucking a graduate student named Betsy. Gandhi was a carnivore. He came of age in Samoa. He traversed a subcontinent in blue suede shoes. Maybe this is the truth.

I buy apples and bananas in the cafeteria and eat them furtively in my room. I'd prefer a cave, a desert, a more complete solitude.

I light my candle. The bath turns a clear green from the herbs. It has the sharp scent of an open field in spring. When I pour it on my hair, I feel a sticky cold like dry ice, then a soporific heat. I'm walking naked as a beam of light along brick paths and squares of grass, phosphorescent and clean.

At midnight, I awake and paint a large canvas ignited with reds and whites, each color betraying the other. I do this for eight more nights.

On the ninth day of my baths, I call my mother and tell her we're going to Cuba.

Talking to the Dead

JUDITH ORTIZ COFER

My grandfather is a *Mesa Blanca* spiritist. This means that he is able to communicate with the spirit world. And since almost everyone has a request or complaint to make from the *Other Side*, Papá once was a much sought-after man in our pueblo. His humble demeanor and gentle ways did much to enhance his popularity with the refined matrons who much preferred to consult him than the rowdy *santeros* who, according to Papá, made a living through spectacle and the devil's arts. *Santería*, like voodoo, has its roots in African blood rites, which its devotees practice with great fervor. *Espiritismo*, on the other hand, entered the island via the middle classes who had discovered it flourishing in Europe during the so-called "crisis of faith" of the late nineteenth century. Poets like Yeats belonged to societies whose members sought answers in the invisible world. Papá, a poet and musician himself when he was not building houses, had the gift of clairvoyance, or *facultades*, as they are called in spiritism. It is not a free gift, however: being a spiritist medium requires living through *pruebas*, or tests of one's abilities.

Papá's most difficult *prueba* must have been living in the same house with Mamá, a practical woman who believed only in what her senses recorded. If Papá's eyes were closed that meant that her lazy man was sleeping in the middle of the day again. His visionary states and his poetry writing were, I have heard, the primary reasons why Mamá had, early in their married life, decided that her husband should "wear the pants" in the family only in the literal sense of the expression. She considered him a "hopeless case," a label she attached to any family member whose drive and energy did not match her own. She never changed her mind about his poetry writing, which she believed was Papá's perdition, the thing that kept him from making a fortune, but she learned to respect his *facultades* after the one incident that she could not easily dismiss or explain.

Although Papá had been building a reputation for many years as an effective medium, his gifts had not changed his position in Mamá's household. He had, at a time determined by his wife, been banished to the back of the house to pursue his interests, and as for family politics, his position was one of quiet assent with his wife's wise decisions. He could have rebelled against this situation: in Puerto Rican society, the man is considered a small-letter god in his home. But, Papá, a gentle, scholarly man, preferred a laissez-faire approach. Mamá's ire could easily be avoided by keeping his books and his spiritist practice out of her sight. And he did make a decent living designing and building houses.

In his room at the back of the house he dreamt his dreams and interpreted them. There he also received the spiritually needy: the recent widows, the women who had lost children, and the old ones who had started making plans for the afterlife. The voices were kept low during these consultations. I know from having sat in the hallway outside his door as a child, listening as hard as I could for what I thought should be taking place—howlings of the possessed, furniture being thrown around by angry ghosts—ideas I had picked up from such movies as *Abbot and Costello Meet the Mummy,* and from misinterpreting the conversations of adults. But, Papá's seances were more like counseling sessions. Sometimes there were the sounds of a grown person sobbing—a frightening thing to a child—and then Papá's gentle, persuasive voice. Although most times I could not decipher the words, I recognized the tone of sympathy and support he was offering them. Two or more voices would at times join together in a chant. And the pungent odor of incense seeping through his closed door made my imagination quicken with visions of apparitions dancing above his table, waiting to speak through him to their loved ones. In a sort of trance myself, I would sometimes begin softly reciting an *Our Father,* responding automatically to the familiar experience of voices joined together in prayer and the church-smell of incense. What Papá performed in his room was a ceremony of healing. Whether he ever

"Talking to the Dead" is reprinted with permission from the publisher of *Silent Dancing: A Partial Remembrance of a Puerto Rican Childhood,* by Judith Cofer Ortiz (Houston: arte Publico Press—University of Houston, 1990).

communicated with the dead I cannot say, but the spiritually wounded came to him and he tended to them and reassured them that death was not a permanent loss. He believed with all the passion of his poet's heart, and was able to convince others, that what awaits us all after the long day of our lives was a family reunion in God's extensive plantation. I believe he saw heaven as an island much like Puerto Rico, except without the inequities of backbreaking labor, loss and suffering which he could only justify to his followers as their prueba on this side of paradise.

Papá's greatest prueba came when his middle son, Hernán, disappeared. At the age of eighteen, Hernán had accepted a "free" ticket to the U.S. from a man recruiting laborers. It was a difficult time for the family, and reluctantly, Mamá had given Hernán permission to go. Papá, on the other hand, had uncharacteristically spoken out against the venture. He had had dreams, nightmares, in which he saw Hernán in prison, being tortured by hooded figures. Mamá dismissed his fears as fantasy-making, blaming Papá's premonitions on too much reading as usual. Hernán had been a wild teenager, and Mamá felt that it was time he became a working man. And so Hernán left the island, promising to write to his parents immediately, and was not heard from again for months.

Mamá went wild with worry. She imposed on friends and relatives, anyone who had a contact in the U.S., to join in the search for her son. She consulted with the police and with lawyers, and she even wrote to the governor, whose secretary wrote back that the recruiting of Puerto Rican laborers by mainland growers was being investigated by the authorities for the possibility of illegal practices. Mamá began to have nightmares herself in which she saw her son mistreated and worse. Papá stayed up with her during many of her desperate vigils. He said little, but kept his hands on his Bible, and would often seem to be speaking to himself in a trance. For once, Mamá did not ridicule him. She may have been too wrapped up in her despair. Then one night, Papá abruptly rose from his chair and rushed to his room where, with his carpenter's pencil, he began drawing something on the white cloth of his special table. Mamá followed him, thinking that her husband had gone mad with suffering for their child. But seeing the concentration on his face—it seemed to be lit with a light from within, she later told someone—she stood behind him for what seemed a long time. When he finished, he held a candle over the table and began explaining the picture as if to himself. "He is in a place far north. A place without a name. It is a place that can be found only by one who has been there. Here, there are growing things. Fruit, maybe. Sweet fruit. Not ready to be picked yet. There are lights in the distance. And a tall fence. Hernán sleeps here among the lights. He is dreaming of me tonight. He is lonely and afraid, but not sick or hurt."

Mamá began to see the things Papá described in the rough pencil lines on that tablecloth. Her mind turned into a map of memories, scraps of information, lines from letters she had received over the years, Christmas cards from strange places sent by a dozen nephews, or the sons of neighbors—young men for whom she had been a second mother—until she remembered this: a few years before Hernán's departure, Alicia's (Mamá's older sister) son, had also been "recruited" as a laborer. Like Hernán, he had not been informed as to exactly where he was going, only that it was in another Nueva York, not the city. Unlike her own son, her nephew had written home to say that he had been picking strawberries and did not like the job. Soon after, he had moved to a city near the farm where he had worked for a season. There he had married and settled down. Alicia would know the name of the place. But Papá had said it was a place without a name. Mamá decided to follow up on the only premonition she had ever allowed into her practical mind.

At that early hour, not quite dawn, the two of them set out for the country, where Alicia lived; Papá was armed with his Bible and the symbol of his calling: a mahogany stick he had carved into a wand. Every spiritist must make one and take it with him on house calls. It is hollow and sometimes filled with Holy Water in order to keep "evil influences" at a distance, but Papá had put a handful of dirt from his birthplace in his, perhaps because his calling as a medium was more than anything a poet's choice of missions: a need to accept mortality while struggling for permanence. Anyway, that earthfilled stick was the only weapon I ever knew Papá to carry. That morning he and his wife walked together in silence, a rare occurrence: to Mamá, long silences were a vacuum her nature abhorred. They came home with hope in the form of a telephone number that day.

After sending for the high school English teacher to interpret, they called the city of Buffalo, New York. Mamá's nephew told them that he would start looking for Hernán at the farm right away. He said, everyone just called it "the farm."

It turned out that Hernán was at the farm. The situation was very bad. The workers had been brought there by an unscrupulous farm worker who kept the men (most of them very young and unable to speak English) ignorant as to their exact whereabouts. They lived in tents while they waited for the fruit to be ready for picking. Though they were given provisions, the cost was deducted from their paychecks, so by the time they were paid, their salary was already owed to the grower. The workers were told that mail was not picked up there and it would have to be taken to the nearest city after the harvest. Though Hernán and many of the other men protested their situation and threatened to strike, they knew that they were virtual prisoners and would have to wait for an opportunity to escape. Mamá's nephew had connections in Buffalo and was able to convince a social worker to accompany him to the farm where he found Hernán eager to lead the exodus. It was not as easy as that, though. Many days passed before an investigation was started which revealed the scheme behind the farm and many others like it based on the recruitment of young men under false pretenses. But Hernán had been found. And Mamá learned to respect, if not quite ever to publicly acknowledge, her husband's gift of clairvoyance.

She paid her tribute to him in her own way by embroidering a new cloth for his *mesa blanca* in a pattern based on his drawings of that night. She did it with white thread on white cloth, so that to see it one had to get very close to the design.

Mestizaje as a Locus of Theological Reflection (1983)

VIRGILIO ELIZONDO

The Hispanic Catholics of the United States have experienced a long history of neglect and oppression not only by society at large, but by the very church that is supposed to be our mother. We had somewhat been ministered to but we had never been invited to be active ministers in our own church. The church was so foreign to us that many felt that priests came only from Ireland or Spain, but it was unthinkable that we would become a priest or a religious.

Quite often we were scolded because we were not sure what the foreign missioners expected us to be as measured by the standards of the Catholicism in their place of origin. But hardly ever were we confirmed in our faith and helped to grow and develop in our pilgrimage of faith. Yet it was the deep faith and simple home practices of our *abuelitas* and *abuelitos* (grandparents) that sustained us in the faith and maintained us loyal to the Catholic tradition.

Church institutions had been so oppressive to us that when the Chicano movement started in the 1960s, the leaders often told priests and religious who tried to join them to get lost. They felt that the only way to help Hispanics get ahead was to get rid of Catholicism. It was painful to hear their insults, but as painful as their accusations were, we had to admit that they were true—if not totally, at least 95 percent of what they were saying against the church was correct. The church had kept us out and had by its silence approved the ongoing exploitation and oppression of Hispanics.

The Chicano movement gave inspiration to the Chicano clergy and later on to all the Hispanic clergy in this country. We began to organize and to work for change within our own church. It was quickly evident that it was not sufficient simply to use Spanish in the liturgy, create our own music, and get more people involved in the work of the church. Much more was needed. We needed both practical know-how so that we could make the structures of our society work in favor of our people and we needed to have a new knowledge about ourselves, our social situation, and our religious beliefs. Until now, others had been telling us who we were. Nobody had bothered to ask us "Who are you?" Until now, all kinds of experts had studied us, but no one had even sought to enter into conversation with us so that they might truly understand who we see ourselves to be. This was the very root of our oppression. We were not allowed to be who we were. We were never allowed to simply say: "I am."

It was at this moment of the struggle that we met Gustavo Gutiérrez and became aware of his method of doing theology. It was God-sent! He was conceptualizing and expressing perfectly what we felt had to be done but had no idea of how to do it or even that we were on the right track. From the documents of Vatican II and our own experience of exclusion, we pretty well sensed what had to be done, but it was not yet clear. Reading Gustavo's work was like turning on the light switch.

The first thing we learned from Gustavo was that theology is important and we cannot leave it to the theologians alone—and much less to theologians who are foreigners. Theology cannot be imported. Neither can it be developed in isolation from the believing and practicing community. It is a joint enterprise of the believing community, which is seeking the meaning of its faith and the direction of its journey of hope lived in the context of charity. Great theologies were coming out of other parts of the world, but no one could do our theologizing for us. We had both the privilege and the responsibility! What follows is an attempt to do our own interpretation of our Christian existence.

The Human Situation of Mexican Americans

The ancestors of today's Mexican Americans have been living in the presentday United States since the early 1600s. Our group did not cross the border to come to the United States; rather the United States expanded its borders and we found ourselves to be a part of the United States. Since the early beginnings, many generations have crossed the Rio Grande to come over to the other side of family lands. Yet we have always been treated as foreigners in our own countryside—exiles who never felt at home. The Mexican Americans are a people twice conquered, twice colonized, and twice mestisized. This is our socio-historical reality!

Mestizaje: *Undefined Identity and Consequent Margination*

Mestizaje is simply the mixture of human groups of different makeup determining the color and shape of the eyes, skin pigmentation, and makeup of the bone structure. It is the most common phenomenon in the evolution of the human species. Scientists state that there are few, if any, truly "pure" human groups left in the world and they are the weakest, because their genetic pool has been gradually drained. Through mixture, new human groups emerge and the genetic makeup is strengthened. Biologically speaking, *mestizaje* appears to be quite easy and natural, but culturally it is usually feared and threatening. It is so feared that laws and taboos try to prevent it from taking place, for it appears as the ultimate threat to the survival of the species itself.

Mestizaje could certainly come in various ways, but it is a fact of history that massive *mestizaje* giving rise to a new people usually takes place through conquest and colonization. This has certainly been the case of the Mexican and the Mexican American *mestizaje*. The first one came through the Spanish conquest of Mexico beginning in 1519, and the second one started with the Anglo-American invasion of the Mexican northwest beginning in the 1830s. The French biologist Ruffie states that, since the birth of Europe thirty-five thousand years ago when the invading Cro-Magnons mated with the native Neanderthals, no other event of similar magnitude had taken place until the birth of European Mexico some five hundred years ago. I would add that a similar event of equal magnitude is presently taking place in the southwest of the United States—an area larger than Western Europe and populated by several million persons.

Conquest comes through military force and is motivated by economic reasons. Yet, once it has taken place, conquest is totalitarian. It imposes not only the institutions of the powerful, but also a new worldview in conflict with the existing one. This imposition disrupts the worldview of the conquered in such a way that nothing makes sense anymore. In many ways, the ideas, the logic, the wisdom, the art, the customs, the language, and even the religion of the powerful are forced into the life of the conquered. Although the conquered try to resist, the ways and worldview of the powerful begin to penetrate their minds so that, even if political and economic independence come about, the native culture can never simply return to its pre-conquest ways.

Yet there is not only the obvious violence of the physical conquest, but the deeper violence of the disruption and attempts to destroy the conquered's inner worldview, which gives cohesion and meaning to existence. The conquered's fundamental core religious symbols provide the ultimate root of the group's identity because they mediate the absolute. They are the final tangible expressions of the absolute. There is nothing beyond them that can put us in contact with God. They are the ultimate justification of the worldview of the group and the force that cements all the elements of the life of the group into a cohesive, meaningful, and tangible world order. When such symbols are discredited or destroyed, nothing makes sense anymore. The worldview moves from order to chaos, from significant mystery to meaningless confusion.

Hence, the ushering in of new religious symbols, especially when they are symbols of the dominant group, are in effect the ultimate conquest. In a nonviolent way, missioners were the agents of a deeper violence. They attempted to destroy that which even the physical violence of the conquerors could not touch—the soul of the native people. In spite of the missionary's conscious opposition to the cruel and bloody ways of the conquistador, the nonviolent introduction of religious symbols of the Spanish immigrant in effect affirmed and justified the way of the powerful, and discredited and tried to destroy the way of the powerless. This same process has taken place with the predominantly Irish-German clergy and religious who have ministered to Mexican American Catholics.

The most devastating thing about the conquest is that it established a relationship so concrete and so permanent that it took on the nature of a metaphysical reality. In many ways, it determines the behavior and the characteristics of the members of each group. It even influences theological reflection as the members of the conquistador group will appeal to scripture and theology to explain and legitimate the relationship. In his classic book *The Righteous Empire*, Martin Marty gives an excellent exposition of how theology and biblical studies can be used to legitimize oppression. The powerful now establish their own version of truth as objective truth for everyone and impose it through their various means of power.

The image of the conquistador as "superior" and of the conquered as "inferior" will be imposed and interiorized by all the media of communications: dress, food, manners, language, modes of thinking, art, music, bodily gestures, mannerisms, entertainment, and all the institutions of society, such as the family, economics, school system, politics, and church, and most of all the religious imagery and mythology. It is now the gods of the powerful who preside over the new world order. The totalitarian image that colonizing Europe established and implanted in the colonized peoples as the universal model for everyone continues to have a determining influence around the world. This "normative image" of Western civilization continues to be reinforced and projected through television and movies, books, periodicals, universities, and the European/United States-controlled religions. Only the white Western way appears as the truly human way of life; all others continue to be relegated to an inferior status. This is not necessarily a conscious effort, but it takes place all the time.

Yet, in spite of the difficult situation of inequality, the very seeds for the destruction of this dichotomy of colonizer-superior vs. colonized-inferior are physically implanted by the conquistador himself. Through his very bodily intercourse with the women of the conquered group, a new biological-cultural race is born, a race that will be both conquistador and conquered, superior and inferior, at one and the same time: he or she will be a real blood sister/brother of both, without being exclusively either. Furthermore, because the mother is the fundamental transmitter of deep cultural traits, it is the culture of the conquered that will gradually triumph over the culture of the conquistador in providing the dominant and deepest personality characteristics of the new group.

Mestizos are born out of two histories and in them begins a new history. The symbolic and mental structures of both histories begin to intermingle so that out of the new story which begins in the *mestizo* new meanings, myths, and symbols will equally emerge. They will be meaningful to the *mestizo* as the firstborn of a new creation, but will remain incomprehensible to persons who try to understand them through the meanings, mythologies, and symbols of either of the previous histories alone. Yet from birth to maturity, there is a long period of painful search.

The deepest suffering of the *mestizo* comes from what we might call an "unfinished" identity or, better yet, an undefined one. One of the core needs of human beings is the existential knowledge that regardless of who I am socially or morally, I am. The knowledge of fundamental belonging—that is, to be French, American, Mexican, English—is in the present world order one of the deepest needs of persons. When this need is met, it is not even thought about as a need; but when it is missing, it is so confusing and painful that we find it difficult to even conceptualize it or speak about it. We strive "to be like" but we are not sure just which one we should be like. As Mexican Americans, we strive to find our belonging in Mexico or in the United States—only to discover that we are considered foreign by both. Our Spanish is too Anglicized for the Mexicans and our English is too Mexicanized for the Anglos.

In the case of Mexico, it was the *mestizo* image of Our Lady of Guadalupe that provided the beginning of the new socio-cultural synthesis. It was not merely an apparition, but the perfect synthesis of the religious iconography of the Iberian peoples with that of native Mexicans into one coherent image. This marks the cultural birth of a new people. Both the parents and the child now have one common symbol of ultimate belonging. For the first time, they can begin to say "we are." As the physical birth of Mexicans had come through conquest, cultural birth came through the new image. It is only after the apparition that those who had wanted to die now wanted to live and to celebrate life. In and through Our Lady, new meanings, myths, and symbols will begin to emerge that will be truly representative and characteristic of Mexico.

Struggles for Accepting and Belonging

In the first stages of the struggle to belong, the *mestizo* will try desperately to become like the dominant group, for only its members appear to be fully civilized and human. This struggle includes every aspect of life, because the whole world structure of the dominant will have been assimilated and made normative for human existence. It equally involves a violent rejection of the way of the conquered, because that now appears to be inferior. Only the scholars of the dominant group will appear as credible, only their universities as prestigious, their language as civilized, their medical practices as scientific, and their religion as true religion. The dominated will sometimes attempt to keep some of their original folklore, but, in every other way, they try to become like the dominant.

Some of the well-intentioned and kind members of the dominant group will help the brighter and more promising ones (according to their own standard of judgment) to better themselves by "becoming like us." They will privilege them with scholarships to the best universities in Europe or the United States and help them to learn the European or American way of life and language.

Some of the marginated will make it into the world of the dominant society, only to discover that they will never be allowed to belong fully, and furthermore that down deep inside they are still somewhat "other." Yet it is this very pain of not being able to belong fully that also marks the beginning of a new search.

In the first stages of the search, the ones who choose not to join the struggle to become like the dominant ones will tend to reject the world of the dominant in a total way: absolutely nothing good can come of it. They will not only reject it but will hate it passionately. The only way to treat the dominant ones is to get rid of them. They are the ones who are guilty not only of the individual sin of homicide, but of the collective sin of ethnocide.

Throughout all these struggles, there is something radically new beginning to emerge. Even though the seeds are planted from the very beginning and biologically this new life begins from the very start, it will take time for cultural identity to emerge as a distinct identity of its own. This new identity does not try to become like someone else, but it struggles to form its own unique individuality. It accepts from both parent cultures without seeking to be a replica of either. It is like the maturing child who no longer tries to be like the mother or like the father, nor to simply reject both of them, but is simply himself or herself. Through the pains and frustrations of trying to be what we are not, the uniqueness of our own proper identity begins to emerge. It is an exciting moment of the process and usually the most creative state in the life of the group.

It is at this moment that the quest to know ourselves begins to emerge in a serious way. In the beginning, knowledge of ourselves will be confused because we see ourselves through a type of double image—that is, through the eyes of the two parent groups. As the group develops, its own proper image will begin to emerge and it will be easier to study ourselves more critically. It is this new and more clearly defined self-image of who we are as Mexican Americans that is presently beginning to take shape. As usual, it is the poets, the artists, and the musicians who are beginning to point and to sing and to suggest the new identity. It is now the critical thinkers who are coming in and beginning to deepen, conceptualize, verbalize, and communicate the reality of our identity. And it is only now that for the first time we begin to ask ourselves about our Christian identity, about our church, and about our religion. What does it really mean? Who are we as Mexican American Christians?

The Human Situation: Divisions and Collective Self-Protection

When one looks at the history of humanity, wars, divisions, and family fights appear more natural than do peace, unity, and harmony. This is evident from the global level down to the family cell. It appears more natural for brothers and sisters to fight one another than to love one another. We struggle to protect ourselves against each other and to conquer others before they conquer us. We prepare for peace by preparing for war. Only violent means appear to help us control or curb violence. Might makes right because power establishes its views as objective truth so as to justify its own position of privilege. The survival of the fittest appears to be the first law of individuals and of society—the survival of the powerful at the cost of the weak.

From this struggle for survival at the cost of others, certain anthropologico-sociological characteristics and behavioral laws appear. The members of the dominant group in power see themselves as pure, superior, dignified, well-developed, beautiful, and civilized. They see themselves as the model for all others. They see their natural greatness as the source of their great achievements. Even the least among them consider themselves superior to the best of the dominated group.

On the other hand, they look upon the conquered and colonized as impure, inferior, undignified, under-developed, ugly, uncivilized, conservative, backward. Their ways are considered childish and their wisdom is looked upon as superstition. Because might is subconsciously assumed to be right, everything about the weak is considered to be wrong and unworthy of being considered human. The conquered are told that they must forget their backward ways if they are to advance and become human. Acculturation to the ways of the dominant, in every respect whatsoever, is equated with human development and liberation.

Even the best among the dominant group find it very difficult to truly accept the other as other: to enjoy their foods, learn from their wisdom, speak their language, dress in their styles, appreciate their art and their music, interpret life through their philosophies, live in their ways, even worship through their forms of cult. Even though many go out, even heroically, to be of service to the poor and the oppressed, and really love them, there is still an inner fear and rejection of their otherness. The way of the powerful as the normative human way for all persons is so deeply ingrained that it takes a dying to oneself to break through the cultural enslavements that keep the dominant from appreciating the inner beauty, the values, the worth, and the dignity of the ways of the conquered.

Because of the image imposed upon them about themselves, some of the conquered will begin to think of themselves as inferior and good for nothing. This develops a type of domesticated, happy-go-lucky, subservient attitude in relation to the dominant. It is a very dehumanizing existence, but the powerless have no choice—either conform to the status assigned by the powerful or be eliminated physically. Law and order work in favor of the rich against the poor. Whereas the rich tend to be considered innocent until proven guilty, the poor are usually considered guilty until proven innocent. They are blamed for all the problems of society and are considered to be the source of all evil and crime. Thus, the very victims of the institutionalized violence of power are labeled by the establishment as the causes of this violence! The powerful can define the image and status of the oppressed as "guilty of all evil" and force them to live accordingly. The poor and the oppressed thus serve as scapegoats for the crimes of the establishment, which can continue to think of itself as pure and immaculate. However, as long as the traditions of the oppressed continue, especially their deepest religious traditions, they may be forced to live as dirt, but they cannot be forced to perceive themselves as such. Through their traditions, perfectly understood by them but incomprehensible to foreigners, they continue to perceive themselves as they truly are: free human beings with full human dignity who, although dominated through external powers, nevertheless remain free and independent in the innermost core of their being.

The in-group will defend tradition, law, and order because its members are the privileged ones of the establishment. National and personal security will be among the top priorities of this group as it strives to maintain the status quo. For the powerful, tradition protects their position of privilege; for the powerless, their own traditions are the ultimate rejection of the status quo of the dominant—their bodies might be dominated but not their souls.

Tradition functions in a diametrically opposed way for the powerful and for the powerless. For the powerless, tradition is the affirmation of inner freedom, independence, and self-worth. It is the power for the radical transformation of the existing order. For the moment, it might appear as a tranquilizer, but we should not underestimate its power in keeping a people alive as a people. As long as their traditions are alive, they are assured of life and ultimate liberation. If their traditions disappear, they will no longer have to work for integral liberation because they will have ceased to exist as a people.

In attempting to analyze the dynamics between the oppressor in-group and the oppressed out-group, three constants seem to function as anthropological laws of human behavior.

First, when one studies the human story across the ages, the tendency of group inclusion/exclusion—that is, to protect our own by keeping others out—appears to be one of the most consistent and fundamental anthropological laws of nature. Dominant groups will struggle to curtail outside influences in a multiplicity of ways, and weaker or dominated ones will likewise fear and resist any type of intrusion. The purity of the group must be maintained. Human barriers of race, class, language, family name, education, economic status, social position, and religion are regularly used as signals to distinguish "our own" from "the others."

The second tendency that appears as an anthropological law of nature is: others can be used and enjoyed, but a social distance must be maintained. Deep friendships might develop and even strong love relationships, but the social barriers are so deeply interiorized and assimilated that they are very difficult to do away with. There are not just laws that keep peoples apart, but also sustain the relationship of superior-inferior that is established, projected, transmitted, assimilated, and even sacralized by religion. This keeps persons from truly appreciating each other as fully equal and from seeing the true human dignity of one another. Even the best among the dominant group tend to see and treat the others as inferior and "different." We can even do good things for the lesser others, but they remain lesser. They can be exploited legitimately, because the culture and the laws of the dominant sanction the superior-inferior relationship. This gives the "master" the right and the obligation to use and "protect" the lesser ones.

This law of social distance is probably the hardest one to break through, because it is not only enforced by external laws and the economic-political mechanisms of the land, it is also interiorized in a number of ways. For example, in ordinary commercials we see blacks waiting on whites, but I have never seen a commercial with a white serving a black. Blacks, but never racially mixed families, appear in commercials. Brown skins do not even appear at all. Social barriers of separability are drilled into a people through all the media of communication and education. Even religious education material and religious images in our churches exhibit a definite racial preference, thus indirectly telling the others that they cannot be reflected in the sacred.

Finally, the third constant that appears as an anthropological law of nature is: anyone who threatens to destroy or annul the barriers of separation will be an outcast—an impure untouchable who must be eliminated.

As should be evident by now, *mestizaje* is feared by established groups because it is the deepest threat to all the humanly made barriers of separation that consecrate oppression and exploitation. It is a threat to the security of ultimate human belonging—that is, to the inherited national/cultural identity that clearly and ultimately defines who I am to myself and to the world. It is even a deeper threat to established societies because the *mestizo* cannot be named with clarity and precision. So much is in the mystery of a name! I am comfortable when I can name you for, in many ways, it indicates that I am somewhat in control of the situation. I may not like what I know, but at least I have the comfort of knowing what it is. But there is a nervousness when I do not know who you are—your name and your cultural nationality are so important, for they tell me who you are personally and fundamentally. They give me your immediate and ultimate human identity.

Because of their hyphenated identity, *mestizos* cannot be named adequately by either group's categories of analysis. They do not fit into the single-history set of norms for testing and identifying persons. This is threatening to both groups—we can name them and even study them, but they cannot name us or even figure out how to really study us. It is threatening for anyone to be in the presence of one who knows us very well, even in our innermost being, but we do not know who they are. To be an outside-insider, as the *mestizo* is, is to have both intimacy and objective distance at one and the same time. Insofar as we are in Mexico, we are outside the United States; but insofar as we are in the United States, we are distant from Mexico. As such we can see and appreciate the aspects of both, aspects which neither sees of themselves or each other. In this very in-out existence lies the potential for our creativity: to pool the cultural genes and the chromosomes of both so as to create a new being!

The potential for newness will not be actualized automatically. The *mestizo* can simply become like one of the parent groups and continue to do unto others as they have done unto us. However, they can equally, although with more hidden difficulties than anyone suspects, choose to live out the radical meaning of their new being. This is exciting but difficult because, even though the dominant way may be rejected totally and explicitly, subconsciously the oppressed will strive to become like the oppressor, for they have already assimilated many of the dominant group's characteristics. Will the group simply obtain power and acceptance by reverting to the ways of the parent group or will they initiate new life? That is the key question.

As a Mexican American Christian, I am convinced that the full potential of *mestizaje* will be actualized only in and through the way of the Lord, which brings order out of chaos and new life out of death. It is in the Lord's way that the salvific and liberating role of our *mestizo* humanity finds its ultimate identity, meaning, direction, and challenge.

The Concrete Historical Meaning of God's Saving Way
The Human Identity of the Savior

The racial-cultural identity of a person is the very first and immediate revelation of who one is. We all have stereotype prejudices about certain colors, accents, languages, features, regions, and religions. There is a natural tendency to categorize persons according to our stereotypes of them and to prejudge them as to their human worth and potential even before they have said or done anything. Looks are all-important and they are the first revelation, according to the standards of the world, of the person's worth and dignity. Persons from the outer regions of any country are usually looked down upon as rustics, whereas those from urban centers look upon themselves as sophisticated.

What was the racial-cultural identity of Jesus? What did others think of when they first saw or heard of him, before they even heard him speak or saw his actions? These are all-important questions, for we know from the New Testament itself that it is in the human face and heart of Jesus that God has been self-revealed to us. It is through the full humanity of Jesus that God has allowed us to see God in a human way.

There is no doubt that, during his lifetime, Jesus was regularly known as a Galilean, that most of his disciples were from Galilee, and that most of the things we remember best of his activity took place in Galilee. There is no doubt that Galilee plays a key role in the life and mission of Jesus as presented in the Gospels.

The full human signification of the *kenosis* of the Son of God becomes evident when we look at the image of Galilee in Jesus' time. First of all, if it had not been for Jesus, Galilee would probably remain an unknown region of the world. Jerusalem, Greece, and Rome were all important with or without Jesus, but not Galilee. It was an outer region, far from the center of Judaism in Jerusalem of Judea and a crossroads of the great caravan routes of the world. It was a region of mixed peoples and languages. In Galilee the Jews were looked down upon and despised by the others as they were in the rest of the world. They were considered to be stubborn, backward, superstitious, clannish, and all the negative stereotypes one could think of. Furthermore, the Jews of Judea looked down upon the Galilean Jews, for they considered them ignorant of the law and the rules of the temple, contaminated in many ways by their daily contacts with pagans, and not capable of speaking correct Greek, for their language was being corrupted by admixture with the other languages of the region. In short, their own Jewish relatives regarded them as inferior and impure. Because of their mixture with others, they were marginated by their own people. There were no doubts about the cultural *mestizaje* that was taking place and, knowing the ordinary situation of human beings, a certain amount of biological *mestizaje* was equally taking place. Culturally and linguistically speaking, Jesus was certainly a *mestizo* between Judaism and the other cultures that flourished throughout Galilee. And we know from the early Jewish charges that tried to discredit Jesus that he was even accused of being the bastard son of a Roman soldier named Pantera, which could also be a colloquial term simply meaning "a Roman," which could have made of him a biological *mestizo* as well. I am, of course, in no way denying or even questioning that Jesus was conceived by the Holy Spirit. What I am saying is that in his human appearance, as viewed by those who knew him only in a worldly way and not through the eyes of faith, he certainly appeared to be of mixed origins. The New Testament itself gives clear evidence that nothing good was expected to come out of Galilee.

The point of bringing out all this is to appreciate the human beginnings of God's mission. God becomes not just a human being, but the marginated, shamed, and rejected of the world. He comes to initiate a new human unity, but the all-important starting point is among the most segregated and impure of the world. Among those whom the world has thrown out, God will begin the way to final unity. It is among those whom the world labels as "impure" that a new criterion for real purity will emerge.

Although the world expected nothing good to come out of Galilee, God chose it to be the starting point of God's human presence among us. The principle behind the cultural image of the Galilean identity is that God chooses what the world rejects. What is marginal to the world is central to God. It is through those whom the world has made nothing that God will reduce to nothing the power and wisdom of the world. It is through the poor and non-persons of the world that God continues to reveal God's face and heart in a human way and among them—the Galilees and Galileans of today—salvation continues to begin for all the peoples of the world.

The Cultural Function of His Mission

The mission of Jesus is not some sort of esoteric or aesthetic truth. He comes to live out and proclaim the supreme truth about humanity, which will have immediate and long-term implications in everyday life and in the history of humanity. Those who hear his word and are converted to his way will see themselves and will equally see all others in a radically new way. This new image of self and others will allow everyone to relate with each other as never before.

Because of his concrete human identity, Jesus had personally suffered the pains of margination and dehumanizing insults. He was concerned with the pains of hunger, sickness, bad reputation, rejection, shame, class struggles, loneliness, and all the real sufferings of humanity. His concern was not abstract, but real and immediate. He spoke with the Samaritan woman, ate with the rich, the tax collectors, and sinners alike. He did not feel repelled by the leper; he enjoyed the company of women and little children. Jesus was truly at home with everyone and it is evident that everyone felt at home with him. This is nowhere more evident than in his ability to enjoy himself in table fellowship with everyone without exception.

Out of the cultural suffering of rejection, Jesus offers a new understanding of the kingdom. He did not come to restore the kingdom of David for the Jewish people but to initiate the reign of God who is the Father of everyone. The innermost identity of Jesus was his life of intimacy with God-Father. It is this living relationship with the absolute that cuts through and relativizes all human images of importance or non-importance, be they dignified or undignified. When we know the ultimate origins of a person—that he is really the son of the king—the superficial appearances are no longer important. It is the ultimate origins and name of a person that give us his or her true worth. It is precisely this intimacy with God-Father which is the basis of the innermost identity of Jesus. It is not the labels that the world places on persons that count, but one's own innermost identity and image of oneself as reflective of the likeness of God.

By discovering that God is our Father we begin to see everything in a new way. No longer will I see others as superior or inferior to me, but as brothers and sisters of the same Father. In this realization is the basis for a totally new value system for humanity. In fidelity to God, Jesus refuses to conform to any human law or tradition that will dehumanize and make appear as inferior any human being whatsoever. The truth of Jesus will upset humankind's criteria of judgment. Because one is, one is a child of God. But precisely because everyone can now belong, those who have set up and guarded the multiple barriers of separation will not only refuse the invitation but will discredit the new way and try to prevent it from coming into existence. This allows them to enjoy the privileges of being "in" at the cost of keeping the so-called inferior ones "out."

But it is not sufficient to invite the rejected into the kingdom. It is not sufficient to tell the exploited and marginated of society that they are truly free human beings who are equal to all others. One must go to the roots of the human mechanisms, both to the external and the internal structures of society, to make known the segregating and dehumanizing evil that has been institutionalized and is now hidden in the various structures of the group. Jesus makes known that he must go to Jerusalem, where the sufferings of his people are highlighted. Truth in the service of love must bring out clearly the evil hidden in human structures, evil which passes as good. Such confusion allows the evils of power to appear as the good of society, while the sufferings of the marginated appear as the cause of all evil. Criminals appear as good; victims appear as criminals. This is the ongoing confusion of Babel, which continues to mask and confuse both the evil and the good of the world.

Jesus appears in the New Testament as the aggressive prophet of nonviolent love who refuses to endorse the violence of the structures and remains faithful to the tradition of the God of his people, of the God who sees the suffering, who hears the cries of affliction, and who wills to save. He questions the human traditions that oppress or destroy a people. Jesus must go to Jerusalem, because that is the center of institutionalized power. When he arrives he goes to the very core of Judaism: the temple. In Jerusalem we see Jesus who does not hesitate to question the very legitimacy of the structures that were enslaving the masses of the people. The house of the God of compassion and justice had become the place that now legitimized and covered up the evil ways of the establishment. The same story is found in all human institutions. We need institutions in order to live in an orderly and peaceful way. Yet, all institutions have the tendency to become self-serving to the benefit of those in control. They are set up to serve persons, but persons end up serving them. It is this very tendency to absolutize that must be confronted and made known.

As institutions, customs, and traditions become absolutized, they function as the idols of the group. Whether we call them God or not, they function as the real gods of the group. To question them is the same as questioning God. And when we challenge them, we will be accused of blasphemy. Yet to the degree that these ways dehumanize or reject any human being, they must be questioned in the name of God. But Jesus does not confront the power of the world with a power of the same order. He does not give in to the ways of humanity. He confronts the power of the world and human violence with a power of an entirely different order: the power of unlimited love which will not engage in violence to eliminate violence.

The nonviolent way of Jesus worked in a diametrically opposed way to the nonviolent way of the missioners of the power countries. First of all, he begins by assuming the way, the language, and the worldview of Galileans—the non-persons of the world. The all-powerful God, in becoming a Galilean, converts to become the marginated, the rejected, and the non-person of the world. Second, he not only denounces the accepted practices of the powerful, as good missioners often do, but, unlike the average traditional missioner, he even denounces and desacralizes their ultimate authority as enshrined in their religious symbols, for it is the religious symbols of the powerful that ultimately legitimize their way as God's way. Third, the radical difference between the missionary activity of Jesus and that of missioners who are culturally and nationally members of the powerful countries is apparent in the response of officials.

Official Judaism condemned Jesus and got rid of him. His accusers disowned him to the Romans because he questioned their ultimate authority and the ultimate legitimacy of their structures. The officials of mission-sending countries support and reinforce the missionary endeavor because it in effect affirms and perpetuates the legitimacy of their own world order. In supporting the missions, they affirm their own ultimate authority and the divine legitimacy of their ways. Let me be clear on this point: this is not necessarily done in an intentional or malicious way. In fact, I would say that quite often it is done with the best of intentions; however, the final result remains the same. The Spanish missioners did not hesitate to chastise openly and consistently the crimes and abuses of the conquest; however, they legitimized the way of the conquerors by affirming their ultimate symbol as superior and true in relation to the captured peoples' symbols of ultimate reality.

The way of Jesus to Jerusalem and the cross is the challenging task of those who are on the margins of society. Their temptation will always be to become simply the powerful themselves, as even the disciples wanted to do. But the challenge is to be willing to die so that a new way will truly be ushered in. The authorities kill Jesus but they cannot destroy him. He remains faithful to his way to the very end. He came to reject every type of human rejection and, even when all appear to have rejected him, even his God, he rejects no one. He dies in perfect communion with his people and his God. He came to tear down barriers of separation and, no matter what humans tried to do to stop him, they were not able to break him down. As he lived his life in communion with everyone—so he died. All had rejected him, but he rejects no one.

God's love in and through Jesus triumphs over all the divisive hatreds and consequent violence of humanity. Jesus passes through death to life. In resurrecting him, God rejects the rejection of humanity, destroys all the charges of illegitimacy, and demolishes the idolized structures. In the resurrection, God ratified the entire way and message of Jesus. It is from the resurrection that the entire way of Jesus and every aspect of his life takes on a liberating and salvific signification.

It is in the resurrection that the new life initiated and offered to everyone by Jesus is now fully and definitively present. No human power will be able to destroy it or slow it down. Jesus is the firstborn of the new creation, and in his followers a new human group now begins. It is definitely a new human alternative now present in the history of humanity.

First of all, those who had nothing to offer now have the best thing to offer to everyone: new life. It is the rejected and marginated Galileans who receive the Spirit and, without ceasing to be Galileans, now see themselves in a new way as they begin to initiate the new humanity. Everyone is invited, but it is the very ones who had been excluded who now do the inviting. It is obvious from the history of the early church how quickly the new way spread to all peoples. It crossed all boundaries of separation. Without ceasing to be who they were culturally, people nevertheless saw themselves in such a new way that the ordinary human barriers were no longer obstacles to the new fellowship.

It is equally evident that the crossing of cultural boundaries was not easy, for each group had its own unsuspected idols, yet the miracle is that it took place. Cultural-national groups which had been totally separated, now can come together—no longer Jew or gentile, master or slave, male or female, but all one in Christ. They continued to be who they were, but they lived their nationality and religion in a radically new way. Their identity was affirmed but their exclusiveness was destroyed. This openness led them to discover new values and criteria of judgment: from competition to cooperation, from divisions to unity, from strangers to a common family, from a superior or inferior status to common friends and all children of the same Father.

The radical all-inclusive way of Christianity started among the rejected and lowly of society. This is the starting point. In the Spirit, they struggle to build new human alternatives so that others will not have to suffer what they have had to suffer. It is they who first hear the invitation to the new universal family of God, and it is the converted poor and suffering of the world who see themselves in a new way, who now go out and invite—by deeds and words—all others into the new society. God continues to begin where humanity would never suspect. Out of the Nazareths and Galilees of today, salvation continues to reach the entire world.

The God-Meaning of Our Mexican American Identity and Mission

"God chose those whom the world considers absurd to shame the wise." (1 Cor. 1:28)

It is in the light of our faith that we discover our ultimate identity as God's chosen people. It is in the very cultural identity of Jesus the Galilean and in his way from Galilee to Jerusalem that the real ultimate meaning of our own cultural identity and mission to society become clear.

For those who ordinarily have a good sense of belonging, the idea of being chosen is nothing special. But for one who has been consistently ignored or rejected, the idea of being noticed, accepted, and especially chosen is not only good news, but new life. For in being chosen, what was nothing now becomes something, and what was dead now comes to life. In the light of the Judeo-Christian tradition, our experience of rejection and margination is converted from human curse to the very sign of divine predilection. It is evident from the scriptures that God chooses the outcasts of the world not exclusively but definitely in a preferential way. Those whom the world ignores, God loves in a special way. But God does not choose the poor and the lowly just to keep them down and make them feel good in their misery. Such an election would be the very opposite of good news and it would truly be the opium to keep the poor quiet and domesticated. God chooses the poor and the marginated of the world to be the agents of the new creation.

The experience of being wanted as one is, of being needed and of being chosen, is a real and profound rebirth. Those who had been made to consider themselves as nothing or as inferior will now begin to appreciate the full stature of human beings. Out of the new self-image, new powers will be released, powers which have always been there but have not been able to surface. Through this experience, the sufferings of the past are healed though not forgotten, and they should not be forgotten. For it is precisely out of the condition of suffering that the people are chosen so as to initiate a new way of life where others will not have to suffer what the poor have suffered in the past. When people forget the experience of suffering, as has happened to many of our immigrant groups in this country, such as the Irish in Boston, then they simply inflict the same insults upon others that had previously been inflicted upon them. The greater the suffering and the more vivid the memory of it, the greater the challenge will be to initiate changes so as to eliminate the root causes of the evils which cause the suffering. It is the wounded healer, the one who has not forgotten the pain of wounds, who can be the greatest healer of society's illnesses.

It is in our very margination from the centers of the various establishments that we live the Galilean identity today. Because we are inside-outsiders, we appreciate more clearly the best of the traditions of both groups, while equally appreciating the worst from the situation of both. It is precisely in this double identity that we in effect have something of unique value to offer both. The very reasons for the margination are the bases of our liberating and salvific potential not only for ourselves but for the others as well. In a privileged way, God is present in the marginated, for distance from the powers of the world is closeness to God. It is consistently in the borderlands regions of human belonging that God begins the new creation. The established centers seek stability, but the borderlands regions can risk to be pioneers. It is the borderlands people who will be the trailblazers of the new societies. "The stone which the builders rejected has become the keystone of the structure. It is the Lord who did this and we find it marvelous to behold" (Matt. 21:42).

"I have chosen you to go and bear much fruit." (John 15:16)

God chooses people not just to make them feel good, but for a mission. "I have chosen you to go and bear much fruit" (John 15:16). To accept God's election is not empty privilege, but a challenging mission. It is a call to be prophetic both in deeds and in words. It is a call to live a new alternative in the world, to invite others into it, and to challenge with the power of truth the structures of the world that keep the new alternative from becoming a reality.

Our Mexican American Christian challenge in the world today is not to become like someone else—Mexicans or Americans—but to combine both into a new way. It is through the very mechanisms of forging a new and more cosmopolitan identity that new life begins to emerge. It must be worked at critically, persistently, and creatively, for the temptation will always be there to become simply one or the other of the previous models. The temptation will always be there to restore the kingdom rather than to usher in the kingdom of God. In our present powerlessness we may think that this is stupid but, in our faith, we know that we must take the risks and begin to initiate new ways of life that will eliminate some of the dehumanizing elements of the present one. We know that we will not eliminate them all, nor will this come about easily and without much effort, organization, and frustration, but nevertheless the efforts must be made to introduce new forms and new institutions that will continue some of the best of the past while eliminating some of the worst. We will not build the perfect society, but we must do our part to at least build a better one. We must begin with the grassroots, but we must equally go to the very roots of the problems.

This is our "divine must"! We, too, must harden our faces and go to Jerusalem. We must go to the established centers of power, whether political, economic, educational, or religious, to confront their sacred idols which prevent them from truly serving all the people. It is the idols of society which function in favor of the rich and the powerful, and against the poor and powerless. It is they which mask the hidden viciousness and manipulations of the wise of the world who find many ways of exploiting the poor and the simple of the world.

We really do not have a choice if we want to be disciples following Jesus on his way to the cross. It is this road from Galilee to Jerusalem which has to be continued if evil is to be destroyed, not with new forms of evil, but with the power of truth in the service of love. We have no choice but to speak the truth which brings to light clearly the evil of the world, knowing full well that the powers of darkness will not stop at anything in order to put out the light.

"Your grief will be turned to joy." (John 16:20)

It is in our fiestas that our legitimate identity and destiny are experienced. They are not just parties; in fact they are the very opposite. They are the joyful, spontaneous, and collective celebrations of what has already begun in us even if it is not recognized by others or verbalized even by ourselves. It is the celebration of the beginning of the ultimate eschatological identity where there will be differences but not division. It is the celebration of what has already begun in germ but is yet to be totally fulfilled. The fiesta is a fore-taste and experience, even if for a brief moment, of the ultimate accomplishment. It is a result of who we are and a cause of what is yet to become. For just as it is true that the celebrations of the people can be used to drug the people and keep them in their misery, it is equally true that the fiestas can be used as rallying moments that not only give the people an experience of togetherness, but can also nourish the movements of liberation. In the fiestas, we rise above our daily living experiences of death to experience life beyond death. They are the moments of life that enable us to survive, come together, rally, and begin anew. The spirit not only to survive but to bring about a new existence can be enkindled in the fiestas so as to ignite the people to action.

Fiestas without prophetic action easily degenerate into empty parties, drunken brawls, or the opium to keep the people in their misery. But prophetic action without festive celebration is equally reduced to dehumanizing hardness. Prophecy is the basis of fiesta, but the fiesta is the spirit of prophecy. It is in the combination of the two that the tradition of faith is both kept alive and transmitted to newcomers. It is through the two of them that the God of history who acts on our behalf, on behalf of the poor and the lowly, continues to be present among us, bringing the project of history to completion.

Thus it is precisely through our fiestas that we are kept together as a people. It is through them that we have continued to maintain our identity and sense of belonging. They are the deepest celebrations of our existence—meaningful to those who belong and incomprehensible and folkloric to outsiders. They are the lifeline of our tradition and the life sources of our new existence.

Popular Religiosity, Spanish, and *Proyecto Histórico*—Elements of Latinas' Ethnicity

ADA MARÍA ISASI-DÍAZ

When the present is limiting—oppressive—one looks to the future to find a reason for living. Historically, religion has been used to encourage the poor and the oppressed to postpone hopes and expectations to "the next world." But liberation theologies turn the focus of the hopes and expectations of the poor and the oppressed from "the next world" to this world. For this reason liberation theologies are feared and opposed by those interested in maintaining the status quo.

In this chapter we will explore the hopes and expectations of Latinas grounded in our reality and aimed at historical fruition. It is the contention of *mujerista* theology that the *proyecto histórico*, historical project, of Latinas is one of the key elements in constructing our reality. We will then analyze popular religiosity and the role it plays in Latinas' struggle for survival, and how the Spanish language functions as part of Latinas' self-understanding and ethnic identification.

Latinas' Preferred Future: Our *Proyecto Histórico*

Mujerista theology uses the term *proyecto histórico* to refer to our liberation and the historical specifics needed to attain it. Though the plan is not a blueprint, it is "a historical project defined enough to force options."[1] It is a plan that deals with the structures of our churches, as well as with social, political, and economic institutions of society. The articulation of Latinas' *proyecto histórico* presented here is not only an explanation but also a strategy: it aims to help shape Latinas' understandings in our day-to-day struggle to survive, and our identity as a community. This articulation springs from our lived-experience and is a prediction of "our hopes and dreams toward survival,"[2] of our *lucha*—struggle.

Latinas' *proyecto histórico,* is based on an understanding of salvation and liberation as two aspects of one process. This is grounded in the belief that there is but one human history that has at its very heart the history of salvation. By "history of salvation" we refer to what we believe are divine actions—creation, incarnation, redemption—as well as our human responses to them, whether positive or negative. For us Latinas, salvation refers to having a relationship with God, a relationship that does not exist if we do not love our neighbor. Our relationship with God affects all aspects of our lives, all human reality. As Latinas become increasingly aware of the injustices we suffer, we reject any concept of salvation that does not affect our present and future reality. For us, salvation occurs in history and is intrinsically connected to our liberation.[3]

For Latinas, liberation has to do with becoming agents of our own history, with having what one needs to live and to be able to strive towards human fulfillment. Liberation is the realization of our *proyecto histórico*, which we are always seeking to make a reality while accepting that its fullness will never be accomplished in history. Liberation is realized in concrete events which at the same time point to a more comprehensive and concrete realization.[4] For Latinas to talk about salvation, liberation, and the coming of the kin-dom of God are one and the same thing. Historical events are never clearly nor completely the fulfillment of the kin-dom of God, but they affect such fulfillment; they are "eschatological glimpses," part of the unfolding of the kin-dom which we do not make happen but which requires us to take responsibility for making justice a reality in our world.

The realization of the kin-dom of God—liberation—is related to our present reality. Our *proyecto histórico* is not divorced from the present but rather is rooted in it, giving meaning and value to our daily struggle for survival. The present reality of Latinas makes it clear that in order to accomplish what we are stuggling for, we need to understand fully which structures are oppressive, denounce them, and announce what it is that we are struggling for.[5] Our struggle for liberation has to start with an analysis of the root causes of our oppression. Such an analysis shows our oppression to be multifaceted—an intersection of ethnic prejudice or racism, sexism, and economic oppression—all of which are intrinsic elements of patriachal and hierarchical structures. Analysis of oppression must then lead to effective denunciation.

Denunciation as part of Latinas' *proyecto histórico* is a challenge to understand and deal with present reality in the name of the future. Such a challenge does not consist only in criticizing, reproaching, and attacking those who maintain the structures that oppress us. Denunciation also has to do with repudiating such structures—not aspiring to participate in them—and refusing to benefit from them.[6] Therefore, *mujerista* theology is not to be only a resource for social criticism from the perspective of Latinas but is also socio-critical at its point of departure.[7] This means that we insist on our preferred future from the very beginning and insist that our *proyecto histórico* grounds our theological task, which we understand to be a liberative praxis.

To denounce oppressive structures without having a sense of what we believe our future should be is irresponsible. For Latinas' denunciation of oppression to be effective, we must also announce, that is, proclaim what is not yet but what we are committed to bringing about. In this context, annunciation, like analysis and denunciation, is indeed a liberative praxis, an exercise that is intended to yield tangible results. Denunciation and annunciation have to contribute effectively to the creation of new structures that make possible the liberation of Latinas and of all humanity. To announce is an intrinsic part of our insistence on fullness of life against all odds and in spite of all obstacles. Such insistence is incarnated in the concrete daily struggle of Latinas, a struggle which makes tomorrow a possibility. Whether that tomorrow is for ourselves or for our children makes no difference to us. Our annunciation becomes reality in our struggle to find or create spaces for self-determination, a key factor in the struggle for liberation. The challenge to be agents of our own history is what pushes us on to do the analysis, denounce those who oppress us, and engage in building a future society with alternative values, no matter how foolish our efforts appear to those with power.[8]

Liberation is a single process that has three different aspects or levels[9] which must not be confused or identified in any simplistic way. Each one maintains its specificity; each is distinct but affects the other; none is ever present without the others. None of those aspects exists in isolation from the others.[10] These three aspects of liberation also serve as points of entry for Latinas into the struggle for liberation because they are concrete aspects of our *proyecto histórico*. We refer to these different aspects of liberation as *libertad, comunidad de fe*, and *justicia*: freedom, faith community, and justice.

Libertad has to do with acting as agents of our own history. This aspect of liberation involves the process of conscientization, with how we understand ourselves personally in view of our preferred future. *Libertad* has to do with a self-fulfillment that renounces any and all self-promotion while recognizing that commitment to the struggle and involvement in it are indeed self-realizing. *Comunidad de fe* is the aspect of liberation that makes us face sin, both personal and social sin. *Comunidad de fe* is both our goal (rejecting sin) and the community that makes rejecting sin possible. *Justicia* here refers to the political, economic, and social structures we struggle to build that will make oppression of anyone impossible. *Justicia* has to do with the understandings that guide us, challenge us, and enable us to survive daily.

Since these three aspects of liberation are interconnected and happen simultaneously, it is difficult to speak about them separately. We do so to distinguish each from the other, to explain and understand how they interrelate without confusing them. The specifics we discuss as part of each of these three elements are not to be understood as relating only to a single element. Each of the specifics has implications for and relates to all three elements.[11]

The first element we will consider is that of *libertad*. In Latinas' struggle for survival we must take great care not to oppose structural change to personal liberation. What is "personal" for us Latinas is neither individual nor necessarily private. For us the term "individual" carries a pejorative meaning, a sense of egocentrism and selfishness that we believe to be inherently bad since it works against what is of great value to us, our communities. Our sense of community keeps us from arrogating a sense of privacy to all aspects of the personal. Therefore, for us, *libertad* involves being aware of the role we play in our own oppression and in the struggle for liberation. It includes being conscious of the role we must play as agents of our own history. *Libertad* has to do with being self-determining, rejecting any and all forms of determinism, whether materialistic, economic, or psychological.[12] It has to do with recognizing that the internal aspiration for personal freedom is truly powerful, as both a motive and a goal of liberation.[13]

Libertad as an element of liberation for us Latinas happens, then, at the psychological and the social level. The two main obstacles to *libertad* among Latinas are apathy and fear.[14] As an oppressed group within the richest country in the world, Latinas view our liberation as such an immense task that a common response is apathy. We often think of our task as beyond accomplishment, and apathy appears as a protection against frustration. For those of us for whom the *proyecto histórico* becomes a motivational factor strong enough to enable us to shake off our apathy, our next struggle is with fear. Our fear is not mainly the fear of failing—fear of trying and not accomplishing what we set out to do—but rather the fear of being co-opted by the status quo.[15]

A central and powerful myth in the U.S.A. tells all those who come here, as well as everyone in the world, that, because this is the best of all societies, whether one accomplishes what one wants or not depends on the individual. It depends on whether one is ambitious enough, gets a good education (which the myth maintains is available to everyone), and is willing to work hard and sacrifice oneself.[16] This myth is promulgated constantly in the most pervasive way possible. It contributes significantly to the negative self-image of Latinas who cannot get ahead, not because we do not try hard, but because of socio-economic realities that militate against us in all areas of life. If a negative self-image is oppressive, the fact that this myth fills us with fear, often robbing us of even envisioning our *proyecto histórico*, is insidious.

In order to counteract apathy and fear, we have to continue to elaborate our vision of the future at the same time that we work to articulate the details of our *proyecto histórico*. Making our preferred future a reality needs much more than vague generalities. Latinas' *proyecto histórico* has to be specific enough for each of us to know how we are to participate in the struggle to make it a reality, and what our task will be when it becomes a reality. All Latinas must know what it is we are being asked to contribute. Our *proyecto histórico* must have concreteness and specificity. Only when we know the concrete details can we face our shortcomings and the tremendous obstacles that we find along the way. Knowing concrete details can also help us face and conquer the fear that an unknown future brings. We can mitigate our fear by insisting on particulars, by being precise, by concretizing our vision of the future. The more tangible our *proyecto histórico* becomes, the more realizable it will be, since once it moves from vision to implementable plan, we will be able to transfer to this task of building our preferred future all the skills we do have—those skills we use effectively to survive every day.

Our explanation of *comunidad de fe* as an element of liberation starts by recognizing that Latinas' relationship with the divine is a very intimate one. It is not only a matter of believing that God is with us in our daily struggle, but that we can and do relate to God the same way we relate to all our loved ones.[17] We argue with God, barter with God, get upset with God, are grateful and recompense God, use endearing terms for God. This intimate relationship with the divine is what is at the heart of our *comunidad de fe*. For Latinas, it makes no sense to say one believes in God if one does not relate to the divine on a daily basis.[18]

Because Latinas relate intimately to the divine, we know that sin hurts such a relationship. We know that sin, while personal, is not private, for it is something that affects our communities negatively. The reflections of grassroot Latinas about evil give a clear sense of their understanding of sin:

> Sin is not a matter of disobedience but of not being for others. Not going to church is not a sin. But not to care for the children of the community—that is a sin, a crime! And the women take direct responsibility for what they do or do not do. Though they have a certain sense of predestination, they do not blame anyone but themselves for what goes wrong, On the other hand, God is given credit for the good that they do, the good that occurs in their lives.[19]

The analysis that our *proyecto histórico* demands can help us deepen our understanding of how sin affects those around us by helping us to understand "structural sin" and the role it plays in our oppression. We need to recognize that there are structures that have been set up to maintain the privilege of a few at the expense of the many and that those structures are sinful. Our analysis of oppressive structures will help us understand that sin is "according to the Bible the ultimate cause of poverty, injustice, and the oppression in which [we] . . . live."[20]

To understand the structural implications of sin, Latinas need to actualize our sense of *comunidades de fe* by setting up communities which are praxis-oriented, which bring together personal support and community action, and which have as a central organizing principle our religious understandings and practices as well as our needs.[21]

We have to accept, however, that most of the time we will not be able to depend on church structures and personnel to help us develop our communities. Once again we are going to have to depend on ourselves and, perhaps, we will be able to find help in the few national Latina organizations that claim to be committed to the struggle for liberation. Our *comunidades de fe* must also find ways of relating to community organizations. Where there are no Latina community organizations, the *comunidades de fe* need to fulfill that function. We must resist the temptation to let our *comunidades de fe* become "support groups" that separate our lives into realms: the personal from the communal, the spiritual from the struggle for justice.

Our *comunidades de fe* must also be ecumenical. We must embrace the grassroot ecumenism practiced by many Latinas who relate to more than one denomination because of their need to avail themselves of help no matter what its source. For others of us, our ecumenicism has to do with our belief that the struggle for liberation—and not the fact that we belong to the same church—must be the common ground of our *comunidades de fe*. Our ecumenism must take into consideration and capitalize on our *religiosidad popular*, popular religiosity.

Finally, the *comunidades de fe* have to develop their own models of leadership, communal leadership that recognizes and uses effectively the gifts of Latinas. Characteristics emerging from our historical reality will make it possible for the *comunidades de fe* to contribute effectively to the building of our *proyecto histórico*.

The third element of liberation is *justicia*. Justice as a virtue does not refer only or mainly to attitudes but to a tangible way of acting and being; it involves not only personal conduct but also the way social institutions—the building blocks of societal structures—are organized, the way they operate, prioritize issues, and use resources. Justice is not only a matter of taking care of the basic needs of the members of society, nor is it a utilitarianism that insists on the greatest happiness for the majority of people.[22] Justice is not a matter of "to each according to one's needs," as Marxist principles proclaim.[23] For *mujerista* theologians justice is all of this and much more. Justice is a Christian requirement: one cannot call oneself a Christian and not struggle for justice.

Our understanding of justice is based on the lived-experience of Latinas, an experience that has as its core multifaceted oppression. In *mujerista* theology *justicia* is a matter of permitting and requiring each person to participate in the production of the goods needed to sustain and promote human life. It has to do with rights and with the participation of all Latinas in all areas of life. Justice is indeed understood as the "common good." But striving for the "common good" can never be done at the expense of anyone. The "common good" is to be judged by the rights and participation of the poorest in society; it never places the rights of individuals against or over the rights and participation in society of others, particularly of the poor. It understands "welfare" in a holistic way and not just as limited to the physical necessities of life. In *mujerista* theology *justicia* is concretely expressed by being in effective solidarity with and having a preferential option for Latinas.[24]

Effective solidarity with Latinas is not a matter of agreeing with, being supportive of, or being inspired by our cause. Solidarity starts with recognizing the commonality of responsibilities and interests that all of us have despite differences of race or ethnicity, class, sex, sexual preference, age. Solidarity has to do with recognizing and affirming, valuing and defending a community of interests, feelings, purposes and actions with the poor and the oppressed. The two main, interdependent elements of solidarity are mutuality and praxis. Mutuality keeps solidarity from being a merely altruistic praxis by making clear that, if it is true that solidarity benefits the poor and the oppressed, it is also true that the salvation and liberation of the rich and the oppressors depend on it. Solidarity is truly praxis, because in order for a genuine community of interests, feelings, and purposes to exist between the oppressed and the oppressor, there must be a radical action on the part of the oppressors that leads to the undoing of oppression. Thus, for solidarity to be a praxis of mutuality, it has to struggle to be politically effective; it has to have as its objective radical structural change.[25]

Effective solidarity with Latinas demands a preferential option for the oppressed. This preferential option is not based on our moral superiority. It is based on the fact that Latinas' point of view,

> *pierced by suffering and attracted by hope, allows them, in their struggles, to conceive another reality. Because the poor suffer the weight of alienation, they can conceive a different project of hope and provide dynamism to a new way of organizing human life* for all.[26]

Solidarity with Latinas as oppressed people is a call to a fundamental moral option, an option that makes it possible and requires one to struggle for radical change of oppressive structures even when the specifics of what one is opting for are not known. As a matter of fact, only opting for a radical change of oppressive structures will allow the specifics of new societal structures to begin to appear.

The ability of Latinas to conceive "another reality" a different kind of social, political, and economic structure, is greatly hampered, as explained above, by the powerful U.S.A. myth regarding the possibility of success in this country for everyone. Poor and oppressed women in the shanty towns that surround Lima, Perú, for example, know very well that they will never be able to live—except as maids—in San Isidro, one of the rich neighborhoods in that city. Knowing that they cannot benefit from the present societal structures helps them to understand the need for radical change and to work for it. But it is not unusual to find Latinas living in the most oppressed conditions in the inner cities of the U.S.A. who think that if they work hard and sacrifice themselves, their children will benefit from the present order, and that they will eventually have the material goods and privileges this society claims to offer to all. I believe that this possibility, which becomes a reality for only the tiniest minority of Latinas and their children, hinders our ability to understand structural oppression. It keeps us from understanding that if we succeed in the present system, it will be because someone else takes our place at the bottom of the socio-economic-political ladder.

In order to overcome the temptation to leave behind oppression individually and at the expense of others, Latinas need to continue to set up strong community organizations. Such organizations are most important in constructing our own identity and strengthening our moral agency. Community organizations are fertile settings for supporting our liberative praxis. They provide spaces for us to gather our political will and power to help us question the present structures. Community organizations provide or help us to move into spaces that can bring together different political projects. These projects enable us to participate in the creation of a different kind of society—a participation that must be present if socio-economic transformation is to happen. Without community organizations that make it possible for us to analyze our reality and to explore alternatives, we will not be able to participate politically, socially, or economically at all levels of society; we will not be able to be agents of our own history, to make our *proyecto histórico* a reality.[27]

Our community organizing will be helped if those with privileges in this society are willing to stand in solidarity with us. To be in solidarity with Latinas is to use one's privileges to bring about radical change instead of spending time denying that one has privileges. For our part, Latinas must embrace the mutuality of solidarity; we have to be open to the positive role that those who become our friends by being in solidarity with us can play in our struggle for liberation. By culture and socialization Latinas are not separatists; we do not exclude others from our lives and from *la lucha*, nor do we struggle exclusively for ourselves. We extend this same sense of community to those who are in solidarity with us. They can enable us in our process of conscientization; they can help us see the deception behind the U.S.A. myth. They can assist us in getting rid of the oppressor within who at times makes us seek vengeance and disfigures our *proyecto bistórico* when we seek to exchange places with present-day oppressors.[28]

At present the unfolding of our *proyecto histórico* requires that Latinas organize to bring about an economic democracy in the U.S.A. that would transform an economy controlled by a few to the economy of a participatory community. Concretely, we must insist on a national commitment to full employment, an adequate minimum wage, redistribution of wealth through redistributive inheritance and wealth taxes, and comparable remuneration for comparable work regardless of sex, sexual preference, race, ethnicity, or age. Radical changes in the economics of the family that will encourage more "symmetrical marriages, allow a better balance between family and work for both men and women, and make parenting a less difficult and impoverishing act for single parents," the majority of whom are women, are a must.[29] We need a national health care plan with particular emphasis on preventive health care. Latinas call for a restructuring of the educational system so that our children and all those interested can study Latino culture and Spanish. We also call for a restructuring of the financing of public education so that its quality does not depend on the economics of those who live in the neighborhood served by a given school but is the responsibility of the whole community of that area, region, or state. Latinas must have access to political office to insure adequate representation of our community. Access to public means of communication including entertainment TV and movies is necessary so that the values of Latinas can begin to impact the culture of the nation at large.

Working for these changes in the U.S. system might not be considered radical enough. But we believe that these kinds of changes within the present system do strike at the

> essential arrangements in the class-power-ideology structure. To respond to these . . . [demands] would necessitate such a fundamental change in the ownership, and use of domestic and international wealth as to undercut the ruling class's position in American society and in the world, a development of revolutionary rather than reformist dimensions.[30]

These reforms demanded by Latinas significantly modify economic structures, gender, cultural relationships, and social and political institutions. Working for such changes also enhances our ability to build coalitions with other oppressed groups struggling for liberation. Thus we can have the numbers we need to be politically effective. Working for these changes strengthens our communities of struggle and makes our survival possible by enabling us to be self-defining and to strengthen our moral agency.[31]

Latinas' *proyecto histórico* is based on our lived-experience, which is mainly one of struggle against oppression. It has been argued that the subjectivity of lived-experience makes it impossible to consider it an adequate normative base. But the fact is that so-called adequate normative bases, such as different theories of justice, spring from the understandings of men, understandings that are based on and are influenced by *their* experiences. The liberative praxis of Latinas, having as its source our lived-experience, is an adequate base for moral norms and values because it enables our moral agency and empowers us to understand and define ourselves—to comprehend what our human existence is all about and what its goal is.[32]

Popular Religiosity as an Element of *Mujerista* Theology[33]

The starting point for a study of the popular religiosity of Latinas is our struggle to survive.[34] Popular religiosity for us is a means of self-identification and our insistence on it is part of the struggle to exist with our own characteristics and peculiarities. Popular religiosity allows religion to remain central to our culture in spite of the neglect we suffer as a people from most organized religions in this country.[35]

It should not be surprising that Latinas, as persons who are "vitally engaged in historical realities with specific times and places,"[36] and as persons who have to struggle for survival, are involved with and reflect on matters of ultimate concern. This reflection includes religious considerations that form "a system of symbols which acts to establish powerful, pervasive, and long-lasting moods and motivations . . . by formulating conceptions of a general order of existence and clothing these conceptions with such an aura of factuality that the moods and motivations seem uniquely realistic."[37]

Many of these powerful symbols arise from a certain kind of "official" Christian tradition. "Official" here refers to "those prescribed beliefs and norms of an institution promulgated and monitored by a group of religious specialists,"[38] the clergy and, in particular, the hierarchy of the church. Without question Christianity is the religion of Latinas—Catholicism being the specific form of Christianity which about 80 percent claim and pass on to our children. But the Christianity to which we relate, our way of relating with the divine and expressing such connection, is not "official" Christianity, nor does it necessarily have the church—either Catholic or Protestant—as its main point of reference. The Christianity of Latinas is of a very specific variety because of its history in the countries of our ethnic roots.

Christianity came to Latin America at the time of the *conquista*, the conquest. It came not only, or even primarily, in the form of organized religion, but as an intrinsic part of the conquering culture. Theology was indeed "the main discourse in the ideological production of the sixteenth century."[39] This is why the *conquistadores*, the conquerors, planted crosses to symbolize their taking possession of the land, and named the territories and the natives in the same way as species and persons are named or renamed in the Bible—to indicate having authority over them.[40] The *conquista* was not just a political conquest, but a conquest in which even the religious world of the conquered suffered total devastation. Christianity was not only imposed on the natives but also played a very important role as moral justifier in the whole process of the *conquista*.

When the Spanish world and the world of the indigenous people of what was to become the Americas met, a process of acculturation was set in motion during which the culture of the conqueror was imposed unilaterally on the conquered people. Real enculturation—"the process of making personal the traditional culture of the society," that is, the society of the *conquistadores*—did not take place because education was not made available to the vast majority of the population. Instead, what resulted was a "culturization" of Christianity; Christianity became culture. It has become a cultural expression in a continent in which the Spanish and the indigenous cultures have come together to give birth to a new culture.[41]

The Christianity that became and is an intrinsic part of Latino culture is one that uses the Bible in a very limited way, emphasizing instead the traditions and customs of the Spanish church.[42] Therefore, the Bible, biblical truth, and revelation are not repudiated by Latinas but, for the majority of Latinas, they are not central, they are not considered very important, they do not play a prominent role in our lives. Most of us seldom read the Bible and know instead popularized versions of biblical stories—versions Latinas create to make a point. One can consider these versions to be distortions, but for us they are "valid" interpretations, albeit imaginative ones, insofar as they contribute to the liberation of Latinas.[43]

The Christianity of Latinas also includes religious traditions brought to Latin America and the Caribbean by African slaves, and the Amerindian traditions bequeathed by the great Aztec, Maya, and Inca civilizations, as well as other Amerindian cultures, such as Taino, Siboney, Caribe, Araucano. The mingling of sixteenth-century Spanish Catholicism with religious understandings and beliefs of the African and Amerindian religions in these regions is what has given birth to Latino popular religiosity.[44]

Popular religiosity refers to the religious understandings and practices of the masses, in contrast to "official" Christianity or the Christianity of certain minorities that eschew popular religiosity. Popular religiosity is

> the set of experiences, beliefs and rituals which more-or-less peripherical [sic] human groups create, assume and develop (within concrete socio-cultural and historical contexts, and as an answer to these contexts) and which to a greater or lesser degree distance themselves from what is recognized by the Church and the society within which they are situated, striving through rituals, experiences and beliefs to find an access to God and salvation which they feel they cannot find in what Church and society have regulated as normative.[45]

Concretely we can say that the popular religiosity of Latinas has five general characteristics. First, it is a real religious subculture in the sense that it is a way of thinking and acting in their religious sphere not as individuals but as a group of persons. As a religious subculture, popular religiosity includes beliefs, attitudes, values, rituals, and so forth, that express the religiosity of Latinos. Second, insofar as rituals are concerned, central position is given to certain aspects of the Catholic tradition considered marginal, for example, "sacramentals."[46] Third, popular religiosity, as I have already begun to suggest, is syncretic for it invests Catholic religious practices with meaning from other religious traditions. Fourth, "official" religious practices are reinterpreted and given a different meaning. For example, Baptism and First Communion become rituals of passage; the Mass becomes a public ceremony used to solemnize the most important moments in the life of a person or a group of people. Fifth, all these behaviors are transmitted as part of the Latino culture in contrast to being personal options.[47]

In *mujerista* theology we see popular religiosity as an essential part of popular culture and, therefore, as a part of the identity of and central to the lived-experience of the people. It is an essential part of our deepest constitutive element.[48] In many ways popular religiosity is one of the most creative and original parts of our heritage and our culture, being a significant element in providing *fuerzas para la lucha*, strength for the struggle. In this sense popular religiosity is valuable not only culturally but also "in relation to its capacity for strengthening the political consciousness and mobilization of the people."[49]

Mujeristas take popular religiosity very seriously, then, finding it to be an essential source of our theology because it is operative in the lives of Latinas as a "system of values and ideas, and a complex of symbolic practices, discursive and non-discursive, enacted in ritual drama and materialized in visual images," relating us to the sacred, originated and maintained in a large measure by Latinas as poor and oppressed people.[50] But this does not exempt popular religiosity from being examined through the critical lens of the liberation of Latinas. As *mujerista* theologians we recognize that the popular religiosity of Latinas has its failings and ambiguities, as do other cultural forms of Catholicism and Christianity.[51] Using a liberative lens, *mujerista* theology recognizes that popular religiosity has elements that legitimize the oppression of Latinas. However, this does not lead us to minimize or dismiss it.

The evangelizing role that popular religiosity has had and continues to have among Latinas and within the Latino community is instrumental in the struggle for liberation because it is a major force in preserving the Latino community. "The historical neglect to which Latinos have been submitted in this country, by Church and society, added to the constant pressure to become 'anglicized,' would have long ago done away with Catholicism among Latinos and with Latino culture in general."[52] Instead, Latino Christianity and culture are alive today thanks to the evangelizing role of popular religiosity through which Latinas transmit the religious, cultural, and social values of our people. Moreover, it has provided common ground for the great variety of Latinos who live in the U.S.A., thus binding the different Latino communities together.[53]

For Latinas, popular religiosity also has another important role: it allows us to experience the sacred in our everyday lives. In many ways it makes it possible for us to live out religiosity as an intrinsic element of who we are and all that we do; it makes it possible to integrate the sacred and the secular. It is through the practices of popular religiosity that Latinas are aware of the sacred in the private as well as the public, in the personal as well as the social.[54]

"Official" churches, instead of seeing popular religiosity as a positive element,[55] either denounce it and work actively against it, or look for ways of purifying it, of "baptizing" it into Christianity—accepting only those elements that can be Christianized.[56] In *mujerista* theology we will not dismiss "the normative, graced, and even universal dimensions of the 'salvific' manifestations of non-Christian religions."[57] As *mujerista* theologians we are suspicious of an imperialistic approach that refuses to recognize and accept as true, good, and life-giving any and all religious understandings and practices that do not directly relate to a magisterial understanding and interpretation of the gospel, that do not have Christ as center, model, and norm.[58] We take exception to such refusal because it does violence to a valid understanding of Jesus as portrayed in Scripture: Jesus clearly indicated that his mission was not to point to himself, but rather to point the way to God.

This imperialistic attitude on the part of "official" churches, particularly vis-à-vis the Amerindian and African strands in popular religiosity, is anti-cultural, and in this case, anti-Latino. To insist on imposing the divinity of Jesus as the only true and relevant expression of the divine on people who because of cultural factors either believe differently or for whom such claim is irrelevant, shows a lack of respect for a people whose religion includes other claims, and whose religion is central to their culture.[59] Is this imperialistic attitude not one of the main reasons for the lack of pastoral care and inclusion of Latinos in the life of the church in the U.S.A.?

Latinas' Christianity is indeed a mixture, a fusion of different religious strands. In this regard it follows in the footsteps of "official" Christianity. For example, Christmas is celebrated at the time of the year when the Feast of the Unconquered Sun took place at Rome in the late third and early fourth centuries;[60] pagan buildings such as the Pantheon were turned into churches; civil offices and the garbs of different periods and cultures have become religious offices and liturgical garb; Greek philosophical concepts of substance are used by Catholics to talk about the Eucharist. Once this syncretism became official, however, it has been used as an orthodox norm which has excluded and continues to exclude other syncretisms.

But such an exclusion does not obliterate syncretism from the Latinas' *religiosidad popular*, popular religiosity. Is Our Lady of Guadalupe the Mother of Jesus, or is she Tonantzin, the Aztec goddess, Mother of the Gods on whose pilgrimage site, the hill of Tepeyac, Our Lady of Guadalupe appeared?[61] In their hearts, and often quite openly, Latinas with Caribbean roots who pray to St. Barbara are identifying her, directly or indirectly, with Chango, the Yoruban God of Thunder. The hierarchy's decision to declare the story of St. Barbara a legend and the improbability that such a person ever existed is irrelevant to them.

The history of Christianity shows that orthodox objections to syncretism have less to do with the purity of faith, and more with who has the right to determine what is to be considered normative and official. For the articulation of religious understandings, beliefs, and practices to be an act of liberation, it has to be an act of self-determination, not an attempt to comply with what the "official" church says, with what it considers to be orthodox. This is why *mujerista* theology does not shrink from claiming that the fusion of Christian, Amerindian, and African religious strands operative in the lives of Latinas may be good and life-giving.

Popular religiosity as a subculture pervades the lives of Latinas. Perhaps because of the precariousness of our lives, perhaps because our variety of Christianity is an intrinsic part of our culture, and because we are keenly aware of our culture since it is different from the dominant one, religion, religious thinking and practices, provide for us the moods and motivations operative in our day-to-day life. Questions of ultimate meaning, understandings of the divine and of ourselves and of our relationship to the divine are not matters for religion experts only. No, they are matters which preoccupy, touch, and affect everyone. "*Si Dios quiere*," God willing, is not an empty phrase for us. The belief that the divine cares about us and participates in our lives is something very real for us, something constantly taken into consideration. There is no doubt for us that what we are able to accomplish is due to much hard work; but it is also a fact that God has had something to do with it, and due credit is given to the divine by fulfilling promises at any physical or monetary cost.[62]

The day-to-day acknowledgment of the role the divine plays in our lives as well as a firm belief in the ongoing revelation of God in the midst of and through the community of faith is what leads us to claim the lived-experience of Latinas as the source of *mujerista* theology. This belief continues the long tradition very much present in the Hebrew Scriptures that God's revelation happens in and through the history of Israel's people. Salvation history *is* not something different from what actually happened to the Jewish people. Salvation history *is* precisely what happened to them; it has to do with how they interpreted what happened to them, with the role that God played in their struggles and accomplishments. Our claiming Latinas' lived-experience as the source of our theology is firmly rooted in this biblical understanding of the revelation of God. Knowing that as Latinas we have indeed been created in the image and likeness of God, trusting that our struggle to be faithful to our understandings of the divine make us worthy members of the Christian community of faith, we believe that God's revelation happens in the day-to-day living of Latinas.

Spanish: "The Language of the Angels"[63]

The Spanish language functions for Latinas not only as a means of communication but as a means of identification. Spanish has become "the incarnation and symbol" of our whole culture, making us feel that here in the U.S.A. we are one people, no matter what our country of origin is. The Spanish language identifies us by distinguishing us from the rest of society. It gives us a specificity that we need to be a certain kind of people within a culture not our own.[64]

White Americans are willing to accept Latinos who are "white enough" as one of them when we become sufficiently middle-class and sufficiently "Anglicized." Many African Americans are also ready to claim black Latinos. But Latinas in general consider ourselves neither white nor black:[65]

> . . . *for Hispanics the prime identifier is not color, but language, and so the Hispanic, whether black or white, tends to think that those who speak Spanish are 'his [sic] people' no matter what their color, while those who speak English (whether black or white) are 'the others'. For Hispanics the 'Anglo' is not the Anglo-Saxon, but the Anglophone.*[66]

The Spanish language for us Latinos here in the U.S.A. has become "the bearer of identity and values."[67] Our attachment to it is such that even those Latinos born and raised in the U.S.A. who understand a little Spanish and can speak only a few words insist on saying that they do know Spanish. Since the importance of Spanish for Latinas is not so much to be able to communicate but to be able to identify each other, grammatical and pronunciation correctness is totally secondary. For us Spanish is indeed a social construct and, therefore, we do not use Spanish to exclude from our communities those who know little Spanish or use it improperly.[68]

In a market study done in 1981 for the SIN National Spanish Television Network, 90 percent of Latinos claimed they knew at least enough Spanish to get by. Only 1 percent of Latinos said they knew only English. Twenty-three percent said they knew only Spanish, 20 percent said they knew Spanish and enough English to get by, 47 percent consider themselves bilingual, and 9 percent know English and enough Spanish to get by. Based on data gathered by the 1980 census and considering that any undercounting probably happened among undocumented Latinos who speak mostly Spanish, one can conclude that only in 10 percent of Latino homes is Spanish not used.[69]

The numbers of those who speak Spanish and use it at home go hand in hand with our sense of national allegiance: 88 percent consider themselves Latinos, 46 percent claiming they are Latino first, American second, and 42 percent saying that they are equally Latino and American. They also are in line with the 89-percent that either agree or strongly agree with the statement, "we should pass on to our children a sense of belonging to our religious and national tradition."[70]

The study also presented an open-ended question asking for the aspect of Latino culture and traditions that we feel is most important to preserve. Eighty one percent mentioned the Spanish language as the most important—83 percent of Puerto Ricans, 77 percent of Mexicans, and 95 percent of Cubans.[71]

Yet maintaining usage of and fluidity in Spanish is no easy task for Latinas. In the U.S.A. the governing principle in this regard continues to be "one population—one language . . . [and it] has assumed overtones of moral, social, and psychological normalcy."[72] The recent successful attempts in several parts of the U.S.A. where Latinos are numerous to pass a law declaring English *the* official language make this obvious. At the same time this insistence on having an English-as-official-language law indicates that Spanish is used widely in certain states in the U.S.A. Laws will not stop Latinas from using Spanish, because it is a social construct that has enormous importance in maintaining our identity, and we will do everything in our power to continue to speak it and teach it to our children. We are aware that as an oppressed group we are not able to preserve the use of Spanish because we are "limited in being able to establish and control institutions of language monitoring, language ideologization [sic] and, most particularly, language use via the establishment and control of significant political and economic bases of . . . [our] own."[73] It is our hope, however, that the constant flow of new Spanish speaking people into the U.S.A. plus the frequent return to their country of origin of Latinos will help us preserve Spanish.

Latino Ethnicity: Social Construct

In these two first chapters I have analyzed the main elements of Latino ethnicity. Our ties with Latin America and the Spanish speaking Caribbean, *mestizaje*, our multilayered oppression and struggle for survival, popular religiosity, the insistence on speaking *español*, Spanish, and our *proyecto histórico*—all of these are pieces that together constitute and shape Latinas' ethnicity. It is the intersection and interplay of all of these elements that give us our pecularities and distinctiveness as Latina Women. In other words, the shared cultural norms, values, identities, and behaviors that form the core of our ethnicity are linked to these six elements we have explored.

At the same time we know that these cultural norms, values, identities, and behaviors are irreversibly impacted by the prejudice and discrimination to which we are subjected in this society.[74] This means that the oppression we suffer as Latinas has become an integral part of our ethnicity—of Latino ethnicity—and, therefore, it impacts every aspect of our lives as does our daily struggle to survive.

Notes

1. José Míguez Bonino, *Doing Theology in a Revolutionary Situation* (Philadelphia: Fortress Press, 1975), 38–39. Chap. 3 of this book is perhaps the most detailed description of the meaning of *proyecto histórico* by a Latin American liberation theologian. *Mujerista* theology appropriates this term critically according to our lived-experience.

2. Audrey Lorde, "Poems Are Not Luxuries," *Chrysalis* 3 (1977): 8.

3. See Gustavo Gutiérrez, *A Theology of Liberation.* (Maryknoll: Orbis Books, 1988), xxxix, 83–91. See also Gustavo Gutiérrez, *The Truth Shall Make You Free* (Maryknoll: Orbis Books, 1990), 14–16, 116–21.

4. Gutiérrez, *Theology of Liberation*, 94.

5. Using Paulo Freire, Gutiérrez sees the relationship of what he calls "utopia" to historical reality as appearing under two aspects: denunciation and annunciation. See Gutiérrez, *Theology of Liberation*, 136–40.

6. This is why we avoid using the terms "minority" or "marginalized." These labels communicate the way the dominant group sees us and not the way we see ourselves; they imply that what we want is to participate in present structures that are oppressive. We see ourselves as a group that has a significant contribution to make precisely because we demand radical change of oppressive structures.

7. See "Larry Rasmussen," *Christianity and Crisis*, 22 October 1990.

8. For the effectiveness of this understanding of struggling to build a preferred future see Renny Golden, *The Hour of the Poor, The Hour of Women* (New York: Crossroad, 1991).

9. We have appropriated Gutiérrez's understanding of the three levels or aspects of the process of liberation. The specifics of each of these aspects arise from our lived-experience as Latinas.

10. Gutiérrez refers to the "Chalcedonian Principle," and uses the Chalcedonian language regarding the two natures of the one person Jesus, in order to clarify the distinctiveness and intrinsic unity of the three aspects of liberation. In this, *mujerista* theology follows Gutiérrez quite closely. The distinctiveness of Latinas' struggle, however, will come in the "content" of each of the three aspects of the process of liberation. See Gutiérrez, *The Truth Shall Make You Free*, 120–24.

11. Following the venerable tradition refered to in Acts 1:26, we cast lots to decide the order in which we would deal with these three aspects of liberation! We know some will try to see in the order we use a certain priority of importance or relevance. That is indeed not our intention.

12. The only reason a *balsero*, a young man who escaped from Cuba in a makeshift raft, could give me for risking his life in such a way was the lack of *libertad* he experienced in Cuba. I assumed that for him, influenced by U.S.A. propaganda, *libertad* had to do with accessibility to consumer goods, with a better material life. But I was wrong. For him *libertad* had to do with self-determination, with wanting something different and being able to work towards making it a reality. Whether I agree or disagree with his assessment of the present Cuban situation, his understanding of *libertad* and his willingness to risk his life for it has helped me to understand what I and other Latinas mean by *libertad*.

13. Cf. Gutiérrez, *The Truth Shall Make You Free*, 132–34.

14. Since psychology is not my field of expertise, my attempt here is only to describe apathy and fear and to locate them in reference to the historical situation Latinas face.

15. This fear is compounded by the fact that seeing ourselves as different from the status quo is an intrinsic element of what it means for us to be Latina.

16. The best proof of this mindset is the name of the U.S.A. government program for Puerto Rico in the middle decades of this century: "Operation Bootstrap." The Puerto Ricans understood very clearly the American expression that was behind that title and they responded painfully and cleverly, "How do you expect us to lift ourselves by our bootstraps when we do not even have boots!"

17. I use the word "God" here not to refer to one divine being but rather as a collective noun that embraces God, the saints, dead ones whom we love, manifestations of the Virgin (not always the same as manifestations of Mary, the mother of Jesus), Jesus (not very similar to the Jesus of the Gospels), Amerindian and African gods, and so forth.

18. To the accusation that this places us in the neo-orthodox ranks, we answer that Latinas have not been part of the "modern experiment"; that the kind of belief in the divine that for the enlightened, scientific mind signifies a lack of autonomous, critical, rational thought, is for us a concrete experience that we use as a key element in the struggle for liberation. See Christine Gudorf, "Liberation Theology's Use of Scripture—A Response to First World Critics," in *Interpretation—a Journal of Bible and Theology*. (January 1987): 12–13.

19. Ada María Isasi-Díaz and Yolanda Tarango, *Hispanic Women: Prophetic Voice in the Church* (Minneapolis: Fortress Press, 1992), 90.

20. Gutiérrez, *Theology of Liberation*, 24.

21. Though indeed we have much to learn from the Base Ecclesial Communities that are at the heart of the Latin American liberation struggle, our *comunidades de fe* have to develop their own characteristics based on our lived-experiences and needs. For a concise articulation of what Base Ecclesial Communities are and the role they play in Latin America, see Pablo Richard, "The Church of the Poor in the Decade of the 90s," *LADOC* XXI (Nov./Dec. 1990): 11–29.

22. See John Stuart Mill, *Utilitarianism* (New York: Bobbs-Merrill, 1957).

23. See also Acts 4:35.

24. For an excellent short analysis of six main justice theories see, Karen Lebacqz, *Six Theories of Justice* (Minneapolis: Augsburg, 1986).

25. For a more comprehensive analysis of the meaning of solidarity see Ada María Isasi-Díaz, Solidarity: Love of Neighbor in the 1980s," in *Lift Every Voice—Constructing Christian Theologies from the Underside*, ed. Susan Brooks Thistlethwaite and Mary Potter Engels (San Francisco: Harper and Row, 1990).

26. José Míguez Bonino, "Nuevas tendencias en teología," *Pasos* (1985): 22

27. Fernando Romero, "Sentido práctico y flexibilidad popular," *Páginas* 111 (Octubre 1991); 43. See also, Arthur F. McGovern, *Liberation Theology and Its Critics* (Maryknoll: Orbis Books, 1990), 177–212.

28. For an amplification of this theme see Isasi-Díaz, "Solidarity," 37.

29. Teresa L. Amott and Julie A. Matthaei, *Race, Gender & Work* (Boston: South End, 1991), 346–48.

30. Michael Parenti, *Power and the Powerless* (New York: St. Martin's, 1978), 226.

31. Romero, "Sentido práctico," 45–47.

32. Isasi-Díaz and Tarango, *Hispanic Women*, 77–80, 109–10; see below chap. 6

33. We set the basis for this section in chap. 3 of Isasi-Díaz and Tarango, *Hispanic Women*.

34. Though popular religiosity among Latinas is suffused with Catholic rituals and understandings, there begins to be a Protestant perspective regarding popular religiosity. See Tito Paredes, "Popular religiosity: A Protestant Perspective" *Missiology* XX, no. 2 (April 1992): 205–20; see also Juan Sepúlveda, "Pentecostalism as Popular Religiosity," *International Review of Mission* 78 (January 1989): 80–88.

35. Juan José Huitrado-Rizo, MCCJ, "Hispanic Popular Religiosity: The Expression of a People Coming to Life," *New Theology Review* 3, no. 4 (November 1990): 43–54.

36. Gutiérrez, *Theology of Liberation*, 13.

37. Clifford Geertz, *The Interpretation of Culture* (New York: Basic Books, 1973), 90.

38. Robert J. Schreiter, *Constructing Local Theologies* (Maryknoll: Orbis Books, 1985), 87–88.

39. Luis N. Rivera Pagán, *Evangelización y violencia—la conquista de América* (San Juan, Puerto Rico: Editorial Cemi, 1991), 1.

40. Ibid., 14–21. Rivera Pagán carefully explains how the discovery was accompanied by the juridical act of taking possession.

41. This definition of enculturation is found in Paulo Agirrebaltzategi, *Configuración eclesial de las culturas* (Bilbao, España: Universidad de Deusto, 1976), 82. The author explains the three terms acculturation, enculturation, and culturization on pp. 81–82. He indicates that what has become cultural expression is what is transcultural or transcendent. It also means the form in which culturally the Gospel message is realized in the Church. I use the term here in a narrower sense to mean simply that which has become a cultural expression.

42. Juan Luis Segundo, *The Liberation of Theology* (Maryknoll: Orbis Books, 1982), 185. Though it is true that an increasing number of Latinas are participating in denominations and churches that give great importance to the Bible, the majority of Latinas still relate to the Catholic church and do not use the Bible often. *Mujerista* theologians are concerned with the way the Bible is imposed on Latinas by some churches since it is done in a way that often threatens rather than enhances our moral agency.

43. The same is often true of sermons we hear on Sundays. Imaginative interpretations are not considered "good theology" when Latinas do it, but it is all right when priests and/or pastors do it.

44. Sixto J. García and Orlando Espín are doing very exciting work on developing a Hispanic American theology using popular religiosity as its key element. In 1987 and 1988 they gave workshops at the Catholic Theological Society of America Conferences. Only synopses of the papers they presented there have been published. See Orlando Espín and Sixto Garciá, "Hispanic-American Theology," *Catholic Theological Society of America Proceedings* 42 (1987): 114–19, and "The Sources of Hispanic Theology," *Catholic Theological Society of America Proceedings* 43 (1988): 122–25. In 1989 they gave a full presentation that has been published. See Garcia and Espín, "'Lilies of the Field'," *Catholic Theological Society of America Proceedings* 44 (1989): 70–90.

45. Espín and García, "Toward a Hispanic-American Theology," unpublished notes of workshop presented at *The Catholic Theological Society of America.* (1987): 6–7. All quotations from Espín and García's presentation at the CTSA conferences in 1987 and 1988 will be from unpublished notes the authors passed out which are much more complete than the published synopses.

46. Sacramentals in the Roman Catholic tradition are things or actions—candles, processions—used as reminders of God's effective presence in the world. The laity has access to the use of sacramentals without having to depend on the priests.

47. Manuel M. Marzal, "La religiosidad popular en el Perú" in *Panorama de la teología latinoamericana*, I, ed. Equipo Seladoc (Salamanca: Ediciones Sígueme, 1975), 28–29. These are adaptations of elements presented by Marzal that I have translated in such a way as to exclude the judgmental tone of his analysis, which I believe limits the value of popular religiosity.

48. See Segundo Galilea, "The Theology of Liberation and the Place of 'Folk Religion,'" in *What Is Religion: An Inquiry for Christian Theology.*, ed. Mircea Eliade and David W. Tracy, *Concilium* 136 (Edinburgh: T. & T. Clark, 1980), 43.

49. Ibid, 44.

50. Michael R. Candelaria, *Popular Religion and Liberation* (Albany: State Univ. of New York Press, 1990), 13.

51. Ibid., 43.

52. Espín and García, "Sources of Hispanic Theology," unpublished notes of workshop presented at the Catholic Theological Society of America (1988): 4.

53. García and Espín, 'Lilies of the Field,' 72.

54. María Pilar Aquino, *Nuestro Clamor par La Vida* (San Jose, Costa Rica: Editorial D.E.I., 1992), 218–22.

55. See Isasi-Díaz and Tarango, *Hispanic Women*, 67, where we indicate that popular religiosity could offer needed correctives to some of the religious understandings of "official" Christianity.

56. Ibid., 14–26. See also II Consulta Ecuménica de Pastoral Indígena, *Aporte de los pueblos indígenas de América Latina a la teología cristiana* (Quito, Ecuador, 1986). Espín and García, "Toward a Hispanic," 4. Jaime R. Vidal, "Popular

Religion among the Hispanics in the General Area of the Archdiocese of Newark," in *Presencia Nueva* (Newark: Office of Research and Planning, Archdiocese of Newark 1988), 250–54.

57. Espín and García, "Toward a Hispanic-American Theology," 17. On this point Espín and García contradict themselves. In spite of the assertion they make here, they make only one reference to Amerindian and African religions and not in a very positive light. They place the Amerindian and African religious elements operative in popular religiosity in what they call a "second constellation" with which they seem to deal only insofar as it goes hand in hand with the "first constellation," which they call "popular catholicism." See pp. 4–6.

58. Tom F. Driver, *Christ in a Changing World* (New York: Crossroad, 1981), 32–81.

59. See Isasi-Díaz and Tarango, *Hispanic Women*, 13–55.

60. John F. Baldovin, S.J., "The Liturgical Year: Calendar for a Just Community," in *Liturgy and Spirituality in Context*, ed. Eleanor Bernstein, C.S.J. (Collegeville: The Liturgical Press, 1990), 104.

61. Compare the difference in interpretation and explanation of Guadalupe between Elizondo and Lafaye. See Virgilio Elizondo, *La morenita* (Liguori, MO: Liguori Publications, 1981), and J. Lafaye, *Quetzalcoatl et Guadalupe* (Paris: Gallimard, 1974).

62. One of my earliest memories has to do with fulfilling a promise my father had made to Our Lady of Charity, the title under which Mary is patroness of Cuba. During World War II my father tried to produce glucose from yucca starch. As a chemical engineer he knew that this could be done, but the process is an industrial secret and he had to start from scratch. To be sure he would succeed, he promised Our Lady of Charity a visit to her sanctuary by the whole family if she would help him, enlighten him in his research. He was able to get glucose from yucca starch, something needed and, therefore, profitable during the war. It was not until a few years later that he was able to keep the promise. We traveled over twelve hours by car and then walked up the hill on the top of which the sanctuary sits. Thus we all honored the divine intervention in the life of my family. I was about seven years old at that time.

63. This is exactly what my grandmother always said!

64. A few years ago I arrived at the very southern tip of Manhattan for a 7 PM meeting. I could not find the building where we were to meet, so I decided to park my car and find someone who could help me. Since there are no homes in that area, at that hour of the evening it is not unusual to see not a single soul. Finally I saw a man who was emptying trash cans in the back entrance of one of the huge office buildings. I approached him a little apprehensively and asked him for directions. Apologetically, he started in a very broken English to tell me he did not understand me. I stopped him by repeating the question in Spanish. His eyes lit up, he squared his shoulders, and told me he did not know where that building was. He then looked into my eyes and said, *"Venga aca, usted es cubana?"* (Listen here, are you Cuban?) When I told him I was, he became all the more helpful. Talking to me as you do to an old friend, he let me know that the doorman around the corner was also Cuban and that he surely knew the answer to my question. Without thinking much, because he spoke Spanish and was a Cuban, I put aside all the cautions I should have been taking and asked him if he thought my car was safe there. *"No hay problema, no hay problema"* (No problem, no problem). I smiled broadly, thanked him, and went to get directions from the Cuban doorman, whom I was sure would help me because I was his *compatriota* (compatriot), and he did!

65. I am not claiming that there is not racism in our culture, and certainly in our countries of origin, skin color, though dealt with in a different way from the way it is operative in the U.S.A., plays a role in societal stratification.

66. Vidal, "Popular Religion among the Hispanics," 257.

67. Ibid.

68. See Eldin Villafañe, "The Socio-Cultural Matrix of Intergenerational Dynamics: An Agenda for the 90s," *Apuntes* Year 12, no.1 (Spring 1992): 13–20.

69. Justo Gonzdlez, *The Theological Education of Hispanics* (New York: The Fund for Theological Education, 1988), 12. Notice that there is a difference between "knowing" Spanish (the question investigated by the SIN National Spanish Television Network), and "using" Spanish in the home (the focus of the 1980 U.S.A. Census study used by Gonzdlez).

70. *Spanish USA—A Study of the Hispanic Market in the United States*, by Yankelovich, Skelly & White, Inc. (New York: Yankelovich, Skelly & White, 1981), 7, 16.

71. The same table in this study gives a quick handle on what Latinos consider the most valuable elements of our culture which we wish to preserve. Here they are in descending order of importance: care of and respect for elders, music, religion, family/commitment to family, art/literature, food and beverages, love for life/know how to enjoy life, happy people, holidays/celebrations.

72. Joshua A. Fishman, "Language Maintenance," in *Harvard Encyclopedia of Ethnic Groups*, ed. Stephan Thernstrom (Cambridge, MA: The Belknap Press of Harvard Univ. Press, 1980), 631.

73. Ibid., 636.

74. Nelson and Tienda, "The Structuring of Hispanic Ethnicity: Historical and Contemporary Perspectives," in *Ethnicity and Race in the U.S.A.—Toward the Twenty-First Century*, ed. Richard D. Alba (London: Henley Routledge & Kegan Paul, 1985), 53.

The Asian American
Religious Experience

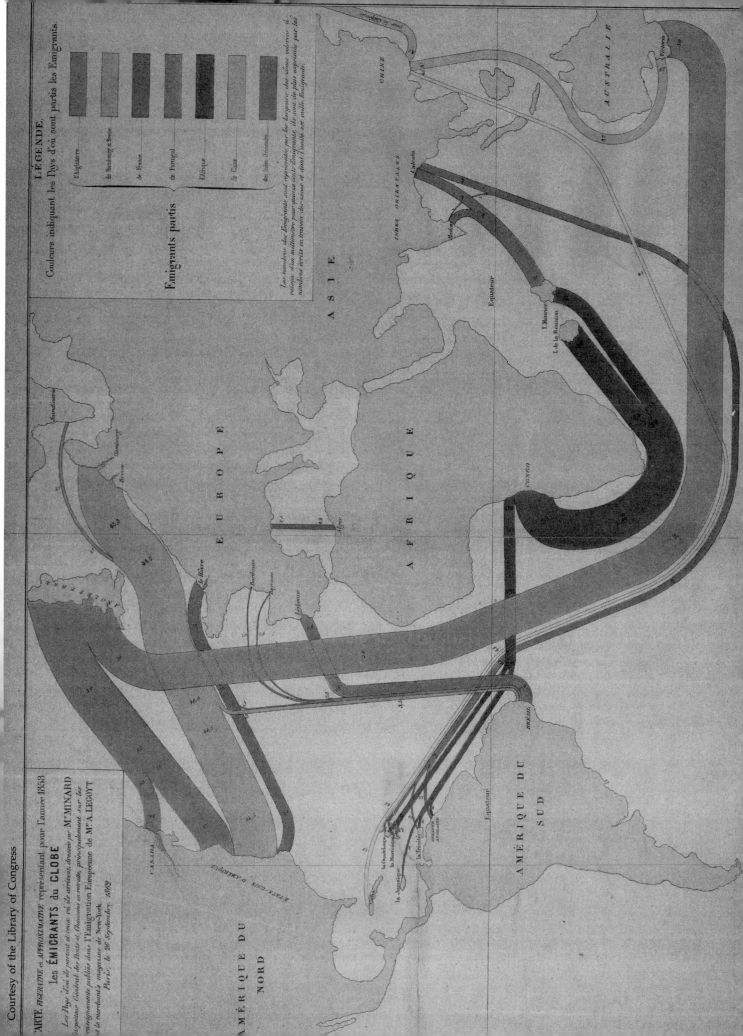

CARTE FIGURATIVE et APPROXIMATIVE représentant pour l'année 1858
les ÉMIGRANTS du GLOBE

Les Pays d'où il partit et ceux où il arrivent dressée par Mr MINARD
Inspecteur Général les Ponts et Chaussées en retraite, principalement sur les
renseignements publiés dans l'Emigration Européenne de Mr A. LEGOYT
et le marchande magasine de New-York.

Paris, le 26 Septembre 1862.

LÉGENDE.

Couleurs indiquant les Pays d'où sont partis les Émigrants.

l'Angleterre

de Hambourg et Breme.

de France.

de Portugal.

l'Afrique.

de Chine.

des Indes Orientales.

Émigrants partis

Les nombres des Émigrants sont représentés par la largeur des zônes colorées à
raison d'un millimètre pour quinze cent Émigrants, ils sont de plus exprimés par les
nombres écrits en travers des zônes et dont l'unité est mille Émigrants.

EUROPE

ASIE

AFRIQUE

CHINE

INDES ORIENTALES

Calcutta

Madras

Equateur

CONGO

I. Maurice
I. de la Réunion

AMÉRIQUE DU SUD

BRÉSIL

Equateur

AUSTRALIE

S. Victoria

AMÉRIQUE DU NORD

CANADA

ÉTATS-UNIS D'AMÉRIQUE

le Havre

Bordeaux

Bayonne

Lisbonne

Alger

Hambourg

Breme

Angleterre

Readings in Asian American Religious Traditions: A Foretaste

Cultural and religious diversity characterize the peoples broadly defined as Asian American. In terms of immigration to and settlement in the United States and elsewhere in the Americas, the first Asian peoples arrived from China in the mid-nineteenth century, followed later by the Japanese, Filipinos, and Koreans, and then by peoples from India and elsewhere in South Asia. By the 1920s, the flow of immigration from Asia became a trickle, due in large part to changes in immigration laws. After these laws were liberalized in the 1960s, new waves of immigrants not only reached the Western Pacific shores, but continued inland beyond the Rockies. After the Vietnam War, larger communities of Asian immigrants began to establish themselves in or near the cities of Boston, Chicago, Pittsburgh, Philadelphia, Houston, and Dallas, as well as Minneapolis and elsewhere throughout the Midwest. Within a generation, these Asian settlements would begin to transform the very character of many suburban American communities.

Historically, the existence of Asian enclaves, such as Chinatowns, Koreatowns, and Little Tokyos, have tended to create concern among long-standing Anglo-American residents. But, the experiences of alien sojourners, if not the ethnic enclaves that they created, were not at all new to Americans. Little Italies, as well as Polish, Jewish, Irish, and Scandinavian neighborhoods, had been carved out of places like Philadelphia, Boston, New York, Chicago, and other major cities across the United States. What was different, however, was the *discontinuity* of cultural and religious traditions that characterized these Asian neighborhoods. Unlike immigrants from Europe, from the standpoint of culture and in most cases religion, Asian Americans were both aliens among as well as alienated from their Anglo-American neighbors. As an example, although both Irish and Chinese immigrants were greeted by harassment and discrimination at nearly every turn, the Irish from Western Europe and the Chinese from East Asia did not inhabit the same cultural or religious worlds, nor did they share similar views regarding the sacred.

Thus, while the readings that comprise this section bear witness to discrimination, at the same time the Asian American experience has also been defined by cultural misunderstanding, suspicion, race hatred, and by the disruption of family life, as well as by alienation, not simply alienation of the Asian immigrant from "white" Protestant culture, but increasingly of the immigrant or first generation from their progressively Americanized children and grandchildren. To these, and perhaps others, within the first generation, the greatest tragedy of immigration may not have been their heroic struggle to keep their religious and cultural traditions alive like a flickering lamp on a storm-tossed boat, but has been the lack of interest their children have often expressed in tending to such traditions. In this instance, the opposite of faith may not be doubt or disbelief, but indifference.

The difficulty that presents itself in discussing Asian American histories and religious traditions is one of tracing multiple story-lines that seldom intersect. Therefore, because of their size and long histories in the United States, for this section of the reader we have selected the Chinese and Japanese communities as two representatives of the Asian American religious experience generally. In addition, to allow for some comparison of fictional literature produced broadly by Asian Americans, we have included a short story by Chitra Divakaruni on a young Indian woman's own ambivalence toward agreeing to the custom of an arranged marriage. We have also included two additional readings that give voice to the more recent experiences of immigrants from Southeast Asia. To orient readers to the reading selections from these two communities, we offer as a "foretaste" the following brief outline of Chinese and Japanese experience in the United States and the role the religion—Buddhist and Christian—appears to have played historically in defining and maintaining these distinct communities.

Like many immigrants, the Chinese traveled to America seeking fortune. After gold had been discovered at Sutter's mill in California in January 1848, hundreds of Chinese sailed for "Gum Shan/Chin Shan," or Gold Mountain, to stake their claims. By 1850, there were close to 800 Chinese immigrants in America, most coming from Canton (Guangdong) Province in coastal southern China. Within a decade, there were as many as 35,000 Chinese in the United States. By 1880, the number would climb to over 100,000. While gold had brought the Chinese to California, not all of these immigrants worked the sluices or dug in mines. Some opened businesses, including general stores, laundries, and restaurants. Others fished and shrimped along the Pacific coast and the inland waters. By the 1860s, when mining became less profitable, the Chinese turned to other types of labor. For example, between 1865 and 1869, Union Pacific employed as many as 15,000 Chinese, and a number of Sikhs, to help complete the transcontinental railroad. During this and other periods, harassment of Chinese workers was typical. Anti-Chinese agitation eventually led to passage of the Chinese Exclusion Act in 1882, which suspended immigration of Chinese laborers for ten years. The act was subsequently renewed in 1893, and was in force until its repeal in 1943, when China and the United States were allies against Japan during World War II.

As with most early immigrants, the Chinese did not intend to remain in the United States but saw themselves as sojourners. Those who came were young bachelors or newly married men attracted by the prospect of gaining easy wealth. Few could afford passage for their wives and children but would regularly send a portion of their earnings to their families in China. Most lived in the crowded and squalid conditions of the Chinatowns and low-priced boarding houses. Few, if any, were concerned with establishing long-term communities. Indeed, early bachelor immigration patterns, combined with anti-Chinese laws, prevented Chinese men from fulfilling traditional duties to their ancestors. Many, realizing that they might not return to China, arranged for their remains to be returned to their ancestral villages. As Shin-Shan Henry Tsai explains, the Chinese immigrant "believed that if his body was buried in a strange land, untended by his family, his soul would never stop wandering in the darkness of the other world" (1986:10). In fact, to serve the social and religious needs of Chinese immigrants, a number of associations were established. These became known as the Six Companies, and membership was based on the regional dialect that the Chinese immigrant spoke. Not only did these companies act to protect the interests of their members, but each company set aside a place for honoring homeland gods. Moreover, leaders of the Six Companies saw conversion to Christianity "as a threat to Chinese culture and Chinese social institutions," and thus sought to dissuade their fellow Chinese from visiting Christian missions. "On a few occasions," writes Tsai, "they made desperate moves, using harassment and social ostracism to discourage the increase of Chinese Christians" (1986:45).

As early as the 1850s, Protestant missionaries had entered the mining camps, intent on converting Chinese laborers. A number of missionaries set up medical clinics, offered English language classes, and published bilingual newspapers. Several others, such as Reverend Otis Gibson, aided the poor, established shelters for run-away prostitutes, and sought to improve the welfare of Chinese immigrants. Though few Chinese were converted, those that did, such as Reverend Ng Poon Chew, would later lament the lawless state of the Chinese American community. Gambling, prostitution, and rampant lawbreaking came to characterize the typical Chinatown. "Opium," Chew warned, "is the devil's curse and device for creating misery" (Chew, in Irwin 1893:51). Sadly, he added, while the churches have brought hope to the Chinese, only a handful have accepted the Gospel. "Many things have to be overcome and endured before a Chinaman can be a Christian. He has to discard all the former beliefs and superstitions and ancestral worship which every Chinaman holds dear; and in addition he has to suffer ill-treatment and separation from his former friends and relatives" (1893:54). Despite the efforts of Chew and other evangelists, the Chinese Americans who did convert—and the number of converts before the 1950s continued to remain small—retained some of their traditional practices, such as honoring their ancestors, following prescribed rituals for weddings and funerals, and visiting Chinese temples to pay "occasional respect to Taoist gods" and, of course, to socialize with fellow sojourners (Tsai 1986:44).

The selections of readings in this section that concern the Chinese religious experience in America document both traditional Chinese and recent Christian expressions. These readings include a turn-of-the-century serialized set of profiles written by Sui Sin Far to correct false impressions and stereotypes of the Chinese, an historical overview of traditional Chinese religious beliefs and practices by L. Eve Armentrout Ma, a social scientific study of Chinese Christian churches as a vehicle for preserving Chinese culture, and an excerpt from Amy Tan's book, *The Kitchen God's Wife*, which examines the continuing, if inconvenient, hold of tradition on a modern Chinese American woman. There is also a selection on Chinese temples in the city of Honolulu published in 1937 in the journal *Social Process in Hawaii*.

Though economic opportunities had brought the Chinese to America, it was the vast and fertile agricultural lands that attracted Japanese immigrants to Hawaii and the Pacific coastal regions of the United States. But, while most of the Japanese who first immigrated to the United States in the 1880s were young men, one major difference from the Chinese sojourner was that Japanese Buddhist missionaries accompanied the first waves of Japanese immigrants to America. Nearly 90% of immigrants from Japan were Buddhist, and most were members of Jodo Shinshu, or the Pure Land sect of Mahayana Buddhism. In fact, it was mostly an accident of history that Jodo Shinshu became predominant among the Japanese in America.

First, most Japanese immigrants to Hawaii and California in the 1880s and 1890s—about 60–65%—came from Pure Land regions in southern Japan. Second, Jodo missionaries and priests were among the first to arrive in the United States. Third, those Japanese immigrants who were not originally affiliated with Jodo were drawn to this sect largely because of the opportunity to socialize with other Japanese as well as to fulfill abiding spiritual needs.

The North American Buddhist Mission, later the Buddhist Churches in America (BCA), was officially founded in San Francisco on September 1, 1899. By late December, a second mission had been established in Sacramento, followed in 1901 by a third mission in Fresno and a fourth in Seattle. At that time, the Japanese community numbered just over 2,000. In 1905, the mission headquarters was renamed The Buddhist Church of San Francisco, perhaps to make the English translation of *bukkyokai* (literally "Buddhist association") more Western sounding. In time, the Buddhist temple/church became a central focus of the Japanese immigrant community, most especially during the period of internment during World War II. As Tetsuden Kashima has observed, "[b]y offering a central locale for the Japanese congregation, through its picnics, religious services, Japanese language schools, Japanese cinema, and so on, the church provided a friendly environment for an ethnic group that often encountered hostility from the society at large" (1977:7).

Interestingly, while the Chinese immigrants tended to define themselves by their families, regions, and dialects, the Japanese located themselves by their generation in America: Issei (first), Nisei (second), and Sansei (third). In addition to generational identities, the transformations that took place within the Japanese community's central organization—the Buddhist church—were principally aimed at holding onto the loyalty of the Nisei, and later the Sansei, who were becoming increasingly more Americanized. For instance, to combat the influences of American culture on the Nisei, the BCA established its own youth clubs and sports leagues patterned after such organizations as the Boy and Girl Scouts and Little League Baseball.

The destruction caused by Imperial Japan's attack on Pearl Harbor in December 1941, and its subsequent offensives throughout Asia and the Pacific in 1942, created heightened suspicion of Japanese communities in America and made them a cause for concern during the U.S. mobilization to defend the homeland from possible invasion. In 1942, President Roosevelt ordered the forced evacuation of persons of Japanese descent from the Pacific coastal regions and their placement in "relocation centers" or internment camps. Of the 110,000 Japanese Americans sent to these camps in desolate areas of the country, 70,000 were Nisei. Even so, whether Issei or Nisei, all Japanese Americans were considered potential saboteurs. During the Relocation period, it is estimated that the Japanese Americans lost properties, possessions, businesses, and earnings valued at half a billion dollars. But, despite these losses, one unintended consequence of wartime internment was a renewal of Buddhism among Japanese in the camps. As Gary Okihiro notes, "the large majority of confined Japanese openly espoused Buddhism, and in some camps, Buddhism gained new adherents" (1985:223; reprinted below). The camps also saw "a resurgence of Japanese folk beliefs and practices," most notably at Tule Lake on the California–Oregon border (1985:230). As Okihiro notes further, "Nisei, who were previously drifting away from Japanese culture, were drawn back to the family unit. Discrimination and the denial of their rights disillusioned many Nisei. They now looked more to their families and ethnic community for security and acceptance" (1985:224). After the war, rebuilding the Japanese American community was among their first priorities. But, because many Japanese did not return to their previous homes and businesses, and instead settled and worked elsewhere in the United States, Buddhist churches came to be established in cities across middle America, such as Minneapolis, Cleveland, and Detroit.

Accordingly, the additional readings in this section include several personal reminiscences of Buddhist observance in the temple as well as in the home, and autobiographical stories by Lydia Minatoya that reflect differences in generational perspectives among Japanese Americans. Also, because generational tensions typify other Asian American communities, the pieces by Minatoya and the short story by Chitra Banerjee Divakaruni, titled "The Unknown Errors of Our Lives," provide interesting examples of these tensions and testify to the strangely powerful pull that cultural and religious traditions continue to have upon those whose lives and experiences in modern America would be altogether foreign to their immigrant grandparents or great-grandparents. The final two readings represent examples of religious oral histories, one of a Vietnamese Buddhist nun and the other of a former Cambodian Buddhist monk.

All in all, the readings in this section—though only a thumbnail sketch of the entire Asian American experience—provide the reader with a glimpse of the place that religion and traditional culture have occupied and continue to occupy in most Asian immigrant communities. These readings likewise give voice to the struggles that all immigrant peoples have encountered as settlers or sojourners in this most culturally and religiously diverse nation in the world today.

Sources and Selected Works in Asian American History, Literature, and Religions

[* indicates works of fiction]

Alumkal, Antony W. *Asian American Evangelical Churches: Race, Ethnicity, and Assimilation in the Second Generation.* New York: LFB Scholarly Publishing, 2003.

Bautista, Veltisezar B. *The Filipino Americans from 1763 to the Present: Their History, Culture, and Traditions,* 2nd ed. Naperville, IL: Bookhaus Publishers, 2002.

Bonus, Rick. *Locating Filipino Americans: Ethnicity and the Cultural Politics of Space.* Philadelphia: Temple University Press, 2000.

Buddhist Churches of America (BCA). *Buddhist Churches of America (Vol. 1): 75-Year History, 1899–1974.* Chicago: Nobart, 1974.

———. *Buddhist Churches of America: A Legacy of the First 100 Years.* San Francisco, CA: Buddhist Churches of America, 1998.

Bulosan, Carlos. *America Is in the Heart: A Personal History.* Seattle, WA: University of Washington Press, 1974.

——— (Epifanio San Juan, Jr., ed.). *On Becoming Filipino: Selected Writings of Carlos Bulosan.* Philadelphia: Temple University Press, 1995.

Burns, Jeffrey M., Ellen Skerrett, and Joseph M. White (eds.). *Keeping Faith: European and Asian Catholic Immigrants.* Maryknoll, New York: Orbis Books, 2000.

Carnes, Tony, and Fenggang Yang (eds.). *Asian American Religions: The Making and Remaking of Borders and Boundaries.* New York: New York University Press, 2004.

Cassel, Susie Lan. *The Chinese in America: A History from Gold Mountain to the New Millennium.* Walnut Creek, CA: AltaMira Press, 2002.

Chan, Sucheng. *Asian Californians.* San Francisco: MTL/Boyd and Fraser, 1991.

——— (ed.). *Entry Denied.* Philadelphia: Temple University Press, 1991.

——— (ed.). *The Vietnamese American 1.5 Generation: Stories of War, Revolution, Flight and New Beginnings.* Philadelphia: Temple University Press, 2006.

Chen, Jack. *The Chinese of America.* San Francisco: Harper & Row, 1980.

Cheung, King-Kok (ed.). *An Interethnic Companion to Asian American Literature.* New York: Cambridge University Press, 1997.

——— (ed.). *Words Matter: Conversations with Asian American Writers.* Honolulu, HI: University of Hawai'i Press, 2000.

The Chinese Historical Society of America. *The Life, Influence, and the Role of the Chinese in the United States, 1776–1960: Proceedings, Papers of the National Conference Held at the University of San Francisco, July 10, 11, 12, 1975.* San Francisco: The Chinese Historical Society of America, 1976.

Choy, Bong-Youn. *Koreans in America.* Chicago: Nelson-Hall, 1979.

Daniels, Roger. *Asian America: Chinese and Japanese in the United States since 1850.* Seattle, WA: University of Washington Press, 1988.

——— *Concentration Camps, North America: Japanese in the United States and Canada during World War II.* Malabar, FL: R. E. Krieger, 1981.

*Divakaruni, Chitra Banerjee. *The Unknown Errors of Our Lives.* New York: Anchor Books, 2002.

Do, Hien Duc. *The Vietnamese Americans.* Westport, CT: Greenwood Press, 1999.

Espiritu, Yen Le. *Filipino American Lives.* Philadelphia: Temple University Press, 1995.

———. *Home Bound: Filipino American Lives Across Cultures, Communities, and Countries.* Berkeley, CA: University of California Press, 2003.

Far, Sui Sin (Amy Ling and Annette White-Parks, eds.). *Mrs. Spring Fragrance and Other Writings.* Urbana, IL: University of Illinois Press, 1995.

Farber, Don, and Rick Fields. *Taking Refuge in L.A.: Life in a Vietnamese Buddhist Temple.* New York: Aperture Books, 1987.

Fields, Rick. *How the Swans Came to the Lake: A Narrative History of Buddhism in America*, 3rd ed. Boston: Shambhala, 1992.

Freeman, James M. *Changing Identities: Vietnamese Americans, 1975–1995*. Boston: Allyn & Bacon, 1996.

Fugita, Stephen, and David J. O'Brian. *Japanese American Ethnicity*. Seattle, WA: University of Washington Press, 1991.

Gibson, Rev. O[tis]. *The Chinese in America*. Cincinnati, OH: Hitchcock & Walden, 1877.

Gillenkirk, Jeff, and James Motlow. *Bitter Melon: Stories from the Last Rural Chinese Town in America*. Seattle, WA: University of Washington Press, 1987.

Hayashi, Brian Masaru. *'For the Sake of Our Japanese Brethren': Assimilation, Nationalism, and Protestantism among the Japanese of Los Angeles, 1895–1942*. Stanford, CA: Stanford University Press, 1995.

Henkin, Alan B., and Liem Thanh Nguyen. *Between Two Cultures: The Vietnamese in America*. Saratoga, CA: Century Twenty-One Publishing, 1981.

Hing, Bill Ong. *Making and Remaking Asia America through Immigration Policy, 1850–1990*. Stanford, CA: Stanford University Press, 1993.

Hunter, Louise M. *Buddhism in Hawaii: Its Impact on a Yankee Community*. Honolulu, HI: University of Hawaii Press, 1971.

Hurh, Won Moo, and Kwang Chung Kim. *Korean Immigrants in America: A Structural Analysis of Ethnic Confinement and Adhesive Adaptation*. Rutherford, NJ: Fairleigh Dickinson University Press, 1984.

Ichihashi, Yamato. *Japanese in the United States: A Critical Study of the Problems of the Japanese Immigrants and Their Children*. Stanford, CA: Stanford University Press, 1932.

Irwin, Rev. D. Hanson (ed.). *The Pacific Coast Pulpit*. New York: Fleming H. Revell Co., 1893.

Iwamura, Jane, and Paul Spickard (eds.). *Revealing the Sacred in Asian and Pacific America*. New York: Routledge, 2003.

Jensen, Joan M. *Passage from India: Asian Indian Immigrants in North America*. New Haven, CT: Yale University Press, 1988.

Jeung, Russell. *Faithful Generations: Race and New Asian American Churches*. New Brunswick, NJ: Rutgers University Press, 2005.

Joshi, Khyati Y. *New Roots in America's Sacred Ground: Religion, Race, and Ethnicity in Indian America*. New Brunswick, NJ: Rutgers University Press, 2006.

Kanzaki, Kiichi. *California and the Japanese*. San Francisco: Japanese Association of America, 1921.

Kashima, Tetsuden. *Buddhism in America: The Social Organization of an Ethnic Religious Institution*. Westport, CT: Greenwood Press, 1977.

Kibria, Nazli. *Becoming Asian American: Second-Generation Chinese and Korean American Identities*. Baltimore: The Johns Hopkins University Press, 2004.

———. *Family Tightrope: The Changing Lives of Vietnamese Americans*. Princeton, NJ: Princeton University Press, 1993.

Kim, Ai Ra. *Women Struggling for a New Life: The Role of Religion in the Cultural Passage from Korea to America*. Albany, New York: SUNY Press, 1996.

Kim, Byong-Suh (ed.). *Koreans in America*. Memphis, TN: Association of Korean Christian Scholars in North America, 1977.

Kim, Byong-Suh, and Sang Hyun Lee (eds.). *The Korean Immigrant in America*. Montclair, NJ: Association of Korean Christian Scholars in North America, 1980.

Kim, Elaine H., and Eui-Young Yu (eds.). *East to America: Korean American Life Stories*. New York: The New Press, 1996.

Kim, Ilpyong J. *Korean-Americans: Past, Present, and Future*. Elizabeth, NJ: Hollym International Corp., 2004.

Kim, Kwang Chung, R. Stephen Warner, and Ho-Youn Kwon (eds.). *Korean Americans and Their Religions: Pilgrims and Missionaries from a Different Shore*. University Park, PA: Pennsylvania State University Press, 2001.

Kingston, Maxine Hong. *China Men*. New York: Alfred A. Knopf, 1980.

Kitano, Harry. *The Japanese Americans*. New York: Chelsea House Publishers, 1987.

Kitano, Harry, and Roger Daniels. *Asian Americans: Emerging Minorities*. Englewood Cliffs, NJ: Prentice Hall, 1988.

Kurashige, Lon. *Japanese American Celebration and Conflict: A History of Ethnic Identity and Festival, 1934–1990*. Berkeley, CA: University of California Press, 2002.

Kwon, Okyun. *Buddhist and Protestant Korean Immigrants: Religious Beliefs and Socioeconomic Aspects of Life.* New York: LFB Scholarly Publishing, 2003.

Larson, Louise Leung. *Sweet Bamboo: Saga of a Chinese American Family.* Los Angeles: Chinese Historical Society of Southern California, 1990.

Layman, Emma McCoy. *Buddhism in America.* Chicago: Nelson-Hall, 1976.

Lee, Leo O., and R. David Arkush (trans. and eds.). *Land without Ghosts: Chinese Impressions of America from the Mid-Nineteenth Century to the Present.* Berkeley, CA: University of California Press, 1989.

Lee, Li-Young. *The Winged Seed: A Remembrance.* New York: Simon & Schuster, 1995.

Lee, Mary Paik (Sucheng Chan, ed.). *Quiet Odyssey: A Pioneer Korean Woman in America.* Seattle, WA: University of Washington Press, 1996.

Lee, Rose Hum. *The Chinese in the United States of America.* Hong Kong: Hong Kong University Press/Oxford University Press, 1960.

Lessinger, Johanna. *From the Ganges to the Hudson: Indian Immigrants in New York City.* Boston: Allyn & Bacon, 1995.

Lim, Shirley Geok-lin, and Amy Ling (eds.). *Reading the Literatures of Asian America.* Philadelphia: Temple University Press, 1992.

Ling, Amy. *Between Worlds: Women Writers of Chinese Ancestry.* New York: Pergamon Press, 1990.

Lydon, Sandy. *Chinese Gold: The Chinese in the Monterey Bay Region.* Capitola, CA: Capitola Book Co., 1985.

Lyman, Stanford M. *Chinatown and Little Tokyo: Power, Conflict, and Community among Chinese and Japanese Immigrants in America.* Millwood, New York: Associated Faculty Press, 1986.

Matsuoka, Fumitaka. *Out of Silence: Emerging Themes in Asian American Churches.* Cleveland, OH: United Church Press, 1995.

Melendy, H. Brett. *Chinese and Japanese Americans: Their Contribution to American Society.* New York: Hippocrene, 1984.

Min, Pyong Gap (ed.). *Asian Americans: Contemporary Trends and Issues,* 2nd ed. Thousand Oaks, CA: Pine Forge Press/Sage Publications, 2006.

———— (ed.). *Second Generation: Ethnic Identity among Asian Americans.* Walnut Creek, CA: AltaMira Press, 2002.

Min, Pyong Gap, and Jung Ha Kim (eds.). *Religions in Asian America: Building Faith Communities.* Walnut Creek, CA: AltaMira Press, 2002.

Minatoya, Lydia Yuri. *Talking to the High Monks in the Snow: An Asian American Odyssey.* New York: HarperCollins, 1992.

Montero, Darrel. *Japanese Americans: Changing Patterns of Ethnic Affiliation over Three Generations.* Boulder, CO: Westview Press, 1980.

————. *Vietnamese Americans: Patterns of Resettlement and Socioeconomic Adaptation in the United States.* Boulder, CO: Westview Press, 1979.

Nee, Victor G., and Brett de Bary Nee (eds.). *Longtime Californ': A Documentary Study of an American Chinatown.* Stanford, CA: Stanford University Press, 1986.

Ng, David (ed.). *People on the Way: Asian North Americans Discovering Christ, Culture, and Community.* Valley Forge, PA: Judson Press, 1996.

Ng, Franklin (ed.). *The History and Immigration of Asian Americans.* New York: Routledge, 1998.

Numrich, Paul David. *Old Wisdom in the New World: Americanization in Two Immigrant Theravada Buddhist Temples.* Knoxville, TN: University of Tennessee Press, 1996.

O'Brian, David J., and Stephen Fugita. *The Japanese American Experience.* Bloomington, IN: Indiana University Press, 1991.

Patterson, Wayne. *The Korean Frontier in America: Immigration to Hawaii, 1896–1910.* Honolulu: University of Hawaii Press, 1988.

Prebish, Charles S. *American Buddhism.* North Scituate, MA: Duxbury Press, 1979.

Prebish, Charles S., and Kenneth K. Tanaka (eds.). *The Faces of Buddhism in America.* Berkeley, CA: University of California Press, 1998.

Purkayastha, Bandana. *Negotiating Ethnicity: Second-Generation South Asian Americans Traverse a Transnational World.* New Brunswick, NJ: Rutgers University Press, 2005.

Richardson, E. Allen. *East Comes West: Asian Religions and Cultures in North America*. New York: The Pilgrim Press, 1985.

Root, Maria P. (ed.). *Filipino Americans: Transformation and Identity*. Thousand Oaks, CA: Sage Publications, 1997.

Rutledge, Paul J. *The Role of Religion in Ethnic Self-Identity: A Vietnamese Community*. Lanham, MD: University Press of America, 1985.

———. *The Vietnamese Experience in America*. Bloomington, IN: Indiana University Press, 1992.

San Juan, Epifanio, Jr. *From Exile to Diaspora: Versions of the Filipino Experience in the United States*. Boulder, CO: Westview Press, 1998.

Sano, Roy I. (ed.). *The Theologies of Asian Americans and Pacific Peoples: A Reader*. Berkeley, CA: Asian Center for Theology and Strategies, Pacific School of Religion, 1976.

Saran, Parmatma. *The Asian Indian Experience in the United States*. Cambridge, MA: Schenkman Publishing Co., 1985.

Saran, Parmatma, and Edwin Eames. *The New Ethnics: Asian Indians in the United States*. New York: Praeger, 1980.

Seager, Richard Hughes. *Buddhism in America*. New York: Columbia University Press, 1999.

Shattuck, Cybelle T. *Dharma in the Golden State*. Santa Barbara, CA: Fithian Press, 1996.

Smith-Hefner, Nancy J. *Khmer American: Identity and Moral Education in a Diasporic Community*. Berkeley, CA: University of California Press, 1999.

Spickard, Paul R. *Japanese Americans: The Formation and Transformations of an Ethnic Group*. New York: Twayne Publishers, 1996.

Sung, Betty Lee. *Mountain of Gold: The Story of the Chinese in America*. New York: Macmillan, 1967.

Takaki, Ronald. *Strangers from a Different Shore: A History of Asian Americans*. Boston: Little, Brown and Company, 1989.

*Tan, Amy. *The Joy Luck Club*. New York: G.P. Putnam's Sons, 1989.

*———. *The Kitchen God's Wife*. New York: G.P. Putnam's Sons, 1991.

Tri-State Buddhist Church. *A History of Fifty Years of the Tri-State Buddhist Church, 1916–1966*. Denver, CO: Tri-State Buddhist Church, 1968.

Tsai, Shih-Shan Henry. *The Chinese Experience in America*. Bloomington, IN: Indiana University Press, 1986.

Tuck, Donald R. *Buddhist Churches of America: Jodo Shinshu*. Lewiston, New York: Edwin Mellen Press, 1987.

Tweed, Thomas A., and Stephen Prothero (eds.). *Asian Religions in America: A Documentary History*. New York: Oxford University Press, 1999.

Williams, Duncan Ryuken, and Christopher S. Queen (eds.). *American Buddhism: Methods and Findings in Recent Scholarship*. New York: Routledge/Curzon, 1999.

Williams, Raymond B. *Religions of Immigrants from India and Pakistan*. Cambridge, UK: Cambridge University Press, 1988.

Wong, K. Scott, and Sucheng Chan (eds.). *Claiming America: Constructing Chinese American Identities during the Exclusion Era*. Philadelphia: Temple University Press, 1998.

Wu, Jean Yu-wen Shen, and Min Song (eds.). *Asian American Studies: A Reader*. New Brunswick, NJ: Rutgers University Press, 2000.

Yanagisako, Sylvia Junko. *Transforming the Past: Tradition and Kinship among Japanese Americans*. Stanford, CA: Stanford University Press, 1985.

Yang, Fenggang. *Chinese Christians in America: Conversion, Assimilation, and Adhesive Identities*. University Park, PA: Pennsylvania State University Press, 1999.

Yoo, Boo-Woong. *Korean Pentecostalism: Its History and Theology*. New York: Peter Lang, 1988.

Yoo, David K. *Growing Up Nisei: Race, Generation, and Culture Among Japanese Americans of California, 1924–1949*. Urbana, IL: University of Illinois Press, 2000.

——— (ed.). *New Spiritual Homes: Religion and Asian Americans*. Honolulu, HI: University of Hawaii Press, 1999.

Yung, Judy, Gordon Chang, and Him Mark Lai (eds.). *Chinese American Voices: From the Gold Rush to the Present*. Berkeley, CA: University of California Press, 2006.

Zhou, Min, and James V. Gatewood (eds.). *Contemporary Asian America: A Multidisciplinary Reader*. New York: New York University Press, 2000.

Some Suggested Questions for Discussion

1. Compare the differing experiences of the Chinese and Japanese. Besides the anti-Asian discrimination that both of these groups have experienced, how similarly or differently did these communities develop in America? What role did or does the observance of traditional cultural and religious practices appear to play in building and uniting an immigrant community? How do such traditions reinforce ethnic and religious identity? At the same time, how might such traditions hinder a community's development?

2. Generally speaking, there do not appear to be many differences in the experiences of those immigrating to the United States. All appear to struggle with maintaining their religious beliefs and observing traditional religious practices. What is it about religious and cultural pluralism that makes maintenance of one's particular homeland traditions difficult, if not impossible? Are accommodation and compromise—and eventual assimilation—inevitable?

3. Given the readings by Eve Ma and Amy Tan, reflect upon the domestic concerns that religion addresses. What do these concerns tell us about gender roles, both in their customary forms as well as their modern evolving forms?

4. One interesting aspect of the Asian immigration to America has been the cultural and religious *discontinuity* that has informed that experience. List and discuss several of these discontinuities between Asian and Western traditions. In what ways have Asian Americans—including the authors and researchers whose works are reprinted in this section of readings—sought to *reduce* or even to *heighten* these discontinuities?

The Chinese in America

Intimate Study of Chinese Life in America.
Told in a Series of Short Sketches—An Interpretation
of Chinese Life and Character.

SUI SIN FAR

In these days when the future of China is being discussed by all thinking people, one reads much in the papers and magazines about Chinese diplomats, Chinese persons of high rank, Chinese students, both boys and girls, Chinese visitors of prominence, scholars and others, who by reason of wealth and social standing, are interesting to the American people, but of those Chinese who come to live in this land, to make their homes in America, some permanently, others for many years, we hear practically nothing at all. Yet these Chinese, Chinese-Americans I call them, are not unworthy of a little notice, particularly as they sustain throughout the period of their residence here, a faithful and constant correspondence with relations and friends in the old country, and what they think and what they write about Americans, will surely influence, to a great extent, the conduct of their countrymen towards the people of the United States. For the Chinese on the Pacific Coast are numbered by the thousands. There is scarcely a city that does not have its local Chinatown or a number of Chinese residents. Many of these men are possessed of fine business ability, some are scholars; those of them who are laborers are stalwart, self-respecting countrymen from the district around Canton city and province, or are American-born descendants of the pioneer Chinamen who came to this Coast long before our transcontinental railways were built, and helped the American to mine his ore, build his railways and cause the Pacific Coast to blossom like the rose. In the romantic past of this western country, the figure of the Chinaman stands forth conspicuously, and every true Westerner will admit that the enlarged life in which he is participating today could not have been possible without the Chinese.

Their reasons for exile, apart from the "fortune" question, are individually interesting; the observations of the most intelligent on American life and manners are pertinent and instructive. If the Chinese can learn much from the Americans, the former can also teach a few lessons to the latter. No one, who, without prejudice, goes amongst the Chinese people in America and converses with them in friendly fashion but will find food for thought.

My father, who lived in China for many years, who married a Chinese lady, and who was a personal friend of Li Soon, Li Hung Chang's secretary, is of the opinion that one has a much better opportunity to study Chinese character in this country than in China, for here the Chinese are naturally more communicative than when in their own land. As for me, my interest in them has been keen and perpetual since the day I learned that I was of their race. And I have found them wherever I have wandered. In New York are some of my best Chinese friends; nearly every mail brings me news from Chinese Canadians, both east and west. Down in the West Indies I met a Chinese whose intelligence and active heroism in a moment of danger and distress will cause him and his compatriots to be ever remembered with gratitude and a warm feeling of kinship. In Los Angeles, San Francisco and the Puget Sound cities I know Chinese, both men and women, whose lives, if written, would read like romances, and whose qualities of mind and heart cannot help but win the interest and respect of all who know them understandingly.

It is true that they—these Chinese people—like other nationalities, have their own peculiar customs, manners and characteristics; but in a broad sense they are one with the other peoples of the earth. They think and act just as the white man does, according to the impulses which control them. They love those who love them; they hate those who hate; are kind, affectionate, cruel or selfish, as the case may be. I have not found them to be slow of intellect and alien to all other races in that "they are placed and unfeeling, and so custom-bound that even their tears are mere waters of ceremony and flow forth at stated times and periods." Thus a European traveler some centuries ago described the Chinese people, and travelers ever since, both men and women, have echoed his words and sentiments, while fiction writers seem to be so imbued with the same ideas that you scarcely ever read about a Chinese person who is not a wooden peg. There are a few exceptions, but the majority of writers on things Chinese echo those who enter before, which is a very foolish thing to do in these revolutionary days. The Chinese may be custom-bound—no doubt they are—but they are human beings, nevertheless. In this country they are slow to push their individual claims, and when with strangers, hide the passions of their hearts under quiet and peaceful demeanors; but because a man is indisposed to show his feelings is no proof that he has none. Under a quiet surface the Chinaman conceals a rapid comprehension and an almost morbid sensitiveness; he also possesses considerable inventive power and is more of an initiative spirit than an imitative one, whatever may be said to the contrary by those who know him but superficially. The pleasures of life he takes quietly; there is a melancholy trait in the characters of most Chinamen, as in all people of old civilizations. His mysticism and childlike faith in the marvelous is also an inheritance from his ancestors. Yet we are not without the Chinaman, merry and glad and full of exuberant animal spirits. Indeed, there is no type of white person who cannot find his or her counterpart in some Chinese. Therefore the following sketches of Chinese in America:

The Story of Wah

Wah was a leading member of the Chinese Reform party, whom I met in this city some years ago. He was an alert-minded young fellow, full of enthusiasm for the Reform cause and ambitious to learn the ways of the western people. His father, as he informed me, was a school teacher. "Then," I said, "you, being but a merchant, are not as much in the eyes of your people as your father was." Wah smiled. "We do not think in China as we did in the old days," said he. In Canton we have as much esteem for the clever man of business as we have for the scholar. When my father was a boy it was different." And he went on to compare his father's China with the China of his own remembrance, demonstrating in a surprisingly clear and convincing manner the progress that had been made.

"Why did you come to this country?" I inquired. "To make money and to learn western ways quicker than I could at home," he answered. Picking up an English paper lying on the table and pointing to a picture of an antique book which was advertised for sale, he inquired why it was marked at such a high price as $500. A lady explained that its age made it valuable. He thought for a moment, then said, "Why, then, is the Bible so cheap? It is very old book."

After a while he remarked that it might be a good plan to send to China for some old things for his store. "They will not be so expensive as newly manufactured goods," said he, "and if I can sell them at a higher price, I shall certainly make my fortune in a very little while."

Wah was a practical man of business, but his principles would have done honor to the noblest philanthropist. He had opportunities of making a great deal of money through the smuggling of opium from Canada into the United States. A safe and secret way was open to him through one of his own cousins. But Wah refused to have anything to do with the business. "No," he answered. "I wish for my countrymen to rise, not to fall, and when I speak at the Reform Club I advise that the pipe should be cast out. How, then, can I place it in their hand? Would that not be inconsistent?"

A Chinese Book on Americans

"I think," said Go Ek Ju, "that when I return to China I will write a book about the American people."

"What put such an idea into your head?" I asked.

"The number of books about the Chinese by Americans," answered Go Ek Ju. "I see them in the library; they are very amusing."

"See, then, that when you write your book, it is likewise amusing."

"No," said Go Ek Ju. "My aim, when I write a book about Americans will be to make it not amusing, but interesting and instructive. The poor Americans have to content themselves with writing for amusement only because they have no means of obtaining any true knowledge of the Chinese when in China; but we Chinese in America have fine facilities for learning all about the Americans. *We go into the American houses as servants; we enter the American schools and colleges as students;* we ask questions and we think about what we hear and see. Where is there the American who will go to China and enter into the service of a Chinese family as a domestic? We have yet to hear about a band of American youths, both male and female, being admitted as students into a Chinese university."

Scholar or Cook?

"You seem to enjoy your work," I remarked to Wang Liang, who was making cake in the hotel kitchen, meanwhile crooning a low song.

"It is very pleasant work," was his reply.

"What did you do when you were in China?" I inquired.

"I was a scholar."

"A scholar?"

Wang Liang went on making his cakes.

"Why," I mused aloud, "I thought a scholar in China was not supposed to know anything about work."

"True," answered Wang Liang; "a scholar must be helpless in all ways in spite of his learning. But my mother was ill and needed ginseng and chicken broth, and my father was getting old, and we were poor. All the time my heart was sad, for my parents had always been very good and kind to me and I loved them much. Then one day I read in my Classics, 'Those who labor support those who govern,' and I reasoned that if those who labored supported those who governed, then the laborer must in no wise be inferior to him who governs. So I decided to work with my hands, and in order that my parents might not be made to feel ashamed, I came to America. Since I have come here, with my labor I have supported myself, paid back my passage money to the agent who loaned it to me, kept my father and mother in comfort at home and have placed some part of every month's wages in a bank. When I have enough to live on for the rest of my life I will return to China and again take up my studies and do honor to my parents as a scholar."

Wang Liang rubbed his hands together and laughed softly and gleefully.

—*Westerner*, May 1909

The Chinese in America, Part II
The New and the Old

The following story of youthful business enterprise is told by Lu Seek, a prosperous Chinese merchant and the owner of many shares in a Mexican railway.

"I came to this country at an early age. I first worked for my Uncle who gave me food, lodging and clothing in return for my services. I attended Mission schools of all denominations, Presbyterian, Episcopal, Baptist, Methodist and Roman Catholic. I learned the English language with little difficulty. From the American youth I also learned that a young person's time in America is quite as valuable as any elderly person's, and that eighteen years of age was a far superior age to forty-eight. Imbued with this knowledge I began to assume airs of dignity. When my Uncle bade me do this or that I would answer negligently—sometimes with hauteur. Whereupon my Uncle was one morning led to try the gentle persuasion of a stick. I objected. I said to him, 'Honorable Uncle, you do not respect me as you should nor do you consider that we are living in America, where a man instead of looking backward and admiring one's parents and uncles, fixes his mind on himself, thinks for himself and so acts that his parents and uncles, instead of wishing and requiring him to admire them wonder at and admire him.'

"'Admire you,' exclaimed my Uncle, with an expression of furious contempt and another well aimed blow at my head, which, however, I successfully dodged.

"'That is what they believe in the west,' I persisted, 'and that is why they of the west progress and those of the east stand still.'

"My Uncle's reply conveyed the impression that there was a difference of opinion between us, and as a difference of opinion is a very sad thing to have between those who live under the same roof, I suggested to my Uncle that he hand over to me the sum of money which he held in trust for me from my father, and I would walk my way which was evidently not his way.

"My Uncle considered for fifteen minutes, then he went to his till, took therefrom fifty silver dollars, the amount of my inheritance, and threw them down on the counter. I quickly pocketed them, and with what few personal belongings I possessed rolled up under my arm, started out in the world to seek my fortune.

"I had not gone very far when I met some of my white acquaintances. I informed them that I had been putting into practice the principles they had inculcated, and they cheered me on and told me that I would not take very long for me to become a real American of free and independent spirit. I showed them my fifty dollars and invited them to lunch with me. This invitation they accepted. The fifty dollars soon became ten. Half of that I spent in buying a present for my Sunday school teacher.

"I then tried to earn my own living as a cook or laundryman, but was not successful. I had no experience in the kitchen, neither was I learned in the lore of the laundry, and though I have known many of my countrymen, who as inexperienced as I, have yet made many successes of these callings, it was plain to be seen that as my American friends observed, I had a soul above domestic service. One day, my Sunday school teacher, who was unaware that I had left my Uncle's store, asked me if I knew of a good Chinese boy who could act as a general servant. I mentioned the names of several and she thanked me, remarking that I was better than an Employment Bureau. That put an idea into my head. I would start such an office and provide help for the American ladies. Though I could not secure employment myself I might obtain it for others. I was acquainted with many Mission and Sunday school ladies, whom I knew would bring their friends to me when they needed servants, and for all my estrangement from my Uncle, I was quite popular with the youth of Chinatown.

"But to start a business a little capital is necessary, and that I lacked. I was musing on this fact and a hungry stomach, when I met a second cousin of mine who did business as a fortune teller near the corner of Dupont and Kearney streets. 'Have you eaten your rice?' he exclaimed. That is a simple Chinese greeting but I took it literally and humbled myself to explain that I had no money with which to buy rice. He stroked his chin reflectively, and remarked that it was a pity that my forefathers had not bequeathed to me the spirit of divination; for if such had been the case, he himself would have been glad to adopt me as an assistant in the expounding of mythical lore.

"As we talked together, he in his long silken robes, I in my exceedingly shabby American store clothes, I envied him his prosperity, his calm and affable manners, his pleasing reposeful face. I knew that his elegantly furnished office was quite a resort for the perplexed of Chinatown's four hundred, and moreover, that many unsettled white people also surreptitiously visited him in the hope of having light thrown on certain difficult questions. I knew that through the fortunate reading of her father's horoscope, he had won as wife the prettiest American born Chinese girl in the City of the Golden Gate. Yet, curious fact—for all my envy of his accomplishments and attainments, I had not the slightest desire to be as he—reader of the stars. It was too ancient a business, and though my cousin had found it practical enough for all his purposes, it did not appeal to me in any sense as a business. I wanted a business which would call for a telephone and electric lights; not candles, incense, tortoise shells and diagrams.

"My cousin was both good hearted and good natured. After dining me, he himself proposed that he set me up in a small Chinese drug store. The herbs with which Chinese doctors' prescriptions are usually filled would not cost much; and the dried nuts, lily bulbs, fish eggs, and other stock necessary, could also be obtained without much outlay. In particular, he advised this business, as a Chinese fortune teller often acts as physician, and it would be in his power to occasionally send me customers.

"But I had in mind the Employment Bureau and nothing else would do for me. I said to my cousin: 'Since you are so kind as to propose to set me up in a business to your liking, perhaps you will be a little kinder still and help me to start a business to my liking.' And I told him of my dreams of the Employment Bureau. For a time my cousin scoffed. For one who was unable to find work for himself to seek to make a living by obtaining it for others seemed too absurd. It would be a case of the blind leading the blind.

"Thus he argued. My arguments are unnecessary to relate. Suffice it to say, however, that they won, and when I left my cousin I was furnished with the necessary funds to launch myself on the business career I had chosen.

"I set up my office near the Plaza. From my doorway I could see the drinking fountain which is put up as a memorial to your great writer, Robert Louis Stevenson. Well, to my great satisfaction, it was not long before I found myself standing under an electric light with a green shade answering a call from a society lady on Nob Hill. She was desiring a boy accomplished in the art of cooking. After that the calls came frequently— and I had dozens of Chinese boys ready to answer. Sometimes my customers would interview me several times before deciding on a boy. From their conversations I derived much benefit.

"That was the beginning of my good fortunes. I found that by maintaining a pleasant demeanor and an affable tongue I could manage to get along very well in the finding of employment for my countrymen in America. Because I was reminded of your great writer by the fountain in the Square or Plaza I bought all of his works from a book agent on the installment plan and read them between the hours of business. I admired much his 'Treasure Island,' and the reading thereof furnished me with good conversation whenever the ladies came to my office. Of course I used my discretion. There were some ladies who did not read Robert Louis Stevenson, you understand. There were other ladies who did. I am of opinion that taken all around Robert Louis Stevenson improved much my business.

"When I had made a few thousand dollars I decided to go to live in New York and sell out my business to my third cousin, Lu Wing. He was the adopted brother of the Fortune Teller cousin who had loaned me the money with which to start business and whose debt I had repaid with interest out of what I made my first year. Just before leaving for the big city I called upon my Uncle, and after making a most humble and contrite apology for my past conduct and the improper speeches connected therewith, persuaded him to pay me a visit at my office. There I smoked with him the pipe of peace, and there the old man, after speaking through the phone with some friend in San Jose, acknowledged that it was true—the days were over for young people to wonder at and admire their parents and the time had come for the old people to wonder at and admire them.

"'That is progress,' I replied.

"'When it is not carried to extremes.' supplemented my wife, an American Chinese girl."

—*Westerner*, June 1909

The Chinese in America, Part III
Like the American

When Tin-a came over the sea to be wife to Sik Ping, there were great rejoicings in Chinatown, for Sik Ping was very popular. Many dinner parties were given, some very brilliant affairs indeed. The one that I attended was on the top floor of a Chinatown building. The dining room was elegantly furnished with black teak wood tables and carved chairs inlaid with mother of pearl; screens adorned the partitions between rooms, and there were couches along the wall where after dining one could lie at ease and smoke; the place was brilliantly illuminated with electric lights and red Chinese candles, and a large incense burner suspended from the ceiling in the middle of the room, filled the air with a truly Oriental fragrance.

Though it is not the custom for Chinese women to sit at meat with men, Sik Ping was Americanized enough to seat his wife by his side. The wife of Go Ek Ju, his friend, gave face to Tin-a as the Chinese say.

The tables were loaded with dishes of chicken, bamboo shoots and confections of all kinds known to the Chinese. Both men and women were attired in gorgeous silk robes, the latter wearing flowers in their hair and in front of their tunics. Each and every one of the Chinese guests presented Sik Ping with a sum of money, as is the custom amongst the Chinese on such occasions.

There was a strange scene at the close of the evening. The little bride, who throughout dinner had sat with downcast eyes, scarcely touching a morsel of food, upon leaving the table was seen to be weeping. Mrs. Go Ek Ju sought to discover the source of her tears, and after a murmured conversation with Tin-a reluctantly informed Sik Ping that his bride had confessed to being afraid that he would be angry with her.

"Afraid that I be angry with her!" exclaimed poor Sik Ping bewilderedly. "Ah No!"

Whereupon Amoy hung her head and shed more tears.

It came out at last that Ping's bride was not the girl whom a cousin had married for him by proxy and for whom he had sent the passage money from China to America. That girl had formed an attachment for her proxy husband, who reciprocated the feeling, they having reaped in the rice fields together. She accordingly prevailed upon Tin-a, her friend, who was an orphan of adventurous spirit, and whose name was the same as her own, to undertake the long ocean journey from which she shrunk and become in reality wife to Sik Ping.

But Tin-a no sooner beheld Ping's kind face when she became conscience stricken, and that feeling so overwhelmed her when he had placed her beside him at the dinner table that she had been unable to restrain her tears.

"Ah!" she cried, falling on the ground at his feet. "You are so good and kind and I so deceitful and evil." But Ping, who had never seen the girl to whom he was married by proxy and who had conceived an affection for the little Tin-a, instead of upbraiding her with hard words, comforted her with loving ones, and the day following bought a marriage license and was married over again by the Chinese missionary.

"I do as the Americans do," said Ping proudly. "I marry the woman I love."

The Story of Forty-Niner

"Why did you come to America?" I asked a Chinaman who was beating a gold ring into shape. He was a manufacturing jeweler.

"Why did I come? Oh, it is so long ago since I came that I am not sure that I can remember the reasons."

And Hom Hing, being a good-natured fellow, began:

"My father had two boys, myself and my brother. I was the eldest, so my father chose me to be the scholar. Therefore, while I was clothed in the best style which the family circumstances would allow, my little queue tied neatly with a string, an embroidered cap on my head, and the whitest of white-soled shoes on my feet, fed on the best which the house afforded and kept in idleness save for study, my brother roamed about the village, bare-footed, bare-headed, and almost bare-bodied. He gathered the wood for fuel, hoed the ground, reaped in the rice fields and grew healthy and handsome. My mother and sisters treated me with respectful politeness, but to my brother they were always careless in manner. As I did nothing but study, naturally my body was weak and I suffered from the slightest exertion or exposure to heat or cold. I was kept at my books from morning till night while I was at home and attended the village school, and when I was old enough to be sent to the university I studied even harder. I was imbued with ambition to become a great scholar and do honor to my parents, but for all that I unconsciously envied my brother, whose lusty arms could fell an ox. When my sisters were given as wives for sons of other families, it became necessary that my brother and myself should marry in order that my mother should have a girl to help her in the house. I was accordingly married by proxy while still in the university. My brother also married, and when I returned home, there was a little son of his crawling about the floor. Our family had become impoverished during my university years, my father was old and unable to do much; almost the whole burden of supporting the family, including myself, fell upon my brother's shoulders.

That year agents of certain Chinese Companies came around our village bribing men to go to America. They offered my father quite a large sum for my brother, Hom Ling, and my father, after talking the matter over with my mother, decided to accept the money and send my brother, Hom Ling, to work in the country across the sea. My parents had no doubt, from what was told them, that Hom Ling's labor would soon repay those who advanced his passage money to America and then he would be free to send his wages home.

"Now, my brother, Hom Ling, loved his wife and child, and the thought of being separated from them filled his heart with sorrow. He spoke to me about it with many sighs, for, though the course of our lives ran in such different channels, we were brothers in affection as well as in blood. While he was lamenting his fate, an inspiration came to me. He was to leave the village at night in company with some other youths. In the darkness it would be impossible to distinguish one lad from another, and though I was weak and he strong, we were of the same build. The cause of this inspiration was the fact that, despite the respect that was paid me, I found home life unbearable. After having lived away from home for several years, my mother, my wife and my sister-in-law's tongues sounded discordantly in my ears. My sedentary life had made me nervous and irritable. Moreover, the wife that had been chosen for me was most repulsive to my taste.

"Why not, then," I suggested to my brother, "that I be the one to go and you be the one to remain?"

"But my parents have placed all their hopes on you," demurred my brother, albeit with brightening eyes.

"Fiddlesticks!" I answered in Chinese, "I shall be doing better by my parents by leaving them you than by remaining with them myself. It will be years before I can earn even my own living as a school teacher and you can help them straight along."

"So I came to America. On this side the change of brothers was never discovered. As for me, the new life brought with renewed health and strength. In the old California days the Chinese lived and worked in the open air, and the work of a laborer in America is easy compared to that of a laborer in China. I had better food and more than I had ever had in my life, and the sunshine and freshness of this western country transformed me both physically and mentally. It is living, not studying that makes a man. Adventures and hairbreadth escapes from death were frequent; hard times, too, but I managed to pull through after fifteen years of it with a nice little bag of gold with which I returned to China. My parents were still living and my brother was surrounded by a large family; my first wife had died. I married a pretty tea picker whom I met while rambling among the hills. She was a slave girl, but I paid her price, and in spite of my parents' opposition, brought her back with me to America. This business I learned after my mining days were over. I have two sons and one daughter, all married and living in this country."

The Story of Tai Yuen and Ku Yum

Tai Yuen was Ku Yum's lover; but whereas Tai Yuen was a See Yup, Ku Yum's father was a Sam Yup. A See Yup is a man from the fourth district of the Province of Kwangtung, a Sam Yup a man from the Third district. Some time before the tale of Tai Yuen and Ku Yum was told, a Sam Yup murdered a See Yup. This was in Southern California. All the See Yups knew that one of their number had been killed by a Sam Yup; but though they thirsted for revenge they could not discover the murderer. It therefore became a case, not of man against man, but of district against district, and as a result a Sam Yup soon went the way of the murdered See Yup. The Sam Yups, however, proved better detectives than their enemies, and traced the crime so that the actual murderer, a man belonging to one of the See Yup's Secret Societies, was convicted and punished by the law of the land. At this the See Yups became so bitterly incensed that notice to boycott all Sam Yups was sent by their chiefs to the See Yups all over the continent. The boycott spread and became a serious matter, for the See Yups are much more numerous than the Sam Yups, the See Yups being chiefly laundrymen and laboring men, and the Sam Yups merchants who depend for the success of their business upon the trade of the See Yups.

Now Tai Yuen was an Americanized Chinaman, having come to this coast at a very early age, and Ku Yum was American born. So when Tai Yuen and Ku Yum met, they fell in love with one another, just as any American boy and girl might have done, and after some more meetings became engaged in true American fashion. It was shortly after they became engaged that the boycott between the Sam Yups and the See Yups became established.

"Do not venture to see me any more," bade poor Ku Yum, fearful for her lover's safety.

But Tai Yuen, being imbued with the American spirit, heeded not her warning, and one night when on his way to see his sweet heart, trusted emissaries of the See Yups' secret society dogged his footsteps. And Ku Yum still looks for her lover.

Wah Lee on Family Life

Wah Lee had left his home when a youth of fifteen with a company of strolling actors who had pitched camp in his home village for a week. From what I learned from a clansman of his, his father's family was a very large one, and home had been full of strife and contention. One day I asked him if he did not wish to return to China. His face sobered at once.

"I love my parents," he answered. "I send to them some part of what I make every month; but when I am at home I am unhappy. Too many tongues in the house interfere with peace." His brothers and sisters numbered fourteen.

"Quite a Rooseveltian family," I observed.

"I think President Roosevelt likes a joke," was his quick reply. "He declares to his people that the best thing for a country is big families, and then he commands them to teach our people to be like them."

Lee had lived for some years in Eastern Canada, and as he had worked in families both there and in the United States, being smuggled backwards and forwards across the line whenever the fancy pleased him, his observations on family life and some of his comparisons were to me quite illuminating. "The French Canadians," he remarked, "are more like the Chinese at home than are the Americans. The parents boss and the children obey; but there is not as much affection of the heart between them as I see in some American families—some not at all. There is also much form of religion with the Canadians and the Chinese. In America it is different. I have been in some families where the religion is not seen at all; but it is felt. That is what makes the heart glad; and to see the father and mother the true friend of the son and daughter, not the boss. The poorer families in Canada have many children, just as in China.

"It makes me sad," said he, "to see a poor little niece of ten years old carrying in her slender arms her uncle or aunt of four or five months. Yet that is what I see very often in Eastern Canada. Some of the little girls never have time to play nor to go to school; there are so many babies to be carried. And if they are not carrying babies, then they must go to work, for the father has too big a family of younger children to support them. And the mother is so cross with so many, and hard words and cruel blows drive the children into the street to steal and do other things for which the priest and the Sunday school teacher scold them. And there is much noise and confusion all the time just like in the big families in China. I think it is better in America, where the family is not so large, but where the children have a happy time and are well brought up. When I was in Montreal I read that more babies die in that city than in any other city in the world. Yet, the men in the black dresses who do not have any children themselves go around to the poor man and advise him all the time, 'Have plenty children, Have plenty children!' The poor little children. I feel so sorry for them!"

The Bonze

I came across Ke Leang in a Joss house. He was a Bonze, or Chinese priest, and a remarkably handsome man. I used to enjoy wandering about the Joss houses, admiring the quaint carvings and images, pondering and wondering over the mysterious hieroglyphics, and now and then confiscating a piece of sandal wood. At that time I had a rage for sandal wood. One day, having possessed myself of a larger piece than usual, I was about to move quietly away from the green bowl or jar from which I had taken it, when a quiet voice just behind me said: "If you like the wood you can take some more." I started guiltily. It was the priest, Ke Leang. He had placed his hand on the bowl and was tipping it towards me. I had the grace to demur, but blunderingly, I said, "Oh, I don't like to take any more. It is sacred, isn't it?" "Not at all," he answered. Then, calmly, and I fancied sarcastically, "Is it so to you?"

I felt ashamed, and feeling ashamed, began to talk of other things. I told him that my mother was Chinese, but because my father was an Englishman and I had been born in England and brought up in Canada, and by choice, lived in America, I was unable to speak my mother tongue. He did not at first pay much attention to my chatter, but when I brought forth a letter of introduction from Chinese friends in my home city to Chinese in other parts of the world, he became more communicative, and I had quite a long chat with him about Chinese religion. He told me that it was error to think that the Chinese bow down in spirit to wood or stone or anything made of such materials. It is true the Chinamen prostrates himself bodily before his ancestral tablets, his images of male and female divinities, but he worships in spirit only the spirit that is supposed to dwell in the image, and not the image itself, which is nothing more to him that what it is—a piece of wood or stone. He declared emphatically that the Chinese worship spirits, not images. "We worship," said he, "in the same way that I have seen American people worshiping in Catholic churches. We kneel before Mother (Ahmah, a Chinese goddess) as the Catholics kneel to the Virgin Mary."

He shook his head gravely when I asked him, in my ignorance, if he were a Confucianist. He admitted, however, that Confucianism, pure and simple, was the religion of most of the learned men of China.

Before I left San Francisco an American friend of mine who occasionally told a true story told me this one of Ke Leang, the Chinese priest.

Ke Leang lived in the province of the Happy River. That was when he was young, happy and not a priest. There also lived Mai Gwi Far. Their parents' houses were close together, the gardens being separated by high stone walls. There was a hole in the separating wall. Mai Gwi Far and Ke Leang looked through the hole. Moreover, they spoke—sighed—smiled. When Ke Leang went to the university in another province he carried within his sleeve one of Mai Gwi Far's little red shoes. Just before the examination for the second literary degree Ke Leang received a letter from Mai Gwi Far. She was in great distress. The leaves of her rose geranium were withering and the night before she had heard the cry of an owl, now near, now far away. These signs meant sorrow and trouble. She feared, she knew not what. Was Ke Leang forgetting her and laughing and jesting with the Sing Song girls—they who sung and danced and painted their faces? Would he be interested to know that her parents had betrothed her to the son of a friend, and that she was to prepare for marriage within five months? The engagement was short because she was beyond the age for betrothing, being seventeen. She was so troubled and sad. What should she do? She awaited his reply with a beating heart. On that same day Ke Leang also received word from his parents that they had betrothed him to the daughter of their neighbor, Mai Gwi Far, she who was called the Pearl of Honan. In the exuberance of his joy at this news Ke Leang lost wisdom and, seeing by Mai Gwi Far's letter that she was as yet in ignorance of the name of her future husband, the spirit of mischief prompted him to sit down and pen the following message to the girl: "Marry the one whom your parents have chosen." When his carrier dove reached Mai Gwi Far it was night. The little bird tapped at her pane as it was wont to do, and she arose and, bringing it in, untied from under its wing her lover's message.

In the morn her parents found her cold in death, the jesting note beside her. It had certainly been her death blow. That is the reason why Ke Leang was a priest in San Francisco's Chinatown. All ambition to attain his literary degree perished with Mai Gwi Far. He entered a monastery and ten years later was ordered by his Abbott to cross the sea to minister to the Chinese people in San Francisco.

—Westerner, July 1909

The Chinese in America, Part IV
Yip Ke Duck and the Americans

"I do not like the Americans," quote old Yip Kee Duck. "They do not speak the truth; they are hypocrites; they think only of money; they pretend to be your friends, to admire you, to like you; but for all their smiles and soft words, they mean to swindle you and do you harm. Behind your back they laugh and sneer; they make amusement for themselves out of all the Chinaman says and does. When they come to trade with him, they expect their goods for next to nothing. Around Christmas time, there are always plenty of Sunday School teachers ready to teach the Chinese. They know the Chinese boys never forget to give presents. Whenever a white man does a little business with or throws business into the way of a Chinese, he looks for a bonus bigger than any profits that the Chinaman may gain. I have been fooled by them too often. 'He that hath wine has many friends.' Now they can fool me no more. Moreover, I shall warn all the Chinese boys that believe in the American Sunday school and the American Sunday school teachers. I shall tell my people in China that Americans are not only devils when they call you names and throw stones at you; but they are worse devils still when they come to you and say, 'Oh, Mr. Yip Kee Duck, how quaint and curious and beautiful is your store. What wonderful people you Chinese are! I wish I were one!' and all that fool talk."

Poor old Yip Kee Duck! Like some others of his race in this country, the treatment accorded him by the Americans had made him very bitter and cynical. For, in spite of all the honest endeavors and good work of some of the Christian missionaries and church women there are those amongst them who are wolves in sheep's clothing, and who bring disrepute upon their cause.

It is almost unbelievable the shameless way in which some white people will act towards the Chinese. This was brought to my attention in many very pointed ways when I was in San Francisco. I was very hard up at that time, and in order to obtain bread and butter put in some time canvassing Chinatown for the San Francisco Bulletin. For every subscription that I secured the paper was to pay me thirty cents. When soliciting from the Chinese merchants I simply asked them to sign their name to the voucher setting forth that they agreed to take the paper. Many of these merchants in answer to my request that they subscribe for the paper, would offer me the amount of the subscription for my own use. "Never mind about sending the paper. Just keep the money yourself," said one. I had difficulty indeed in impressing upon them that I was collecting autographs, not money. One fellow, when reluctantly returning the cash asked, "Perhaps you take it next time you come."

It seems that women who would sooner jump into the fire than ask a white man for money or presents will boldly demand such things of a Chinaman, and I have myself seen American women enter a Chinese store, take up some trinket they fancy, and ask the Chinaman to give it to them. He can hardly refuse, and boldly she walks off with her prize. But she has made a mistake. If a woman sinks low in the eyes of a white man by acting that way, she sinks lower still in the eyes of a Chinaman. To retain the respect of the Chinese, both at home and abroad, one must be careful to keep themselves perfectly independent of them. The respect of the Chinese has been worth much more than mere cash or a few trinkets to me.

At the same time the Chinaman is naturally a very kind, generous and open-hearted fellow, slow to think evil, appreciative of goodness, and respectful to every woman who deserves respect. That is why it is such a pity that they do not always see and know the genuine American, the sincere Christian. They are anxious to learn the best that America can teach them, they are so quick to discern truth and goodness to admire it. Very few of them are Yip Kee Ducks. I have known Chinamen to lose faith in person after person, and yet retain his faith in the American people as a whole. Although the scholars and students who come to our shores are properly conservative when pressing themselves concerning things American, the simple yet intelligent Chinamen who are with us gladly acknowledge that many of the ways of the white man are better than the ways of the Chinese.

New Year as Kept by the Chinese in America

Have you ever noticed how very happy looking the American Chinese are from Christmas to the end of their New Year? They are happy because during this topsy turvy season they can indulge their heart's content in the pleasure of giving. Not indiscriminately, of course; but to those who during the year have won, sometimes designedly, sometimes unconsciously, their liking or their gratitude. The Chinese never think of telling you that "it is more blessed to give than to receive." Perhaps their minds have not yet been educated to grasp the meaning of the saying, but they prove its truth. Give a Chinaman a present and he will thank you gratefully, but very calmly. No emotion disturbs his countenance. There is no visible pleasure. But allow him to give you something and watch his face as you receive it from his hand. You will see expressed real, true solid happiness. Never refuse to accept a Christmas present from a Chinaman unless you wish to offend him. You need not feel that you are bound to return the compliment. A Chinaman gives for the sake of giving, not in the hope of receiving. A poor laundryman will sometimes spend a couple of months' hard earned wages and more in a Christmas present for some friend, say a Sunday school teacher. If he has two teachers, he may spend four months' wages, and so on. Such are known facts. But do not blame him for extravagance, do not pity him as a fool for so doing. He is not a fool; he is a wise man, for he receives more than his money's worth of pleasure in believing that he is giving pleasure.

The Chinese New Year is different from the English year; their months being lunar, that is, reckoned by the revolution of the moon around the earth, are consequently shorter. They have twelve, say, instead of January, February, etc., Regular Moon, Second Moon, Third Moon. Each third year is a leap year and has an extra month so as to make each of the lunar years equal to a solar year. Accordingly, the time of their New Year varies between January and February. The week or ten days during which they keep it is a season of relaxation and rest from the cares of business. There is a great deal of mutual giving and receiving and not even the poorest beggar goes hungry. Those of the American Chinamen who have children celebrate with more than ordinary glee. Little Fat One, Little Black One, Tiny Spring Fragrance and Gentle Peach Blossom are all very happy. Red Chinese candles and punk sticks are burning and the quaint little Chinese people are having a good time, eating all manner of good things, dressing in all the colors of the rainbow, having their little hands and pockets filled with all sorts of trinkets, nuts, and sweets, and best of all, watching the fire-flowers. The fire-flowers are called fireworks by the Americans. The fathers and mothers, and all the grown up aunts, uncles and cousins of Little Fat One and Little Black One are also enjoying themselves. They are taking parts in religious ceremonies, listening to Chinese music, dressing, feasting, resting, laughing, enjoying everything. Red, the good luck color, is much in evidence. You see it all over in bright splashes of long narrow strips of paper pasted upon buildings with inscriptions in Chinese. The restaurants, with their deep balconies ornamented with carved woodwork, brightly colored or gilded, and set off with immense lanterns and big plants in china pots, are distinctively picturesque.

Ceremonies too numerous to be particularized are performed. The name of some of these ceremonies might cause a humorist to smile and the sober-minded to sigh. One is "Keeping company with the gods during the night," a ceremony which consists of making offerings and feasting before a collection of gods or images. The spirits of these gods are supposed to graciously receive the spirit of the food spread before them, while the devotees in order to be sociable with and agreeable to their august company of spirits, represented by the Gods, which, let it be understood, are not themselves worshiped, demolish the substance of the viands.

The Chinese are exceedingly fond of stories and story telling, their favorite themes being magic and enchantment. It is popular also to portray the blessings which fall to the lot of the filial son and the terrible fate of the undutiful. Some of their stories are very pretty. For instance, there is the story of the Storm Dragon, who began life as a snake, but having the misfortune to lose its tail, and, therefore, being unable to enter another world, retired to a mountain spring, whose clear never-failing fountain proved a safe hiding place. There he lived through several centuries, and was the cause of all the storms that came from the southwest. When he became very angry he was said to work fearful destruction through bringing about evil winds and tornadoes. His end, however, was peaceful. In the form of a silkworm's egg, he ventured one day to lie on a palm leaf waving on a tree above the spring. A little girl named Choy found him, and wrapping him in brown paper, placed him within her bosom, hoping by the warmth of her body to hatch him, a silkworm. In that pure and peaceful resting place, the dragon repented of his misdeeds, and when finally he became a silkworm, and from a silkworm to a butterfly, he soared far away on golden wings into the bright heavens, and throughout the region in which he had dwelt there were no more storms.

Another example is the story of the fairy fish. The fairy fish loved a fairy bird, but sacrificed itself for the sake of a poor old woman who had no grandchild to feed her. The fairy fish jumped into a frying pan full of boiling oil and allowed itself to be cooked and eaten by the old lady who was thereby much strengthened. The spirit of the fairy fish, however, entered into a little bird, which little bird became the mate of the fairy bird loved by the fairy fish.

Some Chinamen take advantage of the holiday season to patronize our theatres. I inquired of a well-informed Chinaman if the plays in Chinese theatres resembled those he saw acted on the American stage. He replied that the stories played in Chinese theatres are very much like the stories played here, but nearly all the actors are men, even the female parts being personated by men in the garb of women. He said that a Chinese audience showed its appreciation, not by clapping hands, but by calling out "Good, Good."

Gambling and opium smoking are somewhat indulged in by our black sheep Chinamen during New Year. In some of the gambling places may be found an image made of wood on which is painted a tiger with wings. This image is the God of Gamblers, and is called "The Grasping Cash Tiger." The gamblers light incense and candles before it and cast lots with bamboo sticks.

Chinese-American Sunday Schools

Chinese-American Sunday School festivals are very popular with the exiled Chinamen during the festive season. I was present one time at a gathering of thirteen Chinese Sunday schools, and the crowded room, decorated with Chinese flags and banners, beautifully wrought in various colors, Chinese lanterns, flowers and native plants, presented a very picturesque appearance. The festival was given, not by the teachers, but by the Chinese themselves, and was an expression of the gratitude which Chinamen feel towards those who try to benefit them, and as well, an evidence that these foreign laborers, practical working men for the most part, have buried deep in their hearts, a love and appreciation of the beautiful.

The American preacher who was Chairman said that it gave him great pleasure to see so many of his Chinese brothers, and only regretted that he could not speak to them in their own language and tell them how sorry he was that they had met with experiences which might perhaps cause them to think meanly of the Christian faith. He wished to say that he and all the friends there assembled would endeavor to give them a different impression of Christianity.

The Chinamen who helped in the entertainment betrayed very little embarrassment and acted their parts creditably. One spoke in a very bright direct manner, thanking the American friends for the interest in himself and his fellow countrymen. Another sang the hymn, "Precious Name," and a Chinese orchestra delighted the audience. There was the fiddler with his fiddle, the flutist with his flute, the banjo man with is banjo, and the kettledrummer with his kettledrum. A European gentleman present who could speak Chinese explained that one of the pieces of music was taken from a play in a Chinese theatre. The singer, a man with a falsetto voice, was supposed to be a maiden soliloquizing whilst her lover was in battle. The Chairman remarked with a humorous smile that a piece of such character was not usually chosen for a Sunday school entertainment; but they must "take the will for the deed" and enjoy it in spite of its impropriety. This speech, of course, added to the evening's enjoyment. A little spice is needed, even at Chinese Sunday school festivals.

Chinese Food

Speaking of feasting and festivities brings us to the question of Chinese food. I have partaken of many Chinese dishes, all of which were good and nutritious, many dainty and delectable.

There is, of course, a difference between European and Chinese cooking. For one thing, Chinese use neither milk nor butter in the preparation of food. In their soups they use mostly sundried comestibles and one may observe in their stews various kinds of dried nuts, fruit and vegetables. Their chief article of diet is, as is well known, rice, and the Chinaman cooks it so beautifully that if you will watch him as he manipulates his chopsticks, you will see that nearly every grain rolls separate.

There is nothing on a Chinaman's table to remind us of living animals or birds—no legs, heads, limbs, wings or loins—everything is cut into small pieces. The Chinaman comes to the table to eat, not to work—his carving is done in the kitchen.

At a Chinese banquet, to which I was invited, there were so many fragrant and appetizing dishes passed before me that I thought, even if I could not taste of all, I would take a list of the names. Here it is:

Sin Lip Ap Gang (Duck soup prepared with lotus seeds and flavored with ham)

Foo Yung Dan (Chinese omelette with herbs)

Ham Sun Goey (Sweet and sour fish)

Hung Yan Gaiding (Fried chicken with almonds, bamboo shoots, etc.)

Mo Kwo Bark Gop (Fried mushroom squab)

Jah Tau Goey (Fried fish in fancy)

Mo Kw Gai Tong (Spring chicken soup with mushrooms)

Gai Yong Goey Chee (Fried sharks' fins with chicken and egg)

Choong Taw Chee Yok (Pork with onion)

Foo Yong Har (Lobster omelette with herbs)

Ngow Yok Chop Suey (Chop Suey of beef)

Yin Wah Guy Ga (Chicken chopped with bird's nest)

Gai Yong Wong Ye Taw (Brain of yellow fish with minced chicken)

Hop Howe Gai Nip (Fried walnut and chicken)

Mut Geong (Ginger in syrup)

Mut Kim Ghet (Golden Lime)

Bor Lor (Preserved pineapple)

Mut Ching Moy (Green apricots)

Kwa Ying (Mixed sweet chow chow)

Know Mine Lie Chee Gon (Chinese nuts)

Far Sang Toy (Chinese peanut candy)

Hang Yen Soo (Almond cakes)

Lok Dow Go (Green bean cakes)

Long Sue tea.

A favorite dish is rice flour dumplings filled with mince meat. Another is shark fins boiled to the softest consistency and preserved ducks' tongues—something very gelatinous. Balls of crab and tripe boiled to a tenderness hard to express are also very tempting to the jaded appetite.

A peculiarity of the Chinese table to Europeans and Americans is that although furnished with sauces of every flavor and strength, salt itself is never in evidence.

As a diet for dyspeptics and men of sedentary habits Chinese food is recommended. It is mucilaginous and nutritious.

The Bible Teacher

A lady who had a Chinese pupil in her Bible class lectured him one day for not attending more regularly.

"I am sorry, Miss M—," he replied, "but I myself instruct at that hour two American young men."

"Instruct two American young men! Pray, Sir, in what do you instruct them?"

"In all that you have instructed me."

"From the Bible? Do you mean to say that there are American young men who do not know the Bible?"

Liu Wenti smiled. "There certainly are," he answered. "One day, these two came to my store. I was busy reading a story in the Bible. I told them so. They laughed and asked me if it was a good one. I read it to them. They said they would come again to listen to further stories. They cannot read much themselves and wish me to illuminate them.

Americanizing Not Always Christianizing

It will be seen from the above sketches that some of the Chinamen in our midst are much more Americanized than others, and those who are Americanized are not always those who have been with us the longest. Americanizing does not always mean improving or even civilizing. It ought to, but it does not. Some Chinese are not nearly as fine men after coming in contact with Western civilization as they were before. The majority, however, it is safe to say, benefit by stepping into the Westerner's light, more particularly those who have met with genuine Christian people and have had the privilege of entering into and seeing something of the beauty of the truly Christian American home. I lay great stress on the word "genuine," because an insincere Christian or one to whom religion is but a form, does great harm to the cause of Christianity. This has been repeated over and over again, but there is still reason for its repetition.

The Reform Party

The Chinese of the Reform Party in America are acutely conscious, and have been for many years, of the necessity of a new way of living for the Chinese—and not only a new way of living—a new way of thinking. They are also keenly alive to what is taking place in their own country. Indeed, they may be said to be the only Chinese here who are so. In nearly every city of any importance in America, there are a number of these Reform men, and they are amongst the most influential and enterprising. Not a few of them are graduates from American colleges. Nearly all of the Chinese married to white women in America belong to the Reform party, and they may truly be said to be living revolutionized lives as compared with the lives of their ancestors. Yet their hope and belief in the future of their own country is vital, and nothing causes their eyes to glisten more than to know that China is encouraging educational and industrial reforms, while those of them who have become Christians look forward with bright faith to China's religious reformation.

—*Westerner,* August 1909

Chinese Traditional Religion in North America and Hawaii

L. Eve Armentrout Ma

When Chinese first began arriving in North America and Hawaii in the nineteenth century, they brought with them a religious tradition not previously known in America. For reasons of convenience we may call it Chinese traditional religion, or Chinese popular religion. Today few if any native-born Chinese Americans or Chinese Canadians adhere to this religion, but many recent immigrants of Chinese ethnic background do follow it. In fact, in certain of California's cities a decline in the religion's vitality from the 1920s through the 1960s has been followed by a small upsurge.

Few people who are not ethnically Chinese, and not even all Chinese Americans, have a very clear understanding of this religion. Yet it is an essential part of the history of Chinese Americans and therefore also of the history of Hawaii and North America's west coast. In the 1870s and 1880s in California alone there were more than twenty-five Chinese temples, and the religion had thousands of adherents. The first section of this essay characterizes the religion, particularly as it was practiced in southern China (the area from which almost all ethnically Chinese immigrants to North America and Hawaii trace their origins). The second section discusses temples, festivals, and some of the practices of this religion as followed in North America and Hawaii.

A cautionary note: This religion is discussed here as it has actually been practiced. Its more profound philosophical or even religious bases will not be discussed. Nor are the many regional variations to the practice of Chinese religion analyzed here. In spite of these limitations this article will give the reader an idea of the basic characteristics of the religion, along with some particulars concerning its history in North America and Hawaii.

Chinese Traditional Religion

Chinese traditional religion is immediately distinguishable from most religions of the West and the Near East, such as Christianity, Judaism, and Islam, on two grounds. In the first place it is not monotheistic. Second, a follower is not called upon to participate in regular group worship with a temple, a priest, and a set religious service. Not withstanding the above, the religion does have temples, priests (relatively few in number), and written services derived from holy books.[1]

More to the point, Chinese popular religion is the religion followed (except when the government has intervened) by the average individual in China for the past several hundred years. In the nineteenth century it had more adherents than any other religion in the world. In this century the Communists on mainland China have controlled it, modified it, and at times discouraged its practice. But in places such as, Taiwan and Hong Kong, it continues to be an important force, with tens of thousands of adherents. Many Chinese immigrants, including those to America and to Southeast Asia, have maintained it in their adopted country. The descendants of Chinese immigrants to Southeast Asia have often followed the religion as well, which is of interest here since many of them have recently emigrated from Southeast Asia to the United States and Canada. However, American-born descendants of Chinese immigrants to America rarely adhere to the religion. Many modern Chinese intellectuals shun it as well.

Chinese traditional religion combines Buddhism, Taoism, local cults, and certain elements of Confucianism to form one syncretic whole. It honors a profusion of gods, goddesses, bodhisattvas, and immortals and encourages the belief in fairies, devils, and the like. It makes use of both Buddhist and Taoist clergy, although private religious connotations are just as important as formal services performed in a temple.

The religion's diverse origins, long development, and lack of central hierarchy have meant that its practice varies significantly from region to region. It teaches certain constants, however: Man should follow good and shun evil. There is an afterlife for which we should prepare and which exercises great influence over the mortal world. A large part of virtue consists in maintaining family obligations, including obligations to deceased family members (the latter usually performed by male members of the family group). Fate and chance have a great influence over people's lives. Finally, supernatural beings must be placated, and for the most part, they help to uphold the traditional morality.

Religious Rites Practiced by the Family

Chinese popular religion involves many rites performed in the home. Some are simple daily observances. Others, performed on special occasions such as births, marriages, and death, are much more elaborate. In general these rites serve to define the family unit and bind it together. They also uphold moral tenets and provide an avenue whereby family members can ask for divine assistance.

Worship of deceased ancestors is an essential element of the religion, and a most important aspect of this worship takes place in the home. A small shrine containing an ancestral tablet dedicated to the deceased parents of the male head of the household is set up in the home. Worship at this shrine is supposed to take place daily, although today this is often done only once a week or so. Ordinarily one need only light incense before the shrine, but on special occasions the rites are more elaborate. At festival time, for example, the shrine is presented with offerings of food.

The ancestral tablet is not the only thing in the home that gets an offering of incense. The Kitchen God watches the family all year long to see whether family members behave properly. He is also supposed to receive an incense offering every day, although today this may only be done once a week or even twice a month. Just before Chinese New Year this God, along with several others, is sent up to heaven, where he makes a report to heaven's Jade Emperor. Sometimes the Kitchen God's mouth is sweetened by smearing honey on it right before sending him up so that he will make a "sweeter," better report. (Based on the Kitchen God's report, the Jade Emperor will see to it that family members' good behavior is rewarded and their evil punished.)

Even if an individual behaves properly, he or she cannot completely rule out the possibility of incurring bad luck. In order to find out what lies in store, he or she can purchase an almanac/book of divination that not only predicts the weather and offers little homilies on how to live but also offers astrological calculations and the like to predict one's fortune. A person can also try to influence fate. A charm obtained from a temple, when hung in the home, will give the divine protection of the deity to which it is dedicated. The same charm, if it is burned and the ashes made into a tea, can sometimes cure disease if medical remedies fail. Various paper figures of animals and people can be used in the home to ward off bad luck. Some of these need to be displayed; some should be burned. Mirrors, if surrounded by certain Taoist symbols, are also very effective, as are certain deities.

As might be expected, marriage is considered very important in China. Much of the actual marriage ceremony takes place in the home of the groom and includes worship of heaven and earth, as well as of the groom's ancestors. Certain magical objects are supposed to enhance wedded bliss and harmony; for example, swords made out of old Chinese copper coins ("copper cash") are hung over the connubial bed. Just as Christians may display pictures of Jesus or the Virgin Mary, Chinese often hang pictures of deities, bodhisattvas, Taoist immortals, and the like on their walls. Some of these can help in one of the ultimate aims of marriage—the production of sons.

The family and religious rites carried on by the family are so important in China that several of the most influential types of social organizations act as larger family units. Organization members consider each other to be blood brothers. They establish an "ancestor" (not always in fact a blood relative of members)[2] who is worshiped by the organization. The organizations also worship a variety of other deities, but the principal religious tie among members is the "ancestor" whom the group worships. Organizations of this type include clan, lineage, and surname associations and secret societies.

Festivals with Religious Connotations

Chinese celebrate many festivals throughout the year. Almost all of these festivals have religious connotations, even though most contain important secular elements as well. Among these festivals are Chinese New Year, Ch'ing-Ming, Chung Yuan (Chinese All Souls), Tuan Wu, the Mid-Autumn Festival, and the Mid-Winter Festival (Tung Chin).[3] In addition, annual "birthday" celebrations for the most important deity of a temple provide the occasion for a public celebration that often lasts two or three days.

The Chinese New Year season officially lasts for two weeks—from the first day of New Year until the fifteenth, or Shang-yuan. Even before New Year's Day the devout perform important rites in their homes. The New Year season is a time of natural and cosmic renewal. The house gets a thorough cleaning and family members get new clothes. The family partakes of a feast on New Year's Eve or New Year's Day, while organizations, businesses, and associations offer feasts to members and employees in the days that follow. Children, incidentally, are not to be scolded on New Year's Day, for this portends family disharmony and can bring bad luck.

A visit to a nearby temple for the purpose of worship and fortune telling is another important aspect of the New Year's celebration. It is important to shoot off firecrackers during this season—they frighten away evil spirits. Lion dances perform the same task and bring good fortune, so every organization, association, and business establishment tries to arrange for one before the New Year's season comes to a close. Dragons (who bring water and hence fertility) are often paraded through the streets. Homes, associations, offices, and business establishments paste New Year's couplets next to their doors to bring good fortune and set the tone for the coming year.

The New Year season is also a time for visiting and renewing relationships. First, the family gets together. Later the clan or lineage group will have a feast and meeting. Then even more distant relatives, friends, and business associates are visited. On these visits children are presented with red envelopes containing money for good luck.

The New Year season ends with the lantern festival, at which time a pastry called *yuan-hsiao* (*t'ang-yuan* in Guangdong) is eaten. The lantern festival is not the only one to have its special food; many of the dishes of the family New Year's feast are prescribed to accord with religious practice and bring good fortune. Other festivals, such as the Mid-Autumn Festival and Tuan Wu, require the eating of one particular food: moon cakes in the case of Mid-Autumn Festival, *tsung-tzu* (a rice preparation wrapped in bamboo leaves) for Tuan Wu, *yuan-hsiao* again for the Mid-Winter Festival.

The Tuan Wu festival commemorates the suicide of a Chinese statesman named Ch'u Yuan who lived in the third century B.C. The statesman committed suicide by throwing himself into a river. In the annual celebration religious elements have been added to what was basically a secular historical event. Dragon boat races are an important element of the festival. The dragons—water gods—race to see which can reach the statesman to save his life. *Tsung-tzu*, the food special to this festival, have magical properties that supposedly enable them to float to the body and provide it with nourishment.

The Chung Yuan (Chinese All Souls) festival—brought to China by Buddhist missionaries during the T'ang dynasty (A.D. 618–907)—aims to placate the souls of those who died and did not receive proper burial because they died far from home, left no descendants, or the like. Surely, it is felt, it is both good and appropriate that the believer invite these deceased to come home with his or her family. In addition, elements of the celebration help the souls along the road to the Buddhist heaven. Not surprisingly, much of this celebration involves elaborate ceremonies in Buddhist temples performed by Buddhist monks.

Finally, the annual "birthday" celebration of a local temple's chief deity has been one of the most important events in rural China before the mid-twentieth century. The celebration includes a procession in which the deity is paraded through the streets, a dramatic performance (to please the deity, as well as the mortal audience), and a fair, in which goods from throughout the immediate countryside can be bought and sold. Craftsmen (herbalists, practioners of Chinese medicine, garment workers, porters, even prostitutes) traditionally worshiped a patron deity, and this deity was also given an annual celebration similar to the "birthday celebration" of a temple deity.

Religion in the Temple for the Ordinary Worshiper

Worship in the average Chinese temple is not as organized as that in Christian churches or Moslem or Jewish temples. That is, there are no regular weekly services, professional clergy, or Sunday school classes. Chinese temples are for the most part looked after by temple caretakers. These men often have only slightly better than a layperson's grasp of the essentials of the religious tradition. For special occasions the devout will turn to the trained Buddhist monks or Taoist priests, but for ordinary temple worship the practitioner will rely upon his or her own knowledge of religious practices, as learned from parents and others.

The average Chinese temple houses a variety of deities: Buddha forms, Taoist immortals, gods, goddesses, and figures from Chinese history and legend. The temple will be dedicated to one deity who will be considered the chief god (or goddess) of the temple. In southern coastal China the three most popular deities have been Kuan Kung (Kuan Yu or Kuan-ti, the God of War who values honor, fidelity, valor, and learning), Kuan Yin (a female bodhisattva of great mercy and compassion), and T'ien-hou (the Empress of Heaven, who has special powers to help fishermen and those who travel over the ocean). In addition, many laypersons worship the Buddha.

Ordinary worship in the temple can consist of no more than lighting a stick of incense or a candle and saying a prayer. Rather than relying on one authoritative text, such as the Bible, Talmud, or Koran, Chinese religion draws upon many permissible texts (referred to as "classics," or *ching*), principally either Buddhist or Taoist works. As noted earlier, many of the ideals embodied in these texts come from the Confucian tradition, although Confucius is not considered a god and pure Confucianism is not a religion.

Another common activity in a Chinese temple is the casting of fortunes. The worshiper considers the temple deities to have chosen the fortune obtained. One common method of fortune telling is for the worshiper to kneel and hold one of the temple's large bamboo containers filled with numbered bamboo strips. The worshiper shakes this container until one strip eventually falls out. (If more than one falls out, he or she must start all over again.) The worshiper then takes this strip and gives it to the temple caretaker, who provides a printed fortune that corresponds to the number on the bamboo strip. (The fortunes come from a standard Chinese religious/magical work.)

Death and Burial Practices

As in the case with most of the world's religions, the rites and practices associated with death and burial are of special importance in China. Through these rites and practices the soul of the departed attains its just rewards in the afterlife. The Chinese religious tradition also teaches that the proper observance of burial and postburial rites shows that the living still regard the deceased with respect and love. In addition, the rites help ensure that the dead do not come back to haunt the living. The family of the deceased sees to it that the spirit body of the departed will have better than adequate "material" goods (food, lodging, servants, money) in the spirit world. The living, through prayers, can also atone for many, perhaps all, of the transgressions the departed committed before dying.

The public burial rites are as opulent as financially feasible to bring honor and comfort to the departed as well as to those left behind in the land of the living. Perhaps the most important of these public rites is the funeral procession. As a bare minimum, the procession includes the coffin with the deceased, followed by mourners who travel on foot. The mourners most closely related to the deceased walk closest to the coffin.

If finances permit, the funeral procession will be quite elaborate. The coffin (put on bamboo poles and carried or in more modern days placed in a cart or hearse) is preceded by Buddhist monks chanting sutras, Taoist priests reciting prayers, several musical troupes playing funeral music, and carts with funerary objects: rolls of cloth (given to the immediate relatives by friends of the deceased), paper houses for the deceased to use in the afterlife, and so forth. These days, at least in Taiwan and Hong Kong, elaborate flower arrangements are also much in evidence. Occasionally a family is wealthy enough to hire people to dress as supernatural beings to help the deceased through the different stages of hell and on up into heaven. A painting or photograph of the deceased travels with the coffin or sometimes in a cart or car ahead of it. Behind the coffin comes the family of the deceased, then more distant relatives, then, finally, friends.

For several days preceding the procession and burial, elaborate rites need to be performed. Other rites take place after the burial. Taoist priests perform a large proportion of these rites, including magical incantations on behalf of the deceased to direct him or her to the underworld and prevent him or her from returning to haunt the living. In addition, a paper house is burned to give the departed spirit a home for the afterlife. By the same token much "spirit" money (special paper money) is burned to give the departed enough money to take care of his or her needs. The departed is also provided with food (the odor of real food is enough to satisfy a spirit), a horse to ride on, and perhaps servants. The gods of the underworld are offered gifts so that they will treat the departed well: wine, horses, money, incense, and the like. The departed must pass through all the levels of hell before getting into heaven. ("Hell pictures" hanging in temples show the justice with which sins are punished.)

Religious ceremonies for the deceased do not end with the burial. The official mourning period lasts for days, months, or traditionally even years, depending upon one's family relationship to the deceased. At certain intervals throughout the period, specific religious rites must be performed. As time passes, the individual mourner can perform more and more of these rites without the help of priests or monks. Even later, nothing more is required than that the ancestral tablets be properly honored in the home and that the family visit the grave once a year at the Ch'ing-Ming festival. During this annual visit the family is to sweep and clean the grave site and offer the departed, food, wine, and incense.

Traditional Religion as Practiced in North America and Hawaii

During the nineteenth and the early twentieth centuries, the practice of Chinese popular religion in North America and Hawaii did not vary too much from its practice in southern China. Altars to deities, including the Kitchen God, were set up in the home, as were tablets and altars to ancestors. The Chinese immigrants established Chinese temples, celebrated most of the usual festivals in the usual fashion, and buried the dead with elaborate rites.

The lack of regularly functioning family units and the urban setting in which most Chinese have lived since the 1880s did force some modifications, however, as did the very fact that the immigrants were living far from their native land. Clan and lineage rites could not be established and maintained in the overseas environment, for example, since most members of the clan and lineage groups resided in China. Instead, people of the same surname organized surname ("family") associations. Ancestral rites had to be maintained with the knowledge that in most cases the bones of the deceased ancestors lay across the ocean. In addition, the paucity of wives in this country meant fewer sons to carry on the worship. The urban setting served to undercut the importance of deities associated with agriculture and with location. The lack of Chinese governmental control meant no altars to the City God.

In addition, as early as 1910 the religion began a large-scale decline in both North America and Hawaii. This was due to several factors: the modernization of China, then undergoing a series of revolutionary changes; the Western, rationalistic education that native-born Chinese Americans received; and the low opinion with which the majority (non-Chinese) population regarded Chinese popular religion. This decline has been only partially offset in recent decades by a small revival due to the influx of new immigrants.

We learn from Marianne Kaye Wells, Stewart Culin, and others that from the late 1880s through the turn of the century there were at least thirty functioning Chinese temples in California, several in Nevada, one in Montana, one in Wyoming, and at least three in the eastern part of the United States.[4] There were also at least six Chinese temples in Hawaii during the same period, most of them located in Honolulu. Information about Canada is somewhat harder to come by, but the province of British Columbia, where most of Canada's Chinese population lived, contained at least three Chinese temples (in Vancouver and Victoria). The inland city of Calgary also had at least one temple, and several other locations where Chinese were relatively numerous almost surely did as well. I am including in this list Chinese temples maintained by the Chee Kong Tong Association (also known as Chinese Freemasons), since in many locales (particularly in the continental United States and in Canada) these temples functioned as community-wide religious institutions. In the continental United States, cities that contained Chinese temples included San Francisco (which had about fifteen in the 1890s), Oakland, San Jose, Monterey, Los Angeles, Bakersfield, Marysville, Weaverville, Lewiston, Oroville, Sacramento (all in California), Butte (Montana), Philadelphia, and New York.

In the continental United States some of the temples dated back to the 1850s, including at least three in San Francisco and the one in Weaverville. The greatest period of temple building, however, was in the 1880s and 1890s. Most of the temples in California, as well as those in the eastern part of the United States, were built during those two decades. As for Hawaii, although it is difficult to get any precise information, two of Hawaii's Chinese temples may date from the 1860s or 1870s, when large numbers of Chinese were being brought to the islands as indentured laborers. Certainly all Honolulu's Chinese temples that were still functioning in the 1920s had been built before the turn of the century. The same is true of the three Chinese temples in Canada.

In addition to the regular temples, Chinatown associations ("family" associations, regional associations, and so forth), maintained altars with deities for the protection of members and to give members a place to worship. In this they were simply following the example of their counterparts in China. Even today, when there are probably no more than ten functioning Chinese temples in San Francisco and somewhat fewer in all other North American and Hawaiian communities combined, many of the old-style organizations and associations maintain their altars and deities. For example, in San Francisco and Oakland surname associations for the Lees and Mas, along with multi-surname associations such as the Lung-kong and Soo-yuan, continue to maintain altars.

Not only are there regular temples open to the public and altars in association buildings, but in addition, most businesses in the Chinatowns (and many Chinese-owned businesses in other areas) maintain small altars, a tradition that has existed since the nineteenth century. A favorite deity for this altar is Kuan Kung. Most businesses also post images of the God of Wealth (Ts'ai-shen). In the 1890s the opening of a new business required an elaborate ceremony in the name of this God of Wealth. Today staging a lion dance, setting up the altar, and displaying congratulatory couplets and gifts of fruit are often sufficient.

Judging by numbers, the deities favored by Chinese immigrants to North America and Hawaii have been the Kitchen God (for the home), the God of Wealth (for a place of business), and, in temples, Kuan Kung, Kuan Yin, Hua-t'o (patron God of doctors and pharmacists, and a healer), Pei-ti (who helps protect against floods), Tu-ti (God of the place, the physical location), T'ien-hou, and, in Hawaii, How Wong (a fishermen's God who also protected travelers over the ocean and brought business success). Most of these deities (especially the Kitchen God, the God of Wealth, Kuan Yin, and Kuan Kung) have retained a certain amount of popularity among those Chinese in North America and Hawaii who still practice the traditional religion. In addition, in San Francisco, Oakland, and Honolulu today there are purely Buddhist temples that have been established by Chinese. (In the older Chinese temples, although images of the bodhisattva T'ien-hou were often present, images of the Buddha himself were not common.) All three of these Buddhist temples date from post-1950. The temple in San Francisco does not revere the Buddha as a deity but organizes its functions as a religious institution.

Many Chinese festivals have also been celebrated in North America and Hawaii. From the 1850s through the present, Chinese New Year's has been honored. In the nineteenth century the celebration was quite traditional and included dragon parades, lion dances, feasts, offerings to the deities, firecrackers, the purchase of new clothes, distribution of red envelopes, paper cuttings, the eating of special foods, and the like. Lion dances are still performed in most urban areas that have a large Chinese population, red envelopes are still distributed, and feasts, firecrackers, and the eating of special foods are still important. Many communities, like the one in San Francisco, had dragon parades for the Chinese New Year, and a number also maintained the traditional lantern festival on the last day of the New Year season, in which elaborate lanterns shaped like animals and the like are displayed and taken to temples. Since the 1920s these lanterns are no longer to be seen. In addition, there has been a general decline in some of the more obvious manifestations of the New Year celebration, along with a certain amount of secularization and commercialization of that which is left. As examples of the latter we have the modern version of San Francisco's dragon parade and the Miss Chinatown contest.

Chinese immigrants to North America and Hawaii brought with them other traditional festivals, which were celebrated most noticeably and most traditionally during the last quarter of the nineteenth century and the first decade or two of the twentieth. These included Tuan Wu; in Sacramento Chinese even held dragon boat races in the 1850s, and dragon boat races were also in evidence on San Francisco Bay in the late nineteenth century; tsung-tzu, the food special to the festival, are still eaten. Still other festivals celebrated in the New World were Ch'ing-Ming, Chung Yung, and the Mid-Autumn and Mid-Winter festivals.

Some of the "birthday" celebrations held for deities in North American have been quite as elaborate as anything held in China. Theatrical performances of Chinese opera were not uncommon at these celebrations. In San Jose the traditional parade included the giant figures mentioned so often in the literature concerning religion in southern China. A "birthday" celebration for T'ien-hou held in San Francisco in the mid-nineteenth lasted three days. In Watsonville parades were held in the late 1890s. In Monterey, Marysville, San Jose, and San Francisco, "bombs" (hempen rings) were often shot off during the celebration. The Chinese temple at Marysville, one of the few still functioning outside of Honolulu, Vancouver, or San Francisco, still maintains this practice in honor of the "birthday" of Pei-ti. In most other cases, however, by the 1920s the celebration of these festivals had largely fallen into disuse or had been reduced to little more than the eating of special foods associated with the festival.

Worshipers in the Chinese temples of North America and Hawaii today still light incense before the deities and use fortune-telling sticks. For the latter a small fee is required, usually one dollar. Religious texts can be purchased at most temples, and some of the faithful still offer fruit and other foodstuffs on special occasions. In Hawaii as late as the 1930s, the caretaker of one of the temples was also a faith healer.

Probably even more prevalent than temple worship, however, is the honoring of ancestors. Currently all of the surname and most of the district associations in San Francisco maintain altars that contain the tablets of deceased ancestors. These ancestors are honored on special occasions, most notably during the Chinese

New Year. In addition, in the Bay Area a significant number of native-born Chinese Americans of the second generation, along with a majority of the China-born, go out to the cemeteries at Ch'ing-Ming, either with their families or with an association. There they clean the graves, bow to the departed, burn incense and "spirit" money, and perhaps offer the three cups of wine, some pork, and some fruit.

Up until the 1950s most Chinese immigrants who died in the continental United States or in Canada had their bones sent back to China for "proper" burial. This did not mean that they had no funeral here. Aside from the fact that close family members were sometimes lacking (in which case, surname association brethren or the like would substitute as family members), Chinese funerals in North America and Hawaii before the middle of this century closely resembled what one would expect in China. The later reinterment in China took place because of the feeling that one's final resting place should be in one's native land (and actually, native county and village).

Due to prejudice against Chinese in North America, during most of the nineteenth and the early part of the twentieth centuries, Chinese were usually forbidden to bury their dead in cemeteries where people of other races were buried. As a result Chinese cemeteries were started. A few major Chinese cemeteries remain in use. In addition, there are many smaller cemeteries in many other communities, particularly but not exclusively in California. There are also Chinese sections of other, larger community cemeteries.

Most of these cemeteries no longer contain any human remains, since the bones have long since been disinterred and sent back to China. Other than the cemeteries in Colma, these cemeteries themselves have pretty much fallen into disuse, and most are overgrown and obviously unkept. However, altars and monuments still remain in most. At the Chinese cemetery in Fresno a fifty-five-gallon oil drum is used to burn "spirit" money. One of the most impressive monuments is the remains of a stone temple with altar located in San Francisco's Lincoln Park, formerly a Chinese cemetery. Athough these cemeteries are for the most part no longer used, in many of them mounted photographs of the deceased still remain at the grave sites, attached to the tombstones. This practice of placing the deceased's photo at the grave site is not unique to the Chinese; other groups in the United States that have followed the same practice include Armenians, Serbians, Jews, Greeks, and Italians.

Chinese traditional religion has been much misunderstood in this part of the world. For many decades its practice in North America and Hawaii differed little from its practice in China in the nineteenth century and in today's Taiwan and Hong Kong. During more recent times to the ranks of the devout have been added those for whom the religion itself no longer has much meaning, but for whom participation in at least some aspects of the festivals has cultural significance. The devout, on the other hand, have shown most interest in maintaining the more private aspects of religious practice. In addition, they have established new temples; one was just opened this year in Vancouver. As noted above, some of these temples are more purely Buddhist than the older temples, but others are not. In their performance of the more private aspects of the religion, Chinese devotees in North America and Hawaii tend to differ little from traditional practice.

Chinese popular religion forms an integral part of the study of the history of this part of the world. After all, Chinese were numerically the largest minority on the west coast of North America and the largest Asian minority in Hawaii for several decades of the nineteenth century. Some of the more public forms of the practice of the religion are interwoven with the broader history of numerous American communities. Reaching its height in the latter part of the nineteenth century, in recent years Chinese traditional religion has enjoyed a partial revival in the United States due to the renewed influx of immigrants from China and ethnically Chinese immigrants from elsewhere in the world (especially Southeast Asia). However, even these immigrants take less interest than did nineteenth century Chinese in deities such as Hua-t'o or Pei-ti, who have been rendered anachronistic by modern science—few Chinese immigrants to the United States would prefer these gods to modern medicine and flood control projects.

Notes

1. The material in this section appeared in substantially the same form in L. Eve Armentrout Ma's "Chinese Popular Religion," a booklet published by the Chinese and Chinese American History Project (now Association). Funded by Chevron, U.S.A., the booklet was written to accompany a museum exhibit of the same name.

2. Clans and lineages kept genealogies that did establish a direct blood tie between the worshipers and most of the ancestors worshiped. Some of the genealogies, however, went back beyond the verifiable ancestors to the dawn

of Chinese history and included individuals such as Hsuan-hsiao (a "son" of the mythical Yellow Emperor), who were to be honored as the surname and hence, in a sense, lineage progenitor. In surname associations the tie between association members and the original ancestor worshiped was often quite tenuous. Lao-tsu (putatively surnamed Li, or Lee) is the original ancestor for the Lee Family Association in North America; one ancestor worshiped by the multi-surname Soo Yuan Benevolent Association is a brother-in-law of the Yellow Emperor, and so forth. Secret societies do not pretend to actual blood descent. Instead they become blood brothers through an elaborate initiation ritual. In the Chee Kong Tong and many of the other tongs in America, Kuan-ti is worshiped as if he were an ancestor. In addition, the Chee Kong Tongs worship the five tiger generals and other mythic figures.

3. Other names for these festivals are as follows: Chung Yuan is also called the Yu-lan Festival, or Shao-i; Tuan-Wu can be called Wu-yueh chieh (Festival of the Fifth Moon); and the Mid-Autumn Festival is sometimes called Pa-yueh shih-wu (Fifteenth Day of the Eighth Moon).

4. Marianne Kaye Wells, *Chinese Temples in California* (San Francisco: R and E Research Associates, 1971); Stewart Culin, "Chinese Secret Societies in the United States," *Journal of American Folklore* 3, no. 8 (Jan–March. 1890); Stewart Culin, "Customs of the Chinese in America," *Journal of American Folklore* 3, No. 10 (July–September 1890); and Stewart Culin, "The Practice of Medicine by the Chinese in America," pamphlet, reprinted from *Medical and Surgical Reporter*, March 19, 1887.

In addition to the above, material for this section of the essay comes principally from the following: Leonard Austin, *Around the World in San Francisco* (San Francisco: Abbey Press, 1955); Hubert Howe Bancroft, *Essays and Miscellany*, vol. 38 of *The Works of Hubert Howe Bancroft* (San Francisco: The History Co., 1890); Rev. Ng Poon Chew, "The Chinese in San Francisco," in *The Pacific Coast Pulpit*, ed. Rev. D. Irwin Hanson (New York: Fleming H. Revell Co., 1893), 49–56; Vyolet Chu, "Folk Religion in Hawaii," paper in the author's collection; Richard F. Hough, "Ethnic and Religious Cemeteries in California, U.S.," paper delivered at the National Council for Geographic Education, Mexico City, Mexico, 1979; Rose Hum Lee, *The Chinese in the United States of America* (Hong Kong: Hong Kong University Press, 1960); Sandy Lydon, *Chinese Gold: The Chinese in the Monterey Bay Region* (Capitola: Capitola Book Co., 1985); Edgar Wickberg et al., *From China to Canada: A History of the Chinese Communities in Canada* (Toronto: McClellan and Stewart, Ltd., 1982); Sau Chun Wong, "Chinese Temples in Honolulu," *Social Process in Hawaii* 3 (May 1937): 27–35; Nancy Foon Young, *The Chinese in Hawaii: An Annotated Bibliography* (Honolulu: Social Science Research Institute of the University of Hawaii, 1973); Harry H. Zeigler and Bernhard Hormann, "A Religious and Cultural Calendar for Hawaii," *Social Process in Hawaii* 16 (1952): 59–67.

Preserving Chinese Culture

Fenggang Yang

According to Will Herberg, immigrants in the United States would give up everything but their traditional religion:

> Sooner or later the immigrant will give up virtually everything he had brought with him from the "old country"—his language, his nationality, his manner of life—and will adopt the ways of his new home. Within broad limits, however, his becoming an American did not involve his abandoning the old religion in favor of some native American substitute. Quite the contrary, not only was he expected to retain his old religion, as he was not expected to retain his old language or nationality, but such was the shape of America that it was largely in and through his religion that he, or rather his children and grandchildren, found an identifiable place in American life. (1960, 27–28)

However, for Chinese immigrants who have even forsaken their traditional religion and converted to Christianity, what is left for them to preserve? This question is especially important for Chinese immigrants because of the historical conflicts between Christianity and Chinese culture and between Christian and Chinese identities (see Chapter 2). For immigrant converts, the Chinese church is not a transplant from the old country but a new invention in American soil. These immigrants are uprooted socially, culturally, and religiously as well. Chinese Christian churches in the United States are self-defined as *Chinese* churches. In what sense do Chinese Christians in America claim their Chinese identity? What Chinese traditions does the church preserve?

Many scholars believe, as reviewed in Chapter 2, that the nature of the Chinese culture was fundamentally defined by Confucian values and notions, or by the Confucian orthodoxy (correct belief); whereas some anthropologists argue that orthopraxy (correct practice) reigned over orthodoxy as the principal means of attaining Chinese identity and maintaining cultural unity among the Chinese. In this chapter I will examine the CCC's preservation of traditional praxes (what people do), including the Chinese language and traditional rituals and symbols, and then analyze the church's different attitudes toward traditional value systems of Confucianism, Daoism, and Buddhism. Generally speaking, when they are able to de-religionize a specific Chinese tradition, these Chinese Christians claim it as compatible with the Christian faith; when it seems impossible to de-religionize a tradition, they reject it; when it looks possible but difficult to separate the religious dimension from the cultural dimension in a tradition, they manifest ambivalent anxiety and tend to avoid it. Overall, the Chinese church helps its members to selectively preserve certain aspects of Chinese culture with transformative reinterpretation.

* * * * *

Chinese Rituals and Symbols

Traditional rituals and cultural symbols are important in defining Chineseness because of the historical orthopraxy that united Chinese people in diverse local cultures and plural religions. Chinese Christians have tried to differentiate traditional symbols and rituals of religious nature from those of secular nature, and have rejected religious ones while accepting secular ones.

Funerals and Weddings

Anthropologists have written intensively about Chinese funerals and weddings (see Watson and Rawski 1988). The argument about Chinese orthopraxy as the core of Chinese identity was largely based on studies of Chinese funerals, which they found quite uniform in structure across the vast land of China. I did not have a chance to observe funerals at the CCC during my field work period, but from interviews and informal conversations I learned that their funerals generally followed Western Christian styles. For example, there would be memorial services both at the church or the funeral parlor and in the cemetery. A pastor would officiate at the funeral. His speeches would honor the dead and comfort the relatives and friends. Following the funeral people would be invited to have a dinner at a Chinese restaurant. Many of the Chinese traditional funeral rites were lacking—no performative wailing, no donning of white mourning attire, no burning of "paper moneys" or other offerings, no setting up ancestral tablets, and so forth. The lack of traditionally Chinese rites is common in Chinese Christian funerals in other churches, as my interviews with Chinese Christians in other metropolitan areas revealed. A study of a Chinese Christian community in Hong Kong finds the same phenomenon (Constable 1994). A Chinese pastor in Houston was willing to conduct a funeral for a non-Christian as long as the family invited him. However, he would use this opportunity to comfort the family *and* to evangelize by explaining the Christian beliefs about the meaning of life. He saw the funeral as an unusual opportunity to challenge non-Christian Chinese who otherwise might never step into a church or talk to a pastor.

The weddings I observed at the CCC and other Chinese churches were all in Western Christian style. At a special wedding service, commonly held on a Saturday at the sanctuary, the bride and the groom would take vows and exchange rings in front of the pastor. Then a reception would follow at the fellowship hall and/or a dinner banquet in a Chinese restaurant. There were no traditionally Chinese wedding rites of kowtowing to the Heaven and the Earth (*bai tiandi*), to the husband's parents, and between the groom and the bride. An interesting comparison was a "Buddhist wedding" that I observed in 1994 at a Chinese Buddhist temple in Chicago. The groom wore a Western style suit and tie, and the bride was in a long white wedding gown. Seeing the Western-style wedding dress, it was surprising for me to watch their kowtowing to the Buddha statue and making three prostrations in front of the monk. The bride seemed to have a hard time because of her high-heeled shoes.

Chinese Christians in America do not follow Chinese traditional ways in weddings and funerals because they do not believe that the traditional orthopraxy in weddings and funerals defines Chineseness. Actually, many non-Christian Chinese have stopped practicing the traditional rites as well. In mainland China those traditional rites have been viewed as feudal superstitions, and the Communist government has made great efforts to abolish them (*yifeng yisu*). In Taiwan and Hong Kong many people have followed similar modernist reasoning against "feudal superstitions" and abandoned them as well. In the construction of Chinese identity, besides the Chinese versus non-Chinese dimension, there is also the premodern versus modern dimension. Many Chinese, both Christian and non-Christian, regard giving up traditional funeral and wedding rites as giving up something backward, rather than as giving up the Chinese identity.

The Chinese New Year and the Mid-Autumn Festival

The Chinese New Year and the Mid-Autumn Festival are the two most important traditional festivals.[1] Both are based on the traditional Chinese calendar system, which is a system of lunar months adjusted to the solar year.[2] This system has been used for many centuries in China and thus has many cultural and religious meanings attached to special holidays, just as the cycles of weeks and seasons in the Western calendar system bear Judeo-Christian meanings. China officially adopted the Western solar calendar after the founding of the Republic in 1911. Some political holidays were set according to the solar calendar, such as the National Day on October 10 (or October 1 for the PRC since 1949). However, Chinese people continue to observe festival days according to the traditional calendar. Consequently, the Chinese today have a bi-calendar system, following the solar calendar (*gongli* or public calendar) in public life—government, school, and work schedules—and the traditional calendar (*nongli* or farm calendar, or *yinli* or lunar calendar) in private life—family, cultural, and religious activities. Chinese calendars are commonly printed with both systems.

Christian Chinese, like other Chinese, maintain the bi-calendar system. The week-cycle and Christian seasons bear significant meanings for their religious faith and practice. At the same time, observing Chinese festivals is habitual and also important for them to assure their Chinese identity. However, Chinese Christians celebrate only certain traditional Chinese festivals that do not have the overtones of traditional religious meanings. With a history of several thousand years, China has many traditional festivals, most having some religious meanings or implications. For example, *Qingming Jie*, which is around the Easter time, is a day to remember dead ancestors by visiting and cleaning their tombs. The Ghost Festival on the fifteenth day of the seventh month, like the Buddhist *Yulan Jie*, is a day to "feed" the vagrant ghosts. Traditional practices on these days include burning "paper moneys" and making other offerings to the dead.[3] Chinese evangelical Christians do not observe these holidays. On the other hand, Chinese Christians in America have no problem in celebrating Chinese New Year and the Mid-Autumn Festival. These days are not religious holidays, although different people may attach various religious meanings to them. The Chinese New Year's Day (*xin nian*), also called Spring Festival (*Chun jie*), marks the beginning of a year and the coming of spring; it usually falls in the early part of February in the Western solar calendar. In Chinese societies Spring Festival is a holiday season that, like Thanksgiving and Christmas in America, extends to many days before the New Year's Day and ends around the *Yuanxiao Jie* on the fifteenth day of the first month (*zhengyue shiwu*). Traditionally, Chinese families have all family members get together on this day, and many community activities are held during this season.

At the CCC the climax of the Chinese New Year celebration is a grand *jiaozi* (boiled dumplings) banquet. *Jiaozi* is *the* traditional New Year's food, as are turkeys for the American Thanksgiving day. The Chinese in America have to adjust their communal celebration day because they do not have paid holidays for celebrating the Chinese New Year. The *jiaozi* party at the CCC is always on a Saturday nearest to the Chinese New Year's Day or the *Yuanxiao Jie*. On that day in the years when I did my research, church members and invited friends would gather at the Fellowship Hall of the church and make lots of *jiaozi* together. Preparing dough and stuffing, making wrappers, wrapping, and boiling, everybody participates in this collective cooking. It provides an opportunity for people to chat and enjoy themselves, and it also creates a jolly family-like atmosphere. The "*jiaozi* banquet" is followed with entertainment programs, including performing Chinese dances, playing musical instruments, and singing gospel songs.

New Year's celebration is a nostalgic time for immigrants to remember the past, a joyfully educational time for the American-born children to learn about Chinese customs and cultural traditions, and a wonderful time to get non-Christian Chinese into the church. Chinese New Year is celebrated as a cultural festival, not a religious holy day. Unlike Christmas, which is celebrated in the sanctuary with special musicals, worship services, and thematic sermons, the entire celebration of Chinese New Year takes place outside the sanctuary. These Protestant Chinese celebrate Chinese New Year in a significantly different way than do other Chinese. I did not see "red-pockets" with lucky money for children. The church did not put up red paper couplets outside the doorways or burn incense or make ritual offerings to dead ancestors, nor did they make dragon and lion dances. Anything with any possible religious implications is omitted on this occasion in this evangelical Protestant church. They exercise great caution to avoid anything non-Christian and deliberately try to distance themselves from the possibility of pagan practices. This practice is common in other Chinese evangelical Protestant churches in the United States and also in a conservative Chinese church in Hong Kong (Constable 1994).

In comparison, I observed a very different celebration of Chinese New Year at a Chinese Catholic church in the Washington area, which adopted more traditional Chinese symbols and practices. At a special ceremony of the New Year's Day, these Chinese Catholics offered sacrificial pig heads and fruits to venerate ancestors, burned incense sticks in front of a memorial tablet labeled for "all Chinese ancestors" (*zhonghua liezu liezong*), and gave out red pockets to small children. These practices would not be acceptable to Chinese evangelical Protestants. In the past, the Roman Catholic Church forbade practicing ancestral veneration, causing the "rites controversy" in the early eighteenth century. However, it reversed this policy two hundred years later in 1939 (Ching 1993, 192–95), so that Chinese Catholics today integrate many Chinese traditional rites into their Catholic practices. On the Protestant side, the attitudes of mainline Chinese Christians toward Chinese traditional practices may be changing too. In a recent book (Ng 1996), a group of Asian-American ministers and seminary professors of mainline Protestant denominations explore ways to integrate elements of East Asian traditions with their Christian faith. The book shows greater acceptance toward many Chinese (and Korean and Japanese) traditional practices. In sharp contrast to Catholics and mainline Protestants, Chinese evangelical Protestants today deliberately distance themselves as much as possible from any possible "pagan" practices in Chinese traditions. How these evangelical Chinese Christians change (or not change) will be interesting to watch. Nevertheless, the various attitudes among Chinese Christians suggest that the religious (or nonreligious) meanings of many Chinese traditional practices are elastic and are subject to various interpretations from different people in different times.

The Mid-Autumn Festival (*Zhongqiu Jie*) on the fifteenth day of the eighth month (usually in September of the solar calendar) is another important traditional Chinese festival. The moon on this day is said to be at its roundest and brightest. "Roundness" symbolizes the whole family being united together. It is a time for family reunion. The round moon-cake is the special food for this day.

In its early years, the CCC often held a special gathering in the night of the Mid-Autumn Day. The gathering was not purely for preserving the cultural tradition, however. It was transformed and attached with Christian meanings. For instance, the announcement about the celebration of the Mid-Autumn Festival in 1966 reads,

Come to our Moonlight Prayer Meeting: During this good festival time when we are missing our family members and relatives, let us come together to pray for our dear family members and relatives, and to pray for our mainland compatriots in the sufferings [under the Communist rule]. After the prayer we will have moon-cakes and fruits, and a time for moon-appreciation.

In the 1990s, however, the celebration of the Mid-Autumn Festival has become less formal and less regular. It has become more a time for family reunion than for gathering the church community. Sometimes the church combines the celebration of the Mid-Autumn Festival with a welcome party for new students. These evangelical Christians regard it, like the Chinese New Year, as an opportunity to bring non-Christian Chinese into the church, especially lonely students who have just left their families in Asia.

Family Altars, Artworks, and Dragons

Traditionally, many Chinese families had family shrines, either to venerate ancestors or to worship certain gods, or both. However, I did not see any family shrines at CCC members' homes, neither ancestral tablets nor religious altars. In fact, the conversion to Christianity was sometimes marked by an act of removing a family altar. One example is the Zhao family, a couple with three teenage sons, who immigrated from Fujian, China, in the mid-1980s. The Zhao family owned a Chinese restaurant in Washington, D.C., and worked seven days a week, fourteen to fifteen hours a day. They lived in constant fear of black robbers in the neighborhood. The Zhao family used to have a home altar dedicated to *Guanyin*, a popular female Bodhisattva in China, and other gods. In 1994 the family was invited to the church to attend a dinner party for mainland Chinese. After that they attended some Sunday services and other activities. One year later the couple and their three sons were baptized. Mrs. Zhao wrote this testimonial on behalf of her family:

We used to be very superstitious, like to worship idols and burn incense in front of Guanyin. After we began to come to the church, I stopped worshiping the idols. However, then I sometimes had visions of suddenly stumbling down or my hair burning. One night I had a horrible dream in which I was chased by lots of demons. I was extremely horrified and became almost breathless. Suddenly I remembered the Lord Jesus, so I cried out: "Jesus come to save me!" Immediately, I saw an angel wearing a white robe appearing in the sky, holding a shining cross. The demons were all scared away. In such a wonderful moment I woke up. I prayed to the Lord Jesus and all worked, so I came to know that Jesus Christ is good. He protects me and my family. He is more powerful than ghosts and demons.

Immediately, they got the pastor to their home and demolished the family altar, and soon the whole family was baptized.

Traditional Chinese paintings and sculptures sometimes have religious implications. However, in many cases it is not easy to differentiate the artistic values from religious elements. Many CCC members decorate their houses with Chinese traditional paintings and calligraphic scrolls, often with Christian themes and biblical verses. Most sculptures I saw at members' homes were of a modern artistic nature, and I saw very few Chinese traditional figures. I did see the "triple stars" of good luck (*fu*), officialdom (*lu*) and longevity (*shou*) at the home of a church member who was a restaurant owner. However, whether these statues have religious implications or not depends upon the personal beliefs of the owners. Chinese restaurants often have an altar of certain gods, sometimes including the triple stars; however, these figures can be appreciated solely as artistic works. One young couple had a small china statue of the "Happy Buddha" as an ornament on a table in the living room. The Happy Buddha, a popular legendary figure in China, has a grinning face and a round belly, which signifies lack of worry and broad-mindedness. The wife's parents came to visit them and lived with them. The wife's mother, in her late fifties, had no religion; however, she began to express some revering attitudes toward this statue. Once the young couple noticed this, they removed the statue.

The dragon has been an important Chinese symbol. Chinese people often call themselves "Dragon Descents" (*long de zisun*, or *long de chuanren*). A song written by a young man in Taiwan in the 1970s, "*Long de Chuanren*," became a popular song among many Chinese in Taiwan, Hong Kong, mainland China, and the diaspora. In 1988 a TV commentary series, *The River Elegy*, criticized Chinese traditions and vilified the symbols of the dragon and the Great Wall. This caused emotional rejections by many Chinese people, including overseas Chinese, because they still regard the dragon as a totemic symbol for the Chinese people. The dragon is also a popular decorative image.

However, this sacred Chinese symbol presents some problems for Chinese Christians. In ancient Western cultures, the imaginary dragon is a vicious monster, as depicted in the New Testament book of Revelation and in stories of St. George the dragon slayer. I did not hear CCC people talking about the dragon; I saw no paintings or decorative images of the dragon at members' homes; and no dragon dances were held by these Chinese Protestants to celebrate the Chinese New Year. One lay leader, upon my enquiry, said this:

> *The Chinese dragon and the dragon in the Revelation are totally different things. Their features and their characters are completely different. The Chinese dragon is a cultural symbol, which can be just like the eagle to Americans. Only when someone worships the dragon as an idol it becomes a problem. I once jokingly said to [church] people: if you have a rug with a dragon image, don't throw it away. Give it to me. When someone wears a dragon-shape tie pin, some Christians would say no-no. What is the problem? It should not be a problem.*

However, he acknowledged that some Chinese Christians did not agree with him.

In 1996 a Taiwanese Presbyterian pastor published an article in the newsletter of the Taiwan Christian Church Council of North America in which he distinguished the evil dragon in the Bible from the auspicious dragon of the Orient. He attributed the problem to mistranslation of the Bible and said that the dragon in the Bible should be translated as beast (*guai shou*) instead of dragon (*long*). However, "a group of concerned readers" wrote a letter to the newsletter, which was published in the following issue, in which they insisted that the Oriental dragon was the dragon in the Bible, the image of Satan. No further discussions were published. Apparently the dragon symbol is still problematic for many Chinese Christians. While some people believe that the two dragons are completely different symbols, others insist that they are the same. Most Chinese Christians, however, hold no clear position either for or against the dragon. They simply avoid the image of dragon as much as possible.

Confucianism: Its Compatibility with Christianity

Many scholars hold that Confucianism was the Chinese traditional orthodoxy and that Confucian values still broadly define the nature of Chinese culture and Chinese identity. Understandably, Chinese Christians do not hesitate to claim Confucianism as their cultural heritage. They see most Confucian values as compatible with Christianity and regard them as valuable complements for life in contemporary American society. This positive attitude toward Confucianism is pervasive at the CCC and other Chinese churches.

The Living Water

In 1982 the CCC started a quarterly magazine for publishing testimonials and sharing ideas among church members. They named the magazine *Living Water* (or *Living Spring*) in reference to the biblical verses where Jesus says,

> *Whoever drinks the water I give him will never thirst. Indeed, the water I give him will become in him a spring of water welling up to eternal life. (John 4:14)*

> *If anyone is thirsty, let him come to me and drink. Whoever believes in me, as the Scripture has said, streams of living water will flow from within him. (John 7:37–38)*

Interestingly, the editorial foreword of the very first issue also introduced the magazine with a poem by Zhu Xi (A.D. 1130–1200), the great Neo-Confucian master in the Song Dynasty:

A square pond opens up like a mirror
In it glowing light and white clouds are waving together
No wonder this lagoon is so clear
Because from the springhead comes the living water

The editorial foreword continued,

The Word of God is the living water for our hearts. His love is encompassing. Would you open up your heart
like the pond to receive the light and reflections of the love of God?

Quoting a poem by a Neo-Confucian master in the opening remarks of the church magazine is a clear indication of the profound influence of Confucian heritage in the hearts and minds of these Christian Chinese. What is more interesting is that there seems to be a perfect fit between this Confucian poem and the biblical verses. Zhu Xi likens the heart to the water in his philosophical writings, analogically stating that the clearness and cleanness of the heart/mind depend on the living water. What is the living water? It seems unclear in Zhu Xi's poem and other writings. However, when Chinese Christians read the biblical verses quoted above, they find a definite answer—the living water is Jesus Christ. They find not contradiction, but compatibility.

Love and Filial Piety

A core concept of Confucianism is *ren*, which may be translated as humanity, benevolence, or love. Confucianism regards *ren* as the foundation of goodness and all virtues. Following the Confucian phrase *ren zhe ai ren* ('*ren* is to love people'), Chinese Christians equate *ren* to *ren-ai* (love) and regard this *ren-ai* as the quintessence of Confucianism. They see this Confucian core principle as very close to Jesus' new command of love. Jesus said to his disciples, "A new command I give you: Love one another" (John 13:34). Other New Testament passages say, "God is love. Whoever lives in love lives in God, and God in him" (1 John 4:16); and compassion, kindness, humility, gentleness, patience, and forgiveness, "over all these virtues put on love, which binds them all together in perfect unity" (Colossians 3:14). Apparently, both Confucianism and Christianity regard love as the foundation of all virtues. Citing these biblical verses and Confucian texts, these Chinese Christians firmly believe in the compatibility of Confucian *ren* with Christian love.

The foremost virtue in Confucianism is filial piety (*xiao*), which requires children to respect their parents and elders, to take care of them when in need, to honor them in deed by achieving successes, and to venerate them after death. In sermons, lectures, and interviews these Chinese Christians stress the importance of filial piety. They often cite the fifth of the Ten Commandments: "Honor your father and your mother, so that you may live long in the land the Lord your God is giving you" (Exodus 20:12). They like to point out that this is the only commandment that has a promise of worldly blessing, since Paul said, "Children, obey your parents in the Lord, for this is right. Honor your father and mother—which is the first commandment with a promise—that it may go well with you and that you may enjoy long life on the earth" (Ephesians 6:1–3). Several articles on filial piety have appeared in *Living Water*. One article in 1995 clearly manifests the fusion of Christian beliefs and Confucian teachings to justify the necessity of filial piety:

Some Westerners misinterpret Genesis chapter two verses 23 and 24, and say that "husband and wife are the
one bone and flesh; they two are one flesh and the dearest persons. After marriage they are united into one, so
they should leave their parents and no longer live together with their parents." The first half of these words is
right, but the second half is wrong. We should know that Lord Jesus Christ never said that you should take care
of your wife more than your parents. The purpose of husband and wife being united together is to love each
other and to learn to live a holy life. "To leave parents" does not mean to dismiss or get rid of the parents, but
only means to live not under the same roof. This is reasonable if the wealth allows and if the parents wish to
live separately. It is also natural that in American society children often live far away from their parents because
of the job. However, if one insists that old parents must live separately, that is a misinterpretation of the teach-
ing of the Bible and forsakes the obligation of children to take care of the parents. We Chinese are a people who
highly appreciate filial piety. We must think again and again over this issue. Mark 15:4 says, "For God said,
'Honor your father and mother' and 'Anyone who curses his father or mother must be put to death.'" If you
are a Christian, you ought to take care of your parents, because taking care of the parents is one of the three

behaviors of filial piety. Furthermore, the Bible also tells us this very clearly. Therefore, we must remember this all the time. . . . When we worship God the Creator we should remember our parents for their grace of giving birth to us and rearing us. . . . We who are parenting should be role models for our children. God is watching us from above. If we can do this every generation, our Chinese traditional principle of filial piety (xiaodao) will be forever preserved.

The "Westerners' misinterpretation" was a target of criticism. This essay also clearly shows the author's conviction of the complete compatibility of biblical teachings and Confucian notions.

The emphasis on filial piety is often accompanied by an emphasis on family life, including harmonious relationships between husband and wife, between parents and children, and among siblings. Living in modern American society and following the biblical traditions, Chinese Christians tend to regard the nuclear family as the basic unit of family life. This is different from the traditional Chinese way in which the family often means the extended family or even the clan. On the other hand, these Chinese Christians disapprove of what they perceive as the "breakdown" of the family in American society. They underscore the need to extend family life beyond the nuclear family. As shown in the above quotation, they regard taking care of old parents as part of the good Chinese tradition that Chinese Christians should preserve.

The Philosophy of Life

Chinese Christians believe that Confucianism and Christianity share many other social and moral values as well. Chapter 4 described several moral values that CCC members cherish and promote, which could be called the "Protestant ethic." Actually, most of these values are Confucian too. Both Protestantism and Confucianism maintain "this-worldly asceticism"—success, thrift, delayed gratification, practical rationalism, and so on. Indeed, Christians at the CCC claim that the Confucian and Christian philosophies of life are very much alike. An article published in *Living Water* in 1989 reads:

Learning to be a human person (xue zuoren) is the emphasis of Confucianism. To be a human person is to be free and independent. Wealth and rank will not make him wallowing, poverty and lowness will not make him shaking, and coercive forces will not make him bending. He will not give up moral principles no matter in what circumstances. The true freedom is not to be determined by circumstances. This central view of Confucianism is consistent with a biblical principle. Paul said in the Philippians 4:11–13, "I have learned to be content whatever the circumstances. I know what it is to be in need, and I know what it is to have plenty. I have learned the secret of being content in any and every situation, whether well fed or hungry, whether living in plenty or in want. I can do everything through him who gives me strength." . . . Therefore, no matter in what circumstances, we should always strive forward and upward, with full confidence, dynamism and strong will. We should trust the Lord to lead our life and receive His grace and gifts with joy and hope.

Here the compatibility of Confucianism and Christianity is affirmed with no doubt.

Confucian Deficiency and the Remedy

While pointing out many compatible teachings in Confucianism and Christianity, these Chinese Christians never say that they are the same. In fact, they frequently note various differences between Confucianism and Christianity. The fundamental difference, or the root of other differences, they claim, is the lack of a clear view of God and the spiritual world in Confucianism.

Confucius himself does not deny the existence of God or gods;[4] however, he is agnostic, believing that man cannot know things beyond this world. Confucius talks about no supernatural things and declares that "without knowing life, how can you know death" (*wei zhi sheng, yan zhi si*)! Most Confucian followers in dynastic China moved farther and farther away from acknowledging the existence of God or gods. However, agnosticism is not an essential element in Confucianism, these Chinese Christians argue. They point out that Confucius was fond of ancient classics and that in the classics that Confucius edited, there is no lack of the notion of God. All of the most ancient Chinese classics, including *Shi Jing* (the Book of Songs), *Shu Jing* (the Book of History), *Yi Jing* (the Book of Change), and *Li Ji* (the Book of Rites) have many verses about *Shangdi* or *Tian*. This idea of a supreme ruler who has power and personality is very close to the notion of God in the Judeo-Christian tradition.

Many contemporary Neo-Confucian scholars praise the agnosticism in Confucianism. To Chinese Christians, however, this lack of religious dimension is a fatal deficiency of Confucianism. Although it is true that Confucius cared little about the spiritual world and death, these questions have to be answered. Precisely because Confucianism failed to provide consistent answers concerning God, death, and the spiritual world, these Chinese Christians argue, various human-invented wrong religions have filled China ever since the Han Dynasty (206 B.C.–A.D. 220), when Confucianism became the orthodoxy. Religious Daoists developed a system of gods, spirits, and immortals. Buddhism brought China the doctrine of "soul transmigration." For these Chinese Christians, only Christian beliefs provide the right answer to the questions that Confucianism failed to address. As a member wrote in the church magazine,

Confucianism did not negate the existence of the spiritual world. Daoist and Buddhist superstitions filled the empty space left by Confucianism, but the [Buddhist] soul transmigration is just absurd. Thank God for giving us a clear answer: after death there will be resurrection for Christians. We trust what the Bible says, that we will be resurrected.

To remedy what they perceive as the deficiency of Confucianism, these Chinese Christians call for a restoration of ancient Chinese culture prior to Confucius. They see that the pragmatic rationalism after Confucius blocked Chinese people from the transcendent or *Shangdi* (God), just like ancient Jews who sometimes betrayed Jehovah, God of their ancestors. Once we are reconnected with God as believed by our ancient ancestors, they say, we can expect the revival and revitalization of Chinese culture in the modern world. These Chinese Christians want to show that God is no alien to Chinese spirituality. Ancient Chinese ancestors believed and worshiped God, who is a universal God and is thus the Chinese God too. By pointing out the verses about God in the most ancient Chinese texts and by arguing that this God is the same God whom Christians believe in and worship, these Chinese Christians want to prove that believing in God is indeed very Chinese, very traditional (in ancient roots), rather than at odds with Chinese identity and Chinese traditions.

Moreover, Confucianism has to be complemented by Christianity in the modern world. These Chinese Christians believe that without believing in the living God many Confucian moral values would be devoid of meaning or impossible to practice. For example, *ren-ai* (love) is an ideal in Confucian morality. But people often fail to love others. This is because of the lack of godly love, these Christians believe. They claim that only if one receives love from God can one love others without utilitarian purposes. "We love because he [God] first loved us" (1 John 4:19) and "since God so loved us, we also ought to love one another" (1 John 4:11). Loving others has to be sustained by the love of God. In this sense, only through Christianity can Confucian moral ideals be fulfilled.

More important, Confucianism has to be complemented with Christianity in the modern world. Modernity has challenged the authority of traditions. In the past the Confucian orthodoxy was maintained by the dynastic state, but the dynastic state has collapsed. Another source of authority for Confucianism is traditionalism—upholding Confucian morals because the ancestors held them. In modern society, however, no traditional values can be preserved intact without passing rational reexamination. Appealing to tradition alone is insufficient to carry on Confucian moral values. In this regard, the absolute notion of God in Christianity can be a powerful source of authority. Because these Chinese Christians find the main Confucian values compatible with conservative Christianity, they find it natural to complement Confucianism with Christian beliefs and to maintain these values through the Christian institution. Christian beliefs provide the absolute foundation for the moral principles of Confucianism in the modern world, and this foundation has well survived various modern or postmodern challenges. Also, living in the United States as a minority, they see that no institution has better resources to implement and pass on Confucian values than the church.

Chinese Christians believe that without the Christian faith, Confucianism alone cannot protect the Chinese people from the rising tide of unhealthy developments in modern society. This is true both to Chinese as a minority in America and to Chinese societies in Asia. The so-called greater China has been in an economic boom. But social anomie and moral chaos are rampant along with the rise of materialism, consumerism, and eroticism. Many Chinese Christians in America share this burning concern about the breakdown of Chinese society and consequently strive hard to evangelize Chinese compatriots. In this process, they do not intend to replace Confucianism with Christianity. Rather, they want to revitalize Confucianism through Christianity.

Confucian Orthodoxy Versus Christian Orthodoxy

The description above shows that these Chinese Christians are integrating Confucianism and Christianity. Their efforts have touched upon many Christian theological questions. To attain the Christian identity, these Chinese Christians adhere to evangelical Christianity. Meanwhile, to retain their Chinese identity, they want to inherit the Confucian orthodoxy. Because syncretism has been regarded as a danger to the Christian faith in the orthodox Christian theology, an unavoidable question is: Is it syncretic to mix Confucianism and Christianity?

How do these Chinese evangelical Christians uphold orthodox Christian beliefs while remaining truthful to the Confucian orthodoxy? Theological judgment is not the purpose of this sociological study. On the other hand, an empirical study of a Christian church cannot avoid asking questions with theological significance. "Syncretism" worries theologians and the subjects of this ethnographic study. The Chinese Christians at the CCC have made great efforts to prove the authenticity of their Christian faith as well as their Chinese identity.

First, for these Chinese Christians, Confucianism is a system of moral values, whereas Christianity provides transcendent beliefs and spiritual guidance. In other words, they regard the core of the Confucian orthodoxy as on the level of moral values or social ethics, whereas the essence of Christianity is on the level of spirituality concerning the transcendent. This is to say that Confucianism and Christianity do not compete on the same level. Therefore, these Chinese evangelical Christians can claim that they remain truthful to both Christianity and Confucianism without being syncretic. A frequent statement in talks and articles at the church is "Worship Jesus Christ as God, revere Confucius as a sage, and honor ancestors as human beings."

An article in *Living Water* tried to clarify proper names for the birthday of Christ and that of Confucius. The conventional Chinese translation of the word *Christmas* is *Shengdan* (*sheng*: sage, saint, holy, sacred; *dan*: birth, birthday). In the 1980s some newspapers in Taiwan adopted a new translation of *Christmas—Yedan* (birthday of Jesus). The article reads:

> *Some Confucian apologists [in Taiwan] even have suggested calling the birthday of Confucius* Shengdan *and claim that only the birthday of Confucius deserves to be called* Shengdan. . . . *Actually, the conventional use of the word "Shengdan" for the birthday of the Lord Jesus Christ has no competition with that of Confucius. The character* sheng *in* Shengdan *is not the* sheng *in* shengren, *but is the* sheng *in the word* shensheng, *which means Holy, Godly, or Divine. The* sheng *in the word* shengren *means sages or saints, who are persons of noble virtues and high prestige. [Chinese] Christians also revere Confucius as a sage, and have the greatest esteem for this great Chinese sage. However, he is a man, not God. He is a sage, but not the Holy Divinity. Jesus Christ differs categorically. He was given birth by the virgin Mary whom the Holy Spirit conceived. Jesus Christ is the incarnation of the Word (Dao), the Son in the triune Persons of God. Although He was a person when he was in the world, He was also God. Therefore, His birthday is and should be called* Shengdan, *the Holy Birth.*

This article may look tedious, but is indicative that assuring the authenticity of both their Chinese identity and their Christian identity is important for these Chinese Christians. For them, calling Confucius a sage, rather than a god, is a restoration of Confucianism to its primary form. Confucius never claimed himself a god, or even a sage. Worshiping Confucius as a god is thus against Confucius himself. The feudal dynasties made Confucius a god for the purpose of social control. Chinese Christians call for going back to the original Confucianism and getting rid of the corrupted practices developed in dynastic times. They assert that only with this restoration can Confucianism be revived in the modern world.

Second, in their attempts to integrate Confucianism and Christianity, these Chinese Christians have simultaneously tried to differentiate primitive or essential Christianity from Western theologies. Western theologies have adopted Greek and Roman philosophies to understand and explain Christian notions. However, the Greek and Roman philosophies are only certain means to approach God and the gospel, not the essence of Christianity. Those theologies have helped Western Christians to understand God; they may be helpful for Chinese Christians; but they are not necessarily essential to the Christian faith. Chinese traditional philosophies are very different from Greek and Roman philosophies. These Chinese Christians hope that Chinese theologians will adopt thoughts of Chinese sages to develop a Christian theology so that Chinese people can easily accept Christian beliefs. In their view, an indigenous Chinese Christian theology should be rooted both in continuity with the historical church and in Chinese culture. They argue that the original Hellenic philosophies are not Christian but pre-Christ.

If Westerners could successfully integrate Greek and Roman philosophies with their Christian faith, the Chinese may do something similar by integrating Chinese philosophies with Christianity. A Chinese Christian thinker, who was a popular speaker at the CCC and other Chinese churches, proposed that Chinese theologians should pay more attention to the Chinese philosophical category of "relation" than the Western philosophical categories of "substance and attribute," pay more attention to the Chinese conviction of the goodness of human nature, and talk less about predestination and eschatology. When such a Chinese theology is established, it will be quite different from existing Christian theologies.

Traditional Chinese Heterodoxies: Daoism and Buddhism

Although Confucianism was the orthodoxy in China, Daoism (Taoism) and Buddhism had pervasive influences among the populace. As two major heterodoxies, Daoism and Buddhism complemented Confucianism and made lasting imprints in Chinese culture. Therefore, Chinese Christians must deal with them and take positions.

Appreciating Philosophical Daoism While Rejecting Religious Daoism

Daoism is a Chinese indigenous tradition with roots in ancient Chinese classics. Whereas philosophical Daoism emphasizes knowing or comprehending the Dao and reaching the Dao through inaction (*wu wei*) and spontaneity (*zi ran*), religious Daoism has a system of gods and spirits, religious rituals and symbols, and monasticism. For Chinese Christians the distinction between philosophical Daoism and religious Daoism is important. Generally speaking, Chinese evangelical Christians reject religious Daoism but selectively accept some notions of Daoist philosophy. They regard the Daoist rituals, spirits, and monastic system as superstitious and wrong, although they appreciate some life wisdom in *Dao De Jing* (*Tao Te Ching*) and other Daoist classics. A Chinese pastor stated the Christian position clearly:

> I accept Daoism like I accept Confucianism. I respect Laozi as the founder of Daoism, although I disagree with Daoist religionists who made Laozi the god Taishang Laojun.

The main link between Daoism and Christianity is the word *Dao*. In *Dao De Jing*, Dao is a mystic force. Many philosophers and religionists have tried to understand and interpret the meaning of this mystic Dao, which seems to be very close to the notion of Logos in Greek philosophy. Interestingly, the word *Logos* also appears in the beginning of the gospel of John in the New Testament. The English Bible translates *Logos* as 'Word,' whereas the most commonly used Chinese Bible translates *Logos* as 'Dao.' Therefore, the first verse of the gospel of John in Chinese reads like this:

> In the beginning was the Dao, and the Dao was with God, and the Dao was God. (Tai chu you Dao. Dao yu Shen tong zai. Dao jiu shi Shen).

To Chinese people who are familiar with *Dao De Jing*, reading these biblical verses can be enlightening. They seem to directly address the important question of Dao and to provide a clear interpretation of the mystic Dao. In light of the Christian scriptures, the Dao is a person of the Triune God. This Dao is God, who later was incarnated as Jesus Christ. The Chinese translation of *incarnation* is "the Dao took up the body of flesh" (*dao cheng rou shen*).

Rev. Moses Chow, the first pastor of the CCC, tells the story of how his Daoist father became Christian (1995, 8–12). After his clandestine conversion to Christianity, Moses brought home a copy of the gospel of John in Chinese, hoping his father, a fervent Daoist follower, would read it. At first his father angrily tossed the book aside because it was a book of a *foreign* religion. Later, when he was alone, he opened the book out of curiosity. Young Moses, hiding from his father's sight, watched closely his father's reactions. Upon reading the first verses, his father murmured, "Why, this book talks about *Taoism*!" "The Holy Spirit began to enlighten his heart as he read on," Chow reported. "I hardly dared breathe while watching father read through the gospel of John at one sitting" (1995, 9–10). Then, the senior Chow called Moses and asked to be taken immediately to the pastor. His father had a long conversation with the Chinese pastor. Chow reported that for the next few months after his father read the gospel of John, "he spent every waking hour intensely studying the Word [Dao] of God" (1995, 10). This was followed by the conversion of the whole family. Not surprisingly, Rev. Moses Chow continues to speak positively about the affinity between Daoism and Christianity.

The Dao as a link to the Christian gospel makes a reinterpretation of *Dao De Jing* possible. Yuan Zhiming, a popular speaker at the CCC and many other Chinese churches, has developed a systematic reinterpretation of *Dao De Jing* in light of Christianity. The manuscript, entitled *The Light of God* (*Shen Guang*), was circulated among CCC members before its formal publicatron.[5] To Yuan Zhiming, a Christian convert, God is a universal God of all humankind, and the Dao (Word or Way) of God is the universal Dao. In his book, Yuan comes to the conclusion that more than twenty-six hundred years ago, when God prophesied the coming of Jesus Christ through the prophet Isaiah, God also shed light to ancient China through Laozi. Before the gospel came to China in more recent times, the Dao in *Dao De Jing* had been a myth puzzling generations of people. It was like a gorgeous cloud in the sky. Watching from below, many people have sensed the great superhuman wisdom in it, but they could not see the light above the cloud. The light was from God, Yuan asserts. It has always been there, but people could not see it; therefore, they could not understand Laozi in his own terms. Now with the light of God we can finally understand Laozi.

According to Yuan, Laozi prophesied the Dao of God. The Dao in Laozi is the same as the Dao (Word) in the Bible. Through interpreting various verses in the book, Yuan argues that *Dao De Jing* clearly articulates that the Dao is God, is Who He Is (YHWH), is infinity, eternity, the creator, the transcendent, revelator, and savior. *Dao De Jing* also reveals that the Dao would be incarnated as a *Shengren* (sage), who would be a prophet, a priest, a king, and a savior. Because God's revelation to Laozi was only a "general revelation" (*yiban qishi*), *Dao De Jing* could not prophesy the incarnation of Dao as clearly as Isaiah in the Old Testament, for only Isaiah received God's direct and specific revelation (*zhijie tebie qishi*) at about the same time of Laozi. *Dao De Jing* is not a part of the Holy Scripture. However, reading *Dao De Jing* would help Chinese people to understand God and Christ. Simply put, the Dao of God is not alien to Chinese culture.

This reinterpretation of *Dao De Jing* by Yuan Zhiming is a novel one. It will stimulate debates both among Chinese Christians and among non-Christian scholars of Daoism. Reactions from CCC members during my field work there were positive and accepting, although Yuan has also been challenged at various Chinese Christian meetings. If his reinterpretation can be accepted, this may mark a new era in the development of Chinese Christian theology.

Rejecting Buddhism without Reservation

Buddhism came to China about two thousand years ago. Chinese Christians acknowledge the great impact of Buddhism on Chinese culture and the continuous influence of Buddhism among Chinese people. However, they generally reject Buddhism without reservation. An article in *Living Water* in 1986 listed and articulated ten irreconcilable contrasts between Buddhism and Christianity:

(1) Buddhists worship many gods, whereas Christians worship the "One True God."

(2) Buddhists believe the world is meaningless and has no purpose, whereas Christians believe the world was created by God and it has God's wonderful purpose.

(3) Buddhists hold pessimistic and negative views of life, regard life as sufferings, whereas Christians hold optimistic and positive views of life, regard life as serving the family, the society, the country and the world [note the Confucian tone!] and to glorify God.

(4) Buddhists want to withdraw and escape from the world, whereas Christians affirm and engage in the world.

(5) Buddhists believe in fatalism—causes in the previous life have consequences in this life, whereas Christians seek God's will that can change our fate.

(6) Buddhists regard every and any being as equal, the soul transmigrates [through the forms of god, spirit, human, animal, ghost, and devil] according to cause-consequence retribution, whereas Christians regard man as the best of all beings who is created in the image of God.

(7) Buddhists advise people to do good for the purpose of escaping from the cause-consequence retribution, whereas Christians advise people to do good for the purpose of breaking away from evil by knowing God.

(8) Buddhists cultivate themselves by relying on their own virtuous work, whereas Christians regard man as unreliable. Just as a strong man cannot lift himself up, every person has to rely on God for salvation.

(9) Buddhists are vegetarians because they fear killing animals may cause retribution in the coming life, whereas Christians eat food to keep health.

(10) Buddhists cultivate themselves for the purpose of entering nirvana, whereas Christians believe in the Lord for the purpose of achieving eternal life. Buddhists cannot explain what nirvana is, which may simply mean nonbeing; whereas Christians have a clear explanation about life after death—eternal life and resurrection.

The writer of this article was not a trained theologian, but a lay believer whose profession was hydraulic engineering. His views on Buddhism are commonly shared by CCC members and other Chinese evangelical Christians. These Chinese Christians feel uncompromising competition with Buddhism. Some church members are adult converts from Buddhist backgrounds. They consistently criticize Buddhist beliefs and practices and try to persuade Chinese people to give up Buddhism for Christianity. In fact, some members even helped to convert a Buddhist abbot. In 1989 six or seven CCC members visited a Chan (Zen) Buddhist Center in the Greater Washington area. A person who had both Christian relatives and Buddhist relatives initiated and arranged this visit. The head monk of the Chan center and several Buddhist nuns welcomed these Christian visitors with a sumptuous vegetarian dinner. At the table they freely exchanged views about life and religion. The monk gave the guests some volumes of Buddhist Sutras and expressed a hope for more conversation in the future. As a reciprocal courtesy the guests later mailed the abbot some books on philosophy, Christianity, and Buddhism written by Christian scholars. Several months later this Buddhist head monk cast off his monastery *jiasha* and was baptized at a Christian church. He gave several testimonies at fellowship group meetings and a Sunday worship service at the CCC before moving to California. This event encouraged many CCC members to further evangelize Chinese Buddhists. Doubtless, the competition with Buddhist religion will continue.

Reflection: Types of "Chinese" Christians

To affirm their Chinese identity, CCC members have been making choices in their inherited Chinese cultural traditions. Overall, they consistently preserve Confucian moral values, selectively accept some Daoist notions, and categorically reject Buddhism. However, this general summary is not applicable to all individuals. First of all, many people change their attitudes toward traditional culture over time. A common pattern for Chinese converts is to at first distance themselves from Chinese cultural traditions as much as possible, and then gradually return to some traditions. Immediately following their conversion, their Christian identity takes priority. Anything that may jeopardize their newly achieved Christian identity is cast off. After they achieve a sense of security in their Christian identity, Chinese cultural traditions become less of a threat to their faith. Then they may look to the traditions for cultural values and religious inspiration. Secondly, Chinese cultural traditions are diverse. Depending on circumstances and personal choices, a Chinese Christian may inherit some Confucianism or some Daoism or some Buddhism or a mixture of elements from all three. I have been able to distinguish three types of "Chinese" Christians.

Most CCC members accept Confucianism, or Confucian moral values. Normally these "Confucian" Christians are conservative in theology, traditionalist in ethics, reserved in behavior, and rationalistic in beliefs. They emphasize family life, moral education of children, and successes in the world. Their religious life is very much family-centered or community-oriented. However, they would object to being called "Confucian" Christians for two reasons. First, Confucianism for them simply means "Chinese." They often refer to certain values as "Chinese" rather than "Confucian." An important reason for this is that the term *Confucianism* is a misnomer coined by Westerners. The Chinese term for Confucianism is the "scholarly tradition" (*rujia*), which is synonymous with Chinese culture. Second, they do not intend to preserve Confucianism per se. Their preservation is selective: preserving Confucian moral values while rejecting Confucian agnosticism. They also reject the ritualistic and state-sanctified version of Confucianism, such as worshiping Confucius and emphasizing imperial loyalty.

Some Chinese Christians at the CCC explicitly accept or appreciate some notions of Daoism. These "Daoist" Christians tend to place emphasis on spiritual cultivation through devotional prayers, direct relationship with God, and personal salvation through grace. Compared with "Confucian" Christians, these people are more pietistic than ethicistic, more individualistic than collectivistic, and more experientialistic than rationalistic. Some may have charismatic tendencies and like to be filled by the Holy Spirit, speak in tongues, conduct spiritual healing, and practice exorcism. "Daoist" Christians are few, less than ten percent at the most. In the Washington area, two of the twenty Chinese churches are obviously charismatic; their members might have more Daoist tendencies.

Buddhism is generally rejected by Chinese evangelical Christians. However, for some converts from Buddhist backgrounds, some habits of the heart may continue to affect their Christian practices. Some "Buddhist" Christians are very otherworldly oriented and like to proclaim the "void" of the world and worldly life. Furthermore, the habits of the heart with Buddhist traditions may have two different manifestations. Chan (Zen) Buddhism emphasizes enlightenment through one's own efforts; Pure Land Buddhism believes in "salvation" through the "other-power" and religious work (*gongde*, including religious observances and moral behaviors). Chan Buddhists prefer simplicity, whereas Pure Land Buddhists like elaborate rituals. At the CCC, very few members like elaborate rituals and observances. One may find more of this type of Christian in Chinese Catholic churches. Meanwhile, I have not seen any Chan-like Christians at the CCC who would favor simple methods (*fangbian famen*) and self-nourished enlightenment. However, some may exist outside the church. For example, since the late 1980s some Chinese intellectuals in China have been called "cultural Christians" (*wenhua jidutu*). These people are scholars of Christian studies who may not join any church or participate in Christian rituals. Nonetheless they accept some Christian notions and beliefs. Some unchurched Chinese in the United States who nevertheless claim the Christian faith may be of this type as well. Overall, "Buddhist" Christians are very few, if any, in the evangelical Chinese churches.

The construction of Chinese identity is a complex process for Chinese immigrants in the United States because of the long history of Chinese civilization and its diverse cultural traditions, because of modern conflicts and divisions in Chinese society, and because of their migrating away from China. This is simultaneously a process of deconstruction and reconstruction.

Notes

1. Bernard Wong provides brief illustrations of festivities in New York Chinatowns (1982, 88–90).

2. It is inaccurate to call the traditional Chinese calendar system a lunar system and the Chinese New Year a Lunar New Year.

3. Francis L. K. Hsu described Qingming activities among the Chinese in Hawaii: "In front of graves both new and old are clusters of Chinese men, women, and children paying homage and making offerings to their dead. The offerings may be slim or abundant, including pigs and chickens roasted whole or simply sliced meats and plates of fruit. But cups of alcohol are poured on the ground in front of the tombs, bundles of burning incense placed before them, and large or small quantities of specially made paper money and papier-mâché life-like figures are burned for the benefit of the dead. The entire assemblage kneels down in twos and threes to kowtow to the dead. There are always offerings of flowers. And finally, in front of many of the tombs, a large string of firecrackers is exploded" (1971, 60). In contrast, these traditional Chinese rituals were not seen in a Chinese Christian cemetery in Hawaii: "Instead there is more of the usual type of observance common among white Christian Americans such as flowers and silent prayers on Easter, Memorial Day, Christmas, birthdays of the dead, Father's Day, Mother's Day, and so on" (1971, 63).

4. "Respect gods and spirits, but keep a distance from them" (*jing guishen er yuan zhi*) is a commonly quoted saying of Confucius.

5. Yuan's book was later published in Taiwan in 1997, entitled *Laozi vs. The Bible: A Meeting Across Time and Space*.

The Kitchen God's Wife

AMY TAN

As I turn down Ross Alley, everything around me immediately becomes muted in tone. It is no longer the glaring afternoon sun and noisy Chinatown sidewalks filled with people doing their Saturday grocery shopping. The alley sounds are softer, quickly absorbed, and the light is hazy, almost greenish in cast.

On the right-hand side of the street is the same old barbershop, run by Al Fook, who I notice still uses electric clippers to shear his customers' sideburns. Across the street are the same trade and family associations, including a place that will send ancestor memorials back to China for a fee. And farther down the street is the shopfront of a fortune-teller. A hand-written sign taped to the window claims to have "the best lucky numbers, the best fortune advice," but the sign taped to the door says: "Out of Business."

As I walk past the door, a yellow pull-shade rustles. And suddenly a little girl appears, her hands pressed to the glass. She stares at me with a somber expression. I wave, but she does not wave back. She looks at me as if I don't belong here, which is how I feel.

And now I'm at Sam Fook Trading Company, a few doors down from the flower shop. It contains shelves full of good-luck charms and porcelain and wooden statues of lucky gods, hundreds of them. I've called this place the Shop of the Gods ever since I can remember. It also sells the kind of stuff people get for Buddhist funerals—spirit money, paper jewelry, incense, and the like.

"Hey, Pearl!" It's Mr. Hong, the owner, waving me to come in. When I first met him, I thought his name was Sam Fook, like the shop. I found out later that *sam fook* means "triple blessing" in old Cantonese, and according to my mother—or rather, her Hong Kong customers—*sam fook* sounds like a joke, like saying "the Three Stooges."

"I told him he should change the name," my mother had said. "Luckier that way. But he says he has too much business already."

"Hey, Pearl," Mr. Hong says when I walk in the door, "I got some things for your mother here, for the funeral tomorrow. You take it to her, okay?"

"Okay." He hands me a soft bundle.

I guess this means Grand Auntie's funeral will be Buddhist. Although she attended the First Chinese Baptist Church for a number of years, both she and my mother stopped going right after my father died. In any case, I don't think Grand Auntie ever gave up her other beliefs, which weren't exactly Buddhist, just all the superstitious rituals concerning attracting good luck and avoiding bad. On those occasions when I did go up to her apartment, I used to play with her altar, a miniature red temple containing a framed picture of a Chinese god. In front of that was an imitation-brass urn filled with burnt incense sticks, and on the side were offerings of oranges, Lucky Strike cigarettes, and an airline mini-bottle of Johnnie Walker Red whiskey. It was like a Chinese version of a Christmas crèche.

And now I come to the flower shop itself. It is the bottom floor of a three-story brick building. The shop is about the size of a one-car garage and looks both sad and familiar. The front has a chipped red-bordered door covered with rusted burglarproof mesh. A plate-glass window says "Ding Ho Flower Shop" in English and Chinese. But it's easy to miss, because the place sits back slightly and always looks dark and closed, as it does today.

So the location my mother and Auntie Helen picked isn't exactly bustling. Yet they seem to have done all right. In a way, it's remarkable. After all these years, they've done almost nothing to keep up with the times or make the place more attractive. I open the door and bells jangle. I'm instantly engulfed in the pungent smell of gardenias, a scent I've always associated with funeral parlors. The place is dimly lit, with only one fluorescent tube hanging over the cash register—and that's where my mother is, standing on a small footstool so she can see out over the counter, with dime-store reading glasses perched on her nose.

She is talking on the telephone in rapid Chinese and waves impatiently for me to come in and wait. Her hair is pulled straight back into a bun, not a strand ever out of place. The bun today has been made to look thicker with the addition of a false swatch of hair, a "horse's tail," she calls it, for wearing only on important occasions.

Actually, now I can tell—by the shrillness of her pitch and the predominance of negative "vuh-vuh-vuh" sounds—that she's arguing in Shanghainese, and not just plain Mandarin. This is serious. Most likely it's with a neighborhood supplier, to judge from the way she's punching in numbers on a portable calculator, then reading aloud the printed results in harsh tones, as if they were penal codes. She pushes the "No Sale" button on the cash register, and when the drawer pops forward, she pulls out a folded receipt, snaps it open with a jerk of her wrist, then reads numbers from that as well.

"Vuh! Vuh! Vuh!" she insists.

The cash register is used to store only odds and ends, or what my mother calls "ends and odds and evens." The register is broken. When my mother and Auntie Helen first bought the store and its fixtures, they found out soon enough that anytime the sales transaction added up to anything with a 9 in it, the whole register froze up. But they decided to keep the cash register anyway, "for stick-'em-up," is how my mother explained it to me. If they were ever robbed, which has yet to happen, the robber would get only four dollars and a pile of pennies, all the money that is kept in the till. The real money is stashed underneath the counter, in a teapot with a spout that's been twice broken and glued back on. And the kettle sits on a hot plate that's missing a plug. I guess the idea is that no one would ever rob the store for a cup of cold tea.

I once told my mother and Auntie Helen that a robber would never believe that the shop had only four dollars to its name. I thought they should put at least twenty in the cash register to make the ruse seem more plausible. But my mother thought twenty dollars was too much to give a robber. And Auntie Helen said she would "worry sick" about losing that much money—so what good would the trick be then?

At the time, I considered giving them the twenty dollars myself to prove my point. But then I thought, What's the point? And as I look around the shop now, I realize maybe they were right. Who would ever consider robbing this place for more than getaway bus fare? No, this place is burglarproof just the way it is.

The shop has the same dull gray concrete floor of twenty-five years ago, now polished shiny with wear. The counter is covered with the same contact paper, green-and-white bamboo lattice on the sides and wood grain on the top. Even the phone my mother is using is the same old black model with a rotary dial and a fabric cord that doesn't coil or stretch. And over the years, the lime-colored walls have become faded and splotched, then cracked from the '89 earthquake. So now the place has the look of spidery decay and leaf mold.

"*Hau, hau*," I now hear my mother saying. She seems to have reached some sort of agreement with the supplier. Finally she bangs the phone down. Although we have not seen each other since Christmas, almost a month ago, we do none of the casual hugs and kisses Phil and I exchange when we see his parents and friends. Instead, my mother walks out from around the counter, muttering, "Can you imagine? That man is cheating me! Tried to charge me for extra-rush delivery." She points to a box containing supplies of wire, clear cellophane, and sheets of green wax paper. "This is not my fault he forgot to come last week."

"How much extra?" I ask.

"Three dollars!" she exclaims. I never cease to be amazed by the amount of emotional turmoil my mother will go through for a few dollars.

"Why don't you just forget it? It's only three dollars—"

"I'm not concerned about money!" she fumes. "He's cheating me. This is not right. Last month, he tried to add another kind of extra charge too." I can tell she's about to launch into a blow-by-blow of last month's fight, when two well-dressed women with blond hair peer through the door.

"Are you open? Do any of you speak English?" one of them says in a Texas drawl.

My mother's face instantly cheers, and she nods, waving them in. "Come, come," she calls.

"Oh, we don't want to bother y'all," one of the ladies says. "If you might could just tell us where the fortune cookie factory is?"

Before I can answer, my mother tightens her face, shakes her head, and says, "Don't understand. Don't speak English."

"Why did you say that?" I ask when the two ladies retreat back into the alley. "I didn't know you hated tourists that much."

"Not tourists," she says. "That woman with the cookie factory, once she was mean to me. Why should I send her any good business?"

"How's business here?" I say, trying to steer the conversation away from what will surely become a tirade about the cookie woman down the street.

"Awful!" she says, and points to her inventory around the shop. "So busy—busy myself to death with this much business. You look, only this morning I had to make all these myself."

And I look. There are no modern arrangements of bent twigs or baskets of exotica with Latinate-drooping names. My mother opens the glass door to a refrigerator unit that once housed bottles of soda pop and beer.

"You see?" she says, and shows me a shelf with boutonnieres and corsages made out of carnations, neatly lined in rows according to color: white, pink, and red. No doubt we'll have to wear some of these tonight.

"And this," she continues. The second shelf is chock-full of milk-glass vases, each containing only a single rosebud, a fern frond, and a meager sprinkling of baby's breath. This is the type of floral arrangement you give to hospital patients who go in for exploratory surgery, when you don't know yet whether the person will be there for very long. My father received a lot of those when he first went into the hospital and later right before he died. "Very popular," my mother says.

"This, too, I had to make," she says, and points to the bottom shelf, which holds half a dozen small table sprays. "Some for tonight. Some for a retirement dinner," my mother explains, and perhaps because I don't look sufficiently impressed, she adds, "For assistant manager at Wells Fargo."

She walks me around to view her handiwork in other parts of the shop. Lining the walls are large funeral wreaths, propped on easels. "Ah?" my mother says, waiting for my opinion. I've always found wreaths hideously sad, like decorative lifesavers thrown out too late.

"Very pretty," I say.

And now she steers me toward her real pride and joy. At the front of the shop, the only place that gets filtered daylight for a few hours a day, are her "long-lasting bargains," as she calls them—philodendrons, rubber plants, chicken-feet bushes, and miniature tangerine trees. These are festooned with red banners, congratulating this business or that for its new store opening.

My mother has always been very proud of those red banners. She doesn't write the typical congratulatory sayings, like "Good Luck" or "Prosperity and Long Life." All the sayings, written in gold Chinese characters, are of her own inspiration, her thoughts about life and death, luck and hope: "First-Class Life for Your First Baby," "Double-Happiness Wedding Triples Family Fortunes," "Money Smells Good in Your New Restaurant Business," "Health Returns Fast, Always Hoping."

My mother claims these banners are the reasons why Ding Ho Flower Shop has had success flowing through its door all these years. By success, I suppose she means that the same people over the last twenty-five years keep coming back. Only now it's less and less for shy brides and giddy grooms, and more and more for the sick, the old, and the dead.

She smiles mischievously, then tugs my elbow. "Now I show you the wreath I made for you."

I'm alarmed, and then I realize what she's talking about. She opens the door to the back of the shop. It's dark as a vault inside and I can't make out anything except the dense odor of funeral flowers. My mother is groping for the piece of string that snaps on the light. Finally the room is lit by the glare of a naked bulb that swings back and forth on a cord suspended from the high ceiling. And what I now see is horrifyingly beautiful—row after row of gleaming wreaths, all white gardenias and yellow chrysanthemums, red banners hanging down from their easels, looking like identically dressed heavenly attendants.

I am stunned by how much hard work this represents. I imagine my mother's small hands with their parchmentlike skin, furiously pulling out stray leaves, tucking in sharp ends of wire, inserting each flower into its proper place.

"This one." She points to a wreath in the middle of the first row. It looks the same as the others. "This one is yours. I wrote the wishes myself."

"What does it say?" I ask.

Her finger moves slowly down the red banner, as she reads in a formal Chinese I can't understand. And then she translates: "Farewell, Grand Auntie, heaven is lucky. From your favorite niece, Pearl Louie Brandt, and husband."

"Oh, I almost forgot." I hand her the bundle from Sam Fook's. "Mr. Hong said to give you this."

My mother snips the ribbon and opens the package. Inside are a dozen or so bundles of spirit money, money Grand Auntie can supposedly use to bribe her way along to Chinese heaven.

"I didn't know you believed in that stuff," I say.

"What's to believe," my mother says testily. "This is respect." And then she says softly, "I got one hundred million dollars. Ai! She was a good lady."

* * * * *

"Here we go," I say, and take a deep breath as we climb the stairs to the banquet room.

"Pearl! Phil! There you are." It's my cousin Mary. I haven't seen her in the two years since she and Doug moved to Los Angeles. We wait for Mary to move her way through the banquet crowd. She rushes toward us and gives me a kiss, then rubs my cheek and laughs over the extra blush she's added.

"You look terrific!" she tells me, and then she looks at Phil. "Really, both of you. Just sensational."

Mary must now be forty-one, about half a year older than I am. She's wearing heavy makeup and false eyelashes, and her hair is a confusing mass of curls and mousse. A silver-fox stole keeps slipping off her shoulders. As she pushes it up for the third time, she laughs and says, "Doug gave me this old thing for Christmas, what a bother." I wonder why she does bother, now that we're inside the restaurant. But that's Mary, the oldest child of the two families, so it's always seemed important to her to look the most successful.

"Jennifer and Michael," she calls, and snaps her fingers. "Come here and say hello to your auntie and uncle." She pulls her two teenage children over to her side, and gives them each a squeeze. "Come on, what do you say?" They stare at us with sullen faces, and each of them grunts and gives a small nod.

Jennifer has grown plump, while her eyes, lined in black, look small and hard. The top part of her hair is teased up in pointy spikes, with the rest falling limply down to the middle of her back. She looks as if she had been electrocuted. And Michael's face—it's starting to push out into sharp angles and his chin is covered with pimples. They're no longer cute, and I wonder if this will happen to Tessa and Cleo, if I will think this about them as well.

"You see how they are," Mary says apologetically. "Jennifer just got her first nylons and high heels for Christmas. She's so proud, no longer Mommy's little girl."

"Oh, Mother!" Jennifer wails, then struggles away from her mother's grasp and disappears into the crowd. Michael follows her.

"See how Michael's almost as tall as Doug?" Mary says, proudly watching her son as he ambles away. "He's on the junior varsity track team, and his coach says he's their best runner. I don't know where he got his height or his athletic ability—certainly not from me. Whenever I go for a jog, I come back a cripple," Mary says, laughing. And then, realizing what she's just said, she suddenly drops her smile, and searches the crowd: "Oh, there's Doug's parents. I better go say hello."

Phil squeezes my hand, and even though we say nothing, he knows I'm mad. "Just forget it," he says.

"I would," I shoot back, "if she could. She *always* does this."

When Phil and I married, it was Mary and Doug who were our matron of honor and best man, since they had introduced us. They were the first people we confided in when we found out I was pregnant with Tessa. And about seven years ago, Mary was the one who pushed me into aerobics when I complained I felt tired all the time. And later, when I had what seemed like a strange weakness in my right leg, Phil suggested I see Doug, who at the time was an orthopedist at a sports medicine clinic.

Months later, Doug told me the problem seemed to be something else, and right away I panicked and thought he meant bone cancer. He assured me he just meant he wasn't smart enough to figure it out himself. So he sent me to see his old college drinking buddy, the best neurologist at San Francisco Medical Center. After what seemed like a year of tests—after I persuaded myself the fatigue was caused by smoking and the weakness in my leg was sciatica left over from my pregnancy—the drinking buddy told me I had multiple sclerosis.

Mary had cried hysterically, then tried to console me, which made it all seem worse. For a while, she dropped by with casserole dishes from "terrific recipes" she "just happened to find," until I told her to stop. And later, she made a big show of telling me how Doug's friend had assured her that my case was really "quite mild," as if she were talking about the weather, that my life expectancy was not changed, that at age seventy I could be swinging a golf club and still hitting par, although I would have to be careful not to stress myself either physically or emotionally.

"So really, everything's normal," she said a bit too cheerfully, "except that Phil has to treat you nicer. And what could be wrong with that?"

"I don't play golf," was all I told her.

"I'll teach you," she said cheerily.

Of course, Mary was only trying to be kind. I admit that it was more my fault that our friendship became strained. I never told her directly how much her gestures of sympathy offended me. So of course she couldn't have known that I did not need someone to comfort me. I did not want to be coddled by casseroles. Kindness was compensation. Kindness was a reminder that my life had changed, was always changing, that people thought I should just accept all this and become strong or brave, more enlightened, more peaceful. I wanted nothing to do with that. Instead, I wanted to live my life with the same focus as most people—to worry about my children's education, but not whether I would be around to see them graduate, to rejoice that I had lost five pounds, and not be fearful that my muscle mass was eroding away. I wanted what had become impossible: I wanted to forget.

I was furious that Doug and his drinking-buddy friend had discussed my medical condition with Mary. If they had told her that, then they must have also told her this: that with this disease, no prognosis could be made. I could be in remission for ten, twenty, thirty, or forty years. Or the disease could suddenly take off tomorrow and roll downhill, faster and faster, and at the bottom, I would be left sitting in a wheelchair, or worse.

I know Mary was aware of this, because I would often catch her looking at me from the corner of her eye whenever we passed someone who was disabled. One time she laughed nervously when she tried to park her car in a space that turned out to be a handicapped zone. "Oops!" she said, backing out fast. "We certainly don't need that."

In the beginning, Phil and I vowed to lead as normal a life together as possible. "As normal as possible"—it was like a meaningless chant. If I accidentally tripped over a toy left on the floor, I would spend ten minutes apologizing to Tessa for yelling at her, then another hour debating whether a "normal" person would have stumbled over the same thing. Once, when we went to the beach for the express purpose of forgetting about all of this, I was filled with morbid thoughts instead. I watched the waves eating away at the shore, and I wondered aloud to Phil whether I would one day be left as limp as seaweed, or stiff like a crab.

Meanwhile Phil would read his old textbooks and every medical article he could find on the subject. And then he would become depressed that his own medical training offered no better understanding of a disease that could be described only as "without known etiology," "extremely variable," "unpredictable," and "without specific treatment." He attended medical conferences on neurological disorders. He once took me to an MS support group, but we turned right around as soon as we saw the wheelchairs. He would perform what he called "weekly safety checks," testing my reflexes, monitoring the strength of my limbs. We even moved to a house with a swimming pool, so I could do daily muscle training. We did not mention to each other the fact that the house was one-story and had few steps and wide hallways that could someday be made wheelchair-accessible, if necessary.

We talked in code, as though we belonged to a secret cult, searching for a cure, or a pattern of symptoms we could watch for, some kind of salvation from constant worry. And eventually we learned not to talk about the future, either the grim possibilities or the vague hopes. We did not dwell on the past, whether it had been a virus or genetics that had caused this to happen. We concerned ourselves with the here and now, small victories over the mundane irritations of life—getting Tessa potty-trained, correcting a mistake on our charge-card bill, discovering why the car sputtered whenever we put it into third gear. Those became our constants, the things we could isolate and control in a life of unknown variables.

So I can't really blame Phil for pretending that everything is normal. I wanted that more than he did. And now I can't tell him what I really feel, what it's like. All I know is that I wake up each morning in a panic, terrified that something might have changed while I slept. And there are days when I become obsessed if I lose something, a button, thinking my life won't be normal until I find it again. There are days when I think Phil is the most inconsiderate man in the world, simply because he forgot to buy one item on the grocery list. There are days when I organize my underwear drawer by color, as if this might make some kind of difference. Those are the bad days.

On the good days, I remember that I am lucky—lucky by a new standard. In the last seven years, I have had only one major "flare-up," which now means I lose my balance easily, especially when I'm upset or in a hurry. But I can still walk. I still take out the garbage. And sometimes I actually *can* forget, for a few hours, or almost the entire day. Of course, the worst part is when I remember once again—often in unexpected ways—that I am living in a limbo land called remission.

That delicate balance always threatens to go out of kilter when I see my mother. Because that's when it hits me the hardest: I have this terrible disease and I've never told her.

I meant to tell her. There were several times when I planned to do exactly that. When I was first diagnosed, I said, "Ma, you know that slight problem with my leg I told you about. Well, thank God, it turned out *not* to be cancer, but—"

And right away, she told me about a customer of hers who had just died of cancer, how long he had suffered, how many wreaths the family had ordered. "Long time ago I saw that mole growing on his face," she said. "I told him, Go see a doctor. No problem, he said, age spot—didn't do anything about it. By the time he died, his nose and cheek—all eaten away!" And then she warned me sternly, "That's why you have to be careful."

When Cleo was born, without complications on my part or hers, I again started to tell my mother. But she interrupted me, this time to lament how my father was not there to see his grandchildren. And then she went into her usual endless monologue about my father getting a fate he didn't deserve.

My father had died of stomach cancer when I was fourteen. And for years, my mother would search in her mind for the causes, as if she could still undo the disaster by finding the reason why it had occurred in the first place.

"He was such a good man," my mother would lament. "So why did he die?" And sometimes she cited God's will as the reason, only she gave it a different twist. She said it must have been because my father was a minister. "He listened to everyone else's troubles," she said. "He swallowed them until he made himself sick. Ai! *Ying-gai* find him another job."

Ying-gai was what my mother always said when she meant, I should have. *Ying-gai* meant she should have altered the direction of fate, she should have prevented disaster. To me, *ying-gai* meant my mother lived a life of regrets that never faded with time.

If anything, the regrets grew as she searched for more reasons underlying my father's death. One time she cited her own version of environmental causes—that the electrician had been sick at the time he rewired our kitchen. "He built that sickness right into our house," she declared. "It's true. I just found out the electrician died—of cancer, too. *Ying-gai* pick somebody else."

And there was also this superstition, what I came to think of as her theory of the Nine Bad Fates. She said she had once heard that a person is destined to die if eight bad things happen. If you don't recognize the eight ahead of time and prevent them, the ninth one is always fatal. And then she would ruminate over what the eight bad things might have been, how she should have been sharp enough to detect them in time.

To this day it drives me crazy, listening to her various hypotheses, the way religion, medicine, and superstition all merge with her own beliefs. She puts no faith in other people's logic—to her, logic is a sneaky excuse for tragedies, mistakes, and accidents. And according to my mother, *nothing* is an accident. She's like a Chinese version of Freud, or worse. Everything has a reason. Everything could have been prevented. The last time I was at her house, for example, I knocked over a framed picture of my father and broke the glass. My mother picked up the shards and moaned, "Why did this happen?" I thought it was a rhetorical question at first, but then she said to me, "Do you know?"

"It was an accident," I said. "My elbow bumped into it." And of course, her question had sent my mind racing, wondering if my clumsiness was a symptom of deterioration.

"Why this picture?" she muttered to herself.

So I never told my mother. At first I didn't want to hear her theories on my illness, what caused this to happen, how she should have done this or that to prevent it. I did not want her to remind me.

And now that so much time has gone by, the fact that I still haven't told her makes the illness seem ten times worse. I am always reminded, whenever I see her, whenever I hear her voice.

Mary knows that, and that's why I still get mad at her—not because she trips over herself to avoid talking about my medical condition. I'm mad because she told *her* mother, my Auntie Helen.

"I had to tell her," she explained to me in an offhand sort of way. "She was always saying to me, Tell Pearl to visit her mother more often, only a one-hour drive. Tell Pearl she should ask her mother to move in with her, less lonely for her mother that way. Finally, I told my mother I couldn't tell you those things. And she asked why not." Mary shrugged. "You know my mother. I couldn't lie to her. Of course, I made her *swear* not to tell your mother, that you were going to tell her yourself."

"I can drive," I told Mary. "And that's not the reason why I haven't asked my mother to live with me." And then I glared at her. "How could you do this?"

"She won't say anything," Mary said. "I made her promise." And then she added a bit defiantly, "Besides, you should have told your mother a long time ago."

Mary and I didn't exactly have a fight, but things definitely chilled between us after that. She already knew that was about the worst possible thing she could have done to me. Because she had done it once before, nine years ago, when I confided to her that I was pregnant. My first pregnancy had ended in a miscarriage early on, and my mother had gone on and on about how much coffee I drank, how it was my jogging that did it, how Phil should make sure I ate more. So when I became pregnant again, I decided to wait, to tell my mother when I was in my fourth month or so. But in the third month, I made the mistake of confiding in Mary. And Mary slipped this news to her mother. And Auntie Helen didn't exactly tell my mother. But when my mother proudly announced my pregnancy to the Kwongs, Auntie Helen immediately showed my mother the little yellow sweater she had already hand-knit for the baby.

I didn't stop hearing the laments from my mother, even after Tessa was born. "Why could you tell the Kwongs, not your own mother?" she'd complain. When she stewed over it and became really angry, she accused me of making her look like a fool: "Hnh! Auntie Helen was pretending to be so surprised, so innocent. 'Oh, I didn't knit the sweater for Pearl's baby,' she said, 'I made it just in case.'"

So far, Auntie Helen had kept the news about my medical condition to herself. But this didn't stop her from treating me like an invalid. When I used to go to her house, she would tell me to sit down right away, while she went to find me a pillow for my back. She would rub her palm up and down my arm, asking me how I was, telling me how she had always thought of me as a daughter. And then she would sigh and confess some bit of bad news, as if to balance out what she already knew about me.

"Your poor Uncle Henry, he almost got laid off last month," she would say. "So many budget cuts now. Who knows what's going to happen? Don't tell your mother. I don't want her to worry over us."

And then *I* would worry that Auntie Helen would think her little confessions were payment in kind, that she would take them as license to accidentally slip and tell my mother: "Oh, Winnie, I thought you knew about your daughter's tragedy."

And so I dreaded the day my mother would call and ask me a hundred different ways, "Why did Auntie Helen know? Why did you never tell me? Why didn't you let me prevent this from happening to you?"

And then what answer could I give?

Grand Auntie Du's Funeral

My mother left the house two hours ago with Auntie Helen so they could decorate the funeral parlor. And now Phil and I are going to be late for Grand Auntie's service, thanks to a spat between Tessa and Cleo that resulted in eggs over easy being flung onto Phil's only good shirt and tie. While we searched for replacements along Clement Street, Phil suggested that we shouldn't bring the girls to the funeral.

"They might be disruptive," he said. "And they might not appreciate seeing someone who is D-E-A-D."

Tessa grinned and said in a singsong voice, "Daddy's saying a naughty word."

"Maybe I could wait with them outside in the car," said Phil.

"They'll be fine," I assured him. "I already asked my mother if it's closed-casket and she said it is. And I've explained to the girls it's like that time we went to Steve and Joanne's wedding—grownup time. Isn't that right, girls?"

"We got cake after," said Cleo.

"All right," said Phil. "But after the service, let's make the usual excuses and go home."

"Of course."

At twenty minutes after two, the four of us walk into the reception area of the funeral parlor. My cousin Frank hands us black armbands to wear. As I put mine on, I feel somewhat guilty, this pretense of grief. I realize now that I knew almost nothing about Grand Auntie Du, except that she smelled like mothballs and was always trying to feed me old Chinese candies and sugared beef jerky, pulled out of dusty tins stored on top of her refrigerator.

Bao-bao is there to greet us as well. He's smiling broadly. "Hey, man, glad to see you guys finally decided to make it." He hands each of us a piece of foil-wrapped candy and a small red envelope of lucky money.

"What are we supposed to do with these?" Phil whispers. "Offer them to Grand Auntie Du?" He pulls out a quarter from the lucky-money envelope.

"How should I know?" I whisper back. "I've never been to a Buddhist funeral, or whatever this is."

"My mom says it's like insurance in case you pick up bad vibes here," says Bao-bao. "You eat the candy for luck. You can buy more luck later with the money."

"I'm gonna eat mine now," announces Tessa.

Cleo waves her candy for me to unwrap. "Mommy, me too, me too!"

Phil flips his quarter. "Say, if I buy chewing gum with this, will my luck last longer?"

We turn toward the main parlor. Suddenly we are blinded by the glare of a spotlight. I'm surprised to see Tessa is now walking down the aisle in the manner of a coquettish bride. And Cleo—she's preening and blowing kisses like a movie star. I can't believe it: Uncle Henry is standing in the middle of the aisle—videotaping the funeral! Who's going to watch this later?

Through the haze of the incense-blurred light, I can barely see my mother. She's gesturing for us to come sit with her in the second row. Phil corrals the girls. As the camera continues to roll, we walk quickly down the aisle, past what must be only a dozen or so mourners—Mary, Doug, and their children, some people from the church, all Chinese. I also see several old ladies I've never met before. They look like recent immigrants, to judge from their undyed cropped hair and old-style brown padded jackets.

As we slide into our seats, Auntie Helen turns around in the front row. She squeezes my hand, and I see she has tears in her eyes. My mother is dry-eyed. "Why so late?" she asks crossly. "I told them to wait until you came."

Suddenly Cleo starts laughing and points. "Daddy, there's a lady sleeping up there! And her dinner's on fire!" Tessa is staring too, only her eyes are big, her mouth dropped open.

And then I see it too—God!—Grand Auntie Du lying in her casket, with glasses perched on her emotionless waxy face. In front of the casket is a long, low table overflowing with food—what looks like a nine-course Chinese dinner, as well as an odd assortment of mangoes, oranges, and a carved watermelon. This must be Grand Auntie's farewell provisions for trudging off to heaven. The smoke of a dozen burning incense sticks overlaps and swirls up around the casket, her ethereal stairway to the next world.

Phil is staring at me, waiting for an explanation. "This has to be a mistake," I whisper to him, and then turn to my mother, trying to keep my voice calm. "I thought you decided on closed-casket," I say slowly.

She nods. "You like? Clothes, I chose for her, all new. Casket, I also helped decide this. Not the best wood, but almost the best. Before she is buried, we take the jewelry off, of course."

"But I thought you said the lid would be down."

My mother frowns. "I didn't say that. How can you see her that way?"

"But—"

"Do we have to eat here?" Tessa asks fearfully. She squirms down low in her seat. "I'm not hungry," she whispers. I squeeze her hand.

"Tell that lady to wake up," Cleo squeals, giggling. "Tell her she can't sleep at the dinner table. It's not nice!"

Tessa slaps Cleo's leg. "Shut up, Cleo, she's not sleeping. She's dead, like Bootie the cat."

And Cleo's bottom lip turns down, dangerously low. "Don't tell me that!" she shouts, and then pushes Tessa's shoulder. I am trying to think of what I can say to comfort the girls, but—too late—they are pushing each other, crying and shouting, "Stop it!" "You stop!" "You started it!" My mother is watching this, waiting to see how I will handle it. But I feel paralyzed, helpless, not knowing what to do.

Phil stands up to lead both of the girls out. "I'll get them some ice cream over on Columbus. I'll be back in an hour."

"Make it forty-five," I whisper. "No more than that. I'll meet you out front."

"Daddy, can I have a chocolate and a rocky road?" asks Cleo.

"And sprinkles on top?" adds Tessa.

I'm relieved to think this may be all the damage that will remain, a ruined appetite and sticky hands. Over on the other side of the pews, Mary's son, Michael, is snickering. As I throw him a scowl, I notice something else: Uncle Henry still has the videocamera going.

After Phil and the girls leave, I try to regain my composure. I look ahead to avoid glaring at my mother or Uncle Henry. No use arguing, I tell myself. What's done is done.

In front of the pews is a large picture of Grand Auntie. It looks like a blown-up version of a passport photo taken fifty years ago. She's not exactly young, but she must have had most of her teeth back then. I look at Grand Auntie in her casket. Her mouth looks caved in, her thin face like that of a wizened bird. I is so still, yet I feel we are all waiting for something to happen, for Grand Auntie suddenly to transform and manifest herself as a ghost.

It reminds me of a time when I was five years old, that age when anything was possible if you could just imagine it. I had stared at the flickering eyes of a carved pumpkin, waiting for goblins to fly out. The longer

I waited, the more convinced I became that it would happen. To this day, I can still vividly remember the laughing ghost that finally poured out of the pumpkin's mouth. My mother had come rushing into the room when I screamed. I was babbling tearfully that I had seen a ghost. And instead of comforting me, or pooh-poohing that it was just my imagination, she had said, "Where?" and then searched the room.

Of course, my father later assured me that the only ghost was the Holy Ghost, and He would never try to scare me. And then he demonstrated in a scientific way that what I must have seen were smoky fumes created when the candle inside the pumpkin burned too low and extinguished itself. I was not comforted by his answer, because my mother had then stared at me, as if I had betrayed her and made her look like a fool. That's how things were. She was always trying to suppress certain beliefs that did not coincide with my father's Christian ones, but sometimes they popped out anyway.

"The *jiao-zi*, I made them," my mother is now telling me. "Grand Auntie always said I made the best-tasting." I nod and admire the steamed dumplings on the banquet table. She really does make the best ones, and I think it's a pity that these are just for show.

"Auntie Helen made the chicken and green peppers dish," she says, and after I nod, she adds, "Very dry-looking." And I nod again, wondering if Grand Auntie is appreciating this culinary postmortem in her honor. I scan the other dishes and see they have even added the cake left over from last night.

Above the casket, a white banner made out of ten feet of butcher paper is stuck to the wall with masking tape. The banner is covered with large black characters, and the whole thing ends with an exclamation point, just like political billboard slogans I once saw in magazine photos of China.

"What does that say?" I ask my mother quietly.

"'Hope that your next life is long and prosperous.' Nothing too special," my mother replies. "I didn't write it. This is from people with the Kwong family association. Maybe Helen gave them a donation."

I see all the wreaths perched on their easels. I search for mine, and I'm about to ask my mother where it is, when Uncle Henry turns the spotlight on again and starts filming Grand Auntie Du, lying at center stage. He waves to someone at stage left.

The next moment, I hear hollow wooden knocking sounds, followed by a persistent *ding-ding-ding*, as if someone were impatiently ringing for the bellhop in a hotel lobby. These sounds are joined by two voices, chanting a tune that seems to consist of the same four notes and syllables. It repeats so many times I'm sure it's a record that has become stuck.

But now, emerging from the left alcove are two Buddhist monks with shaved heads, dressed in saffron-colored robes. The older, larger monk lights a long stick of incense, bows three times to the body, then places the incense in the burner and backs away, bowing again. The younger monk is sounding the wooden clapper. Then they both begin walking down the aisle slowly, chanting, "Ami-, Ami-, Amitaba, Amitaba." As the older monk passes by, I see one cheek is flattened, and the ear on the same side is badly misshapen.

"He must have been in a terrible car accident," I whisper to my mother.

"Cultural Revolution," she says.

The smaller monk, I can see now, is not a monk at all, but a woman, a nun with three or four small scabs on her skull.

"She must have been in the Cultural Revolution too," I tell my mother.

My mother looks. "Too young. Flea bites, maybe," she concludes.

"Amitaba, Amitaba," they drone. And now the old ladies in the old-style jackets begin moaning and wailing, waving their arms up and down, overcome with grief, it seems. Uncle Henry turns the camera toward them.

"Are they Grand Auntie's good friends?" I ask my mother.

She frowns. "Not friends, maybe Chinese people from Vietnam. They came early, later saw we didn't have too many people to mourn Grand Auntie. So they talked to Auntie Helen, she gave them a few dollars. And now they're doing the old custom, crying out loud and acting like they don't want the dead person to leave so fast. This is how you show respect."

I nod. Respect.

"Maybe these ladies can do two or three funerals every day," my mother adds, "earn a few dollars. Good living that way. Better than cleaning house."

"Um," I answer. I don't know if my mother has said this to be disdainful or simply to state a matter of fact.

The wooden clapper and the bell sound again, faster and faster. Suddenly the white paper banner tears away from the wall, and the family association wishes for lucky and long life spiral down and land draped across Grand Auntie's chest like a beauty pageant banner. My mother and several of the older women jump up and cry, "Ai-ya!" Mary's son shouts, "Perfect landing!" and laughs hysterically. The monk and nun continue chanting with no change of expression. But my mother is furious. "How bad!" she mutters. She gets up and walks out of the room.

In a few minutes, she comes back with a young Caucasian man with thinning blond hair. He is wearing a black suit, so he must be with the funeral parlor. I can tell my mother is still scolding him, as she points to the disaster-ridden banner. People are murmuring loudly throughout the room. The old ladies are still wailing and bowing stiffly; the monk and nun keep chanting.

The blond man walks quickly to the front, my mother follows. He bows three times to Grand Auntie Du, then moves her casket, which glides forward easily on wheels. After another bow, the man ceremoniously plucks the banner off Grand Auntie's chest and carries it in both arms as if it were holy vestments. As he tapes the banner back up, my mother is fuming, "That corner, put more tape there! More there, too. How can you let her luck fall down like that!"

Once he has finished, the man pushes the casket back in place and bows three times to the body, once to my mother, who huffs in return, then quickly retreats. Did he bow to show genuine respect, I wonder, or has he learned to do this only for his Chinese customers?

Now Frank is passing out lit sticks of incense to everyone. I look around, trying to figure out what to do. One by one, we each get up and join the monk and nun, everyone chanting, "Amitaba! Amitaba!"

We are circling the coffin 'round and 'round, I don't know how many times. I feel silly, taking part in a ritual that makes no sense to me. It reminds me of that time I went with some friends to the Zen center. I was the only Asian-looking person there. And I was also the only one who kept turning around, wondering impatiently when the monk would come and the sermon would begin, not realizing until I'd been there for twenty minutes that all the others weren't quietly waiting, they were meditating.

My mother is now bowing to Grand Auntie. She puts her incense in the burner, then murmurs softly, "Ai! Ai!" The others follow suit, some crying, the Vietnamese ladies wailing loudly. Now it is my turn to bow. And I feel guilty. It's the same guilt I've felt before—when my father baptized me and I did not believe I was saved forever, when I took Communion and did not believe the grape juice was the blood of Christ, when I prayed along with others that a miracle would cure my father, when I already felt he had died long before.

Suddenly a sob bursts from my chest and surprises everyone, even me. I panic and try to hold back, but everything collapses. My heart is breaking, bitter anger is pouring out and I can't stop it.

My mother's eyes are also wet. She smiles at me through her tears. And she knows this grief is not for Grand Auntie Du but for my father. Because she has been waiting for me to cry for such a long, long time, for more than twenty-five years, ever since the day of my father's funeral.

I was fourteen, full of anger and cynicism. My mother, brother, and I were sitting by ourselves in an alcove, a half-hour before the service was supposed to begin. And my mother was scolding me, because I refused to go up to the casket to see my father's body.

"Samuel said good-bye. Samuel is crying," she said.

I did not want to mourn the man in the casket, this sick person who had been thin and listless, who moaned and became helpless, who in the end searched constantly for my mother with fearful eyes. He was so unlike what my father had once been: charming and lively, strong, kind, always generous with his laughter, the one who knew exactly what to do when things went wrong. And in my father's eyes, I had been perfect, his "perfect Pearl," and not the irritation I always seemed to be with my mother.

My mother blew her nose. "What kind of daughter cannot cry for her own father?"

"That man in there is not my father," I said sullenly.

Right then my mother jumped up and slapped my face. "That bad!" she shouted. I was shocked. It was the first time she had ever struck me.

"Ai-ya! If you can't cry, I make you cry." And she slapped me again and again. "Cry! Cry!" she wailed crazily. But I sat there still as a stone.

Finally, realizing what she had done, my mother bit the back of her hand and mumbled something in Chinese. She took my brother by the hand, and they left me.

So there I sat, angry, of course, and also victorious, although over what, I didn't know. And perhaps because I didn't know, I found myself walking over to the casket. I was breathing hard, telling myself, I'm right, she's wrong. And I was so determined not to cry that I never considered I would feel anything whatsoever.

But then I saw him, colorless and thin. And he was not resting peacefully with God. His face was stern, as if still locked in his last moment of pain.

I took so many small breaths, trying to hold back, trying not to cry, that I began to hyperventilate. I ran out of the room, out into the fresh air, gasping and gulping. I ran down Columbus, toward the bay, ignoring the tourists who stared at my angry, tear-streaked face. And in the end, I missed the funeral.

In a way, this is how it's been with my mother and me ever since. We both won and we both lost, and I'm still not sure what our battle was. My mother speaks constantly of my father and his tragedy, although never of the funeral itself. And until this day, I have never cried in front of my mother or spoken of my feelings for my father.

Instead, I have tried to keep my own private memories of him—a certain smile, a coat he wore, the passion he exuded when he stood at the pulpit. But then I always end up realizing that what I am remembering are just images from photos. And in fact, what I do remember most vividly are those times when he was ill. "Pearl," he would call weakly from his bed, "do you want help with your homework?" And I would shake my head. "Pearl," he would call from the sofa, "come help me sit up." And I would pretend I didn't hear him.

Even to this day I have nightmares about my father. In my dreams, he is always hidden in a hospital, in one of a hundred rooms with a hundred cots filled with sick people. I am wandering down long hallways, looking for him. And to do so, I must look at every face, every illness, every possible horror that can happen to one's body and mind. And each time I see it is not my father, I shake with relief.

I have had many variations of this dream. In fact, I had one just recently. In this version, I have gone to the hospital for a checkup, to see if the multiple sclerosis has advanced. Without explanation, a doctor puts me in a ward with terminally ill patients. And I'm shouting, "You can't treat me this way! You have to explain!" I shout and shout and shout, but nobody comes.

And that's when I see him. He is sitting in front of me, on a dirty cot, in soiled bedclothes. He is old and pathetically thin, his hair now white and patchy after years of waiting and neglect. I sit next to him and whisper, "Daddy?" He looks up with those helpless searching eyes. And when he sees me, he gives a small startled cry—then cries and cries, so happy!—so happy I have finally come to take him home.

Grand Auntie's memorial service is finally over. We are all standing outside and the bay wind has already started to blow, cutting through our thin jackets and causing skirts to whip up. My eyes are stinging and I feel completely drained.

My mother stands quietly next to me, peering at me every now and then. I know she wants to talk about what happened, not about all the disasters at the funeral, but why I cried.

"All right?" my mother asks gently.

"Fine," I say, and try to look as normal as possible. "Phil and the girls should be here any minute." My mother pulls a balled-up Kleenex from her sweater sleeve and hands it to me without a word, pointing to her own eye to indicate I've smudged my mascara.

Right then, Bao-bao comes up. "Boy, that was sure weird," he says. "But I guess that's the kind of funeral the old lady wanted. She always was a bit *you-know*," and he taps his finger twice to the side of his head.

My mother frowns. "What is *you-know*?"

Bao-bao grins sheepishly. "You know, uh, different, unusual—a *great* lady!" He looks at me and shrugs. And then relief springs to his face. "Whoa! There's Mimi with the car. Gotta run. You guys going to the cemetery?"

I shake my head. My mother looks at me, surprised.

Bao-bao walks over to a shiny black Camaro, and Mimi slides over so he can drive. "I don't got a choice. Mom roped me into being one of the pallbearers." He flexes his arm. "Good thing I've been pumping iron." He turns the radio way up and flexes his arm faster in rhythm with the vibrating music. "Well, nice seeing you again, Pearl. Catch you later, Auntie." The car rumbles off.

And now I hear Auntie Helen calling from behind. "Pearl! Pearl!" She waddles over, dabbing a tissue to her eyes at the same time. "You going to the cemetery? Nice buffet afterward, our house. Lots of good food. Your mother made the potstickers. I made a good chicken dish. Mary and Doug will be there. You come."

"We can't. Tomorrow's a work day, and it's a long drive."

"Oh, you kids," she says, and throws her hands up in mock frustration, "always too busy! Well, you come visit me soon. No invitation needed. You come, so we can talk."

"Okay," I lie.

"Winnie-ah!" Auntie Helen now calls loudly to my mother, even though they are standing only five feet apart. "You come with us to the cemetery. Henry is getting the car now."

"Pearl is taking me home," my mother answers, and I stand there, trying to figure out how she manages to catch me every time.

Auntie Helen walks up to my mother, a worried look on her face. She asks her quickly in Chinese: Not coming? Are you feeling sick?

I can't understand all the Mandarin words, only the gist of them. It seems my mother doesn't want anyone to worry, nothing is wrong, only a little discomfort here—and she points to her chest—because something-something has been bothering her. She mentions something-something about the banner falling down, and how her whole body has been aching ever since.

Auntie Helen rubs my mother's back. She tells my mother she can visit Auntie Du when something-something is more quiet, not running around all over the place. And then Auntie Helen laughs and tells my mother that Auntie Du will wait, of course she will wait for her visit, she has no choice. And my mother jokes back that maybe Auntie Du has already become mad-to-death about what happened today and has flown off to something-something place where she doesn't have to do something-something anymore with such a crazy family.

They are laughing hysterically now, laughing so hard that tears sprout from their eyes and they are barely able to catch their breath. My mother covers her mouth with her hand, giggling like a schoolgirl.

Uncle Henry drives the car up, and as Auntie Helen climbs in, she sternly reminds my mother to drink plenty of hot tea. They take off, beeping the horn twice.

"Aren't you feeling well?" I ask my mother.

"Ah?"

"You told Auntie Helen you couldn't go to the cemetery because you were sick."

"I didn't say sick. I only said I didn't want to go. I did my duty. I sent Auntie Du to heaven. Now it's Helen's duty to put her inside the ground."

That's not what they said. And although I'm not sure I understood most of their conversation, apparently there's a lot I don't know about my mother and Auntie Helen.

As we drive across town to my mother's house, Phil drops hints: "I hope we're on the freeway before the weekend rush hour to get back home."

My mother is making small talk. She tells me that Bao-bao may lose his job soon. This gossip she heard at the dinner from Uncle Loy, who heard it from his son. She tells me that Frank is now working the day shift as a security guard, but he is breaking Auntie Helen's heart, spending all his extra time and money at a pool hall on Geary Street.

As we get closer to her house, she points to a place on Clement Street, Happy Super, where she always does her grocery shopping. It's one of the typical Asian markets in the neighborhood, people standing outside, pinching and poking through piles of fruits and vegetables, hundred-pound bags of rice stacked like giant bricks against the window.

"Tofu, how much do you pay?" asks my mother, and I can tell she's eager to outdo me with a better price, to tell me how I can save twenty or thirty cents at her store.

But I can't even oblige her with a guess. "I don't know. I've never bought tofu."

"Oh." She looks disappointed. And then she brightens. "Four rolls of toilet paper, how much?"

"One sixty-nine," I answer right away.

"You see!" she says. "My place, only ninety-nine cents. Good brands, too. Next time, I buy you some. You can pay me back."

We turn left onto Eighth Avenue and head toward Anza. Auntie Helen and Uncle Henry live one block up, on Ninth. The houses in this area all look the same to me, variations of two-story row houses built in the twenties, differing mostly in what color they are painted and whether the front has been modernized in stucco, asbestos shingles, or aluminum siding. Phil pulls into my mother's driveway. The front of her place is Day-Glo pink, the unfortunate result of her being talked into a special deal by a longtime customer, a painting contractor. And because the outside is bumpy stucco, the whole effect looks like Pepto-Bismol poured over cottage cheese. Amazingly enough, of all the things my mother complains about, the color of the house is not one of them. She actually thinks it's pretty.

"When will I see you again?" she asks me as she climbs out of the car.

"Oh, soon," I say.

"Soon like Auntie Helen's soon?" she says.

"No, *soon*. Really."

She pauses, looking as if she doesn't believe me. "Oh, anyway, I will see you at Bao-bao's wedding next month."

"What? The wedding is next month? I didn't hear that."

"Very fast," my mother says, nodding. "Edna Fong from our church said she heard this from her daughter. Mimi washes her hair at that beauty shop. Mimi told Edna Fong's daughter they are in a big hurry to get married. And Edna Fong said to me, Maybe because something else is hurrying to come out. Auntie Helen doesn't know this yet. Don't tell her."

So there goes Auntie Helen's theory about Bao-bao's getting married because she's going to die soon. Something's growing all right, but it's not a tumor in Auntie Helen's head.

My mother climbs out of the car. She turns back and gives Tessa a cheek to kiss, then Cleo. My mother is not the cheek-kissing type, but she knows we have taught the girls to do this with Phil's parents.

"Bye-bye, Ha-bu!" they each say. "We love you."

"Next time you come," my mother says to the girls, "I make potstickers. And you can eat moon cakes for Chinese New Year's." She takes a tissue out of her sleeve and wipes Cleo's nose. She pats Tessa's knee. "Okay?"

"Okay!" they shout.

We all watch my mother walk up the steps to her front door, all of us waving the whole time. Once she's safe inside, we wave once more as she peers out the window, and then we take off.

"Whew!" Phil sighs. "Home." And I too sigh with relief. It's been a difficult weekend, but we survived.

"Mommy?" Tessa says at the first stop sign.

"Yes, sweetie."

"Mommy," she whispers. "I have to go to the bathroom."

"Me too," says Cleo. "I have to go oo-oo *real* bad."

My mother is standing outside the house when we return.

"I tried to chase you, but you were too fast," she says as soon as I get out of the car. "And then I knew you would remember and come back." Tessa and Cleo are already racing up the stairs.

"Remember what?"

"Grand Auntie's farewell gift. Remember? Two three days ago I told you not to forget. Yesterday I said, Don't forget. You forgot?"

"No, no," I say. "Where is it?"

"In back, in the laundry room," she says. "Very heavy, though. Better ask your husband to carry it." I can just imagine what it must be: the old vinyl ottoman Grand Auntie used to rest her feet on, or perhaps the set of chip-proof Melmac dishes. As we wait for Phil to come back with the girls, my mother hands me a cup of tea, waving off my protests. "Already made. If you can't drink it, I only have to throw it away."

I take a few quick sips. "This is really good." And I mean it. I have never tasted tea like this. It is smooth, pungent, and instantly addicting.

"This is from Grand Auntie," my mother explains. "A few years ago she bought it for herself. One hundred dollars a pound."

"You're kidding." I take another sip. It tastes even better.

"She told me, 'If I buy myself the cheap tea, then I am saying my whole life has not been worth something better.' So she decided to buy herself the best tea, so she could drink it and feel like a rich person inside."

I laugh.

My mother looks encouraged by my laughter. "But then she thought, If I buy just a little, then I am saying my lifetime is almost over. So she bought enough tea for another lifetime. Three pounds! Can you imagine?"

"That's three hundred dollars!" I exclaim. Grand Auntie was the most frugal person I knew. "Remember how she used to keep all the boxes of See's candies we gave her for Christmas, telling us they were too good to eat? And then one year, she gave a box back to us for Thanksgiving or something. Only it was so old—"

My mother was nodding, already laughing.

"—all the candies were white with mold!"

"Bugs, too!" my mother adds.

"So she left you the tea in her will?" I say.

"Already gave it to me a few months ago. She was thinking she was going to die soon. She didn't say, but she started to give things away, good things, not just junk. And one time we were visiting, drinking tea. I said, 'Ah, good tea!' same as always. This time, Grand Auntie went to her kitchen, brought back the tea.

She told me, '*Syau ning*, you take this tea now.' That's what she called me, *syau ning*, 'little person,' from the old days when we first knew each other.

"I said, 'No, no! I wasn't saying this to hint.' And she said, '*Syau ning*, you take this now so I can see how happy you are to receive it while I am still alive. Some things can't wait until I'm dead.' How could I refuse? Of course, every time I came to visit, I brought back her tea."

Phil returns with Cleo, Tessa is right behind. And now I am actually sorry we have to leave.

"We better hit the road," says Phil. I put the teacup down.

"Don't forget," my mother says to Phil. "Grand Auntie's present in the laundry room."

"A present?" Cleo says. "Do I have a present too?"

Phil throws me a look of surprise.

"Remember?" I lie. "I told you—what Grand Auntie left us in her will."

He shrugs, and we all follow my mother to the back.

"Of course it's just old things," says my mother. She turns on the light, and then I see it, sitting on the clothes dryer. It is the altar for Grand Auntie's good-luck god, the Chinese crèche.

"Wow!" Tessa exclaims. "A Chinese dollhouse."

"I can't see! I can't see!" Cleo says, and Phil lifts the altar off the dryer and carries it into the kitchen.

The altar is about the size of a small upturned drawer, painted in red lacquer. In a way, it resembles a miniature stage for a Chinese play. There are two ornate columns in front, as well as two ceremonial electric candles made out of gold and red plastic and topped by red Christmas tree bulbs for flames. Running down the sides are wooden panels decorated with gold Chinese characters.

"What does that say?" I ask my mother.

She traces her finger down one, then the other. "*Jye shiang ru yi*. This first word is 'luck,' this other is another kind of luck, and these two mean 'all that you wish.' All kinds of luck, all that you wish."

"And who is this on the inside, this man in the picture frame?" The picture is almost cartoonlike. The man is rather large and is seated in regal splendor, holding a quill in one hand, a tablet in the other. He has two long whiskers, shaped like smooth, tapered black whips.

"Oh, this we call Kitchen God. To my way of thinking, he was not too important. Not like Buddha, not like Kwan Yin, goddess of mercy—not that high level, not even the same level as the Money God. Maybe he was like a store manager, important, but still many, many bosses above him."

Phil chuckles at my mother's Americanized explanation of the hierarchy of Chinese deities. I wonder if that's how she really thinks of them, or if she's used this metaphor for our benefit.

"What's a kitchen god?" says Tessa. "Can I have one?"

"He is only a story," answers my mother.

"A story!" exclaims Cleo. "I want one."

My mother's face brightens. She pats Cleo's head. "You want another story from Ha-bu? Last night, you did not get enough stories?"

"When we get home," Phil says to Cleo. "Ha-bu is too tired to tell you a story now."

But my mother acts as if she has not heard Phil's excuses. "It is a very simple story," she says to Cleo in a soothing voice, "how he became Kitchen God. It is this way."

And as my mother begins, I am struck by a familiar feeling, as if I am Cleo, again three years old, still eager to believe everything my mother has to say.

"In China long time ago," I hear my mother say, "there was a rich farmer named Zhang, such a lucky man. Fish jumped in his river, pigs grazed his land, ducks flew around his yard as thick as clouds. And that was because he was blessed with a hardworking wife named Guo. She caught his fish and herded his pigs. She fattened his ducks, doubled all his riches, year after year. Zhang had everything he could ask for—from the water, the earth, and the heavens above.

"But Zhang was not satisfied. He wanted to play with a pretty, carefree woman named Lady Li. One day he brought this pretty woman home to his house, made his good wife cook for her. When Lady Li later chased his wife out of the house, Zhang did not run out and call to her, 'Come back, my good wife, come back.'

"Now he and Lady Li were free to swim in each other's arms. They threw money away like dirty water. They slaughtered ducks just to eat a plate of their tongues. And in two years' time, all of Zhang's land was empty, and so was his heart. His money was gone, and so was pretty Lady Li, run off with another man.

"Zhang became a beggar, so poor he wore more patches than whole cloth on his pants. He crawled from the gate of one household to another, crying, 'Give me your moldy grain!'

"One day, he fell over and faced the sky, ready to die. He fainted, dreaming of eating the winter clouds blowing above him. When he opened his eyes again, he found the clouds had turned to smoke. At first he was afraid he had fallen down into a place far below the earth. But when he sat up, he saw he was in a kitchen, near a warm fireplace. The girl tending the fire explained that the lady of the house had taken pity on him—she always did this, with all kinds of people, poor or old, sick or in trouble.

"'What a good lady!' cried Zhang. 'Where is she, so I can thank her?' The girl pointed to the window, and the man saw a woman walking up the path. Ai-ya! That lady was none other than his good wife Guo!

"Zhang began leaping about the kitchen looking for some place to hide, then jumped into the kitchen fireplace just as his wife walked in the room.

"Good Wife Guo poured out many tears to try to put the fire out. No use! Zhang was burning with shame and, of course, because of the hot roaring fire below. She watched her husband's ashes fly up to heaven in three puffs of smoke. Wah!

"In heaven, the Jade Emperor heard the whole story from his new arrival. 'For having the courage to admit you were wrong,' the Emperor declared, 'I make you Kitchen God, watching over everyone's behavior. Every year, you let me know who deserves good luck, who deserves bad.'

"From then on, people in China knew Kitchen God was watching them. From his corner in every house and every shop, he saw all kinds of good and bad habits spill out: generosity or greediness, a harmonious nature or a complaining one. And once a year, seven days before the new year, Kitchen God flew back up the fireplace to report whose fate deserved to be changed, better for worse, or worse for better."

"The end!" shouts Cleo, completely satisfied.

"Sounds like Santa Claus," says Phil cheerfully.

"Hnh!" my mother huffs in a tone that implies Phil is stupid beyond words. "He is not Santa Claus. More like a spy—FBI agent, CIA, Mafia, worse than IRS, that kind of person! And he does not give *you* gifts, you must give *him* things. All year long you have to show him respect—give him tea and oranges. When Chinese New Year's time comes, you must give him even better things—maybe whiskey to drink, cigarettes to smoke, candy to eat, that kind of thing. You are hoping all the time his tongue will be sweet, his head a little drunk, so when he has his meeting with the big boss, maybe he reports good things about you. This family has been good, you hope he says. Please give them good luck next year."

"Well, that's a pretty inexpensive way to get some luck," I say. "Cheaper than the lottery."

"No!" my mother exclaims, and startles us all. "You never know. Sometimes he is in a bad mood. Sometimes he says, I don't like this family, give them bad luck. Then you're in trouble, nothing you can do about it. Why should I want that kind of person to judge me, a man who cheated his wife? His wife was the good one, not him."

"Then why did Grand Auntie keep him?" I ask.

My mother frowns, considering this. "It is this way, I think. Once you get started, you are afraid to stop. Grand Auntie worshipped him since she was a little girl. Her family started it many generations before, in China."

"Great!" says Phil. "So now she passes along this curse to us. Thanks, Grand Auntie, but no thanks." He looks at his watch and I can tell he's impatient to go.

"It was Grand Auntie's gift to you," my mother says to me in a mournful voice. "How could she know this was not so good? She only wanted to leave you something good, her best things."

"Maybe the girls can use the altar as a dollhouse," I suggest. Tessa nods, Cleo follows suit. My mother stares at the altar, not saying anything.

"I'm thinking about it this way," she finally announces, her mouth set in an expression of thoughtfulness. "You take this altar. I can find you another kind of lucky god to put inside, not this one." She removes the picture of the Kitchen God. "This one, I take it. Grand Auntie will understand. This kind of luck, you don't want. Then you don't have to worry."

"Deal!" Phil says right away. "Let's pack 'er up."

But now I'm worried. "Are you sure?" I ask my mother. She's already stuffing the plastic candlesticks into a used paper bag. I'm not exactly superstitious. I've always been the kind who hates getting chain letters—Mary used to send them to me all the time. And while I never sent the duplicate letters out as instructed, I never threw the originals away either.

Phil is carrying the altar. Tessa has the bag of candlesticks. My mother has taken Cleo back upstairs to find a plastic neon bracelet she left in the bathroom. And now my mother comes back with Cleo and hands me a heavy grocery sack, the usual care package, what feels like oranges and Chinese candy, that sort of thing.

"Grand Auntie's tea, I gave you some," my mother says. "Don't need to use too much. Just keep adding water. The flavor always comes back."

Fifteen minutes after leaving my mother's home, the girls fall asleep. Phil has chosen to take the 280 freeway, which has less traffic and longer stretches between speed traps. We are still thirty-five miles from home.

"We're not really keeping that altar thing?" Phil says. It is more a statement than a question.

"Um."

"It sure is ugly," he adds. "Although I suppose we could let the girls play with it for a while, until they get tired of it."

"Um." I look out the car window, thinking about my mother, what kind of good-luck god she will get for me. We rush past freeway signs and Sunday drivers in the slow lane. I look at the speedometer. We're going nearly eighty miles an hour.

"What's the rush?" I say.

Phil slows down, then asks, "Do we have anything to snack on?"

And now I remember the care package my mother gave us. It is stowed at my feet. I look in the bag. Inside are a few tangerines, a roll of toilet paper, a canister of Grand Auntie's tea, and the picture of my father that I accidentally knocked over last month. The glass has been replaced.

I quickly hand Phil a tangerine, then turn back toward the window so he does not see my tears. I watch the landscape we are drifting by: the reservoir, the rolling foothills, the same houses I've passed a hundred times without ever wondering who lives inside. Mile after mile, all of it familiar, yet not, this distance that separates us, me from my mother.

Chinese Temples in Honolulu

SAU CHUN WONG*

The religion of the Chinese combines the beliefs of Buddhism, Taoism and Confucianism. The objects of worship are the forces of nature, ancestors, ancient heroes, and patron deities. Religion, as observed by the uneducated masses, is handed down from generation to generation chiefly through ceremonial practices and tradition and differs greatly from the philosophies and moral systems propounded by the sages.

The Chinese temple in Honolulu, like many other immigrant institutions, arose in response to the need for security and confidence in a strange land. Almost every Chinese mutual aid society had its special altar room for worship of the familiar deities of the homeland, and special temples with sacred idols and priests from China appeared more than fifty years ago. This paper will attempt to describe six of the temples now existing.

The Temples.—1. The oldest and most frequented of the various Chinese temples in Honolulu is the **"Goon Yum" (Kwan Yin) Temple** or the Goddess of Mercy temple on Vineyard Street. Established first in the early eighties and later rebuilt several times, it is now situated near the river and stands as a guardian over it. Only a narrow gate with three large characters painted on it informs the visitor of the temple's existence. It is a two story structure, the lower portion of which is used to house the caretaker, and the priest. On the upper floor, reached by an outside stairway, are the four shrines clustered about the central figure of Kwan Yin. Bedecked with paper flowers on either side, with gilded detailed carvings framed about her, and gorgeous embroidered fans on either side, Kwan Yin reposes calm and serene in the center of lesser gods and goddesses. The heaven table is directly in front of her and is laden with copper kettles of sand, drum and gong, incense, candles, "chi-chi"[1] cylinders, and offerings.

As legend tells us, Kwan Yin was the youngest and most beautiful daughter of an ancient king of China. As she grew older she observed the many trials and tribulations that humanity had to endure. In spite of the loud protests of her father, the king, she vowed that she would never marry. In order to escape the punishments threatened by her father, she renounced the world and became a nun. The gods took pity upon her and made her the Goddess of Mercy. Worshippers pray to her for long life, for many sons and children, for fortune, and for strength. Four holidays are celebrated in her name: February 19, her birthday; September 19, her baptismal day; November 19, her ascension to heaven; and June 19, her death. It is believed that Kwan Yin can transform herself into any imaginable form. People call her the woman with a million eyes and hands. Usually her disguises are used to help those in distress.

The shrine situated on the right of Kwan Yin's is the shrine of the Seven Sisters. There are seven figures seated in the shrine, one of which, as legend discloses, returns to her mortal husband on the seventh day of the seventh month, and remains for seventeen days during which time she washes chopsticks and bowls for every day in the year. Girls especially who desire to be skilled in embroidery work come to worship her.

Other shrines in the same temple are the Wah Tow or Doctor's shrine,[2] famed for helpfulness to the sick and diseased, the Quan Dai or war god, worshipped for life and strength, and the shrine of the "king of gods, king and ruler of earth and heaven." Still another in the corner of the room is the shrine of Choy Sun, the god of fortune, worshipped particularly by merchants, housewives, and sons.

Each figure is brightly decorated, and small oil lamps are kept burning before them constantly. Soot-covered lanterns hang humbly down, and strands of crepe paper flowers waver in the heavy air. Worshinpers kneel on the badly worn mats and cushions before all the separate shrines, but it is evident that most prayers are made before the image of Kwan Yin.

"Chinese Temples in Honolulu", by Sau Chun Wong, Toshimi Yoshinaga, Katsumi Onishi, *Social Process in Hawaii*, Vol. 3, 1937. Reprinted by permission of Social Process in Hawaii.

The caretaker is a middle-aged, wizened-looking man and is usually clad in a pair of soiled woolen trousers, a grimy can, and Chinese shirt and slippers. Several assistants help with the preparation of images and the care of the shrines.

The temple is supported by donations from the Chinese pubic and by the sale of ceremonial papers, candles, and incense. The caretaker and his staff receive their wages from fees given by the worshippers. Other sources of income are few.

2. Another important temple is the **How Wong Temple** on Fort Street opposite the Y.M.B.A. The founder even as a child was considered to be a living god as she healed people with her miraculous power and the potions which she concocted. In all her life, a span of some eighty years, she had never partaken of any solid food. Her diet consisted only of fruit juices, citron water, small lemons, and carambulas. When she left China to come to Hawaii, she brought with her the How Wong god after whom the temple was named. Later, after the temple was built, she had the Bak Sak or White Mountain Temple in China send the other gods. All the money for the temple was earned by this priestess, and today the temple is one of the few that are self-supporting. The present caretaker is unmistakably proud of her mother who, she claims, prayed with such concentration that even the entrance of bandits did not break her trance. She is credited with predicting the Chinatown fire in 1900, even disclosing the number of days of the fire. This increased her popularity tremendously.

There are five different shrines in this temple. Several of them are similar to those of the Kwan Yin Temple. The center shrine is reserved for the How Wong, or the fisherman's god. Legend discloses that once, when a fisherman was fishing out at sea, a white rock kept coming up to him. Sensing some unseen power at work, the fisherman picked up the stone and said that he would take it ashore and erect a shrine for it if it would give him more power and more fish. The shrine, originally for fishermen, has gradually expanded in use, until today people of any profession or trade may petition the god for good fortune, protection, business success, and safety in travel to China. On either side of the god are seated his two assistants still and solemn in their dignity.

To the left of How Wong is hung a piece of white cloth with small black characters of the thirty-six gods, "Jung Sun". The worshippers must not forget this small shrine, as it represents all of the gods. He must be careful not to invoke the anger of any god through negligence.

Directly in front of the How Wong shrine is a high table with two large copper incense burners, a pair of kidney-shaped wooden blocks and a cylindrical box with "chi-chi" sticks, and oil burners which are kept burning constantly. The copper burners were presents from a rich Chinese merchant and philanthropist.

To the right of the fishermen shrine is the abode of the Zeus of the Chinese gods, "Yuk Wong Dai Dei," the king and ruler of heaven and earth, while to his right is the doctor's god with a round pill in his outstretched hand. The shrine to Kwan Dei, the war god, has smaller incense burners but no oil burners or "chi-chi" or blocks.

To the left of the fishermen's shrine is the maternity shrine, consisting of three figures. The central figure is of course the mother god with a baby in her arms; on her left is the father who presents the child, and on her right is the nurse who holds a pair of scales to weigh the baby. This shrine is naturally endowed for expectant mothers who pray for a good son, good luck, and happiness.

Each of the side walls has a shrine. "Hin Tan", the tiger keeper and trainer with tigers by his sides, has control of thunder and lightning.[3] On the other side wall is the life sized figure of "Choy Sun" the god of fortune. He is arrayed in his mourning clothes, as his mother had died, and is leaning on a frilled paper stick which he uses as a cane. He is bowed in grief, and the stick helps him to hold his head bowed, as holding his head up, which signifies happiness, is unfilial. In his left hand, he carries a fan which is supposed to fan away evil. A collection of fans reclines behind him. His ceremonial day is January 26 according to the lunar calendar.

The present caretaker of this How Wong Temple is Hawaiian born and has a fair education in Chinese and a little in English. Her knowledge in ceremonial procedures was received from her mother.

The temple is supported by donations from the public and through the sale of offerings of candle, punk and ceremonial papers. A worshipper pays twenty-five cents for a sheaf of ceremonial papers with two candles, a sheaf of incense, and punk, so the profit is very little. As she has to keep the oil lamps burning day and night she is glad when some one donates a bottle or two of oil.

This temple is popular with mothers who bring their month old babies to the temple to thank the gods for their safe delivery and to celebrate their birthdays which makes them one year old. The mother brings with her some form of meat, usually a succulent roast pig, wine, tea, incense, sweet bread, and rice. The caretaker helps her pray after the mother pays her a fee wrapped in red paper.

3. A very picturesque temple is the **How Wong Temple** on School Street, beyond Liliha Street. It is surrounded by small residential cottages and is itself a rented cottage made over for temple purposes. It is quite colorful with its bright red fence, cement incinerators and shrines. As one enters the gates, he notices a remodeled garage enclosing a large shrine immediately on his left. No idols can be seen, but two large rocks stand imposingly with red paper arrayed about them and incense and candles burning before them. These gods guard the premises of the temple.

The temple is a one-room affair with the gods facing the door and a pair of guardian gods near the door. In the center is the How wong or fishermen's shrine. Two additional shrines, for Wah Tow, or the god of doctors, and Choy Sun, or the god of fortune, are also worshipped at this temple.

The offerings of worshippers are placed on the table in front of the center shrine. These offerings include sweetmeats, to sweeten the god's palate, rice for food, wine and tea for drink, and ceremonial paper as money for the gods. Although ancient in atmosphere, the temple carries a few modern touches as electric lights, electric clock, telephone, doorbell, and a license for operation artistically framed. Even the young caretaker, clothed in American style, is modern and radical in some of his ideas, derived from a western education.

The caretaker states that he came from China to Hawaii, attended the St. Louis College until the seventh grade, then had to return to China. At that time he had no belief in any religion and used to disfigure the idols and the temples. Then suddenly, one day, the spirit entered his body. He could not study, eat, or sleep for seven days and nights. He acquired the power of healing the sick, and his conquests over disease and death were famous. Many came to him for healing. Even the insane and epileptic benefited from his power. He came back to Hawaii with no intention of continuing his healing practice, but his relatives and friends insisted, so he did whatever he could. He became a priest and took charge of the temple. He secured another job but was unable to keep it. Some misfortune always stalked him whenever he was away from the temple. He states that he remained in good health only when he was healing people.

This caretaker laments that because of ignorance, people in China and in the islands are superstitious over small matters. Take the subject of hair washing. Chinese people insist that there are only certain ordained days when they can wash their hair, so they look it up in the "tung see", a horoscope-like book. The caretaker shakes his head and laughs. "What difference does it make when you wash your hair. When it's dirty, you know it is, so wash it when necessary, not upon the advice of a book!" He says that as long as the "heart is good", there is no use in offering a huge roast pig to the gods, as the gods do not care. A little incense is as big a thought as roast pig. Only ignorant people do such unnecessary acts. He laughingly says, "If fate determines your life, why do so much unnecessary worship to curb its whims?"

4. **The Quan Dai** or **War God's Temple** is situated in a dark, musty room over a row of grocery stores on Vineyard Street near the river. An old man, about seventy years old, a retired vegetable vendor, is the present caretaker. He bought it from the former owner, and although he did not know much about the procedure, "the gods taught him". In a week's time he learned practically "the whole business." The Quan Dai shrine is black from the fumes of the candles and is shaded in the background by many high tables laden with copper kettles filled with sand and ashes. Quan Dai is worshipped for life and strength.

5. A slightly different temple is located on River Street, near the Japanese produce markets. In the center of the upstairs rooms is the shrine of Leong Ma, the goddess of safety, who was a beautiful woman, as one can see from the clear-cut features of the idol. She has bound feet and holds a mirror in her hand. She is surrounded by lesser goddesses, and many have mirrors in their hands which help to light their paths. This temple was built by the "Lum" clan and supported by it. Scattered about the walls of the room are pictures of famous Lums and photographs of Lum gatherings. The caretaker, a toothless gentleman clad in an undershirt and a pair of trousers, is also a Lum. He has a small room adjoining the big room and one can spy a tiny sink, dishes, and an iron bed within. This temple is not often frequented by worshippers but is chiefly used for clan meetings and gatherings.

6. Another temple is the **Sing Wong Temple** located on Kukui Street. The temple proper occupies one side and the proprietor's home the other, where ceremonial papers and offerings are sold and where the proprietor sits and gossips with frequent cronies. This temple was founded at Hanapepe, Kauai, by the present caretaker, who is educated in Chinese history and language. The temple houses "guardian gods" who keep watch over the temple, "Choy Sun" or god of fortune. The center shrine holds the "Eight Great Spirits" while on the right are the King of gods, and the "Fut Mu," the teacher of Kwan Yin. The caretaker is also a spiritual medium and a chanter at funerals, both these occupations being better sources of income than the temple. The temple is not supported by public donations but is supported through sale of ceremonial offerings.

Procedure of Worship.—The ceremonials in all of the temples tend to be chiefly of a magical character designed to coerce the gods and spirits to grant the expressed desires of the worshippers. Among the recurrent values sought are: sons, happiness for departed spirits, family happiness, long life, wealth and health, and security against accident and misfortune.

A worshipper usually brings with him on special holidays, and celebrations, a basket of food composed of some form of animal flesh, as pork, chicken, or fish, (or if he is rich, all of the above) wine, tea, and three bowls of cooked rice, and a vegetable dish, as tofu or "jai."[4] As he enters, he hits a panel and a drum several times to arouse the gods to listen to his supplication and also to chase away the evil spirits that are lurking near. The priest may assist if the worshipper desires. He endeavors to get all the information he can as to the desires of the worshipper. Then he chants in a sing-song manner, all the while kneeling in front of the shrine on the mat or cushion. (If information is sought as to the future of sons and daughters, their names and birthdays are written on a piece of paper.) He picks up the pair of kidney-shaped blocks and answers to questions are secured by the throw of the blocks. If both fall with the curved side up, it is a good sign; if one is flat and the other curved, it is also good, but if both fall on the flat side, the future is not propitious and one should take care. The priest may also secure answers to questions through the "chi-chi" sticks or the "chim".

This is the procedure followed by a young Chinese who has had an American education, has all the external marks of a westerner, and who is praying for some member of her family who is suffering from a headache. She buys incense from the caretaker, lights it and distributes it among the gods. The caretaker helps her light candles and takes up the tea leaves, after which both kneel down before the shrine and ask the gods for help. Then the caretaker takes up the "chim" and shakes them up and down until one drops out, chanting while he is doing this. He then looks up the predictions for the number in his case book. Gathering up the ceremonial papers he burns them and then dusts the incenseash into the tea leaves and wraps both in red paper. He rings the gong and beats the drum. The girl departs after paying and giving thanks with the thought that after drinking the tea the headache will disappear. If it does not, she will come again to pray.

Caretakers.—Every caretaker seems to think of his task as ordained by the gods. As one caretaker said, "I didn't like religion at first; I used to draw mustaches on the gods and mark the temples. But suddenly, I was "gong" (the spirit entered my soul) and I became a priest. The gods wanted me to be a priest, so I had to become one or I would he unlucky and have many accidents." This fatalistic viewpoint is rather common.

Pride of position prevents the caretakers from seeking other more remunerative tasks. As one caretaker says, "I tried to look for a job, but after securing one for a while, I would get sick and couldn't go back to work; so I have to stay in the temple." Another caretaker who has been a vegetable vendor says, "I couldn't make much money selling vegetables. Too much competition. When I heard of this chance to take care of the temple, I took it so that when I get old, I can still make a little money without too much effort."

The caretakers and priests, of course, must make a living, and that is one of the chief concerns of some. All lament that too many people come with their own ceremonial papers instead of buying them from the temples, and also do their own praying instead of paying the priest a fee to do it for them. But as the temple is supposedly public, the priests can do nothing.

Each caretaker assumes that his temple is the one truly ordained by the gods and that other temples and priests are fakes. There is not much cooperation among them and no guild to protect and raise their interests.

Worshippers.—The worshippers at the temples are chiefly first generation women who most strongly adhere to the traditional religious values and observe the ancient ceremonies, both at home and at the temples. They pin their faith on one or more experiences which have coincided with the priests' predictions.

Most worshippers visit the temples on holidays, as neglect would invite misfortune. Some more devout, however, visit on any good day of the lunar calendar. Some, thrifty, or miserly, bring their own offerings and chant their prayers instead of buying them from the temple or securing the priest's services; others do not visit the temples at all, as they say they can pray to the gods just as effectively at home. The gods, they add, are everywhere.

Some believe in going only to one temple as their faith has strength and security in that certain temple, not because of the sect, but because of the priest who might have a greater influence on the person than would the other priests, and who might have predicted some truth or facts which strengtened the person's faith.

Ceremonies.—Altogether there are thirteen definite times for worship. The first and fifteenth of every month are also considered as worship days. Other important days of worship and the items of food usually offered are listed below:

1. New Year's Day—vegetables.

2. Second day of New Year—meat and vegetables.

3. Twelfth day of New Year—pork, chicken, and fish.

4. Tsing Ming—anything.

5. Fifth day of fifth month—pork and sweets.

6. Fourteenth day of seventh month—anything.

7. Fifteenth day of eighth month—pork and moon cakes.

8. Winter of the eleventh month—pork and sweets.

9. Last day of old year—fish, chicken, and pork.

10–13. Birthdays and death days of fathers and ancestors.

Changing Functions.—Religious devotion to spirits and natural objects has controlled the life and activities of the Chinese people to a great extent. It was the center about which their life revolved as they believed that the spirits controlled and motivated their activities; in other words, no differentiation was made between fate and the will of the spirits. Ancestor worship was adhered to closely as an example for future generations to follow in respect to the departing generation. Ancestor worship considered the fami

Now, since the advent of Christianity, modern science, and public education, the older type of Chinese worship has ceased to control the life of a large part of the second and third generations of the Chinese community of Honolulu. The first generation go to the temples on feast days, a few consistently, while the younger generations seldom do. The same practices, however, tend to persist, with the exception that ancestor worship has been neglected in the temples but not in the homes. Once a year at about Easter time, "Tsing Ming" is held at the ancestral graves and this is a time when even babies are taken.

Notes

* This was originally a term paper submmited by Chew Young Wong, Florian Wong, Sally Sun, and Sau Chun Wong for an introductory course in Sociology.

1. The "chi-chi" cylinders contain one hundred "chim". Each of these "chim", which has a number written on it, refers the worshipper to one of the many printed answers given by the gods—for sickness, he refers to the set of prescriptions, for perplexing problems, he looks up the set which gives him the god's advice.

2. Wah Tow was a famous surgeon living during the time China was divided into three kingdoms under the Tartar king. One day the king received a scalp wound during battle. When Wah Tow recommended that the king be given a head operation, the cowardly king thinking that some treachery was afoot, commanded that the doctor be put to death. The gods took pity upon the unfortunate victim and made him a god.

3. Legend says that long ago there was neither thunder nor lightning. The world was peaceful, and food was plentiful, but people began to waste rice and food, and the gods were angry. So in the dead of the night, the gods came and tried to kill the wasteful people, but in the darkness they killed the wrong people. Feeling very abject, the gods thought of a plan. They appointed the special tiger keeper, gave him the duty of scattering thunder and lightning so that the people would know by the sound of thunder that the gods were angry, and through the lightning the gods might be able to see the people they were punishing.

4. "Jai" is a rich vegetable dish eaten during the New Year fast by some Chinese and it is also the food of monks and nuns who abstain from eating meat all their lives.

Japanese Buddhist Temples in Honolulu[1]

Toshimi Yoshinaga

When the Japanese immigrants came to Hawaii, they brought with them, along with other cultural institutions, several of the principal sects of Japanese Buddhism.[2] Six of these Buddhist sects, Shin, Nichiren, Shingon, Tendai, Jodo, and Zen, are represented by temples or organized groups in Honolulu. When all the sub-sects and branches are included in the enumeration, there are 19 Buddhist temples in Honolulu.

Honpa Hongwanji

All of the sects have been affected more or less by the American setting. Perhaps the most westernized temple in Honolulu is the Honpa Hongwanji,[3] located on upper Fort Street. Here the influence of the west is reflected in the architecture of the temple as well as in the religious rites.

Regular services of the Honpa Hongwanji are held every Sunday at the temple for different age groups, and here also the innovations from the west are apparent. The most obvious innovations are found in the four sections of pews which fill a large portion of the spacious hall, and in the western pipe organ choir, and pulpit located to the right of the highly ornate Buddhist altar. Beginning at 6:00 A.M. on Sundays, there is a sunrise service at the temple for adults. The children's ceremony for grade children begins at 8:40 A.M. for half an hour and serves as a brief gathering in the temple hall of all the Sunday School children prior to an instructional period which is conducted at the Fort Street Japanese Grammar School. The High School group's service which is conducted immediately after the children's service is mainly for young people between the ages of twelve and eighteen years. Student boarders at the high school dormitories are required to attend this service, which consists of several chants, responses, and hymns. The noisy conversations of the boys in the left section and the girls in the right section of the temple quickly subside as the organ begins to play and all bow their heads and press the palms of their hands together in silent meditation. The next hour is devoted to the young people's service. The addition of a sermon makes this service slightly different from the preceding high school service. Occasionally the sermon is delivered in English, but more often it is given in Japanese. Congregational singing, accompanied by the organ, gives these services a distinctly western atmosphere.

The older people, mainly those between the ages of forty and sixty, gather at 1:30 in the afternoon to worship. This service is conducted entirely in Japanese and retains more of the Oriental flavor. Most of the women are dressed in the traditional ceremonial kimonos and many have their ceremonial "haoris" or coats. The entire congregation averages about seventy-five elderly men and women. Many arrive at the temple before the hour to enjoy a bit of visiting.

The service is begun by the striking of the gong—at first slow and loud with the tempo gradually increased and the volume decreased. This is repeated several times. The congregation sits in silence until the sound from the gong has died away. Then the priests, seated before and to the side of the image of Buddha, begin to chant, followed by the people, some aided by books and some from memory, while still others remain silent. After twenty minutes of chanting, the priests lift to their faces the books from which they have been reading, and then replace them on the small desks in front of them. Then rising, they all leave. Later the head priest or a visiting priest reappears alone, and delivers his sermon from the pulpit.

In addition to the regular services, there are numerous other activities which the Honpa Hongwanji undertakes. One of its major projects is the maintenance of the largest Japanese language school in the territory.[4] Two young people's organizations, the Young Men's Buddhist Association with a membership of 485, and the Young Women's Buddhist Association, are sponsored by the temple. Three dormitories, one for the boys, one

---

"Japanese Buddhist Temples in Hawaii", by Sau Chun Wong, Toshimi Yoshinaga, Katsumi Onishi, *Social Process in Hawaii*, Vol. 3, 1937. Reprinted by permission of Social Process in Hawaii.

for the girls and women, and a third for young men are supervised by the Hongwanji. A priest of the Honpa Hongwanji visits Oahu prison every Sunday morning and conducts a service there. The women of the Y.W.B.A. make regular visits to Leahi Home, a sanitorium for tubercular patients, in order to cheer up the Japanese patients there. Besides these visits, every Monday evening a religious service for the patients is conducted.

The Higashi Hongwanji

This sect is strikingly similar in its activities. The main temple, located on North King Street, is a two story wooden structure—the lower floor consisting of a receiving room and quarters for the priests; the entire second floor comprising a worship hall. As one enters, there is a little room designated as "office" on the left end of a very small porch. On both extremities of this porch are stairways leading to the worship hall. At the head of both of these stairs are small **Saisen Bako** (offering box) attached to the wall.

Three sections of twelve long benches with backs are found in the main worship hall. An elaborate altar is found on a raised platform in the front. In addition to a large altar house in the center, there are four smaller ones, two on each side of the center altar. The altar is beautifully decorated with fresh flowers contributed by members of the congregation. Within the center altarhouse is a standing image of "Amida." Another much larger **saisen bako** is located on the right center of the platform. Just below this raised platform is a speaker's stand where the sermon is delivered.

This temple is maintained mainly through generous donations from its members and by the profits from benefit shows and movies. Donations are received at the office and the name of each donor, his or her address, and the amount donated are written on a long strip of white paper. This paper is then taken upstairs and hung on cords along the walls of the hall during festivals.

This temple sponsors such organizations as the **Fujin Kai** for the older women, Y.W.B.A. for local-born girls and women, and weekly Sunday schools for little children, in addition to regular Sunday afternoon services.

Kempon Hokke-Shu

Although western ideas are noted in the Hongwanji practices, there is a branch of Japanese Buddhism which, because of its brief contact with the West, is still decidedly eastern in customs and traditions. This temple is the Kempon Hokke-shu, one of the most interesting of the sects represented here. Kempon Hokke-shu belongs to the Nichiren sect,[5] the only Japanese Buddhist sect that bears the name of its founder. Though there are in all nine branches, only two of them are found in Honolulu. They are Kempon Hokke-shu and the Nichiren Mission. Nichiren means "Sun Lotus" and this name was selected in association with the sayings, "nothing is more brilliant and fairer than the sun and the moon," and "nothing is purer than the lotus." The sacred call of this sect is **"Namu Myoho-Renge-Kyo"**, meaning "Adoration to the Lotus of Perfect Truth".[6]

The Hokke-shu temple, located in Nuuanu Valley on Laimi Road, was established in Hawaii very recently (1931), but it has become very popular, with a large following, especially on Oahu. Its congregation of 300 is made up chiefly of Honolulu residents but it also draws from the rural districts such as Wahiawa, Waipahu, and Aiea.

Every worshipper, as he enters the chapel, removes his shoes, or clogs, or slippers and goes to a sink in a concealed corner of the narrow veranda to purify himself. Then, sitting on his knees at the entrance of the main worship hall, each person throws a coin or two into a saisen bako and, with finger tips of both hands touching the floor, bows toward the elaborate gold-plated altar. Each takes his rosary and puts it around the second finger of each hand, presses his palms together, followed by a "vow to carry on the work of this sect." Then lifting his head, he murmurs the sacred call **"Namu-Myoho-Renge-Kyo"** thrice, bowing after each call. Finally he removes his rosary and claps his hands together five times and ends the ceremonial with another bow. This is a ritual peculiar only to this temple and is practiced nowhere else in Honolulu.

Now every one is free to seek his place in the hall—men usually the left side and the women the right. There are no pews in the temple but **zabuton** or floor cushions are placed at intervals on the mat-covered floor for the use of worshippers.

As the time for the service approaches, the seven members, of the temple staff—a Chief Priest, two nuns, a girl, and three boys who are in training, all with heads closely shaved (**bozu**), and dressed in ceremonial robes, enter the chapel and proceed to their places at the front in a straight line before the congregation. The chief priest strikes a bell and every member in the congregation, even the youngest children, join in a chant.

After the chant, the priest sits down on a slightly raised seat, while his assistants sit on either side of him—three boys on his left and three nuns on his right. All face the altar. The service consist almost wholly of chants at various tempos. Sometimes the chant is slow and solemn and at other times it picks up speed and volume to a grand crescendo of chanting and the rapid beating of the gong, drums, and a bell. This continues for about 45 minutes, then the priest and his assistants leave.

For several minutes now the people have time to exchange a few words of greeting with their friends. During this period of intermission, some of the members busy themselves by getting the hall ready for a sermon. They pull a blackboard into the center of the room and also bring in a table. The priest returns and everyone sits attentively for a long sermon averaging about an hour and a half in length. After this seemingly interminable sermon, **O-set-tai** or refreshments, including hot tea with candies, **manju,** and other Japanese delicacies are often served.

Every day of the week is a "holy day" at this temple, although the service described above occurs typically on Sunday night, but from Monday to Saturday, there are three services daily—at 5 A.M., 9 A.M., and 7 P.M. On Sunday there is a slight change with a 9 A.M. Sunday school service for boys and girls and a single general service at 7 P.M. for the whole congregation, which incidently is open to all visitors. Week day services are open only to members and to others who have formally expressed their desires to join the membership. At these ceremonies, the congregation is usually very small and each person sits on the bare floor near the altar—no mat, no cushion. It is at these services that ceremonies for curing the sick and afflicted are performed.

The people who go to this temple believe staunchly that the priest and the nuns have the power to cure them of their illnesses by praying. There are many miraculous incidents to which the members point as being adequate proofs that faith healing in this temple has been successful. One cannot understand how strongly these people believe in faith healing until he has attended one of the temple's annual sunrise services[7] which are held on the 28th of April at Hanauma Bay. At four in the morning, members from all over the city, as well as from the rural districts gather at the temple and from there drive out to the service on the mountain. The people climb up the rocky mountain sides, and hold the service on some level spot. A small mat is spread on the ground and two large lighted candles are placed on both sides of a bowl of burning incense. This represents the altar in the temple. With this altar in the foreground, all the people stand close together facing the sun and commence to chant. For more than a half hour everyone continues chanting and drumming until the sun has risen. People who have had attacks of paralysis, the blind, the infirm, and the aged, all are present for this service. Those who are unable to climb the mountain due to illness or weakness are carried up on the backs of young men.

According to one of its members the chief aim of the Hokke-shu temple is to offer fellowship and to help and cure those who are weak and sick. All these things, they claim, can be accomplished by vigorous prayer and faith.

The Nichiren Mission

Although it belongs to the same sect as Kempon Hokke-shu, [it] is quite different in its practices. Services are held less frequently, and the congregation is relatively small. The Nichiren-shu of Honolulu is situated on School Street just off Nuuanu Avenue, and, although introduced in Hawaii in 1900, was not established at this spot until 1914. It claims a membership of 300 households in Honolulu and rural Oahu. Services are held on the first and third Sunday afternoons and on the evenings of the 12th and 23rd of each month. The priest also conducts ceremonies every night of the week from Monday to Friday.

An attractive yard surrounds the temple which is built in Japanese style with a verandah extending around the three sides. A few chairs are arranged on the veranda for guests, but most of the members use only the **zabuton.** Within the temple are the altar to Buddha, low lacquered tables for incense, large drums, gongs, containers of holy water, boxes for the Sacred Sutras, and a considerable floor space for worshippers. The Sunday services are largely devoted to chanting, accompanied by the drum, and to sermons by the priest. A language school is maintained by this temple, as well as several semi-religious and social organizations.

The Jodo Sect

This sect, the second largest group of Buddhists in Hawaii,[8] has a new and spacious temple on Makiki Street. As in the Shin shu temples noticeable accommodations to western values have been made. To the left of the temple is a tennis court which is extensively used by the members. The first floor is reserved for social purposes, and the second floor, which houses the figure of Buddha, has chairs for its worshippers, and a pulpit for the priest.

This temple is quite active in the community. Its first girls' school, giving courses in sewing and Japanese morals, was opened in 1910. Two dormitories for school children in Honolulu and a Sunday school for children are maintained by this sect. Regular radio broadcasts are likewise conducted.

Shingon

Among the other sects of Buddhism represented in Honolulu, the Shingon, or True Word sect, is one of the most influential. The doctrine of this sect was introduced into Japan by Kobo Daishi in A.D. 806 and includes a great deal of mystical ritualism, lapsing often into magic. The first Shingon-shu was established in Honolulu in 1914 and at present the main temple is located on Sheridan Street, below King. Another official temple is located in Liliha and there are many small private O-Daishi scattered throughout Honolulu, which are not officially recognized. The main temple claims a membership of 1,000.

Regular services are held three evenings of every month, on the first, tenth, and twenty-first. The bishop, in a brilliant orange robe and his four assistants in black robes chant some of the Buddhist Sutras accompanied at times by the congregation and the music of bells and wood blocks. Certain ceremonies conducted by the bishop, as well as a sermon, are included in these services. The distribution of holy water to the worshippers also occurs afterwards.

Sunday school for children and clubs for young women and men are also provided through the Shingon-shu. But its most spectacular service is in the curing of illness, for which Shingon-shu is noted among its followers. One of the reputed cures involves a student who met with an accident which left her unconscious for several days. The family assembled at the Temple where a special service, called the reading or chanting of **Sengan Shingyo,** was performed for the daughter. This consists chiefly in the repetition of a brief prayer a thousand times. According to the story, when the choir finished the last chant, there was a telephone call from the hospital saying that the patient had just regained consciousness.[9]

The Tendai Sect

With its one temple located on Young Street near Alapai since 1915, this sect is historically older than any of the other Buddhist sects represented in Honolulu. Noted for its eclectic tendencies, this movement in Japan has given birth to the Nichiren, Amida, and Zen sects of Buddhism, and it is not surprising that the small group of Honolulu worshippers at the Tendai temple should also be affiliated with other sects. The chief object of worship in the Honolulu temple is Fudo, god of wisdom, although other deities are also worshipped. The worship is entirely in Japanese and the temple indicates little of western influence. Much emphasis is placed upon healing services.

The Soto Mission

Representing the Zen sect of Buddhism, the Soto Mission was established in Honolulu in 1903 and is located at the corner of School and Nuuanu streets. The temple is an impressive structure of conventional Japanese temple architecture. An elaborate altar is designed to assist in the "silent meditation and abstract contemplation"[10] by which the worshippers seek to penetrate into reality. Chairs are provided for the worshippers and a small organ also is used.

The Soto branch of Zen places considerable emphasis upon "book learning as a subsidiary aid to silent meditation on the truth,"[11] and it supports a Sunday school for children and a vocational school for girls where sewing and embroidery are taught.

Notes

1. Because of limitation of space, this article covers only some of the external features of Buddhist temples in Honolulu. The original study from which this article is extracted, dealt with (1) the history of the sect; (2) a description of the temple; (3) the type of congregation; (4) a description of a service; and (5) the activities of the temple.

2. See Brinkley, Cap't Frank: A History of the Japanese People, New York, 1915, pp. 369–372 for short commentaries on the nature and significance of the different sects in the Buddhist thought system.

3. Since its introduction to Honolulu in 1897, this temple has grown steadily both in prestige and membership, until today it has the largest membership (1000) in the Territory of Hawaii.

   Honpa Hongwanji is a subdivision of the strong Shin sect founded by Shinran Shonin in 1224 A.D. Of its ten sub-sects in Japan, the Hongwanji branches, Nishi Honpa and Higashi, are the only ones represented in Hawaii. As preaching centres of Shinran Shonin's teachings, the Honpa Hongwanji has a central temple and seven small district branches located throughout the city. The Higashi Hongwanji has two sub-branches in addition to its central temple.

4. The Hongwanji mission maintains three separate language schools in Honolulu, one known as the Fuoto Gakuen or the Fort Grammar School, another as the Palama Gakuen, and the third as the Hawaii Chujokakko or the Hawaii Boys' and Girls' Middle School. The grade schools, covering the first six years of elementary education in reading and writing are preparatory schools for the high school which offers a diversified cultural education of four years. A graduate of the high school may complete two more years in the Kotoka or the College Preparatory School. A Kotoka graduate may enter the Shihanka or Teachers College for an extra-year, practicing in the grade schools.

   Faculty members, with the aid of a few teaching cadets in the grade schools, teach the students of their respective schools on Sundays.

5. This sect was founded by Nichiren in 1253. The doctrine is based on "the sutra Myoho-renge-kyo, which contains the last instruction of Buddha . . . preached in Japan for the first time by Nichiren. It is the doctrine of the three great secrets; adoration (honzon), law (daimoku) and moral (kaidan), which resume all the discourses of Shaka: It is however so profound that only the Buddha and the highest Bosatsu can comprehend it. The followers of Nichiren have always been the most turbulent and fanatic Buddhists in Japan. Little by little the sect split into nine branches which at present have 5,194 temples, about 3,700 bonzes, chiefs of tera and 1,283,600 adherents." E. Papinot, Historical and Geographical Dictionary of Japan, pp. 43p–40.

6. Sansom translates it as "Homage to the Scripture of the Lotus of the Good Law" (See Sansom: Japan, A Short Cultural History, New York, 1936, p. 326). Members of the Nichiren Sect worship the above revered scripture, the utterance of which they believe brings salvation. The principal book upon which the teachings of the sect is based is the Saddharma-Pundarika-sutra, In Japanese, the Hokkekyo.

7. The origin of this service is explained as follows: "Early on the morning of the 28th of the 4th month in the 5th year of Kencho-he (meaning Nichiren) stood on the summit of Kivesumi and gazing intently at the sun which had just begun to rise in all its resplendent majesty above the horizon that united the heaven and the mighty Pacific in the far away distance, sonorously uttered for the first time, the title "'Namu Myoho-Kenge Kyo'" G. Umata, Footsteps of Japanese Buddhism, Part 1, "Life and Teaching of Saint Nichiren'", p. 6.

8. Tajima, Japanese Buddhism in Hawaii, p. 24.

9. This student attends a Christian church and her parents are devout members of the Zen sect, yet every month they all attend Shingon-shu.

10. A. K. Reischauer, Studies in Japanese Buddhism, p. 116.

11. Ibid.

The Second Generation Japanese and the Hongwanji

KATSUMI ONISHI

The first missionary priest of the **Honpa Hongwanji,** the largest sect of Buddhism in Japan, arrived in Hawaii in 1897. In spite of early difficulties, this (Shin-shu) sect has grown into the most powerful of the Buddhist sects in the Islands. It numbers among its adherents some 15,000 members, 10,000 Sunday school children and about 3,500 Young Buddhist Association members. Thirty-six temples, some twenty-one language schools, and thirty-nine Y.B.A. organizations scattered throughout the Islands are evidence of the influence of the Hongwanji among the Japanese population of Hawaii. Of the 28,000 odd adherents, more than half are second generation Japanese with American citizenship.

The success achieved by this movement in Hawaii in due in part to the mere persistence of old country values and in part to the sympathetic attitude of the leaders toward Americanization. The first bishop of this sect in Hawaii expressed his attitude as follows:

> *I take here the liberty of announcing in no ambiguous terms that our mission as a whole advocates Americanizing the people of this territory in every possible way. I, more than anybody else, am aware of my incompetency in carrying on this work. Born a Japanese, brought up as a Japanese, I am a Japanese through and through. Whatever honest intention and pure motive I may have, this sense of incompetency has always kept me from pushing to the front as an active participant in this work of Americanization. . . . Our mission in the islands is, in a sense, a cradle of future Americans.*[1]

A similar attitude has been maintained by the leaders of this sect throughout its history in Hawaii.

Youth and Buddhism

The child in the average Buddhist family in Hawaii comes under the influence of the parental religion at an early age. He sees his parents go into the garden to pick the daily **"o-hana"** (flowers) for the **butsudan** (Buddha's shrine). He watches his mother reverently offer fresh rice to the shrine and soon learns that no rice is to be eaten unless some of it is first offered on the altar. With the flowers and rice before the shrine and two small candles lighted on either side of the **butsudan,** the mornning worship begins. He may join in the service, imitating his parents as they offer the prayer of thanksgiving (**Namu Amida Butsu**), burn incense, and bow in deep reverence before the altar. He gazes interestedly at the flickering candles, delights in the melodious "ching-ching" of the tiny gong and plays aimlessly with the beads on the rosary. When father lets him light the candles and burn the incense, he is delighted. He asks his father to let him blow out the candles after the worship. Everything is mysterious, an endless wonder to the young child. He does not understand exactly what it is all about, but he sits with the family, watches the candles, hears and repeats the prayer. The service which is held before breakfast is repeated in the evening just before bed time.

Long before the child enters either the public or the language school, he starts attending Sunday school with his elder brother or sister or a neighboring friend. The temple beautifully decorated with flowers, candles and much gold lacquer work, impresses him far more than his own family shrine. He listens to the organ, to

"The Second Generation Japanese & the Hongwanji", by Sau Chun Wong, Toshimi Yoshinaga, Katsumi Onishi, *Social Process in Hawaii*, Vol. 3, 1937. Reprinted by permission of Social Process in Hawaii.

the **gathas** (hymns) and learns to sing them in his own childish way. He listens to the tales of Buddha, of Shinran the founder of his sect, to exciting adventure stories, fables and myths. He meets new faces, makes new friends, learns to revere and respect the Buddha. He anxiously looks forward to the **o-sagari-mono,** usually candy distributed to the pupils after it has been offered on the temple altar. Sunday is a day of joy, of fun, and of new and exciting experiences for him.

When the boy approaches junior high school age, Sunday school often loses its charm, and as he gets older, he drifts away more and more. The stories are not interesting enough, or other attractions, usually athletics, demand his time and attention. He may also consider the family worship as something childish and neglect to join in the services. Approximately two thirds of the boys lose touch with the temple when they drop out of Sunday school at adolescence. Only the most conscientious remain with the temple.

On the other hand, the Sunday school has a firmer hold on the average adolescent girl. She continues to attend regularly, often even after she has finished school and may join a girls' club, sponsored by the Sunday school. The more capable of the girls are chosen to help the priest conduct his classes. Later, with increasing duties at home, the girls likewise tend to drop out of Sunday school.

A substantial number of the more interested young people continue their affiliations with the Hongwanji by joining the Y. B. A., an organization similar to the YMCA and the YWCA. They attend the meetings occasionally and participate in the different activities of the organization to their best advantage. At marriage, they may transfer affiliations to the **kyodan,** the active supporting congregation, or may continue as members of the Y. B. A. An eldest son who is fulfilling the obligations of his deceased father, is more likely to cast in his lot with the **kyodan.** Should his father be still living, he remains with the Y. B. A. as long as he sees fit. Only a few are members of both organizations at the same time.

With the gradual decline in the number of first generation Japanese through death and departure to Japan, the active support and the control of the Hongwanji temples with their Y. B. A.'s, language and Sunday schools are passing into the hands of the second generation. The first generation declare that they wish to turn over the temple affairs to the younger set, but they continue to exercise their authority and power. Of the second generation that are elected to the board of directors, only a few take an active interest in the management of affairs. The majority confine their chief activities to the Y. B. A. and postpone joining the older and more conservative **kyodan.** In one community where the first generation have actually retired in favor of the second generation, fears of the elders that the younger set was incapable of continuing the support of the temples have proven groundless. The process is very slow, as those in power are reluctant to relinquish their hold upon the organizations, but the trend is inevitable.

Buddhist Festivals

Among the numerous Buddhist festivals and ceremonies, none has more appeal and glamour than the **Bon** festival, celebrated in Hawaii during the months of July and August, depending upon the use of the solar or the lunar calendar. The approach of this festival, which honors the ancestors and the dead, is eagerly anticipated by all sects and by both young and old. It is a time of gaiety, of dancing, fine clothes, feasts and general merrymaking. With New Year's Day, it is one of the two important days in the year for the Japanese when the scattered members of the family circle reunite to celebrate the occasion.

At **Bon,** the altar of the **butsudan** is decorated more carefully than ordinarily. Instead of the usual offering of rice, special candy, oranges or mochi are substituted. The daily **o-hana** from the back garden is missing and in its place may be a beautiful bouquet from the florist's. A **cho-chin** or lantern, hung before the shine, continues to be lighted a week prior to and for the duration of the **Bon** season.

The most attractive feature of the festival to the second generation is the dance, known as **Bon-odori.** Usually held in the temple yards, these **Bon-odori** attract hundreds of followers who travel long distances to attend them. Even in the strictest of families, the bars of discipline are let down and the children are allowed to participate in the merrymaking. **Bon** without the **Bon-odori** is like Christmas without the Christmas tree.

The most noticeable feature of these **odori** is the almost complete absence of the first generation, especially among the ranks of the dancers. Most of them are content to be merely spectators. The more active and capable ones may help beat the drums or chant in the shed built for the musicians and the drummers. All do their share by contributing towards the dance fund from which must be paid the drummers and the singers. With the retirement of the first generation from active participation in the **Bon-odori,** their places are being rapidly filled by the second generation who today sponsor the majority of these dances through special committees of the Y. B. A. The element of play, the youthful urge for activity, and the fascination of the rhythmic dance can largely explain the eagerness with which the younger group relieve the older generation of the responsibility. It may be noted that in the majority of the cases, the latter are helping behind the scenes in the planning and the preparation of the dance.

Besides the **Bon** festival, **Hanamatsuri,** or the Flower Festival celebrating the birth of Buddha is observed by all Buddhists. Curiously enough, **Hanamatsuri** in Hawaii has never attained the significance of the **Bon** festival. It was not until some ten or twelve years ago when Buddha's birthday was first celebrated as a joint affair under the auspices of all the Buddhists irrespective of sect, that the second generation Japanese became actively conscious of **Hanamatsuri.**

Like **Hanamatsuri, Bodhi Day,** the day of Buddha's enlightenment, was scarcely known among the second generation a few years ago. After the day was called to the attention of the delegates at a Pan-Pacific Y. B. A. conference some eight years ago, the practice of observing **Bodhi Day** has become increasingly popular among the second generation Buddhists who observe it more religiously than their parents who are disposed to neglect Buddha for St. Shinran the founder of the sect. This special emphasis on **Bodhi Day** and **Hanamatsuri** has sharply focused the attention of the second generation on original Buddhism which is more logical and appealing to the American educated Buddhist than the teaching of faith in **Amida-Buddha** by St. Shinran. As the young Buddhist studies original Buddhism, the task of reconciling the teachings of Buddha and the creed of St. Shinran becomes increasingly difficult. It is a problem now facing the Hongwanji priests.

Young Buddhist Associations

Of the many young people's organizations existing among the second generation Japanese in Hawaii, the Y. B. A. is one of the strongest and the most influential. The thirty-nine units scattered throughout the Islands play an important role in the Japanese community. Organized along the lines of the YMCA, they perform a variety of duties and activities in connection with the missions with which they are affiliated. Among the activities engaged in by a typical Y. B. A. unit may be mentioned the following: religious—lectures and classes in Buddhism; educational—night classes in English and Japanese; dramatics and oratorical contests, arts and crafts, etiquette; social—welfare work as cleaning cemeteries, picnics, socials and dances, participation in the Territorial Y. B. A. conventions; athletic—sponsoring and participating in American and Japanese sports.

The Y. B. A. hall affords a convenient place for lectures, educational movies, discussions and parties for the use of the community. Through this organization, the second generation have helped break down some of the traditional customs and prejudices of the older generation. The introduction of social dancing into the Y. B. A. and some slight modifications in the marriage customs, as having a Buddhist instead of a Shinto priest unite a couple, may be mentioned as a possible influence of the Y. B. A. on the first generation. As an active socializing agent in the athletic, educational, religious, and social fields, the Y. B. A. occupies a conspicuous position in the lives of the second generation Buddhists.

Religious Accommodations

Realizing the difference in the background and the education of the rising generation and the inadequacy among them, of the methods that proved so successful in spreading Shinran's teachings among the first generation, the Hongwanji has tried to adapt itself to meet the needs of the young Japanese Americans. The adjustment to the new Hawaiian environment was not begun early enough to cope effectively with the situation today, but a definite beginning has been made to meet changing conditions. In order to spread the gospel of Buddha more effectively among the Hawaiian-born, publications explaining the fundamental tenets of Buddhism have been issued in English. An English division was established and services in English have been developed to replace the Japanese rituals. This change is particularly welcomed by the rising generation as the services become more meaningful and understandable. Five second generation priests trained in Japan under a special scholarship created by the Hongwanji are now engaged in mission work among the young men and women. Three more studying in Japan will soon return to assist those in active service now.

One of the outstanding features of Japanese Buddhism in contrast with most western religions is the absence of a hymnology. To cope with this deficiency, the Hongwanji has undertaken the task of composing hymns in Japanese and English suitable for the different occasions like **Bon** and **Hanamatsuri.** The result is a repertoire of Buddhist music sufficient to meet the immediate needs of the day. Those actively engaged in the development of new **gathas** and music are pioneering in a field quite foreign to Buddhism.

According to Japanese custom and tradition, wedding rites are properly the function of the Shinto priest, and funerals are properly officiated by the Buddhist minister. In the new environment of Hawaii, Buddhism, especially the Hongwanji sect, has invaded the field of Shintoism and has taken part of its function in the marriage ceremonies. The number of weddings among the second generation that are officiated by a Buddhist priest is increasing year by year. A common practice to-day, it was considered a novelty only a decade ago. This invasion into a field, formerly forbidden by age-long customs, is clearly the influence of the second generation Japanese who, educated in American ideals and practices, wish to have their wedding solemnized in the temples of their faith. Buddhism, flexible and adaptable to new situations, has struck a new note of optimism and happiness in Hawaii and promises to undergo still further changes to meet the conditions and demands of the rising generation.

Language Schools

No discussion of the second generation Japanese in Hawaii is complete without a note on the language schools. The twenty-one language schools[2], a vital factor in the support and maintenance of the Hongwanji temples, are attended by some 8,500 young Japanese Americans. Besides the regular instruction in the Japanese language, these schools lay great emphasis on ethics, especially filial piety and respect to elders. The low proportion of personal disorganization among the second generation Japanese in Hawaii has often been credited to the close attention given to the moral and character training of the students by these schools. It is generally conceded among the first generation Japanese that the solidarity of the Japanese family in Hawaii has been maintained in part through the instruction in ethics and language in these schools. The ability to read, speak, and write the language of his parents has been a vital factor in the economic life of many a second generation Japanese. Through his knowledge, he has been able to secure a more lucrative position, a higher social status among his associates and a greater self-respect. Despite the dwindling numbers of first generation Japanese, a poor command of the Japanese language is still an obstacle in getting a good position. The language schools are attempting to meet this situation. The practice among the second generation of going to Japan to continue or round out their education can often be traced to the influence of the language school, although other factors such as parental influence and economic advantage are also involved. Despite the growing reluctance of the local born to attend the language schools, their careers will continue to be influenced by these schools for some time to come.

That the Hongwanji plays a vital and important role in the lives of the second generation Buddhist is evident. In the home, at school, at work, in his social, educational and religious life, through marriage and through death, the Honwanji helps to direct and shape his future. He in turn is breathing new life and vigor into the Hongwanji, freeing it from the shackles of narrow sectarianism, creating and evolving a new Buddhism, peculiar and native to Hawaii.

Notes

1. Y. Imamura: "A Short History of the Hongwanji Buddhist Mission in Hawaii", p. 7.

2. The language schools maintained by the Hongwanji constitute only a portion of the total. In 1936, 178 Japanese language schools with a total enrollment of 41,173 pupils and teaching staff of 705 were reported to the Department of Public Instruction.

Religion in Our Family

MASAKO TANAKA*

Religion has for several generations played an important role in our family. My grandfather and grandmother (my father's parents) had always been devout Buddhists who spent much of their time praying and attending services in temples and in other people's homes. Religious faith had a great influence upon Father from his early youth, and also upon Mother after she got married and came to live with them. And now we in turn are under the strong influence of our parents.

Although my parents do not make a lot of fuss about dances, dates, and acquiring a higher education, like many other Japanese parents, they are very particular when it comes to religious customs and traditions which are ignored in many homes.

Every morning before breakfast, each member of the family is expected to pray before the altar. We must also thank God for the food before and after each meal.

In the morning, each person usually prays individually, since we all rise at different times and are not ready for breakfast at the same time. However, in the evening the whole family gathers before the altar to pray before going to bed. No one is allowed to go to bed before praying, so usually when a member of the family wishes to go to bed early, he lights the candles, burns some incense and taps the little gong that is on the altar. No matter who rings the gong, whether it be Father or the baby of the family, all members of the family will quickly assemble in the room, where our nearly a century old altar is placed.

Then Father sits at the head of the group before the altar and leads the family in prayers. The prayers are difficult and we children do not understand anything we are saying. However, we have been saying them since we were very young, even before we started for school. Everyone in our family knows them so well that we can say them without even thinking.

Every morning Mother places newly cooked rice and fresh flowers on the altar. Also whenever we have anything good to eat, like fruits and candies, or when we make anything special, like mochi or cakes, something is always placed on the shrine. We have been taught since we were very young never to eat anything that is given to the family or that is specially made without first offering some to God. Although pastries, fruits and candies are offered, meat, fish, eggs and other flesh of living things are not offered. It is against our religion to do so.

The offering of food to God isn't such a bad idea after all, for in the evening after the prayers are over, it is taken down from the altar and divided among the members of the family. Therefore the younger children always light the candles and assemble the family early, so that they can enjoy the nice things.

On Sundays, with other children of the neighborhood, my brothers and sisters and I all walk to the Community Sunday school which is located about a mile away. Every child feels it is his duty to go to Sunday school, so fortunately, my parents do not have to coax us, as parents of other families do.

In a recent disaster, I was able to observe the important role of religion in the family. On April 1, 1946, my fourteen-year-old brother Fred was lost in the tidal wave with twenty-five other students and teachers of X school. When the disaster occurred, everyone in the community was upset and there was much disorganization in the community. This was the first time that I could clearly see the difference between one family which had great faith in God and others which had very little faith.

At the time of the disaster, families which were less religious and had very little faith in God cried and cried, blamed their loss upon the waves, the principal of the school, seismologists, and anybody else whom

---

*This is a pseudonym used, at the request of the writer, in order to prevent embarrassment to persons involved.

"Religion in Our Family", by Masako Tanaka, Margaret Miki, Dorothy Yashima, *Social Process in Hawaii*, Vol. 12, 1948. Reprinted by permission of Social Process in Hawaii.

they could possibly accuse. They damned God for making them lose their sons and daughters while other people's children were spared. Of course my parents felt the loss just as keenly and greatly as anyone else. I'm quite sure Fred was just as dear to them as the other children were to their parents, and that the thought must have occurred to them, "Why did our son have to go when the neighbors' children returned safely?" However, they did not blame others for our misfortune, nor did they curse against God for taking away a member of our family. Instead they prayed very hard and tried to make themselves and the rest of the family understand that God wanted it that way, that Brother Fred had only been loaned to us, and that that was the day set for his return to God's land. They shed many, many tears but they were not hysterical like many other parents. It was not because they did not love their child as much as other parents, but because they had such great faith in God. They felt that Fred was safe and that we need not worry for God would take care of the rest. My parents were much more self-possessed than many other parents who had lost their children.

When I first found out that Fred was missing, I was very much afraid to notify my parents for fear that my mother might lose her mind or something dreadful might happen to her from the great shock. But much to my surprise I found that my mother and father acted much more sensibly than many other parents whom I had seen. For the first time I was very grateful that my parents and family had great faith in God, which guided them and gave them great comfort during those dark and grievous moments when we were most in need of help.

Like most true Buddhists, we held an elaborate service for Fred. Since we could not find his body, we only had his picture at his service. We went through all the proper rituals regarding the dead. Our family and close relatives attended the temple the following day and on the seventh day we had another service at our home. On the forty-ninth day, we gave two packages of coffee to all the families who had extended their sympathy during our bereavement. We also had a service at our home that night. When one year passed by, another service was held for Fred. After these services, we always served food, but no meat, fish, or eggs were used. Also, an even number of different kinds of foods were prepared. We held all of the required services, hoping to help the spirit of the dead one to follow the right road to heaven.

Like a majority of the Buddhists, our family has always adhered very closely to the customs of Bon.[1] Every Bon festival, we decorate our family plot with lanterns, flowers, and food. We also pour some water on the tombstone, meant to soothe the thirst of the dead. Then we light the candles, burn some incense, and all pray together. After our family plot has been taken care of, we place candles, incense, and flowers on our friends' graves, and especially on the graves of those that have no one to decorate them. We also place incense and flowers on a huge tombstone which has an opening at the bottom in which are placed the bones that have been accidently dug up. Then we usually attend a service or the gala Bon dance, if any is held. I usually went to a Bon dance not with the intention of dancing, but to try to get as many towels as I could to have Mother make an attractive blouse for me. Of course that was not the right spirit to go with to a Bon dance.

Another significant thing about Bon, before the war, was that we always gave lanterns to the family who had lost members of their family in the preceding war.

Our family has always participated in the monthly services conducted at one house after another. Each family takes a turn holding the service at their house and all the people go to their home to hear the priest. After the service, food is served and people indulge in gossip and discuss community problems. Food at this type of service includes meat and fish. Also each month, the families take turns in collecting money to pay for the priest.

Most of the community's young children attend these services to enjoy the food. That is how a typical monthly service is held in our community.

As I compare the customs in our home when my grandparents were living with the family customs of our home today, I can clearly see the changes that are gradually taking place. But I do not mean that because we are adhering less and less to the traditions and customs our religious faith is weakening.

One of the first changes which I notice is that our daily prayers are much shorter than they used to be when Grandpa led the family. He always used to chant prayers that took at least one hour and a half to complete. So, we often got bored and would sneak away and go to bed. Of course, Grandpa used to be furious with us. Nowadays, our prayers are only about five minutes long. Only on special occasions are longer prayers chanted.

The practice of offering cooked rice twice a day is reduced to once a day now.

Another change which I notice concerns the fasting on the death days of anyone of our family or a close kin. On those days our grandparents fasted and refrained from meat and fish for the three meals of the day, for forty-nine days. They were very particular about the tradition. However, when Fred died, Dad excused the family from fasting after the seventh day. He felt that with all the worries, shock, and disappointment we would ruin our health. He believes that we should eat everything to bring back our health to normal.

As one of the traditions, our family always fasts on the first, twelfth, and seventeenth of the month in honor of Fred, Grandpa, and Grandma respectively. We used to fast three meals a day but now we refrain from fish and meat only one meal a day. These are some of the changes that have taken place in our traditions and will continue to change from generation to generation.

I believe that religion has a great deal to do with maintaining happiness in the family. As yet, although our family is large, we have very few serious problems concerning the members of the family. Religion seems to help keep the children out of trouble.

Judging from our family, although ours is far from a perfect family, I believe that if more families would worship God and had more faith in Him, there would be fewer conflicts, delinquences, crimes, and broken homes, today. Religion to some people has helped a great deal in times of disaster and sorrow, and to many others it has given hope. It helps make this world a happier and a more comfortable place to live in.

Notes

1. The memorial celebration during the seventh month when the spirits of the dead are said to return to earth.

Mother and Her Temple

MARGARET MIKI

Mother is a devout Buddhist. It has never occurred to her to doubt the existence of a Supreme Being. That to others this Being is personified in the figure of Christ or Mohammed or any other "one" seems to be of no concern to her. Buddha personifies God for her and that is all that matters.

To one whose faith is centered in the temple, it was a blow to have all communications halted with the coming of the war. December 7th, 1941 not only curtailed many privileges for aliens but it closed the doors of the temple to Mother and many others like her. It was not only a black-out during the evenings but a total black-out of Mother's spiritual life.

For days I remember Mother was too engrossed in other immediate activities to be openly concerned with the question of her temple and the priests residing there. But as the passing of the days brought back a bit of equilibrium, one day I heard her calling her friend. As though she already sensed the deep disapproval of society of anything Japanese, she carried on her conversation in a low pitch. I was openly eavesdropping. Part of it went as follows:

> *Kinoshita san, what do you think happened to* our *temple? Do you think that they (the priests) were all taken into internment camps? I wonder if Mrs. M is still there. I want to go so very much but I'm afraid.*

The answer from the other end seemed to be one of discouragement for Mother heaved a great sigh and there were signs of tears in her eyes. This brought to me the realization that the prospect of years without the right to pray aloud in the language she understood was to Mother one of the most personal losses from the war. It did not matter to her or to the older generation whether or not they understood all of the prayers they uttered. What mattered was the strong feeling of belonging together that they experienced on Sundays. Mother's we-group was torn apart and she felt lost. Perhaps if the Buddhist temples had remained open during the war years, the older generation could have found some form of relief from their feelings of insecurity.

Week days were not very bad since other activities crowded the day and there was no time to waste in brooding. But on Sundays, when others dressed to attend their church services, the lost look on Mother's face was pitiful. The behavior pattern of twenty-one years so suddenly destroyed could not be replaced by another in such a short while. Often I would see her take out her Japanese prayer book and thumb her way through it, her lips moving to denote that she was praying.

Before the war, funerals of friends had been times when Mother and her friends gathered to express their sympathy together in the form of Buddhist prayers and rituals. Now it was no longer possible to do so. After attending several funeral services for friends, I heard her say to this same friend of hers:

> *Don't you think it's a pity to die now? One can't even be buried decently.*

The friend replied:

> *It just doesn't seem final without the smell of the incense, the temple gong, and the chanting of the prayers at funerals. These haole services are so incomplete and cold. There almost seems to be no respect for the dead. What is this world coming to?*

"Mother & Her Temple", by Masako Tanaka, Margaret Miki, Dorothy Yashima, *Social Process in Hawaii*, Vol. 12, 1948. Reprinted by permission of Social Process in Hawaii.

Mother and her friend obviously missed the elaborate rituals that accompanied Buddhist funerals. To her a person was not really dead and properly buried until there were services of *O-tsu-ya* and the chanting of prayers by black or red robed priests. That perhaps sorrow might be eased and emotions controlled by the calm services of the Christian religion did not seem to occur to them. She ended this phase of her conversation by saying:

> *I don't want to die until the temples are reopened and the priests return from the internment camps. Then I'll be assured of a* decent *funeral.*

With the decrease of the community's suspicion towards the aliens, it was gradually possible for a few of the women to at least help in the upkeep of the physical appearance of the temple. This occasion came once a month. Knowing the resistence we youngsters showed to anything associated with Japan, Mother did not try to share her experience with us. Somehow we, her children, had become an out-group so far as the temple question was concerned. Nothing was said but the barrier was there.

The jubilation of V-J Day was not complete for Mother until the news came that the priests were returning once more and that the temples would be reopened. This was the real end of the war for her.

It has taken months to reconvert the dismantled temple, but the speed with which the older generation organized themselves was amazing. As I saw the effectiveness of the united labor of the members of the temple I could understand the feeling of suspicion, bordering on hostility, that many non-Orientals felt towards the Japanese. I could also understand why politicians still harp on the question of bloc-voting. Granting that in this instance the energy of this group was being used in constructive avenues and for religious goals, nevertheless, the intense we-group feeling the older members nurtured was a thing that gave me food for thought.

With the reopening of the temple, however, I have seen Mother regain many of her values and her purpose of living. What was during the war quite a bleak existence with a strong under-current of insecurity is now once more a more meaningful existence. The days of a week, no matter how burdensome, seem to become a thing of the past when she goes to the temple.

Sometime ago on the way home from school, I was seated in the front of the bus. Next to me was an elderly woman of about fifty-five years. She, evidently, was one of these women who are hired by the day by Caucasians to do the laundering or house cleaning. About two bus stops after she had gotten on the bus, another Japanese woman boarded the bus. I gathered she was a friend of the first woman. After the usual exchange of courtesies in such a loud tone of voice that I felt uncomfortable, I heard the first woman say to the second:

> *My only pleasure now is to go to the temple on Sunday morning and to the movie after that. All my troubles seem to "fall off my shoulders" on Sunday. The temple, the movies, and perhaps some day a grandson are the only interests in my life.*

This woman, my mother, and many others like them have once more been able to pick up the threads of a stable life.

One Sunday afternoon I went to the temple to satisfy my curiosity as to what really happens there to give the aliens this feeling of stability. Contrary to the feeling of restfulness that one receives upon entering some churches, the atmosphere was one of festivity. The worshippers chanted their prayers loudly, Mother not the least among them. I knew that ninety per cent of them did not know the meaning of the prayers they were repeating so enthusiastically after the priest. I doubt if they ever stopped to wonder about the meaning. The thought that prayer is really a way in which one communes with a Supreme Being and tries to face the realities of life, to adjust oneself to the Supreme Being, and to understand oneself, appears to be entirely foreign to them. To chant prayers (difficult words that are just words to them) with their hands together was and is sufficient for them. This they all sum up as being *a-ri-ga-tai*. (In a sense this denotes appreciation or thankfulness.)

After the services were over all the old women clattered downstairs chatting loudly in Japanese. It was the first time in four years that I had heard genuine chuckling that came without any restraint from the throats of the older women. They nudged each other at times, exchanged the latest gossip, and actually let out sounds that we would classify as giggling. These women were actually youthful on Sunday afternoons.

To me it meant more than that. It meant that there in the temple Mother and the older generation are once more able to rebuild their self-respect. The war, among other things, took away much of the authority that they held in the home. Much of what they did and said was brushed aside by the younger generation, namely their own children, as being "Japanesey" or "Bobura-ish". They have had to restrain themselves in the matter of self-expression due to the silent reprimands from the society at large and the general forbidding atmosphere symbolized by the slogan, "Speak American".

At the temple they are in a sense, "free". They may converse, laugh, and think together in Japanese. There are no impatient answers or frowns, but rather congeniality. There, they are not the "old lady" and "old man" of some young citizen but personalities whose ideas are respected. There, they count as human beings.

I am not advocating the indefinite retention of the Buddhist temples. Left alone, and ignored by the younger generation, they gradually will be reduced to a mere skeleton. But at present they do have a vital function in the lives of our older generation. One may add an emotional appeal by saying, "The old folks have worked so hard. Why deny them the satisfaction that their temple worship gives them?" If the temples can continue to rehabilitate many others like Mother, can somehow make them feel comfortable in this new atomic age, then Buddhism has accomplished its greatest good in Hawaii.

I have seen the war cause Mother and her friends to lose their footing in the family and in society. I have sensed their feeling of inadequacy and insecurity. For these reasons I do feel that we can accept the temples and their rituals.

Mother is a devout Buddhist. She accepts the existence of a Supreme Being and is contented with her conception of It in the form of Buddha. Her faith centered in the temple gives her happiness and after all that is the thing that counts, for is not happiness in life the ultimate goal of every human being?

My Family

DOROTHY YASHIMA

My family consists of seven persons: Father, Mother, two boys and three girls. Father is 58, Mother is 55, and the children's ages are: Big Sister, 30; Big Brother 25; Second Sister, 24; myself, 20; and Little Brother, 14. No one has married, and all live at home.

Father is head of the house, and his opinions are respected by all. He runs a little grocery store owned by Big Sister. Mother is a housewife, and her functions are feeding, caring for, clothing, and worrying about the family. She is physically weak, and all the members of the family protect her, and try to ease her burden. Big Sister manages the store and dominates the family's business affairs. Big brother works at Hickam Field as a carpenter and contributes his pay check to the family. He is the quiet member of the household, but is an important figure in family affairs because he is the eldest son. Second Sister works at the store. Little Brother and I attend school. We help at home or at the store.

Father and Mother together discipline the family and the older children have a hand in the discipline of the youngsters. If Little Brother and I are scolded by Big Sister, we "talk back" and try to justify our actions, but if Mother scolds us, we seldom do, and if Father is the one doing the scolding, we don't dare "talk back".

Both my parents are Japan-born, and had only a Japanese elementary school education. They respect our opinions for there is much that they can learn through us, just as they can teach us. The three older ones out of school have all graduated from high school. Second Sister has graduated from business school, Big Brother went to vocational school before serving in the Army, and Big Sister has had correspondence courses and taught at an island Japanese school for two years. When Father has difficulty in reading the newspaper, he asks one of us, "What is this word? What does it mean?" Mother neither reads nor writes much English, but since the war we have taught her the alphabet and to write her name in English, and to recognize words like LILIHA, KALIHI and KAIMUKI, so that in going from place to place she wouldn't be too greatly inconvenienced.

Father and Mother consult each other a great deal. For example when Little Brother asks permission to go to a show:

Little Brother: Mama—I can go to movies? (Mother is always asked first).
Mother: See what Oto-san *says.*
Little Brother: Oto-san, *I want to go show.*
Father: You just went last time. Too often is no good. Did you ask Mama? What she say?
Little Brother: She said ask you.
Father: If she says all right you may go. But not next week again if you go today.
Little Brother: Mama, Oto-san *said ask you and if you say all right, I can go.*
Mother: All right, but come home early.

Evening mealtime is the only time during the day when the whole family sits at the table together. During the day, Father and the girls eat at home in shifts, the youngsters are in school, and Big Brother at work. The family saves its choicest bits of gossip, anecdotes, and the day's experience to relate to the members at this time. These dinner sessions have helped greatly in maintaining the feeling of group solidarity in our family.

"My Family", by Masako Tanaka, Margaret Miki, Dorothy Yashima, *Social Process in Hawaii*, Vol. 12, 1948. Reprinted by permission of Social Process in Hawaii.

Religion plays an important part in our lives. In those days when we attended language school at Fort Gakuen and at Hongwanji, regular attendance at the Buddhist Sunday School there came naturally to us. When the Buddhist churches were closed as a result of the war, our religious education stopped. During the war years we three sisters visited a Methodist church now and then but somehow we felt we didn't "belong". The director of Christian Education of this church encouraged us to join their groups and sent us cordial letters. We still kept back. Then the letters changed in tone and expressed regret and sorrow in the director's failure to "convert" us. We kept away completely after that. During this irregular "Christian interlude" in our lives, my parents never lifted a finger against our seeming to "change" religions, and we felt that we were free to choose as we wished.

About this time also, Little Brother changed from a public school to a private one. At St. Louis College, he got, and is still getting heavy doses of Catholicism. He wants to become a Catholic, which is the only religion he is familiar with, and to him no other religion exists. In his immature mind, he believes that we are all atheists and will go to purgatory. He is unhappy because we tell him to wait until he is older and knows his own mind before joining the Catholic church. "If I die, I cannot be saved," he says.

Buddhism has been our family religion for many generations. My Issei parents are deeply religious and teach us what they learned from their parents. Through religious stories we have got our lessons in honesty, patience, peace, respecting our elders, and of an awareness of our everlasting obligations (o-n) to them.

Every morning when Father gets up he lights a candle or incense at the family shrine. Then he taps the little bronze bowl that has a clear, ting! ting! sound, and prays to the ancestors. When Mother wakes up she also pays homage. This ritual is gone through every morning, but we children are not forced to do so.

Certain religious days call for special rituals. In our small family shrine, we have three small wooden sticks with the names of my three dead sisters. This morning is the day on which the younger of the three died. Mother said, "Today you must light some *sen ko* (incense) for Yae-san and pray for her." I obediently did as she said. I stood in front of the *hotoke sama* and put the palms of my hands together. I lighted two sticks of incense and said, "*na mu ami da butsu*", three times to myself. I don't understand the meaning of the words, but I know that everybody says them. Today we will eat no meat or fish but only tofu, vegetables, and rice.

Sometime, on a death day the whole family goes to the temple where the bones of two of the girls are kept in small sealed boxes. These boxes are all in a large room where hundreds of such boxes are put. I have the impression that the priests guard them with their lives. The priest on duty brings out the box of the one we have come to pray for, and chants long prayers and hits the gong. At the front of the temple there is a large wooden bowl with burning embers and next to it a small box with fragrant incense which feels and looks like ground tobacco. While the priest is still chanting, Father walks to the front, stops a few feet before the bowl, prays with his palms together, and then steps up to the bowl. He prays again, pinches a bit of the ground incense between his thumb and forefinger, brings it up to his forehead, and drops it in the bowl from which thin smoke is slowly rising. Then he prays again and returns to his seat. After him Mother goes up and then the others one by one do the same.

We observe another ritual every New Year's Day. When the old year draws to a close, it is the busiest time of the year. The whole house must be cleaned. On New Year's Eve, we all wait for 12:00 o'clock, when *so-ba* (black noodles) is served. *So-ba*, unlike noodles and saimin, breaks easily into short bits. This signifies that all the last year's bad luck is broken up and gotten rid of. In the morning a special breakfast of *zo-ni*, a soup made of *mochi* (rice dumpling), abalone or fish, and vegetables, is served. On this day everything has a special touch to it. Mother formally addresses each one individually: "*Oto-san, o me de to go zai masu, Nii-chan, o me de to*," and so on *around* the table. And then she makes a little speech to this effect: "We have again greeted a new year. May we all have good health and happiness. You children will be obedient to *Oto-san* and *Oka-san*. Let us hope that we have a good year." She serves Father a tiny cup of Japanese sake (rice liquor) and the cup is passed around to every one of us. I remember that Mother used to dab a little sake on our forehead when we were young.

Marriage is another institution strongly bound by tradition. When Big Brother marries, his wife must come to live with us. This is an understanding that goes without saying. If Big Sister marries, she would go away to live because Big Brother is home to carry on the family name and to look after Mother and Father. Mother hears much gossip about young brides being mean to their mothers-in-law, and feels distressed about such behavior. "In Japan," she say, "there are many stories about mean mothers-in-law, but here the situation is usually just the reverse."

Religion and Resistance in America's Concentration Camps*

GARY Y. OKIHIRO

Religion, imbedded in the psyche, folklore, and identity of immigrants, gave meaning and order to the individual, the family, and community, and helped them survive.[1] Religion has also been both a mobilizer for, and an expression of, resistance to colonialism, slavery, and exploitation.[2] While many authors have written on the resistance function of religion in African, Afro-American, and Native American societies, relatively few have explored that theme among other American ethnic minorities, especially among Asian Americans. That neglect is particularly notable because of the central role of religious belief in the Asian cultural heritage.[3]

This essay examines the role of ethnic religion in resistance among the Japanese confined primarily at Tule Lake concentration camp during World War II. The resurgence of ethnic religious belief is seen as part of a wider network of cultural resistance after the Manzanar model of resistance.[4] Cultural resistance was directed against the camp administrators' efforts to "Americanize" the Japanese, and was effective in preserving Japanese American families from total disintegration and in maintaining ethnic identity and solidarity.

There are two basic historical interpretations of Japanese reaction to life in America's concentration camps. The orthodox view characterizes the Japanese as defenseless, dependent, and abiding victims of circumstance. This image was fostered by the paternalistic War Relocation Authority (WRA) which administered the camps.[5] "The outstanding feature of the evacuation process was the complete absence of disturbance from the evacuees. Accepting without public protest the military orders, the evacuees appeared when called and got themselves on the trains without any compulsion by the public authorities."[6] Consequently, resistance by the "submissive" Japanese was depicted as sporadic and uncharacteristic.[7] The orthodox interpretation dismissed the various mass resistance movements in the camps as mere "incidents," and proposed that resistance was fomented by a small minority of pro-Japan agitators and constituted a necessary release of tension. After the outburst, "normalization" was restored resulting in a peaceful, "happy" camp.

In contrast, revisionist historians regard the concentration camps as the culmination of nearly a century of anti-Asian agitation and racial discrimination in America, the essential thrust of which was exclusionism and cultural hegemony. Resistance for the pre-war Japanese, according to that interpretation, was a means of survival to maintain their physical presence and culture in the face of white supremacy. That historical struggle continued in the camps when the Japanese, stripped of their civil liberties and the bulk of their property, resisted manipulation of their lives and the administration's attempt to erase their ethnic identity. Two models of resistance were proposed by a revisionist historian.[8] The Poston model of resistance is protest which results in acceptable responses from the administration. Japanese resisters, in the Poston model, realize their goals and achieve greater camp stability. The Manzanar model, on the other hand, is protest which results in unacceptable responses from the administration. Resistance, in the Manzanar model, did not end with administrative intransigence but continued either in open defiance of the WRA or in "the redirection of resistance into new forms which would be para-administration."[9]

Cultural resistance is seen not as unique to the camp experience but as an intensification and revival of past modes of resistance from the pre-war Japanese experience in America, as Frank Miyamoto put the issue, "to most evacuees but especially to the Issei who frequently reminisced about their experience in America, the evacuation was only the most recent and most outrageous expression of the long history of anti-Japanese agitation on the Pacific Coast." Continuing, Miyamoto noted that, "The historical reaction of the immigrant Japanese to instances of anti-Japanese action has been one of very strong resentment against

*The author gratefully acknowledges the research and editorial assistance rendered by Debra May Ushijima.

the attitudes of white supremacy, and one motivation behind their economic struggles in America has been the aim of showing the white majority group that they are a group to contend with as equals and not to be treated slightingly."[10] It appears, thus, that anti-Japanese activity frequently resulted in an upsurge of Japanese American ethnicity.

That phenomenon during World War II paralleled the rise of Buddhism within the Japanese American community during the 1920s and 30s in reaction to the anti-Japanese movement of those decades. Kashima, in his *Buddhism in America,* made that observation, citing a study of the Gardena, California Buddhist church.

> *After the passage of the Immigration Law of 1924 discriminating against the Japanese, the number of Buddhists increased rapidly, and so did that of the Buddhist churches. Before that event, some of them had been hesitant in declaring themselves Buddhists, considering such an act impudent in a Christian country. But the immigration law made them more defiant and bold in asserting what they believed to be their rights; it made them realize the necessity of cooperation for the sake of their own security and welfare, and naturally sought the centers of their communal activity in their Buddhist churches.*[11]

The WRA program for the camps ostensibly included three principal goals. The first was to provide for the physical upkeep of the internees; the second was a longer range objective to relocate the Japanese out of the camps into "normal" communities; and the third was to deal with hostile anti-Japanese elements, especially in the national press.[12] All three objectives emphasized the importance of the WRA "Americanization" program—to demonstrate the loyalty of the Japanese in acquiescing to camp confinement, to enable assimilation into American life, and to refute the accusations of Japanese disloyalty by a hostile press. The WRA saw the camps as a critical trial period for the Japanese in America. "The entire future of the Japanese in America is dependent on their deeds during the emergency," noted the WRA deputy director. "If the Japanese assist in the war effort and prove by constructive deeds, that they are loyal Americans, the public will recognize this fact."[13] Thus, to the camp administrators, the "Americanization" of the Japanese was an essential element in their program.[14]

However, the concentration camps and the WRA's "Americanization" program were progressions in the anti-Asian movement and attacked the basis of Japanese American ethnicity. "Americanization," noted Berkson, meant Anglo-conformity, and sought to disperse the minority communities and alter their ethnic identities and culture including the family, language, and religious belief.[15] Within that context, then, the maintenance of ethnic culture constituted a form of resistance. "When cultures are whole and vigorous," wrote Blauner, "conquest, penetration, and certain modes of control are more readily resisted."[16] Despite the WRA's "Americanization" program, the Japanese retained ethnic beliefs and values, many rooted in religion, and sought to preserve the ethnic community in the face of cultural hegemony. A camp analyst observed that "the assembly of fairly large numbers of Japanese tended to revive some of the practices which had fallen somewhat into disuse. The emotional upheaval which was the inevitable consequence of the disruption of familiar ways of life manifested itself, for many Issei at least, in a return to religion."[17]

For the majority of Japanese in the camps, that efflorescence of formal religion meant Buddhism along with "informal" Shintoism.[18] "The camp administrators could not suppress the religious needs of the Japanese people by encouraging the growth of Christianity and not of Buddhism," observed Horinouchi. "The masses of the Japanese people still identified with Buddhism in name, if not in practice."[19] A WRA survey in 1942 revealed that 61,719 or 55.5 percent listed themselves as Buddhist, while Protestants numbered 32,131 or 28.9 percent.[20] The designation *Buddhist* was politically significant because Buddhism was viewed as pro-Japanese and subversive and Christianity as American.[21] In the days immediately following Pearl Harbor, Shinto and Buddhist priests, along with Japanese language school teachers, were summarily arrested and interned in detention camps administered by the Justice Department. Christians, both white and Japanese, denounced these religions as "pagan," and many Japanese, fearful of being suspect, destroyed all traces of Shintoism and Buddhism such as the *kamidana* and *butsudan* (Shinto and Buddhist family shrines), scrolls, Japanese flags, and pictures of the emperor and royal family.

While the label *Buddhist* made one vulnerable, *Christian* seemed to offer a measure of security. "Many Nisei Buddhists," wrote Kashima, "apparently were afraid to attend the religious institution of their parents: thousands listed 'no preference' in their religion, and many even became Christians."[22] Remarked a Japanese internee, "Buddhists and Shintoists went to the Christian churches because they felt that there would be more protection for them."[23] Those nominal Christians were ridiculed as "Christians of convenience" by both

Buddhists and Christians alike.[24] Still, despite the pressure to conform, the large majority of confined Japanese openly espoused Buddhism, and in some camps, Buddhism gained new adherents. Kitagawa, a Christian minister at Tule Lake concentration camp, reported a "profoundly significant" revival of interest in Buddhism even among those previously disinterested,[25] while Gordon Brown, a community analyst at Gila River concentration camp, reported:

> It is said that the Christians lost in numbers during life in the center. At the time of registration, a well-known Japanese-American minister spoke publicly supporting volunteering for the Army. He incurred the wrath of many and was labelled a "dog." This opprobrium was extended to all Christians and some extremists even today say that "all Christians are dogs." Many half-hearted Christians ceased to identify themselves as such and would not permit their children to attend Christian Sunday school. They were afraid of the consequences of being considered dogs.[26]

It would be simplistic, however, to characterize Buddhism as "pro-Japanese" and resistant to assimilation and Christianity as "pro-American" and indicative of Anglo-conformity. While nativistic and "traditional" revivals might clearly be seen as assertions of ethnicity, adaptations and acculturated beliefs could also comprise aspects of an ethnic identity. For example, Buddhism underwent situational changes in America,[27] and a few Japanese Christian ministers advocated the ethnic church in the face of integrationist sentiment among the parent white churches. Further, those ministers linked their support for Japanese Christian churches with the wider struggle for ethnic community survival. "The ministry in the relocation centers," wrote Suzuki,

> . . . was pregnant with the seed of the theology of pluralism. The emergence of that theology was being pressed down. The articulation and implementation of this concept was still in the future, but there was a feeling for it. The Japanese people had a self-consciousness as an ethnic people. They were trying to demand self-definition but their voices were not heard. They were trying to assert their dignity and humanity in the intrinsic worth of their own traditions and cultural inheritance . . . but they were being pressed down at every turn. The ministry tried to affirm their pride as a people of God, and show fidelity to their peculiar peoplehood as a part of God's intention in a pluralistic community.[28]

Spencer suggests that this resurgence of religious practice was attributable to the increased amount of leisure time in the camps.[29] In contrast, Horinouchi proposed that a more basic consideration was the psychological stress of the camp situation. "Students of religion," noted Horinouchi, "recognize that religious activity increases in relationship to the stresses of the uncontrollable, the threatening, and the unknown. The Buddhistic rituals of repeating and chanting the *sutras*, the offering of incense, and other ritualistic movements are part of the anxiety release or a reaction formation to the uncertainties of the future. Thus, the increased religious behavior in detention camps may be primarily a psychological behavior response to a unique situation and less attributable to the increased leisure time of the internees.[30] Perhaps even more fundamental, Japanese religious belief permeated the culture which in turn gave meaning to the lives of the internees and which stood in opposition to external hegemony and control. This is not to deny the cathartic function of ritual and belief; it simply proposes that in addition to that role, ethnic religious belief comprised a means to resist "Americanization" and anti-Japanese racism, and formed the basis for a wider network of cultural resistance in the camps. Wrote Brown of Buddhists confined at Gila River:

> When asked what particular contribution Buddhism has for America the usual answer is "democracy." The Lord Buddha believed all men to be . . . spiritual equals. He attempted to break down the caste system of India. . . . Buddhism disregards race.
>
> This pat answer . . . is clearly a response to the particular situation in which Japanese Buddhism finds itself. Many priests are still excluded from California, some are interned. They belong to an "oppressed group." Buddhism is "against discrimination." Hence, both to aid themselves and to meet a hostile world, they must concentrate upon that particular interpretation of their religious teachings. . . .[31]

Buddhist church membership was simply one indication of ethnic religious belief. Religion in Japanese culture cannot be defined narrowly, but must be broadly defined as a people's beliefs and practices concerning their place in the universe and moral code of conduct. "The difference between the American view of religion and the Japanese view," wrote Hirano, "is that the Japanese did not compartmentalize religion. Religion was a part of and inseparable from life."[32] Thus, although it could be said that most Issei did not concern themselves with formal religion, religious belief, nonetheless, permeated their culture and daily activities. Japanese religious belief was syncretistic, containing elements of Shintoism, Buddhism, Confucianism, and Taoism. The nature of this religious belief was compared by Prince Shotoku to the root, stem and branches, and flowers and fruits of a tree:

> *Shinto is the root embedded in the soil of the people's character and national traditions; Confucianism is seen in the stem and branches of legal institutions, ethical codes, and educational systems; Buddhism made the flowers of religious sentiment bloom and gave the fruits of spiritual life. These three systems were molded and combined by the circumstances of the times and by the genius of the people into a composite whole of the nation's spiritual and moral life.*[33]

There are two fundamental features of Japanese religious belief. The first is filial piety and ancestor worship, and the second is the closeness of man, gods, and nature. Filial piety, as expressed in Confucian status ethics, was the cornerstone of Meiji Japan, and while the family unit may have arisen out of economic or political necessity, filial piety has its origins in religion.[34] This hierarchical system of moral and social conduct was codified in the New Civil Law of 1891 which stressed that (a) the family is the basis of society; (b) the family centers around the father; and (c) Japanese hereditary succession is to be strictly maintained (ancestral spirits dwell in the family house and the head of the household is the living embodiment of those spirits).[35] In that way, ancestor worship was simply an extension of filial piety, and both constituted religious belief and ethical morality. The spiritual basis of ancestor worship was enunciated by Bishop D. Ochi, a Buddhist leader at Gila River concentration camp, in his unpublished manuscript, *The Spiritual Life of the Japanese Evacuees.*

> *By devoting himself to the ancestral cult, a person may appear to be idolatrous. Yet the fact cannot be overlooked that by doing so he is adoring the Buddha in his heart. Buddhist philosophy holds that the Buddha essence melts into the spirit of one's ancestors. . . . On this basis, ancestral worship and the Buddha constitute an inseparable unit. Through sutras and services the ancestor is one with the Buddha. To the Buddhist in America the Buddha and the ancestors exist together as a meaningful part of the life of the individual.*[36]

The other basic feature of Japanese religious belief is the closeness of man, gods, and nature. Neither Shintoism nor Buddhism claimed a monotheistic or transcendent god. In fact, Shintoism stressed a love for the land where the ancestors repose and where gods (*kami*) abound, while Buddhism, especially Zen, emphasized enlightenment and harmony with the cosmos. That view of the natural world and of a person's place within the universe formed the basis for various Japanese cultural expressions such as *bonsai, ikebana* (flower arrangement), landscape gardening, the tea ceremony, and *haiku* poetry.[37]

The WRA's "Americanization" policy threatened one of the most basic Japanese cultural institutions, the family. Filial piety—the respect for elders and the role of the father as head of the household and embodiment of the ancestral spirits—was disregarded by the WRA in its "Americanization" of camp government. The WRA maintained that "since the objective of the WRA was to create a community as nearly American in its outlook and organization as possible, policy should conform with American practice, and only citizens should vote and hold office."[38] Further, the WRA gave the Nisei special privileges and recognition because of their American citizenship. "In addition to making elective offices open only to evacuees who are citizens of the United States," stated the WRA national director, "it is our intention to give them preference in considering application for leave from relocation centers, in assignment of work opportunities, and in other respects. . . ."[39]

Although most studies point to this WRA policy as having caused or at least accelerated the generational breach between Issei and Nisei,[40] there is suggestive evidence which points to Japanese success in resisting such a split. This struggle for the control of the children was poignantly described in a WRA report. "But during their stay at the centers they continued their previous practices of religious worship, tried to achieve some semblance of order and dignity in their broken lives, and frequently showed an almost pathetic eagerness to hold their families together and to work back toward their prewar social and economic status."[41]

Revisionist historians have pointed to countervailing forces which worked against the "Americanization" of the Nisei. Hansen and Hacker, for example, enlarge upon the lead provided by Yatsushiro's thesis which maintains that pre-war Japanese culture contained several basic values and beliefs which governed behavior and promoted ethnic solidarity.[42] These, according to Hansen and Hacker, were "strengthened by the pre-evacuation discriminatory practices, reinforced by the evacuation crisis, and expressed within the concentration camp culture."[43] Filial piety, ancestor worship, and family and ethnic collectivity were cultural values which were emphasized in the home and stressed in the Buddhist churches and Japanese language schools.[44] Those internal values were reinforced by external forces such as anti-Japanese agitation, barriers to Nisei assimilation and restrictive employment opportunities, and the concentration camps themselves which were pointed reminders to the Nisei that they were not considered to be "true Americans."[45]

The dislocation caused by the evacuation and the conditions of camp life reinforced the need for group solidarity and mutual aid. There is evidence to suggest that the traditional family roles were strengthened with the Issei father as the hierarchical head. The Issei, from the beginning, resented the WRA "Americanization," which threatened the group's traditional family structure. Nisei, who were previously drifting away from Japanese culture, were drawn back to the family unit. Discrimination and the denial of their rights disillusioned many Nisei. They now looked more to their families and ethnic community for security and acceptance. Evidence of this was seen in the reasoning of Nisei who answered "No-No" to the loyalty questions, 27 and 28. Two brothers were closely questioned on why they had renounced their American citizenship:

Board Member:	"You want to be American citizens?"
Subject #1:	"Well, there's our parents."
Board Member:	"You are over 20 years old."
Subject #1:	"But the parents come first no matter how old you are."[46]
	(Emphasis added.)

As time progressed, the block, a camp residential unit consisting of fourteen barracks, emerged as a primary unit of ethnic solidarity. Although many families within the block were from different geographical areas prior to evacuation, living in close quarters resulted in a degree of cohesiveness through group endeavors in improving conditions around their blocks and in self-governance. Solidarity was evident, for example, in boasts of talented chefs or well landscaped grounds within a block. The Issei, respected for their knowledge which comes with age, became the central core of block leadership. That was in direct conflict with the WRA mandate on internal camp government which had disenfranchised the Issei but in harmony with traditional Japanese culture. The success of resistance against that aspect of WRA rule has been documented elsewhere.[47] The block eventually became equated with the extended family in the common camp expression, "My block is like my family."

The block took on the characteristics of the family in stressing conformity of the individual to the collective will. Thus, block residents disciplined children who lacked parental control and brought discredit to the collective. The slogan, "Keep Children Within the Block," was widely circulated. The Young People's Association, a block organization, was initiated and supervised by the Issei as a means of promoting morals and obligations through social activities. With group conformity a policy, members within the block were required to subject their individual wishes to the will of the majority. Rumors and gossip were oftentimes used as tools to maintain conformity and solidarity.[48] Rebels were ostracized from the group and branded *inu*.

The block community merged into a camp-wide group identity by referring to such phrases as the *Japanese spirit* and *We're all Japanese*. On the few special cultic occasions such as New Year's Day and *Obon*, Japanese of all ages observed and participated in the rituals. Traditional speeches extolled the people's Japanese ties. Such occasions were "a means whereby members renewed their solemn allegiance to the group, reaffirmed the established themes in their center culture, and thereby nourished the solidarity of the group."[49] Phrases which exemplified that Japanese spirit were not essentially nationalistic or anti-American. Instead, the phrases sought to remind the internees of the virtues of their cultural ancestry and to enable them to resist the forces of "Americanization" which threatened their existence as a people. The following is a typical exhortation for ethnic solidarity: "It is not possible to be an informer as we are all Japanese. We should have loyalty to our own group. A Japanese cannot kick another Japanese. . . ."[50] The excerpt below exemplifies the use of ethnic cultural values to promote ethnic solidarity, and at the same time illustrates its neutral nationalistic content. *Yamato damashii* or "Japanese spirit" was a patriotic rallying cry for Japanese militarists and an expression of anti-Americanism for the WRA camp authorities; within this context, however, it was employed to depict customary virtues of perserverance, loyalty, forbearance, and sacrifice for the common good. The speaker was a Nisei at Minidoka and the occasion a farewell banquet for the volunteers of the all-Nisei combat team.

We have been kicked around and kicked around. We have lost most of what we had. We have been stuck here in these centers. And we don't feel too good about it. But we know our future will depend on what these boy volunteers will do. They have had the courage to risk their lives in spite of this. We know that they will go in there and fight and we know that they will never do anything to dishonor the spirit of Yamato damashi.[51]

Camp life had achieved a degree of security in the retention of such virtues as filial piety and ancestor worship, in the family unit, and in the ethnic community. In a speech delivered in San Francisco, Dillon Myer, WRA national director, categorically stated: "The bulk of Nisei or second generation groups are wholehearted Americans . . . and have absorbed Americanism almost as naturally as they breathe. To claim otherwise is equivalent to asserting that American institutions exercise a less potent influence over the youthful mind than the transplanted institutions of the Orient. I deny that assertion. I have faith in the strength of American institutions. . . ."[52] In contrast, in a report filed by Myer's own agency, a camp high school principal noted the realities of the "struggle with family institutions for the possession of the future of the child. . . ." The principal wrote of the difficulty in combating the language problems of the students. The Nisei were said to have been greatly influenced by their ties with the ethnic community, thus affording little opportunity to speak English. The report went on to point to "regressive tendencies in the Issei community" as the cause for the decline in the students' English vocabulary "by as much as four full grades since Fall of 1942."[53] In contrast to the languishing English medium schools, the Japanese language schools flourished. For example, at Tule Lake, there were three established Japanese schools with branches dispersed "in all corners of the camp." The schools enrolled 5,355 students and maintained a teaching staff of 160. The English schools, on the other hand, enrolled only a total of 2,529 students from preschool to high school, with a staff of just over fifty-five.[54] Along with the deterioration of English, the Nisei invented a camp jargon called *Evacuese* which reflected the bitterness and irony of camp life. *Evacuese* combined English and Japanese with an underlayer of resistance humor. The term *barracks*, for example, became *buraku* in *Evacuese*; *buraku* to these Nisei implied a primitive, tribal colony. The word *foreman* was substituted for the *Evacuese* term, *foeman*.[55] Suzuki, in his study of the ethnolinguistics of the camps, concludes: "the total camp experience became embedded in a matrix of words used to circumscribe a segment of their lives, of which the images and memories conjured up by some of the slang terms and phrases to account for that experience, although latent for many Nisei, even today evoke powerful emotions that cannot be readily dissociated from a unique phase of Japanese American history."[56]

Besides the revival of formal organized religion in Buddhism, there was a resurgence of Japanese folk beliefs and practices at Tule Lake.[57] Marvin Opler, a community analyst at the camp from 1943 to 1946, observed the rise of a "nativistic cultural revivalism" during that period and documented its swift decline after the closing of that camp in 1946. Following Linton's analysis of nativistic movements,[58] Opler distinguished between perpetuative-magical movements or ones invoked to perpetuate a culture or group, and revivalistic-magical movements or ones in which "revival is a part of a magical formula designed to modify the society's environment in ways which will be favorable to it" and thus take on more intense forms. At Tule Lake, according to Opler, all 19,000 internees participated in this folkloristic revival which took the form of Linton's revivalistic-magical movement. "Folklore which had been remembered by a handful of Issei," wrote Opler, "and perpetuated in a small circle, was seized upon by Issei and Nisei alike in a broadening sphere where it was deemed important to strike back at administrative pressures, programs, and policies with the dignified weapons of Japanese culture."[59]

One of the more prevalent beliefs was the *hidama* or "fireball" which was an omen of bad luck, and the *hinotama* or "ghost seen as a fireball presaging death." These were reportedly seen by Issei and Nisei alike signifying impending death. Two accounts of *hinotama* are excerpted below.

There are ghosts seen over there, hinotama. *Greenish lights, they say, bigger than a fist. Last winter, I heard only one story of light coming out of the camp smoke above the field on a foggy morning, but now all sorts of stories are going around. We wouldn't go near too early in the morning or at night around that barrack. It's the worst place.*

A young girl . . . was walking back to her apartment . . . when something prompted her to look over her shoulder. She glanced up and was chilled by a strange glow hovering over the latrine roof. She shivered violently and hurried home to tell her mother, fully expecting her not to believe it. But her mother look worried, opens the door, looks out, but says nothing. The girl insisted on knowing what it was and her mother told her she must have seen hinotama. *A few days later an elderly bedridden block resident died.*[60]

Another folk belief made popular in the camps was of the fox, cat, and badger. These animals were connected with the widespread and important cult of the rice goddess Inari, who descended from heaven to Japan during a time of famine riding on a white fox and holding in her hand sheaths of grain or cereal. Inari was a bearer of food, and thus was not only connected with agriculture and farming but also with commerce. The worship of Inari in Japan, particularly in the agricultural regions from whence most of the Issei derived, was so widespread that it was nearly a distinct cult and religion.[61] The Inari cult was revived in the camps and a number of shrines were maintained by Japanese families in their apartments.[62] The fox on which Inari rode had white hair, denoting age and wisdom, and had the ability to see into the future. Farmers consulted the Inari shrine master before undertaking any important event such as a long journey; thus, many Issei immigrants had in their possession a little image of a fox which had been blessed by the Inari shrine master upon leaving for America. Besides being prescient, the fox, cat, and badger were tricksters and could take possession of a person's mind and body. Although the Inari shrine master could exorcise the victim, the person would nonetheless have a shorter life because fox possession supposedly ate away some of the life force (*ki ga nukeru*, "spirit leaks out").[63] A Tule Lake internee recalled the prevalence of stories of fox, cat, and badger possession.

I had never heard much of Fox, Badger, or Cat until this camp. Back in Gilroy, where I was born, I had heard it only once and forgot it until here. Then it was a newcomer had arrived and the old people found he kept several foxes on his farm. They talked about it until it became a choice story among the young that he could set these foxes to bewitch anyone he didn't like. It started when he threatened an oldtime resident. . . .[64]

The functional usefulness of this revival of ethnic folk belief during the period of camp confinement was evidenced in its rapid decline once the camps had been disbanded. Commented a former Tule Lake internee: "Oh, those fox and badger stories back in the Center; well, people used to believe a lot of things in the Center they never believed before and haven't believed since!"[65]

Other cultural resistance manifestations, rooted in religious belief, included the revival and resurgence of study groups and clubs which promoted such cultural activities as *shibai* and *kabuki* (drama), *utai, shigen*, and *nanaewabushi* (song), *haiku* and *senryu* (poetry), various dance forms and the playing of traditional musical instruments, *ikebana, bonsai*, and rock gardens, and *sumo* and *judo*. Orthodox writers point to the rise of these activities to illustrate internee recreation and the great amount of leisure time available in the camps.[66] Revisionist historians, in contrast, see these not merely as recreation but also as a means of cultural resistance. Like Japanese religious belief itself, however, the ethnic arts, including poetry clubs, did not arise situationally in the concentration camps but flourished in the pre-war Japanese American community.[67] The social and political context of the camps, nonetheless, highlighted their resistance function and meaning to the confined ethnic culture.

Perhaps the most expressive of these cultural resistance forms which we have today and which distills the sensitivity of the people and the bleakness of the camp experience is the *senryu* poetry produced at Tule Lake by members of the Tule Lake *Senryu Kai*.[68] "To understand the poetry," wrote Opler, "one must understand the people. In general, they are all, except the very young, embittered and disaffected by the journey inland."[69] The poetry captures that mood and records the barren landscape of camp life: the barbed wire fence, watchtowers and sentries, the searchlights, fingerprinting and cataloguing, mass feeding, interrogations on loyalty-disloyalty, and a dull, regimented life. Of the 558 *senryu* poems written between January 4 and August 31, 1943, only about seventeen dealt with camp life. That, concluded Opler, pointed to the essentially escapist nature of the poetry. "It may . . . be assumed that they desired to forget the drab existence of the Center, and as a matter of fact sought in Senryu a method of escape from it. Cultural revivalism and folk expression are, then, the prime purposes of Senryu poetry. The cultural form itself provides the refuge, the recreation, and the escape."[70] Nonetheless those poems which did speak to the conditions of camp life were eloquent, reflecting protest, disenchantment, sorrow, and dreams of a better tomorrow. No poem directly attacked the U.S. government or the WRA, but *senryu*, through its techniques of "restraint, suggestiveness, and studied understatement," was clearly an expression of cultural resistance. Examples of such *senryu* follow below.

Original	Literal Translation	Free Translation
Onaji Yane	The uniform roofs,	Here, reminiscence comes
Nagamete shinobu	Looking at, lost in	When looking at
Shyu-yo-sho	reminiscence	The endless rows of
	In the Center	barracks' roofs
Kibana naki	With few natural flowers	Here, where natural flowers
Haru o zoka ni	Spring is seen in the	are rare,
Miru haisho	artificial flowers,	Spring is seen
	In the Center	In artificial ones
Henka naki	Changeless	Here in the exile's
Haisho ni henka	In the place of exile	Monotonous life
Aru kion	Is the temperature	Only the seasons change
Mata shimon ka to	Again, the fingerprints	"So, the finger-printing again!"
Oyaji no	The old man's	See the old man's
Nigai loa	Bitter face	Bitter face
		(We are not criminals)
Chyu, fuchyu	Loyalty, disloyalty	"Loyalty," "disloyalty"
Mojiga men-shimu	The words make eyes sore	Such words to plague us
Kino-o, kyo	Yesterday, today	yesterday, today
		In eyes made red with weeping
Yume dakega	Dreams only	Only in dreams
Jiyu no ten chi	Of freedom and earth	In a world of freedom
Kake meguri	and sky	Earth-bounded, we walk
	Running about	(And here, the fence)

The America of "freedom and earth and sky" was "dreams only"; what was reality was "here, the fence."[71] A satirical wedding song portrays a similar mood. The song deals with the seagulls which fly to Tule Lake in the summer, and the chorus translates as follows.

The sea-birds fly inland to the dry and waterless desert. They stop here, but will not stay. Too dry, too weary here. They fly away. Even the sea-birds find no reason to remain.[72]

Cultural resistance was a reality within the concentration camps and ethnic religious belief provided an ideological basis for that resistance. The pattern of cultural resistance was established even before the creation of the camps largely in reaction to white supremacy. The concentration camps and "Americanization," manifestations of racism and cultural hegemony, reinforced that historical pattern. Before World War II, the various Japanese institutions such as the ethnic church, language schools, and mutual aid and economic associations served to preserve the ethnic identity.[73] Those pre-war institutions were temporarily shattered in the removal and confinement, a process which not only separated family members but also dismantled entire communities. The former means of resistance in the camps were thus lost, though not completely. The ethnic church, language schools, and even unofficial "unions" persisted in the camps; indeed they flourished. The traditional values of filial piety, the primacy of the family, and ethnic solidarity continued to be upheld as cardinal virtues. The family unit merged into the block collective which in turn merged into the wider camp community of the "Japanese spirit" of cooperation, loyalty to the collective, and community participation in cultural activities. Formal religion prospered, as evidenced in the growth of the Buddhist churches and revival of magical and cultic beliefs—perhaps because of the pervasive feeling of insecurity, but also because religious belief constituted the core of Meiji Japanese culture and ethics. The ideals of filial piety and ancestor worship, and of the closeness of man, gods, and nature, were manifested in the wider network of cultural resistance in the various aesthetic expressions through music, drama, and poetry. Resistance was rechanneled away from open rebellion into ethnic beliefs and practices, which, because of the nature of the oppression, themselves constituted resistance. Japanese religious belief, therefore, was both a vehicle for and an expression of the people's resistance.

Notes

1. See e.g., Randall M. Miller and Thomas D. Marzik, eds., *Immigrants and Religion in Urban America* (Philadelphia, 1977).

2. T.O. Ranger and Isaria Kimambo, eds., *The Historical Study of African Religion* (Berkeley, 1972); Vincent Harding, "Religion and Resistance Among Antebellum Negroes, 1800–1860," in: August Meier and Elliott Rudwick, eds., *The Making of Black America*, I (New York, 1969), pp. 179–97; and Anthony F.C. Wallace, *The Death and Rebirth of the Seneca* (New York, 1969).

3. See e.g., Frederick W. Mote, *Intellectual Foundations of China* (New York, 1971); and Masaharu Anesaki, *Religious Life of the Japanese People* (Tokyo, 1970).

4. Gary Y. Okihiro, "Japanese Resistance in America's Concentration Camps: A Re-evaluation," *Amerasia Journal* 2 (Fall 1973): 20–34.

5. Edgar C. McVoy, "Social Processes in the War Relocation Center," *Social Forces* 22 (December 1943): 188–90.

6. Family Welfare Orientation Program, mss. in Barnhart Papers, Box 49, Folder 6, Japanese American Research Project (JARP) Collection 2010, University of California, Los Angeles (hereafter referred to as JARP Collection).

7. See Okihiro, "Japanese Resistance"; and Arthur A. Hansen and David A. Hacker, "The Manzanar Riot: An Ethnic Perspective," *Amerasia Journal* 2 (Fall 1974): 112–57.

8. Okihiro, op. cit.

9. Ibid., 25–6.

10. Frank Miyamoto, "The Structure of Community Relationships," Folder R 20.42, 6–7, in the Bancroft Library collection of material relating to Japanese American evacuation and resettlement, University of California, Berkeley (henceforth referred to as Bancroft Collection). See also, "B.B.," "Caucasian Staff at Tule Lake," Folder R 20.15, 8, Bancroft Collection.

11. Tetsuden Kashima, *Buddhism in America* (Westport, Conn., 1977), p. 37.

12. Dillon S. Myer, *Uprooted Americans* (Tucson, 1971), p. 29. See also, interview with Dillon Myer, May 20, 1968, Oral History Tapes, Box 397, No. 300, JARP Collection.

13. War Relocation Authority, *WRA, A Story of Human Conservation* (Washington, D.C., 1946), p. 76.

14. "Comments by the War Relocation Authority On Remarks of Representative John M. Costello Made in the House of Representatives June 28, 1943," U.S. War Relocation Authority Miscellaneous Publications, vol. 1, Documents Department, Main Library, University of California, Berkeley; and War Relocation Authority, *Community Government in War Relocation Centers* (Washington, D.C., n.d.), p. 10.

15. Isaac B. Berkson, *Theories of Americanization* (New York, 1920).

16. Robert Blauner, *Racial Oppression in America* (New York, 1972), p. 67. See also Michael Hechter, *Internal Colonialism: The Celtic Fringe in British National Development* (Berkeley, 1975), p. 37.

17. Robert Francis Spencer, "Japanese Buddhism in the United States, 1940–1946: A Study on Acculturation" (Ph.D. dissertation, University of California, Berkeley, 1946), p. 164.

18. E.g., the Inari cult, fox, cat, and badger stories, and *sumo*.

19. Isao Horinouchi, "Americanized Buddhism: A Sociological Analysis of a Protestantized Japanese Religion" (Ph.D. dissertation, University of California, Davis, 1973), p. 210.

20. War Relocation Authority, *The Evacuated People—A Quantitative Description* (Washington, D.C., 1942), p. 79.

21. Spencer, op. cit., pp. 127–8. Official WRA policy, nonetheless, declared religious freedom in the camps.

22. Kashima, op. cit. p. 54.

23. Alexander H. Leighton, *The Governing of Men* (Princeton, 1945), p. 35.

24. Spencer, op. cit., p. 127.

25. Daisuke Kitagawa, *Issei and Nisei: The Internment Years* (New York, 1967), pp. 107–8. At the same time, the Buddhist church itself was undergoing fundamental change in leadership from Issei to Nisei and orientation from Japan to America. Kashima, op. cit., pp. 57–59.

26. G. Gordon Brown, "Final Report on the Gila River Relocation Center as of May 20, 1945," Carr Papers, Box 55, Folder 5, JARP Collection. See also, Kitagawa, op. cit., p. 120; and Lester E. Suzuki, *Ministry in the Assembly and Relocation Centers of World War II* (Berkeley, 1979), pp. 34, 130.

27. Horinouchi, op. cit., Cf. Kashima, op. cit., pp. 217–20.

28. Suzuki, op. cit., pp. 40–1, 345.

29. Spencer, op. cit., pp. 141–2.

30. Horinouchi, op. cit., p. 216. See also Brown, op. cit.

31. Ibid.

32. David Y. Hirano, "Religious Values Among Japanese Americans and Their Relationship to Counseling" (D.M. dissertation, School of Theology at Claremont, 1974), p. 2. See also Anesaki, op. cit.

33. Masaharu Anesaki, *History of Japanese Religion* (London, 1930), p. 8. *Sei-cho No Ie*, a popular cult in California especially among the Issei during the 1930s, combined Buddhist belief with some of the teachings of Mary Baker Eddy on health and healing. The cult reemerged at Granada concentration camp. Carr Papers, Box 55, Folder 1, JARP Collection; and Suzuki, op. cit., 212.

34. Hirano, op. cit., p. 12.

35. Ibid., p. 13; and Hideo Kishimoto, *Japanese Religion in the Meiji Era* (Tokyo, 1956). Filial piety and Confucian ethics were also taught in the public schools in a course known as *Shushin* where students learned warrior ethics (*Bushido*), filial piety, and loyalty to Emperor and country. Horinouchi, op. cit., pp. 33–4.

36. Spencer, op. cit., p. 172.

37. Okakura Kakuzo, *The Book of Tea* (Tokyo, 1956); and Daisetz T. Suzuki, *Zen and Japanese Culture* (Princeton, 1959).

38. WRA, *Community Government*, p. 7.

39. Ibid., p. 27.

40. See e.g., Leonard Broom and John I. Kitsuse, *The Managed Casuality: The Japanese-American Family in World War II*, Berkeley, 1973; Anne Umemoto, "Crisis in the Japanese American Family," *Asian Women*, Berkeley, 1971, 31–34; and Kitagawa, *Issei and Nisei*, 86–88.

41. WRA, *WRA, A Story*, 95.

42. Toshio Yatsushiro, "Political and Socio-Cultural Issues at Poston and Manzanar Relocation Centers: A Themal Analysis," (Ph.D. dissertation, Cornell University, 1953).

43. "Manzanar Riot," 121.

44. See e.g., Marian Svensrud, "Attitudes of the Japanese Towards Their Language Schools," *Sociology and Social Research*, 17:3 (January-February 1933), 259–64; and Chotoku Toyama, "The Japanese Community in Los Angeles," MA thesis, (Columbia University, 1926).

45. Hansen and Hacker, "Manzanar Riot," 121–22. See also John Modell, "Class or Ethnic Solidarity: The Japanese American Company Union," *Pacific Historical Review*, 38:2 (May 1969), 193–206; and Jere Takahashi, "Japanese American Responses to Race Relations: The Formation of Nisei Perspectives," *Amerasia Journal*, 9:1 (1982): 29–57.

46. Yatsushiro, "Political and Socio-Cultural," 364. See also, Roger Daniels, *Concentration Camp U.S.A.*, New York, 1971, 104–29; Morton Grodzins, *The Loyal and the Disloyal*, Chicago, 1956, 131; and David A. Hacker, "A Culture Resisted, a Culture Revived: The Loyalty Crisis of 1943 at the Manzanar War Relocation Center," MA thesis. (California State University, Fullerton, 1979).

47. Okihiro, "Japanese Resistance"; and Hacker, "Culture Resisted."

48. Toyama, op. cit., p. 29.

49. Yatsushiro, op. cit., pp. 513–14.

50. Yatsushiro, op. cit., p. 529. Kitagawa sees the subordination of the family to the collective will as an indication of the breakdown of Japanese society in the camps, which he termed "primitive tribal community" and an "ostrichlike community." *Issei and Nisei*, p. 106.

51. Quoted in Peter T. Suzuki, "The Ethnolinguistics of Japanese Americans in the Wartime Camps," *Anthropological Linguistics* 18 (December 1976): 422.

52. Dillon Myer, "The Truth About Relocation," mss. in McGovern Papers, Box 119, Folder 1, JARP Collection.

53. Family Welfare Orientation Program, Barnhart Papers, Box 49, Folder 6, JARP Collection. See also Suzuki, op. cit., pp. 416–27.

54. Austin Papers, Box 44, Folder 9, Document 2, JARP Collection. See also, "Letter to friend from a teacher in Tule Lake (Oct. 30, 1944)," Austin Papers, Box 44, Folder 6, Document 7.

55. *The Pen*, mss. in Barnhart Papers, Box 49, Folder 7, JARP Collection. See also Suzuki, op. cit., pp. 416–27.

56. Suzuki, op. cit., p. 423.

57. This was not the only such camp. See e.g., Spencer, op. cit., pp. 173–75.

58. R. Linton, "Nativistic Movements," *American Anthropologist* 45 (April-June 1943): 230–40.

59. Marvin K. Opler, "Japanese Folk Beliefs and Practices, Tule Lake, California," *Journal of American Folklore* 63 (October-December 1950) 385–87.

60. Ibid., pp. 388–89.

61. Morris E. Opler and Robert Seido Hashima, "The Rice Goddess and the Fox in Japanese Religion and Folk Practice," *American Anthropologist* 48 (January-March 1946): 50.

62. Opler, "Japanese Folk Beliefs," pp. 389–90.

63. Opler and Hashima, "Rice Goddess," pp. 43–50.

64. Opler, "Japanese Folk Beliefs," p. 391.

65. Ibid.

66. Myer, op. cit., pp. 56–7; and Michi Weglyn, *Years of Infamy* (New York, 1976), p. 82.

67. Peter T. Suzuki, "Wartime *Tanka*: Issei and Kibei Contributions to a Literature East and West," *Literature East and West: Journal of World and Comparative Literature* 21 (July 1977): 242–54.

68. See Suzuki, op. cit., for similar expressions of the people in other poetic forms such as *haiku* and *waka*.

69. Marvin K. Opler and F. Obayashi, "Senryu Poetry as Folk and Community Expression," *Journal of American Folklore* 58 (January-March, 1945): 2.

70. Ibid., p. 7.

71. Ibid., pp. 8–9.

72. Ibid., p. 11.

73. See e.g., Shotaro Frank Miyamoto, *Social Solidarity Among the Japanese in Seattle* (Seattle, 1939); and Kashima, op. cit.

The Role of the Buddhist Church in the Ethnic Adjustment of the Japanese American

TETSUDEN KASHIMA

Not all the Japanese who came to America in the late 1900s espoused Eastern religions; some were Christians. There were obvious differences between the two groups, in terms of cultural continuity and adaptation to the new social environment. The Buddhist missionaries who began arriving in 1899 were able to offer the immigrants a cultural tie to the world they had left behind, in a way the missionary Christian church could not. In any case, social intercourse with the American populace was as limited for the Japanese Christians as for the Japanese Buddhists:

> Not only the Buddhist but also the Methodist churches were strictly for Japanese and services were conducted in the Japanese language. Of the two religions, Buddhism provided an important link with Japan in ways Christianity did not. Buddhism was the religion of the ancestors of the Japanese immigrants, and when a man died, his ashes were preserved in the church until ready to be taken back to Japan by one of his relatives or friends.[1]

To offset some of the inevitable "sociological death,"[2] the Japanese created or modified their processes and organizations within the United States. It does not come as a surprise that as the numerically stronger Japanese religious institution, Jodo Shinshu Buddhism was able to retain its Japanese adherents and to attain an importance that far surpassed its original position in Japan. In Japan, the temples in the community are viewed predominantly as religious organizations; in America, the NABM served as a place not only for religious solace, but also for social gatherings that preserved communal ethnic ties.

Life for the early immigrant was full of hardships. Without a surrounding social support to aid and bolster the young men living and working in a foreign environment, such conditions could easily have lead to alienation and loneliness. The following description of the relationship of the church to the immigrants suggests the importance of the social aspects of the religious organization:

> Instead of trying to drown out their unhappiness with mere pleasure seeking, they [the young immigrants] turn to the church and religion to afford them comfort and relief from their economic and social misery, and they hold a cheaply optimistic, goody-goody idea that if they stay in their place, work hard and please the Americans and remain happy in the position where God has placed them, surely the Christian Americans, out of the generosity of their hearts, will throw out to them a few more crumbs to ease their condition.[3]

The important point here is that the church was able to offer this necessary spiritual and social solace for those immigrants who desired it.

Most of the elements within the NABM and BCA were brought to America and utilized by the Buddhists, but certain inimical events made it more tactful and judicious to downplay or suppress various constituent parts of the organization that could become controversial or injurious to the Buddhist religion. The story of the Buddhist swastika is one example of a social change within the Buddhist institution in America.

The sauvastika or swastika[4] has long been a traditional Indian symbol for Buddhism. In most Buddhist temples and churches before World War II, the swastika was exhibited ornamentally. The Buddhist church in Seattle, Washington, for example, displayed the symbol on an archway above the front entrance upon a temple building built in 1906.[5]

Abridgement of "The Role of the Buddhist Church in the Ethnic Adjustment of the Japanese American," *Buddhism in America* by Tetsuden Kashima. Copyright © 1997 Greenwood Press. Reproduced with permission of Greenwood Publishing Group, Inc., Westport, CT.

It is clear today that the sign of the swastika, constructed either in a counterclockwise Buddhist fashion or clockwise as used in Nazi Germany, remains a symbol of Nazism for most Americans. Long before the 1940s, however, the swastika was regarded as a symbol representing a foreign tradition:

> *One might pass the Buddhist temple in Portland a hundred times a day, and unless one's eyes were quick to spy the modest Swastika ꕔ on the door glass, and the neat gold letters BUDDHIST CHURCH on the transom, one would never suspect the square brick house of being other than an old-time domicile, or a present-day rooming house; but there it is, a heathen temple on American soil.*[6]

Madden described the swastika as the symbol of Buddhism in America. Her main objection as a non-Buddhist was the presence and threat of this religion to America: "Who shall rule America, Christ or Buddha? Just outside your church door is the sign of the Swastika, what will you do about it?"[7]

Despite anti-Japanese sentiment in America during the 1920s, the swastika did not become as overt an issue at that time as it did in the 1940s. Until the advent of World War II, the Buddhist churches continued to utilize and to display the swastika as a religious emblem. Then, just after the attack on Pearl Harbor, not only things Japanese, but especially Buddhist artifacts and writings, became immediately suspect in the minds of Americans. Some Japanese Americans, cognizant of the suspicions generated by war hysteria, attempted to divest themselves of their Buddhist religious possessions.

> *Those who had little confidence in their own religious beliefs believed that any association with a Buddhist organization would be to their disadvantage. Possession of Japanese writings became suspect and a source of concern; thus, the fearful ones removed their Buddhist altars, destroyed their sutra books and burned their family albums containing photos of relatives or friends in uniform.*[8]

The use of the Buddhist swastika as a symbol was repressed during the war. The attendant meanings that non-Buddhists could attach to the swastika created a crisis for the Buddhists. Hence, from that time, other Buddhist symbols were given more emphasis: the "Wheel of Law," an eight-spoked wheel representing the "eightfold noble path," became, and remained, the accepted logo for the American Buddhists. However, one recently formed Jodo Shinshu Buddhist group in Los Angeles, the Kinnara, now utilizes the swastika as its logo.[9]

The BCA as a Cohesive Force: 1945–1975

To be sure, the swastika is a mere symbol, and the resemblance between the Buddhist and Nazi emblems was ultimately a historical accident. But the repression and degradation inflicted upon all Japanese Americans during World War II was not an accident of history.

The immediate problem after the relocation of the Japanese was the reopening of the dormant temple structures. Most temples were initially used as hostels, with all available space converted to makeshift bedrooms, except the kitchens, which were used to prepare communal food. These hostels also served as job placement offices and community centers for all Japanese and Japanese Americans.

Upon their return, many ministers found that their temples had been vandalized and religious articles destroyed or stolen.[10] Religious services were at first given secondary consideration, since the personal needs of the Japanese Americans were paramount and acute. The ordeal inherent in their return, especially with regard to employment and housing, became another complete dislocation process for the returnees.

Along the West Coast, people of Japanese descent did not return to precisely the places they had left. Before the war, the Bakersfield Buddhist Church had a membership of approximately fifty families, with a resident minister; the only Japanese who returned were those who owned agricultural lands. With only a handful of families to support it, the temple was forced to close. The Guadalupe Buddhist Church also lost many members, although a sufficient number did return eventually to support a resident minister and an active church organization. The Buddhist Church of Salinas lost about a third of its previous membership families, but it retained enough members to continue supporting a resident minister. The Oakland Buddhist Church, an urban temple that had once enjoyed a large membership, also experienced a large decrease. The Placer Buddhist Church and the West Los Angeles Buddhist Church had stable membership numbers only because new families moved in to replace those who did not return.

On the other hand, churches and temples in Berkeley, Palo Alto, Reedley, Gardena, San Diego, Oxnard, and San Jose, and in Denver, Colorado (Tri-State Buddhist Church), experienced a small to large increase in membership. Many new churches or temples were constructed to meet the needs of the new Japanese population; by December 1946, organizations were established in Cleveland, Ohio; Detroit, Michigan; Idaho-Oregon (Ontario, Oregon); Spokane, Washington; Minneapolis, Minnesota (Twin Cities); and Monterey, California. From 1950 to 1971, seven new churches or temples were constructed: at Mountain View, Union City (Southern Alameda County Buddhist Church), Anaheim (Orange County Buddhist Church), Marin, and Fowler, California; Seabrook, New Jersey; and Honeyville, Utah. The last church to become independent was Venice, California, on March 1, 1976.

Since 1945, the Issei population has grown older and fewer in number, while the Nisei and Sansei population has increased. Because the Nisei have continued to move into nonagricultural occupations, rural Buddhist churches have suffered the most from resettlement. Although some ministers who would have returned with their adherents to the West Coast took over the new temples and churches in the Midwest and on the Eastern seaboard, from 1948 onward a continuous flow of new ministers, both Nisei and native Japanese, has entered the BCA.[11]

Conflicts between the Issei and Nisei, within the temples, continued after the war. The Issei and Nisei both desired decision-making powers within the church organization. Most temples had their own constitutions and eventually incorporated under the laws of their respective states whereby the elected board of directors controlled their finances. The Issei ministers with their bishop continued to dominate the BCA, but at the local temples the Nisei continued to gain in ascendancy. Income was difficult to generate since the members were readjusting to life outside the camps. The prewar language schools, which had augmented the salaries of the ministers and temples, were not immediately reestablished to any large extent. Only after the BCA Buddhist adherents started to overcome their financial losses from the evacuation, in the late 1950s, were the churches and temples able to provide substantial increases in the ministers' salaries and other necessary church expenditures. During the readjustment period, large-scale financial projects such as the NABM *Zaidan* (Endowment Fund) were tabled because of insufficient funds; however, two important centers were created to fill the need for more English-speaking ministers.

A Ministerial Training Fund was emphasized through a BCA Special Project Fund in 1966 to further the training of Nisei ministers, through scholarships for prospective ministerial candidates studying here or in Japan, and to aid active ministers desiring to continue their study of English.[12] The BCA established a Ministerial Training Center at the Hompa (Nishi) Hongwanji in Kyoto, Japan. A plan to initiate the training of the priests in the United States resulted in the American Buddhist Academy in 1948 under the Reverend Hozen Seki and the New York Buddhist Church; and the Berkeley Study Center in 1965 under the BCA Bishop Enryo Shigefuji, the Reverend Kanmo Imamura, and the Berkeley Buddhist Church.

The period from 1945 to 1965, with the start of the Institute of Buddhist Studies in Berkeley, can be characterized as a consolidation era, with the BCA reevaluating the Issei priorities and anticipating the changing needs of Buddhists. However, the Buddhist religion remained tied to those of Japanese ancestry, in the Nishi Hongwanji sect as embodied in the BCA.

The Present Crisis

Changes in the BCA in the 1960s have resulted in a more vocal organization than previously existed. An important issue entered into by the BCA concerned the California State Curriculum Committee's approval of a textbook entitled *Japanese Americans: The Untold Story*.[13] The textbook, aimed at the third to fifth grade grammar school level, was written by a team of twelve authors (Nikkei school teachers and citizens) forming the Japanese American Curriculum Project (JACP). The JACP had previously produced a television program in San Francisco on Japanese Americans, which had drawn criticism from some individuals who felt it made "inaccurate representations of the Japanese American Community."[14] After writing the short book in four months, the JACP submitted it to various Japanese organizations for prepublication approval. Instead, the textbook was overwhelmingly denounced by the Japanese American Citizens League, the Southern California Buddhist-Christian Clergy Fellowship, and various Asian American student organizations, as well as parents, educators, and ministers.

On October 7, 1970, in a letter signed by the bishop, the president of the board of directors, and the chairman of the Ministerial Research Committee, the BCA stated that there were "overtones to the book which were racial, consistently anti-Buddhist and pro-Christian biased, and a gross misrepresentation of the true picture of the lives of Japanese Americans. . . . The preface of the book is written as though the authors have acquired the endorsement of the Buddhist Churches of America, but actually the Buddhist Churches of America have not endorsed the book, whatsoever."[15] Through a series of meetings and public presentations, the BCA and other organizations and individuals were able to convince the California State Curriculum Committee to reject the book. The authors now have plans to rewrite some portions of the text and to submit the revised version for reconsideration.

Regardless of the outcome of the television program and textbook controversies, the BCA in 1970 clearly stepped out of what many had considered an insular, conservative community position. The BCA perceived the book to be a threat to the future Buddhists of America. In an unsigned but BCA-sponsored letter distributed to the members of the Buddhist churches to elicit written support of the BCA's position, the concern for the Buddhist child's self-image is very apparent:

> This book reflects unfavorably upon the Japanese American Buddhists and has a pervading religious bias. We feel that this religious bias could be very detrimental to the Buddhist identity of our children. It can only serve to make our children feel insecure about being Buddhists, but also can serve to make a critical change in their thoughts and minds about their Buddhist identity and heritage. How it will affect the thinking of others about Buddhists and Japanese Americans is an equally disturbing thought.[16]

The BCA's and their adherents' willingness to come forward to speak in defense of their position had a precedent in Bishop Uchida's testimony at the Immigration Commission meetings in the 1920s. The crisis concerning the textbook was a perceived threat to the image of Buddhism presented to the adherents' children. It was important enough to involve the headquarters and the member churches and temples in a lobbying and letter-writing campaign to help avert the State Education Committee's adoption of the book.

Another issue on which the BCA took an active position concerned the inclusion of the Divine Creation Theory in California public school textbooks.[17] The Reverend Hogen Fujimoto, director of the Bureau of Buddhist Education, BCA, testified before the State Board of Education that this "Divine Creation" represented a religious interpretation; it was therefore a subject for churches—not schools. Reverend Fujimoto quoted from various sources and explained that Buddhists did not subscribe to the ideas inherent in the theory: "According to Buddhism, human beings and all living things are self created or self creating. The universe is not homocentric, it is a creation of all beings. Buddhism does not believe that all things come from one cause, but holds that everything is inevitably created out of more than two causes."[18]

Thus, by 1972 the BCA was willing to enter into debates in secular areas, utilizing its religious doctrines in defense of its stand on public issues. The YBA has demonstrated a similar initiative by passing an antiwar resolution deploring the destruction of human life in the Vietnam conflict[19] and by giving Buddhists guidelines for becoming more involved in protest against racism and other forms of social oppression.[20]

The BCA and some BCA member churches have also sponsored housing projects to assist the elderly Issei. With the cooperation of the San Francisco Redevelopment Agency and the Japanese community, the Japanese American Religious Federation (JARF) has begun construction of a thirteen-story, 272-unit apartment building for low-income residents.[21] This joint undertaking of the BCA, the Buddhist Church of San Francisco, and nine other Japanese and Japanese American member churches[22] is but one example of the ability of religious organizations to work together on a project of mutual benefit.

The 1970s has been explicitly proclaimed a period for broadening Sansei involvement in the BCA. As the past president of the BCA board of directors has stated, "With the coming of the 75th Anniversary, we must begin the new era of American Buddhism. The area of youth is a challenging area."[23] The Sansei represent the important problems of the present and the future. There is some reason to suppose that some Sansei perceive themselves as outside the mainstream of American life.[24] Many are now, in one sense, returning to their Japanese cultural and associational roots, refusing to forget their Asian past. Of the third generation Marcus Lee Hansen has written that "what the son wishes to forget, the grandson wishes to remember."[25] The creation of Asian American Studies Centers, Yellow Brotherhood, and Asian American Anti-Drug Groups, as well as the Relevant American Buddhists and Kinnara groups within the Buddhists of America, indicates that the Sansei are not only willing to stay in the Buddhist religion, but also to form new organizations tailored to their needs.

To facilitate communication with the Sansei, the BCA board of directors authorized the creation of the Relevant American Buddhists (RAB), with eight youth coordinators' positions within the BCA districts to aid the YBA and their programs and to insure that the youths' needs and demands would be given an official channel of communication to the BCA ruling bodies. Since the older YBA members, parents of the third generation, have now formed the Adult Buddhist Association (ABA), the Sansei have desired to expand their activities to aid the aging Issei, allow other racial groups within the Junior and Senior YBA, become involved in social and political issues, and initiate changes in the presentation of their religion.

The Kinnara, a Southern California-based Buddhist organization, was formed, in the main, by a group of Nisei and Sansei BCA ministers and the Sansei membership to change the format of religious teachings. The Kinnara group, as was mentioned previously, has incorporated traditional Japanese music (*gagaku*), sutra chanting, and meditation techniques to allow for a diversity of methods in Buddhist services and ceremonies. For instance, the group has instituted Buddhist retreats, daylong celebrations of important Buddhist days of reverence, and interchurch gatherings to sustain and generate new interest in Buddhism among the Nisei's children. It would be premature at this time to estimate the longevity of this new organization. However, it can be stated that the membership is growing. Moreover, since more Nisei and Sansei ministers are entering, while maintaining their particular churches for the Issei and Nisei, there is reason to believe that the Kinnara group represents one vital and important alternative to the existing BCA organization.

There is some evidence too that some of the Sansei are returning to their Buddhist religion.[26] They are still young, in their teens and twenties. The BCA ministers have had difficulty attracting them to existing church organizations[27] primarily because the ministers are still largely Issei, the member churches are controlled by a Nisei board of directors, and the Sansei have not clearly communicated the type of changes they desire.

The Sansei would appreciate a stronger voice in the activities of the church or temple organizations, but they have not yet articulated a positive program that the churches could accept or reject. Most churches have included sports and other social activities, but Buddhist study groups or religious-oriented activities have not met with overwhelming success in attracting the Sansei.[28] The future of the Sansei in the BCA is still uncertain. Programs and activities will continue to be modified to attract the Sansei and non-Japanese; upon their success or failure rests the future of the BCA.

The Continuity of Buddhism and the Problem of Language

The strongest force for continuity in the member temples has, of course, been the Jodo Shinshu Buddhist religion itself. Throughout its history, the basic religious tenets, practices, and ceremonies have constituted the major continuous and unchanging focal point for the membership. An Issei minister was asked in an interview:

INT: What is the difference between Issei Buddhism and Nisei Buddhism, and then Sansei Buddhism?

RESP: That definition would be based on majority membership, and so, of course, [on the] accompanying psychological or other cultural differences.

INT: But they are all Buddhist?

RESP: All Buddhists, yes.

INT: Now, is Jodo Shinshu Buddhism different between the Issei, Nisei and Sansei?

RESP: I don't think so, and the doctrine, of course, never changes. Buddhism you know consists of the triple jewels: [the Buddha], the teaching of the Buddha, and the Sangha [brotherhood of Buddhists]. . . . The Sangha may be changing. Even many of the vocabularies must be carefully used. This is a funny example, but the lady's breast is a symbol of mother's love in Japan. So we often refer to *Ochichi o nomaseru* [literally: to allow someone to drink from the breast], but some Issei ministers came to this country and explained [this concept] pointing [to the breast region] causing laughter among the [non-Japanese speaking] audience. So we have to adapt ourselves to this particular situation even linguistically. So from that standpoint, maybe our way of presentation must be changed.

INT: But not the doctrine.

RESP: Not the doctrine.

INT: What are the purposes of the Buddhist church for the Issei?

RESP: Of course, to retain, to keep the Jodo Shinshu [for] themselves and also through their capacity as the leader of the family to transmit the teaching to the children, the grandchildren. . . .

INT: What is the purpose of the Buddhist Church for the Nisei?

RESP: Niseis of course accept this precious gift of Dharma of Buddha from their parents and transfer [it] to their children. So nowadays, Issei and Nisei are not young anymore. So in spite of linguistic differences, language differences, from their chronological experiences they are becoming closer to the Issei. . . .

INT: Now what is the purpose of the Buddhist church for the Sansei?

RESP: Not very much difference from Issei, Nisei propagation. But if I [could] add a point, it is [that it] makes them missionary agents to all other non-Japanese Americans, because they are at a good position to do that. . . . They have the same language as the American people in general, so they are in a good position to introduce Buddhism, explain Buddhism to others.[29]

This Issei minister, like many others, emphasized the continuity of religious doctrine within a modified form of presentation. The most important modification is the use of English, with the attendant problem of adequately translating Buddhist terminology to make the religious concepts understandable to the membership.
    Another minister, a Nisei, seconds the points raised by the Issei *kaikyoshi*:

INT: What do you think are the purposes of the Buddhist Churches in America?

RESP: The first purpose is to keep on propagating the Jodo Shinshu to the Nisei and Sansei and Yonsei and Gosei.[30]

All ministers appear to agree that the roots of the Buddhist tree have been kept healthy in America. They also agree that there are many methods of presentation:

INT: It has been said that the BCA and North American Buddhist Mission stem traditionally from Japan. Can you name some things that are purely Japanese that are still carried on in the 1970's?

RESP: Oh yes, the teaching of the *Nembutsu* (Dharma), the Jodo Shinshu teaching has been the same all the way through, and lately, we have realized that, in some ways, the presentation has to be changed to compromise with our younger youngsters.

INT: What do you mean by compromise?

RESP: Well, in, not to compromise with their wishes all along, but to make them understand, have them enjoy our religion.

INT: Although the Buddhist doctrine comes from Japan, has it changed because we've had to use English as the main language for the Japanese Americans?

RESP: Yes, we have had a language barrier there. The translation of Buddhist teaching into English is very difficult. That is, sometimes we lose the essence of the teaching.

INT: And how is that being counteracted, or is it being counteracted?

RESP: Well it has been brought out by the Sansei and the Nisei. However, I don't think we have found a solution to that yet.[31]

The problem of adequate English translations has yet to be resolved. Thus far, the translations have been handled on a utilitarian or expedient basis—a past course presently undergoing criticism by ministers and lay members alike. There has been no attempt to change the basic doctrines or precepts of Buddhism. Instead, the adaptations have been made to render Buddhism more comprehensible to an English-speaking audience. Transmission and preservation of the tenets of Buddhism has been the paramount goal of the Buddhist institution.

Services and Ceremonies

The most important components of any religious organization are the religious services and ceremonies. From the start of Jodo Shinshu Buddhism in America to the present, important religious observances have continued. Although the format of the religious services may have changed in varying degrees over the years, especially with the prevalent use of English in the services, consistency and continuity in the content of the services are very apparent in the observances of Buddhist religious ceremonial days.

There are eleven important days and ceremonies within the Jodo Shinshu sect. The BCA ritually observes these occasions:

Shusho-E: January 1 (New Year's Service). A dedication service for the start of the new year.

Ho onko: January 16 (Shinran Shonin's Memorial Day). A special service to honor the founder of the Jodo Shinshu sect of Buddhism.

Nehan-E: February 15 (Nirvana Day). A service to memorialize the passing away of Sakyamuni Buddha.

Higan-E: March 21 *and* September 23 (Spring and Autumn Equinox). The equinox day, where the nights and days are of equal length, symbolizes the harmony pervading the universe. "Therefore we gather before the sacred shrine of Amida Buddha and meditate on the harmony of nature and devote ourselves to the realization of this harmony in our inner lives."[32]

Hanamatsuri: April 8 (Wesak Day). A day to commemorate the birth of Sakyamuni Buddha.

Gotan-E: May 21 (Shinran Shonin's Birthday). Commemoration to honor the birth of Shinran Shonin.

Ura Bon-E: July 15 (Obon Festival). A Buddhist memorial day for all who have passed away.

Beikoku Bukkyo Kaiyo Kinenbu: September 1 (BCA Founding Day). September 1, 1899, is accepted by the BCA as the date of its inception, and a service is held to honor the occasion.

Jodo-E: December 8 (Bodhi Day). A special service to commemorate the day that Sakyamuni Buddha finished his meditation under the Bodhi tree and became enlightened.

Joya-E: December 31 (New Year's Eve Service). A service to meditate on the events of the past year.

These eleven special ceremonies (*Higan-E* is observed twice a year) are observed by the member churches of the BCA. Except for the BCA Founding Day, the services have always been a part of Jodo Shinshu services in America. Most temples and churches have taken a very flexible attitude toward the actual date for these observances. Many schedule the ceremonies for the "usual" weekly services or observe them on a more convenient day close to the ritually prescribed date. For instance, the observance of *Ura Bon-E*, or *Obon* for short, usually includes not only a religious service, but also a "dance for the deceased." This celebration is inspired by a legend concerning a disciple of Buddha who performed a dance of joy when his mother was given entrance into Nirvana after her death. The entire congregation, dressed in traditional Japanese attire, enters into the *Obon* dance; it is a time for gaiety and enjoyment. Since *Obon* is very colorful, in many locales the event draws both Buddhists and non-Buddhists as onlookers and as participants. Besides the *Obon* dance, many churches feature booths and counters to sell Japanese foods and other refreshments. For many churches, the revenue generated by the booths augments regular income. In areas where there are many geographically close Buddhist churches, the individual churches will space out the observance of the event over a month's time, so that participants from one church may attend another's celebration. Scheduling also allows for guest speakers in the area to give special sermons at several churches.

At other ceremonies the bishop, as well as other speakers, may be asked to participate. These occasions are reserved for the more important services such as *Shusho-E, Ho onko, Nehan-E,* or *Hanamatsuri*. In order to make his presence available to as many temples as possible, the celebration days are often negotiated with the bishop or other church dignitaries. The spacing of the special services is an example of one form of change within the BCA. Where the special observance days in the Buddhist temples in Japan are more ritually followed, the absence of a large pool of available guest speakers or Buddhist priests outside the BCA has required that the temples accommodate the dates of observances to coincide with the availability of desired speakers. The priests within the BCA often travel to other temples to give guest lectures. This allows each church to hear priests other than the resident minister. However, for the special services, prior coordination must be accomplished with the minister to preclude conflicting engagements.

Aside from these ceremonial occasions, each temple or church conducts funeral, memorial, and wedding services. Among the most important of these services is the *hoji* or memorial service for the departed, which is observed in a very formal manner. For example, just after the death, a *makura-gyo* or bedside service may be held at the home of the deceased. Then an *otsuya* or wake service is held one day prior to the funeral service for the family of the deceased. At the *soshiki* or funeral service, a posthumous Buddhist name (*homyo*) may be given to the deceased if he or she has not previously been granted one. The officiating priest will place the Buddhist name inside the casket, and another copy is given to the family to keep within their family shrine. Family memorial services (*hoji*) are then held on the seventh day after the death, and if the family is very devout, also on the fourteenth, twenty-first, twenty-eighth, thirty-fifth, and forty-ninth day. Ceremonies after the forty-ninth day service are observed on the hundredth day, then on the first anniversary, and thereafter in the seventh, thirteenth, seventeenth, twenty-fifth, thirty-third, and fiftieth year. At most temples and churches, a collective monthly memorial service (*shotsuki hoyo*) is held, and the names of those families with relatives who have passed away during that month are printed in the church bulletin.

Each church or temple also has regularly scheduled services. These include the children's Sunday Schools and the adult services on a weekly, biweekly, or monthly basis, depending upon the number of adherents. The typical adult service may start with an opening address by the chairman. "Meditation" follows, in which the members bow their heads, placing an *ojuzu* (a Buddhist rosary) over their hands with palms together, while the priest gives a Buddhist invocation. The meditation concludes with a thrice-given recitation of an homage to the Buddha, "Namu Amida Butsu." Then a sutra (Buddhist scripture) is chanted by all, followed by the singing of a Buddhist *gatha* or hymn. The minister then gives a sermon, after which another *gatha* may be sung. The conclusion of the service includes another meditation, followed by an "incense offering," where the members may go to the front of the altar to bow, offer incense, recite the homage to the Buddha, and return to their seats. If there are any announcements they are given here; otherwise, the members leave the worship hall (*hondo*) by bowing to the shrine and departing.

The sermons given by the priests are usually of an emotional or analytic type. In the former, the priest starts with a story, usually of a personal nature, introducing an appropriate Buddhist interpretation, and usually concludes with the thought that all human events, be they tragic or comic, can be understood from the Buddhist perspective. The analytic sermon generally starts with a Buddhist concept such as *karma* or *shinjin* (faith). This is exemplified, expounded upon, and interpreted in everyday language. One priest has stated that priests can be typified according to the type of sermon they give. The Issei congregation prefers an emotional appeal, but the sermons given to the Nisei and Sansei vary.[33] For a Sansei audience from a university community, the analytic approach is most common; in an agricultural area, the emotional sermon may be better received. For a regular service, the priest's everyday activities apparently serve as a source for his sermons. The topics may range from mercury poisoning in a village in Japan[34] to the deathbed statements of an eighty-year-old Issei lady.

For special ceremonies, the sermon topic usually revolves around the reasons for the service. For example, *Hanamatsuri* sermons often discuss events surrounding the birth of the Buddha, and *Joya-E* or year-end service may recount the events of the past year as they have affected the temple or its members. For these ceremonies an outside priest or speaker is invited to give a sermon. Having a visiting priest always signals a special event for any temple, for he gives his most effective sermon, having pretested it at his home temple. Thus, there is usually a larger than average attendance during these occasions.

Buddhist Weddings

Another important service conducted by the Buddhist priests in America is the Buddhist wedding ceremony. The wedding ceremony in Japan is traditionally performed by the Shinto priests; however, the Jodo Shinshu sect of Buddhism has had a long history of performing weddings—both in Japan and in America.[35] When a marriage occurred within the family of a Buddhist priest in Japan, the wedding ceremony was almost always performed by another Buddhist official.[36] Reverend Koju Terada stated that the marriage ceremony conducted in front of the Buddhist altar was not an uncommon occurrence, especially if the participating families were strong believers in Buddhism. He also stated that the prevalent view that weddings in Japan are performed solely by Shinto priests is an idea that has developed in America since World War II.[37]

The Buddhist wedding ceremony in Japan is rather uncomplicated. The nuptial couple appears before the family Buddhist shrine, performs a *gassho* (bow) before the shrine, and recites the *Nembutsu*. A sutra may or may not be chanted, although usually there is an exchange *ojuzu* (Buddhist rosary) between the couple. The name of the new bride is then recorded in the groom's family register. Finally, the couple goes to the reception, where part of the ceremony is to sip *sake* three times each (called *sansankudo*).[38]

The American Buddhist wedding ceremony is somewhat more complex. As in Euro-American ceremonies, the American ceremony includes the use of wedding gowns, the playing of a wedding march (Mendelssohn's "Wedding March"), the exchange of rings, and the witnessing of a wedding license. All officiating ministers must be sanctioned by the respective state legal body and empowered to perform a ceremony binding to the laws concerning the rights, privileges, and responsibilities inherent in the marriage contract. The groom wears a formal tuxedo, especially for the picture-taking portion of the wedding ceremony. (This custom, by the way, has been followed in Japan since the Meiji era and was utilized by the Japanese prior to the arrival of the Jodo Shinshu institution in America.) The marriage license is also a part of the Japanese wedding ceremony; the erasure of the bride's name from her family register and the recording of her name in the groom's register is in effect a legal sanction of the marriage ceremony.

Despite all the Western innovations, the American Buddhist wedding ceremony does retain some elements peculiar to the Buddhist faith. The couple offers incense at the Buddhist altar, affirms their faith in the Buddhist religion, and have placed over their hands the *ojuzu*, the string of beads symbolic of the Buddhist faith. The *ojuzu* is given to both participants as an affirmation of their partnership and of their commitment to the Buddhist "way of life."

An important part of the wedding is the postceremony reception. At many of the receptions, a thrice-called salute to the couple ("*Banzai*") is often given by the guests. The reception features the singing of Japanese *No* songs (*yokyoku* or *utai*) by the guests, along with felicitations in both Japanese and English. There was a time when the nuptial couple would toast each other with *sake*, a custom similar to the *sansankudo*; however, this practice is now less frequently seen at the Sansei weddings.

The social forms of the wedding ceremony in America are now undergoing some changes. For example, some of the young have their ceremonies outside of the temples—in a wooded glen or at home; the guitar is sometimes played instead of the piano; and wedding gowns and tuxedos are becoming optional items of apparel. Such changes will undoubtedly continue in the future.

Sutras and Appurtenances

Other elements besides the religious ceremonies, services, and weddings are intrinsic to Buddhism in America. The most important of these concerns the religious sutras, the sermons of the Buddha. The sutras used by the BCA are in Chinese with Japanese pronunciations. The members chant with the priest. Only a few sutras are used in the Buddhist churches today, although the collection of the original sermons of the Buddha has been estimated at about thirty volumes.[39] The most important for the BCA are: *Shoshin-ge* (the Hymn of Faith), *San Sei-ge* (the Three Sacred Vows), *San Butsu-ge* (the Praises of the Buddha), and *Junirai* (the Twelve Adorations).[40] In a technical sense these four are not sutras since they are not authored by the Buddha. However, the Nikkei Buddhists call them sutras, and we will follow their convention. The sutras are not comprehensible to the American-born Japanese, although they have been translated into English.[41] They are still chanted in the traditional language, however. No service or ceremony is conducted without the chanting of at least one sutra. Although there have been attempts to chant them in English, the cadence and intonations have not been successfully adapted to this idiom.

Besides the sutras, elements that have persisted since the start of Buddhism in America include the shrine (*onaijin*), candles, incense, floral offerings, and gongs, bells, and drums. The shrines are often ornate gold-gilt, elaborate structures. In the center is a statue or picture of the image of the Buddha or a scroll with the sacred writings ("*Namu Amida Butsu*"). The candles are used both to symbolize the impermanence of all material objects and to shed light upon the teachings of Buddha. The incense, which symbolizes a technique of purification, is used to expunge unfavorable odors and to burn and extinguish impure thoughts. The flowers also symbolize the impermanence of living things. The gongs and bells are used to punctuate pauses within the sutras, but the fading tones also symbolize the impermanence of all material beings. All of these appurtenances have been part of the services and ceremonies of the Buddhist churches and temples both in Japan and America. All have continued throughout the years of the NABM and BCA, and have not been altered in content to adapt to a non-Buddhist environment. The Buddhist services, ceremonies, sutras, and appurtenances have remained unchanged for Jodo Shinshu adherents in America.

Problems of Ethnicity

Aside from teaching the precepts and practices of Buddhism, the NABM and BCA have attempted to sustain ethnic community solidarity—for the creation and enjoyment of group cohesiveness through racial, ethnic, and religious ties. Throughout its history, the BCA has been predominantly an organization by and for the

Japanese and Japanese Americans.[42] As one Nisei father stated, "The Buddhist church is a place for the Japanese to meet other Japanese." The pressures created by prejudice and oppression during the early 1920s, and especially during the relocation in World War II, drove the Japanese to look to their own group for solace and companionship. The NABM and BCA have been religious institutions, for all Japanese and Japanese Americans, and together with the Japanese Association, the *kenjinkais* (prefectural associations), and the Japanese American Citizens' League, they have offered their members a social haven in a hostile environment.

In 1945, even the Japanese Christians were subjected to anti-Oriental prejudices, the roots of which are traceable to the early 1920s: "The Japanese feel that they are not wanted in the American churches. . . . Some who have attended the Occidental churches have experienced a warm reception, only to find later, as their numbers increased, that they were no longer welcome. Apparently, their presence in white American churches, arouses opposition as soon as there is danger of a Japanese invasion."[43] Thus, since the Japanese Christians also felt the effects of anti-Oriental sentiment, it can be stated that the basis for the prejudice was racial and only partly religious or cultural in origin.

A problem of religious differences between the Japanese and Caucasians occurred even in the 1960s. Situated in an agricultural community near the coast above Los Angeles County, which has a sizable Japanese American population, is a town with both a Nikkei Christian (Methodist) and a Buddhist church. The Methodist organization had a Japanese minister, a predominantly Japanese congregation, and a Japanese-dominated board of directors. A nearby Caucasian Methodist church approached the Japanese Methodist church with a proposal to merge the two churches for their mutual benefit. Part of the benefit involved selling the Japanese church building, making $45,000 available for the downpayment on a new structure. The agreement which was accepted included integration of the membership, combination of the boards of directors, and retention of the Japanese American minister in the combined church. The retention of the Japanese American minister, which later caused some concern, was the result of an informal agreement:

> It was an understanding that a Japanese minister would be employed at the merger church. The assumption was [for] forever, I think. Nothing was written on paper. Being a church, I think things were done in "good faith.". . . I think the Japanese never raised this issue [of who would be head minister] but accepted whatever the Caucasians said. There is an interesting followup on this when the confrontation occurred on the head minister position. It was not raised by the Japanese members. It was raised by the second Japanese minister (by second, I mean the one succeeding the first). He was quickly reassigned to a small church in Piru [California], largely a migrant labor community. There were no more ministers of Japanese extraction thereafter. (I suppose that Caucasians here didn't think a Japanese could service their needs.)[44]

A new church building was financed, with substantial monetary contributions from the Japanese and the Nikkei. After the structure was completed in 1963, for a number of years the social relations within the church continued without incident. H. Kajihara explains the nature of the interaction: "I don't feel that there was any harmonious or disharmonious social relationship after the merger. You just went to church. You didn't have in-depth socialization which is common in all-Buddhist or all-Japanese membership church. In fact, the Japanese-Americans formed the Nisei Fellowship. To some Caucasians and Japanese this was strange, because the purpose of the merger was to integrate, so why have a segregated organization?"[45]

A series of events soon disturbed the existing relationship. The initial event was the transfer of the second Japanese American Methodist minister, which was followed by discussions as to his replacement. Although the initial church board had been composed of both Japanese and Caucasians, most decisions were now being made by the Caucasians because the Japanese were outnumbered (by twenty to three)—and apparently because the Japanese were reticent in making their position known. The Asian board members began to skip the board meetings. The general Japanese membership also declined to attend, although they generally never resisted openly, nor did they bring the disagreement into the open. Instead, person by person, they began to drop out of the church. The replacement minister was a Caucasian, and in time the board of directors also became a Caucasian-dominated group.

Subsequent board decisions had further effects on the Japanese and Nisei congregation. For example, the social hall had been reserved for some time, on one Saturday night per month, for meetings or social activities for the Japanese. Suddenly they found that that night was filled with social activities for the Caucasian Methodist Youth Fellowship. A *"shikataganai"* (literally, "cannot be helped") or stoical attitude prevailed among the Japanese Americans, and they expressed few words of protest. One Japanese American board member approached the bishop of the southern district with a plea to improve the situation—but to no avail. The

Caucasian church members made no direct attempts to change the deteriorating interracial relationship. The Japanese American congregation gave up and stopped participating in church activities; they perceived the situation as an attempt to give them second-class membership status and to drive them out of the church. Since the Caucasian group had originally introduced the idea of a merger, and since the Japanese had donated funds for the construction of the new structure, the Japanese were troubled. Nonetheless they meekly accepted the situation.

Many Nisei left the church and attended no other religious institution. Others left the church and started to participate in the activities of the nearby Buddhist temple; this group was especially interested in maintaining some institutional ties with a Japanese American religious organization. They apparently believed that the retention of ethnic ties was of paramount importance, since the Caucasians, as a group, had indicated the unacceptability of the Japanese Americans as full members of their religious institution. One member who came from the Methodist church stated: "I started to attend the Buddhist temple for the sake of my children. There, they could meet other Japanese Americans and meet other boys and girls with whom they could play and eventually date. And then I started to learn about Buddhism. It has really been a great help to me and my family."

Racial differences between the Caucasians and Nikkei have not occurred in many other instances, perhaps because the Japanese Americans have been able to retain control over all facets of church organizations, monies, and programs in other churches.

The Buddhist Sunday Schools

The Buddhist Sunday Schools are an important part of the NABM-BCA organization. Along with the Buddhist services, the Sunday Schools have been a strong factor in keeping Japanese American children within the Buddhist religion.

With the start of the Nisei births in the 1920s, the members and ministers of the NABM experienced a crisis that would remain a continuing problem. This crisis concerned the proper education of the Nisei to insure their adherence to Buddhism. The Buddhist Sunday School was thus created, "to make Buddhism an American religion by educating the children of the church members in the ideas and atmosphere of Buddhism; to insure a happy religious life for the individual and the family."[46] The continual problem of perpetuating Buddhism in America was long ago recognized by Ogura: "As the future of Buddhism in the United States depends almost entirely upon the second generation Japanese, the Sunday Schools fill an important position in the work of the Buddhist mission.[47]

Creating and sustaining this educational portion of the NABM was recognized as vitally important to the organization. The Sunday Schools, though, were not without precedent in Japan *prior* to their incorporation within the temples in America. Contrary to other researchers' writings on the BCA, the Buddhist Sunday Schools did not originate in the United States after the arrival of the Japanese immigrants.[48] The Sunday Schools, Young Men's Buddhist Associations, and other such institutions were already in Japan by the late nineteenth and early twentieth centuries. The reasons for the adoption of the Euro-American forms of religious propagation are instructive.

Even before the Jodo Shinshu Buddhist religion was established in America, Japan's Buddhist leaders had sent priests to Europe to study Western religions and their activities. Other Buddhist priests visited the United States to observe religious conditions there through the 1870s, as a result of which changes within the Japanese religious institution occurred.[49] After the Tokugawa era (1601–1868), the Meiji authorities attempted to suppress Buddhism and to make Shintoism the state religion. This move could have resulted in the "complete expulsion of Buddhism from Japan."[50] Aided by reports and observations about the West, the lord abbots of the Nishi and Higashi Hongwanji petitioned the Meiji authorities to allow the Japanese people the right to practice any religion they chose. This petition was accepted in 1876, and as a result the Jodo Shinshu sect, in particular, was able to reassert itself in Japanese national life. Freedom of worship, coupled with the insights brought back from Europe and America, helped revitalize and reorganize Buddhism in Japan.

The Jodo Shinshu Buddhists in Japan adopted certain European and American techniques of religious dissemination. Thus, in the late 1800s and early 1900s, not only the Sunday Schools, but also Buddhist women's societies, orphanages, and Buddhist homes for ex-convicts were instituted. During this phase of Japanese infatuation with Western ideas, some Buddhist sects inaugurated street preaching, "evangelical" campaigns, sermonizing, and hymnals along "Christian" lines.[51] The changes were made primarily to resolve problems that Buddhist organizations were having with the Meiji authorities. For one thing, the government then favored Occidental ideas and practices, and for another, the changes alleviated the problem of membership losses resulting from the apparent complacency of the Buddhist leaders during the Tokugawa era.

The Japanese model was resurrected in the United States with the birth of the Nisei, when the need for some form of educational institution became apparent. As Ogura states, "All the Sunday Schools are modeled after those of Japan, which are conducted by the Shin sect."[52] The first Sunday School in America was established in 1913 by the San Francisco headquarters.[53] The early teachers were the *kaikyoshi* and their wives; later, with more students attending the classes, YMBA and YWBA members were trained and assisted the priests in conducting classes. The various Sunday Schools from the early 1920s to the middle 1930s were affected by conditions at the member temples. The programs and quality of instruction varied according to the talents of resident ministers and interested lay leaders. Mrs. Kiyo Kyogoku gives her impression of the early Sunday Schools: "I was disappointed in the first Sunday School session I attended on my arrival [from Japan] forty years ago [1912]. It consisted of practicing a few secular songs and listening to fairy tales."[54] At that time, the lessons and tales were given in Japanese and were apparently copied from the Jodo Shinshu Sunday Schools of Japan.

For the Buddhist churches in America and for the Buddhists themselves, the designation of Sunday as the day to hold services has no religious significance. Sunday was chosen as a matter of convenience, since in the United States most individuals and families do not work on that day. However, at some churches, the term *Sunday School* is a misnomer. Localities where the members were predominantly agricultural workers often held their services on Saturdays. Sunday was a workday for these people, as they prepared farming produce for distribution to the urban markets for Monday sales.[55]

Aware of the possibility that the Buddhist Sunday Schools might be mistaken for Christian Sunday Schools, some Buddhist churches have changed the old designation to Dharma Schools.[56] Others have instituted monthly Saturday night family services[57] to encourage the children and their parents to attend services together. The Sunday Schools, like many other activities and programs in the Buddhist churches, are best understood as having arisen to meet the demands of the Buddhist members.

The Sunday School was the first organization under the NABM to be directly affected by transplantation to America. The Buddhist education of the Nisei was an immediate challenge to the Issei because the Nisei manifested the immediate influence of their new homeland. As K. Kyogoku states:

> *The strongest reason all of us tried to build up the Sunday School came from a remark my husband overheard at a non-religious function of leaders of the Japanese community. At the meeting, a non-Buddhist minister chanced to say, "Oh, Buddhism will quietly fade away." My husband asked, "Why do you think so?" He replied, "The Issei may be members of your church, but they're sending their children to our Sunday Schools." My husband made a survey right away and was awestruck at the discovery that what the minister said was true.*[58]

The Buddhist institution recognized this possibility in the 1920s with reference to the Nisei. The immediate problem concerned the appropriate method of education to counteract the loss of future members. The initial approach was to examine American religious educational techniques to ascertain those methods most suitable and adaptable for the NABM. One important source of information in the 1920s was a group of four ministers studying at the University of Southern California.[59] A few were majoring in religious education, and all helped the Southern California Buddhist churches on weekends, especially in developing the embryonic Sunday Schools.

Beginning in the middle 1930s, English became the primary means of communication within the Sunday Schools, although the *kaikyoshi* continued to give sermons to the children in Japanese. Sunday School lesson cards, initially printed in Japanese, were later modified for the English-speaking children. The cards, of varying sophistication based on an age-graded system, had religious pictures that the preschool children could color and paste into books. For the advanced children, religious stories were used for instruction and discussion.

An annual NABM summer workshop (*kaki koshukai*) was inaugurated in about 1924 to coordinate and train Sunday School teachers more systematically. The workshops, held throughout California until the outbreak of the war in 1941, were attended by YMBA and YWBA members. The YMWBA teachers were taught by a team of resident area ministers. After the war, the use of picture cards and the more centralized training centers resulted in the development of a BCA Sunday School Department to coordinate most aspects of the religious education of Buddhist children.

By 1959, the training of the young was regarded as important enough to warrant a Bureau of Buddhist Education (BBE). Created by the BCA in 1959, the BBE became an umbrella bureau supervising the Youth Department, Sales Department (e.g., bookstore), Audio-Visual Departments, Boy Scout Committee, and public programs. The Sunday School Department came under the Bureau in 1963; until that time, it had been supervised by the Ministerial Association. This responsibility had been vested in the ministers because the Sunday Schools were primarily viewed as places for religious services. As more sophisticated educational methods were introduced, there was an increasing need to centralize control of the Sunday Schools for more efficient dissemination of materials such as films. Thus, in 1963, a full-time minister-director position was created to oversee the program; this resulted in a cohesive and integrated educational system for preschool to college-aged students.

In interviews, many reverends and lay leaders indicated that the future of the Buddhist churches lies in the children. Despite this view, the Sunday Schools and Junior YBA are often given secondary consideration in the face of economic issues confronting individual temples. For example, the annual food bazaar at one small (198-member) southern California Buddhist church,[60] with a gross receipt of about $5,400 in 1974 and a net gain of about $3,000, is discussed at the board meetings for four months prior to the event, and in the last month before the bazaar is held it almost monopolizes the attention of the temple's leaders and members. The bazaar is important to the financial stability of the church; consequently, the Sunday School, with forty-eight students, is left solely to the Sunday School superintendent, the minister, and the teachers. The future members of the church are often given less consideration than present needs.

The problems of the smaller churches in sustaining an active Sunday School program are different from those of large churches. With fewer members, there are fewer volunteer-teachers, a smaller pool from which new teachers can be recruited, and fewer financial resources to subsidize new methods and techniques of presenting Buddhist materials. If the children are forced to attend Sunday Schools, the atmosphere will hardly be conducive to effective religious training. The first issue that must be resolved is the children's apparent disinclination to attend Sunday services; resolution of this problem will probably necessitate the closer attention of BCA leaders, member ministers, and interested family members. If, as the church leaders state, the future of the church depends upon these youngsters in the Sunday Schools, then the BCA as it is known today faces a bleak and uncertain prospect.

Notes

1. Befu, op. cit., p. 212.

2. The term *sociological death* was used to describe the process whereby blacks attempted to portray themselves as white. "For the negro to pass socially means sociological death and rebirth. It is extremely difficult, as one loses in the process his educational standing (if he has gone to a Negro school), intimate friends, family and work references." St. Clair Drake and Horace Cayton, *Black Metropolis* (New York: Harper and Row, 1945), p. 163.

3. Kazuo Kawai, "Three Roads and None Easy: An American Born Japanese Looks at Life," *Survey Graphics* (May 1, 1926): 165.

4. The Buddhist swastika extends in a counterclockwise fashion 卐, while the symbol associated with Nazi Germany extends clockwise 卍.

5. Munekata, op. cit., p. 166. The swastika is noticeable on the older structures, either embedded within the structure (see Los Angeles Betsuin, constructed in 1925), on the front windows as in San Francisco (Munekata, p. 145), or as a design on the front wall as in Sacramento (Munekata, p. 151).

6. Maude W. Madden, *When the East Is in the West* (New York: Fleming H. Revell Co., 1923; reprint ed., San Francisco: R and E Research Associates, 1971), p. 120.

7. Ibid., p. 128.

8. Reverend Arthur Takemoto, "The War Years," in Munekata, op. cit., p. 61.

9. *Kinnara Newsletter*, Los Angeles, September 1972.

10. "Part of the loss the evacuees suffered during their detention in camps was in communal religious property. Of the twenty-eight temples in Los Angeles, twenty-two were damaged, some almost beyond repair; in Seattle the Navy took over the temple for its use." William Petersen, *Japanese Americans* (New York: Random House, 1971), p. 178.

11. From 1948 to 1971, eighty-five new priests entered the BCA. Of that number, twenty-one have subsequently withdrawn, leaving sixty-four priests still active. There were, in addition, nineteen priests in active service from before 1948. BCA, *Annual Report, 1970*, pp. 1–4; the figures do not reflect changes since 1970.

12. Manimai Ratanamani, op. cit., p. 86.

13. Japanese American Curriculum Project, *Japanese Americans: The Untold Story* (New York: Holt, Rinehart and Winston, 1971).

14. Ethnic Studies Committee, Asian American Alliance, Stanford University, "Critical Reviews of *Japanese Americans: The Untold Story*," mimeographed, March 1971, p. 1; also a letter written to the San Francisco Station (KQED) objecting to the telecast, signed by the bishop of the BCA, the president of the board of directors, and the chairman of the Ministerial Research Committee, dated October 5, 1970, in the personal possession of the author.

15. Ethnic Studies Committee, op. cit., "Documentary Appendices," p. 10. Critiques by the other organizations did not always focus on religious bias, but on the pro-Japanese, anti-Chinese, Anglo-conformity, "model-minority" perspective.

16. Mimeographed letter dated October 6, 1970, in possession of the author.

17. "State Textbook Body Hears Buddhist Viewpoint Concerning 'Divine Creation,'" San Francisco *Hokubei Mainichi*, November 14, 1972, p. 1.

18. Ibid.

19. "Young Buddhists Pass Anti-War Resolution," Los Angeles *Kashu Mainichi*, May 25, 1971, p. 1.

20. The Reverend La Verne Senyo Sasaki, "Buddhism and Social Activism," a lecture presented at the Western Young Buddhist League Conference, March 31, 1973, Los Angeles.

21. "JARF Gets Federal Approval for Apartment Construction," San Francisco *Hokubei Mainichi*, December 2, 1972. The Parlier Buddhist Church has also started a housing project for low-income persons.

22. The other participating churches are: Christ Episcopal Mission, San Francisco Independent Church, Konko Church, Nichiren Church. St. Xavier Mission, Zen Sokoji Mission, Seventh Day Adventist Church, Pine United Methodist Church, and Christ United Presbyterian Church.

23. "New Era of American Buddhism with Youth in Focus Emphasized," San Francisco *Hokubei Mainichi*, February 29, 1972, p. 1.

24. See Amy Tachiki, et al., *Roots: An Asian American Reader* (Los Angeles: UCLA Asian American Studies Center, 1971); and Joe R. Feagan and Nancy Fujitaki, "On the Assimilation of Japanese Americans," *Amerasia Journal* 1, no. 4 (February 1972): 13–31.

25. Marcus Lee Hansen, "The Third Generation in America," *Commentary* 14 (November 1952).

26. Yuki Yanagita, "Familial, Occupational, and Social Characteristics of Three Generations of Japanese Americans," Master's thesis, University of Southern California, Los Angeles, June 1968, pp. 35–37. "On the other hand, among the Sansei generation the percentage of Buddhists has increased, and the percentage of Protestants has decreased."

27. Most conferences on the ministerial and affiliated Buddhist organizational levels have included topics on the problem of the Sansei. Author's personal observation from 1970 to 1974.

28. Personal interview with BCA ministers.

29. Interview with Reverend Masami Fujitani, Oxnard Buddhist Church, Calif., June 14, 1974.

30. Interview with the Reverend Seiko Okahashi, Santa Barbara, June 6, 1974. Reverend Okahashi was formerly with the Seattle Buddhist Church and is one of three active women ministers in the BCA. Yonsei refers to the fourth generation or great-grandchildren of the Issei; Gosei are the fifth-generation Japanese Americans.

31. Ibid.

32. Reverend Osamu Fujimoto, "Nembutsu," in BCA, *Shin Buddhist Handbook*, p. 118.

33. Personal interview with Reverend S. Sakow, Santa Barbara, December 4, 1973.

34. Reverend J. Yanagihara, sermon given at a Buddhist conference, October 21, 1973, Los Angeles.

35. One researcher is in error when he states, "We can conclude that Buddhism as an indigenous religion from Japan had no formal experience with performing weddings in Japan." Isao Horinouchi, "Americanized Buddhism:

A Sociological Analysis of a Protestantized Japanese Religion," Ph.D. dissertation, University of California, Davis, 1973, p. 164.

36. Personal interview with Reverends S. Sakow, December 4, 1973, Santa Barbara, and K. Terada, January 1, 1974, San Diego. Both Reverends Sakow and Terada had their marriage ceremonies performed in a Buddhist temple in Japan.

37. Interview with Reverend Terada.

38. Ibid.

39. Eidmann, *Young People's Introduction*, p. 40.

40. BCA., *Shin Buddhist Handbook*, pp. 125–136; and BCA, *Buddhism and Jodo Shinshu* (San Francisco, 1955), pp. 179–186.

41. Ibid., and Shoyu Hanayama, op. cit., pp. 12–29.

42. There have been a few non-Japanese members and ministers. The non-Asian membership has always been very small, however, usually limited to isolated but dedicated individuals and the spouses of Asian members. The non-Asian Buddhist priests have played an important role, especially in influencing the Nisei priests. Within the non-Japanese membership and ministerial group, Caucasians are most widely represented. There are few black, Chicano or native American Buddhists within the BCA, although at the 1972 BCA ministers' conference, three blacks did address the ministers, at least one of whom was singled out as a Buddhist. See "Black Buddhists Speak at BCA Ministers' Seminar," San Francisco *Hokubei Mainichi*, August 28, 1972, p. 1.

43. Forrest E. La Violette, *Americans of Japanese Ancestry: A Study of Assimilation in the American Community* (Toronto: Canadian Institute of International Affairs, 1945), p. 48.

44. Interview with Mr. and Mrs. Harry Kajihara, May 11, 1974; and personal correspondence, June 29, 1974. I am indebted to Mr. and Mrs. Kajihara for this example and for their observations about the Japanese American reactions to the situation.

45. Ibid.

46. Ogura, op. cit., p. 19.

47. Ibid.

48. Both Spencer and Horinouchi appear to be in historical error on this point. Spencer has stated, "As a means of maintaining a Nisei interest in Buddhism, the Sunday School was inaugurated. It is of interest to note that this concept spread back to Japan from America, the Buddhist Sunday Schools or its equivalent now having become part of the organizational program of the Shin sect there." Spencer, op. cit., p. 212.

    Horinouchi states that "Sunday schools were created like the Christian Sunday Schools" and credits a Hawaiian Buddhist adoption of the Christian educational format. Horinouchi, op. cit., p. 100.

49. Hideo Kishimoto, *Japanese Religion in the Meiji Era* (Tokyo: Obusha, 1956), p. 137.

50. Utsuki, op. cit., p. 34.

51. August K. Reischauer, *Studies in Japanese Buddhism* (New York: AMS Press, 1917, 1970), p. 154.

52. Ogura, op. cit., p. 19.

53. Chonen Terakawa (ed.), *Hokubei Kaikyo Enkakushi* [History of the North American Buddhist Mission], (San Francisco: North American Buddhist Mission Publication, 1936), p. 48.

54. Munekata, "BCA Sunday School Department," op. cit., p. 101. 55. Thus, prior to 1942 and after 1946, the Orange County Buddhist Church held its Sunday School on Saturdays, until the population changed from an agricultural occupational base to a suburban housing area in the late 1950s. Munekata, "Orange County Buddhist Church," op. cit., p. 44.

56. The term *Dharma School* is used, for instance, by the Southern Alameda Buddhist Church, Union City, Calif., and the Oxnard Buddhist Church, Oxnard, Calif.

57. Title used by the San Diego Buddhist Church.

58. Munekata, "BCA Sunday School Department," op. cit., p. 101.

59. Reverends Kenjo Kurokawa, Ryugyo Fujimoto, Nishi Utsuji, and Ryuchi Fujii. From Munekata, op. cit.

60. BCA census, 1972.

Glossary

TETSUDEN KASHIMA

J. = Japanese, P. = Pali, Skt. = Sanskrit.

ABA.   Adult Buddhist Association, an organization within the BCA.

Amida (Buddhism).   A division of Buddhism founded in Japan. Amida is a transliteration of the Sanskrit word *a-mita*, a shortened form for *a-mitabha* (infinite light) or *a-mitayus* (infinite life).

***Baishakunin* (J.).**   Marriage match maker or go-between.

Bankoku Bukkyo Taikai.   Literally: World Buddhist Conference.

BBA.   Buddhist Brotherhood of America.

BBE.   Bureau of Buddhist Education.

BCA.   Buddhist Churches of America. See *Hokubei Bukkyo Dan.*

BCCF.   Buddhist-Christian Clergy Fellowship.

***Beikoku Bukkyo Dan* (J.).**   Japanese translation of Buddhist Churches of America.

***Betsuin* (J.).**   Literally: Special temple. In America, this is an honorific designation given by the Hongwanji in Japan for an American Buddhist temple with a large congregation and administrative responsibilities for a cluster of dependent branch temples. The chief minister is called a *rimban.*

***Bhikshu (Bhikkhu)* (Skt.) (P.).**   An Indian word for a male Buddhist monk.

***Bhikshuni (Bhikkhuni)* (Skt.) (P.).**   An Indian word for a female Buddhist monk.

***Bodhisattva* (Skt.).**   A Buddha to be. One striving for enlightenment not only for oneself but for the aid of others.

***Bonsan* (J.).**   Literally: Mr. Temple. A colloquial Japanese term for a priest. Phonetic corruption from *Bo* (temple) and *San* (Mr., Mrs., etc.). Same as *Obosan.*

***Buddhadharma* (Skt.).**   Buddhism

Buddhist Mission of North America.   See *Hokubei Bukkyo Dan.*

***Bukkyo* (J.).**   Literally: Teachings of Buddha. A formal term for Buddhism.

***Bukkyokai* (J.).**   A Buddhist temple or sangha (assembly). A term used by the Issei to designate a Buddhist temple or church.

***Bukkyo Kyudo Kai* (J.).**   Literally: Buddhist-searching-for-the-way association. A Buddhist study group.

***Bukkyo Seinen Kai* (J.).**   Young Men's Buddhist Association or YMBA.

***Bussei* (J.).**   An abbreviation of *Bukkyo Seinen Kai* or YMBA.

***Chokuzokujiin* (J.).**   Literally: Belonging-directly (mother) temple.

***Dana* (Skt.).**   Literally: Charity or offering.

***Dharma* (Skt.).**   The teaching, doctrines, or ultimate law of the Buddha. May apply to any religion, for example, *Khrishtiyadharma* (Christianity).

***Dojo* (J.).**   Literally: The place where the Way is cultivated. The term may refer to a religious or secular institution.

***Enryo* (J.).**   Undue restraint or reticence.

***Fuho* (J.).**   The simplest black robe worn by Jodo Shinshu priests while officiating in religious ceremonies. In Japan, *fuho* is often the usual daily attire for a priest.

***Fujinkai* (J.).**   Literally: Women's association.

***Fuku-rimban* (J.).**   Literally: Vice-rimban. See *Rimbun.*

Abridgement of "The Role of the Buddhist Church in the Ethnic Adjustment of the Japanese American", *Buddhism in America* by Tetsuden Kashima. Copyright © 1997 Greenwood Press. Reproduced with permission of Greenwood Publishing Group, Inc., Westport, CT.

Fukyoshi **(J.).** Literally: Gospel messenger. A Jodo Shinshu title given to a person passing the *kyoshi* rites and having two to five years of experience.

Gagaku **(J.).** Literally: Graceful music. Ancient Japanese court music derived from Chinese and Korean music and dance.

Gassho **(J.).** Literally: Join the palms. A Buddhist bow of respect.

Gathas **(Skt.).** Buddhist hymns.

Goingesan **(J.).** Literally: Resident priest at a temple.

Goinjusan **(J.).** Literally: Resident priest at a temple. Synonymous with *goingesan* but more frequently used in Japan.

Gomonshu **(J.).** Literally: School or denomination chief. It is usually translated as the lord or chief abbot in the BCA.

Gotan-E **(J.).** A religious service to honor the birth of Shinran Shonin, founder of Jodo Shinshu Buddhism. May 21.

Guntai Fukyoshi **(J.).** Naval or army chaplain. See *Fukyoshi*.

Hanamatsuri **(J.).** A religious service to honor the birth of the Buddha. April 8 is the accepted date among Japanese Mahayana Buddhists.

Higan-E **(J.).** A Buddhist religious service held on the spring and autumn equinox. March 21 and September 23.

Higashi Hongwanji **(J.).** Literally: The East School of the Original Vow of Amida Buddha. One sect of the Japanese Jodo Shinshu Buddhism. See also *Nishi Hongwanji*.

Hoji **(J.).** Memorial service or services.

Hokubei Bukkyo Dan **(J.).** North American Buddhist Mission. Original Japanese immigrants' term to designate their Japanese Jodo Shinshu Buddhist Institution in America. The name was changed to the Buddhist Churches of America (BCA), *Beikoku Bukkyo Dan*, in 1944.

Hompa Hongwanji **(J.).** See *Hongwanji-ha Hongwanji*.

Homyo Juyo **(J.).** Literally: Giving of a posthumous Buddhist name.

Hondo **(J.).** Literally: Main hall. The main worship hall of a temple or church.

Hongwanji **(J.).** Literally: Temple of the Original Vow. Applies to two subdivisions of Jodo Shinshu Buddhism. See *Hongwanji-ha Hongwanji*.

Hongwanji-ha Hongwanji **(J.).** Literally: School of the Temple of the Original Vow of Amida Buddha. One of the subdivisions of Jodo Shinshu Buddhism. The BCA is identified with this division. Often abbreviated as *Hompa Hongwanji* or *Nishi Hongwanji*.

Honzan **(J.).** Literally: Principal mountain. Translated as the headquarters of the *Hongwanji* found in Kyoto, Japan.

Ho-onko **(J.).** A religious ceremony to express gratitude; the memorial service for Shinran Shonin, founder of Jodo Shinshu Buddhism. January 16.

Howakai **(J.).** Literally: Sermon meeting. A Buddhist gathering to hear Buddhist sermons, often in homes rather than in a temple.

IBS. Institute of Buddhist Studies, Berkeley, California.

ICSC. Interreligious Council of Southern California.

Ippan-ji-in **(J.).** Literally: General temple. Part of the organizational structure of the *Hompa Hongwanji* and different from *Honzan* and *Betsuin*.

Issei **(J.).** Literally: First generation. Term for original immigrants from Japan to America. See also Nisei and Sansei.

JARF. Japanese American Religious Federation, San Francisco, California.

Jiin **(J.).** Literally: Temple.

Jodo (Buddhism) (J.). Literally: Pure Land. A sect of Japanese Amida Buddhism founded by Honen Shonin (1133–1212), teacher of Shinran Shonin.

Jodo-E **(J.).** Bodhi day. A religious service to commemorate the day that Shakamuni Buddha became enlightened. December 8 according to Mahayana Buddhists.

Jodo Shinshu (Buddhism) (J.). Literally: True Pure Land Sect. A sect of Japanese Amida Buddhism founded by Shinran Shonin (1173–1262). There are ten subsects in Japan; however, in America, the main division is between *Nishi* and *Higashi Hongwanji*. The *Nishi Hongwanji* is represented by the BCA.

Joya-E **(J.).** New Year's eve service. A religious service to close the present year. December 31.

Jugunso (J.).   Literally: Engaging in a military Buddhist mission. A Jodo Shinshu term for a missionary traveling with the armed forces.

Junirai (J.).   The Twelve Adorations. An important Jodo Shinshu gatha.

Jushoku (J.).   Literally: Resident office. Chief resident priest at a Jodo Shinshu Japanese temple.

Kaikyoshi (J.).   Literally: Open-teaching messenger. A Jodo Shinshu term for a priest completing the *kyoshi* course and qualified to work as an overseas missionary.

Kaki Koshukai (J.).   Literally: Summer seminar. An NABM summer workshop to train Dharma school teachers.

Kantoku (J.).   Literally: Supervisor or director. A title used by the NABM to designate its leader until 1918, when the title was changed to *socho*, or bishop.

Karuna Award.   A recognized Campfire Girls religious award for Buddhist youths. Karuna is translated as "kindness" or "compassion."

Kenjinkai (J.).   Literally: Prefectural associations.

Kibei (J.).   A person born in and returning to America after spending part or much of his or her early life in Japan.

Kieshiki (J.).   Literally: Taking-refuge ceremony. A Buddhist confirmation ceremony performed by the BCA bishop. Also called a Sarana Affirmation Ceremony.

Kikyoshiki (J.).   Literally: Taking-refuge-in ceremony. A Buddhist confirmation ceremony performed by the chief abbot of the Jodo Shinshu Nishi Hongwanji Buddhist sect.

Kinnara.   An incorporated nonprofit religious organization founded by BCA priests and followers but not formally within the BCA organization.

Koroma (J.).   Literally: Robe or clothing. Buddhist robe worn by priests.

Koshukai (J.).   Literally: Seminar. An NABM designation for a teacher's training program.

Kumi (J.).   Literally: Class or division. Same as *So*.

Kyokai (J.).   Literally: Teaching association. Also the place or temple.

Kyokaishi (J.).   Appelation for prison chaplain.

Kyoku (J.).   Literally: Parish. Similar to a diocese in the *Nishi Hongwanji* in Japan.

Kyoshi (J.).   Literally: Teacher. The level of Jodo Shinshu ordination above the *tokudo*. Qualified to give sermons. Roughly equivalent to monsignor in the Roman Catholic Church.

Mahayana (Buddhism) (Skt. and P.).   The Great Vehicle. One of the two major divisions of Buddhism, found in Northern Asia.

Makura-gyo (J.).   Literally: Pillow sutra or chant. A religious service for the deceased performed just after death.

Mikado (J.).   Emperor.

Monshu (J.).   Literally: Gate master. Abbreviation of *gomonshu*.

NABM.   North American Buddhist Mission or Buddhist Mission of North America. See *Hokubei Bukkyo Dan*.

Namu Amida Butsu (J.).   Literally: Homage to the Amida Buddha.

Nehan-E (J.).   Nirvana day. A religious service to memorialize the passing away of Shakamuni Buddha. February 15.

Nembutsu (J.).   Literally: Thinking of Buddha. The recitation of the Amida Buddha. In Jodo Shinshu Buddhism, this is *Namu Amida Butsu*, or Homage to the Amida Buddha.

Nichiren (Buddhism) (J.).   A denomination of Buddhism in Japan founded by Nichiren (1222–1283).

Nikkei (J.).   Americans of Japanese ancestry. Synonymous with Japanese Americans.

Nirvana (Skt.).   Enlightenment, salvation, or emancipation.

Nisei (J.).   Literally: Second generation. Term for the children of the original immigrants from Japan. See Issei and Sansei.

Nishi Hongwanji (J.).   Literally: The West School of the Original Vow. of Amida Buddha. One sect of Jodo Shinshu Buddhism in Japan. Represented in America by the BCA.

North American Buddhist Mission.   See *Hokubei Bukkyo Dan*.

NYBA.   National Young Buddhist Association.

Obasan (J.).   Aunt or if *obasan*, then old woman.

Obon (J.).   A religious service and festival to memorialize those who have passed away. The formal term is *Ura-Bon-E*. July 15.

Obosan (J.).   A priest.

Ojoraisan (J.).   Literally: Praise for Rebirth. Hymns by Zendo.

Ojuzu (J.).   Religious rosary or beads.

Okusama (J.).   Literally: Madam. An informal honorific title used by Japanese or Japanese Americans to address the wife of a person with higher status, such as a minister or professor. Synonymous with *Okusan*.

Onaijin (J.).   Literally: Inside of the altar. The most sacred place within the temple.

Ondobo or *Ondogyo* (J.).   Literally: Fellow man or fellow traveler.

Oseibo (J.).   Literally: End of year. An informal term for a gift, "thank you" present, or recognition award.

Oshieru (J.).   To teach.

Oshoko or *Shoko* (J.).   Literally: Burning of incense. Offering of incense.

Otera (J.).   Literally: Temple.

Oterasan (J.).   Literally: A priest living at a temple.

Otsuya (J.).   Wake service.

Prefectures (J.).   A territorial division in Japan similar to a state in America.

RAB.   Revelant American Buddhist. One organization within the BCA.

Renraku (J.).   Literally: Liaison. Organization of NABM priests.

Renraku Bukkyo Dan (J.).   A term for an early NABM priest's association.

Rimban (J.).   Literally: Wheel-taking turn. Rotating temple keeper for the abbot in Japan. An honorific title bestowed by the BCA for a priest heading a *betsuin*.

Sake (J.).   Japanese rice wine.

San Butsu-ge (J.).   "The Praises of the Buddha." An important Jodo Shinshu Buddhist gatha in the larger *Sukhavati-vyuha* sutra.

Sangha (Skt.).   A Buddhist assembly or community or a brotherhood of Buddhists.

Sangha Award.   A recognized American Boy Scouts religious award for Buddhist youths.

Sanji (J.).   Literally: Counseling affairs office. Counselors of the NABM.

Sansankudo (J.).   Part of the Japanese wedding ceremony in which the nuptial couple sip Japanese rice wine in a prescribed manner (three sips, three times).

Sansei (J.).   Literally: Third generation. Term for the grandchildren of the original immigrants from Japan. See Issei and Nisei.

San Sei-ge (J.).   "The Three Sacred Vows." An important Jodo Shinshu gatha in the larger *Sukhavati-byuha* sutra.

Sarana Affirmation Ceremony. See *Kieshiki*.

Senbei (J.).   Japanese cookies.

Sensei (J.).   Teacher.

Shashinkekkon (J.).   Literally: Picture marriage. This term designates the picture-bride era from 1908 to about 1921.

Shikataganai (J.).   Literally: Cannot be done; otherwise translated as "cannot be helped."

Shingon (Buddhism) (J.).   A denomination of Japanese Buddhism founded by Kobo Daishi (744–835).

Shinjin (J.).   Literally: Believing mind. Usually translated as "faith."

Shomyo (J.).   Traditional Buddhist music or chanting.

Shotsuki hoyo (J.).   Literally: Right monthly memorial. Monthly memorial service for the deceased.

Shu-e (J.).   Legislative body of the *Nishi Hongwanji* in Japan. See *Shukai*.

Shugyo (J.).   Literally: Take action. Directors of the *Nishi Hongwanji* in Japan within the ecclesiastical headquarters. Appointed by the chief abbot.

Shuji (J.).   Literally: Take-office-affairs. Main secretary of the NABM.

Shukai (J.).   The present term for the legislative body of the *Nishi Hongwanji* in Japan. The former term was *Shu-e*.

So (J.).   Similar to a subparish or middle parish in the *Nishi Hongwanji* in Japan. Temples grouped under a particular administrative jurisdiction.

Soshiki (J.).   Literally: Funeral. A formal funeral ceremony.

Shoshin-ge (J.).   "The Hymn of Faith." An important Jodo Shinshu gatha.

Shusho-E (J.).   A religious service dedicated to the start of a new year, January 1.

Socho (J.).   Literally: Chancellor. Popularly translated as "bishop." A title used by the NABM to designate its leader after 1918.

Soryo (J.).   A priest or qualified minister in Jodo Shinshu Buddhism.

Sushi (J.).   Japanese rice flavored with various seasonings.

Sutra (Skt.).   Holy words, sermon, or discourse of the Buddha.

Tanomoshi **(J.).**   Rotating credit system.

Tendai (Buddhism) (J.).   A Buddhist denomination founded by Chih-i (538–597) in China and introduced to Japan by Dengyo Daishi (767–822).

Theravada (Buddhism) (Skt.).   The Doctrine of the Elders. One of the two major divisions of Buddhism. Found especially in Southern Asian countries and formerly called Hinayana Buddhism.

Tokudo **(J.).**   Literally: Reaching the other shore. Shortened form of *Tokudocho*. The initial level of Jodo Shinshu ordination in the priestly ranks of this branch of Buddhism. The term means to "receive one's enrollment in the book of the laws [priest's sangha]."

Wagesa **(J.).**   Literally: Ring Buddhist robe. A Jodo Shinshu religious lapel cloak which is placed around the neck. The term is a modified form of *kesa*.

YABL.   Young Adult Buddhist League.

YBA.   Young Buddhist Association.

YWBA.   Young Women's Buddhist Association.

Zaidan **(J.).**   Literally: Nonprofit treasury or finances group.

Zen (Buddhism) (J.).   A Buddhist denomination established in Japan in the thirteenth century after importation from China.

Ghosts

LYDIA YURI MINATOYA

It was in Okinawa where I first began to feel the presence of ghosts. Oh, maybe not *ghosts* per se, not the white diaphanous things that rise from graveyards in a Halloween's tale. But it was in Okinawa that I first began to believe in things I could not see.

Sometimes, in different places at different times, different spirits, different *moods* if you will, tugged insistently at my awareness. A sense of sorrow here, of gentleness there, of confusion, or tranquility, or vengeance would rise and assume a felt form and a known weight. It was not a scary thing. It was a familiar dimension of daily life.

I lived amidst ancient souls: of people and events, of storms and trees, of lost buttons and broken sewing needles. I would walk into a coral cave and find a wartime agony still cowering. I would enter an old wooden house and be warmed by the faithful glow of generations of household appliances. In Okinawa, the supernatural became a familiar presence, like a stout uncle dozing over the evening papers after a heavy meal.

Perhaps I am overly fanciful. I have been accused of owning a preindustrial mind. To me, it is a mysterious thing that bridges do not crumble atop their spindly legs of steel. To the mathematical formulations that undergird such structures, I grant only my grudging trust. It is far easier for me to believe that a gentle prayer, written and fastened to the branch of a tree, will find its way to heaven.

I am not a religious person. For my father, religion was a practical matter: a need to be educated more than a need to believe.

"Since you live in a Judeo-Christian society," he said when I was six years old, "you will need to understand the assumptions within that society."

"Yes, Daddy," said I.

My father studied the religious choices available to my sister and me. He made the selection of Judaism.

"The family is important to American Jews," I heard him tell my mother, "as is the tradition of education. These beliefs are shared by Japanese Americans."

But although there were advantages of cultural congruency, the deciding factor was practical.

"Besides," said Father as he shifted his gaze to Misa and me, "the Jewish Community Center has a pool. The girls will learn to swim."

When my father shared his decision with his Gentile colleagues, they dissuaded him; and eventually, my sister and I went to Methodist Sunday school. The church was within walking distance from our home.

I was disappointed. The AME Zion Church had been my choice. It too was close to where we lived; its back lot adjoining ours. If proximity was to be the test, surely it fit the bill.

I loved the AME Zion Church. Each Sunday the sounds of the gospel choir would wash across our yard. Rich, soaring voices knowing both joy and pain. Voices that could wrap each note in such transcendent faith, in such perfect reverence, that the purity touched me clear to the bone. "Through many dangers, toils and snares, I have already come. Tis grace that's brought me safe this far. And grace will lead me home." To me, it was the song of angels.

* * *

When I was in Japan and beginning to feel the nudging of things metaphysical, I asked Dr. Kinjo if I could attend his course on Japanese religion. Besides much scholarly reading, the course included field trips to Zen masters, ecstatic healers, and other ascetic beings. During these field trips, some in the class reported sightings of auras and waves of light shooting forth from holy fingertips. I saw nothing. It was fascinating, but I found no answers, no formal faith to embrace. Somehow, I was relieved.

Dr. Kinjo and I were interested in character: cross-cultural, national, individual. Distilling such an interest into a researchable topic was a long process of glorious grieving. It was an exultant, ongoing wake, in which all the ideas we could not pursue were lovingly examined before they were laid to rest.

Once, I dabbled with ideas of grandiose projects.

"Wouldn't it be interesting," I mused, "to gather people's stories? Maybe to videotape them as they recalled some key historical event that had shaped their lives? Collectively, it could illuminate the consequences of history."

"What do you mean?" Dr. Kinjo looked at me strangely.

"Well, for example, the American Wartime Relocation. The survivors are all aging. Soon their stories will be lost. Or, in Japan, what was the Battle of Okinawa like for real people? Most of us depersonalize history. We cannot learn its lessons because it does not seem to have occurred to real people, to people we can care about and suffer with . . ." I was swept away by the boldness of my vision.

"Perhaps that is one of the purposes of art," gently interrupted Dr. Kinjo, "to teach without exploiting."

"Exploiting?"

"A videotape? Of individual people? As they relive the horrors that they knew?"

I flushed.

"My father was an engineer in Taiwan," said Dr. Kinjo. "During the war, I did not live in Okinawa, but my wife did. The war is the only subject that is taboo in our marriage. Once, when our boys were in high school, they casually asked her what it was like. 'Tell us about the Battle of Okinawa, Mom,' they said. 'What was it like for you?' My wife grew still and remote. It is the only time I have ever seen her act with coolness toward her sons."

We sat in silence. Then, Dr. Kinjo spoke.

"My wife lost both her parents. Still in early elementary school, she took her brother and sister by their hands and walked through the battle. She walked and walked, toward the north, toward the mountains where she thought they might be safe."

Dr. Kinjo paused, then gently shook his head. "I cannot imagine what she saw."

When I lived in Boston, I did not like my job. Such a small disappointment, really, but the bitterness made me twisted and shorn. Like a tree that is hit by lightning, I darkened and shrank.

I am not a person of great or specific faith, but I thought of Mrs. Kinjo, of her transcendence and goodness and warmth; and somehow I understood. The lessons I had learned in the backyard of the AME Zion Church came home to me at last. Somewhere, there is a force called Grace.

Karma

LYDIA YURI MINATOYA

When I was in graduate school, the miniseries *Shogun* was aired on television. And for a while things Japanese became the national rage. For days, people arrived at work talking about the characters: the proud noble shogun, the brave beautiful interpreter, the handsome resourceful Englishman. But when the series was over, people felt betrayed. "What kind of ending was that?" they demanded of one another. "The lovers are parted. The woman dies. The man spends his life in futility. After we've invested all this time getting to know and care about them, what the hell kind of ending was that!"

That was what Asians call karma. What Turks call kismet. What we call fate. Often, it is not very satisfying.

Cultures make virtues out of necessities. Americans—immigrants from distant lands, fleeing the past, setting sail from the familiar, from the beloved—built a national ethos based on the future. Based on belief in the goodness of going it alone, on the need for an ultimate happy ending. But Nepalis live in a landlocked country. With mountain avalanches on one end and jungle tigers on the other. From poverty and sadness, they cannot sail away.

On Tuesdays, at Dakshinkali there are blood sacrifices to Kali, the mother goddess. Before dawn, families begin the climb through quiet forested hills, to a natural recess where rivers run between steep jagged mountains, to a place of extraordinary beauty. They carry an animal. Usually it is a chicken. If the family is wealthy enough or the prayer heartfelt enough, the sacrifice might be a goat. After the blood-letting, the carcasses are cleaned in the river. They will be cooked and eaten as a picnic or carried home to feed the family. By 10 A.M., the shallow river is pink. Women sell garlands of holy marigolds. Fallen petals mix with splattered blood forming a mosaic.

The Himalayas are called the abode of the gods and, in Nepal, their presence is potent. Here the sacred mingles with the mundane. But the Hindu gods do not end with lofty creator Brahma—who rides a swan and stays away from worldly affairs. Or with noble naughty Vishnu—whose duty is to preserve the world and whose incarnations include both Rama, the enduring husband, and Krishna, the inventive cowherd who once appeared to a group of girls in as many embodiments as there were women so that he could make love to each in the ways she most secretly desired. No, the Hindu gods also include the destroyer, Shiva, and the bloodthirsty mother, Kali. And in Nepal, it is they who are most revered.

A parking lot overlooks ancient Dakshinkali. It is for tourist minivans. In the thin air of 7,000 feet, skirting the endless line of worshippers and their animals to get to the important spot—the killing spot—feeling the crush of blossoms under your feet while watching one man deftly slash the throat of animal after animal: the colors and sounds and scents begin to hang heavily. Tourists largely come for this experience. It produces a giddiness, a near nausea that many find exhilarating.

It is not death that is being worshipped. Asians do not rejoice in destruction. They believe that life, no matter how joyous, includes pain and loss and sorrow. From endings come beginnings. From separation comes joining. From wrenching pain comes fulfilling pleasure. Think of childbirth and perhaps you will understand.

Beyond the killing spot, down by the banks of the pink river, the atmosphere is very different. Adults clean the carcasses. Children play by their sides. Faced with the quiet dignity of people matter of factly performing their weekly tasks, most tourists hurry past. If you stop and search the scene for too long, you begin to feel intrusive—like a voyeur. The boundaries between which group is engaging in barbaric rituals and which is not begin to blur uncomfortably. The children pause in their play to gaze at the tourists with wonder. Their eyes are rimmed with kohl. Some tourists take pictures; but the parents do not glance up. They know kohl will protect their children from the evil eye.

On Tuesdays, there is a children's pilgrimage to the parking lot of Dakshinkali. The pilgrims are not the kohl-eyed children of the worshippers. They are children with the copper hair of malnutrition. They pertly greet each person disembarking from each van. The cutest, the luckiest, the most tenacious may earn a few rupees, a stick of gum, a cigarette. A man is trying to evade three of these children. He plunges past me on his descent to the shrine. The birdlike children hop by his side. "Hullo, hullo," they chirp. They peer sideways up at him. "Hullo?" they inquire with hope.

The man does not look down at the children. The tension of remaining deliberately unmindful makes him clumsy. He takes the descent in long strides, each stride ending with a downward skid. Small avalanches of dust and stones radiate in his wake. A camera swings wildly from his neck and ricochets against his thorax. Thunk, thunk, thunk, thunk. The sound reminds me of a racing heart.

As the children try to meet his eyes, the man stares desperately ahead. It is painful to meet the gaze of a hungry child.

Then another man begins to lope easily down the trail. "Say," he calls, "what's the rush? We're on vacation!" It must be a friend, for the first man smiles in relief. With one hand, he stills the swinging camera; and in that moment an idea is formed.

Wordlessly, he transfers his camera to his friend. Slowly, he reaches into his coat pocket. Now the children and I are mesmerized. I am aware that it is strangely silent. Then, in a flash, something flicks from the pocket and is brandished in the air.

The man dances a few paces down the trail. Suddenly he is nimble. He holds the object aloft, posing like the Statue of Liberty with her torch. In a common instant, we all recognize it. It is a package of crackers. It is a waxed papered, half-eaten stack of Saltine crackers.

"Hullo!" The children are shrill. "Hullo, hullo!" They leap for the crackers. More children stampede down the trail. They rush the man. "Hullo, Hullo, Hullo!" Again and again, they leap for the crackers. The man laughs. Avoiding the eyes of the children, he beams into the eye of the camera.

"Click."

I think of Venice, of snapshots of feeding the pigeons in Piazza San Marco. The man drops the package and steps unnoticed from the scramble of children.

I board the van. I sit alone. I do not want to chat. Perhaps it is the altitude.

I am an American. I have no patience with fatalism, no regard for the gift of forbearance. Often Asia disconcerts me. She has lured me back. She has willed me into the investment of my time and caring. And again and again, she shows me scenes that I am powerless to change. I sit on the van and rail. What kind of ending is this? What the hell kind of ending is this?

Epilogue

LYDIA YURI MINATOYA

My uncle has spent years tracing the fate of his mother. As eldest son, it is he who travels again and again to Japan, who initiates family reunions, who has traced and located his long lost half-brother. In his seventies, his cancer in remission, my uncle travels to Japan to meet this half-brother. On his return, he flies to Albany. He arrives on my wedding day.

It has been two years since I returned to America. On this day I have married Robert Stone, the man with whom I taught in China and traveled in Nepal.

We have returned from the wedding luncheon and are sitting around the dining room table. The table is honey maple, Early American style. It looks odd against the Japanese shoji screens that separate dining from family room; but my parents are very proud. The table is a recent acquisition, purchased from a mail-order catalog. We sit at this new table, pouring over photographs of the mysterious brother.

"I have learned terrible secret," says my uncle to Okaa-chan. "Our mother tried to kill us."

Okaa-chan says nothing. She picks up a stack of travel snapshots and begins to shuffle them unseeingly.

"Forgive me," says my uncle, "Perhaps you would rather not know. You were only a toddler. Perhaps you have forgotten our mother."

Okaa-chan lays the photos aside. She gazes wistfully at the piles of my uncle's omiyage—specialties from here to take there—which are scattered across the table. Seaweed, forest mushrooms, tiny dried sardines. They smell sharp and salty, like a seaside memory. Strangely, she begins to sing.

"*Miyeko enkara ochite hana utsuna.*" Miyeko do not fall from the veranda, do not fall and bump your nose. She touches her nose and smiles. "Our mother used to sing this to me," she says, "a silly song, to commemorate some childhood mishap of mine. It was a game she played; the whole point was to kiss her baby's nose."

Okaa-chan absentmindedly fans herself with a cellophane bag of dried cuttlefish. "Oh, no," she says. "I have not forgotten."

"You never speak of her. You were close to our father. I was afraid I am asking for feelings you simply could not share," my uncle's voice cracks.

This is my beloved, gentle uncle—the tea master. A sentimental and contemplative man, he is mildly disappointed in himself. He lacks drive, rage, the sublime self-confidence of a samurai. It is his younger brother, Koji—the sword master, the No No Boy—who has inherited all the warrior bushido.

"Once, I recall awakening," muses Okaa-chan, "and I think the house is haunted. Through the cool tatami, echoing under polished wooden floors, comes the scent of incense and the sound of muffled sobbing."

"When Father demanded divorce," my uncle explains, "our mother went to the temple. She spent hours saying sutras. She was longing for some spiritual sign." He hesitates.

"Tell me," my mother's voice is calm and certain.

"On a night selected for auspiciousness," says my uncle, "Mother mixed rodent poisoning in a gruel of tea and rice. She could not bear separation from us and murder-suicide was considered an honorable act. She placed the gruel on the table and gathered us around her. A growing boy, Koji eagerly reached for the bowl."

My uncle pauses. He reaches for his tea. His elegant fingers cup the base. His eyes close. His face disappears behind the earthenware rim as he takes a long draft. I feel a twinge of fear.

"Perhaps the poisoning had a scent, perhaps a not natural aroma. A willful child, Koji thrust the bowl away. He made a face of disgust. In his roughness, the bowl overturned and the gruel spread across the table. Mother sprang up and rushed us from the room. It was as if the spill was fire."

"Do you remember this?" asks Okaa-chan.

"Perhaps a tremble in Mother's fingers, a muffled cry in her throat. Perhaps a confusing rush from an innocent spill in a familiar room. But no, I did not know she intended our deaths."

There is a silence. Misa and I hover like vapors, like forecastings, at the end of the table. We are the future; we are not part of this gathering of ghosts and elders. I look at Okaa-chan with curiosity. I picture her as a little girl, in a summer kimono on an ordinary night. Her singing mother has carefully plotted her murder.

"Our half-brother says that Mother took it as a sign from Buddha," continues my uncle. "She saw the spill as divine intervention. Buddha told her to let us go. From that point on, she busied herself with preparations. She stopped weeping and started to plan for our futures."

We sit in stillness while, somewhere in the past, my grandmother packs her children's belongings.

"Our half-brother had a present for us," my uncle suddenly says. "Something that Mother wanted us to have."

He rises and goes to the guest bedroom. Once, it was Misa's teenaged home. Now, in the family room, Misa's children watch television. Her youngest, her daughter, sits on my sleeping father's lap. My husband sits by his side.

I finger my sleeve, stroking the rich wine-toned silk. I am wearing my mother's kimono. Long ago, it had been a coming-of-age gift from her father. All day, my mother and uncle have been staring at me. They have been seeing her younger self. This gives me pleasure, knowing that I have my mother's face.

I look into my green tea. A stem floats perpendicularly. The Japanese say that this is an omen of luck.

My uncle returns with a gift. "I had copies made for each of us," he explains. The gift is an aging photograph tucked into a silver frame.

Okaa-chan holds the frame in both hands. "Ahhhh," she says. She bows her head.

Misa and I move forward. We peer over her shoulder at the picture. My young kimono-clad grandmother is in a photographer's studio. Around her are her children. Her sons are soldierly in their school uniforms. Her eldest daughter, poised on the brink of womanhood, is astonishingly lovely. Her youngest, my mother, slouches forlorn and pouting.

It is the first time I have seen the photograph but I recognize it immediately. "It's that time, before the parting, when you caught your mother crying into her kimono sleeve!"

Okaa-chan nods her head. "*Saa neh,*" she murmurs. A tear slides down her cheek.

From the family room comes a roar of laughter. My father starts from his sleep. "What is it?" he cries, alarmed.

"It is us, Grandpa," reassures Misa's husband.

In the dining room Okaa-chan speaks. "Today is most joyous," she pronounces. "Today, I gain son and find half-brother."

She swallows and looks again at the photograph. "And here is *my* Okaa-chan," she proclaims almost fiercely, "come home to see it all!"

"*Neh, neh, honto neh,*" croons my uncle's wife. Yes, yes, truly yes. She scatters soothing little syllables across the table, like a benediction.

The Unknown Errors of Our Lives

CHITRA BANERJEE DIVAKARUNI

Ruchira is packing when she discovers the notebook in a dusty alcove of her apartment. It is sandwiched between a high school group photo in which she smiles tensely at the camera, her hair hacked short around her ears in a style that was popular that year, and a box of brittle letters, the sheets tinged with blue and smelling faintly of sweet betel nut, from her grandmother, who is now dead. For a moment she fingers the book's limp purple cover, its squished spiral binding, and wonders what's inside, it's been that long since she wrote in it. Then she remembers. Of course! It's her book of errors, from her midteens, a time she thinks back on now as her Earnest Period.

She imagines telling Biren about it. "I was a gawky girl with a mouth full of braces and a head full of ideas for self-improvement."

"And then?" he would ask.

"Then I turned twenty-six, and decided I was perfect just the way I was."

In response, Biren would laugh his silent laugh, which began at the upturned outer edges of his eyes and rippled through him like wind on water. He was the only person she knew who laughed like that, soundlessly, offering his whole body to the act. It made her heart feel like a popcorn popper where all the kernels have burst into neon yellow. She'd respond with a small smile, the kind she hoped made her appear alluring and secretive, but inside she'd be weak with gratitude that he found her so funny.

That, and the way he looked at her paintings. Because otherwise she doesn't think she could have agreed to marry him.

To think that none of this would have happened, that she wouldn't be sitting here this beautiful rainy morning, pale blue like jacarandas, packing, getting ready to move out of her Berkeley apartment into their newlywed condo in San Francisco in two weeks, if she hadn't mumbled an ungracious agreement when her mother said, "Why don't you meet him, Ru? Kamala Mashi writes so highly of him. Meet him once and see how you like each other." Ruchira shudders when she realizes how close she had come to saying No, she wasn't interested, she'd rather use the time to go to Lashay's and get her hair done. Just because Aunt Kamala had written, *Not only is the boy just two years older than our Ruchira and handsome looking, 173 centimeters tall, and holds a fast-rising job in the renowned Charles Schwab financial company, he is also a nephew of the Boses of Tullygunge—you recall them, a fine, upright family—and to top it all he has intelligently decided to follow our time-tested traditions in his search for a bride.* It would have been the worst error of her life, and she wouldn't even have known it. It saddens her to think of all the errors people make (she has been musing over such things lately)—the unknown errors of their lives, the ones they can never put down in a book and are therefore doomed to repeat.

But she had shown up at the Café Trieste, sullen in old blue jeans and a severe ponytail that yanked her eyebrows into a skeptic arch, and met Biren, and been charmed.

"It's because you were so wary, even more than me," she told him later. "You'd been reading—wasn't it one of those depressingly high-minded Russians?"

"Dostoyevsky. Brought along for the precise purpose of impressing you."

"And for the first fifteen minutes of our conversation, you kept your finger in the book, marking your place, as though you couldn't wait to get back to it."

"You mean it wasn't my suave Johnny Depp looks that got you? I'm disappointed."

"Dream on," she said, and gave him a little push. Actually, she'd been rather taken by the stud he wore in his ear. Its small, beckoning glint in the smoke-fogged café had made him seem foreign and dangerous, set him apart from the Indian men she knew, at least the ones who would have agreed to meet a daughter-of-a-friend-of-a-distant-relative for late-afternoon coffee with matrimony in mind. But most of all she liked that he admitted up front to feeling sheepish, sitting like this in a café after having declared, for all those arrogant years (just as she had), that *he'd* never have anything to do with an arranged marriage.

"But the alternative—it doesn't seem to work that well, does it?" he would say later, shrugging, and she'd agree, thinking back on all the boys she had dated in college, Indian boys and white boys and black boys and even, once, a young man from Bolivia with green eyes. At a certain point they had all wanted something from her, she didn't know what it was exactly, only that she hadn't been willing—or able—to give it. It wasn't just the sex, though that too she'd shied away from. What throwback gene was it that stopped her, a girl born in America? What cautionary spore released by her grandmother over her cradle when Ruchira's parents took her to India? Sooner or later, the boyfriends fell away. She saw them as though through the wrong end of a telescope, their faces urgent or surly, mouthing words she could no longer hear.

Thumbing through her book of errors, Ruchira thinks this must be one of life's most Machiavellian revenges: one day you look back at your teenage self and realize exactly how excruciatingly clueless you were, more so even than you had thought your parents to be. And pompous to boot. Here, for example, is the quotation she'd copied out in her tight, painstaking handwriting: *An unexamined life is not worth living.* As if a fourteen-year-old had any idea of what an examined life was. The notion of tracking errors possesses some merit, except that *her* errors were so puerile, so everygirl. The time she told Marta that she thought Kevin was cute, only to have that information relayed back to her, with crude anatomical elaborations, from the walls of the girls' bathroom. The time she drank too many rum-and-cokes at Susie's party and threw up on the living room carpet. The time she believed Dr. Vikram, who wore maroon suspenders and gave her a summer job in his dental office, to be so cool—and then he made a groping pass at her.

She tosses the purple notebook onto the growing pile of things to be recycled. (Recycling mistakes, now that's a thought!) She's come to terms with misjudgments and slippages, she's resigned to the fact that they'll always be a part of her life. If there are errorless people in the world, she doesn't want to know them. She's certain they'll be eminently disagreeable. That's something else she likes about Biren—all the mistakes he has already admitted to. How he dropped out of college for a semester during his freshman year to play electric guitar with a band aptly named The Disasters. How late one night, coming back to the city from Sausalito, he gave a ride to a hitchhiker of indeterminate sex only to have him/her try to throw him/herself from the car and off the Golden Gate bridge. How, for a short time last year, he got involved with a woman who had a knife tattooed on her chest, even though he knew she did drugs.

Ruchira was shocked and enthralled. She wasn't sure why he was telling her all this. To impress her? To start clean? To gain her (or was it his own) forgiveness? Small disquiets nipped at the edge of her mind like minnows; she let them slip away. Questions filled her mouth. What had he lost by jilting Tina Turner for Standard and Poor? What had he said to the hitchhiker to stop her—Ruchira was sure it was a woman—from jumping? (He *had* tried to stop her, hadn't he?) What made him break up, finally, with the knife-woman?

She pushed the questions into a corner of her cheek like hard candy, saving them for later. Meanwhile, he was the most exciting man she knew. His was a geography of suicide bridges and tattoo parlors, night concert alleys and skyscrapers rising into the sky like blocks of black ice. A galaxy far, far away from the blandness of auto-malls and AMC cinemas which she'd never really escaped, not even by moving from her parents' suburban house to Berkeley. But now conjugality would confer that same excitement on her.

He saw the paintings when he came to pick her up for a concert. They'd discovered a common interest in classical Indian music, and Chaurasia was playing at the Zellerbach. She had not intended for him to come up to the apartment—she felt she didn't know him well enough. She was going to meet him downstairs when he rang the buzzer. But one of the other tenants must have let him in because here he was, knocking on her door. For a panicked moment she thought of not opening it, pretending she wasn't there, calling him later with a fabricated disaster.

He was severely suave in a jacket with a European cut and, although the sun had set already, dark glasses in which she could see herself, convex and bulbous-headed. She felt mortified. Behind her, she knew, paint rags were strewn across the floor. A cereal bowl left by the armchair, swollen flecks of bran drowning in bluish milk. A half-eaten packet of Cheetos on the counter. Jelly jars of turpentine with brushes soaking in them on the coffee table. The canvas she'd been working on (and which was totally wrong, she knew it already) was the only thing she'd managed to put away.

"Very nice," he said, lightly touching the sleeve of her short black cocktail dress. But already he was looking beyond her at the canvases hanging on the wall.

"You didn't tell me you paint," he said accusingly.

This was true. She had told him a lot of things about herself, but they were all carefully chosen to be shielding and secondary. Her work as events coordinator in an art gallery, which she liked because the people she met had such intense opinions, mostly about other people's art. Her favorite college class, "Myth and Literature" in junior year, which she had picked quite by chance because "Interpersonal Communication" was full. The trip she took two winters back to New Zealand to stay for a few nights in a Maori village—only to discover that it had water beds in the more expensive rooms and a Jacuzzi strategically positioned among the lava rocks. She felt bad now about her duplicity, her reluctance to give of herself, that old spiral with her boyfriends starting again.

He'd moved close to the wall and was standing very still. It took her a moment to figure out that he was examining her brushstrokes. (But only artists did that. Was he a closet artist, too?) Finally he moved back and let out a long, incredulous breath, and it struck her that she had been holding hers as well. "Tell me about your work," he said.

This was hard. She had started painting two years ago, and had never talked to anyone about it. Even her parents didn't know. When they came for dinner, she removed the canvases from the wall and hid them in her closet. She sprayed the room with Eucalyptus Mist and lit incense sticks so they wouldn't smell the turpentine. The act of painting was the first really risky thing she had done in her life. Being at the gallery, she knew how different her work was from everything in there, or in the glossy art journals. Her technique was crude—she hadn't taken classes and didn't intend to. She would probably never amount to much. Still, she came back from work every evening and painted furiously. She worked late into the night, light-headed with the effort to remember. She stopped inviting people over. She made excuses when her friends wanted her to go out. She had to force herself to return their calls, and often she didn't. She ruined canvas after canvas, slashed them in frustration and threw them into the Dumpster behind the building. She wept till she saw a blurry brightness, like sunspots, wherever she looked. Then, miraculously, she got better. Sometimes now, at 2.00 A.M., or 3:00, her back muscles tight and burning, a stillness would rise around her, warm and vaporous. Held within it, she would hear, word for word, the stories her grandmother used to tell.

Ruchira has seen her grandmother no more than a dozen times in her life, once every two or three years during summer vacation, when her parents visited India. She loves her more than she loves anyone else, more than her parents. She knows this to be unfair; they are good parents and have always done the best they can for her in their earnest, Quaker Oatmeal way. She had struggled through the Bengali alphabet, submitting to years of classes at that horrible weekend school run by bulge-eyed Mrs. Duttagupta, just so she would be able to read her grandmother's letters and reply to them without asking her parents to intervene. When a letter arrived from India, she slept with it for nights, a faint crackling under her pillow. When she had trouble making up her mind about something, she asked herself, What would Thakuma do? Ah, the flawed logic of loving! Surprisingly, it helped her, although she was continents and generations apart, in a world whose values must have been unimaginable to a woman who had been married at sixteen and widowed at twenty-four, and who had only left Calcutta once in her entire life for a pilgrimage to Badrinath with the members of her Geeta group.

Someday she plans to tell Biren all this.

When her grandmother died two summers back of a heart attack, Ruchira spent an entire week in bed. She refused to go to India for the funeral, though maybe she should have, because she dreamed over and over what she had thought she couldn't bear to look at. The hard orange thrust of the flames of the cremation pyre, the hair going first, in a short, manic burst of light, the skin warping like wood, the eyeballs melting, her grandmother's face blackening and collapsing in on itself with terrible finality. It didn't help that her parents told her that the event, which occurred in a modern crematorium rather than the traditional burning ghats, was quick and sanitary and invisible.

She started the paintings soon after that.

"It's a series." Ruchira stammered now, speaking too fast. "Mythic images from Indian legends. I've only managed to complete three so far. The first is Hanuman, the monkey god, carrying the magic herb that can bring you back to life—you know the story? When Lakshman was hurt in battle, and Hanuman plucked up an entire mountain because he wasn't sure which herb he was supposed to bring back . . . ?" She'd painted Hanuman in purples and blues and looped his tail in an elegant, gentlemanly manner over an arm. In his right hand he held a miniature mountain the way one might hold a box of chocolates when paying a visit.

She had given him a human face, her father's (unexpectedly, she'd turned out to be good at portraits), his expression of puzzled kindness. She remembered the ecstatic day when the idea had first swooped down on her like a taloned angel. Now the painting looked fanciful, garish. It made her blush.

"But it's brilliant. They're all brilliant," Biren said. "An amazing concept. I've never seen anything like it. This next one, isn't that the magic cow, what's her name, who possesses all the riches of the world—"

"Kama dhenu," she supplied shyly, delighted by his recognition. The cow in the painting reclined on a cloud, her chin resting on demure, folded forelegs. A shower of gold coins fanned out from her hooves, carpeting the earth below. Her white wings were as tidily pleated as a widow's sari. Around her head, words from old stories arched in a rainbow. *Long long ago. Beyond the fields of Tepantar. Once there was a poor brahmin who had a clever wife. And the snake carried a jewel on its head.* Her stubborn, alert face was that of Ruchira's grandmother.

By the time they got to the third painting, it was too late to go to the concert and Ruchira no longer stammered. With precise gestures she explained to Biren that the huge eagle creature was Jatayu, who died trying to save Sita from the evil ten-headed Ravana as he was abducting her. In Ruchira's painting Jatayu's feathers were saffron and white and green, the colors of the Indian flag. His face was that of her grandfather, whom she only knew from sepia photographs because he died long before she was born—in the Andaman prisons, where the British used to send freedom fighters. Her grandmother had told her the story. They had caught him making bombs, he'd been part of a conspiracy to assassinate Lord Minto, the hated governor-general. In Ruchira's painting, Ravana, pasty-faced and with a prominent overbite, was clearly British, and Jatayu had knocked off all his bowler hats with one giant swipe of his claw.

"I love it!" said Biren. "I just love it!"

They kissed their first kiss soon after that. He tasted of salted sunflower seeds (his secret weakness, she would learn later). His tongue was thin and pointy and intelligent. She doesn't remember leading him to the bedroom, only that they were there already, lying on the crumpled blue bed-cover, his fingers, her fingers, the small hollow inside his elbow and the vein pulsing in it. She thought she could see a faint radiation of heat where their skins touched. Did his hair smell of lemons? In her hurry she tore a loose button off his shirt. (Later they would laugh about that.) The back of his ear stud rasped her hand, raising a weal. He brought it to his mouth and licked it. The small mirrors embroidered into the bedcover pressed their cool disks against her bare back, then against his. His nipples were brown and hard as apple seeds in her mouth.

Then his hands were on hers, tight, stopping her as she tugged on his zipper.

"Don't. It isn't safe. I didn't expect this. I don't have anything with me. And I take it you don't either. . . ."

The blood rocked so hard in the hollows of her body, she feared she'd break open. He had to repeat himself before she could understand the words. She shook her head vaguely, not caring. She wouldn't let go. Her body, thwarted so long, had seized on wildness like a birthright. A part of her cried, *You're insane, girl.* She pushed her face against him, his chest hairs wiry against her tongue, until finally his hands were gone. She could feel fingers, their drowning grip on her hair. She heard him say something. The words were too close, out of focus. Later she would think they had started with *God.* As in *God I hope you know what you're doing.*

Just three days left before her wedding, and Ruchira thinks, Does anyone ever know what they're really doing? What the tightening of certain muscles and the letting go of others, the aspiration of certain vowels and the holding back of others, will lead to? What terrifying wonder, what injured joy? But she *had* known one thing that night, even before he asked her to marry him and she said yes. She'd known what this, the next and final painting in her Mythic Images series, would be.

She adds a last stroke of burnt sienna to the painting and stands back to examine it. It's her best one so far, and it's ready now, at least this phase of it. Just in time, because it's to be her surprise wedding gift to Biren. She thinks how she'll do it—steal into their new condo the evening before the wedding—she has the key already—and hang it in the foyer so that he will see it first thing when they enter together as husband and wife. Or maybe she'll hang it opposite their bed, so they can look at it after lovemaking, or in the morning, waking each other up. The tree with its multicolored jewel leaves, its branches filled with silky birds. It's the kalpa taru, the wish-fulfilling tree, and the birds are shalikhs, those bold, brown creatures she would find everywhere when she visited Calcutta, with their clever pin eyes and their strident cry. Her grandmother used to call them birds of memory. Ruchira had meant to ask her why but never got around to it. Now she doesn't want to ask anyone else. She has given the birds the faces of the people she loves most dearly. And Biren too—she borrowed one of his photo albums, secretly, for this purpose. She has put him and herself, feathers touching, at the very center of the tree. (Why not? It's her right as artist to be egoistic if she wants.) Below them she has left empty branches, lots of them, for the birds she will paint in. New friends, children. Is it sentimental to be thinking about grandchildren already? She'll fill every space, and more. Maybe she'll never be done.

Then Biren's knocking, and she lifts the easel into the closet and rushes to the door and opens it. But it's not him, of course not, it's the middle of the afternoon, he's at work. She really should be more careful and keep the chain on while she checks who's outside, though this person doesn't look particularly dangerous. It's a young woman—well, maybe not so young, once you take in the cracked lines at the corners of her eyes—very thin and very pregnant, with spiky blond hair and a pierced eyebrow, wearing a shapeless pink smock that looks borrowed and a studded black leather jacket that she can no longer button over her belly. There's a look on her face—determined? resigned? exhilarated? Ruchira gets ready to tell her that she has come to the wrong address. Then she sees it, above the smock's meandering neckline, against the too-pale freckled skin. Red and blue. A bruise, or a half-healed wound. No. It's the hilt of a tattooed knife.

Ruchira sits awkwardly at her kitchen table, knees pressed together, as though she were the visitor here, and stares at the knife-woman. She had realized, right away, that she shouldn't let her in. But she couldn't just shut the door in the face of a pregnant woman who looked like she was starving, could she? It was not, however, a totally altruistic act. Ruchira knows this, though she is unable to articulate what it is that she hopes to gain from Biren's ex-lover. Now she stares at the woman, who is sitting in a chair opposite her and crumbling, with self-possession, the muffin that Ruchira has given her into a small anthill. Ruchira tries to be angry with her for being here. But she feels like someone who drowned a long time ago. In the underwater world she inhabits, there are no emotions, only a slow, seaweedy drifting. She asks, "Why did you come?"

The woman looks up, and the light slip-slides over her hungry cheekbones. What is she hungry for? She's finished demolishing the muffin, but her fingers continue to twitch. Ruchira suspects scars under the leather, puckered fang marks in the dip inside the woman's elbow, the same place she loves to kiss on Biren's arm. Where she has chewed away the lipstick, the woman's lips are papery, like palest cherry blossom. Then she speaks, an unexpected dimple appears in her cheek, and Ruchira is shocked to discover she's beautiful. "My name's Arlene," she says.

Ruchira wants to ask how she knew about her and Biren, about this apartment. Did she see them on Telegraph Avenue, perhaps, late one night, returning from a movie at the Pacific Film Archives? Did she follow them back? Did she watch from the shadows as they kissed under a street-lamp, their hands inside each other's coats? Ruchira wants to ask if she loved him, too.

But she knows enough to wait—it's a game of silences they are playing—and after a while Arlene says, "It'll be born in a month, in February." She narrows her eyes and stares as though Ruchira were a minor fact she's memorizing for a future test, one she'd rather not take.

This time Ruchira loses the game because she can't bear not to know.

"Does he know about the baby?"

"Yes."

Ruchira holds this new, trembling knowledge like a too-heavy blob of paint at the end of a brush, threatening to ruin the entire painting unless she finds the right spot to apply it.

"He gave me the money for an abortion. But I didn't."

Ruchira closes her eyes. The insides of her eyelids are like torn brown silk, like hundreds of birds taking flight at a killing sound. When she opens them, Arlene lifts her shoulders in a shrug. The knife hilt moves up and down over the bumpy bones of her thin chest. The blade is curved in the shape of a Nepali kukri. Ruchira wonders how much it hurt to get the tattoo done, and how the tattooer knew about Nepali knives, and if Arlene ever looked in the mirror and thought of it as a mistake.

"He doesn't know I kept it," Arlene says. She grins suddenly, for the first time, with gamine charm, a kid who's just won at kickball. There's a small, neat gap between her front teeth. A famous poet—who was it?— had proclaimed gap-toothed women to be sexy. Why is it that Ruchira can never remember crucial information when she needs to?

Arlene stands up with a decisive scrape of her chair.

"Wait," Ruchira cries. "Where do you live? Do you have health insurance? Do you need money?" She reaches for her purse and digs frantically in it, coming up with all the bills she can find, ones and fives and a twenty, and extends them to Arlene.

"I'm going to Arizona," says Arlene. She doesn't offer further details. She doesn't stretch out her hand for the money. She does a little pirouette (was she a dancer, before?) and from the door she calls out, "Think of me in February, in Arizona."

The first thing Ruchira does after she is sure Arlene is gone is to run down the stairs to the garbage area. There it is, next to the Dumpster: the blue recycling bin with its triangle of arrows. In her mind she's seeing the garbage bag, white, with a red tie, that she upended over it—was it just two days back?—freeing a tumble of papers and books. In her mind she's already dug past the discards of other people's lives—term papers and love letters and overdue bills—to grab it. She's opened its purple cover and has started writing, she isn't done writing even when her hand begins to cramp up, she fills her book of errors all the way to the back cover and has more to put down, that's how much she's learned in this one hour.

But the bin is empty.

Ruchira leans into the wall, pressing her forehead against the fake stucco. It smells of sour milk and diapers, and its bumps leave indentations on her skin. Behind her she hears footsteps approach.

"Arlene," she calls, turning wildly, as though hoping for instructions. But it is a different woman, one of Ruchira's neighbors, who looks vaguely alarmed. She carries a Hefty bag in one hand and holds on to a little boy with the other.

"Mommy," the boy asks, "what's wrong with the lady?"

It's very late now, and Ruchira has packed everything, even the bedsheets, even the pillow. She lies down on the bare mattress and watches the shadows on the wall. She's chilled, but inside her brain it feels hot and spongy. *What would you do, Thakuma?* Inside her brain, her grandmother says, Why do you ask me? Can you live your life the way I lived mine? She speaks with some asperity. Or maybe it's sorrow she feels for the confused world her granddaughter has inherited. Ruchira recalls a prayer her grandmother used to chant in the mornings after her bath, in her raspy, sugarcane voice, as she waved a stick of incense in front of the brightly colored pictures on her altar. *Forgive us, O Lord Shiva, all our errors, both the known and the unknown.* It had seemed impossible to Ruchira that her grandmother could commit any errors. Now she knows better, but she is still unsure what those errors might have been. *Errors that took your life between their thumb and forefinger, Thakuma, and crumbled it like a muffin until you were alone, separated by oceans and deserts and a million skyscrapers from the people you loved, and then you were dead.* Ruchira wants to say the old prayer, but she has forgotten most of it. Does a fragmented prayer merit a fragmented forgiveness? On the wall the shadows move like sleepy birds. If there really were a kalpa taru, what would she wish for?

She had called Biren at home and got his answering machine. But how could you tell a machine, You lousy jerk, you son of a bitch, forget about the wedding? How could you explain to metal and plastic why you needed to grasp the promises a man had made to you and break them across the middle, snap-snap, like incense sticks?

At his work, his secretary informed her he was at a lunch meeting. Could she call back in an hour?

No, she could not. She rummaged through her phone book. Here it was, his cell phone number, written in his expansive, looped hand.

On this machine, his voice sounded huskier, sexy in a businesslike way. Against her will, she found herself listening as he asked people to leave a message at the tone. But the tone didn't come on just yet. Instead, the voice said, "And in case this is Ruchira, I want you to know I'm crazy about you."

There were three short, impatient beeps. She held the phone pressed to her ear until the machine disconnected her. He hadn't informed her about that voice mail greeting, which was a kind of public avowal of his love. He trusted that one day, at the right time, she would find out.

Was that trust enough to outweigh a lifetime of imagining, each time she kissed Biren, that Arlene's papery lips had bloomed there already? He had never pretended Ruchira was his first. How could she blame him for a past he had admitted to right at the start, just because it had come to her door wearing a pierced eyebrow, an implosive, elfish smile? And the baby, smooth and oval in its ivory sheath, its head pushing up against the echo of a knife. The error its father had paid to erase. She couldn't blame Biren tor that either. Could she?

She won't tell Biren about Arlene and the baby, Ruchira knows this as she watches the shadows detach themselves from her walls to flap their way across the ceiling. And she won't be sad for him. The baby, she means. A boy. She knows this inside herself as surely as though she were his mother. A boy—she whispers this to herself—named Arizona. There are many ways in the world to love. With luck he'll find one.

And with luck Ruchira will, too. But what is she thinking? She already loves Biren. Isn't that why all evening she has been folding and stuffing and tearing strips of tape and printing words on brown cartons in aggressive black ink? *Books: living room. China: dining alcove.* Their lives are already mixed, like past and future, promise and disappointment, linseed oil and turpentine. Like the small exhalations of birds on a wish-fulfilling tree. Maybe they can be separated, but she doesn't have the expertise for it, even if she wanted to. Marriage is a long, hobbled race, learning the other's gait as you go, and thanks to Arlene she has a head start.

The wind has dropped. On Ruchira's window sill the shadows lie stunned, as though they've been shot. She wonders if Biren and Arlene did drugs together. It wouldn't have been a needle, he was too fastidious for that. Maybe pills. Ecstasy? Dexedrin? It annoys her suddenly that she doesn't know enough about these things. *Clothes: master bedroom. Medicines: bathroom cabinet. Paints: studio.* Because Biren wants her to have a studio in their new condo, on the airy top floor with its view of Coit Tower, next to the balcony where they're planning to sit in the evenings and drink jasmine tea and talk. (But what will they talk about?) Until one day in February the wind will be like cherry blosssoms, and she'll take down the painting she hung in the foyer and go into the studio and add in a bird with a boy-face and spiky gold hair, with Biren's square chin and an unsuspected dimple. And if Biren asks about him . . . ? This is what Ruchira wants from the kalpa taru: that when Biren asks, she'll know how to ask him back.

Narrator 5: North Vietnamese Buddhist Nun

from *Hearts of Sorrow*

The first time I saw the Vietnamese nun, in the spring of 1982, she was performing a ceremony at her pagoda, located in a predominantly Hispanic neighborhood in a West Coast American city. The small lawn in front of the pagoda was festooned with brightly colored Buddhist flags; the exterior walls were covered with paintings and decorations, transforming what had once been a modest five-room house into a miniature island of Vietnamese culture. Throughout the day, the transformative image was perpetuated by the hollow, measured beats of the wooden bell; the drone of chanting; the super-sweet smell of burning incense; the subtle flavors of specially pre-pared rice cakes and other delicacies; and the kaleidoscope of dazzling yellow, green, and blue women's tunics, contrasted with the drab-colored suits of the men. Older women, wearing subdued browns, spoke to each other with animation; they smiled widely, revealing red-and-blackened betel-stained teeth.

Most striking of all was a slight, youthful-looking woman with a shaven head who wore a plain brown robe—the nun. Only later would I learn that she was over 50 years old. Somehow, through simplicity, she projected a commanding presence, at once both lively and dignified, personal yet distant, an individual with whom each follower could identify in his or her own way: the nun was a mother-figure for children, a coun-selor for troubled adults, a mentor for older women, a ritualist for those celebrating weddings or funerals, a spiritual master for those wishing to enter the monastic life, and a narrator for the anthropologist.

When we met, I told her of my project, and she said she would be happy to tell me about the Buddhist way and her own experiences as a nun in Vietnam and America (see also Freeman 1987). Our sessions began around seven in the evening, and lasted from three to five hours. One of my Vietnamese friends helped as an inter-preter, but also participated as a third discussant. While talking, we drank tea and occasionally ate oranges, persimmons, or other fruits and snacks donated to the pagoda. I taped the interviews and also wrote notes throughout the evening. On occasion, other persons stopped by to visit the pagoda or the nun. Often she would leave to attend to these persons, but sometimes they joined us and expressed their views of the Buddhist way.

The direction of the interviews was structured, yet flexible; interwoven with the details of her life story is the nun's own exposition of the principles of Buddhism, along with her interpretation of some of the formative events of contemporary Vietnamese history.

The interviews began in October 1982 and continued almost weekly until May 1983. After a three-month break, we met for the final time in September 1983. Earlier I had told her that for our final session I wanted her to discuss how her masters had influenced her life. I figured that this was an appropriate way to culminate our 64 hours of interviews. With vivid anecdotes, the nun described how her master both taught and lived the Buddhist way. Her greatest master was Dam Soan, whom she described as "successful in all respects." Then she concluded, "She was no less than others," a designation which I believe aptly fits the nun herself.

As we were parting, the nun said, "When we began this evening, I had no idea what I would say; not until I heard your questions did I know what to say; it just came out of my unconscious."

I replied, "My questions, too, came from the same source; I had no idea what to ask you until I heard you speak; then I just let it flow. If we do something in a natural way, it is much better."

She nodded, "Yes, much better."

The position of a nun in Vietnamese society is an ambivalent one. Parents often object to and try to dissuade a son or daughter who wishes to choose the monastic life, for it removes them from family ties and commit-ments. At the same time, Buddhist monks and nuns are given great respect for developing those very traits that enable them to disengage from ordinary society.

In many respects, the life story of the nun highlights the opposition between religious and secular spheres in Vietnamese society. The Buddhist monastic life chosen by the nun is aimed to prepare a person for a new mode of being, achievement of enlightenment. This reverses the principles and life-styles of ordinary, hierarchical, secular society. Ordinary social identities are removed. A monk or nun is known only by the religious names conferred upon them by their religious masters, and later by the names of the pagodas in which they temporarily reside. A novice is shorn of hair, given plain food and garments, and taught to devalue personal attachments. At the same time the novice is enjoined to be compassionate, knowledgeable, and involved for the betterment of other people, all of whom should be treated equally.

In this chapter, the nun describes how she was drawn to the monastic life at the age of five and how the simple lessons she learned while a child remained with her as the foundation of her faith.

I was born in 1932 in a village of about 400 people located in a province of North Vietnam. My father was a farmer and a seller of oriental medicines. My mother took care of my father, my elder sister, and myself.

My earliest memory is that of going to our village pagoda with my parents. I remember that I felt so comfortable there; the pagoda attracted me, I cannot explain why. I now realize that I was predestined for the pagoda. When I was five years old, I told my parents that I wanted to go and live in the pagoda. This was an unusual request from one who was so young, but they did not resent or resist my going there. They figured that I was too young to know what I was doing, and that I'd soon get tired of it. I never returned home again.

When I was young, my daily tasks at the pagoda, which housed six nuns, consisted of house chores such as sweeping and cleaning the house, watering the vegetables, and watching the water buffalo to keep it from eating the rice. At the evening service, I would listen to the nuns reciting the Buddhist prayers. In this way, when I was very young, I learned it by heart.

At the pagoda, we awakened around 4:30 or 5:00 A.M. After breakfast, most of us worked in the rice fields. During the dry season, we cultivated sweet potato and peanuts, while the master remained at the pagoda and cleaned it.

Between the ages of six and twelve, I attended school, where I learned Chinese characters with Vietnamese meanings. While at school, I played with other children, but I had no attachments to them. After school, I'd simply return to the pagoda to do my chores.

One day, when I was still very young, I came from school and found that lunch was unappetizing. A nun said to me, "I'll give you an additional dish; it's a very special one for the master."

I replied, "If I have the right to eat it, give it; if you are doing me a favor, don't." I didn't eat.

Three hours later, the nun took away the special food, saying, "You didn't want the food, so now go hungry." That night I went to bed without food.

That incident taught me a lesson that has stayed with me all my life. I had become angry at first because the nun hadn't served the special dish, then resentful when she brought it as a favor. It was an insignificant event, yet I attached too much importance to it. I failed to keep an even outlook, and the result was that I suffered for it. What I learned from this was never to be angry, nor disappointed; I use that lesson to teach others.

In 1944, when I was 12 years old, I moved with my master to another pagoda. For the next six years we were frequently on the move because of war. I saw the flooding of Hadong city in 1945, and the Japanese invasion of North Vietnam, when they dragged French soldiers through the streets to humiliate them.

But my most vivid memory of that time was the terrible starvation of the people. [See also Chapter 11.] I saw many people die in the villages. The Japanese were losing the war, so they didn't let people cultivate rice, and they threw the rice from storehouses in the river. People streamed into the cities looking for food, stealing whatever they could find, even taking it out of the hands of other people. Ravenous people overate and died of indigestion; the Japanese executed others for stealing, but many simply died of starvation.

When we traveled during these days of turmoil, I was afraid, but my master reassured me, "If something happens, accept fate, but not passively. If there is danger, we should try to escape."

After the defeat of the Japanese in 1945, the Viet Minh and the French fought for control of the country. Again for safety we had to move from one village to another. Finally in 1948, we walked to Hanoi, passing right through the Viet Minh into French-controlled territory. We settled in a large pagoda.

In those troubled days, my master taught me one important lesson. "If you can do something of benefit for others," she said, "try to do your best not only for yourself but for them. Don't be disappointed if you fail; don't be overjoyed if you are successful, for success or failure depends on many circumstances. You may succeed because you are lucky. If you fail, don't feel bad. The main thing is devotion. Failure or success is of no importance."

When I was ten years old, I received my religious name. My master conferred it on me when I participated in the first of three ceremonies that we call "Acceptance of Restraints." At the first or lowest level, we are received as novices. In the ceremony, we commit ourselves to sacrifice things, to follow the rules, to study the Buddha-teachings and canon every day, to wear Buddhist dress, to hold no property, to eat no meat but only vegetables, and to devote our lives for the benefit of others, with an attitude of disinterest, or rather, without self-interest. In other words, we develop less ties for self-attachment, but greater concern for others. For example, if I have a child, I must love it, but since I have no child, I can love my neighbor's child without attachment.

For the same reason, we don't eat meat. The Buddha-teaching is that of cause and effect. If we do harm to somebody, it causes harm to us; we are responsible for our own actions. If we eat meat, we have lost love for the animals. We should show love; the more we eat meat, the more we destroy our love.

So we are taught to consider the seat of love. Our expression has two parts. The first means to bring happiness to somebody other than yourself, while the second refers to the relief of suffering of somebody else. This is a Buddha-expression, the combination of both. If somebody drives me downtown, it makes me happy, since it saves me from walking, so that is happiness and the relief of suffering for the person who offers it.

Before I went through this first-stage ceremony, I was given formal preparation. I had to learn a prayer that I recited when washing my hands, "I use water to wash my hands. I pray for everybody to have clean hands and to understand the Buddha-teachings." When I washed my face, I uttered a different prayer, and so on.

Then I was subjected to a review and tests, not formal tests as in school, but observations through our normal routine. I had to learn the Buddhist canon and rules, but in addition, the master watched my behavior, and tested me to see how I would react. Once, she left a certain amount of money nearby when I was sweeping the floor. She wanted to see if I would keep it or return it, indicating that I was not attracted to desire. She watched to see if I took fruit from the trees in front of the pagoda. Sometimes she would create an incident such as accusing me of making a mistake and would observe my reaction. She also evaluated how I conversed with other people, in a normal way or with flattery to make them happy.

When my master decided I was ready, she announced, "My disciple deserves to be raised to a higher rank. I am responsible for her." The other nuns and monks didn't examine me directly, but they had observed my behavior. They had to approve me unanimously, or I would not be raised to a higher status.

The first-stage ceremony marked my official entrance into the Buddhist religious community. It was a big ceremony presided over by three senior monks.

At the age of 20, I went through the second-stage ceremony, which raised us to a new level. At this stage, monks had to observe 250 rules, while nuns had to follow 348 rules. [Editor's note: Some monks say that the required number of rules for nuns is 290.] Ten senior monks conducted this ceremony for some 15 to 20 other new nuns drawn from many pagodas. It was a big event attended by hundreds of people. The monks, dressed in saffron robes, conducted a ceremony, and the superior monk delivered a sermon on the meaning of the ceremony as well as the ten major rules we had to observe. The description of each rule was ten words long, and consisted of prohibitions such as not to lie, steal, or have lewd ideas. Then we made our vows.

After this ceremony, I was sent to a nun-training school in Hanoi. This was a more formal, detailed, and advanced training than I had received before. In my earlier training, I learned the everyday activities, such as cleaning rooms, prayer, washing hands, and all of the regular services, plus elementary reading and learning of the canon. But at the school we went more in detail, more in depth with the study and explanation of the canon. The first half of the day basically was for myself. I studied for my own improvement, knowledge, and personality. The second half of the day was devoted to economic activities for the self-support of the pagoda. These included handicrafts such as knitting sweaters, making mats, operating hand looms for cotton cloth, all sold to people, and working in the rice fields.

Each year, we also went into a period of retreat for three months. To hold a retreat, at least four nuns or monks agreed to attend. This was an even more intense period for religious activity, with an even stricter regimen than our ordinary routine. On the retreats, we slept only five and a half hours a night. Unlike our ordinary routine, we spent more time in study and prayer, less time in work. Particularly if we went to large pagodas for our retreats, we became involved in a much more intense experience for religion, for we came into contact with people who were much more advanced, and that inspired us to learn more.

From this training, I have learned to distinguish superstitions and obsessions from Buddha-nature. Dreams, for example, reflect our obsessions. If we want to have a car, we dream about that car. This has no significance. I don't believe in the interpretation of dreams. Similarly, a lot of people say that some days are good days, and others are bad, or unlucky. But according to the Buddha, all days are good days, for it depends on us. A lot of people follow the superstition of lucky or unlucky days. Others believe in those ideas which come from Taoism, not Buddhist teaching.

We are responsible for our own deeds; nobody can be responsible for our own deeds but ourselves. The Buddha cannot make us good or bad; he can advise or show us, but then it is our own choice. If a medical doctor gives you a prescription and you throw it away, how can the doctor cure the illness? The Buddha is like a guide; if he shows the way and you don't follow it, the fault is not his, but yours. He cannot make us good, but he can help us. He loves people equally, and gives all people the same opportunity to use, to apply his help. Then it is up to the person, female or male, to develop their Buddha-nature.

That is why in our Buddhist tradition, unlike that of the Catholics, a nun can fulfill all the responsibilities of a monk. I can offer any kind of service, worship, or teaching of the Buddha to people, anything that a monk can do, except for one thing. At the second level of the "Acceptance of Restraints" ceremony, a monk can give exams to other monks, but a nun requires the participation of a monk.

In order simply to preserve harmony, we have eight rules for the social behavior of nuns with monks. These are basically rules of respect and deference, and avoidance of conflict and criticisms of monks.

Feminists in the West have found the teachings of the Buddha easy to criticize, particularly that men should have some control over the behavior of women. But the feminist criticisms greatly misunderstand us. A nun should be restrained simply to avoid disruption. But likewise, the monk must treat the nun with respect. The eight rules are created to assure a harmonious relationship between monks and nuns. This does not mean that monks are superior to nuns. In religious activities, both are equal, just as they are equal in spirit, soul, and capability. [Editor's note: This is the nun's personal interpretation of the rules, even though many of them explicitly require nuns to defer to monks without any alteration or distortion of the regulations. (See Narada Maha Thera 1982: 166–167.)]

Buddhism Under Communism: 1975–1978

In the view of the Buddhist nun, the Communists proclaim that they allow religious freedom, while in fact they undermine it. She describes how the Communists denounced Buddhist monks, disrupted religious traditions, and constricted religious and social freedoms.

The Closing of the Orphanage

Fifteen days after the fall of Saigon, the Communists sent four people to visit the orphanage that I ran. First they asked me questions about my activities, the financial situation of the orphanage, and about all of the property belonging to the orphanage. They addressed me not with terms of respect, but as "Elder Sister," which was less respectful.

One month later, they sent five men to mix with the children and ask them questions: "Are you satisfied?" They tried to find if the children were unhappy with me, if I had anything to hide, if I had exploited them. They needed evidence to accuse me and evict me. Then the men made an inventory of all the items in the warehouse, and from that time took over control of the orphanage. They let me stay, but would not let me do anything. They kept the key; I became just an employee without any authority. I was not even allowed to speak with the children.

The Communists would not allow me to hold a ceremony on the anniversary of the death of the Buddha, nor to preach at gatherings. Twice they did let me invite a senior monk to give a talk. The first time was about three months after I was relieved of authority; the second was one week later. On a third occasion, the Communist with the key did not show up to unlock the pagoda. The monk and the audience waited outside for a half-hour, and then returned home.

The man with the key appeared long after. I asked him, "Where were you?"

He replied, "I was down over there."

I said, "This is Thursday, and the monk came. Why didn't you open the door?"

He did not respond.

When I complained to the Director of Social Services, who supervises all orphanages, he agreed to let a monk come and preach, provided that he submit his text in advance for approval, that those who attend leave their names and addresses, and other restrictions. People would be afraid to leave their names. It was impossible, so I canceled the talk.

This is typical of how the Communists treated us. They claimed that they respected religious freedom and that they did not forbid religion, but in hidden ways they disrupted and prevented religious gatherings and worship.

Soon after, the Communists separated the children according to age, and moved many of them out gradually to other orphanages in the countryside. They removed the food from our warehouse. Then they moved out the machinery for making bags and ampules. We had used these machines for earning income to make the orphanage economically self-sufficient. The Communists offered to hire me as an employee to continue to run the machines. I refused, saying that the government has few resources, and it should spend its money for others. My actual reason was that I did not want to be ensnared in their trap, under their control, and subject to their orders. I wanted to remain free.

"Narrator Five: North Vietnamese Buddhist Nun: Buddhism Under Communism: 1975–1978", *Hearts of Sorrow: Vietnamese-American Lives* by James M. Freeman. Copyright © 1993 by the Board of Trustees of the Leland Stanford Jr. University. All rights reserved. Used with permission of Stanford University Press, www.sup.org.

Monks Denounced

One day I was told to attend a ward meeting. When I arrived, a Communist official handed me a piece of paper and said, "We brought you here to denounce the six senior monks we have arrested. Write your opinions!" He did not address me by my title as a Buddhist nun, but in a more familiar, less respectful way.

I hesitated, but a monk near me wrote, "Buddhist monks contribute to the well-being of society."

After reading it, the Communist official said, "No! Write it to accuse the *traitors* who have been arrested!"

The monk wrote another general statement. "Be calm. The government will only punish those who commit crimes and reward those who meet government goals." This monk wouldn't betray his teacher, who was one of the six arrested monks.

Then the Communists brought in their agents who claimed to represent various groups: a woman's association, Catholics, and a Buddhist association. One after another they stood up and said, "Those monks are traitors. They have plotted revolution against the government. Punish them!"

For their third and final step, the Communists handed around a people's petition, prepared in advance, which enumerated all types of wrongdoing the accused traitors were said to have made. Then the officials asked, "Do all the people agree?" Everybody at the meeting automatically raised their hands. "Then sign the petition!"

My heart was beating wildly. I feared that the Communists would insist that the first and most important signature be that of the monk whom they had ordered to write the denunciation. If he signed first, he would betray not only Buddhism, but his own teacher, who was like his father. If he refused to sign, he would break up the meeting and himself be condemned. But the Communists asked an old man to sign first. He was said to represent senior citizens. Next, they asked a representative of veterans. The monk was placed tenth. This is how the petition received its signatures.

In this atmosphere, the Vietnamese Communists declare that they allow freedom of religion, while in fact they discourage it. They encourage sons to denounce fathers, students to accuse teachers, and novices to betray their monks. This is very difficult. If you press the trigger of a gun, at least you kill someone fast. But this other way is a slow death, much more terrible. After three years of living under Communist rule, I realized that they intended to destroy religion. It was then that I decided to escape.

The majority of those who escape do so not to improve their economic or material life but because life in their homeland has become unbearable. They spend a fortune to escape, even though life for most of them is not easier in America. They come here for freedom. They wanted to stay in Vietnam, to help rebuild the country after years of war, but they were not accepted.

Whenever people visited me, they complained about the Communist invasion of their privacy. They were especially upset that nobody could trust anybody, for Communist agents were everywhere in disguise. The agents would say something critical about the government, and if you agreed, they would report you. If they went to your home and saw you talking with another person, they would immediately separate you and ask you both to write on a piece of paper what topic you had discussed, and turn you in if your reports were in disagreement. So whenever we began a conversation, we first agreed on a fictitious subject that we would describe if we were forced to report it. If Communists suddenly appeared, we would switch to that topic. Parents dared not talk to their own children, for the next day the children might involuntarily reveal something to their friends at school. Even husbands and wives became wary of one another.

I had lost all freedom. I could not talk. I could not circulate freely. This was no life at all.

The Communist take-over of South Vietnam in 1975 and the consequent suppression of religious and personal freedoms prompted the nun to flee the country. Under Communism, although her activities were curtailed, her identity remained unchallenged. As a Buddhist nun who could attract followers, she was feared as a potential source of dissent. As a refugee, however, she found herself to be considered powerless and worthless. Her social role changed from respected teacher to displaced boat person.

In Vietnam, the nun's image of herself had been reinforced by prevailing cultural values and practices, and by the society of monks and nuns of which she was a part. While she faced uncertainty regarding her success in spiritual development, the general direction of her quest was clear. As a refugee, she and others faced serious threats to their identities. Their status, the social importance they had had in Vietnam, was denied by fellow refugees as well as by refugee-camp guards. Frequently she heard people say, "All people are equal here; everybody is out for himself." She rightly comments that this was the most trying time of her life, when uncertainty and the potential for disintegration were at their greatest.

Becoming a Refugee

We escaped at twilight on August 19, 1978, with perhaps 150 or 200 people in our small boat. We were so crowded that we were cramped. While I sat on a barrel of water, with my knees bunched up, the girl who accompanied me sat on the floor, with no place to stretch her legs.

As we pulled away from shore, I thought, "Destiny, I have no control over it; what will be will be."

That first night, everybody was very tense. We all worried that the Communist officials, whom we had bribed to let us escape, would now report us. Some people became seasick; others prayed that we would escape. Soon the children fell asleep, while the rest of us sat quietly. No one ate that night, but from time to time people drank water.

Throughout the next day, we remained obsessed with the fear of being caught before we reached international waters. Our minds were not free to think of anything else—except the children: they asked for oranges. People now ate, those who had brought food with them. The others were out of luck. I had not brought food, but the captain of the boat shared his provisions with me and the girl.

Because we slept crowded on the boat for several days, we soon recognized who was good and who was bad. We could not move around the boat, but we could turn around in one place. From time to time, high waves swept over the boat, drenching us if we were outside. Those on the inside were suffocating with insufficient air. People didn't know or care whether the person next to them lived or died. Maybe they were too tired, maybe they concentrated on their prayers, or had a lot of problems on their minds, but the way they sat conveyed the message "Don't bother me."

On the second day, the boat reached international waters; now we worried about not seeing any commercial boats that might pick us up. Since we had no nautical map or compass, we feared that we might be lost.

On the third day, the boat owner and captain told us that for the past day we had been going in the wrong direction, and he didn't know exactly where we were. Now we began to panic. People complained, "We're lost, the boat is lost!" Some people talked of the dreams they had had the night before. Particularly disturbing were the dreams about owls, and those in which one person got others to follow him. Both of these are signs of death. Night birds, especially the owl, are considered inauspicious and are greatly disliked by the Vietnamese people. If someone in a family is seriously ill and at midnight an owl sings, the family says that the person will die. We have an expression, "Wicked like the owl."

On the fourth day, some 30 or 40 ships passed us without stopping. Now we were really scared. Some people made large S.O.S. letters with cloth while others burned cloth to attract attention. Unlike the first day, the people were noisier now. They talked about the boats that passed us by, the fish they saw in the water, or the fact that we were lost and going in the wrong direction.

We felt that our situation was hopeless, that we would die. The passengers blamed the boat owner: "He did not know anything. We trusted him and he is incapable, and now we are lost. He took us to sea and dumped us." Others complained about the boats that passed us by: "They are inhuman." Most of these complaints were from women, but the men also spoke harshly: "I told the captain what to do, but he didn't listen, so look at us now." Whoever spoke tried to show that he was right and the others wrong.

Near the end of this day, a Thai fishing boat approached us. One of their people asked in English what had happened to us. Through an interpreter, our captain explained that we had lost our way. He asked that we be allowed to board their boat. The Thais offered some fuel, along with cigarettes and drinking water.

We took the 5-gallon containers of water. People stood around waiting to drink that water. There was only one cup. I stood next to the container and asked for the cup. A man gave it to a family who were his friends; then they gave it to other friends. Since I did not belong to any group, I was ignored. The container was emptied; then the next. Still, no one gave me water, but passed the cup to others.

In the meantime, after our captain pleaded with them, the Thais let two-thirds of our people transfer to their boat. Now began a mad scramble; those who understood the offer rushed over without consideration of women or children. Families were divided. I lost track of the girl who was traveling with me. It was everybody for himself. I ended up in the Thai boat, where we could circulate freely. The Thais provided food.

A woman of our group washed her handkerchief and put down her bar of soap. I picked it up and asked, "Could I use it?"

She replied angrily, "Why do you use my soap?" I put it down silently.

After another two days and a night, the Thai captain told us that we were close to Malaysia. He told us to return to our boat, and he showed us the direction to the shore. Early the next morning, we arrived, but we were immediately stopped by a patrol boat. We found that we were near Kuching, Borneo. The patrol guards searched us, then forced us to wait all day at the mouth of a river. During the search, my religious vestments and books were found, so people discovered I was a nun. Before that, they had not known; I had disguised myself as a layperson by wearing a wig and ordinary clothes.

That day, the children played, but everybody else became agitated. They talked a lot without making any sense. As they bumped against each other in the cramped quarters, they fell into irritable arguments, "Why did you touch me!" The children ran back and forth, making the boat tip; parents called to them to be quiet.

A Malaysian came by and gave us a message written by Vietnamese refugees in the nearby camp. It warned us that the Malaysians would tow our boat out to sea and send us away unless we destroyed the boat. The owner's brother made a big hole in the boat. When the owner started the engine, water rushed in and the boat collapsed. People jumped into the water, which was only about four feet deep, and waded to shore.

The authorities took us to a stable for cows, and we remained there for four days. The Red Cross provided rice and cooking utensils.

I felt humiliated because they put us in an abandoned stable along the river, a place for cows and animals. The officials were not hospitable. I felt rejected. This was the time of most suffering for me.

Life in a Refugee Camp

One morning, we were taken to a large barge and sent down the river on a journey that lasted about an hour. When we arrived at our destination, we were both surprised and discouraged. We had expected something better. We had left a country in which we had lived in brick houses; now we were put in makeshift huts of palmtree leaves and bamboo. We slept on the floor and in some cases in the open air. The next day, the Red Cross brought some tents.

We were desperate; we never imagined that we would live in such an unbelievable place, surrounded by barbed wire, prevented from leaving or entering by armed guards. Every four days they gave us rice, but it lasted us only three days. We had to adjust to this low ration. Sometimes we received canned fish and meat. I did not eat these, but for others these items were important. Not until four months later did the people of the camp receive fresh meat and vegetables, given twice a week. Probably they changed the contractor.

Once a week a medical doctor visited our small clinic, but for the most part we were not ill, outside of occasional headaches.

But we had to stay too long in one place with no exercise. Life was monotonous. We had nothing to do. We had the same food every day. We had no water for bathing, just for drinking, so we swam in the sea. A lot of people had scabies, and they were bothered a great deal by mosquitoes, since only a few people had mosquito nets. At first, two or three people would crawl under one net together. In order to maximize their use, people threw the nets over tables: one person would sleep on top, the other below. Later, more nets were given out, and as people left the camp, they gave their nets to others.

At first the Red Cross was involved in transmitting mail. After three months, when they refused to do it, the police took over this task, but they told us that for the purposes of control, we would be allowed to write letters only in English or Chinese, not Vietnamese. This was another humiliation for us, but even worse, we had a hard time sending out mail. Sometimes a few guards would take out the mail. In return for this, we hired them to buy things in the market, and we let them overcharge us and make a profit. We knew they were poor and needed the extra income.

I had carried a small address book with me from Vietnam. Immediately upon arriving in the camp, I wrote to the Catholic charity organization that I knew from the time I had lived in West Germany for five years. I told them that I needed a watch and a radio. They promptly sent me about $500. When I received it, I decided not to buy things, but save the money. I wrote also to a family in Washington, D.C., and asked them to forward a message to some monks in the United States. Within three weeks, the monks had sent me $200 and the offer to sponsor me and anyone else who sent them papers.

Before the money and letter arrived, people did not treat me well. I had brought no money with me from Vietnam. After arriving in the camp, I borrowed a small sum from a woman. Later, the girl who had accompanied me from Vietnam asked me for some fruit. I told her, "There is a very good lady who lent me a little money; ask her for a little more."

The woman spoke harshly to the girl, "This is the second time you want to borrow!"

Now that I had money in my hand and a sponsor who would help others, suddenly people came to me for help. The woman who had once refused to give me a piece of soap now was enthusiastic, warm, and friendly to me. Suddenly, too, everybody claimed to be Buddhists, as were their fathers. Whenever they had some vegetables or extra food, they gave it to me. The person who had refused me water and had completely ignored me now gave me warm and polite greetings. She often brought me gifts. "We just offer you," she would say, using respectful words.

When we had transferred to the Thai boat, people had looked down at me in a strange way and said, "Why should she get on the Thai boat? Why her? She should stay with her master." They thought that I was the servant of the boat owner. These same people now inquired about my health with a great show of interest, "Did you sleep well last night? How do you feel today?"

From the ordinary point of view, the behavior of those people was not good. But from the religious, the Buddhist point of view, what they did is normal. People just act or behave according to their interests, what they see as beneficial for themselves. People don't judge a person in their true value or depth, but judge just appearance. If a person is introduced to you as of low status, you may treat him as of less value than if you thought he were of higher status. Not long ago, I was a religious leader with high status in Vietnam, the director of an orphanage. Suddenly, I was brought down to earth, I had nothing. In good times, it is very easy to adjust with the situation; you can gradually move up or down. But when the move is sudden, it becomes very difficult.

In these circumstances, I had to struggle to show my real personality. In the refugee camp, everybody had lost their former positions and their constraints. The refugees said, "All people act alike. Everybody is the same. If you strip the uniform off a colonel and a private, they are the same." But I disagree. It depends on one's true personality. I am different in the quality of my person. I show care to people, all people. I do not run after power. Some people if hungry simply grab food. If you really care, even if you are hungry, you still look and give the food to a person weaker than you.

Experience has taught me a lesson that if someone is in need, we have to share with them. Times may change, but don't act nasty. Be nice, be helpful to everyone in all cases. According to the Buddha, charity should be done according to the following principle: ignore the giver, ignore the receiver, ignore the quality [value] of the gift. If you want to help me, just do it, but without attaching value to the gift.

Each day we would hear an announcement of people who would leave the camp. One day, the Red Cross announced my name as one who had been accepted for the United States. Perhaps if that had happened after only a couple of months in the camp, I would have been excited. But by the time it came, after I had been there for one year, I felt no excitement. I knew it would happen. I left the next day for a transit camp. After a few days for health screening, I boarded a plane for America. When I landed, I was met by the monk who had sponsored me. He took me back to his pagoda, where I remained for nine months.

They Tell Me Their Troubles: 1979–1984

Social, family, and religious patterns that were maintained in Vietnam are rapidly changing in the new American environment. The Buddhist nun's description of this provides insights into the dilemmas faced by Vietnamese people attempting to adjust. Though some Vietnamese Buddhist monks, faced with problems of survival in America, have abandoned their monastic activities, the nun has not. Her solution to this newest, most unpredictable, and most complex change in her life has been to provide a haven of Vietnamese culture where lonely refugees can retreat to rekindle old memories, maintain cultural traditions, and feel comfortable for a while before returning to the pressures of American life. The services provided by the nun are by no means traditional; they are themselves adjustments to a strange new environment. The nun's activities reflect her remarkable flexibility in adjustments that does not diminish her steadfast identity and commitment to seek what she calls "permanence, not the impermanence of this world."

Why Vietnamese Are Not at Ease

In February, around the Vietnamese New Year, the Vietnamese of a midwestern city invited me to visit them. I went there for four days and performed religious ceremonies for them. They had a pagoda, but no full-time religious person, so they were happy to have me there. Most of them had come to America in 1975, and most now had jobs at the automobile plant. At first they had encountered many difficulties in this foreign land, but through much effort they had overcome them. Now they had secure jobs, money, and the ability to provide material needs. Nevertheless, the people who were 30 years and older did not feel satisfied, they did not feel comfortable. They said that if they could return peacefully to their country, they would. Their children do not wish to go back, nor to learn Vietnamese, for they have no attachment, no memories of Vietnam as do the older people.

For the elders, life is unbearable because it is not the way life used to be. Here they just work every day without being "at ease." "In our country," they said, "when we return home from work, we have friends, neighbors, sentimentality, the family, the environment: we feel secure, we feel relaxed physically and emotionally. In Vietnam, you work, but you also can ask to take off a couple of days. If you do that in America, you will be fired. Here you have to work, have to eat, have to run; you must, you have no choice."

We Vietnamese have grown up and lived in a period of continuous war for over a century, ever since the French came to our country. I, too, was uprooted and forced to move many times because of war. That's why I and many others never had long-range plans. We lived day by day. One government after another rose and fell, with no continuity. Family life, too, was not consistent. First it was based on Buddhism, then on Confucianism; when the French arrived, we turned to the French, then the Japanese. When the Americans came, we learned American ways.

Despite all of this, we have an absence of pressure in Vietnam that you do not have here. In America, we are never free of pressure, never free of worrying. There is permanent pressure here because you don't feel "at ease." That's why you cannot enjoy life.

The concept of "at ease" does not mean not doing anything at all. You may work very hard day and night, but you enjoy working, you have an enjoyment of life, and a sense of security. So it means, "free of worry," or rather, we may still worry, but we feel relaxed. If someone tells you how to do something, makes you do it his way, then you do not feel "at ease," but when you do a task freely, when it is not another person's assignment, then it is "at ease." In that sense, the term means "comfortable," and that is what is lacking in America. People frequently say, "Life is not comfortable."

Now you can understand why people have left Vietnam after the Communists took over. What exists there now is not Vietnamese; it is a Russian import. It is inconceivable that "at ease" could exist when people control your life day and night, when your neighbors watch you, and your children spy on you, when you are controlled by the rationing of your food, by restrictions on your travel, and by prohibitions on what you are allowed to say. If we had felt "at ease" in Vietnam, we would not have passed through death as boat people to come here. We came to America not for material gain but for freedom.

We have another important belief, that of suffering. The Buddhists believe that you suffer if you do not have a cause or purpose. But if you believe, as do the Buddhists, that "nothing is permanent," that you are born, grow up, and die, then you see nothing abnormal when someone in your family dies, so why suffer? If something wrong happens, again there is no need to suffer if you believe in the Buddha-teaching of causality. If bad happens to me, I realize that maybe I did a sin in an earlier existence. If good comes my way, I am not overjoyed, because that may just be a reward for my earlier good behavior in another life. So to understand is not to be too happy or unhappy.

There is also no need to feel hopeless. If we suffer, we can correct the cause of that suffering. We can redeem ourselves; we have that chance, for we are solely responsible for our acts. Nobody can save us but ourselves. The Buddha is like a medical doctor who can show us the way but cannot save us if we choose not to take the medicine.

These ideas have been very important for the refugees who have lived under Communism and who are trying to adjust to America. One man whom I know spent three years in a Communist reeducation camp. It just happened, and he had to accept it. Not only did he not feel miserable or suffer, he felt satisfied because he had the opportunity to share suffering with other people. Suffering or enjoyment, it depends on our state of mind, how we conceive it.

Here, too, when refugees arrive in America, they experience a lot of hardship. If they sit down and think about their past, they suffer, they worry, and it does them no good. They destroy themselves after two or three years. Regret destroys the self. If they temporarily forget, not forever, and look forward to the future, they will not feel so bad. For example, unemployment is universal, but it is temporary. If you are unemployed, spend less money, manage, survive, until you can find employment.

Some people are in really dire need. When I find this out, I call on people to help. We do not have any organization to do that. Rather, we do it for each case as it comes up. I just help them personally. I prefer that; I believe that it is not good to have an organization. I do not want to be under the influence of others. If someone is in need, I do not want to have to ask permission of a group to help that person. I decide right there, and if I cannot do it alone, then I ask others.

That's why this pagoda was founded. Three to four months after my trip to the midwestern city, a group of people, mostly women, requested that I establish a pagoda for them in their city. To show respect to the monk who had sponsored me, I told the people to ask him. He agreed to their request.

I rented a house on a corner, next to an elementary school, so only one family lives next to us. When we have large ceremonies, we use the school auditorium next door. Our one neighbor is very friendly. When he saw that I did not have a lawn mower, he came over and mowed my lawn. Later I bought a lawn mower. If I want to plant something in the yard, he offers to help me. From time to time I borrow implements from him. The landlord also is a good person. He is not Vietnamese, but he often brings his friends and relatives to see the pagoda. I pay him the monthly rent in cash which comes from donations.

We have no regulations. Those who worship and wish to give donations do so. Those who wish to help in other ways do so. Everybody is treated the same. Those who come to worship are completely free; nobody asks anybody anything. We have no president or organization, no fighting between factions. Even for big or great ceremonies, we have no organization. People come, they help as they will, spontaneously. Women know in advance what to expect. After talking to each other, they make informal, casual arrangements on what foods to bring.

The pagoda has grown by word of mouth. I did not advertise much because the pagoda is too small. If too many people come to our ceremonies, we will be too crowded, and the neighbors might complain.

I had been in foreign countries, so I knew the importance of retaining one's native language. When I established the pagoda, the first thing I thought of was starting language classes for children. I asked several of the parents to bring children for the classes. At first, only a few did so, but they did not see it as important. They had to drive their children here on the weekends, an additional burden.

The first classes began two weeks after the pagoda opened. Only four or five children attended, sometimes only two. In the summer vacation time, we offered classes from 1:00 to 4:00 P.M. on Monday through Thursday. People gradually learned of the classes, taught by volunteers, heard they were free, and realized the need. Now during the school year we have six classes totaling 75 students ranging in age from five to middle teens.

They meet on Sundays from 10:00 to 12:00 A.M., have lunch provided free by the pagoda; then from 1:00 to 3:00 P.M. they participate in activities which we call the Buddhist family. It's like scouts.

In the Buddhist family activities we teach a three-word motto: compassion (to others); knowledge (to determine needs); and involvement (acting courageously based on knowledge). If you have no compassion, you will not treat others well; without knowledge you are blind; but without involvement, your knowledge is useless. Knowledge without action is useless; you cannot just sit.

That is what I taught my children in the orphanage in Saigon. We lived in the spirit of those three words. And I try to teach the same things here. The older children can understand about Buddhism; the younger ones cannot, but they can follow these simple words each day. I want them to help others, to bring a cup of water to a child who is sick, to share a piece of cake, to help with chores, always with this spirit. When they get into arguments, I try to resolve them by reminding the children of those three words. If they have jealousies, I explain that they lack involvement; if they have rancor, I point out that they lack knowledge. In this way, I show them that events of their everyday lives revolve around these three words, all of which are concerned with helping people, sharing.

The children study Buddhist teaching, they play games, and they learn camping skills and handicrafts. At the end of the lunar year, we have a big event for the children. They give musical performances and receive prizes, while their parents prepare a feast. Rather than hire professional singers, I prefer to encourage the children to perform and to make their own costumes and props so that they develop confidence in themselves.

For adults, however, we have the main altar where they can worship. On it we have many images that are designed to remind us of Buddhist teachings. These include representations of the Sleeping Buddha, who reaches Nirvana, and of the Bodhisattva Kuan Yin [or Quan The Am; see Chapter 12], who helps those in distress.

Also at the altar, we have fortune sticks. These are of Chinese influence. Some people who are doubtful of their ability to make a decision pray to the Buddha to give them some guidance; they think it helps to select a stick. It has a number. They consult a paper with that number on it. The paper contains a Vietnamese poem, written in Chinese characters, with explanations in Vietnamese, providing guidance on how to behave. The fortune paper might tell you to be satisfied with what you have, or to start new activities on particular days. But the main thing is that it tells you to do good things.

The fortune sticks do not belong in a Buddhist pagoda, but we have to satisfy the needs of people. The sticks are used mainly by women, particularly old women. Whenever they come here, they look for and use the fortune sticks. If we didn't carry them, they'd go to another pagoda. Sometimes young men in distress turn to the sticks. And even some Catholics and other Christians come here to use them.

People in great distress depend not on fortune sticks, but on Kuan Yin. She is part of the Mahayana tradition. Some people say they have received miracles from her.

I have had a miracle of Kuan Yin. Usually I dry my clothes at the laundry, but on this day, for the first time, I decided to dry clothes on a line outside the pagoda. Suddenly, I saw a fire in the house next door. I intended to call the fire department, but the fire was too close, so I put a hose of water on it, called a boy nearby, and he and others put out the fire. If we hadn't, the pagoda would have burned. When the landlord heard of this, he said the pagoda had been saved by the Buddha.

Many people come to the pagoda, where they remain for two to three hours. They have many things in their hearts. They talk to me, and I speak to them about the Buddha teachings, to set their minds at rest. In a sense this is like counseling therapy, and it clarifies and helps them to deal with their problems, marital and economic, as well as those of loneliness.

Buddhists come here for help because they feel at home here. Everything looks like their home in Vietnam, the atmosphere, the furniture. Furthermore, things here are informal and not expensive, so they are not too removed from their own experience.

Some people come here to meet others. When they see old people here, it reminds them of their parents in Vietnam. When they see young people, it reminds them of their younger brothers and sisters in Vietnam. They see the figure that they miss and compare them with the letters from their own people, and that makes them feel better. They eat vegetable dishes like those prepared by their mothers in Vietnam. This relieves them. At the pagoda they don't have to face an actual reality in this country. Some people say that the sound of the bell lightens their sorrow. By coming here, their memories are revived. When they lived in Vietnam, they heard their mothers reciting the canon, but they never paid attention. Now they visit the pagoda and appreciate its value.

Many young adults in the ages of 20 to 25 have no family in this country. They are very lonely. Often they come by themselves to the pagoda. I cook for them. I provide some family for them, like a sister figure. If they need something and I have the possibility, I help to show them that somebody cares about them, pays attention to them.

People visit me with two different types of problems. The first is that of specific crises such as bad news at home, illnesses, or the need for specific services such as dealing with various agencies, or performing ceremonies at funerals or at the anniversaries of deceased family members.

The second kind of problem involves people who want to talk. Usually they do not go directly to the point because their problem cannot be expressed in an explicit way. First they go to the main shrine to worship. Many of them consult the fortune sticks. Then they bring them to me and ask me what it means. I select the paper, read the poem, and explain it to them. When that person sees the relationship between the explanation of the poem and their personal problems, they volunteer more detail.

At first, they don't say anything in particular. Normally they wait until nobody else is here before they volunteer more information. Sometimes they come back two or three times but just talk indirectly, "My family has some problems; I'd like to talk with the master; since she's busy, I'll come back." It is not good manners to go directly to the point. To warm up the conversation, I use all the information people have told me, for example, how much rent people pay. I use all the clichés to encourage them to talk about themselves and their difficulties: the weather; how many relatives are in Vietnam and how many in America; if married, how many children there are; and so on.

I see that people have problems, so I try to give them the time. Most of their problems involve their adjustment in this country. For example, a relative comes to live with a family, but the family does not know how to tell the relative to share costs. Not to tell is bad, but telling directly also is bad. Sometimes children don't want to go to school, or they want to get married, or they want to live separately from the family. Parents worry about this because they fear the children are not mature enough, but also because it involves extra costs. Some of the elderly people complain that they are made to baby-sit over weekends; they do not want to do this, but they do not know how to say no. This is made more difficult because the children never say to their parents that they are going out for fun, only that they need to go out.

The problem for the elderly is that they want to go to the pagoda, but they depend totally on their children, who are reluctant to take them. So the elderly are unhappy. In Vietnam they were not dependent on their children; they used taxis, pedicabs, or they rode with friends, but here that is impossible.

People also complain about the difficulties they have with the English language and their difficulties in getting jobs. They never mention discrimination, but they frequently complain about the stress of living in America, running all the time, with no time to relax physically and mentally. There is too much to do in learning how to survive and not enough time to do it.

They wake up early, work all day, return home tired, then get up early the next day. So do Americans, but Americans do not have to learn a new language at the same time. This is a continual task and a continual strain. People are very insecure. In Vietnam, a person could depend on parents and relatives, and so not go hungry. Here if you do not do everything yourself, you go hungry. People also send much of their earnings back to Vietnam. Two days of average American wages enables a family to live for three months in Vietnam. If one's brother is in a concentration camp and his wife and children are starving, how can a person not send them money? Previously in Vietnam, people didn't have those worries; a person could earn and easily support a family of ten.

On occasion, young men come here who say they want to become monks. Often they are sad and lonely; rarely do they show any strength or determination. If they believe that they want to live the religious life, I explain to them that at the monastery where they will be sent for their training, the path will be very difficult to follow: one meal a day, very isolated, and cold, so they may feel even more lonely. And they will not be able to communicate easily with the monks because most of them are English-speaking Americans. The young men are often too enthusiastic, I think, and also of volatile temperament, showing excessive determination, and then losing heart. Very few people here have the even temper and perseverance to live successfully in the religious life. You cannot be successful if you want to run away from ordinary life because you are lonely.

Sometimes people talk to me about some injustice they have endured. I usually tell them to forget it, not pursue it, or they will simply become more personally involved, but nothing will come of it. Everything is unjust. Instead of using their time for more useful activities, they will be wasting it on a lost cause. Injustice is greater now than it used to be because now that society is modernized, injustice is much wider. Missiles can kill many more people than do spears.

A lot of people complain that they are suffering and that they do not want to live. In one month, for example, ten people told me that they were considering suicide, and three people attempted it. I try to convince people that life is precious, and that others suffer much more. Often the complaints are not really serious, such as when an old lady said to me that she wanted to die because her children didn't treat her as well as in Vietnam.

The quarrels in her family follow a cycle. Her children did not treat her well; now the grandchildren treat the children badly. The grandson says he doesn't want to recognize his parents anymore. The old lady says, "See, the cause and the effect!" She moved to the pagoda for a while and lived here, and her 27-year-old grandson said, "Since you have left, I too have not gone back home."

When they live in American society, the behavior of the children changes. They do not have a connection with their country, and the old teachings and customs disintegrate, for there is nothing to hold them together. Furthermore, every day people work hard under pressure; they are tense, fatigued. They have no time to think of how to act, behave, treat parents. The old woman suffers because she stays home all day long, so has no means of communication outside, no one to take her outside. She is isolated, a recluse, as are most of the older women and men.

One old man told me that fortunately he has one grandchild, so he has the means to communicate. If not, he would become mute, remaining home alone, while his son works all day. When his son returns home at 6:00 P.M., he eats dinner, reads the newspaper, and goes to bed.

Although old people like that are depressed, they are not the ones who attempt to take their lives; mostly it is younger men and women in their middle twenties and early thirties, people who have no family and who have felt lonely; they have had no one with whom to talk. In Vietnam, it was much easier. They mixed with their countrymen. But here people feel isolated. They have no support. Life has no meaning. Whether they die today or later makes no difference. To prolong life is simply to prolong suffering.

In Vietnam, we have had some unhappy and frustrated people, but at least when they came home, they saw their parents and relatives, who made them forget all unhappiness and also made them feel some responsibility to their family. In Vietnam, if a person commits suicide, he hurts his family a great deal. People say that the family is very unfortunate, that they must have committed a sin in the past, so now they are paying that debt. People who commit suicide or have mental health problems are viewed as people guilty of religious sins in the past, so now the family must pay the price. This is a great stigma to the family.

But in America, people do not have any connection, they do not hurt anybody, so they feel free to commit suicide.

A Vietnamese woman married to a Mexican-American came to complain about her long-standing marital and family problems, that her husband acted polite to his work partners, but rude at home.

Because this was a personal family problem, I would not make any comments about what is right and wrong. Instead, I tried to explain to her about the role of women. "As women," I said to her, "we cannot expect to be getting our way all the time. We should show some abnegation, some flexibility. If the husband is angry and will not pay attention to the wife's illness, the wife must accept that. Maybe it is fate, and we cannot escape that."

I advise not only women, but also men to show abnegation. I advised this woman to look at the bright side of her husband, for example, that he brings in a check, gives it to her, lets her handle the financial aspects of the household. If the man shows nice behavior with his co-workers, but not with his wife, perhaps it's her fate that she got that kind of husband. If he does not show love and affection to his child, then the child will follow his mother.

Many Vietnamese complain of headaches. They work very hard in their jobs, then return home to find a peaceful time to relax, but receive a letter from Vietnam, and it's always bad news, followed by a request for money and gifts, or just complaints of the miserable life, arrests, harassment, and jailing of relatives. Often the people cannot solve the problems mentioned, such as requests for $500, or relatives who are stuck for years in refugee camps, or even undisciplined, uncontrollable children. So they get headaches. They are unable to sleep.

Insomnia is widespread among the Vietnamese. If they tell a doctor, he tells them to see a psychiatrist or a counselor. When they go to these people, they find that they receive advice that is not related to their problems.

In some families, husbands have become quite uncontrollable in their anger and hit their children until they bleed. In one case, the husband would refuse to talk to the wife if she tried to interfere or if she would talk back to him. For two weeks or more, he would talk through the children to communicate with her. The more silent he became, the more she talked to him trying to get him to respond. When he could no longer stand it, he left for a friend's house.

In Vietnam, it's much easier. When a woman raises her voice and tries to dominate her husband, he goes out to see friends and they may go to the movies or theater. You might stay with the friend for a few days, until the wife has to go looking for you and beg you to return. The children can go to school by themselves, so the absence of their father does not disrupt their routines.

In America, it's much more difficult; first, because friends are not as close here; second, because housing is much more restricted, and there may be no room for a friend; and finally, because if an angry husband is late for work, he is fired. So there is a lot of pressure in the United States that Vietnamese didn't feel back home. There is no safety valve. In Vietnam, after the husband has stayed away for a few days, his parents and relatives can intervene; they can take his side so he doesn't lose face, and they can mediate for him. A wife's parents would tell her to go to her husband and that helps her to save face. She says to him, "My parents ordered me to ask you to come back."

But in America, there are no parents, and no place to go.

One time, a lady with two small children under three years of age came to the pagoda, worshiped, and threw the fortune sticks. I asked her why.

She said, "I plan to move away."

Again I asked her why.

She replied, "I came here with two children. I live with another family, but they are not helpful. I don't have transportation, a car. I plan to move away."

I asked, "You want to move to another state, but whom will you live with?"

She said, "I know someone."

I said, "Here you have good weather, better than other states. Adjustment will be difficult. With whom will you live?"

"A man. I was engaged to him before 1975. After 1975 he left, and he is married now. After he went, I married another person, and I have two children. In the refugee camp, my husband met another woman and abandoned me and the children. That man in the other state has invited me to come there and be with him, even though he's married to another."

When I heard this, I feared that the woman would be putting on make-up, looking for another man, and she might neglect her children. I felt that she was unstable, and that if she went there, the man would be emotionally divided in two and could not support all of them. There she would have to live alone, with no money, and lots of troubles. She'd have to get a job. Here she has friends. The only thing I advised was, "Don't go; you'll destroy happiness."

The woman replied, "You are like my mother; I listen to you."

She has to baby-sit her two children, so maybe she can baby-sit other children and make some money. When she came to the pagoda and looked at the fortune sticks, I knew she was lonely and isolated. I said, "Now you have a pagoda. You can stay here." She stayed through the afternoon because she had nothing to do at home and she's not happy there, sharing it with other people. Living together with people who are not your relatives has problems, mostly that the children fight or are noisy, or that they have too many visitors, or the children mess up the house and won't clean it. The television may be on all day loudly. The days become long. The old people have a different character. They complain about small things; they are meticulous; they criticize and don't let things go. Living together is quite difficult. All of this is a consequence of the problem of divided families, some in Vietnam, some in America.

Even if families are later united, there may be problems. I heard today about a lady who had come to the United States with her child while her husband remained in Vietnam. He just arrived in America to find that his wife went to work every day, drove the car, took the child to the baby-sitter, and he simply stayed home, feeling neglected that his wife did not pay attention to him. Sometimes she returns home in a bad mood, so he suffers a lot. When she comes home with an unpleasant attitude, he suspects that she has a boyfriend. He lives in hell, and he wants to leave for another country.

A woman came by who complained that her American husband didn't love her. Yet he had learned Vietnamese, sent their children to Vietnamese language lessons, and took them to the pagoda. So I said to her, "Your husband shows he loves you by learning your language and raising your children in your tradition." We see that people always complain, and their complaints range from the truly serious to the banal.

Particularly when people are suffering, they often misunderstand the Buddhist view of events. They expect that an immediate cause will produce an immediate effect, so they wonder, "Why did I receive unfortunate results when I did good?"

Such a view distorts Buddhism. For an orange seed to grow into a tree, you need many causes: soil, sun, rain. The effect may be different at different times. We have to pay attention to different circumstances. When we were boat people, our seat on the boat was considered a good place to sit; when we reached shore, we no longer found the boat seat comfortable. In the refugee camp, we used small sticks with which to eat our rice. They were very precious to us, as were empty cans. But when we arrived in the United States, do we use those things? Life in the refugee camp was better than in Vietnam, but who is satisfied with the camp? We expected to go to another country and have a better life. So too, this life is a false and temporary life, not a true life. If we would like to elevate ourselves to a higher one, we must still depend on our false life, our body.

Buddhism aims at something higher, but people distort that by saying our goal is disinterest. Not so, for our goal is to go for something that is permanent. So if we live here, we cannot do simply nothing. We should do something. The next 20, 30, or 40 years, we act, then we die. If we do nothing, it's just a waste of our life. We should do something, try to help, sacrifice our time because we believe that we can help. If we use our time just to enjoy, that's a waste. If we see a person is hungry, we should give him cake to satisfy his hunger, but it is not good enough if we do not also teach him to avoid sins, not to steal, but to earn the food.

We try to elevate ourselves over and above all the normal passions: anger, selfish stupidity, and greed. If we let our emotions disturb us, we are never happy, never elevated. So according to Buddhism, we must ignore all those passions, get rid of all passion and desire.

The person who achieves this is happy, enlightened. Such a person does not regret this work, is ready to enter another world. This person is very rare, for he is close to being a Buddha.

My master knew in advance that she would die. She told her followers who had come to see her to return in one week to see her die. They did not believe her, did not take her statements literally. One week later, she asked to be cleaned for death. After hot water was boiled and herbs were thrown in to make a scent, she died.

Permanence through Change: Influence of the Master

In earlier Buddhist periods, many people became enlightened, but in our present era, of one million persons, not even one will gain enlightenment. I am not discouraged to see others fail, but am discouraged about myself. If you say something flattering, I am happy; if you criticize, I am sad. I become discouraged when I cannot control my emotions. I try to convince myself like the Buddha had done thousands of years ago that the body is just temporary, that nothing lasts, that nothing is durable, all is temporary. The more we realize that, the more we can neutralize every passion, not become angry, overjoyed, or jealous. It is like food: it's delicious, we appreciate it, but after two or three hours of digesting it, do we dare to touch it? Three hours earlier we took very good care of it. If someone takes some of it, and we have one piece less, we feel bad. But three hours later, who wants it?

One time, I lost $50 I was given for being at a wedding. I was in a hurry; I bought some tofu, and on the way back, I lost the money. I felt bad. But a few hours before, that money belonged to another person; it wasn't mine. When they contributed it, I didn't expect it, and yet one hour later when I lost it, I felt bad. I try to get rid of attachments like this, but this happened. I felt unable to control my feeling. And that is my main concern.

The most important influence on my life was my master, the Reverend Dam Soan. My master always advised me to do everything; she was the best. My master was a woman, but her knowledge was very wide; she knew almost everything. She always said, "Be modest, even though you do something. Don't be pretentious. If you don't keep modest, if you are haughty, people will dislike you, and it will be very difficult to succeed. You will not be able to do anything wisely. If you don't have a correct point of view, if you are no longer impartial, you will think you are superior, and you won't respect the ideas of others. You will feel that your own ideas are better than everybody else's. Then other people will hate you."

We know that sometimes a person has good ideas, sometimes bad. Sometimes an illiterate person has better ideas than a learned person. So my master emphasized that we should not think our ideas are better.

My master also taught that we should not establish close relationships with others because then you begin to depend on them. She stated that we should not depend on anybody, but rather just keep open with everybody, be concerned about everybody. If you develop a close relationship with anyone, then another person hates you and becomes unhappy. I personally am not caught into anything. *I am free.*

When I was about 17, I developed a special friendship with a nun in her early twenties. If a person is just a usual friend, you don't develop deep emotional attachments. Because our friendship became very close, we developed *resentment*. If I don't know you well, I don't care, and I don't develop resentment. But if you are my close friend, I pay special attention to how you react to me. That happened with us.

The master recognized that, saw the backfire of a close friendship, so she told us to stay apart. If we would be distant, we wouldn't develop like this. If you have a special affection, you cannot share with all; if you have $100 and give it to one, you cannot share it with others. If you choose one person as a close friend, you ignore the others, even if they try to treat you nicely.

We treat everybody with the same standard, not too close and not too far. If you are too close one day and too far the next, that person will become jealous and will develop hatred. The next time, he is your enemy. That's why we try to develop equal distance between all.

My master taught us to help people as long as we live, that we live to help others, not to enjoy life, not to drink, not to be involved in the pleasures of the world. "Do something useful," she said. "Don't just let time pass."

Once in Vietnam, after the Communists had taken over, I went to visit a nun. About halfway there, I saw a lot of people collecting wood, splitting it, tying it, and selling it. I thought, "They work very hard to make a living, they suffer, while I go to visit someone." I continued my visit, but I was not happy. I just didn't feel right wasting time.

So in conclusion, don't depend, don't be emotionally attached to others. Do everything the right way; don't be haughty, but modest. I try to follow that, but sometimes it is difficult to control. Even if one tries, it is impossible. But you cannot wait until you are perfectly successful. I follow my master, who said, "Start to do something; don't wait until you have all the necessary means. Just do it."

My master was of medium stature, not thin, not fat. I am very proud of her, that she was of good appearance, not abnormal. Her spiritual, intellectual power, her knowledge and activity were superior to others. *I prefer to say no less than others rather than superior*. That's an example, like a mirror reflected. There are two things, one physical, the other spiritual. She was a mirror-mold [exemplary] person.

Her voice was soft, mild. She was not impulsive, but calm. Her speech was like that. Even though her speech was soft, her rules were very strict. She did not want attachment. I used to think that her way was too strict, but I now realize that hers was the logical way to act.

I thought that my master required us to just work without enjoyment. But from the teaching of my master, now I have achieved something, that people love me and show me consideration and respect. If I led a free life, maybe we would not sit today to talk. I did not tell this story to intend to expose something that is good. It comes naturally. My working spirit, my way of life leads to this.

When I think about my master, I feel very grateful. I benefited a lot from her teaching; she helped my personal growth and my achievement of becoming a *person spiritually successful in all respects*. Parents raise their children with the expectation that they become successful. I am very happy, very lucky to have had a master like that. Had I met another master in a different situation, I might not be here today.

Look Tha: A Former Buddhist Monk

Usha Welaratna

Look Tha and his wife live with their daughter's family in a three-bedroom stucco dwelling situated in a cul-de-sac of unpretentious houses. From the outside, Look Tha's home, with its brown shutters and faded lawn, looks like any other in the neighborhood. But the visitor who peers through the oval glass pane on the front door sees a different world inside. The wall facing the door is lined with a bookshelf, but there are no books on it. Instead, it is adorned with a framed poster of the Buddha placed beside a large painting of the Angkor Wat. A brass container with three sticks of incense stands to the right of the Buddha, and a brass vase with pink and yellow plastic flowers stands on the left. At either end of the painting of the Angkor Wat are deep maroon roses preserved in sealed glass bowls.

I first met Look Tha, which is a polite term for "grandfather," at a Cambodian wat or temple ceremony, where, at 5'2", he was one of the shortest men around. As the day went by, however, I became increasingly aware of his presence; his pleasant, unhurried demeanor projected a certain dignity, and he was treated with much respect by the community who had gathered that day to offer alms to the monks in memory of their dead relatives and friends. I requested the friend who had invited me to the ceremony to introduce me to him. When he discovered I was a fluent English speaker, Look Tha told me of his great desire to learn English. Delighted, I asked him if he would teach me Khmer in exchange for English lessons, and over the next two years we met a couple of times a week at his house to learn languages from each other.

Every time I step across Look Tha's threshold, I leave American culture behind. After greeting me with hands clasped in the traditional manner, Look Tha carries my bag and books to the coffee table, to indicate his respect for me as his teacher, even though I am twenty years younger than he. We begin our lessons only after he serves me a glass of soda, or a cup of coffee prepared by his wife, sometimes accompanied with home-made sweets or tropical fruits. Although I am accustomed to the warm hospitality Cambodians extend to their visitors, I am particularly touched by Look Tha's thoughtfulness and concern for me because he is an elder.

The first time I visited him, Look Tha's actions took me back to my childhood in Sri Lanka, where we stood up when the teachers entered the classroom, greeted them with clasped hands, and carried their books to the teachers' room at the end of the lesson. At the end of my first lesson with Look Tha, I found myself taking his leave as I would from a teacher in Sri Lanka, and I did so almost unconsciously. I bade him farewell first, with my hands clasped, and allowed him to walk to the door ahead of me; I have done that ever since.

I chose Look Tha as a narrator because he appeared to embody many of the characteristics of traditional Khmer culture. But I soon realized that while he agreed enthusiastically to tell me his life history, he was reluctant to recount the Khmer Rouge atrocities in detail, even though he never said so directly. When I asked him about those experiences, he replied that he could not relate them because his English was not good enough. When I asked him to tell me in Khmer, his answer was that my Khmer was not good enough. Despite my knowledge of the regime's atrocities and the immense pain they cause survivors and my firm intention not to probe for information that the narrators did not wish to convey, I was deeply disappointed at his reticence.

Compassion had to come before knowledge, and I did not press him for information on the Khmer Rouge period. Instead, I talked about his culture, traditions, and Buddhism. Recounting these gave him immense pleasure, but Look Tha was by no means a passive narrator. To be sure that I understood Buddhism and his views and experiences, he once tested my knowledge and understanding of Buddhism by asking me to define a list of 30 Buddhist terms.

Because Look Tha displayed such a deep respect for religious teachings and ideals, I was curious to find out if and how he lived a Buddhist way of life; in this way, Look Tha came to mention some events about the Pol Pot era without any coercion from me. Even more important, I discovered he continues to cope with the Pol Pot trauma largely by following Buddhist teachings and practices. He departed from his ideals, however, when it came to his relations with the Vietnamese; here events in his country's history became much more significant.

Since, in the Buddhist outlook, old age and death are as much a part of life as birth and youth, I felt quite at ease talking with Look Tha about his remaining years in this life. His extension of not only his present life but also the lives of the Khmer Rouge soldiers to future rebirths shows how deeply the belief in karma (kamma) and rebirth is ingrained in the Buddhist worldview.

I have presented Look Tha's narrative first in this book for two reasons. First, his explanations of and insights about Cambodian history, society, culture, and Theravada Buddhist doctrines help to clarify information presented in the other narratives. Second, as an elder and a former monk, Look Tha occupies a primary place in his community.

Early Years

I was born a child of a farmer in November 1926, and I am now 62 years old. My father was a strong, handsome man. He was tall and big like an American. My mother was just about five feet tall; that is why I am small. Still, when I was younger, I was strong like my father.

When I was growing up, I lived with my parents, two brothers, and three sisters in a village of about five hundred people, in Battambang province. Many of our relatives, including our grandparents, Mother's older brother, and Father's older sister, lived in our village too. Most of the villagers, including my parents, were good people who went to the Buddhist temple every holy day. We call the Buddhist holy days "*Sila* days."

Almost everybody in my village was a farmer. Rich farmers had big fields all together in one place, and a lot of oxen. Poor farmers had no land, and perhaps just two oxen, so they usually worked for other people.

My father came from a very poor family, but after marriage, he worked very hard and became more prosperous. When I was growing up he was a middle-level farmer, neither rich nor poor. His fields were scattered in different places, and he had only six oxen. But he had a big house, two bicycles, and a motorcycle.

In the village, the only people who were not farmers were the twenty or so Vietnamese families that lived on the riverbank. They were fishermen. They spoke to each other in Vietnamese, but they spoke to us in Cambodian. Since Cambodians were not regular fishermen, we never became close friends with them. We did not like to fish for a living because we did not want to kill, but we fished occasionally when people got together to chat, or when rice fields were far away from the market.

When the rainy season started, Father cultivated about 70 ares of rice fields and orange gardens [100 ares = 1 hectare]. He hired labor only during transplanting and harvesting seasons. After harvesting the rice, he grew beans, peanuts, potatoes, mustard, white pepper, cucumber, chili, corn, and pumpkin in the fields. My father sold some of his harvest to people who came to the farm. Mother and I took the rest to sell in the market.

During the dry season, Father went in his ox cart to distant villages in the countryside to sell clothing, food, and medicines to people who lived there. Those people always looked dirty and ragged, and spoke in a different dialect. They also knew Khmer, so they could deal with us; from them, Father bought tobacco and reeds to make chairs, which he sold in Battambang. Mother helped him in the farm, and also went with him to the countryside whenever possible. Sometimes they hired people to help them, and about thirty ox carts trundled toward the countryside for two weeks or more. My older sisters looked after the family then. After my sisters got married and moved to their houses, I took care of my younger sister and brother. When I grew up and accompanied my parents, somebody from the village took care of them.

My mother never had any free time. When she was not working in the farm, she went to the countryside. During the rainy season she made cakes and sold them at a small stand she built near the river. When she returned home in the evenings, she prepared cakes for the next day. Like other women in the village, Mother cooked on a wood fire, and except for the rice pot, which was made of copper, all her cooking pots were made of clay. Later on, however, people used aluminum pots because the clay ones broke so easily.

When I was a child, I liked to play marbles with my friends.

"Now don't play in the sun, it's too hot. Play in the shade," Mother would say, as I ran out. And, "Don't climb those tall trees, you'll fall and break your legs!"

I also loved to play in the clear, fast-flowing river near my home, and my mother constantly worried that I might drown in it, especially when it was swollen after the rains.

"You are not to go near the river while I am gone," she would tell me whenever she had to go somewhere.

Although I obeyed her much of the time, sometimes when she was gone I could not stop myself from going to the river when friends called me. If I got caught, she or Father caned me for disobeying her.

As I grew older, I had to help Mother cook and take care of younger children, so I did not have much time to play. Still, whenever I could, I went to the river with my friends to swim or fish. Sometimes we brought food to share with each other. In Cambodia we had all kinds of fruits—oranges, grapefruits, papayas, mangosteens, pineapples, bananas, and sugar cane—my favorites were mangoes and young green coconuts, which have delicious water in the center.

My aunt and uncle who lived closest to our house had no children. We visited them often, and looked after them. We also frequently visited other neighbors. In Cambodia, unlike in America, we did not keep our doors closed. They were always left open so we could go to each other's home. If a new person came to the village, people talked to him and introduced him to others. People from my village went to other villages too. Even though our villages did not have paved roads, it was easy to go to other places because many of us had Honda motorcycles.

The happiest time for us in the village was during New Year, which we celebrated in mid-April. In the morning everybody took food to the monks in the temple and made merit. In the night, we played lots of different games in the temple grounds, which would be beautifully lit. Even though New Year came in the dry season, we felt cool and comfortable because we celebrated in the night.

My favorite game was called *chung*. To play chung, we first made a ball with a *kramar* [a large multipurpose scarf]. Then, girls and boys about fifteen to twenty years of age divided into two teams, and they threw the chung to each other, singing:

> Boys: *When I throw the chung,*
> *The chung will break into four pieces.*
> *Any girl who gets the chung,*
> *Can then catch me.*
> Girls: *When I throw the chung,*
> *The chung will break into five pieces.*
> *Any boy who has my kamma,*
> *Can wait to wed with me.*

Another festival we celebrated was Pchum Ben, in memory of our dead relatives. We believe that when people die, they are born in different places, and that once a year, the spirits of the dead come to visit all the children. So every November, we made floats with banana-tree trunks, and decorated them with 40 or 50 candles, incense, many kinds of foods, cigarettes, and betel leaves, and sent them down the river, saying, "I send all these good things to release you, every spirit, every living thing. So if you are searching for food, take whatever you can eat and be happy!"

Many people gathered on the riverbank to see the floats go down, and we felt very happy as we watched them go. We believed they also made the spirits happy, so that they could go back to their dwellings.

Schooling in the Temple

There were only two government schools in Battambang when I was little, so most villagers taught their children at home until the children could read and write some, after which the boys continued their education at the temple.

When I was about six years old, my father taught me to read and write Khmer, just as he had taught my sisters. Father did not have a high education because he had not gone to school, and after some months had gone by he said, "It is time for you to go and live in the temple and learn from the monks; there is nothing more I can teach you." I was eight or nine years old when my father took me there.

"You must behave well in the temple and not do anything unreasonable or disrespectful," my mother advised me before I left. "Don't speak harshly to the monks, or to the old men and women who come to the temple. Don't steal anything or harm anyone. Listen to the monks and do as they say."

The temple was across from the river, and Father carried my clothes, a blanket, and a pillow, tied up in a bundle. There were 60 or 70 boys of various ages already living there. I was the youngest. Father handed me over to the monks, and before he left, he too advised me to always obey the monks. After he left, I did not want to stay. I missed my parents, brothers, and sisters terribly, and always asked the monks to go back home. They allowed me to go home about seven or eight times the first year, but after that, the monks did not allow me to return home so often.

In the temple, everyone got up at half-past five. The older boys prepared rice gruel for breakfast, plucked ripe fruits from the many fruit trees in the temple yard, and served the monks their breakfast. The younger boys swept the dry leaves off the temple grounds and watered the plants.

When they finished breakfast, some monks walked from house to house with their bowls, and villagers gave them rice to use at lunchtime. After we finished breakfast, those monks who remained in the temple taught us Sanskrit, using long-leaf books. They also told us stories of the Buddha and other great people in our history.

We studied until about nine-thirty, when the villagers started arriving with different kinds of soups, meat and fish, vegetables, fruits, and sweetmeats to offer the monks at lunchtime. We always had enough left over for dinner as well, but the monks had only two meals a day; after the noon hour, they only drank tea or juices. Sometimes, instead of bringing food to the temple, people invited the monks to their houses.

After lunch, the younger monks went to a nearby temple to study because our temple did not have learned monks. The older monks read Dhamma books, studied Pali and Sanskrit, or rested.

We went swimming in the river, and for the next two hours, the river was filled with screaming, yelling children. When we returned we studied Sanskrit again till five o'clock, when we had dinner. In the evening all of us, the monks and students, washed again at the river. Later on the villagers installed a water machine [spigot] in the temple, so the monks did not go to the river to wash. Because we wanted to play, we continued to go to the river, and after we came back we had some free time.

In the night, the monks taught us Dhamma until ten o'clock. At this time they did not give us any books; we had to listen and memorize everything they taught. When it was time to sleep, the monks slept in the bedrooms, and the boys slept outside on the verandah.

Although we were fond of the monks, we were also afraid of them because they were strict disciplinarians. When we misbehaved or did something wrong, the monks first advised us using moral proverbs; if we continued to do wrong things, they beat us two or three times with the switch. However, they did so only to scare us, and to teach us good behavior.

One time a monk beat me too. We went to bathe in the river, and saw some Vietnamese men catching fish. When they finished, the fishermen took with them the big fish, and threw away the little ones, which we picked up and took back to the temple.

"Why did you catch those fish?" asked a monk who saw them.

"We did not catch them, we just picked them up because the Vietnamese threw them out," we told him.

However, the monk did not believe us. Thinking we caught the fish ourselves, he beat us, because in the Buddhist religion we are told not to kill animals.

There were about 30 or 40 monks in my temple, but I liked Sankharaja, the head monk, best. He was 75 years old, and was tall and fair-skinned. Oh, he was handsome! He was also a very good man. When he spoke to the pupils, he always smiled. He never scolded anybody. When he lay down and rested after lunch, he sometimes called me to fan him to keep him cool, or to massage his legs.

When I was fourteen years old, I decided to go back home because I wanted to go to government school. Sankharaja said, "When you go back home, obey your parents just like you did when you were a little boy," and gave me permission to leave. I returned home with my father's approval.

The government school was very different because about 30 percent of the 50 or 60 students in my class were female; but we did not become friends with them. At recess girls played on one side of the schoolyard and boys played on the other side. We talked to each other only if we needed any help with our lessons.

In the classroom, about five students of the same sex sat on a long bench at each table. We learned French as well as Cambodian, but we did not learn English. We used regular books instead of the long-leaf books the monks used in the temple, and since ballpoint pens did not exist in those days we used dip pens for writing. When I came home after school, I continued to help my parents on the farm and with household chores.

When I was about seventeen, my sisters were married, and had left with their husbands to live on their own. Father said to me, "You are a big man and you had your education. Now you must stay at home and look after your younger brother and sister while they go to school."

Although I did not want to stop my schooling I had to obey my father and I remained at home. But whenever I had free time I tried to learn the Thai language from a monk who knew it well, because at that time, Battambang was ruled by the Thai. Two years later I left home again to become a monk.

A Novice Monk

When I was young, it was the tradition for all peasant boys who could do so to become monks. If a boy did not enter monkhood, he would not know the Buddha's teachings and would have wrong thoughts; the villagers did not consider such a person a good man. So when my parents told me to become a monk at age twenty, I returned to the temple in which I had studied, this time to be ordained as a monk, just as my grandfather and father had done.

Five other boys joined the monkhood with me, and this was marked by a big ceremony. A layperson shaved our heads. We were given white kramars to cover our shoulders and special *sarongs* [worn by men and women] to wear, but not the kind that monks wore. When we were ready, musicians, dancers, my parents, and hundreds of other people escorted us into the temple in a procession. There, Sankharaja ordained us as novice monks.

Although I had learned some Dhamma when I lived in the temple before, now I had much more to learn about *dana* [giving], *seela* [disciplinary precepts], and *bhavana* [meditation]. As a monk, I had to strive continually to purify my mind and do good deeds.

The Buddha said:

Sabbha papassa akaranam
Kusalassa Upa Sampada
Sachitta pariyodapanam
Etam Buddhanu Sasanam.

This means:

Avoid all evil,
Do what is good,
Purify your heart,
This is the advice of all the Buddhas.

When monks have seela, or are disciplined, they bring happiness to people. The disciplinary precepts taught us how to behave so we could control our thoughts and actions, and not lose our concentration. For instance, when I went to people's houses I could not laugh or speak loudly; and when I walked, I was required to look ahead, and not glance around. If I behaved otherwise, it led to loss of concentration and discipline.

We spent much of our time teaching Dhamma to laypeople, because if people did not know about dana, seela, and bhavana, they would not know about good and bad; then they would be like animals. To teach people about life experiences, we told them Jataka stories, which are about the Buddha's past lives.

In return for our guidance, the people looked after our needs since we had little time to cook, and we lived in the temple without parents or family. They gave us food, robes, bedding, and other items we needed.

In addition to receiving moral guidance, they also received much merit, or good karmic results for their actions. For instance, when someone gave food to us, or to those who were destitute, or to animals, they enabled us to live one more day. We believe that this act of giving to others brings merit to those who gave, and helps them to attain worthy lives in future rebirths. In Buddha's language merit is called *punya*. Even though we believe it is meritorious to give to others and we encouraged people to do so, no one was forced to give anything; it was up to the people to do so if they wished.

In Buddhism, we also believe that we can transfer merit we acquire to those who are deceased, and who may not yet be reborn in a good place. So after lunch, we prayed that those dead relatives of the people who had offered food or other items to us would benefit from those good deeds.

I learned Dhamma at my village temple for three years. There was a great deal to learn, and I wished to study for at least seven years, but after my third year, I was sent to a temple in Phnom Penh to teach for a year. After that I returned to my own temple because it needed a teacher.

I was much happier as a monk than as a layperson, because as a monk, I became a good person. But I was still young and strong, and when I was 26, I decided to return home because I wanted to work. I knew I could return to monkhood when I grew older. I obtained my father's approval to go back home.

Before I left, Sankharaja advised me on how to be a good layperson again. He then blessed me, and sprayed holy water on my head. I removed my robes and put on a normal sarong, and cried as I worshipped Sankharaja and bade him farewell. After returning home, I did what my parents asked me to do, but for a long time, I felt sick in my heart because I wanted to return to the temple.

A few months after I came back, I started working for a Chinese businessman, overseeing about 300 loggers working in the jungles near the Thai-Cambodia border. That work was done in the dry season only. During the rainy season, I supervised coolies building the railway lines in Battambang. Three years later, I got married.

An Arranged Marriage

When I was 16 or 17 I liked a certain girl, but I never told her of my feelings; in those days, boys and girls did not talk about love and romance. She got married when I became a monk, so when I was 29 years old, I got married to a girl chosen for me by my parents, as was our custom.

In Cambodia, when a man's parents found a girl whom they considered a suitable bride for their son, they first asked her neighbors about her character. If those neighbors said, "She never had a boyfriend. She cooks well, and she knows how to look after a house. She will make a good wife!" the groom's parents approached her parents. If the girl's parents found the proposition agreeable, they in turn inquired from the groom's neighbors about his conduct and character. To be considered suitable, a man had to be a good worker who did not drink, gamble, or engage in cockfighting.

When both families were satisfied, the groom's parents came to the girl's house bearing trays with gifts of fruits, a whole head of a pig, two hens, new clothes, and other things. If the young couple agreed to the marriage, a wedding date was set. The night before the wedding monks visited the bride's home and advised the couple to always speak respectfully to each other, not to commit adultery, to take care of one another, and so on, so the two would have a harmonious marriage. Then festivities continued for three days.

I never saw her before my parents arranged my marriage, but everybody who knew the girl that my parents chose for me said she was a very good person. My parents told me she had never had a boyfriend; if it had been otherwise, I would never have married her. I did not worry about how she looked; whether she was beautiful, or whether she was dark or light-skinned, because I trusted my parents' judgment. When I saw her I thought, "That girl is the right person for me."

After the wedding, I went to live with my wife's parents. I had to show my parents-in-law that I would be a good husband to their daughter. I worked with my father-in-law on his farm, and planted mangoes, oranges, grapefruits, coconuts, and many other fruit trees, but because they would not bear fruit for a few years, I also planted vegetables such as cucumber, corn, and eggplant, for faster yields.

After about a year, my wife's parents said, "We see you can do things for yourself, and we think you make a good husband for our daughter. It is time for you to live on your own."

In Cambodia, as people became prosperous, they bought furnishings to decorate the house, or land and other gifts for their children. Parents did not sell things to children as they do in America. When children married, parents gave gold necklaces, earrings, and bracelets to daughters, and rings and necklaces to sons. When newly married couples went to live on their own, their parents gave them land and various household items.

When my wife and I moved from her parents' house, my father-in-law gave me about three ares of land in the countryside and tools for my new farm. It was a very small parcel of land, but sufficient for us to begin our new life. Also, because I had no farm machinery I could not have managed a bigger farm.

Every morning I went to my farm at half-past six, and about an hour later my wife brought me freshly cooked hot rice and grilled fish for breakfast. Sometimes she stayed on and helped me with the work, but I did not think she was strong enough to do farm work. Besides, she had to look after our house and the children. My wife had eleven pregnancies, but she had five miscarriages. Of the other six children, a boy and a girl died just after birth, and a daughter died of disease when she was seven. So we were left with only three children.

After breakfast I worked till about noon, plowing the land with the oxen, or cultivating by hand. Some mornings I drew about 150 buckets of water from the well and watered my plants. When the sun became too hot, I bathed in the river, and went home to eat a full plate of rice, fish, soup, and vegetables my wife cooked for our noon meal. Then I slept for an hour or two, and returned to my fields and worked until five or six in the evening.

Like my parents, I too worked seven days a week. "You work too hard; why don't you take a rest?" some people would say to me, but I did not like to stop working even for a day because things piled up. Besides, I could see the results of my work. We had nice clothes to wear and good food to eat. My family had a good life, and I had a good marriage.

After we had been married for about seven years, the fruit trees I planted in my father-in-law's land started to produce bountiful harvests. Every year, I earned about six or seven thousand *riel* [Cambodian currency] selling fruit, and I gave that money to my parents for safekeeping. All of us in the village kept our savings in our homes. Only the big people [rich people] in the city kept money in the bank. Later, as I became more experienced, I bought more land in other places, but I was careful to buy only as much land as I could manage.

Peasants in Cambodia were different from government people who were born in Phnom Penh. The city people went to good schools and got a high education; they were rich, high-class people. As a child of a farmer, I knew I could never become rich like the people in Phnom Penh, but I did not feel angry that I was poor, because I knew what I could do for myself. I could plant, sell, and do good things for my family, and for other people in the village.

I never fought with anybody in the village; even if someone made me angry I usually kept quiet, not because I feared others or surrendered to them, but because I did not want to lose control of myself. My village was generally a peaceful place, though, because even if two people disagreed about something, a third person would say gentle words to both and help to resolve their problem.

Although I avoided arguments and physical fights, I knew how to defend myself if someone confronted me, because an elder who liked me taught me martial arts; and once I almost fought with some Vietnamese who tried to steal the food from the floats we had sent downstream to honor our dead relatives. When they heard us shouting and running toward them they turned back, so we never went after them.

Another time, I used my wit to fend off two Laotians who tried to accost me in the countryside. I had gone there with a lot of gold to buy some goods from the villagers when two hefty men closed in on me, asking, "Well, what's your business here?" I knew I was strong, and I carried a knife tucked into my sarong, but I did not want to fight two people. So even though I spoke some Laotian, I pretended not to understand what they said. Instead, I smiled broadly and carried on with my journey, and to my relief, they stopped following me.

In 1970, the year my father died, I was struck with a serious illness. My legs became numb, and at harvesttime I had to hire people to gather my crops. My wife and children too had to work hard. For about six months, I had to crawl on the floor, but finally, some medicine made with tree roots helped me to get better.

About the time I was using a cane and walking a little, Lon Nol soldiers and the Khmer Rouge started fighting close to our village. When bombs started to destroy the houses and farms in my village, we were forced to go to live in the town. There, my wife and daughters earned a living by selling cooked food and sweetmeats in the market.

Life and Death Under the Khmer Rouge

On April 17, 1975, Khmer Rouge came to Battambang. Two days later Pol Pot soldiers came to my brother-in-law's house in the night and said, "We want you to come with us to get something to eat." When they reached the store they shot my brother-in-law, right on the sidewalk. The next day the soldiers came and ordered us to bring his body to the temple for cremation. Since I was still unable to walk, my wife and his wife did so. In the next two or three days they also killed my father-in-law, brother, another brother-in-law, and my wife's uncle. The soldiers did not say why they were killed, but all of the victims had worked in the previous regime.

The Pol Pots also killed the head monk of Battambang, who was my relative. He was a very kindhearted man and everybody loved him. He was also very intelligent; he spoke French, Cambodian, Thai, and Vietnamese, and he also knew Sanskrit and Pali. Later, a woman told me that before he was killed, the Pol

Pots ordered the monk to dig a big hole. They then bashed his head with a hoe, and pushed him into it. But, she said, they did not even cover his body properly; after the soldiers left, the monk's legs protruded from the grave.

A week after they came to Battambang, the Pol Pots chased all of us from our houses to the countryside. They talked by the gun: OUT, OUT, OUT. SHOOT.

Like other villagers, my family too kept large supplies of rice and dry fish in our home. When the soldiers ordered us to leave, we wanted to take the food with us, but they said, "Take only enough food for three days. You will come back to your houses after three days, when we have cleaned up the city."

However, we did not believe them, and took as much food as we could carry, and all the money and gold we had collected.

The street was packed with thousands of people. Some even took their pigs, cattle, and chickens with them, and those who had to carry young children as well as their goods could barely walk. But the soldiers did not care. They forced us to hurry, with threats and random shootings.

I brought my family back to my farm in the countryside, only to find that my house and land had been taken over by other people. The Pol Pots gave us a small hut nearby, and that night, I hid my gold inside the bamboo steps leading to that hut, and buried the money in the ground.

A few months after evacuation, the Pol Pots took my older daughter and son to live with other young people in youth camps. For the next several months, we did not know where our children were, or if they were alive. My wife and I felt sick with worry, but there was nothing we could do; the soldiers told us our families belonged to Angka. Finally, after about six months my daughter came to visit us, but only for two days. We did not see our son for a whole year.

My younger daughter who lived with us had to look after small babies because their parents, along with my wife, had to work in the rice fields.

Because I still could not walk without using a cane, the soldiers ordered me to sit on the ground and cut grass, or weave baskets. I worked very slowly because I was old and ill, and the Pol Pots often accused me of pretending to be sick. "We will kill you if you lie to us," they would threaten me often. I knew they would do so; I saw many people who were beaten or killed for such crimes.

We worked all day, under the sun and in the rain, with no medicine and hardly any food. I was so hungry that I caught every snail, lizard, frog, and fish I saw, even though I had stopped fishing after I was about 40 years old, because I did not want to kill living beings anymore. Other people did the same, but we were very careful not to let Pol Pots see us when we foraged for food because they would have punished us severely for "stealing."

Once they killed a handicapped person in my village who ate the stem of a cassava that was left on the ground after the cassava was dug up. Another time I saw a man tied up and beaten with hefty bamboo poles because he had plucked an orange. There was a thundering noise every time they beat him, and blood gushed out of his head and back. Oh, it was terrible! I also saw a soldier return an ax he had borrowed from a boy who lived near my hut, and it was covered with blood. I don't know who was killed. At that time, we all lived with great fear; every moment we expected the soldiers would come to take us away to be killed.

I didn't want to die during the Pol Pot time because the Buddha said that humans who did not purify their minds at the time of death would be born in a bad place. But how could I purify my mind then? I was very angry with the Pol Pots; they did not give us enough clothes or food, and forced us to do hard labor. So because I did not have good thoughts, I did not want to die at that time.

Although I was angry with the Pol Pots, I never said or did anything to get revenge; if I did so, I would also be bad like them. The Buddha said, "If someone does wrong to another person and that person takes revenge, the result will never end."

Whenever I was tempted to take revenge on the soldiers, I thought of those words, and also of my past lives. I believed that if I had acted badly in a previous life, something bad will happen to me in this life. But if in a previous life I had not killed, stolen, or done bad things to other people, I would escape being killed by the Pol Pots.

To help me control my anger, I recited Dhamma in my mind every night, and prayed to the Ratana Thrai [the Three Jewels]. I prayed over and over,

Khadesa, khadesa
Kang karana khadesa
Ahang petthang cha na mi

This means, "Even if anybody does me any wrong, I will never take revenge."

That was all I could do. I had so little food or possessions that I could not give dana [alms] to anybody. I had no seela because I killed. The only thing I could do was meditate.

I believe my meditation also helped my son. When he was assigned to a youth camp close to our village, he came over to our hut whenever he could, in the night. One night Pol Pot soldiers saw him and arrested him. A man who saw my son being taken away came and told me what had happened. I was terrified that my son would be killed. So while my hands worked, my mind meditated on Buddha, Dhamma, and Sangha on behalf of my son. My son was not killed. Someone had told the Pol Pot leader that my son was a good worker, and the leader had released my son after warning him not to disobey their orders again.

I believe that when people die, they are reborn, and that those who observed *Panchaseela* [the Five Precepts] and led good lives will be reborn in the heavens or in the universe. Those who did bad things will be born in hell or as animals. Therefore, in the future, the result of kamma (karma) will not bring Pol Pot soldiers to a good place. Someday they too will suffer and be killed, either in this life or in a future life. Already they have had to suffer in this life; I saw them living in the jungle like animals, after the Vietnamese came.

When the Vietnamese Came

After the Vietnamese liberation, my family and I went back to our farm because the people who lived there in the Pol Pot time had gone back to their own place. We planted sweet potatoes, corn, chili, and other vegetables, and we were in control of our lives when the Vietnamese ordered my eighteen-year-old son and the husband of my older daughter, who married during the Pol Pot regime, to join the army. They did not want to do so, because though it was the Cambodian army, it was controlled by the Vietnamese. We heard that those who did not follow orders were forcibly taken away to the army, and we decided then to leave our country because we knew that whether they were Cambodian or Vietnamese, under Communists we had no freedom.

In November 1979 we left our home for the Thai-Cambodia border. We carried very little food and clothing with us because we did not want to attract the attention of Vietnamese soldiers. Because I walked so slowly, my son and son-in-law helped me by carrying me on their backs, but soon my wife too had problems walking: her soles cracked, became bloody, and caused her severe pain. After five days we had made little progress because we were ill, tired, and had little to eat. We had no choice but to pay some gold and hire a motor trailer [a trailer pulled by a motorcyclist] to take us to the border. When we reached the border, we discovered that it was too dangerous to stay there because the Khmer Rouge and the Vietnamese continued to fight close to our camps, and we left for Khao-I-Dang camp in Thailand on December 8, 1979.

The United Nations gave my family a single room in a long shelter, and rations of bean sauce, fish sauce, salt, and rice. Although we ate sparingly, the rations were not sufficient for our family, and I sold gold for *baht* [Thai currency] and bought food from vendors. Still, I felt happy; even though our living conditions were bad and we did not have enough to eat, things were now much better than in the Pol Pot time.

In the camp I studied English using a Thai-English dictionary because I did not have enough money to pay a teacher. I did not know much Thai, but I could speak and read enough to look up English words in the dictionary. I would then write them in Thai, and memorize them. My son-in-law didn't know Thai, but knew a little English and a lot of French, and we helped each other to learn English, using *English for Today, Book III*.

Thousands of new refugees continued to come to Khao-I-Dang, and I met several people from my village. From them I heard that the Vietnamese soldiers had begun to commit many robberies in my village, although they had not done so before I left. One friend said, "You know what happened to your good friend Prov? He went back and forth between the border and the village selling things, and every time he traveled, the Vietnamese soldiers checked his bags and took whatever they wanted. One time because the soldiers did not find anything they liked, they kicked him so badly that they broke three ribs, and he died."

I decided I would not return to Cambodia until the Vietnamese left.

I had not planned to come to America when I left my country; I knew nothing about America then. I went to the refugee camp only to move far away from the fighting. There, however, I discovered that many people, including my mother, brother, and sister, and their children who had also escaped, had gone to America, and I thought I will also come here. My brother sent a letter saying he would sponsor us, but before I applied to come, I received orders from the camp officials to move with my wife to another camp.

When we first went to Khao-I-Dang, the officials told us that we would not be separated from our children; later, they ordered my wife and me to move. We had no choice in the matter. I do not know why we were moved. After twenty months, with no explanation, they sent us back to live with our children. By then, our children had applied to come to America and they left a few months later. We also applied to come, and finally, in 1982, the Americans called us for an interview. We passed the interview, but we lived in Khao-I-Dang for two more years before being moved to a transit camp in the Philippines. In that camp, we went to school to learn English, and how to live in America. We arrived here in 1984.

An Old Man in America

When we came, my daughter and son-in-law were living in a small apartment, and we too lived with them. My son-in-law showed me how to get to the grocery store, to the International Rescue Committee, which helps refugees, to the hospital, and to various other places. During my first year in America, I went to the hospital often because I still had problems with numbness. In this country, I like the hospital best because the receptionists, nurses, and doctors always speak nicely to me, which makes me feel happy.

Sometimes I think Americans don't like refugees. One time a young American man climbed into the bus ahead of me, but instead of moving forward, he stood still. I waited for a while, and climbed up behind him. Suddenly, he shoved me with his elbow; if I had not been holding the handrail I would have fallen on the street. I did not say or do anything. I kept quiet because I am an old man, and I am not American. The driver and many people in the bus saw what happened, but they didn't say anything. I wonder why that young man did that? America is a capitalist country, not a Communist country, so why do people behave like that?

I miss my homeland. I liked living in my village because I had relatives and friends, and the freedom to go about whenever and wherever I liked. Here, I don't even know my neighbors. During the day they go to work, and in the evening, they keep their doors closed. In America, people wait for Saturday or Sunday to talk to others.

I also miss my rice fields and my big garden with all the fruits and vegetables. There, I worked hard and ate a lot more food than I eat here; in Cambodia we didn't have diets. Now, because I don't do any work, I eat only what I need to keep me from starvation. Otherwise I will get fat, and lose my health.

My biggest problem is that I do not know much English. The first time I heard some white people speak English in Cambodia, I knew it was not French, but I did not know what language it was. When I heard it again in the refugee camp, I remembered the sounds of the unknown language that I had heard before, and realized that it was English!

I wish I could go to school to learn English, but because my children have to go to work they don't have too much time to take us around. My ambition now is to learn to drive, buy an old car, and go to school to learn English. Some people say, "You are an old man. Why do you want to go to school?" I tell them I want to be able to speak to American people.

Sometimes I try to learn English by watching television, but usually the man speaks too fast for me to understand. When I read the English newspaper, I understand only about half of what I read. If I learn more English I will be able to improve my mind because I will have new things to think about, and new people to talk to.

Reflections

When I am lonely I think of Cambodia; but then I think of Pol Pot, and I get so upset. I think, "Why did they kill so many people? They all had the same religion, the same nationality, the same dress; they were all Cambodians!"

I do not cry when I think of what the Pol Pots did to my country and my people, but when I think of those times my head feels very tight, and I feel sick in my chest. At such times, I go to my room, shut the door, and meditate. I concentrate on my breathing, and it helps to relax me. When I breathe in, I concentrate on the cool air that touches the nostril. When I breathe out, I am conscious of the hot air that touches the nostril. I do not think about anything else. When I finish meditating I read newspapers, historical books, or Buddha stories, to forget about Cambodia and my people's troubles.

But when I sleep, I dream of my country. Some nights I dream I am working in my rice fields like I used to, but some nights I dream I am working for Pol Pot, and it is very upsetting. I almost never dream of my life here.

I think Cambodia fell to the Communists because of two major reasons. First, the people in the countryside did not have much education. Most of them went to the temples and became monks, but their temples may not have had highly educated monks who were good teachers. Then, if the people did not go to another temple to study, they would not have learned Dhamma properly, and therefore would not have known what was good and what was bad. When the Khmer Rouge told untruths to such ignorant people, they believed them and became Communists.

Sihanouk's wrong politics was the second reason for Cambodia's fall. I know about Sihanouk's political ideals because when he came to Battambang, soldiers made the people listen to his speeches. Sometimes he spoke for two or three hours.

In 1953, Sihanouk fought for Cambodia's independence and Cambodia became independent in 1954. At that time we all thought Sihanouk was glorious. He kept Cambodia in the middle [politically neutral]. Around 1964–66, however, Sihanouk visited China and his politics changed. He thought that the Communists will triumph over the capitalists, and he formed a friendship with Ho Chi Minh, even though we despised Ho Chi Minh. When Sihanouk left the United Nations in 1966 and started to lean toward socialism, I began to dislike him. Only stupid people in the countryside liked him. The government of Thailand brought progress and peace to their country, but the leader of Cambodia governed the wrong way, and the result he got was Pol Pot.

I had a lot of property in Cambodia. My children would have had good jobs there because we sent them to school and gave them a good education. But we don't think of going back because Cambodia is no longer a peaceful country, and the Khmer Rouge wants to control it again. They have all kinds of weapons they get from China. Even if Pol Pot did not come back, our country is still under Vietnamese Communists, and I don't trust them.

Under Communists, nobody can do what they want. My older sister and her children still live there. She did not escape with us because my nephew wanted to have all our property, but now he has to work as a soldier. His wife works too, in the bank, but their salaries are too small to feed all their children. Since my sister is very old and cannot work, she does not have enough to eat. I wish I had money to spare so I could send some to them every month, but I don't, because I am on welfare. So even though I feel sad about my relatives and I get homesick, I do not think about going back.

Here in America, I have Vietnamese neighbors, but I cannot trust them because I have read the chronicles of Cambodia, and I know that Cambodians and Vietnamese have been enemies through history. Buddha said to treat all people equally, but I cannot become close friends with them. I only say "Hi" to my Vietnamese neighbors, and they say "Hi" to me.

When Cambodian women who live here marry Vietnamese men, I get very angry. I don't know what I would do if my grandchildren married Vietnamese; I don't even want to think about it. I like Chinese people though, they are the same as Cambodians. I would like it if my grandchildren married Chinese people. But I hope my children or grandchildren will not marry American or Spanish people because we have different cultures.

I did not know how different the Cambodian and American cultures were until I came here. When I went to school in the Philippine camp, my teacher was an American Mormon Christian. She told me, "When you come to America, you must not forget your Cambodian culture. Teach your culture to all your children and grandchildren." I could not understand why she said that, because to me it seemed that people will always like the culture of the country they were born in.

I also thought that in America, the government let refugees keep their natural cultures, because in this country there is freedom. Now I know it is not so.

In Cambodian culture, teachers tell the students, "When you go back home, you must never do anything that your parents dislike. You must always obey them." At home, our parents reminded us often to obey our teachers and although we disobeyed them sometimes, we usually did what our parents and teachers told us. However, in America, teachers teach children about their freedom to do what they want, so they don't obey their parents, and many Cambodian refugees have problems with their children.

Some Cambodian youth in this country do not even know about our culture or customs. They grew up in Pol Pot time, and then when they came here, they went to school here; so they know only the American customs. For example, they shout and they jump when they talk to each other, and even if older people tell them not to, they do not listen. Although everybody likes their freedom, it is not good to disturb others by loud and noisy behavior.

I don't dislike everything about American culture, but I dislike people kissing on the road, or on the sidewalk. In Cambodian culture, it is shameful to kiss so all the people can see. I never saw people kiss in public in Thailand, or in the movies we used to get from India. When I wait for the bus, young men and women kiss at the bus stand. I am an old man and I feel ashamed when I see them. If my granddaughters kiss like that I will tell them not to do it, but I do not know if they will listen to me because they grew up here. Also, I can only tell them what is right and wrong. It is up to them to choose what they want to do. Some TV programs have naked people and sex, and then I switch it off. I feel embarrassed to watch them because those stories are for young people.

I want my grandchildren to learn about our history, language, and culture. For instance, when people come to our house, they must greet them respectfully with their palms together, and treat them well. When the people leave, they must again show respect. When we go to another house, they must respect the owner of that house. I am happy to say that my daughter and son-in-law have taught their children these customs.

I would like to teach my grandchildren to read and write our language, but the Cambodian language has many sophisticated words that they don't understand yet because they are too young. Also, the choice is up to their parents. Before I teach Cambodian to my grandchildren, I will ask my daughter and son-in-law if they will allow me to do so. I am their grandfather and I take care of them, but if my daughter and son-in-law do not want them to learn Cambodian, I will not teach them because I do not like to do things that others dislike.

I believe that people must have the freedom to say if they dislike something. For example, if I dislike going to church, nobody should force me to go to church as some people try to do. I think wherever I live, if nobody forces me to do anything, I will have no worries.

Some Cambodians are unhappy here because they came with no education, cannot get jobs, and so cannot have a good life. They do not have enough money to go to Lake Tahoe, Las Vegas, Disneyland, Santa Cruz, Monterey, and other places, like those who came in 1979 with a good education and got good jobs.

As for me, I am neither happy nor unhappy. I am an old man and I am not strong enough to work. The government gives me enough money to get by from month to month, I have a place to live, and I feel contented. I have no desire to go to the cinema or to concerts. I have seen all that in Cambodia. I am happy staying at home, watching TV, reading books. In that respect, I am different from old men in America. They visit places to find ways to happiness. As long as I have the freedom to meditate, to talk about Dhamma, to read, go to the temple, and purify my mind, I will be happy.

All men and women grow old, and I think I am ready to die when the time comes. I do not worry about death because I didn't harm anybody or do anything that others disliked. After I die, I wish to be reborn in a place where I will know Buddhism because the Buddha's word is true.

The Christian religion says, "If you lie, kill, or commit any other sin, you can wash away the sin," but I don't believe that. If people do wrong, they receive bad results. If they do good, they receive good results. For example, if I say bad words to you, you will get angry with me, but if I say good words to you, you will be happy. If somebody touches the fire, they will be burnt, but if they do not touch the fire, they will not burn.

I don't know where I will be reborn, but I will do good in this life because when people are jealous, greedy, steal, lie, or take intoxicants, the results of kamma will not be very good in another life. My only wish is to be reborn anywhere that has Buddhism, so I can listen to Dhamma, study Dhamma, and purify my mind.

Index